57th

Annual of Advertising, Editorial, and Television Art and Design

The 57th Annual of Advertising, Editorial,
and Television Art and Design

Published by the Art Directors Club, Inc.
488 Madison Avenue, New York, N.Y. 10022
I.S.B.N. 0-916800-20-2
United States Trade Distribution by
Louis J. Martin Associates
95 Madison Avenue, New York, N.Y.

Contents

The Gold Awards

Newspaper Advertising

Newspaper Editorial

Magazine Advertising

Magazine Editorial

Promotion & Graphic Design

Posters

Books & Jackets

Art & Illustration

Photography

Television

Hall of Fame

Club Activities

Index

Gold
Awards

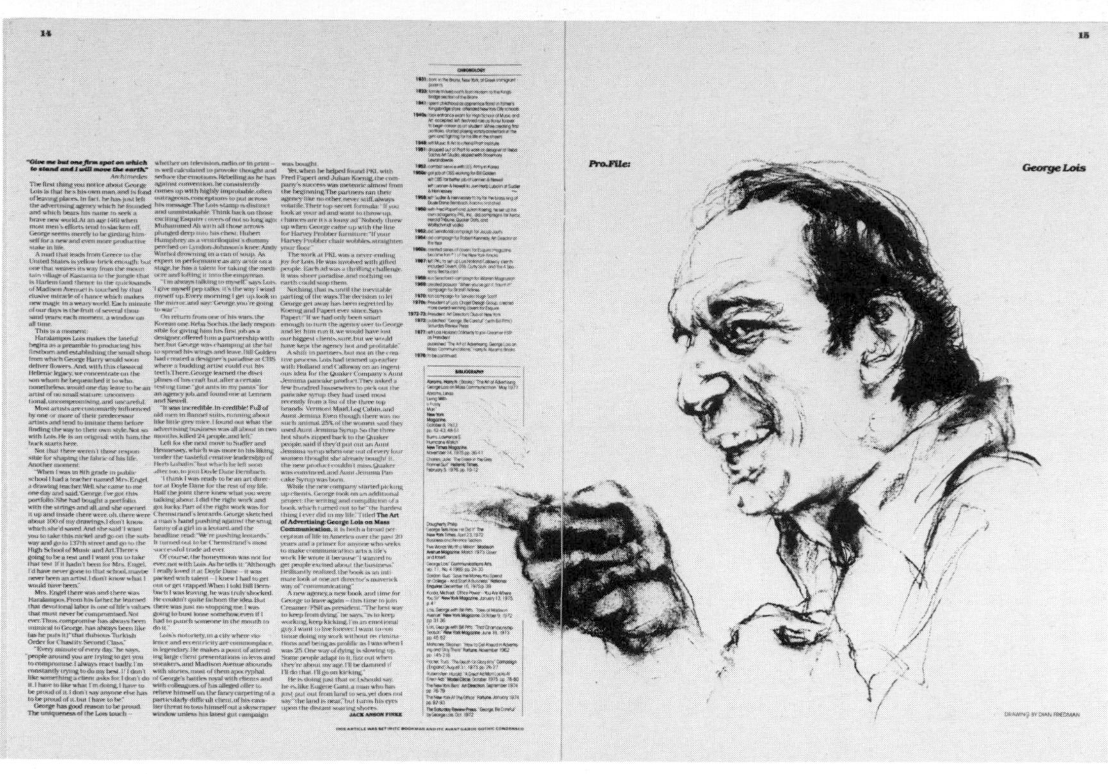

14 15

Pro.File: George Lois

"Give me but one firm spot on which to stand and I will move the earth."
Archimedes

JACK ANSON FINKE

DRAWING BY DIAN FRIEDMAN

10 11

Pro.File: Paul Rand

DRAWING BY DIAN FRIEDMAN

GERTRUDE SNYDER

346

Art Director	Herb Lubalin
Writers	Jack Anson Finke
	Gertrude Snyder
Designer	Herb Lubalin
Artist	Dian Friedman
Publisher	International Typeface Corp.
Agency	LSC&P Design Group
Client	International Typeface Corp.

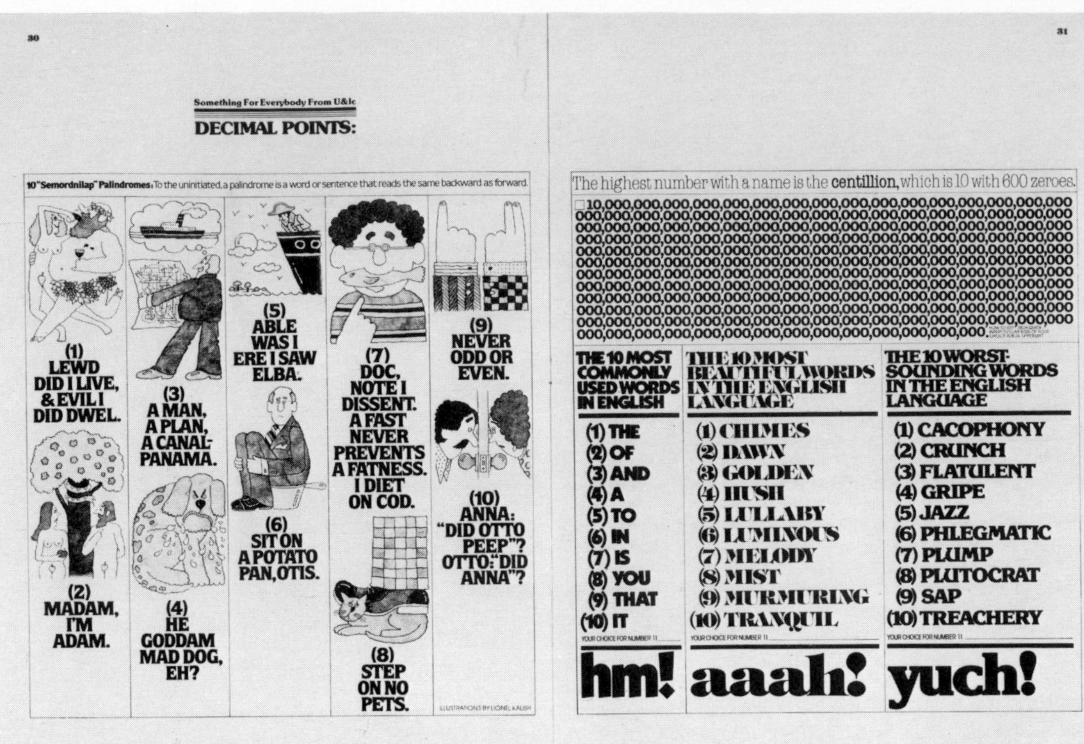

30

Something For Everybody From U&lc

DECIMAL POINTS:

10 "Semordnilap" Palindromes: To the uninitiated, a palindrome is a word or sentence that reads the same backward as forward.

(1) LEWD DID I LIVE, & EVIL I DID DWEL.

(2) MADAM, I'M ADAM.

(3) A MAN, A PLAN, A CANAL-PANAMA.

(4) HE GODDAM MAD DOG, EH?

(5) ABLE WAS I ERE I SAW ELBA.

(6) SIT ON A POTATO PAN, OTIS.

(7) DOC, NOTE I DISSENT. A FAST NEVER PREVENTS A FATNESS. I DIET ON COD.

(8) STEP ON NO PETS.

(9) NEVER ODD OR EVEN.

(10) ANNA: "DID OTTO PEEP"? OTTO: "DID ANNA"?

ILLUSTRATIONS BY LIONEL KALISH

31

The highest number with a name is the **centillion**, which is 10 with 600 zeroes.

THE 10 MOST COMMONLY USED WORDS IN ENGLISH	THE 10 MOST BEAUTIFUL WORDS IN THE ENGLISH LANGUAGE	THE 10 WORST-SOUNDING WORDS IN THE ENGLISH LANGUAGE
(1) THE	(1) CHIMES	(1) CACOPHONY
(2) OF	(2) DAWN	(2) CRUNCH
(3) AND	(3) GOLDEN	(3) FLATULENT
(4) A	(4) HUSH	(4) GRIPE
(5) TO	(5) LULLABY	(5) JAZZ
(6) IN	(6) LUMINOUS	(6) PHLEGMATIC
(7) IS	(7) MELODY	(7) PLUMP
(8) YOU	(8) MIST	(8) PLUTOCRAT
(9) THAT	(9) MURMURING	(9) SAP
(10) IT	(10) TRANQUIL	(10) TREACHERY
YOUR CHOICE FOR NUMBER 11	YOUR CHOICE FOR NUMBER 11	YOUR CHOICE FOR NUMBER 11
hm!	aaah!	yuch!

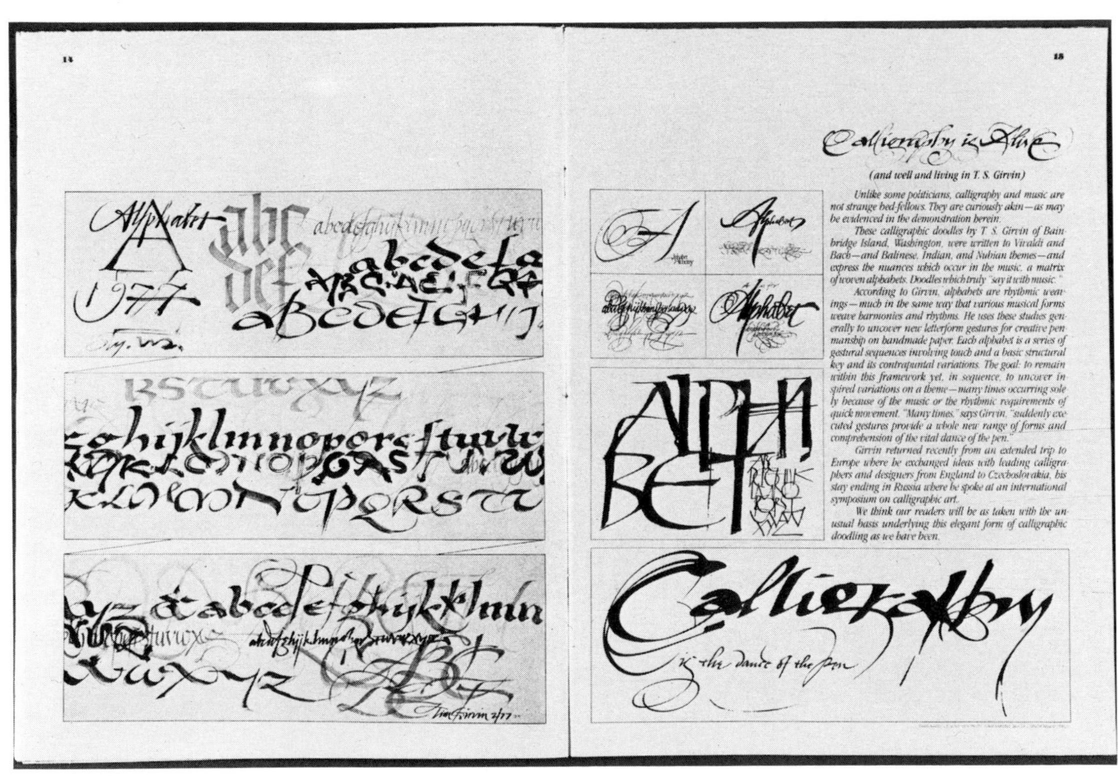

14

15

Calligraphy is Alive

(and well and living in T. S. Girvin)

Unlike some politicians, calligraphy and music are not strange bed-fellows. They are curiously akin—as may be evidenced in the demonstration herein.

These calligraphic doodles by T. S. Girvin of Bainbridge Island, Washington, were written to Vivaldi and Bach—and Balinese, Indian, and Nubian themes—and express the nuances which occur in the music, a matrix of woven alphabets. Doodles which truly "say it with music."

According to Girvin, alphabets are rhythmic weavings—much in the same way that various musical forms weave harmonies and rhythms. He uses these studies generally to uncover new letterform gestures for creative penmanship on handmade paper. Each alphabet is a series of gestural sequences involving touch and a basic structural key and its contrapuntal variations. The goal: to remain within this framework yet, in sequence, to uncover inspired variations on a theme—many times occurring solely because of the music or the rhythmic requirements of quick movement. "Many times," says Girvin, "suddenly executed gestures provide a whole new range of forms and comprehension of the vital dance of the pen."

Girvin returned recently from an extended trip to Europe where he exchanged ideas with leading calligraphers and designers from England to Czechoslovakia, his stay ending in Russia where he spoke at an international symposium on calligraphic art.

We think our readers will be as taken with the unusual basis underlying this elegant form of calligraphic doodling as we have been.

504

Art Director Herb Lubalin
Writers Herb Lubalin
Jack Anson Finke
Gertrude Snyder
Designer Herb Lubalin
Agency LSC&P Design Group
Client International Typeface Corp.

1062

Art Director Bob Engel
Writer Charlie Ryant
Director Bob Giraldi
Agency Producer Bob Engel
Production Company Bob Giraldi Productions
Agency McCann-Erickson, Inc.
Client Miller Lite (Miller Brewing Co.)

1156

Art Director John Plucinski
Writer Mara Blum
Director Bob Giraldi
Agency Producer Angelo Antonucci
Music Lucas-McFaul
Production Company Bob Giraldi Productions
Agency Leo Burnett, Inc.
Client Royal Crown Cola

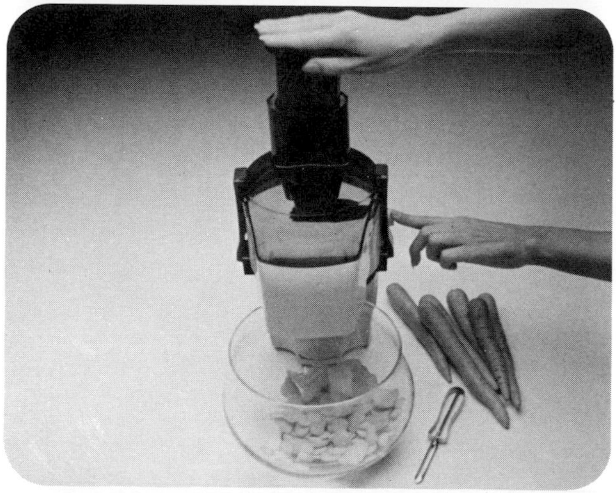

1165

Art Director	Joe Sedelmaier
Writer	Jeff B. Gorman
Editors	Peggy De Lay
	Henry Hoda
Director/Cinematographer	Joe Sedelmaier
Production Company	Sedelmaier Film Productions
Agency	Marketing Communications International
Client	Moulinex/La Machine

1167

Art Directors	Bob Ryzner (Elmo & Neato)
	Jeff Whitchel (Butter Pecan)
Writers	Jean Zerries (Elmo & Neato)
	Harold Kaplan (Butter Pecan)
Producers	Ted Storb (Elmo & Neato)
	Ed Pollack (Butter Pecan)
Production Company	Bianchi
Agency	Young & Rubicam
Client	General Foods/Jell-O Pudding

1194

Art Director	Robert Lenz
Writer	Robert Meury
Director	Bob Gaffney
Producers	Linda Mevorach
	Sally Smith
Production Company	Bob Gaffney Productions
Agency	McCann-Erickson, Inc.
Client	Miller Brewing Company

290

Art Director Noel Werrett
Writer Tony Jones
Designers Noel Werrett
Bart Drury
Publisher Ambassador International
Cultural Foundation
Client Quest/77

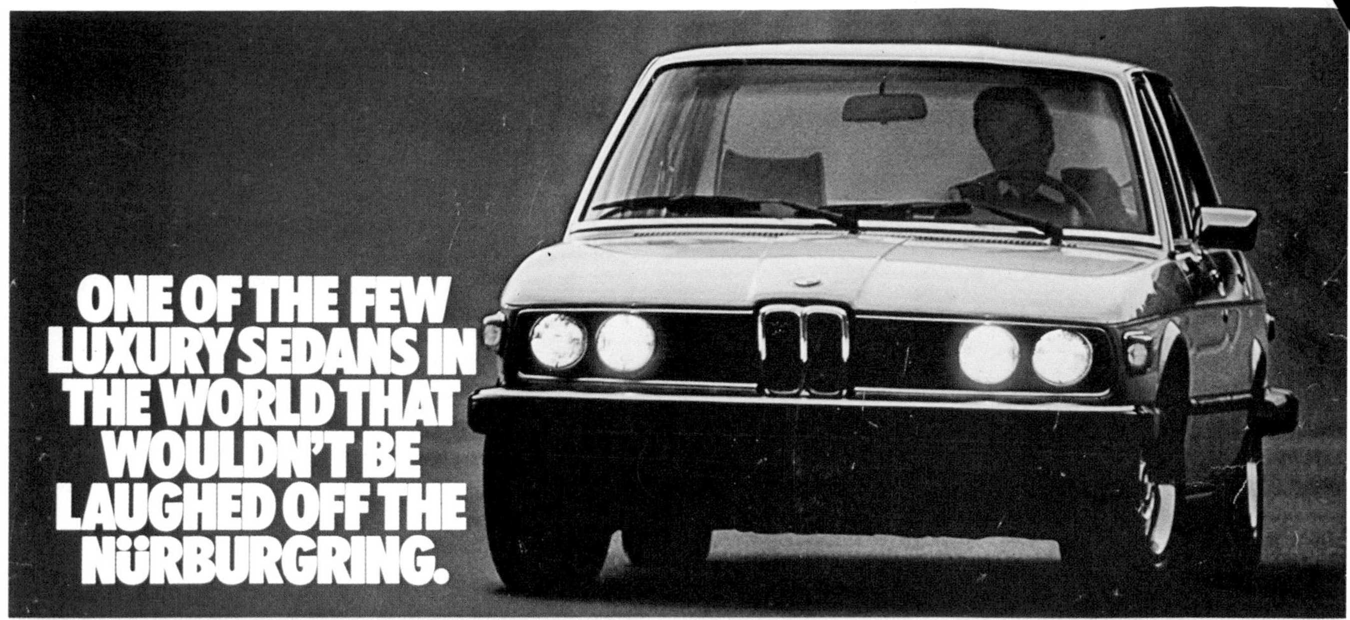
ONE OF THE FEW LUXURY SEDANS IN THE WORLD THAT WOULDN'T BE LAUGHED OFF THE NÜRBURGRING.
In the heart of Germany there is a race course called the Nurburgring.
An awesome giant of a track, generally acknowledged to be the most arduous test of both cars and men.
All of the world's great high-performance cars have raced there—most have had their day.
Yet, few cars—and certainly no luxury sedans—have achieved a more impressive record on the Nurburgring than those built by the Bavarian Motor Works of Munich, Germany.
Luxury sedans? Yes. But luxury sedans built by racing engineers. German engineers who believe that extraordinary performance is the only thing that makes an expensive car worth the money.
PERFORMANCE PERFECTED ON THE RACE TRACK
While it is, of course, feasible to develop an acceptable automobile in the relative vacuum of the test track and the laboratory, it is virtually impossible to simulate the perfection demanded by motor racing.
Motor racing enables BMW engineers to develop ideas and experiment without the inhibiting constraints of economics or the cost of production—a crucial role in the development of a true high-performance automobile.
And the BMW 530i is a direct reflection of this cache of engineering intelligence.
Its suspension—independent on all four wheels—is quick and clean through the corners; its steering sharp and accurate.
Its four-speed manual transmission (automatic is available) slips precisely into each gear. And its acceleration comes up smoothly, with the turbine-like whine so characteristic of the justifiably renowned 3-liter BMW engine.
PARTICIPATION NOT ISOLATION
The interior of the conventional luxury sedan is deliberately engineered to isolate the driver from the mechanical workings of the automobile, the world outside and the road beneath.
The interior of the BMW 530i is carefully engineered to include the driver as one of the integral, functioning parts of the car itself—the human part that completes the mechanical circuit.
Careful study has been made of the critical interrelation between seat location, visual position, steering wheel, pedals and controls.
Luxurious? Yes. Yet all functions have been assiduously planned to facilitate total, precise control at all times, under all conditions.
So successful is this integration of man and machine that when you drive the BMW 530i for the first time, you will experience an almost total oneness with the car. A unique feeling of effortless control which, if you're accustomed to conventional luxury sedans, will be completely and pleasantly new to you.
Surprising? Only to those who have never driven a BMW.
As the editors of Motor Trend magazine observed, "The reaction to a BMW is always the same. The first time driver takes the wheel and after a few minutes no other automobile will ever be the same again."
If the thought of owning such a car intrigues you, call us anytime, toll-free, at 800-243-6000 (Conn. 1-800-882-6500) and we'll arrange a thorough test drive for you at your convenience.
B M W
THE ULTIMATE DRIVING MACHINE.
Bavarian Motor Works, Munich, Germany
© 1977 BMW of North America, Inc.

73

Art Director Clem McCarthy
Writer Martin Puris
Photographers Dick James
David Thorpe
Agency Ammirati Puris AvRutick
Client BMW of North America, Inc.

A TEST DRIVE ONLY
A BMW DEALER WOULD HAVE
THE NERVE TO SUGGEST.

The BMW 530i is a luxury sedan designed by racing engineers—and perfected in places like Le Mans, Monte Carlo and the Nurburgring.

A car built to be driven on high-speed autobahns and over the tortuous roads of the Bavarian Alps.

So, while the conventional once-around-the-block test drive is perhaps ideally suited to the performance capabilities of the conventional luxury sedan, in the case of the BMW 530i, we suggest you consider something a bit more challenging.

THE INNER-CITY-SLALOM.

What better place to test the extraordinary handling characteristics of the BMW than the streets of the city.

As you weave nimbly through traffic and around the potholes, you will discover that the suspension of the 530i—independent on all four wheels—is quick and clean through the corners; its steering sharp and accurate.

THE TURNPIKE SPRINT.

As you no doubt know, turnpike traffic pauses for no man. Surely, one could ask for no more valid test of acceleration than attempting to enter one. And when you press the accelerator of the BMW 530i, you will note that the three-liter, L-Jetronic, fuel-injected engine—the same basic engine that powers the BMW race cars—responds instantly. Without the nerve-jangling lag one experiences in the average four-door luxury sedan.

THE PANIC STOP.

When one drives, inevitably, one is faced with a situation that calls for rapid braking—our third and final test.

If you're accustomed to conventional braking systems, you'll find the front-vented, four-wheel power disc-braking system of the BMW 530i most reassuring. Particularly its ability to come to a complete, rapid stop in a straight line, time after time, with a minimum amount of brake fade and wheel pull.

IF YOU'RE GAME, WE'RE GAME.

The editors of Motor Trend magazine once observed, "The reaction to a BMW is always the same. The first time driver takes the wheel and after a few minutes no other automobile will ever be the same again."

If you'd care to test drive the BMW 530i for yourself, simply phone your BMW dealer and he'll arrange a thorough test drive for you at your convenience.

BMW

THE ULTIMATE DRIVING MACHINE.

Bavarian Motor Works, Munich, Germany.

73

Art Director Clem McCarthy
Writer Martin Puris
Photographers Dick James
David Thorpe
Agency Ammirati Puris AvRutick
Client BMW of North America, Inc.

MAYBE YOU WOULDN'T BE SO ANXIOUS TO TRADE IN YOUR PRESENT CAR IF YOU ACTUALLY ENJOYED DRIVING IT.

If one can judge from the plethora of "late model", "hardly driven" luxury sedans that grace the used car lots of America, it would seem that the average American's love affair with his car is surprisingly brief.

Social observers may well attribute this curious phenomenon to some sort of inate fickleness.

We at the Bavarian Motor Works, however, choose to point our finger in another direction.

Put as charitably as possible, the majority of the world's luxury cars—while lacking nothing in the area of luxury—are considerably lacking in the area of performance.

The one thing, in our view, that makes an expensive car worth the money.

WHY PEOPLE WHO OWN A BMW ENJOY DRIVING MORE THAN YOU DO.

While the BMW 530i provides all the creature comforts one could sanely require of an automobile, it also provides a driving experience so unusual, so exhilarating, that people who have never before enjoyed driving find themselves seeking out long sweeping curves and twisting back roads.

Its acceleration comes up smoothly—with the turbine-like whine characteristic of the renowned 3-liter, fuel-injected BMW engine.

Its four-speed transmission (automatic transmission is available) slips precisely into each gear.

Its suspension—independent on all four wheels—is quick and clean through the corners; its steering sharp and accurate.

And on the inside, where the average luxury sedan leans heavily toward the frivolous, the BMW 530i has been biomechanically engineered to facilitate total, precise control at all times, under all conditions.

Actually designed to include the driver as an integral, functioning part of the mechanical workings of the car itself.

All seats are orthopedically molded; front seats infinitely adjustable. Controls are within easy reach and all instruments are instantly visible.

So successfully is all this accomplished that one automotive expert wrote "...the 530i does so much so well we are hard pressed to think of a car that can even come close to matching it".

If the thought of owning such a car intrigues you, call us anytime, toll-free, at 800-243-6000 (Conn. 1-800-882-6500) and we'll arrange a thorough test drive for you at your convenience.

B M W

THE ULTIMATE DRIVING MACHINE.
Bavarian Motor Works, Munich, Germany.

161

Art Director Clem McCarthy
Writer Martin Puris
Photographers Dick James
David Thorpe
Agency Ammirati Puris AvRutick Inc.
Client BMW of North America, Inc.

THE BMW COUPE. AS CLOSE TO AN ALL-OUT RACING MACHINE AS A PASSENGER CAR SHOULD EVER COME.

If one peers beneath the sporty facade of even the most expensive luxury coupes, one often finds that the promise of performance far exceeds the reality.

In the case of the new BMW 630CSi, the opposite is true.

Beneath its tastefully restrained exterior, the BMW Coupe is, in fact, the direct evolutionary descendant of the BMW Coupes that have dominated international motor racing since the early 1960's.

A car that exemplifies our contention that extraordinary performance is the one thing that makes an expensive car worth the money.

PERFECTED ON THE RACE TRACK, NOT MERELY THE TEST TRACK.

The majority of the world's automobiles are developed in the relative vacuum of the laboratory and the test track.

The BMW is perfected in places like Le Mans, Monte Carlo and the Nürburgring, where precision is crucial and agility and durability meet their ultimate test.

Under the hood of the BMW 630CSi is the same basic three-liter, fuel-injected masterpiece of engineering that powers the BMW race cars.

An awesome source of turbine-smooth power that the editors of Road & Track magazine unhesitatingly call "...the most refined in-line six in the world."

Its suspension system is independent on all four wheels (McPherson struts and coil springs in front, semi-trailing arms and coil springs in back). And this, combined with a multi-jointed rear axle, provides a total control, an effortless response to every driving and road condition that will spoil you for any other car.

LOGIC CLEVERLY COUCHED IN LUXURY.

"...once a knowledgeable and experienced driver has driven a BMW, any BMW, nothing else feels quite as good as it did before." So writes Motor Trend magazine.

Part of the explanation for this phenomenon lies inside the car.

Traditionally the domain of the stylist, the interior of the BMW 630CSi—while richly upholstered in supple leathers—is ergonomically engineered to the nth degree.

All seats are orthopedically molded; all individual seats are infinitely adjustable. Controls are within easy reach and all instruments are instantly visible in an innovative three-zone control panel that curves out toward the driver in the manner of an airplane cockpit.

So thorough is the integration of human and machine that the driver literally functions as one of the car's working parts—the human part that completes the mechanical circuit.

Intriguing? "...my feeling goes beyond mere respect...," writes the European automobile journal, Car, of the BMW Coupe.

"This one, for me, is the definitive BMW, the epitome of the character that the Bavarian company set out to develop and to market."

If you'd care to judge for yourself, we suggest that you telephone your BMW dealer and arrange to take a thorough test drive.

THE ULTIMATE DRIVING MACHINE.
Bavarian Motor Works, Munich, Germany

161

Art Director Clem McCarthy
Writer Martin Puris
Photographers Dick James
David Thorpe
Agency Ammirati Puris AvRutick Inc.
Client BMW of North America, Inc.

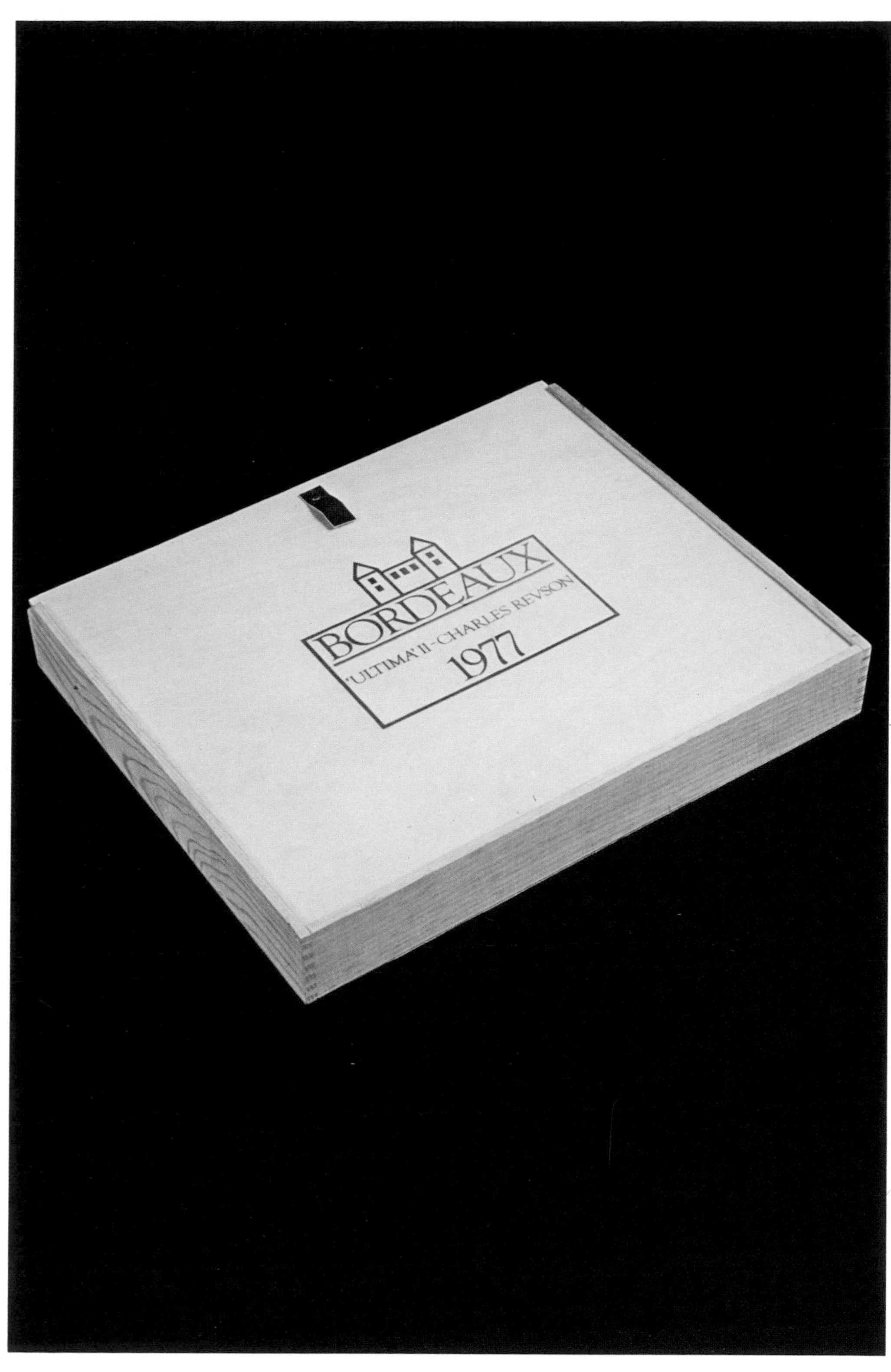

453

Art Director	David M. Griffing
Writer	Sandi Burrows
Artist	Richard Giglio
Photographers	Dan Wynn
	Joel Brodsky
Agency	Revlon, Inc.
Client	Revlon, Inc.

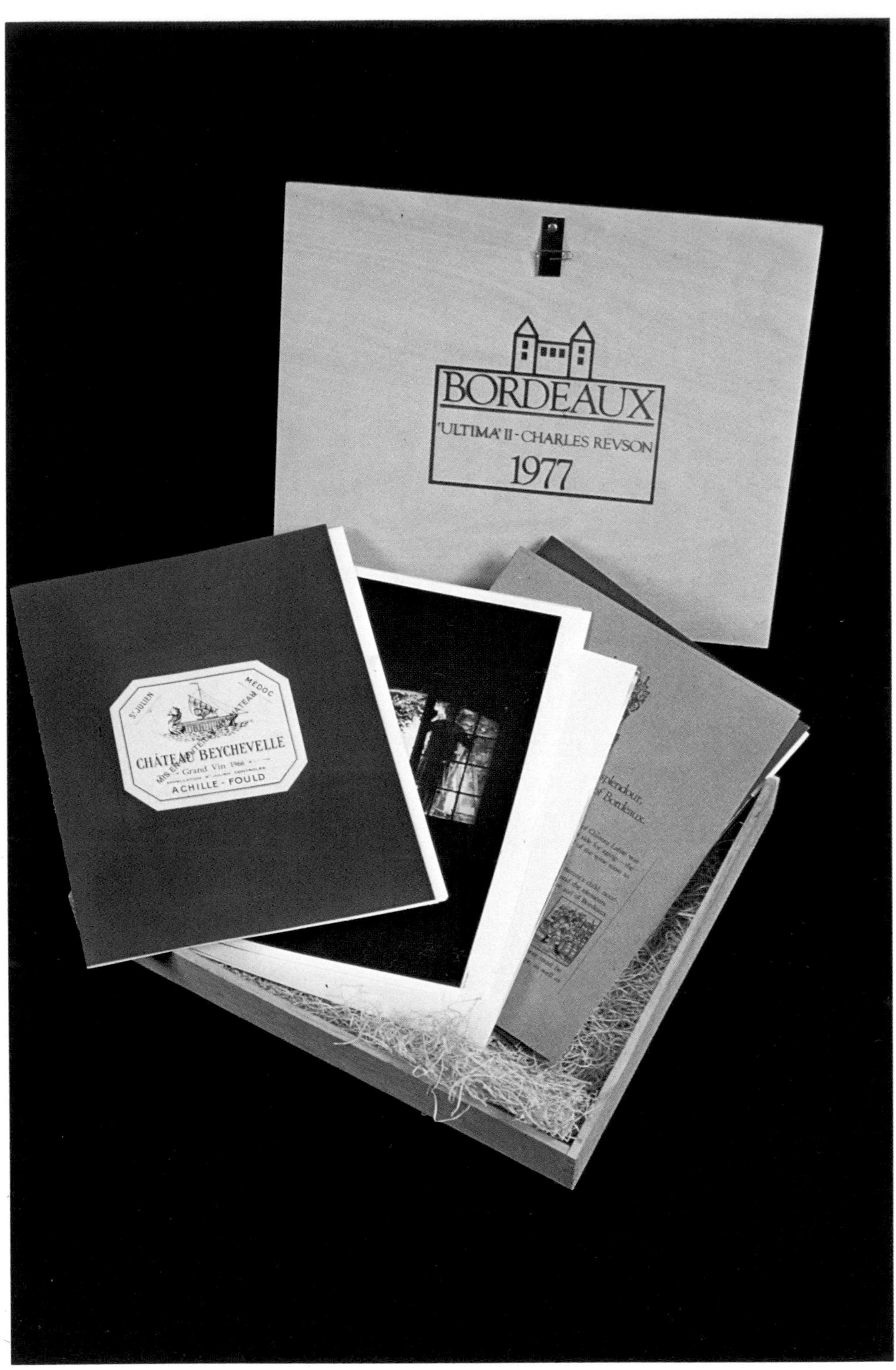

453

Art Director	David M. Griffing
Writer	Sandi Burrows
Artist	Richard Giglio
Photographers	Dan Wynn
	Joel Brodsky
Agency	Revlon, Inc.
Client	Revlon, Inc.

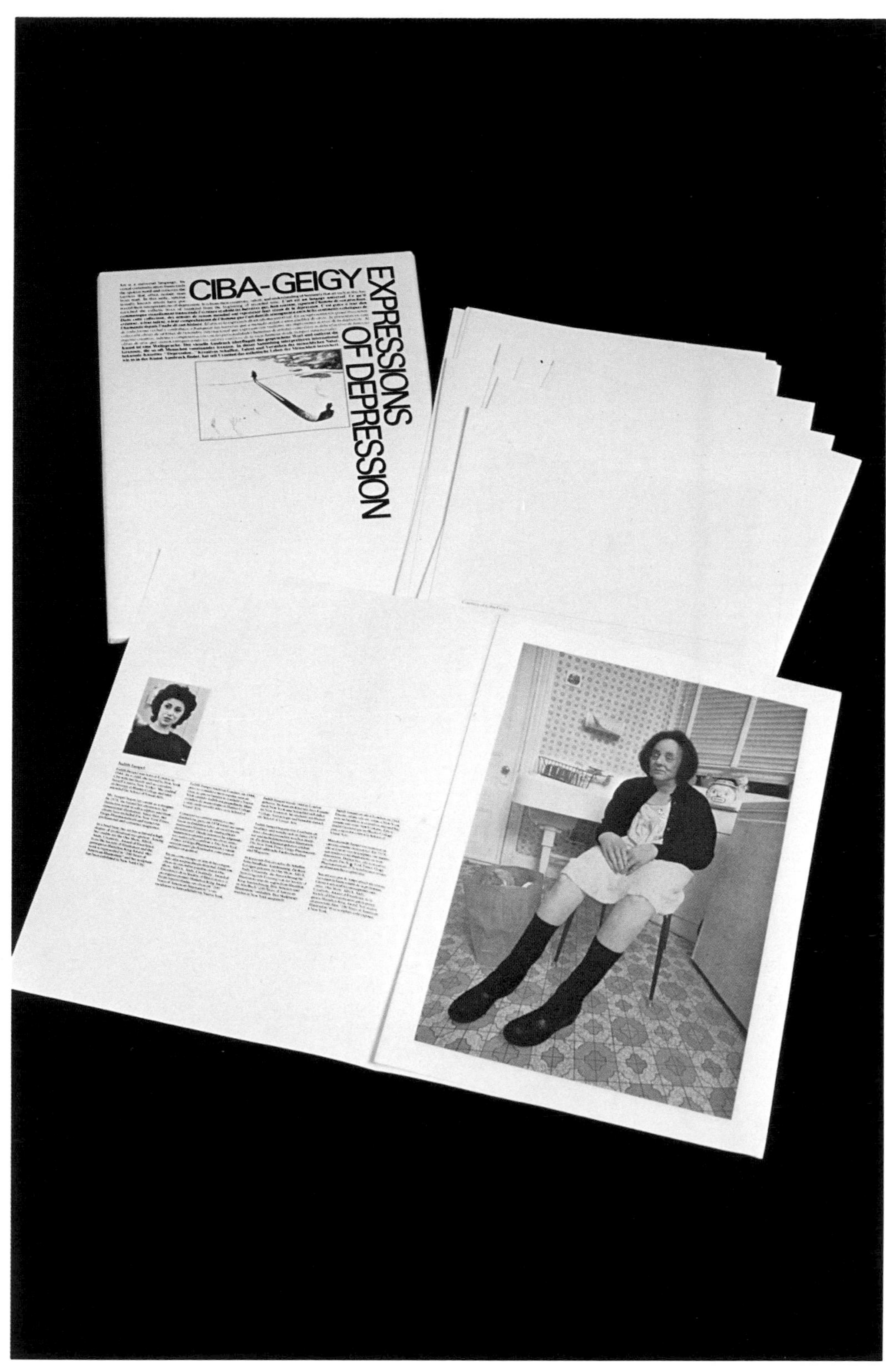

594
Art Director John deCesare
Designer John deCesare
Client Ciba-Geigy Corporation

COUPLES
NOW. THE COUPLE TAKES ITS RIGHTFUL PLACE IN THE SUN.

855

Art Directors	Alan Murphy Heather Cooper
Designers	Heather Cooper Lawrence Finn
Artist	Heather Cooper
Agency	Alan Murphy & Associates
Client	Couples Hotel—Jamaica

THE ART AND POLITICS OF
GEOFFREY MOSS

With a Foreword by Dan Rather

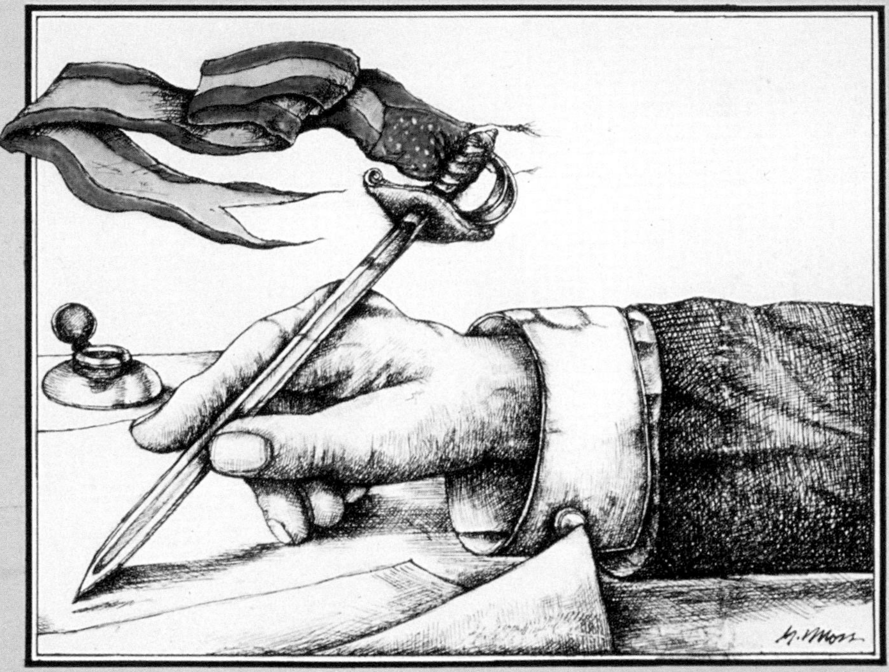

A Washington Post Book

933

Art Director	Geoffrey Moss
Editor	Sandra Choron
Designer	Stanley Drate
Artist	Geoffrey Moss
Publisher	Hawthorn Books Inc.
Client	Hawthorn Books Inc.

933

Art Director Geoffrey Moss
Editor Sandra Choron
Designer Stanley Drate
Artist Geoffrey Moss
Publisher Hawthorn Books Inc.
Client Hawthorn Books Inc.

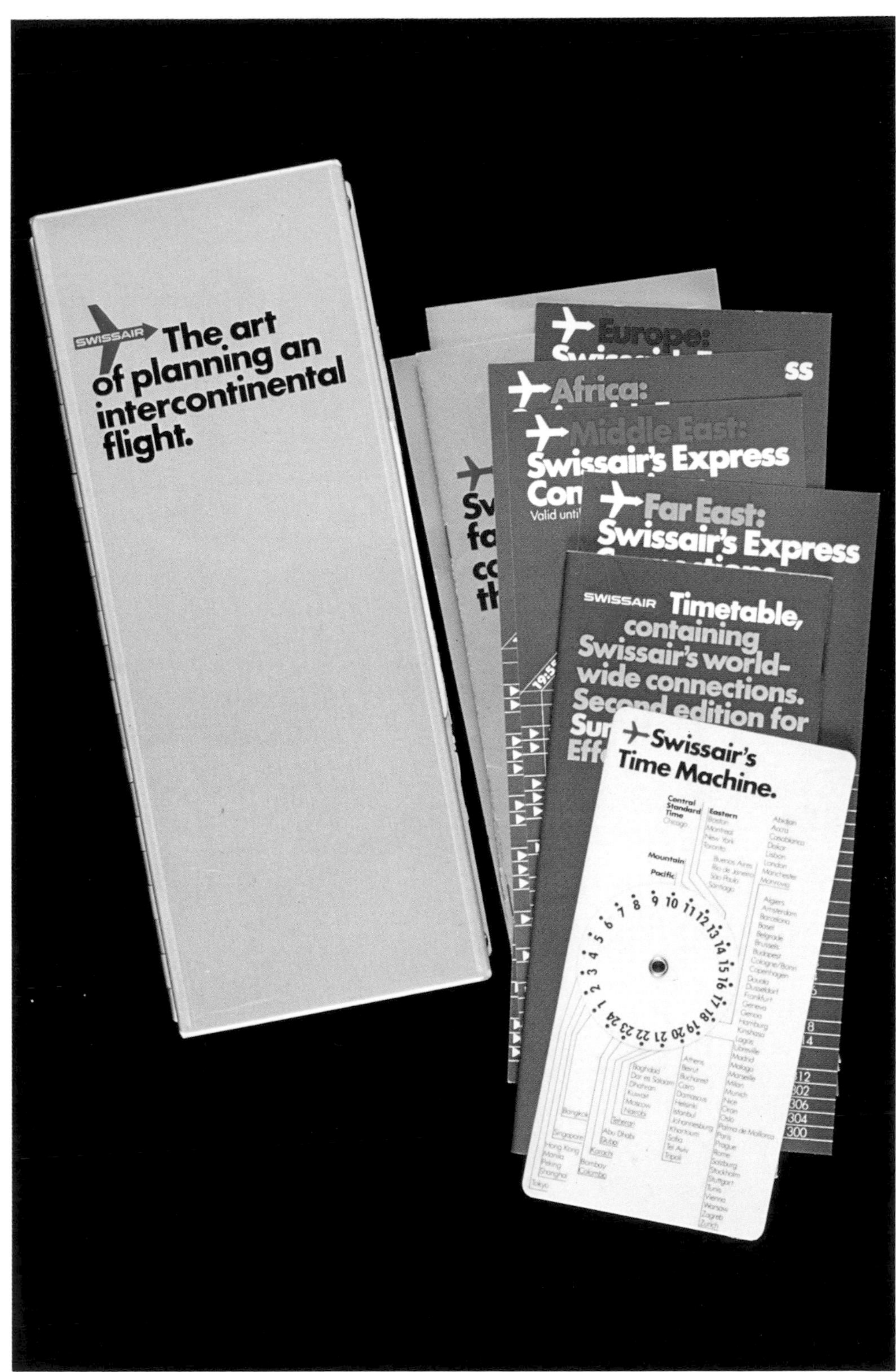

511

Art Director Christine Sauers
Writers Wolf Rogosky
Phil Becker
Agency GGK America, Ltd.
Client Swissair

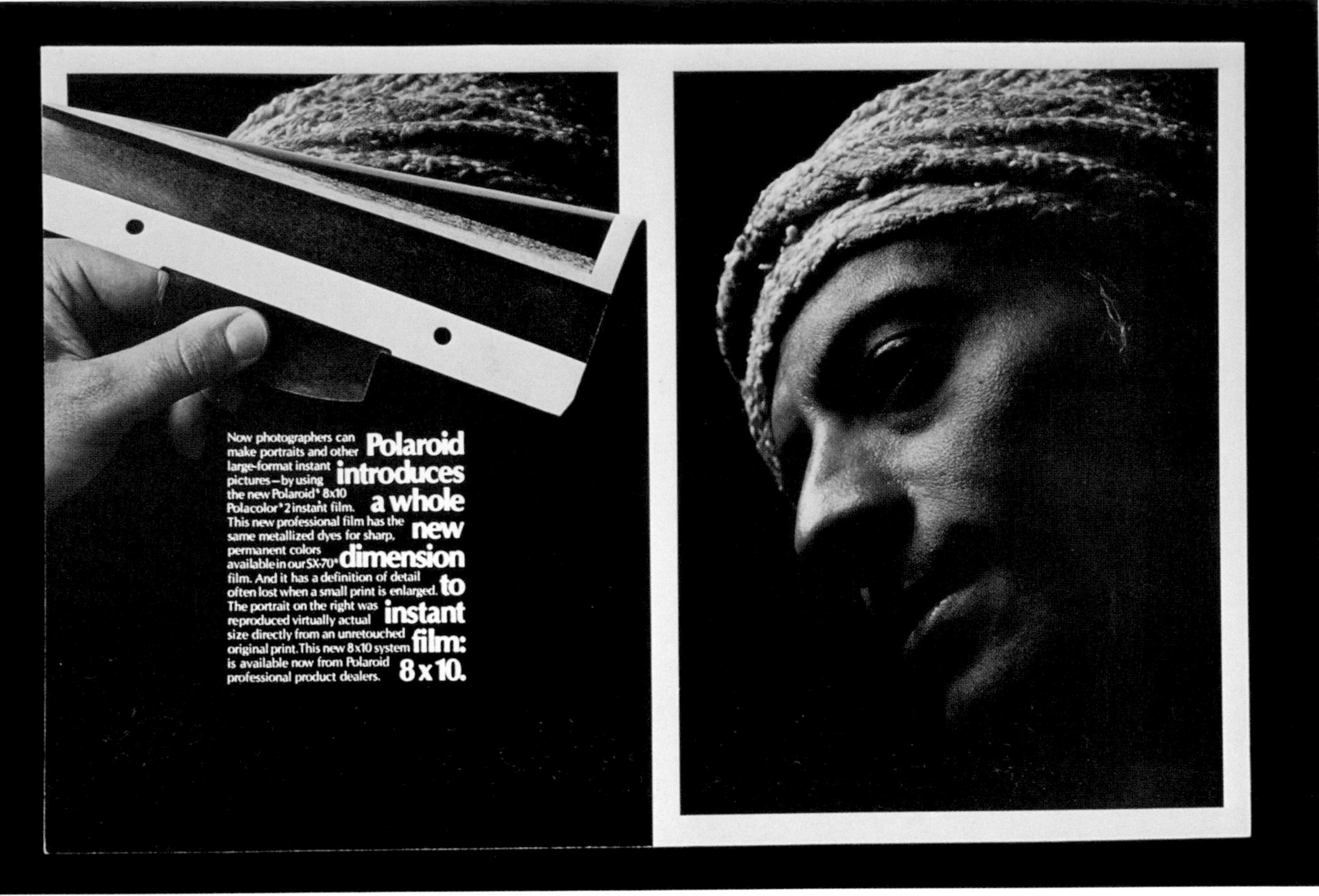

Polaroid introduces a whole new dimension to instant film: 8 x 10.
Now photographers can make portraits and other large-format instant pictures—by using the new Polaroid* 8x10 Polacolor* 2 instant film. This new professional film has the same metallized dyes for sharp, permanent colors available in our SX-70* film. And it has a definition of detail often lost when a small print is enlarged. The portrait on the right was reproduced virtually actual size directly from an unretouched original print. This new 8x10 system is available now from Polaroid professional product dealers.

147

Art Director Helmut Krone
Writers Ed Smith
George Rike
Photographer Carl Fischer
Agency Doyle Dane Bernbach
Client Polaroid

934

Art Directors	Marilyn Hoffner	Edmond Casarella	Milton Glaser
	Albert Greenberg	Remy Charlip	Dimitri Hadzi
Writer	Marilyn Hoffner	Seymour Chwast	Lionel Kalish
Designers	Marilyn Hoffner	Ray Cruz	Alex Katz
	Albert Greenberg	Lillian Delevoryas	William King
Artists	John Alcorn	Lois Dodd	R. B. Kitaj
	Harold Altman	Lou Donato	Lee Krasner
	Al Blaustein	Audrey Flack	George Leavitt
	Tom Boutis	Gerry Gersten	Herb Lubalin
	Gretna Campbell	Gregory Gillespie	Richard Lytle

NOV
GREGORY GILLESPIE has been included in all of the Whitney Museum Annuals and is in the collections of the Whitney, Hirshhorn Museum, Georgia Museum of Art, N.J. State Museum and others. In 1977 his sixth one-man exhibition was held at Forum Gallery, as well as a one-man retrospective exhibit at the Hirshhorn Museum. He is the recipient of a Fulbright, Prix de Rome, Medaglio d'Oro and other awards.
Sunday
November 5
Monday
November 6
Tuesday
November 7
ELECTION DAY
Wednesday
November 8
Thursday
November 9
Friday
November 10
Saturday
November 11
LANDSCAPE WITH BIRCH TREES, mixed media, courtesy Forum Gallery

934

Peppino Mangravite
Kenneth Munowitz
Norman Narotzky
William Negron
Elliot Offner
Clare Romano
Richard Rosenblum
John Ross
Reynold Ruffing
George Segal

Alan, Arthur & Judy Singer
Robert Slutzky
Ed Sorel
Raphael Soyer
Simms Taback
Louis Trakis
Gary Viskupic
Hilde Weingarten
Tom Wesselmann
Christopher Wilmarth

Photographers Carl Fischer
Norman Griner
Art Kane
Jay Maisel
Irving Schild
Neal Slavin
Ben Swedervsky

Publisher The Cooper Union Alumni Association
Client Cooper Union

277

Art Director Emma Landau
Writer Elinor Reichlin
Designer Emma Landau
Credit The President and Fellows of Harvard College, Peabody Museum, Harvard University
Publisher American Heritage Publishing Co.

430

Art Directors David November
Ed Sobel
Writer Peter Moreau
Designers Ed Sobel
David November
Photographers Jerry Darvin
Pete Mecca
Mel DiGiaccomo
Agency CBS Entertainment Division/Advertising and Promotion
Client CBS Television Network

Newspaper Advertising

Insuring Complex Risks

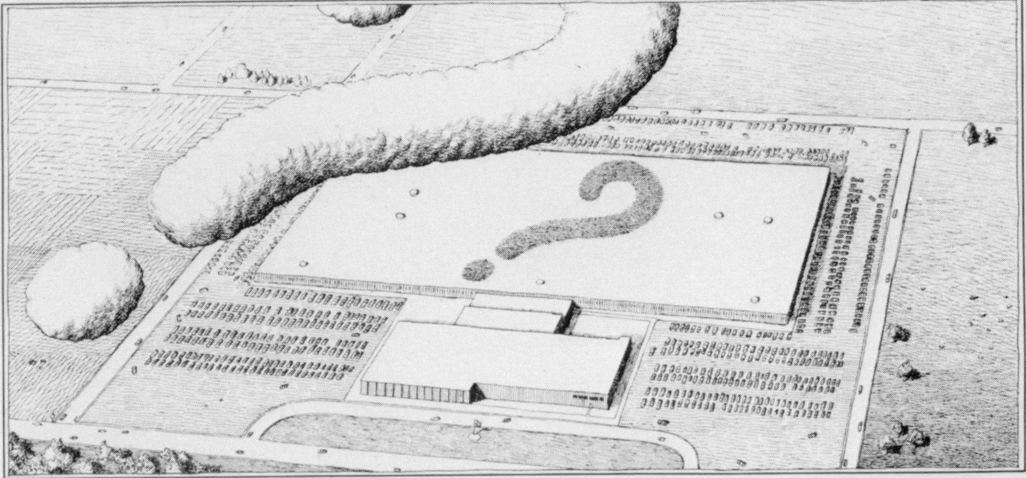

By any standard, today's business organizations are more complex and have more difficult-to-meet insurance needs than at any time in the past.

Typically, a modern company offers a variety of products and services, with a number of offices, factories and warehouses at widely separated locations. Its markets are international and its distribution patterns complex. Its exposures to risk of loss are correspondingly widespread.

For some firms, the dollar magnitude of potential losses can have a significant impact on corporate profitability, and the mounting cost and complexity of insurance coverage has reached the point where it can add substantially to the cost of doing business.

Under these circumstances, corporate risk managers and financial executives are seeking new alternatives in structuring programs to protect their companies' assets.

The importance of risk retention

In today's markets, insurance coverage often hinges upon the retention by the insured of some part of the risks involved—whether through high deductibles or outright self-insurance. Many companies find that the higher cost of insurance in itself justifies increased risk retention. Determining what part of what risks might be self-insured is one of the most important single moves a company can make toward efficient overall protection.

Those risks with high loss frequency but low severity are good candidates for partial or complete retention. The company's capacity to finance risk retention must be considered in every case, with large exposures above certain limits often placed with an insurance carrier.

Any program of risk retention should also make provision for the services usually furnished with insurance coverage. They include loss control, claims handling, record keeping, rehabilitation, salvage and subrogation (the right of the company to succeed to a claimant's rights after satisfying the claims). Such services, which may be financed through funds saved on premium payments, can be furnished internally or provided by an outside supplier.

Confronted with increasingly complicated risks and exposures, together with a rise in insurance costs, business organizations today are seeking new approaches to insuring their assets.

A brief review by INA of an insurance topic of interest to business executives.

If a corporation is able to handle sizable risks, it might also consider the formation of a company-owned "captive" insurance or reinsurance company, with services provided in part from the outside.

A comprehensive approach

The range of corporate insurance needs frequently includes both standard risks, for which insurance usually can be readily obtained, and high risks, which can be more difficult to place. Generally speaking, a company with a wide range of risks might find it advantageous to treat all of its exposures together. Working through an insurance broker or agent, the company can then approach insurance carriers with a comprehensive picture of its overall needs and invite them to propose solutions that best fit the firm's requirements.

This could result in all coverages being placed with the insurer that offers the best proposal.

Alternatively, the difficult-to-place risks may have to be handled by "layering"—placing coverages in layers with different carriers. In unusual high-risk situations, all or part of the coverages may have to be placed with surplus lines or excess lines carriers.

Many firms face complex alternatives in meeting their insurance needs. Comprehensive analysis of all available options by risk managers and financial executives, working closely with agents and brokers and the insurance companies they represent, can generate the most cost-effective solutions.

As an objective discussion of the insurance needs of business today, INA has prepared a booklet entitled, "Insuring Complex Risks: Some Professional Considerations." Copies may be requested by writing INA Corporation, 1600 Arch Street, Philadelphia, Pa. 19101.

* * *

The Insurance Company of North America was founded in Independence Hall, Philadelphia, in 1792. Today INA and its affiliated companies operate around the world with major interests in property and casualty insurance, marine and aviation insurance, life and group insurance, reinsurance and risk management services.

INA insurance products and services are made available through selected independent agents and brokers—professionals with a comprehensive knowledge of insurance needs and solutions.

Insurance Professionals

1

1

Art Director Richard Kline
Writer John Jackson
Designer Richard Kline
Artist Mel Furukawa
Agency Geer, DuBois Inc.
Client INA (The Insurance Company of North America)

OROWEAT
Bran'nola
a natural food fiber bread
OROWEAT
Bran'nola
natural food fiber muffins
WHAT MAKES BRAN'NOLA BREAD AND MUFFINS SO UNCOMMONLY GOOD-TASTING? THE INGREDIENTS THEY HAVE IN COMMON.

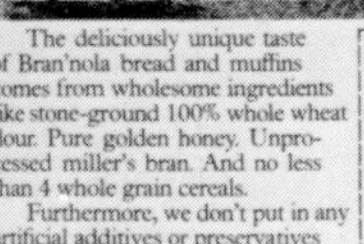

The deliciously unique taste of Bran'nola bread and muffins comes from wholesome ingredients like stone-ground 100% whole wheat flour. Pure golden honey. Unprocessed miller's bran. And no less than 4 whole grain cereals.
Furthermore, we don't put in any artificial additives or preservatives which would take away from the delicious effect, either.

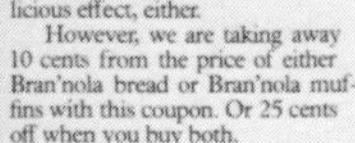

However, we are taking away 10 cents from the price of either Bran'nola bread or Bran'nola muffins with this coupon. Or 25 cents off when you buy both.

10¢ OFF ON OROWEAT BRAN'NOLA BREAD OR MUFFINS. 10¢
25¢
SAVE ON BRAN'NOLA BREAD AND MUFFINS.
STORE COUPON
VOID
10¢
25¢ OFF IF YOU BUY BOTH BRAN'NOLA BREAD AND MUFFINS. 25¢

2

HAPPILY, AMERICAN AIRLINES NOW FLIES TO CLUB MED GUADELOUPE.
UNHAPPILY, WE ALSO FLY BACK.
It's never easy to leave Club Med Guadeloupe.
But it's certainly easy to get there.
Thanks to American Airlines direct flight service to Guadeloupe.
Once you get there you'll find two beautiful Club Med villages. A weeks stay at Caravelle, with its famous Antilles beach, costs as little as $280.* And a week at the smaller, more intimate Fort Royal, with kids mini-club, costs $525.**
And Club Med's prices include many activities that cost extra on other vacations.
For more information about Club Med Guadeloupe call your travel agent. Or fill in the coupon below.
American Airlines to Club Med Guadeloupe. This year enjoy a little rest and relaxation on your way to your vacation.
Name
Address
City State Zip
AMERICAN AIRLINES/ CLUB MED GUADELOUPE

3

2
Art Director Al Colello
Writer W. Weiss
Photographer Robert McCabe
Agency Isidore Lefkowitz Elgort
Client Oroweat Foods Co.

3
Art Director Bob Phillips
Writer Frank Anton
Artist Whistlin Dixie
Agency Levine, Huntley, Schmidt, Plapler & Beaver
Client Club Mediterranee

THE PROFIT MOTIVE BUILT THIS BUILDING. IT ALSO BURNED IT DOWN.

Arson is our fastest growing crime. Its most significant motivation: the dollar, of course.

From people looking for insurance to bail them out from financial difficulties to arson rings that peddle their services to businessmen.

The alarming thing is that the conviction rate for these crimes is abysmally low. (They destroy the evidence along with the building, according to one arson detective.)

Recently, an aroused insurance industry took a very important step to try to improve the poor conviction rate.

It started something called the Property Insurance Loss Register. It's a computerized file which can instantly cross-check policyholders and claimants.

Without going into the mechanics, we can tell you that it will make it infinitely harder for a potential arsonist to collect on the same property from more than one insurance company, set up phony ownerships, falsify claims, or, if he's been successful at arson before, get away with it again.

It's one more effort to control insurance costs. If we're successful, you'll save the money that has been profiting the arsonists.

We'd like to know what you think. Just write our Office of Consumer Information, One Tower Square, Hartford, Conn. 06115. Or dial, toll-free, 800-243-0191. In Connecticut, call collect, 277-6565.

THE TRAVELERS
Raising our voice, not just our rates.

The Travelers Insurance Company, The Travelers Indemnity Company, and Affiliated Companies, Hartford, Conn. 06115.

4

Isn't it about time you learned how to watch the other kind of football?

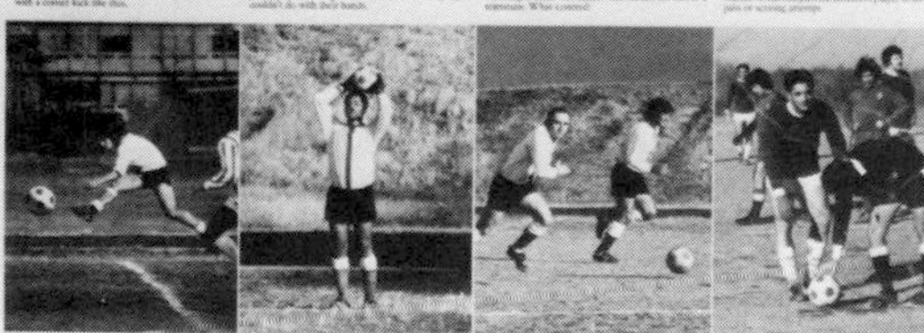

Sports Illustrated
We are sports in print.

5

It's worth hunting for.

Boar's Head
Seen only in the best places.

6

4
Art Director Michael Tesch
Writer Tom Messner
Designer Michael Tesch
Photographer Fire Dept. Files
Agency Ally & Gargano, Inc.
Client The Travelers Insurance Company

5
Art Director Bob Czernysz
Writer Dick Olmsted
Photographer Co Rentmeester
Agency Young & Rubicam
Client Sports Illustrated

6
Art Director Robert Reitzfeld
Writer Dick Jackson
Designer Robert Reitzfeld
Artist Robert Reitzfeld
Photographer Henry Sandbank
Agency Altschiller, Reitzfeld & Jackson, Inc.
Client Boar's Head Provisions

"Have you ever met anybody who actually reads this magazine?"

JOHN H. SWEET, PRESIDENT & PUBLISHER, U.S. NEWS & WORLD REPORT

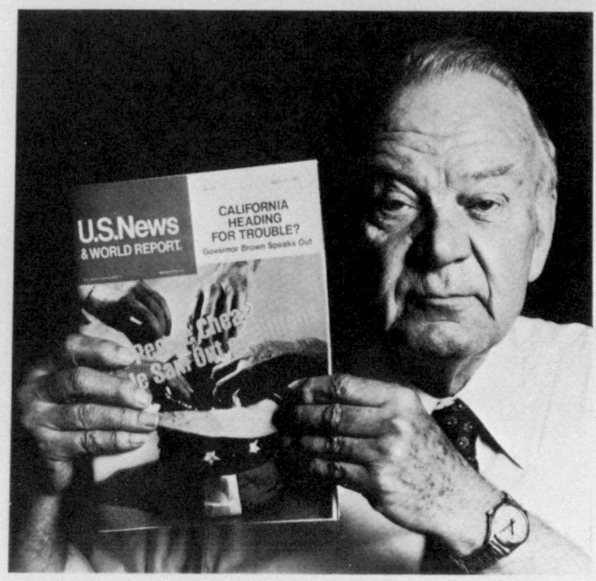

Only 8 million very, very selective people do read it.

Because this magazine contains no cute pictures.

No cute writing.

No gossip.

No entertainment.

No stylishly warmed-up old news.

None. Ever. This magazine isn't pretty.

Does that mean it's designed to repel non-serious readers? Definitely.

For amusement, you simply have to go elsewhere.

We spare our readers unimportant news.
We spare our advertisers unimportant readers.

7

7

Art Director	J. Ryder
Writer	D. Staley
Photographer	Mick Pateman
Agency	Ted Chin & Company, Inc.
Client	U.S. News & World Report

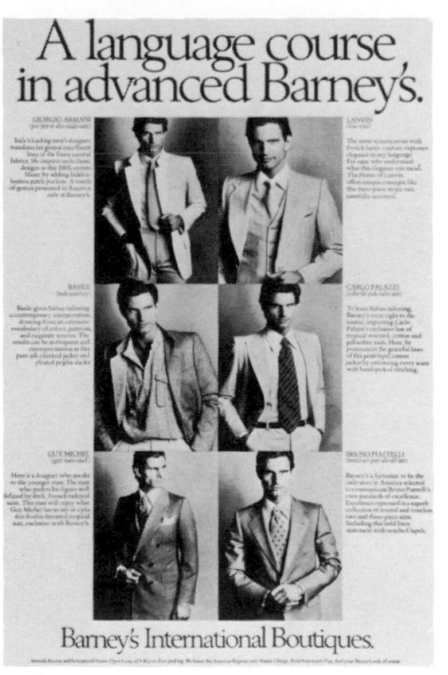

8

Go to your room.

Imagine a place where "Go to your room" is a welcome expression. The place is Barney's, and the rooms comprise an entire block—a men's store without equal anywhere in the world.

You can browse by yourself, or with a personal guide, throughout five floors of elegant fashions.

You see, at Barney's, the nicest thing about going to your room is having so many rooms to go to.

The Oak Room.

The man who can afford a custom made suit will find The Oak Room's standards equal to his own.

What could be more luxurious than choosing from elegant silks, linens and lightweight worsteds. Each superbly tailored by such ranking makers as Oxxford, Hickey Freeman, Chester Barrie, and GGG's.

The English Room.

If British fashion is your cup of tea, there's one place that boasts a selection to rival even London itself. Barney's English Room.

It's the only shop in the New World where you'll discover the bespoke tailors of Kilgour, French and Stanbury.

Along with not just partial, but complete collections of Burberry, Daks, Aquascutum and Rodex.

The New Yorker Room.

Barney's New Yorker Room is for the man who wants to be in the forefront of fashion. But won't compromise when it comes to quality.

It's here you'll find American styling unmatched for value in its price range.

The Madison Room.

Nowhere else in New York will you find so many interpretations of tradition.

Limited only by their allegiance to natural shoulder styling. Compare this spring's concepts by Norman Hilton, H. Freeman, Hart, Schaffner & Marx, and Scott Thomas.

International Boutiques.

There's no need to venture abroad to discover which designer is for you. Because they're all here. Many of them exclusively with Barney's.

You might prefer the superbly tasteful designs of Giorgio Armani, Bruno Piattelli, or Basile. Or, try Yves St. Laurent, Cardin or Lanvin's French versions.

All within the boundaries of our International House.

Barney's

7th Avenue and 17th Street. Open 9 a.m. til 9:30 p.m. Free parking. We honor the American Express card, Master Charge, BankAmericard/Visa. And your Barney's card, of course.

9

8
Art Directors Allen Kay
Tony Angotti
Writers Lois Korey
Steve Penchina
Agency Needham, Harper & Steers Adv. Inc.
Client Barney's

9
Art Directors Allen Kay
Tony Angotti
Writer Lois Korey
Photographer Ron Demilt
Agency Needham, Harper & Steers Adv. Inc.
Client Barney's

10

Today, the one-billionth passenger boarded a Boeing 727.

11

10

Art Director Bill Sweney
Writer James P. Cole
Designer Bill Sweney
Photographer Randy Miller
Agency Cole Henderson Drake, Inc.
Client Omni International Hotels, Inc.

11

Art Director Bob Tanaka
Writer Hal Newsom
Artist Norm Hansen
Agency Cole & Weber
Client Boeing Commercial Airplane Co.

IF YOU COULD
TEST-DRIVE YOUR NEW HOUSE,
WOULD YOU STILL BUY IT?

If you're going to spend 20 or 30 years paying for a house, there are probably a lot of things you'd like to know before you buy.

Like whether you'll be stuck with a wet basement every time it rains. Or how effective the insulation is when it's really cold.

And how about the way things are put together? Are you getting your money's worth—or are there structural shortcuts that will show up later as leaky pipes and sagging walls?

Unfortunately, there's no way to take a split level out for a spin and see how it performs. Which is why it's so important to buy from a builder you can trust—Poretsky and Starr, for instance.

QUALITY RUNS IN THE FAMILY.

Martin Poretsky and Jack Starr are third-generation Washington builders with a deep concern for quality. They know that a home is the biggest and most important purchase most families ever make. So they build each one of theirs from scratch—as if *they* were going to live there.

From the insulated windows and money-saving heat pump to the solid wood cabinets and double-track closet doors, everything you see in a Poretsky and Starr home is designed to give years of trouble-free service.

And they don't skimp on what you can't see either. They put a full six inches of batted insulation into the ceilings. They use kiln-dried lumber to prevent buckling and warping. They glue *and* nail joists and dry wall. And they specify only the top grade of copper wiring to keep your family safe from fire.

AN A+ FROM THE EXPERTS.

In fact, their houses are so well constructed they can afford to back them up with more than just words. So in 1975, Martin Poretsky spearheaded a drive to bring the Home Owners Warranty program to this area. And thanks to his efforts, every Poretsky and Starr community is now covered by this 10-year buyers' protection plan.

With all this going for them, you might expect Poretsky and Starr houses to cost a bundle. But actually, the opposite is true.

In the past two years, the Metropolitan Washington Builders Association has voted them nine awards for things like the "Most Affordable Home," the "Best Single-Family Home Under $55,000," and the "Most Efficient Use of Energy."

And that's not all. Four of these were *overall* awards for their consistently good design, sound construction, environmental planning, and reasonable price.

Those are pretty impressive results for the first two times they entered the competition. Especially when you consider that the judges were builders, architects, and professional engineers who knew exactly what to look for.

NOT A LEMON IN THE LOT.

But you don't have to take the word of an association. Instead, do what the U.S. government recommends: Talk to some people who have already moved in.

Whether you check a townhouse priced in the 40's or a single-family luxury home selling for over $100,000, you'll find the story is always the same.

Poretsky and Starr owners are satisfied owners. People who didn't have to test-drive their homes to keep from getting a lemon.

And that's something to think about when *you're* house-hunting.

PORETSKY & STARR
A COUPLE OF GUYS WHO BUILD A BETTER HOUSE.

12

WAS YOUR NEW HOUSE SHIPPED IN FROM THE FACTORY LAST NIGHT?

You may not realize it, but a lot of houses being built these days are prefabricated.

Everything from the railings to the roof trusses is shipped in on a flat-bed truck and unloaded at the construction site.

All that's left for the workmen to do is fit the pieces together.

Well, that's fine if the builder takes the time to see that the job's done right. But all too often that just doesn't happen.

The walls are thrown up overnight to keep labor costs down. The detail work is treated as an unnecessary extra. And the finished house is a slapdash, slipshod affair that's full of compromises and shortcuts.

QUALITY RUNS IN THE FAMILY.

Martin Poretsky and Jack Starr think that when you invest your hard-earned money in a home, you have a right to expect more. Which is why they do things a little differently.

As third-generation builders, Poretsky and Starr take pride in how well their homes are constructed—not how quickly. So each one is built from scratch by experienced craftsmen.

If it takes a little longer to make sure the wall seams match and the closet doors don't stick, they make that extra effort. If they spot a window or a weather strip that doesn't look quite right, they tear it out and start over.

And they don't skimp on what you *can't* see either. They put a minimum of six inches of batted insulation into the ceilings. They use kiln-dried lumber to prevent buckling and warping. They glue *and* nail joists and dry wall. And they specify only the top grade of copper wiring to keep your family safe from fire.

In fact, their homes are so well constructed they can afford to back them up with more than just words. So in 1975, Martin Poretsky spearheaded a drive to bring the Home Owners Warranty program to this area. And thanks to his efforts, every Poretsky and Starr community is now covered by this 10-year buyers' protection plan.

AN A+ FROM THE EXPERTS.

With all this going for them, you might expect Poretsky and Starr houses to cost a bundle. But actually, the opposite is true.

In the past two years, the Metropolitan Washington Builders Association has voted them nine awards for things like the "Most Affordable Home," the "Best Single-Family Home Under $55,000," and the "Most Efficient Use of Energy."

And that's not all. Four of these were *overall* awards for their consistently good design, sound construction, environmental planning, and reasonable price.

Those are pretty impressive results for the first two times they entered the competition. Especially when you consider that the judges were builders, architects, and professional engineers who knew exactly what to look for.

NOT A LEMON IN THE LOT.

But you don't have to take the word of an association. Instead, do what the U.S. government recommends: Talk to some people who have already moved in.

Whether you check a townhouse priced in the 40's or a single-family luxury home selling for over $100,000, you'll find the story is always the same.

Poretsky and Starr owners are satisfied owners. People whose homes reflect all the care and attention that went into them.

And that's something to think about when *you're* house-hunting.

PORETSKY & STARR
A COUPLE OF GUYS WHO BUILD A BETTER HOUSE.

13

12
Art Director Charlie Clark
Writer Jean Hall
Designer Charlie Clark
Artist Kenny Higdon
Agency Weitzman & Associates, Inc.
Client Poretsky & Starr

13
Art Director Charlie Clark
Writer Jean Hall
Designer Charlie Clark
Artist Kenny Higdon
Agency Weitzman & Associates, Inc.
Client Poretsky & Starr

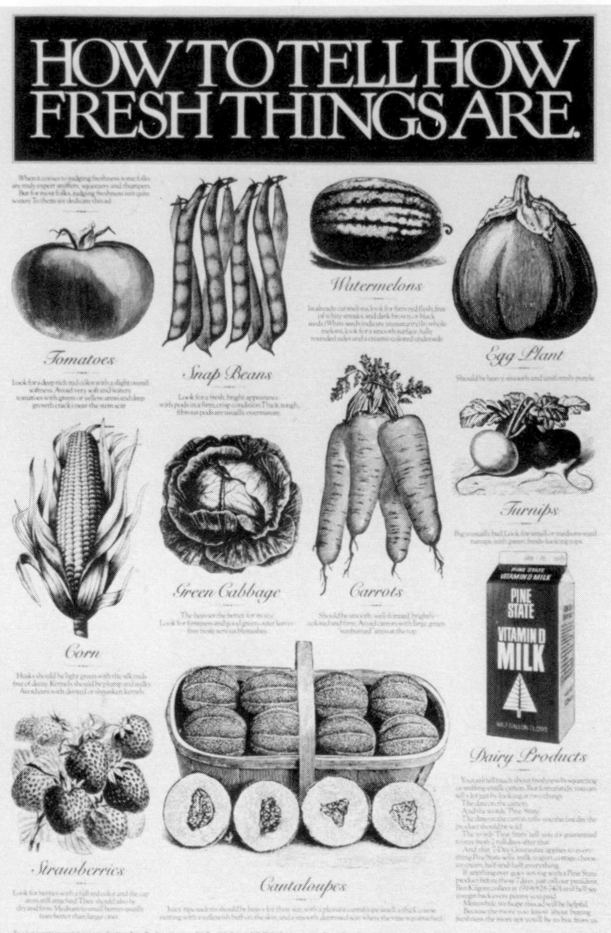

14

15

14

Art Director	Michael Winslow
Writer	Rich Maender
Designers	Michael Winslow Larry Bennett
Artists	Bettman Archives Harlan Scheffler
Agency	McKinney Silver & Rockett
Client	Pine State Creamery Company

15

Art Director	Jim Clarke
Writers	Jim Pappademas Jennifer Berne
Designer	Jim Clarke
Agency	Martin Landey, Arlow Adv., Inc.
Client	Putnam Trust

16

17

16

Art Director	Clem McCarthy
Writer	Martin Puris
Photographer	David Thorpe
Agency	Ammirati Puris AvRutick Inc.
Client	BMW of North America, Inc.

17

Art Director	Clem McCarthy
Photographers	Dick James
	David Thorpe
Agency	Ammirati Puris AvRutick Inc.
Client	BMW of North America, Inc.

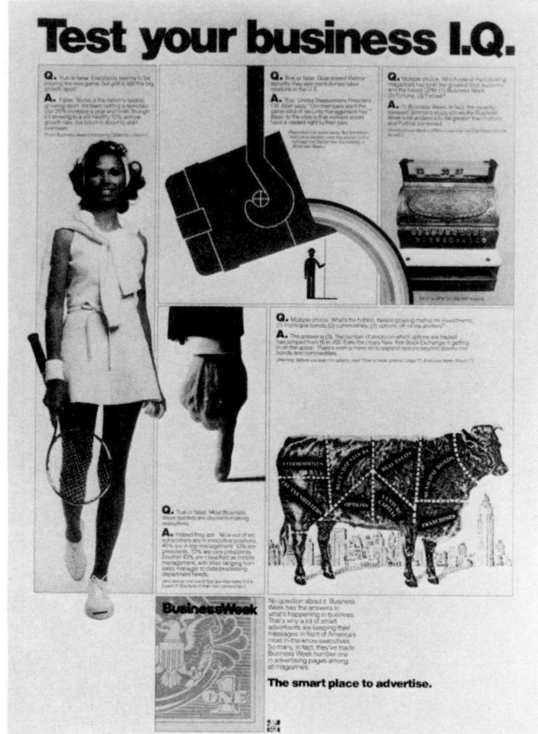

18

19

20

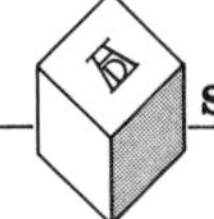

SILVER

18
Art Directors Phil Gips
Diana Graham
Writer Robert Fearon
Designers Phil Gips
Diana Graham
Artists Murray Tinkelman
Tetsuya Matsuura
Photographer Jean-Marie Guyaux
Agency Robert Fearon Associates Ltd.
Client Business Week

19
Art Director John Eding
Writer Doug Houston
Photographer Larry Robins
Agency Doyle Dane Bernbach
Client Volkswagen

20
Art Director Michael Tesch
Writer Tom Messner
Designer Michael Tesch
Photographer Bill Stettner
Agency Ally & Gargano, Inc.
Client Barney's

ORGANIZED CRIME IS NOW THE BIGGEST CAR THIEF. AND THEY'RE NOT GOING FOR JOYRIDES.

Organized crime has found a new bonanza.

The stolen cars they don't send abroad for profits in the black market or peddle in "steal-to-order" circles are broken down and sold here for parts. (And we all know what parts go for.) Others are used as transportation in robberies or in the drug traffic.

The magnitude is frightening, too.

Last year, alone, 1,000,000 cars were driven away by people who didn't own them. (About 1/10 as many as were bought.) Oddly, 15% of the cars stolen had their keys in a very convenient place: the ignition.

The future may be a little less bleak, though. Thanks to the cooperation of government agencies under a Federal Interagency Committee and to the National Automobile Theft Bureau and local committees backed by the insurance industry. They've been giving help to the public on ways to protect their cars. And trying to get the public to cooperate in the apprehension of car thieves. The Travelers Office of Consumer Information would be glad to put you in touch with the National Automobile Theft Bureau to help set up a committee in your area. Just write our Office of Consumer Information, One Tower Square, Hartford, Conn. 06115. Or dial, toll-free, 800-243-0191. In Connecticut, call collect, 277-6565.

Maybe we can get some of those car thieves behind bars instead of behind the wheels of our cars.

THE TRAVELERS

Raising our voice, not just our rates.

The Travelers Insurance Company, The Travelers Indemnity Company, and Affiliated Companies, Hartford, Conn. 06115.

21

Municipal Liability

In many ways, cities today have interests and activities as diversified as those of a sizeable corporation.

As with cities at state and county governments, municipalities may be engaged in generating electricity, running hospitals, putting on fireworks exhibitions, operating airports, broadcasting radio and TV programs, maintaining roadways and bridges, providing buildings and constructing housing. Most of the services they provide, including police and fire protection, present high probabilities of producing claims for bodily injury and property damage.

But traditionally such exposures seldom resulted in any serious financial loss to the municipalities. That's because governments were long shielded from damage claims and lawsuits by the doctrine of sovereign immunity, which derives from the concept that "the king can do no wrong."

Starting about two decades ago, however, the immunity doctrine has been substantially changed by the courts. Now in some states the immunities are gone, and with a few exceptions the governments in those states are as much exposed to damage claims as are private organizations.

Given the reach of the news toward more lawsuits, and higher court awards, the outcome was predictable.

Across the country, municipal liability lawsuits have proliferated. In 1965, Los Angeles paid $2,000 for claims against the police; in 1975 they totaled $1,455,205. In California, liability claims against cities nearly doubled between 1973 and 1975, while settlement costs almost tripled. An award of $4,700,000 for a single case confronted cities with the potential dimensions of the problem.

Many observers believe, however, that the longer range solution lies in legal restrictions on municipal liability—a partial return to the immunity principle.

With their traditional immunity to damage suits largely a thing of the past, state, city and local governments have been hard hit by high jury awards and a consequent rise in insurance costs.

A brief review by INA of an insurance topic of general interest.

A $4.7 million judgment

Limiting civic liability today, INA has prepared a booklet entitled, "Municipal Liability: Some Professional Considerations." Copies may be requested by writing INA Corporation, 1600 Arch Street, Philadelphia, Pa., 19101.

The Insurance Company of North America was founded at Independence Hall, Philadelphia, in 1792. Today INA and its affiliated companies operate around the world with many strengths in property and casualty insurance, marine and aviation insurance, life and group insurance, reinsurance and risk management services.

INA insurance products and services are made available through selected independent agents and brokers—professionals with a comprehensive knowledge of insurance needs and solutions.

INA

Insurance Professionals

22

October 31, 1977. Another men's stronghold bites the dust.

Ever since Barney's first opened its doors back in 1923, it's been a place where a man who wears the pants in the family could shop for them.

Women have always been welcome here, of course. But their primary purpose in coming was to offer an opinion or to buy something (asked).

Through the years, though, women came to Barney's so often that they began to appreciate what a terrific place it was to shop in much as men did. And wondered why there couldn't be a women's store like Barney's.

A year ago, we gave them a hint of what it could be like. A small department on the third floor that contained the work of some of the world's important designers.

But it wasn't enough. It seemed that once women had a foot in the door they wanted more.

So today, 54 years after opening what has became the world's largest men's store, Barney's is happy to announce the women's movement has finally arrived at 7th Avenue and 17th Street.

And not through any back door, either.

Housed on two newly constructed floors atop our International House, Barney's new women's department will be, from both an architectural and fashion point-of-view, unlike anything ever seen before.

It's set on spectacular split levels with hanging plants, trees, and a picturesque skylight to top things off. And contains the creations of the foremost makers of women's fashions in the world today.

The soft, subtly-suits-tailored suits of Giorgio Armani, the more classic styling of Burberry, the elegance of Halli's Harp, the far-Eastern disphracements of Kenzo, the impeccable tailoring of Cerruti.

(Not to mention, of course, the work of Robert Nelson, John, Olympia Saint Angelo, Halston, John Anthony, Geoffrey Beene, Camelback and Daniel Hechter.)

This fall, even the most fashion-conscious of women will make this discovery to all the world there isn't a more impressive collection of impressive collections than the one you'll find at A Woman's Place at Barney's.

On the seventh floor, of course.

Because as we all know, you can't keep a good woman down.

Barney's introduces A Woman's Place, two floors of the world's finest designer fashions.

23

21

Art Director Michael Tesch
Writer Tom Messner
Designer Michael Tesch
Photographer Bill Stettner
Agency Ally & Gargano, Inc.
Client The Travelers Insurance Co.

22

Art Director Richard Kline
Writer John Jackson
Designer Richard Kline
Artist Mel Furukawa
Agency Geer, DuBois Inc.
Client INA (The Insurance Company of North America)

23

Art Director Ron Becker
Writer Ron Berger
Designer Ron Becker
Photographer Harold Krieger
Agency Ally & Gargano, Inc.
Client Barney's

24

25

24
Art Director Steve Juliusson
Writer John Schmidt
Designer Steve Juliusson
Artist Alan E. Cober
Agency N W Ayer/Chicago
Client WLS-TV

25
Art Director Kirk Hinshaw
Writer Rhonda Gunderson
Designer Kirk Hinshaw
Artist Chuck Eckhart
Agency Dancer, Fitzgerald, Sample Inc./SF
Client Celestial Seasonings

HOW NOT TO GET PLUCKED AT THE POULTRY COUNTER.

by Frank Perdue

Every day thousands of women go to stores thinking they know how to select a fresh chicken. Read on, and learn how little you know.

When you shop for chicken, you like to think you're getting the freshest chicken possible. Unfortunately, what you think you're getting isn't always what you get.

Not like the good old days.

Years back, it was easier to check out a chicken. Most women shopped in butcher shops where they could give their prospective dinner a pretty thorough going over.

But today most women shop in supermarkets. And approaching the modern supermarket poultry counter can be a bewildering experience. The consumer is faced with a sea of chickens. Chickens in a multitude of sizes, shapes, types and parts. All tightly wrapped in shiny plastic packages. And plastic can cover a multitude of sins.

Proceed with caution.

At a self-service supermarket poultry section, there is rarely a knowledgeable person standing by who you can turn to for advice. So when it comes to picking out a fresh chicken what do you do? Too many shoppers operate on blind faith. To them, Frank Perdue offers this advice: Don't. Use this information to guide you. And you'll always end up with a fresh chicken instead of a freshly defrosted one.

Ladies, please squeeze the chicken.

Many chickens are processed with a quick chilling system. Chickens that undergo this treatment are blasted with temperatures of 40° below zero. Between the wind and temperature, the chickens are exposed to a wind-chill factor of 80° below zero.

This often results in chickens with frozen or semi-frozen outer extremities. The wings for example. And the thin layer of meat on the chicken's back. So poke around and squeeze. If you hear or feel the chicken "crackling" it isn't from freshness.

Beware of borderline cases.

Sometimes frozen chickens aren't so obvious. They can arrive at your supermarket frozen like rocks. But after a few hours out in the open air, they'll defrost and feel completely fresh. So feeling isn't always believing.

If you have doubts about a chicken, go find someone and ask if the chicken was frozen or chilled when it arrived. Most supermarket personnel should be completely honest and open with you. Your continued business is more important than the sale of one chicken.

Watch out for stale chickens hiding in fresh wrappers.

Some chickens are wrapped at the processing plant and will appear on your poultry counter with a brand name printed right on the plastic wrapper.

If you regularly shop in a supermarket that carries this type of chicken, keep a close watch on them. If chickens in plain clear wrappers start turning up among the others it could mean a couple of things. Neither are in the best interest of you getting a fresh chicken.

It could mean that the chickens have been sitting around so long or handled so often that the packages began to look messy and dog-eared. And had to be re-wrapped. Or it could mean that the chickens went beyond the expiration date that was printed on the label. So the store dressed up the stale chickens in fresh clothes.

If you catch your supermarket pulling stunts like that you'd do well to find yourself a new place to shop.

Or just look for Perdue.

When you buy Perdue, you don't have to know all the ins and outs of the chicken business. Or be wise to any tricks of the trade.

Whether you buy Perdue chicken, Perdue Pedigreed Chicken Parts, the Perdue 'Oven Stuffer' Roaster, or the Perdue Fresh Cornish Game Hen, there's one thing you can always be sure of.

No matter which one of them you get, you'll be getting the finest, freshest poultry obtainable. Frank Perdue makes sure of that.

Just because his money-back quality guarantee is prominently displayed on every product he makes doesn't mean he wants you to take advantage of it.

IT TAKES A TOUGH MAN TO MAKE A TENDER CHICKEN.

If you'd like a handy purse-sized reprint of this advertisement write: Reprint, Perdue Farms Inc.
Box 1537, Salisbury, Maryland, 21801
NAME
ADDRESS
CITY
STATE
ZIP

26

26

Art Director Sam Scali
Writer Ed McCabe
Designer Sam Scali
Artist Larry Ross
Agency Scali, McCabe, Sloves
Client Perdue Farms Inc.

27

28

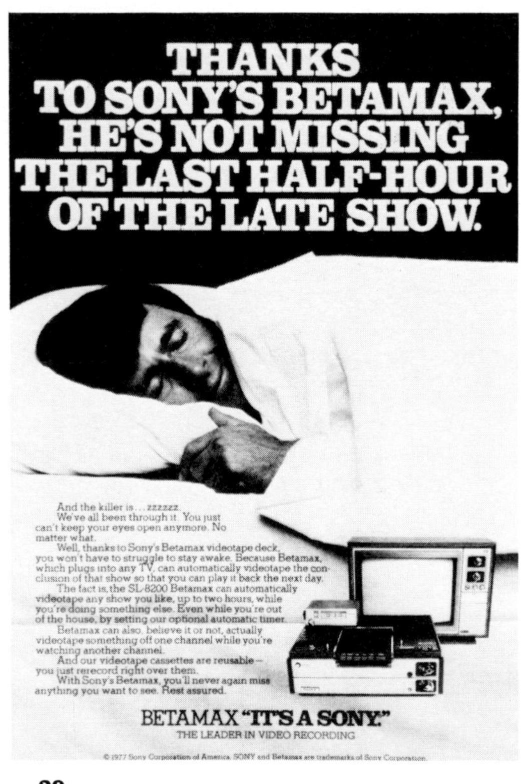

29

27
Art Director Dan Fauver
Writer Vivian Henoch
Designer Dan Fauver
Artist Dave Fitch
Producer Wally Piascik
Agency Wyse Advertising
Client The East Ohio Gas Co.

28
Art Director Steven Ong
Writer David Levy
Photographer Leon Kusmanoff
Agency Young & Rubicam
Client Eastern Airlines

29
Art Director John Caggiano
Writer Mike Mangano
Designer John Caggiano
Photographer George Hausman
Agency Doyle Dane Bernbach
Client Sony

30

31

30

Art Director	Tony Romeo
Writer	Richard Goodman
Designer	Tony Romeo
Artist	Robert Weber
Agency	Scali, McCabe, Sloves
Client	Waldenbooks

31

Art Director	Richard Kimmel
Writer	Martin Cooke
Photographer	Dennis Manarchy
Agency	N W Ayer/Chicago
Client	Illinois Bell Telephone

When James Earl Ray was recaptured, this is what was in his pocket.

The once-confessed killer of Dr. Martin Luther King was after an Eyewitness News reporter. Nancy Becker.

Before his escape, he had spent a couple of hours in an exclusive interview with her. At the conclusion, Nancy told Ray how to reach her should he want to speak further.

A month later, he tried his escape. When he was captured, he was carrying a state road map. And in his pocket were the instructions for contacting Nancy. He had hoped she would help him reach Attorney General Griffin Bell to make a deal. A deal to surrender in exchange for a jury trial.

Why would he turn to a local news person when he could have contacted a better-known national news figure?

Probably because he trusted her. To be fair. To try to get both sides of the story. He felt she was one reporter that seemed more concerned with what he wanted to say than what the news producers wanted to hear.

We're proud of Nancy. Of course, we don't always expect this sort of thing from our reporters.

But we do expect them to be like Nancy in many ways.

Involved. Concerned. Professional. And human.

More people watch Eyewitness News than any other news in Chicago.

7

5, 6 & 10

32

Fat Chance

Fat Kids. The last to be picked and the first to be picked on.

What's it like to be so painfully "different" at the time in life when everyone wants to be the same? John Drury talks with some experts on the subject of fat. A kid who lives it, a psychologist who explains it, a doctor who treats it, and some former fatties who've beat it.

Fat Kid on the Block
Eyewitness News Close-up Tonight at 10 pm.

If it's important to Chicago, it's on Eyewitness News.

7

33

32

Art Director	Gary Johns
Writer	Mike Faems
Designer	Gary Johns
Photographer	Dennis Manarchy
Agency	N W Ayer/Chicago
Client	WLS-TV

33

Art Director	Marcus Kemp
Writer	Mary Jo Leverette
Designer	Marcus Kemp
Photographer	Jean Moss
Agency	N W Ayer/Chicago
Client	WLS-TV, Chicago

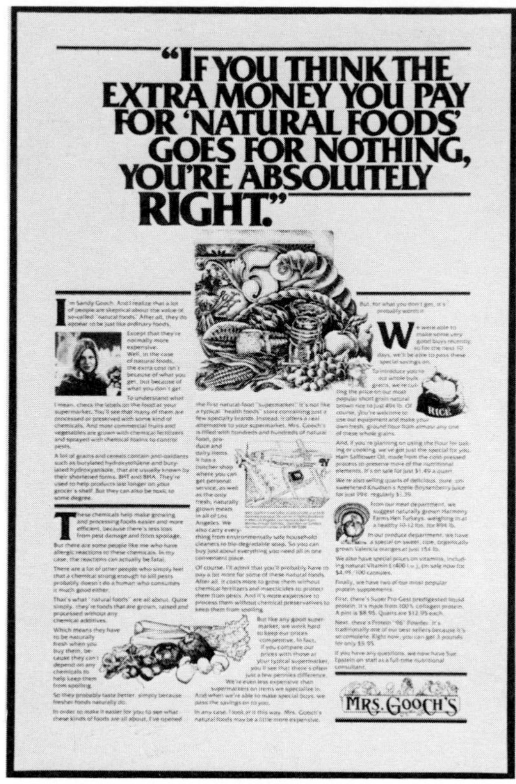

34

1. Do you feel your spouse appreciates you for who you are?	yes	no
2. Do you feel comfortable about the way you and your spouse communicate with each other?	yes	no
3. Do you feel that you and your spouse are generally able to settle your differences?	yes	no
4. Do you feel that a marriage takes energy and effort?	yes	no
5. Would you say that you are more happy in your marriage than unhappy?	yes	no
6. Are you comfortable with your spouse's expectations and demands?	yes	no
7. Do you and your spouse agree on what kinds of activities and relationships are permitted outside the marriage?	yes	no
8. Do you feel free to ask your spouse for what you would like?	yes	no
9. Are you and your spouse sometimes able to laugh together about some of your difficulties?	yes	no
10. Are you as forgiving and understanding of your spouse as you were before?	yes	no
11. Do you and your spouse generally agree on the handling of your children?	yes	no
12. Do you feel that you and your spouse are affectionate enough toward one another?	yes	no
13. Do you and your spouse spend enough pleasurable time together?	yes	no
14. Do you and your spouse generally agree on how your money should be handled?	yes	no
15. Are you comfortable with the amount and type of sex you and your spouse have?	yes	no

To find out what your answers mean, tune in the final segment of Terry Murphy's special report on divorce. It should help you figure out if your marriage is earning passing marks.

Divorce: Can you beat the odds?
Eyewitness News Close-Up Tonight at 10 pm.

7

If it's important to Chicago, it's on Eyewitness News.

35

34

Art Director **Douglas Hoppe Stone**
Writer **Terry Taketa**
Designer **Douglas Hoppe Stone**
Artists **Abe Gervin**
Rob Sprattler
Joe Taylor
Photographer **Stan Sholik**
Agency **Douglas Stone & Associates (Newport Beach, Ca.)**
Client **Mrs. Gooch's Natural Food Store**

35

Art Director **Steve Juliusson**
Writer **John Schmidt**
Designer **Steve Juliusson**
Agency **N W Ayer/Chicago**
Client **WLS-TV**

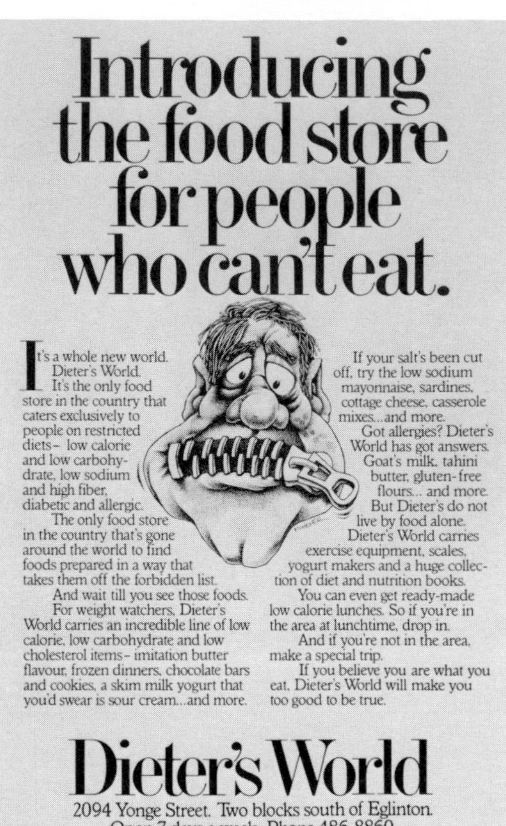

Introducing the food store for people who can't eat.
It's a whole new world. Dieter's World.
It's the only food store in the country that caters exclusively to people on restricted diets– low calorie and low carbohydrate, low sodium and high fiber, diabetic and allergic.
The only food store in the country that's gone around the world to find foods prepared in a way that takes them off the forbidden list.
And wait till you see those foods.
For weight watchers, Dieter's World carries an incredible line of low calorie, low carbohydrate and low cholesterol items– imitation butter flavour, frozen dinners, chocolate bars and cookies, a skim milk yogurt that you'd swear is sour cream...and more.
If your salt's been cut off, try the low sodium mayonnaise, sardines, cottage cheese, casserole mixes...and more.
Got allergies? Dieter's World has got answers. Goat's milk, tahini butter, gluten-free flours... and more.
But Dieter's do not live by food alone. Dieter's World carries exercise equipment, scales, yogurt makers and a huge collection of diet and nutrition books.
You can even get ready-made low calorie lunches. So if you're in the area at lunchtime, drop in.
And if you're not in the area, make a special trip.
If you believe you are what you eat, Dieter's World will make you too good to be true.
Dieter's World
2094 Yonge Street. Two blocks south of Eglinton.
Open 7 days a week. Phone 486-8860.

36

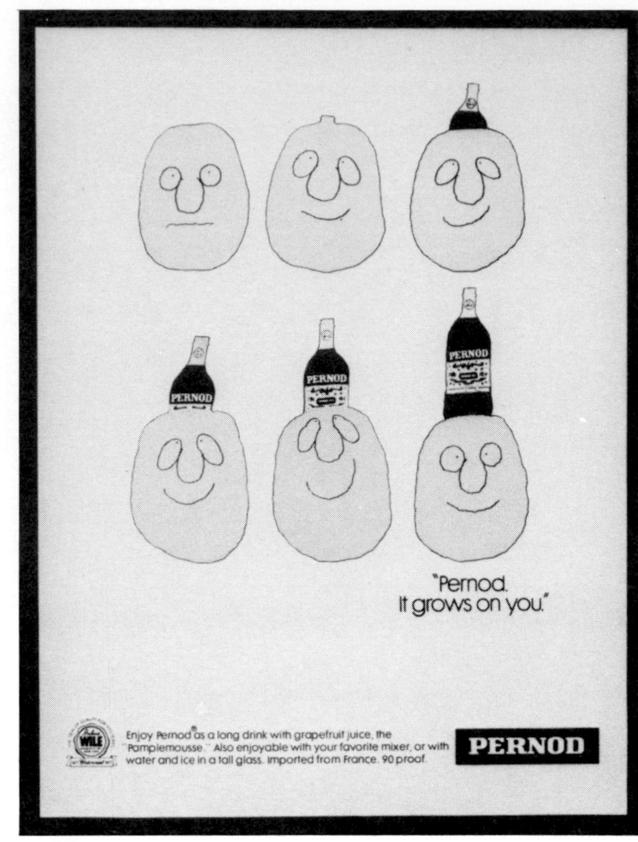

PERNOD
"Pernod.
It grows on you."
Enjoy Pernod® as a long drink with grapefruit juice, the "Pamplemousse." Also enjoyable with your favorite mixer, or with water and ice in a tall glass. Imported from France. 90 proof.
WILE
PERNOD

37

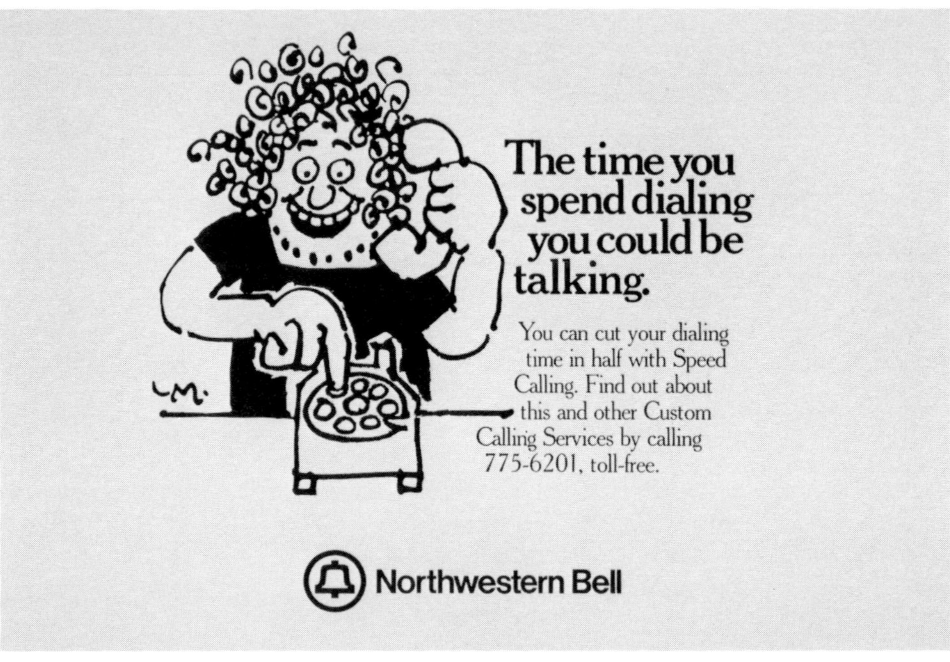

LM.
The time you spend dialing you could be talking.
You can cut your dialing time in half with Speed Calling. Find out about this and other Custom Calling Services by calling 775-6201, toll-free.
Northwestern Bell

38

36

Art Director	John Cruickshank
Writer	Heather Chisvin
Designer	John Cruickshank
Artist	Ted Michener
Agency	Heather Chisvin Creative Services
Client	Dieter's World

37

Art Director	Bob Bidner
Writer	Ray Baker
Designer	Bob Bidner
Artists	Bob Bidner Tony Toscano
Agency	Ted Bates & Co., Inc.
Client	Julius Wile Sons & Co., Inc.

38

Art Director	Ron Anderson
Writer	Tom McElligott
Artist	Lou Myers
Agency	Bozell & Jacobs/Mpls
Client	Northwestern Bell

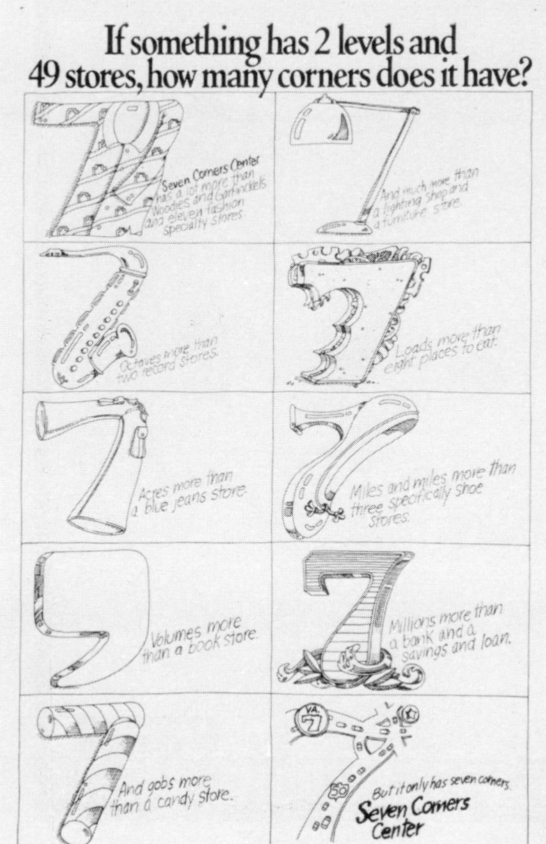

39

There's more to bad employee attitudes than meets the eye.

An employee attitude survey should do more for you than point out obvious problems. It should give you an accurate basis for comparison to help you understand how important the problems really are.

The SRA Attitude Survey is a measurement tool that gives you just that, with all-new statistical norms for 1977 based on surveys with over a thousand companies and hundreds of thousands of employees. These norms allow you to compare your employee attitudes (guaranteeing anonymity to employees) with those of other companies your size, in your business.

Put into proper perspective by these standardized norms, an attitude problem that seems severe may be found to be relatively normal, or conversely, seemingly insignificant problems may be revealed to be serious ones requiring immediate attention.

In addition, The SRA Attitude Survey can be tailored to your specific needs, using custom-built questions. Results may be compared by department, sex, or any other variable. The survey is computer scored for prompt results, and SRA offers complete planning assistance.

Special editions are available for Spanish, French, and other employee groups.

For more information, write today or stop by SRA's Booth 101 at the "Training '77" Convention November 30—December 2 at the Statler-Hilton in New York.

Or, simply contact us today to arrange to have The SRA Attitude Survey administered to your employees.

It could be an eye-opening experience.

*SRA SCIENCE RESEARCH ASSOCIATES
259 E. Erie, Chicago, Illinois 60611
A subsidiary of IBM

Call 800-621-6488 or 312-266-5191.

40

39
Art Director Dan Rosenthal
Writer Dan Rosenthal
Designer Dan Rosenthal
Artist Jean Pidgeon
Agency Earle Palmer Brown And Assoc.
Client Seven Corners Center

40
Art Director David Kennedy
Writer John Scott
Photographer Hauser-D'Orio Photography
Agency John Scott and Others
Client Science Research Asociates, Inc.

Try walking into Merrill Lynch and asking for Mr. Lynch.

Try going into Thompson McKinnon and asking for Thompson or McKinnon. Try calling Chase Manhattan and asking for Mr. Chase.

You won't get them.

Instead, you'll often end up talking to someone who's thinking as much about his own job outlook as your financial outlook.

Try calling Goldberg Polen & Co.

At Goldberg Polen & Co., we operate on a different principle.

When you deal with Goldberg Polen & Co., you'll be dealing directly with Goldberg and Polen themselves. Benefiting directly from their years of experience on Wall Street and in every area of the financial field.

What's more, you can rest assured that when you deal with any member of our staff, you'll be dealing with someone who has met our rigorous standards and is more than fully qualified to serve your needs.

You can also rest assured that you'll continue to have access to Goldberg and to Polen. They're committed to a close, long term personal relationship with their clients. They won't suddenly disappear, because their names are on the door.

We do more than just recommend stocks.

As we've said, Goldberg Polen & Co. operates on a different principle.

We believe in total financial planning. Although few people seem to understand this idea, it's the only way important financial goals have a chance of being achieved.

At Goldberg Polen & Co. we do more than recommend which stock to buy or which stock not to buy. We slowly and carefully formulate a balanced financial program based on your own special needs and goals, whether you're an individual or a corporation. Including not just stocks and bonds, but estate planning, insurance, annuities, and most important, tax planning, the cornerstone of any soundly conceived financial plan.

Every decision or recommendation we make is determined solely by what's in your best interest. Long term as well as short term. Not by how much we can make on the transaction. Because we know that putting your interest ahead of our own is better for us both in the end.

Goldberg Polen & Co. is located at 14 East Central Avenue, Spring Valley, N.Y. Our number is 914-356-2900. If you're genuinely and seriously interested in forging a sound financial program for yourself, give us a call.

Just ask for Mr. Goldberg or Mr. Polen.

GOLDBERG POLEN
AND COMPANY, INC.

41

WHY SHOULD CAR COMPANIES STOP BUILDING DISAPPOINTING CARS? YOU'RE STILL BUYING THEM.

If everytime you buy a new car, you get the distinct feeling that you're paying more money for less quality, join the crowd.

According to a recent survey conducted in the U.S., 64% of the people feel that in the past ten years the quality of new cars has declined.

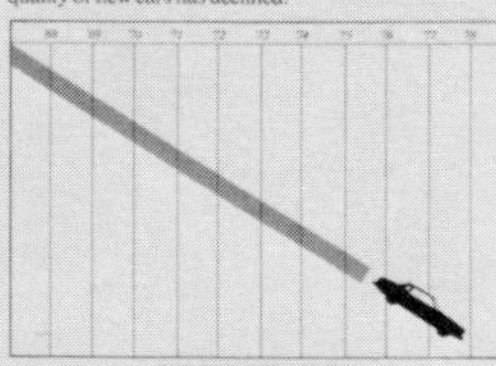

THE PUBLIC'S OPINION OF NEW CAR QUALITY TEN YEARS AGO VS. TODAY.

And yet, despite this, Detroit is planning to sell more new cars this year than ever before.

But before you automatically go out and buy one of them, maybe you should give some thought to a car you've never bought before. A Volvo.

A Volvo has things you may think have disappeared from cars altogether.

Things like workmanship. There's a definite feeling you get when you ride in a Volvo that this car has been fit together instead of slapped together. A strong, unitized body construction helps eliminate squeaks and rattles. And if you're old enough to remember when a paint job was actually a feature you could point to in a new car, you'll admire Volvo's. It's five coats deep.

If what you look for in a car is comfort, come and sit in a Volvo. (And bring four big friends.) There's enough leg, hip, shoulder and headroom in a Volvo for five six-footers. The air around you is kept continuously fresh by Volvo's 12 outlet ventilation system. And up front, you'll find Volvo's famous orthopedically-designed bucket seats that adjust in ten different ways, including from "soft" to "firm" against the small of your back.

Many people who buy Volvos rediscover something else they'd thought was a thing of the past: the sheer pleasure of driving a car. In an era of shrinking engines and power-robbing pollution controls, Volvo has refused to produce a car that's boring to drive. Instead, we've developed overhead cam engines that meet all clean air requirements without sacrificing essential mid-range torque and acceleration.

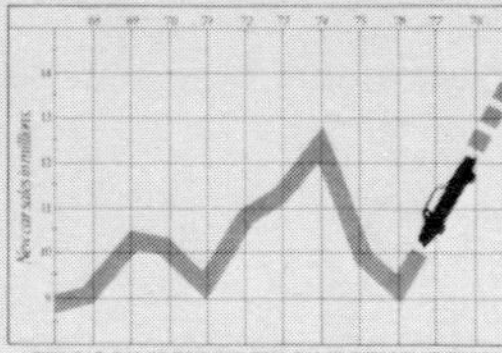

NEW CAR SALES DURING THE SAME TEN YEAR PERIOD.

Volvo also has rack and pinion steering, for precise, responsive control. An advanced spring-strut suspension system for a smooth, stable ride. And power-assisted disc brakes on four wheels, instead of just two.

Of course, with a Volvo, you also get all those things that Volvo is famous for. The legendary strength and durability (the average life expectancy of a Volvo in Sweden has increased by 37% in the last ten years). And safety features so advanced, they're being studied by the U.S. government.

Your Volvo dealer has a whole selection of Volvos to choose from. 2-doors, 4-doors and station wagons from either our Volvo 240 series or from our luxurious series of Volvo 260's.

Volvos start at $7,195.*

Which may sound like a lot. Until you realize what you're getting is a terrific car.

Instead of a disappointment.

VOLVO. A CAR YOU CAN BELIEVE IN.

42

41	
Art Director	Paul Jervis
Writer	Marc Shenfield
Designer	Paul Jervis
Photographer	Paul Jervis
Agency	Direct
Client	Goldberg/Polen

42	
Art Director	Jim Perretti
Writers	Ray Freidel
	Larry Cadman
Designer	Jim Perretti
Photographer	David Langley
Agency	Scali, McCabe, Sloves
Client	Volvo Canada Ltd.

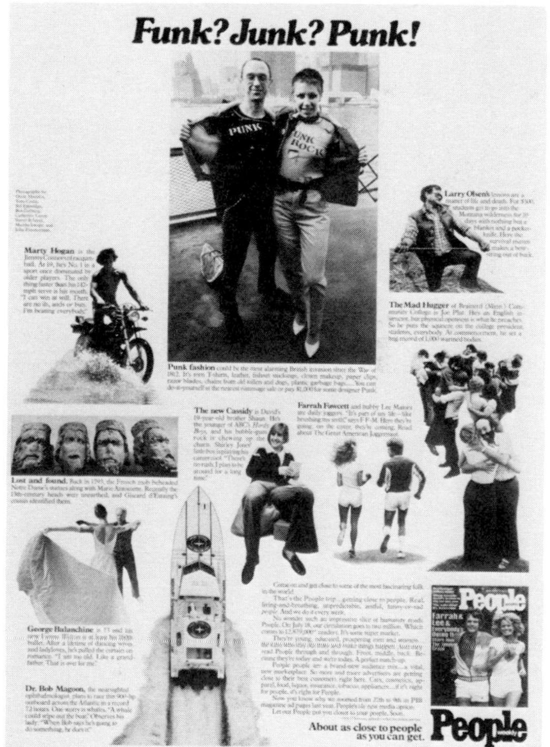

43

43

Art Director	Bob Czernysz
Writer	Dick Olmsted
Photographer	Editorial Photography
Agency	Young & Rubicam
Client	People Magazine

I've been dressing him since he was 6'2."
From his shirts to his B.V.D.'s—women are making more than half of all the purchases in men's furnishings. In men's toiletries, the figures for women making the purchases are even higher.
In fact, she's increasingly wearing the pants in all the areas of purchase that used to be male dominated.
A whole new mass market. But—a very different kind of shopper.
She's the comparison shopper.
The label reader. The feel-and-compare expert. And that's good.
But, here's the snag. She's more skeptical. Critical. Scrutinizing. And you have to do more than reach her. You have to engage her confidence.
One of the most certain ways to gain that confidence is to place your ads in Good Housekeeping.
Traditional advertisers will tell you that.
Survey after survey will tell you that.
Because it's been proved—an ad in the editorial environment of Good Housekeeping stimulates more consumer confidence than it does in any other woman's magazine.
Good Housekeeping. It's like placing your merchandise in the most respected store in the neighborhood.
She's a tougher customer than ever. You never needed Good Housekeeping more.

44

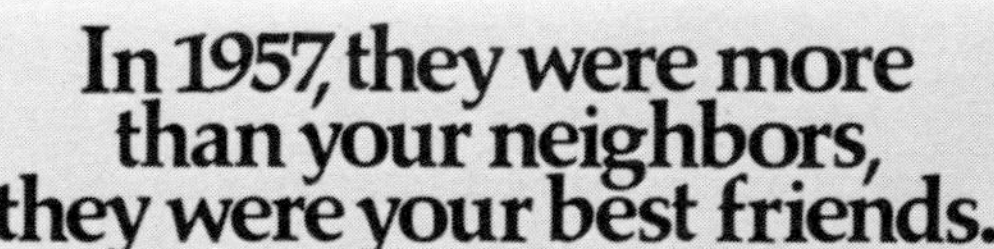

In 1957, they were more than your neighbors, they were your best friends.

St. Paul Home Bldrs '57
ANNUAL DINNER DANC
Isn't it worth $1.50 to spend 5 minutes with them again?
Remember the great times you had together? Staying in touch regularly with old friends and loved ones costs less than you think.
For example, for under $1.50* you can talk for a full five minutes on the telephone to New Orleans, New York, or Seattle, evenings after 5 PM and anytime on weekends.
So go ahead, relive those old memories and plan for new ones. On the telephone.
Northwestern Bell

In 1959, your sister gave you her first dance.
Isn't it worth $1.50 to spend 5 minutes with her again?
Remember the great times you had together? Staying in touch regularly with old friends and loved ones costs less than you think.
For example, for under $1.50* you can talk for a full five minutes on the telephone to New Orleans, New York, or Seattle, evenings after 5 PM and anytime on weekends.
So go ahead, relive those old memories and plan for new ones. On the telephone.
Northwestern Bell

45

44

Art Directors	Keith Rabedeau Carol Moser
Writers	Phillip Geraci Geraldine Newman
Designer	Gus Scheuer
Photographers	Francesco Scavullo Bob Stone
Agency	Advertising to Women
Client	Good Housekeeping

45

Art Director	Ron Anderson
Writer	Tom McElligott
Photographers	Rick Dublin Tom Berthiaume
Agency	Bozell & Jacobs/Mpls MN
Client	Northwestern Bell

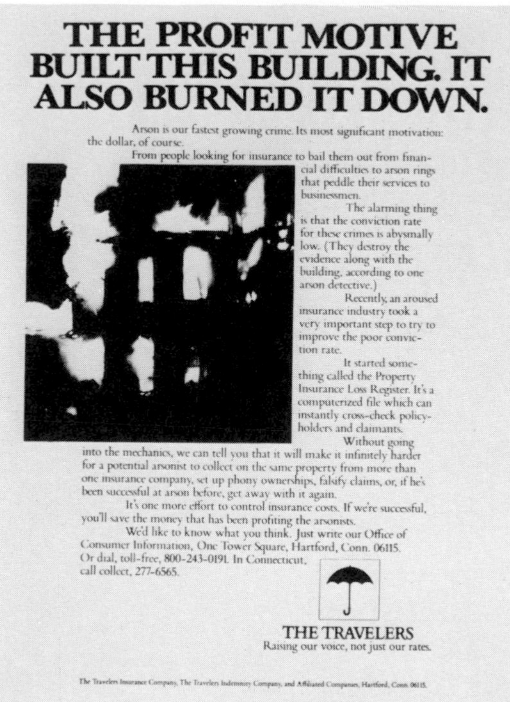

46

"Let's just do what we did last year. It worked, didn't it?"
Give him a Zero.
Zero-Base Media Planning.
Ask Newsweek.

47

"No recipes."
CRAIG CLAIBORNE, FOOD CRITIC. A READER SINCE 1972.
U.S.News & WORLD REPORT
We spare our readers unimportant news.
We spare our advertisers unimportant readers.

48

SILVER

46

Art Director	Michael Tesch
Writer	Tom Messner
Designer	Michael Tesch
Photographers	1) Fire Dept. Files
	2,3) Bill Stettne
Agency	Ally & Gargano Inc.
Client	The Travelers Insurance Co.

47

Art Director	Barry Littmann
Writer	Bob Linderman
Designer	Barry Littmann
Artist	Lee Lorenz
Photographer	John Bechtold
Agency	Foote, Cone & Belding
Client	Newsweek

48

Art Director	J. Ryder
Writer	D. Staley
Photographer	Mick Pateman
Agency	Ted Chin & Company, Inc.
Client	U.S. News & World Report

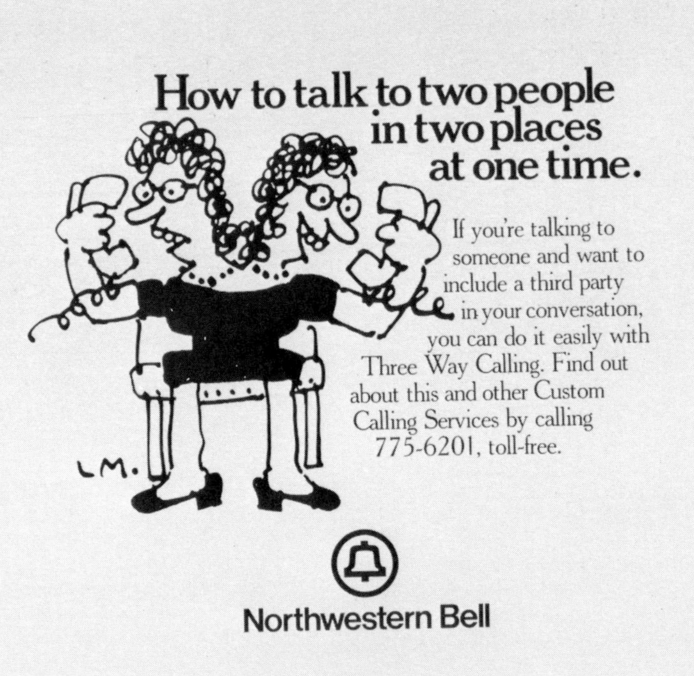

49

49
Art Director **Ron Anderson**
Writer **Tom McElligott**
Artist **Lou Myers**
Agency **Bozell & Jacobs/Mpls MN**
Client **Northwestern Bell**

Doctors lik
our operation
KNX NEWSRADIO 10.70

50

"How did you feel when you bought a skirt at Hit or Miss, then saw it at a department store for twice the price?"

"delighted."

Hit or Miss
Name brand fashions for 30% to 50% less.
Opening Thursday in the Delco Plaza in Groesbeck and on Dixie Highway in Ft. Wright.

"How would you feel if you bought pants, then saw them at Hit or Miss for 1/3 less?"

"sick."

Hit or Miss
Name brand fashions for 30% to 50% less.
Opening Thursday in the Delco Plaza in Groesbeck and opening soon on Dixie Highway in Ft. Wright.

51

50
Art Director Dick Bell
Writer Fred Bergendorff
Designer Dick Bell
Artist Hank Hinton
Client KNX Newsradio

51
Art Director Bill Gustat
Writer Sara Rosenberg
Designer Bill Gustat
Agency Ingalls Associates
Client Hit or Miss

52

53

52
Art Director Theodore Duquette
Writer Betsy Clark
Designer Theodore Duquette
Artist Gunn Studios
Agency Ingalls Associates
Client Charlestown Savings Bank

53
Art Director Charlie Clark
Writer Jean Hall
Designer Charlie Clark
Artist Kenny Higdon
Agency Weitzman & Associates, Inc.
Client Poretsky & Starr

54

55

ELIZABETH ARDEN CLINIQUE PIER AUGE CHRISTIAN DIOR ESTEE LAUDER GERMAINE MONTEIL DU BARRY ULTIMA II MAX FACTOR SANS SOUCIS LOVE HELENA RUBINSTEIN LANCOME EDITH SEREI GEMINESSE REVLON JUVENA ELECTA & CORRADO YARDLEY LANCASTER JEAN D'AVEZE ANNE MARIE COTY CHARLES OF THE RITZ MARY QUANT ALMAY FERNAND AUBRY PAYOT CEDIB BONNIE BELL ORLANE SHISEIDO LISE WATIER at EATON

Oh yes, when it comes to beauty, Eaton's has the big names and one of the biggest departments in the city

56

54

Art Director Eugene Turner
Writer Mark D. Goldstein
Designer Eugene Turner
Artists Graphics Group
Kenny Higdon
Jean Pidgeon
Agency Earle Palmer Brown and Assoc.
Client Country Legend, Inc.

55

Art Director Michael Leon
Writer Daryl Warner
Designer Michael Leon
Artist Lee Lorenz
Agency Doyle Dane Bernbach
Client Sylvania

56

Art Director Harriet Golfos Santroch
Writer Mary McLean
Designer Virginia Poisson
Artist Virginia Poisson
Agency T. Eaton Co. Montreal

58

The great restaurants all have proud histories.
Even when they're brand new.

57

Fannie May wishes you a Merry Christmas and
offers many ways you can express it.

59

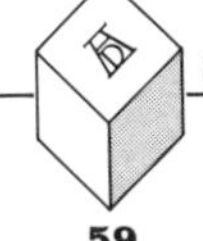

SILVER

57
Art Director Dick Athey
Writer Mike Hughes
Designer Harold Tench
Photographer Ron Seichrist
Agency Webb & Athey, Inc.
Client Kingsmill on the James

58
Art Director Steve LaGattuta
Writer Jim Dale
Artist Don Ivan Punchatz
Agency W.B. Doner & Co.
Client United Brands/Chiquita

59
Art Director Bob Sherman
Writer Arnold Paley
Designer Bob Sherman
Photographer Michel Ditlove
Agency Brand Advertising
Client Fannie May Candies

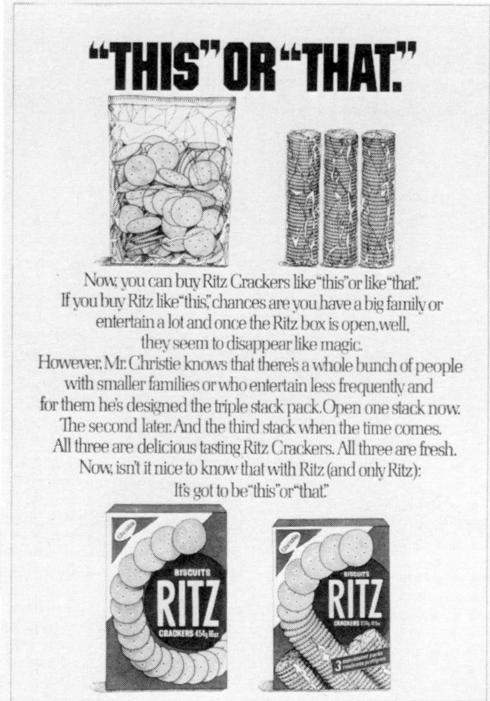

"THIS" OR "THAT."
Now, you can buy Ritz Crackers like "this" or like "that."
If you buy Ritz like "this," chances are you have a big family or
entertain a lot and once the Ritz box is open, well,
they seem to disappear like magic.
However, Mr. Christie knows that there's a whole bunch of people
with smaller families or who entertain less frequently and
for them he's designed the triple stack pack. Open one stack now.
The second later. And the third stack when the time comes.
All three are delicious tasting Ritz Crackers. All three are fresh.
Now, isn't it nice to know that with Ritz (and only Ritz):
It's got to be "this" or "that."
BISCUITS
RITZ
BISCUITS
RITZ

60

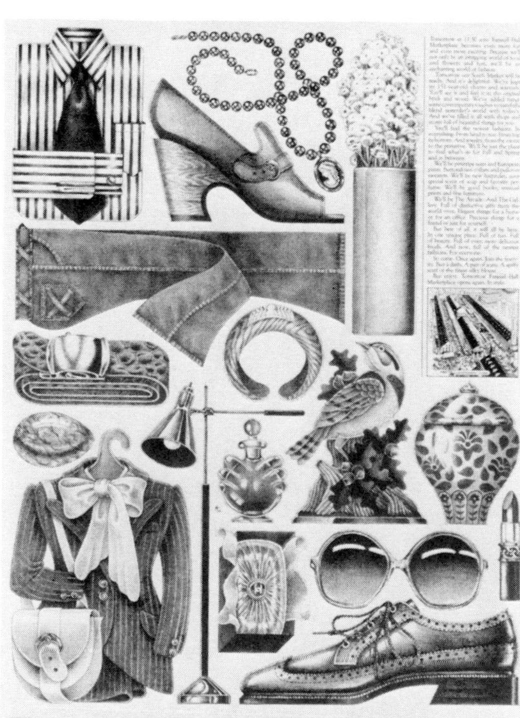

61

THE CLOSEST THE PAPER TOWEL HAS EVER COME TO CLOTH.

Introducing Bolt. A disposable paper towel so close to cloth, in laboratory tests it actually stood up to a washing machine.

At last there's a disposable paper towel that actually performs – even feels – like cloth.

It's called Bolt (like in a bolt of cloth). And what makes it so much like cloth is the way it's made.

Unlike conventional paper towels made from what is known as the "water-laid" process, Bolt is made from a unique "air-laid" process. Producing a far stronger, fluffier and more absorbent paper towel.

To demonstrate just how close to cloth Bolt comes, in laboratory tests we put a sheet of Bolt, Bounty and Viva in a washing machine. The rather lopsided results are pictured above.

To demonstrate just how close to cloth Bolt performs, we also put a sheet of Bolt, Bounty and Viva in a kitchen. Even we were slightly amazed at the results.

Bolt proved to be three times more absorbent than Bounty. Had more than twice the wet-strength of Viva. And absorbed four times faster than them both.

Which means that Bolt will not only vastly out-perform other paper towels around your kitchen, but a roll could last you a lot longer.

But you don't have to use Bolt to appreciate just how close to cloth it is. All you have to do is touch it. Bolt is so soft and fluffy, you'll use it for jobs you wouldn't dare use other paper towels for. Such as polishing silver, dusting fine furniture, even wiping an infant's face.

So instead of putting up with paper towels that have all the disadvantages of conventional paper, pick up a roll of Bolt.

The world's most cloth-like paper towel.

BOUNTY BOLT VIVA

NEW
Bolt
Does more jobs better

62

60

Art Director Brian Harrod
Writer Allan Kazmer
Artist Tony Kew (Portfolio Studio)
Agency McCann-Erickson Canada
Client Christie-Brown

61

Art Director Bob Dennard
Writer Bob Dennard
Designers Bob Dennard
Dick Mitchell
Artists Dick Mitchell
David Kent
Don Grimes
Mary McDowell Keck
Mike Washlesky
Agency The Richards Group, Inc.
Client The Rouse Company

62

Art Director John Danza
Writer Mike Drazen
Designer John Danza
Photographer Phil Mazzurco
Agency Scali, McCabe, Sloves
Client American Can Company

Are you paying filet prices but eating sole?
All steak today costs a small fortune.
But when was the last time you can remember eating a steak that was worth what you paid for it?
Our steaks cost a little more than you're paying now.
But you should know you cannot buy a more tender, better tasting steak than a Prime-Pak steak. At any price.
A fact we're willing to guarantee, unconditionally, in writing.
We can make this guarantee, fearlessly, because we buy only the best beef money can buy.
This means paying top-dollar for our steaks and charging top-dollar for them.
But in return, you get a steak that has been fed only expensive corn and grain.
A steak that is rich in crucial marbling.
A steak that has been through a costly aging process.
A steak that has been trimmed of all but a quarter-inch of fat, the proper amount for cooking.
A steak that is the best-eating piece of meat you've ever bought anywhere at any price.
In addition, each Prime-Pak steak we sell must not only meet USDA standards, it must meet our own. And our standards are a lot harder to meet than the government's.
We also *blast freeze* our steaks at 50° below zero to seal in all the tenderness, flavorfulness and juiciness we've paid so dearly for.
Then we ship them individually wrapped, vacuum sealed in heavy-gauge film and packed in a carton overstuffed with dry ice.
Naturally, all this adds up to a lot of money. But at least when you promise your friends the best steak they've ever tasted, you won't feel like you've put your foot in your mouth.
Prime-Pak

63

Polaroid's SX-70 Alpha 1
Its electronics and optics make it the world's finest instant camera.
The SX-70® Alpha 1 Land camera has the most advanced optical and electronic system ever integrated into one camera. The SX-70 is the world's only folding single-lens reflex camera. Its four-element glass lens provides razor-sharp focusing from infinity to 10.4 inches. You see details clearly, even in dim light, because the SX-70 has one of the brightest SLR viewfinders. And its electronics automatically calculate all exposures, using a unique variable shutter and aperture combination which even makes split-second flash corrections. The SX-70 Alpha 1. So advanced, it frees you to do the creative thinking.

64

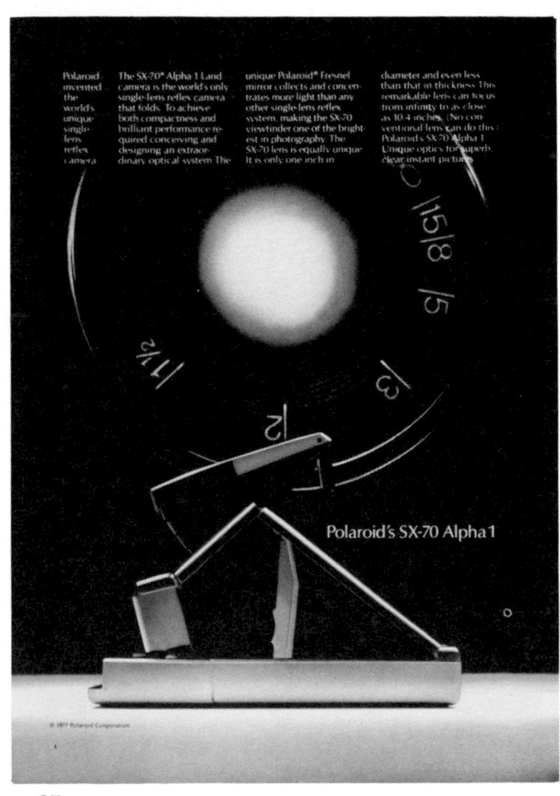

Polaroid invented the world's unique single-lens reflex camera
The SX-70® Alpha 1 Land camera is the world's only single-lens reflex camera that folds. To achieve both compactness and brilliant performance required conceiving and designing an extraordinary optical system. The unique Polaroid® Fresnel mirror collects and concentrates more light than any other single-lens reflex system, making the SX-70 viewfinder one of the brightest in photography. The SX-70 lens is equally unique. It is only one inch in diameter and even less than that in thickness. This remarkable lens can focus from infinity to as close as 10.4 inches. (No conventional lens can do this.) Polaroid's SX-70 Alpha 1. Unique optics for superb, clear instant pictures.
15
8
5
3
2
1½
Polaroid's SX-70 Alpha 1

65

63	
Art Director	Jim M. Cox
Writer	Jeff B. Gorman
Designer	Jim M. Cox
Photographer	Charles Gold
Agency	Epiphany, Inc.
Client	Prime-Pak, Inc.

64	
Art Director	Helmut Krone
Writer	Ed Smith
Photographer	Helmut Krone
Agency	Doyle Dane Bernbach
Client	Polaroid

65	
Art Director	Helmut Krone
Writer	Ed Smith
Photographer	Helmut Krone
Agency	Doyle Dane Bernbach
Client	Polaroid

INTRODUCING
THE UNIVERSITY OF CHIQUITA
The U of C: A handling and merchandising seminar to help increase banana profits.
Remember what your mother told you, "You can't get ahead without an education." Well, it isn't too late to go back to school. You can go to the University of Chiquita. In fact, U of C will come to you. We'll give you and your produce people the most intensive education in growing, shipping, ripening and selling of bananas ever offered.
You'll master every aspect of the business from handling techniques to the most sophisticated merchandising methods. You'll learn how to promote and display better... how to reduce seasonality and make more money year round.
Now, if you're worried because you slept through Trig or counted the seconds in study hall, don't. The entire program, from freshman to grad, takes only one session. And as for tuition, forget it. Consider it a scholarship, on Chiquita. (After all, if you sell more bananas, so do we.)
So if you or any of your people are interested, contact your Chiquita* representative. Enroll in the University of Chiquita. You'll make more money in bananas and you'll make your mother proud. (Tell her you've got your MBA... Masters of Banana Art.)
Chiquitas sell better than bananas
Chiquita

66

67

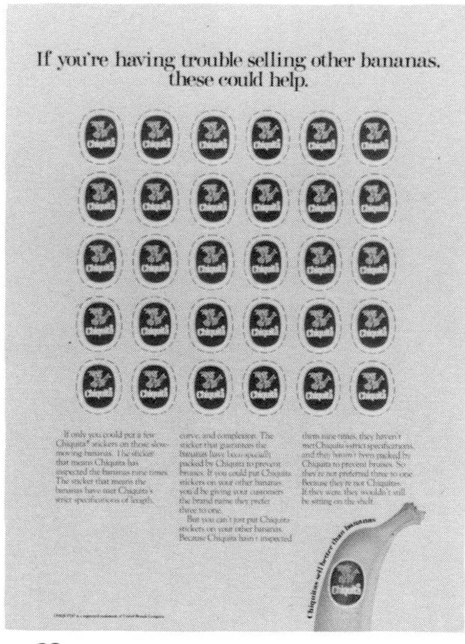

68

66
Art Director Steve LaGattuta
Writer Jim Dale
Artist Sean Early
Agency W.B. Doner & Co.
Client United Brands/Chiquita

67
Art Director Bob Sherman
Writer Arnold Paley
Designer Bob Sherman
Photographer Michel Ditlove
Agency Brand Advertising Inc.
Client Fannie May Candies

68
Art Director Steve LaGattuta
Writer Jim Dale
Agency W.B. Doner & Co.
Client United Brands/Chiquita

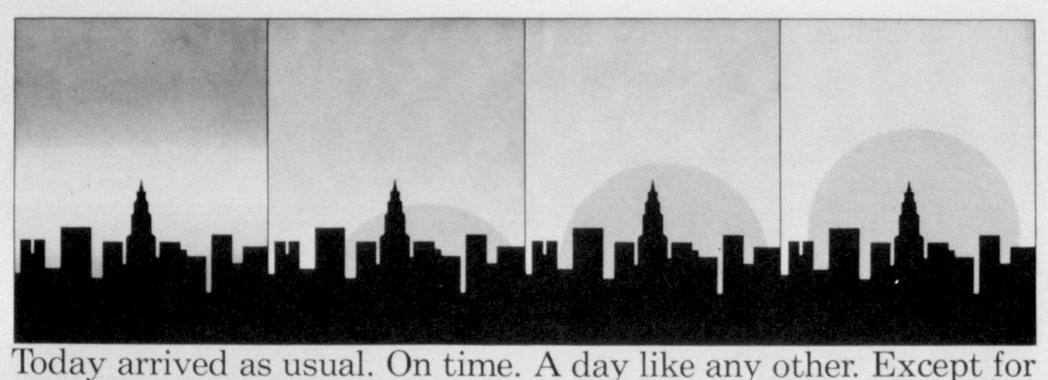

Today arrived as usual. On time. A day like any other. Except for

its own individual sunrise. And it will come and go, passing its

memories along, and leaving us with the promise of another new

day, another New Year. May it be a happy one. **Higbee's**

69

69
Art Director Rick Seich
Writer Vivian Henoch
Designer Rich Seich
Artist Art Plant
Agency Wyse Advertising
Client The Higbee Co.

OUR LEVI'S ARE DOWN.

But we're not embarrassed. We've dropped our prices on 2,000 pairs of Levi's for guys. $12.50 covers it. So pull yourself together, and get into our basic bells and straight-leg and boot-cut jeans . . . . 2,000 pairs in cotton denims and corduroy and pre-washed denims. You name it, if the name is Levi's, we've got it. Regularly 15.75 to 19.50

Now $12.50

Higbee's

Young Men's Shop, Street Floor.

70

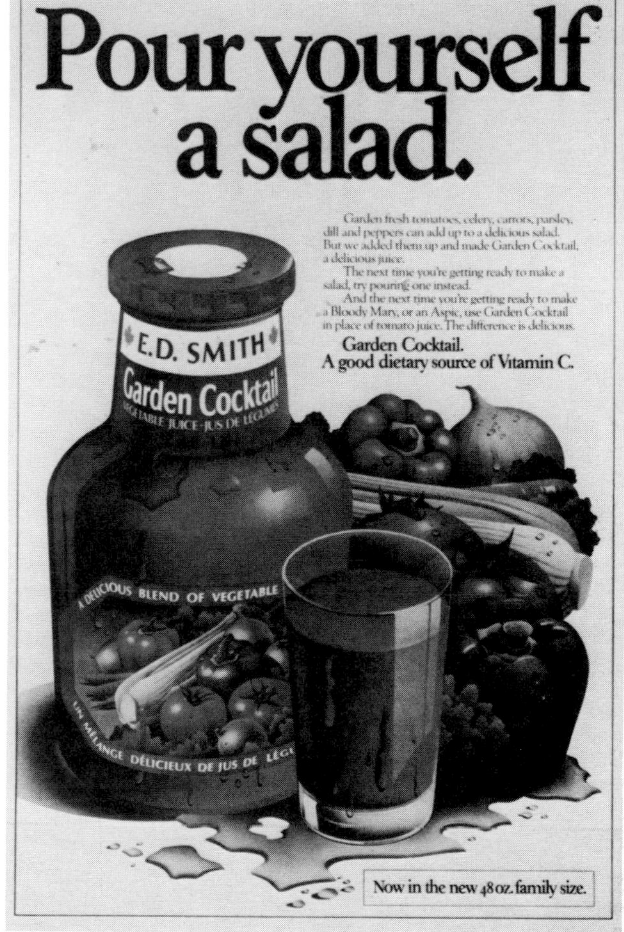

Pour yourself a salad.
Garden fresh tomatoes, celery, carrots, parsley, dill and peppers can add up to a delicious salad. But we added them up and made Garden Cocktail, a delicious juice.
The next time you're getting ready to make a salad, try pouring one instead.
And the next time you're getting ready to make a Bloody Mary, or an Aspic, use Garden Cocktail in place of tomato juice. The difference is delicious.
Garden Cocktail.
A good dietary source of Vitamin C.
E.D. SMITH
Garden Cocktail
Now in the new 48 oz. family size.

71

70

Art Director Rick Seich
Writer Vivian Henoch
Designer Rick Seich
Artist Ron Van Buskirk
Agency Wyse Advertising
Client The Higbee Co.

71

Art Director Bill Yip
Writer Tom Hicks
Designer Bill Yip
Artist Roger Hill
Agency Case Associates Advertising Ltd.
Client E.D. Smith & Sons Limited

Fannie May wishes you a happy Valentine Day
and offers you many ways to express it.

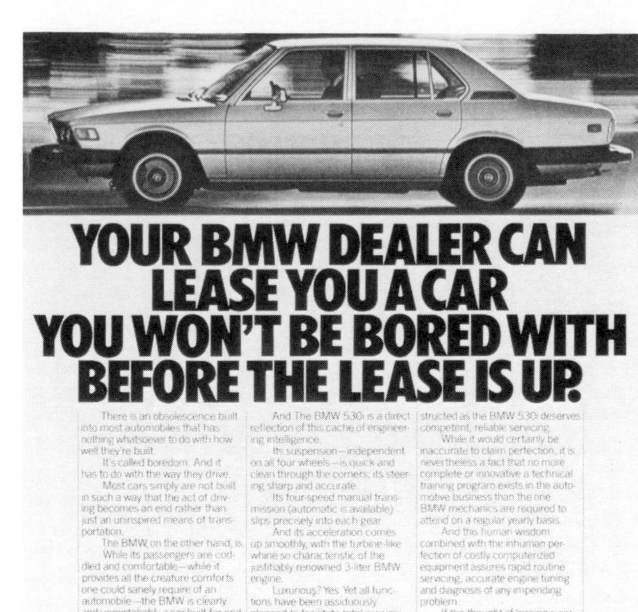

YOUR BMW DEALER CAN LEASE YOU A CAR YOU WON'T BE BORED WITH BEFORE THE LEASE IS UP.
There is an obsolescence built into most automobiles that has nothing whatsoever to do with how well they're built.
It's called boredom. And it has to do with the way they drive.
Most cars simply are not built in such a way that the act of driving becomes an end rather than just an uninspired means of transportation.
The BMW, on the other hand, is.
While its passengers are coddled and comfortable—while it provides all the creature comforts one could sanely require of an automobile—the BMW is clearly and unmistakably a car built for and around the driver.
PERFORMANCE PERFECTED ON THE RACE TRACK.
While it is, of course, feasible to develop an acceptable automobile in the relative vacuum of the test track and the laboratory, it is virtually impossible to simulate the engineering perfection demanded by motor racing.
And The BMW 530i is a direct reflection of this cache of engineering intelligence.
Its suspension—independent on all four wheels—is quick and clean through the corners; its steering sharp and accurate.
Its four-speed manual transmission (automatic is available) slips precisely into each gear.
And its acceleration comes up smoothly, with the turbine-like whine so characteristic of the justifiably renowned 3-liter BMW engine.
Luxurious? Yes. Yet all functions have been assiduously planned to facilitate total precise control at all times, under all conditions. Engineered to include the driver as one of the functioning parts of the car itself—the human part that completes the mechanical circuit.
SERVICE AS EFFICIENT AND RELIABLE AS THE CAR ITSELF.
An automobile as thoroughly engineered and meticulously constructed as the BMW 530i deserves competent, reliable servicing.
While it would certainly be inaccurate to claim perfection, it is nevertheless a fact that no more complete or innovative a technical training program exists in the automotive business than the one BMW mechanics are required to attend on a regular yearly basis.
And this human wisdom combined with the inhuman perfection of costly computerized equipment assures rapid routine servicing, accurate engine tuning and diagnosis of any impending problem.
If the thought of leasing a car you can actually enjoy driving intrigues you, we suggest you phone your BMW dealer. Not only can he arrange a thorough test drive at your convenience, he can make available a variety of convenient leasing plans as well.
BMW
THE ULTIMATE DRIVING MACHINE.
Bavarian Motor Works, Munich, Germany

72

ONE OF THE FEW LUXURY SEDANS IN THE WORLD THAT WOULDN'T BE LAUGHED OFF THE NÜRBURGRING.
In the heart of Germany there is a race course called the Nürburgring.
An awesome giant of a track, generally acknowledged to be the most arduous test of both cars and men.
All of the world's great high-performance cars have raced there—most have had their day.
Yet, few cars—and certainly no luxury sedans—have achieved a more impressive record on the Nürburgring than those built by the Bavarian Motor Works of Munich, Germany.
Luxury sedans? Yes. But luxury sedans built by racing engineers. German engineers who believe that extraordinary performance is the only thing that makes an expensive car worth the money.
PERFORMANCE PERFECTED ON THE RACE TRACK.
While it is, of course, feasible to develop an acceptable automobile in the relative vacuum of the test track and the laboratory, it is virtually impossible to simulate the perfection demanded by motor racing.
Motor racing enables BMW engineers to develop ideas and experiment without the inhibiting constraints of economics or the cost of production—a crucial role in the development of a true high-performance automobile.
And the BMW 530i is a direct reflection of this cache of engineering intelligence.
Its suspension—independent on all four wheels—is quick and clean through the corners; its steering sharp and accurate.
Its four-speed manual transmission (automatic is available) slips precisely into each gear. And its acceleration comes up smoothly, with the turbine-like whine so characteristic of the justifiably renowned 3-liter BMW engine.
PARTICIPATION NOT ISOLATION.
The interior of the conventional luxury sedan is deliberately engineered to isolate the driver from the mechanical workings of the automobile, the world outside and the road beneath.
The interior of the BMW 530i is carefully engineered to include the driver as one of the integral, functioning parts of the car itself—the human part that completes the mechanical circuit.
Careful study has been made of the critical interrelation between seat location, visual position, steering wheel, pedals and controls.
Luxurious? Yes. Yet all functions have been assiduously planned to facilitate total, precise control at all times, under all conditions.
So successful is this integration of man and machine that when you drive the BMW 530i for the first time, you will experience an almost total oneness with the car. A unique feeling of effortless control which, if you're accustomed to conventional luxury sedans, will be completely and pleasantly new to you.
Surprising? Only to those who have never driven a BMW.
As the editors of Motor Trend magazine observed, "The reaction to a BMW is always the same. The first time driver takes the wheel and after a few minutes no other automobile will ever be the same again."
If the thought of owning such a car intrigues you, call us anytime, toll-free, at 800-243-6000 (Conn. 1-800-882-6500) and we'll arrange a thorough test drive for you at your convenience.
BMW
THE ULTIMATE DRIVING MACHINE.
Bavarian Motor Works, Munich, Germany.
© 1977 BMW of North America, Inc.

73

GOLD

72
Art Director Bob Sherman
Writer Arnold Paley
Designer Bob Sherman
Photographer Mike Ditlove
Agency Brand Advertising Inc.
Client Fannie May Candies

73
Art Director Clem McCarthy
Writer Martin Puris
Photographers Dick James
David Thorpe
Agency Ammirati Puris AvRutick
Client BMW of North America, Inc.

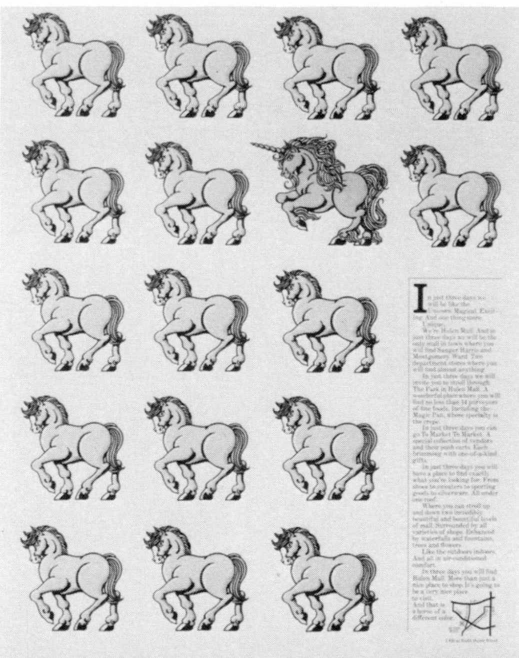

**Hulen Mall Opens in Three Days.
Look for Something Unique.**

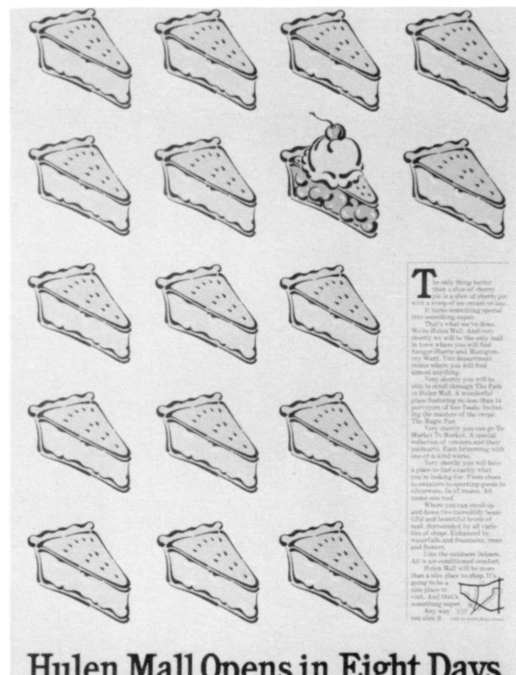

**Hulen Mall Opens in Eight Days.
Look for Something Super.**

74

Soon the PLO may have its own country to land hijacked planes in.

The fact that the PLO has already made itself infamous for hijacking, murder, and turning the country of Lebanon into a bloodbath is bad enough.

But can you imagine what would happen if this same organization became the governing body of a Palestinian state?

Not only would the PLO have a place to land hijacked planes in —it would have a country from which it could launch a lot more than terrorist attacks.

It could easily, with a little nuclear help from you know who, launch World War III.

Is it any wonder, then, that Israel cannot sit down at the Geneva Conference with the PLO?

It would be ludicrous for any nation—the United States, Israel or anyone else—to bargain with a gang of terrorists bent on destroying it.

What has to be done, then, is pretty obvious: keep the PLO out of the Geneva Conference and that will keep Israel in.

Unless that happens, there can be no peace in the Middle East.

And until the Arab states stop supporting the PLO, there can be no peace in the world.

So, what's more important? A handful of PLO terrorists? Or the human race?

The birth of Palestine may be the death of us all.

75

For two years, this man had a steady job, a place to stay, and enough to eat. Then they let him out of prison.

Two years behind bars and he didn't start losing hope until he got out. Because then he found out that nobody wanted to hire him or extend him credit. Lots of people didn't even want to talk to him.

If we keep ignoring him, he'll go away. Probably right back to prison. And that'll cost the taxpayer about as much per year as it would cost to send two people to Harvard University.

Damascus Way is a better alternative. We're a halfway house that goes the whole distance helping people re-enter society after they've been in trouble. Whether they're ex-prisoners, or recovering from chemical dependency, or have some other serious problem.

Damascus Way gives them intensive day-by-day counseling, guidance and vocational training, all in a Christian atmosphere. The approach is as tough and disciplined as it is kind and compassionate.

Above all, it works. Our record so far has been excellent. Now we want to expand our facilities so we can help a few more people out.

Please give to Damascus Way. Your contribution is tax deductible. Just phone us your pledge now, or mail your contribution along with this coupon.

Here is my contribution to Damascus Way.
NAME
ADDRESS
CITY
STATE ZIP

Dial a donation: 920-8147

Damascus Way Halfway House
Helping people out.

76

74
Art Director Jim Hradecky
Writer Jim Hradecky
Designer Jim Hradecky
Artists Woody Pirtle, Jerry Jeanmard
Agency The Richards Group
Client The Rouse Company

75
Art Director Rosenwasser
Writer Bob Veder
Agency Grey Advertising
Client Anti-Defamation League

76
Art Director Bill Hogan
Writer Dick Thomas
Designer Bill Hogan
Photographer Tom Berthiaume
Agency Bozell & Jacobs/Mpls.
Client Damascus Way

FILL IN SOMEBODY'S LIFE.

The Salvation Army fills the needs and the hopes of thousands of people right here in New York.

When people are homeless, we give them shelter. When they are sick, we help them heal. When they feel hopeless, we share our faith.

In our work, every day counts. And every dollar counts. We need your help.

The checklist shows just some of the ways your contribution to The Salvation Army can help.

$.60 buys lunch for a kid in a Day-Care Center. $_____

$1.00 gives a youth a month of supervised athletics at a Corps Community Center—a month off the streets. $_____

$2.25 brings one more needy child to a Merry Christmas party right in his or her neighborhood. $_____

$11.00 will cover a day's room, meals, laundry, and other services for a disabled woman at the Anthony Residence. $_____

$15.00 pays for an hour of professional rehabilitative counseling at a Salvation Army Center. $_____

$25.00 helps feed, house and counsel a girl trying to kick her drug habit at Stuyvesant Square Narcotics Center. $_____

$30.00 gives a student who needs extra assistance with his or her studies a special tutor for a week. $_____

$37.92 is an entire week's room and board for one person at a Salvation Army Rehabilitation Center. $_____

$55.00 takes a lonely senior citizen to the country for a companionable week at a Vacation Center. $_____

$100.00 contributes to the costs of a Family Counseling Center, to help troubled families stay together. $_____

$150.00 helps The Salvation Army prison visitation program, helps prisoners remember they're still people. $_____

$175.00 takes one child off the steamy city streets and to summer camp for 12 days. $_____

$275.00 feeds a child for a year at a Day-Care Center. $_____

$759.00 buys a 16mm. sound projector for films to be used in a Rehabilitation Center. $_____

$1,000.00 sponsors a year of Operation Toy-Lift, a program to bring toys to children of prisoners in Nassau County. $_____

$47,331.00 operates all The Salvation Army programs and services in Greater New York for one day. $_____

I know The Salvation Army will use my contribution in the way it's needed most. Enclosed is my total tax-deductible contribution of $________

Please make checks payable to The Salvation Army of Greater New York.

Mail to Lt. Col. Walter C. French, Divisional Commander, The Salvation Army, Suite 600, 50 West 23rd Street, New York, New York 10010.

Name ________________

Address ________________

City ________________

State ________ Zip ________

This message contributed by **Avon Products, Inc.**

The Salvation Army is a partner of the United Fund of Greater New York and the United Way of Long Island and Westchester.

77

77

Art Director	**Tom Wolsey**
Writers	**Tom Wolsey**
	Suzette Prigmore
Designer	**Tom Wolsey**
Photographer	**Joe Toto**
Agency	**Ogilvy & Mather**
Client	**Avon Products**

AFTER YOU GIVE THAT LITTLE BIT EXTRA, GIVE YOURSELF A PAT ON THE BACK.

YOU JUST SAVED SOMEBODY'S LIFE.

Every year at this time, United Jewish Appeal canvassers are busy knocking on doors.

Every year at this time they're faced with the same old problem.

You see, a lot of people out there could give a little more than they do. The problem is they don't think it'll make much of a difference.

The fact is, that little bit extra you're holding back can mean the difference between life and death.

If you think we're being a little melodramatic, tell it to the Jew imprisoned in a Soviet Gulag. To him that little bit extra can mean his sheer physical survival.

To the Soviet Jew immigrating to Israel, that extra push you make can mean a full year of university training and that does more than improve his life, it breathes a little more life into Israel.

To that Moroccan Jewish family living in a moshav, that little bit extra can mean a lot of things most of us take for granted. Things like beds instead of dirt floors to sleep on.

To the wounded soldier who laid his life on the line for Judaism, those few extra bucks we could all give can pay for months of the medical attention he so badly needs and deserves.

And to the unskilled and jobless, that little bit extra can mean new skills, new jobs and a productive life. Not to mention the chance at pride and accomplishment.

The fact is, that when we all hold back that little bit extra, thousands of Jews suffer a lot.

So when the time comes to give, dig a little deeper. Give that little extra that you always thought was meaningless.

Then go pat yourself on the back.

We know a lot of Jews who, given the opportunity, would do it for you.

We are one
UNITED JEWISH APPEAL / ISRAEL SPECIAL FUND

150 Beverley Street, Toronto, Ontario M5T 1Y6 Phone 869-3811

78

78
Art Director Jerry Ginsberg
Writer Terry Bell
Agency Vickers & Benson Ltd.
Client United Jewish Appeal

KIEFER

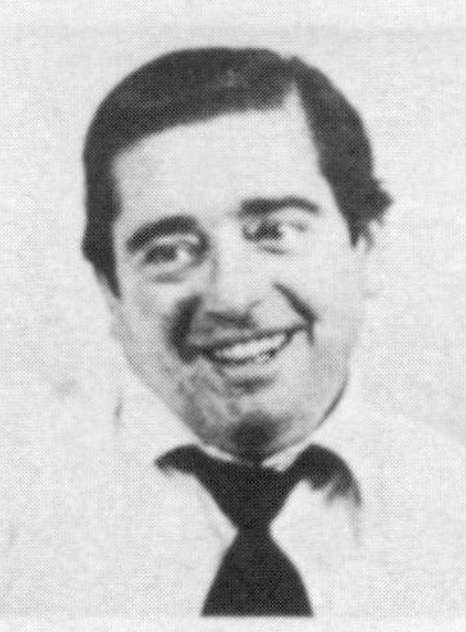

80

80

Art Director	Tom Varisco
Writer	Rusty Cantelli
Designer	Tom Varisco
Photographers	John McRoberts
	B. Coleman
	Varisco
Agency	The Swigart Co., Tom Varisco
Client	Nat Kiefer Campaign for Mayor

Newspaper Editorial

BREAD: A Toast to Ethnic Bakeries, And Noble Loaves of Splendor

Best Buys

By the Numbers

BREAD

81

Caesar's Wife on Lance

By James Reston

Indeed, 'the Moral Equivalent of War'

Mr. Lance Is Not A Crook

By Tom Wicker

IN THE NATION

The report raises nothing but questions about his competence.

"Catch-22" in Turkey

FOREIGN AFFAIRS

The United States has really replaced Greece as the most disliked country in Turkey today.

WASHINGTON

Q. If you had borrowed money on the old man's power and reputation, what would Julius have done?
A. He would have tossed me to the lions

82

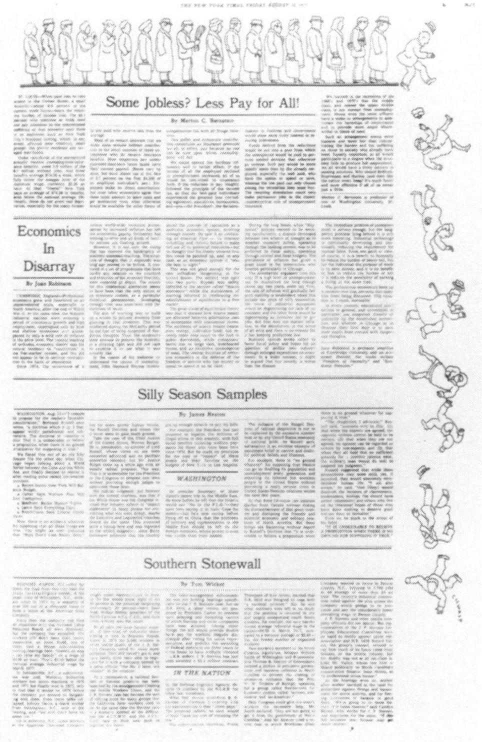

Some Jobless? Less Pay for All!

Economics In Disarray

By Joan Robinson

Silly Season Samples

By James Reston

WASHINGTON

Southern Stonewall

By Tom Wicker

IN THE NATION

83

81
Art Director Jerelle Kraus
Editor Annette Grant
Designer Jerelle Kraus
Photographer Al Wegener/The New York Times
Agency The New York Times
Client The New York Times

82
Art Director Pamela Vassil
Editor Charlotte Curtis
Designer Pamela Vassil
Artist Jacqueline Chwast
Agency The New York Times
Client The New York Times

83
Art Director Pamela Vassil
Editor Charlotte Curtis
Designer Pamela Vassil
Artist Seymour Chwast
Agency The New York Times
Client The New York Times

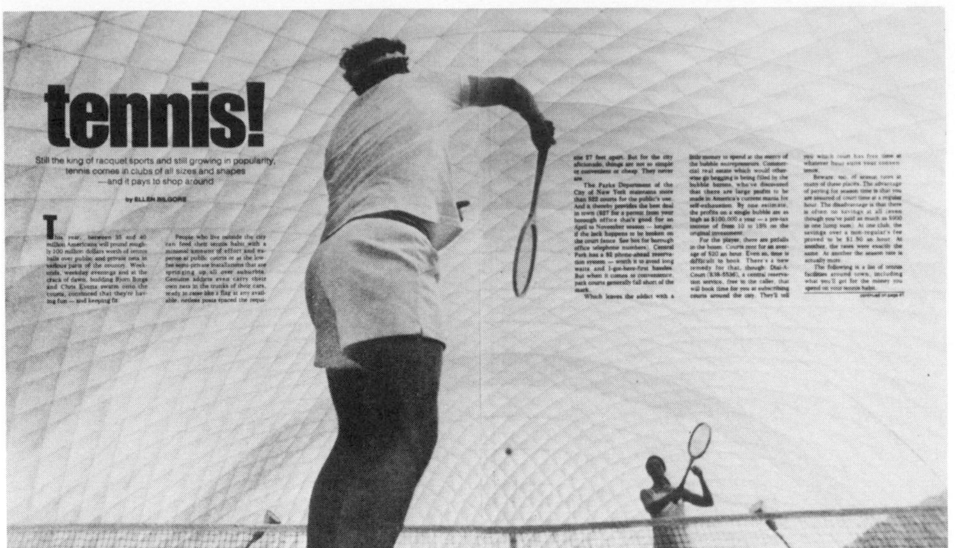

tennis!

Still the king of racquet sports and still growing in popularity, tennis comes in clubs of all sizes and shapes —and it pays to shop around

by ELLEN BILGORE

85

The Living Section

Savoring the Best Of French Cookery

Habit de Cuisinier

Charting Life With a Daughter

A Survivor of the 60's Recalls the Decade

The New Disco: Life Begins At Midnight, Page C10

84

Book World

THE BOOKS OF CHRISTMAS

2

86

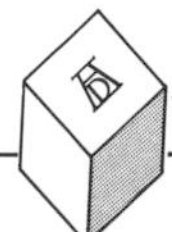

SILVER

84
Art Director Jerelle Kraus
Editor Annettee Grant
Designer Jerelle Kraus
Artist Pillow by Miriam Wosk
Photographers Cook by Bettman Archive
Disco by Bill Cunningham
Agency The New York Times
Client The New York Times

85
Art Director Robert Clive
Writer Ellen Bilgore
Designer Tom Ruis
Photographer Roy Morsch
Agency New York Daily News
Client Sunday News Magazine

86
Art Director K. Francis Tanabe
Writer William McPherson
Designer Michael David Brown
Artist Michael David Brown
Client The Washington Post Book World

Magazine Advertising

"How the Xerox 9200 improved our figures."

"With two 9200s and one operator, we can complete crucial rush jobs totalling more than 1 million copies a month at a savings of 96 man-hours."
Floyd Bowman, Chief
Bureau of Administrative Services
Department of Public Aid
State of Illinois

"Because of the Xerox 9200's capability to automatically feed, print and sort simultaneously, I find it's five times faster than our two offset presses."
George W. Cook
Production Manager
General Research Corporation
McLean, Virginia

"On an average job, the Xerox 9200 turned out to be 100% faster than offset. Why? No original plating. No collating slowdown. And no cleanup."
Barbra Cooper, Manager
Communications Center
Miller & Paine, Lincoln, Nebraska

"Now we rarely have difficulty meeting short delivery requirements of our customers. In our business, there is no tomorrow. With the 9200 we've improved our turnaround time by 50%." John Kirincich
Vice President & Treasurer
Mathias & Carr, Inc., New York, N.Y.

The Xerox 9200 Duplicating System, with its computerized programmer, can automatically feed, cycle, reduce and sort a limitless number of complete sets at the incredible rate of 2 pages a second. It can help you and your budget look a lot better.

XEROX

87

I'll promise you anything, but give me Arpege
LANVIN
from five to a thousand dollars

88

87
Art Directors Anthony Angotti
Allen Kay
Writers Anthony Angotti
Steve Penchin
Agency Needham, Harper & Steers Adv. Inc.
Client Xerox Corp.

88
Art Director Keith Rabedeau
Writer Phillip Geraci
Photographer Eugenia Louis
Agency Advertising to Women
Client Charles of the Ritz —Arpege

A Candle Can Tell You a Lot About Great Wine. Or Great Whisky.

You can prove Old Forester has a unique taste without even putting it to your lips. The same way experts prove it with wine, by color.

For example, when held to a candle, a Burgundy should glow a deep purple. A Bordeaux, brick red. Two different colors, two different tastes.

When held to a candle, a great whisky should be rich, burnished gold. The color of Old Forester.

The golden glow assures you Old Forester will taste like no other whisky in the world. That every sip will be mellow, full-bodied and perfectly smooth.

What's more, Old Forester gets this color and taste solely from the unique way it's matured in our charred oak barrels.

It's made naturally, like Great Wine.

But there's another way to test Old Forester's superiority that's even more conclusive. Taste it.

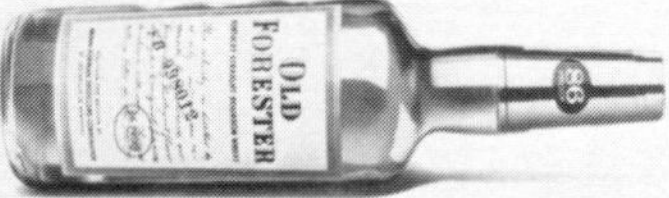

The Great Whisky Made Like Great Wine.

89

Do you keep running into your office on the late show?

It's one thing to have an office furnished with antiques. It's another to have an antiquated office.

If your office strikes your customers and clients as old and worn-out, your business may strike them the same way.

The Itkins are in the business of making business look good, any business, small, medium or large. As New York's largest office furnishings firm, The Itkins have the decorating skills, the enormous selection and the sensible prices that make decorating your office a practical idea, not just a good one.

So, if your office could be used to shoot a remake of "The Maltese Falcon", call The Itkins today.

You can't do today's business in yesterday's office. **The Itkins**

90

The look.
The fragrance.
Ambush
PERFUME
Dana
Ambush by Dana.
Now the look of freshness has a fragrance all its own.

91

89	
Art Director	Mark Shap
Writers	Joe Tantillo
	Ken Majka
Designer	Tom Wai-Shek
Agency	DKG Advertising, Inc.
Client	Brown Forman

90	
Art Director	Steve Ohman
Writer	Murray Klein
Designer	Steve Ohman
Photographer	Cailor/Resnick
	7 stock photos
Agency	Smith/Greenland, Inc.
Client	Itkins Office Furniture

91	
Art Director	Gary Carlisle
Writer	Cynthia Johnson
Designers	Martin Lipsitt
	Gary Carlisle
Photographer	Patrick DuMarchelier
Agency	DKG Advertising, Inc.
Client	Dana Perfumes

DON'T SMEAR YOUR OWN GOOD NAME.
When copies go out of your office with your letterhead, they have to make a good first impression.
If they don't, you may not get a second chance.
So any copy you send out has to arrive sharp, dry and unsmearable.
That's why Toshiba created the BD-601 copier.
Toshiba's BD-601 is an economical, compact, precision plain paper copier that delivers clean, sharp, *dry* impressions with extraordinary consistency.
Unlike others in its price range, the Toshiba uses *dry toner*. No messy liquids. No special-finish duplicating paper.
Toshiba's BD-601 is a *true plain paper copier*.
This means that like other Toshiba copiers, it'll make completely dry copies of just about anything on letterhead, colored stock, graph paper—just about any paper in your office.
The BD-601 is fast (first copy in 11 seconds) and handy (it fits on a desk). Perfect for a small firm. Or a larger one ready for a decentralized copying system.
Business is competitive. And if your correspondence looks better than the competition, it could be the edge you need.
The Toshiba BD-601. For $3,150* no other copier copies all its features.
TOSHIBA
FAGUNDO & TEICH
CERTIFIED PUBLIC ACCOUNTANT
600 FIFTH AVENUE
NEW YORK, NEW YORK 10019
Hogue, Pennette and Nathan, Inc.
Precision Engineering
1271 Avenue of the Americas
New York, New York 10020
Gentlemen:
We have comp
records and
GET THE TOSHIBA BD-601. IT MAKES DRY COPIES ON JUST ABOUT ANY PAPER.

92

"Dear General Foods, Imitation this. Artificial that. Synthetic this. What's wrong with real food?"
"THERE MUST BE A REAL EGG HERE SOMEWHERE!"
Actually, there's nothing wrong with "real" food. Or with any foods, natural or man-made, that you're likely to come across in the supermarket.
But there *is* some confusion regarding imitation eggs or artificial bacon, or any of those foods variously called synthetic or man-made. Now, the more you know about what you eat, the better. So toward that end, we'd like to clear up some of that confusion and provide a few explanations here.
Man-made foods: who needs them?
As with everything else you can buy, it's consumers who determine whether or not man-made foods exist. If people are willing to buy these foods, supermarkets will sell them. So when we're asked who wants these man-made foods, it isn't a glib answer to say that people do.
Okay. People need them. But why?
Because, for one reason, they can save you money. You actually spend less of your income on food than most people in other countries. Man-made foods are part of the reason. They usually cost less to produce, and therefore to buy, than many of the fresh foods they may replace.
Another reason for man-made foods is simply that they taste good—not occasionally, but consistently. Since they can be made under conditions more controllable and predictable than the weather, man-made foods don't fluctuate in quality quite the way natural foods do. And, of course, they're produced and available year-round, winter *and* summer.
Then, too, most man-made foods store for a long time without spoiling and are usually easy to prepare—points so obvious we sometimes overlook them.
Finally—and maybe most important—man-made foods will help make sure the world has enough to eat. We're producing more and more people, and conserving less and less farmland to feed them. In a world with some 4 billion mouths to feed, man-made foods perform an important role now, and will perform an increasingly important one in the future.
How "imitation" butter became "real" margarine.
It's sometimes assumed that there are two kinds of food in the world: (1) real and (2) everything else. Actually, the distinction between "real" and man-made is nowhere near as sharp as it might seem.
Take margarine. It was invented over a century ago as a sort of "imitation" butter. The margarine people couldn't have been very happy with the "imitation" label, suggesting, as it did, some inferior version. But over the years, margarine came to be known as something else: a good-tasting, long-lasting alternative that's especially useful for people concerned about animal fats and cholesterol. It's not "imitation" anything, anymore. It's genuine margarine. Not "imitation" butter, but certainly "real" food.
And that's the point: there are any number of man-made alternatives to natural foods in the supermarket, and these are no less "real" for being alternatives. In fact, the alternatives usually offer some benefit the original doesn't, or else there'd be no need for them.
Take our Dream Whip* Whipped Topping Mix. It isn't whipped cream. But it is a good-tasting alternative that's readily available, low-calorie, certainly long-lasting, and probably more dependable (it virtually always whips). Or take our Tang Instant Breakfast Drink. It's made with natural orange flavor. A 4-fluid-ounce serving gives you a full day's supply of Vitamin C, and not even an orange can give you better Vitamin C than Tang. It won't spoil quickly, and you can mix up as little or as much at a time as you want, without waste.
What's wrong with "real" food? Not a thing. It's just that today it comes in more varieties, and with more alternatives, than even the inventors of margarine ever dreamed.
For more information.
We hope this brief discussion of man-made foods has taken a little of the mystery out of why they're made.
If you have any questions about them, please feel free to ask. Just write to Miss Peggy Kohl, V.P., Consumer Affairs, G.F. Consumer Center, White Plains, N.Y. 10625.
Our reasons for telling you all this are a mixture of helpfulness and pride in our products. The more you understand about food, the better off you'll be. And the more you understand about our foods, the better off we'll be.
GF
©1977 General Foods Corp.

94

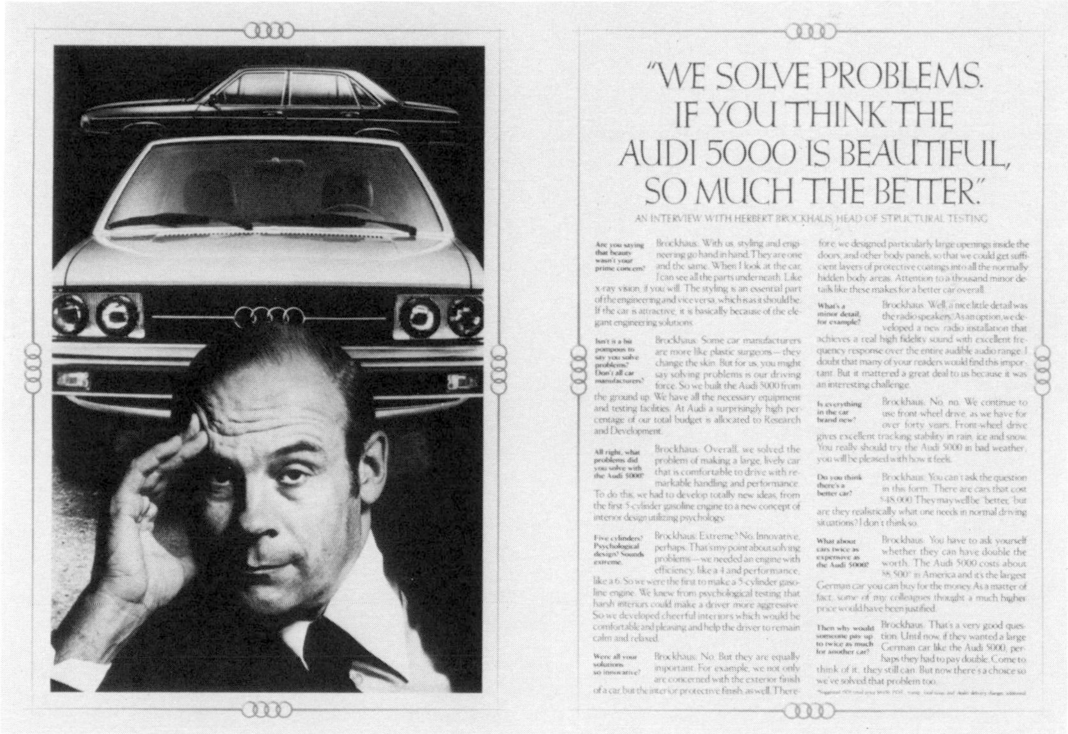
"WE SOLVE PROBLEMS. IF YOU THINK THE AUDI 5000 IS BEAUTIFUL, SO MUCH THE BETTER."
AN INTERVIEW WITH HERBERT BROCKHAUS, HEAD OF STRUCTURAL TESTING
Are you saying that beauty wasn't your prime concern?
Brockhaus: With us, styling and engineering go hand in hand. They are one and the same. When I look at the car, I can see all the parts underneath. Like x-ray vision, if you will. The styling is an essential part of the engineering and vice versa, which is as it should be. If the car is attractive, it is basically because of the elegant engineering solutions.
Isn't it a bit pompous to say you solve problems? Don't all car manufacturers?
Brockhaus: Some car manufacturers are more like plastic surgeons—they change the skin. But for us, you might say solving problems is our driving force. So we built the Audi 5000 from the ground up. We have all the necessary equipment and testing facilities. At Audi a surprisingly high percentage of our total budget is allocated to Research and Development.
All right, what problems did you solve with the Audi 5000?
Brockhaus: Overall, we solved the problem of making a large, lively car that is comfortable to drive with remarkable handling and performance. To do this, we had to develop totally new ideas, from the first 5-cylinder gasoline engine to a new concept of interior design utilizing psychology.
Five cylinders? Psychological design? Sounds extreme.
Brockhaus: Extreme? No. Innovative, perhaps. That's my point about solving problems—we needed an engine with efficiency, like a 4 and performance, like a 6. So we were the first to make a 5-cylinder gasoline engine. We knew from psychological testing that harsh interiors could make a driver more aggressive. So we developed cheerful interiors which would be comfortable and pleasing and help the driver to remain calm and relaxed.
Were all your solutions so innovative?
Brockhaus: No. But they are equally important. For example, we not only are concerned with the exterior finish of a car but the interior protective finish as well. Therefore we designed particularly large openings inside the doors, and other body panels, so that we could get sufficient layers of protective coatings into all the normally hidden body areas. Attention to a thousand minor details like these makes for a better car overall.
What's a minor detail, for example?
Brockhaus: Well, a nice little detail was the radio speakers. As an option, we developed a new radio installation that achieves a real high fidelity sound with excellent frequency response over the entire audible audio range. I doubt that many of your readers would find this important. But it mattered a great deal to us because it was an interesting challenge.
Is everything in the car brand new?
Brockhaus: No, no. We continue to use front-wheel drive, as we have for over forty years. Front-wheel drive gives excellent tracking stability in rain, ice and snow. You really should try the Audi 5000 in bad weather, you will be pleased with how it feels.
Do you think there's a better car?
Brockhaus: You can't ask the question in this form. There are cars that cost $48,000. They may well be 'better,' but are they realistically what one needs in normal driving situations? I don't think so.
What about cars twice as expensive as the Audi 5000?
Brockhaus: You have to ask yourself whether they can have double the worth. The Audi 5000 costs about $8,500* in America and it's the largest German car you can buy for the money. As a matter of fact, some of my colleagues thought a much higher price would have been justified.
Then why would someone pay up to twice as much for another car?
Brockhaus: That's a very good question. Until now, if they wanted a large German car like the Audi 5000, perhaps they had to pay double. Come to think of it, they still can. But now there's a choice so we've solved that problem too.

93

	92
Art Director	Michael Pennette
Writer	Tom Nathan
Designer	Michael Pennette
Photographer	Chuck LaMonica
Agency	DKG Advertising, Inc.
Client	Toshiba America

	93
Art Director	Helmut Krone
Writer	Bob Levenson
Photographer	Carl Fischer
Agency	Doyle Dane Bernbach
Client	Porsche-Audi

	94
Art Director	Gary Carlisle
Writer	Tom Thomas
Artist	Bill Woodman
Agency	Young & Rubicam
Client	General Foods Co.

Don't buy two turkeys for Thanksgiving Dinner.
Buying a turkey at a meat counter is fine. Buying a turkey at a wine counter is not.
But amidst all the choices, how does one avoid a mistake?
French wine is the best.
But even French wine can be a jungle.
There are thousands of chateaus, hundreds of shippers, a dozen different vintage years—perhaps *a million different bottles* from which to choose...what?
We'd like to suggest Grande Marque.
Grande Marque is fine vintage French wine, consistent from year to year. It comes from Bordeaux, that small part of France that produces more great wines than the rest of the world combined.
A large gold seal (literally, a "*grande marque*") on the label makes it easy to spot. And the name is easy to say—just pronounce it "Grand Mark."
There's a Grande Marque red and a Grande Marque white—and a lively debate as to which goes best with a Thanksgiving feast. (The experts say both.)
Grande Marque is good insurance that your Thanksgiving fowl will end up on your plate and not in your glass.
TIP: The bouquet and taste of a great red wine like Grande Marque improves when cork is removed a half hour or so before serving and wine is allowed to "breathe."
GRANDE MARQUE
BORDEAUX
"All the French you need to know." Grande Marque is a product of France, imported by Munson Shaw, New York.

95

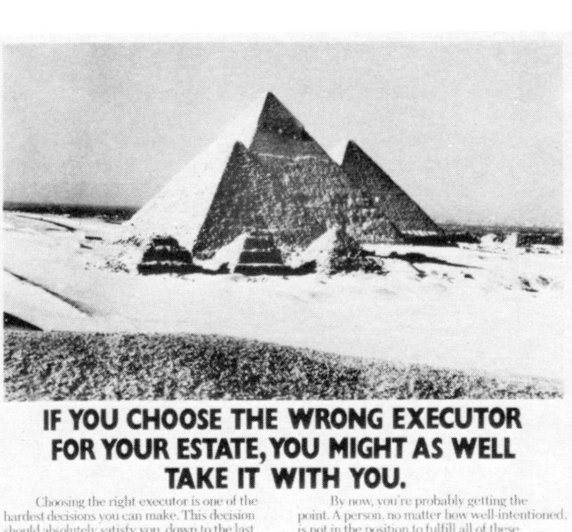

IF YOU CHOOSE THE WRONG EXECUTOR FOR YOUR ESTATE, YOU MIGHT AS WELL TAKE IT WITH YOU.
Choosing the right executor is one of the hardest decisions you can make. This decision should absolutely satisfy you, down to the last detail, and you should demand the highest standards in handling every single one of your requirements.
You should require that your executor is sophisticated and competent in handling financial problems. Your executor should have access to the best legal and financial consultants.
Your executor should have no conflicts between his desires and yours. Your executor should be available to spend every day, all day, if necessary until matters are settled. Your executor should not go away during the settlement. Your executor should be expected not to have emotional reactions which could get in the way of making important decisions. Your executor should not become ill during the settlement. Your executor should have years of experience, knowledge, understanding and training in being an executor.
By now, you're probably getting the point. A person, no matter how well-intentioned, is not in the position to fulfill all of these requirements.
That is why we would like to talk with you about our ability and experience in handling this difficult and demanding task.
You can feel comfortable in knowing that as an executor, or co-executor, we are absolutely competent in handling your complete needs.
Now, at this point it becomes a very personal and individual matter. We will be glad to discuss it with you, with no obligations.
To arrange for an appointment call Donald R. Cowles, Vice President. He will be pleased to assist you in making your decision.
PUTNAM TRUST
The Bank of Greenwich
We're here to make your life a little easier.

96

Mobil 1
Your antifreeze will freeze before our oil will.
We know you'll probably never see temperatures cold enough to make antifreeze freeze up. But it's nice to know that there's an oil that's good enough to flow freely after antifreeze, not to mention ordinary oil, has turned to slush.
Mobil 1 is a new, synthesized motor oil that can actually help a properly maintained engine get started at 35 degrees below zero!
If this were the end of the story Mobil 1 would still be a remarkable buy. But it's only the beginning. Since Mobil 1 reduces friction and drag better than ordinary motor oil, you get better mileage. With Mobil 1 the average car will get up to 10 extra miles out of a tankful of gas.
The oil that saves gas also saves oil. In highway and city fleet tests Mobil 1 cut oil consumption by as much as 25%. The explanation is simple. Mobil 1 doesn't evaporate as rapidly as ordinary motor oil.
Being synthetic, Mobil 1 also gives you better engine protection. To prove it, we put Mobil 1 in a fleet of highway patrol cars for 12,000 miles. But even after all this abuse, we found that Mobil 1 still protected like brand new ordinary oil!
In an age when many products don't seem good enough, it's almost a shock to see one that's this much better than it has to be.
Mobil 1 The oil that saves you gas.

97

95
Art Director: Reinhold Schwenk
Writer: Ilon Specht
Designer: Reinhold Schwenk
Artist: Ed Sorel
Agency: Case & McGrath, Inc.
Client: National Distillers Corporation

96
Art Director: Jim Clarke
Writer: Jennifer Berne
Designer: Jim Clarke
Photographer: Stock
Agency: Martin Landey, Arlow Adv., Inc.
Client: Putnam Trust

97
Art Director: Ron Arnold
Writer: Dodds Musser
Photographer: Henry Sandbank
Agency: Doyle Dane Bernbach
Client: Mobil Oil

WHAT'S REALLY GETTING HIGH HERE IS THE COST OF HEALTH CARE.

Nobody in the world overindulges like we Americans do.

We drink too much. We eat too much. We smoke too much. We work too hard. And we hardly ever relax or exercise enough.

We may be living the good life. But it's not a healthy one.

Of course, everyone knows this. Yet we do it anyway.

We figure America's doctors, hospitals and medical technology are the world's best. If we get sick, we'll be fixed up in no time.

What we don't figure is how much our behavior is costing all of us in health care.

Naturally, it's not just the individual's fault. There's more involved in the high cost of health care than people not taking care of themselves.

Inflation is a big factor. And so is the fact that health care is just plain better.

But all of us—doctors, hospitals, Blue Cross and Blue Shield Plans, and individuals—have to work together to hold down the increasing cost of health care.

Many Blue Cross and Blue Shield Plans, working with doctors and hospitals across the country, have introduced a number of programs designed to slow down rising health care costs.

Programs like outpatient lab tests; quicker discharge from the hospital; surgery on an "in by nine, out by five" basis. And more. As well as programs to promote health education and physical fitness.

With more than 90 million subscribers, not-for-profit Blue Cross and Blue Shield Plans have good reason to want to hold costs down.

But the simple fact is that if we're going to be successful, everybody must help. Including you.

If we take better care of ourselves, we're going to need less health care. And this will slow down the rise in health care costs.

Taking care of yourself is the best kind of health care. An ounce of prevention is still worth a pound of cure. And a lot less costly.

We're not asking you to become a Puritan, to stop enjoying life.

Just to take better care of yourself.

Please don't overeat, don't oversmoke, don't overwork.

And if you're going to drink to someone's health, don't overdo it.

For a free booklet, "Food and Fitness," or for information on how your company can view a special film, "You Can't Buy Health," write Box 8008, Chicago, IL 60680.

ALL OF US HELPING EACH OF US.

98

"WHEN YOU TEST-DRIVE THE AUDI 5000, SAVE IT FOR A RAINY DAY."

AN INTERVIEW WITH DR. FRANZ BEHLES, ASSISTANT AUDI PROJECT DIRECTOR

Why on a rainy day? Behles: In bad conditions, this car shows how good a car can really be. In good weather, nearly every car is good. But in rain, ice, snow or a strong crosswind, it's a different story. That's the time to try the Audi 5000. If you've never driven a front-wheel drive car on a slippery road, you're in for a surprise. The engine over the drive wheels gives excellent traction on rain, ice and snow. The center of gravity is closer to the front; the car is more stable in crosswinds.

Does everything depend on front-wheel drive? Behles: No. But front-wheel drive provides so many advantages that even in the U.S. engineers are using it in their "cars of the future." It's amusing to us since our company has been using this system for over forty years.

You sound very proud of this car. What are you proudest of? Behles: Our 5-cylinder gasoline engine; it's a first. We have achieved the best of both worlds: efficiency like a 4 and smoothness like a 6. And without excess noise or bulk. My colleague, Mr. Hauk, was right to insist, although we smiled when he proposed it.

You mentioned U.S. engineers. Would you hire a Detroit engineer? Behles: Yes, for some things, electronics for example. Cruise control was borrowed from America. But we have it, as standard equipment. Also, we admired American air-conditioning; we developed ours based on one of their best systems. We can always learn from others, but I think our philosophies are different.

Different philosophies? Behles: Yes. Many Americans feel that for a car to hold the road well and be comfortable, it has to be heavy. We feel that weight is wasteful. We can achieve the same degree of roadholding, comfort and safety through advanced engineering. Also, we're not bound by marketing men and stylists.

Can you give me an example? Behles: American engineers had under their noses a theory of elastics by Prof. Timoshenko, of Stanford. He predicted that a steel beam could be made to compress like an accordion and absorb the energy of an impact. The principle: absorb the greatest amount of energy with the lowest weight penalty. We studied this theory and tested it thoroughly, and are first to apply it to an actual car.

If you could start over again, would you do anything different? Behles: Well, maybe I would spend more money on the interior of the car; it could be fancier. It would have been smarter, I suppose. But we spent the money under the hood on engineering innovations. We tried to make it cheerful and calm, so the driver and the passengers would be comfortable and relaxed. I think it is elegant myself.

The interior looks fine to me. Would you do anything else? Behles: I don't know what. There would be no sense in making it bigger. The interior is big enough. The trunk is big enough. It is already the biggest German car you can buy for the money, which is about $8,500.* And certainly not more powerful. The 5-cylinder engine gives you more power than you need.

Thank you, Dr. Behles. Behles: It was very clever of you to photograph me with a raincoat and umbrella. I guess that kind of thing helps publicize the car.

99

SILVER

98

Art Director	Mike Eakin
Writer	Jeff Gorman
Designer	Mike Eakin
Photographer	Carl Fischer
Agency	N W Ayer/Chicago
Client	Blue Cross/Blue Shield

99

Art Director	Helmut Krone
Writers	Dave Reider
	Robert Levenson
Photographer	Carl Fischer
Agency	Doyle Dane Bernbach
Client	Porsche-Audi

HE'S WORKING 12 HOURS A DAY TO INCREASE THE COST OF HEALTH CARE.

In the Horatio Alger story, the hero works day and night to get ahead and everybody looks up to him with admiration.

Now, millions of Americans are following this example: working unreasonable hours, grabbing non-nutritious meals, chain smoking, and never taking time off to relax or exercise.

Of course, everyone knows this isn't very healthy. Yet we do it anyway.

We figure America's doctors, hospitals and medical technology are the world's best. If we get sick, we'll be fixed up in no time.

What we don't figure is how much our behavior is costing all of us in health care.

Naturally, it's not just the individual's fault. There's more involved in the high cost of health care than people not taking care of themselves.

Inflation is a big factor. And so is the fact that health care is just plain better.

But all of us—doctors, hospitals, Blue Cross and Blue Shield Plans, and individuals—have to work together to hold down the increasing cost of health care.

Many Blue Cross and Blue Shield Plans, working with doctors and hospitals across the country, have introduced a number of programs designed to slow down rising health care costs.

Programs like outpatient lab tests; quicker discharge from the hospital; surgery on an "in by nine, out by five" basis. And more. As well as programs to promote health education and physical fitness.

With more than 90 million subscribers, not-for-profit Blue Cross and Blue Shield Plans have good reason to want to hold costs down.

But the simple fact is that if we're going to be successful, everybody must help. Including you.

If we all take better care of ourselves, we're going to need less health care. And this will slow down the rise in health care costs.

Taking care of yourself is the best kind of health care. An ounce of prevention is still worth a pound of cure. And a lot less costly.

We're not asking you to stop working. Just try not to overdo it.

And when you see someone who thinks he's Horatio Alger, don't think of him as a hero. Think of him as a villain.

For a free booklet, "Food and Fitness," or for information on how your company can view a special film, "You Can't Buy Health," write Box 8008, Chicago, IL 60680.

ALL OF US HELPING EACH OF US.

100

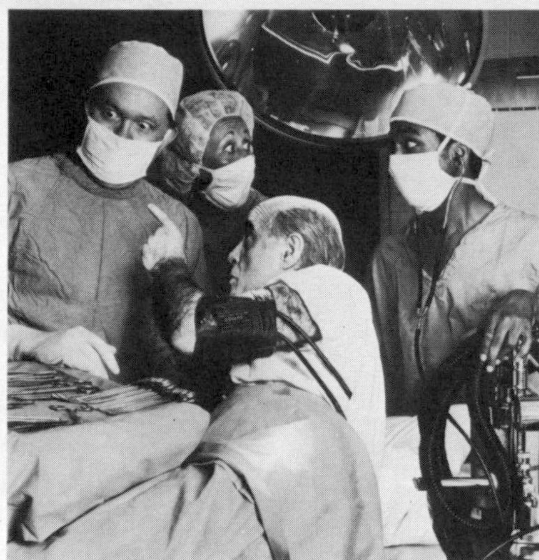

"$1500 for everything... and that's my final offer!"

How absurd it sounds—a consumer of medical care who's actually concerned about the price!

But while he may be greeted with amazement by the hospital staff, it isn't really *he* who's amazing—it's the rest of us, who've been buying health care as if money grew on trees.

The result has been a staggering inflation of the cost of health care and health insurance.[1]

(In 1950, for example, our intrepid bargainer's hospital bill would have run about $15 a day. Today, it'll be close to $175 a day!)

Ætna is working to slow that inflation.

We're going back, claim in hand, to doctors whose charges seem out of line. Ætna did that half a million times last year—and reduced those claims by an average of $50 each.[2]

We're advocating more "same-day surgery,"[3] we're pushing "co-payment," where the actual users of health care pay for a piece of it.[4]

These positions do not always make Ætna popular, but they *do* help make health insurance affordable. Insurance costs *can* be controlled. Don't underestimate your own influence. Use it, as we are trying to use ours.

Ætna wants insurance to be affordable.

[1] "Staggering" is probably too weak a word. The share of the gross national product which goes for health services has virtually doubled in the past 15 years. The Government's share of the national health bill is now $70 billion—a sum second only to national defense.

[2] This requires Ætna knowing what the prevailing charges are for every type of medical service in every area of the country, and examining each claim against that standard. Costs vary wildly from city to city. In Philadelphia, $413 is the average surgeon's charge for the removal of a gall bladder; in Manhattan, the same operation averages $813!

[3] Many minor operations—as many as 20% of all hospital operations—can properly be performed without the patient staying at the hospital overnight. At the now prevailing rate of $175 a day, this could mean enormous savings. Ætna also advocates peer-group review by doctors of cases of improper hospitalization—again, to prevent misuse of hospital facilities.

[4] "Co-payment" reduces premiums; it also gives the consumer a reason to *care* about health costs, and to demand reasonable ones. Today, frankly, too many consumers of health care have too little stake in controlling costs.

101

100
Art Director Mike Eakin
Writer Jeff Gorman
Designer Mike Eakin
Photographer Carl Fischer
Agency N W Ayer/Chicago
Client Blue Cross/Blue Shield

101
Art Director Reinhold Schwenk
Writer Gene Case
Designer Reinhold Schwenk
Photographer Manny Gonzales
Agency Case & McGrath, Inc.
Client Aetna Life & Casualty Company

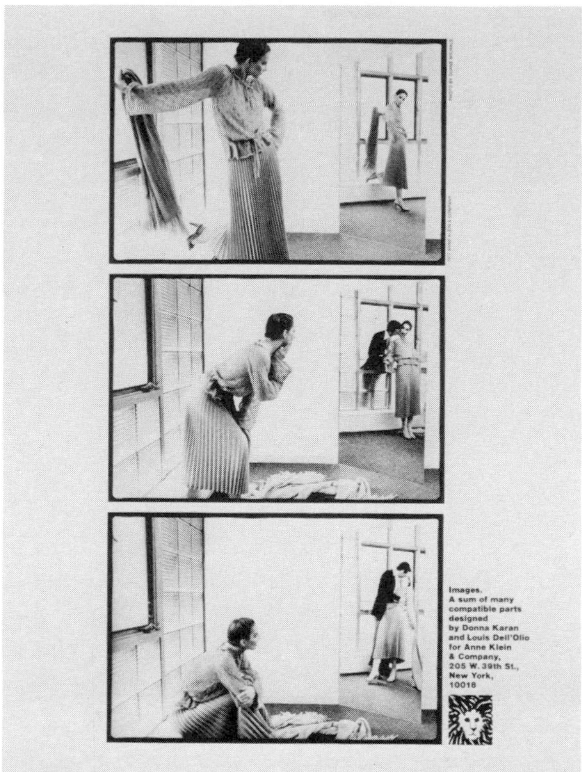

102

103

102	
Art Director	Richard Trask
Copywriter	Ruth Branchor
Agency	Don Wise & Co., Inc.
Client	Anne Klein & Co.

103	
Art Director	Bill Kamp
Writer	John Russo
Photographer	Carl Fischer Photography, Inc.
Agency	Levine, Huntley, Schmidt, Plapler & Beaver
Client	The Sparkomatic Corp.

NO OTHER BUSINESS CALCULATOR CAN MAKE THIS STATEMENT.

The Olivetti Logos 75B is the beginning of a new generation of calculators for businessmen and accountants. With automatic functions that have never been available before at anywhere near this price.

For instance: when you're working to both horizontal and vertical totals, like a journal sheet (also known as crossfooting—CF), the Logos 75B has the ability to automatically accumulate up to 48 downtotals as a by-product of the horizontal computation.

When you're adding figures to a total, finding what percentage each amount is of that total and then allocating an expense, like rent, to each department (better known as proration—PRO—and allocation), the Logos 75B does it for you automatically for up to 52 categories.

And when you want amounts, like sales tickets, added to separate categories, like departments or products, and you want to find the total amount per category, what percent that amount is of the total, and the number of entries in each category (distribution—DIST—for short), the Logos 75B again does it all automatically. And it handles up to 52 categories at random.

The Logos 75B is the first business calculator that automatically performs proration, distribution and crossfooting and has the ability to automatically compare each column to the next, or any specific column, to determine percentages and amount and percent of increase or decrease with a printed record of every step in the calculations.

And the Logos 75B provides these extraordinary functions at an extraordinary price of only $398. If you're already sold, just enclose a check or money order. And, of course, we'd be happy to demonstrate the Logos 75B on some of your own work. Please fill in the coupon below and we'll take it from there.

AUTOMATIC CROSSFOOTING, AUTOMATIC PRORATION AND AUTOMATIC DISTRIBUTION. THE STATEMENTS NO OTHER CALCULATOR CAN MAKE.

Olivetti Corporation of America
500 Park Avenue, New York, N.Y. 10022
Attn: Business Products Division

___Enclosed is my check or money order for______Logos 75B @ $398.00 plus any applicable state and local taxes. (No shipping or handling charge.)

___Please arrange for a demonstration.

Name __________________

Title _________ Company _________

Address __________________

City _________ State ____ Zip ______

olivetti

104

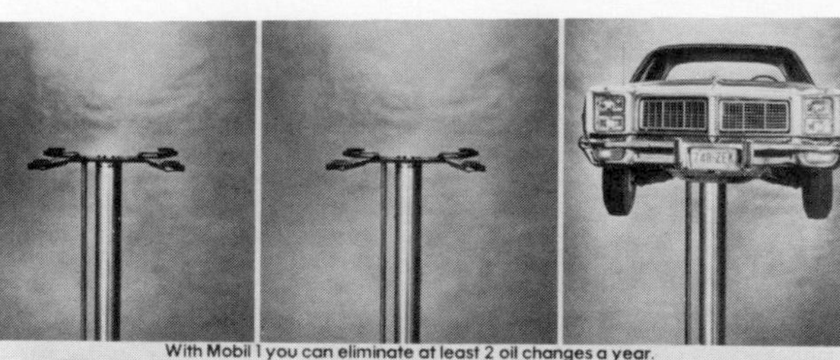

With Mobil 1 you can eliminate at least 2 oil changes a year.

Spend less time in the air.

Switching to Mobil 1 is a good way to keep your car where it belongs. On the ground.

If you've been changing your oil the way most people have (every 4 to 6,000 miles) Mobil 1 could take you much farther and eliminate at least 2 oil changes a year. You could rack up a total of 15,000 miles or go a full year, whatever comes first, before you have to put your car up on the rack for an oil change. (If your car is still under warranty, you should change your oil in accordance with warranty requirements.)

The oil that saves you gas.

Mobil 1 cuts friction so well it actually takes the average car up to 10 extra miles on a tankful of gas.

The oil that saves you oil.

Since Mobil 1 doesn't evaporate as rapidly as ordinary oil you should be using less oil. (Provided, of course, that your engine is in good mechanical condition.)

Better in hot and cold weather.

Mobil 1 is a synthesized engine lubricant that outperforms premium motor oil all seasons of the year. Since Mobil 1 doesn't thicken up as much as ordinary oil in cold weather, you'll be getting easier cold weather starts. Mobil 1 can actually help your car get started in temperatures as low as 35 degrees below zero.

Mobil 1 doesn't thin out the way ordinary oil does in hot weather, either. It continues to spread a better protective film over the moving parts of your engine, even in the hottest days of summer.

Better engine protection.

To prove how good our oil really is we ran Mobil 1 in a car for 15,000 miles, adding oil as needed. Incredible as it may seem, tests showed that after 15,000 miles of driving, used Mobil 1 still protected the engine as well as brand new premium motor oil!

So if you're up in the air about which oil to buy, come down to earth.

Buy Mobil 1.

The oil that saves you gas ...saves you oil changes.

105

104
Art Directors Sam Scali
Peter Kingman
Writer Mike Drazen
Designers Sam Scali
Peter Kingman
Photographer Robert McCabe
Agency Scali, McCabe, Sloves
Client Olivetti Corp. of America

105
Art Director Ron Arnold
Writer Dodds Musser
Photographer Dennis Chalkin
Agency Doyle Dane Bernbach
Client Mobil Oil

Dannon Yogurt may not help you live as long as Soviet Georgians. But it couldn't hurt.

There are two curious things about the people of Soviet Georgia. A large part of their diet is yogurt. And a large number of them live to be well over 100.

Of course, many factors affect longevity, and we are not saying Dannon Yogurt will help you live longer. But we will say that all-natural Dannon is high in nutrients, low in fat, reasonable in calories. And quite satisfying at lunch or as a snack.

Another thing about Dannon. It contains active yogurt cultures (many pre-mixed or Swiss style brands don't). They make yogurt one of the easiest foods to digest and have been credited with other healthful benefits.

Which is why we've been advising this: If you don't always eat right, Dannon Yogurt is the right thing to eat.

By the way, Bagrat Topagua thought Dannon was "dzelian kargia." Which means he loved it.

Dannon Milk Products, 22-11 38th Ave. Long Island City, N.Y. 11101.

106

Of the hundreds of papermakers in the United States, only four or five can match our capacity. We're bigger in paper than Mead, Union Camp, Westvaco, Boise Cascade and many other familiar names.

That comes as a surprise to a lot of bankers, investment advisers, brokers and market analysts. Until recently, they've thought of us as the company we used to be.

But now they are aware that while we own a railroad, a coal mine, a major paper converter and a large paper merchant, we own them because they're directly related to the core of our business: making paper.

They're now aware that we hold leading shares of market in three important areas of the paper business – and that these areas where we're leaders generate 95% of our revenues.

Linerboard and corrugating medium. We make it in one of the industry's largest and most efficient plants and are the nation's number one supplier to the independent box makers, who have 22% of the market.

Business communication papers. Paper for your office copier, computer, letterhead. We're good at making such papers and at selling them – as our leading market position demonstrates.

Uncoated groundwood printing papers. The kinds used in mail-order catalogs and telephone books. We have more uncoated groundwood capacity than any other North American producer, and are diversifying this relatively low-cost product to serve new markets.

In the last five years, our earnings per share have grown at an average annual rate of 30%. Further, our pre-tax return on sales has increased more than 150% to 13.0%, and return on equity has doubled to 14.4%.

Our NYSE ticker symbol is GNN, our newspaper stock listing is GtNoNk, and our chairman is Sam Casey. He wants to send you an annual report, a 10-K and a fact book about GNN. Write to him at Great Northern Nekoosa Corporation, 75 Prospect Street, Stamford, Connecticut 06901.

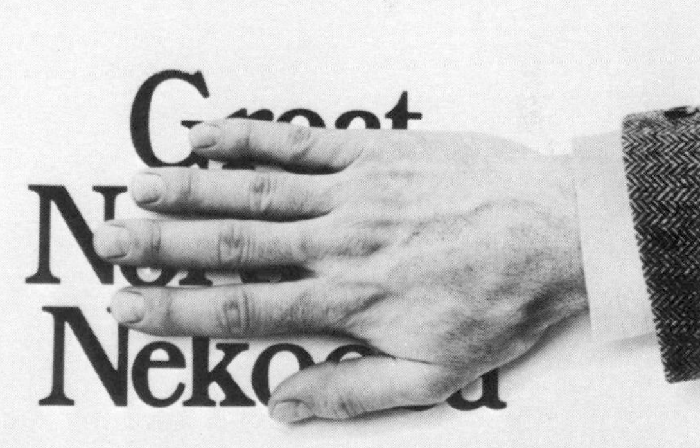

107

106
Art Director Joe Goldberg
Writer Peter Lubalin
Photographer Bob Gaffney
Agency Marsteller
Client Dannon Yogurt

107
Art Director Dick Thomas
Writer Arthur Einstein, Jr.
Designer Kathy Manuelian
Photographer John Paul Endress
Agency Lord, Geller, Federico
Client Great Northern Nekoosa Corp.

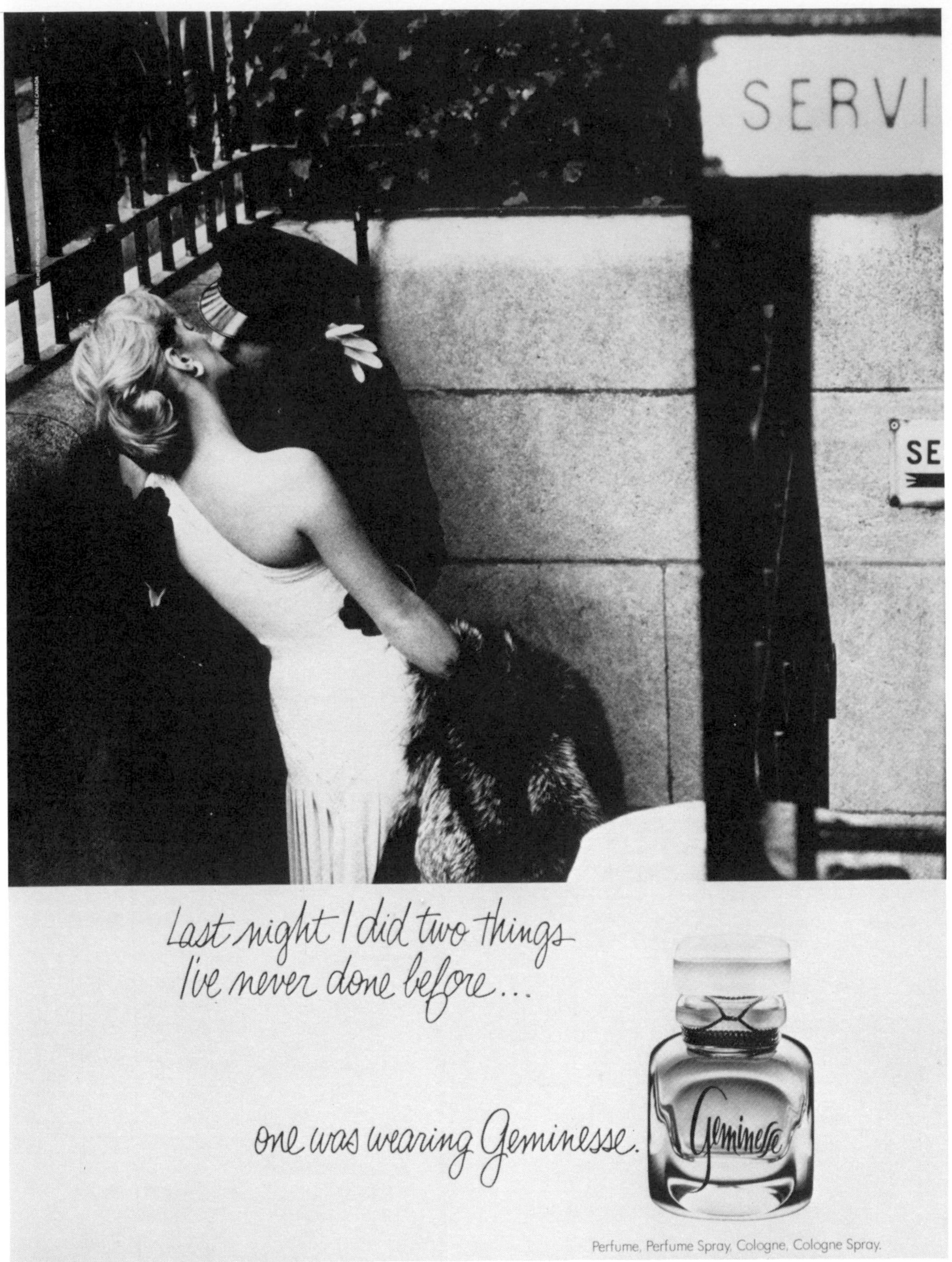

SERVI
SE
Last night I did two things
I've never done before...
one was wearing Geminesse.
Geminesse
Perfume, Perfume Spray, Cologne, Cologne Spray.

108

108

Art Directors	**Frank Kirk**
	Howard Russo
	Bob Kuperman
Writer	**Peter Murphy**
Designer	**Bob Kuperman**
Photographer	**Helmut Newton**
Agency	**Wells, Rich, Greene**
Client	**Max Factor**

THE MUSEUM OF MODERN ART RECENTLY ACQUIRED AN OLIVETTI LEXIKON 82 TO PUT ON DISPLAY.

WHAT A PITY.

While it's certainly an honor to be a part of the Museum of Modern Art's permanent Design Collection, it's also a bit frustrating.

For to appreciate this work of art, you have to do more than look at it, you have to use it.

THE PORTABLE TYPEWRITER WITH MANY FACES.

The Olivetti Lexikon 82 and the more deluxe Lexikon 83 are the only electric portables to use the interchangeable typing ball. A revolutionary advance that actually makes it possible to change type faces in seconds. Simply pop one ball out, and another in, and you can select the type style that most clearly expresses in type what you're trying to express in words.

If, for example, you're writing a blunt letter to the phone company—no-nonsense and to-the-point—a straightforward pica face like this may be called for.

On the other hand, if you're writing a letter of eternal love to the young man or woman you met at last week's game, you may desire a type style with a bit more warmth and affection, such as this graceful script.

In fact no matter what you're trying to say, one of our ten different faces will help you say it even better.

THE PORTABLE TYPEWRITER THAT KEEPS YOU CLEAN.

This odd-looking object is one of the Lexikon 82's interchangeable ribbon cartridges. They're available in five different colors. Can be changed in seconds. And because your fingers never touch the ribbon, you're never left with messy hands.

In addition, extra-sharp mylar film ribbon is available for those times when you want to leave a particularly vivid impression.

THE HOME TYPEWRITER THAT MAKES YOUR FINGERS FEEL MORE AT HOME.

As easy as designer Mario Bellini has made the Lexikon 82 on the eyes, it's just as easy on the fingers. The nearly flat slope of the keyboard makes travelling about the keys a delight. And the keys themselves have been designed to make your fingers feel more at home than they have ever felt on a typewriter.

But, of course, the only way you'll be convinced of all this is to visit an Olivetti dealer (he's in the Yellow Pages).

The Lexikon 82 may look like it belongs in a museum, but once you use one you'll know that the place it really belongs is in your home.

olivetti

The Lexikon 82. The world's most advanced electric portable typewriter.

109

THIS COUNTRY NEEDS MORE AIR CONDITIONING REPAIRMEN. NOT MORE ENGLISH PROFESSORS.

Guys who can fix an air conditioner, map out a highway, or do electrical wiring in a new house are a lot more in demand than someone who can recite the collected works of Shakespeare.

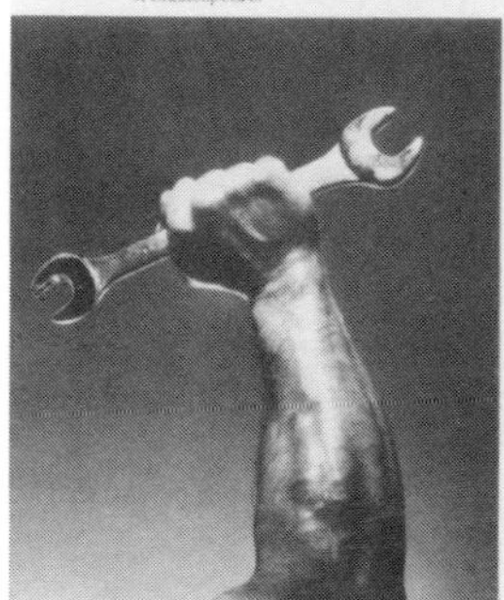

That's why we at ICS specialize in training you for service and technical fields like the ones you see on the right.

We can prepare you for a future in one of these fields at home. In about an hour a day. Without the hassle of a classroom. Without missing a paycheck.

It's not all a piece of cake. But you get the texts it takes, plus help from our instructors every step of the way. Any special questions about your lessons, and our Dial-a-Question® service lets you call us from anywhere in the continental United States. Toll-free.

Since 1890, millions have turned to ICS. We think we're good. And corporations like Bethlehem Steel, 3M, and Union Carbide think we're good enough to use for their own training programs.

We can't guarantee you a job or a raise. No school can. But if you see the value of having a solid skill no man can ever take from you, check the field that interests you. We'll send you a free career booklet and demonstration lesson, with no obligation.

At a time when Ph.D's are driving taxicabs, it's the intelligent thing to do.

I've checked the field that interests me. Send me a free demonstration lesson and career booklet with details on career opportunities and how ICS training works. I understand there's no obligation.

- AIR CONDITIONING & REFRIGERATION
- ELECTRICAL ENGINEERING
- ELECTRICIAN
- AUTOMOTIVE MECHANIC
- ELECTRONICS TECHNICIAN
- TV SERVICE & REPAIR
- DRAFTING
- ACCOUNTING
- SURVEYING & MAPPING
- DIESEL/TRUCK MECHANICS
- BUSINESS MANAGEMENT
- CIVIL ENGINEERING
- CONSTRUCTION ELECTRICIAN
- APPLIANCE SERVICE & REPAIR
- MECHANICAL ENGINEERING
- HIGH SCHOOL
- CHEMICAL ENGINEERING

The ICS Center for Degree Studies is authorized by the Pennsylvania Dept. of Education to offer career programs leading to Associate in Specialized Technology and Associate in Specialized Business degrees.

TECHNOLOGY DEGREES:

- CIVIL ENGINEERING
- MECHANICAL ENGINEERING
- ELECTRICAL ENGINEERING
- CHEMICAL ENGINEERING
- ELECTRONICS
- MECHANICAL DRAFTING & DESIGN

BUSINESS DEGREES:

- ACCOUNTING
- BUSINESS MANAGEMENT

Print name ______ Age ______

Address ______

City ______

State ______ Zip ______

Telephone ______

ICS

International Correspondence Schools
Scranton, Pennsylvania 18515

110

109

Art Directors	Sam Scali
	Peter Kingman
Writer	Mike Drazen
Designers	Sam Scali
	Peter Kingman
Artist	Ted Lodigensky
Photographers	Steve Horn
	Robert McCabe
Agency	Scali, McCabe, Sloves
Client	Olivetti Corp. of America

110

Art Director	Jerry Whitley
Writer	Bill McCullam
Designer	Jerry Whitley
Photographer	Peter Papadopoulos
Agency	Schwab/Beatty, Inc.
Client	International Correspondence Schools

THE TRAVELERS THINKS THAT STAYING ALIVE SHOULDN'T BE AN OPTIONAL EXTRA ON YOUR CAR.

Last year, 46,000 Americans died in car accidents. Another 1,800,000 were injured.

The cars had things like AM/FM radios, air conditioning, reclining bucket seats, and illuminated dashboards.

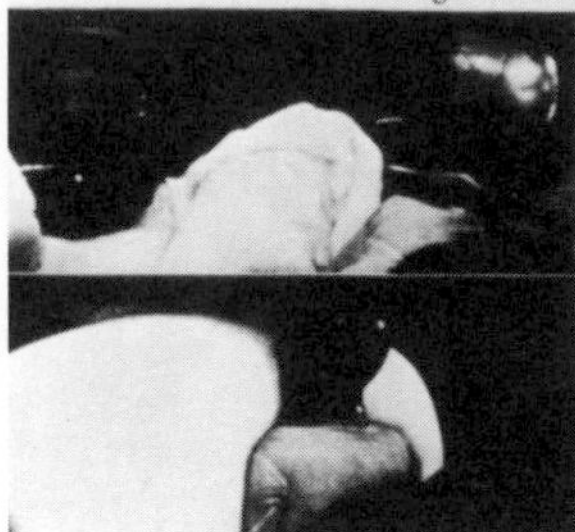

Yet a recent Department of Transportation study concluded that other pieces of standard equipment could help. Air bags and automatically applied seat belts, it said, could save more than 9,000 lives annually and prevent hundreds of thousands of injuries every year.

As an insurance company, The Travelers also realizes that automatic crash protection devices not only save lives and suffering, but also reduce the cost of medical care and the insurance that pays for that care.

That's why we will offer a 30% discount on personal injury protection and medical coverage premiums* on all cars equipped with the air bag protecting all front seat occupants. An appropriate discount will be offered for driver-only air bag systems coupled with passive restraint systems that meet current government standards. And if the study projections are borne out, additional savings may be possible.

We like to find ways to reduce losses. For humanitarian reasons. And also to reflect the savings, when we can, in your rates.

*Pending state regulatory approval.

THE TRAVELERS
Raising our voice, not just our rates.

111

IT UNTYPES AS EASILY AS IT TYPES.

THE TYPER

Typer cartridges come in black, red, blue, green, and brown executive quality film for the sharpest image of any portable; as well as everyday black nylon.

THE UNTYPER

When you make a mistake, just snap out the typer cartridge, and snap in the untyper cartridge.
In seconds, good-bye mistake.

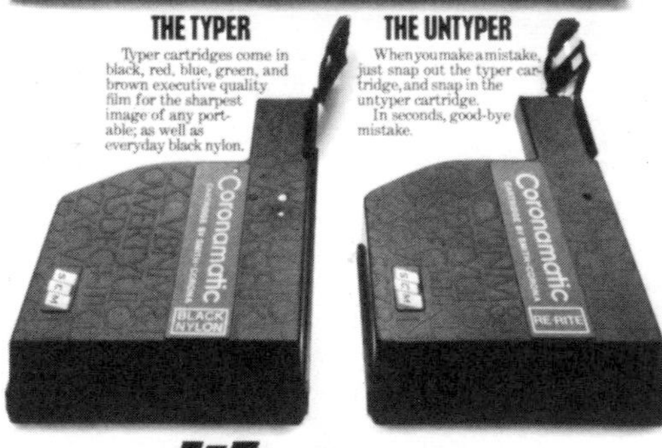

SCM SMITH-CORONA

112

111
Art Director Michael Tesch
Writer Lou Redmond
Designer Michael Tesch
Photographer Stock Photography
Agency Ally & Gargano, Inc.
Client The Travelers Insurance Co.

112
Art Director Lars Anderson
Writer Irwin Warren
Designer Lars Anderson
Photographer Jerry Friedman
Production Company Pioneer Moss
Agency Richard K. Manoff Inc.
Client SCM Corporation

And other revelations about skim milk presented by Alba.

No matter how knowledgeable a dieter you think you are you're probably downright starved for facts when it comes to skim milk. Where does skim milk come from? How is it made? What does it have to offer? Skim over this ad and we promise you'll find the answers.

THE IDEA THAT SKIM MILK COMES FROM SPECIAL COWS IS UDDER NONSENSE.

The truth is cows know how to make only one kind of milk, called whole milk. An average cow produces between 3,700 and 13,950 quarts of it a year. That may sound like a lot but just compare it to the amount of food she takes in: 3,100 to 5,000 pounds of farm grains and seed oil cake, 2½ tons of hay, 6½ tons of silage, a couple acres of grass, and more than 4,000 gallons of water.

Out of stuff practically inedible by man, a cow produces one of man's healthiest foods.

No wonder in ancient times wealth was counted by the cow.

SKIM MILK IS WHOLE MILK THAT WENT ON A DIET.

Simply put, skim milk is whole milk minus the fat. By law it must be pasteurized and fortified with 2,000 IU of vitamin A per quart. And must weigh in with less than 0.5 per cent fat. Some skim milks like Alba, are also fortified with vitamin D.

DAILY RECOMMENDED ALLOWANCE OF MILK	
Children	3 or more glasses (smaller glasses for children under 8)
Teenagers	4 or more glasses
Adults	2 or more glasses
Pregnant and Lactating Women	4 or more glasses

Nonfat dry milk is simply skim milk minus the water. Add the water back and you get the good taste and nutrition of skim milk. Only difference is that it costs less and stays fresher longer since it comes dry.

ONE OF THE MOST PERFECT FOODS MADE MORE PERFECT FOR DIETERS.

Milk has long been called one of the most perfect foods. And for good reason.

It's rich in protein, which helps repair body tissue and forms antibodies to fight infection.

It's also rich in calcium, which is A-OK for bones. And since calcium is continually removed from our body it's important for us to drink milk often.

Protein and calcium though, are only the beginning. Milk also supplies vitamins A, C, B_1, B_2, phosphorus, niacin, magnesium, potassium and sodium.

Unfortunately milk also supplies about 150 calories a glass. So as good as it is for a growing body, it's not so good for a growing waistline. That's where Alba comes in.

HERE COMES THE PITCH.

As the milk maiden on our box symbolizes, Alba provides all the farm fresh flavor and nutrition of whole milk. Yet it provides a whole lot fewer calories (only 80 per glass).

There's good reason for Alba's good taste. Alba is one of the few nonfat dry milks made under continuous USDA government supervision. In fact in a recent independent consumer test, Alba was rated superior to other nonfat dry milks.

In addition to regular Alba, we make a whole family of delicious low calorie drinks that give you all the benefits of nonfat dry milk.

Alba '77 Fit 'N Frosty lets you stir up a rich, thick, chocolatey shake. Alba '66 gives you a creamy cup of hot cocoa. And when you want to lighten coffee or tea, there's Alba Dairy Light.

Now that you know perhaps more than you asked for about skim milk, we hope you'll practice what we've preached and try Alba.

Look, no one wants you to lose that weight more than we do. After all, we stand to gain a steady customer.

113

We build them better.

Take safety. Underneath the hood you'll find a safety feature you wouldn't dream of finding in most cars:

Holes.

They're specially designed using a computer, so the front end will help absorb energy in the event of a collision.

We also developed such things as an "independent stabilizer rear axle," which increases the stability of the car on rough roads.

And for our deluxe Rabbit, we developed special seat belts that actually put themselves on when you close the door.

Hardly a detail escaped our attention. Even the ignition key is padded for safety.

What about room? It's probably not the first thing you think about when you say "VW."

Yet today, Volkswagens actually have more combined interior room and trunk space than most other cars in their class.

Rabbits are so roomy they're being used as taxicabs in Lexington, Kentucky.

In fact, Rabbits have more interior room than 25 other cars you could buy. And more trunk space than a Cadillac Seville.

They're also surprisingly quick, with acceleration from 0 to 50 mph faster than a Triumph Spitfire.

Which brings us to another subject: performance.

Our Scirocco can take you from 0 to 50 in an amazing 7.5 seconds. And last year it was the Trans Am Champion in the under-2-liter class.

What's more, our newest Volkswagens are among the few cars in the world that combine front-wheel drive (for improved tracking), fuel injection (for smooth acceleration), an overhead cam engine (for sportier performance), front disc brakes (for controlled stopping), and rack-and-pinion steering (for incredible response).

Do we still sound like the VW you remember?

Well then, take a look at our station wagon.

We never made anything like our Dasher wagon before. With more cargo room than any other wagon in its class. With a plush interior and carpeting all around.

And in our beautifully appointed 2-door or 4-door sedans, Dasher has more room than most American cars in its class.

Yet, with all the changes we've made, some things always remain the same.

We still employ 13,500 inspectors to insure the quality of every car we make.

And much of our work is still done by hand.

Like the paint. It's hand sprayed, over and over. It's hand sanded and hand cleaned. It's even checked by people wearing special mittens. And before it's finished it's put through 29 individual steps of preparation.

There's also that familiar "jingle" you get putting money in the bank. Because all three Volkswagens get 24 MPG in the city. Rabbit and Scirocco get 37 MPG on the highway. Dasher gets 36. (EPA estimates with standard transmission. Actual mileage depends on how and where you drive, optional equipment and the car's condition.)

Volkswagens aren't sounding like Volkswagens of the past.

They're sounding more like cars of the future.

Rabbit

Scirocco

Dasher

Economy without sacrifice

114

113

Art Directors: Ernie Blitzer, Steve Kasloff
Writer: Steve Kasloff
Artist: Bettman Archives
Photographer: Alan Lieberman
Agency: Marsteller
Client: Alba

114

Art Director: John Eding
Writer: Doug Houston
Photographer: Larry Robins
Agency: Doyle Dane Bernbach
Client: Volkswagen

115

116

115

Art Director	Bill Kamp
Writer	John Russo
Photographer	Carl Fischer Photography, Inc.
Agency	Levine, Huntley, Schmidt, Plapler & Beaver
Client	The Sparkomatic Corp.

116

Art Director	Al Calello
Writer	W. Weiss
Agency	Isidore Lefkowitz Elgort
Client	Quest 77

One of Soviet Georgia's senior citizens thought Dannon was an excellent yogurt. She ought to know. She's been eating yogurt for 137 years.

CAMACHICH KVITZINIA. PHOTOGRAPHED IN ATRARA, SOVIET GEORGIA.

117

117

Art Director	Joe Goldberg
Writer	Peter Lubalin
Photographer	Bob Gaffney
Agency	Marsteller
Client	Dannon Yogurt

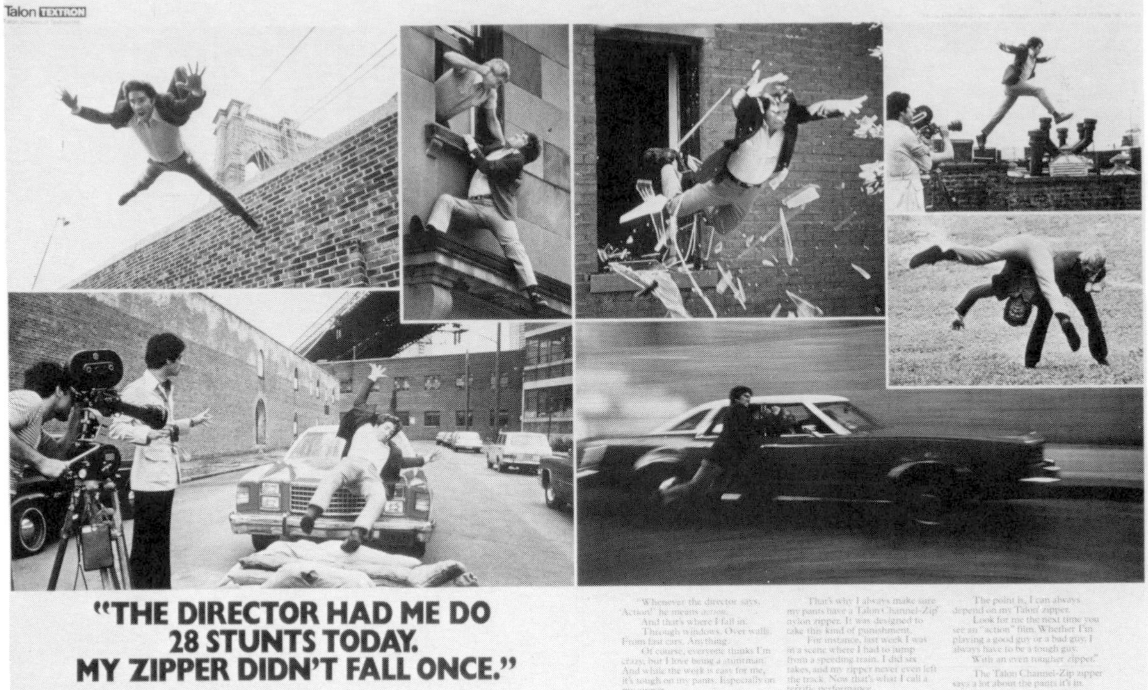

"THE DIRECTOR HAD ME DO 28 STUNTS TODAY. MY ZIPPER DIDN'T FALL ONCE."

"Whenever the director says, 'Action!' he means action.

And that's where I fall in.

Through windows. Over walls. From fast cars. Anything.

Of course, everyone thinks I'm crazy, but I love being a stuntman. And while the work is easy for me, it's tough on my pants. Especially on my zipper.

That's why I always make sure my pants have a Talon Channel-Zip nylon zipper. It was designed to take this kind of punishment.

For instance, last week I was in a scene where I had to jump from a speeding train. I did six takes, and my zipper never even left the track. Now that's what I call a terrific performance.

The point is, I can always depend on my Talon zipper.

Look for me the next time you see an "action" film. Whether I'm playing a good guy or a bad guy, I always have to be a tough guy.

With an even tougher zipper."

The Talon Channel-Zip zipper says a lot about the pants it's in.

118

The earth has a clock all her own when she does things or doesn't. And one of the things she does is make grass grow differently in the fall than it does in the spring. No kidding. Your lawn gets thicker in the fall.
A little Turf Builder in early fall and your grass will grow sideways.
In the spring, everything reaches up for the sun and grass blades do too. They grow up and up. But with the warm days and cool nights of fall, this upward growth is slower and your grass actually grows more sideways and starts new grass growing beside itself. It does this by sending out tillers and rhizomes and these send down new grass roots. You couldn't pick a better time to put down some fertilizer.
So if you spend just a half an hour with a spreader and some Scotts' Turf Builder, what you will get for it is a darker thicker lawn that doesn't take as much mowing as it did in the spring. And that isn't all you get for your half hour's work. You also get a knitting of new roots to take the worst of winter, along with a storage of carbohydrates down in the ground that will get your turf started earlier than most other lawns next spring.
We make Turf Builder so that it lets its nitrogen out a little at a time to keep on feeding your roots for just about 8 weeks. (We have U.S. Patents on the way our Turf Builder is made.) And if you happen to have some weeds and dandelions you want to get rid of at the same time, we also have Turf Builder Plus 2. This gives you a weed control with fertilizer mixed in with it. More grass and good-bye dandelions with one pass of your spreader.
A little Turf Builder right now will keep your lawn full and healthy all through fall, and all it takes is about the same time as a trip to your local car wash and back. We do it ourselves and if you want to see our lawn, just stop by.
We're easy to find. We're the Scotts people and we've been here in Marysville, Ohio, for 100 years.
Scotts
Turf Builder

119

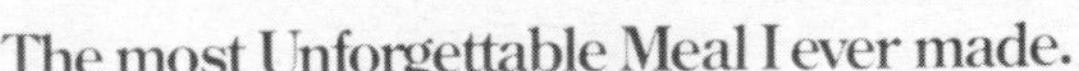

The most Unforgettable Meal I ever made.

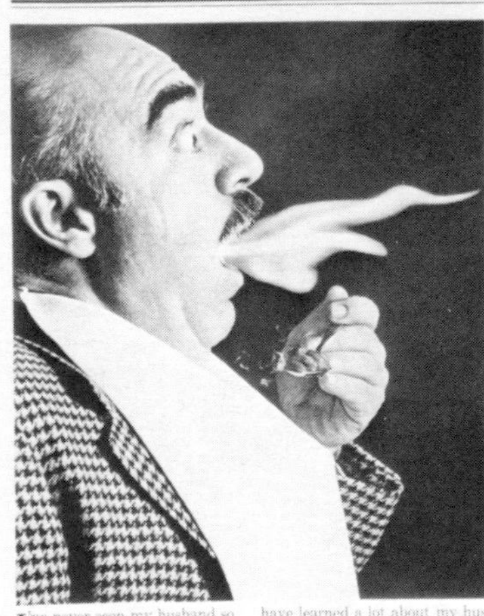

I've never seen my husband so burned up. It was the night I was trying out a new recipe for chili we picked up in a little place on the Mexican border. Of course, the recipe wasn't all we picked up. But that's another story.

At any rate, there we were, sitting down to a nice hot bowl of chili, when my husband took his first bite.

You know, there's an old saying that the best way to learn about people is to watch the way they eat. Well, if you watched the way he ate that night, you could have learned a lot about my husband. Then again, you could've learned a lot about my chili. And believe me, I had a lot to learn.

Anyway, later that night the nurse at the hospital gave me a few words of advice. "McCormick Schilling", she said. Which is the most practical advice a nurse could ever hand you.

You see, McCormick Schilling are the spice and flavor people. So when it comes to chili, tacos, or anything at all where the right blend of seasoning can be critical, it makes good sense to go with McCormick Schilling.

Which is what I did when Ray got home. Of course, when he saw we were having chili again, he turned as white as a sheet. And reached for the Blue Cross card.

I whispered, "McCormick Schilling flavor makes all the difference in the world." And eased a tiny teaspoon past his lips.

No flames. No tears. And no leftovers.

In fact, since we discovered McCormick Schilling, we've tried their Taco Mix, Enchilada Casserole, not to mention their Tamale Pie. And believe me, they make a memorable meal, every single time.

Chili without Tears

Brown one pound ground beef in 2 tablespoons of oil. Add one 15 ounce or two 8 ounce cans of Tomato Sauce, $\frac{1}{2}$ cup hot water, one number 303 can of Kidney Beans, and the contents of one package of McCormick or Schilling Chili Seasoning Mix. Cover and simmer 10 minutes. Makes 4 servings.

McCormick/Schilling flavor makes all the difference in the world.

McCormick/Schilling

120

118
Art Director Ron Becker
Writer Anita Baron
Designer Ron Becker
Photographer Jerry Abramowitz
Agency DKG Advertising, Inc.
Client Talon, Inc.

119
Art Director Helmut Krone
Writer Jack Dillon
Artist Cosgrove Associates
Agency Doyle Dane Bernbach
Client O.M. Scotts

120
Art Director Pete Coutroulis
Writer Jim Weller
Designer Pete Coutroulis
Photographer Menken Seltzer
Agency Clinton E. Frank, Inc.
Client McCorick/Schilling

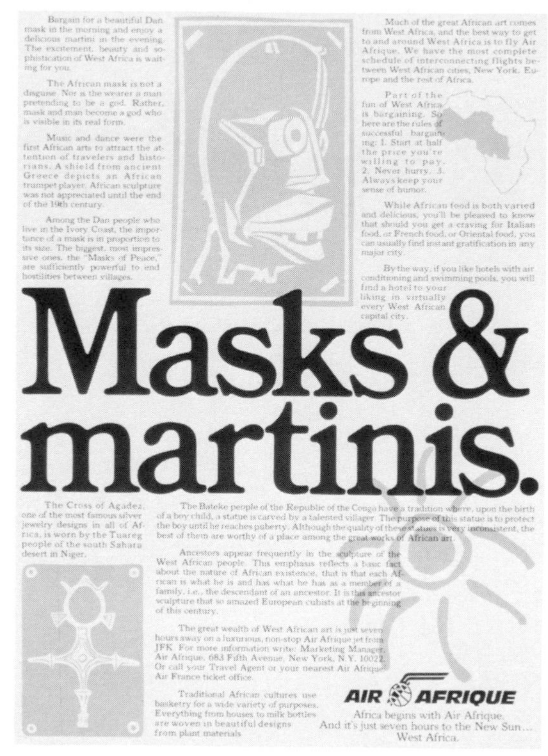

121

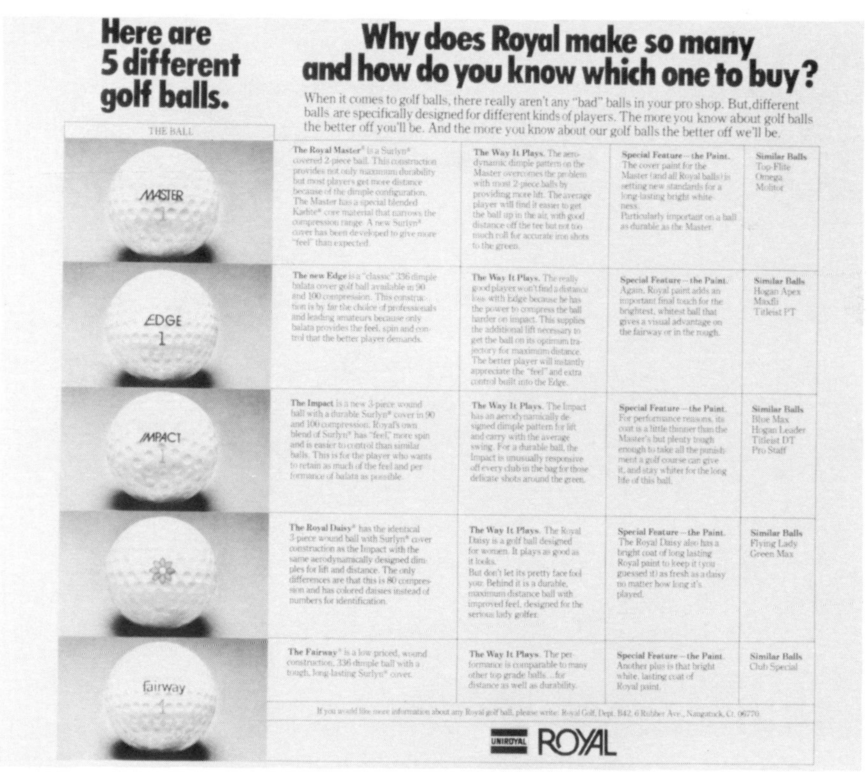

122

121
Art Director Rocco Campanelli
Writer Robert Kilzer
Artist Rocco Campanelli
Agency David Deutsch Associates, Inc.
Client Air Afrique

122
Art Director Herb Jager
Writer Chester Gore
Photographer Ulf Skogsberg
Agency Chester Gore Company Inc.
Client Uniroyal, Inc.

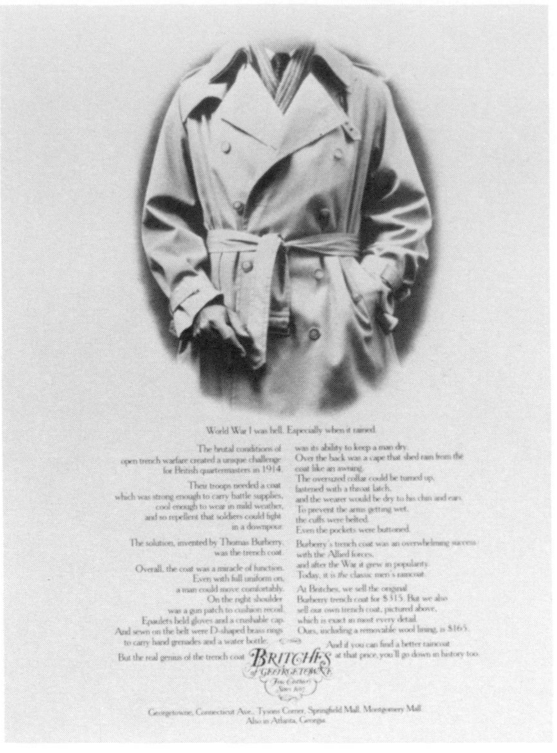

World War I was hell. Especially when it rained.
The brutal conditions of open trench warfare created a unique challenge for British quartermasters in 1914.
Their troops needed a coat which was strong enough to carry battle supplies, cool enough to wear in mild weather, and so repellent that soldiers could fight in a downpour.
The solution, invented by Thomas Burberry, was the trench coat.
Overall, the coat was a miracle of function. Even with full uniform on, a man could move comfortably. On the right shoulder was a gun patch to cushion recoil. Epaulets held gloves and a crushable cap. And sewn on the belt were D-shaped brass rings to carry hand grenades and a water bottle.
But the real genius of the trench coat was its ability to keep a man dry.
Over the back was a cape that shed rain from the coat like an awning.
The oversized collar could be turned up, fastened with a throat latch, and the wearer would be dry to his chin and ears.
To prevent the arms getting wet, the cuffs were belted.
Even the pockets were buttoned.
Burberry's trench coat was an overwhelming success with the Allied forces, and after the War it grew in popularity.
Today, it is the classic men's raincoat.
At Britches, we sell the original Burberry trench coat for $315. But we also sell our own trench coat, pictured above, which is exact in most every detail.
Ours, including a removable wool lining, is $165.
And if you can find a better raincoat at that price, you'll go down in history too.
BRITCHES of Georgetowne
Georgetowne, Connecticut Ave., Tysons Corner, Springfield Mall, Montgomery Mall
Also in Atlanta, Georgia

124

Become a big picture producer.

The picture on the right was made from the slide on the left. In just 33 seconds. On the Xerox 6500 color copier.

With its new slide adapter, the 6500 not only lets you reproduce graphics in vibrant color, but it now lets you reproduce slides in photographic-like color. If you'd like to become a big picture producer, write Cary J. Nolan, Xerox Corporation, Rochester, New York 14644 and we'll send you more information. When people see the big pictures you and Xerox produce, we'll both get rave reviews.

XEROX

Same size reproduction of Xerox 6500 color copy.

125

124

Art Director Joe Carri
Writer David Levy
Designer Joe Carri
Artist Bennett Hall
Photographer Fred Maroon
Agency Weitzman & Associates, Inc.
Client Britches of Georgetowne

125

Art Directors Allen Kay, Tony Angotti
Writers Lois Korey, Steve Penchina
Photographer Steve Steigman
Agency Needham, Harper & Steers Adv. Inc.
Client Xerox Corp.

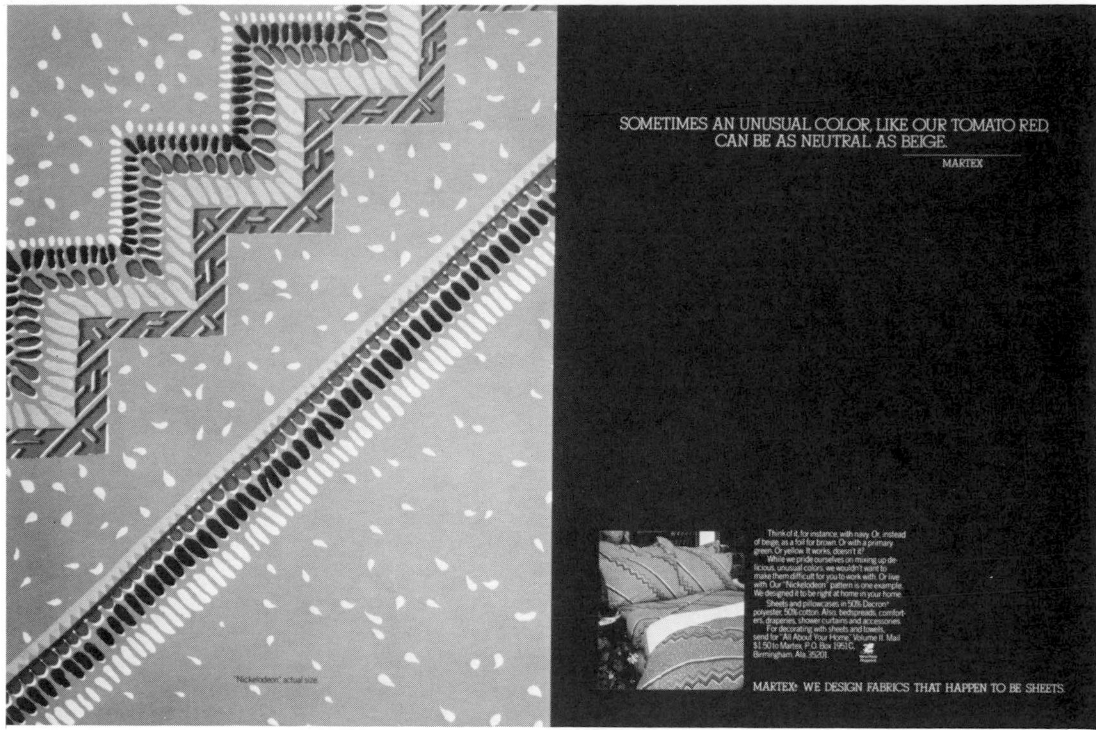

126

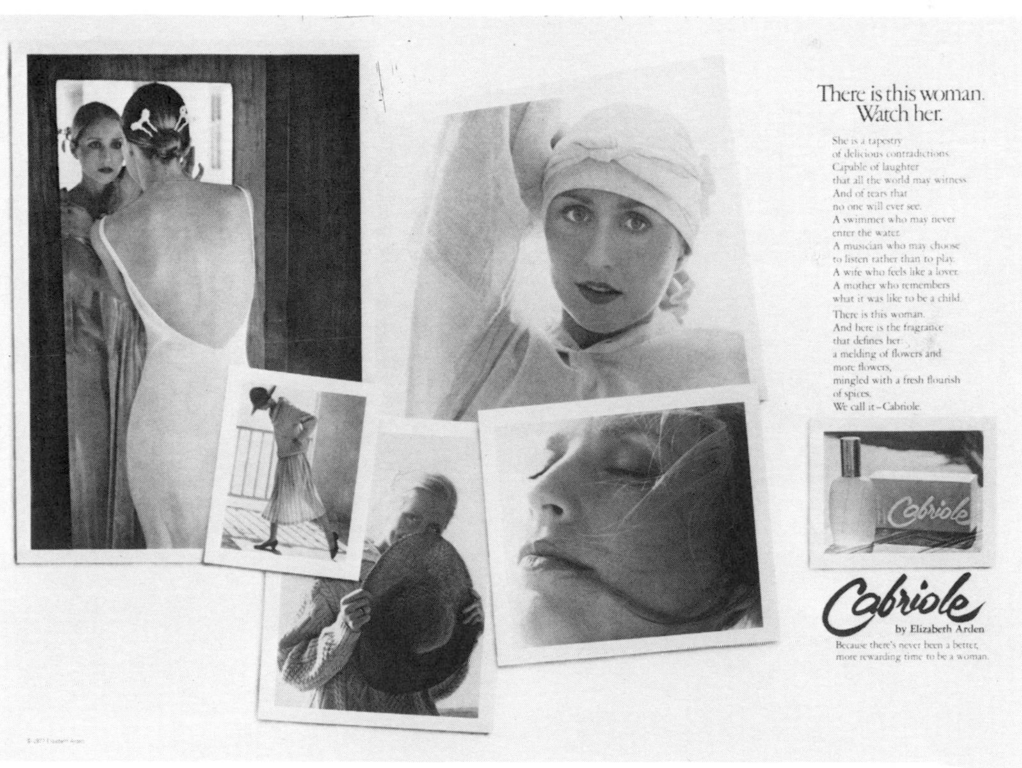

127

126

Art Directors Gary Carlisle
Martin Lipsitt
Writer Susan Schermer
Designers Martin Lipsitt
Gary Carlisle
Photographer Armen Kachaturian
Agency DKG Advertising, Inc.
Client West Point Pepperell

127

Art Director Robert Pasqualina
Writer Dorothy Friedman
Designer Janet Pasqualina
Photographer Debbie Turbeville
Agency Cohen Pasqualina Timberman
Client Elizabeth Arden

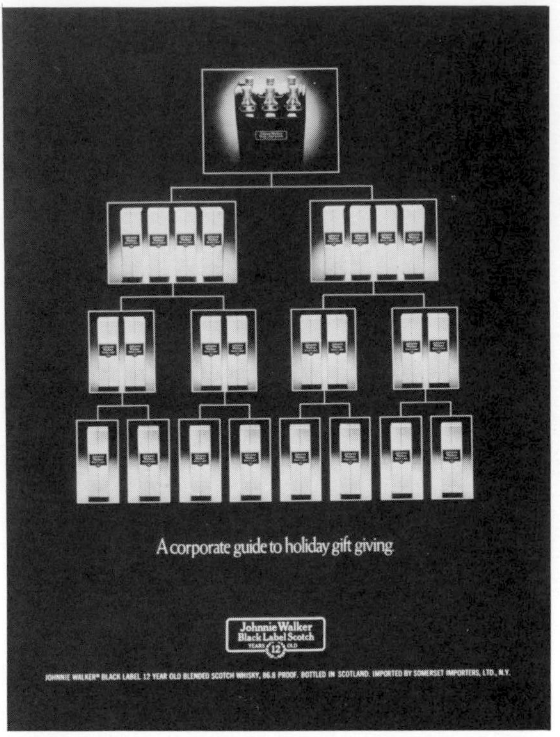

128

129

128

Art Directors Steve Ohman
Stuart Pittman
Writers Murray Klein
Faith Popcorn
Designer Steve Ohman
Artist Steve Ohman
Photographer Jerry Friedman
Agency Smith/Greenland, Inc.
Client Somerset Importers, Ltd.

129

Art Director Bob Phillips
Writer Frank Anton
Photographers Pete Turner
Cailor/Resnick
Agency Levine, Huntley, Schmidt,
Plapler & Beaver
Client Mem Company, Inc.

DO YOU RATE YOUR CAR AS HIGHLY AS A VOLVO OWNER RATES HIS?

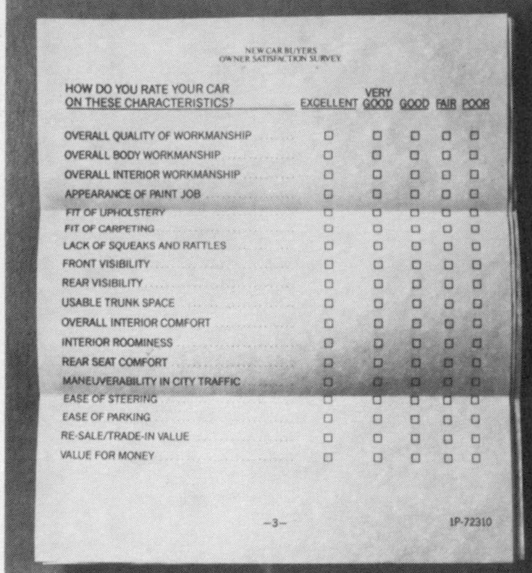

NEW CAR BUYERS
OWNER SATISFACTION SURVEY

HOW DO YOU RATE YOUR CAR ON THESE CHARACTERISTICS?	EXCELLENT	VERY GOOD	GOOD	FAIR	POOR
OVERALL QUALITY OF WORKMANSHIP	☐	☐	☐	☐	☐
OVERALL BODY WORKMANSHIP	☐	☐	☐	☐	☐
OVERALL INTERIOR WORKMANSHIP	☐	☐	☐	☐	☐
APPEARANCE OF PAINT JOB	☐	☐	☐	☐	☐
FIT OF UPHOLSTERY	☐	☐	☐	☐	☐
FIT OF CARPETING	☐	☐	☐	☐	☐
LACK OF SQUEAKS AND RATTLES	☐	☐	☐	☐	☐
FRONT VISIBILITY	☐	☐	☐	☐	☐
REAR VISIBILITY	☐	☐	☐	☐	☐
USABLE TRUNK SPACE	☐	☐	☐	☐	☐
OVERALL INTERIOR COMFORT	☐	☐	☐	☐	☐
INTERIOR ROOMINESS	☐	☐	☐	☐	☐
REAR SEAT COMFORT	☐	☐	☐	☐	☐
MANEUVERABILITY IN CITY TRAFFIC	☐	☐	☐	☐	☐
EASE OF STEERING	☐	☐	☐	☐	☐
EASE OF PARKING	☐	☐	☐	☐	☐
RE-SALE/TRADE-IN VALUE	☐	☐	☐	☐	☐
VALUE FOR MONEY	☐	☐	☐	☐	☐

–3– 1P-72310

If you put your car to the test on the left and discover it rates a lot of "poors" and "fairs," maybe you should own a Volvo.

Recently, Volvo owners were sent a similar questionaire as part of a nationwide survey among new car owners. They were asked to rate their new Volvos on these, and several other points.

The results were very enlightening.

They showed that Volvo owners overall were more satisfied than the owners of Impalas, LTDs, Cutlasses, Sevilles, Regals, Cordobas and 42 other cars from G.M., Ford, Chrysler and AMC.*

Volvo owners rated their cars higher on a whole range of things.

Quality of workmanship (something you may think has vanished from cars altogether).

Comfort and roominess (on that score, Volvo owners rated Volvos higher than Cadillac owners rated Cadillacs).

Safety, maneuverability, handling and value for the money.

So if you're interested in a car that's recommended by the experts—namely the people who have bought it and owned it—consider a Volvo.

They start at $6,645.†

Which to some people may seem like a lot of money to pay for a car.

But to others, it's a small price to pay for satisfaction.

VOLVO. A CAR YOU CAN BELIEVE IN.

130

TAKE AWAY THEIR UNIFORMS AND WHO ARE THEY.

JOCKEY® BRAND

131

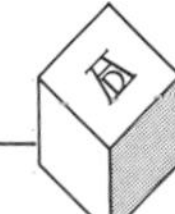

SILVER

130
Art Director Jim Perretti
Writer Larry Cadman
Designer Jim Perretti
Photographers David Langley
Cailor/Resnick
Agency Scali, McCabe, Sloves
Client Volvo of America

131
Art Director Allan Beaver
Writer Larry Plapler
Photographer Carl Fischer Photography, Inc.
Agency Levine, Huntley, Schmidt, Plapler & Beaver
Client Jockey International, Inc.

"Pernod.
It grows on you."

Enjoy Pernod® as a long drink with grapefruit juice, the "Pamplemousse." Also enjoyable with your favorite mixer, or with water and ice in a tall glass. Imported from France. 90 proof.

132

132

Art Director Bob Bidner
Writer Ray Baker
Designer Bob Bidner
Artists Bob Bidner
Tony Toscano
Agency Ted Bates & Co., Inc.
Client Julius Wile Sons & Co., Inc.

133

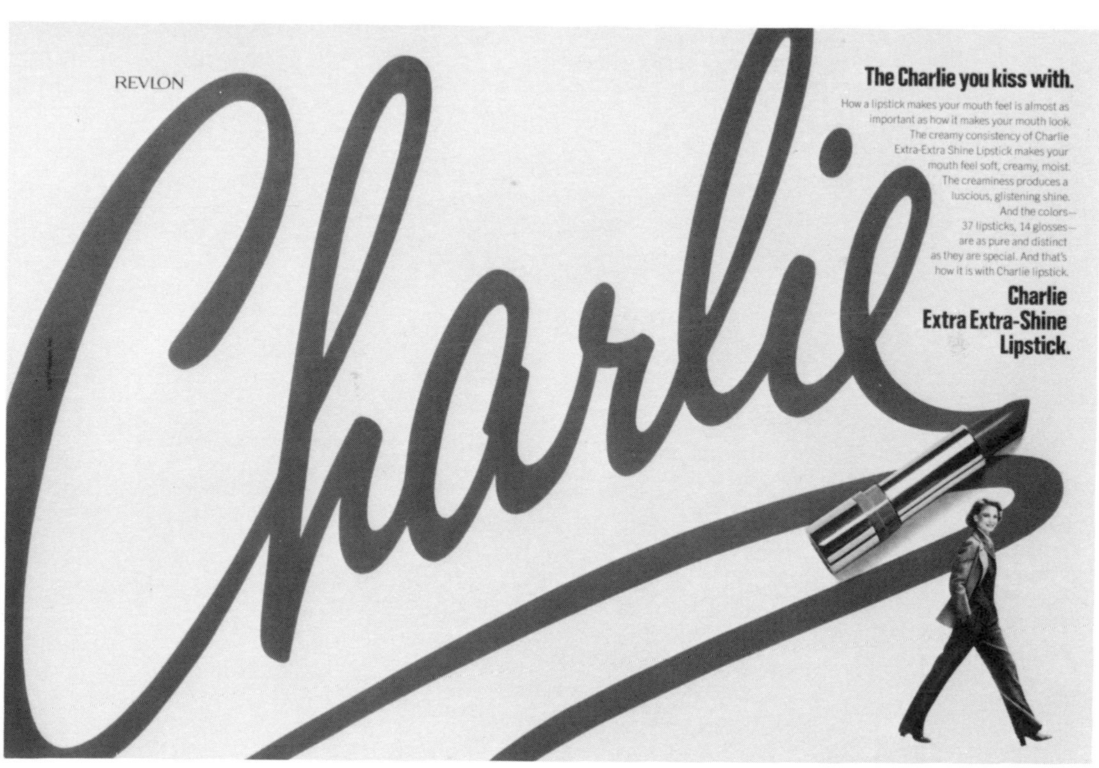

134

133
Art Director Martin Stevens
Writer Rita Connor Grisman
Designer Martin Stevens
Photographer Richard Avedon
Agency Revlon—50th Floor Workshop
Client Ultima II

134
Art Director Constance von Collande
Writer Joan LaMell
Designer Constance von Collande
Photographer Jerry Friedman
Agency Revlon Creative Workshop
Client Revlon, Inc.

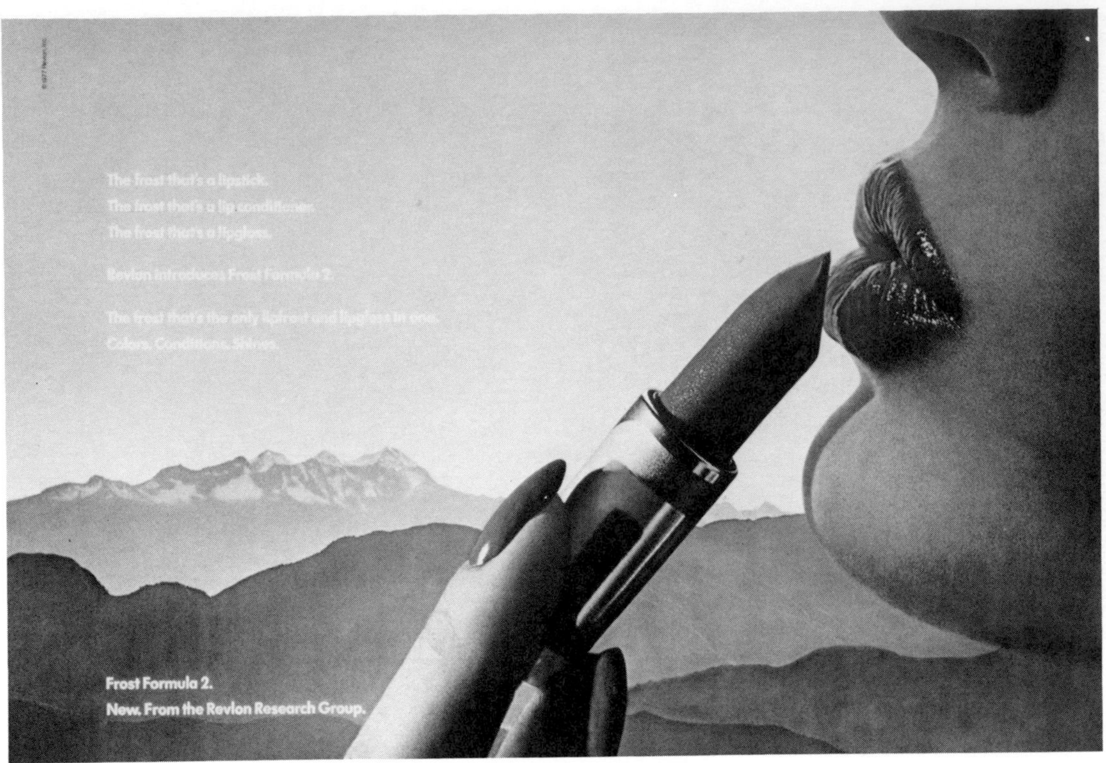

135

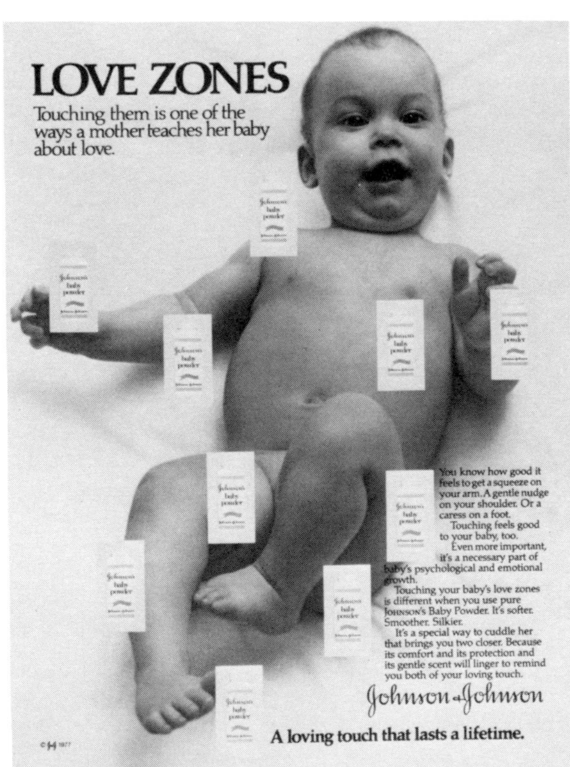

136

135
Art Director Martin Stevens
Writer Rita Connor Grisman
Designer Martin Stevens
Photographer James Moore
Agency Revlon—50th Floor Workshop
Client Revlon Formula II

136
Art Director Arvale Rogers
Writer Mara Connolly
Photographer Steve Horn
Agency Young & Rubicam
Client Johnson & Johnson

"Dear American Tourister: Now I believe your crazy ads."

Frank Bishop used to think we were kidding. Until the day he left his American Tourister in the back of his dump truck, and proceeded to load the truck with tons and tons of rock.

Later, when Mr. Bishop dumped the rocks, there was his American Tourister. One side was bent, but it was still usable. (Fact is, Mr. Bishop's still using it.)

A word of caution however. We do not recommend that you drop rocks on your American Tourister, or do anything crazy like that. Because that's not why we make American Touristers the way we do.

We mold each piece from the toughest materials we can find.

We wrap each case with a strong stainless steel frame.

We even install special nonspring locks designed not to spring open on impact.

We do everything we can to help your American Tourister survive the everyday torment of everyday traveling. Mile after mile of it. Trip after trip.

You don't have to be in a crazy American Tourister ad to appreciate an American Tourister.

American Tourister

137

"Dear American Tourister: I fell flat on my attache."

This true story comes from a lawyer in San Diego, California.

Rushing off to work one morning, he tumbled down a flight of stairs, landing squarely on his American Tourister attache. Naturally he was shook up (so was his attache). But his wife writes that we saved him from a cracked tailbone, and that both he and his attache made it to work that day.

Well, it's wonderful to hear we protected someone's most valuable possessions. But if you think you have to land on an American Tourister to appreciate an American Tourister, you're missing the point.

That's not the reason we choose the toughest materials we can find for our attaches and every piece of our molded luggage.

That's not why we wrap each case with a strong stainless steel frame.

And that's not why we install special nonspring locks designed not to spring open on impact.

There's just one reason why we do all these things: to help protect your luggage (and what's inside your luggage) from the ordinary pressures of ordinary travel. Trip after trip, mile after mile.

We want you to understand, you don't have to fall down to prove an American Tourister holds up.

American Tourister

138

Wrangler
has more styles than Heinz has varieties.

139

SILVER

137
Art Director John Mariucci
Writer Marcia Grace
Photographer Casimo
Agency Doyle Dane Bernbach
Client American Tourister

138
Art Director John Mariucci
Writer Marcia Grace
Photographer Casimo
Agency Doyle Dane Bernbach
Client American Tourister

139
Art Director Merv Shipenberg
Writer Austin Hamel
Designer Merv Shipenberg
Photographer David McCabe
Agency Altman, Stoller, Weiss
Client Wrangler

THE SHIP THAT BROUGHT AMERICA ITS TASTE FOR SCOTCH.

December 5, 1933 was a noteworthy day for Scotch drinkers. For it was the first time in 13 years that drinking it was legal. Prohibition was repealed.

Perhaps even more noteworthy: it was the day Cutty Sark landed in America. A Scots Whisky already legendary in other civilised parts of the world.

Scotch had been imported into this country before, but had also been largely ignored. Cutty Sark, however, with its particular smoothness, soon captured a large and loyal following of Americans with good taste.

Today, wherever you go in America, you will find the bottle with the famous ship "Cutty Sark" on the label. And the distinctive Scots Whisky inside.

Who would have thought back in 1933 that someday people would be able to cross the United States without changing ships?

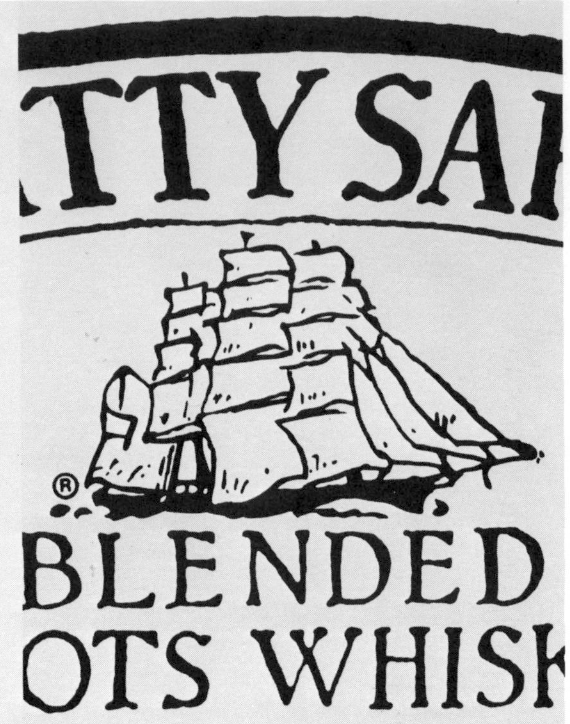

140

The Purist.
Perhaps you've noticed how many of your favorite products have been miraculously "improved" lately. They've been lemon-freshened, hyped up with ingredients to make them last longer, changed into exotic shapes and colors. Purity and quality, those old-fashioned absolutes, have become harder and harder to find.
Take heart. There are a few stubborn purists still around. And when it comes to sensitive skin care, count us among them.
Neutrogena proudly announces nothing new or improved about our soap.
We don't tamper with the Neutrogena® formula by adding new ingredients just to keep reviving your interest. Our soap's made with pure, natural ingredients, the finest we can buy. Without artificial hardeners or coloring or additives or free alkali that potentially could irritate sensitive skin.
We don't crank out Neutrogena by the usual mass production methods, either.
We make our soap the way you'd make a gourmet dinner because we're just as finicky about quality as you are. Individual batches are carefully controlled and "cooked" for six hours. During that time they're checked time and time again by our chemists.
All in all there are 22 separate tests for quality and purity during manufacture.
And independent dermatology laboratories, adhering to strict FDA standards, have also tested Neutrogena eight different ways to make sure it's as careful with your face as it should be.
That's why so many doctors recommend Neutrogena. It cleans your skin thoroughly, but not drastically, leaving it immaculately fresh, but not dry.
We don't promise you miracles or magical ingredients or exotic fragrances. We don't make claims we can't live up to. All you get from us is a safe, pure bar of amber soap that won't irritate even the most sensitive skin.
If you've gotten a little skeptical of change for change's sake, you should try Neutrogena.
It's a purist. And we think your complexion will enjoy going back to these old-fashioned basics, purity and quality.
Neutrogena
for sensitive skin care.

141

140
Art Director Dick Lopez
Writer Ed McCabe
Designer Dick Lopez
Agency Scali, McCabe, Sloves
Client Buckingham Corp.

141
Art Director Mary McInerny
Writers Joan Levine
Sharon O'Connor
Designer Mary McInerny
Photographer Arthur Beck
Agency Hall & Levine
Advertising Inc.
Client Neutrogena Corporation

142

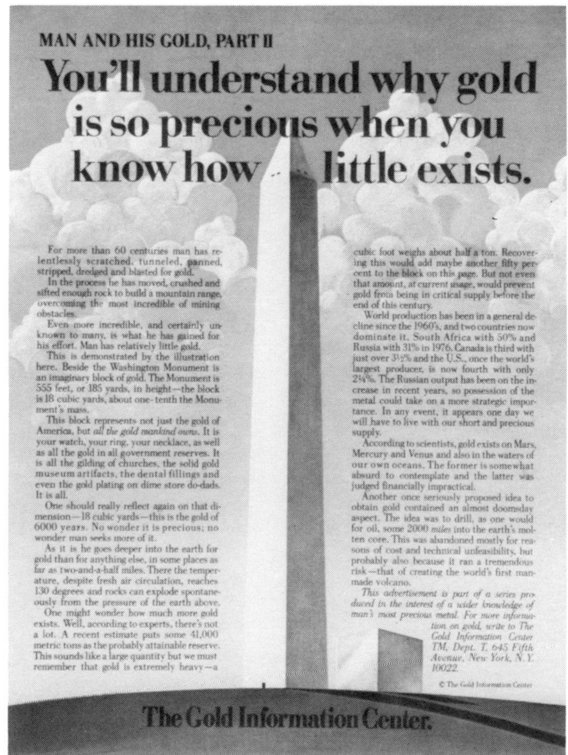

143

142

Art Director Nick Rice
Writers Bill Miller
Duane Johnson
Designer Nick Rice
Photographer Jim Marvy
Agency Carmichael-Lynch, Inc.
Client Normark Corporation

143

Art Director William Taubin
Writer Paul Zoellner
Designer William Taubin
Artist Isadore Seltzer
Agency Doyle Dane Bernbach
Client Intergold

144

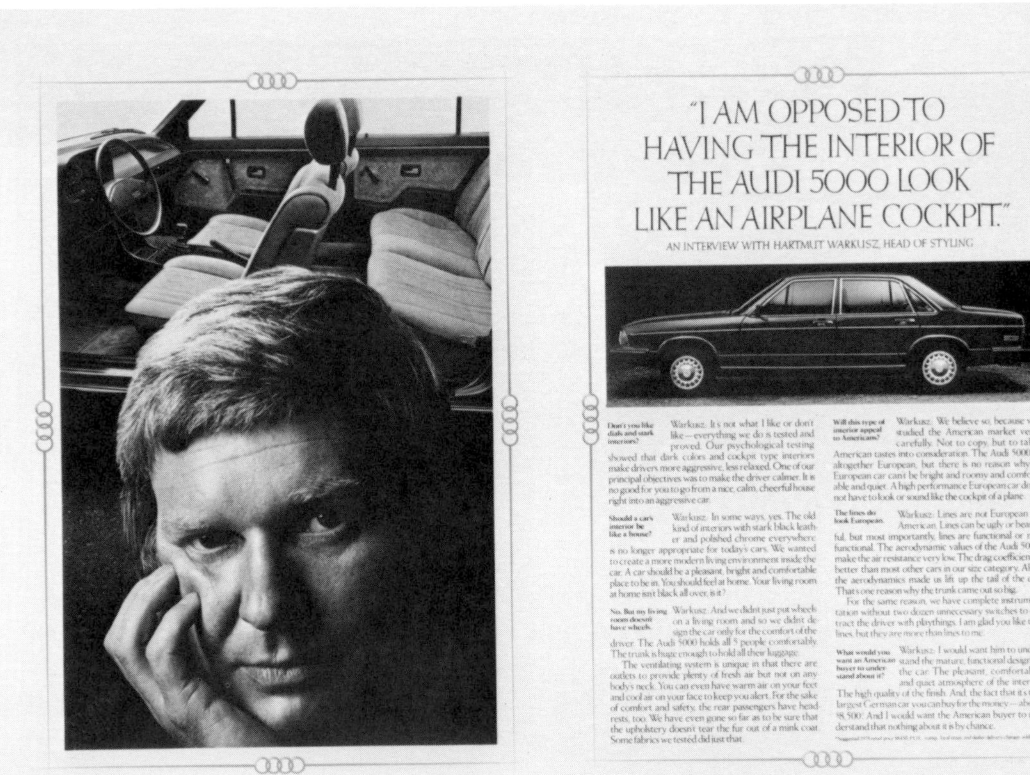

145

144	
Photographer	Rosemary Howard
Agency	William Seltzer 'Advertising
Client	Adolpho

145	
Art Director	Helmut Krone
Writers	Dave Reider Robert Levenson
Photographer	Carl Fischer
Agency	Doyle Dane Bernbach
Client	Porsche-Audi

146

147

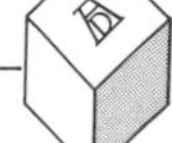

GOLD

146	
Art Director	Helmut Krone
Writers	Ed Smith
	George Rike
Photographer	Carl Fischer
Agency	Doyle Dane Bernbach
Client	Polaroid

147	
Art Director	Helmut Krone
Writers	Ed Smith
	George Rike
Photographer	Carl Fischer
Agency	Doyle Dane Bernbach
Client	Polaroid

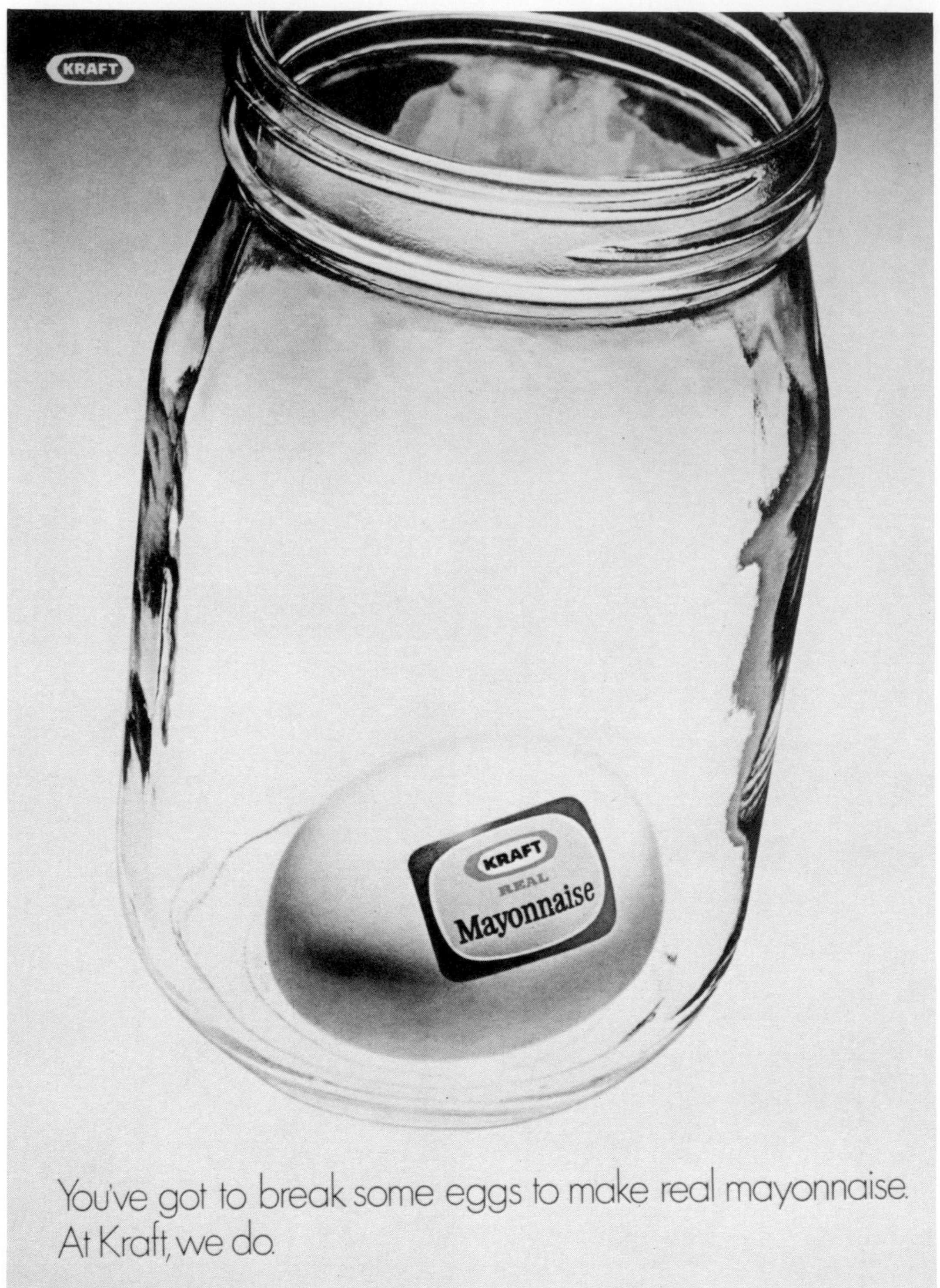

KRAFT
KRAFT
REAL
Mayonnaise
You've got to break some eggs to make real mayonnaise.
At Kraft, we do.

148

148
Art Director John Koelle
Writer Charlie Martell
Designer John Koelle
Photographer Clay Taylor
Agency J. Walter Thompson
Client Kraft

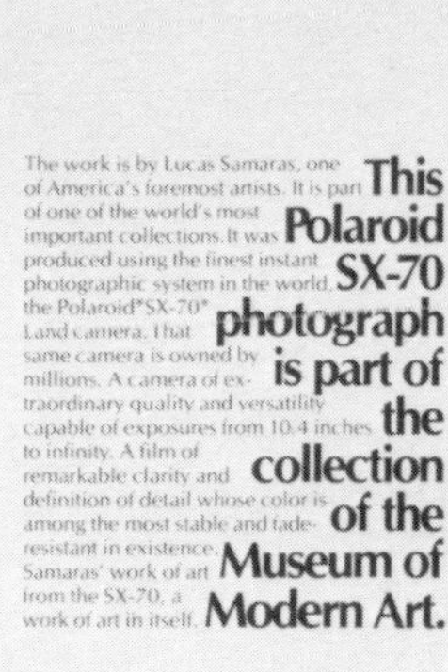

149

RABBIT. THE #1 SELLING IMPORT IN JAPAN.
The Japanese obviously know a good thing when they see one.
And so more people in Japan are buying Volkswagen Rabbits than any other imported car.
Fascinating. But not astonishing.
The Rabbit has more total room than any Japanese car in its class.
The Rabbit hops from 0 to 50 mph in 8.3 seconds.
Most Japanese cars don't.
If you're interested in superior handling and maneuverability, you'll get them in a Rabbit, because the Rabbit has front-wheel drive.
Most Japanese cars don't.
If you're interested in economy, a VW Rabbit with a diesel engine got the highest mileage of any car in America for 1978. 53mpg on the highway, 40mpg in the city.
The gasoline Rabbit is no slouch, either, with 38mpg on the highway, 25mpg in the city.
(EPA estimates, with standard transmission. Your own mileage may vary, depending on how and where you drive, your car's condition and optional equipment.)
In short, the Rabbit delivers precisely what thoughtful people anywhere want in a car: performance, room, handling, economy.
So next time you have a yen for a terrific sukiyaki dinner, drive to the restaurant in a Rabbit. And enjoy the best of both worlds.
VOLKSWAGEN DOES IT AGAIN

150

PEUGEOT
RUGGER KEEPS ON ROLLING. MOVING ALONG TOGETHER. IT'S AS ACTIVE AND ALIVE AS YOU ARE. NEVER SITTING BACK, BUT ALWAYS GOING AND ALWAYS DOING. IT'S RUGGER BY GANT FOR MEN OR BOYS. FOR FATHER OR SON. GANT, INCORPORATED, NEW HAVEN, CONN. 06509.
THE GANT ATTITUDE

151

149
Art Director Helmut Krone
Writers Ed Smith
Edith Stevenson
Photographer Helmut Krone
Agency Doyle Dane Bernbach
Client Polaroid

150
Art Director Bert Steinhauser
Writer Robert Levenson
Designer Bert Steinhauser
Photographer Bert Steinhauser
Agency Doyle Dane Bernbach
Client Volkswagen

151
Art Director Howard Title
Writer Chuck Cohen
Designer Howard Title
Photographer Gary Bernstein
Agency Waring & LaRosa
Client Gant, Inc.

THIS IS AN AD FOR PEOPLE WHO THINK ALL THE LITTLE COUNTRY INNS ARE IN OTHER PEOPLE'S COUNTRIES.

They seem to have been lifted, setting and all, out of some other place. The French countryside, an English village, the Swiss Alps.

North Carolina's country inns. You see them standing tall on the mountaintops, tucked into green and yellow valleys, set back in the trees beside a winding road.

And, while the feeling may be European, the hospitality is strictly Southern. One innkeeper says it's "like having company all the time."

You'll find fresh flowers and four-poster beds. Music boxes and dinner bells. Long tables loaded with steaming platters of home-grown, home-cooked food.

And outside your window, and off the wide verandahs, scenery like you thought you could only find on picture postcards.

The famous and the obscure have warmed themselves at the great stone fireplaces of the inns. Aaron Burr. John C. Calhoun. Woodrow Wilson. F. Scott Fitzgerald. William Jennings Bryan.

George Washington never slept at any of them, of course. But Cornwallis (a gentleman who reportedly caused him to lose quite a bit of sleep) did.

The inns, in a way, are North Carolina in miniature. Because the warmth of the people, the reverence for nature, the deep sense of history, are everywhere you go. Everywhere the inns are. From the mountains to the sea.

So come, this year. Bring your camera, your heartiest appetite, and your comfortable shoes. And spend your vacation in a fascinating country. Yours.

NORTH CAROLINA

THE CHEROKEE CALLED THEM "THE GREAT BLUE HILLS OF GOD." THE NAME HAS CHANGED. THE MOUNTAINS HAVEN'T.
NORTH CAROLINA

COME SEE THE STATE THAT KEPT THE WORLD'S SECOND OLDEST RIVER FROM DYING OF UNNATURAL CAUSES.
NORTH CAROLINA

152

152

Art Director	**Michael Winslow**
Writer	**Harriet Frye**
Photographer	**Jay Maisel**
Agency	**McKinney Silver & Rockett**
Client	**North Carolina Department of Commerce**

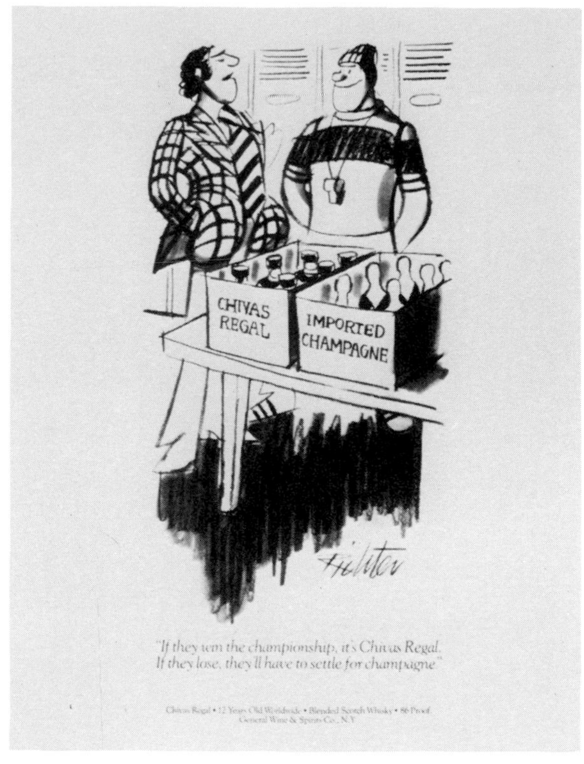

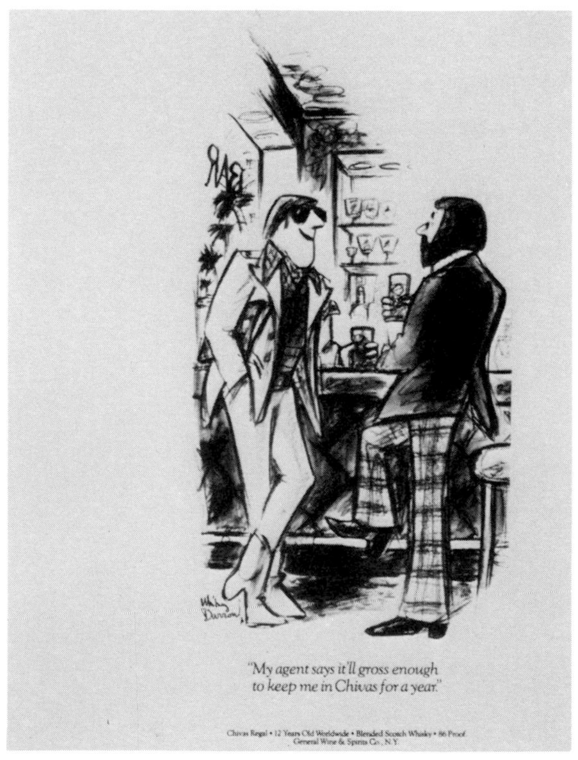

153

153

Art Director	**Charles Abrams**
Writers	**George Rike**
	Howard Brookstein
Artists	**Charles Saxon**
	Mischa Richter
	Whitney Darrow, Jr.
	Frank Modell
Agency	**Doyle Dane Bernbach**
Client	**General Wine & Spirits Co.**

Don't let the energy crisis squeeze you into a small car.
Well friends, you heard what the man said. Some sacrifices will have to be made.
But getting into a Volkswagen won't be one of them.
Volkswagens may look like small cars, but only on the outside.
Inside is another story altogether.
A VW Rabbit, for example, has (incredibly!) more space for people than 19 other cars in its class, including Monza, Mustang, Pinto, Sunbird, Datsun F-10, and Toyota Celica.
The Rabbit also has (shockingly!) more trunk space than 34 other cars, including Cadillac Seville, Thunderbird, Camaro, Monza, Nova, Comet, Starfire, Firebird, Skylark and Ventura.
These are official U.S. Government statistics, by the way, published in the official Environmental Protection Agency 1977 Gas Mileage Guide.
The Rabbit also goes like a bat out of you-know-where. From 0 to 50 in 7.7 seconds is sports car performance.
Moving along smartly to our Dasher. We hope you'll be floored to learn that the VW Dasher Wagon, according to the same EPA guide, has more trunk space than any wagon in its class made by any other manufacturer. Meaning General Motors, Ford, Chrysler, Datsun, Toyota.
And if your family doesn't need quite that much space, Dasher also comes in a beautifully appointed 2-door Hatchback and 4-door Sedan. Yet both Dashers have way more passenger room and trunk room than any Japanese car in their class and more than most American cars in their class.
Finally, Scirocco. The VW Scirocco is a true sports car that can bring home 16 cubic feet of stuff on Saturdays and racing trophies on Sundays.
Scirocco is just something else, beating everything in its class (and a lot of other classes). Yet it has more trunk space than any—repeat—any car in its class made by any—repeat any—manufacturer.
All the new Volkswagens were made for the times that are on us now. All three get 24 MPG in the city. Rabbit and Scirocco get 37 MPG on the highway. Dasher gets 36. (EPA estimates with standard transmission. Actual mileage depends on how and where you drive, optional equipment, and the car's condition.)
Yet even with all this economy, there is nothing quite like them for their combination of handling, performance, reliability, safety, space and just plain wisdom of design.
You're going to appreciate them. Better still, you're going to love them.
Dasher
Rabbit
Scirocco

154

The work is by Lucas Samaras, one of America's foremost artists. It is part of one of the world's most important collections. It was produced using the finest instant photographic system in the world, the Polaroid®SX-70® Land camera. That same camera is owned by millions. A camera of extraordinary quality and versatility capable of exposures from 10.4 inches to infinity. A film of remarkable clarity and definition of detail whose color is among the most stable and fade-resistant in existence. Samaras' work of art from the SX-70, a work of art in itself.

This Polaroid SX-70 photograph is part of the collection of the Museum of Modern Art.

155

154	
Art Director	John Eding
Writer	Doug Houston
Photographer	Larry Robins
Agency	Doyle Dane Bernbach
Client	Volkswagen

155	
Art Director	Helmut Krone
Writers	Ed Smith
	Edith Stevenson
Photographer	Helmut Krone
Agency	Doyle Dane Bernbach
Client	Polaroid

156

157

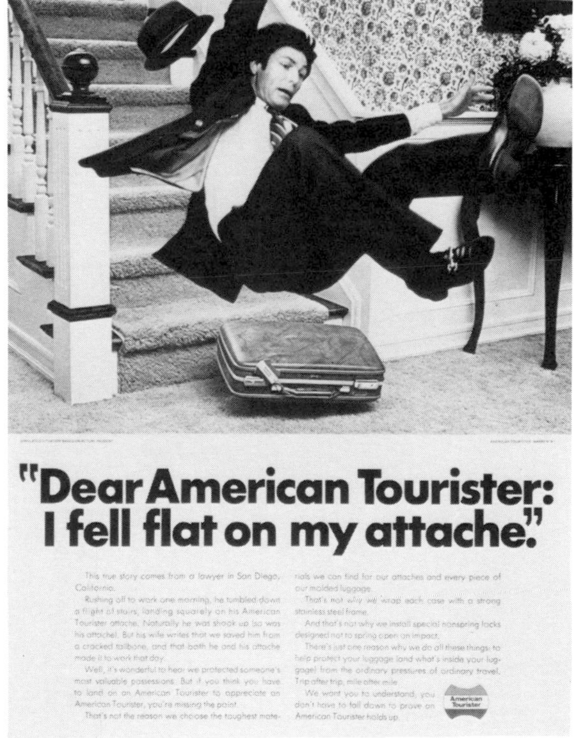

158

SILVER

156
Art Director Kurt Haiman
Writers Ed Hannibal
Frank Izzo
Bobbie Kaplan
Designer Kurt Haiman
Photographer Phil Marco
Agency Grey Advertising
Client Renfield Importers Ltd.

157
Art Director Helmut Krone
Writer Ed Smith
Photographer Helmut Krone
Agency Doyle Dane Bernbach
Client Polaroid

158
Art Directors John Mariucci
Roy Grace
Writer Marcia Grace
Photographer Casimo
Agency Doyle Dane Bernbach
Client American Tourister

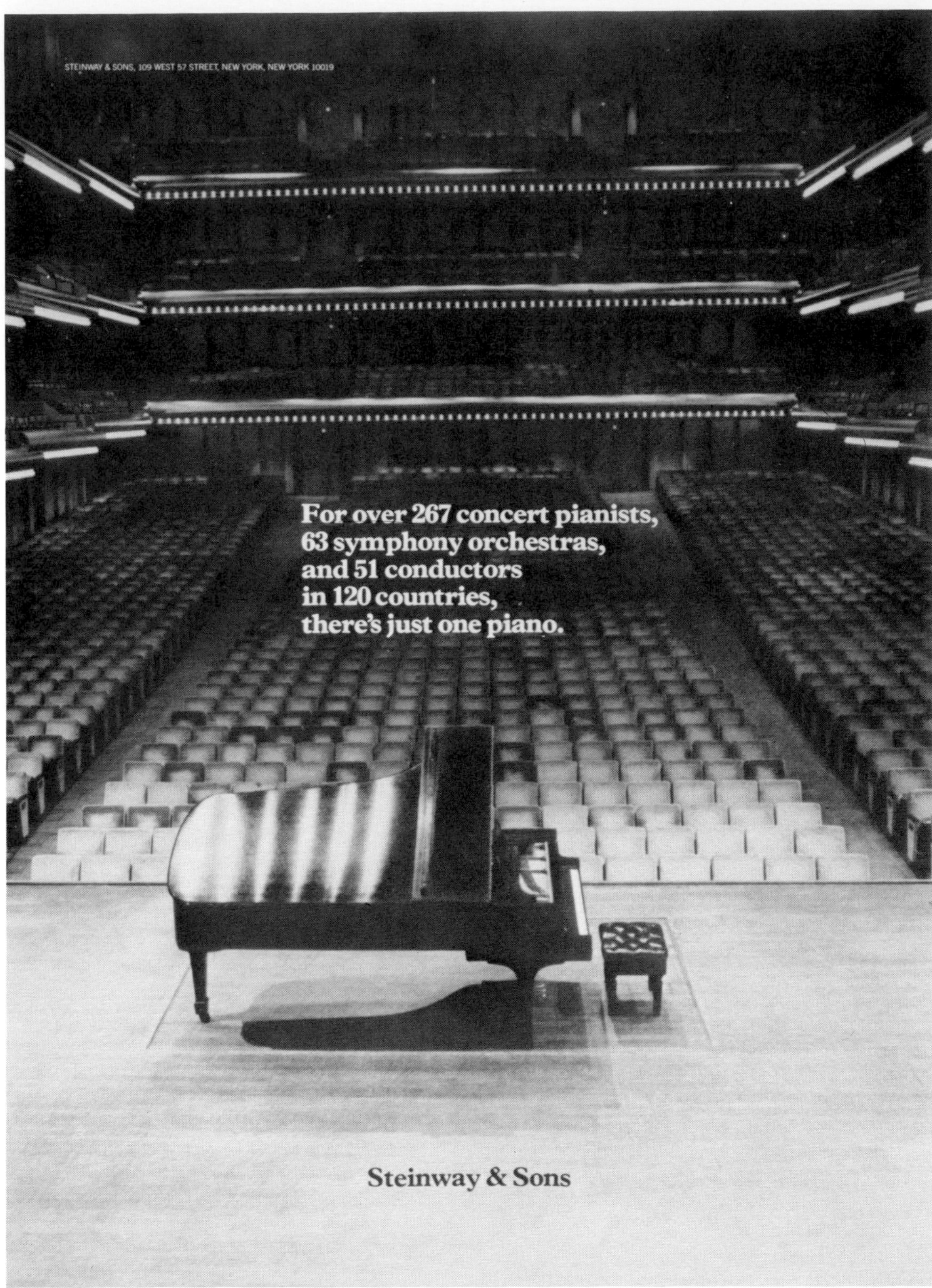

STEINWAY & SONS, 109 WEST 57 STREET, NEW YORK, NEW YORK 10019
For over 267 concert pianists,
63 symphony orchestras,
and 51 conductors
in 120 countries,
there's just one piano.
Steinway & Sons

159

159

Art Directors	Cathie Campbell
	Sirje Helder
Writer	Charles Griffith
Photographer	Dave Langley
Agency	Lord, Geller, Federico, Inc.
Client	Steinway & Sons

THE SHIP THAT BROUGHT AMERICA ITS TASTE FOR SCOTCH.

December 5, 1933 was a noteworthy day for Scotch drinkers. For it was the first time in 13 years that drinking it was legal. Prohibition was repealed.

Perhaps even more noteworthy: it was the day Cutty Sark landed in America. A Scots Whisky already legendary in other civilised parts of the world.

Scotch had been imported into this country before, but had also been largely ignored. Cutty Sark, however, with its particular smoothness, soon captured a large and loyal following of Americans with good taste.

Today, wherever you go in America, you will find the bottle with the famous ship "Cutty Sark" on the label. And the distinctive Scots Whisky inside.

Who would have thought back in 1933 that someday people would be able to cross the United States without changing ships?

160

THE BMW COUPE. AS CLOSE TO AN ALL-OUT RACING MACHINE AS A PASSENGER CAR SHOULD EVER COME.
THE ULTIMATE DRIVING MACHINE.
Bavarian Motor Works, Munich Germany

161

GOLD

160	
Art Director	Dick Lopez
Writer	Ed McCabe
Designer	Dick Lopez
Agency	Scali, McCabe, Sloves
Client	Buckingham Corporation

161	
Art Director	Clem McCarthy
Writer	Martin Puris
Photographers	Dick James
	David Thorpe
Agency	Ammirati Puris AvRutick Inc.
Client	BMW of North America, Inc.

162

162
Art Director Mel Rustom
Writers Mel Rustom
Chuck Griffith
Designer Mel Rustom
Photographer John Stember
Agency Ogilvy & Mather
Client American Express Co.

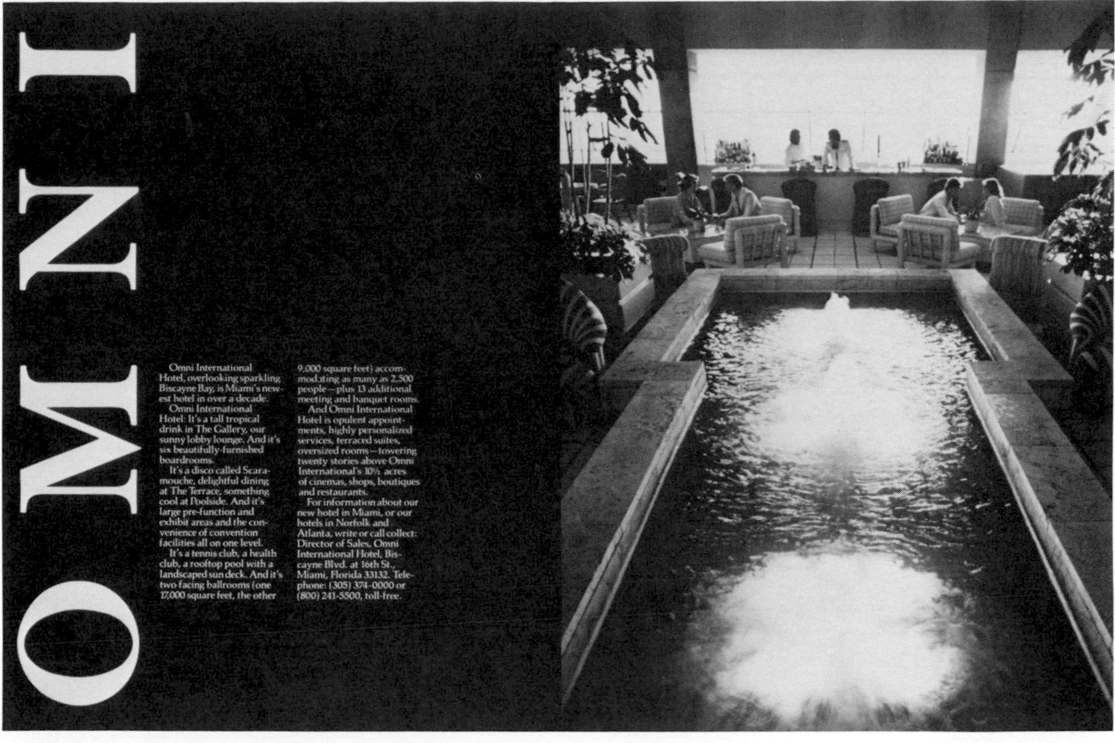

163

164

163
Art Directors Dick Henderson
Bill Sweney
Writers Brian McKenna
James P. Cole
Designers Dick Henderson
Bill Sweney
Photographers Jamie Cook
Randy Miller
Agency Cole Henderson Drake, Inc.
Client Omni International Hotels, Inc.

164
Art Director Sal Lombardo
Writer David F. Willis
Designer Sal Lombardo
Photographer Rudy Tesa
Agency Wilson, Haight & Welch
Client BMW of North America

In Saronno, all we think about is love.

For it was here that Amaretto, the drink of love, began 450 years ago. When a beautiful young woman created an extraordinary liqueur for the man of her heart. To be known for the way you make love in Italy. . . believe us, that is no small matter.

So here in Saronno, we do not fool around with love. We still make Amaretto di Saronno as we have for centuries. We allow the flavor to develop until it is soft and full. We take our time—can love be hurried?

Sip it as it is, on the rocks, in a mixed drink. Just bear in mind: only Amaretto di Saronno is *originale*. There are other amarettos you can buy. But true love comes only from Saronno.

Love-On-The-Rocks.

Amaretto di Saronno. Originale.
From the Village of Love.

In Saronno, Amaretto is our bambino.

It was in our little town that Amaretto, the drink of love, was born 450 years ago. When a beautiful young woman created an extraordinary liqueur to please the man she loved.

Here we still make Amaretto di Saronno as we have for centuries. We allow the flavor to develop until it is soft and full. We take our time—can love be hurried?

Enjoy Amaretto di Saronno as it is, or on the rocks, or with coffee. Try it in any number of exciting mixed drinks. With love, anything goes.

But a word of caution. There is only one Amaretto di Saronno. Remember this. Because if it is not Amaretto di Saronno that you drink, it may not be love after all.

Amaretto di Saronno. Originale.
From the Village of Love.

165

There is a tide
in the affairs of women.

KINGSMILL
on the James

166

165
Art Director Thomas W. Heck
Writer Marcia Bell Grace
Designer Thomas W. Heck
Photographer Anthony Edgeworth
Agency Wells, Rich, Greene
Client Foreign Vintages

166
Art Director Dick Athey
Writer John Hartmann
Designer Dick Athey
Photographers Bob Llewellyn
John Whitehead
Agency Webb & Athey, Inc.
Client Kingsmill on the James

We're among the six largest papermakers in the United States.

We have more capacity than Mead, Union Camp, Westvaco, Potlatch, Boise Cascade and many other fine and familiar names.

But, a lot of the bankers, investment advisers, brokers and market analysts we are just beginning to reach thought of us until recently as the company we used to be.

But now they are aware that while we own a railroad, a coal mine, a major paper converter and a large paper merchant, we own them because they're directly related to the core of our business: making paper.

They're now aware that we hold commanding shares of market in three important areas of the paper business—and that these areas where we're leaders generate 95% of our revenues.

Linerboard and corrugating medium. We make it in one of the industry's largest and most efficient plants and are the nation's number one supplier to the independent box makers, who have 22% of the market.

Business communication papers. Paper for your office copier, computer, letterhead. We're good at making such papers and at selling them—as our leading market position demonstrates.

Uncoated groundwood printing papers. The kinds used in mail-order catalogs and telephone books. We have more uncoated groundwood capacity than any two other United States producers combined, and are diversifying this relatively low-cost product to serve new markets.

In the last five years, our earnings per share have grown at an average annual rate of 30%. Further, our pre-tax return on sales has increased more than 150% to 13.0%, and return on equity has doubled to 14.4%.

Our NYSE ticker symbol is GNN and our chairman is Sam Casey. He wants to send you an annual report, a 10-K and a fact book about GNN.

Write to him at Great Northern Nekoosa Corporation, 75 Prospect Street, Stamford, Connecticut 06901.

167 A

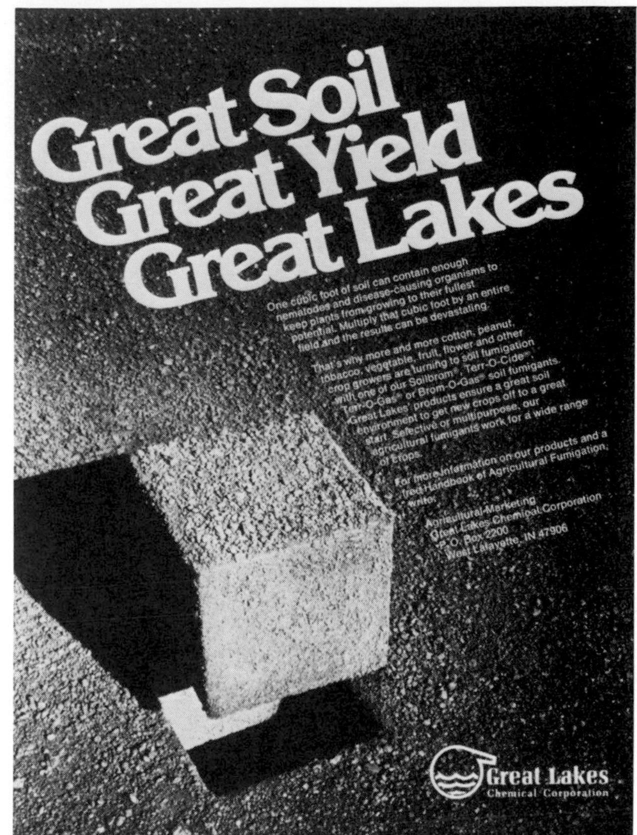

Great Soil
Great Yield
Great Lakes
One cubic foot of soil can contain enough nematodes and disease-causing organisms to keep plants from growing to their fullest potential. Multiply that cubic foot by an entire field and the results can be devastating.
That's why more and more cotton, peanut, tobacco, vegetable, fruit, flower and other crop growers are turning to soil fumigation with one of our Soilbrom®, Terr-O-Cide®, Terr-O-Gas® or Brom-O-Gas® soil fumigants. Great Lakes' products ensure a great soil environment to get new crops off to a great start. Selective or multipurpose, our agricultural fumigants work for a wide range of crops.
For more information on our products and a free Handbook of Agricultural Fumigation, write:
Agricultural Marketing
Great Lakes Chemical Corporation
P.O. Box 2200
West Lafayette, IN 47906
Great Lakes
Chemical Corporation

167 B

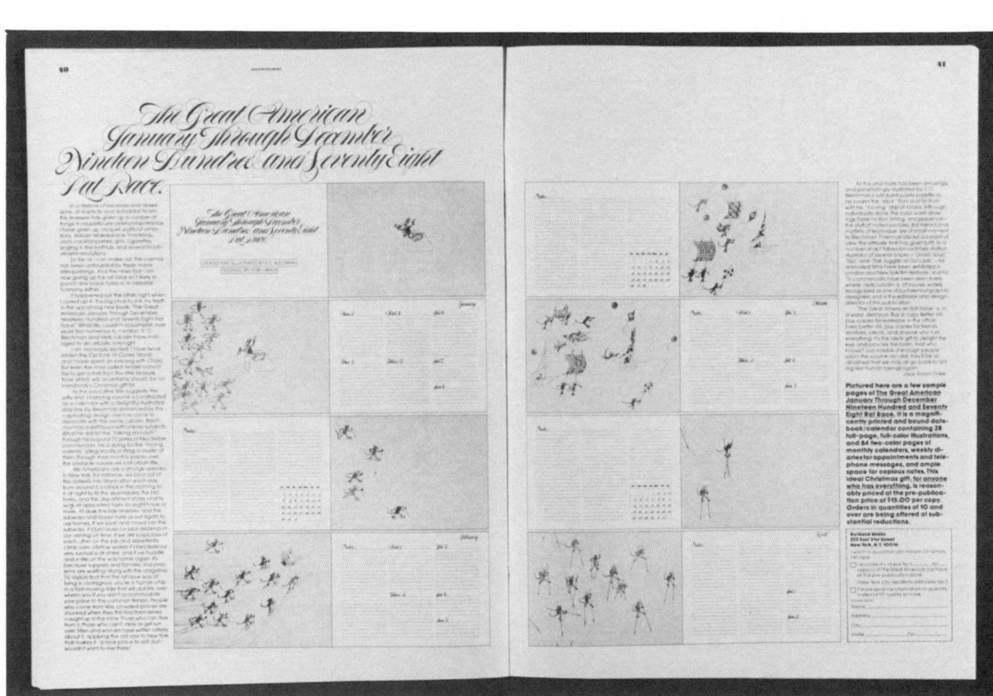

168

167A
Art Director Dick Thomas
Writers Arthur Einstein, Jr.
Robert Higbee
Designer Kathy Manuelian
Photographers John Paul Endress
Robert Grant
Agency Lord, Geller, Federico, Inc.
Client Great Northern Nekoosa Corp.

167B
Art Directors Kendall S. Smith
Robert J. Kennedy, Jr.
Writer Dennis Lange
Designer John Bugg
Photographer Mark Fitch
Agency Indiana Design Consortium
Client Great Lakes Chemical Corporation

168
Art Director Herb Lubalin
Writer Jack Anson Finke
Designer Herb Lubalin
Artist R.O. Blechman
Agency LSC&P Design Group
Client RatRace Books

169

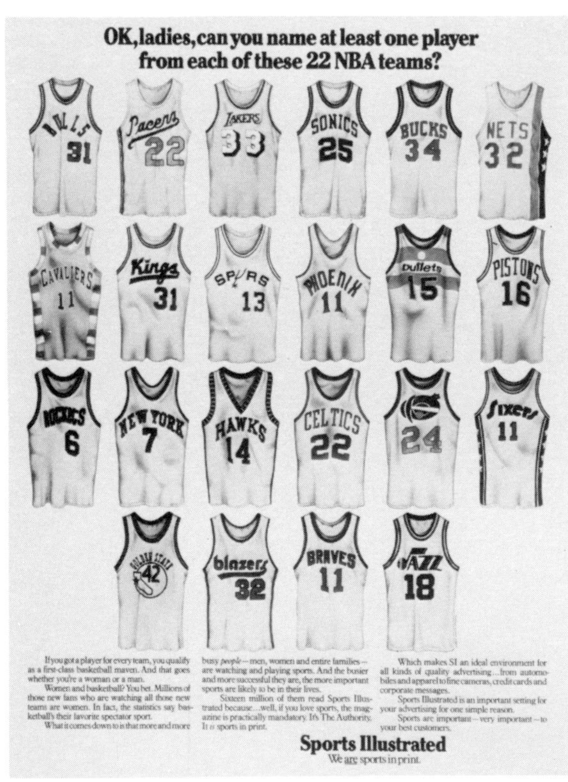

170

CLASS OF 78

Japanese Brides. Order Now!

parade

It wouldn't be Sunday without a Parade

171

169
Art Director Ernie Smith
Writer Ernie Smith
Designer Ernie Smith
Agency LSC&P Design Group, Inc.
Client Alphatype Corporation

170
Art Director Bob Czernysz
Writer Dick Olmsted
Artist Hernandez and Kinstrey
Agency Young & Rubicam
Client Sports Illustrated

171
Art Director Tony Mandarino
Writer Karl Vollmer
Designer Tony Mandarino
Photographer Tony Mandarino
Agency Frankfurt Comm.
Client Parade Magazine

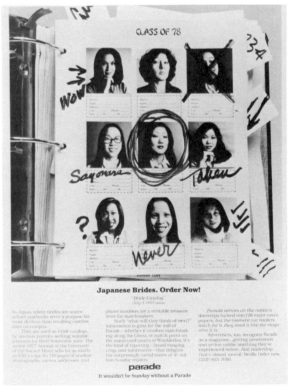

172

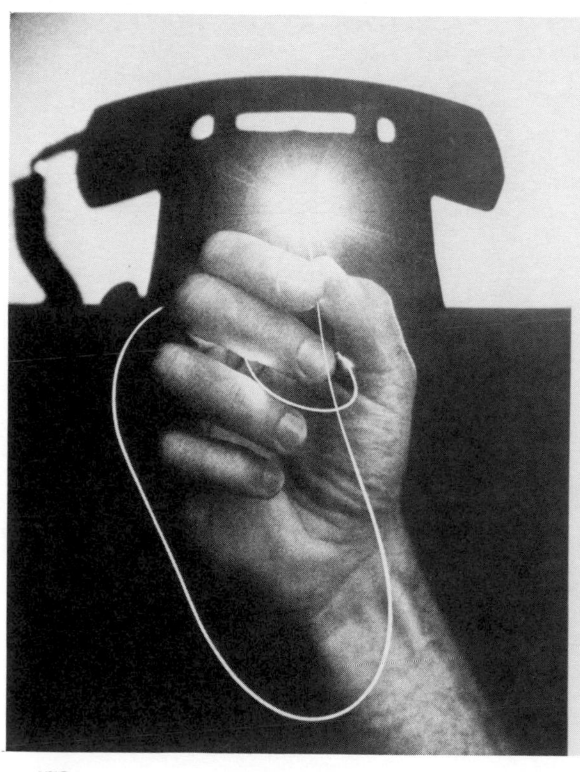

Hear the light.

Today, communications may be at the threshold of another revolution in technology.

Someday soon, when you make a phone call, your voice may be carried between telephone offices as pulses of light over a hair-thin glass fiber.

We call this new technology lightwave communications.

Less Cost, Less Space:

Lightwave communications has the potential for carrying enormous quantities of information—from phone calls to business data to TV programs—at low cost. And it can do it in much less space.

Right now, we're testing an experimental system that can carry nearly 50,000 phone calls in a cable of glass fibers not much thicker than a clothesline. It could do the work of several copper cables, each as thick as your arm.

That will allow us to save space in the crowded cable ducts under the streets of many of our cities. Which in turn will lessen the need to add new cable ducts to expand service.

But even carrying that many calls uses only a fraction of a light beam's capacity.

So it will give us plenty of room to grow.

To make lightwave communications possible, the people at Bell Labs and Western Electric attacked a number of problems simultaneously.

What Had to be Done:

What kind of problems?

Creating some of the most transparent glass the world has ever known.

Developing techniques to draw the glass into highly precise fibers which, despite their tiny size, have a complex internal structure that keeps the light from leaking out.

Devising ways to protect the delicate fibers from damage, to make them into cables strong enough to pull through underground ducts, and to splice them—a hundred or more at a time.

To generate the light carried by the fibers, they developed a tiny, solid-state laser smaller than a grain of salt. (Today's design is expected to operate continuously for ten years or more.)

To put information onto the light beam, they designed equipment that turns the tiny laser on and off millions of times a second.

And they developed repeaters to regenerate the light signal along its way, as well as photodetectors at the receiving end to convert the light back into an electrical signal that can travel throughout the telephone network.

We think lightwave communications may prove a long step forward in the development of communications.

We may put it to use in the early 1980's to relieve cable congestion between major switching centers. For special applications, we may use it even sooner.

And it may someday carry business data, visual communication services and facsimile transmission into your home and office.

Seeing to It:

Innovations from Bell Labs and Western Electric are put to work by your Bell telephone company. That's another reason you have the most reliable, least expensive telephone service in the world.

To keep it that way, one of the things we're doing is seeing to it that before long you'll be hearing the light.

One of a series of messages to keep you informed of how telecommunications technology is changing our world—and the part Bell Labs, Western Electric and your Bell telephone company are playing in it.

Bell Laboratories/Western Electric

173

172

Art Director	Wally Arevalo
Writer	Walt Hampton
Photographer	Ed Centner
Agency	Doyle Dane Bernbach
Client	Unistrut Corp.

173

Art Director	Joe Frederick
Writers	Ted Littleford
	Roger Levinsohn
Designer	Joe Frederick
Photographer	Carl Fischer
Agency	Foote, Cone & Belding
Client	Western Electric

She stole the shirt off his back. Took the pants off his legs. Now, she's walked off with his closet full of suits.

Today a woman is discovering what a man always knew. That a suit makes sense. She can put it on in minutes. Throw on everything from a cowl neck to a silk shirt. And voila. She's fashionable and comfortable all day long.

But one suit makes as much sense as one pair of shoes. Like him, she needs an eight suit wardrobe. For every work day. And play day.

Now, she'll find it. In the biggest, busiest, most exciting closet she (and you) have ever seen: "The Suit Closet." The island that will soon be coming to your store. Where one great pants suit leads to another. And another.

With Happy Legs/Jazzie, hundreds of busy customers will soon walk off with your closet full of suits.

Happy Legs/JAZZIE
1407 Broadway, New York, N.Y. 10018.
A Spencer Company.

Happy Legs/Jazzie
A whole new way of dressing.

174

Goodbye Yves St. Laurent, Pierre Cardin, Nino Cerruti.

Hello Oscar de la Renta.

American men have had it with the harsh, extreme European silhouette. (Most of them couldn't squeeze into it anyway.)

They're going back—for keeps, we think—to classic, understated, elegant, wearable clothing.

And no one is more closely or favorably identified with that kind of clothing than Oscar de la Renta.

The Spring '78 line he just completed for us proves that he is, indeed, the king of classic designers.

The line is, in a word, magnificent. The best expression of the traditional soft shoulder British silhouette we've ever seen.

And we're not the only ones who think so. Almost everyone who's seen it has bought it. Usually in depth.

Superb styling. Exquisite detailing inside and out. Oscar de la Renta signature lining and label. Fabulous fabrications that are ours and ours alone.

Based on a keystone plus markup, the suits will retail from $185 to $225, sport coats from $125 to $150. But everything looks like it costs a lot more.

If we sound excited it's because we are. And you will be too, when you've seen the line.

Because you won't just be looking at Oscar de la Renta's superb work.

You'll be looking at the future of men's clothing.

Oscar de la Renta
DESIGNS FOR LOUIS GOLDSMITH
1290 Avenue of the Americas, New York City. (212) 581-9513.

175

174
Art Director Millie Sachs
Writer Marty Friedman
Designer Millie Sachs
Photographer Hal Davis
Agency Ferber and Strauss Inc.
Client Happy Legs/Jazzie

175
Art Director Jack Anesh
Writer Ned Viseltear
Designer Jack Anesh
Photographer Hal Davis
Agency Anesh, Viseltear, Hirschberg, Inc.
Client Louis Goldsmith, Inc.

176

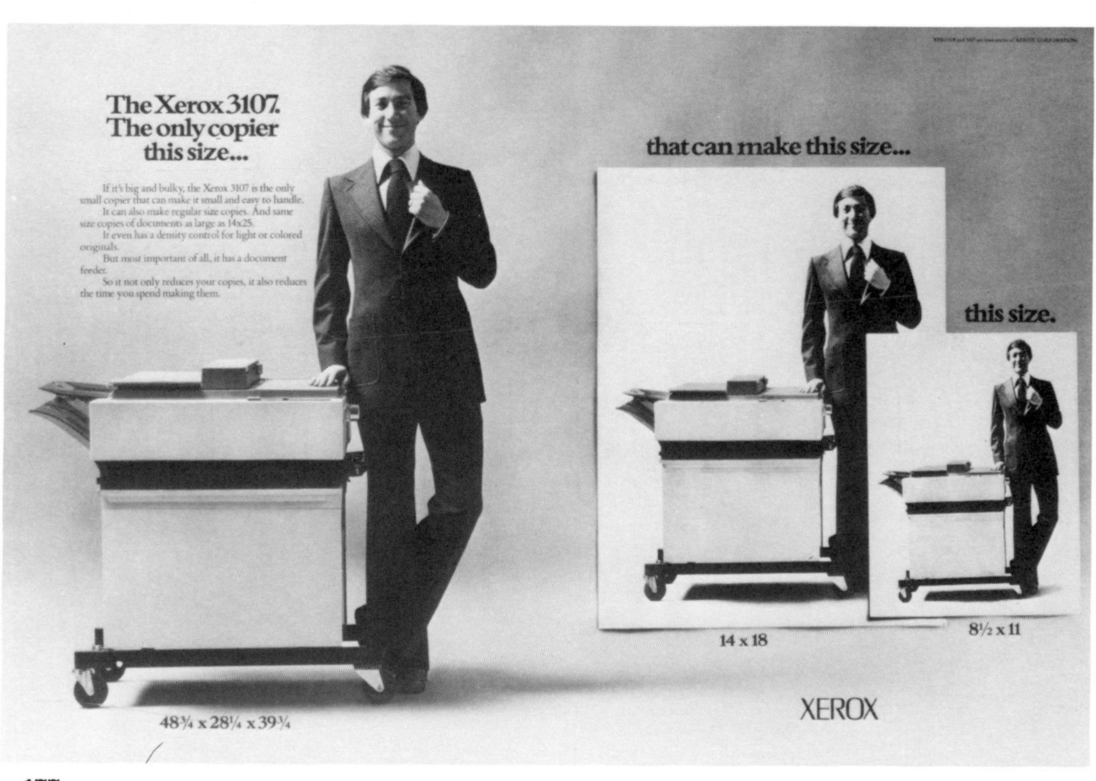

177

176
Art Director Tony Mandarino
Writer Karl Vollmer
Designer Tony Mandarino
Photographer Hoffman (stock photo)
Agency Frankfurt Comm.
Client Parade Magazine

177
Art Director Allen Kay
Writers Lester Colodny
David Cantor
Photographer Harold Krieger
Agency Needham, Harper
& Steers Adv. Inc.
Client Xerox Corp.

"No gossip."
ANDY WARHOL, ARTIST. A READER SINCE 1968.
U.S.News & WORLD REPORT
We spare our readers unimportant news.
We spare our advertisers unimportant readers.

178

MEET YOUR MAKER.
Jerell Inc.

179

178

Art Director	J. Ryder
Writer	D. Staley
Photographer	Mick Pateman
Agency	Ted Chin & Company, Inc.
Client	U.S. News & World Report

179

Art Director	Arthur Eisenberg
Writer	Arthur Eisenberg
Designer	Arthur Eisenberg
Agency	Eisenberg & Pannell
Client	Jerell Inc.

Mother's finest.
"Baby Love." It's catching on. The hit single from "Another Mother Further." On Epic Records.
Produced by Tom Werman and Mother's Finest for Tara-Ti Productions • Management: Hugh Rodgers, c/o Ram International, Box 76436, Atlanta, Ga. 30328 (404) 992-1050

180

Contact Sports

This isn't the only activity where contact lenses have proven to be a boon.

As Yankee outfielder Roy White can attest (and he does, in a testimonial advertising campaign for Bausch & Lomb, the optical manufacturers)—baseball is another contact sport where eyeglasses just won't do.

In fact, as a recent article in Forbes Magazine points out, there are 115 million Americans—one in two—who wear glasses or who sport contacts. But contact wearers are a surprisingly small percentage of the total potential market. The soft lens type of contacts, that hug the eye comfortably, would seem to be the answer to the visual problems of some 35 million Americans. Yet just 1.5 million contact lens wearers buy them. Why? Because the purchase and fitting of contact lenses (especially the soft, more expensive kind) averages $300.

But the Federal Trade Commission may change that. In the Forbes article (called "Shifting Channels") it's reported that the F.T.C. is proposing rules that could put a whole new focus on the market. Doctors would be required to give their patients a copy of the prescription, thus providing the option of buying lenses from the less costly optician. The potentials of the market would also open wider to such companies as Warner-Lambert, Dow Corning, Revlon and 15 others, scanning and planning for their share of this eye-opening business volume.

In its coverage of a product as tiny, yet hugely significant as contact lenses, Forbes gives its readers a clear-sighted perspective on what's up and what's ahead. And the same is true for all of its business, industrial, financial and governmental news. That's why Forbes stays in first place in the measured reading preferences of America's key executives. Those at the very top. And those determinedly on their way there.

The research firm of Erdos & Morgan made a reconfirming study of this among the corporate officers of 1300 of America's largest companies. The results of this study showed Forbes to be read by more of these top management executives than any other major business or news magazine.

No wonder Forbes was the only magazine in its field last year to register a second record breaking year in a row for advertising page gains.

No wonder Forbes is the clear winner as the fastest-growing business or news magazine of the past decade, with an advertising page gain for that period of 72%. Compare that, for example, with Business Week—down 28%. Or Fortune—down 20%.

And in the first five months of 1977, Forbes gained 11% in ad pages. Set new highs in 7 of the first 10 issues. Achieved, in the May 15th issue, a record $2 million of advertising.

Look to Forbes in the coming year for more of the same kind of editorial vitality and quality of audience that makes all this possible. You don't need glasses to know that's where you'll find your relevant audience of decision makers.

Your market. Your customers. Your prospects. Your contacts.

FORBES: CAPITALIST TOOL

181

180

Art Director	Hillary Vermont
Writer	Mark Levitt
Designer	Hillary Vermont
Photographer	Lawrence Robbins
Agency	CBS Records
Client	Epic Records

181

Art Directors	Tom Van Steenbergh
	Gene Gramm
Writer	Gene Gramm
Photographer	Alan Dolgins
Agency	Doremus Uptown
Client	Forbes Magazine

182

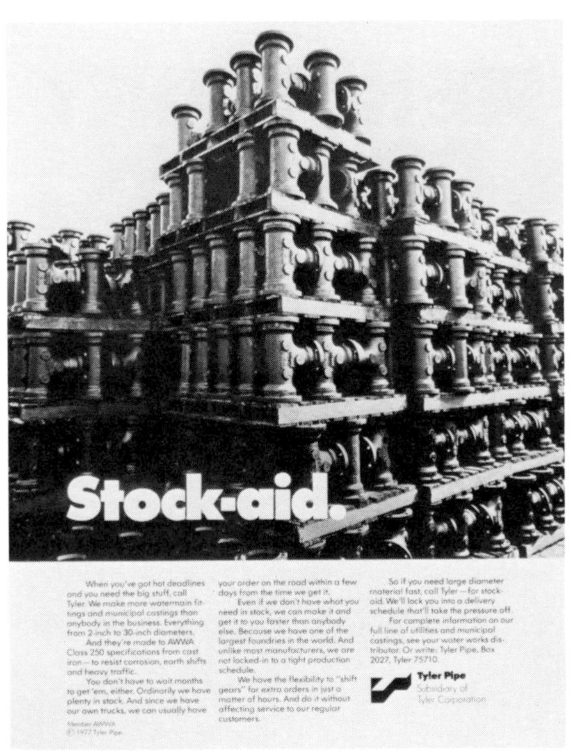

183

182
Art Directors Bob Czernysz
Barbara Gemza
Writer Dick Olmsted
Photographer Editorial Photography
Agency Young & Rubicam
Client People Magazine

183
Art Director Rob Lawton
Writer Ben Vergati
Designer Rob Lawton
Photographer Eric Lindstrom
Agency Crume & Associates, Inc.
Client Tyler Pipe

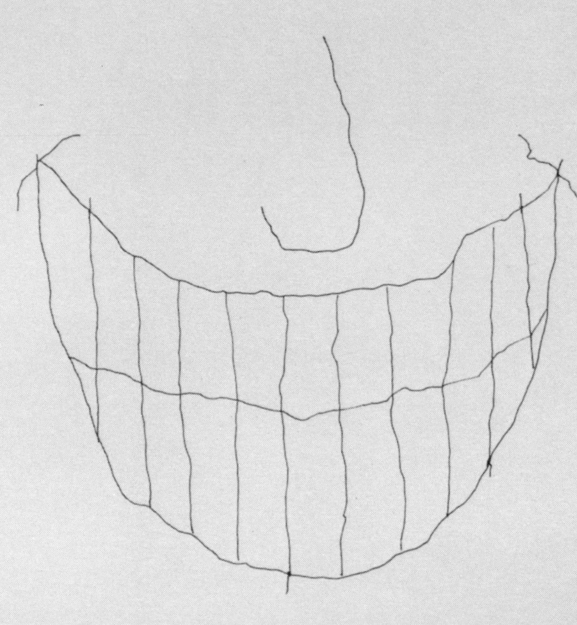

Is your agency too agreeable for your own good?

Somebody once said that if two people agree on everything, one of them isn't necessary.

It seems that applies to advertising.

One of the most valuable services an agency can perform is to provide you with objective counsel on whether your advertising strategy is really going to take your company on to glory.

An agency that specializes in smiling isn't going to give you that.

And when was the last time your agency dared to present something a little out of the ordinary?

If it's been awhile, perhaps they've become more concerned with keeping themselves successful than they are with making you successful.

After all, real live customers don't always get excited about the same advertising that thrilled top management.

If your agency relationship has become so comfortable it's making you uncomfortable, may we make a suggestion?

Hire Cole & Weber, Inc.

You may find our recommendations occasionally hard to swallow. But don't worry. You'll feel much better when the results are in.

184

SEE HOW THEY DON'T RUN.
See how the protective colloid function of CELLOSIZE Hydroxyethyl Cellulose thickener is fighting to reduce dripping, splattering and glooping.
See how nicely pigment dispersion and suspension are maintained even during prolonged storage. And how water layering in the can is minimized or eliminated entirely.
See how easily solutions of CELLOSIZE HEC are prepared using simple mixing equipment with hot or cold water.
See how well it works with a wide variety of colorants and latexes, giving you good color stability and uniform color in the applied film.
See your nearest Union Carbide salesman and ask him about CELLOSIZE HEC.
And see for yourself why the thickener that's been so good at stopping runaway paint has been such a runaway success.
PEOPLE PLANNING THE FUTURE.
UNION CARBIDE
Coatings Materials
CELLOSIZE is a Registered Trademark of Union Carbide Corporation USA.

185

184
Art Director Bill Bowman
Writer Dave Newman
Artist Bill Bowman
Agency Cole & Weber
Client Cole & Weber —PAF Directory

185
Art Director Duane Plants
Writers Allen Kay, David Cantor
Photographer Steve Eisenberg
Agency Needham, Harper & Steers Adv. Inc.
Client Union Carbide

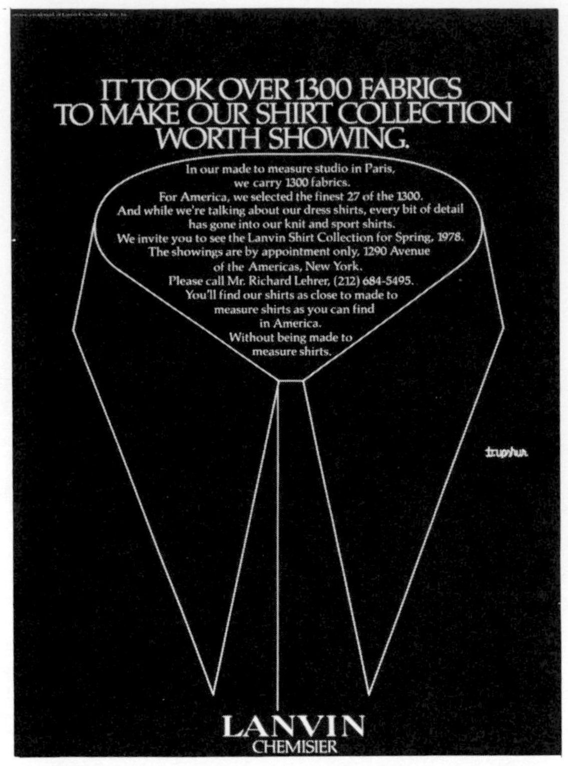

186

187

186
Art Director Richard Brown
Writer George Adels
Designer Richard Brown
Artist Thomas Upshur
Agency D'Arcy-MacManus & Masius
Client Lanvin

187
Art Director Herb Lubalin
Writer Jack Anson Finke
Designer Herb Lubalin
Photographer Carl Fischer
Agency LSC&P Design Group
Client Alphatype Corporation

189

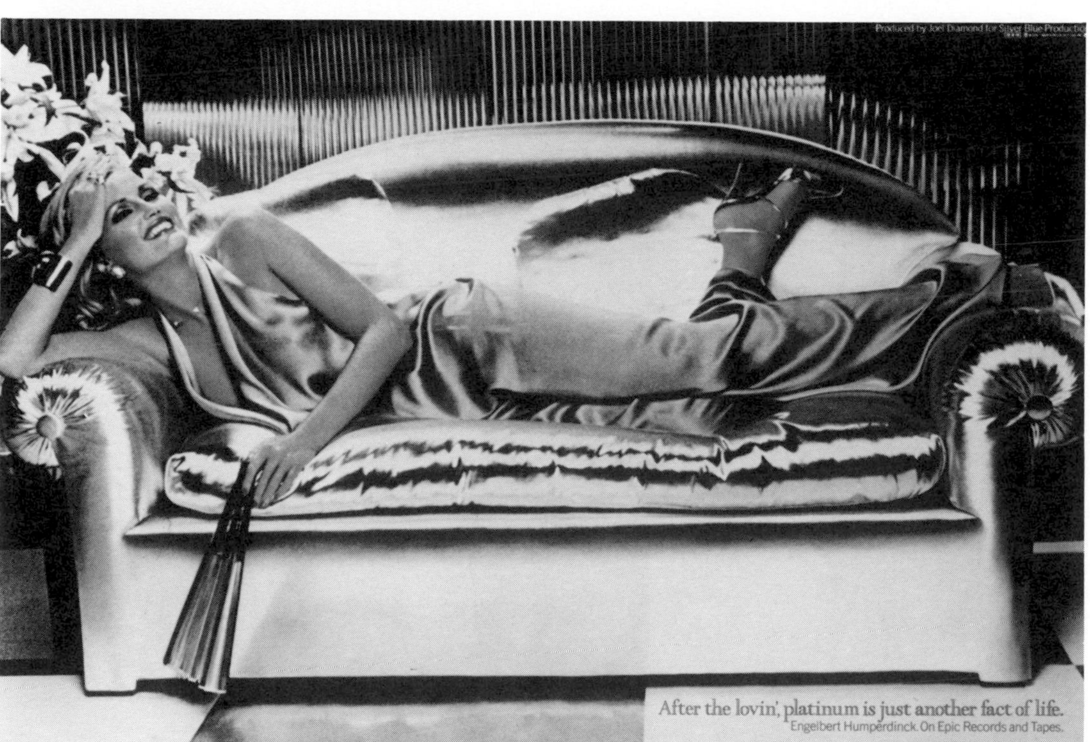

After the lovin', platinum is just another fact of life.
Engelbert Humperdinck. On Epic Records and Tapes.

190

189	
Art Director	Bruce Day
Writer	Patricia Kennely
Designer	Bruce Day
Photographer	Ronald G. Harris
Agency	CBS Records
Client	Columbia Records

190	
Art Director	Bruce Day
Writer	Rick Lyon
Designer	Bruce Day
Photographer	Ladner-Blake
Agency	CBS Records
Client	Epic Records

A fortune in double platinum.
Heart on Portrait™ Records and Tapes.
Produced by Mike Flicker

191

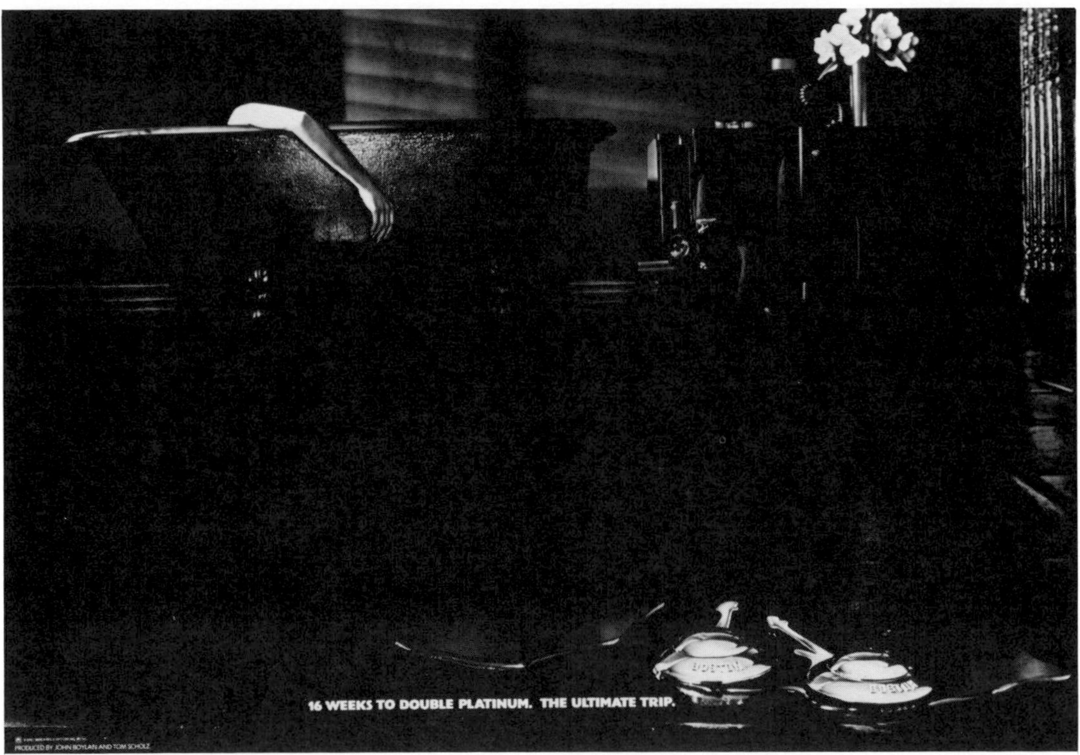

192

191

Art Director	Bradley H. Olsen-Ecker
Writer	Marty Pekar
Designer	Bradley H. Olsen-Ecker
Photographer	Steve Prezant
Agency	CBS Records
Client	Heart-Portrait Records

192

Art Director	Myron Polenberg
Writer	Barry Levine
Designer	Myron Polenberg
Photographer	Steinbicker/Houghton
Agency	CBS Records
Client	Epic Records

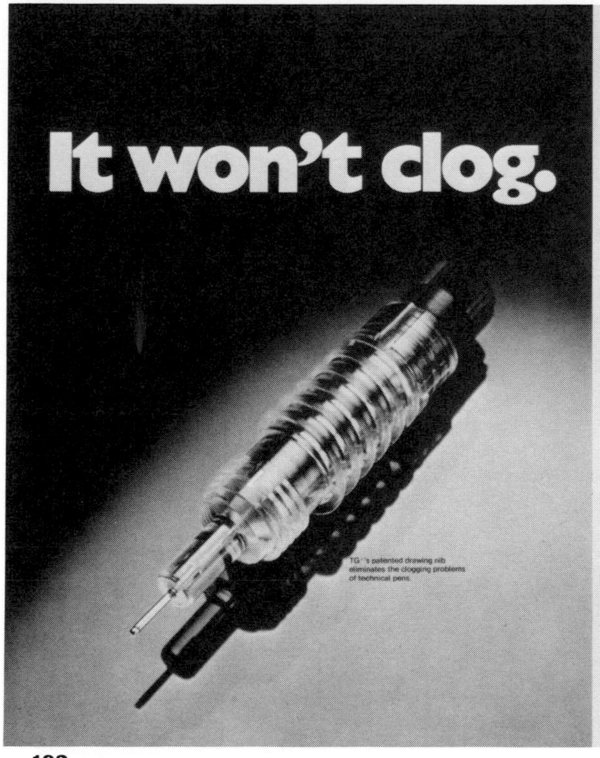

It won't clog.
TG's patented drawing nib eliminates the clogging problems of technical pens.

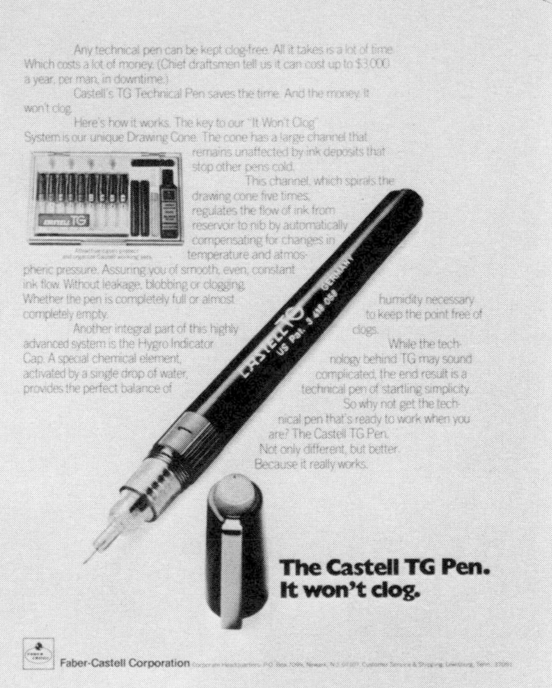

Any technical pen can be kept clog-free. All it takes is a lot of time. Which costs a lot of money. (Chief draftsmen tell us it can cost up to $3000 a year, per man, in downtime.)
Castell's TG Technical Pen saves the time. And the money. It won't clog.
Here's how it works. The key to our "It Won't Clog" System is our unique Drawing Cone. The cone has a large channel that remains unaffected by ink deposits that stop other pens cold.
This channel, which spirals the drawing cone five times, regulates the flow of ink from reservoir to nib by automatically compensating for changes in temperature and atmospheric pressure. Assuring you of smooth, even, constant ink flow. Without leakage, blobbing or clogging. Whether the pen is completely full or almost completely empty.
Another integral part of this highly advanced system is the Hygro Indicator Cap. A special chemical element, activated by a single drop of water, provides the perfect balance of humidity necessary to keep the point free of clogs.
While the technology behind TG may sound complicated, the end result is a technical pen of startling simplicity.
So why not get the technical pen that's ready to work when you are? The Castell TG Pen.
Not only different, but better.
Because it really works.
The Castell TG Pen.
It won't clog.
Faber-Castell Corporation

193

IN 1945, PEACE WASN'T THE ONLY THING AMERICANS BROUGHT TO EUROPE.

They also brought their cigarettes.

And soon the rich American blends had become popular with Western Europeans, as well.

So much so that European cigarette manufacturers started importing the rich, flavorful U.S. leaf to accommodate their own customers' newly-acquired taste.

The very same thing also happened in Asia. And to this day, U.S. leaf remains an important part of European and Asian blends. Just as Monk remains an important supplier of U.S. leaf for those blends.

But today, in order to meet the total requirements of all our customers around the world, we are also major suppliers and processors of flue-cured and burley tobaccos from Korea, Italy, Brazil, Guatemala and other countries.

The tobacco industry has come a long way since 1945. And so, we're happy to say, have we. **MONK**

194

193

Art Directors Shaller Rubin
Howard Grant
Writers Shaller Rubin
Howard Grant
Designers Shaller Rubin
Howard Grant
Photographer Michael O'Neill
Agency WillsGrant Marketing Communications Inc.
Client FaberCastell Corporation

194

Art Director Michael Winslow
Writer Rich Maender
Photographer Bart Harris
Agency McKinney Silver & Rockett
Client A. C. Monk & Company

Rice producers: stop feeding the competition.
First they eat the fertilizer you meant for the rice. Then they use this energy to compete with rice for control of the field.
These are the kinds of problems you can do without. And Modown preemergence herbicide is the way to do without them. Modown controls these early weeds. Prevents fertilizer waste. And does it for up to four to five weeks.
Modown also reduces potential drift problems because both your rice and herbicide go down early before other crops like cotton, sorghum and beans are up. The result is better stands and better yields. The kind of results a rice grower needs these days to show a profit.
So stop feeding the competition. Use Modown herbicide

195

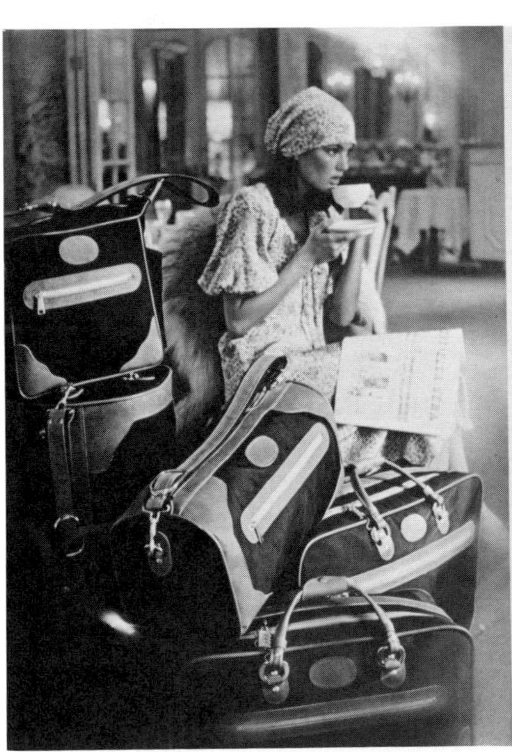

LA DOLCE VITA,
AMERICAN STYLE.
PORTOFINO
BY INVICTA.
Portofino, haunt of the very rich, the famous, the privileged.
It conjures up romantic visions.
A fleet of elegant pleasure craft gliding across the sparkling Mediterranean. Magical, moon-lit evenings.
Now Invicta has translated the leisurely elegance of this exclusive resort into sporty travel wear with the dash of genuine pigskin. Featuring the handsome gold Secur-A-Lock with a combination you set yourself to keep all those valuables safe inside.
Portofino by Invicta.
A hint of foreign intrigue that's made in the USA.
York Luggage Corp. Lambertville, NJ

196

195
Art Director Don Schnably
Writer Bill Evans
Designer Don Schnably
Artist Jean Pidgeon
Agency Richardson, Myers & Donofrio
Client Mobil Chemical Co.

196
Art Director Larry Alten
Writer B. J. Kaplan
Designer Larry Alten
Photographer Robt. Barclay Studio
Agency Alten, Cohen & Naish, Inc.
Client York Luggage Company

But man can give them a reprieve.
The Continental Group
Carrying a better life around the world.
The Continental Group
Nature only gives them
5 days to live.

197

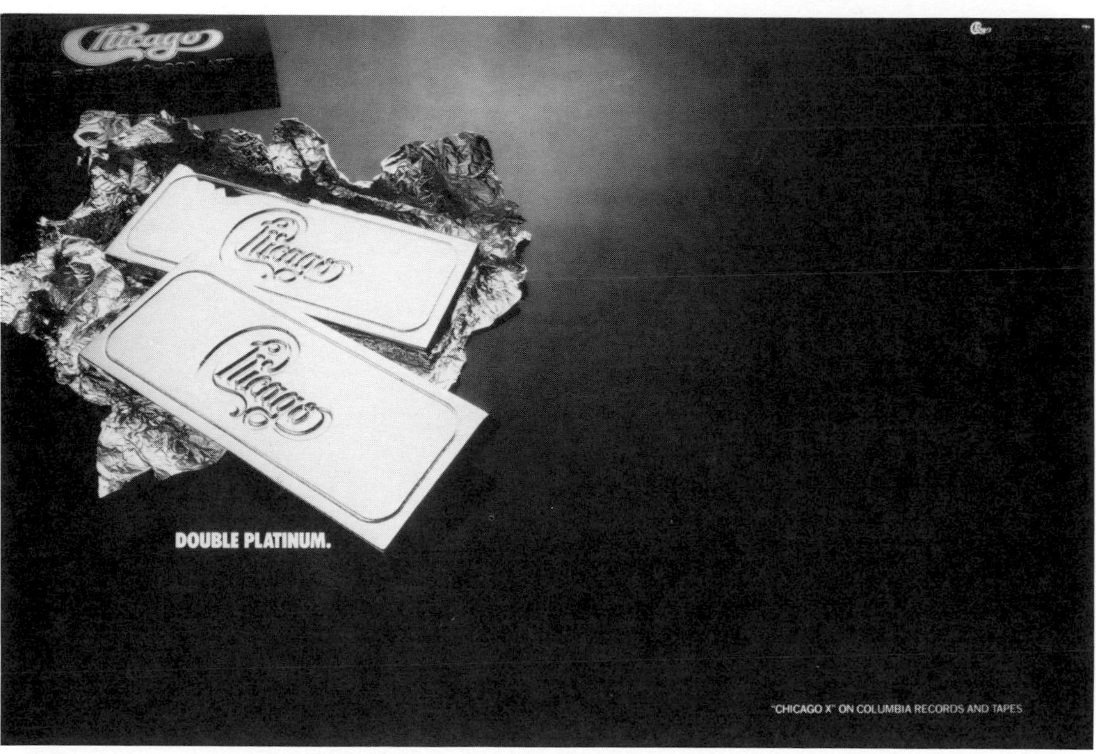

198

197
Art Director Arvale Rogers
Writer William Appelman
Photographer John Paul Endress
Agency Young & Rubicam
Client The Continental Group

198
Art Director Steve Feldman
Writer Marty Pekar
Designer Steve Feldman
Photographer Bill Stettner
Agency CBS Records
Client Columbia Records

A Conoco resin helped a customer
become a success in the flea market.
A new flea collar is now doing well in the market.
But starting from scratch, the maker needed a resin that would be compatible with the collar's pesticides.
Testing of Conoco's 5465 PVC Resin showed a high compatibility.
Also, the resin ran well due to its superb flow properties, blistering was avoided, the reject rate was reduced 5-8%, and the buckle was easy to attach.
So another of our pet projects turned out to be a howling success.
And we can do the same for yours.
Already, we're in everything from sneakers to toys, carpet runners to wall coverings, power cables to appliance wire, and hundreds of other products.
So why not mail the coupon for technical data sheets on our line of resins and compounds?
You'll be barking up the right tree.
Please send information on the materials checked below.
☐ PVC Resins ☐ PVC Powder Compounds ☐ Injection Molding Compounds
☐ Extrusion Compounds ☐ Wire and Cable Compounds ☐ Plasticizers
Name
Address
City State Zip
Company Title
Application
CONOCO CHEMICALS
DIVISION,
POST OFFICE BOX 2197,
HOUSTON, TEXAS 77001,
conoco

199

Wrangler
has more styles than Heinz has varieties.

200

199
Art Director Charles Hively
Writer Bob Miller
Designer Charles Hively
Photographer Carl Fischer
Agency Metzdorf Advertising Agency
Client Conoco Chemicals

200
Art Director Merv Shipenberg
Writer Austin Hamel
Designer Merv Shipenberg
Photographer David McCabe
Agency Altman, Stoller, Weiss
Client Wrangler

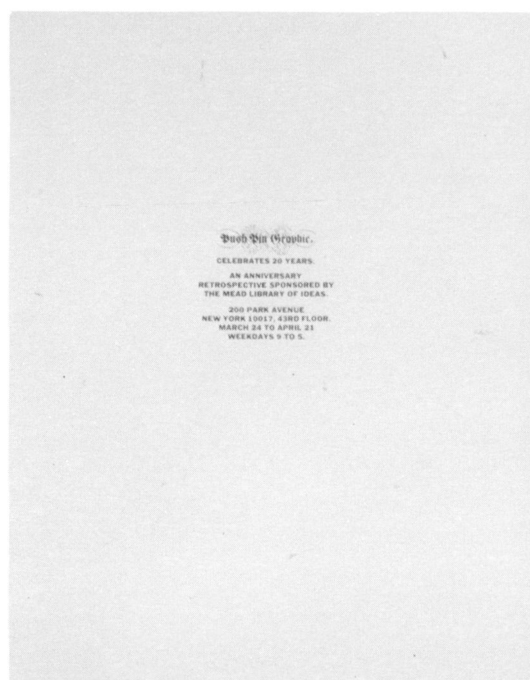

201

202

201

Art Director	Seymour Chwast
Designer	Seymour Chwast
Artist	Leonardo da Vinci
Client	Mead Library of Ideas
Agency	Push Pin Studios

202

Art Director	David A. Cooper
Writer	Patricia Kennely
Designer	David A. Cooper
Photographer	Ronald G. Harris
Agency	CBS Records
Client	Columbia Records

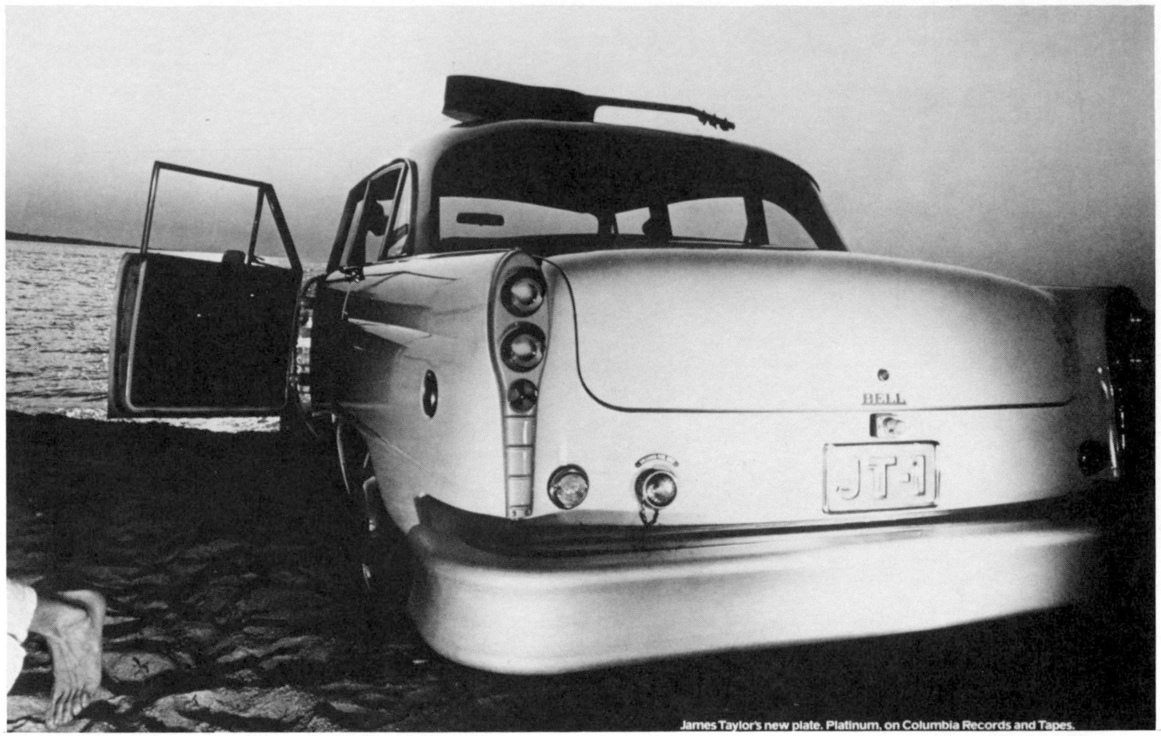

BELL
JT-1
James Taylor's new plate. Platinum, on Columbia Records and Tapes.

203

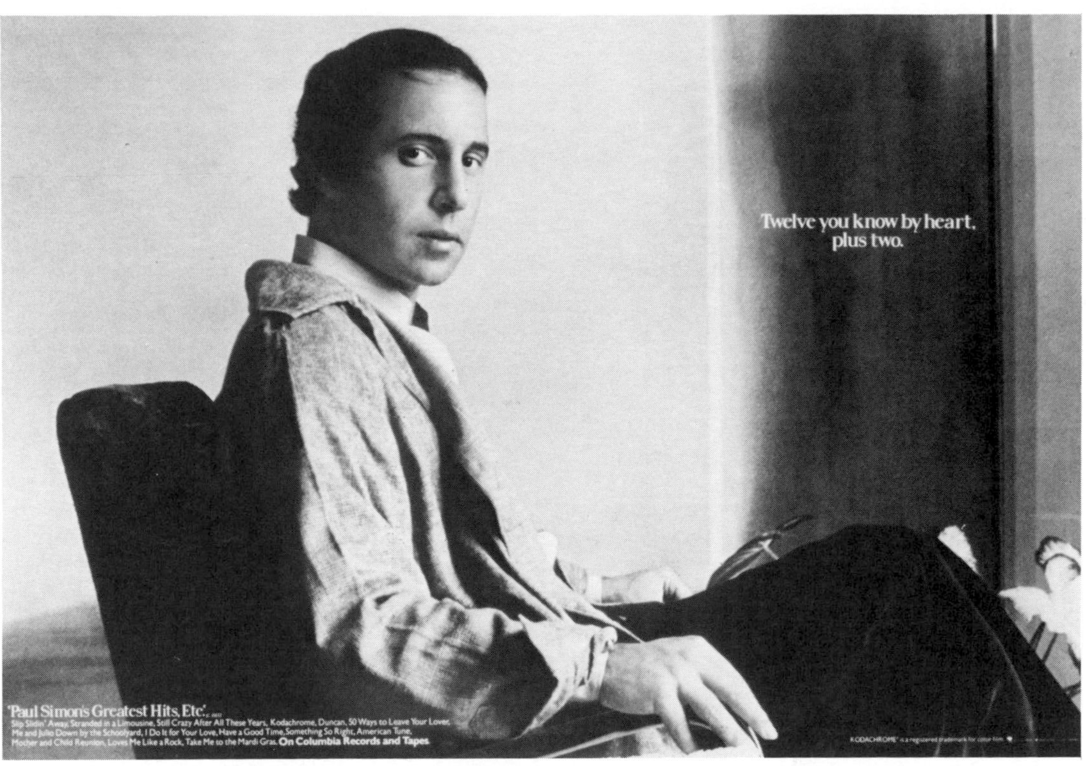

204

203
Art Director Hillary Vermont
Writer Marty Pekar
Designer Hillary Vermont
Photographer Moshe Brakha
Agency CBS Records
Client Columbia Records

204
Art Director Vince Marrapodi
Writer Rick Lyon
Designer Vince Marrapodi
Photographer Marie Cosindas
Agency CBS Records
Client CBS Records

205

206

205
Art Director Bob Tanaka
Writer Hal Newsom
Photographer Bob Peterson
Agency Cole & Weber
Client Boeing Commercial Airplane Co.

206
Art Director Howard Friedman
Writer Marty Pekar
Designer Howard Friedman
Photographer Bill Stettner
Agency CBS Records
Client Columbia Records

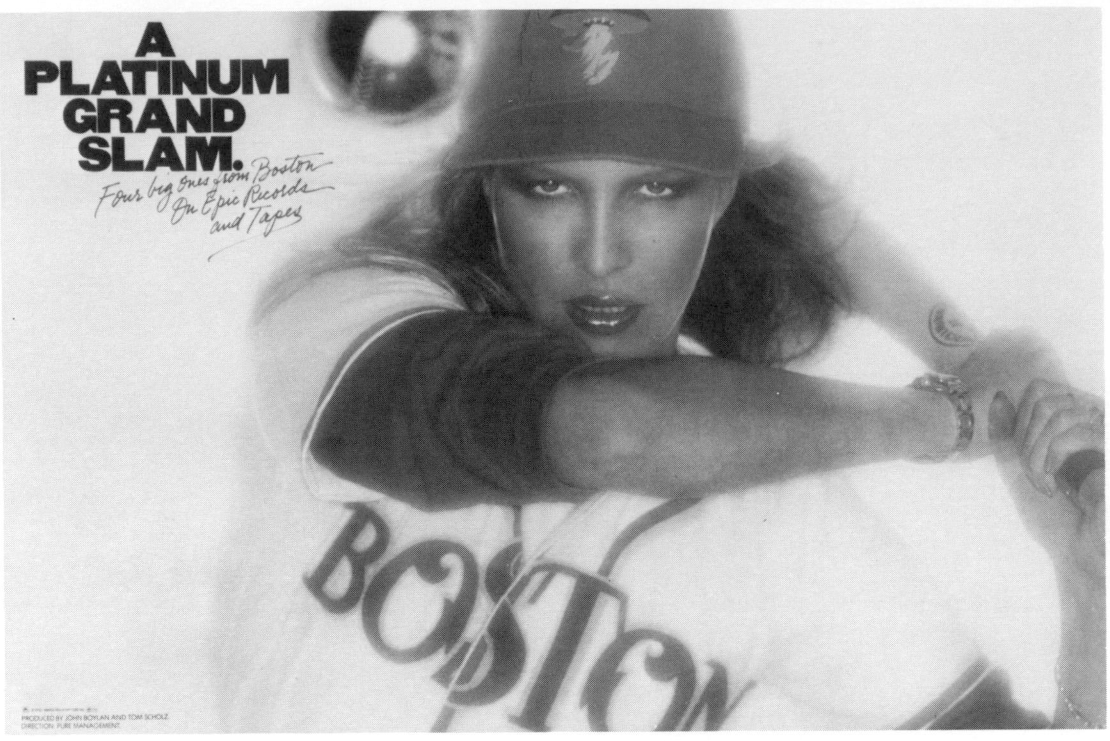

207

What do you see when you look at your newspaper? It depends on your perspective.

You might see a source of information that helps you spend your money wisely, invest your money wisely, act responsibly.

You might see a source of employment for a diversity of people—publishers, printers, journalists, truck drivers, your 12 year old son perhaps.

Or you might see the short-lived ghost of a once-proud tree.

We see all these things, and more. We see a big part of a business our employees and shareholders depend on.

We're one of the world's largest suppliers of paper products: business, writing, printing, publishing, packaging, forms papers, corrugated and, of course, newsprint.

We also see the trees that stand behind these products, and we recognize that, as the song says, you can't have one without the other.

But we can have both.

We strive to manage our forests in a way that reconciles your perspectives and ours, to provide satisfactory jobs, products, profits and thriving trees.

If we succeed, everybody wins. You the consumer, worker, investor and citizen. And we, the employees and shareholders of Boise Cascade.

Reason enough to try, don't you think?

Boise Cascade Corporation

A company worth looking at.

208

207
Art Director Myron Polenberg
Writer Ronnie Finkelstein
Designer Myron Polenberg
Photographer Frank Lafitte
Agency CBS Records
Client Epic Records

208
Art Director Kirk Hinshaw
Writer David Hill
Designer John Casado
Artist Paul Pratchenko
Agency Dancer, Fitzgerald, Sample Inc./SF
Client Boise Cascade Corporation

Now photographers using 8x10 view cameras can make large-format pictures on the spot–by using Polaroid's new 8x10 Polacolor®2 instant film. In just 60 seconds this new professional film delivers all the exceptional detail and sharpness inherent in 8x10 photography. And its brilliant metallized dyes are among the most stable and fade-resistant in photography. The portrait on the right was reproduced directly from an unretouched original print. The new 8x10 system is available now from Polaroid® professional product dealers.
Polaroid introduces a whole new dimension to instant film: 8x10.
For more information or the names of dealers, call us toll free: 800-225-1618. (In Massachusetts call collect: 617-547-5177.)

209

Seventy-five operators now fly 727s. One hundred new 727s have been ordered in 1977, and more than 180 are on order through 1980. Our prediction: The two-billionth 727 passenger will board the aircraft in 1984.

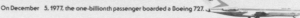

On December 5, 1977, the one-billionth passenger boarded a Boeing 727.

210

209
Art Director Helmut Krone
Writers Ed Smith
George Rike
Photographer Carl Fischer
Agency Doyle Dane Bernbach
Client Polaroid

210
Art Director Bob Tanaka
Writer Hal Newsom
Artist Norm Hansen
Agency Cole & Weber
Client Boeing Commercial Airplane Co.

Robin / Modular Soft Seating

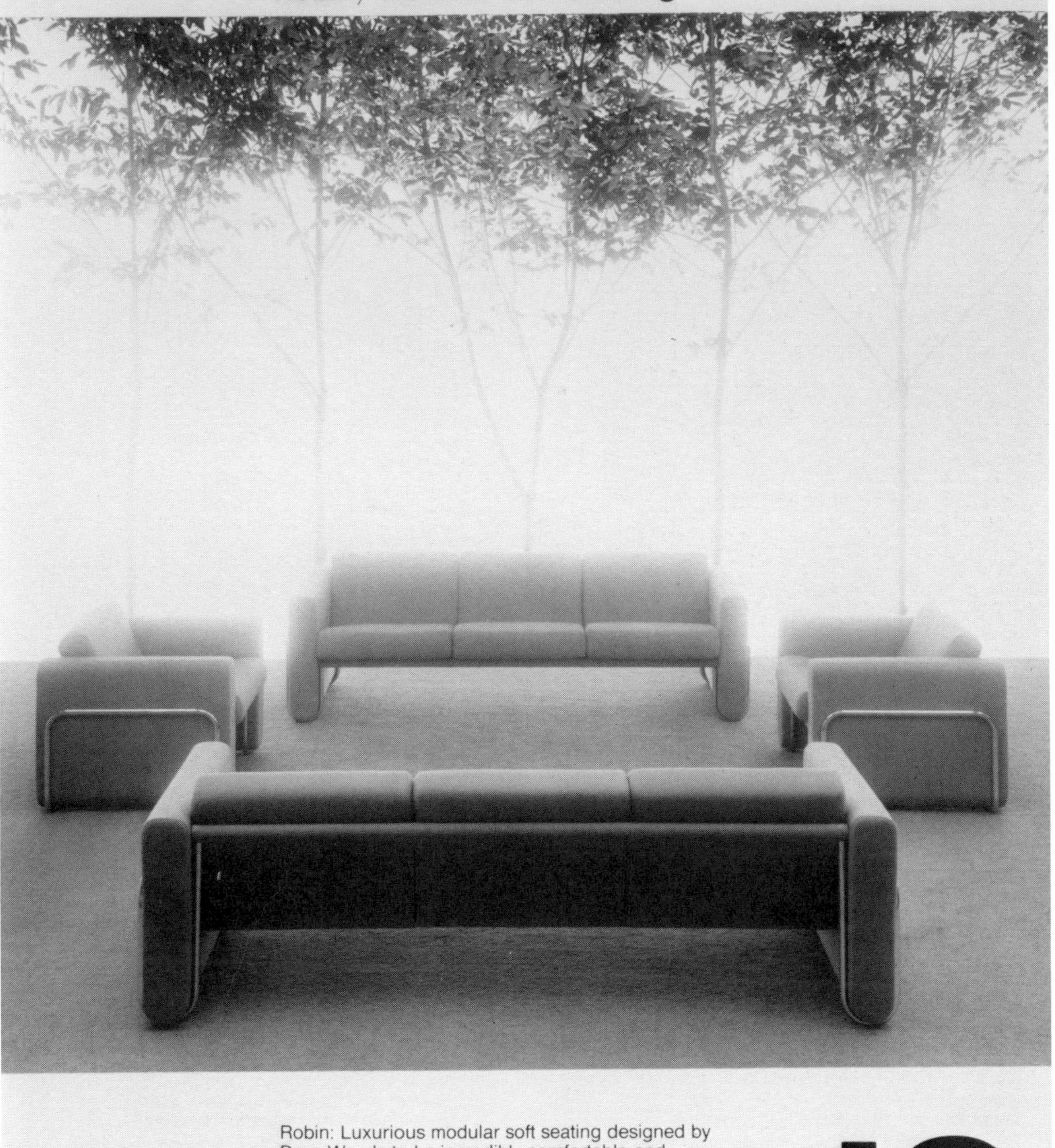

Robin: Luxurious modular soft seating designed by Dave Woods to be incredibly comfortable and remarkably economical. Available in one, two, three and four seat units, Robin is engineered to withstand the most rigorous abuse and can be completely reupholstered in a matter of minutes with stock JG replacement covers. Brochure available on request.
JG Furniture, a Division of Burlington Industries
Quakertown, Pennsylvania, 18951, 215 536 7343

JG

211

211

Art Director	Thomas H. Janicz
Writer	Thomas H. Janicz
Designer	Thomas H. Janicz
Photographer	Roland Falkenstein
Director	Thomas H. Janicz
Producer	Ronald P. Roussell
Production Company	JG Furniture
Agency	In-House
Client	JG Furniture

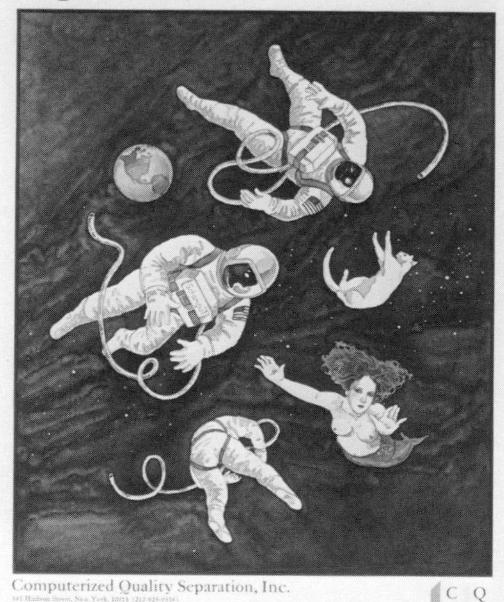

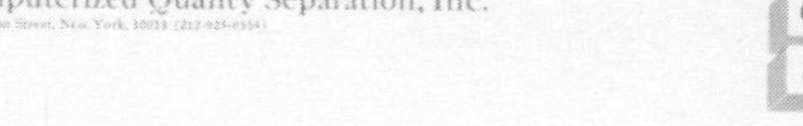

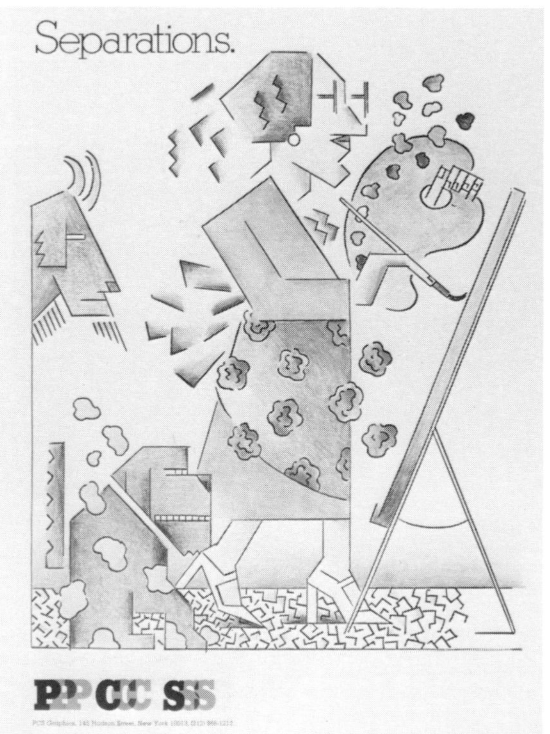

212

212
Art Director Seymour Chwast
Designer Seymour Chwast
Artists Seymour Chwast
Haruo Miyauchi
Richard Mantel
Publisher Push Pin Graphic
Agency Push Pin Studios
Client PCS/CQS Graphics

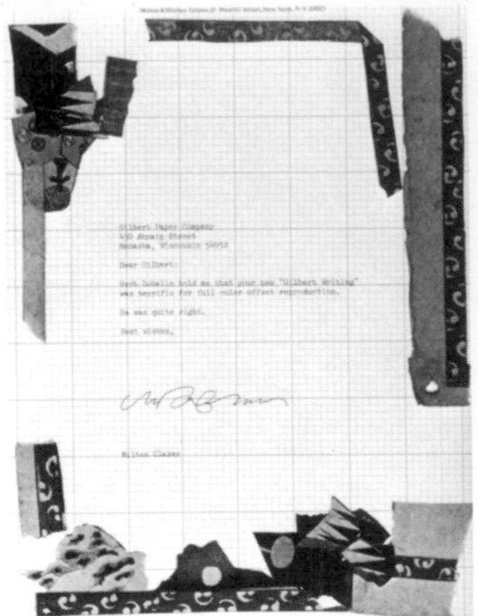

Gilbert Paper Company
430 Ahnaip Street
Menasha, Wisconsin 54952

Dear Gilbert:

Herb Lubalin told me that your new "Gilbert Writing" was terrific for full color offset reproduction.

He was quite right.

Best wishes,

Milton Glaser

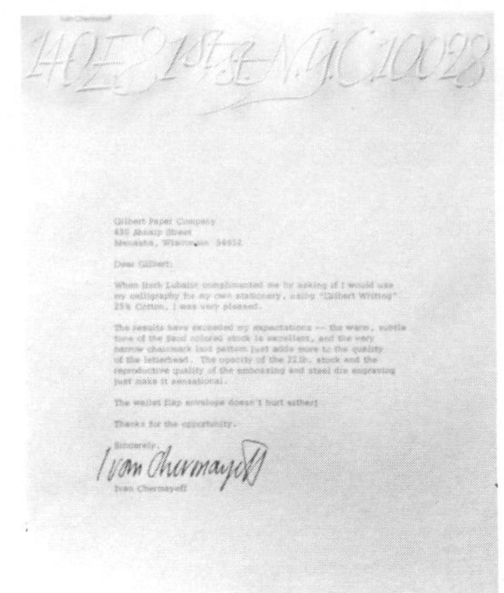

Gilbert Paper Company
430 Ahnaip Street
Menasha, Wisconsin 54952

Dear Gilbert:

When Herb Lubalin complimented me by asking if I would use my calligraphy for my own stationery, using "Gilbert Writing" 25% Cotton, I was very pleased.

The results have exceeded my expectations -- the warm, subtle tone of the Sand colored stock is excellent, and the very narrow chainmark laid pattern just adds more to the quality of the letterhead. The opacity of the 22lb. stock and the reproductive quality of the embossing and steel die engraving just make it sensational.

The wallet flap envelope doesn't hurt either!

Thanks for the opportunity.

Sincerely,

Ivan Chermayeff

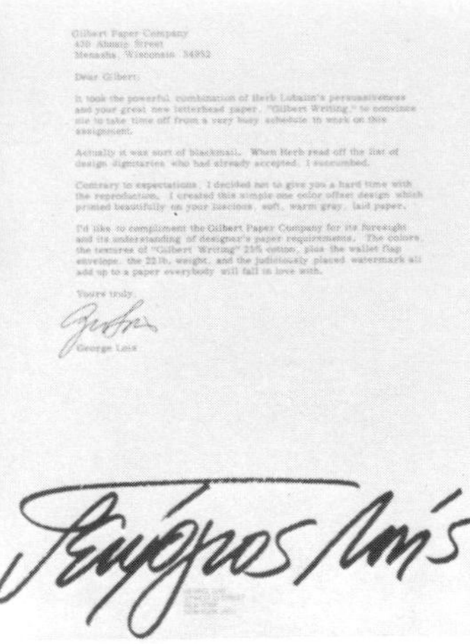

Gilbert Paper Company
430 Ahnaip Street
Menasha, Wisconsin 54952

Dear Gilbert:

It took the powerful combination of Herb Lubalin's persuasiveness and your great new letterhead paper, "Gilbert Writing," to convince me to take time off from a very busy schedule to work on this assignment.

Actually it was sort of blackmail. When Herb read off the list of design dignitaries who had already accepted, I succumbed.

Contrary to expectations, I decided not to give you a hard time with the reproduction. I created this simple one color offset design which printed beautifully on your luscious, soft, warm gray, laid paper.

I'd like to compliment the Gilbert Paper Company for its foresight and its understanding of designer's paper requirements. The colors, the textures of "Gilbert Writing" 25% cotton, plus the wallet flap envelope, the 22 lb. weight, and the judiciously placed watermark all add up to a paper everybody will fall in love with.

Yours truly,

George Lois

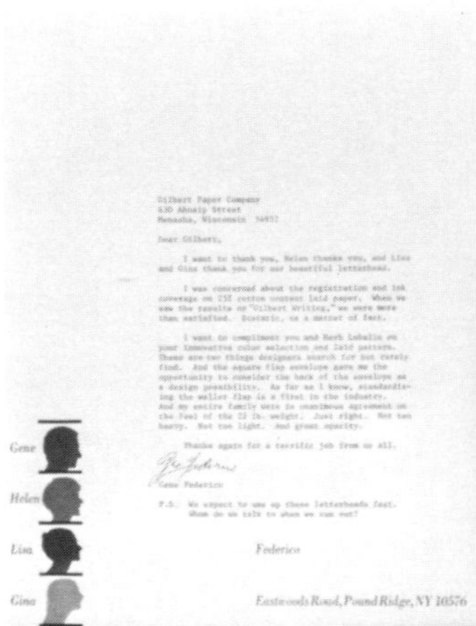

Gilbert Paper Company
430 Ahnaip Street
Menasha, Wisconsin 54952

Dear Gilbert,

I want to thank you, Helen thanks you, and Lisa and Gina thank you for our beautiful letterhead.

I was concerned about the registration and ink coverage on 25% cotton content laid paper. When we saw the results on "Gilbert Writing," we were more than satisfied. Ecstatic, as a matter of fact.

I want to compliment you and Herb Lubalin on your innovative color selection and laid pattern. These are two things designers search for but rarely find. And the square flap envelope gave me the opportunity to consider the back of the envelope as a design possibility. As far as I know, standardizing the wallet flap is a first in the industry. And my entire family were in unanimous agreement on the feel of the 22 lb. weight. Just right. Not too heavy. Not too light. And great opacity.

Thanks again for a terrific job from us all.

Gene Federico

P.S. We expect to use up these letterheads fast. Whom do we talk to when we run out?

Gene
Helen
Lisa
Gina

Federico

Eastwoods Road, Pound Ridge, NY 10576

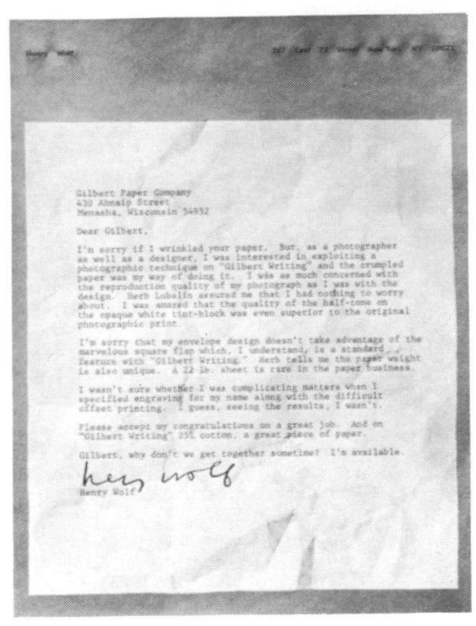

Gilbert Paper Company
430 Ahnaip Street
Menasha, Wisconsin 54952

Dear Gilbert,

I'm sorry if I wrinkled your paper. But, as a photographer as well as a designer, I was interested in exploiting a photographic technique on "Gilbert Writing" and the crumpled paper was my way of doing it. I was as much concerned with the reproduction quality of my photograph as I was with the design. Herb Lubalin assured me that I had nothing to worry about. I was amazed that the quality of the half-tone on the opaque white tint-block was even superior to the original photographic print.

I'm sorry that my envelope design doesn't take advantage of the marvelous square flap which, I understand, is a standard feature with "Gilbert Writing." Herb tells me the paper weight is also unique. A 22 lb. sheet is rare in the paper business.

I wasn't sure whether I was complicating matters when I specified engraving for my name along with the difficult offset printing. I guess, seeing the results, I wasn't.

Please accept my congratulations on a great job. And on "Gilbert Writing" 25% cotton, a great piece of paper.

Gilbert, why don't we get together sometime? I'm available.

Henry Wolf

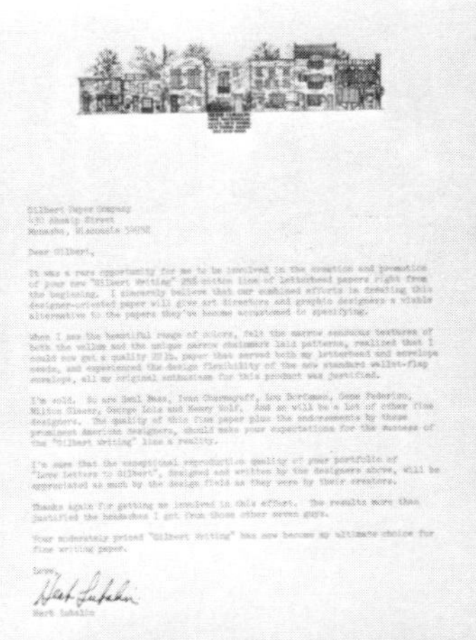

Gilbert Paper Company
430 Ahnaip Street
Menasha, Wisconsin 54952

Dear Gilbert,

It was a rare opportunity for me to be involved in the creation and promotion of your new "Gilbert Writing" 25% cotton line of letterhead papers right from the beginning. I sincerely believe that our combined efforts in creating this designer-oriented paper will give art directors and graphic designers a viable alternative to the papers they've become accustomed to specifying.

When I saw the beautiful range of colors, felt the narrow sensuous textures of both the vellum and the unique narrow chainmark laid patterns, realized that I could now get a quality 22 lb. paper that served both my letterhead and envelope needs, and experienced the design flexibility of the new standard wallet-flap envelope, all my original enthusiasm for this product was justified.

I'm sold. So are Saul Bass, Ivan Chermayeff, Lou Dorfsman, Gene Federico, Milton Glaser, George Lois and Henry Wolf. And so will be a lot of other fine designers. The quality of this fine paper plus the endorsements by these prominent American designers, should make your expectations for the success of the "Gilbert Writing" line a reality.

I'm sure that the exceptional reproduction quality of your portfolio of "Love Letters to Gilbert", designed and written by the designers above, will be appreciated as much by the design field as they were by their creators.

Thanks again for getting me involved in this effort. The results more than justified the headaches I got from those other seven guys.

Your moderately priced "Gilbert Writing" has now become my ultimate choice for fine writing paper.

Love,

Herb Lubalin

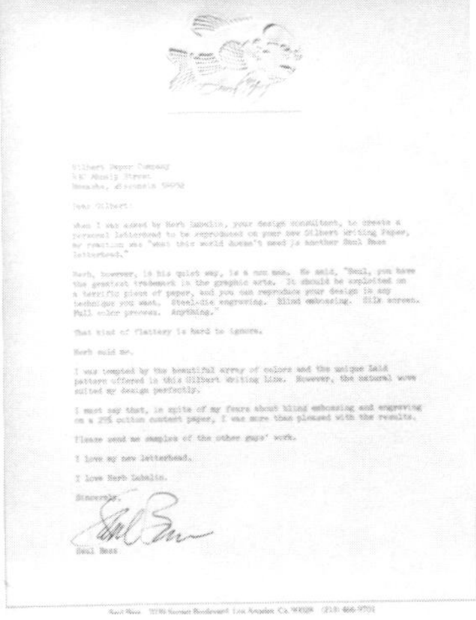

Gilbert Paper Company
430 Ahnaip Street
Menasha, Wisconsin 54952

Dear Gilbert:

When I was asked by Herb Lubalin, your design consultant, to create a personal letterhead to be reproduced on your new Gilbert Writing Paper, my reaction was "what this world doesn't need is another Saul Bass letterhead."

Herb, however, in his quiet way, is a con man. He said, "Saul, you have the greatest trademark in the graphic arts. It should be exploited on a terrific piece of paper, and you can reproduce your design in any technique you want. Steel-die engraving. Blind embossing. Silk screen. Full color process. Anything."

That kind of flattery is hard to ignore.

Herb sold me.

I was tempted by the beautiful array of colors and the unique laid pattern offered in this Gilbert Writing line. However, the natural wove suited my design perfectly.

I must say that, in spite of my fears about blind embossing and engraving on a 25% cotton content paper, I was more than pleased with the results.

Please send me samples of the other guys' work.

I love my new letterhead.

I love Herb Lubalin.

Sincerely,

Saul Bass

Gilbert Paper Company
430 Ahnaip Street
Menasha, Wisconsin 54952

Dear Gilbert,

This project seemed like an appropriate opportunity to test a theory I've been carrying around with me for a long time. It's not that it's a great theory -- it's a money savings one. In short, I see no reason why a complete line of business stationery and forms cannot be designed to cut out of one sheet of paper, i.e., letterheads, envelopes, business cards, shipping labels, note paper, memo sheets and more.

With the advantage offered by the new range of beautiful colors and textures found in the Gilbert Writing line -- I took off. The only trouble was that the most economical part of it all was the paper. Little did the Gilbert Paper Company anticipate the headaches I would give them. Steel engraving! Steel rule perforations separating the various forms! And the tear off perforations on the envelope.

I chose the beautiful Sand color with vellum texture. It worked better for my purpose than the almost irresistible narrow chain laid pattern. The reproduction was superb. I really like the paper and that's from a guy who knows and spends his life with some fancy papers.

I've used a single sheet before for a line of stationery but this one from Gilbert is more economical and has a rich feel. And I'm a big believer in looking rich (if it don't cost money.)

Thank you again.

Lou Dorfsman

Lou Dorfsman
Lou Dorfsman
Lou Dorfsman
Lou Dorfsman
Lou Dorfsman
Lou Dorfsman

213

213

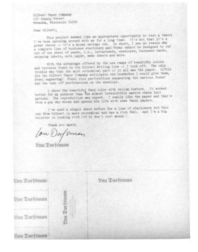

Art Director	Herb Lubalin	Designers	Saul Bass
Writers	Saul Bass		Ivan Chermayeff
	Ivan Chermayeff		Lou Dorfsman
	Lou Dorfsman		Gene Federico
	Gene Federico		Milton Glaser
	Milton Glaser		George Lois
	George Lois		Herb Lubalin
	Herb Lubalin		Henry Wolf
	Henry Wolf	Agency	LSC&P Design Group
		Client	Gilbert Paper Company

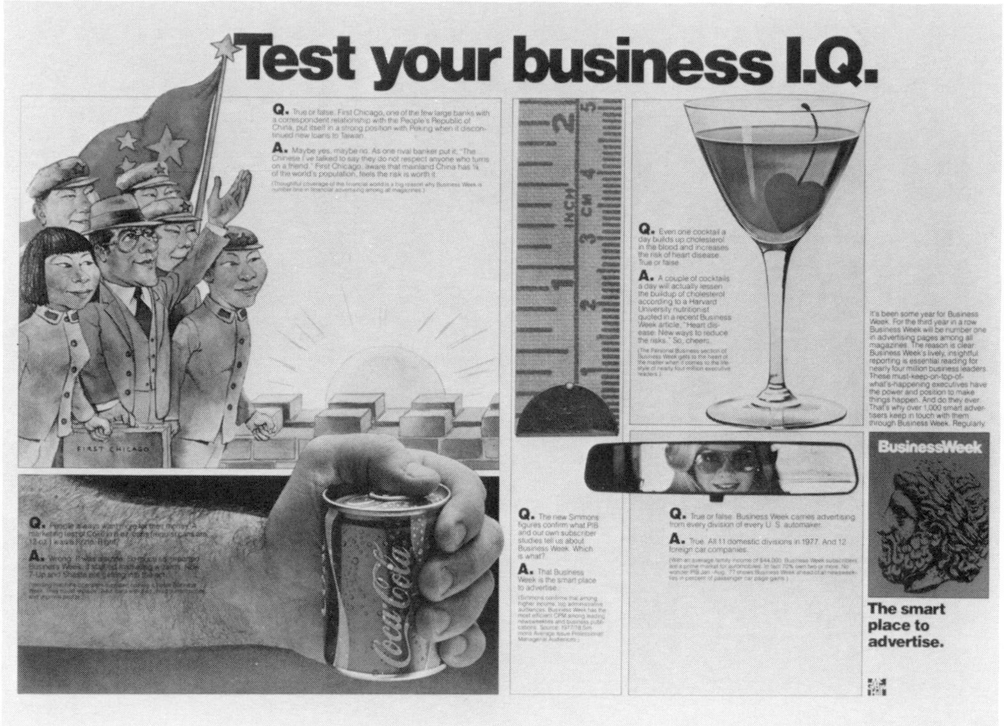

214

215

214

Art Directors Phil Gips
Diana Graham
F.E. Boland
Writer Robert Fearon
Designers Phil Gips
Diana Graham
F.E. Boland
Artists Murray Tinkelman
Tetsuya Matsuura
Diana Graham
Sandy Huffaker
Mario Stasolla
Donald Leek
Rich Grote
Lemuel Line
Photographers Jean-Marie Guyaux
Barry Patmore
Jon Riley
Agency Robert Fearon Associates
Client Business Week

215

Art Director Lee Epstein
Writer Hal Silverman
Designer Lee Epstein
Photographers Henry Sandbank
Malcolm Kirk
Bill Stettner
Agency Doyle Dane Bernbach
Client Polaroid Corp.

We don't love you and leave you.

Xerox won't woo you with sweet promises, deliver a machine, and then disappear in the night.

We're still old-fashioned enough to believe in meaningful relationships. So when you get a Xerox machine, you also get a Xerox commitment.

Xerox technical representatives will keep that equipment in good working condition with tender, loving care.

We'll keep improving our equipment, even after it's yours. And we'll make those improvements right in your office. So the longer you have it, the better it gets.

And you can feel secure in knowing that there'll always be a nearby Xerox service center that you can count on.

Only Xerox gives you a Xerox commitment. And you can get it whether you buy or lease.

At Xerox, we don't love you and leave you. Because anything and everything we do for you is a labor of love.

XEROX

The fastest duplicator in the West.

And the East. And the North. And the South.

The Xerox 9200 Duplicating System.

Just push some buttons and the 9200 will automatically feed, cycle, reduce and sort a virtually limitless number of complete sets at the incredible speed of 2 pages a second. Which means it can get a lot more done in a lot less time.

So now, everyone in your office can have copies of multi-page documents, proposals, even booklets in their hands faster than ever before.

In fact, the Xerox 9200 is so productive on jobs like these there isn't a duplicator in town that can stand up to it.

Whether it's 9 o'clock in the morning or high noon.

XEROX

216

216

Art Directors	Allen Kay
	Anthony Angotti
Writers	Lester Colodny
	Lois Korey
	Steve Penchina
Photographers	Krieger Steigman
Agency	Needham, Harper & Steers Adv. Inc.
Client	Xerox Corp.

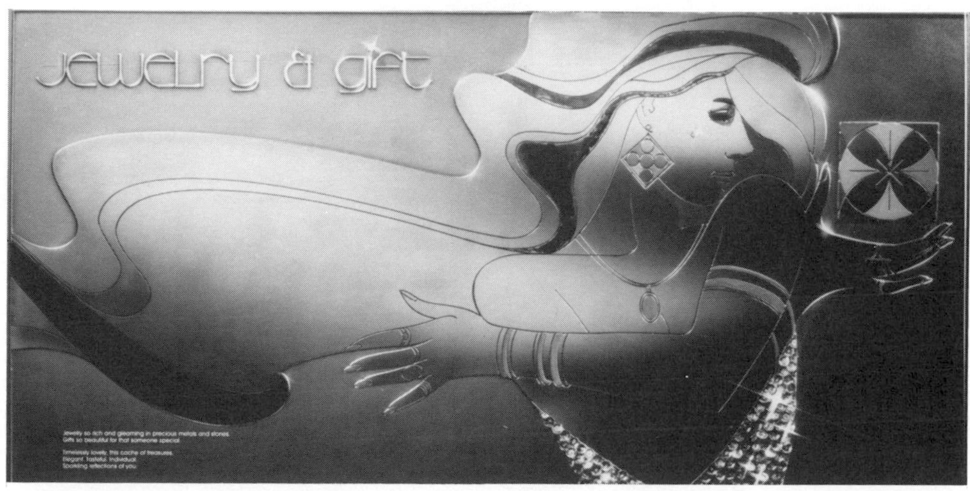

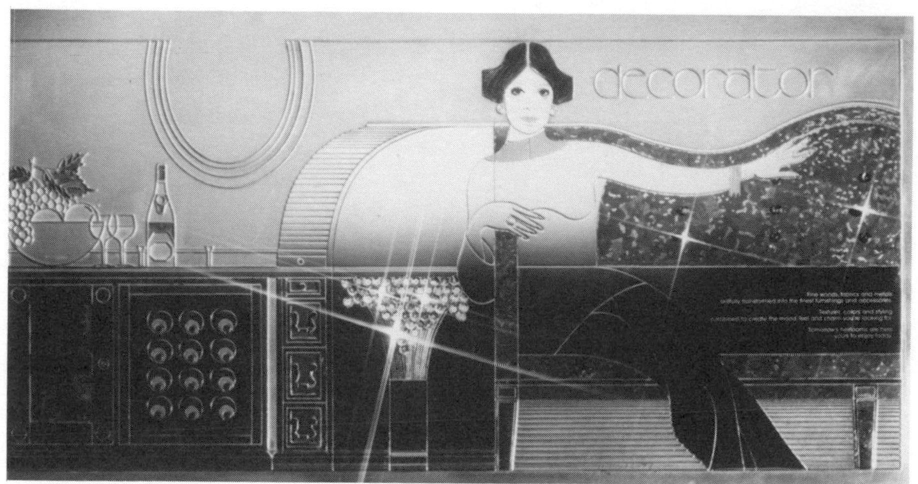

217

217
Art Director Mike Foley
Designer Mike Foley
Artist Mike Foley
Photographer Communico
Client Maritz Inc.

Tolban™ is the preplant herbicide with excellent crop tolerance. Tolban Tolerance.
Which means Tolban won't hold your cotton back.
Even in cool wet weather. Even in poor soils. Even in variable soils. Even at the 2X rate for johnsongrass.
Excellent crop tolerance.
Plus effective control of most annual grasses and certain broadleaf weeds.
That's Tolban Tolerance.
Ciba-Geigy, Ag. Div., Box 11422, Greensboro, NC 27409
Tolban by CIBA-GEIGY
TOLBAN TOLERANCE
CIBA-GEIGY

218

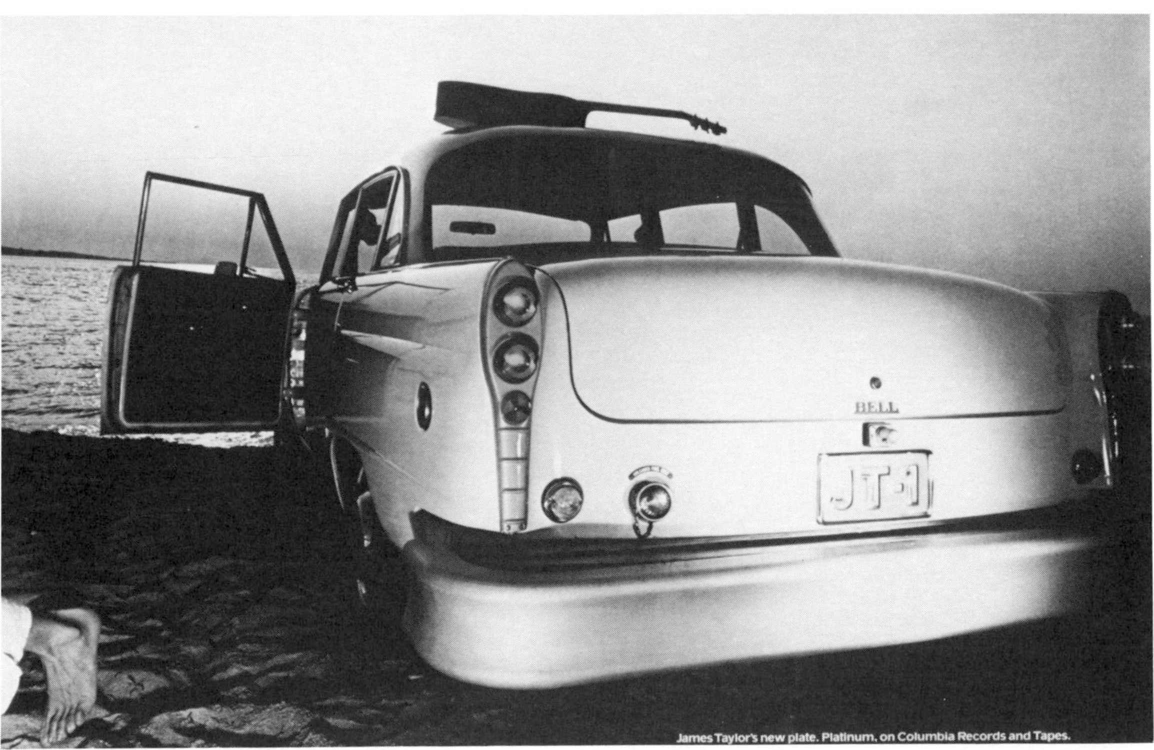

BELL
JT-1
James Taylor's new plate. Platinum, on Columbia Records and Tapes.

219

218

Art Director	Marc Eisenoff
Writer	Ray Bethea
Photographer	Mike Hirst
Agency	Keenan & McLaughlin Inc
Client	CIBA-GEIGY Corporation

219

Art Directors	Stephen Ohler Hillary Vermont Bruce Day
Writers	Mark Levitt Marty Pekar Patricia Kennely
Designers	Stephen Ohler Hillary Vermont Bruce Day
Photographers	Steinbecker/Houghton Moshe Brakha Ronald E. Harris
Agency	CBS Records
Clients	T-Neck Records Columbia Records Columbia Records

221

SAXON
we've got no tanked tigers, but we're high on extra dimension
We're willing to let our competition have their fun, putting tigers in tanks and all that. Our game is not only to keep our customers happy, but to provide extra dimensions to investors.
Dimensions like "Mobil 1," our new synthesized lubricant, give us clear leadership in a big new market. It's a lubricant that actually saves gasoline.
Expensive. But worth the price, for it reduces engine wear even as it improves mileage.
And speaking of gasoline brings to mind another extra dimension: many of our competitors actually depend on us for the gasoline they make in their refineries. The cracking catalysts developed by Mobil research are used, under license, throughout the industry. To squeeze extra gasoline from crude oil. To reduce pollution.
We're much more today than "one of the international oils." A leader in research and marketing, with a strong producing position in the Gulf of Mexico and U.S.-centered diversifications. With around three billion tons of coal reserves, sizable holdings of uranium and shale, and an active commitment to solar energy research.
All this plus a record of rising dividends each year for 16 straight years.
Mobil

222

221
Art Director Seymour Chwast
Designer Seymour Chwast
Artists Seymour Chwast
Haruo Miyauchi
Publisher Push Pin Graphic
Agency Push Pin Studios
Client Pioneer Moss

222
Art Director Walter Ferro
Writer Mobil Public Affairs
Designer Walter Ferro
Artist Charles Saxon
Client Mobil Public Affairs

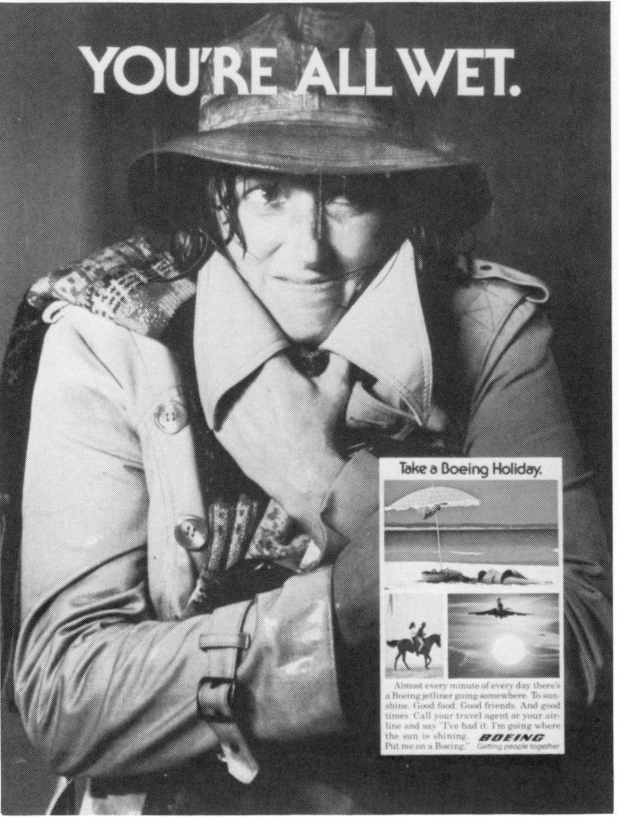

223

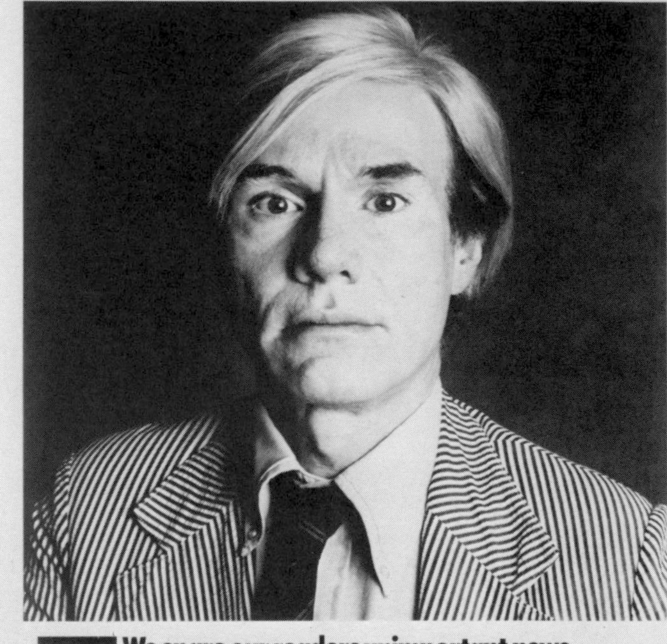

224

223
Art Director Bob Tanaka
Writer Hal Newsom
Photographer Darrell Peterson
Agency Cole & Weber
Client Boeing Commercial Airplane Co.

224
Art Director J. Ryder
Writer D. Staley
Photographer Mick Pateman
Agency Ted Chin & Company, Inc.
Client U.S. News & World Report

225

For the cost of a few apples
we shipped the whole carton.
From Washington to Missouri, 1969 miles for just 96¢ a carton.
Burlington Northern. The Railroad to talk to for efficient freight service.

226

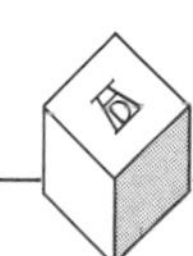

SILVER

225

Art Director	**Seymour Chwast**
Designer	**Seymour Chwast**
Artists	**Seymour Chwast**
	Haruo Miyauchi
Publisher	**Push Pin Graphic**
Agency	**Push Pin Studios**
Client	**Metropolitan Printing**

226

Art Director	**Brian Stewart**
Writer	**Carol French**
Designer	**Brian Stewart**
Artist	**Bob Gadbois**
Photographer	**Jim Marvy**
Agency	**BBDO/Minneapolis**
Client	**Burlington Northern Railroad**

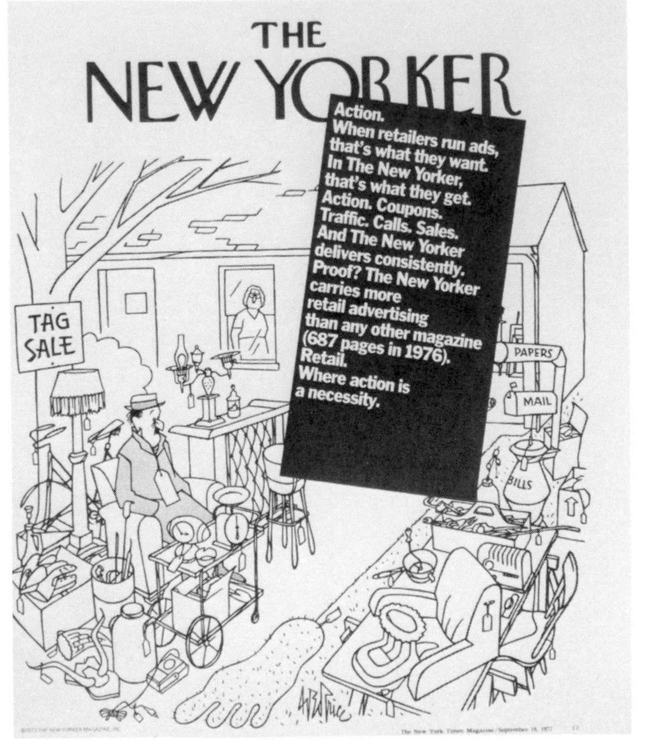

227

228

227
Art Director Gene Federico
Writer Bob Higbee
Designer Gene Federico
Artists Weber, Modell, Koren, Searle, Price
Agency Lord, Geller, Federico, Inc.
Client The New Yorker Magazine

228
Art Director Gene Federico
Writer Bob Higbee
Designer Gene Federico
Artists Booth, Saxon, Addams, Weber, Searle
Agency Lord, Geller, Federico, Inc.
Client The New Yorker Magazine

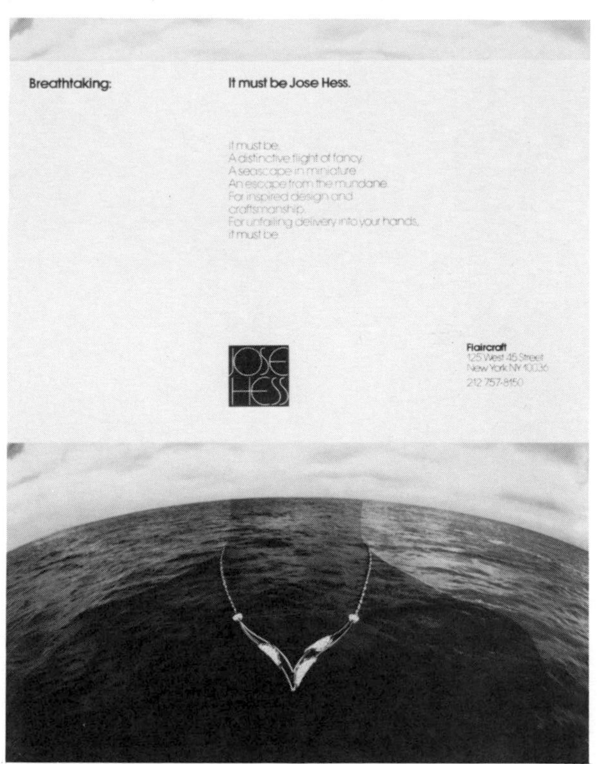

229

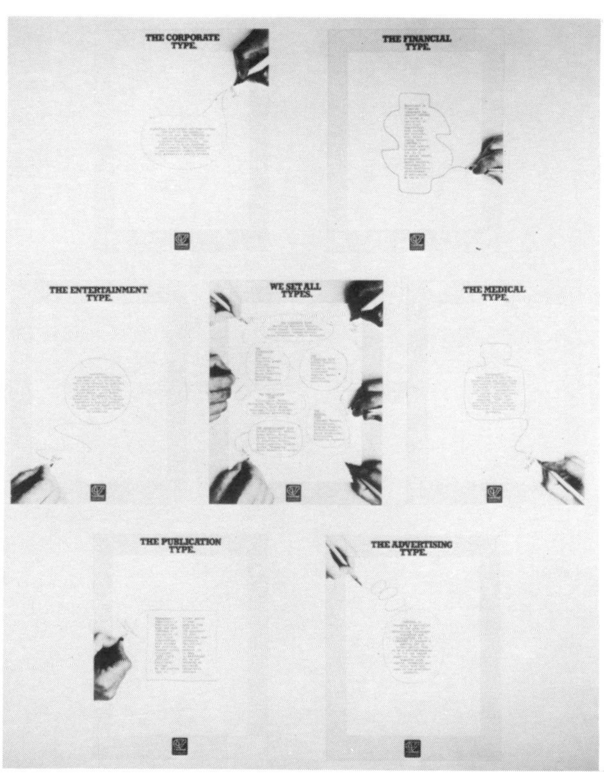

230

229

Art Director Aric Frons
Writers 1 & 2, Frank Mecca; 3, Ted Halaki
Designer Aric Frons
Photographers 1 & 2, Cosimo; 3, Paccione
Agency Haward Peskin & Edrick Inc.
Client Jose Hess/Flaircraft

230

Art Director Don Menell
Writer Allan R. Wahler
Designer Don Menell
Photographer Richard Izui
Client Cardinal Type Service, Inc.

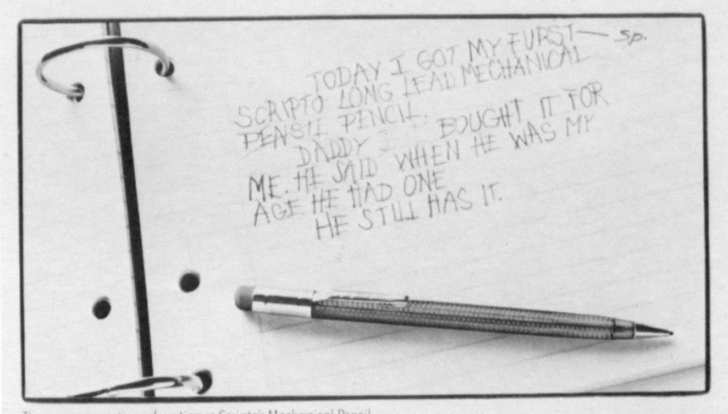

TODAY I GOT MY FURST — sp.
SCRIPTO LONG LEAD MECHANICAL
PENSIL PENCIL.
DADDY BOUGHT IT FOR
ME. HE SAID WHEN HE WAS MY
AGE HE HAD ONE
HE STILL HAS IT.
There are generations of writing in Scripto's Mechanical Pencil.
It's rugged and durable. Each four-inch lead writes about two miles!
And, the no-smudge eraser is replaceable. No wonder this pencil
has stayed in the family for years and years and years.
All the great writers are from Scripto

To my secretary,
Roses are red
Violets are blue
thanks for the great Scripto ballpoints
and all the other terrific things you do.
The Boss
The nicest things happen when you order Scripto disposable ballpoint
pens. The textured carbide ball controls the ink flow to give you over 7,000
feet of effortless writing pleasure. Choose medium or fine point in blue,
black, red or green and prepare yourself for a pleasant surprise.
All the great writers are from Scripto

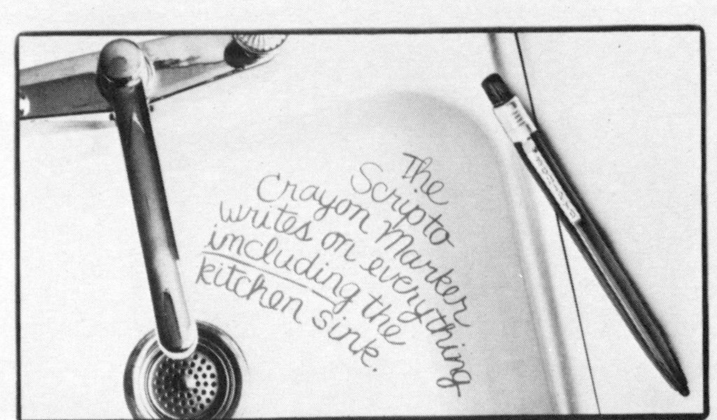

The Scripto Crayon Marker writes on everything including the kitchen sink.
Scripto's crayon marker works on anything!
Even slick surfaces like acetate, glass or porcelain.
It's the marker that twists out to write, twists back to store.
And the Scripto Crayon Marker comes in six colors.
All the great writers are from Scripto

231

231

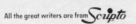

Art Director	Mickey Surasky
Writers	Peggy Flynn
	Charles Blustain
Photographer	John Retallack
Agency	D'Arcy-MacManus & Masius
Client	Scripto

The Futurists...
...Our innovative lending techniques enable industry to channel more funds into research and development—with breakthroughs that mean more jobs and better ways to do business around the world. Consider the source.
MANUFACTURERS HANOVER
The financial source.Worldwide.

The Communicators...
...Through our growing network of overseas facilities—branches, representative offices, subsidiaries and correspondents—Manufacturers Hanover offers international customers direct access to virtually any marketplace in the world. Consider the source.
MANUFACTURERS HANOVER
The financial source.Worldwide.

232

232
Art Director Mario Giuriceo
Writer Neal McMenamin
Designer Mario Giuriceo
Photographer Marvin Koner
Agency Edwin Bird Wilson, Inc.
Client Manufacturers Hanover Trust Company

233

233

Art Directors Larry Pfisterer
Joe Thaler
Writers Margot Bobroff
Mary Ann Quick
Ted Simmons
Designer Bill Budde
Artist Richard Juenger
Photographer Norman Parker
Agency Gardner Advertising Company
Client Lily Div. of Owens-Illinois, Inc.

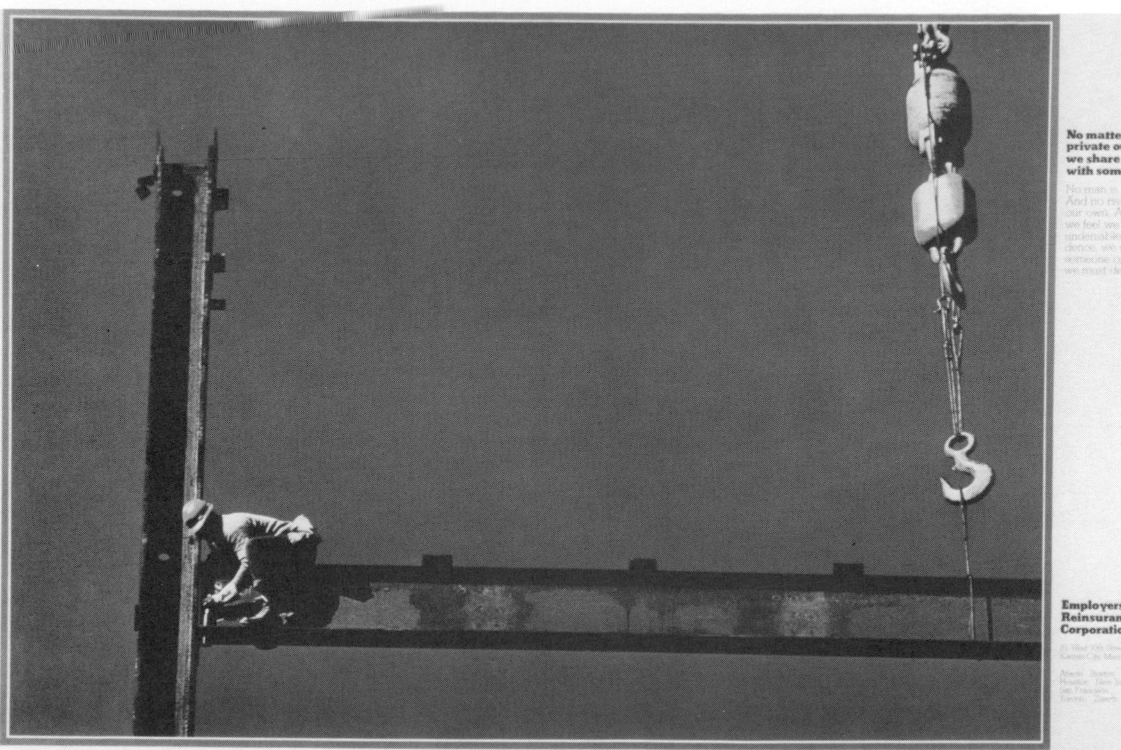

No matter how private our lives, we share our risks with someone else.
No man is an island. And no risk is totally our own. As soon as we feel we have undeniable indepen-dence, we discover someone on whom we must depend.
Employers Reinsurance Corporation

Only by passing through the tunnel can we be sure it isn't a cave.
There are few things in life we experience standing still. We must taste the fruit. Cross over the mountain. Enter the classroom. Pass through the tunnel. And only when we have done these things, do we gain the experience that each offers.
Employers Reinsurance Corporation

234

234

Art Director	Tim Hamill
Writer	Paul Welsh
Photographer	Jay Maisel
Agency	Brewer Advertising
Client	Employers Reinsurance Corporation

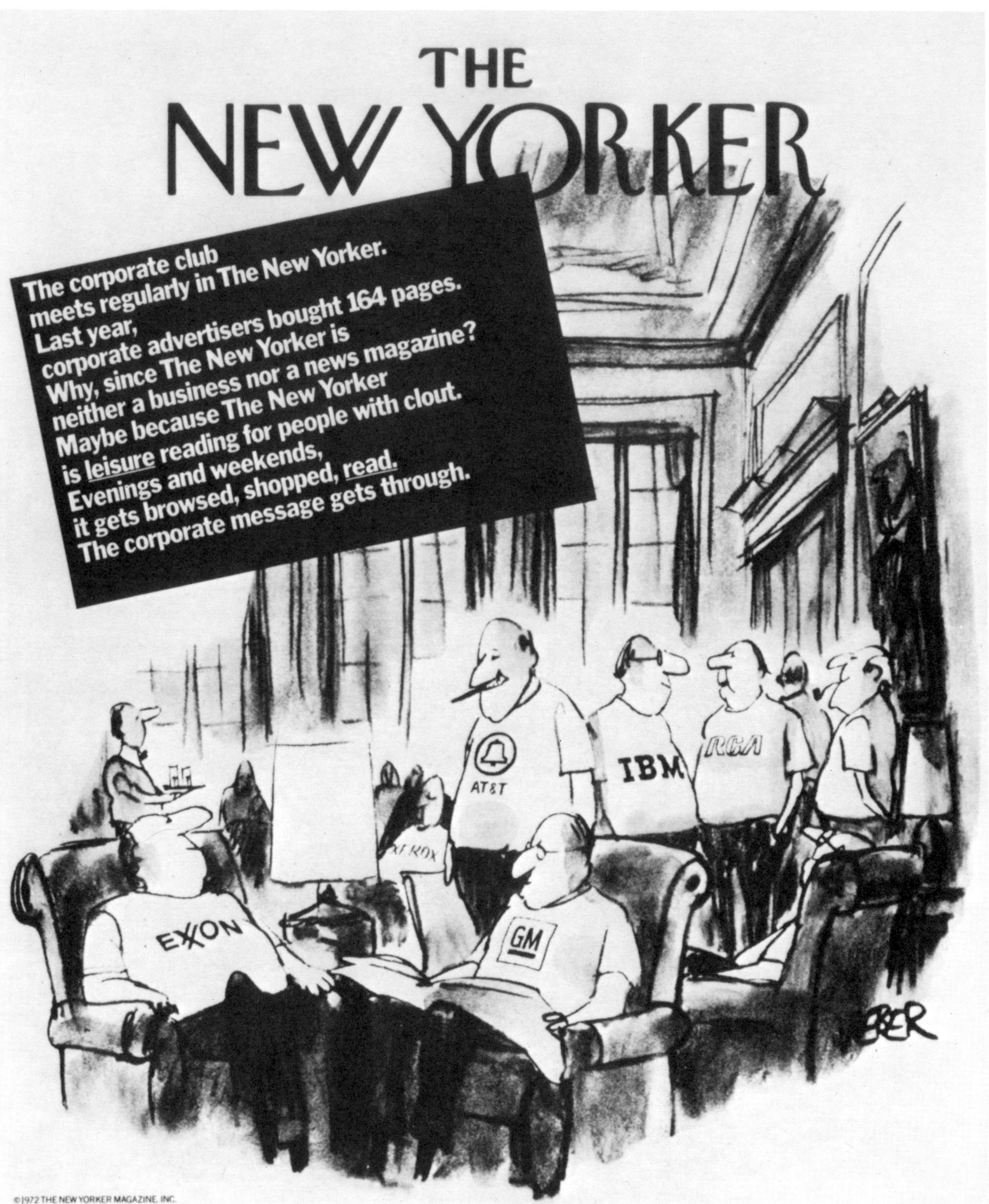

235

235
Art Director Gene Federico
Writer Bob Higbee
Designer Gene Federico
Artists Weber, Koren, Steinberg, Modell, Price, Whitney Darrow, Jr.
Agency Lord, Geller, Federico, Inc.
Client The New Yorker Magazine

How to preserve a Great American Classic.
Freezing food—like hamburger patties—isn't easy. And with the pressures of time, quality, production efficiency, peak loading, economics, freshness, speed, color and flavor—not to mention strict standards and regulations—well, it isn't simple, either.
Which is why the Airco Kryofoods group has developed the kind of expertise you need when you get into cryogenic food freezing.
Our Kryofoods Engineers, for example, have been designing, building, installing and maintaining both nitrogen and carbon dioxide freezing systems for everything from hamburger patties and seafood to pizza and bakery goods for years. So when you encounter a problem, it's probably a lot like one they've solved before.
Our freezing systems—spirals, tunnels, tumblers and chillers of every size, shape and capacity you'll ever need—also represent a considerable development effort. It wasn't easy, for example, coming up with the best spiral freezer in the industry. But it was worth it.
At Airco, of course, the refrigerants practically go without saying. Except that whether you want CO_2 or nitrogen makes no difference to us. We supply both nationally. And we have all the production, storage and delivery facilities and equipment necessary to get them to you whenever, wherever and in whatever quantities you need them.
We also maintain a fully equipped, fully staffed (more food-freezing experts, of course) lab in which you can evaluate and test practically anything freezable you wish.
That's the Airco Kryofoods story. Systems. Refrigerants. Equipment. Facilities. And the people who know how to use them all to make your job a little easier. Airco Kryofoods, 575 Mountain Avenue, Murray Hill, New Jersey 07974. (201) 464-8100.
AIRCO Kryofoods
The food-freezing experts.

How to preserve a Great American Classic.
Freezing food—like this pie—isn't easy. And with the pressures of time, quality, production efficiency, peak loading, economics, freshness, packaging, speed, color and flavor—not to mention strict standards and regulations—well, it isn't simple, either.
Which is why the Airco Kryofoods group has developed the kind of expertise you need when you get into cryogenic food freezing.
Our Kryofoods Engineers, for example, have been designing, building, installing and maintaining both nitrogen and carbon dioxide freezing systems for everything from bakery products and pizza to seafood and hamburger patties for years. So when you encounter a problem, it's probably a lot like one they've solved before.
Our freezing systems—spirals, tunnels, tumblers and chillers of every size, shape and capacity you'll ever need—also represent a considerable development effort. It wasn't easy, for example, coming up with the best spiral freezer in the industry. But it was worth it.
At Airco, of course, the refrigerants are second nature. Whether you want CO_2 or nitrogen makes no difference to us. We supply both nationally. And we have all the production, storage and delivery facilities and equipment necessary to get them to you whenever, wherever and in whatever quantities you need them.
We also maintain a fully equipped, fully staffed (more food-freezing experts, of course) lab in which you can evaluate and test practically anything freezable you wish.
That's Airco Kryofoods. Systems. Refrigerants. Equipment. Facilities. And the people who know how to use them all to make your job easier. Airco Kryofoods, 575 Mountain Avenue, Murray Hill, New Jersey 07974. (201) 464-8100.
AIRCO Kryofoods
The food-freezing experts.

How to preserve a Great American Classic.
Freezing food—like this pizza—isn't easy. And with the pressures of time, quality, production efficiency, peak loading, economics, freshness, packaging, speed, color and flavor—not to mention strict standards and regulations—well, it isn't simple, either.
Which is why the Airco Kryofoods group has developed the kind of expertise you need when you get into cryogenic food freezing.
Our Kryofoods Engineers, for example, have been designing, building, installing and maintaining both nitrogen and carbon dioxide freezing systems for everything from hamburger patties and seafood to pizza and bakery goods for years. So when you encounter a problem, it's probably a lot like one they've solved before.
Our freezing systems—spirals, tunnels, tumblers and chillers of every size, shape and capacity you'll ever need—also represent a considerable development effort. It wasn't easy, for example, coming up with the best spiral freezer in the industry. But it was worth it.
At Airco, of course, the refrigerants are second nature. Whether you want CO_2 or nitrogen makes no difference to us. We supply both nationally. And we have all the production, storage and delivery facilities and equipment necessary to get them to you whenever, wherever and in whatever quantities you need them.
We also maintain a fully equipped, fully staffed (more food-freezing experts, of course) lab in which you can evaluate and test practically anything freezable you wish.
That's Airco Kryofoods. Systems. Refrigerants. Equipment. Facilities. And the people who know how to use them all to make your job easier. Airco Kryofoods, 575 Mountain Avenue, Murray Hill, New Jersey 07974. (201) 464-8100.
AIRCO Kryofoods
The food-freezing experts.

236

236

Art Directors	Pat Hutt
	Mike Rosen
Writer	Jim Carter
Designer	Pat Hutt
Photographer	Tony Garcia
Agency	Hammond Farrell Inc.
Client	Airco Kryofoods

Magazine Editorial

237

237

Art Director	Paul D. Miller
Writer	Dean R. Drury
Designers	Roger Davidoff Keith Helmetag Mike Leon
Photographers	Larry Shmenco Martha Swope
Publisher	WNCN/GAF Broadcasting Co., Inc.
Agency	GAF Corporation Design Services
Client	Keynote Magazine WNCN, a GAF Broadcasting Co.

BY LEONARD FEATHER

JAZZ Goes to College

A FEW MONTHS AGO, at Royce Hall on the University of California campus in Los Angeles, Cecil Taylor, a black, classically trained pianist, offered two hour-long marathons of unremitting sound and fury. Energy predominated; harmony, "melody" in the traditional connotation of the word, and rhythm—in the sense of the old Duke Ellington dictum, "It don't mean a thing if it ain't got that swing"—were all jettisoned in favor of Taylor's commanding, riveting force as he attacked the keyboard demonically. Except for a few brief sequences when his two saxophonists and trumpeter read skeletal arrangements, there was no suggestion of tonality or a home base. Though a number of bemused observers plugged their ears or walked out, the bulk of the predominantly white and youthful audience remained to give Taylor a roaring ovation following the performance.

A few days later, the Southern California Hot Jazz Society held its annual meeting at a stuffy hall in Los Angeles. Ed "Montudie" Garland, born in New Orleans in 1895, twirled his bass fiddle around and slapped the strings as his colleagues, mostly old and black but a couple of them young and white, wove their way around the chords of "Muskrat Ramble," written by the late Kid Ory in 1922. Some of the audience, fortyish, wearing suits, shirts and ties, sang along.

On the same day, the quintet led by Blue Mitchell and Harold Land, a trumpeter and a saxophonist of the second bebop generation, played recognizable themes to an almost entirely black audience at a small club in one of Los Angeles' black neighborhoods.

Meanwhile, an interracial big band led by Bill Berry, a white trumpeter who played with Duke Ellington's band in the early 1960's, brought an excited, racially mixed crowd to its feet in a San Fernando Valley nightclub.

That these four events took place within a brief time span and that all could be defined, by one faction or another, as jazz, is symbolic of the extraordinary diversity that exists today in America's resurgent jazz community. It is hard to imagine any one enthusiast who would attend all four of these performances, relate emotionally to them and concede that all four could be classified as jazz. The polarization takes several forms: generational, racial, intellectual, doctrinaire. To diehard adherents of the New Orleans school of jazz, the music of Cecil Taylor is not merely incomprehensible and deafening; it is not jazz. The avant-gardists for whom Taylor represents the wave of the future probably would (Continued)

238

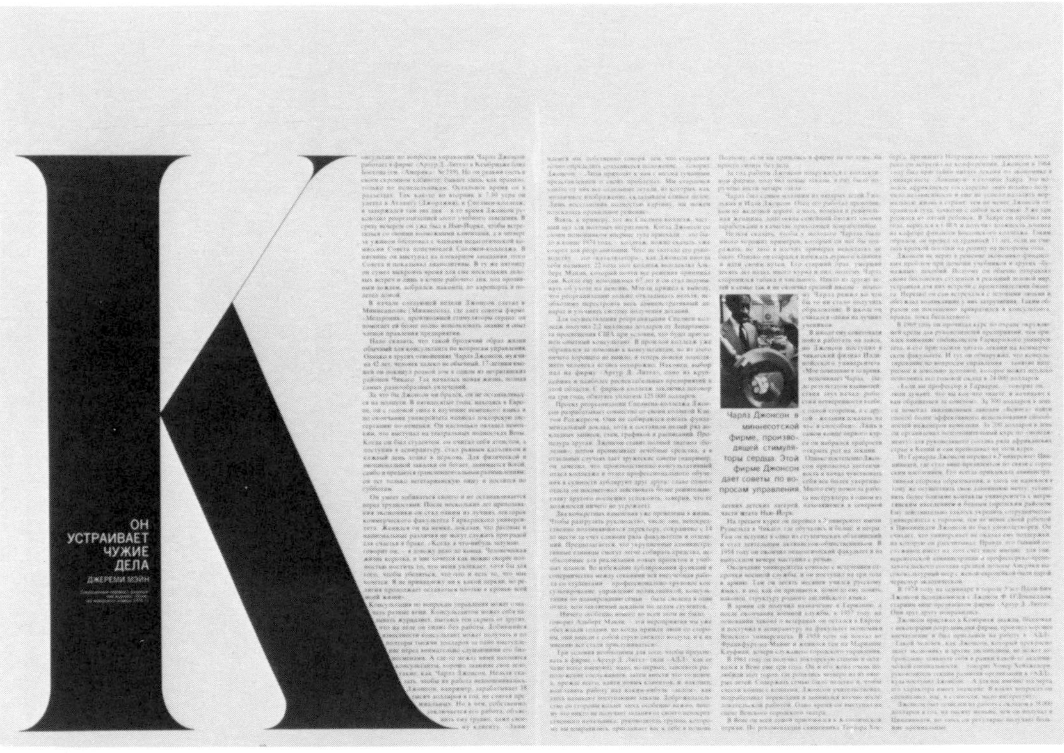

К

ОН УСТРАИВАЕТ ЧУЖИЕ ДЕЛА

ДЖЕРЕМИ МЭЙН

Чарлз Джонсон в миннесотской фирме, производящей стимуляторы сердца. Этой фирме Джонсон дает советы по вопросам управления.

239

238	
Art Director	Thaddeus A. Miksinski, Jr.
Writer	Leonard Feather
Designer	Thaddeus A. Miksinski, Jr.
Photographer	Veryl Oakland
Publisher	International Communication Agency
Agency	International Communication Agency
Client	Topic Magazine

239	
Art Director	David Moore
Editor	Robert Poteete
Designer	Patricia Gipple
Photographer	James H. Karales, Money © Time Inc.
Publisher	U. S. Information Agency
Agency	U. S. Information Agency
Client	America Illustrated Magazine

ONE HELL OF A NEWSPAPER WAR

CAN THE HERALD SURVIVE THE BATTLE WITH ITSELF?

By Bill Kirtz and John Kronenberger The week before Boston's "new-ew" newspaper hit the stands in late October, rumors started tickling ears in the *Globe* city room that the *Herald-American*'s editors were carefully stockpiling major stories—really big ones—for the inaugural week of their redesigned publication. Not only that, went the word, but *Globe* editors were already putting the finishing touches to their counterattack. The third week of the month, in short, would witness the beginning of a great old-fashioned war between the dailies. Pens and blue pencils at the ready, both papers' staffs waited for the imminent call to arms.

The *Herald*'s promotion department, having geared up for nearly a year, let its loudspeakers roar on Monday, October 18: *Okay, folks, this is it. Get ready, get set—Boston has a new-ew newspaper.*

240

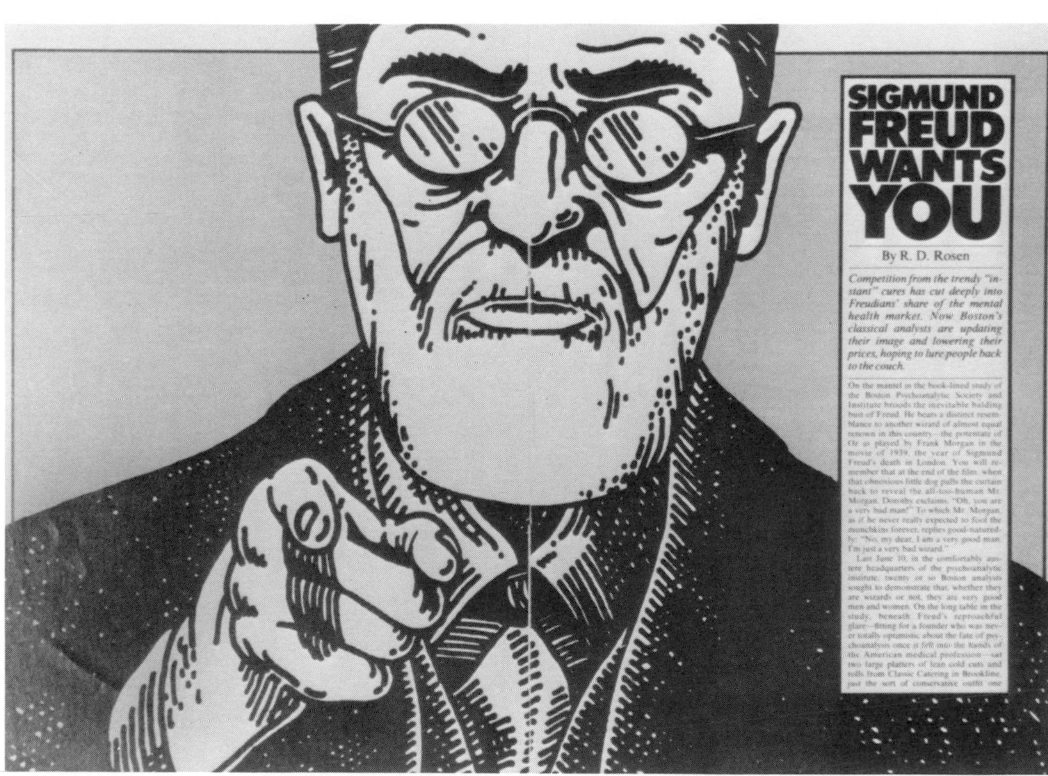

SIGMUND FREUD WANTS YOU

By R. D. Rosen

Competition from the trendy "instant" cures has cut deeply into Freudians' share of the mental health market. Now Boston's classical analysts are updating their image and lowering their prices, hoping to lure people back to the couch.

On the mantel in the book-lined study of the Boston Psychoanalytic Society and Institute broods the inevitable balding bust of Freud. He bears a distinct resemblance to another wizard of almost equal renown in this country—the potentate of Oz as played by Frank Morgan in the movie of 1939, the year of Sigmund Freud's death in London. You will remember that at the end of the film, when that obnoxious little dog pulls the curtain back to reveal the all-too-human Mr. Morgan, Dorothy exclaims, "Oh, you are a very bad man!" To which Mr. Morgan, as if he never really expected to fool the munchkins forever, replies good-naturedly: "No, my dear, I am a very good man. I'm just a very bad wizard."

Last June 10, in the comfortably austere headquarters of the psychoanalytic institute, twenty or so Boston analysts sought to demonstrate that, whether they are wizards or not, they are very good men and women. On the long table in the study, beneath Freud's reproachful glare—fitting for a founder who was never totally optimistic about the fate of psychoanalysis once it fell into the hands of the American medical profession—sat two large platters of lean cold cuts and rolls from Classic Catering in Brookline, just the sort of conservative outfit one

241

240	
Art Director	Ronn Campisi
Editor	George Gendron
Designer	Ronn Campisi
Artist	Charles Waller
Publisher	Boston Magazine
Agency	Ronn Campisi Design
Client	Boston Magazine

241	
Art Director	Ronn Campisi
Editor	George Gendron
Designer	Ronn Campisi
Artist	Mark Fisher
Publisher	Boston Magazine
Agency	Ronn Campisi Design
Client	Boston Magazine

DOCTORS UNDER THE INFLUENCE

Though thousands of doctors are now alcoholics, the medical world maintains its official silence.

242

by Frederick E. Jordan

SURVIVAL IN A CONSERVATIVE PROFESSION

MINORITY ENGINEERS FACE STIFF ODDS

The survival of small consulting engineering firms depends primarily on factors that involve good performance and sound management. However, there is a small group of firms whose position is even more precarious and whose survival depends on factors we cannot always control. We are what has been classified as "minority" firms—companies that are at least 50 percent owned by members of minority groups or, if it is a publicly owned business, 51 percent of its outstanding stock is held by minority group members.

We are scattered across the country in such places as Newhall, California; Anchorage, Alaska; and Window Rock, Arizona, as well as in big cities like Miami, New York, Cleveland, and Los Angeles. By the Federal government definition, minorities include American Indians, Afro-Americans, Spanish-speaking Americans, American Eskimos, American Aleuts, and American Orientals.

Prior to the Federal government's urban redevelopment programs of the 1960's, the so-called minority engineering firm was a myth. It is estimated that fewer than 10 fulltime Black operating engineering firms existed in this country prior to 1960. Our engineering services were, in many instances, only extensions of architectural and construction contracting firms.

In 1976, there are fewer than 50 fulltime Black engineering offices in the U.S., out of nearly 10,000 consulting firms. The number of other minority group firms is even more difficult to estimate, since many such minorities will lay no claim to being minorities if they can avoid doing so. The American Indian Council of Architects and Engineers has estimated that there are fewer than 10 Indian firms currently operating in this country that are identified as native Americans. No estimate is made of the Spanish-speaking and Oriental groups. No Eskimo or Aleut firms are known to exist.

Numbers Don't Add Up

The plight of Black businesses is illustrated by the fact that in 1971 General Motors lost more money than all the Black businesses in the United States had grossed. However, the picture is even more dismal for minority engineering firms. It is safe to say that the aggregated personnel of all the Black engineering firms in the United States would make up less than 10 percent of the staff of Bechtel Corporation. In addition, the largest white firm in this country grossed in 1975, on engineering contracts, more than 20 times the combined amount that all Black engineering firms grossed in 1975.

What is the reason for this miniscule participation of Blacks and other minorities in the consulting engineering profession? Louis Warner, principal of System Architects and Engineers, sees it as a perpetuation of exclusion, since firms are selected for contracts instead of having to submit bids. This exclusion is exemplified by the Federal Insurance Administration, which administers $100 million in fees in 1976 for flood plain studies. The agency's selection board is typical of many agencies in not assigning projects to minority firms because of a purported lack of experience. Yet, in awarding the projects to white firms, which thereby obtain more and more experience, the perpetuation of minority exclusion is continued.

There are many other reasons for the economic disparity between white and minority engineering firms. One reason is that the engineering profession as a whole has traditionally excluded minorities. Less than one percent of the engineers in the profession are Black. Consequently, the number of minority firms is proportionately small. Majority firms, like other economic dominating corporations, have done little in the past to bring about parity for minority firms.

Affirmative Action

Affirmative action is the main force in keeping minority firms alive, although most affirmative action plans relate to construction, totally disregarding the design effort.

Neal McCaleb, president of the American Indian Council of Architects and Engineers and a principal in the firm of McCaleb-Nusbaum-Thomas, of Edmont, Oklahoma, has described the ineffectiveness of affirmative action as follows:

"Indian and other minority-owned professional organizations have not received their proportionate share of government A&E contracts in spite of the lofty objectives given lip service by the bureaucratic agencies regarding their commitment to equal employment opportunities.

Mr. Jordan is president of Jordan Associates, Inc. and president of the National Council for Minority Consulting Engineers. This article contains excerpts from an article published in Consulting Engineer, July 1976.

8 MINORITY BUILDER

243

242

Art Director	Ronn Campisi
Editor	George Gendron
Designer	Ronn Campisi
Photographer	Ralph King
Publisher	Boston Magazine
Agency	Ronn Campisi Design
Client	Boston Magazine

243

Art Director	Del Harrod
Editor	Kay Koplovitz
Designer	Del Harrod
Artist	Del Harrod
Agency	Harrod Associates
Client	Minority Builder Magazine

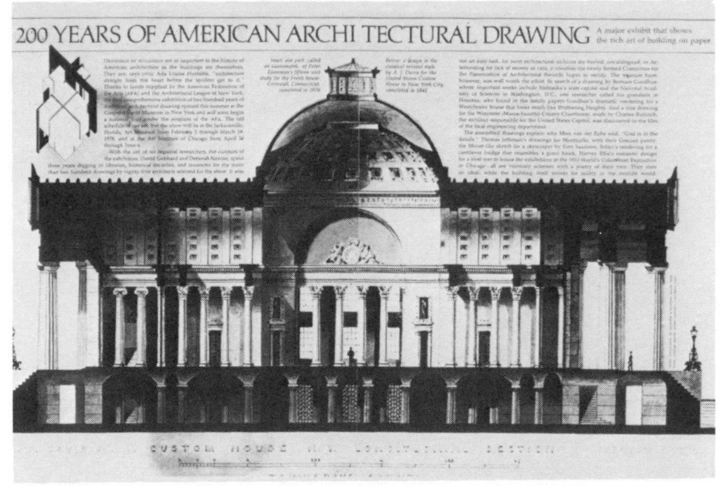

200 YEARS OF AMERICAN ARCHITECTURAL DRAWING A major exhibit that shows the rich art of building on paper

244

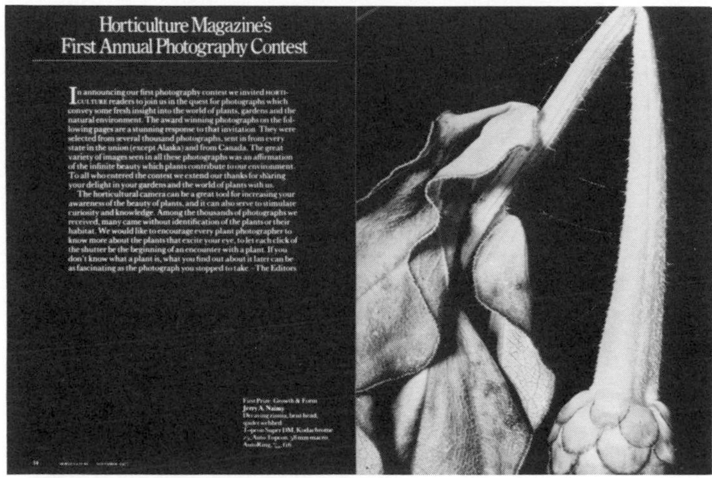

Horticulture Magazine's First Annual Photography Contest

In announcing our first photography contest we invited HORTICULTURE readers to join us in the quest for photographs which convey some fresh insight into the world of plants, gardens and the natural environment. The award winning photographs on the following pages are a stunning response to that invitation. They were selected from several thousand photographs, sent in from every state in the union (except Alaska) and from Canada. The great variety of images seen in all these photographs was an affirmation of the infinite beauty which plants contribute to our environment. To all who entered the contest we extend our thanks for sharing your delight in your gardens and the world of plants with us.

The horticultural camera can be a great tool for increasing your awareness of the beauty of plants, and it can also serve to stimulate curiosity and knowledge. Among the thousands of photographs we received, many came without identification of the plants or their habitat. We would like to encourage every plant photographer to know more about the plants that excite your eye, to let each click of the shutter be the beginning of an encounter with a plant. If you don't know what a plant is, what you find out about it later can be as fascinating as the photograph you stopped to take. –The Editors

245

ALL-TIME TOURNAMENT CROWNS A $1 MILLION CHAMPION

By MARK MULVOY

246

244
Art Director Carmile S. Zaino
Writers Valerie Brooks
Michael Durham
Editors Valerie Brooks
Michael Durham
Publisher American Heritage Pub. Co. Inc.
Agency American Heritage Pub. Co. Inc.

245
Art Director Bruce McIntosh
Editor Paul Trachtman
Designer Bruce McIntosh
Photographer Jerry A. Naimy
Publisher Massachusetts Horticultural Society
Client Horticulture Magazine

246
Art Director Pete Libby
Writer Mark Mulvoy
Artist Jim Sharpe
Publisher Golf Digest, Inc.
Client Golf Digest, Inc.

DEVIL'S FOOD!

Hell hath no flavor like a hot pepper properly prepared

by Marilyn Kaytor

Go ahead, try it; just about everyone else is. The hot pepper is making friends thanks to the many ethnic foods being offered up to us lately, foods high on hot pepper bite: Thai, Vietnamese, Szechwan, Indian, Arab, Spanish and particularly Mexican cooking, our hottest ethnic-food influence at the moment. All have helped dispel prejudice against the savagely hot pepper. We're learning to appreciate the wonderfully lusty flavor hot pepper gives to food when it is used with the proper touch and restraint.

Let's hasten to warn, however, that although no pepper will permanently scorch, some can be treacherous. If you take too big a taste of the fiery little devils, the burn won't dissipate quickly. Treat them with respect. And when working with either fresh peppers or soaked dry ones be careful never to leave their juice on your hands, and never touch the liquid to your face or rub your eyes until your hands are thoroughly washed.

Hot peppers were cultivated for centuries by the Indians of Central America, and they were found there in the late 1400's by Spanish explorers. As the Spaniards were familiar with the taste of black pepper, they compared the multicolor, variform fruit to it and called them peppers, although technically they have no botanical relationship to peppercorns. The Spaniards' name stuck and later became chili peppers (from Nahuatl *chilli*) to most of us. Taken to the Old World, the seeds spread quickly throughout Europe and into the Asian and African tropics. In different soils and climates the pods took on modified characteristics, varying in color, shape and pungency.

The major fresh, canned or dried hot peppers on the market today are known by many varietal names, and no two people, it seems, identify them the same way. These, however, are some forms you are likely to encounter. Tabasco: A bright red elongated and tapered pepper, usually one to one and a half inches in length. Fiery hot, it's found fresh and bottled whole and used for sauces. Cayenne (long pin and long red): Smooth-skinned red peppers with a pungent flavor. The first is short—six inches maximum—and is what our satanic friend at left is eating. The latter runs seven to eight inches and is not as hot. Found fresh and dried on strings. Poblano: A dark green chili pepper similar in shape to a bell pepper but with a tapered end. Mildly hot, it's found fresh and canned. Jalapeño and serrano: These are small green chilies. The jalapeño is up to three inches long, denser in color and hotter than the serrano, which is shorter by an inch. Both have an earthy flavor and are widely used in Mexican cooking. Chili and chilitepines: Whole dry red forms often sold on strings and commonly used in the Southwest in Mexican food.

Because the hotness of peppers varies, and because each person's palate differs in what it can take, the cook must rate hotness for himself. Recipes can give guidelines only, so add hot pepper slowly and taste, taste. Should you use the seeds? It depends on the temperature wanted. The pepper's pungency comes from a substance in the tissues that hold the seeds to the center, so for less heat, discard the seeds. On page 136 you'll find some hot-pepper-sauce recipes and a few ideas for finished dishes.

Photographed by Salomon-Wahlberg

ESQUIRE: FEBRUARY 73

247

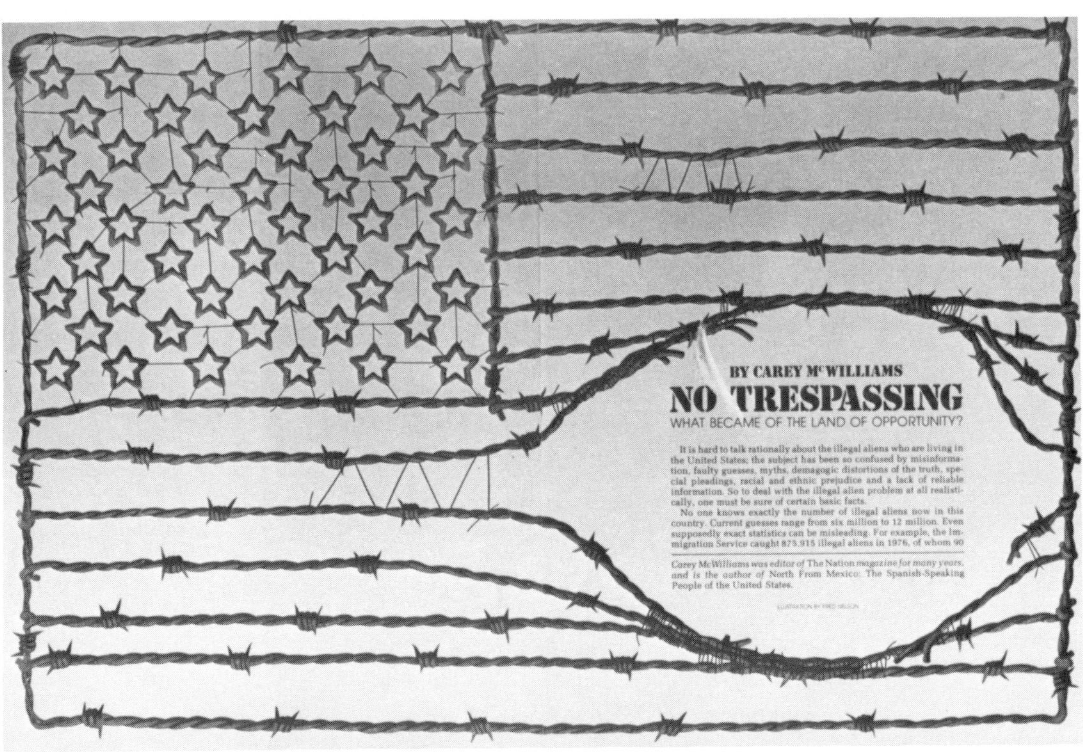

BY CAREY McWILLIAMS

NO TRESPASSING

WHAT BECAME OF THE LAND OF OPPORTUNITY?

It is hard to talk rationally about the illegal aliens who are living in the United States; the subject has been so confused by misinformation, faulty guesses, myths, demagogic distortions of the truth, special pleadings, racial and ethnic prejudice and a lack of reliable information. So to deal with the illegal alien problem at all realistically, one must be sure of certain basic facts.

No one knows exactly the number of illegal aliens now in this country. Current guesses range from six million to 12 million. Even supposedly exact statistics can be misleading. For example, the Immigration Service caught 875,915 illegal aliens in 1976, of whom 90

Carey McWilliams was editor of The Nation magazine for many years, and is the author of North From Mexico: The Spanish-Speaking People of the United States.

248

247	
Art Director	Michael Gross
Writer	Marilyn Kaytor
Designer	Michael Gross
Photographer	Salomon-Wahlberg
Publisher	Esquire, Inc.
Client	Esquire Magazine

248	
Art Director	Gordon Mortensen
Editor	David Sanford
Designer	Gordon Mortensen
Artist	Fred Nelson
Publisher	Politics Today (formerly Skeptic Magazine)
Client	Politics Today (formerly Skeptic Magazine)

BY JOHN F. HELLEGERS

THE CONCORDE IS VERY FAST – ALSO LOUD, DANGEROUS AND FINANCIALLY DISASTROUS

BOOM AND BUST

If you're in business to make a profit, the worst thing you can do is lose money. The Ford Motor Company, after a few unhappy seasons with the Edsel, took the car off the market, cut its losses and hoped that people would forget.

In politics, though, the worst thing is to admit an obviously horrendous multibillion-dollar mistake. The admission is too likely to be thrown back in your face at the next election. Far better to brazen it out and hope that any admission can be postponed for your successor. This is why the world is still struggling with the Anglo-French Concorde supersonic transport, or SST, an aircraft into which the British and French governments say they have sunk $3 billion since 1962. (The real sum is probably much larger.) For their money they'll eventually get 16 copies of a plane that's more than twice as loud on takeoff as the loudest subsonic commercial jet (four times louder than a 747), in addition to being a fuel-guzzling financial disaster and a threat to the stratospheric ozone layer, which filters out solar ultraviolet radiation and thus protects us from skin cancer. The Concorde is also a producer of startling sonic booms that have bedeviled residents of southern England and the islands in the English Channel since commercial Concorde service began last year. Luckily, the British and French have agreed not to build any more than 16 Concordes. But no one can figure out how to get rid of them.

That's not for lack of trying: the Concorde is still around despite strenuous behind-the-scenes efforts by its nominal supporters to kill it. As long ago as 1964, the newly elected British government led by

John F. Hellegers is the attorney for the Environmental Defense Fund in Washington, DC.

249

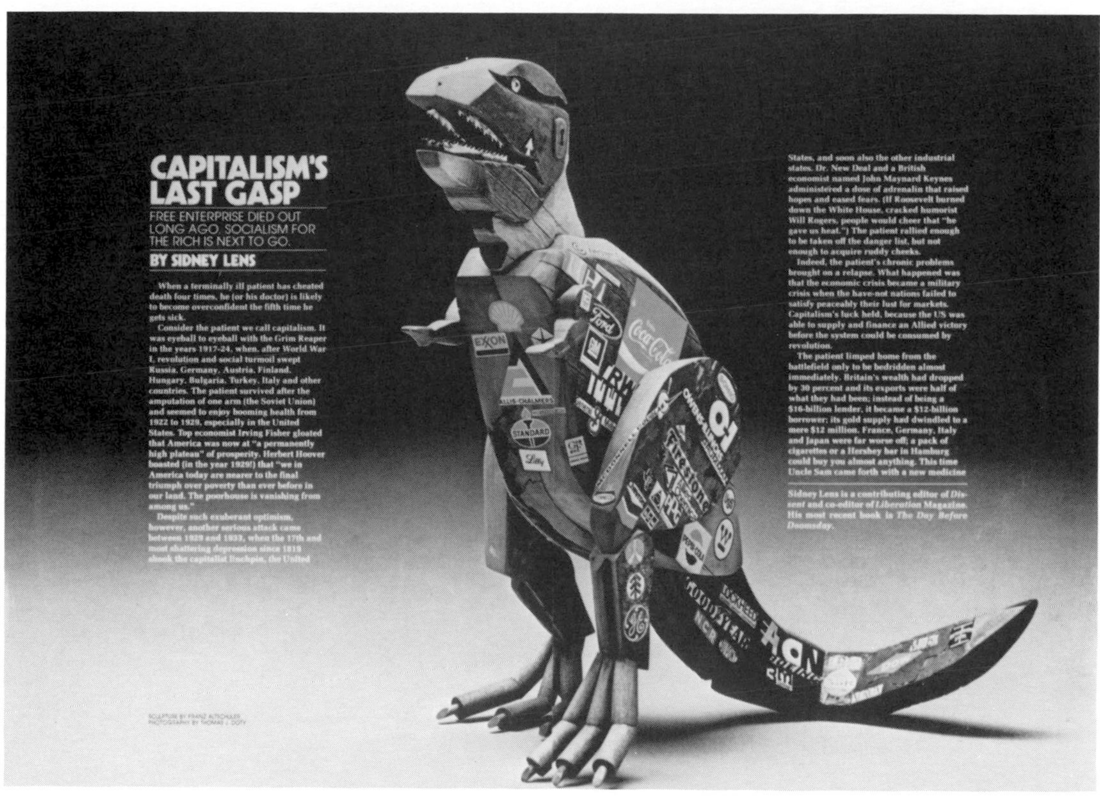

CAPITALISM'S LAST GASP

FREE ENTERPRISE DIED OUT LONG AGO. SOCIALISM FOR THE RICH IS NEXT TO GO.

BY SIDNEY LENS

When a terminally ill patient has cheated death four times, he (or his doctor) is likely to become overconfident the fifth time he gets sick.

Consider the patient we call capitalism. It was eyeball to eyeball with the Grim Reaper in the years 1917-24, when, after World War I, revolution and social turmoil swept Russia, Germany, Austria, Finland, Hungary, Bulgaria, Turkey, Italy and other countries. The patient survived after the amputation of one arm (the Soviet Union) and seemed to enjoy booming health from 1922 to 1929, especially in the United States. Top economist Irving Fisher gloated that America was now at "a permanently high plateau" of prosperity. Herbert Hoover boasted (in the year 1929!) that "we in America today are nearer to the final triumph over poverty than ever before in our land. The poorhouse is vanishing from among us."

Despite such exuberant optimism, however, another serious attack came between 1929 and 1933, when the 17th and most shattering depression since 1819 shook the capitalist linchpin, the United States, and soon also the other industrial states. Dr. New Deal and a British economist named John Maynard Keynes administered a dose of adrenalin that raised hopes and eased fears. (If Roosevelt burned down the White House, cracked humorist Will Rogers, people would cheer that "he gave us heat.") The patient rallied enough to be taken off the danger list, but not enough to acquire ruddy cheeks.

Indeed, the patient's chronic problems brought on a relapse. What happened was that the economic crisis became a military crisis when the have-not nations failed to satisfy peaceably their lust for markets. Capitalism's luck held, because the US was able to supply and finance an Allied victory before the system could be consumed by revolution.

The patient limped home from the battlefield only to be bedridden almost immediately. Britain's wealth had dropped by 30 percent and its exports were half of what they had been; instead of being a $16-billion lender, it became a $12-billion borrower; its gold supply had dwindled to a mere $12 million. France, Germany, Italy and Japan were far worse off; a pack of cigarettes or a Hershey bar in Hamburg could buy you almost anything. This time Uncle Sam came forth with a new medicine

Sidney Lens is a contributing editor of *Dissent* and co-editor of *Liberation Magazine*. His most recent book is *The Day Before Doomsday*.

250

249
Art Director Gordon Mortensen
Editor David Sanford
Designer Gordon Mortensen
Artist Ed Soyka
Publisher Politics Today (formerly Skeptic Magazine)
Client Politics Today (formerly Skeptic Magazine)

250
Art Director Gordon Mortensen
Editor David Sanford
Designer Gordon Mortensen
Artist Franz Altschuler
Photographer Thomas J. Doty
Publisher Politics Today (formerly Skeptic Magazine)
Client Politics Today (formerly Skeptic Magazine)

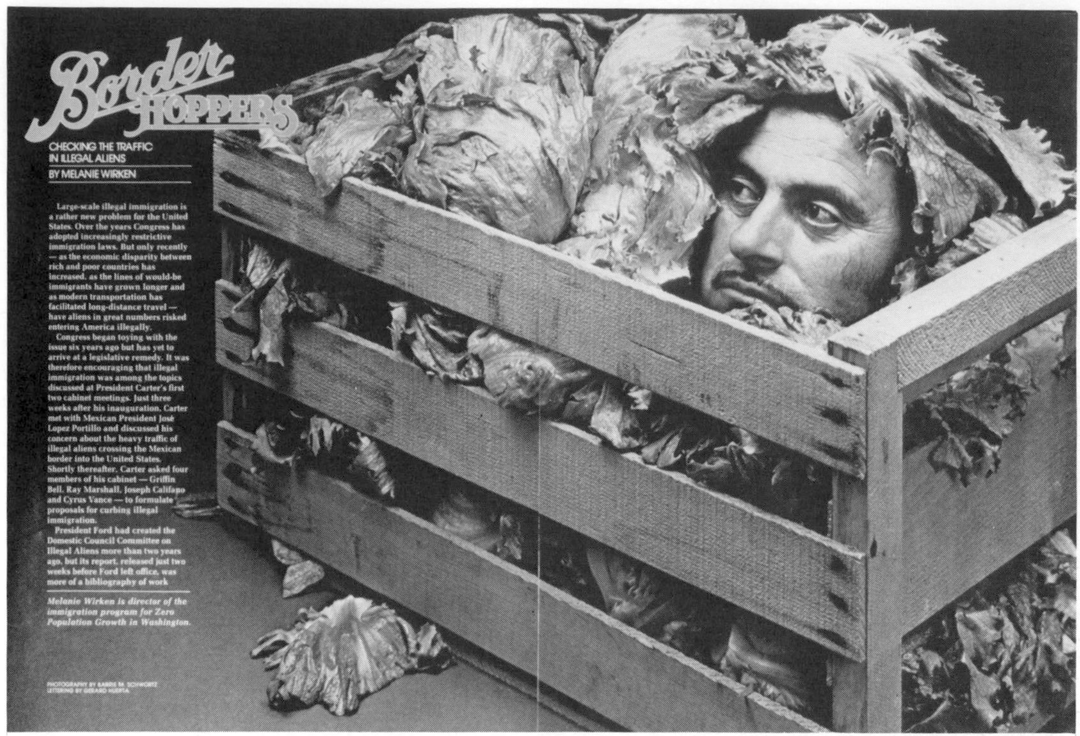

Border Hoppers

CHECKING THE TRAFFIC IN ILLEGAL ALIENS

BY MELANIE WIRKEN

Large-scale illegal immigration is a rather new problem for the United States. Over the years Congress has adopted increasingly restrictive immigration laws. But only recently — as the economic disparity between rich and poor countries has increased, as the lines of would-be immigrants have grown longer and as modern transportation has facilitated long-distance travel — have aliens in great numbers risked entering America illegally.

Congress began toying with the issue six years ago but has yet to arrive at a legislative remedy. It was therefore encouraging that illegal immigration was among the topics discussed at President Carter's first two cabinet meetings. Just three weeks after his inauguration, Carter met with Mexican President José Lopez Portillo and discussed his concern about the heavy traffic of illegal aliens crossing the Mexican border into the United States. Shortly thereafter, Carter asked four members of his cabinet — Griffin Bell, Ray Marshall, Joseph Califano and Cyrus Vance — to formulate proposals for curbing illegal immigration.

President Ford had created the Domestic Council Committee on Illegal Aliens more than two years ago, but its report, released just two weeks before Ford left office, was more of a bibliography of work

Melanie Wirken is director of the immigration program for Zero Population Growth in Washington.

251

ФОТО МАЙКА МИТЧЕЛЛА

ПЕРЧАТКИ ...ДЛЯ НОГ

В мире молодежной моды набирает популярность новый вид носков. На манер перчаток, носки имеют пальцы. Носить их одно удовольствие, хотя бы потому, что в них каждый палец сам себе хозяин и может шевелиться как ему угодно. Некоторые поклонники новой моды даже уверяют, что такой покрой носков способствует кровообращению и придает устойчивость. Так это или не так, очевидно одно: носки необыкновенно практичны.

Изготовляют их из чистой шерсти или из смеси ее с искусственными волокнами, и зимой ногам в них тепло даже в сандалиях.

252

251

Art Director Gordon Mortensen
Editor David Sanford
Designer Gordon Mortensen
Lettering Gerard Huerta
Photographer Barrie M. Schwortz
Publisher Politics Today (formerly Skeptic Magazine)
Client Politics Today (formerly Skeptic Magazine)

252

Art Director David Moore
Editor Robert Poteete
Designer Dorothy Fall
Photographer Mike Mitchell
Publisher U.S. Information Agency
Agency U.S. Information Agency
Client America Illustrated Magazine

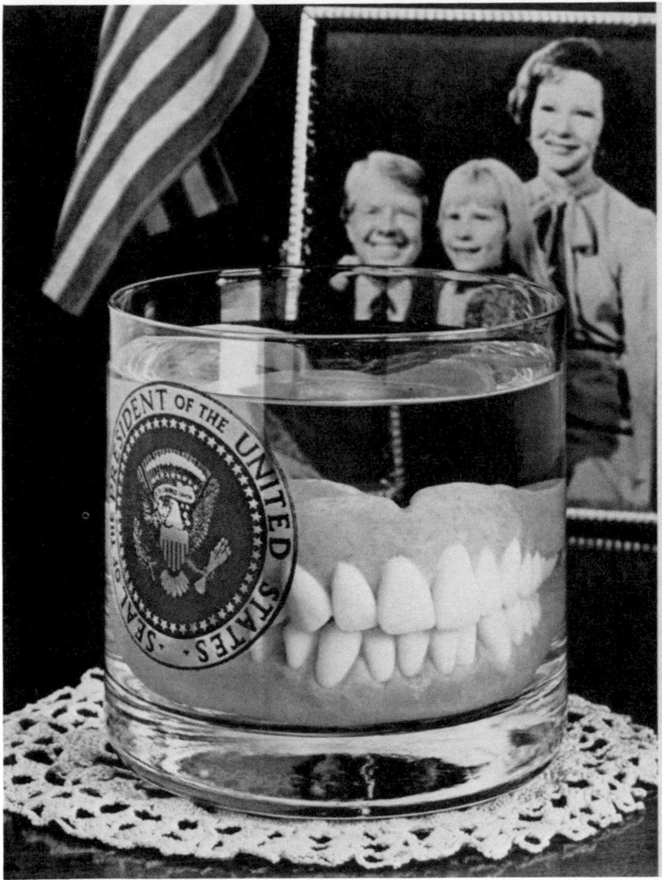

LOOSE GRIP

BY VIC GOLD

THERE'S NO WAY TO PUT A GOOD FACE ON THE CARTER PRESIDENCY

Travel is the last refuge of foundering presidencies. Whenever plagued by problems unsolved and promises unkept at the seat of government, American presidents in the media age have taken to the countryside, to bask in the rays of television and strobes. There is nothing better than an airport crowd, a frenzied motorcade, a political or diplomatic ceremony (however mindless) and a healthy shot of happy-hour TV coverage to help a politician through a funk.

Nixon under siege took to foreign countrysides in a futile effort to shore up his domestic popularity and, he hoped, sensitize a threatening Congress to the awesome image-making powers of the presidency. Jerry Ford, who never enjoyed the working details of the presidency quite as much as he did perquisites like Air Force One, was the most peripatetic of chief executives, traveling here, there, everywhere. Today Peking, China, as one of his congressional friends once said, tomorrow Pekin, Illinois.

Jimmy Carter was elected president chiefly on the theme that he was a puritan among politicians, a man who went about his trade without need of frills. He mocked his opponent's golfing with rich lobbyists and he scorned Ford's reliance on a chief of staff, declaring that in a Carter White House there would be a plaque on the Oval Office desk that said, Truman-like, "The buck stops here."

But he didn't say anything about travel. Even puritanical politicians understand the importance travel has as a presidential frill. There is, first, the need to get away, to give the executive ego breathing room after sustained periods of political stress. But more. There is the symbolism. Overseas, exchanging toasts with foreign heads of state, a president wears the mantle of peacemaker. At home, exchanging smiles and platitudes with the citizenry, a president can be seen as "bringing government closer to the people." Or in the alternative public relations phrase, "taking his case to the grass roots."

True, a mediagenic president can just as easily save the airplane fuel and reach the grass roots by way of television. For this purpose, as Jimmy Carter knew before he came to power, the White House offers some marvelous PR backdrops. Nixon preferred an Oval Office setting, with a bust of Lincoln, a picture of his family, and a flag. Ford's flacks, perhaps eager to spike the rumor that their client was less than intellectual, hit on the idea of a library motif for his first speech on energy. Jimmy Carter's media experts decided on a "fireside chat," wrapping their client in both the mystique of FDR and a sweater that would make the point that while we may have an energy crisis, we have just the leader to see us through it.

Yet, there comes a time for every modern president when staying put in the White House becomes onerous. And when such moments arrive — when stopping the buck means dealing with an intransigent Congress, coping with an unmanageable bureaucracy, trying to satisfy an insatiable press corps — the

Vic Gold was Vice President Agnew's press secretary and is now national correspondent for The Washingtonian.

PHOTOGRAPHY BY BARRIE SCHWORTZ
CARTER FAMILY PORTRAIT: UPI

253

253
Art Director Gordon Mortensen
Editor David Sanford
Designer Gordon Mortensen
Photographer Barrie M. Schwortz
Publisher Politics Today (formerly Skeptic Magazine)
Client Politics Today (formerly Skeptic Magazine)

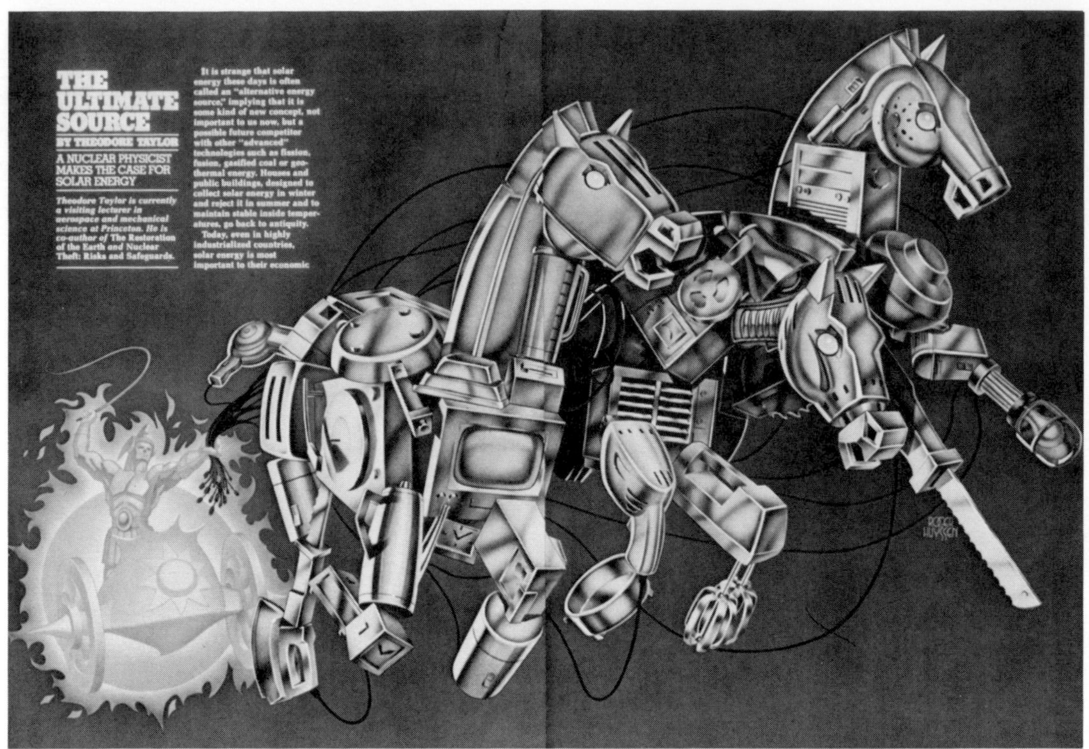

THE ULTIMATE SOURCE

BY THEODORE TAYLOR

A NUCLEAR PHYSICIST MAKES THE CASE FOR SOLAR ENERGY

Theodore Taylor is currently a visiting lecturer in aerospace and mechanical science at Princeton. He is co-author of The Restoration of the Earth *and* Nuclear Theft: Risks and Safeguards.

It is strange that solar energy these days is often called an "alternative energy source," implying that it is some kind of new concept, not important to us now, but a possible future competitor with other "advanced" technologies such as fission, fusion, gasified coal or geothermal energy. Houses and public buildings, designed to collect solar energy in winter and reject it in summer and to maintain stable inside temperatures, go back to antiquity.

Today, even in highly industrialized countries, solar energy is most important to their economic

255

GIDEON ARIEL AND HIS MAGIC MACHINE

If you want to run faster, throw farther or jump higher, call on this electronic mastermind, who will photograph you in action, digitize the moving parts of your body and feed the data into a computer, which in turn will spew out reams of athletic advice no human authority can provide

by KENNY MOORE

256

	255
Art Director	Gordon Mortensen
Editor	David Sanford
Designer	Gordon Mortensen
Artist	Roger Huyssen
Publisher	Politics Today (formerly Skeptic Magazine)
Client	Politics Today (formerly Skeptic Magazine)

	256
Art Director	Richard Gangel
Designer	Geoffrey Gove
Photographers	Geoffrey Gove Jerry Cooke
Publisher	Time-Life Building
Client	Time-Life Building

NOVEMBER 1977 psychology today

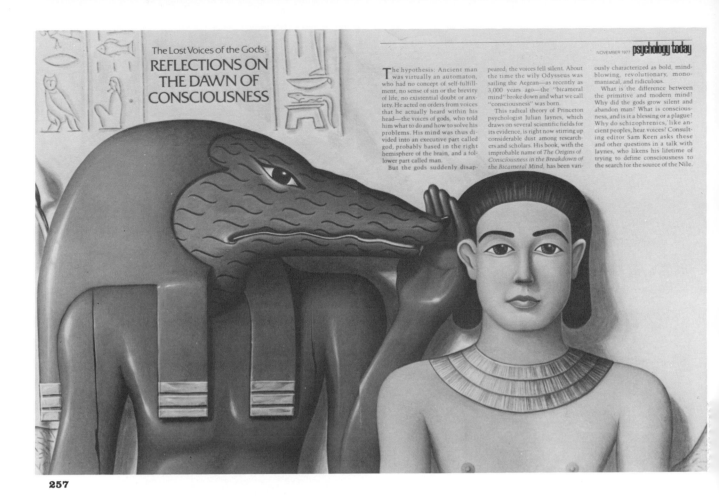

The Lost Voices of the Gods:

REFLECTIONS ON THE DAWN OF CONSCIOUSNESS

The hypothesis: Ancient man was virtually an automaton, who had no concept of self-fulfillment, no sense of sin or the brevity of life, no existential doubt or anxiety. He acted on orders from voices that he actually heard within his head—the voices of gods, who told him what to do and how to solve his problems. His mind was thus divided into an executive part called god, probably based in the right hemisphere of the brain, and a follower part called man.

But the gods suddenly disappeared; the voices fell silent. About the time the wily Odysseus was sailing the Aegean—as recently as 3,000 years ago—the "bicameral mind" broke down and what we call "consciousness" was born.

This radical theory of Princeton psychologist Julian Jaynes, which draws on several scientific fields for its evidence, is right now stirring up considerable dust among researchers and scholars. His book, with the improbable name of *The Origins of Consciousness in the Breakdown of the Bicameral Mind*, has been variously characterized as bold, mind-blowing, revolutionary, monomaniacal, and ridiculous.

What is the difference between the primitive and modern mind? Why did the gods grow silent and abandon man? What is consciousness, and is it a blessing or a plague? Why do schizophrenics, like ancient peoples, hear voices? Consulting editor Sam Keen asks these and other questions in a talk with Jaynes, who likens his lifetime of trying to define consciousness to the search for the source of the Nile.

257

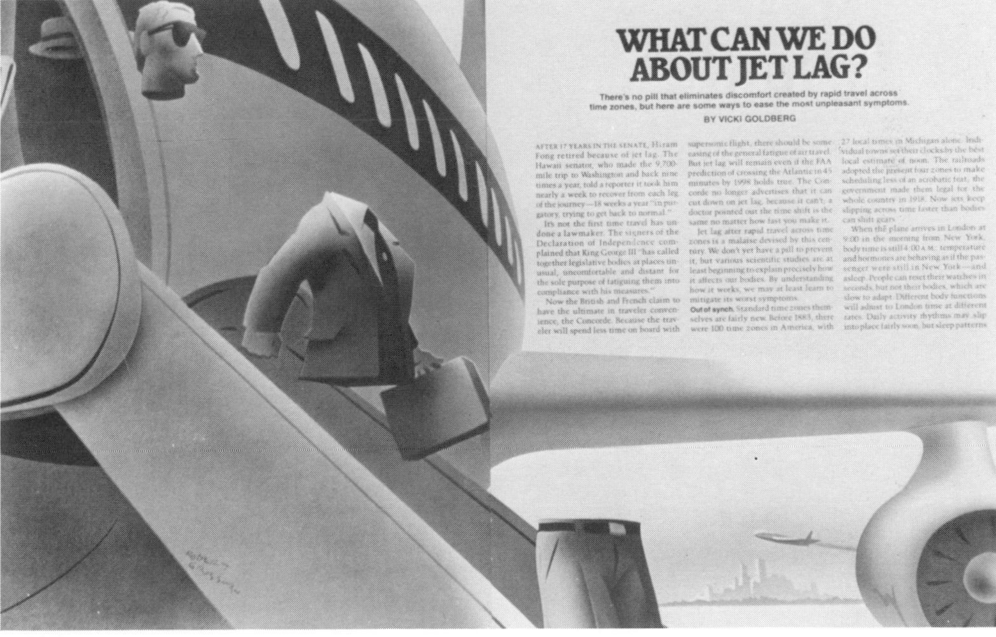

WHAT CAN WE DO ABOUT JET LAG?

There's no pill that eliminates discomfort created by rapid travel across time zones, but here are some ways to ease the most unpleasant symptoms.

BY VICKI GOLDBERG

AFTER 17 YEARS IN THE SENATE, Hiram Fong retired because of jet lag. The Hawaii senator, who made the 9,700-mile trip to Washington and back nine times a year, told a reporter it took him nearly a week to recover from each leg of the journey—18 weeks a year "in purgatory, trying to get back to normal."

It's not the first time travel has undone a lawmaker. The signers of the Declaration of Independence complained that King George III "has called together legislative bodies at places unusual, uncomfortable and distant for the sole purpose of fatiguing them into compliance with his measures."

Now the British and French claim to have the ultimate in traveler convenience, the Concorde. Because the traveler will spend less time on board with supersonic flight, there should be some easing of the general fatigue of air travel. But jet lag will remain even if the FAA prediction of crossing the Atlantic in 45 minutes by 1998 holds true. The Concorde no longer advertises that it can cut down on jet lag, because it can't; a doctor pointed out the time shift is the same no matter how fast you make it.

Jet lag after rapid travel across time zones is a malaise devised by this century. We don't yet have a pill to prevent it, but various scientific studies are at least beginning to explain precisely how it affects our bodies. By understanding how it works, we may at least learn to mitigate its worst symptoms.

Out of synch. Standard time zones themselves are fairly new. Before 1883, there were 100 time zones in America, with 27 local times in Michigan alone. Individual towns set their clocks by the best local estimate of noon. The railroads adopted the present four zones to make scheduling less of an acrobatic feat; the government made them legal for the whole country in 1918. Now jets keep slipping across time faster than bodies can shift gears.

When the plane arrives in London at 9:00 in the morning from New York, body time is still 4:00 A.M.; temperature and hormones are behaving as if the passenger were still in New York—and asleep. People can reset their watches in seconds, but not their bodies, which are slow to adapt. Different body functions will adjust to London time at different rates. Daily activity rhythms may slip into place fairly soon, but sleep patterns

258

	257		258
Art Director	Carveth Kramer	Art Director	Carveth Kramer
Editor	Jack Nessel	Editor	Jack Nessel
Designer	Carveth Kramer	Designer	Carveth Kramer
Artist	Rich Grote	Artist	Robert Grossman
Publisher	Ziff-Davis Publishing	Publisher	Ziff-Davis Publishing
Client	Psychology Today	Client	Psychology Today

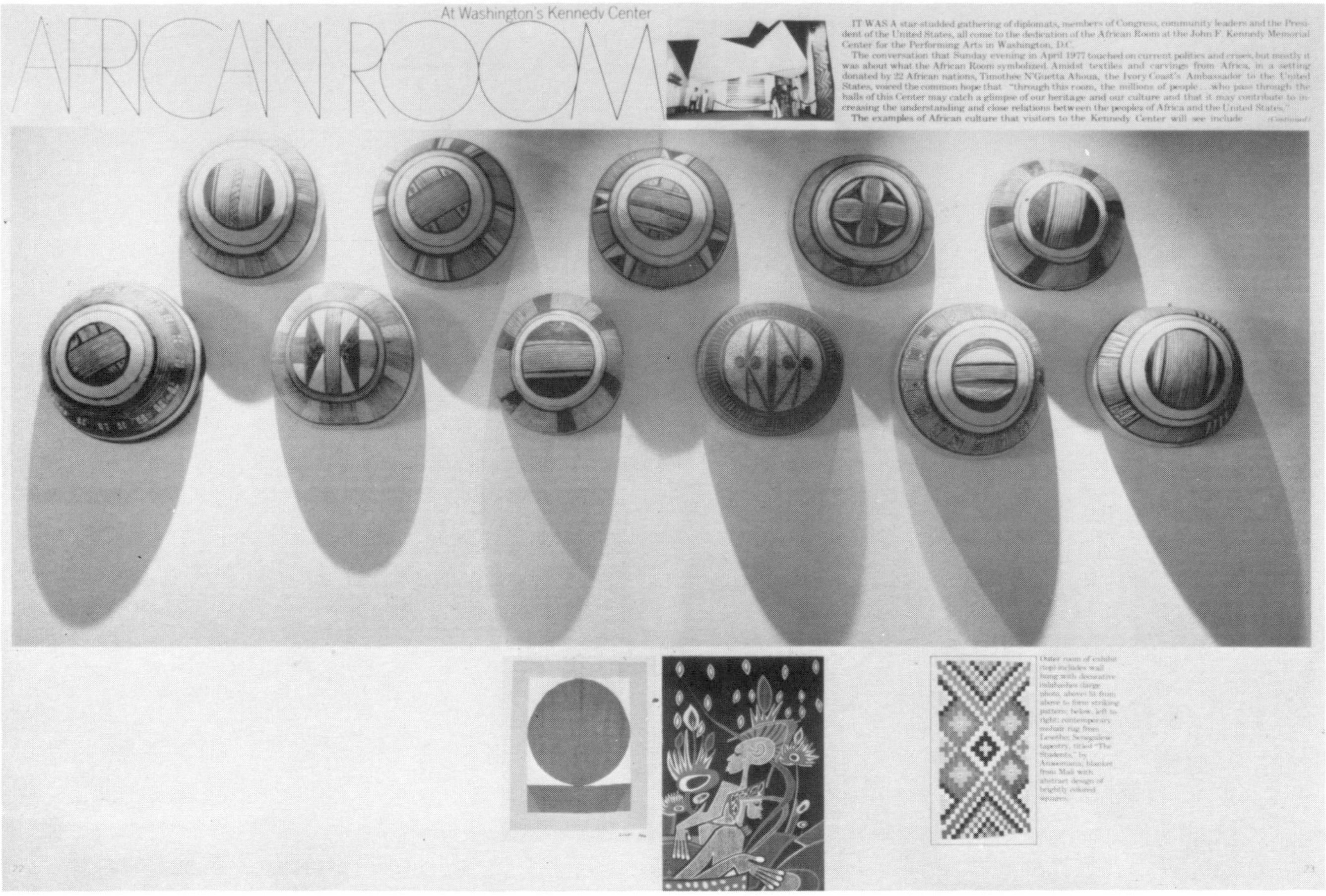

At Washington's Kennedy Center

AFRICAN ROOM

IT WAS A star-studded gathering of diplomats, members of Congress, community leaders and the President of the United States, all come to the dedication of the African Room at the John F. Kennedy Memorial Center for the Performing Arts in Washington, D.C.

The conversation that Sunday evening in April 1977 touched on current politics and crises, but mostly it was about what the African Room symbolized. Amidst textiles and carvings from Africa, in a setting donated by 22 African nations, Timothee N'Guetta Ahoua, the Ivory Coast's Ambassador to the United States, voiced the common hope that "through this room, the millions of people . . . who pass through the halls of this Center may catch a glimpse of our heritage and our culture and that it may contribute to increasing the understanding and close relations between the peoples of Africa and the United States."

The examples of African culture that visitors to the Kennedy Center will see include (Continued)

Outer room of exhibit (top) includes wall hung with decorative calabashes (large photo, above) lit from above to form striking pattern; below, left to right: contemporary mohair rug from Lesotho; Senegalese tapestry, titled "The Students," by Anawenana; blanket from Mali with abstract design of brightly colored squares.

259

16. Flying colors: Geometric pattern distinguishes this 40-year-old cotton 9 ft. 7 in. by 13 ft. 9 in. carpet. It's $6,500 from Doris Leslie Blau, Inc.

17. Florid: This 4 ft. by 7 ft. 1 in. carpet is one of a pair of Pakistani rugs woven in a Bessarabian cabbage-rose pattern. It's $950 at the Pillowry.

18. Let us pray: Rare older Afghan prayer rug is a 2 ft. 3 in. by 4 ft. Kunduz design. It's $1,500 at Artweave Textile Gallery, 924 Madison Ave.

19. In the pinks: Shocking pink predominates in this 2 ft. 7 in. by 6 ft. durrie that's about 75 years old. It's $1,100 from Berge Boghossian.

20. Game show: Late-nineteenth-century, 3 ft. 11 in. by 8 ft. 11 in. carpet has a central game board and stylized birds. It's $4,000 from Artweave.

21. Horsing around: Older cotton durrie on an equestrian theme measures 4 ft. 3 in. by 6 ft. 10 in. and retails for $6,000 at Coury Rugs, Inc.

22. Solid geometry: Brightly colored cotton durrie, about 80 years old, measures 4 ft. 5 in. by 7 ft. It's $1,100 from Vojtech Blau, Inc.

23. Desert song: Camels march around this wool rug, 4 ft. by 6 ft., handmade in India, a copy of an older design. It's $250 at Bloomingdale's.

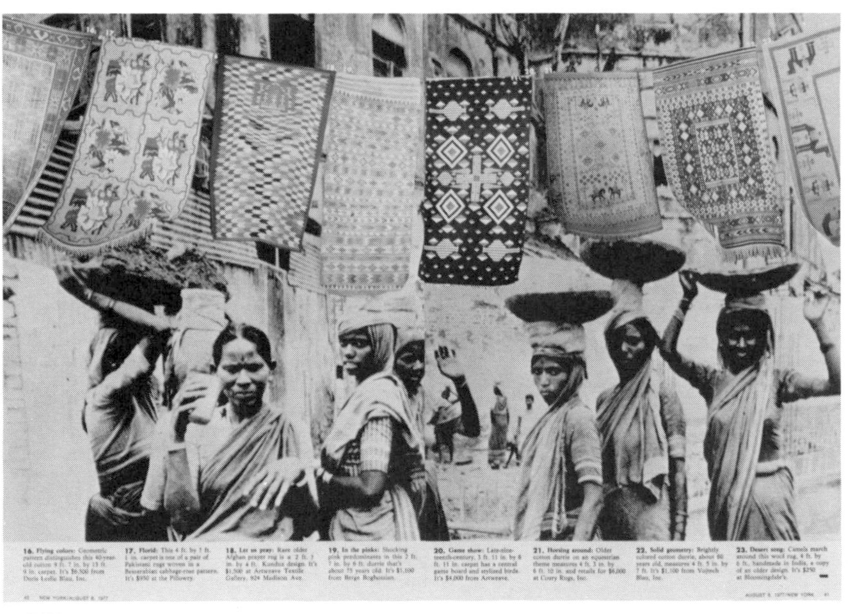

260

259
Art Director Joseph Baumer
Editor Andrew Bardagjy
Designer Joseph Baumer
Photographers Bob Grove
Howard Millard
Publisher International Communication Agency
Agency International Communication Agency
Client Topic Magazine

260
Art Director Joan Dworkin
Writer Suzanne Slesin
Designer Joan Dworkin
Photographers Roberto Brosan
Leo de Wys, Inc.
Publisher New York Magazine

E.B. WHITE VS. XEROX

WHITE'S LETTER TO XEROX

E.B. WHITE is a man of letters whose letters recently stopped the giant Xerox Corporation, the copying machine manufacturer, in its tracks. White didn't like the idea of Xerox sponsoring magazine articles under a plan by which the corporation paid the author, but gave the magazine and the author "full editorial control."

So White wrote a letter to the editor of the Ellsworth *American*, a small newspaper in the state of Maine, taking issue with a 23-page article in *Esquire* magazine called "Travels Through America" by Harrison Salisbury. Salisbury was paid $40,000, plus $15,000 in expenses, and *Esquire* received $115,000 in Xerox advertising.

Salisbury is a former associate editor of *The New York Times*, and *Esquire*, a "reputable sheet," but both should know better, said White—himself a formidably reputable essayist and co-author of the authoritative writing guide, *The Elements of Style*. He warned that *Esquire's* "new idea in publishing" charts a "clear course for the erosion of the free press in America."

The letter was read by W. B. Jones, Xerox director of communications operations. He wrote to White, explaining the detailed ground rules of the arrangement, and why he thought it as legitimate as sponsoring "programs of substance" on television. But Jones wanted to hear more from White: Did a letter writer of his "achievement and insight" still see something sinister in the sponsorship plans?

Here, courtesy of Xerox, is White's reply—and the decision reached by the corporation after considering it.

Dear Mr. Jones:

In extending my remarks on sponsorship, published in the Ellsworth *American*, I want to limit the discussion to the press—that is, to newspapers and magazines. I'll not speculate about television, as television is outside my experience, and I have no ready opinion about sponsorship in that medium.

In your recent letter to me, you ask whether, having studied your ground rules for proper conduct in sponsoring a magazine piece, I still see something sinister in the sponsorship. Yes, I do. Sinister may not be the right word, but I see something ominous and unhealthy when a corporation underwrites an article in a magazine of general circulation. This is not, essentially, the old familiar question of an advertiser trying to influence editorial content; almost everyone is acquainted with that common phenomenon. Readers are aware that it is always present but usually in a rather subdued or non-threatening form. Xerox's sponsoring of a specific writer on a specific occasion for a specific article is something quite different. No one, as far as I know, accuses Xerox of trying to influence editorial opinion. But many people are wondering why a large corporation placed so much money on a magazine piece, why the writer of the piece was willing to get paid in so unusual a fashion, and why *Esquire* was ready and willing to have an outsider pick up the tab. These are reasonable questions.

The press in our free country is reliable and useful not because of its good character but because of its great diversity. As long as there are many owners, each pursuing his own brand of truth, we the people have the opportunity to arrive at the truth and to dwell in the light. The multiplicity of ownership is crucial. It's only when there are few owners, or one owner, that the truth becomes elusive and the light fails. For a citizen in our free society, it is an enormous privilege and a wonderful protection to have access to hundreds of periodicals, each peddling its own belief. There is safety in numbers; the papers expose each other's follies and peccadillos, correct each other's mistakes and cancel out each other's biases. The reader is free to range around in the whole editorial *bouillabaisse* and explore it for the one clam that matters—the truth.

When a large corporation or a rich individual underwrites an article in a magazine, the picture changes; the ownership of that magazine has been diminished, the outline of the magazine has been blurred. In the case of the Salisbury piece, it was as though *Esquire* had gone on relief, was accepting its first welfare payment, and was not its own man any more. The editor protests that he accepts full responsibility for the text and that Xerox had nothing to do with the whole business. But the fact remains that, despite his full acceptance of responsibility, he somehow did not get around to paying the bill. This is unsettling and I think unhealthy. Whenever money changes hands, something goes along with it—an intangible something that varies with the circumstances. It would be hard to resist the suspicion that *Esquire* feels indebted to Xerox, that Mr. Salisbury feels indebted to both, and that the ownership, or sovereignty, of *Esquire* has been nibbled all around the edges.

Sponsorship in the press is an invitation to corruption and abuse. The temptations are great, and there is an opportunist behind every bush. A funded article is a tempting morsel for any publication—particularly for one that is having a hard time making ends meet. A funded assignment is a tempting dish for a writer, who may pocket a much larger fee than he is accustomed to getting. And sponsorship is attractive to the sponsor himself, who, for one reason or another, feels an urge to penetrate the editorial columns after being so long pent up in the advertising pages. These temptations are real, and if the barriers were to be let down I believe corruption and abuse would soon follow. Not all corporations would approach subsidy in the immaculate way Xerox did or in the same spirit of benefaction. There are a thousand reasons for someone's wishing to buy his way into print, many of them unpalatable, all of them to some degree self-serving. Buying and selling space in news columns could become a serious disease of the press. If it reached epidemic proportions, it could destroy the press. I don't want International Business Machines or the National Rifle Association providing me with a funded spectacular when I open my paper; I want to read what the editor and the publisher have managed to dig up on their own—and paid for out of the till.

My affection for the free press in a democracy goes back a long way. My love for it was my first and greatest love. If I felt a shock at the news of the Salisbury-Xerox-*Esquire* arrangement, it was because the sponsorship principle seemed to challenge and threaten everything I believed in: that the press must not only be free, it must be fiercely independent—to survive and to serve. Not all papers are fiercely independent, God knows, but there are always enough of them around to provide a core of integrity and an example that others feel obliged to steer by. The funded article is not in itself evil, but it is the beginning of evil, and it is an invitation to evil. I hope the invitation will not again be extended, and if extended, I hope it will be declined.

About 150 years ago, [French historian Alexis de] Tocqueville wrote: "The journalists of the United States are generally in a very humble position, with a scanty education and a vulgar turn of mind." Today, we chuckle at this antique characterization. But about 50 years ago, when I was a young journalist, I had the good fortune to encounter an editor who fitted the description quite closely. Harold Ross, who founded *The New Yorker*, was deficient in education and had—at least to all outward appearances—a vulgar turn of mind. What he did possess, though, was the ferocity of independence. He was having a tough time finding money to keep his floundering little sheet alive, yet he was determined that neither money nor influence would ever corrupt his dream or deflower his text. His boiling point was so low as to be comical. The faintest suggestion of the shadow of advertising in his news and editorial columns would cause him to erupt. He would explode in anger, the building would reverberate with his wrath, and his terrible swift sword would go flashing up and down the corridors. For a young man, it was an impressive sight and a memorable one. Fifty years have not dimmed for me either the spectacle of Ross's ferocity or my own early convictions—which were identical with his. He has come to my mind often while I've been composing this reply to your inquiry.

I hope I've clarified by a little bit my feelings about the anatomy of the press and the dangers of sponsorship of articles. Thanks for giving me the chance to speak my piece.

Sincerely,
E. B. White

FIRST XEROX REPLY

Xerox officials thought it over . . .

Dear Mr. White:

Thank you for your ringing, strong letter telling me what I didn't want to hear.

We have a couple of Salisbury-like projects now in the works, but your letter has stopped us in our tracks.

We're trying to sort out our dilemma now. When I know what we're going to do, I'll give you a report because we very much appreciate the care you have taken to spell out the issues clearly and forcefully so that we can understand the risks of what we believed would be useful support of substantive journalism.

W. B. Jones

SECOND XEROX REPLY

and decided that White's arguments made good sense: No matter how idealistic the motivation, corporate subsidies for editorial projects were just not right

Dear Mr. White:

I promised you a report on further Xerox-sponsored articles like the Salisbury piece in *Esquire*.

We had two projects in development at the time we received your letter. Since then we've aborted them both, and, although that process involved some discomfort, we now feel better for it.

Your correspondence was a primary factor in our reconsideration, and we do appreciate your help in reaching what I am convinced is the right decision.

Sincerely,
W. B. Jones

Illustration by John Heinly

261

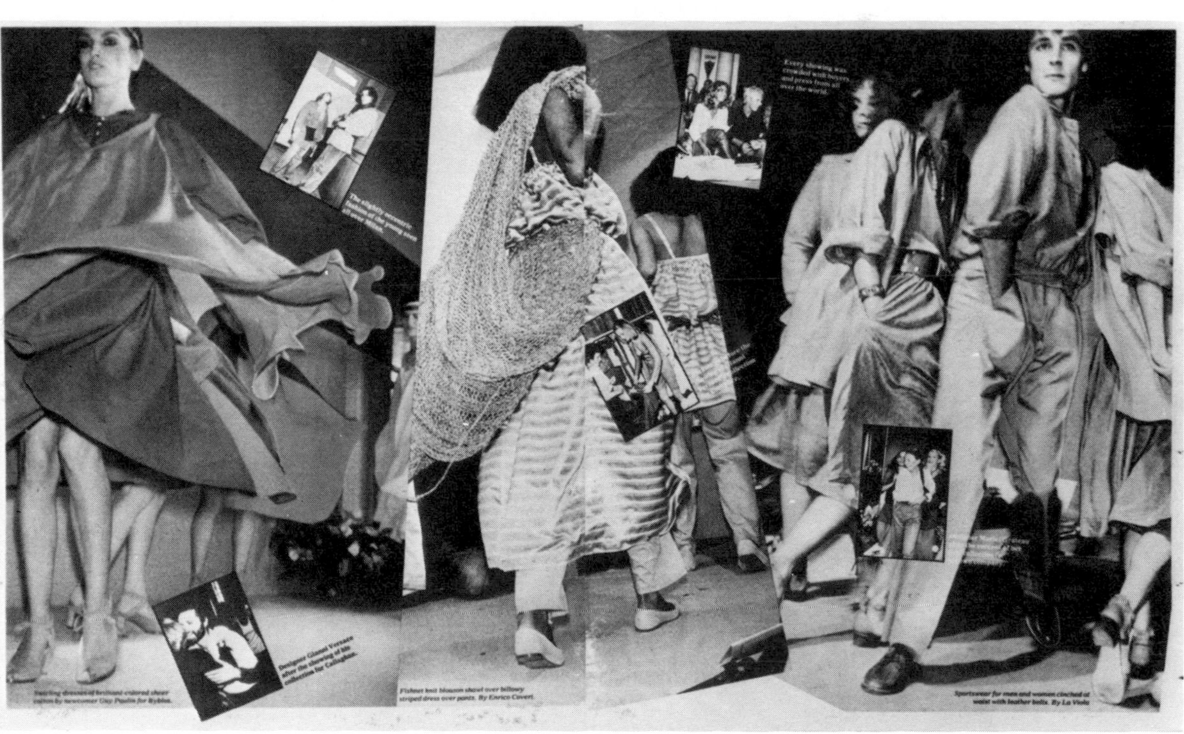

262

261
Art Director Joseph Baumer
Editor Andrew Bardagjy
Designer Pat Eschbacher
Artist John Heinly
Publisher International Communication Agency
Agency International Communication Agency
Client Topic Magazine

262
Art Director Ruth Ansel
Editor Carrie Donovan
Designer Ruth Ansel
Photographer Amanda Sposito
Publisher The New York Times
Agency The New York Times
Client The New York Times

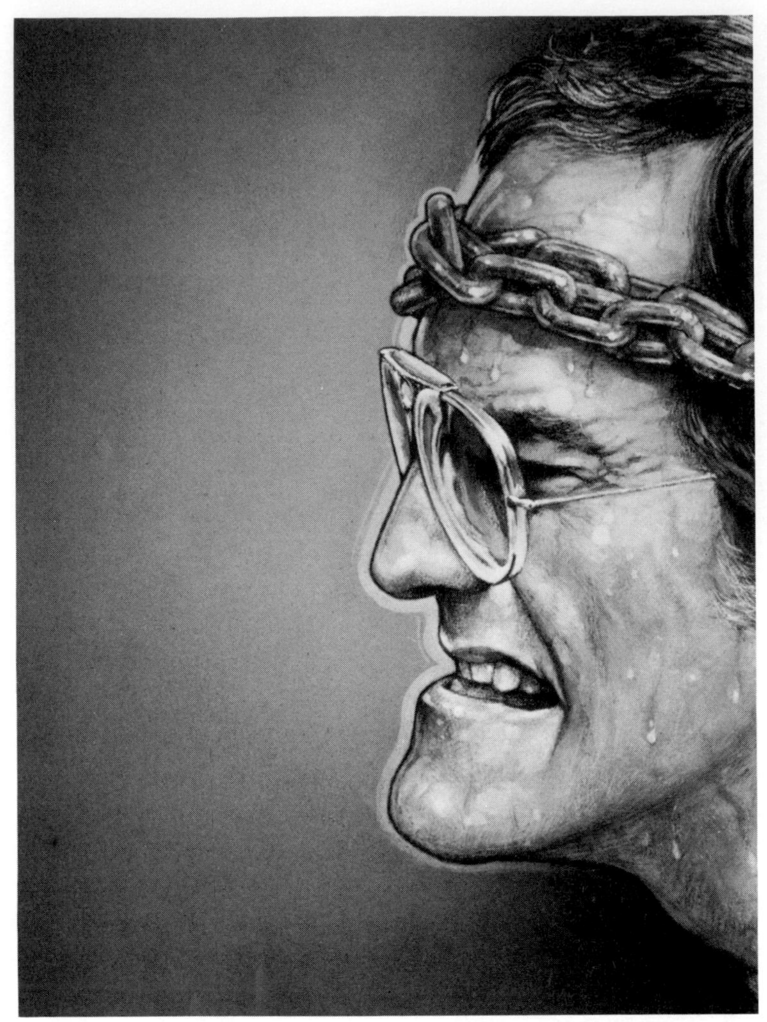

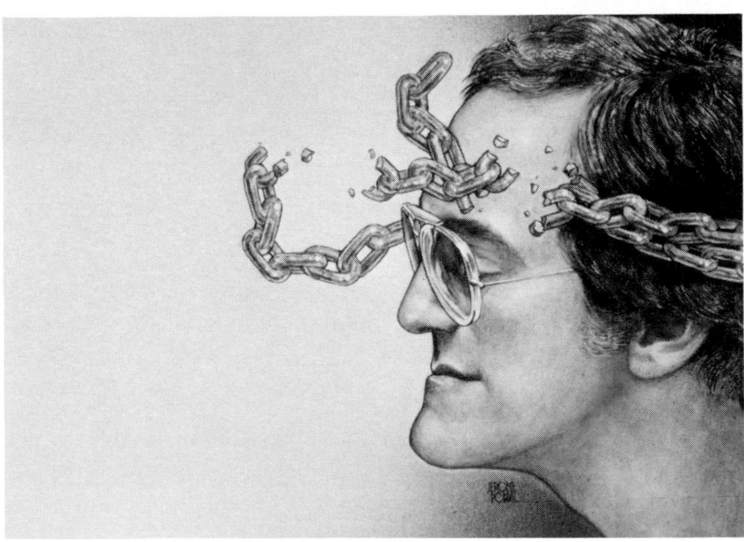

263

263

Art Director	Arthur Paul
Writer	Dan Greenberg
Designer	Roy Moody
Artist	Jerry Podwill
Publisher	Playboy Enterprises, Inc.
Agency	Playboy Magazine

YET ANOTHER EXCERPT STILL FROM

UNPAID BILLS

by Truman Garbage

"There have been more tears shed over unpaid bills than over any others."
—The Author's Accountant

Editor's Note: *For some years now, Mr Garbage has been devoting his time exclusively to the writing of a major novel,* Unpaid Bills. *Several excerpts from this work-in-progress have already appeared in other publications: most notably,* Le Boeuf et Brew, 1965, *which told the tale of a wealthy society matron whose breath was murder, and* Red Desert, *the story of a woman who deliberately left her blind husband in a Michelangelo Antonioni movie. More recently, we have been treated to the appearance in print of* Horrible Icky People, Part of the Middle and Some of the End of My Big New Book, *and* Sky King's Niece, Penny. *Now, the honor of publishing Mr. Garbage's latest segment of* Unpaid Bills *has fallen to the* National Lampoon. *Therefore, without further comment, even though it doesn't seem to be quite finished and really could use a lot of work, we are pleased to present...*

LA RENT EST DUE

"Coco Chanel used to fart in bed and pull the sheets up over her nose." It was Mrs. Important Last Name, "Impy" to her friends, who was doing the talking—a big, breezy, peppy broad built exactly like a man in every detail, and raised on a ranch in Cleveland. We were sitting in the good booth next to the steam table in Le Cafe au Lait. Outside, it was a day filled with [adverb adjective adverb adverb adjective], but inside the hallowed precincts of Le Café, all was [use *tout le monde, art deco,* and *snobbisme*—especially *snobbisme*]. Le Café is owned by Monsieur au Lait, the same fabled restaurateur who for years ran La Côte of Brisket—that landmark of *très chic* where ordinary rich people or garden variety celebrities were merely shown to a comfortable table and served a delicious meal, but where the truly, truly select were made to squat outdoors on the sidewalk and eat offal. Le Cafe is a more casual restaurant—a simple seat close to the men's room is enough to show the esteem in which you're held by its proprietor, and Impy and I could see every inch of the urinals (not that many men pee standing up in Le Cafe).

Lee Radziwill came in the door and was shown to a table with Andrew Mellon, Dick Van Dyke, Garry and Pierre Trudeau, and Baron Rothschild-Lafite. Le Café is a quiet bastion of wealth, a watering hole for the world's great fortunes, a culinary retreat at midday for the well-heeled and the well-fixed. And Impy could afford it. This was her milieu. She had married a doctor.

Brandon De Wilde was seated next to us with Alice Roosevelt Longworth and Countess Maria Ties. Monty Python came in with Houghton Mifflin and Tatum O'Neal. Charo was having cocktails with Anheuser Busch, the young brewery heir. And Merrill Lynch, Pierce Fenner, Jean Shrimpton, and Ralston Purina arrived with a very prominent woman who's the Queen of England. Carol Channing had been there yesterday.

Impy and I were having brunch together—a sort of combination breakfast and lunch—but when Monsieur au Lait glided to our table with menu in hand, Impy regally waved him away, ordering instead bottle after bottle of [call Byron over at *Esquire* and get the name of that really expensive kind of Cold Duck].

My name is P.J. Clarke, and I'm of two minds—whether to skillfully weave my personal history into the warp and woof of a subtle plot structure that evolves through the play and counterplay of mimetic imagery to reveal my narrative point of view as an integral part of this literary work, or whether to just dump my life story into your lap out of sheer lack of writing ability.

I've been peddling my ass since before I could walk. When I was six months old, I was already performing sex acts for money, or even for a change of diapers. I wouldn't shit in my potty unless somebody gave me a quarter. I said, "If you want the kinky stuff, you're going to have to pay." Later, when I was growing up, I wouldn't jack off unless I found money under the couch cushions. I'd suck the legs of a chair just to sit down. There was nothing I wouldn't do, and where I grew up, everybody was queer, too. All the kids in the neighborhood were queer. The nuns at school were queer. A lot of the trees and plants in our yard were queer. My dad was queer—the only way he could get mom preg-

—*more*

264

265

264
Art Director Skip Johnston
Writer P.J. O'Rourke
Designer Skip Johnston
Photographer Ronald G. Harris
Publisher National Lampoon, Inc.

265
Art Director Harry Coulianos
Designer Harry Coulianos
Photographer John Peden
Client GQ

Man of the Year

TIME, JAN. 2, 1978

Anwar Sadat: Architect of a New Mideast

With one stunning stroke he designed a daring approach to peace

He called it "a sacred mission," and history may judge it so. By the trajectory of his 28-minute flight from a base in the Canal Zone to Tel Aviv's Ben Gurion Airport, Egyptian President Anwar Sadat changed the course of Middle Eastern events for generations to come. More emphatically than anything that has happened there since the birth of Israel in 1948, his extraordinary pilgrimage transformed the political realities of a region blackened and embittered by impermeable hatreds and chronic war. In one stroke, the old rules of the Arab-Israeli blood feud no longer applied. Many of the endless hurdles to negotiation seemed to dissolve like Saharan mirages. Not in three decades had the dream of a real peace seemed more probable. For his willingness to seize upon a fresh approach, for his display of personal and political courage, for his unshakable resolve to restore a momentum for peace in the Middle East, Anwar Sadat is TIME's Man of the Year.

"What I want from this visit," Sadat had told TIME Cairo Bureau Chief Wilton Wynn during the historic flight that took him to Jerusalem, "is that the wall created between us and Israel, the psychological wall, be knocked down." The wall fell. The astonishing spectacle was global theater—the images caromed off television satellites to viewers around the world. In a wash of klieg lights, the Egyptian who had hurled his armies across the Suez Canal in 1973 stood at attention next to the old Irgun guerrilla whose name has been a dark legend to Palestinian Arabs for 30 years. An Israeli military band played first the Egyptian national anthem, *By God of Old, Who Is My Weapon*, and then the Israeli *Hatikvah*. In a hushed, deeply moving tableau, Sadat walked along the receiving line with Israeli Premier Menachem Begin to greet the old and resolute enemies: former Premiers Yitzhak Rabin and Golda Meir, Foreign Minister Moshe Dayan, Ariel Sharon, "Israel's Patton," who thrust Israeli armor deep into Egypt in the October War of 1973.

Next day, fulfilling a vow he had made to himself (see *interview*), Sadat prayed in Al Aqsa mosque in the Old City of Jerusalem, one of Islam's holiest places. Then the son of Ishmael stood before the sons of Isaac in the Israeli Knesset and formally declared that the deep, violent enmity between them had somehow passed.

Sadat's demands on Israel, in exchange for peace, were tough and familiar: the return to Arab sovereignty of all territory (including East Jerusalem) conquered during the 1967 Six-Day War; a homeland for Palestinians on the West Bank and in Gaza. Yet far more important were the generous words of acceptance that few Israelis ever expected to hear from an

Egyptian President Sadat standing before the Pyramids of Giza
The old rules of the Arab-Israeli blood feud no longer applied

11

266

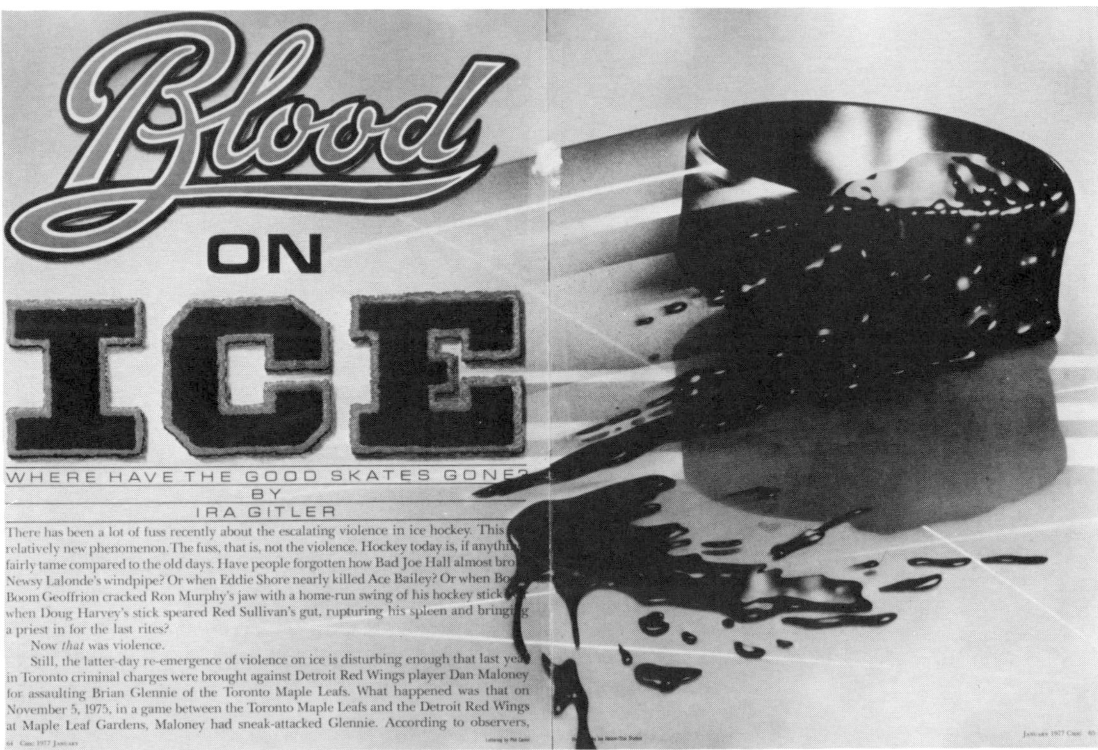

Blood ON ICE

WHERE HAVE THE GOOD SKATES GONE?

BY

IRA GITLER

There has been a lot of fuss recently about the escalating violence in ice hockey. This relatively new phenomenon. The fuss, that is, not the violence. Hockey today is, if anythi fairly tame compared to the old days. Have people forgotten how Bad Joe Hall almost bro Newsy Lalonde's windpipe? Or when Eddie Shore nearly killed Ace Bailey? Or when Bo Boom Geoffrion cracked Ron Murphy's jaw with a home-run swing of his hockey stick when Doug Harvey's stick speared Red Sullivan's gut, rupturing his spleen and bringi a priest in for the last rites?

Now *that* was violence.

Still, the latter-day re-emergence of violence on ice is disturbing enough that last yea in Toronto criminal charges were brought against Detroit Red Wings player Dan Maloney for assaulting Brian Glennie of the Toronto Maple Leafs. What happened was that on November 5, 1975, in a game between the Toronto Maple Leafs and the Detroit Red Wings at Maple Leaf Gardens, Maloney had sneak-attacked Glennie. According to observers,

267

266
Art Director Walter Bernard
Designer Walter Bernard
Photographer David Hume Kennerly
Publisher Time Inc.

267
Art Director Mike Salisbury
Designer Mike Salisbury
Artists Joe Heiner
Star Studios—Phil Carrol
Publisher Larry Flint Publications
Agency Mike Salisbury Design
Client CHIC Magazine

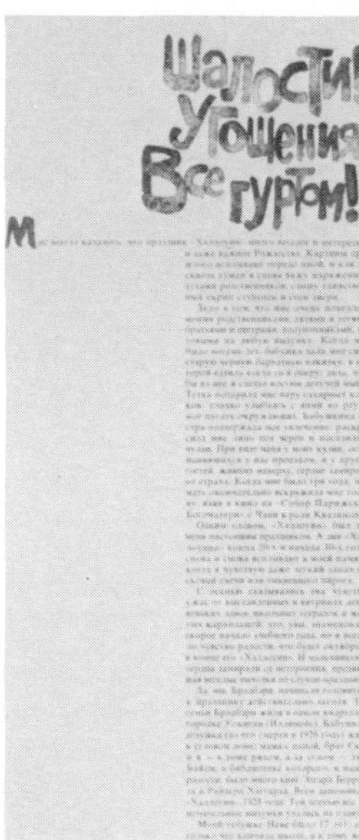
Шалости!
Угощения!
Все гуртом!

268

SAINT COLUMBA'S LEGACY

The Irishness of Irish art

ALEXANDER ELIOT

Up to now the only way to get a sense of medieval Ireland has been to visit the old country's libraries, museums, and remaining ruins. Beginning in October, however, Ireland's chief relics will be on display at Manhattan's Metropolitan Museum, and later in Boston, Philadelphia, Pittsburgh, and San Francisco. Along with 70 metal and precious-stone art works of incalculable importance, the show includes fabulous and fragile illuminated manuscripts. Among them: the *Book of Dimma*, the *Book of Armagh*, the *Book of Durrow*, and one of the four Gospel volumes that comprise the *Book of Kells* in its modern rebinding. Tradition ascribes more than one of these codices to "Himself"—Saint Columba, the patron saint of Irish art and letters. What's so remarkable about these books? Let's examine a single vellum leaf from one of them.

As medieval codices go, the *Book of Durrow* is modest in size, with pages measuring a mere 9½ by 6½ inches. I have selected a page of pure ornamentation called folio 192 verso (*see opposite page*), which seems to me both very beautiful and intensely Irish. Bright-yellow orpiment, glowing lead red, deep-green acetate of copper, a warm black, and the ivory tone of the vellum itself were the artist's main means of expression. What a modern critic might call a vivid "color statement" resulted, and this achieves immediate impact. Yet the ornamentation is not quite so abstract as it seemed at first. In the rectangles at top and bottom, serpents writhe together; and, whether lovingly or in earnest, they bite each other. The serpents appear captive, moreover, loosely tangled in a net of knots like letters running wild. The same curious net reappears in the two flanking rectangles, wherein wolflike creatures bite each other's haunches. What does all this signify? One's thoughts begin wandering with one's glance, baffled and yet aware. This is just the state of mind, I submit, that the artist was aiming to induce. The medallion in the middle of the composition, one now perceives, radiates yellow light from a whirling tangle of colors and snowflakelike figures. At their center appears a tiny Cross—perfectly still.

What a contrast this is to classical aesthetics, which always called for subordination of the parts to the whole. Pull out a coin—a dime, say—and notice how the details are clear and few. Nonrepresentational elements such as lettering stand aside from the main image, which plainly dominates the entire circle. Irish art, however, is the opposite of classical. If one could comb out all the involutions of design to be found in Irish codices, they'd stretch for miles. In these volumes, compression is achieved not by paring away details, but by packing in more and more. This conveys a sense of inhuman energies regressing to infinity, like fine watch springs, or DNA molecules. Here the aesthetic whole—be it a vellum page or even a single initial letter—soon vanishes in contemplation of the parts. It is as if the "little people," the fairies of Irish legend, were casting their spells. Comprehension blurs out as one peers; dreaminess intervenes. These things make one's head spin.

Take the page in question again. Once I've allowed myself to be visually involved, it becomes just as much a tangle of velocities as of colors *per se*. I find myself thinking about the magnetic fields stirred up in cyclotrons, and the millisecond-short lives of particles in flight. Subatomic experiments, however, center on the seeming abyss of the nucleus, whereas the half-abstract representation before us centers on the Cross.

One day in 1868, a Limerick boy went digging for potatoes in the ruins of an old fortified farm called Ardagh. The point of his spade struck something smoother and harder than any spud; the object had a silvery gleam. Falling to his knees, the boy brushed the dirt from the only ancient (*circa* early eighth century) Irish chalice ever found. It is a wide beaten-silver communion cup, ornamented with woven and beaded gold filigree as sinuous as weeds in a rock pool, and inset with fat bronze-veined studs of red and azure glass. To drink from the heavy chalice in Holy Communion, one would have to heave it up in both hands and tilt it toward one's lips. At that moment, but not until then, a rock crystal previously concealed in the hemispheric hollow base of the chalice

ALEXANDER ELIOT, *former art editor of Time magazine and author of many books on art, is a Contributing Editor of Quest/77.*

28 QUEST/77

Book of Durrow's *folio 192 verso is a full-page hand painting that precedes Gospel According to Saint John.*

269

268
Art Director David Moore
Editor Robert Poteete
Designer David Moore
Artist Susan Foster
Publisher U.S. Information Agency
Agency U.S. Information Agency
Client America Illustrated Magazine

269
Art Director Noel Werrett
Writer Alexander Eliot
Designer Noel Werrett
Publisher Ambassador International Cultural Foundation
Client Quest/77

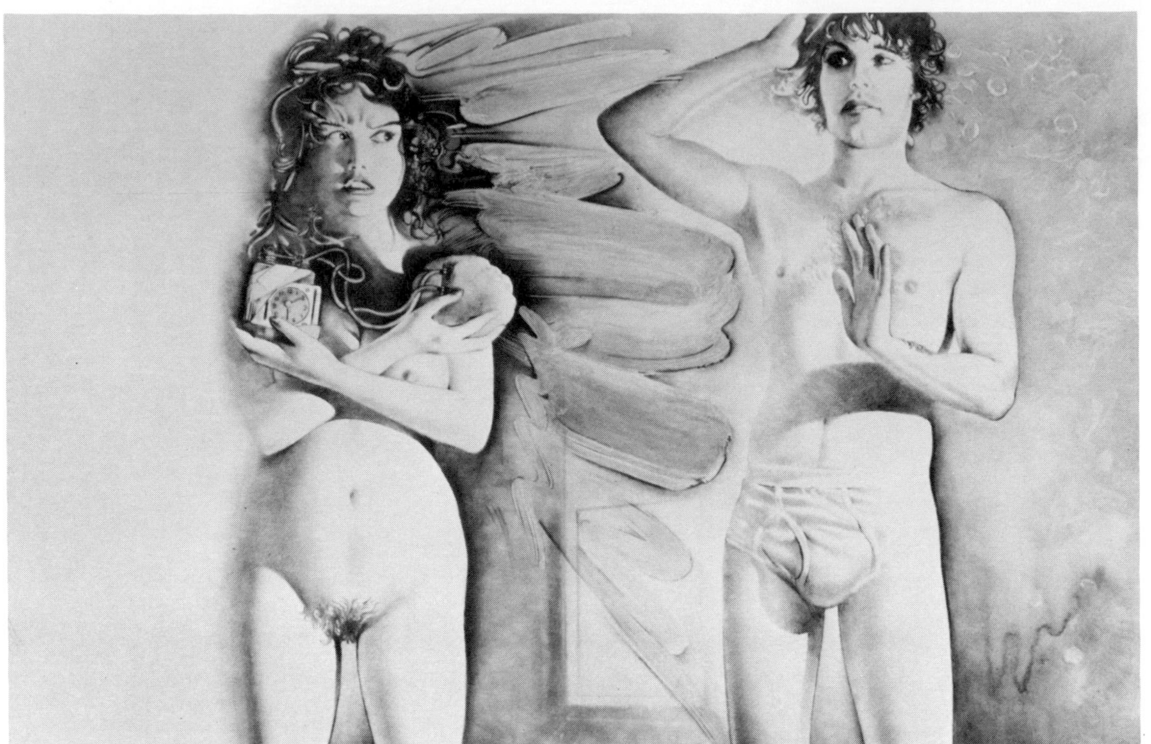

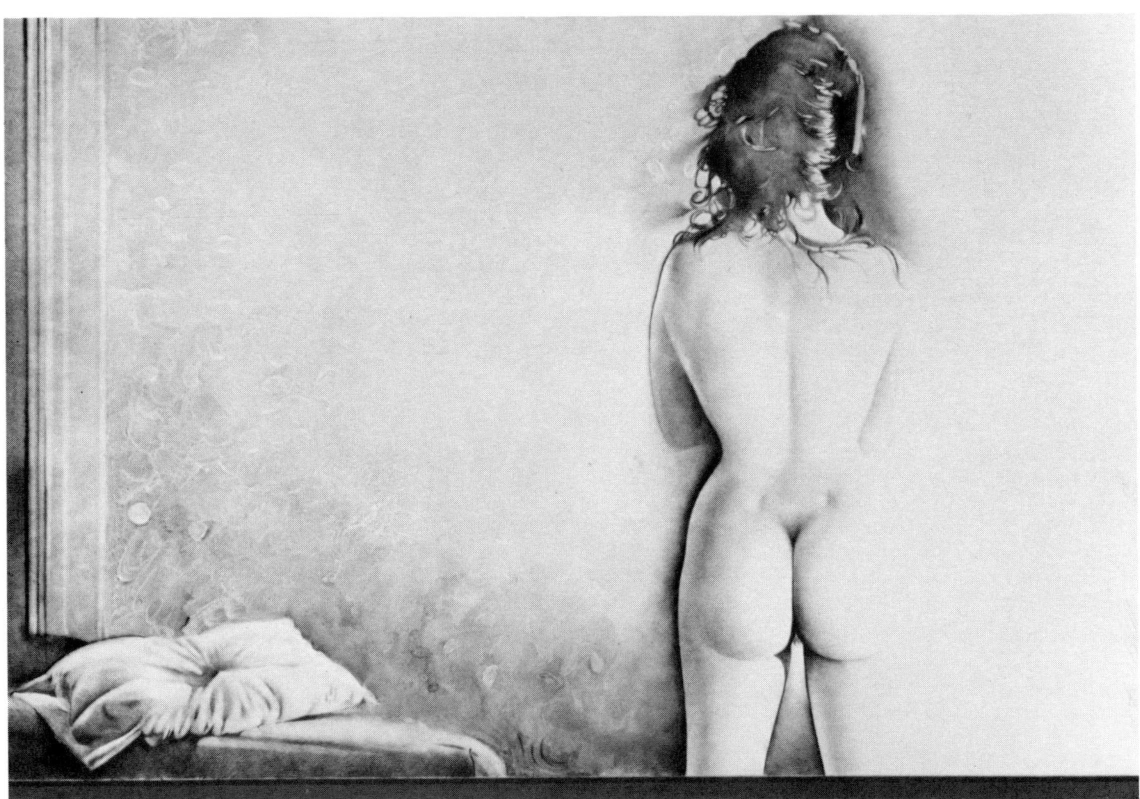

271

SILVER

271

Art Director Arthur Paul
Writer Irwin Shaw
Designer Kerig Pope
Artist Martin Hoffman
Publisher Playboy Enterprises, Inc.
Agency Playboy Magazine

This year's extraordinary Christmas issue was inspired by the man whose self-portrait you will recognize above: Norman Rockwell. And superimposed on the painting (in the same humorous spirit as Rockwell, who often painted his own image into his work) are the two men responsible for this tribute to America's most beloved artist: McCall's art director, Alvin Grossman (immediately to the left), who conceived and planned the entire issue, and photographer Otto Storch, at far left, whose work has often graced our pages.

Grossman's basic idea was to fill this Christmas issue with photographs that would duplicate the spirit of Rockwell's paintings—specifically, to create photographic replicas of the nine favorites you will find on the next page. Storch—who once studied with Rockwell at the Art Students' League in New York and later became his friend (in fact, the studio Storch used for many years had once been Rockwell's)—was the ideal choice to attempt the task. Together, the two men visited Rockwell's hometown of Stockbridge, Massachusetts (which you'll

272
Art Director Alvin Grossman
Designer Alvin Grossman
Photographer Dolores Storch
Publisher The McCall Publishing Company

AMERICA HAS BECOME A DOG RUN

At last year's National Conference on Dog and Cat Control, held in Denver and sponsored by such groups as the American Kennel Club and the American Humane Association, speakers dutifully bemoaned the spiraling public health, safety and ecological hazards created when America became a dog run: An estimated one million citizens are bitten annually, at a cost of \$50–\$75 per bite. Millions of tons of dog waste — dung and urine — are deposited on city streets and lawns, either to be swept away untreated into streams, rivers and other potential sources for drinking water or to lie there to contaminate anyone who might touch it, for instance, children in playgrounds. In Houston alone, the dung of unhealthy dogs — both strays and family pets — seeded the landscape with 178 million hookworm eggs *daily*. Fifteen million dogs and cats are destroyed annually, and 80 percent of them are brought to shelters by their loving owners.

After a rendering of the standard collection of horrors, the conferees issued the inevitable calls for "something to be done." The list of somethings included nothing more than the weary old recommendations trotted out like obedient dogs at every gathering such as this. Pet owners must be told that their friendly beasties are a responsibility. Neutering should be "encouraged." Vets should "counsel" their clients about diseases passed on by their pets. Communities should create "advisory committees" to evaluate the nuisance of stray animals. Lawmakers should be diligent about enforcing regulations. And, of course, people should not let their pets run wild.

Since this gassy conference issued its meaningless recommendations, dogs have continued to bite; defecate; pollute;

SNARL

copulate; cause auto accidents; strain municipal, state and federal budgets; damage property; contaminate and lower the quality of life in immeasurable ways. And dogs are only part of what is clearly both a pet mania and pet menace. Figures offered by one of the so-called humane groups document that America is the world's largest zoo: We have, by conservative estimate, 23 million pet birds, 340 million fish and 125 million exotic pets ranging from monkeys, snakes, turtles and hamsters to iguanas, gorillas and even lions. Together they carry 40 diseases that can be transmitted to humans, devour more than 3.7 million tons of food every year and cost — another conservative estimate — \$500 million annually in control programs.

Little of this would be worth discussing, except that much of the immense cost of this derangement is imposed on people like me who love animals so much that we refuse to own them. The costs are not limited to the medical bills paying for bite treatments, nor the \$500 million for shelters and spaying clinics. They reach also into the budgets of numerous federal agencies. Commercial dog dealers alone, many of which are the puppy mills marketing dogs that will end up in the municipal death mills, involve no less than 16 federal agencies in their regulation: the Departments of Agriculture, Interior, HEW, Labor, Commerce, Treasury, Justice, the ICC, CAB, FAA, EPA, FTC, SBA, the Consumer Product Safety Commission, the Postal Service, and the Occupational Safety and Health Administration. Who is paying for all these bureaucrats to regulate the dog merchants? Citizens are, many of them victimized in more harmful ways than mere wounds to the pocketbook.

The most effective solution to the imbalance costs of this immense crisis is for government agencies to stop pawing at the ground and realize the

Colman McCarthy is an editorial writer for The Washington Post.

BY COLMAN McCARTHY

273

The Clean Sound of Music

by Dave Marsh

Good grooming for your record collection

Because the bulk of my work as a music critic involves listening to records (often, rest assured, more profitably than pleasurably), I can't be overly conscientious in keeping my twelve-hundred-disc collection spick-and-span. Hi-fi buffs recommend that records be cleaned before and after each listening. I'd drive them nuts. Still, I do want my records to last. And since I suspect that most record buyers are more fanatical about pleasure than the absolutes of quality care, the tips I've acquired and the products I've learned about over the years might be more useful than a set of rigid standards.

Records are for listening. But the nature of the device that makes listening possible is disintegrative: the cumulative result of

Dave Marsh is an associate editor and rock critic for Rolling Stone.

Photographed by John Wilkes

274

273
Art Director Gordon Mortensen
Editor David Sanford
Designer Gordon Mortensen
Artist Ed Soyka
Publisher Politics Today (formerly Skeptic Magazine)
Client Politics Today (formerly Skeptic Magazine

274
Art Director Michael Gross
Writer Dave Marsh
Designer Judy Schiern Hecker
Photographer John Wilkes
Publisher Esquire Inc.
Client Esquire Magazine

УЧЕТ ОБЩЕСТВЕННОГО МНЕНИЯ

ДАНИЭЛ Б. МОСКОВИЦ

275

275
Art Director David Moore
Editor Robert Poteete
Designer Dorothy Fall
Artist Barbara Alu
Publisher America Illustrated Magazine
Agency U. S. Information Agency
Client America Illustrated Magazine

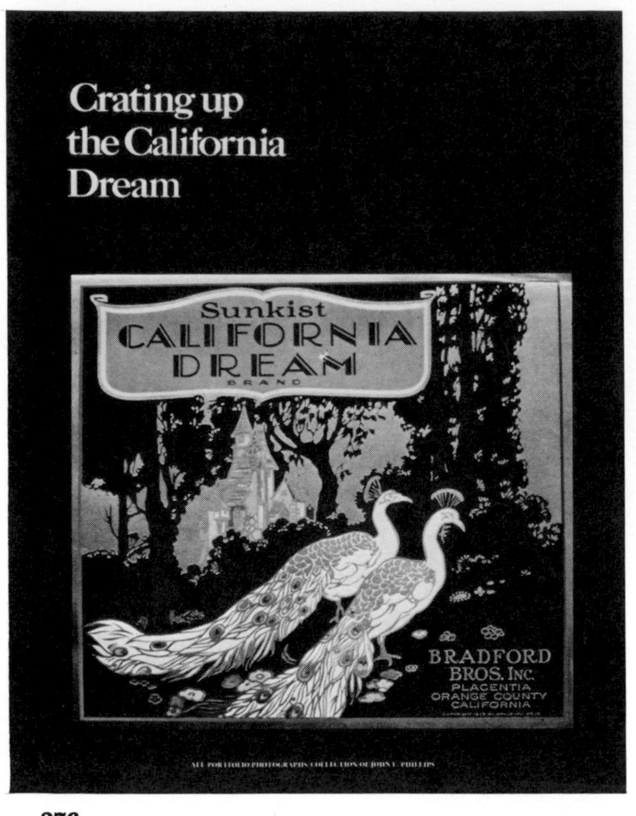

276

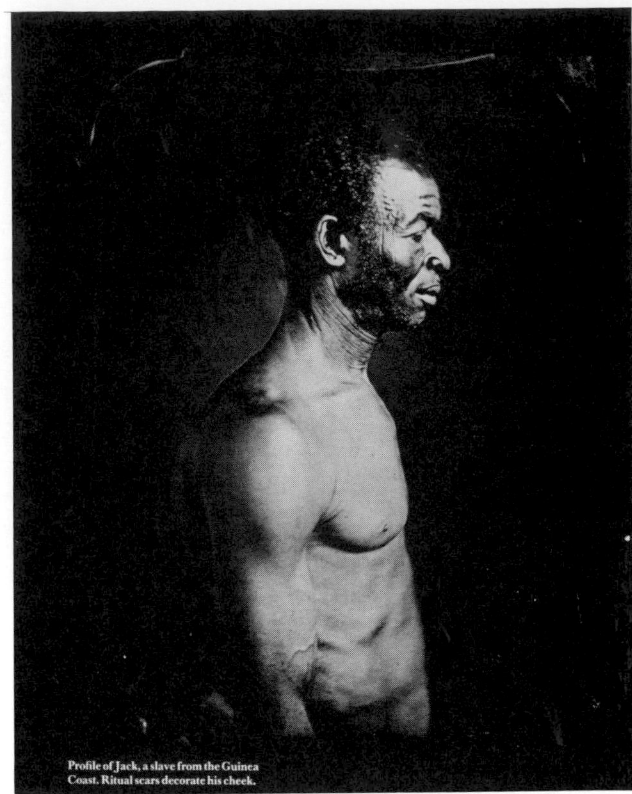

Profile of Jack, a slave from the Guinea Coast. Ritual scars decorate his cheek.

277

In the spring of 1976, Ross Sterling was a lawyer at John Connally's Houston firm. President Ford wanted Connally's help against Ronald Reagan. In April, Ford nominated Sterling to the U.S. district court. In July, Connally endorsed Ford. Ford beat Reagan, but lost in November. Now he plays pro-am golf. And Ross Sterling is still a federal judge.

THE POLITICS OF PICKING FEDERAL JUDGES

by James Goodman

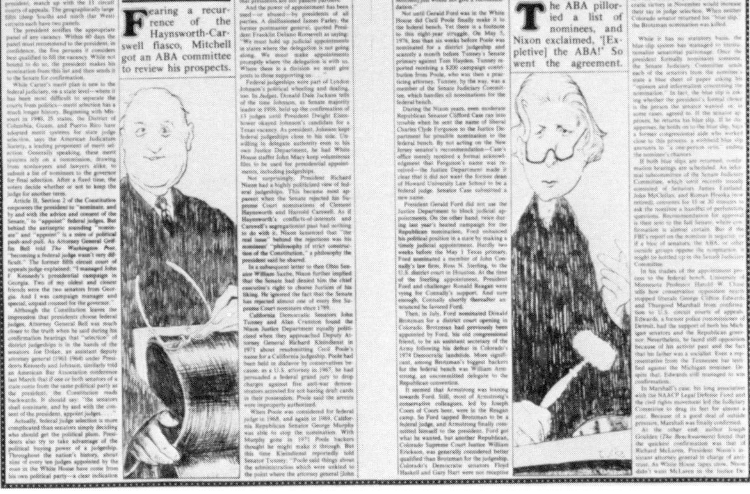

Fearing a recurrence of the Haynsworth-Carswell fiasco, Mitchell got an ABA committee to review his prospects.

The ABA pilloried a list of nominees, and Nixon exclaimed, '[Expletive] the ABA!' So went the agreement.

278

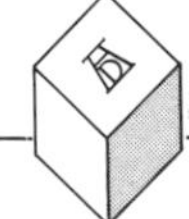

GOLD

276	
Art Director	Emma Landau
Writer	John L. Phillips
Designer	Emma Landau
Photographer	John L. Phillips
Publisher	American Heritage Publishing Co.

277	
Art Director	Emma Landau
Writer	Elinor Reichlin
Designer	Emma Landau
Credit	The President and Fellows of Harvard College, Peabody Museum, Harvard University
Publisher	American Heritage Publishing Co.

278	
Art Director	John C. Jay
Editor	Zachary Sklar
Designer	John C. Jay
Artist	Richard Tulka
Publisher	MBA Communications, Inc.
Client	MBA Communications, Inc.

TREE SENSE

EDITED BY TONY JONES

Trees suffer from familiarity. We take their miracles too much for granted. But indifference to trees is a sign of idiocy. They are sources of joy and calm. Their beauty and shade offer profound pleasures. Yet aesthetics are only the beginning: trees are absolutely essential to human life. They hold the soil in place, clean the air, create watersheds, give food, shelter wildlife, and make weather. They supply lumber and fuel and all the paper we use. Civilization is predicated on the tree. Without trees, there is only desert.

It is vital, then, to attend to tree questions. How can we use trees to stop the march of deserts around the planet? How can we develop their crop potential into an agriculture to replace the orthodox exploitative kind? How can we use biomass plantations to manufacture energy on an indefinitely renewable basis? How might trees teach us about natural rhythms, or enlarge our sense of time, or show that nourishment requires rootedness below and receptivity above?

The following pages discuss these and other possibilities. But the main point is that trees need attention. This is not something that can simply be left to the experts, whoever they may be. Governments and bureaucracies do poorly with living things, trees no exception. We *all* need to be concerned, even if the only space we give trees is in our minds.

A good place to start is with a personal tree census. Count, examine, identify, classify, evaluate, feel the trees you find around you. Try to bring trees more into your consciousness. Then, once you've taken stock, you can decide where and how to add to the totals.

Unchopping a Tree

by W. S. Merwin

Start with the leaves, the small twigs, and the nests that have been shaken, ripped, or broken off by the fall; these must be gathered and attached once again to their respective places. It is not arduous work, unless major limbs have been smashed or mutilated. If the fall was carefully and correctly planned, the chances of anything of the kind happening will have been reduced. Again, much depends upon the size, age, shape, and species of the tree. Still, you will be lucky if you can get through this stage without having to use machinery. Even in the best of circumstances it is a labor that will make you wish often that you had won the favor of the universe of ants, the empire of mice, or at least a local tribe of squirrels, and could enlist their labors and their talents. But no, they leave you to it. They have learned, with time. This is men's work. It goes without saying that if the tree was hollow in whole or in part, and contained old nests of bird or mammal or insect, or hoards of nuts, or such structures as wasps or bees build for their survival, the contents will have to be repaired where necessary and reassembled, insofar as possible, in their original order, including the shells of nuts already opened. With spiders' webs you must simply do the best you can. We do not have the spider's weaving equipment, nor any substitute for the leaf's living bond with its point of attachment and nourishment. It is even harder to simulate the latter when the leaves have once become dry—as they are bound to do, for this is not the labor of a moment. Also it hardly needs saying that this is the time for repairing any neighboring trees or bushes or other growth that may have been damaged by the fall. The same rules apply. Where neighboring trees were of the same species it is difficult not to waste time conveying a detached leaf back to the wrong tree. Practice, practice. Put your hope in that.

Now the tackle must be put into place, or the scaffolding, depending on the surroundings and the dimensions of the tree. It is ticklish work. Almost always it involves, in itself, further damage to the area, which will have to be corrected later. But as you've heard, it can't be helped. And care now is likely to save you considerable trouble later. Be careful to grind nothing into the ground.

At last the time comes for the erecting of the trunk. By now it will scarcely be necessary to remind you of the delicacy of this huge skeleton. Every motion of the tackle, every slight upward heave of the trunk, the branches, their elaborately reassembled panoply of leaves (now dead) will draw from you an involuntary gasp. You will watch for a leaf or a twig to be snapped off yet again. You will listen for the nuts to shift in the hollow limb and you will hear whether they are indeed falling into place or are spilling in disorder, in which case—or in the event of anything else of the kind—operations will have to cease, of course, while you correct the matter. The raising itself is no small enterprise, from the moment when the chains tighten around the old bandages until the bole hangs vertical above the stump, splinter above splinter. Now the final straightening of the splinters themselves can take place (the preliminary work is best done while the wood is still green and soft, but at times when the splinters are not badly twisted most of the straightening is left until now, when the torn ends are face to face with each other).

TREE SENSE
16-page Potentials Section
30 lb. stock/500,000 print run
requires
13 Tons of Paper
69 SPRUCE TREES
36 ASPEN TREES
116 JACK PINES
(Average size: 25' height, 8" diameter)

When the splinters are perfectly complementary the appropriate fixative is applied. Again we have no duplicate of the original substance. Ours is extremely strong, but it is rigid. It is limited to surfaces, and there is no play in it. However, the core is not the part of the trunk that conducted life from the roots up into the branches and back again. It was relatively inert. The fixative for this part is not the same as the one for the outer layers and the bark, and if either of these is involved in the splintered section they must receive applications of the appropriate adhesives. Apart from being incorrect and probably ineffective, the core fixative would leave a scar on the bark.

When all is ready, the splintered trunk is lowered onto the splinters of the stump. This, one might say, is only the skeleton of the resurrection. Now the chips must be gathered, and the sawdust, and returned to their former positions. The fixative for the wood layers will be applied to chips and sawdust consisting only of wood. Chips and sawdust consisting of several substances will receive applications of the correct adhesives. It is as well, where possible, to shelter the materials from the elements while working. Weathering makes it harder to identify the smaller fragments. Bark sawdust in particular the earth lays claim to very quickly. You must find your own ways of coping with this problem. There is a certain beauty, you will notice at moments, in the pattern of the chips as they are fitted back into place. You will wonder to what extent it should be described as natural, to what extent man-made. It will lead you on to speculations about the parentage of beauty itself, to which you will return.

The adhesive for the chips is translucent, and not so rigid as that for the splinters. That for the bark and its subcutaneous layers is transparent and runs into the fibers on either side, partially dissolving them into each other. It does not set the sap flowing again but it does pay a kind of tribute to the preoccupations of the ancient thoroughfares. You could not roll an egg over the joints but some of the mine shafts would still be passable, no doubt, for the first exploring insect who raises its head in the tight echoless passages. The day comes when it is all restored, even to the moss (now dead) over the wound. You will sleep badly, thinking of the removal of the scaffolding that must begin the next morning. How you will hope for sun and a still day!

The removal of the scaffolding or tackle is not so dangerous, perhaps, to the surroundings as its installation, but it presents problems. It should be taken from the spot piece by piece as it is detached, and stored at a distance. You have come to accept it there, around the tree. The sky begins to look naked as the chains and struts one by one vacate their positions. Finally the moment arrives when the last sustaining piece is removed, and the tree stands again on its own. It is as though its weight for a moment stood on your heart. You listen for a thud of settlement, a warning creak deep in the intricate joinery. You cannot believe it will hold. How like something dreamed it is, standing there all by itself. How long will it stand there now? The first breeze that touches its dead leaves all seems to flow into your mouth. You are afraid the motion of the clouds will be enough to push it over. What more can you do? What more can you do?

But there is nothing more you can do.

Others are waiting.

Everything is going to have to be put back.

W. S. Merwin is a poet. This piece of prose is reproduced from The Miner's Pale Children *(Atheneum, N.Y.), copyright © 1970 by W. S. Merwin.*

279

GRAVURE PORTFOLIO

LILO RAYMOND

Photographing the quiet evidence of people

BY ALICIA WILLE

Amidst the multifarious commerce and chaos of New York City's 14th Street, Lilo Raymond has created a haven of quiet domestic beauty and light. The apartment where she lives and works is spacious and unpretentious. Turn-of-the-century walls and moldings that have been painted white one too many times suggest the same soft-tone modulations of white found in the photographer's work. Raymond's setting is an expression of the same warm esthetic which informs her still lifes.

Lilo Raymond lives with and celebrates simple things. Yet, the sense of well-being and calm she evokes through her art is not a simple effect. It denotes the visual sensitivity and craftsmanship of an accomplished camera artist.

It would be true and yet a gross underestimation of the artist's work to say that she photographs inert and commonplace things. She does photograph everyday objects, but she imbues them with an amiability that the objects themselves do not necessarily have. Her subjects are human in scale, "the quieter evidences of people. These are objects people make or put someplace. God makes apples and vegetables, which I love, but I know that I like them because they have something to do with people."

What Lilo Raymond captures is more than the integrity of these objects in and of themselves. Edward Weston celebrated the quintessence of the pepper in all its pepperness. Raymond celebrates both "the pepper" and its place within a human setting. She is photographing a personal rapport with these objects and so inviting us to regard them in a similarly benevolent way.

But Raymond would be the first to say that it

Vase, New York, 1976

280

279
Art Director Noel Werrett
Writer Tony Jones
Designer Miriam Berman
Publisher Ambassador International Cultural Foundation
Client Quest '77

280
Art Director Shinichiro Tora
Writer Alicia Wille
Designer Shinichiro Tora
Photographer Lilo Raymond
Publisher Ziff-Davis Publishing Co.
Client Popular Photography

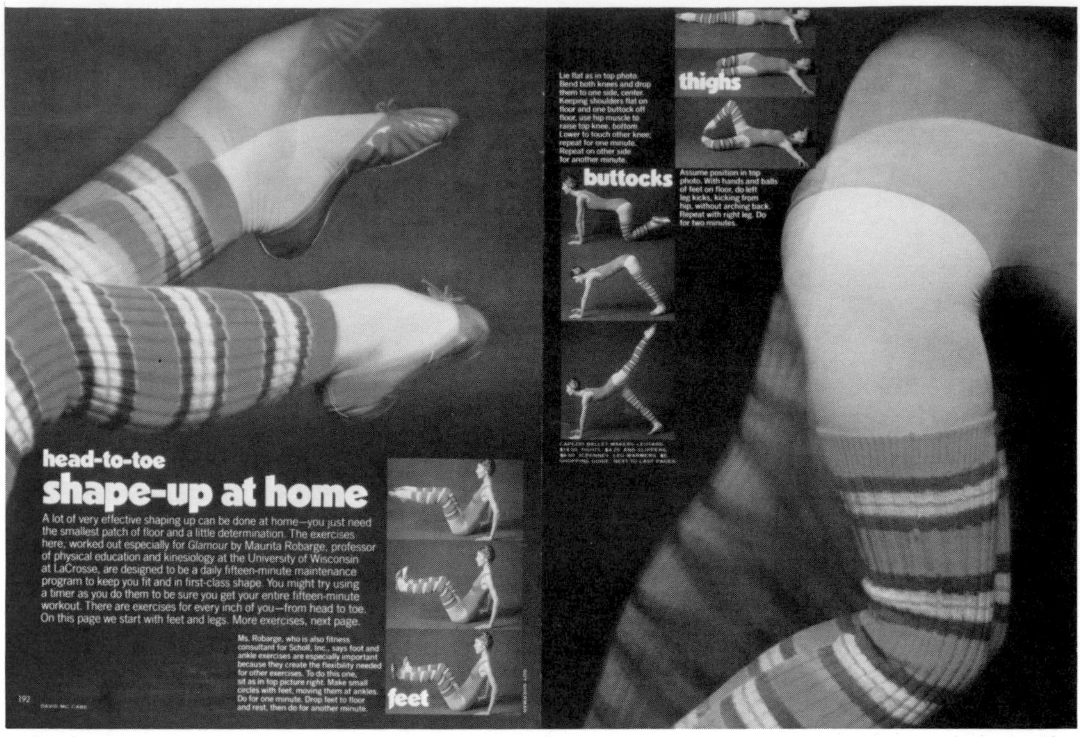

head-to-toe
shape-up at home

A lot of very effective shaping up can be done at home—you just need the smallest patch of floor and a little determination. The exercises here, worked out especially for *Glamour* by Maurita Robarge, professor of physical education and kinesiology at the University of Wisconsin at LaCrosse, are designed to be a daily fifteen-minute maintenance program to keep you fit and in first-class shape. You might try using a timer as you do them to be sure you get your entire fifteen-minute workout. There are exercises for every inch of you—from head to toe. On this page we start with feet and legs. More exercises, next page.

Ms. Robarge, who is also fitness consultant for Scholl, Inc., says foot and ankle exercises are especially important because they create the flexibility needed for other exercises. To do this one, sit as in top picture right. Make small circles with feet, moving them at ankles. Do for one minute. Drop feet to floor and rest, then do for another minute.

feet

192

thighs

Lie flat as in top photo. Bend both knees and drop them to one side, center. Keeping shoulders flat on floor and one buttock off floor, use hip muscle to raise top knee, bottom. Lower to touch other knee; repeat for one minute. Repeat on other side for another minute.

buttocks

Assume position in top photo. With hands and balls of feet on floor, do left leg kicks, kicking from hip, without arching back. Repeat with right leg. Do for two minutes.

281

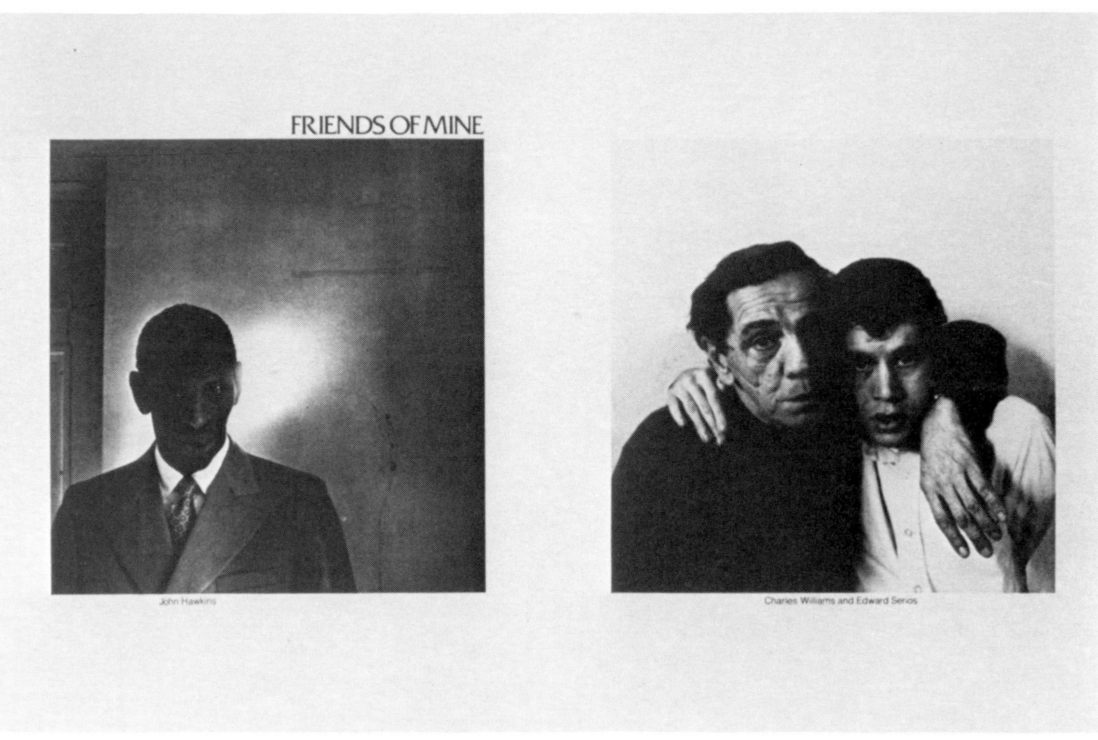

John Hawkins

Charles Williams and Edward Serios

282

281
Art Director George Hartman
Designer George Hartman
Photographer David McCabe
Publisher Condé Nast Publications Inc.
Client Glamour Magazine

282
Art Director Shinichiro Tora
Writer Arthur Gildsmith
Designer Shinichiro Tora
Photographer Richmond Jones
Publisher Ziff-Davis Publishing Co.
Client Popular Photography

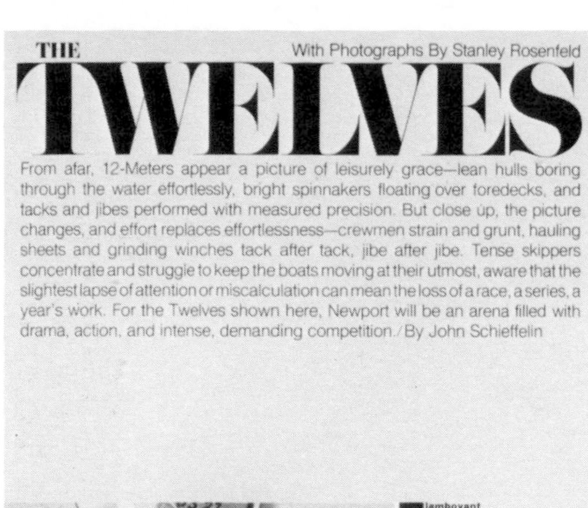

THE

TWELVES

With Photographs By Stanley Rosenfeld

From afar, 12-Meters appear a picture of leisurely grace—lean hulls boring through the water effortlessly, bright spinnakers floating over foredecks, and tacks and jibes performed with measured precision. But close up, the picture changes, and effort replaces effortlessness—crewmen strain and grunt, hauling sheets and grinding winches tack after tack, jibe after jibe. Tense skippers concentrate and struggle to keep the boats moving at their utmost, aware that the slightest lapse of attention or miscalculation can mean the loss of a race, a series, a year's work. For the Twelves shown here, Newport will be an arena filled with drama, action, and intense, demanding competition./By John Schieffelin

Flamboyant baseball tycoon Ted Turner (right) pushed '74 Cup winner *Courageous* to early front-runner position, taking first 12 of 13 trials races. A new deck and rig are the only major changes to S&S-designed boat. Left: Early skirmishes between *Courageous* and *Enterprise* proved embarrassing for *Enterprise*, sailmaker Lowell North's command. The newest design of Sparkman & Stephens, *Enterprise* is largely a West Coast effort, although officially owned by N.Y.'s Maritime College at Fort Schuyler.

66 BOATING

Skipper, sailmaker, and designer Ted Hood had teething troubles, a few successes in early going aboard *Independence* (right). Members of New York Yacht Club Selection Committee (bottom) eye *Independence* and *Courageous* from bridge of motor yacht. Heeling to crisp breeze, *Enterprise* shows off form that made her early favorite.

283

283
Art Director Shelley Heller
Writer John Schieffelin
Designer Shelley Heller
Photographer Stanley Rosenfeld
Publisher Ziff-Davis Publishing Co.
Client Boating Magazine

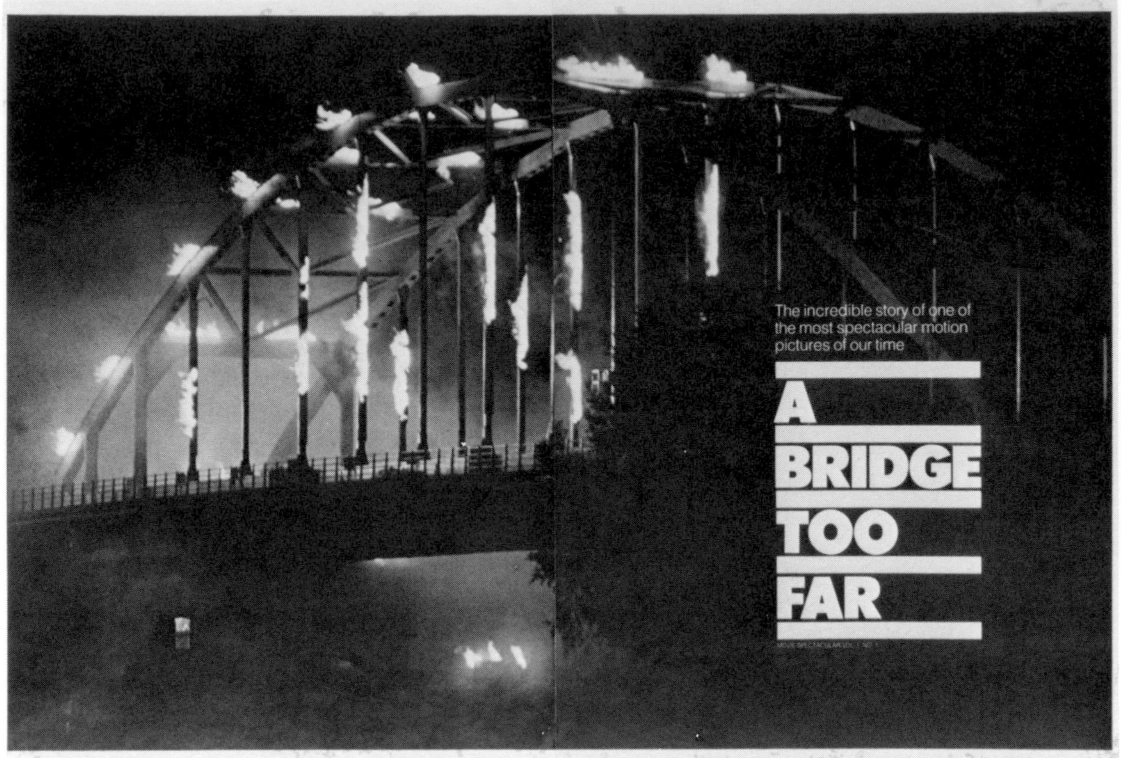

An unknown wounded soldier asks, "My God, why am I still alive?"

284

284
Art Director John Newcomb
Writer Nancy Fitzpatrick
Designer John Newcomb
Photographers Frank Connors
Robert Penn
Producer Porter Bibb
Publisher The New York Times
Client The New York Times

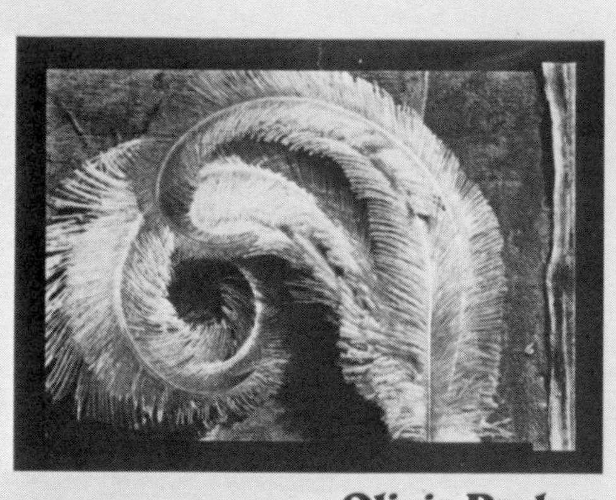

Olivia Parker

This sensitive young photographer searches for both man-made and natural forms that please her and then casts them in silver for posterity, as baby shoes are cast in bronze. Parker describes the process by which she achieves her luminous, metallic two-color effect as "split-toning," or so it was called by the only other person she had ever seen practice it, her view-camera instructor. The toner she uses is selenium; the only other deviation from the norm is that the time for it is longer than the usual 3-5 minutes, but rather for as long as 10. She decides the exact length of time by pulling the print when the desired effect has been reached. Her printing paper (contact) is silver chloride rather than the more common bromide. She points out that darker tones in the images tend to go a deep rust, light tones, bluish.

Parker does free-lance photography out of Manchester, Mass.

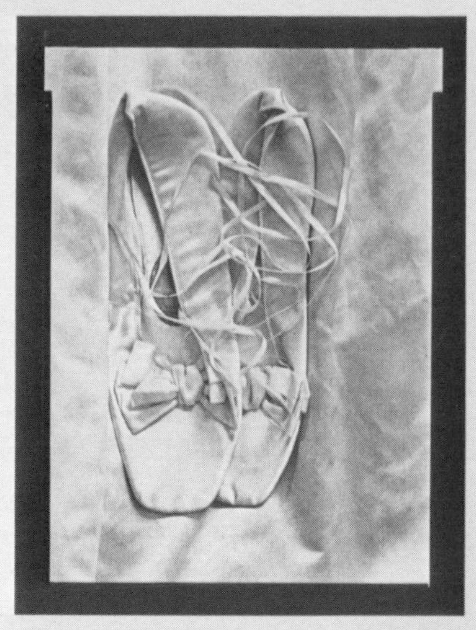

285

МЕНЬШЕ
ЧИЩЕ
БЕЗОПАСНЕЕ

АМЕРИКАНСКИЕ АВТОМОБИЛИ

286

285

Art Director Thomas Ridinger
Writer Jim Hughes
Designer Thomas Ridinger
Photographer Olivia Parker
Publisher Ziff-Davis Publishing Co.
Agency Ziff-Davis Publishing Co.
Client Photography Annual

286

Art Director David Moore
Editor Robert Poteete
Designers David Moore
Dorothy Fall
Patricia Gipple
Artist pp. 40-41 Joseph Farris

Photographers Andrew Sacks
General Motors Corporation
Robert Pelletier
Ford Motor Company
American Motors Corporation
Chrysler Corporation
International Harvester Comp
Joseph Farris
Publisher U. S. Information Agency
Agency U. S. Information Agency
Client America Illustrated Magazine

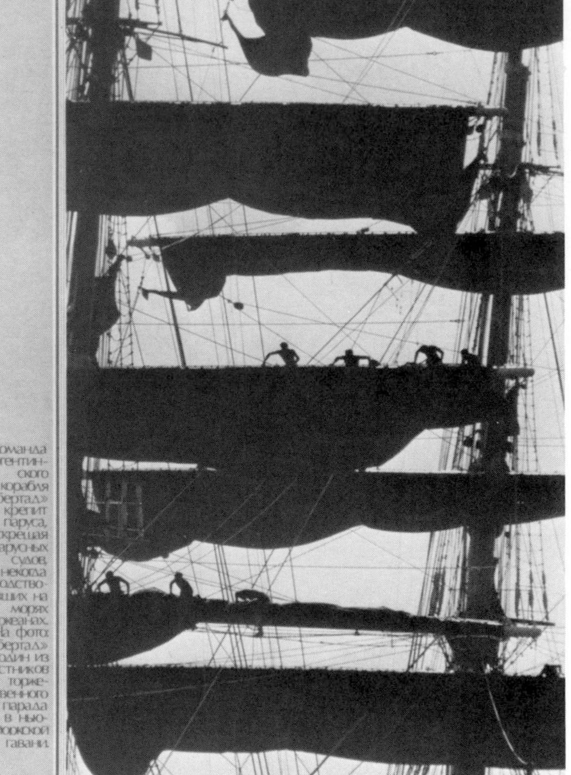

287

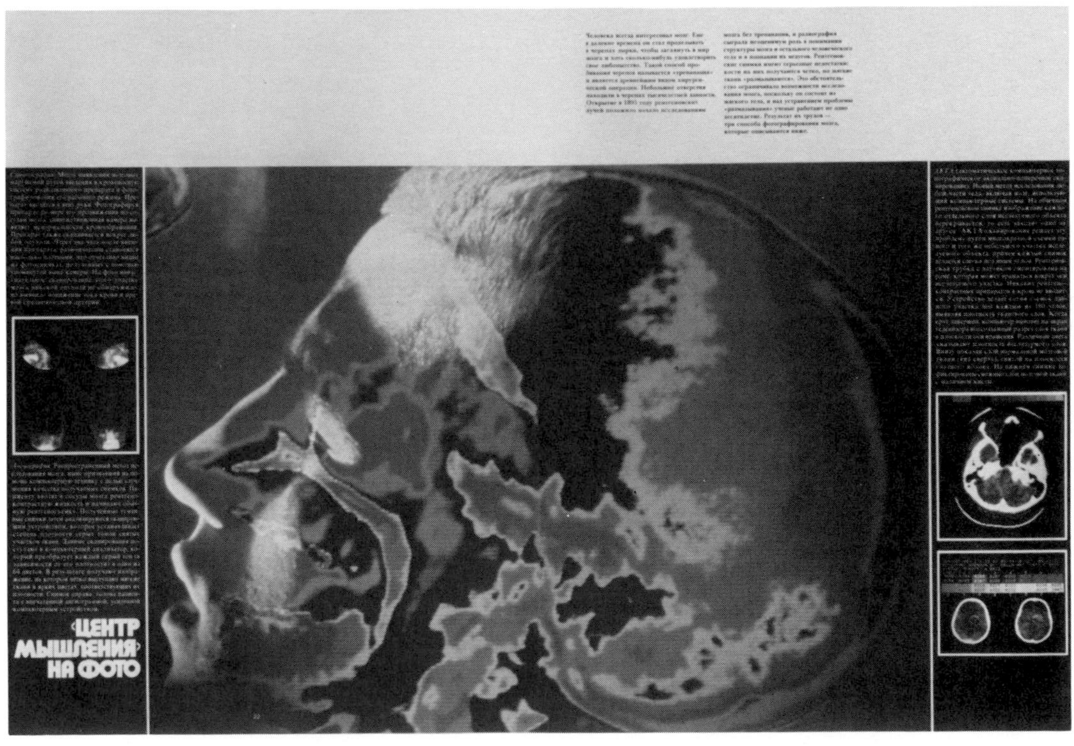

288

287

Art Director	David Moore
Editor	Robert Poteete
Designer	Dorothy Fall
Photographers	Tomas Sennett
	Ortiz/Sander
	John McDermott
	Kenneth Garrett
	John McDermott
Publisher	U. S. Information Agency
Agency	U. S. Information Agency
Client	America Illustrated Magazine

288

Art Director	David Moore
Editor	Robert Poteete
Designer	Patricia Gipple
Artist	Martim Alvillez (from Harper's Magazine)
Photographers	Searle Radiographics Inc.
	Howard J. Sochurek
	Dr. Robert S. Ledley
	Georgetown University Medical Center
	National Biomedical Research Foundation
Publisher	U. S. Information Agency
Agency	U. S. Information Agency
Client	America Illustrated Magazine

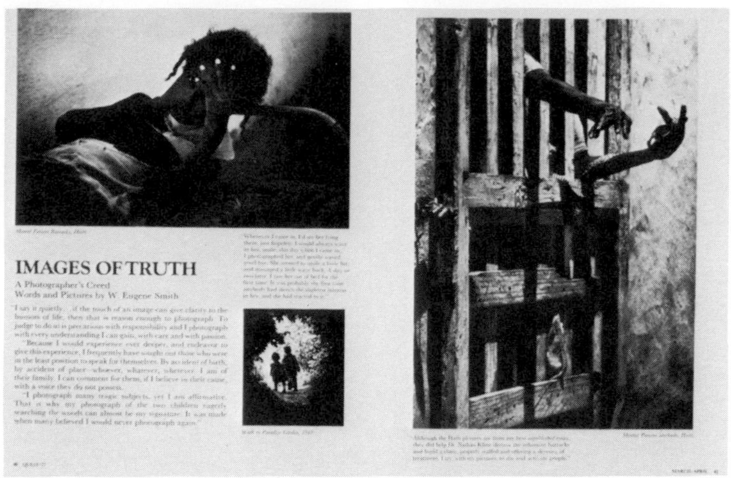

IMAGES OF TRUTH

A Photographer's Creed

Words and Pictures by W. Eugene Smith

289

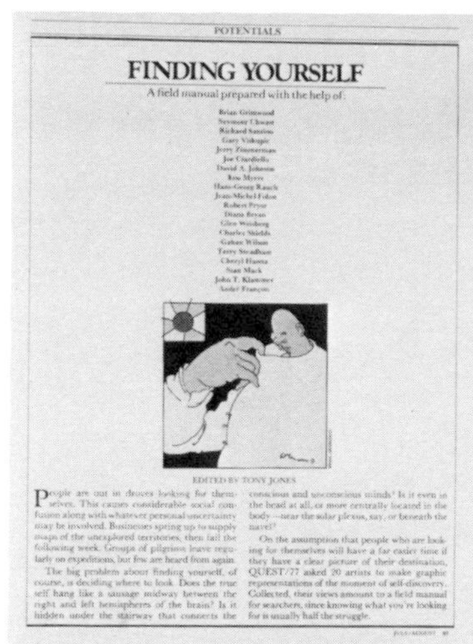

POTENTIALS

FINDING YOURSELF

A field manual prepared with the help of:

EDITED BY TONY JONES

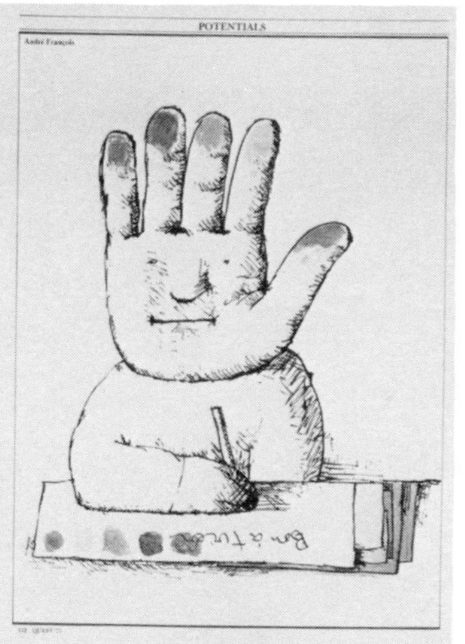

POTENTIALS

290

291

GOLD

289
Art Director Noel Werrett
Writer W. Eugene Smith
Designer Noel Werrett
Photographer W. Eugene Smith
Publisher Ambassador International Cultural Foundation
Client Quest/77

290
Art Director Noel Werrett
Writer Tony Jones
Designers Noel Werrett, Bart Drury
Publisher Ambassador International Cultural Foundation
Client Quest/77

291
Art Director Tamara Schneider
Designer Tamara Schneider
Artist Isadore Seltzer
Publisher Seventeen Magazine
Client Seventeen Magazine

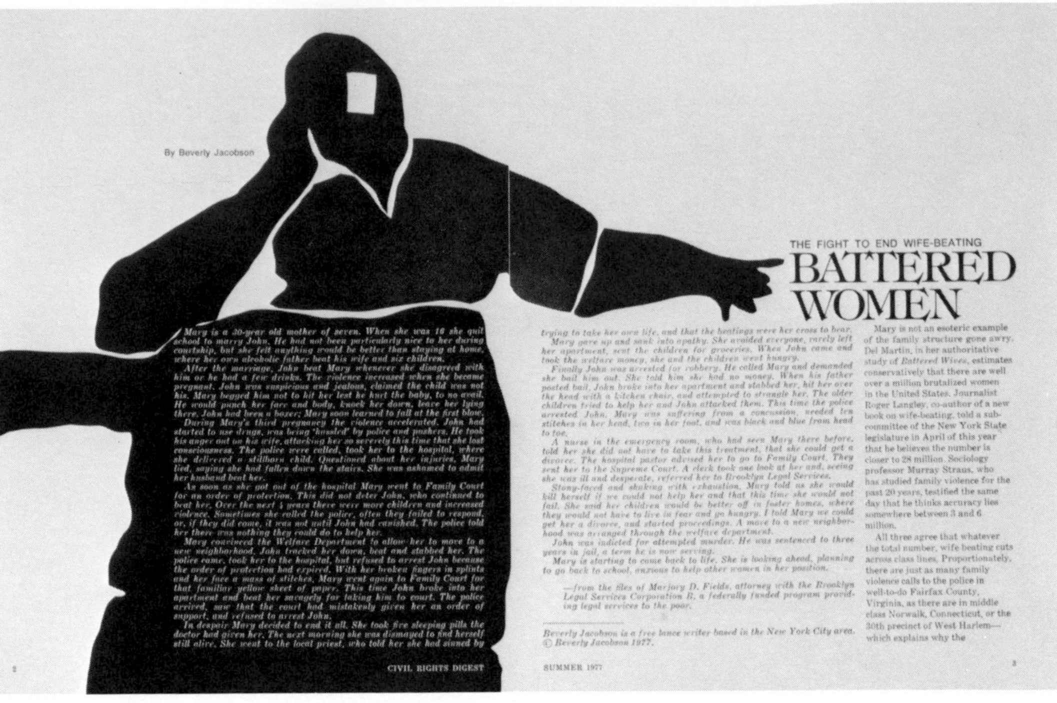

By Beverly Jacobson

THE FIGHT TO END WIFE-BEATING

BATTERED WOMEN

Mary is a 30-year old mother of seven. When she was 16 she quit school to marry John. He had not been particularly nice to her during courtship, but she felt anything would be better than staying at home, where her own alcoholic father beat his wife and six children.

After the marriage, John beat Mary whenever she disagreed with him or he had a few drinks. The violence increased when she became pregnant. John was suspicious and jealous, claimed the child was not his. Mary begged him not to hit her lest he hurt the baby, to no avail. He would punch her face and body, knock her down, leave her lying there. John had been a boxer; Mary soon learned to fall at the first blow.

During Mary's third pregnancy the violence accelerated. John had started to use drugs, was being "hassled" by police and pushers. He took his anger out on his wife, attacking her so severely this time that she lost consciousness. The police were called, took her to the hospital, where she delivered a stillborn child. Questioned about her injuries, Mary lied, saying she had fallen down the stairs. She was ashamed to admit her husband beat her.

As soon as she got out of the hospital Mary went to Family Court for an order of protection. This did not deter John, who continued to beat her. Over the next 5 years there were more children and increased violence. Sometimes she called the police, often they failed to respond, or, if they did come, it was not until John had vanished. The police told her there was nothing they could do to help her.

Mary convinced the Welfare Department to allow her to move to a new neighborhood. John tracked her down, beat and stabbed her. The police came, took her to the hospital, but refused to arrest John because the order of protection had expired. With her broken fingers in splints and her face a mass of stitches, Mary went again to Family Court for that familiar yellow sheet of paper. This time John broke into her apartment and beat her savagely for taking him to court. The police arrived, saw that the court had mistakenly given her an order of support, and refused to arrest John.

In despair Mary decided to end it all. She took five sleeping pills the doctor had given her. The next morning she was dismayed to find herself still alive. She went to the local priest, who told her she had sinned by trying to take her own life, and that the beatings were her cross to bear.

Mary gave up and sank into apathy. She avoided everyone, rarely left her apartment, sent the children for groceries. When John came and took the welfare money, she and the children went hungry.

Finally John was arrested for robbery. He called Mary and demanded she bail him out. She told him she had no money. When his father posted bail, John broke into her apartment and stabbed her, hit her over the head with a kitchen chair, and attempted to strangle her. The older children tried to help her and John attacked them. This time the police arrested John. Mary was suffering from a concussion, needed ten stitches in her head, two in her foot, and was black and blue from head to toe.

A nurse in the emergency room, who had seen Mary there before, told her she did not have to take this treatment, that she could get a divorce. The hospital pastor advised her to go to Family Court. They sent her to the Supreme Court. A clerk took one look at her and, seeing she was ill and desperate, referred her to Brooklyn Legal Services.

Stony-faced and shaking with exhaustion, Mary told us she would kill herself if we could not help her and that this time she would not fail. She said her children would be better off in foster homes, where they would not have to live in fear and go hungry. I told Mary we could get her a divorce, and started proceedings. A move to a new neighborhood was arranged through the welfare department.

John was indicted for attempted murder. He was sentenced to three years in jail, a term he is now serving.

Mary is starting to come back to life. She is looking ahead, planning to go back to school, anxious to help other women in her position.

—from the files of Marjory D. Fields, attorney with the Brooklyn Legal Services Corporation B, a federally funded program providing legal services to the poor.

Beverly Jacobson is a free lance writer based in the New York City area. © Beverly Jacobson 1977.

Mary is not an esoteric example of the family structure gone awry. Del Martin, in her authoritative study of *Battered Wives*, estimates conservatively that there are well over a million brutalized women in the United States. Journalist Roger Langley, co-author of a new book on wife-beating, told a subcommittee of the New York State legislature in April of this year that he believes the number is closer to 28 million. Sociology professor Murray Straus, who has studied family violence for the past 20 years, testified the same day that he thinks accuracy lies somewhere between 3 and 6 million.

All three agree that whatever the total number, wife beating cuts across class lines. Proportionately, there are just as many family violence calls to the police in well-to-do Fairfax County, Virginia, as there are in middle class Norwalk, Connecticut, or the 30th precinct of West Harlem—which explains why the

2 CIVIL RIGHTS DIGEST SUMMER 1977 3

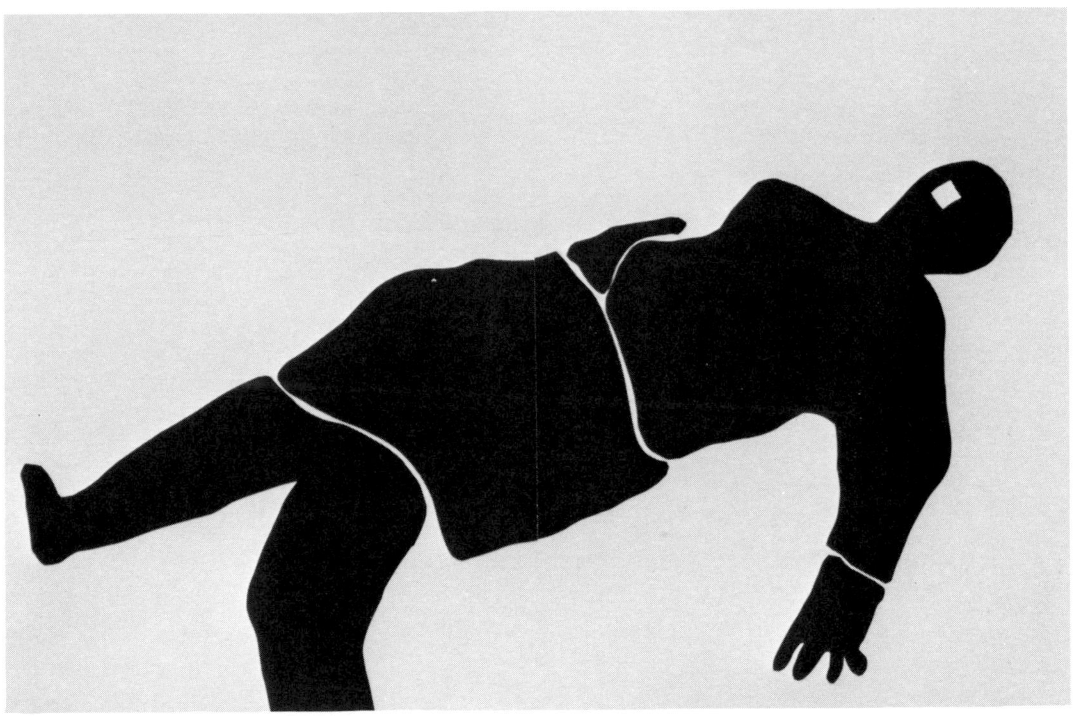

292

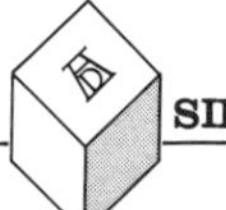

SILVER

292

Art Directors	Del Harrod
	Joseph Swanson
Designer	Del Harrod
Artist	Del Harrod
Agency	U.S. Commission on Civil Rights
Client	Civil Rights Digest

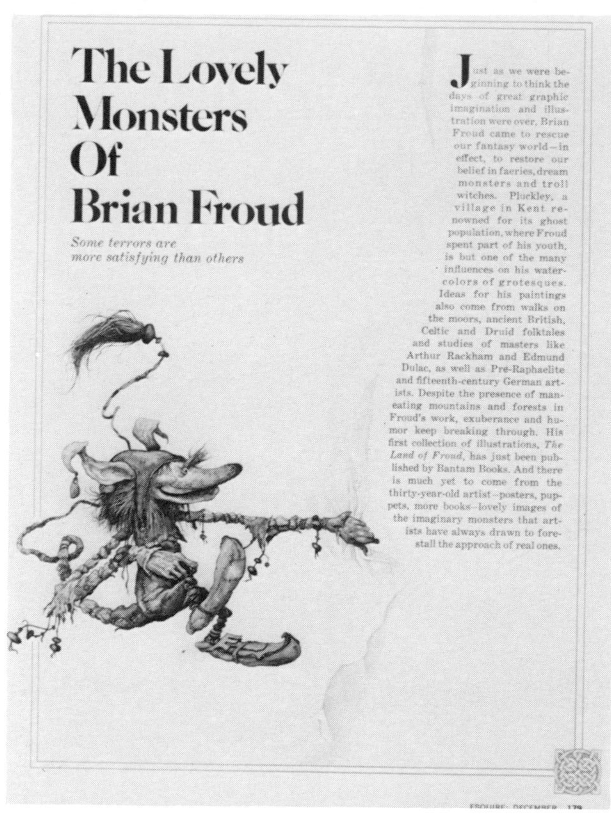

The Lovely Monsters Of Brian Froud

Some terrors are more satisfying than others

Just as we were beginning to think the days of great graphic imagination and illustration were over, Brian Froud came to rescue our fantasy world—in effect, to restore our belief in faeries, dream monsters and troll witches. Pluckley, a village in Kent renowned for its ghost population, where Froud spent part of his youth, is but one of the many influences on his watercolors of grotesques. Ideas for his paintings also come from walks on the moors, ancient British, Celtic and Druid folktales and studies of masters like Arthur Rackham and Edmund Dulac, as well as Pre-Raphaelite and fifteenth-century German artists. Despite the presence of man-eating mountains and forests in Froud's work, exuberance and humor keep breaking through. His first collection of illustrations, *The Land of Froud*, has just been published by Bantam Books. And there is much yet to come from the thirty-year-old artist—posters, puppets, more books—lovely images of the imaginary monsters that artists have always drawn to forestall the approach of real ones.

ESQUIRE: DECEMBER 179

Tree Giant: "I feel that trees are alive," Froud says, "crouching, waiting." In folktales, trees bled when chopped and wreaked revenge on unsuspecting woodsmen.

Dragon Worm: A twelfth-century monster terrorized the countryside with breath "so venomous it could kill cattle at a distance." It was slain by a brave young man who jammed a blazing sword down its throat.

293

293

Art Director	Samuel Antupit
Writers	Byron Dobell
	Lou Ann Walker
Designer	Judy Schiern Hecker
Artist	Brian Froud
Publisher	Esquire Magazine, Inc.

295

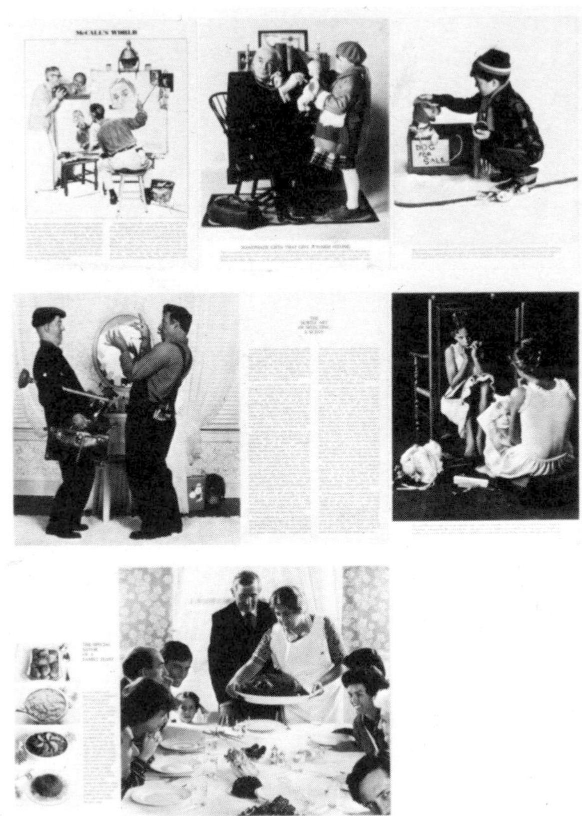

294

295

Art Directors	Robin Rickabaugh
	Heidi Rickabaugh
Writer	Clare Lundell
Designers	Robin Rickabaugh
	Douglas Mitchell
Photographer	B. Frederick Peterson
Publisher	Oregon Rainbow Inc.
Client	Oregon Rainbow Inc.

294

Art Director	Alvin Grossman
Designer	Alvin Grossman
Photographer	Otto Storch
Publisher	The McCall Publishing Company
Client	McCall's Magazine

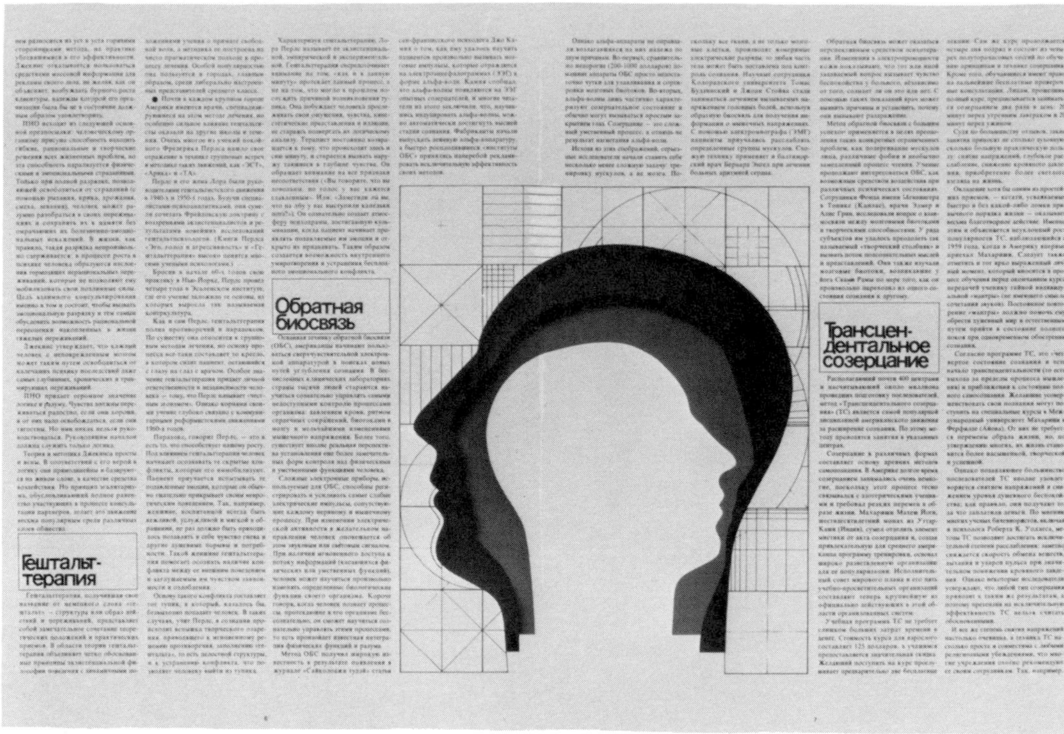

Гештальт-терапия

Обратная биосвязь

Трансцен-дентальное созерцание

296

297

296

Art Director	David P. Moore
Editor	Robert Poteete
Designer	David Moore
Artist	Tom Gould
Publisher	U.S. Information Agency
Agency	U.S. Information Agency
Client	America Illustrated

297

Art Director	David Moore
Editor	Robert Poteete
Designer	Patricia Gipple
Photographers	Peter B. Kaplan
	Elizabeth Friedman
Agency	U. S. Information Agency
Client	America Illustrated

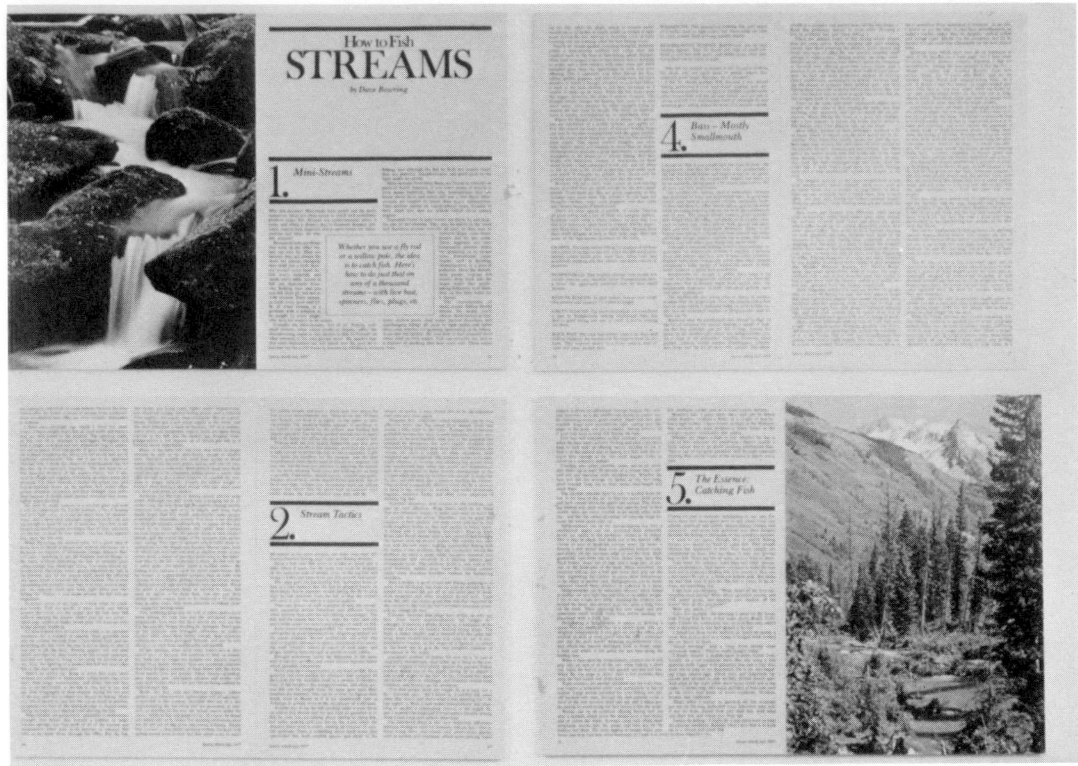

How to Fish
STREAMS
by Dave Bowring

1. Mini-Streams

Whether you use a fly rod or a willow pole, the idea is to catch fish. Here's how to do just that on any of a thousand streams—with live bait, spinners, flies, plugs, etc.

4. Bass—Mostly Smallmouth

2. Stream Tactics

5. The Essence: Catching Fish

298

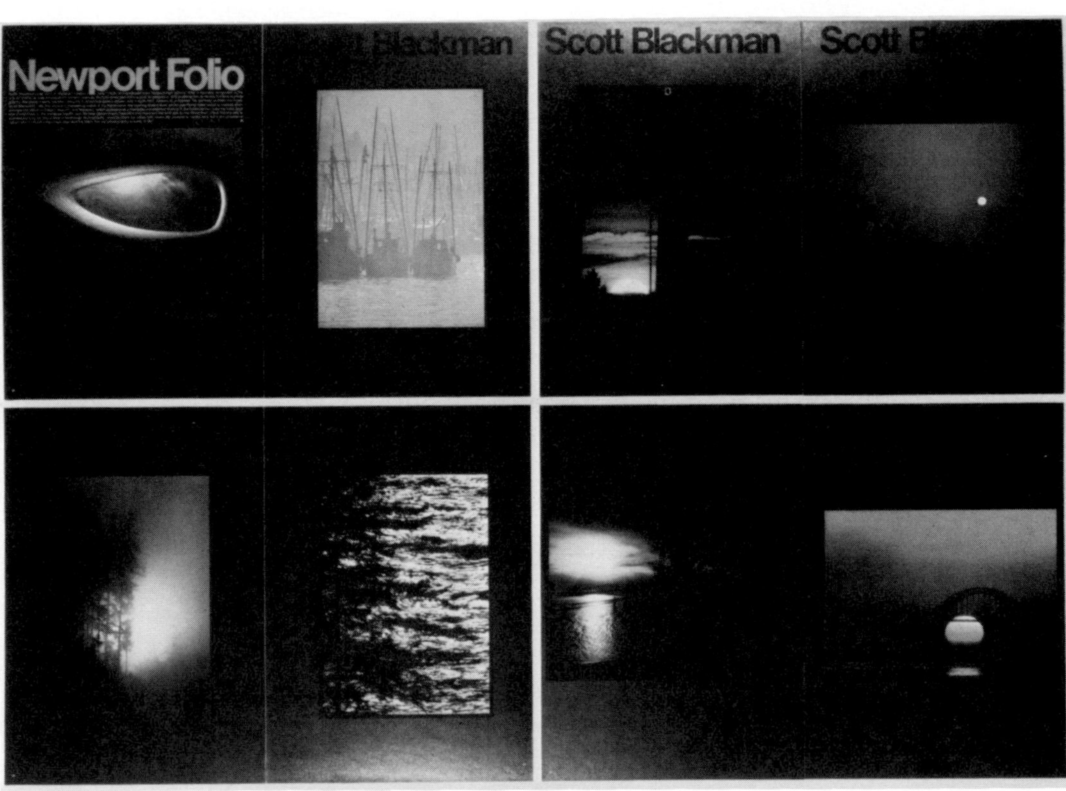

299

298
Art Director James Eisenman
Writer David Bowring
Photographers Frank Miller
Charlie Ott
Photo Reserves
Publisher The Hearst Corporation
Client Sports Afield Magazine

299
Art Directors Robin Rickabaugh
Heidi Rickabaugh
Writer Phil Rickabaugh
Designers Robin Rickabaugh
Heidi Rickabaugh
Photographer Scott Blackman
Publisher Oregon Rainbow Inc.
Client Oregon Rainbow Inc.

300

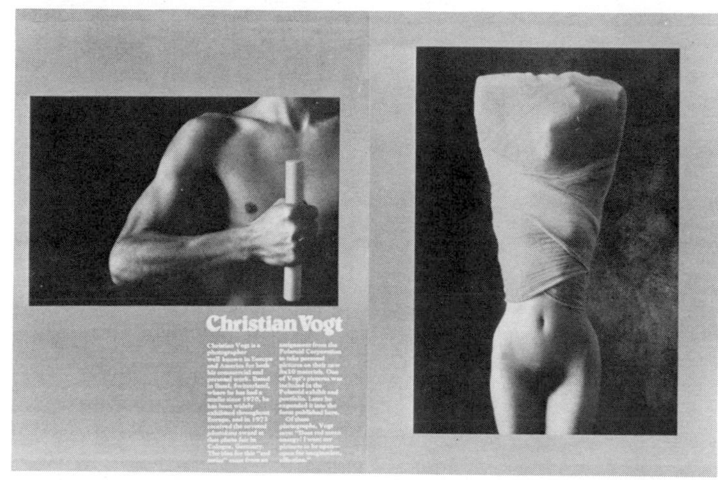

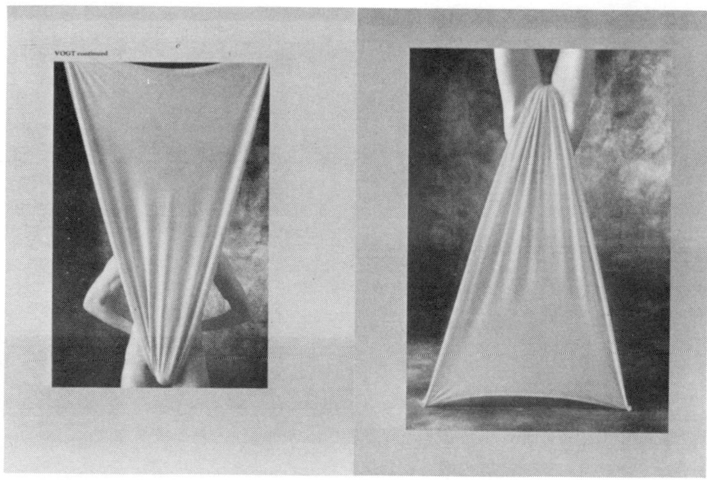

301

300

Art Director Bruce McIntosh
Editor Paul Trachtman
Designer Bruce McIntosh
Photographers Dr. Ensio E. Aalto
Thomas C. Ballantyne
Jerome J. Barry
Pamela Blevins
Jim Haberman
Linda M. Harn
Jerry A. Naimy
Larry L. Scott
David Stone
Emanuel Weiss
Kathy S. Williams
Stephen W. Worrel
Publisher Massachusetts Horticultural Society
Client Horticulture Magazine

301

Art Director Thomas Ridinger
Writer Jim Hughes
Designer Thomas Ridinger
Photographer Christian Vogt
Publisher Ziff-Davis Publishing C
Agency Ziff-Davis Publishing C
Client Photography Annual

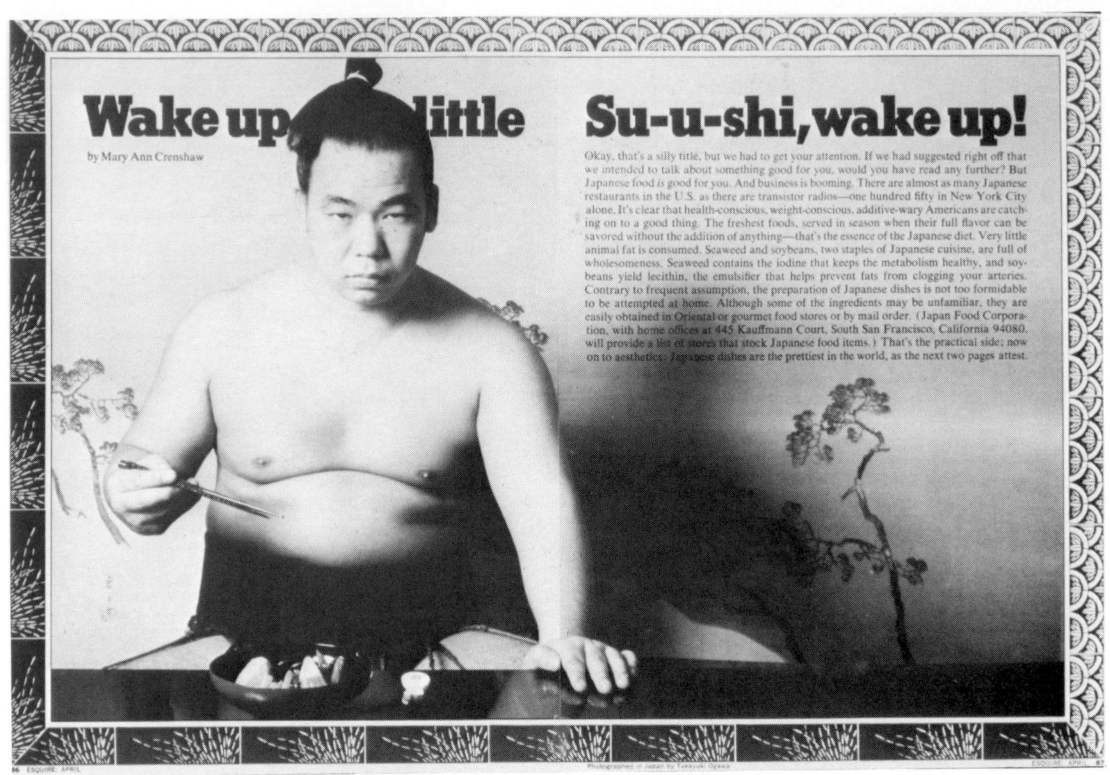

Wake up little Su-u-shi, wake up!

by Mary Ann Crenshaw

Okay, that's a silly title, but we had to get your attention. If we had suggested right off that we intended to talk about something good for you, would you have read any further? But Japanese food *is* good for you. And business is booming. There are almost as many Japanese restaurants in the U.S. as there are transistor radios—one hundred fifty in New York City alone. It's clear that health-conscious, weight-conscious, additive-wary Americans are catching on to a good thing. The freshest foods, served in season when their full flavor can be savored without the addition of anything—that's the essence of the Japanese diet. Very little animal fat is consumed. Seaweed and soybeans, two staples of Japanese cuisine, are full of wholesomeness. Seaweed contains the iodine that keeps the metabolism healthy, and soybeans yield lecithin, the emulsifier that helps prevent fats from clogging your arteries. Contrary to frequent assumption, the preparation of Japanese dishes is not too formidable to be attempted at home. Although some of the ingredients may be unfamiliar, they are easily obtained in Oriental or gourmet food stores or by mail order. (Japan Food Corporation, with home offices at 445 Kauffmann Court, South San Francisco, California 94080, will provide a list of stores that stock Japanese food items.) That's the practical side; now on to aesthetics: Japanese dishes are the prettiest in the world, as the next two pages attest.

86 ESQUIRE: APRIL   Photographed in Japan by Takayuki Ogawa   ESQUIRE: APRIL 87

Bangkok

Cynics sigh and speak of the gentle city that existed only twenty years ago. They mourn the loss of most of the enchanting klongs (canals) that gave the city its Siamese signature, and they grouse at the traffic that now fills these once bucolic byways. **B**ut it's still possible to rise at dawn and hire a boat to join the frenetic traffic on the Chao Phraya River. First to the Floating Market to engage in aquatic commerce, then to the klongs of neighboring Thon Buri, there to glide by the stilted houses as residents carry on their daily business totally impervious to the presence of tourists. **I**t is unlikely that you will sense the underlying unease of the city, for it's difficult to plumb political malaise while you are being dazzled by a succession of wats (chapels or monastic complexes) that are unequaled for collective splendor anywhere else in the world. Wat Phra Keo, the Chapel of the Emerald Buddha, is perhaps the most splendid, though there are three hundred more from which to choose a sight-seeing program. **T**he oldest of Bangkok's substantial hotels is The Oriental, still the city's staunchest bastion of grace and tradition. It is 101 years since a Jewish family from Baghdad opened its first rooms, but the newly built annex keeps it in the forefront of modernity and luxury. The Siam InterContinental is just a hair behind in comfort and cachet, and its Talay Thong Restaurant still serves the best seafood in the city. **C**oin of the Thai realm is the baht, or the tical, and more than one first-timer in Thailand has survived the currency-conversion confusion by memorizing and mumbling "A tical is a nickel" when the bargaining gets most intense. **T**he generally mediocre state of Western cooking in Bangkok forces dedicated gastronomes to rely on the superb Chinese restaurants, and it also reinforces a daring urge to try traditional Thai cooking. One note of warning: Beware the prik-kee-noo, a devilish pepper that is fully capable of rendering you literally speechless. Thai cuisine borrows heavily from the nostril-burning spiciness of Indian kitchens, so it's probably best to cut your teeth on "tourist Thai" food at The Piman or certain of the hotel restaurants. Then, once weaned from the blandness of a conventional Western palate, you may be ready to test your tongue on the true Thai curries at Rung Taw Tollgate or the rough-and-ready Ruen Phae. **T**his taste of Thailand may well whet your appetite for some of the other, farther corners of the Pacific, and there's every reason to give in to the impulse. It is one of the last truly fantastic voyages. #

92 ESQUIRE: AUGUST

Life centers around the network of Bangkok's canals.

Crimson tassels decorate the streets.

The water buffalo is the local beast of burden.

Magnificent temple ruins to the north of Bangkok.

Fishermen's nets at the ready, below.

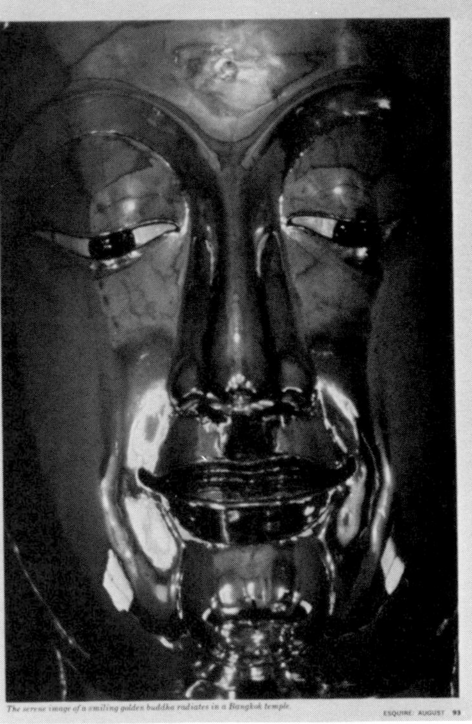

The serene image of a smiling golden buddha radiates in a Bangkok temple.

ESQUIRE: AUGUST 93

303

302	
Art Director	Michael Gross
Writers	Mary Ann Crenshaw
	Anita LeClerc
Designer	Judy Schiern Hecker
Photographers	Takayuki Ogawa
	Tohru Nakamura
Publisher	Esquire Inc.
Agency	Esquire
Client	Esquire Magazine

303	
Art Director	Samuel Antupit
Writer	Stephen Birnbaum
Designer	Judy Schiern Hecker
Photographer	Will McBride
Publisher	Esquire Magazine, Inc.

THE INTREPID FURS

Photographs by Silano

Soft explosions of mink. Color-emboldened lynx. Raccoons of great hardihood and audacity of spirit. All of them warming safeguards against formidable forecasts of severe winters ahead. *Town & Country* tested these new fur fashions in the coldest place on earth—the pristine blue-and-white glacial grandeur of that vast stretch of Greenland that lies north of the Arctic Circle and is a veritable weather factory for the North Atlantic. Our polar adventuress: Susan Hess, a snow-country beauty from Seattle, echoes the shape of an arctic animal, here, in a full-sleeved Russian raccoon coat by Geoffrey Beene for HBA Furs. Beene accessories.

Behind the great ice curtain, above the clouds, on the largest island in the world, where gigantic granite mountains tower to heights of 12,000 feet, Susan finds the ultimate shelter—a thick, light coat of wine-colored fox, lavishly collared and reaching to mid-calf. By John Anthony for Jan Originals. At Bonwit Teller, New York; Woolf Brothers; Sakowitz. Matching chiffon shirt and silk jersey pants, as well as the jet-beaded belt, also by John Anthony. Don Kline turban. Wine suede boots by Ferragamo.

304

304

Art Director	Linda Stillman
Writer	Mary Louise Ransdell
Designer	Linda Stillman
Photographer	Bill Silano
Publisher	The Hearst Corp.
Agency	Town & Country
Client	Town & Country Magazine

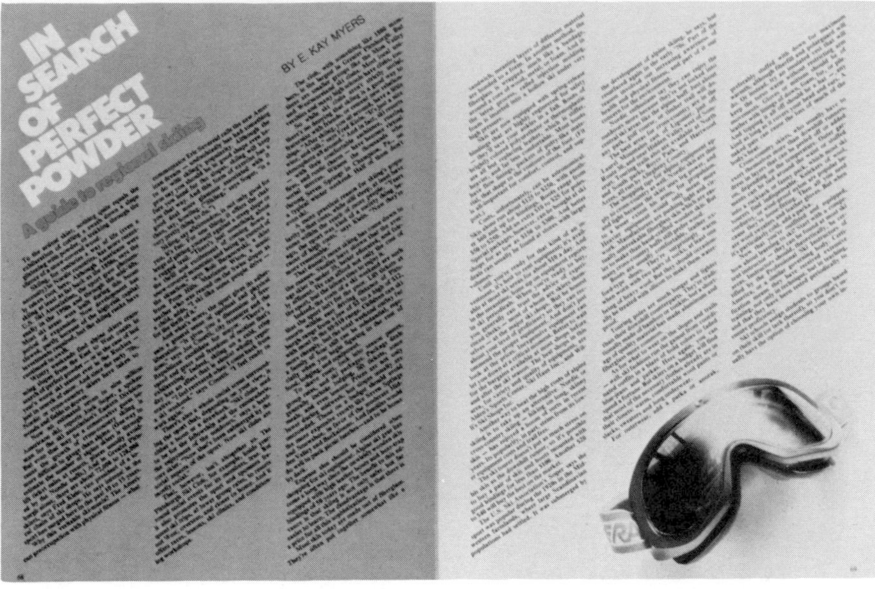

305

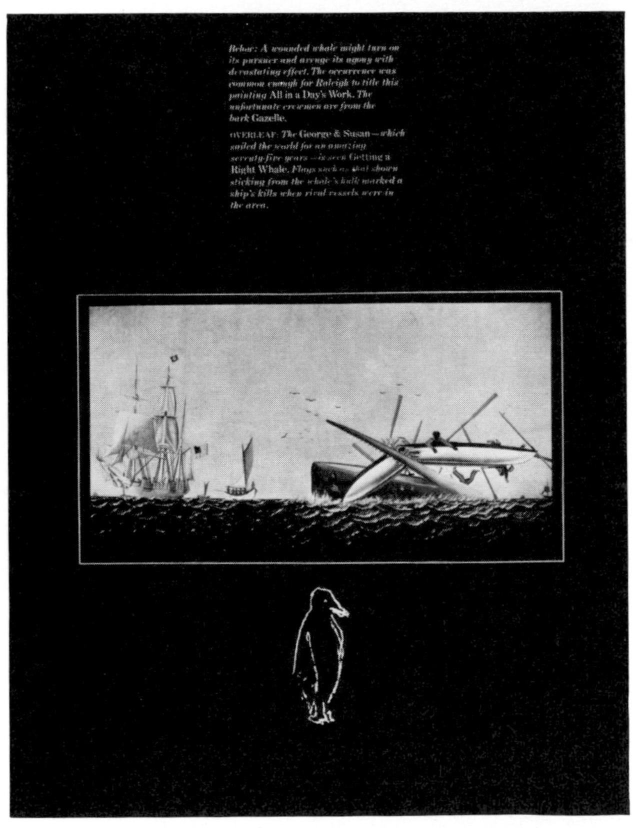

306

305
Art Director Martine Sheon
Writers E. Kay Myers
Andrea Naversen
Editor Pat Minarcin
Designer Martine Sheon
Photographer Tom Cooper
Publisher R. M. Scaile
Client Pittsburgher Magazine

306
Art Director Emma Landau
Designer Massimo Vignelli
Artist Charles S. Raleigh
in 1877 thru 1887
Publisher American Heritage
Publishing Co.

307

309

308

307
Art Director Harry Coulianos
Designer Donald Sterzin
Photographer Barry McKinley
Publisher GQ Magazine, Inc.
Agency Gentleman's Quarterly Magazine
Client GQ

308
Art Director Joseph Baumer
Writer Geoffrey Gould
Designer Jack Lefkowitz
Artist Jack Lefkowitz
Publisher International Communication Agency
Agency International Communication Agency
Client Topic Magazine

309
Art Director Thaddeus A. Miksinski, Jr.
Editor Andrew Bardagjy
Designer Thaddeus A. Miksinski, Jr.
Photographer Peccinotti
Publisher International Communication Agency
Agency International Communication Agency
Client Topic Magazine

310

311

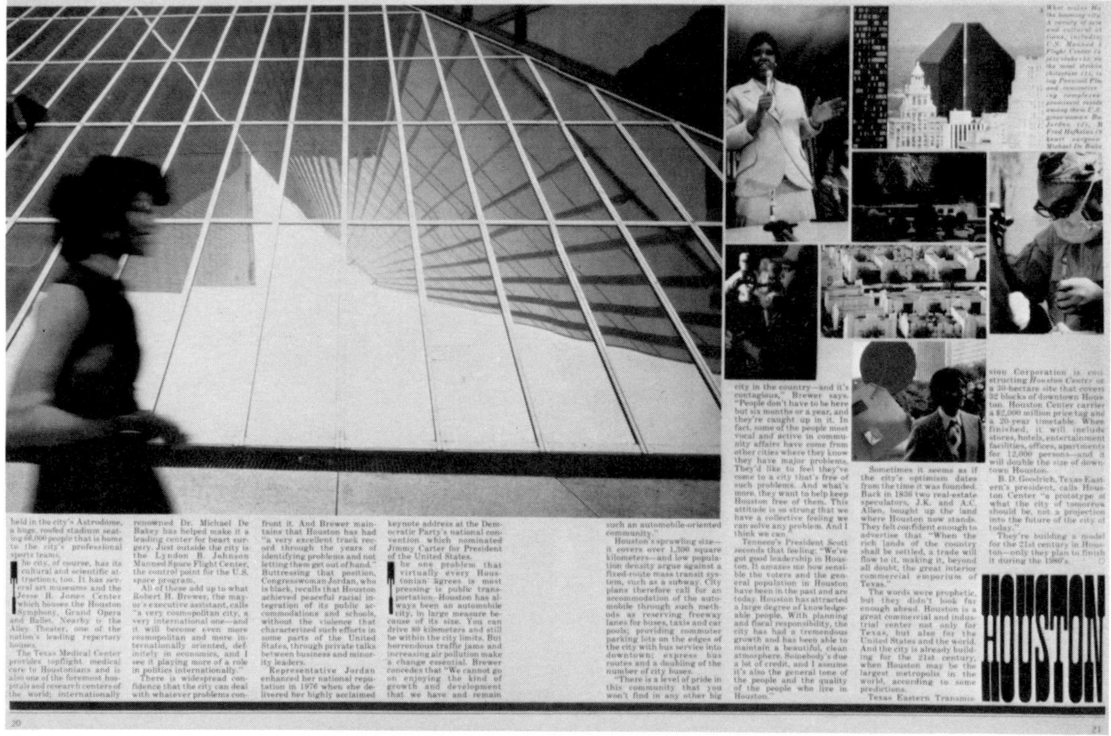

312

310
Art Director Rowan Johnson
Designers Claire Victor
Bob Guccione
Photographer James Moore
Publisher Bob Guccione
Agency Viva International Ltd.
Client Viva International

311
Art Director James Eisenman
Writer Tom Brakefield
Photographer Michael O'Neill
Publisher The Hearst Corp.
Client Sports Afield Magazine

312
Art Director Thaddeus A. Miksinski, Jr.
Writer John F. Coppola
Designer Thaddeus A. Miksinski, Jr.
Photographer Christopher Casler
Publisher International Communication Agency
Agency International Communication Agency
Client Topic Magazine

LITTLE AUTUMN Annie

CAST OF NEW MUSICAL HIT STARS IN FALL FASHIONS

Leapin' Lizards! It's Annie, the smash of Broadway, an All-American musical comedy centered around a handful of spunky kids singin' and dancin' their hearts out. Here, the little troupers model the big hits for girls—some to buy, some to sew. The Apron Look, mixing patterns and layers in muted, pretty colors. The Classics, preppy blazers, shirts and kilts; good-mannered dresses. And all kinds of fun-outdoors clothes. This page: Lovable star, Andrea McArdle as Little Orphan Annie and her loyal pal, Sandy. Arf! By Trudy Owett, Fashion and Home Sewing Editor.

313

Something Special For Everyone

Town & Country presents its annual extravaganza of Christmas goodies, all with the aid of Santa Claus, portrayed by restaurateur Warner Leroy of New York's Tavern on the Green and Maxwell's Plum. When Santa finishes his cigar and gets on with his job, the antique cane and mahogany wheelchair will be available at James II Gallery, New York, for $2,400. Special for your rich gouty uncle.

Photographs by Cy Gross

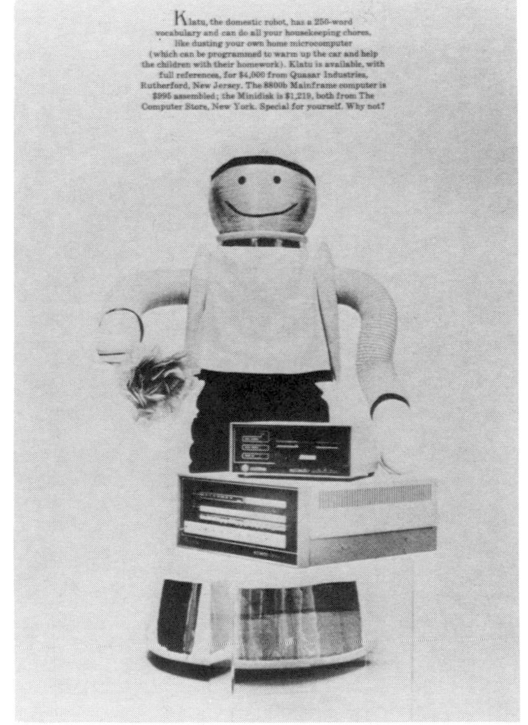

Klatu, the domestic robot, has a 250-word vocabulary and can do all your housekeeping chores, like dusting your own home microcomputer (which can be programmed to warm up the car and help the children with their homework). Klatu is available, with full references, for $4,000 from Quasar Industries, Rutherford, New Jersey. The 8800b Mainframe computer is $995 assembled; the Minidisk is $1,219, both from The Computer Store, New York. Special for yourself. Why not?

314

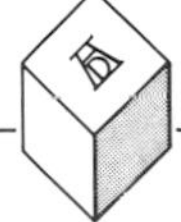

SILVER

313

Art Directors	Bruce Danbrot
	Donald A. Adamec
Writer	Lys Margold
Designer	Bruce Danbrot
Artist	Bruce Danbrot
Photographer	Henry Wolf
Agency	Ladies' Home Journal

314

Art Director	Linda Stillman
Writer	Monica Meenan
Designer	Brad Pallas
Photographer	Cy Gross
Publisher	The Hearst Corporation
Agency	Town & Country
Client	Town & Country

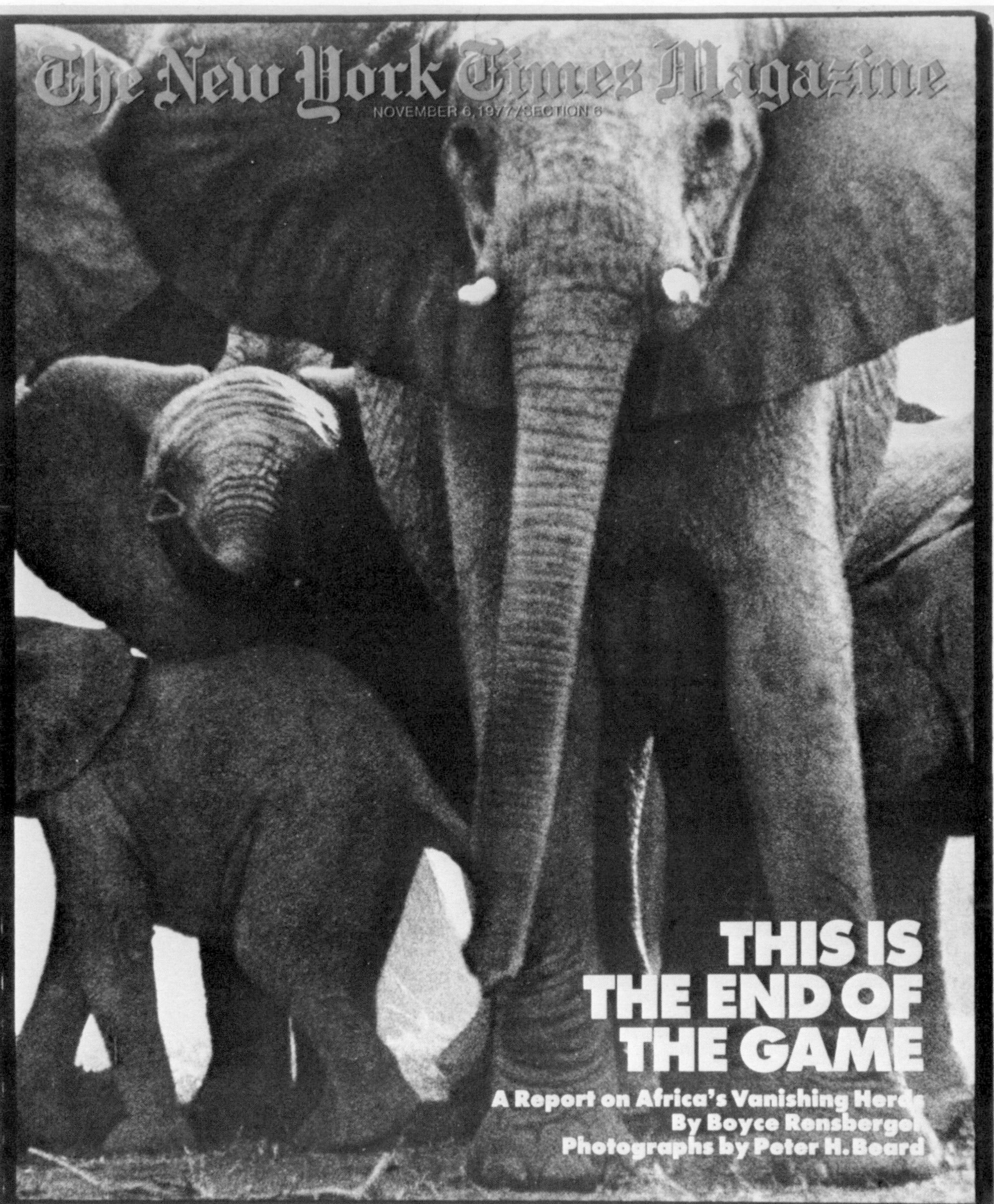

The New York Times Magazine
NOVEMBER 6, 1977/SECTION 6
THIS IS THE END OF THE GAME
A Report on Africa's Vanishing Herds
By Boyce Rensberger
Photographs by Peter H. Beard

315

315

Art Director	Ruth Ansel
Editor	Edward Klein
Designer	Ruth Ansel
Photographer	Peter Beard
Publisher	The New York Times
Agency	The New York Times
Client	The New York Times

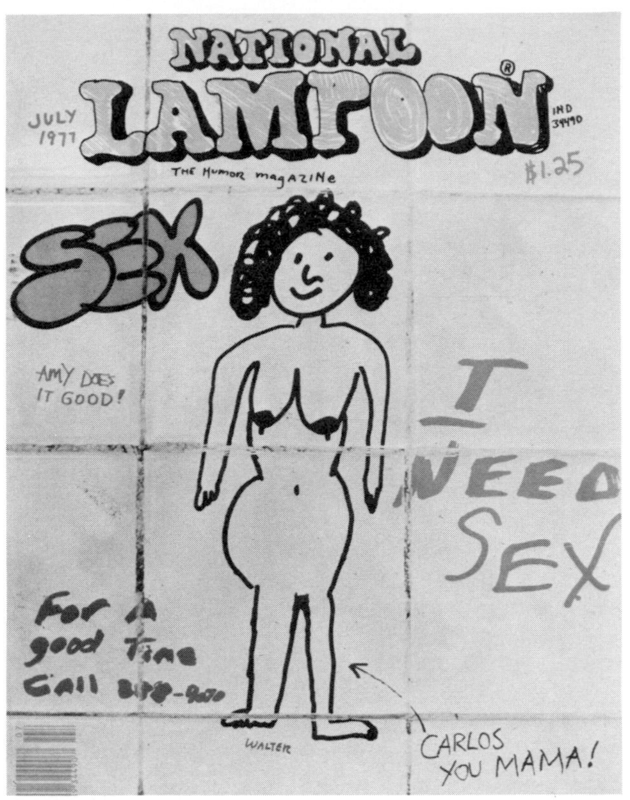

316

317

318

316
Art Director Peter Kleinman
Designer Peter Kleinman
Artist Walter Garibaldi
Photographer Peter Kleinman
Publisher National Lampoon, Inc.

317
Art Director Peter Kleinman
Designer Peter Kleinman
Artist Carter Jones—Sculptor
Photographer John Barrett
Publisher National Lampoon, Inc.

318
Art Director Walter Bernard
Designer Seymour Chwast
Artist Seymour Chwast
Publisher Time Inc.
Agency Time
Client Time Magazine

319

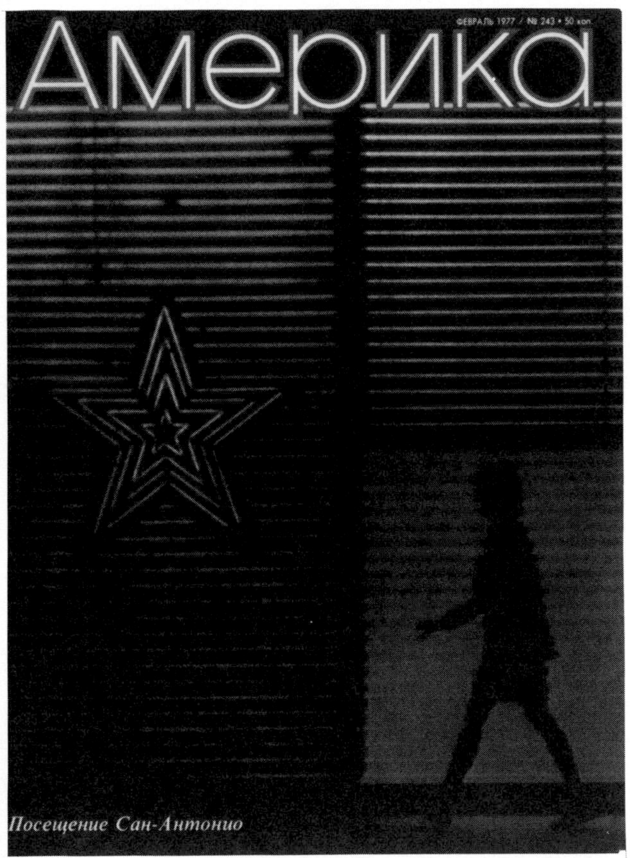

320

321

319
Art Director David Moore
Editor Robert Poteete
Designer David Moore
Artists Stan Mack
Redwood East (logo)
Publisher U. S. Information Agency
Agency U. S. Information Agency
Client America Illustrated Magazine

320
Art Director David Moore
Editor Robert Poteete
Designer Dorothy Fall
Photographer Blair Pittman
Publisher U. S. Information Agency
Agency U. S. Information Agency
Client America Illustrated Magazine

321
Art Director David Moore
Editor Robert Poteete
Designer Patricia Gipple
Artist Fritz Scholder
Publisher U. S. Information Agency
Agency U. S. Information Agency
Client America Illustrated Magazine

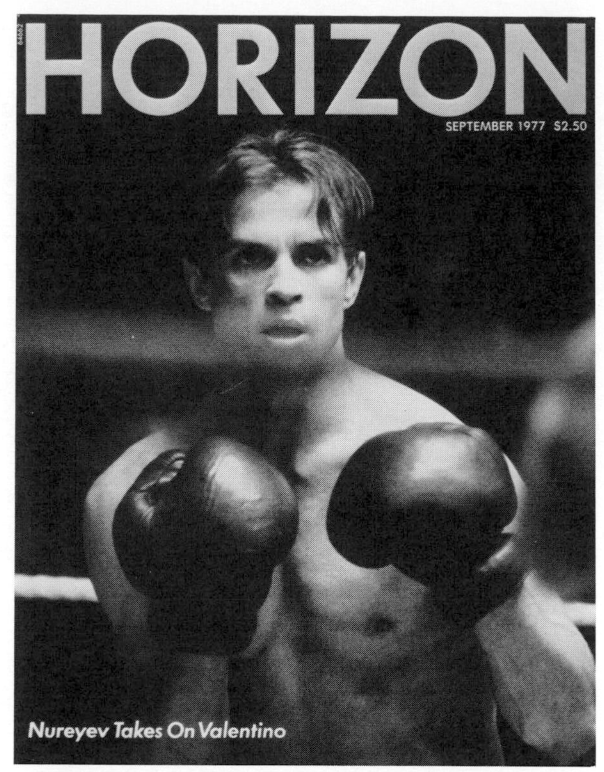

HORIZON
SEPTEMBER 1977 $2.50
Nureyev Takes On Valentino

322

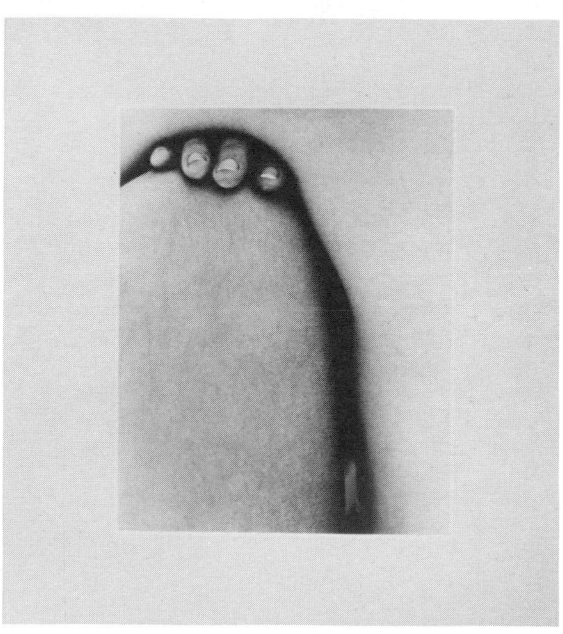

323

322
Art Director Ken Munowitz
Designer Ken Munowitz
Photographer Steve Schapiro/Sygma
Agency American Heritage Publishing

323
Art Director Dave Epstein
Editor Michael E. Hoffman
Designer Dave Epstein
Photographer Walter Chappel
Publisher Aperature Inc.
Client Aperature

324

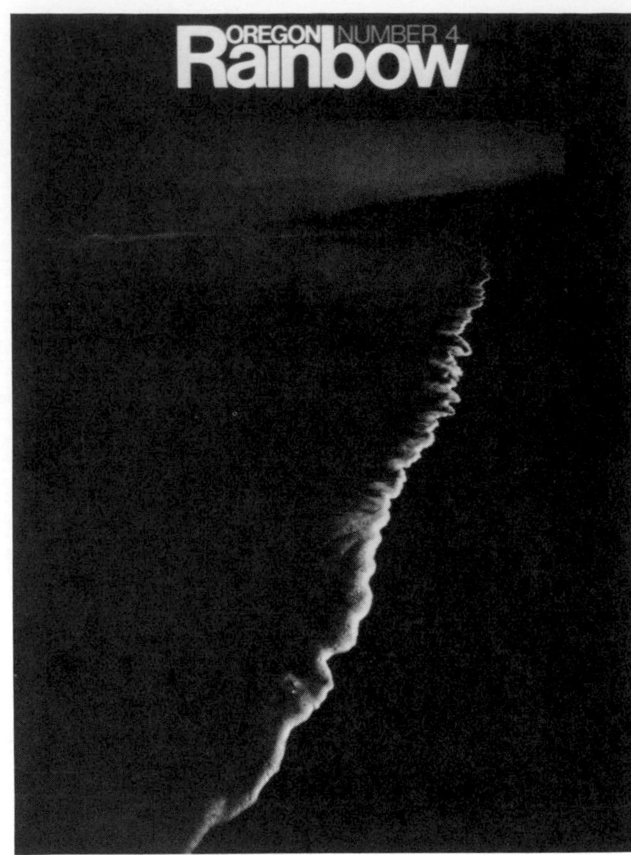

325

326

324
Art Directors Robin Rickabaugh
Heidi Rickabaugh
Designer Robin Rickabaugh
Photographer Gary Braasch
Publisher Oregon Rainbow Inc.
Client Oregon Rainbow

325
Art Directors Robin Rickabaugh
Heidi Rickabaugh
Designer Robin Rickabaugh
Photographer Scott Blackman
Publisher Oregon Rainbow Inc.
Client Oregon Rainbow

326
Art Director Don Owens
Designer Don Owens
Photographer Horst Luedeking
Publisher Owens Publishing Co.
Client Picture Magazine

327

328

329

327
Art Director Seymour Chwast
Designer Richard Mantel
Agency Push Pin Studios
Client Push Pin Graphic

328
Art Director Seymour Chwast
Artist Seymour Chwast
Agency Push Pin Studios
Client Push Pin Graphic

329
Art Director Seymour Chwast
Designer Richard Mantel
Artist Richard Mantel
Agency Push Pin Studios
Client Push Pin Graphic

330

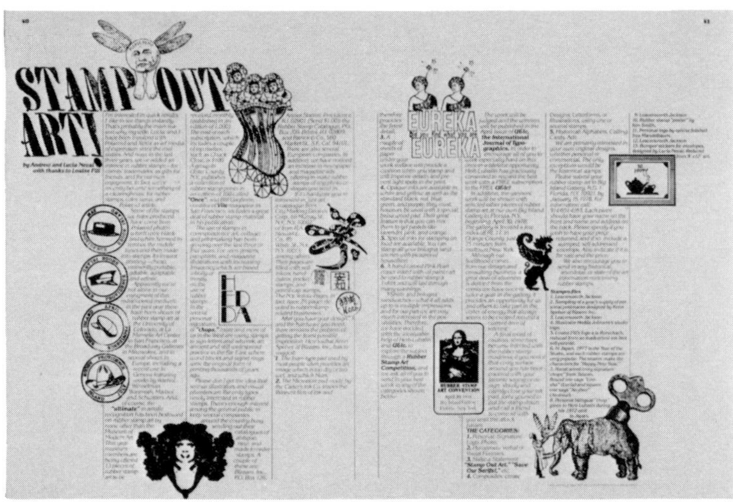

331

SILVER

330

Art Director	Herb Lubalin
Designer	Herb Lubalin
Artist	Lou Myers
Publisher	International Typeface Corp.
Agency	LSC&P Design Group
Client	International Typeface Corp.

331

Art Director	Herb Lubalin
Writers	Andrew Nevai
	Lucia Nevai
Designer	Louise Fili
Publisher	International Typeface Corp.
Agency	LSC&P Design Group
Client	International Typeface Corp.

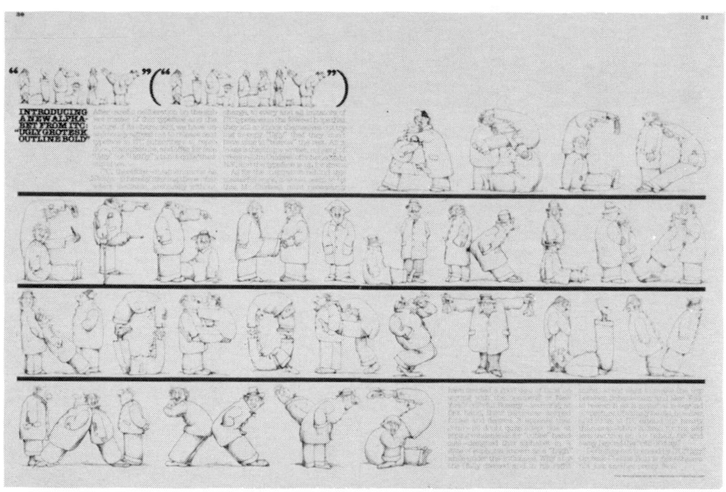

332

333

334

332
Art Director Herb Lubalin
Writer Herb Lubalin
Designer Herb Lubalin
Artist John Caldwell
Publisher International Typeface Corp.
Agency LSC&P Design Group
Client International Typeface Corp.

333
Art Director Herb Lubalin
Writer Jack Anson Finke
Designer Herb Lubalin
Artist Hedda Johnson
Publisher International Typeface Corp.
Agency LSC&P Design Group
Client International Typeface Corp.

334
Art Director Herb Lubalin
Writers Herb Lubalin
Carol Wald
Designer Herb Lubalin
Publisher International Typeface C
Agency LSC&P Design Group
Client International Typeface C

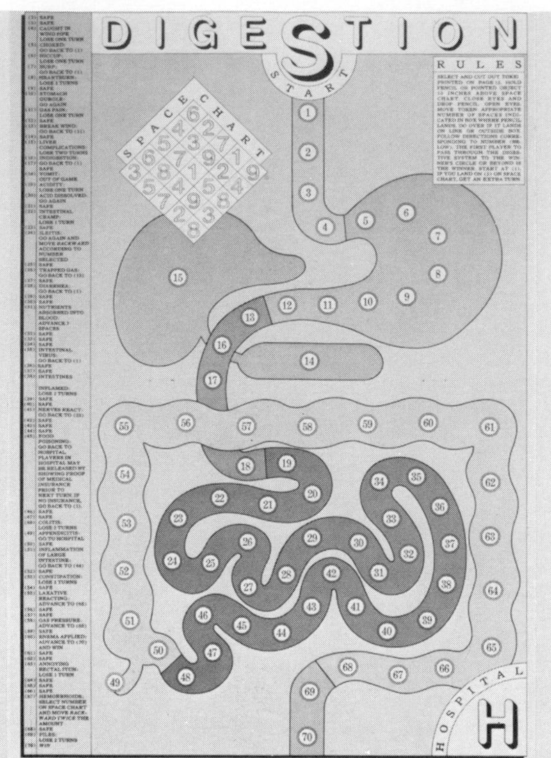

335

336

335

Art Director	Seymour Chwast
Designer	Richard Mantel
Artist	William Sloan
Agency	Push Pin Studios
Client	Push Pin Graphic

336

Art Director	Seymour Chwast
Writer	Paula Scher
Designer	Seymour Chwast
Artist	Seymour Chwast
Agency	Push Pin Studios
Client	Push Pin Graphic

337

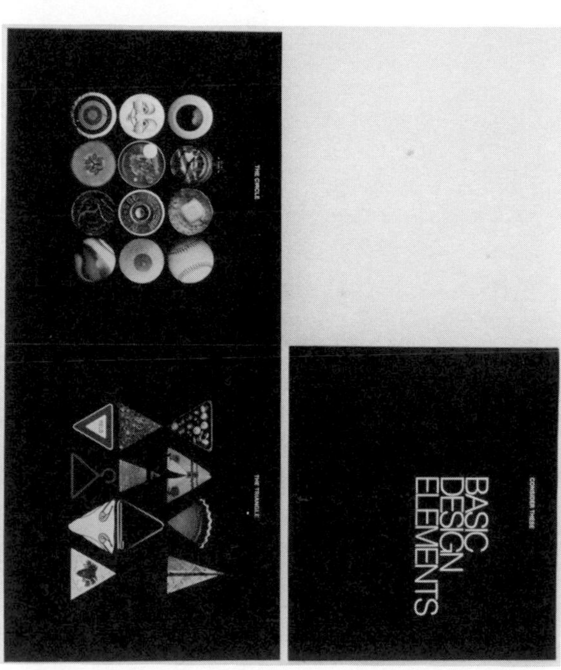

338

337

Art Directors: Robin Rickabaugh, Heidi Rickabaugh
Writers: E. Kimbark MacColl, Clare Lundell, Phil Rickabaugh, Pat Probst, L.S. Dryden, Lionel L. Fisher
Designers: Robin Rickabaugh, Douglas Mitchell, Terry Daline
Photographers: Gary Braasch, B. Fredrick Peterson, Scott Blackman, Edward Gowans, R. Moland Reynolds, Claire Trotter, Jerome Hart
Publisher: Oregon Rainbow Inc.
Client: Oregon Rainbow

338

Art Director: Jim Lienhart
Writer: Jim Lienhart
Designer: Jim Lienhart
Artists: Bobbye Cochran, Jim Lienhart
Photographers: Tom Vack, Von Dorn
Publisher: The 27 Chicago Designers
Agency: Jim Lienhart (Murrie White Drummond Lienhart & Assoc.)
Client: The 27 Chicago Designers

339

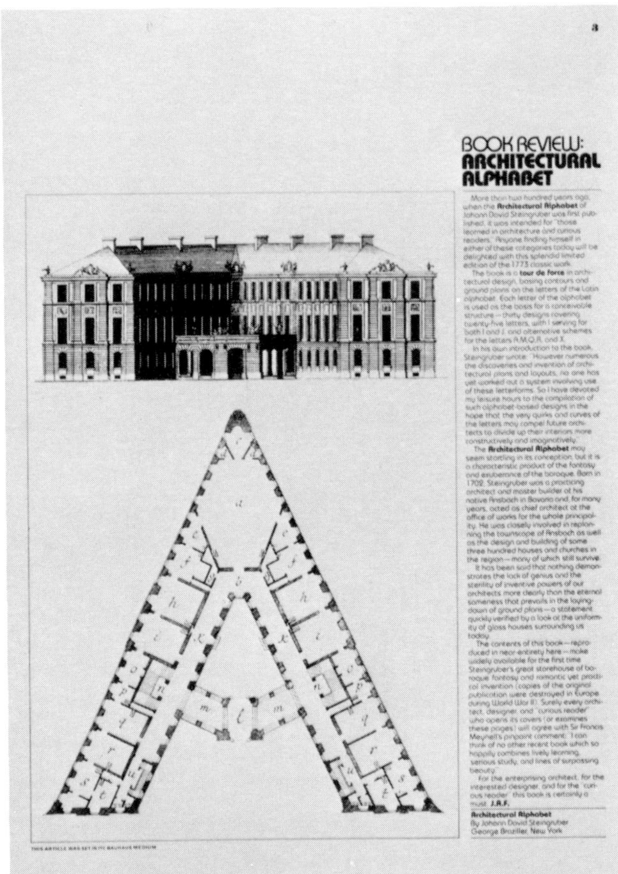

3

BOOK REVIEW: ARCHITECTURAL ALPHABET

More than two hundred years ago, when the **Architectural Alphabet** of Johann David Steingruber was first published, it was intended for "those learned in architecture and curious readers." Anyone finding himself in either of these categories today will be delighted with this splendid limited edition of the 1773 classic work.

The book is a **tour de force** in architectural design, basing contours and ground plans on the letters of the Latin alphabet. Each letter of the alphabet is used as the basis for a conceivable structure—thirty designs covering twenty-five letters, with I serving for both I and J, and alternative schemes for the letters A, M, O, R, and X.

In his own introduction to the book, Steingruber wrote: "However numerous the discoveries and invention of architectural plans and layouts, no one has yet worked out a system involving use of these letterforms. So I have devoted my leisure hours to the compilation of such alphabet-based designs in the hope that the very quirks and curves of the letters may compel future architects to divide up their interiors more constructively and imaginatively."

The **Architectural Alphabet** may seem startling in its conception, but it is a characteristic product of the fantasy and exuberance of the baroque. Born in 1702, Steingruber was a practicing architect and master builder of his native Ansbach in Bavaria and, for many years, acted as chief architect at the office of works for the whole principality. He was closely involved in replanning the townscape of Ansbach as well as the design and building of some three hundred houses and churches in the region—many of which still survive.

It has been said that nothing demonstrates the lack of genius and the sterility of inventive powers of our architects more clearly than the eternal sameness that prevails in the laying-down of ground plans—a statement quickly verified by a look at the uniformity of glass houses surrounding us today.

The contents of this book—reproduced in near-entirety here—make widely available for the first time Steingruber's great storehouse of baroque fantasy and romantic yet practical invention (copies of the original publication were destroyed in Europe during World War II). Surely every architect, designer, and "curious reader" who opens its covers (or examines these pages) will agree with Sir Francis Meynell's pinpoint comment: "I can think of no other recent book which so happily combines lively learning, serious study, and lines of surpassing beauty."

For the enterprising architect, for the interested designer, and for the "curious reader" this book is certainly a must. **J.R.F.**

Architectural Alphabet
By Johann David Steingruber
George Braziller, New York

340

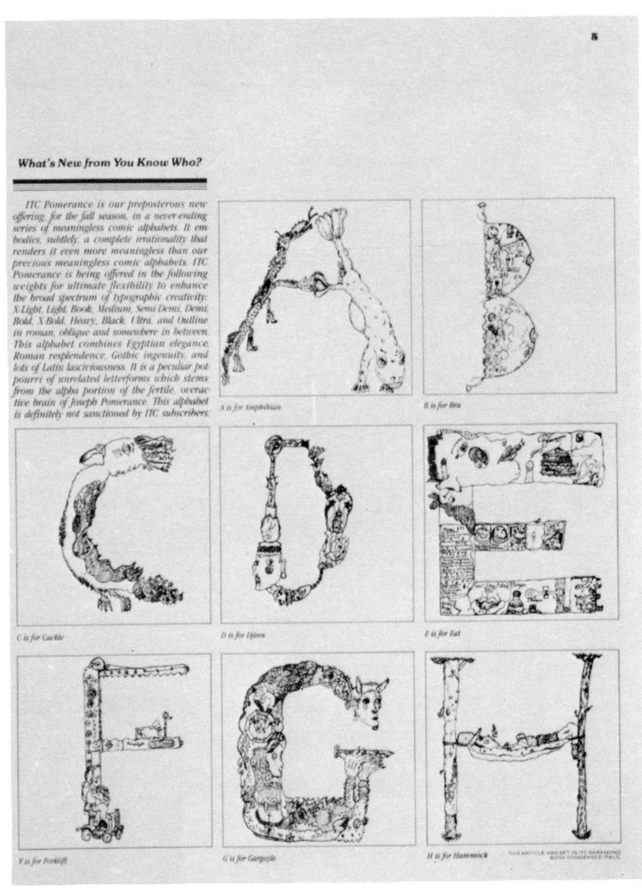

5

What's New from You Know Who?

ITC Pomerance is our preposterous new offering, for the fall season, in a never-ending series of meaningless comic alphabets. It embodies, subtlely, a complete irrationality that renders it even more meaningless than our previous meaningless comic alphabets. ITC Pomerance is being offered in the following weights for ultimate flexibility to enhance the broad spectrum of typographic creativity: X-Light, Light, Book, Medium, Semi-Demi, Demi, Bold, X-Bold, Heavy, Black, Ultra, and Outline in roman, oblique and somewhere in between. This alphabet combines Egyptian elegance, Roman resplendence, Gothic ingenuity, and lots of Latin lasciviousness. It is a peculiar potpourri of unrelated letterforms which stems from the alpha portion of the fertile, overactive brain of Joseph Pomerance. This alphabet is definitely not sanctioned by ITC subscribers.

A is for Amphibian

B is for Bra

C is for Cackle

D is for Djinn

E is for Eat

F is for Forklift

G is for Gargoyle

H is for Hammock

341

339
Art Director Will Hopkins
Editors Edward Klein
Carrie Donovan
Designer Will Hopkins
Photographer Rico Puhlmann
Publisher The New York Times
Agency The New York Times
Client The New York Times Magazine

340
Art Director Herb Lubalin
Writer Jack Anson Finke
Designer Herb Lubalin
Artist Johann David Steingruber
Publisher George Braziller
International Typeface Corp.
Agency LSC&P Design Group
Client International Typeface Corp.

341
Art Director Herb Lubalin
Writer Herb Lubalin
Designer Herb Lubalin
Artist Joseph Pomerance
Publisher International Typeface Corp.
Agency LSC&P Design Group
Client International Typeface Corp.

342

ART FOR THE '70s

THE WHITNEY BIENNIAL

American artists of the 1970s see themselves less and less as participants in major art trends or movements, and increasingly as totally independent beings. Consequently, say the curators of New York's Whitney Museum of American Art, the art of the '70s has "generally emerged from personal experiences rather than ideologies," and therein lies its chief distinction from previous decades.

This concept of the current art scene in America was the guiding influence in the selection by the Whitney Museum of some 40 U.S. artists represented in its 1977 Biennial Exhibition, a sampling of which is presented here.

Indeed, a glance at the highly individualistic models of Charles Simonds (opposite), the super-realism of Chuck Close or the intricate computations of Alfred Jensen (on the following pages) seems to prove the Whitney's contention.

Moreover, according to the Whitney, the current artistic experience has been too personal for any new movements to begin, although groupings and associations are made for the sake of critical clarity.

These are only some of the conclusions to be drawn from the works of art displayed in the Whitney Biennial. Such exhibitions, strictly invitational, have been the museum's forte for the past 45 years. Each has, in its own time, attempted to survey "the current state of American art."

Whitney surveys have not always been universally praised, nor have critics always agreed with the museum's conclusions, but as one of the country's leading art institutions, the Whitney has always been listened to.

Washington, D.C., art critic Benjamin Forgey, for example, agrees that American art today is divergent, that it is not following trends or movements, and that the latest Biennial accurately reflects this. In writing for *Art News* magazine, however, Mr. Forgey wondered if such surveys by museums might not be anachronistic in today's highly complex and efficient art world network of communications. He concluded, however, that the latest Biennial added legitimate emphasis to the divergence of contemporary art.

The New York Times art critic, Hilton Kramer, however, called the exhibition "an unendurable bore." Art lovers and Whitney supporters took offense, and in a deluge of letters to the editor, he was roundly drubbed for his comments, one reader even going so far as to suggest that he be given "a new beat to cover."

Thomas Hess of *New York* magazine, on the other hand, declared the exhibition to be "the best of its kind, at least since 1946" and wrote that the exhibition is filled with "an astonishingly large number of wonderful paintings and sculptures."

In explaining the selection of artists to be included in the current exhibition, Whitney Director Tom Armstrong stated that "the Biennial is devoted for the most part to work by artists who were first decisively influential in the 1970s, and also to comparatively important works of lesser-known artists. Artists who received extensive public attention during the 1960s are not in the exhibition."

Thus, the Biennial was not intended—as some critics would have it—to be a survey of the very best art being produced in America today, but rather to be a study of artists who have become newly and decisively influential. ■

48

"Dwelling," Charles Simonds (size variable, bricks 1.25 cm) 1977

343

342

Art Directors	David Hale
	Bob Bryant
Writer	Carolyn Paine
Designer	David Hale
Artist	Steve Osborn
Publisher	Education Today Co. Inc.
Client	Learning Magazine

343

Art Director	Joseph Morgan
Editor	Ellen F. Toomey
Designer	Sam Burlockoff
Artist	Various
Photographer	Yale Joel
Publisher	U. S. Information Agency
Agency	U.S. Information Agency
Client	Horizons USA

LOFTY PERSPECTIVE

Photographs By Georg Gerster

Ever since 1858, when the first photograph was taken from a flying craft (a balloon), aerial photography has been the domain of scientists, cartographers, military strategists, technicians and others concerned mainly with the gathering of information. Now Georg Gerster, one of the world's foremost aerial photographers, is trying to change all that. Gerster sees his work not as the clinical recording of data, but as a form of art—"a unique vehicle of wonder, vexation, joy, wrath." Two hundred of his best photographs, taken during a 10-year period and over more than 50 countries, have been published in an imposing book, *Grand Design: The Earth From Above* (Paddington Press Ltd., New York, London). The photographs of the United States on the following pages are selected from this collection.

Gerster, who has written eloquent passages to accompany his photos, views his vocation as that of portraying "the patterns and ornaments that man, as he lives and labors, coaxes and bullies out of untouched nature." Through his lens, the mundane is transformed into the captivating: farmers' fields become mosaics; highways, calligraphy; desalinization ponds, the brightly splashed but haphazard canvas of a temperamental artist.

Yet, because distance often lends a quality of beauty where none exists, his art has its drawbacks. From the air, the ugliest of automobile scrapyards may seem a delight of ordered colors and shapes. Gerster accepts this disadvantage, but argues that it is far outbalanced by the benefits that flow from his work. Distance, he contends, clarifies and transforms the single image into a panorama of the possible: "On the ground we worry about an inventory of what is, but the lofty contemplation of the aerial photograph shows us also what might be—it is a stocktaking of our chances." Moreover, he says, aerial photography eliminates the temptation to which many earthbound photographers fall prey—meddling with the subject by an unwise use of props and gimmicks. From on high, there is nothing but the photographer and the surface below. At that moment, Gerster says, "the world is recreated without tears, as fresh and unsullied as in Genesis."

In his views of the United States, the Swiss-born photographer-as-artist brings to the commonplace a feeling of the sublime. Thus, wetted-down old carpets prosaically keeping the moisture in freshly poured concrete for a new bridge are transformed and framed as an arresting, brightly colored abstract painting. But beyond their intrinsic beauty, the photos also represent a unique perspective of U.S. society: the intense circular motion of excavation work at an exposed copper mine in Utah, the procession of autos along sinews of highway coursing through Los Angeles. In his photographs, Gerster has succeeded in capturing not only the natural grand design of America, but its tempo as well. ■

A roundabout way to mine copper

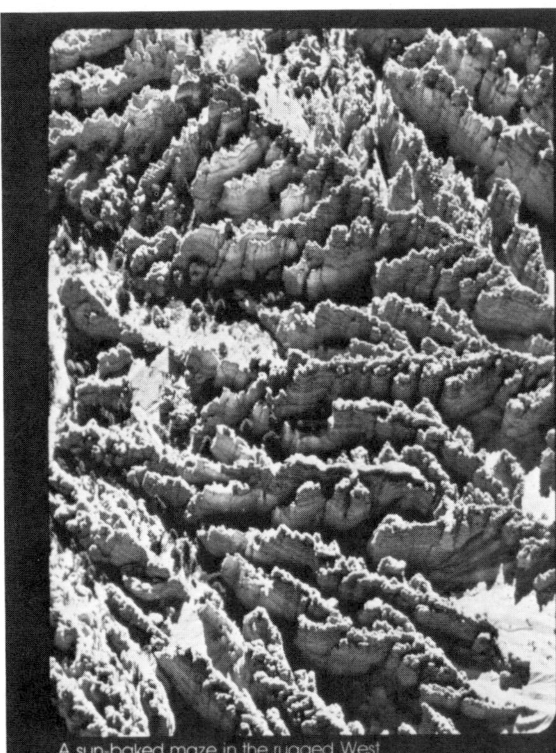

A sun-baked maze in the rugged West

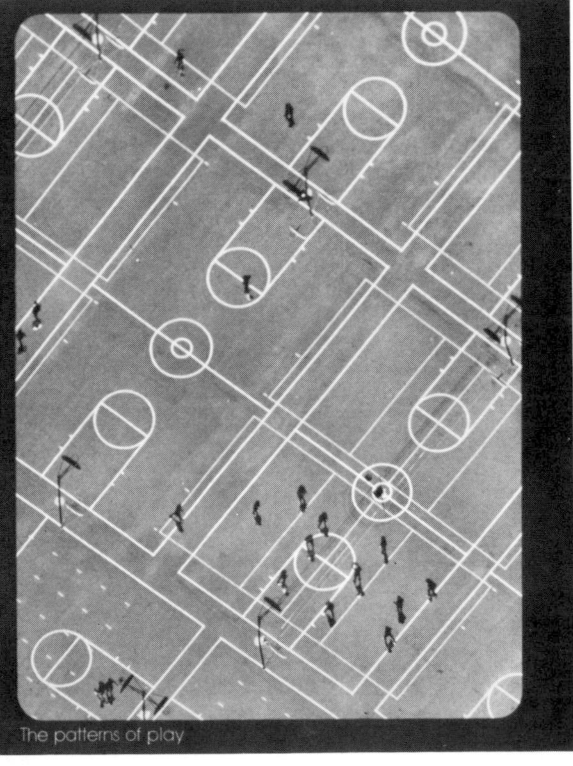

The patterns of play

344

SILVER

344

Art Director	Joseph Morgan
Picture Editor	Ellen F. Toomey
Designer	Sam Burlockoff
Photographer	Georg Gerster
Publisher	U. S. Information Agency
Agency	U.S. Information Agency
Client	Horizons USA

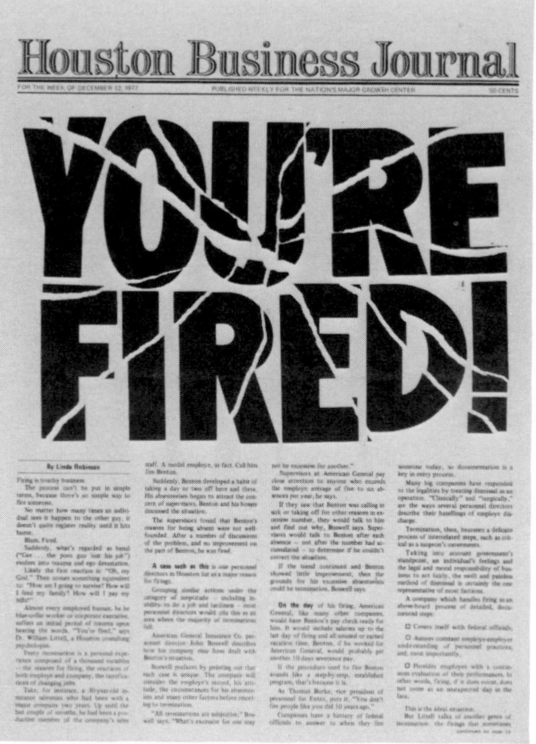

Houston Business Journal

FOR THE WEEK OF DECEMBER 12, 1977 PUBLISHED WEEKLY FOR THE NATION'S MAJOR GROWTH CENTER 50 CENTS

YOU'RE FIRED!

By Linda Robinson

Firing is touchy business.

The process can't be put in simple terms, because there's no simple way to fire someone.

No matter how many times an individual sees it happen to the other guy, it doesn't quite register reality until it hits home.

Blam. Fired.

Suddenly, what's regarded as banal ("Gee . . . the poor guy lost his job") evolves into trauma and ego devastation.

Likely the first reaction is: "Oh, my God." Then comes something equivalent to: "How am I going to survive? How will I feed my family? How will I pay my bills?"

Almost every employed human, be he blue-collar worker or corporate executive, suffers an initial period of trauma upon hearing the words, "You're fired," says Dr. William Littell, a Houston consulting psychologist.

Every termination is a personal experience composed of a thousand variables — the reasons for firing, the reactions of both employe and company, the ramifications of changing jobs.

Take, for instance, a 30-year-old insurance salesman who had been with a major company two years. Up until the last couple of months, he had been a productive member of the company's sales staff. A model employe, in fact. Call him Jim Benton.

Suddenly, Benton developed a habit of taking a day or two off here and there. His absenteeism began to attract the concern of supervisors. Benton and his bosses discussed the situation.

The supervisors found that Benton's reasons for being absent were not well-founded. After a number of discussions of the problem, and no improvement on the part of Benton, he was fired.

A case such as this is one personnel directors in Houston list as a major reason for firings.

Grouping similar actions under the category of ineptitude — including inability to do a job and tardiness — most personnel directors would cite this as an area where the majority of terminations fall.

American General Insurance Co. personnel director John Boswell describes how his company may have dealt with Benton's situation.

Boswell prefaces by pointing out that each case is unique. The company will consider the employe's record, his attitude, the circumstances for his absenteeism and many other factors before resorting to termination.

"All terminations are subjective," Boswell says. "What's excessive for one may not be excessive for another."

Supervisors at American General pay close attention to anyone who exceeds the employe average of five to six absences per year, he says.

If they saw that Benton was calling in sick or taking off for other reasons in excessive number, they would talk to him and find out why, Boswell says. Supervisors would talk to Benton after each absence — not after the number had accumulated — to determine if he couldn't correct the situation.

If the trend continued and Benton showed little improvement, then the grounds for his excessive absenteeism could be termination, Boswell says.

On the day of his firing, American General, like many other companies, would have Benton's pay check ready for him. It would include salaries up to the last day of firing and all unused or earned vacation time. Benton, if he worked for American General, would probably get another 10 days severance pay.

If the procedure used to fire Benton sounds like a step-by-step, established program, that's because it is.

As Thomas Burke, vice president of personnel for Entex, puts it, "You don't fire people like you did 10 years ago."

Companies have a battery of federal officials to answer to when they fire someone today, so documentation is a key in every process.

Many big companies have responded to the legalities by treating dismissal as an operation. "Clinically" and "surgically," are the ways several personnel directors describe their handlings of employe discharge.

Termination, then, becomes a delicate process of interrelated steps, each as critical as a surgeon's movements.

Taking into account government's standpoint, an individual's feelings and the legal and moral responsibility of business to act fairly, the swift and painless method of dismissal is certainly the one representative of most factions.

A company which handles firing as an above-board process of detailed, documented steps:

☐ Covers itself with federal officials,

☐ Assures constant employe-employer understanding of personnel practices, and, most importantly,

☐ Provides employes with a continuous evaluation of their performances. In other words, firing, if it does occur, does not come as an unexpected slap in the face.

This is the ideal situation.

But Littell talks of another genre of termination: the firings that sometimes

continued on page 13

345

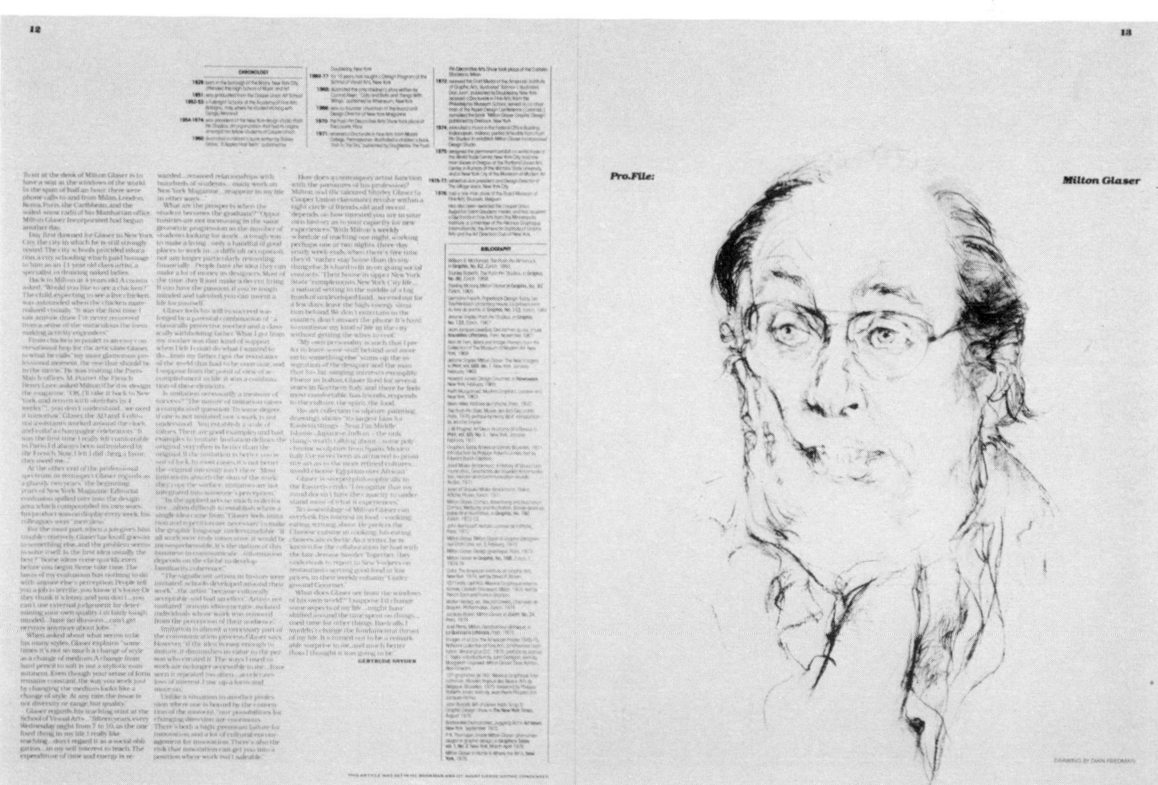

346

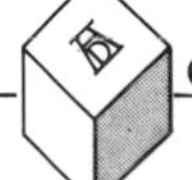

GOLD

345

Art Director Jay Loucks
Designers Jay Loucks
Bill Carson
Artists Jay Loucks
Larry McEntire
Bill Carson
Publisher Bob Gray
Houston Business Journal
(Cordovan Corp. Publishers)
Agency Loucks Atelier
Client Houston Business Journal

346

Art Director Herb Lubalin
Writers Jack Anson Finke
Gertrude Snyder
Designer Herb Lubalin
Artist Dian Friedman
Publisher International Typeface Corp.
Agency LSC&P Design Group
Client International Typeface Corp.

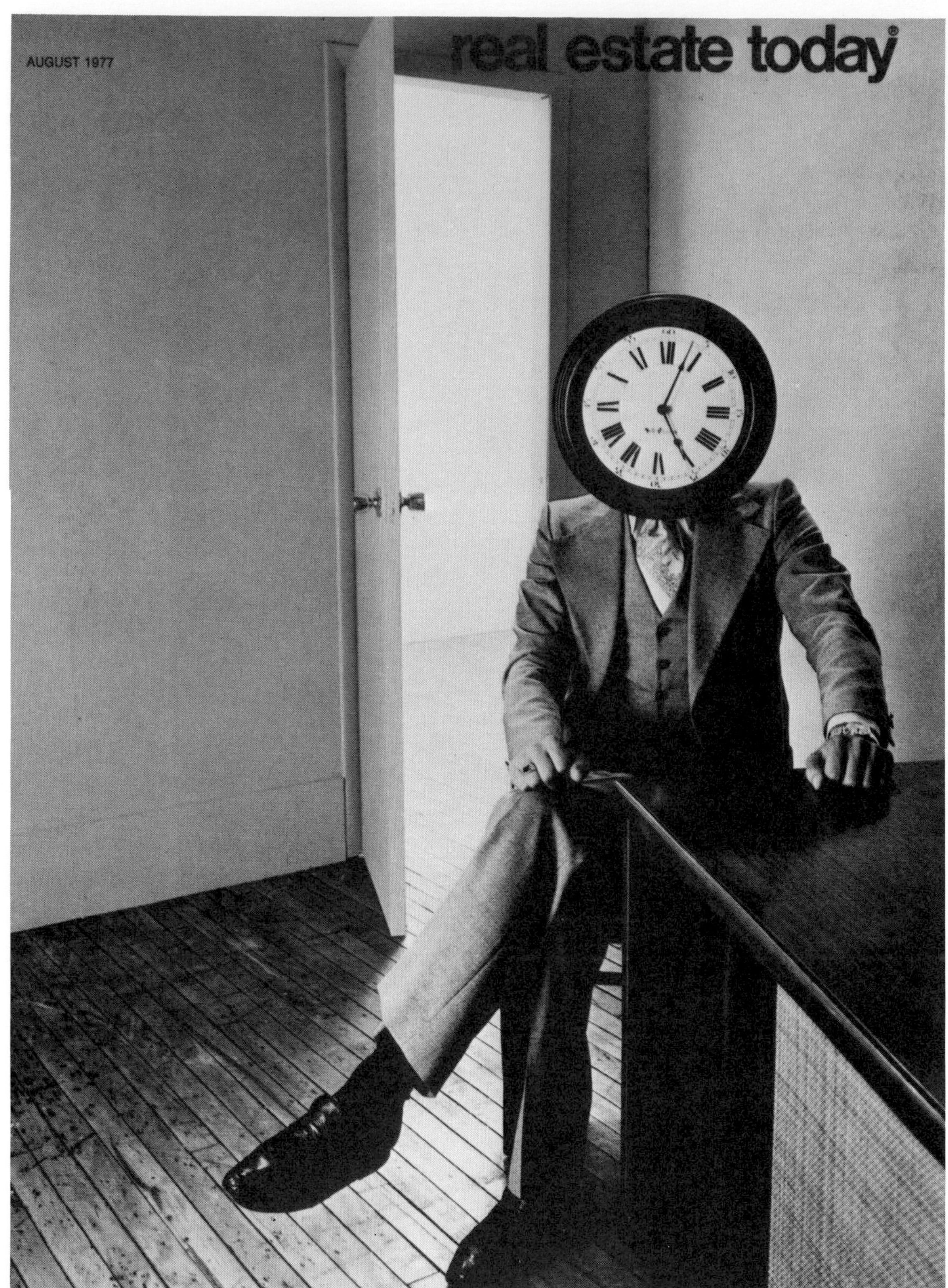

347

347
Art Director Carl Hofmann
Writer Isabelle Zainaldin
Photographer Tom Zamiar
Publisher Realtors National Marketing Institute®

348

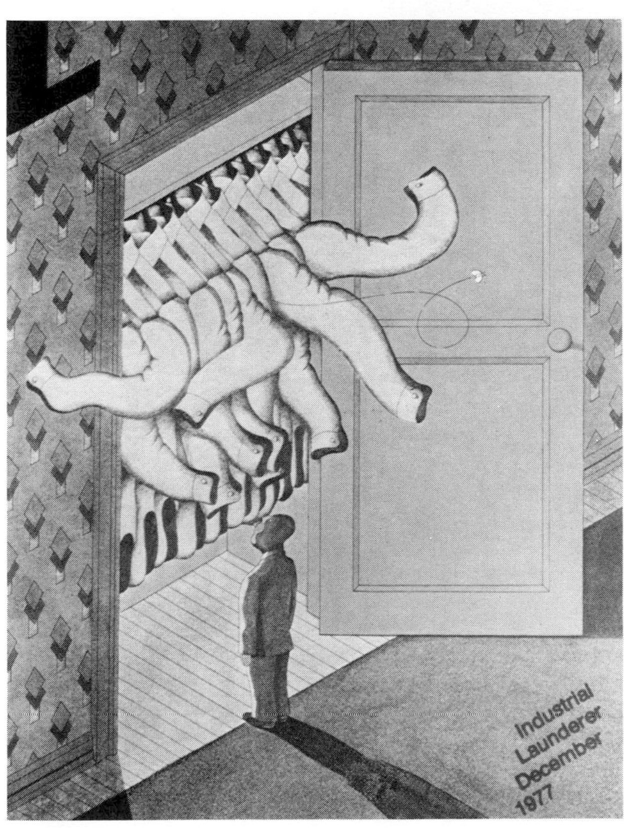

349

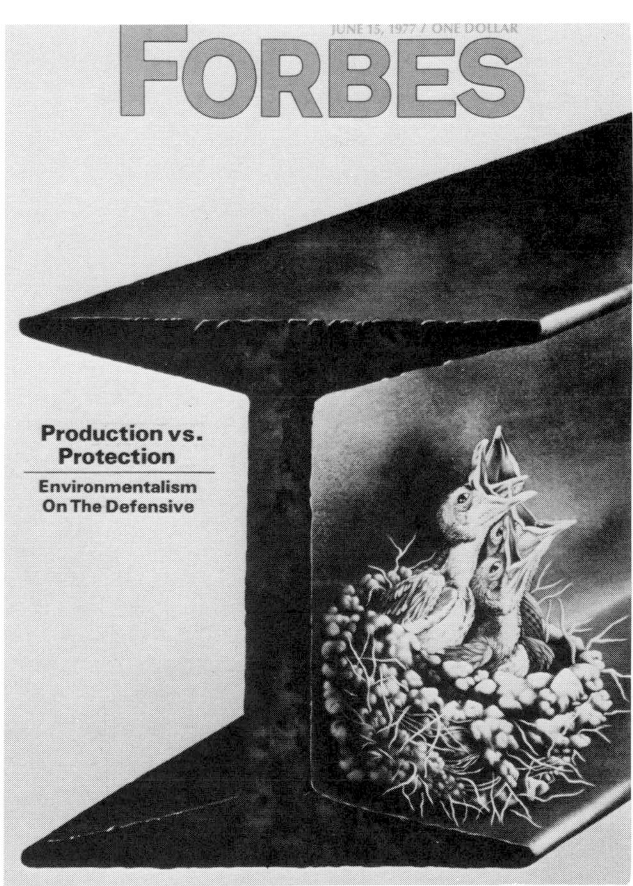

350

348
Art Director Jim Lienhart
Writers Hoyt Mathews
Vanessa Bush
Designer Jim Lienhart
Photographer Ibid
Publisher United States League of Savings Associations
Agency Jim Lienhart (Murrie White Drummond Lienhart & Assoc.)
Client Savings & Loan News

349
Art Director Jack Lefkowitz
Writer Jim Roberts
Designers Jack Lefkowitz
Pam Lefkowitz
Artists Jack Lefkowitz
Pam Lefkowitz
Publisher Institute of Industrial Launderers
Agency Jack Lefkowitz Inc.
Client Industrial Launderer Magazine
Institute of Industrial Launderers

350
Art Director Peter Palazzo
Editor James W. Michaels
Artist Melinda Bordelon
Publisher Forbes Inc.
Client Forbes Magazine

351

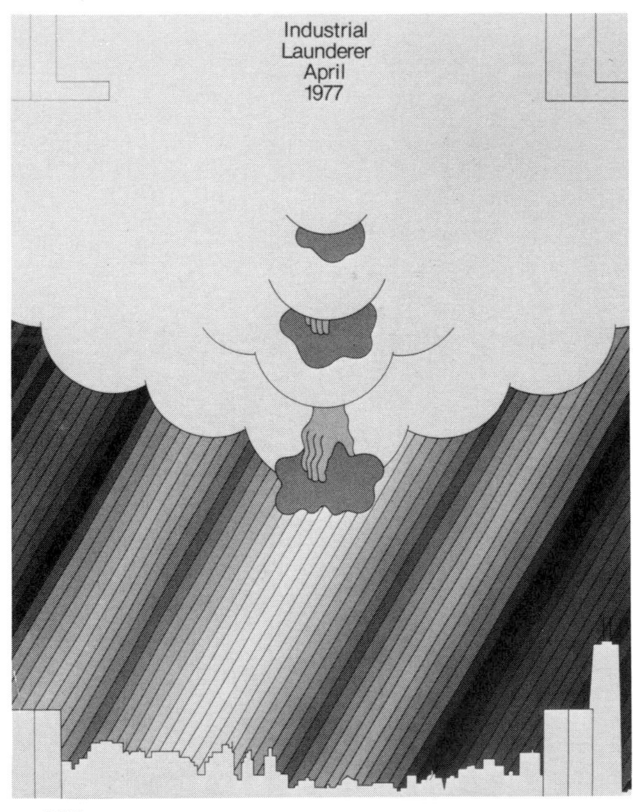

352

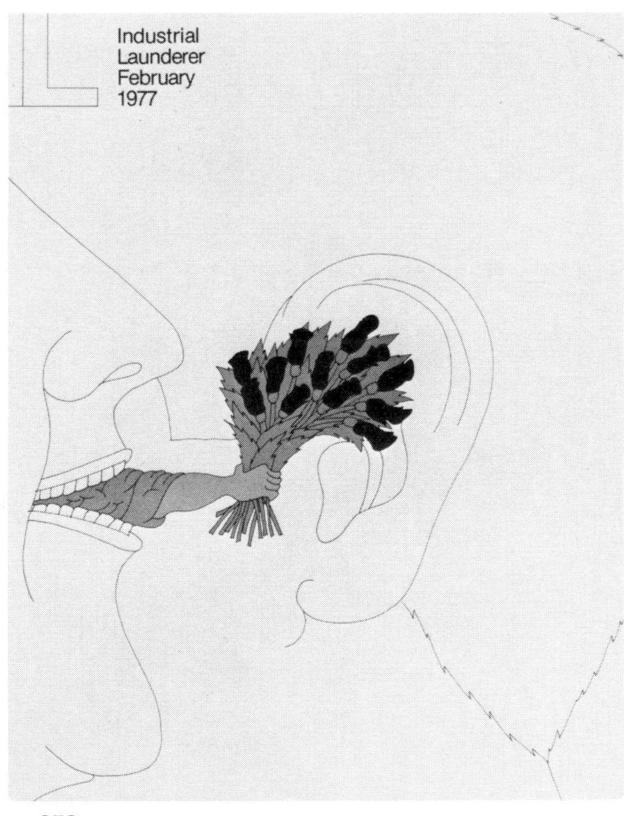

353

351
Director John C. Jay
Writers Marlene Deverell
Van Meter
Designer John C. Jay
Artist Ray Cruz
Publisher MBA Communications, Inc.
Client MBA Communications, Inc.

352
Art Director Jack Lefkowitz
Writer Jim Roberts
Designers Jack Lefkowitz
Pam Lefkowitz
Artists Jack Lefkowitz
Pam Lefkowitz
Publisher Institute of Industrial Launderers
Agency Jack Lefkowitz Inc.
Client Industrial Launderer Magazine
Institute of Industrial Launderers

353
Art Director Jack Lefkowitz
Writer Jim Roberts
Designers Jack Lefkowitz
Pam Lefkowitz
Artists Jack Lefkowitz
Pam Lefkowitz
Publisher Institute of Industrial Launderers
Agency Jack Lefkowitz Inc.
Client Industrial Launderer Magazine
Institute of Industrial Launderers

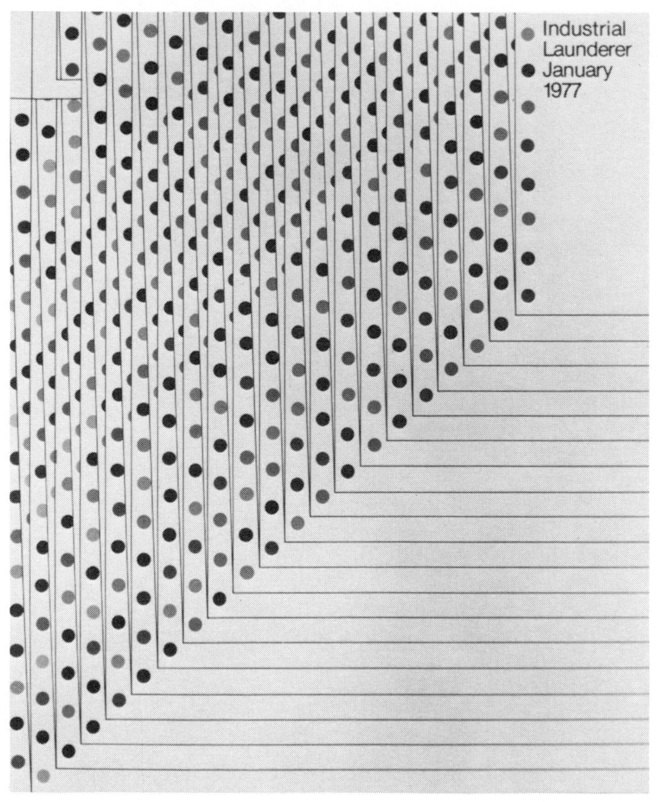

354

355

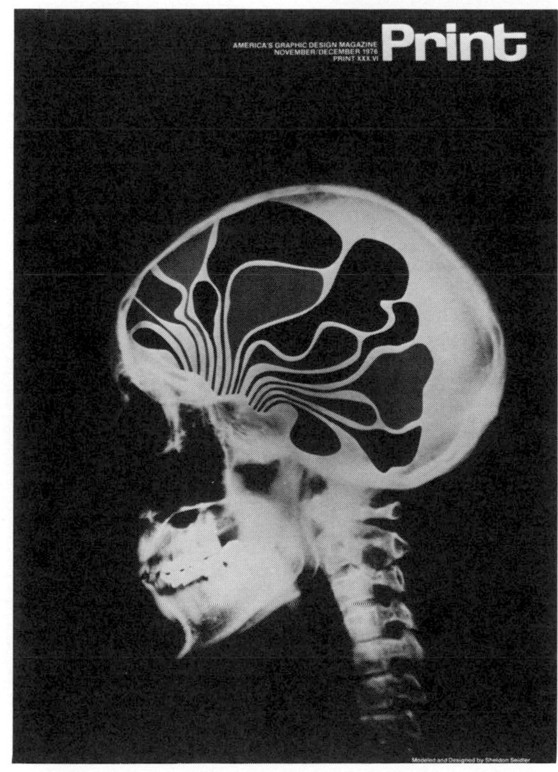

356

354

Art Director	Jack Lefkowitz
Writer	Jim Roberts
Designers	Jack Lefkowitz
	Pam Lefkowitz
Artists	Jack Lefkowitz
	Pam Lefkowitz
Publisher	Institute of Industrial Launderers
Agency	Jack Lefkowitz Inc.
Client	Industrial Launderer Magazine
	Institute of Industrial Launderers

355

Art Director	Ernest Scarfone
Writer	Patricia Maye
Designer	Ernest Scarfone
Photographer	Lloyd Englert
Publisher	Ehrenreich Photo Optical Ind.
Client	Nikon World

356

Art Director	Sheldon Seidler
Designer	Sheldon Seidler
Artists	Sheldon Seidler
	Werner Pfeiffer
Photographer	Dr. Simon
Publisher	R.C. Publication
Agency	Sheldon Seidler
Client	Print Magazine

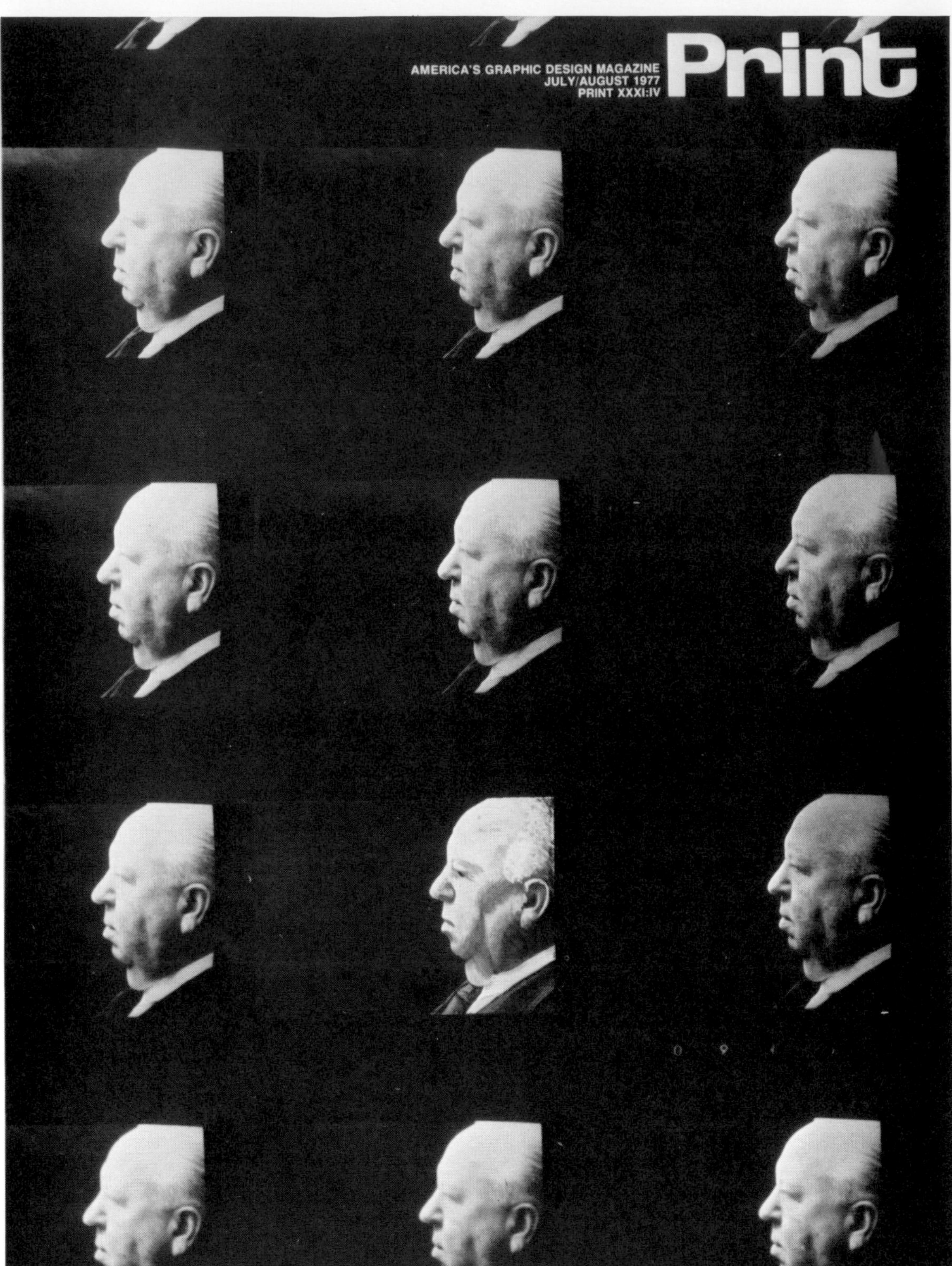

357

357
Art Director Andrew Kner
Writer Martin Fox
Designer Andrew Kner
Artist Andrew Kner
Publisher R.C. Publications
Client Print Magazine

358

359

358
Art Director Mary Sealfon
Writer Fred Schmidt
Designer Mary Sealfon
Photographer Pete Turner
Publisher Ziff-Davis Publishing Co.
Client Photomethods

359
Art Director Carl Hofman
Writer Isabelle Zainaldin
Photographer Tom Zamiar
Publisher Realtors National Marketing Institute®

360

361

360
Art Director W. Chris Gorman
Writer William G. O'Donnell
Designer W. Chris Gorman
Publisher The Baker & Taylor Companies
Client The Baker & Taylor Companies

361
Art Director Chester Peterson Jr.
Designer Craig Ridenour
Artist Craig Ridenour
Publisher Chester Peterson Jr.
Client Simmental Shield

362

363

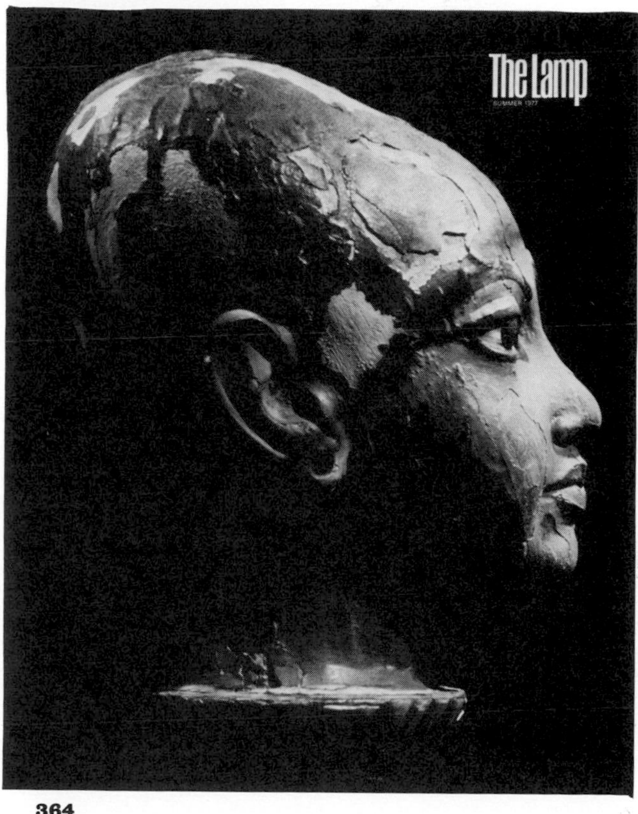

364

362
Consulting Art Director Peter Palazzo
Editor James W. Michaels
Artist Ed Soyka
Publisher Forbes Inc.
Client Forbes Magazine

363
Art Director Marvin Glick
Writer Glen Richardson
Publisher Crow Publications, Inc.
Client Dairy Magazine

364
Art Director Harry O. Diamond
Designer Harry O. Diamond
Photographer Co Rentmeester
Publisher Exxon Corp.
Client The Lamp
Exxon Corp.

365

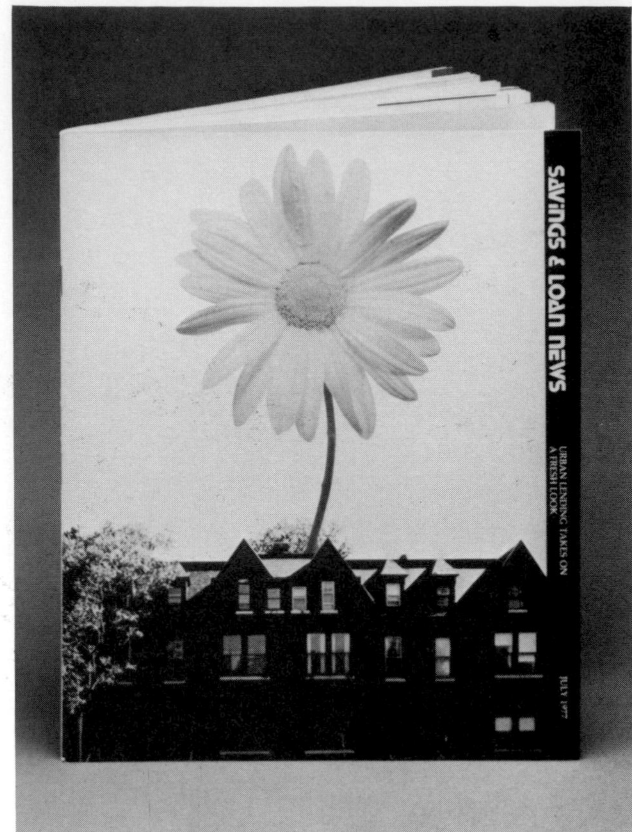

366

365
Art Director Rudi Wolff
Writer Robert Ubell
Designer Rudi Wolff
Artist René Magritte
Director Robert Ubell
Publisher N.Y. Academy of Science
Client The Sciences Magazine

366
Art Director Jim Lienhart
Writers Hoyt Mathews
William Marshall
Designer Jim Lienhart
Photographer Tom Vack
Publisher United States League
of Savings Associations
Agency Jim Lienhart
(Murrie White Drummond
Lienhart & Assoc.)
Client Savings & Loan News

Promotion and Graphic Design

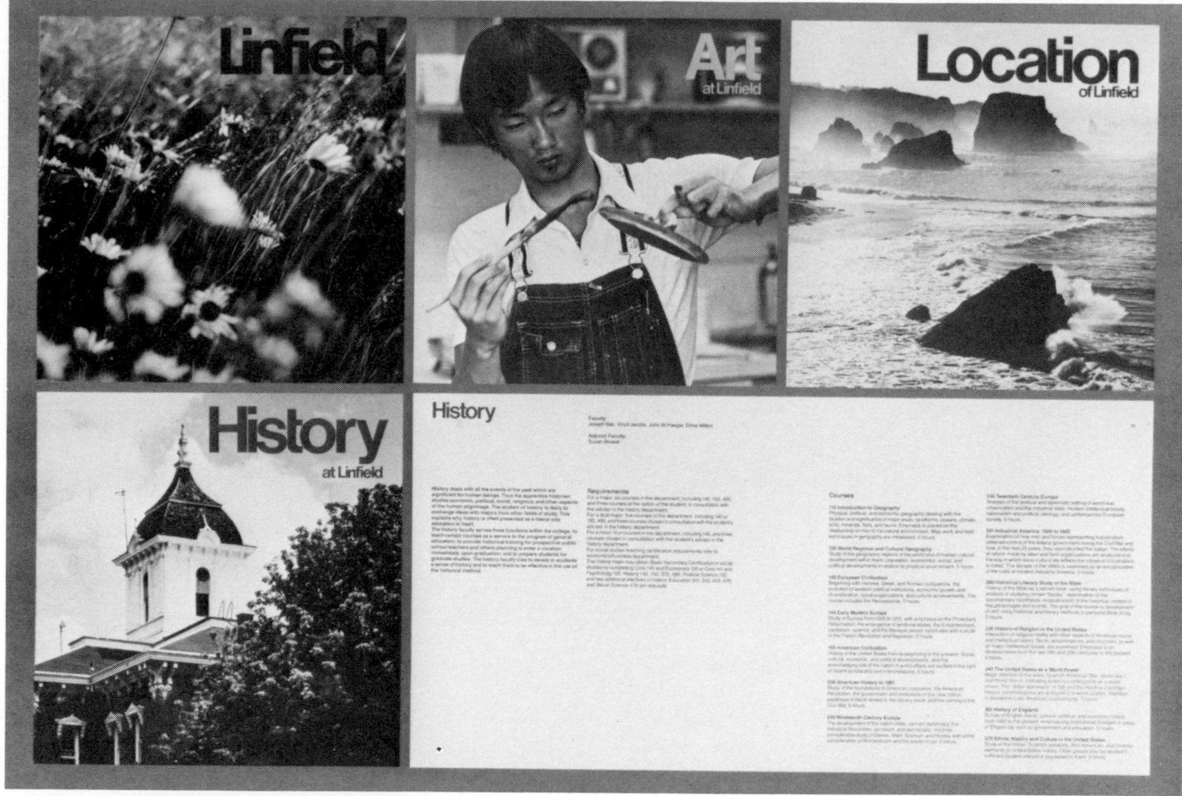

367

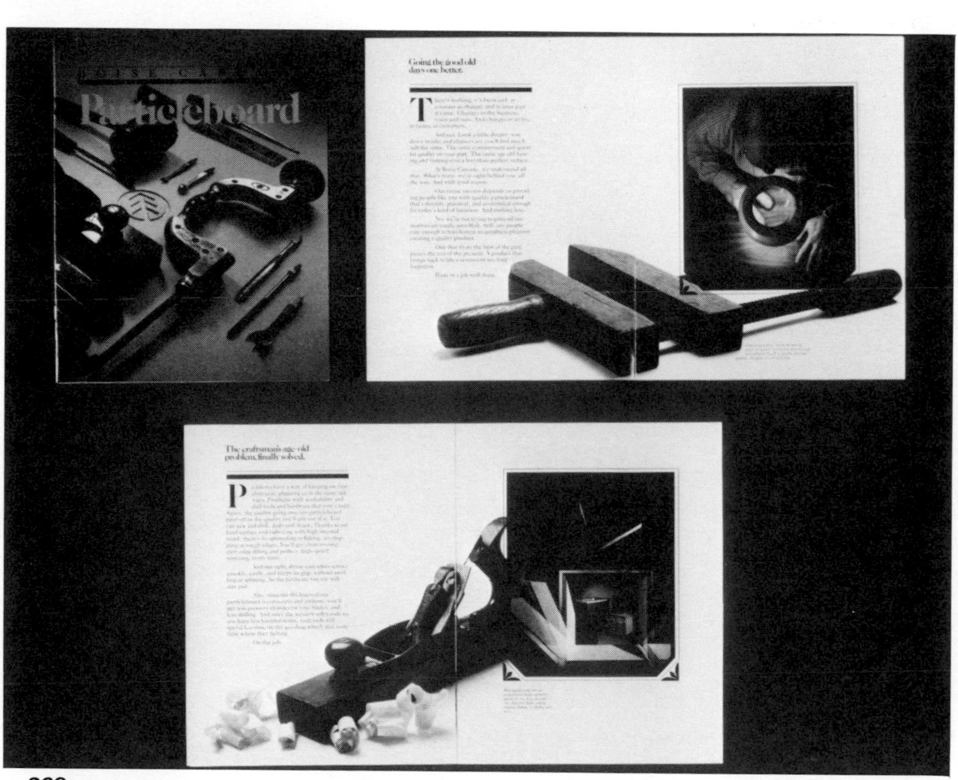

368

367

Art Directors	Robin Rickabaugh
	Heidi Rickabaugh
Editor	Ann Granning Bennett
Designer	Robin Rickabaugh
Artist	Terry Daline
Photographers	Lawrence Hudetz
	Joan Brown
	Mike Lloyd
Client	Linfield College

368

Art Director	Frank Roehr
Writer	JoAnn Lunt
Designer	Frank Roehr
Photographer	Ed Dull
Agency	Young & Roehr
Client	Boise Cascade Timber & Wood Products Group

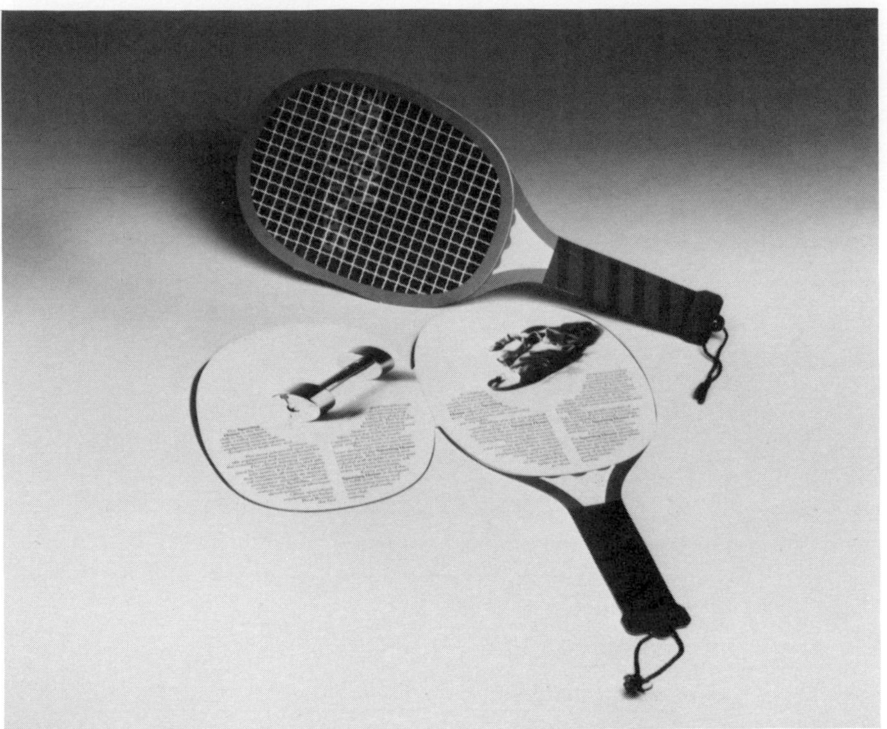

369

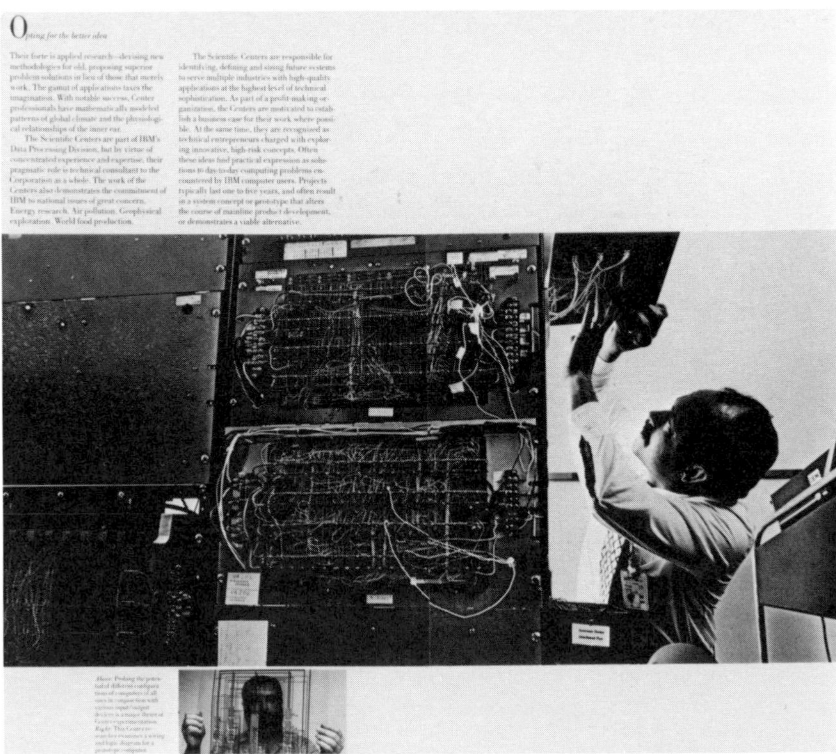

370

369
Art Director Jann Church Advertising & Graphic Design, Inc.
Writer Crowell/Anderson
Designer Jann Church Advertising & Graphic Design, Inc.
Artist Jann Church Advertising & Graphic Design, Inc.
Photographer John Lawder
Agency Jann Church Advertising & Graphic Design, Inc.
Client Sporting Houses of America

370
Art Directors Sal Ilardi
Richard Rogers
Writer Hugh Welborn
Designer Richard Rogers
Artist Richard Rogers
Photographers Paul Fusco
Burt Glinn
Eric Hartmann
Producer IBM Corporation
Agency Richard Rogers Inc.
Client IBM Corporation

The direction in which
knowledge starts a man will
determine his future.

371

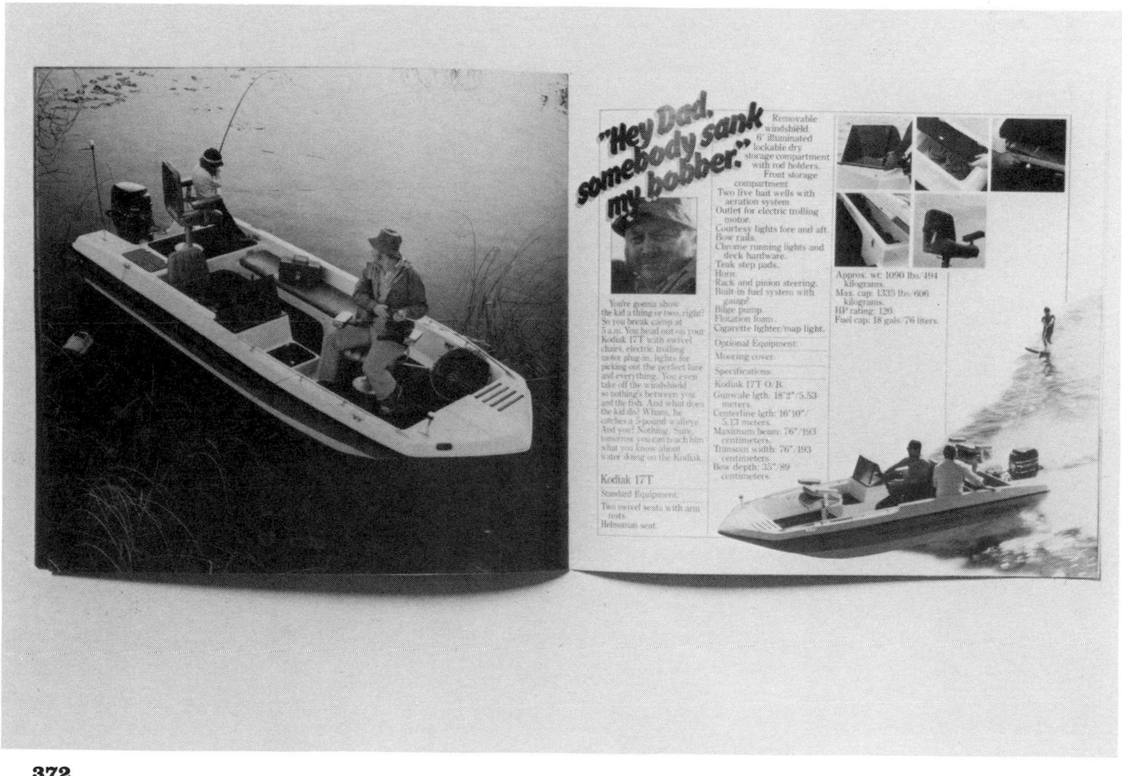
"Hey Dad, somebody sank my bobber."
Kodiak 17T

372

371

Art Directors Roger Cook
Don Shanosky
Writer John Monteleone
Designers Roger Cook
Don Shanosky
Photographers Arthur Beck
Allen Green
Agency Cook and Shanosky Associates, Inc.
Client The Johnson Companies

372

Art Director Frank Haggerty
Writer Bill Miller
Photographer Chuck Schmid
Agency Carmichael-Lynch, Inc.
Client Silverline, Division
of Arctic Enterprises, Inc.

The
SUMMER TIMES
1977 Syracuse University Summer Sessions 1977
When the green grass has replaced winter's white blanket and spring's gentle showers touch the land, a rainbow will appear in the sky. Follow the rainbow to summertime at Syracuse University.

373

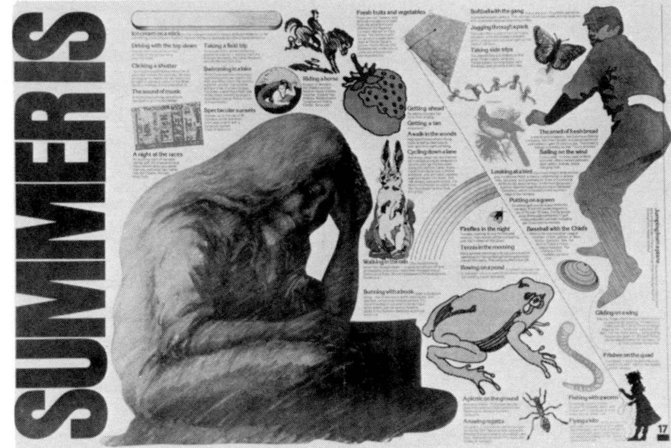

373

Art Director Don Trousdell
Writer Pat Very & Office of Summer Sessions
Designer Don Trousdell
Artists Don Trousdell
Paula Havey
Sandi Glass
Roger Poole
Nancy Stevenson
Cary Smith
Jane Kowalik
Barbara Sablow
Agency Don Trousdell (Freelancer)
Client Syracuse University, Div. of Summer Sessions

374

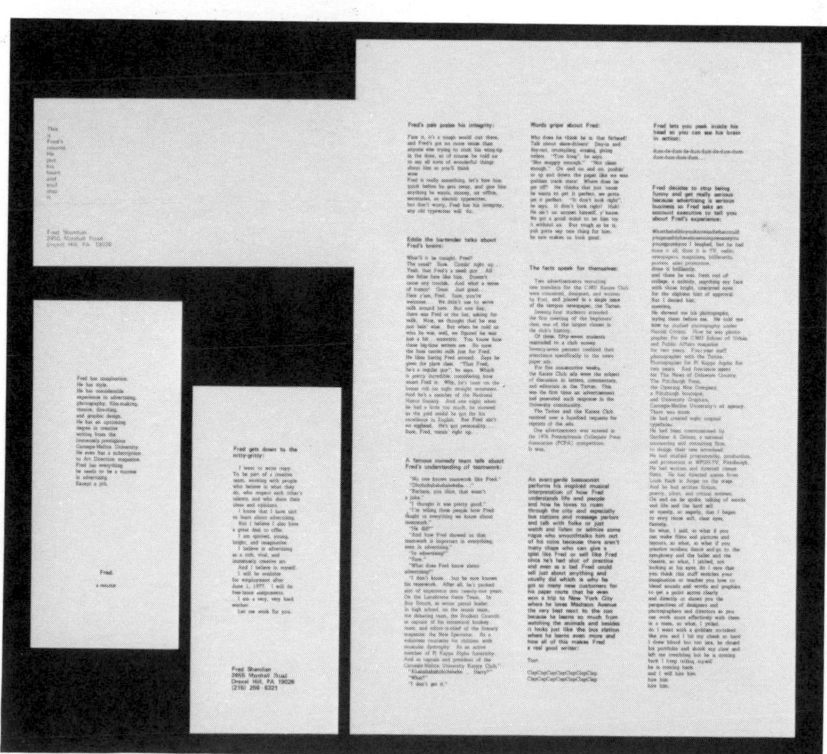

375

374
Art Director Peter Bradford
Writer Larry Hulack
Designer Jennifer Clark
Photographer Nancy Dubin
Agency Peter Bradford and Associates
Client Business Careers Inc.

375
Art Director Fred Shamlian
Writer Fred Shamlian
Designer Fred Shamlian
Agency Fred Shamlian
Client Fred Shamlian

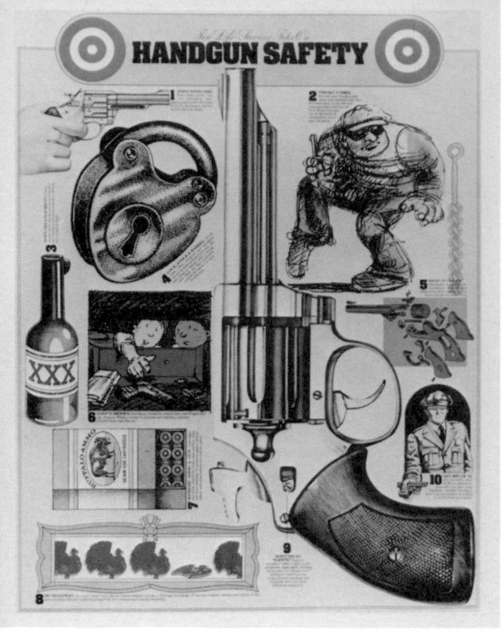

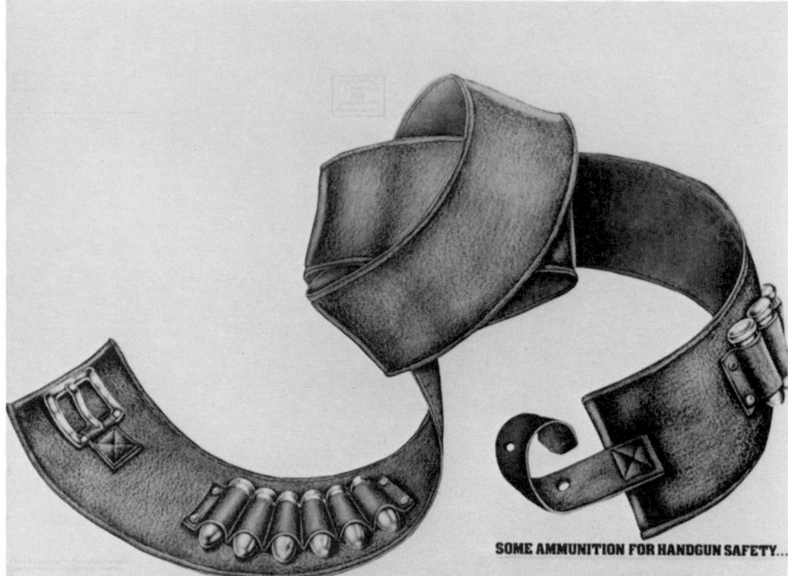

376

377

376

Art Director Carl T. Herrman
Writer Scott Gebhardt
Designer Nancy Hoefig/ Whole Hog Studios Ltd.
Artists Bill Mayer, Pamela Smith, Gail McCrory, Sandra Glass
Agency Super Creato
Client United States Conference of Mayors

377

Art Director B. Martin Pedersen
Writer Carole Lewis
Designer B. Martin Pedersen
Artist Jerry Cosgrove
Agency Jonson/Pedersen/Hinrichs
Client West Point Pepperell

The IBM Office Products Division
The Office Products Division (OPD) is large compared to most independent enterprises with over 180 branch offices spanning the country. And yet, OPD operates like a company-within-a-company. We develop, manufacture, sell and service word processing equipment and systems. Our proud record of growth and stability encourages today's modern office administrators to look to us for leading-edge innovation, technology and products.

The OPD Marketing Representative
In straightforward language, the OPD Marketing Representative markets IBM word processing products and systems. Marketing Representatives begin with some decided advantages.

IBM products are quality products. They make possible efficient, cost-saving solutions to important business problems.

IBM researches and develops a steady stream of new, advanced products and systems for markets anxious to solve word processing problems.

The market is vast and growing. Diverse businesses of all sizes require some form of word processing equipment.

The IBM name is known. Our reputation for superior quality and service is recognized.

OPD Marketing Representatives generally deal with customers at all levels of management, due to the importance of IBM products and systems to their business.

Marketing Representatives sell office products and systems that solve important business problems.

378

378
Art Director Peter McGuggart, Compton Advertising
Writer Compton Advertising
Designers Roger Cook
Don Shanosky
Photographer Arthur Beck
Agency Cook and Shanosky Associates, Inc.
Client IBM, Compton Advertising

379

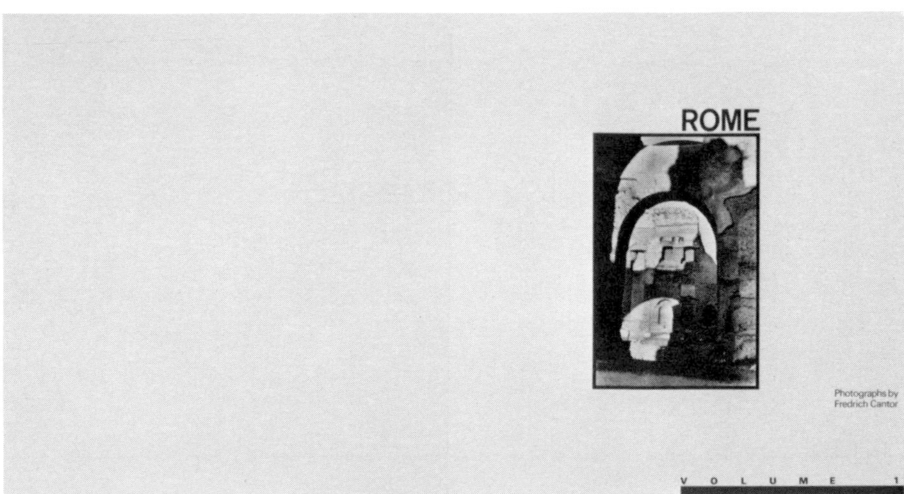

380

379

Art Director	John Casado
Designer	John Casado
Artist	Del Rae Hrubes
Photographer	Various
Agency	Casado, Ltd.
Client	Itel Corporation

380

Art Director	Willi Kunz
Writer	Janet Malcolm
Designer	Willi Kunz
Photographer	Fredrich Cantor
Client	Fredrich Cantor

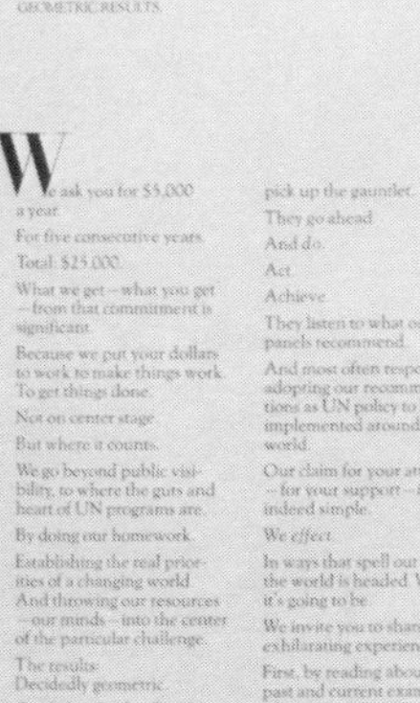

381

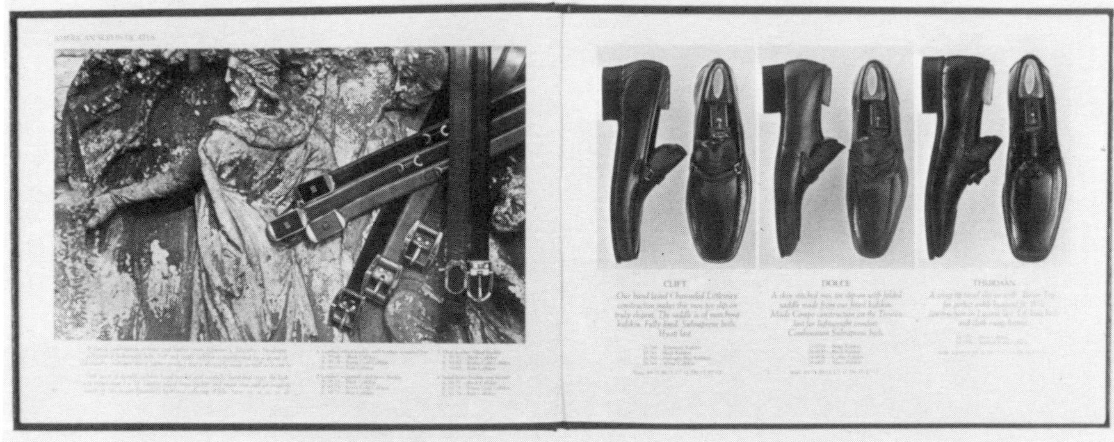

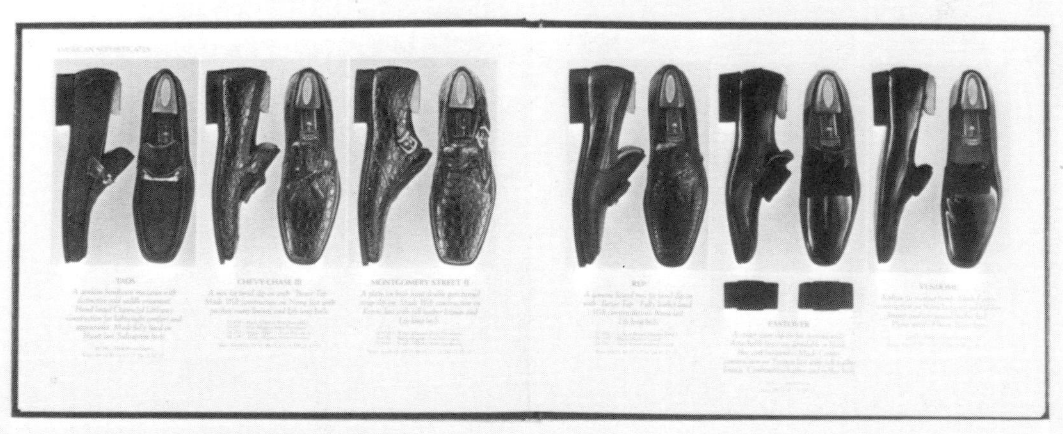

382

381
Art Director Jerry Cosgrove
Writer Emile Pragoff III
Designers Jerry Cosgrove
Vicki Navratil
Artists Vicki Navratil
Gabor Kiss
Photographer (Stock) Pete Turner;
Baldwin/Watriss & various others
Agency Cosgrove Associates Inc.
Client United Nations Association

382
Art Director Brad Whitfield
Designer S. Amjad Habib
Photographer Wolfgang Floge-Bohem
Agency Design Graphics Inc.
Client Johnston & Murphy Shoe Co.

383

384

383

Art Director	John Vandover
Writer	Leigh A. Doxsee
Designer	John Vandover
Photographer	John Vandover
Agency	Obata Design, Inc.
Client	Mercantile Bancorporation

384

Art Director	Steve Jacobs
Writer	Dick Garvin
Designers	Steve Jacobs
	Ed Jaciow
	Norman Orr
Photographers	Bill Arbogast
	Tom Tracy
Production Company	Anderson Litho
Agency	Steven Jacobs Design, Inc.
Client	Peterbilt Motors Company

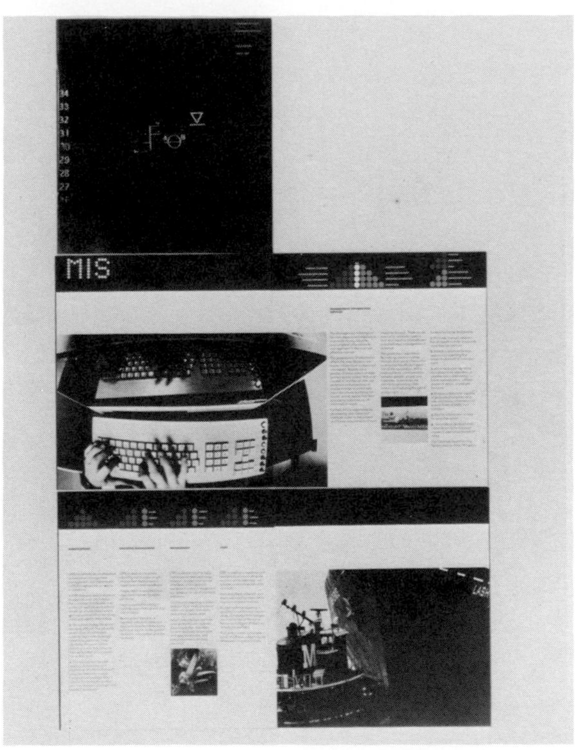

385

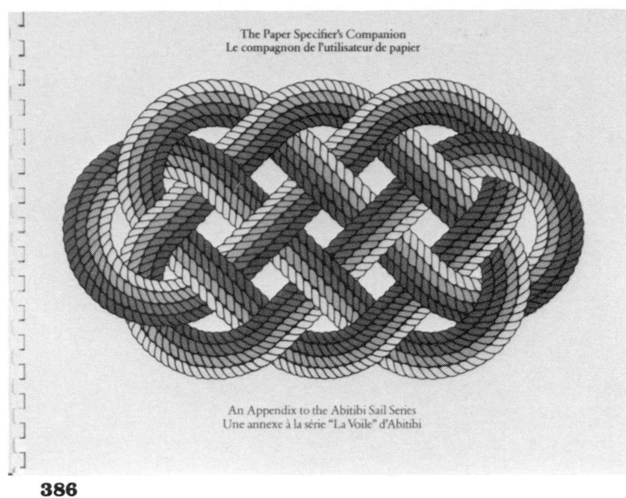

386

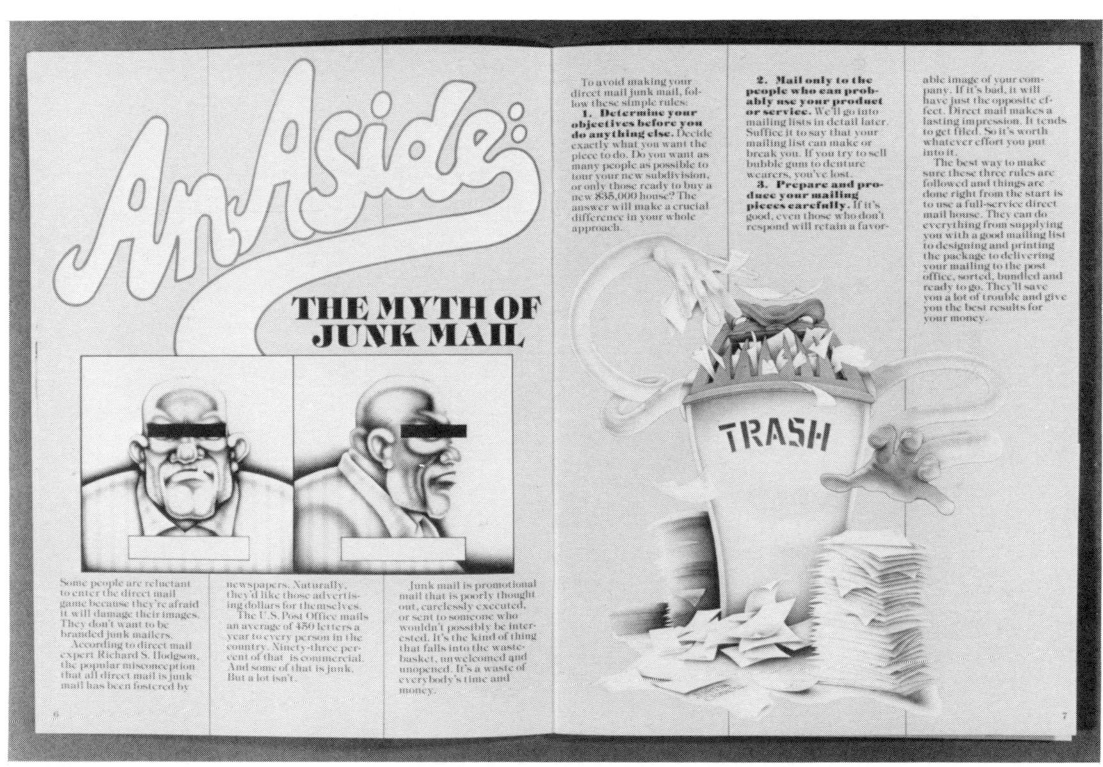

An Aside:

THE MYTH OF JUNK MAIL

Some people are reluctant to enter the direct mail game because they're afraid it will damage their images. They don't want to be branded junk mailers.

According to direct mail expert Richard S. Hodgson, the popular misconception that all direct mail is junk mail has been fostered by newspapers. Naturally, they'd like those advertising dollars for themselves.

The U.S. Post Office mails an average of 450 letters a year to every person in the country. Ninety-three percent of that is commercial. And some of that is junk. But a lot isn't.

Junk mail is promotional mail that is poorly thought out, carelessly executed, or sent to someone who wouldn't possibly be interested. It's the kind of thing that falls into the wastebasket, unwelcomed and unopened. It's a waste of everybody's time and money.

To avoid making your direct mail junk mail, follow these simple rules:

1. Determine your objectives before you do anything else. Decide exactly what you want the piece to do. Do you want as many people as possible to tour your new subdivision, or only those ready to buy a new $35,000 house? The answer will make a crucial difference in your whole approach.

2. Mail only to the people who can probably use your product or service. We'll go into mailing lists in detail later. Suffice it to say that your mailing list can make or break you. If you try to sell bubble gum to denture wearers, you've lost.

3. Prepare and produce your mailing pieces carefully. If it's good, even those who don't respond will retain a favorable image of your company. If it's bad, it will have just the opposite effect. Direct mail makes a lasting impression. It tends to get filed. So it's worth whatever effort you put into it.

The best way to make sure these three rules are followed and things are done right from the start is to use a full-service direct mail house. They can do everything from supplying you with a good mailing list to designing and printing the package to delivering your mailing to the post office, sorted, bundled and ready to go. They'll save you a lot of trouble and give you the best results for your money.

6

7

387

385
Art Director Carla Hall
Writer Cassandra Skouras
Designers Carla Hall, Ellen Shapiro, Ed Marson
Photographer Michael Hirst
Client Prudential Lines, Inc.

386
Art Director Robert Burns
Writer Jim Hynes
Designer Dawn Cooper Tennant
Artist Glynn Bell
Photographer Tim Saunders
Agency Burns, Cooper, Hynes Limited
Client Abitibi Provincial Paper

387
Art Director Marilyn Spears
Writer Sandy Sheehy
Designer Marilyn Spears
Artist Marilyn Spears
Photographer Reagan Bradshaw
Agency Neal Spelce Associates/ Manning, Selvage & Lee
Client Texas Mailing and Printing

388

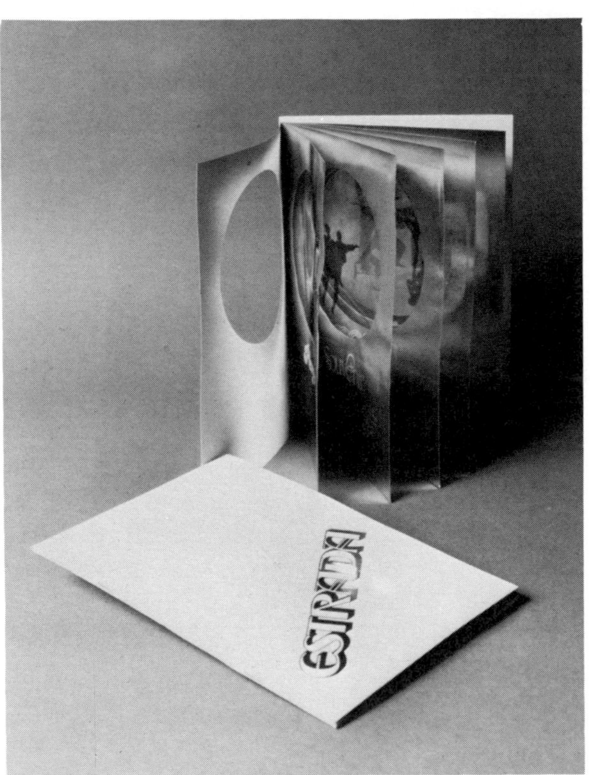

389

388
Art Director Jim Jarratt
Writers Klaus Wust
Norbet Muehlen
Designer Marion Rector
Agency The Creative Department, Inc.
Client National Carl Schurz Association

389
Art Director Don Gordon
Writer Peter Le Donne
Designer Gene Krackehl
Artist Gene Krackehl
Agency Ash/Le Donne
Client United Euram Corp.

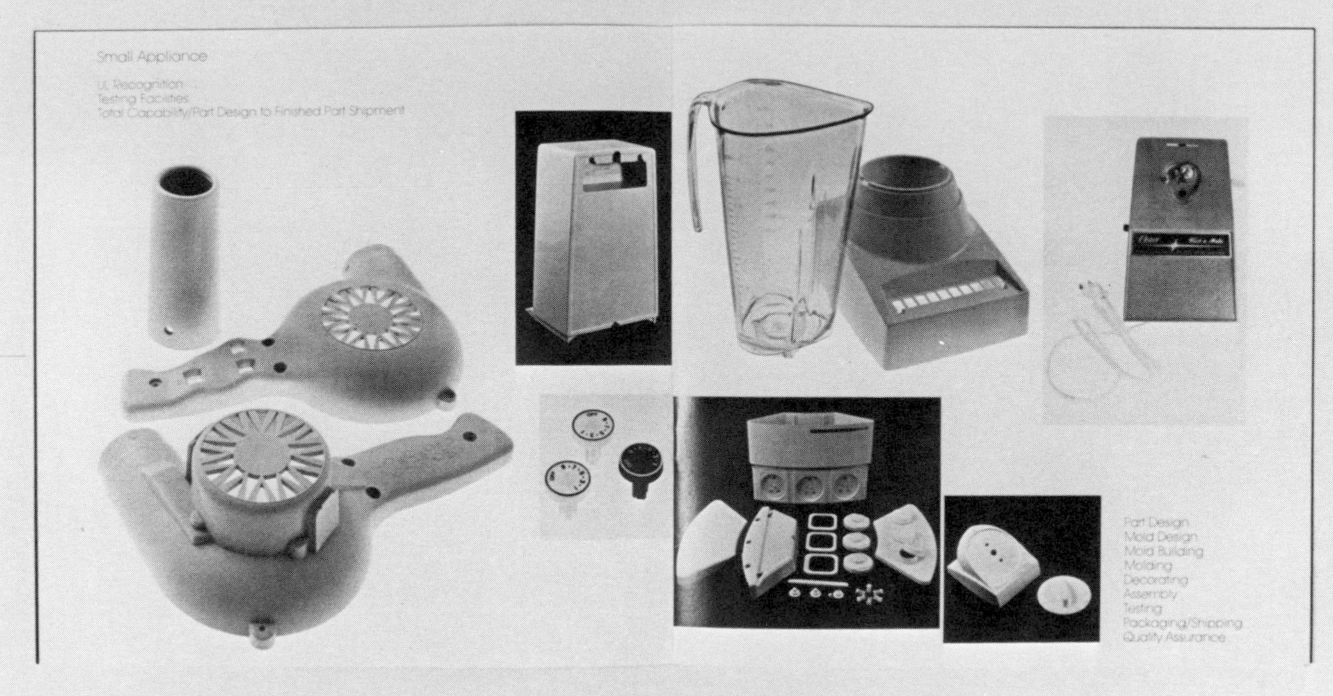

390

391

390
Art Director Brad Whitfield
Designer Brad Whitfield
Artist Charles McAllen
Photographer Chris Kelley
Agency Design Graphics Inc.
Client Kusan

391
Art Director Michael B. Richards
Designer Glade Christensen
Artists Scott Greer
Kerry Gonzales
Agency University of Utah Graphic Design
Client Financial Aids & Scholarships,
University of Utah

392

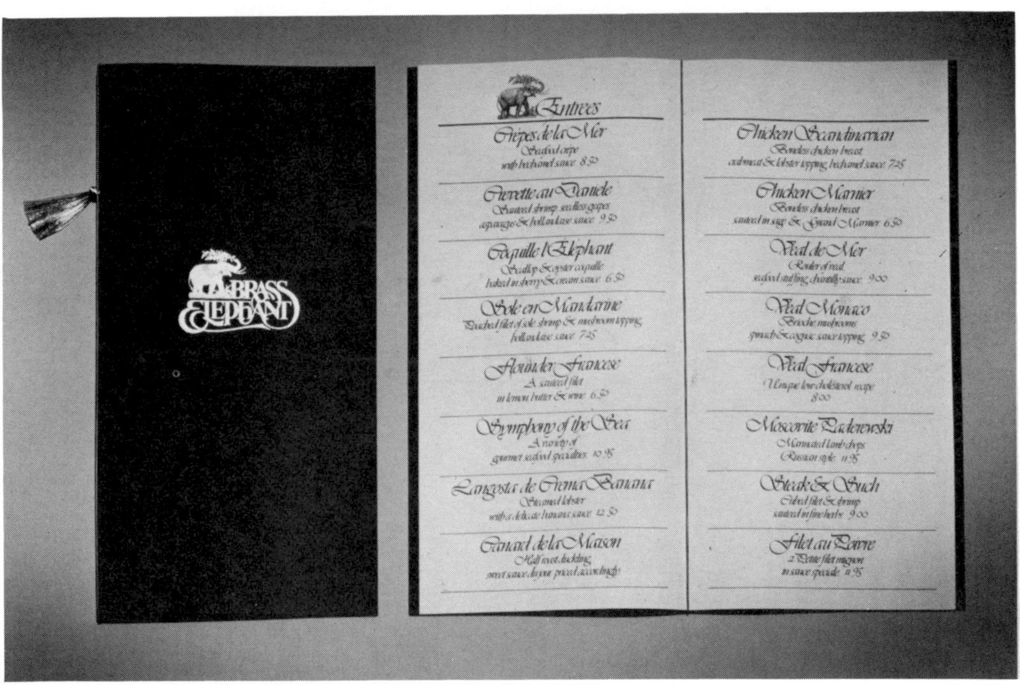

393

392
Art Director Robert Sadler
Designer Robert Sadler
Artist Robert Sadler
Agency Robert Sadler Design
Client Deloitte, Haskins & Sells

393
Art Director Carolyn Wade Frazier Studio
Writer Client
Designer Marilyn Worseldine
Artist Carolyn Wade Frazier
Agency Carolyn Wade Frazier Studio
Client Brass Elephant Restaurant

The first "sugar" revolution began in India.

For thousands of years a tall grass grew in Northern India. Local natives called it "sakcharon" and would cut off a piece and chew or suck it for sweetness.

About 300 B.C. Alexander the Great heard about this special cane plant while battling in India. He took home a sample as a souvenir, proclaiming it *"the reed that drips honey."* Interestingly enough, even in these times, a new sweetener could only be described or measured by comparison with the current sweetener.

The first crystallized sugar, and how it spread.

The first authentic evidence of truly crystalline sugar dates from Persia, in 627 A.D. Mohammed's religious wars spread the word of this new sweetener, *"almost as fine as honey,"* throughout the Islamic empire. People spoke in wonder of *"this curious foreign salt, which looks like salt—but tastes like honey."*

But it was in Egypt that sugar-growing and processing became an art. Egyptians adapted their existing process for the refining of saltpeter to sugar. The result was the finest granulated sugar known in the world at that time.

The spread of cane sugar throughout Europe was hastened by the Holy Crusades. Crusaders found this new sweetener so valuable and profitable, they sometimes quit the holy battles to raise cane for export home.

Columbus was an unsuccessful sugar planter.

It's true. Christopher Columbus set out to build a sugar industry in Santa Domingo in 1493. He failed when cooperative cheap labor could not be found.

Later a successful sugar industry was established on Santa Domingo with the help of imported slave labor. This example was quickly followed elsewhere. Soon sugar cane was cultivated wherever the climate was favorable and cheap labor plentiful.

Sugar Cane (Saccharum officinarum)

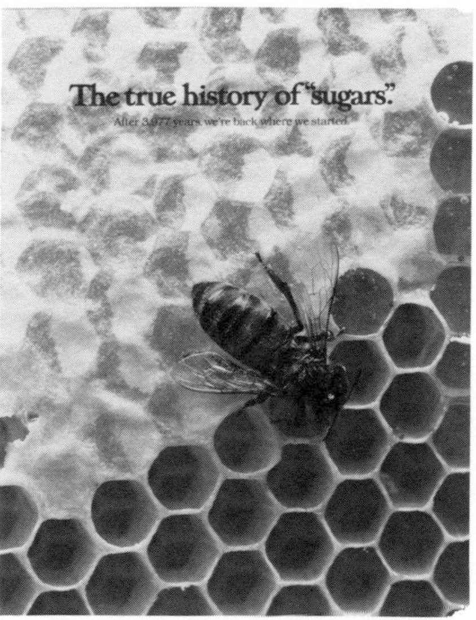

The true history of "sugars."
After 5,977 years, we're back where we started.

Man's first "sugar" is wild honey.

(Chemically fructose/dextrose.)

394

394
Art Director Ken Morrison
Writer Sandra Bucholtz
Designer Ken Morrison
Artist Bob Ziering
Photographer Frank Miller
Agency Martin Williams Advertising
Client ADM Corn Sweeteners

395

396

395
Art Director Lou Dorfsman
Writer Paula Gottschalk
Designers Lou Dorfsman
Ira Teichberg
Cover Concept Lou Dorfsman
Photographers Cover: Ben Somoroff
Inside: Various
Agency CBS/Broadcast Group
Client CBS Inc.

396
Art Director Miho
Writer David R. Brown
Designer Miho
Artist Miho and others
Photographer Miho
Client Champion Papers

398

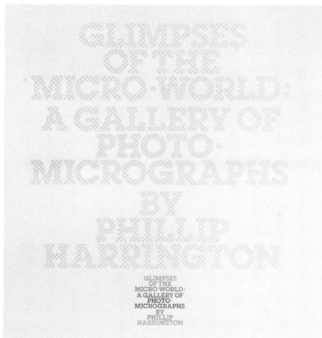

397

399

397
Art Director Frank Satogata
Writers Hal Bowser
Rick Dieringer
Designer Frank Satogata
Photographer Phillip Harrington
Client The Hennegan Printing Co.

398
Art Director Alyssia Lazin
Designer Alyssia Lazin
Artist Alyssia Lazin
Agency Alyssia Lazin Design Studio
Client Yale University
Symphony Orchestra

399
Art Directors Onofrio Paccione
Zane Tankel
Writer Michael Lissauer
Designer Onofrio Paccione
Client Collier Graphic Services

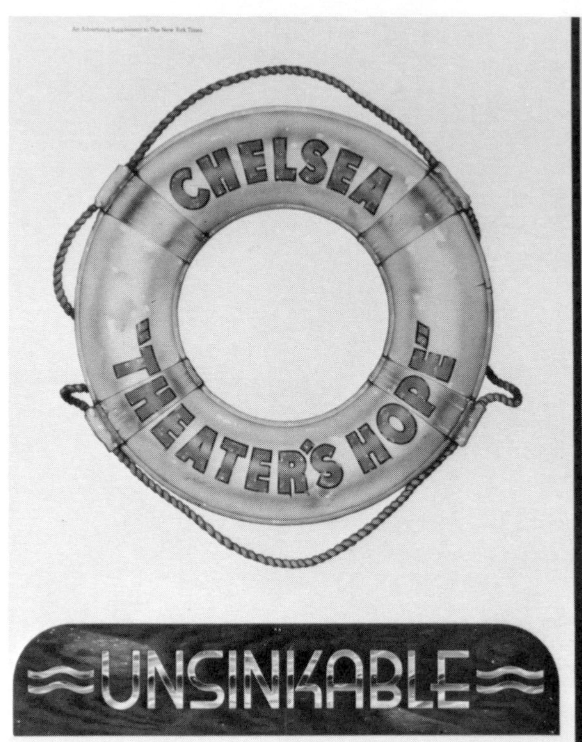

400

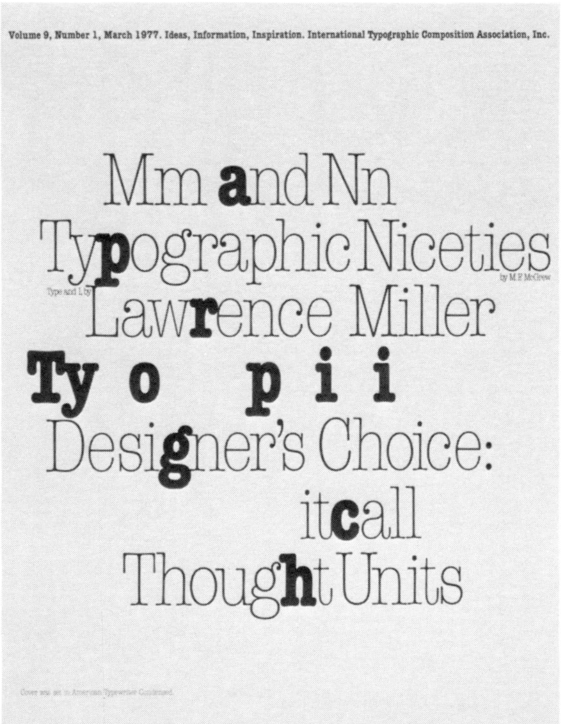

401

400
Art Directors Doug Johnson
Michael David
Designers Doug Johnson
Herb Bossardt
Artists Doug Johnson
Lettering by Gerard Huerta
Agency Performing Dogs
Client Chelsea Theater Center

401
Art Director Lawrence Miller/Design Alliance Inc.
Writer/Editor Edward M. Gottschau
Designer Lawrence Miller
Artist Donald Reilly, Hour Hands Inc.
Agency Design Alliance, Inc.
Client International Typographic
Composition Association

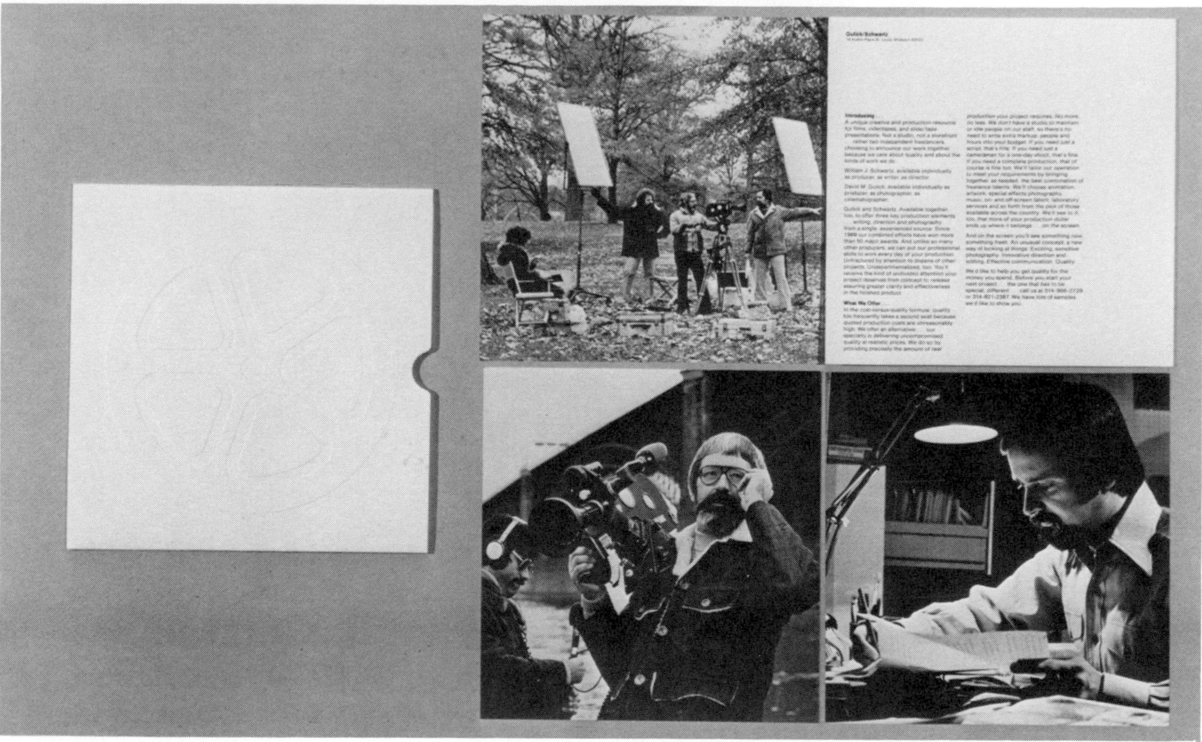

402

403

402
Art Director **Stan Gellman**
Writer **William J. Schwartz**
Designer **Janet Nebel**
Artist **Janet Nebel**
Photographer **David M. Gulick**
Agency **Stan Gellman Graphic Design, Inc.**
Client **Gulick/Schwartz**

403
Art Director **Rick Horton**
Writer **Alan VanDine**
Designer **Rick Horton**
Artist **Dave Roos**
Agency **VanDine Horton McNamara Manges**
Client **The Koppers Company**

The Federal Design Response **American Institute of Graphic Arts**

Designers who have responded creatively to the Federal government's communication needs were invited to submit their work to The Federal Design Response. This is a design competition sponsored by the AIGA in cooperation with the Federal Design Council providing an opportunity to show projects that solve the unique communication problems presented by government agencies. Entries submitted to The Federal Design Response were judged by a distinguished jury consisting of Saul Bass, Bill Lacy and Paul Rand. This catalogue contains 64 selected entries which form an AIGA exhibit scheduled to open at the AIGA gallery in New York City on November 29, 1977. As an AIGA traveling exhibit, the show will travel nationally and internationally during the coming year.

404

404

Art Director	Bob Salpeter
Writers	Erica Udoff
	Mike Gorner
Designer	Bob Salpeter
Calligrapher	Hal Fiedler
Agency	Lopez Salpeter, Inc.
Client	American Institute of Graphic Arts and The Federal Design Council

a company in transition

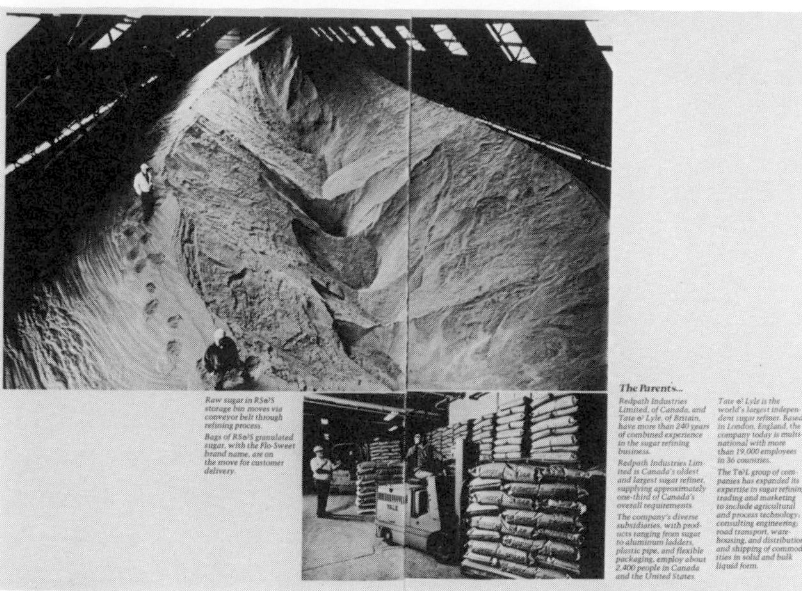

Raw sugar in RS&S storage bin moves via conveyor belt through refining process.

Bags of RS&S granulated sugar, with the Flo-Sweet brand name, are on the move for customer delivery.

The Parents...

Redpath Industries Limited, of Canada, and Tate & Lyle, of Britain, have more than 240 years of combined experience in the sugar refining business.

Redpath Industries Limited is Canada's oldest and largest sugar refiner, supplying approximately one-third of Canada's overall requirements.

The company's diverse subsidiaries, with products ranging from sugar to aluminum ladders, plastic pipe, and flexible packaging, employ about 2,400 people in Canada and the United States.

Tate & Lyle is the world's largest independent sugar refiner. Based in London, England, the company today is multinational with more than 19,000 employees in 36 countries.

The T&L group of companies has expanded its expertise in sugar refining, trading and marketing to include agricultural and process technology, consulting engineering, road transport, warehousing, and distribution, and shipping of commodities in solid and bulk liquid form.

Today Refined Syrups & Sugars Inc. supplies refined cane sugar in solid and liquid form to food and related industries. The company also is developing a full line of sugar products for the consumer market.

While current production is approximately 80% liquid and 20% granulated, RS&S's objective is a reversal of this output. RS&S's capital investment to meet this goal is estimated to be about $15 million.

When this transition is completed, the company will be refining and marketing a full range of sugar products: granulated, liquid, soft (dark and light brown), powdered, and blends of cane and corn sweeteners.

The company's cane/corn liquid blending capabilities are recognized throughout the food industry and it is acknowledged that its systems and its technology are of the first-order.

405

405

Art Director	Carol Vanderhoven Moore
Writer	Richard Stinnette
Designer	Carol Vanderhoven Moore
Artist	(Cover) Jane Hively Barber
Photographer	Dennis Chalkin
Agency	Davis-Delaney-Arrow Inc.
Client	Refined Syrups & Sugars Inc.

406

407

406

Art Directors Bill Bundzak
Larry Goldman
Writer Sybil Carlin
Designer Bill Bundzak
Artists Bill Bundzak
Barbara Montgomery
Agency Larry Goldman
Client Des-Con Interiors

407

Art Director David Lizotte
Writer Leverett Peters
Designer David Lizotte
Photographers Lily Peters
Larry Long
Jim Thomas
Steve Grohe
Agency Gunn Associates
Client Monadnock Paper Mills, Inc.

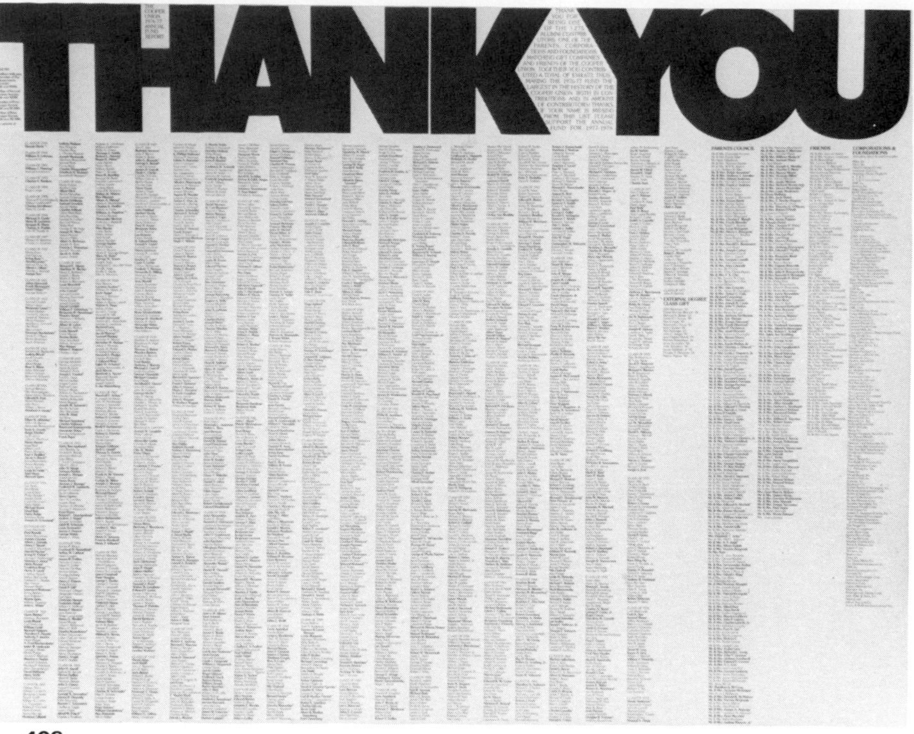

408

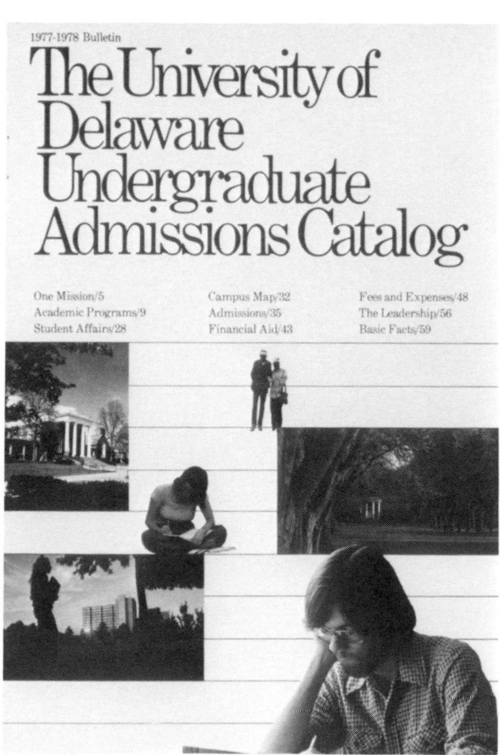

409

408
Art Director Marilyn Hoffner
Writer Marilyn Hoffner
Designer Marilyn Hoffner
Client The Cooper Union Alumni Association

409
Art Director Ed Gold
Writer Dave Treadwell/Client
Designer Barbara Brown
Photographer Dick Durrance/Client
Agency The Barton-Gillet Co.
Client University of Delaware

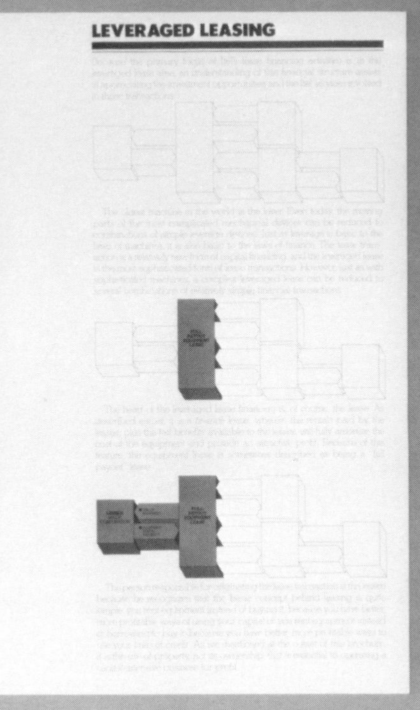

410

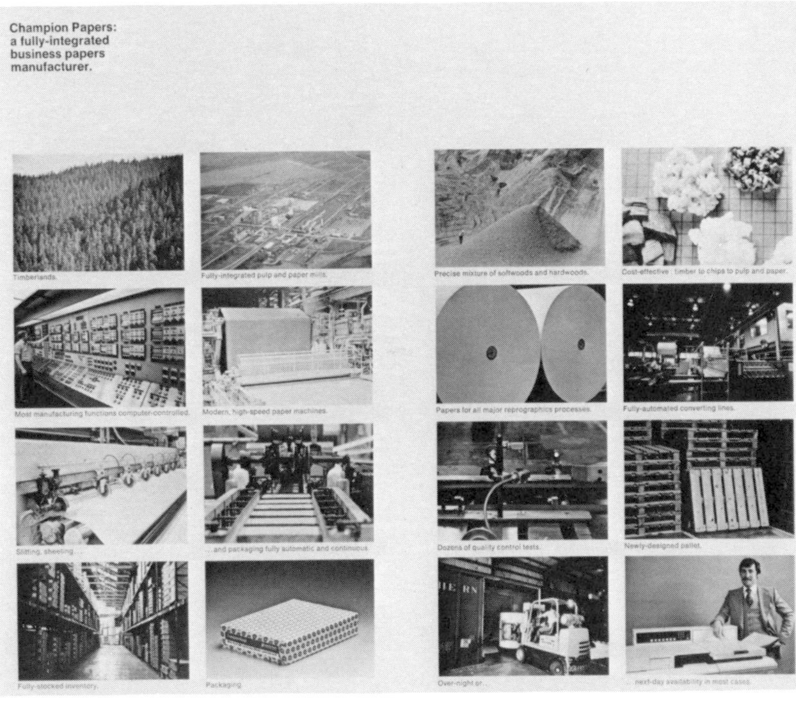

411

410
Art Director Thom Laperle
Writer John Bannister, Jr.
Designer Thom Laperle
Artist Hank Barenz
Photographer Tom Tracy
Production Company Anderson Lithograph Company
Agency Laperle/Assoc., Inc.
Client Itel Corp.

411
Art Director Miho
Writer David R. Brown
Designer Miho
Artist Miho
Photographer Miho
Client Champion Papers

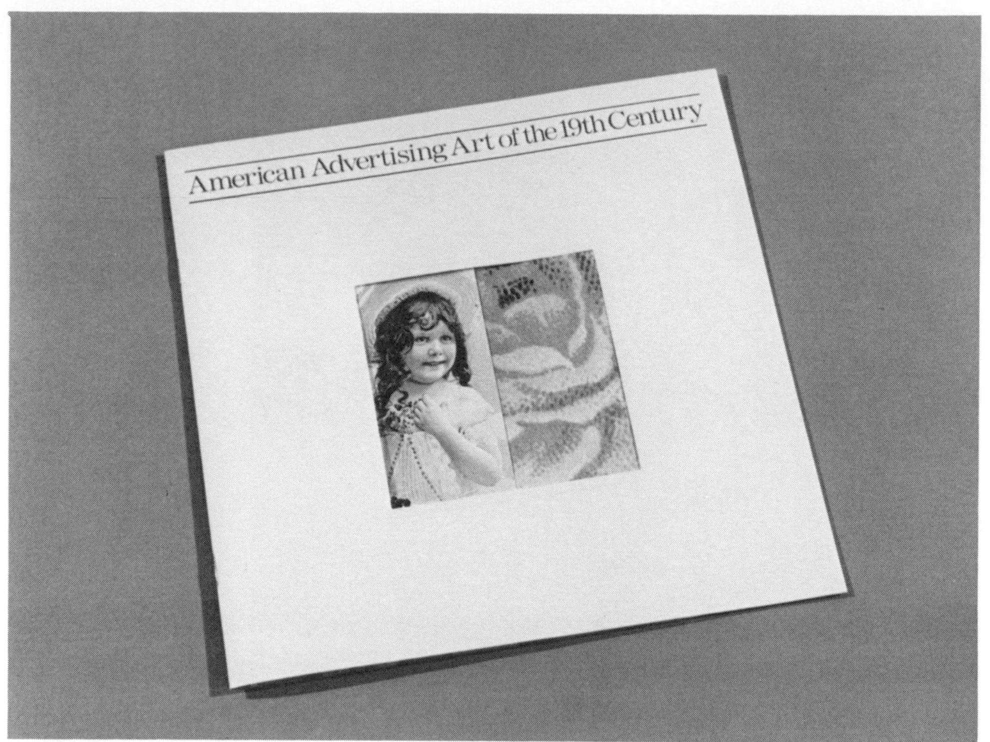

412

413

412
Art Director Duane A. Hammond
Writer Dean Barrett
Designer Hugh E. Bird
Agency Magnificent Art Machine
Client Monadnock Paper Mills, Inc.

413
Art Director Donald A. Adamec
Writers Elaine Simchowitz
Ed Chapman
Designer Donald A. Adamec
Photographer Alan Vogel
Producer Elaine Simchowitz
Agency Adamec Assoc.
Client Fritz & La Rue Co., Inc.

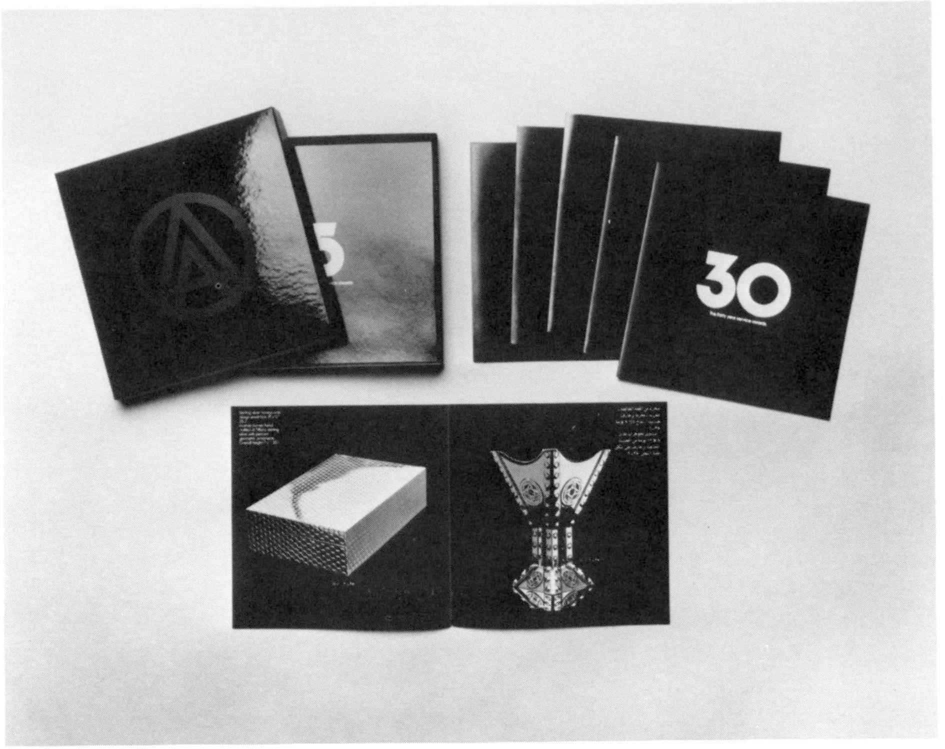

414

415

414
Art Director Frank Schulwolf
Writers Arthur Low
Esam Trabulsi
Designer Frank Schulwolf
Photographer Robert Panuska
Agency Frank Schulwolf
Client Aramco

415
Art Director Herb Lubalin
Designer Herb Lubalin
Artists Hedda Johnson
Seymour Chwast
Photographers Henry Sandbank
Pete Turner
Agency LSC&P Design Group
Client American Showcase

416

Fruit cocktail under glass. If you like fresh fruit, you'll go bananas over this. Bananas. Tree-ripened and fresh picked. Oranges. Bursting with juice and brilliant with flavor. Grapefruit wedges so intensely delicious they need no sugar. And fresh pineapple. Ready to be chopped into small, sweet chunks.

Together, they make a fruit cocktail that kingdoms might fight over. Yet this can become commonplace for you if you select the "fruit cocktail under glass."

We'll build a greenhouse in your backyard big enough to hold a banana tree. Then we'll stock it with a banana tree, a grapefruit tree, a small crop of pineapples and an orange tree (including an inflatable likeness of Anita Bryant).

We'll set it up, but from then on, it's up to you. If you're successful, you may even decide to run off the the South Pacific to become a banana baron.

The vorld's best Oktoberfest. Harvest time just wouldn't seem proper without an authentic festival to celebrate the fruitage of the season's work. Oktoberfest began in that fine land the Rhineland when King Ludwig wanted to celebrate his wedding with a big feast. Everyone came – royalty and peasantry alike.

Over the years, King Ludwig and his Mrs. were forgotten – but the feast lingers on. Today, Oktoberfest has spread around the world. And this winter, that's where you and a friend will celebrate it – around the world.

Once in Milwaukee.

Once in Munich.

And once in Kitchener, Ontario. (Don't knock it. Oktoberfest is very big in Kitchener).

For three consecutive weekends, we'll pay your airfare and foodfare while you enjoy your fair share of the fun.

Farewell.

At your service. Silver service, that is. Now you can impress your butler with how classy you are.

The prize includes a complete silver service for twelve from C.D. Peacock.

Of course, not everyone has a table that will seat twelve people. And since it's hard to find twelve people (and one butler) who will be sufficiently impressed by your expensive silver while eating at TV tables – we'll include a dining room table. The table comes with twelve chairs, of course – all in solid cherry wood from the Ethan Allen Carriage House.

And, since silver doesn't blend well with plastic dinnerware and commemorative juice glasses, we'll throw in a complete set of Wedgwood China and Waterford Crystal.

(Just to make sure no one misses the point, Peacock, Ethan Allen, Wedgwood and Waterford are all very expensive, impressive names).

The entire prize will be delivered to your home (or safety deposit vault) by two armed security guards. The prize includes a one-year paid insurance policy with Lloyd's of London.

417

416

Chairman Susan Jackson Keig
Writers Rhodes Patterson & others
Designers 27 Chicago Designers
Artists 27 Chicago Designers
Producer 27 Chicago Designers
Exhibitor Susan Jackson Keig

417

Art Director Bob Sherman
Writer Craig Fry
Artists Hank Parker
Jackie Geyer
Kinuko Craft
George Joseph Studio
Agency Brand Advertising
Client CR Industries

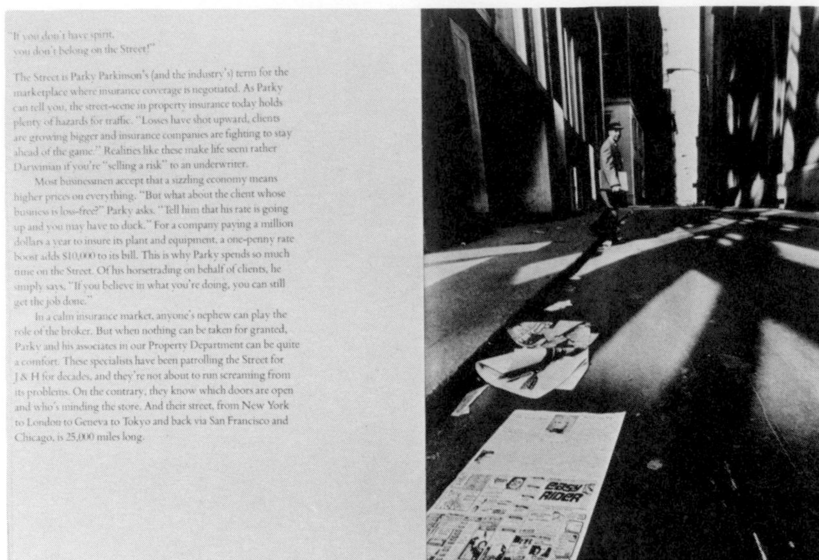

"If you don't have spirit,
you don't belong on the Street!"

The Street is Parky Parkinson's (and the industry's) term for the marketplace where insurance coverage is negotiated. As Parky can tell you, the street-scene in property insurance today holds plenty of hazards for traffic. "Losses have shot upward, clients are growing bigger and insurance companies are fighting to stay ahead of the game." Realities like these make life seem rather Darwinian if you're "selling a risk" to an underwriter.

Most businessmen accept that a sizzling economy means higher prices on everything. "But what about the client whose business is loss-free?" Parky asks. "Tell him that his rate is going up and you may have to duck." For a company paying a million dollars a year to insure its plant and equipment, a one-penny rate boost adds $10,000 to its bill. This is why Parky spends so much time on the Street. Of his horsetrading on behalf of clients, he simply says, "If you believe in what you're doing, you can still get the job done."

In a calm insurance market, anyone's nephew can play the role of the broker. But when nothing can be taken for granted, Parky and his associates in our Property Department can be quite a comfort. These specialists have been patrolling the Street for J & H for decades, and they're not about to run screaming from its problems. On the contrary, they know which doors are open and who's minding the store. And their street, from New York to London to Geneva to Tokyo and back via San Francisco and Chicago, is 25,000 miles long.

418

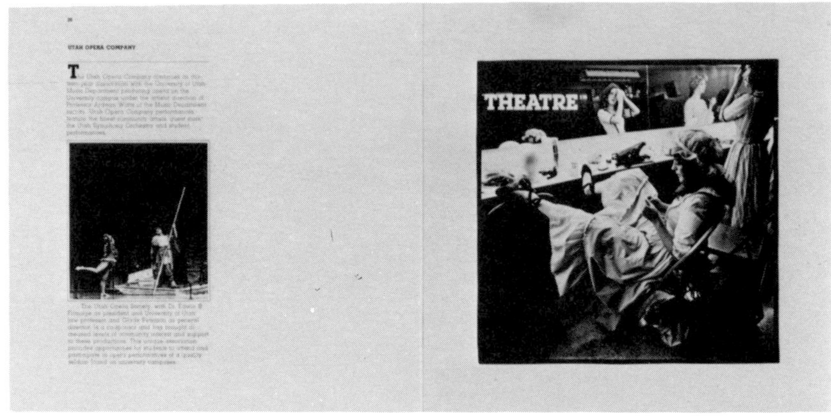

419

418
Art Director Milton Ackoff
Writer Jim Gollin
Designer Milton Ackoff
Artist Milton Ackoff
Photographers Milton Ackoff
Vince Aiosa
Agency Ackoff Inc. & Gollin
Client Johnson & Higgins

419
Art Director Raymond C. Morales
Writer Nancy Haunes
Designer Raymond C. Morales
Artist Karen S. Morales
Photographer George M. Brown
Agency Morales and Friends
Client College of Fine Arts,
University of Utah

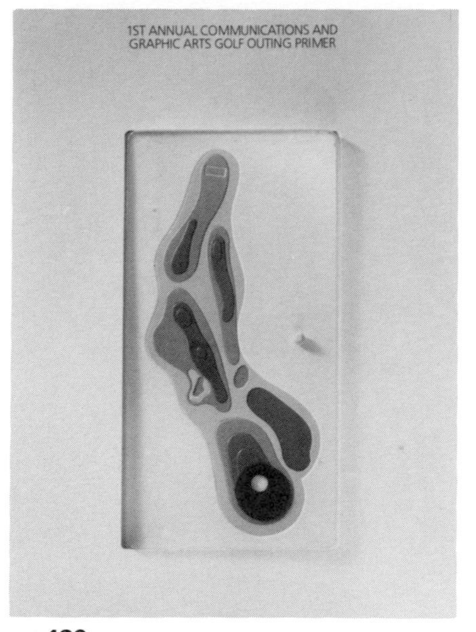

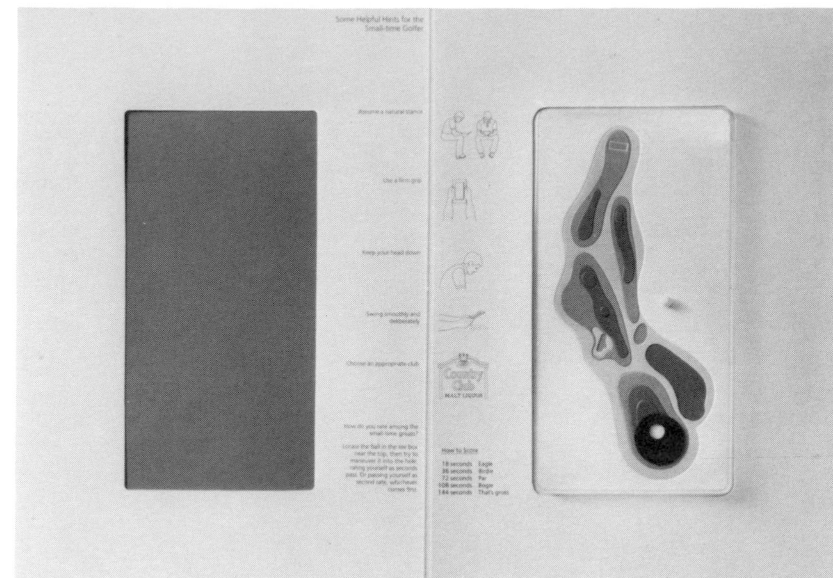

420

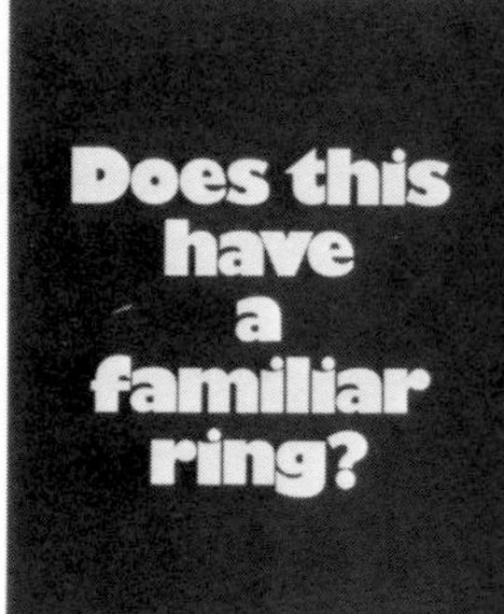

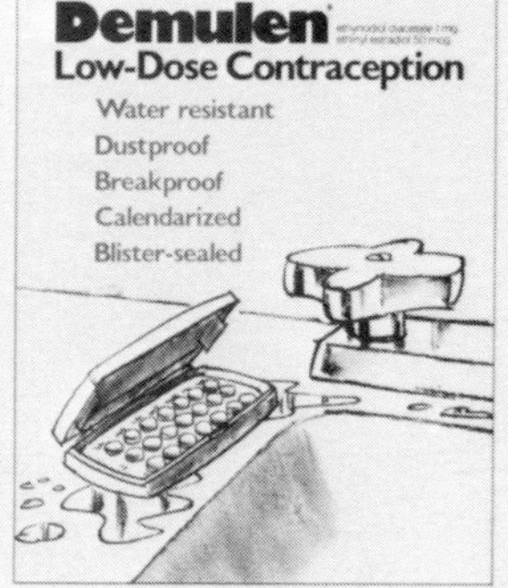

421

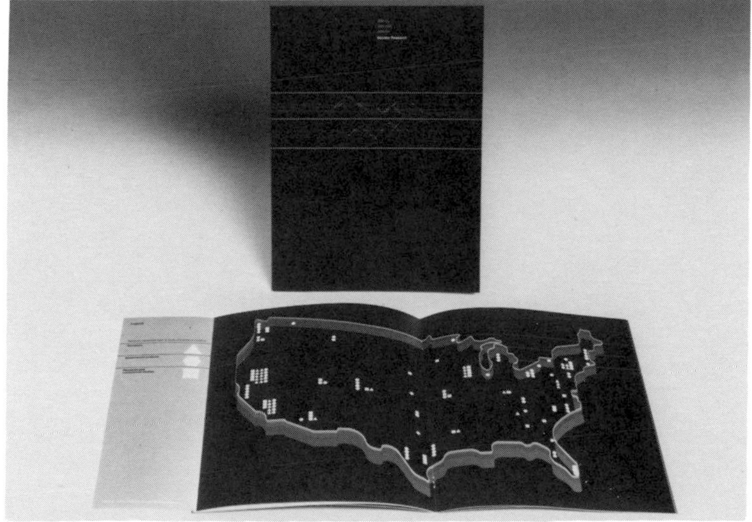

422

420

Art Director Steve Connatser
Writers Rick Harvey
Steve Connatser
Designer Steve Connatser
Artist Dario Badillo
Agency Ad Directors, Inc.
Client Business and Professional Adv. Assoc.

421

Art Director Leslie Sisman
Writers Robert Clark
Bill Butler
Designer Leslie Sisman
Artist Weber
Agency J. Walter Thompson, Deltakos Div.
Client Searle and Co.

422

Art Director Jann Church Advertising & Graphic Design, Inc.
Writers Kathy Dalzen
Ron Hemberger
Designer Jann Church Advertising & Graphic Design, Inc.
Artist Jann Church Advertising & Graphic Design, Inc.
Photographer John Palmer
Agency Jann Church Advertising & Graphic Design, Inc.
Client Decima Research

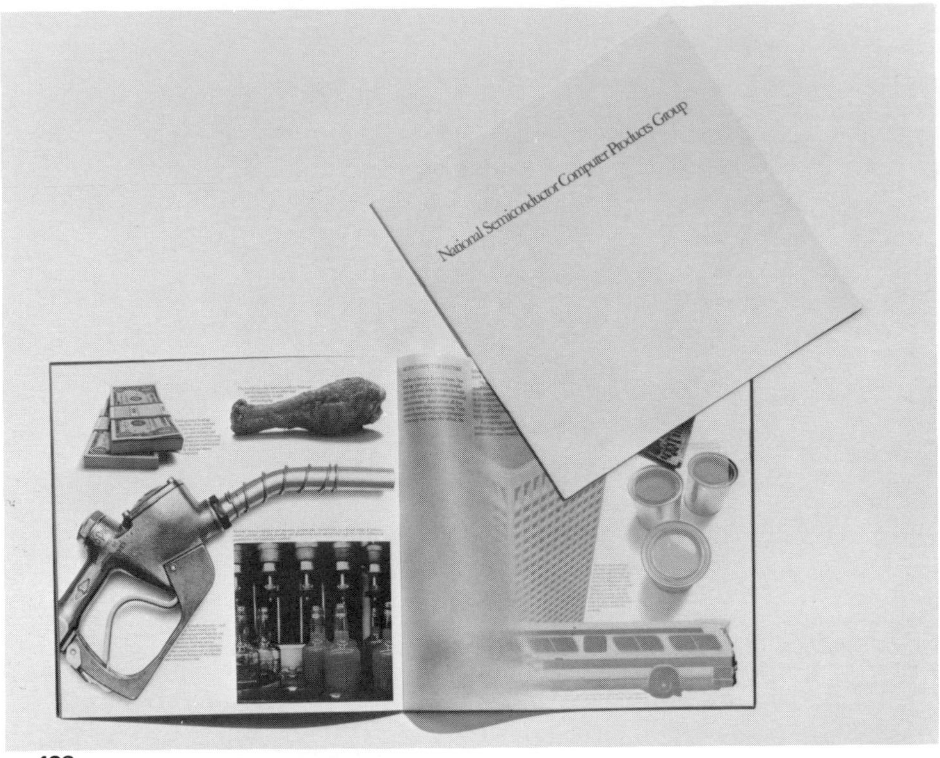

423

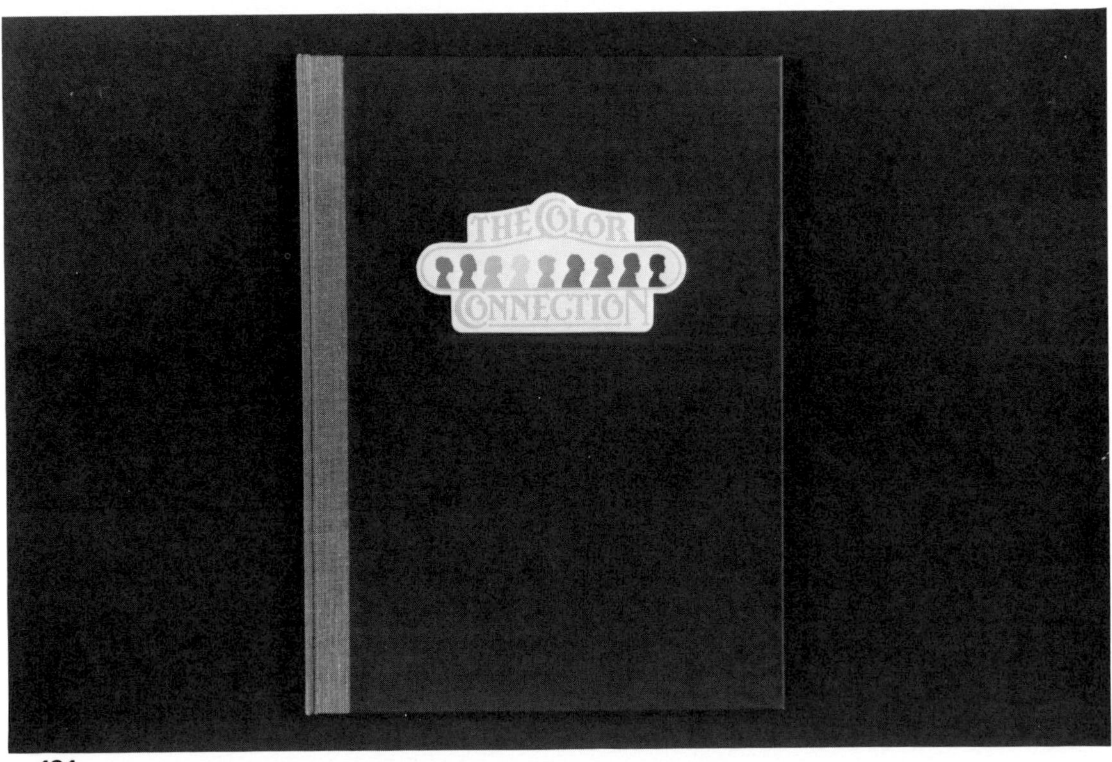

424

423
Art Director Steve Jacobs
Writer Mark Fulton
Designer Hall Kelly
Photographer Tom Tracy
Production Company Continental Graphics
Agency Steven Jacobs Design, Inc.
Client National Semiconductor

424
Art Director B. Martin Pedersen
Designer B. Martin Pedersen
Artist Mary Ann Sterrett
Photographer Armen Kachaturian
Agency Jonson/Pedersen/Hinrichs
Client West Point Pepperell

425

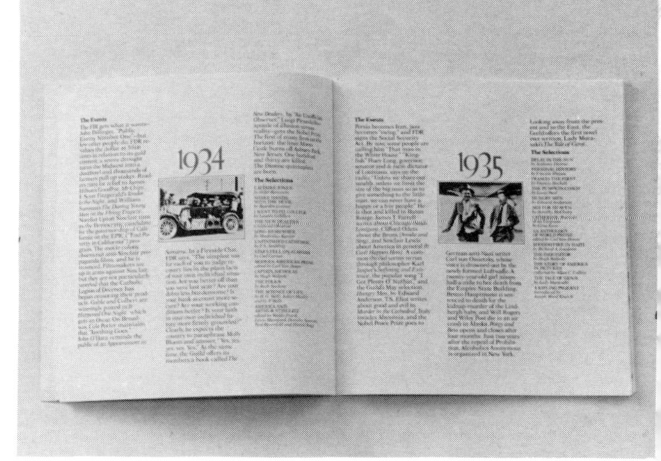

426

425

Art Director Jann Church Advertising & Graphic Design, Inc.
Writers Ron Hagerthy
Julia Chase
Kathy Dalzen
Jim Clements
Designer Jann Church Advertising & Graphic Design, Inc.
Artist Jann Church Advertising & Graphic Design, Inc.
Photographers John Lawder
John Palmer
Harold Birch
Agency Jann Church Advertising & Graphic Design, Inc.

426

Art Directors Larry Ottino
Harvard Toback
Writer Peter Freundlich
Designer Larry Ottino
Artist Larry Ottino
Photographers The Bettman Archive
World Wide Photos—Neal Slavin
Director Victor Zolfo
Producer Thomas Stasink
Client Doubleday—The Literary Guild

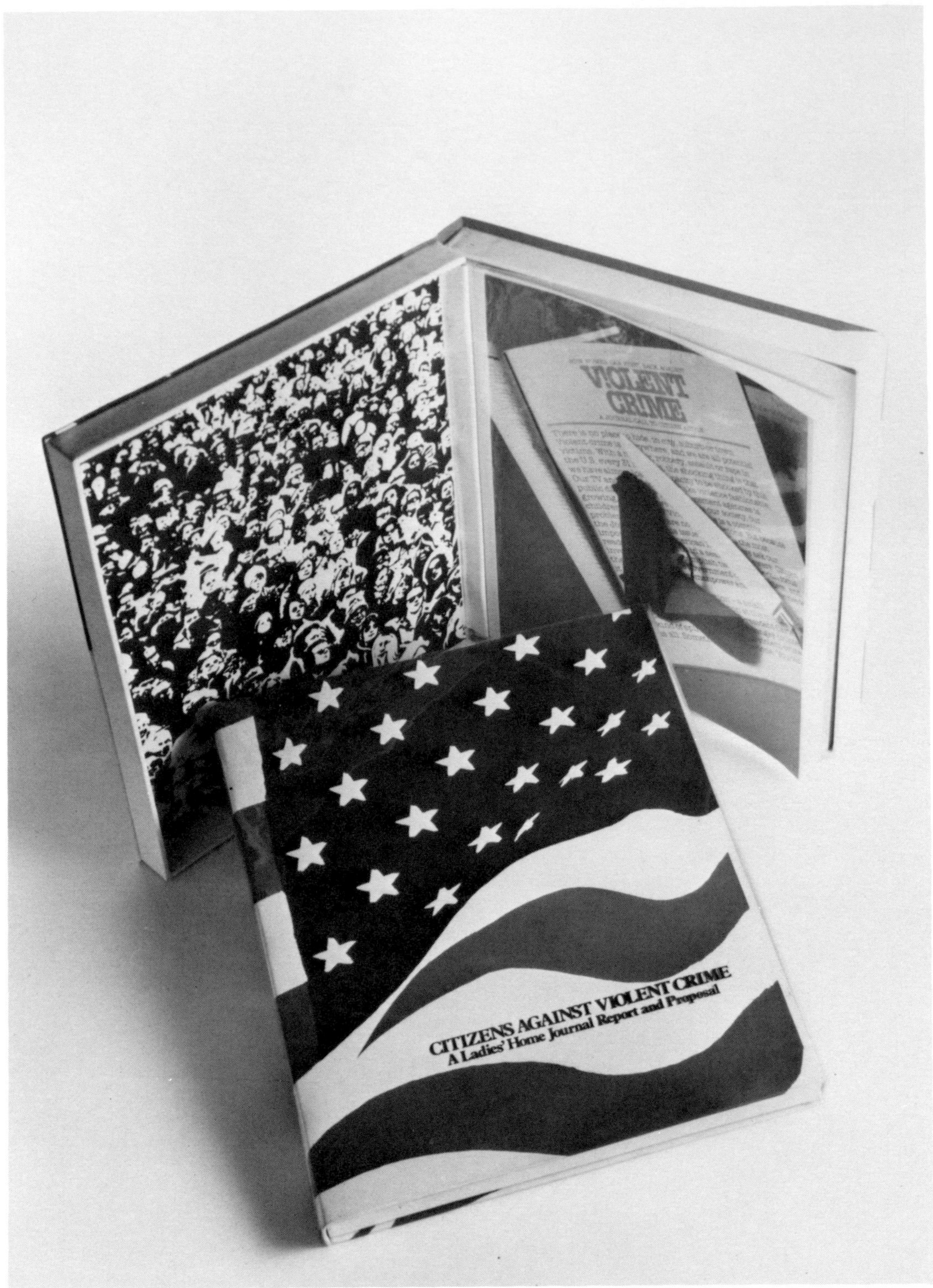

427

427
Art Director Donald A. Adamec
Writer Mary Susan Miller
Designer Donald A. Adamec
Photographer Tasso Vendikos
Agency Ladies' Home Journal
Client Ladies' Home Journal

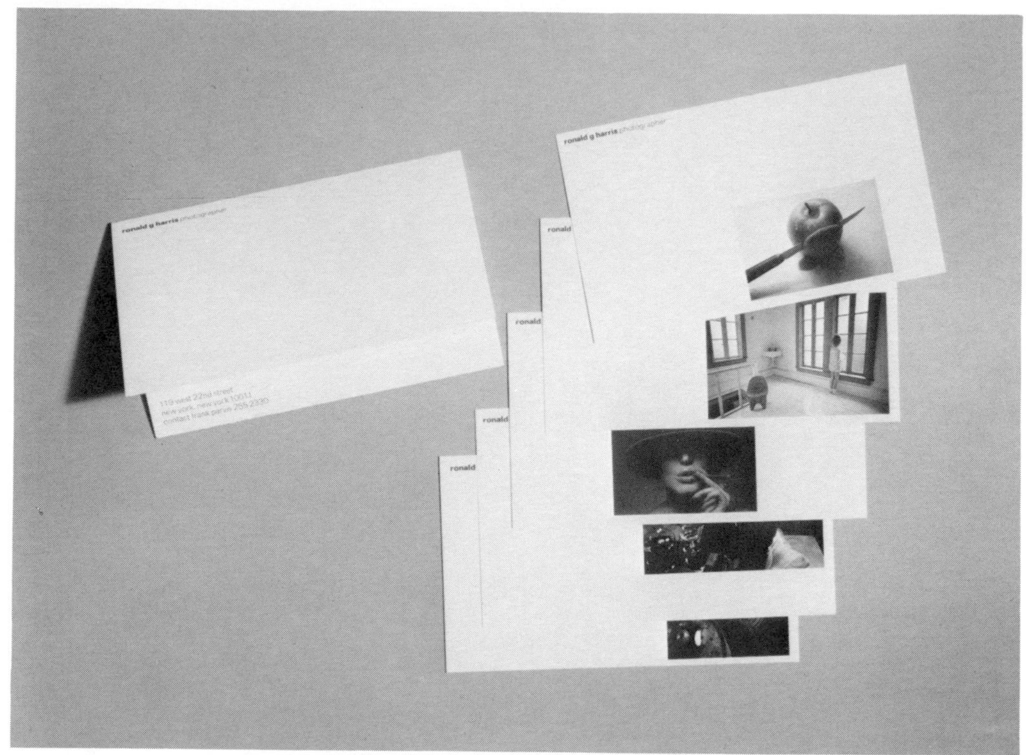

428

429

428
Art Director Arthur Celedonia
Designer Arthur Celedonia
Photographer Ronald G. Harris
Agency Celedonia Design
Client Ronald G. Harris

429
Art Director James Van Noy
Writer James Van Noy
Designer James Van Noy
Artist Van Noy & Company
Photographer Van Noy & Company
Client Van Noy & Company

430

GOLD

430

Art Directors	David November
	Ed Sobel
Writer	Peter Moreau
Designers	Ed Sobel
	David November
Photographers	Jerry Darvin
	Pete Mecca
	Mel DiGiaccomo
Agency	CBS Entertainment Division/
	Advertising and Promotion
Client	CBS Television Network

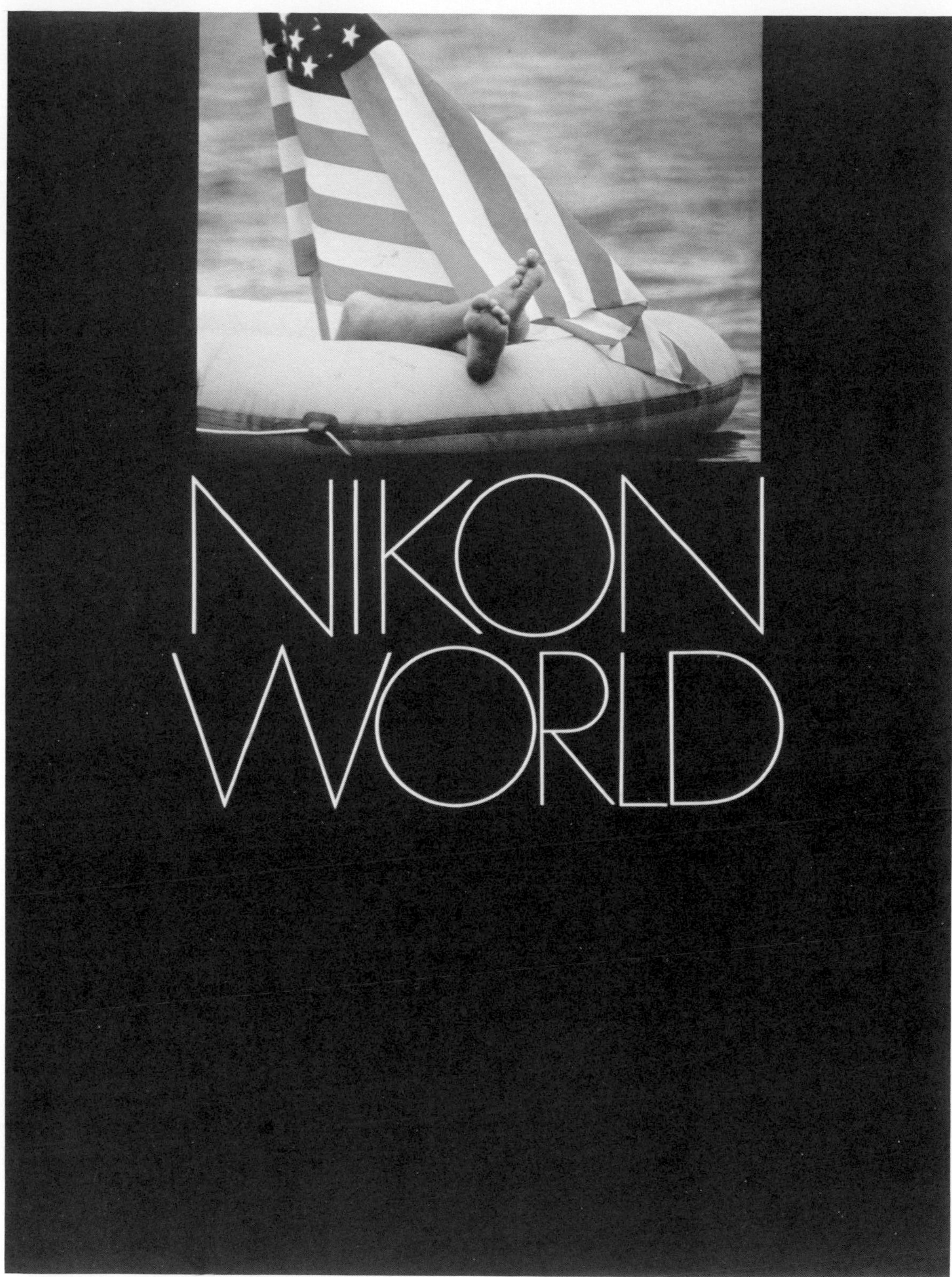

431

431

Art Director	Ernest Scarfone
Writer	Patricia Maye
Designer	Ernest Scarfone
Photographers	Roy Zaletsky Doug Clemmer
Client	Epol Corp. Nikon World

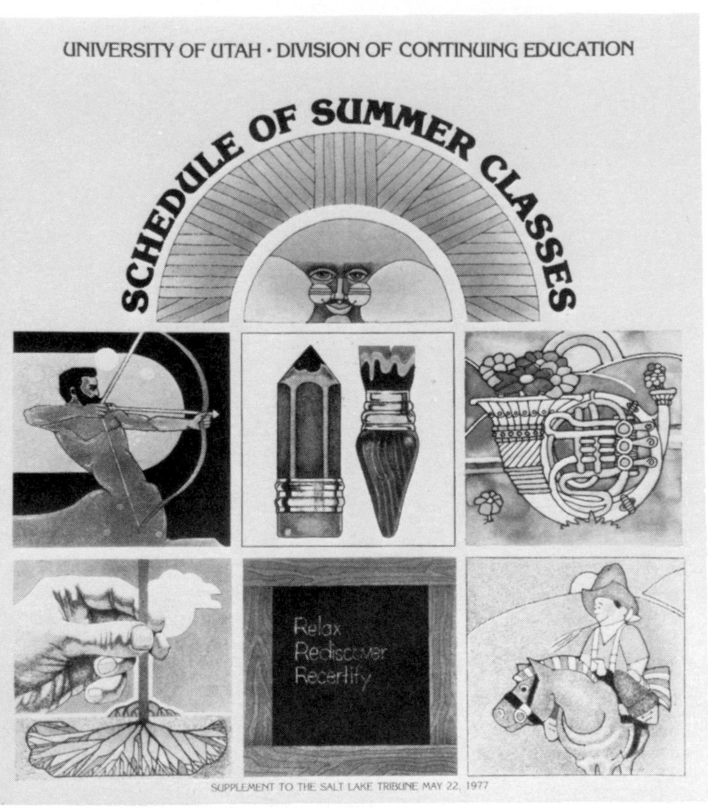

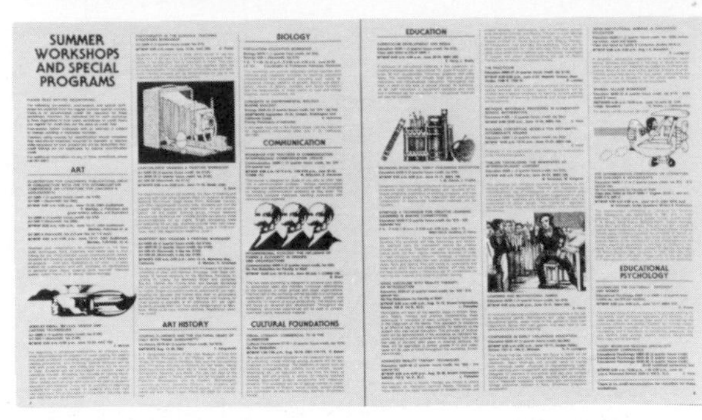

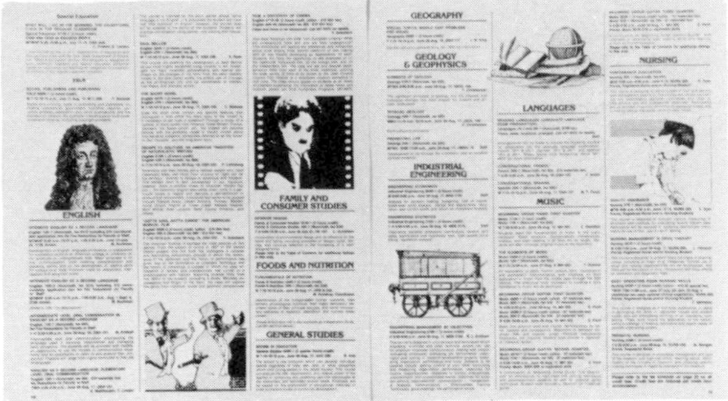

432

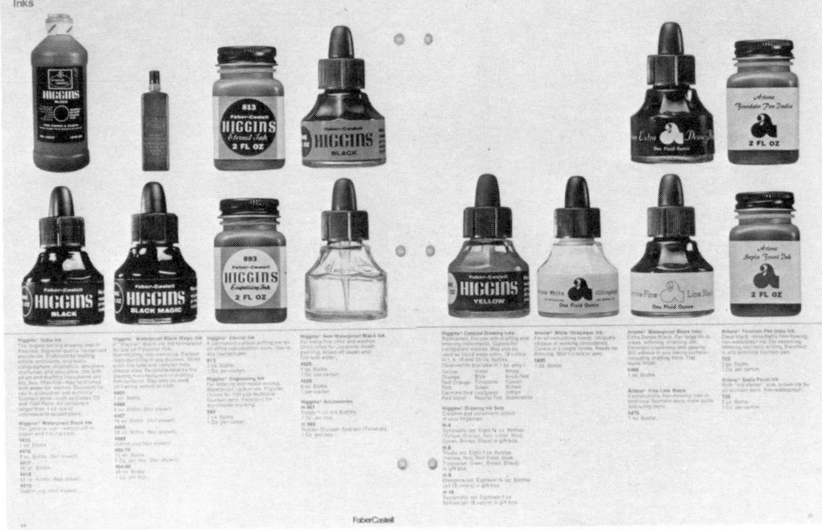

433

432
Art Director Michael B. Richards
Writers Cheryl Baldwin
Ted Phillips
Designer Michael B. Richards
Artists Scott Greer
Kerry Gonzales
Agency University of Utah Graphic Design
Client Division of Continuing Education, University of Utah

433
Art Directors Howard Grant
Kathy Kuhl
Writer Jeff Cramp
Designers Kathy Kuhl
Howard Grant
Photographer George Gelernt
Agency WillsGrant Marketing Communications Inc.
Client FaberCastell Corp.

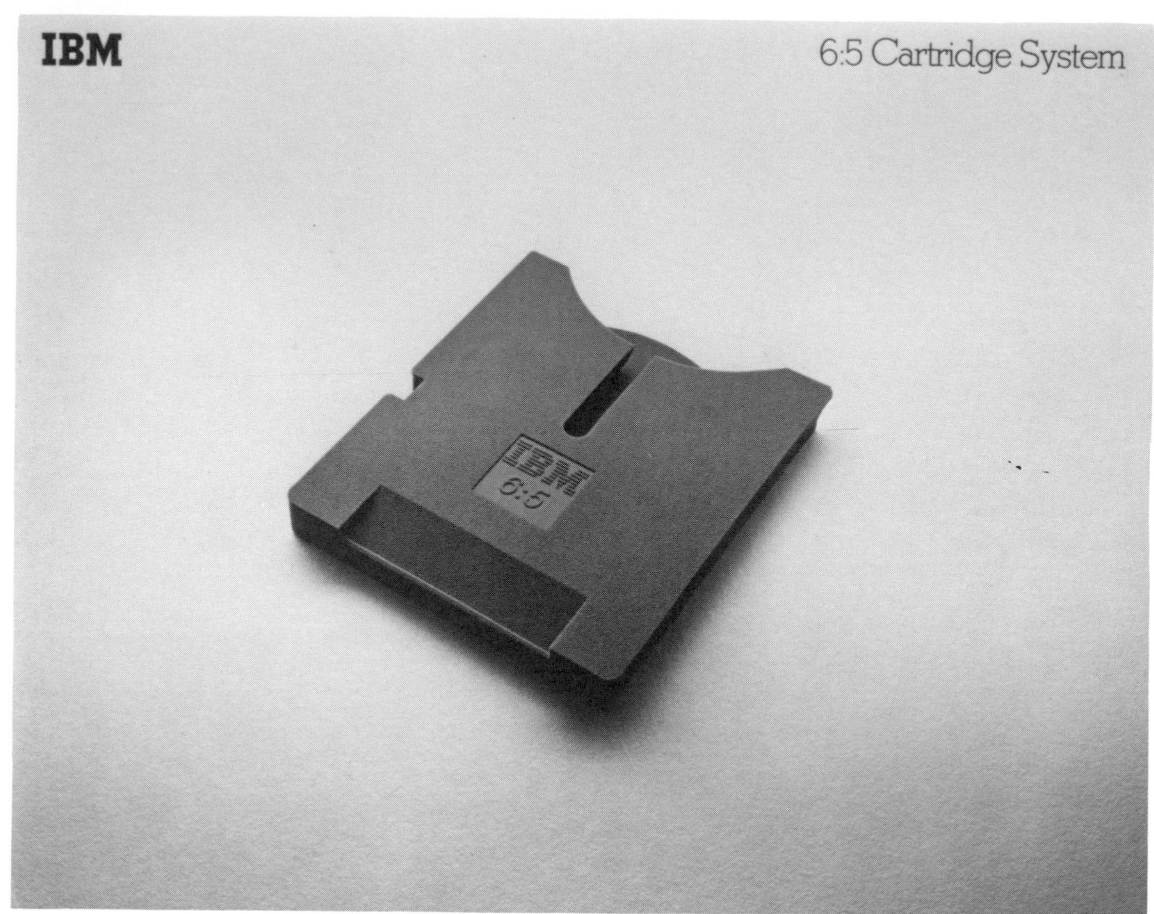

Now you no longer have to choose between tape dictation and belt dictation.

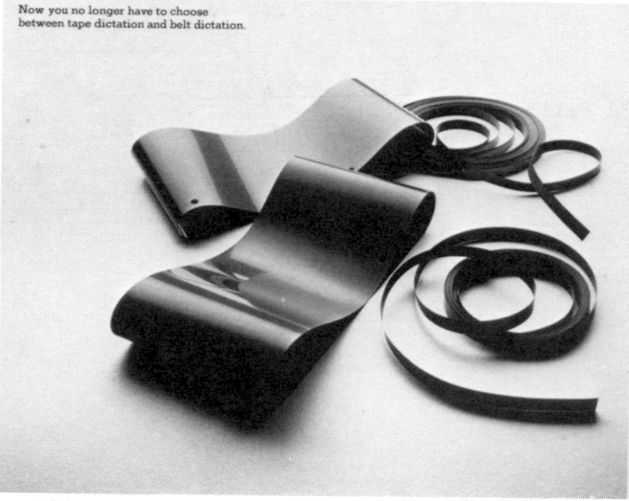

Input processing technology and equipment have been greatly refined and improved in recent years. Still, even the most advanced machines depend on the basic capabilites and limitations of the specific medium used.

In the past, you have had to decide which medium—tapes or belts—offered those features best applied to your uses. Now, the IBM 6:5 Cartridge System offers you the best features of previous alternatives combined in one advanced medium.

434

434
Art Director Peter McGuggart
Designer Cook & Shanoshy Assoc., Inc.
Photographer Arthur Beck
Agency Compton Adv. Inc.
Client IBM Office Products Division

435

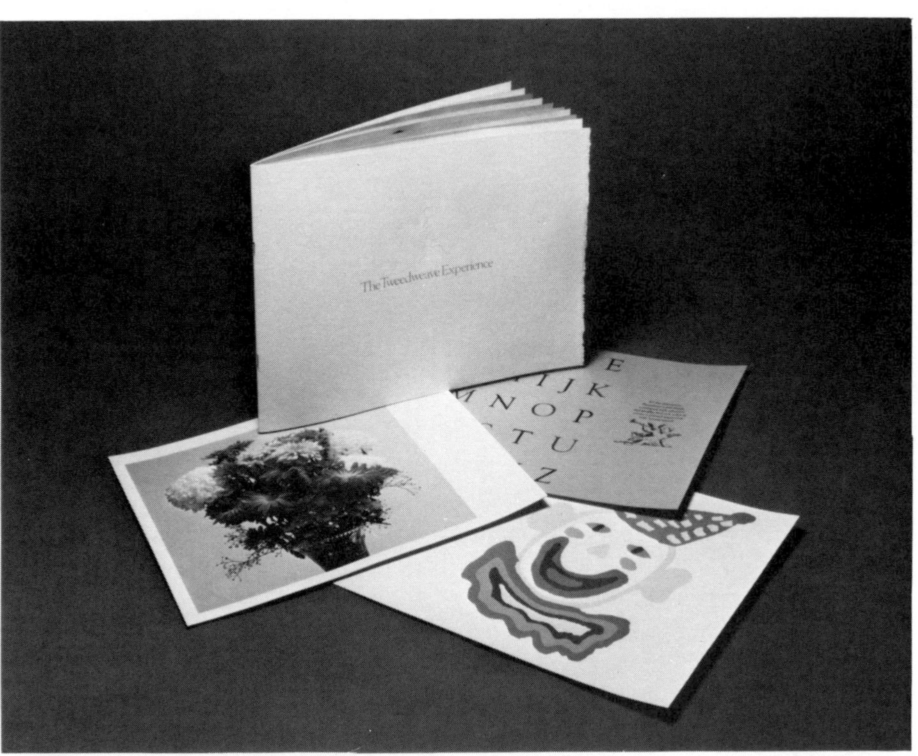

436

435

Art Directors	Onofrio Paccione Zane Tankel
Writer	Michael Lissauer
Designer	Onofrio Paccione
Client	Collier Graphic Services

436

Art Director	Cameron Hyers
Writer	Cameron Hyers
Photographers	Gerald Zanetti John Gairy Frank Guida
Agency	Hyers/Smith, Inc.
Client	Curtis Paper

How Electricity is Made

A stream of moving electrons (infinitesimal particles of atoms), each with a tiny electrical charge, creates electric power. Most of the present and proposed methods of generating electricity for large scale use obtain this electron stream by spinning a magnet inside coils of wire. This magnet/wire combination is known as a turbine generator. When the magnet rotates, its changing magnetic field penetrates the copper wire and releases a stream of electrons. Transmission lines then move these electrons from the power plant to homes, offices, and factories where they are needed.

A number of energy sources can be used to turn the turbines and thus create electricity. Most of these sources are used to create steam which in turn spins the turbines. We can get steam from burning natural fossil fuels or solid waste; we can use the heat from nuclear reaction; we can use the heat in sunlight; we can use the earth's natural steam. Alternatively, instead of steam, we can use the pressure of falling water or wind to turn the turbines.

Electricity can also be produced without turbines through the direct conversion of sunlight (in photovoltaic cells) or fossil fuels (in fuel cells) to electricity.

Since we do not have enough of any one source to furnish all of the energy necessary to satisfy our electric power requirements, we must create an Energy Mix — a combination of the best available sources. In determining this mix, we take into account how much of each source is available, its environmental impact, and its cost.

Benjamin Franklin whose famous kite experiment proved that lightning is a form of electricity.

Michael Faraday, whose research made electric motors possible.

Thomas A. Edison, who invented the first electric light for home use.

3

4

437

437

Art Director Don Weller
Writer Words
Designers Don Weller
Chikako Matsubayashi
Artists Don Weller
Chikako Matsubayashi
Agency The Weller Institute for the Cure of Design
Client Southern California Edison Co.

438

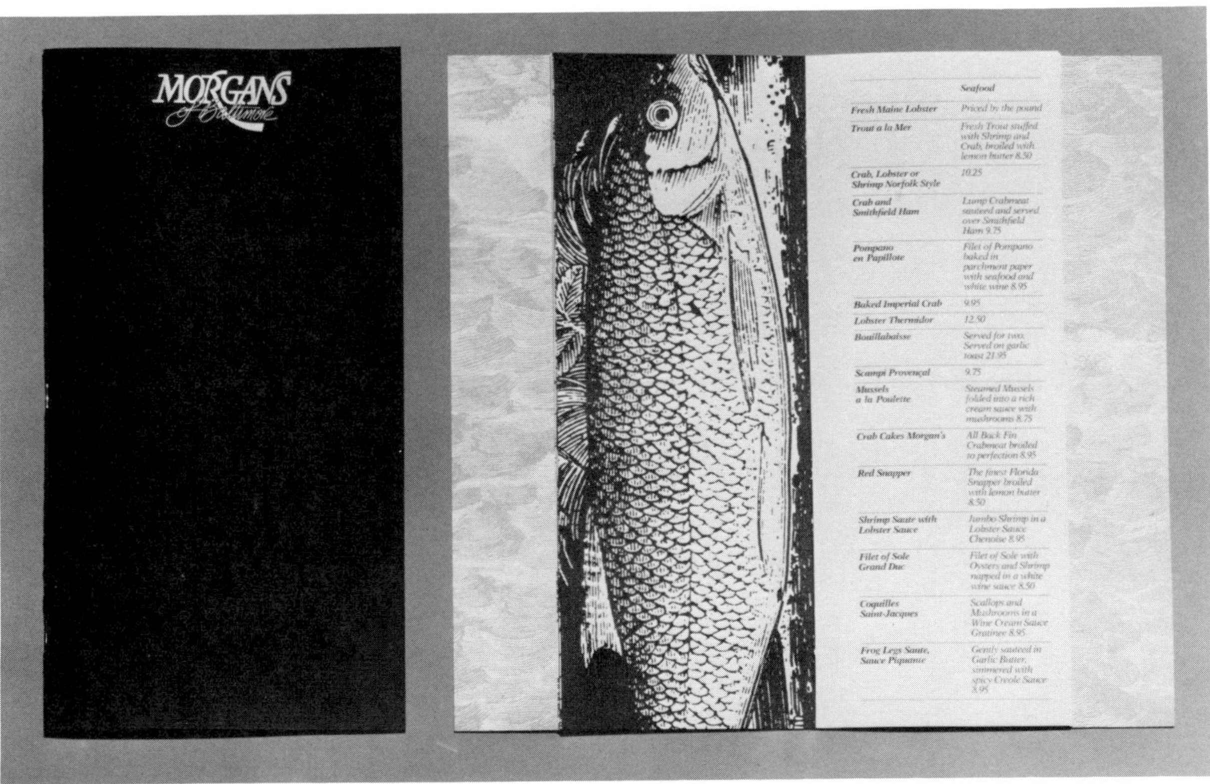

	Seafood
Fresh Maine Lobster	Priced by the pound
Trout a la Mer	Fresh Trout stuffed with Shrimp and Crab, broiled with lemon butter 8.50
Crab, Lobster or Shrimp Norfolk Style	10.25
Crab and Smithfield Ham	Lump Crabmeat sauteed and served over Smithfield Ham 9.75
Pompano en Papillote	Filet of Pompano baked in parchment paper with seafood and white wine 8.95
Baked Imperial Crab	9.95
Lobster Thermidor	12.50
Bouillabaisse	Served for two. Served on garlic toast 21.95
Scampi Provençal	9.75
Mussels a la Poulette	Steamed Mussels folded into a rich cream sauce with mushrooms 8.75
Crab Cakes Morgan's	All Back Fin Crabmeat broiled to perfection 8.95
Red Snapper	The finest Florida Snapper broiled with lemon butter 8.50
Shrimp Saute with Lobster Sauce	Jumbo Shrimp in a Lobster Sauce Chenoise 8.95
Filet of Sole Grand Duc	Filet of Sole with Oysters and Shrimp napped in a white wine sauce 8.50
Coquilles Saint-Jacques	Scallops and Mushrooms in a Wine Cream Sauce Gratinee 8.95
Frog Legs Saute, Sauce Piquante	Gently sauteed in Garlic Butter, simmered with spicy Creole Sauce 8.95

439

438
Art Director Henry Epstein
Writer Joel Graham
Designer Carolyn Lamont
Photographer Steve Fenn
Client American Broadcasting Company (Sales Development)

439
Art Director Carolyn Wade Frazier Studio
Designer Marilyn Worseldine
Artist Carolyn Wade Frazier
Agency Carolyn Wade Frazier Studio
Client Morgan's of Baltimore

440

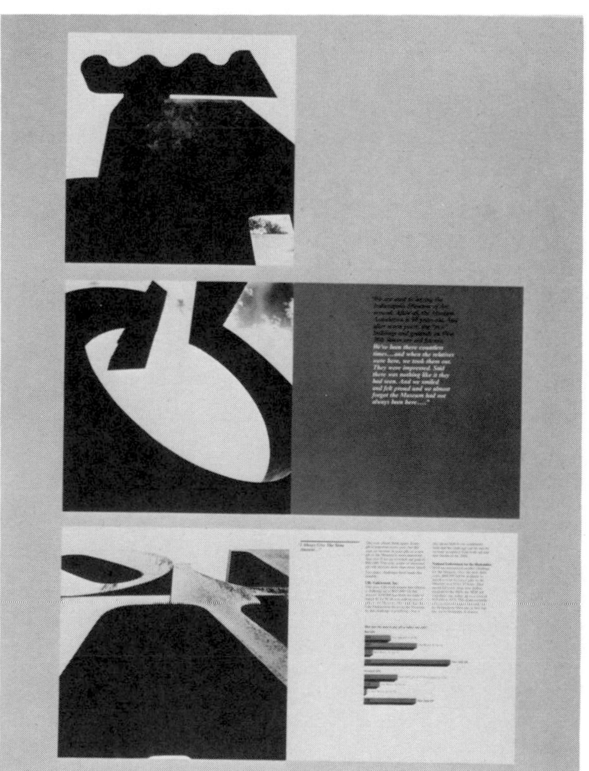

441

440
Art Director W. Chris Gorman
Designer W. Chris Gorman
Client American Business Press, Inc.

441
Art Director Robert L. Willis
Designer Robert L. Willis
Photographer Jack Ward
Client Indianapolis Museum of Art

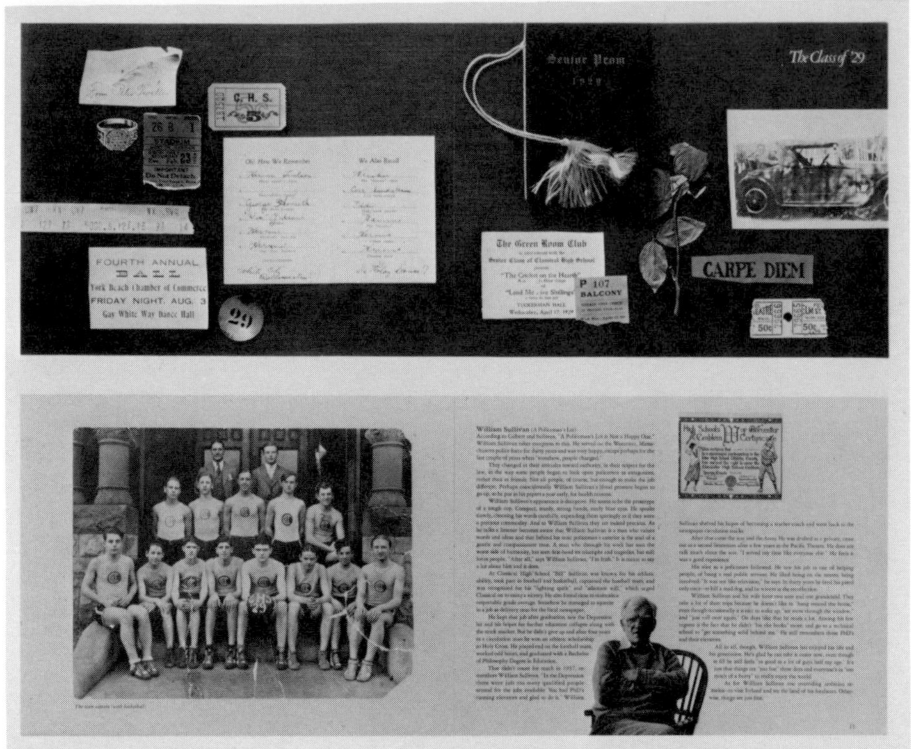

442

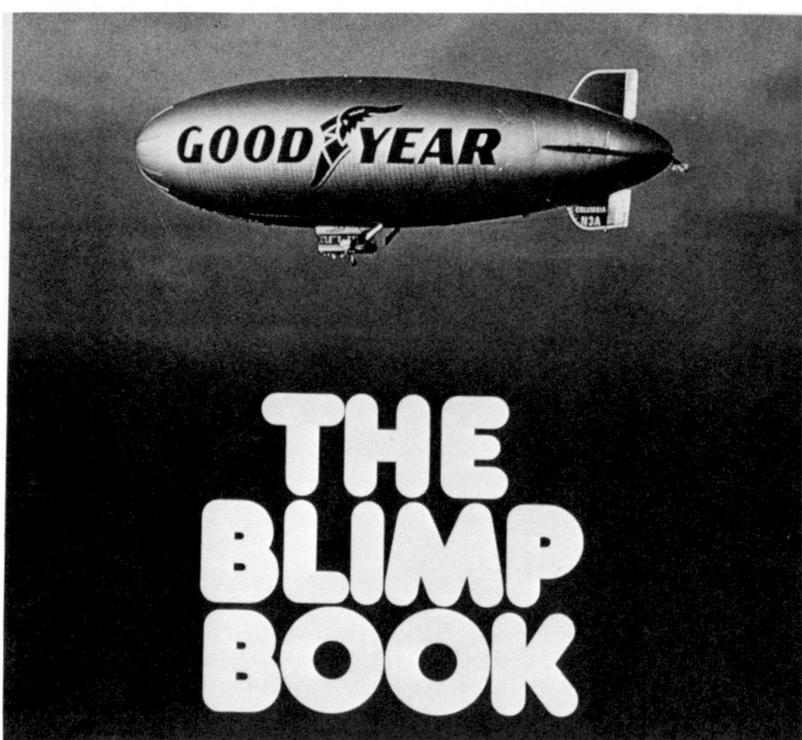

443

442
Art Director George Tscherny
Writer Corporate Affairs Department, Colonial Penn Group, Inc.
Designer George Tscherny
Photographers B.A. King
John Naso and others
Agency George Tscherny, Inc.
Client Colonial Penn Group, Inc.

443
Art Director Neil Shakery
Writer George Larson
Designer Neil Shakery
Photographers George Hall
Baron Wolman
Agency Jonson Pedersen Hinrichs
Client Goodyear

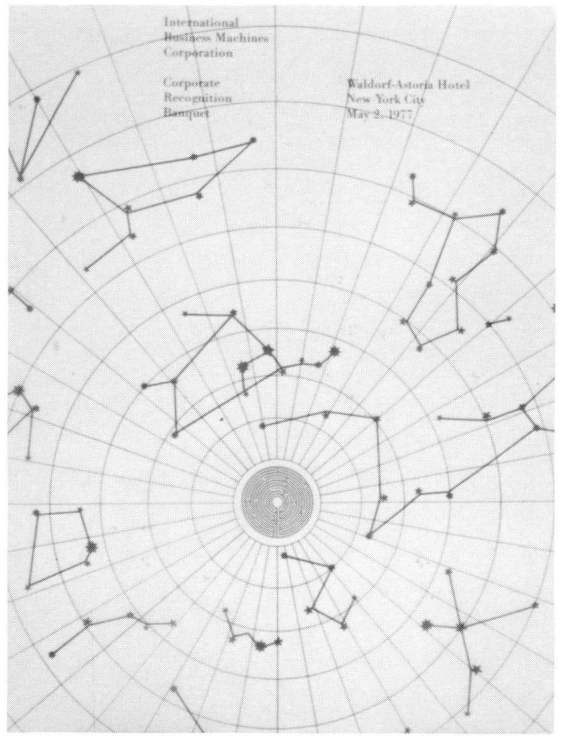

444

445

444

Art Director Richard Rogers
Writer Herb Saxe
Designer Richard Rogers
Artist Richard Rogers
Photographers Herb Levart &
IBM staff Photographers
Director Herb Saxe
Agency Richard Rogers Inc.
Client IBM Corp.

445

Art Director Joe Carri
Writers David Levy
Jean Hall
Stan Levin
Designers Joe Carri
Eduardo Zayas
Jessica Wilson
Artists Bennett Hall
Mitchell Kuff
Photographer Fred Maroon
Agency Weitzman & Associates, Inc.
Client Britches of Georgetowne

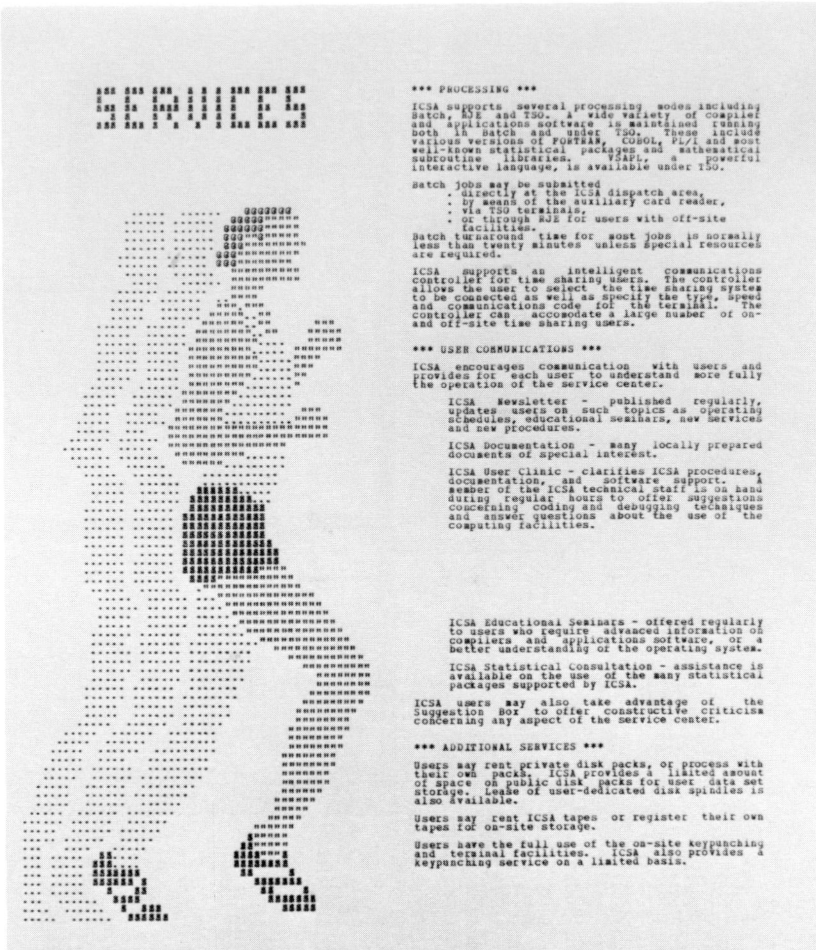

SERVICES

*** PROCESSING ***

ICSA supports several processing modes including Batch, RJE and TSO. A wide variety of compiler and applications software is maintained running both in Batch and under TSO. These include various versions of FORTRAN, COBOL, PL/I and most well-known statistical packages and mathematical subroutine libraries. VSAPL, a powerful interactive language, is available under TSO.

Batch jobs may be submitted
- . directly at the ICSA dispatch area,
- . by means of the auxiliary card reader,
- . via TSO terminals,
- . or through RJE for users with off-site facilities.

Batch turnaround time for most jobs is normally less than twenty minutes unless special resources are required.

ICSA supports an intelligent communications controller for time sharing users. The controller allows the user to select the time sharing system to be connected as well as specify the type, speed and communications code for the terminal. The controller can accomodate a large number of on- and off-site time sharing users.

*** USER COMMUNICATIONS ***

ICSA encourages communication with users and provides for each user to understand more fully the operation of the service center.

ICSA Newsletter - published regularly, updates users on such topics as operating schedules, educational seminars, new services and new procedures.

ICSA Documentation - many locally prepared documents of special interest.

ICSA User Clinic - clarifies ICSA procedures, documentation, and software support. A member of the ICSA technical staff is on hand during regular hours to offer suggestions concerning coding and debugging techniques and answer questions about the use of the computing facilities.

ICSA Educational Seminars - offered regularly to users who require advanced information on compilers and applications software, or a better understanding of the operating system.

ICSA Statistical Consultation - assistance is available on the use of the many statistical packages supported by ICSA.

ICSA users may also take advantage of the Suggestion Box to offer constructive criticism concerning any aspect of the service center.

*** ADDITIONAL SERVICES ***

Users may rent private disk packs, or process with their own packs. ICSA provides a limited amount of space on public disk packs for user data set storage. Lease of user-dedicated disk spindles is also available.

Users may rent ICSA tapes or register their own tapes for on-site storage.

Users have the full use of the on-site keypunching and terminal facilities. ICSA also provides a keypunching service on a limited basis.

446

446

Art Director	Jeffrey DeBevec
Writers	Jim Criswell M. Stuart Lynn
Designer	Jeffrey DeBevec
Photographer	Jeffrey DeBevec
Agency	EVC Group
Client	The Institute for Computer Services and Applications at Rice University (ICSA)

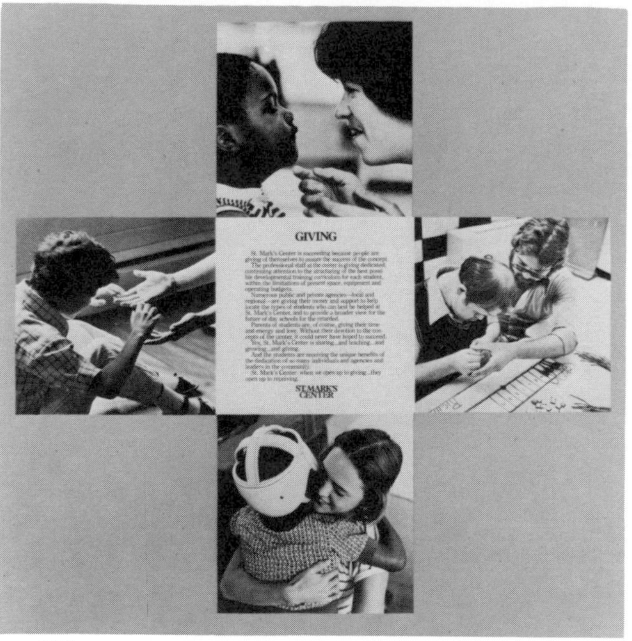

447

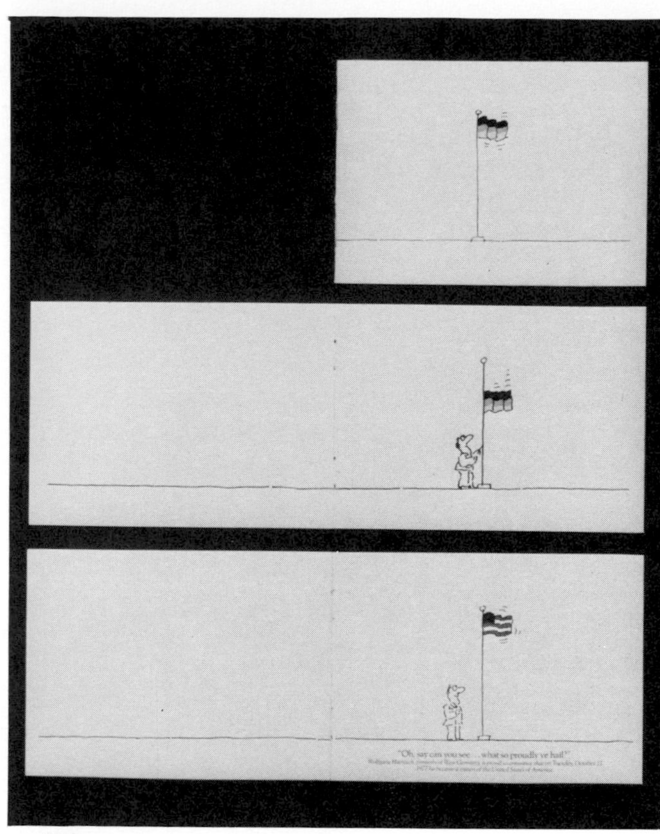

448

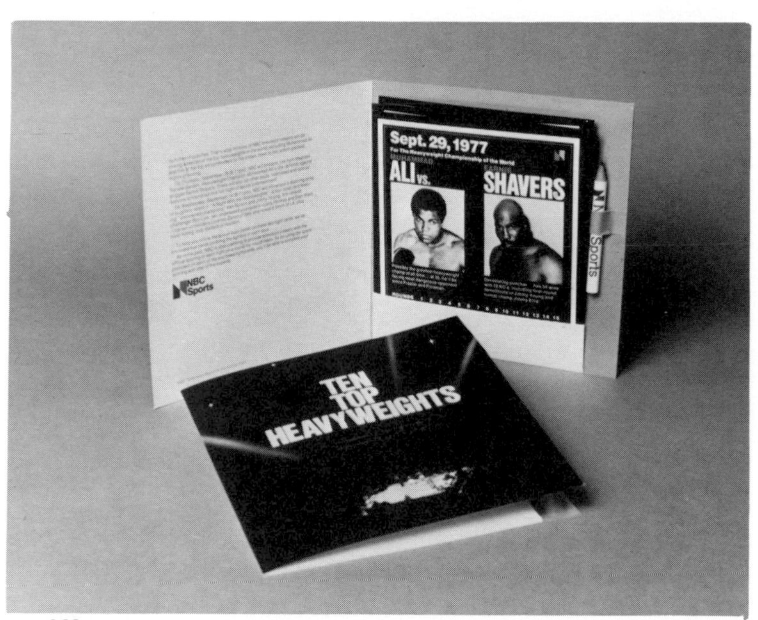

449

447
Art Director Jim Mountjoy
Writers Jack McConnell
Jim Mountjoy
Designer Jim Mountjoy
Photographer Tom Walters
Agency McConnell & Associates, Inc.
Client St. Mark's Center

448
Art Director Dick Henderson
Writer James P. Cole
Designer Dick Henderson
Artist C. K. (Kenny) Higdon
Agency Cole Henderson Drake, Inc.
Client Wolfgang Haenisch

449
Art Director Charles V. Blake
Writer Hal Alterman
Designer Gene Krackehl
Agency NBC TV Network
Client NBC

Goucher Women Have One Thing In Common:

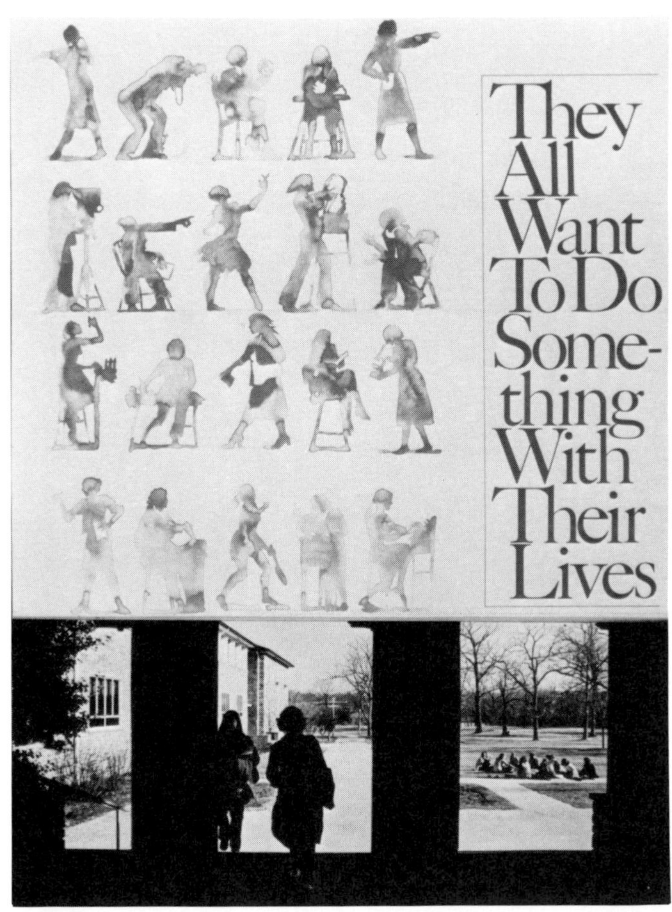

They
All
Want
To Do
Some-
thing
With
Their
Lives

450

450
Art Director Ed Gold
Writer Glorian Dersey
Designers Ed Gold
Barbara Brown
Artist Whitney Sherman
Agency The Barton-Gillet Co.
Client Goucher College

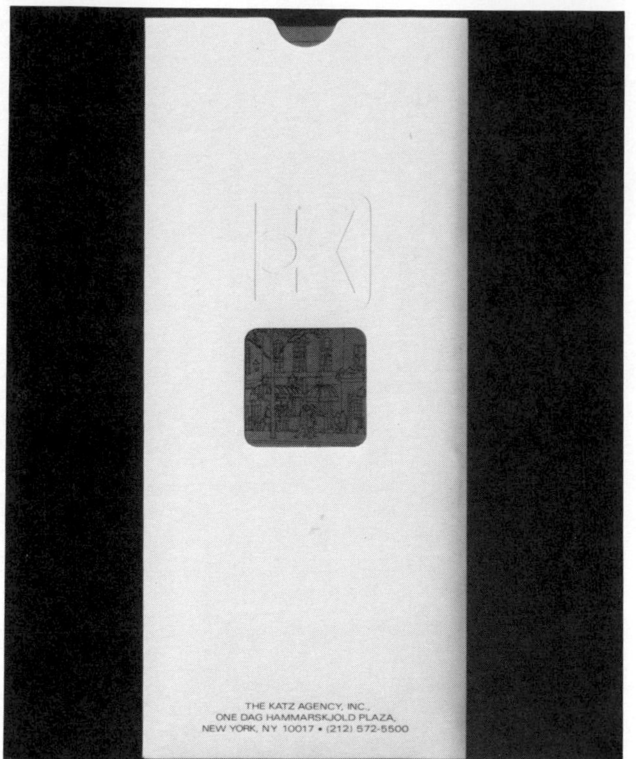

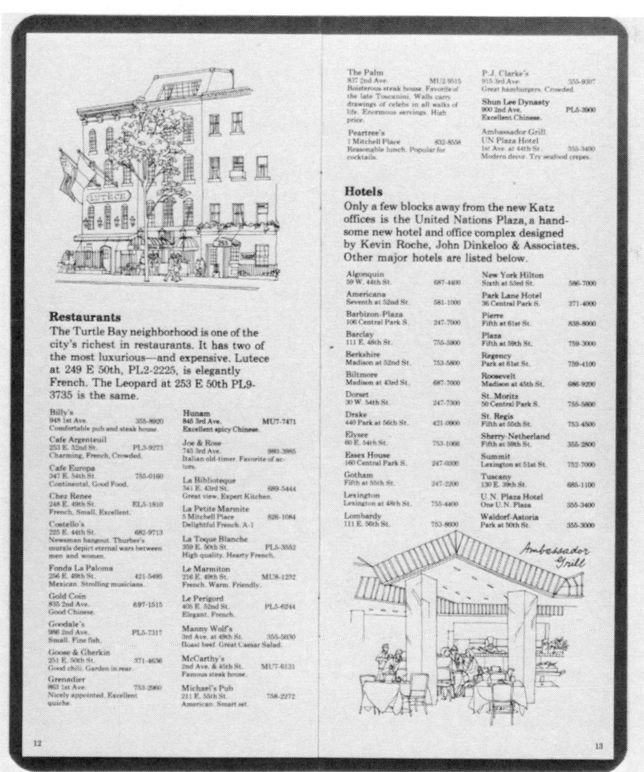

Restaurants

The Turtle Bay neighborhood is one of the city's richest in restaurants. It has two of the most luxurious—and expensive. Lutece at 249 E 50th, PL2-2225, is elegantly French. The Leopard at 253 E 50th PL9-3735 is the same.

Billy's
948 1st Ave. 355-8920
Comfortable pub and steak house.

Cafe Argenteuil
253 E. 52nd St. PL3-9273
Charming, French, Crowded.

Cafe Europa
347 E. 54th St. 755-0160
Continental. Good Food.

Chez Renee
248 E. 49th St. EL5-1810
French. Small. Excellent.

Costello's
225 E. 44th St. 682-9713
Newsman hangout. Thurber's murals depict eternal wars between men and women.

Fonda La Paloma
256 E. 49th St. 421-5495
Mexican. Strolling musicians.

Gold Coin
835 2nd Ave. 697-1515
Good Chinese.

Goodale's
986 2nd Ave. PL5-7317
Small. Fine fish.

Goose & Gherkin
251 E. 50th St. 371-4636
Good chili. Garden in rear.

Grenadier
863 1st Ave. 753-2960
Nicely appointed. Excellent quiche.

Hunam
845 3rd Ave. MU7-7471
Excellent spicy Chinese.

Joe & Rose
745 3rd Ave. 980-3985
Italian old-timer. Favorite of actors.

La Bibliotheque
341 E. 43rd St. 689-5444
Great view. Expert Kitchen.

La Petite Marmite
5 Mitchell Place 826-1084
Delightful French. A-1

La Toque Blanche
359 E. 50th St. PL5-3552
High quality. Hearty French.

Le Marmiton
216 E. 49th St. MU8-1232
French. Warm. Friendly.

Le Perigord
405 E. 52nd St. PL5-6244
Elegant. French.

Manny Wolf's
3rd Ave. at 49th St. 355-5030
Roast beef. Great Caesar Salad.

McCarthy's
2nd Ave. & 45th St. MU7-6131
Famous steak house.

Michael's Pub
211 E. 55th St. 758-2272
American. Smart set.

12

The Palm
837 2nd Ave. MU2-9515
Boisterous steak house. Favorite of the late Toscanini. Walls carry drawings of celebs in all walks of life. Enormous servings. High price.

Peartree's
1 Mitchell Place 832-8558
Reasonable lunch. Popular for cocktails.

P.J. Clarke's
915 3rd Ave. 355-9307
Great hamburgers. Crowded.

Shun Lee Dynasty
900 2nd Ave. PL5-3900
Excellent Chinese.

Ambassador Grill
UN Plaza Hotel
1st Ave. at 44th St. 355-3400
Modern decor. Try seafood crepes.

Hotels

Only a few blocks away from the new Katz offices is the United Nations Plaza, a handsome new hotel and office complex designed by Kevin Roche, John Dinkeloo & Associates. Other major hotels are listed below.

Algonquin
59 W. 44th St. 687-4400

Americana
Seventh at 52nd St. 581-1000

Barbizon-Plaza
106 Central Park S. 247-7000

Barclay
111 E. 48th St. 755-5900

Berkshire
Madison at 52nd St. 753-5800

Biltmore
Madison at 43rd St. 687-7000

Dorset
30 W. 54th St. 247-7300

Drake
440 Park at 56th St. 421-0900

Elysee
60 E. 54th St. 753-1066

Essex House
160 Central Park S. 247-0300

Gotham
Fifth at 55th St. 247-2200

Lexington
Lexington at 48th St. 755-4400

Lombardy
111 E. 56th St. 753-8600

New York Hilton
Sixth at 53rd St. 586-7000

Park Lane Hotel
36 Central Park S. 371-4000

Pierre
Fifth at 61st St. 838-8000

Plaza
Fifth at 59th St. 759-3000

Regency
Park at 61st St. 759-4100

Roosevelt
Madison at 45th St. 686-9200

St. Moritz
50 Central Park S. 755-5800

St. Regis
Fifth at 55th St. 753-4500

Sherry-Netherland
Fifth at 59th St. 355-2800

Summit
Lexington at 51st St. 752-7000

Tuscany
130 E. 39th St. 686-1100

U.N. Plaza Hotel
One U.N. Plaza 355-3400

Waldorf-Astoria
Park at 50th St. 355-3000

Ambassador Grill

13

451

451

Art Director	William O'Day
Writer	Kenn Donnellon
Designer	William O'Day
Artist	Don MacKay
Agency	Lloyd, DuVall & Miller
Client	The Katz Agency Inc.

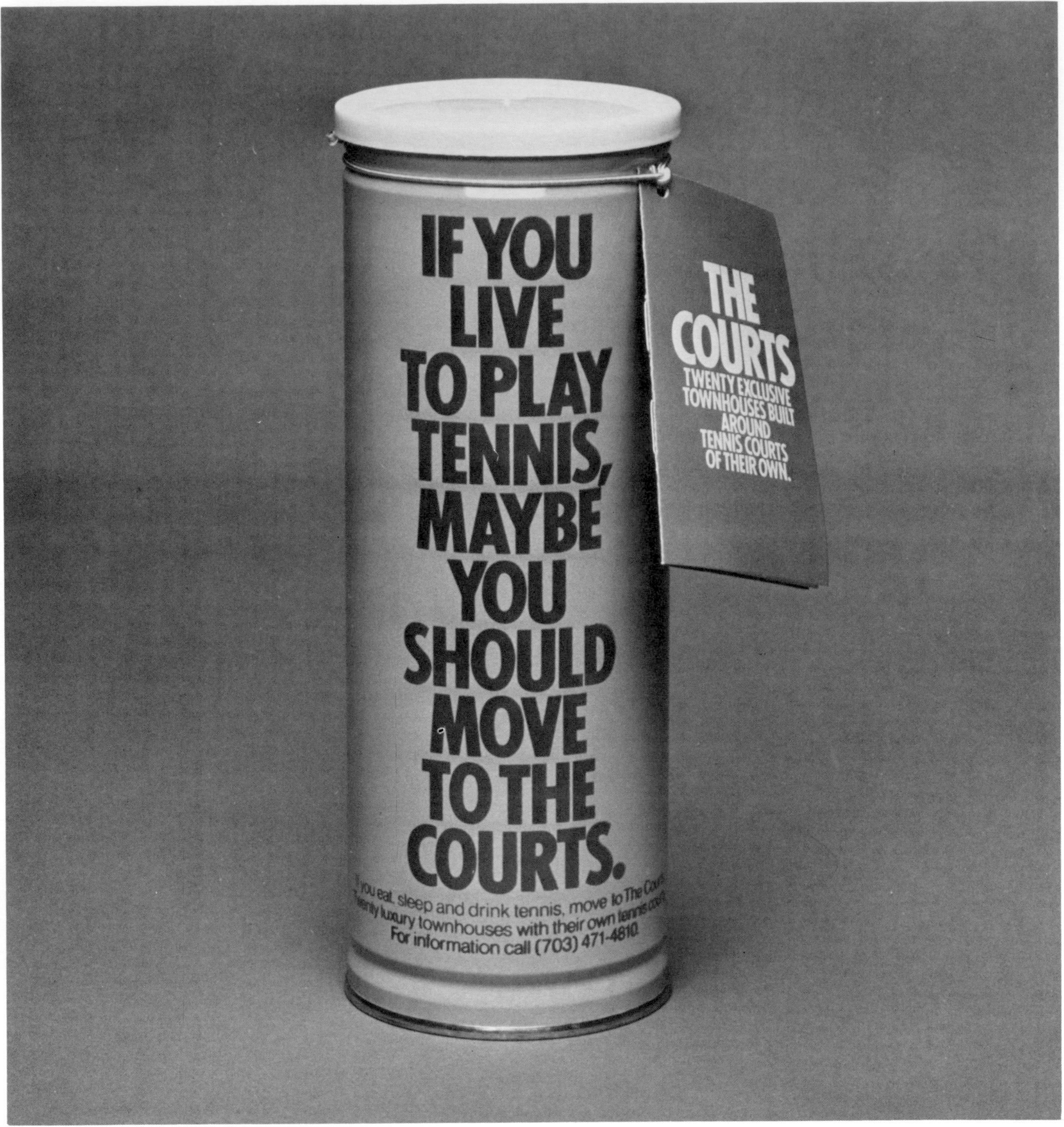

452

452
Art Directors Mark W. Moffett
Diane M. Cook
Writer John N. Siddall
Designer Mark W. Moffett
Artist Rendering: Art Associates Inc.
Agency Siddall, Matus & Coughter Inc.
Client Gulf Reston, Inc.

453

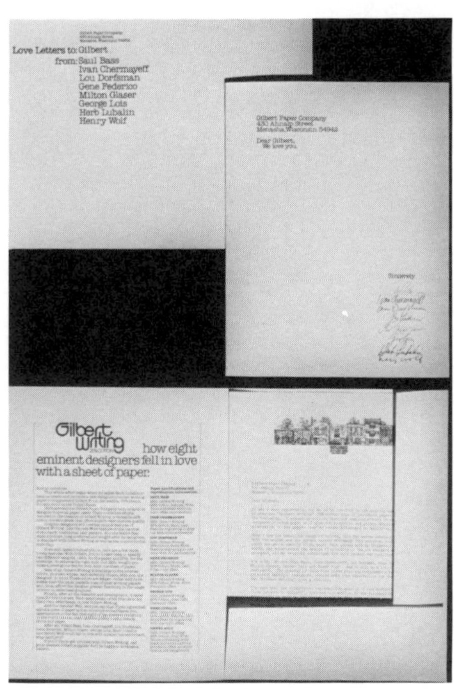

454

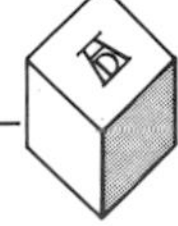

GOLD

453

Art Director	David M. Griffing
Writer	Sandi Burrows
Artist	Richard Giglio
Photographers	Dan Wynn
	Joel Brodsky
Agency	Revlon, Inc.
Client	Revlon, Inc.

454

Art Director	Herb Lubalin
Writers	Jack Anson Finke
	Herb Lubalin
Designer	Herb Lubalin
Agency	LSC&P Design Group, Inc.
Client	Gilbert Paper Company

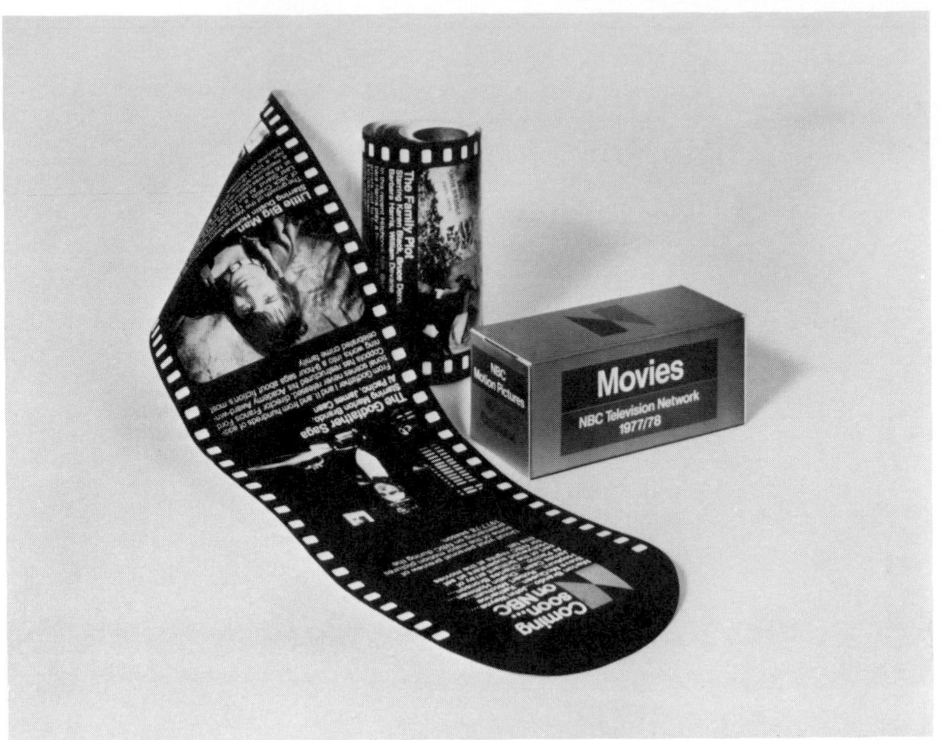

455

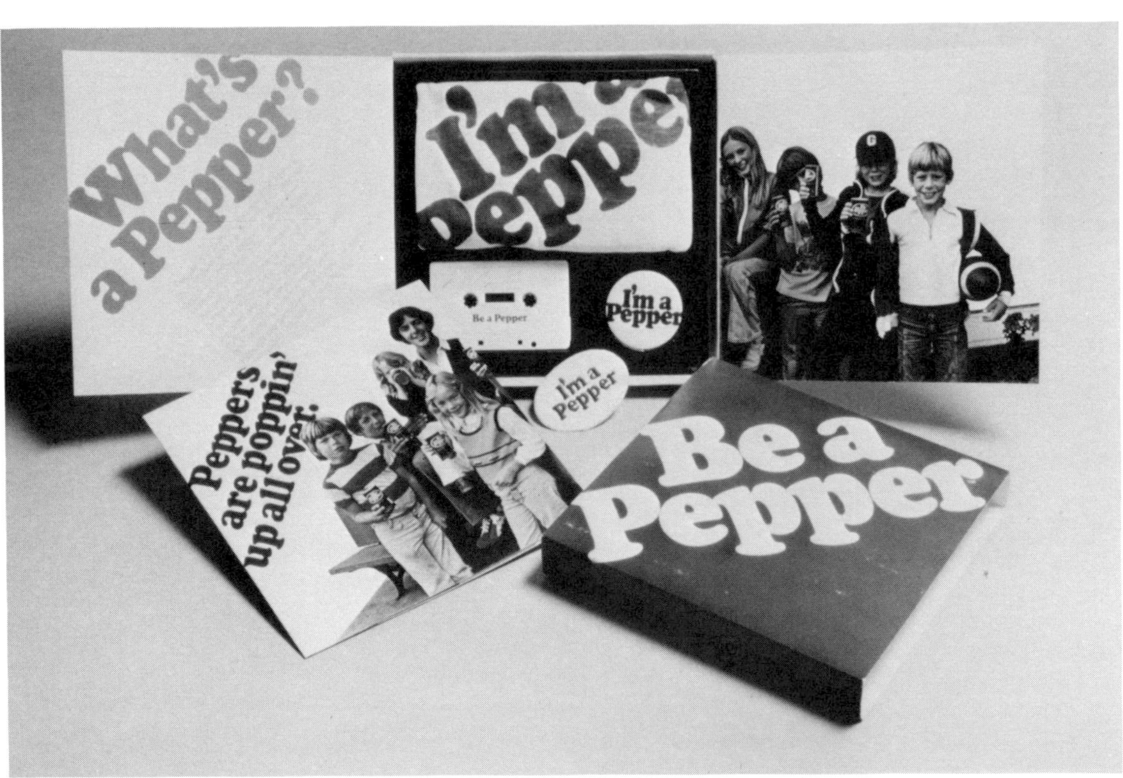

456

455
Art Director Charles V. Blake
Writer Stephen Weinstein
Designer Charles V. Blake
Agency NBC-TV Network
Client NBC

456
Art Director Clark Frankel
Writer Jane Warshaw
Designer Jonson Pedersen Hinrichs
Agency Young & Rubicam
Client Dr Pepper

slighted by other ethnic groups, they tend to become very confused and don't know why it happens. WASPs need greater awareness of and sensitivity to the world outside of their cultural niche.

Dr. Campbell: I think you are quite right that the WASP who has felt that he was the majority all these years is having a very difficult time right now, because all of a sudden the tables are turned and he is quite unprepared to deal with these questions of ethnicity and culture that have suddenly reared their heads. The WASP feels put upon by what has been called reverse discrimination. I think he feels his superior position is being threatened.

Dr. Bartusis: However, we must force a raising of consciousness. If we wait for the natural processes of integration, it's going to take hundreds of years. By forcing it initially, recognizing that it's not the way we want it to be done, we will bring about positive change.

Dr. Adams: But the attitude that you and I have, Dr. Bartusis, is not a very Protestant- or WASP-like attitude. The WASP-like attitude is that all you need to do is to get your heart right with God and proclaim to have no malice against blacks, provided they don't move next door. Then nothing has to be done of a practical nature; nothing has to be done that would bring about some sacrifices on the part of the dominant majority.

I think the crux of the matter is that we can enact institutional change first and then later try to raise consciousness, or we can sit around and take the Protestant attitude that we don't need to make institutional changes, don't need to do anything tangible, as long as we have a change of heart.

Dr. Bartusis: I think attitudinal changes are necessary for ultimate integration, but we need the initiation of the institutional change to get the whole movement going.

Dr. Campbell: One without the other is not going to work, otherwise all our changes will be temporary ones.

25

457

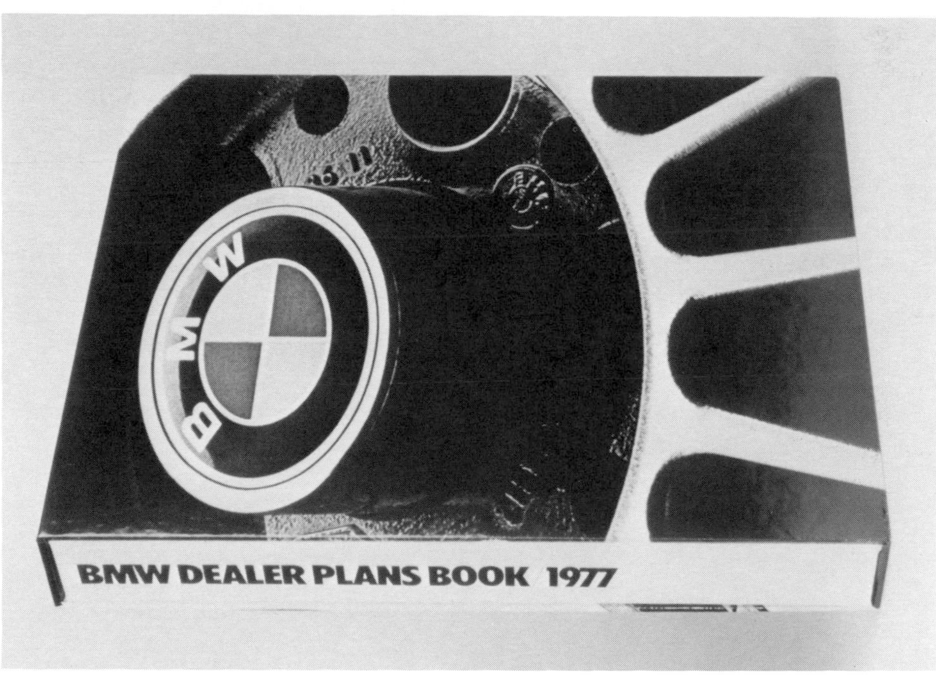

458

457
Art Director Alan J. Klawans
Writer Len Aulenbach
Designer Neil R. Shakery
Artist John O'Leary
Agency Jonson Pedersen Hinrichs
Client Smith Kline and French

458
Art Director Ralph Ammirati
Writer Martin Puris
Designers Ralph Ammirati
Barbara Sharman
Photographer Phil Marco
Producer John Contelmo
Agency Ammirati Puris AvRutick Inc.
Client BMW of North America, Inc.

Administrator's Report

SINCE 1976 WAS the nation's Bicentennial Year, it seems appropriate for us to look back through the eyes of our Administrator, not to 1949 when the Foundation was formed, but to 1965 when growth demanded business administration as well as medical direction.

In 1965 the Radiation Center occupied a concrete and frame building at 2315 Bath Street, on Cottage Hospital property, the total area being approximately 2,160 sq. ft. In that area two physicians provided Radiation Therapy and the beginnings of a new field, Nuclear Medicine.

In 1976 the Radiation Center occupied 13,000 sq. ft. in the Ireland Wing of Cottage Hospital, which The Cancer Foundation helped to finance. Its modern, permanent construction is designed to withstand fire and earthquake. In this complex, six physicians provide Radiation Therapy, Chemotherapy, Clinical Lab, Nuclear Medicine and Thermography. The latter is still an excellent device for early detection of breast cancer in young women, since no radiation is used.

The equipment provided by The Cancer Foundation in its early years was the best available, and in 1965 totalled seven pieces. The Foundation has continued over the years to replace and update capital equipment, some of which had not been invented in 1965. We now have over a dozen of these devices. They are maintained in top condition, with several being calibrated regularly by our Medical Physicist, who also monitors the radiation safety program.

The business office in 1965 had three and one half employees and now has eight, one less than in 1975 due to improvements in technology. Patient billings moved progressively from hand posting in 1965 through a peg-board system, small bookkeeping machine, to a punch card computer service, and finally to an optical scanning computer service with a very low error rate, and

"Every time I see a new patient I say to myself, okay, I'm not going to become emotionally involved. Which is fine as long as you think of some abstract data on a piece of paper. But as soon as they walk in, and they're frightened and anxious, that whole idea of remaining uninvolved goes right out the window."

2

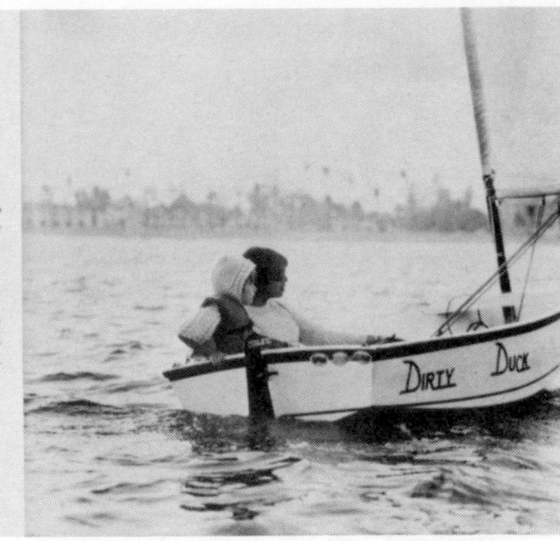

Physics Department

OUR PHYSICS STAFF was reduced in 1976 to one person on three-quarter time, responsible for machine calibrations, dose calculation checks, computerized treatment plans and maintenance of our in-house radiation safety program.

Besides giving routine support to the Therapy Department our physicist has designed and constructed an attachment for the Radiation Center's linear accelerator, which permits routine blocking for beams directed horizontally. Presently under construction are two more wedge filters for the Clinac-6—one of brass and one of lead. When completed, these will require considerable time by the physicist to characterize the resulting beams. However, they will then be available as additional tools for our staff for producing treatment plans which optimize the distribution of the radiation dose—concentrating it in the tumor while protecting the healthy tissue.

Throughout the course of treatment a patient at The Cancer Foundation benefits from our team approach, where physician, physicist and technologist frequently review the patient's progress and evaluate the effectiveness of the therapy program. This can be done at the Radiation Center because the computer, the physics workshop, the Medical Physicist, the highly trained physicians and medical staff all work so closely together.

Radiation Therapy Department

RADIATION THERAPY kills cancer cells—it can also kill or significantly damage normal cells or organs. If the therapeutic ratio can be increased, if we can further the radiation effect in a tumor while decreasing the damage to surrounding normal tissues, the cure rates can be improved with optimal preservation of normal patient function.

"It takes a certain kind of person to work with cancer patients—a certain humanness. When new patients come in, they see this nice waiting room, but they also see a long hallway and worry about where it leads. What I try to do is just talk to them."

Pam Miley, Office Coordinator

10

459

459
Editors Marty Neumeier
Barrie Schwortz
Designer Marty Neumeier
Photographer Barrie Schwortz
Agency Marty Neumeier Design
Client Cancer Foundation of Santa Barbara

460

The Datapoint 1170 *Dispersed Processor adds the practicality of diskette storage to the computing power of the* Datapoint 5500 *Advanced Business Processor. The* Datapoint 1500 *Dispersed Processor, the newest and lowest priced in the family, makes dispersed data processing the Datapoint way practical in many applications where it was not before.*

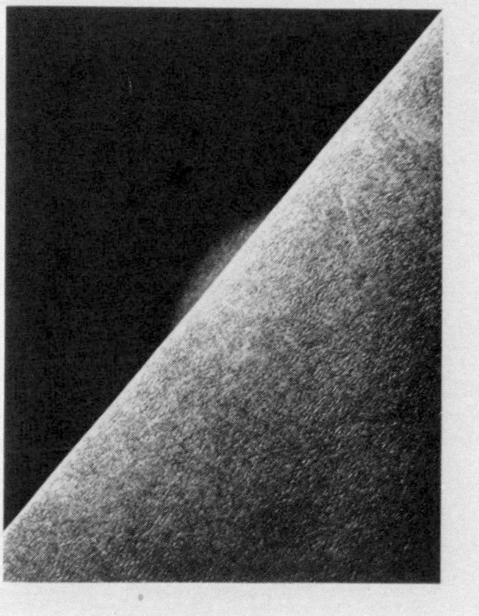

461

460

Art Directors	Robert Miles Runyan
	Dick Rice
Designers	James Guerard
	Claire Denador
Agency	Runyan & Rice
Client	National Medical Enterprises

461

Art Director	Ron Sullivan
Writer	Ed Wattenbarger
Designer	Ron Sullivan
Photographer	Greg Booth
Agency	The Richards Group, Inc.
Client	Datapoint Corp.

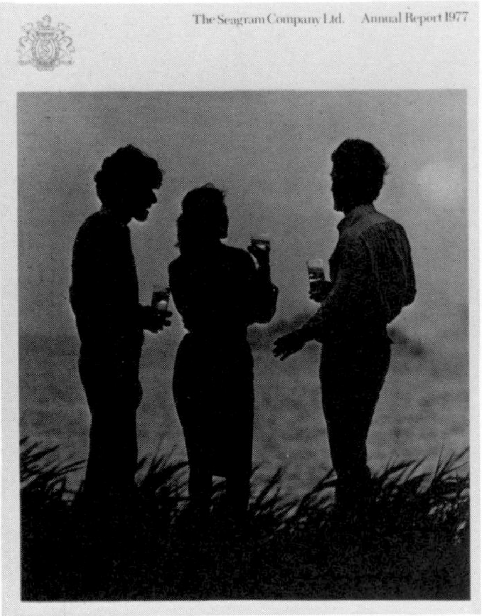

As reported last year, Seagram has adopted a strategy under which certain key brands are receiving added emphasis, while others are being deemphasized. Within the Company's U.S. subsidiary, there was a restructuring of the sales companies to further this strategy. These changes were solidified during the last year and are proving beneficial.

The patterns of consumption in the U.S. market have been shifting significantly in recent years. They reflect certain fundamental changes in the United States population, an understanding of which is essential for future profitability. The Special Report this year focuses on the United States market. From it shareholders can see not only what has happened but how Seagram is positioned to move to satisfy and further stimulate this vital market in the years to come.

On August 2, 1976, Harold Fieldsteel was elected Vice President of The Seagram Company Ltd. Mr. Fieldsteel is also Executive Vice President, Administration and Finance, and a director of Joseph E. Seagram & Sons, Inc., the U.S. subsidiary, as well as Treasurer, Controller, a member of the Executive Committee and a director of The Seagram Company Ltd.

In summary, 1977 was a year of substantial progress on major fronts. A new, aggressive marketing program has already been launched, and we have every indication of gains in the year ahead. Our oil and gas business will benefit from new production coming onstream as well as from somewhat more realistic government attitudes toward oil and gas prices.

Seagram enters the new fiscal year stronger, in a better balanced financial position and with the expectation of continued progress in the year ahead. We gratefully acknowledge the loyal support of our employees and customers, who have made 1977 an outstanding year.

On behalf of the Board,

Edgar M. Bronfman
Chairman

September 19, 1977

Special Report

The United States market, which accounts for some seventy percent of Seagram's sales, is different in many respects from a dozen years ago. Reaching it successfully requires marketing strategies developed from new dimensions of understanding.

462

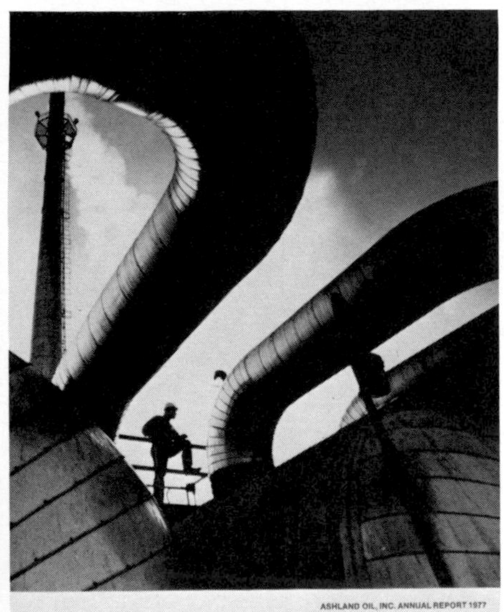

463

462
Art Director Arnold Saks
Writers Jonathan Rinehart, Adams & Rinehart
Designers Ingo Scharrenbroich, Arnold Saks
Photographer Burt Glinn, Magnum
Production Company Canadian Gazette Printing
Client Seagram Company Ltd.

463
Art Director Sheldon Seidler
Writer Teo Nutini
Designers Sheldon Seidler, Edward Broderick
Photographer Cheryl Rossum
Agency Sheldon Seidler Inc.
Client Ashland Oil Inc.

464

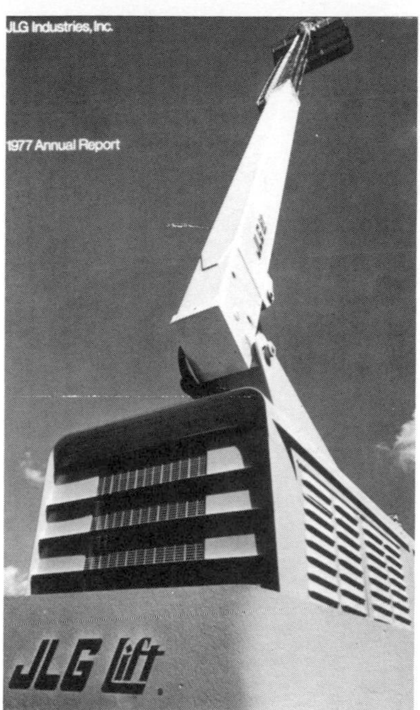

JLG Industries, Inc.
1977 Annual Report
JLG Lift

JLG Industries was conceived when John L. Grove developed the concept of a single-operator, mobile work platform to provide a more efficient and safer working environment than traditional "hi-reach" access devices such as scaffolding and ladders. JLG was incorporated in 1969 and the next year began producing JLG Lifts* through a subsidiary, Fulton Industries, Inc., which was recently merged into JLG. Within the space of eight years JLG has established its position as the largest manufacturer of hydraulically-operated, off-highway, self-propelled lifts with net sales exceeding $25,000,000.

The JLG Lift* is a hydraulically-operated, off-highway, mobile unit that brings a new dimension to "hi-reach" work areas. These platforms are mounted on a motorized mobile four-wheel base either at the end of a telescoping boom or atop a scissors lifting mechanism. JLG Lifts* may be operated by one person from the work platform and are designed to position men, tools or materials easily and quickly in hard-to-reach elevated work areas. The Company's lifts, in many applications, are more versatile, reduce the number of man-hours needed to perform a job, and provide greater safety than scaffolding, ladders and other traditional "hi-reach" devices.

Boom-Type Models The Company's boom-type lifts may be rotated continuously 360 degrees in either direction, raised or lowered from vertical to horizontal, and extended while the work platform remains horizontal and stable. The vehicles on which the booms are mounted may be maneuvered forward or backward and steered in any direction and are designed for stable operation on inclines with grades up to five (5) degrees. JLG boom-type lifts have reach capabilities of up to 80 feet on the largest model. The work platforms vary from 2½ by 3 feet to 3 by 12 feet and have a rated capacity of 500 pounds at any extension and in any position. JLG also offers a 40-foot and 60-foot boom-type lift that is mounted on a truck chassis.

SIZZOR Models The JLG Sizzor* models have larger work platforms and greater lift capacity than the boom-type models. While the Sizzor* lifts may be maneuvered in a manner similar to the boom-type models, the platforms may be

As part of JLG's commitment to manufacturing excellence, all Company welders (shown at the left welding a chassis turntable) are trained and certified. The boom-type lift is produced in various sizes having reach capabilities of 20 to 80 feet. The 40-foot lift at the right is engaged in maintenance of an air-conditioning unit.

465

464
Art Director James Cross
Writer Laurence Pearson
Designer Emmett Morava
Photographer Scott Slobodian
Agency James Cross Design Office, Inc.
Client United California Bank

465
Art Director Barry Ostrie
Writer Donald R. Stevenson
Designer Barry Ostrie
Photographer Burk Uzzle
Client JLG Industries, Inc.

466

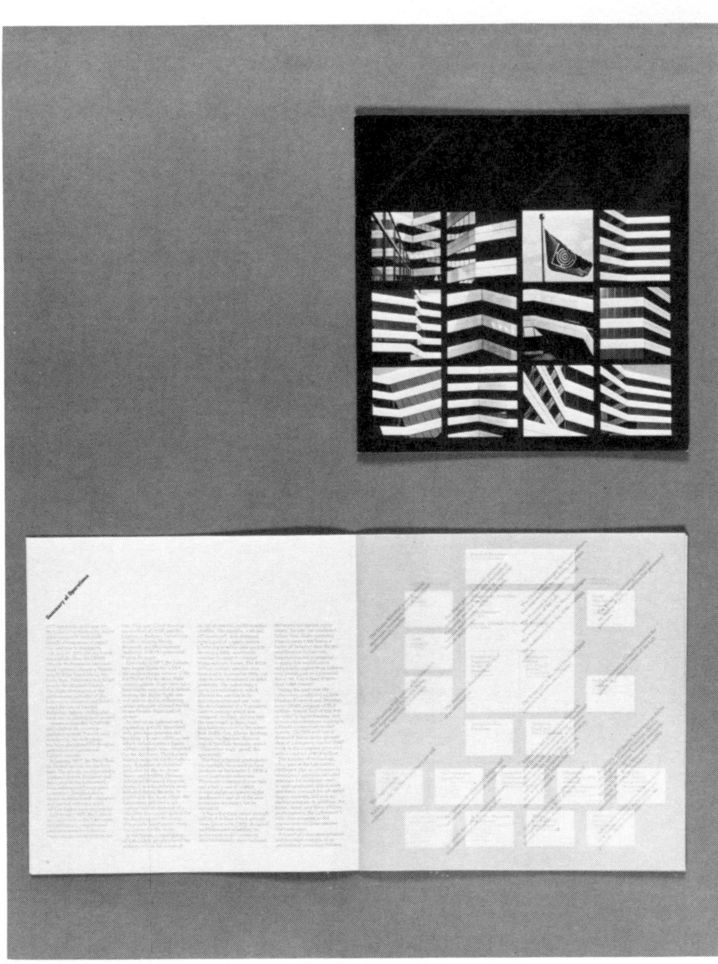

467

466

Art Director Danne & Blackburn
Writer J. Alexander McGhie
Designer Richard Danne
Artists Richard Danne
Claude Saunders
Diane DeLucia
Marlowe Goodson
Photographer Bob Colton
Agency Danne & Blackburn, Inc.
Client Hammermill Paper Company

467

Art Directors Advertising Designers, Inc.
R.L. Steinle
Tom Ohmer
Writers Robert L. Steinle
Joe Ianocci
Joe O'Connor
Designer Jim Marrin
Artist Advertising Designers, Inc.
Photographer Technical Communications
Office of CSDL
Agency Advertising Designers, Inc.
Client Charles Stark Draper Laboratory

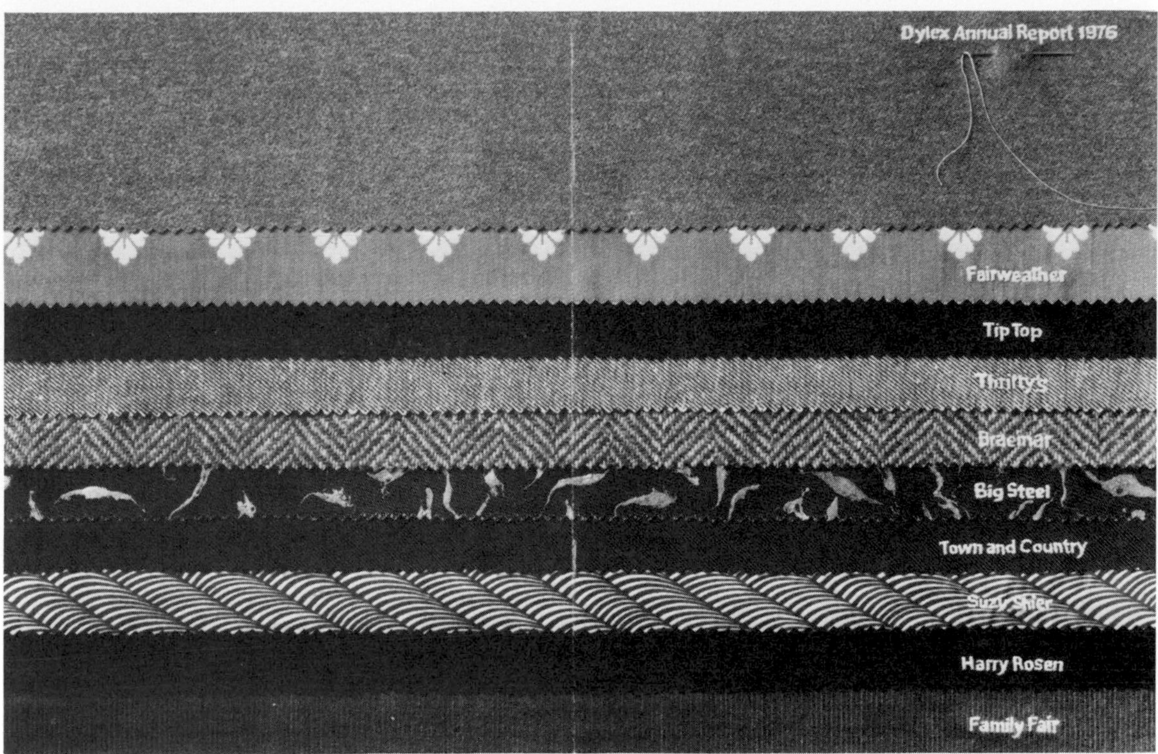

468

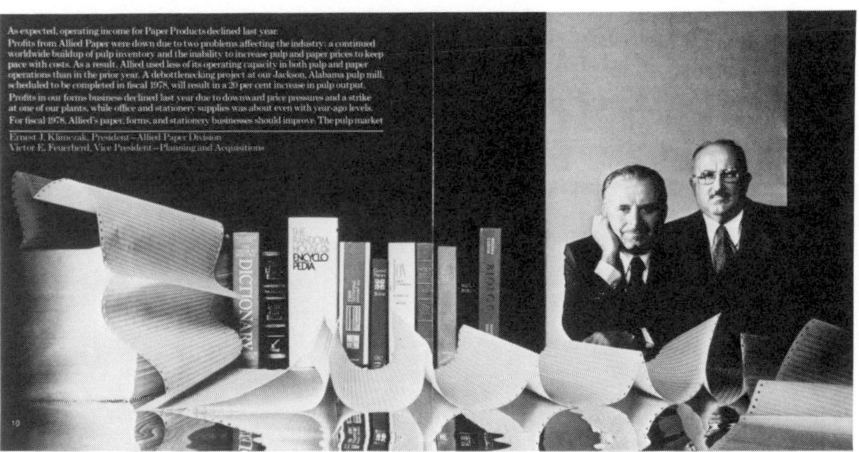
As expected, operating income for Paper Products declined last year.

Profits from Allied Paper were down due to two problems affecting the industry: a continued worldwide buildup of pulp inventory and the inability to increase pulp and paper prices to keep pace with costs. As a result, Allied used less of its operating capacity in both pulp and paper operations than in the prior year. A debottlenecking project at our Jackson, Alabama pulp mill, scheduled to be completed in fiscal 1978, will result in a 20 per cent increase in pulp output.

Profits in our forms business declined last year due to downward price pressures and a strike at one of our plants, while office and stationery supplies was about even with year-ago levels.

For fiscal 1978, Allied's paper, forms, and stationery businesses should improve. The pulp market

Ernest J. Klimczak, President—Allied Paper Division
Victor E. Feuerherd, Vice President—Planning and Acquisitions

10

469

468
Art Director Robert Burns
Designer Ann Ames
Photographer Tim Saunders
Agency Burns, Cooper, Hynes Limited
Client Dylex Limited

469
Art Director Peter Harrison
Writer SCM Corp. PR Dept.
Designer Randee Rubin
Photographer Arnold Newman
Agency Harrison Associates
Client SCM Corporation

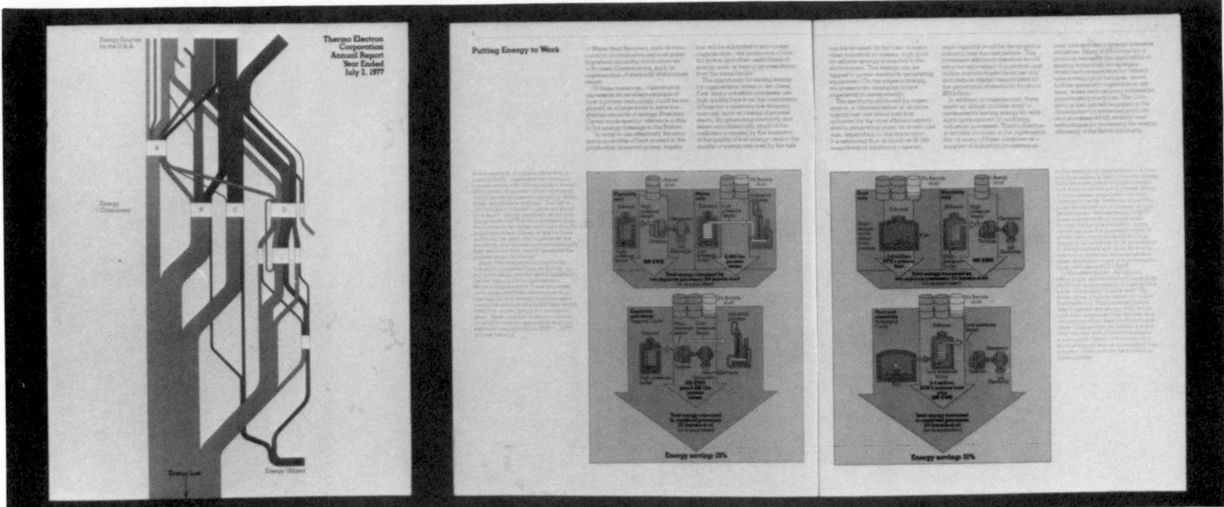

470

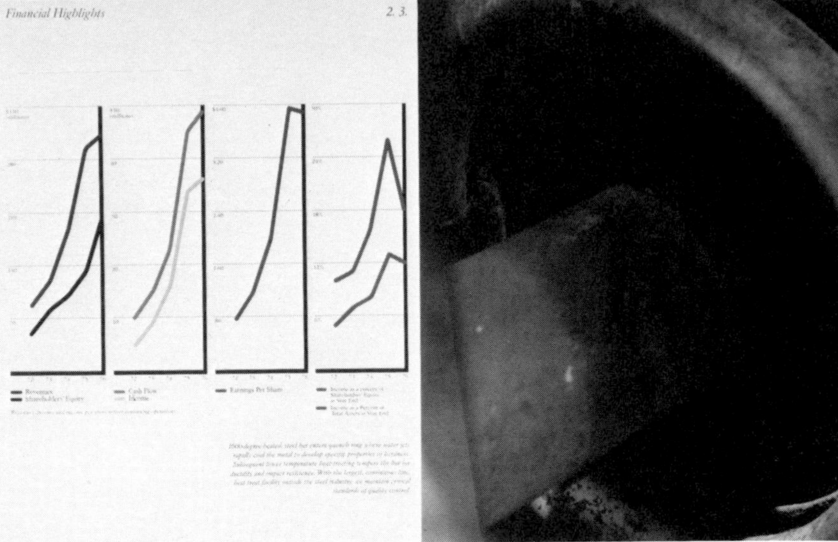

471

470
Art Director Robert Cipriani
Writer Leonard P. Entin
Designer Robert Cipriani
Photographer George Sakmanoff
Agency Gunn Associates
Client Thermoelectron

471
Art Director James Cross
Writer Bruce Russell
Designer James Cross
Photographer Jason Hailey
Agency James Cross Design Office, Inc.
Client Smith International, Inc.

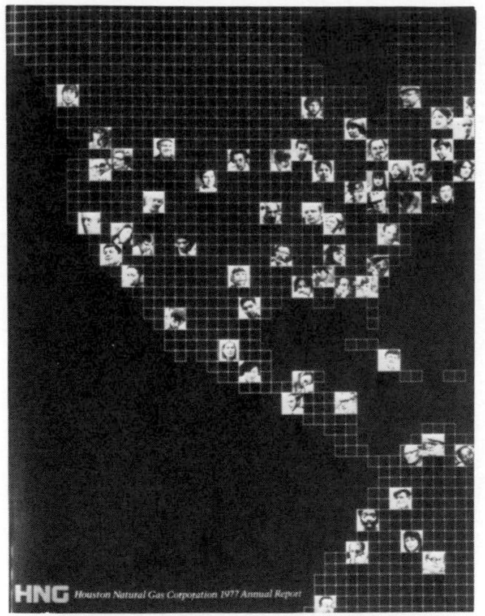

472

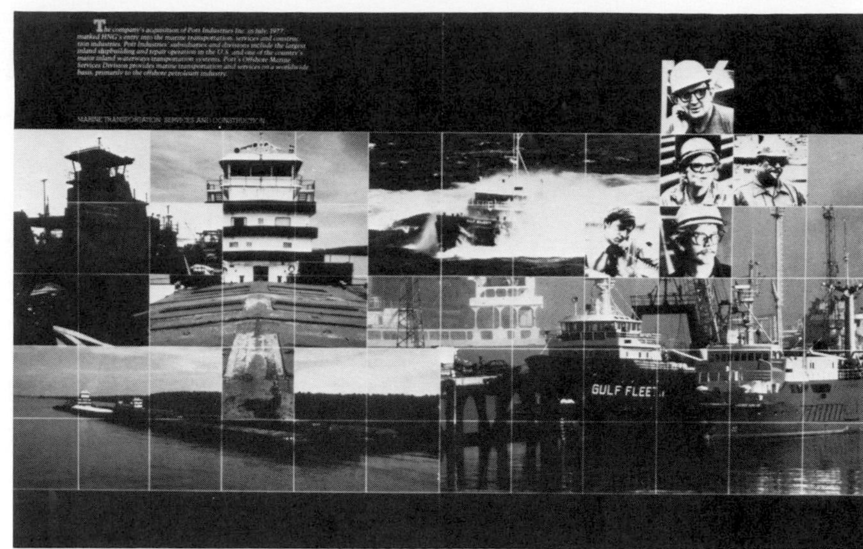

473

Contents

For example, a saturation diving system which uses a team of divers and surface support personnel, would require a day of decompression for each 100 feet of depth. A job performed in 600 feet of water could require six days of decompression and take 15 days to complete. "Jim" has completed the same job in one day with less support people.

Oceaneering now has six "Jim" suits. Development is underway on a new version of the one-atmosphere diving suit which will give the operator even greater freedom of movement.

Subsea Construction

Formed in 1973, Oceaneering's Subsea Construction Division offers one of the greatest opportunities for growth.

Oceaneering combines underwater diving skills with specialized surface support vessels and barges to perform underwater construction for the oil industry, either as a prime contractor or as a sub-contractor to large marine construction firms.

Often Oceaneering can perform many types of marine construction tasks more economically than companies using larger and more expensive equipment.

The Company provides underwater welding services (employing both wet and dry techniques) to produce high quality welds to meet the most stringent requirements of the offshore industry.

Oceaneering's subsea construction services include: connecting flowlines to platform risers and subsea wellheads; burying of flowlines; installing valve assemblies on pipelines; installing cathodic protection systems; installing tanker loading terminals; trenching for large scale pipe; laying and stabilizing power cables and small diameter pipelines; setting platform structures; constructing harbor facilities; and installing Seadomes* (protective shelters for valves).

Long recognized as a pioneer in inspection and maintenance,

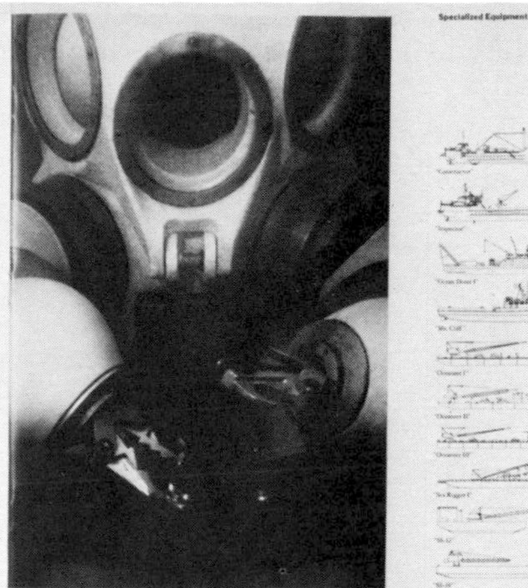

472
Art Director John Weaver
Writer Houston Natural Gas Corporation
Designer John Weaver
Artist Joe Romano
Photographers Mark St. Gill
Mark Judson
Agency Baxter & Korge, Inc.
Client Houston Natural Gas Corp.

473
Art Director Lyle Metzdorf
Writer Lyle Metzdorf
Designer Lyle Metzdorf
Artist Al Bates
Photographers Bob Gomel & others
Agency Metzdorf Advertising Agency
Client Oceaneering International

474

475

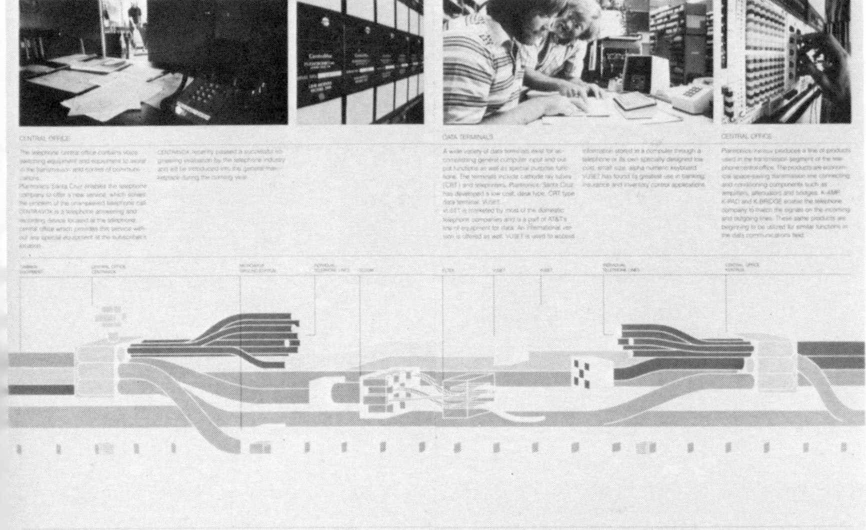

476

474
Art Director Don Weller
Writer Sheldon Weinstein
Designers Don Weller
Chikako Matsubayashi
Artist Don Weller
Photographer Stan Caplan
Agency The Weller Institute for the Cure of Design
Client Standard Brands Paint Company

475
Art Director Brian O'Neill
Designer Victor Gialleonardo
Photographers Cheryl Rossum
Bert Glinn
Agency Doremus & Company
Client The Bank of Tokyo Trust Company

476
Art Directors Robert Miles Runyan
Dick Rice
Designer Claire Denador
Artist Paul Bice
Photographer William Warren
Agency Runyan & Rice
Client Plantronics, Inc.

Growing, building, picking up speed.
Southwest momentum. Mercantile momentum.
These are the themes of this year's report.
Mercantile Texas Corporation Annual Report 1976

"Traffic to and from the Dallas/Fort Worth Regional Airport, and other air centers throughout the Southwest, breaks down traditional time and geographic barriers and opens up a whole new way of looking at the world and doing business. It significantly enlarges great regional distribution centers and centers of wholesale trade, like Dallas, and establishes patterns that will last for many years to come. Here there is economic momentum, and here, too, is Mercantile Texas."

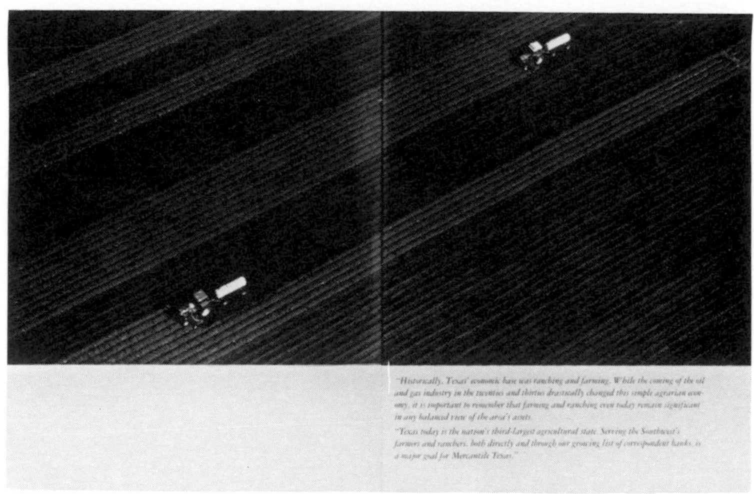

"Historically, Texas' economic base was ranching and farming. While the coming of the oil and gas industry in the twenties and thirties drastically changed this simple agrarian economy, it is important to remember that farming and ranching even today remain significant in any balanced view of the area's assets.
"Texas today is the nation's third-largest agricultural state. Serving the Southwest's farmers and ranchers, both directly and through our growing list of correspondent banks, is a major goal for Mercantile Texas."

477

477
Art Director Jack Summerford
Writer John Stone
Designer Jack Summerford
Photographer Greg Booth
Agency The Richards Group, Inc.
Client Mercantile Texas Corp.

478

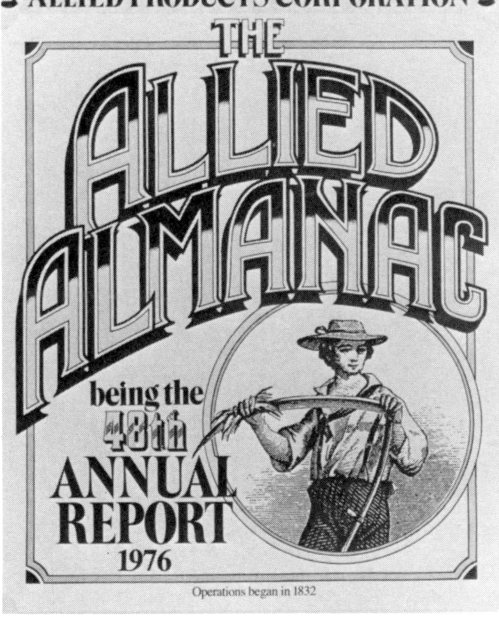

BUSH HOG AGRICULTURAL EQUIPMENT GROUP

479

478
Art Director Sheldon Seidler
Writer Irving Geller
Designers Sheldon Seidler
Irene Liberman
Artist Barry Ross
Photographers Tom Hollyman
Arnold Newman
Agency Sheldon Seidler Inc.
Client Combustion Engineering

479
Art Director Andy DiMartino
Writer Meno Schoenbach
Designer Graphicsgroup, Inc./Atlanta
Artist Graphicsgroup, Inc./Atlanta
Agency Graphicsgroup, Inc./Atlanta
Client Allied Products Corp.

OPERATIONS REVIEW

Menswear A consumer trend toward "dressing up" was capitalized on in 1976 by *The Arrow Company*, largest of Cluett's Divisions. With three-quarters of its volume in dress shirts, Arrow made substantial sales and earnings gains.

The brand did not, however, lose sight of another, longer-term trend—toward more informal lifestyles. Arrow continues to anticipate a growing market for sportswear.

A separate management team devoted solely to sportswear laid the foundation for larger future sales. As a first step it introduced the *Omni* brand of sport shirts for the more sophisticated segment of the market.

Another part of the sportswear picture is covered by the growing volume of *Saturdays in California*, whose shirts and sweaters are merchandised for younger men.

1976 was also a fine year for *J. Schoeneman*. The long-recognized quality of its suits, sport coats and slacks, sold through leading department and specialty stores, helped it reach new highs.

In the second half, merchandise was shipped from a new division of J. Schoeneman, *Halston For Men*. This versatile line is styled by Halston, a top American designer.

Another important target for Cluett is the high volume chain store business. A leading dress shirt supplier to this market is *Alatex, Inc.*, whose sales and earnings rose substantially last year. Alatex is also an important factor in the private label shirt business of large department and specialty stores.

Chain store volume in men's and boys' underwear has grown steadily over the years. In this market the major chains are served by *Spring City Knitting Company*, whose

4

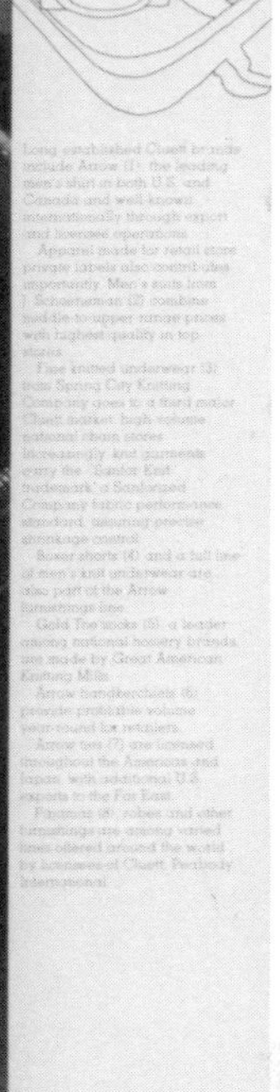

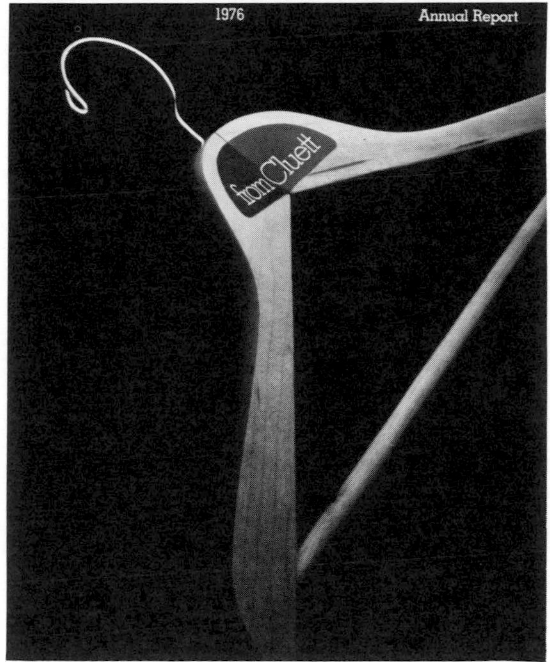

480

480

Art Directors Roger Cook
Don Shanosky
Writer Cochran B. Supplee
Designers Roger Cook
Don Shanosky
Photographer Arthur Beck
Agency Cook and Shanosky Associates, Inc.
Client Cluett, Peabody & Co., Inc.

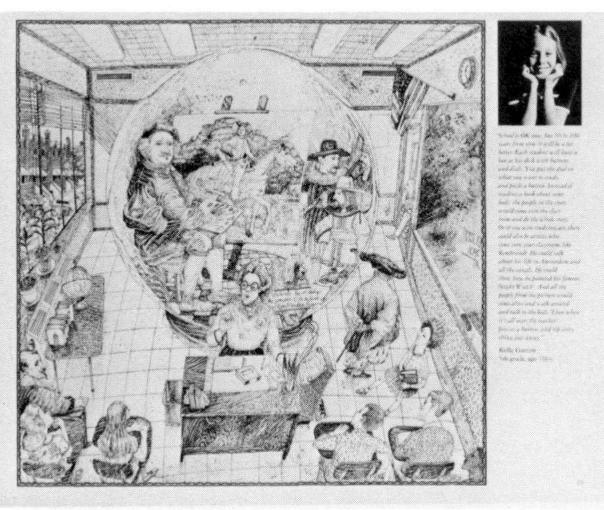

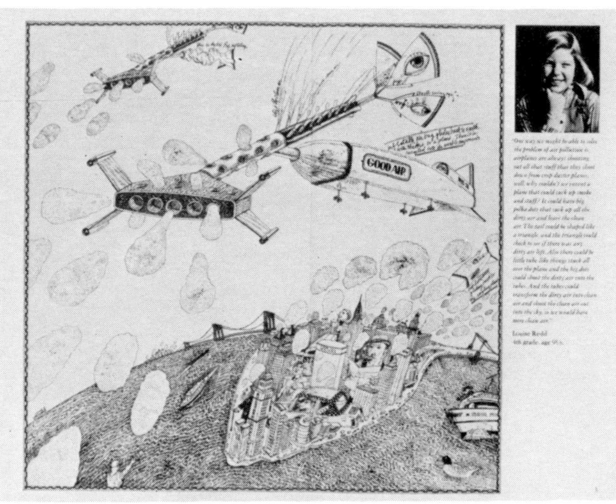

481

481

Art Director Ron Sullivan
Writer John Stone
Designer Ron Sullivan
Artist Jack Unruh
Photographers Keith Wood
Greg Booth
Agency The Richards Group, Inc.
Client Lomas & Nettleton Mortgage Investors

482

482
Art Directors Robert Miles Runyan
Dick Rice
Designer Al Briggs
Photographers Kim Tucker
Marv Silver
Ken Whitmore
Agency Runyan & Rice
Client Denny's Restaurant

483

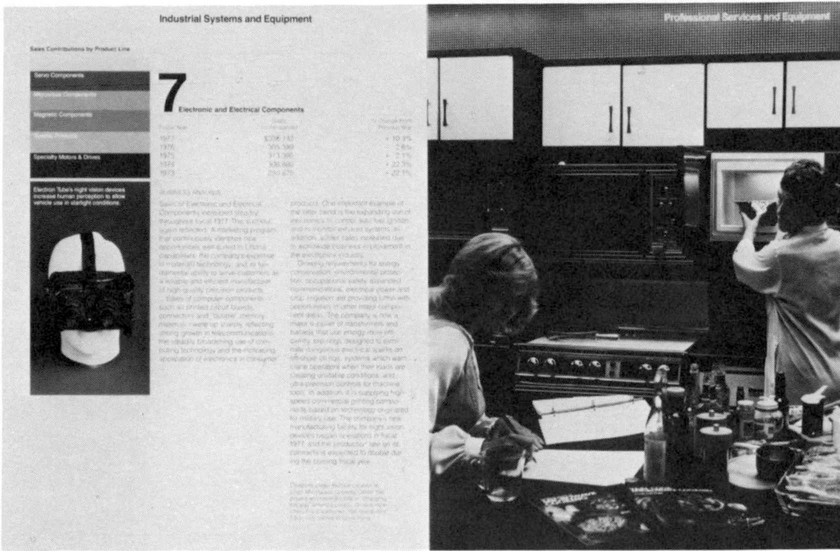

484

483
Art Directors Robert Miles Runyan
Dick Rice
Designer Ronald Jefferies
Photographers Kim Tucker
Marvin Silver
Agency Runyan & Rice
Client Litton Industries

484
Art Directors Robert Miles Runyan
Dick Rice
Designer Al Briggs
Artist Deanna Glad
Photographer Ken Whitmore
Agency Runyan & Rice
Client Levi Strauss & Co.

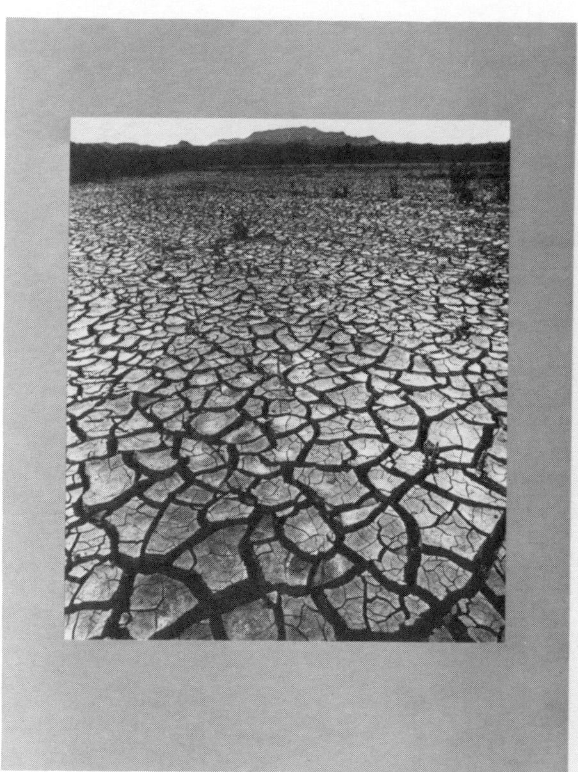

Blyth Eastman Dillon for balanced investment banking.

The position of leadership in municipal finance that Blyth Eastman Dillon has earned through the years is also characteristic of the full spectrum of investment banking services that the firm offers.

The firm's beginnings date back to 1864 when the predecessor to the investment banking business of Union Securities Corporation was founded. Eastman Dillon & Co. was established in Philadelphia in 1912. In 1956, the two merged to form Eastman Dillon, Union Securities & Co.

Blyth & Co. originated in 1914 in San Francisco. That firm specialized in municipal finance, and rapidly became the leading West Coast municipal investment banker, and then a national leader.

The 1972 merger between Eastman Dillon, Union Securities and Blyth created a single firm from three that had been among the most influential in financial history. Stronger than any of its predecessors, Blyth Eastman Dillon manages the investment affairs of the present from a perspective of over a century of combined experience.

A hallmark of Blyth Eastman Dillon's services is the firm's willingness to commit major capital resources on behalf of its clients. Presently capitalization of some $83 million places the firm among the top investment bankers in the country. Augmenting that financial strength is INA Corporation, a Philadelphia-based financial holding company of $4 billion in consolidated assets, which owns 60% of Blyth Eastman Dillon's stock. Additionally, Compagnie Financiere de Suez, France's largest private banking and financial holding company with widespread clientele and facilities throughout Europe and the Middle East, has acquired a 20% common stock interest in our firm. The remaining 20% is held by partners active in the firm.

Blyth Eastman Dillon is a major factor in all sectors of the securities and investment banking business.

Corporate finance.

In corporate finance, Blyth Eastman Dillon is a leading underwriter of negotiated and competitive offerings for both public sale and private placement. During the last year, the

For capabilities in depth.

This brochure was designed to introduce you to Blyth Eastman Dillon's municipal finance capabilities and to the firm's record of meeting pressing public needs with measured, professional response. Yet it is only an introduction. For more detailed information about the firm's expertise in all areas of municipal finance, we invite you to review one or more of these supplementary brochures. Also available are an introduction to the Blyth Eastman Dillon municipal finance professionals, and a comprehensive, current review of the issues the firm has managed or co-managed in all areas of municipal finance.

But the best introduction to our capabilities is a personal meeting or conversation with our people. Because, in the final analysis, it is the quality of the interaction between client and investment banker, underwriter or financial advisor that assures ultimate success in meeting today's need for capital.

We believe that Blyth Eastman Dillon has the professionals to help you meet that need. A telephone call to Mr. Stanley T. Pardo, an Executive Vice President of the firm and the head of its Municipal Bond Division, can put you in touch with them, and in touch with the investment banking, underwriting and advisory expertise that have made Blyth Eastman Dillon an industry leader.

Housing

Health Care

Public Power

Environment and Solid Waste

The Record

McGraw-Hill Building (right), 1221 Avenue of the Americas, New York—as of January 1978, World Headquarters of Blyth Eastman Dillon & Co. Incorporated.

24

485

485
Art Director Edward G. Infurna
Writer Dave Brown
Editor Ed McCarthy
Designer Edward G. Infurna
Co-Designer Gordon C. Baker
Photographer David Plowden (Principal Photographer)
Design Firm Mayo-Infurna Design Incorporated
Client Blyth Eastman Dillon & Co. Incorporated

Virginio Sonvico

Large distribution sales manager responsible for sales to supermarkets and hypermarkets
Plasmon, Milan

Impatiently, Virginio Sonvico hurries up three flights of marble stairs to his neat apartment in Milan. Donning his wife's blue apron, he pushes through double doors to the balcony. There, in stacked wire cages, wait the objects of his passion—English border canaries, 10 couples and their young, chirping at his arrival. / "Yes, it is a passion. I began with a bird called Lizard, because it looks like a lizard. All 20 died. Then someone told me of the English border breed, of a very sweet character, also rare and beautiful." / He arises half an hour early every morning to feed the birds. "It is my own formulation. They eat little quantity, but they need protein. It must be good, I think, because they have won prizes in shows." / Each year, he chooses the best of his collection for further breeding and sells the others. "This intense yellow, it came from a cross between a yellow and a frost-colored. It is like mixing paints." / At the conference table, he is a formidable presence in the chair. He leans his large torso forward, drums his finger pads on the wood surface, wags an admonitory pen, delivers an endless flow of words, his voice rising and falling as he conducts an orchestration of response. It seems an exhausting performance. "You see why I go to the birds. It is my first hobby, although I have others. The birds relax me the most. I have to talk to people so much when I negotiate." He coaxes the bird in his cupped palms to eat. When it does, he strokes its head affectionately. "Bravo!" he cries.

22

Basil A. Celany

Manager-taxes and property accounting
Ore-Ida Foods, Boise

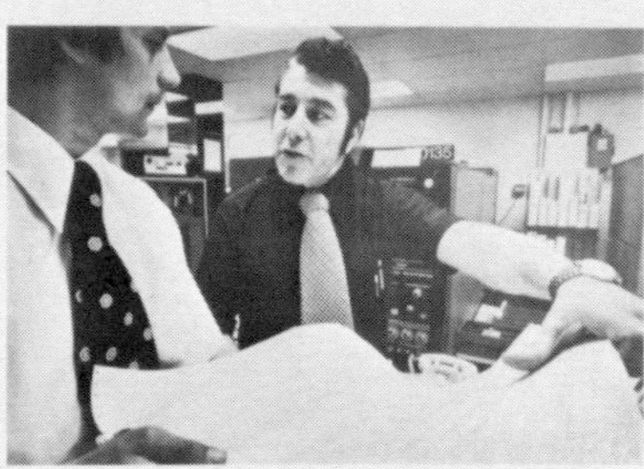

As institutional representative to Boy Scout Troop 4 of the Ore-Ida Scout Council, Basil Celany is the first to arrive at the site. Soon after come the boys, jumping awkwardly, shaking hands all around, clamoring to build the fire and break out the food, their red berets like giant poppies moving through the woods. / "You can call them retarded, yes, but almost every mentally handicapped person is also physically handicapped. We take that into account." / Gently, he warns them not to walk too close to the river. Instantly, gravely, they join hands and edge away from the bank. / The fire is lively now, and beans bubble in the pot. "It touches you, how eager they are to learn. And learn they can, although retention is a problem. We do see a lot of progress. Last year, four of our boys served as color guard at the Governor's Conference on the Handicapped. And two of our boys are ready for 'mainstreaming'—ready to join regular troops of normal boys. That took work and patience, on their part and ours." / Patience. "If a boy can't learn to tie a square knot in four or five tries, we move on to something else. They lose interest fast, and need constant encouragement." / The day-long clouds darken, threatening rain. Quickly the food is gone, every bite. The fire is covered with dirt. The site is cleared, left as nature had it. The boys move out for their homes, shouting repeated goodbyes over their shoulders. This day's challenge has been faced and conquered.

12

13

486

486
Art Director Bennett Robinson
Writer Oscar Schefler
Designer Bennett Robinson
Photographer Bruce Davidson
Agency Corporate Graphics Incorporated
Client H.J. Heinz Company

Missile Technology 21

Northrop's fundamental interest in pursuing low-cost answers to emerging defense needs prompted the company several years ago to begin proprietary work on an all-weather, air-to-air, radar-guided missile light enough to be suitable for our F-5 and other lightweight fighters. While existing all-weather radar-guided missiles can be mounted on some aircraft which are designed for high maneuverability and relatively low cost, such as the F-18, their size and weight make them unsuited to smaller aircraft. Technical advances now provide means to design a missile that in most respects has equal or better performance than current radar-guided missiles, but is smaller, lighter, and lower in cost.

Last year, as a result of its preliminary work, Northrop was one of three firms awarded contracts to formulate design concepts for an advanced, medium-range, air-to-air missile (AMRAAM) under a long-term joint USAF/Navy program. The AMRAAM program supports development of a missile designed from the outset to complement the new generation of U.S. fighters — the F-14, F-15, F-16, and F-18 — in size, weight, and cost. Such a missile would, in addition, be suitable for advanced versions of the F-5. Later this year, two companies will be selected to conduct parallel development of AMRAAM prototypes during the 1978-1979 period. One of these companies ultimately would produce the missile. The potential value of the program, which will extend into the next century, is estimated at $1 billion to $3 billion in view of the large number of possible applications for the missile.

The diversity of Northrop's technical experience is being directly applied to the AMRAAM program. The Electro-Mechanical Division, which designed, developed, and continues to produce, as sole supplier, a significant portion of the U.S. Army's Hawk missile, is managing Northrop's effort and supplying hardware for the missile airframe, launcher, and warhead. The program is also drawing on the guidance and control experience of the Precision Products Division, the electronic countermeasures capability of the Defense Systems Division, and the Aircraft Division's special knowledge of tactical aircraft weapon systems. Northrop has as a principal associate the Government Electronics Division of Motorola, Inc. in Scottsdale, Ariz. In addition, Northrop has access to extensive missile design and performance data accumulated by Societe MATRA of France.

Northrop's AMRAAM design integrates the Precision Products Division's strapdown guidance technology, which makes inertial guidance available for the first time in a small, inexpensive package, with Motorola's compact active-radar seeker, which gives the missile accurate terminal guidance independent of the launch aircraft. With these features, the missile can be effectively deployed at medium stand-off ranges and, because it is small and maneuverable, it is also an effective weapon at short range.

Model of the lightweight medium-range radar-guided air-to-air missile

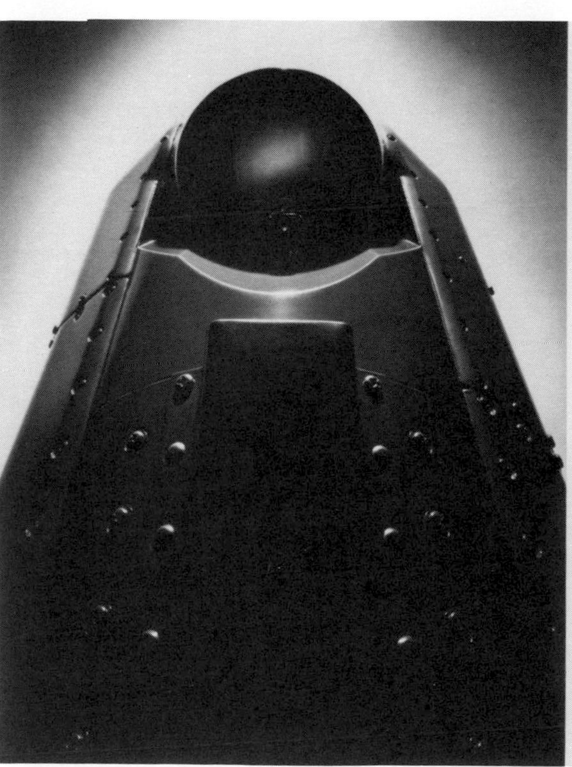

Visionics 17

In March 1977, Northrop was awarded a $29.6 million contract for competitive development of a day and night target designation and pilot's night vision system for the U.S. Army's new advanced attack helicopter. Between 1977 and 1979, the Northrop system and a competing unit will be evaluated, with a production decision expected to follow. The potential value of the production program could exceed $200 million. Northrop's design, which was one of seven competing for the development contract, integrates features of each of Northrop's advanced visionic products into a system particularly adapted to the Army's needs.

Visionics is one of the key technologies supporting modern weapon development and one in which Northrop has built a broad, proprietary expertise. Over the past decade, Northrop's Electro-Mechanical Division in Anaheim, Calif. has developed a family of electro-optical systems, each of which increases the effectiveness and survivability of aircraft and their crews by greatly extending the range at which targets in the air or on the ground can be sighted, identified, and destroyed.

TISEO, the first of these visionic systems, mates a stabilized telescope with closed-circuit television to give a continuous, magnified image of distant objects. It was designed by Northrop to allow pilots approaching a potential target at supersonic speeds to identify it and take the necessary action at the earliest possible moment. The system proved equally effective for air-to-surface missions, enabling a pilot to identify and move on a target quickly, reducing his exposure to hostile fire. To date nearly 440 TISEO units have been ordered or delivered for installation on U.S. Air Force F-4E Phantoms.

The success of TISEO led Northrop to develop similar systems for helicopter use. Using ISTAR, a day system, or LOHTADS, an advanced day and night system, helicopters can stand well away from an area of enemy activity, surveying and selecting prime targets. With the laser designators incorporated in these systems, the helicopter pilot can then spotlight the selected target with a laser beam for an attack helicopter or fixed-wing aircraft to attack with laser-guided weapons.

The newest member of the family is LATAR — for laser-augmented target acquisition and recognition. LATAR is an advanced version of TISEO equipped with both a laser designator and a laser spot seeker and tracker. They permit an aircraft to designate a target for attack by another aircraft or to launch its own laser-guided weapons against a target designated by itself or by another aircraft. LATAR is a compact, lightweight system designed for small, high-performance, single-seat aircraft such as the F-16 and F-18. With LATAR-provided targeting capabilities, a lone pilot has the weapon delivery capability of a pilot and weapons operator team in a two-seat aircraft. The Air Force has successfully tested LATAR for fighter compatibility on a single-seat Northrop F-5E and is now testing it in tactical maneuvers on a two-seat F-4E modified to simulate single-seat operations.

Laser-augmented electro-optical targeting system

487

487
Art Director James Cross
Writer Judith Wheeler
Designers James Cross
Andrew Nawrocky
Photographer Per Volquartz
Agency James Cross Design Office, Inc.
Client Northrop Corp.

Victoria Station Incorporated
150 Chestnut Street
San Francisco, CA 94111
1977
Annual Report
Victoria
Station
Incorporated

Boston—a rich heritage symbolized by the Paul Revere Statue and the Old North Church

The densely populated northeast harbors a number of markets which provide much potential for Victoria Station. With eight restaurants already in Boston, Philadelphia, Darien, Pittsburgh, Alexandria, Wayne, N.J., and Rockville, MD, several more are planned for metropolitan New York, Boston, Albany, and Washington, D.C.

Just as these cities differ greatly in local customs and color, so also do our restaurants—no two are quite alike in this region, although the theme, decor and high standards of quality are consistent.

The ability to operate individual restaurants in different markets is a tribute to our operations skill. All our management personnel receive comprehensive, standardized instruction at one of our two California Training Centers prior to their first assignment. The attention paid to the training of management is a primary reason why we are able to consistently meet our markets' needs.

Our specifications for the purchase, preparation and presentation of our product are monitored closely to achieve the quality control we seek and the excellence our customers expect. Uniformity in all our restaurants is a goal in the areas where it counts most—food and service. From Boston to San Francisco, outstanding execution in the local markets is the hallmark of Victoria Station.

4

5

488

488

Art Director	Reginald Jones
Writer	Harlow White
Designer	Dawson Zaug
Artist	Ellen Smith
Photographers	Paul Fusco & Others
Agency	Unigraphics
Client	Victoria Station Incorporated

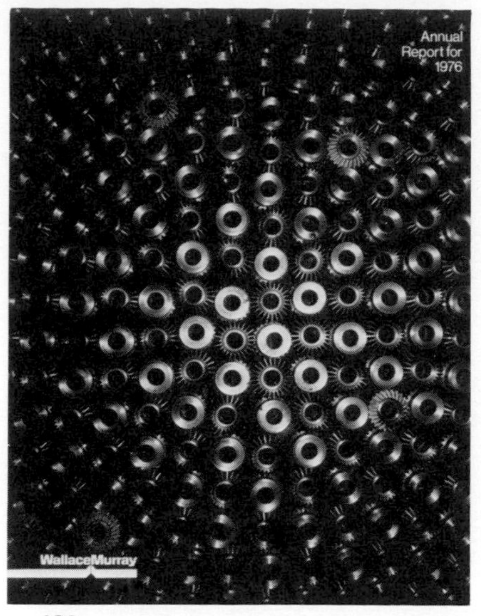

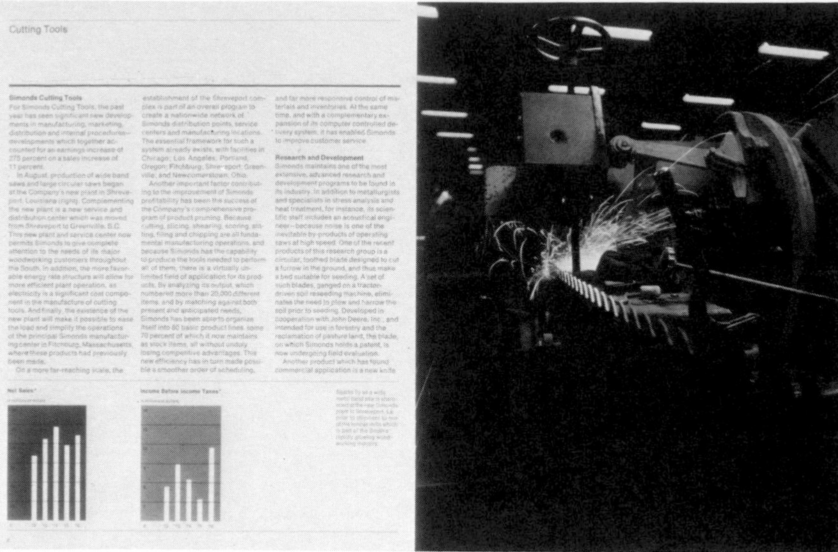

489

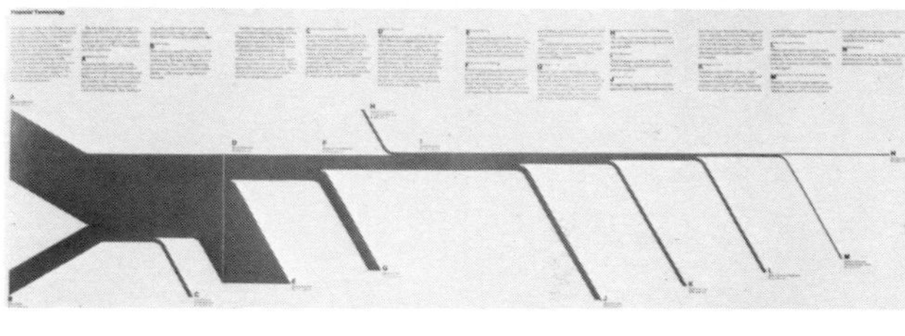

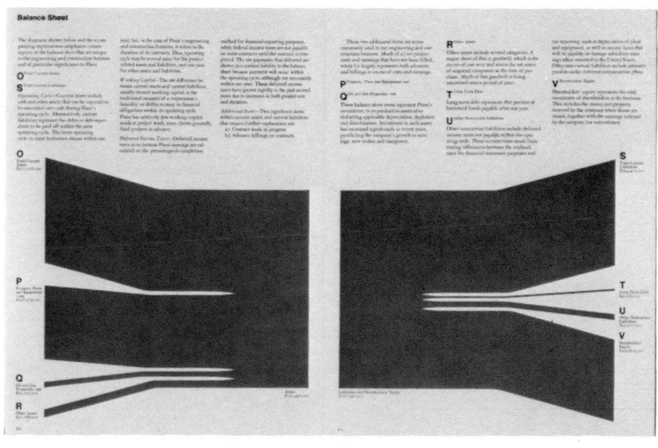

490

489

Art Director	Arnold Saks
Writer	Mark Strage
Designers	Taris Charysyn
	Arnold Saks
Major Photography	Joel Meyerowitz
Other Photography	Burt Glinn, Magnum
	Burk Uzzle, Magnum
Production Company	Sanders Printing Corp.
Client	Wallace Murray Corp.

490

Art Director	James Cross
Writer	Paul Etter
Designer	Emmett Morava
Photographer	Fluor Corporation
Agency	James Cross Design Office, Inc.
Client	Fluor Corp.

491

CYS GUARDIAN

1972 1973 1974 1975 1976

SSI Navigation's dry bulk carriers are generally chartered for periods up to five years. The tanker and product carrier are chartered through 1987 and 1988, respectively. Since SSI Navigation's vessels are generally on relatively long term charters, there is both predictability and stability in the revenue generated from these vessels. It is anticipated that this Division will continue to set new records in revenues and profits in 1977.

492

491

Art Director	Kit Hinrichs
Writer	Carol Hillman
Designer	Kit Hinrichs
Photographer	Arthur Schatz
Agency	Jonson Pedersen Hinrichs
Client	Burlington Industries Inc.

492

Art Director	Thom Laperle
Writer	Kekst & Co., Inc.
Designer	Thom Laperle
Artist	Hank Barenz
Production Company	George Rice & Sons
Agency	Laperle/Assoc., Inc.
Client	Itel Corp.

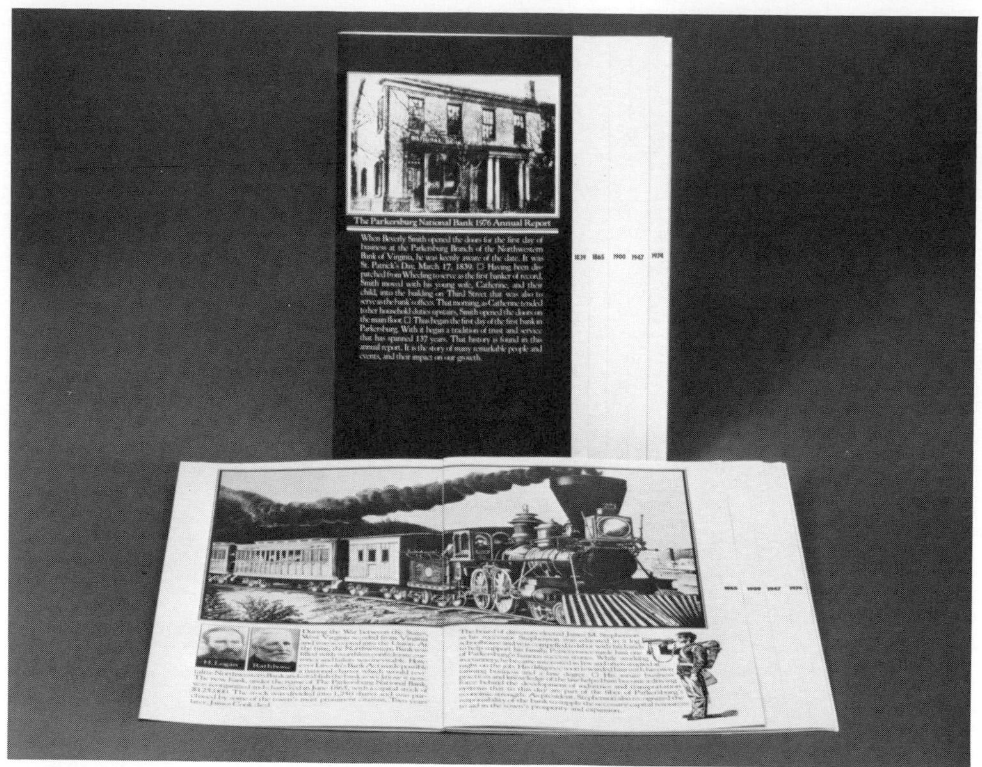

493

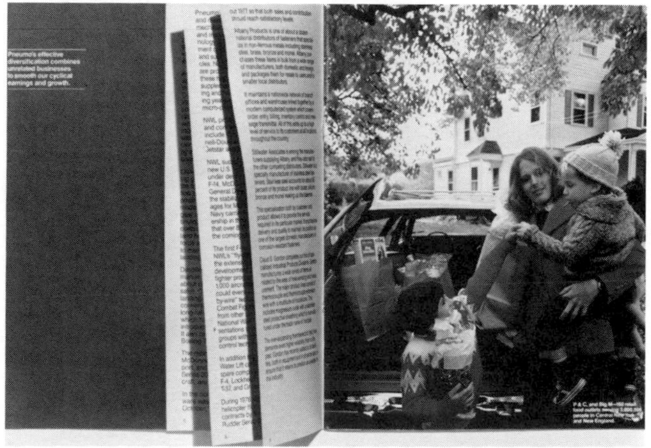

494

493

Art Director George R. Fugate
Writers Sean Burguet
Leslie Trinite
Designer George R. Fugate
Artist Don Woodlan
Agency Lawler Ballard Little
Client Parkersburg National Bank

494

Art Director Barry Ostrie
Writer Michael T.K. Sullivan
Designer Barry Ostrie
Photographer Bruce Davidson
Client Pneumo Corp.

495

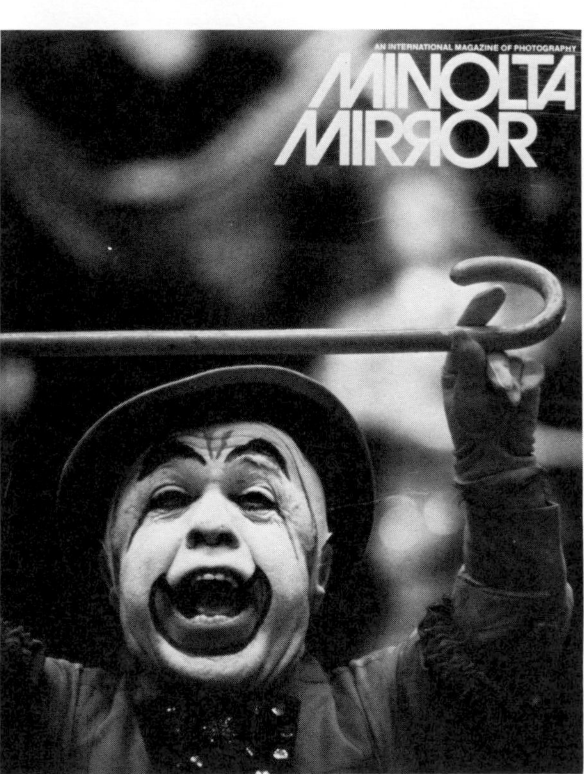

496

SILVER

495
Art Director Len Fury
Writer Robert W. Peckham
Designer Len Fury
Photographer Phil Marco
Agency Corporate Annual Reports, Inc.
Client St. Joe Minerals Corp.

496
Art Director Fred O. Bechlen
Editor Richard V. Bryant
Agency Bozell & Jacobs, Inc.
Client Minolta Corp.

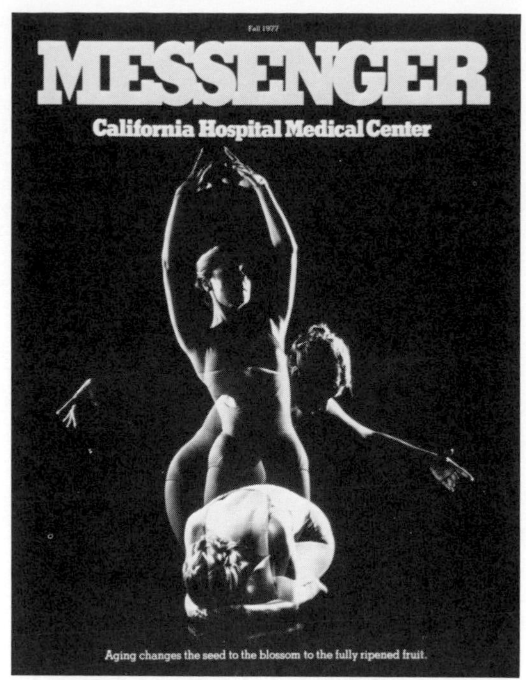

MESSENGER
California Hospital Medical Center
Aging changes the seed to the blossom to the fully ripened fruit.

497

498

497

Art Directors	Advertising Designers, Inc. Bruce Dobson Tom Ohmer
Writer	Merrilee Gerew
Designer	Bruce Dobson
Artist	Advertising Designers, Inc.
Photographer	Mark Coppos
Agency	Advertising Designers, Inc.
Client	Pacific Health Resources, Inc.

498

Art Directors	Len Slonevsky Don Kahn Paul Jerr
Editors	Barbara Slonevsky B.J. Nelson
Designer	Harry Sehring/ Creative Annex, Inc.
Artists	Vol. 1, No. 3— Isadore Seltzer Vol. 1, No. 4—Kaaren Shandro Vol. 1, No. 5—Lou Bory Assoc. Vol. 1, No. 6—Seymour Chwast Vol. 1, No. 7—Lowren West Vol. 1, No. 8—Don Kahn
Photographer	Vol. 1, No. 8—Louis Mervar
Client	Lederle Laboratories

499

500

503

499
Art Director John Casado
Writer Charles Roderman
Designer John Casado
Artists John Casado
Calvin Hom
Del Rae Hrubes
Agency Casado Ltd.
Client Itel Corp.

500
Art Director Herb Lubalin
Writers Herb Lubalin
Jack Anson Finke
Designer Herb Lubalin
Agency LSC&P Design Group
Client International Typeface Corp.

503
Art Director Herb Lubalin
Writers Herb Lubalin
Jack Anson Finke
Gertrude Snyder
Designer Herb Lubalin
Agency LSC&P Design Group
Client International Typeface Corp.

U&lc.

An exploration of the new and merging word processing and typesetting technologies and what they offer the designer, buyer, specifier and other users of printed communications.

Vision '77, a three-day conference sponsored by the International Typeface Corporation and hosted by the Rochester Institute of Technology May 16-19, 1977, addressed itself to the ultimate consumers who work with type. Newspapers, book and magazine publishers, and commercial graphic arts services have been flooded with seminars, exhibits and trade paper reportage, but the ultimate consumers—such as art and production managers, graphic designers, type directors, printing buyers, advertising and sales promotion managers, marketing directors and some editors and publishers—have been under-informed.

Vision '77 attempted to fill this void. U&lc offers in this and its next issue heavy coverage of the information and thinking exchanged at Vision '77. It is impossible, even in the large number of pages of U&lc is devoting to Vision '77, to produce verbatim coverage. Some 1500 slides plus films and even videotapes were needed for the intensive 3-day "crash course." U&lc has edited down the presentations and, in so doing, captured not just Vision '77's highlights but the major viewpoints and conclusions, together with considerable supportive detail. The bulk of U&lc's report is in the words of each speaker. Vision '77, Part I, starts on Page 2. Vision '77, Part II will appear in the next issue of U&lc.

COMMUNICATIONS TYPOGRAPHICS

VISION '77

504

U&lc.

In This Issue:

What America Needs Is More "Music & Art" (High Schools)
No drugs, no violence, no obscenity, no listeness, no absenteeism, no need for discipline. That's the scene at New York's High School of Music and Art, one public high school undimmed by urban chaos. Page 1.

The Abstract Alphabet Of Manuel Bennett
Continuing U&lc's policy of ferreting out unique and unusual new alphabets. Page 6.

The Man With More Faces Than Bodoni
His name is Jim Spanfeller and a good portion of his extraordinary artwork revolves around, well, Jim Spanfeller. Page 8.

Propaganda And Other Photographs
There's much more here than meets the casual eye in the perceptions of Simpson Kalisher from his recent book titled above. Page 12.

Bedtime Stories
Lou Myers on the rampage again with pictorial calamities of the boudoir. As usual, Lou makes us think while we laugh. Where will it all end? Page 14.

What's New From ITC?
ITC Quorum Light, Book, Medium, Bold, Black; & ITC Korinna Kursiv Regular, Bold, Extra Bold, Heavy are the new typefaces this time around. Page 16.

Dian Friedman
Spectacular sports paintings by a very feminine artist selected from her "Landmark Series" for the Virginia Slims Tennis Tour. Page 20.

Something From Everybody
First returns from our readers of letters we asked them to write Congress re the copyright protection law among other things. Page 22.

Thar's Gold (And Silver) In Them Thar Hills
Increasingly in recent years, the annual awards of the Art Directors Show have been going to out-of-town entries. Page 24.

Rewards Of Merit
There's no limit to what people will collect. Happily for us, Carol Wald has been collecting old school merit cards since she was ten. Page 26.

Patterns In Packaging
Take an ordinary detergent box, put it in the hands of Robert Gale, mix gently, and what have you got? Turn to page 30 and see for yourself.

Something For Everybody
Our regular feature returns with a new assemblage of wonderfully irrelevant stuff & nonsense. Page 32.

Great "Pomp" And Much "Ado"
"What Is It? A Mystery," was the title of a famous short story by Fitzjames O'Brien. The same question might well apply to *Le Centre National d'Art et de Culture de Georges Pompidou*, which opened recently in Paris. Hedda Johnson, our roving reporter, was in attendance. Page 34.

What This Country Needs Is More "Music & Art" (High Schools)

EXPERT

505

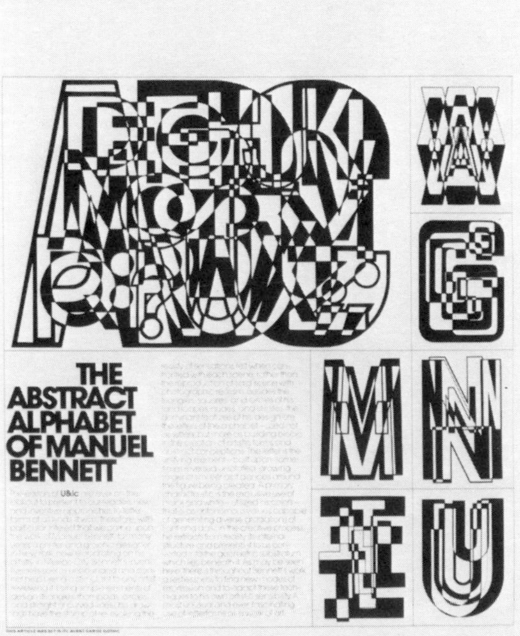

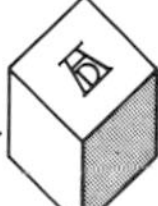

GOLD

504

Art Director	Herb Lubalin
Writers	Herb Lubalin Jack Anson Finke Gertrude Snyder
Designer	Herb Lubalin
Agency	LSC&P Design Group
Client	International Typeface Corp.

505

Art Director	Herb Lubalin
Writers	Herb Lubalin Jack Anson Finke
Designer	Herb Lubalin
Agency	LSC&P Design Group
Client	International Typeface Corp.

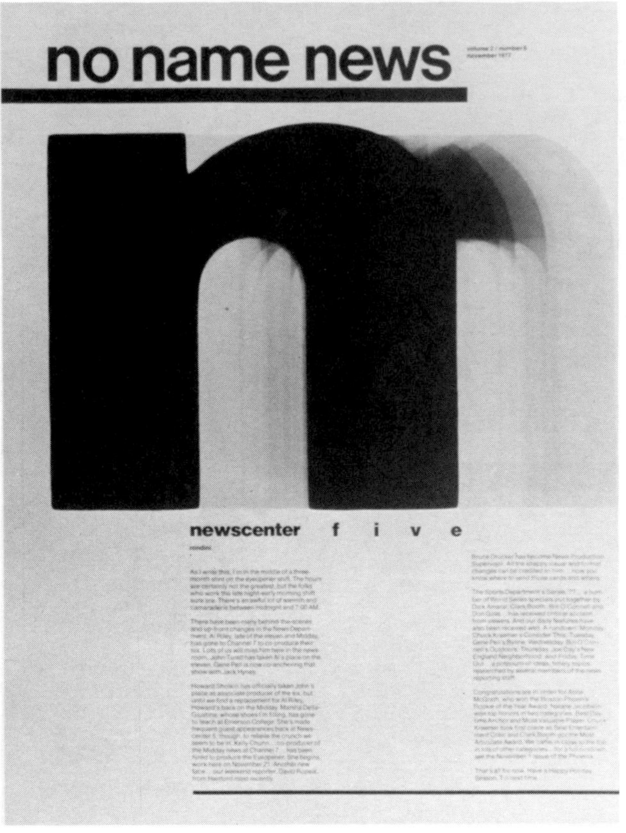

506

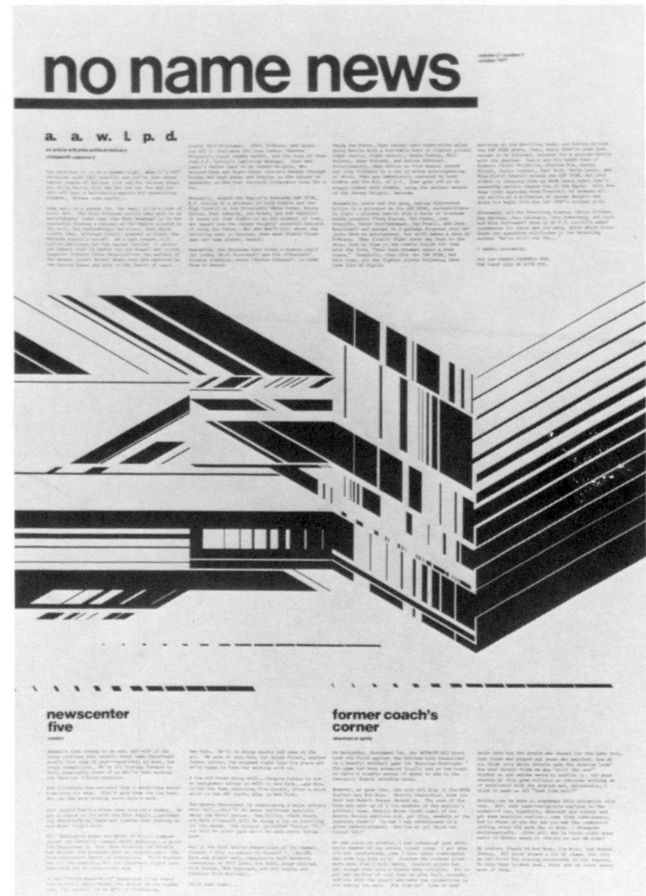

507

506

Art Director	George Canciani
Writer	Larry Pickard
Designer	George Canciani
Artist	George Canciani
Agency	WCVB-TV 5/ Boston Broadcasters Inc.
Client	WCVB-TV 5

507

Art Director	George Canciani
Writer	Larry Pickard
Designer	George Canciani
Artist	George Canciani
Agency	WCVB-TV 5/ Boston Broadcasters Inc.
Client	WCVB-TV 5

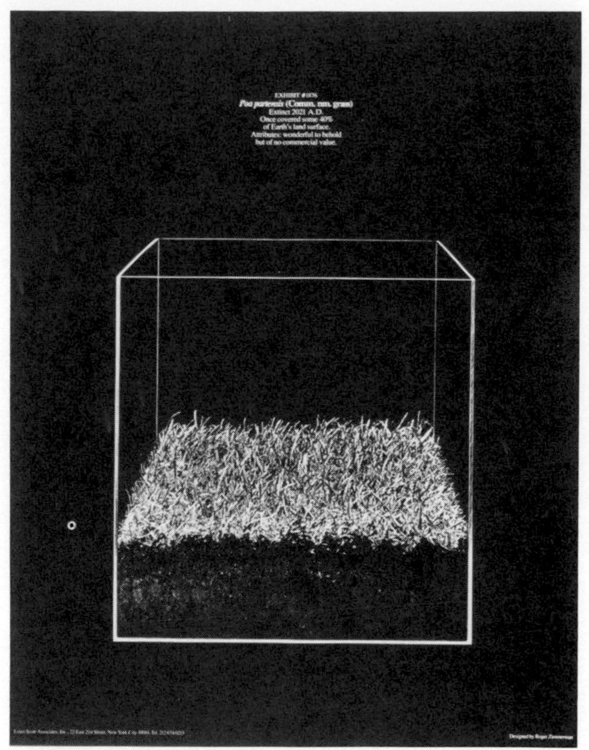

508

509

508

Art Director	Roger Zimmerman
Writer	Roger Zimmerman
Designer	Roger Zimmerman
Photographer	George Gorra
Agency	Louis Scott Associates, Inc.
Client	Louis Scott Associates, Inc.

509

Art Director	Mark W. Moffett
Writer	John N. Siddall
Designer	Mark W. Moffett
Photographer	Bryan Snoddy
Producer	John N. Siddall
Production Company	Alpha Recording Co.
Agency	Siddall, Matus & Coughter Inc.
Client	Gulf Reston, Inc.

510

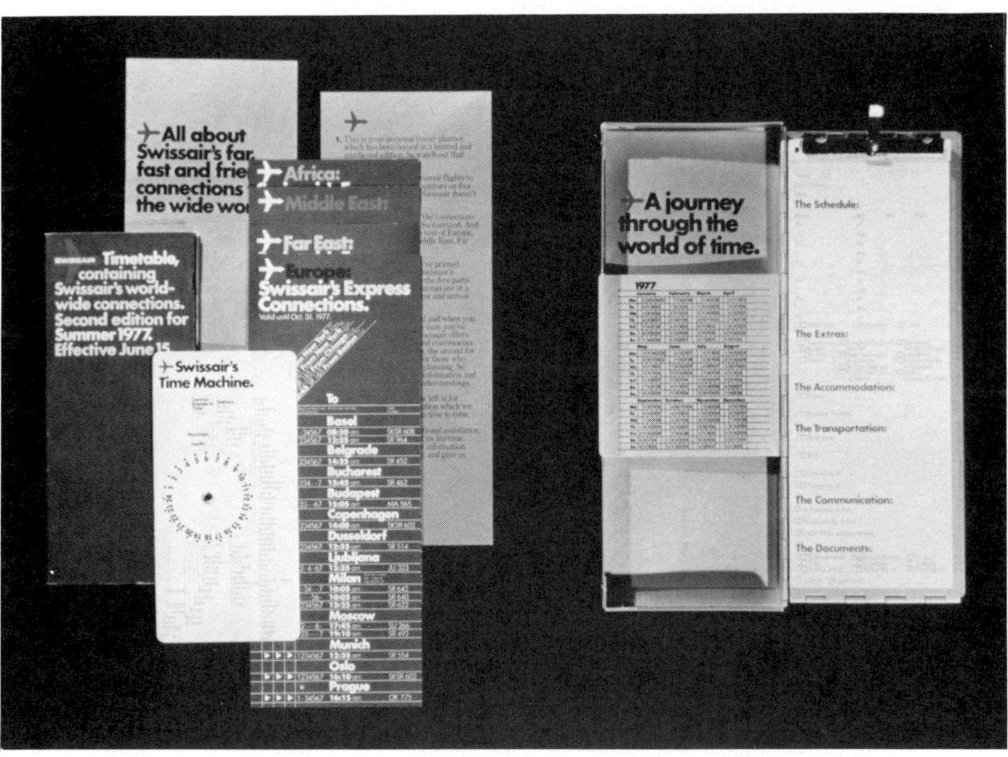

511

GOLD

510

Art Directors Ed Sobel
David November
Writer Peter Moreau
Designers Ed Sobel
David November
Photographers Jerry Darvin
Pete Mecca
Mel DiGiaccomo
Agency CBS Advertising and Promotion Entertainment Division
Client CBS Television Network

511

Art Director Christine Sauers
Writers Wolf Rogosky
Phil Becker
Agency GGK America, Ltd.
Client Swissair

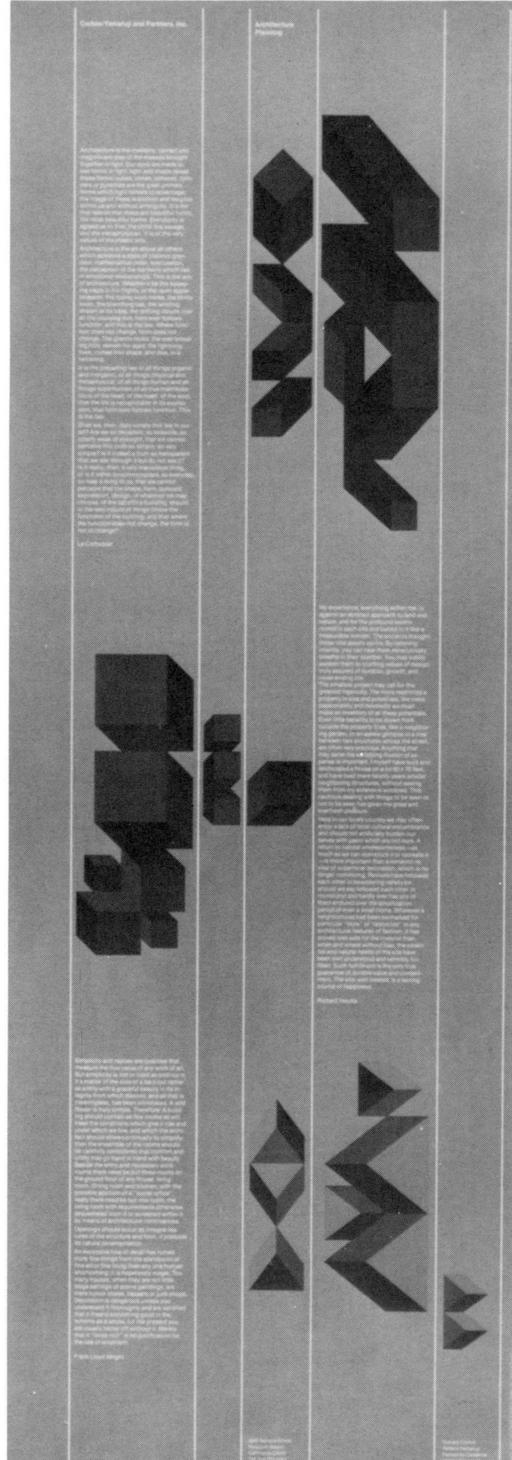

512

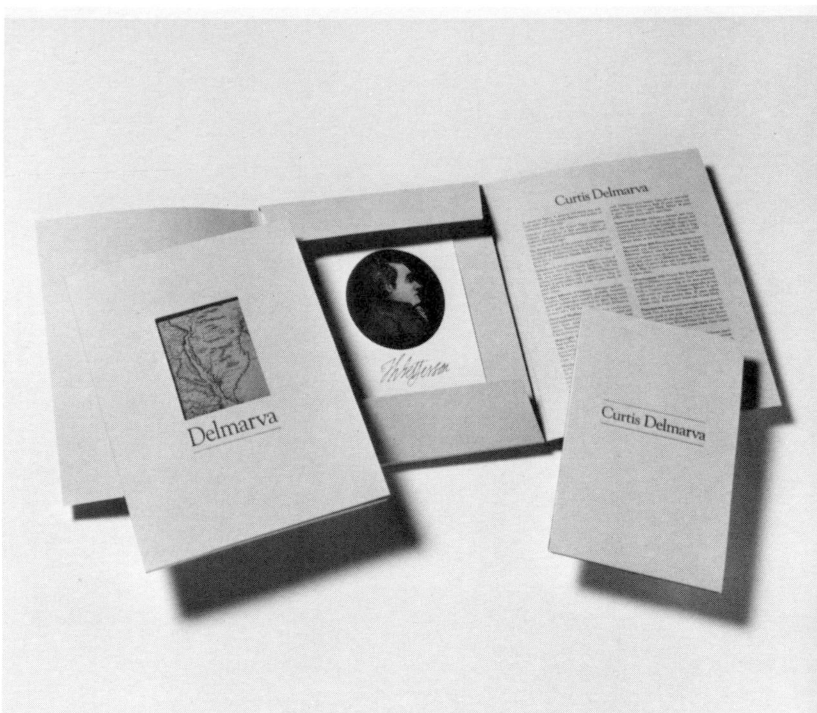

513

512
Art Director Jann Church Advertising & Graphic Design, Inc.
Writers Le Corbusier
Richard Neutra
Frank Lloyd Wright
Designer Jann Church Advertising & Graphic Design, Inc.
Artist Jann Church Advertising & Graphic Design, Inc.
Agency Jann Church Advertising & Graphic Design, Inc.
Client Corbin/Yamafuji & Partners, Inc.

513
Art Director Cameron Hyers
Writer Cameron Hyers
Designer Cameron Hyers
Artist Tom Horbey
Photographer Barry McCormick
Agency Hyers/Smith, Inc.
Client Curtis Paper

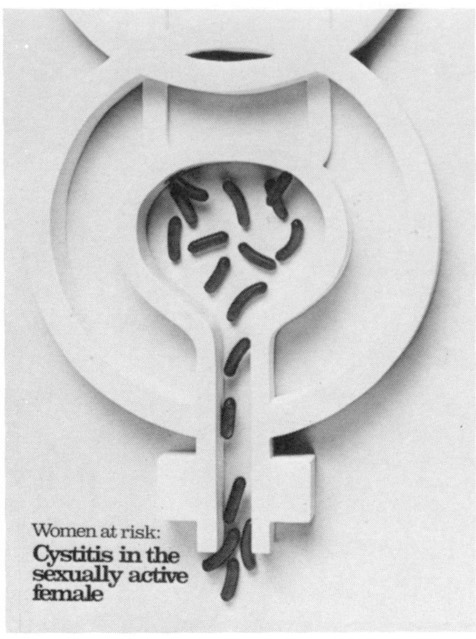

Women at risk:
Cystitis in the sexually active female

514

The phones that drive your business.
Mountain Bell's new communications system for dealers.

515

516

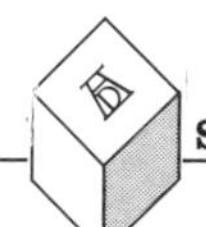

SILVER

514
Art Director Paul Nemesure
Writer Harry Smith
Artist Lou Bory
Agency Lavey/Wolff/Swift Inc.
Client Norwich International

515
Art Director Jerry Murff
Writer Bernie Schmidt
Photographer Phil Marco
Agency Tracy-Locke, Inc.
Client Mountain Bell

516
Art Director Richard Martino
Photographer David Hamilton
Client Bloomingdales

517

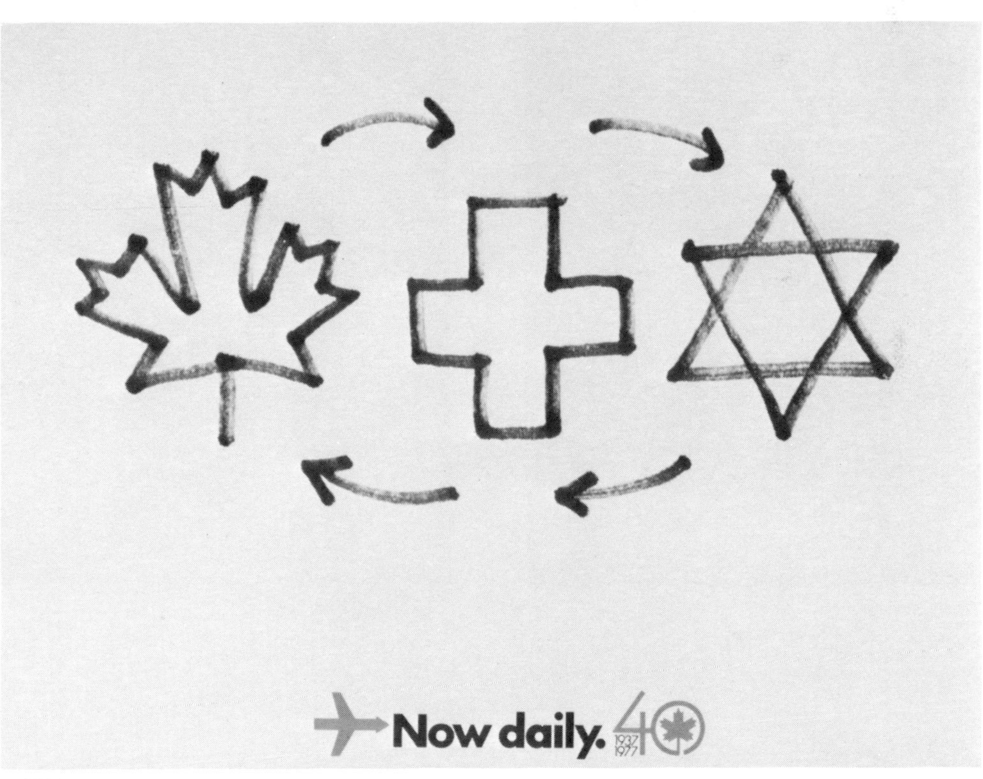

518

517
Art Director Annette Rector
Writer Dick Bueschel
Designer Annette Rector
Artist Annette Rector
Agency Ladd/Wells/Presba Advertising, Inc.
Client Union Tank Car Company

518
Art Director GGK America, Ltd.
Writer GGK America, Ltd.
Agency GGK America, Ltd.
Client Swissair

519

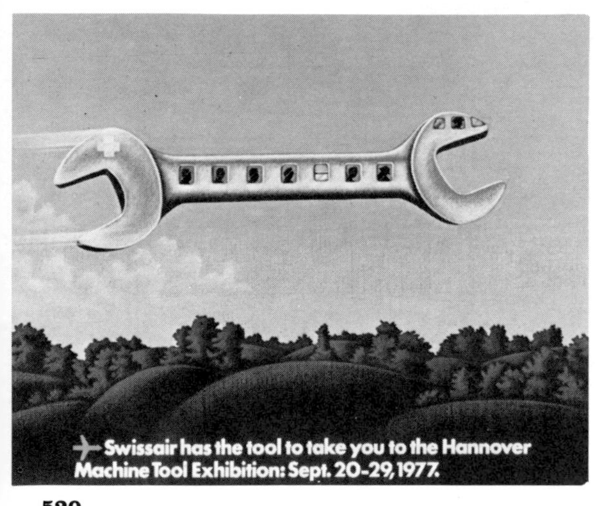

520

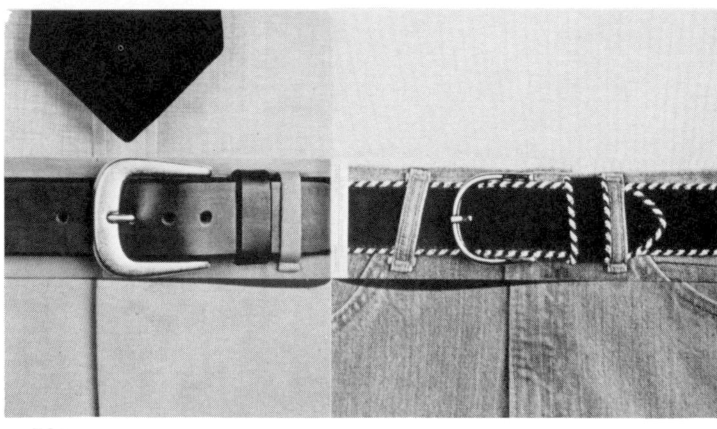

521

519
Art Director Victor Cevoli
Editor Sam Yanes
Designer Victor Cevoli
Artist D&A Studio
Photographers Carl Fisher, William Buckley, Ron Scott, Michael O'Neill, Steve Grohe, R. Twarog, Bruno Joachim, Paul Camello, John Olson, Reinart Wolf
Agency Polaroid
Client Polaroid

520
Art Director GGK America, Ltd.
Writer GGK America, Ltd.
Artist Philip Slagter
Agency GGK America, Ltd.
Client Swissair

521
Art Director Stan Kovics
Writer Joyce Fabian
Designer Stan Kovics
Photographer Avedis Baghsarian
Agency Stan Kovics Advertising
Client Canterbury Belts

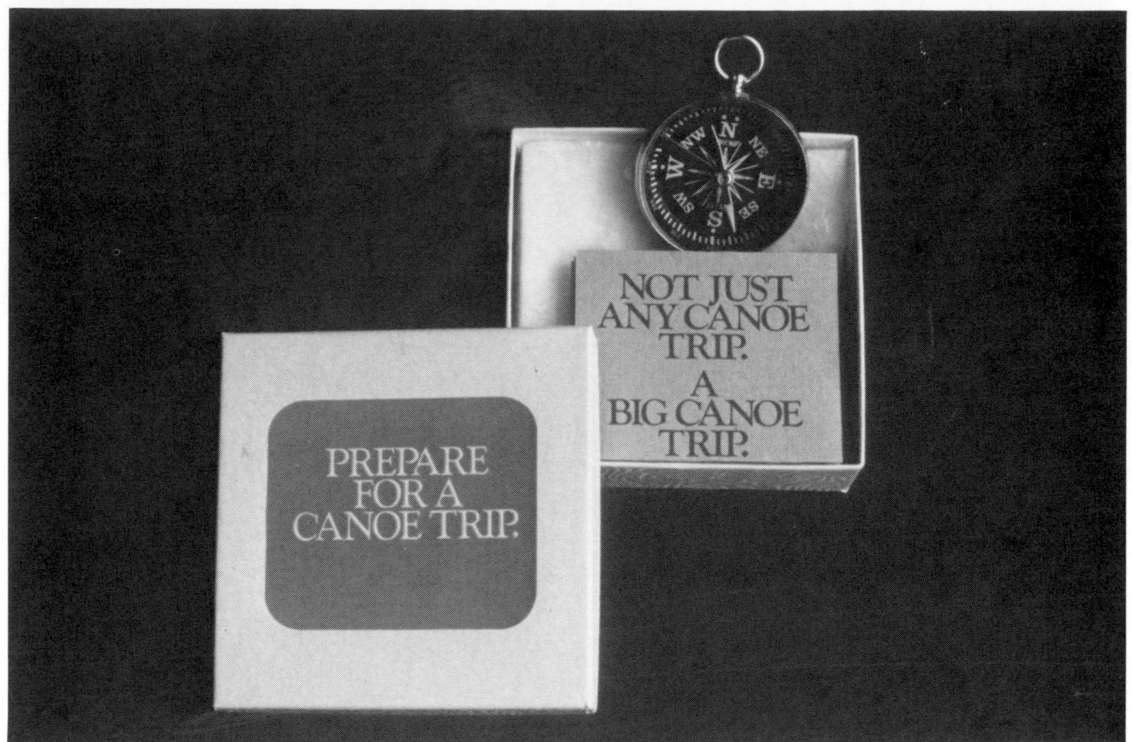

522

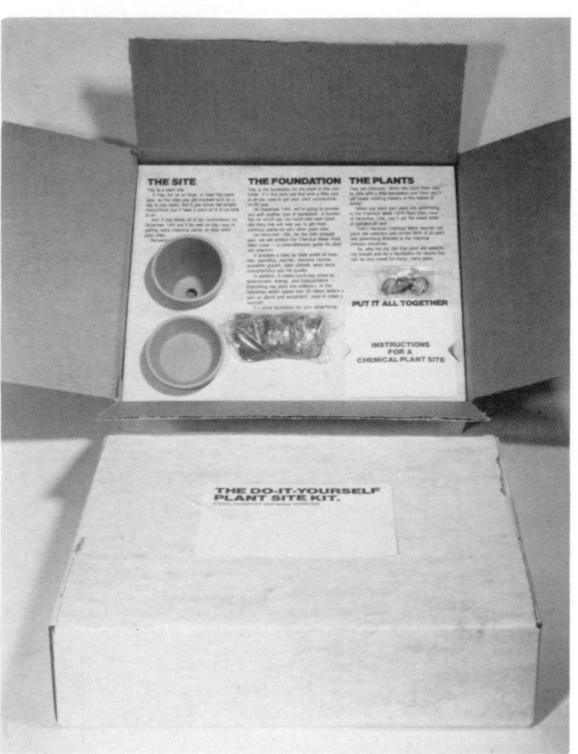

523

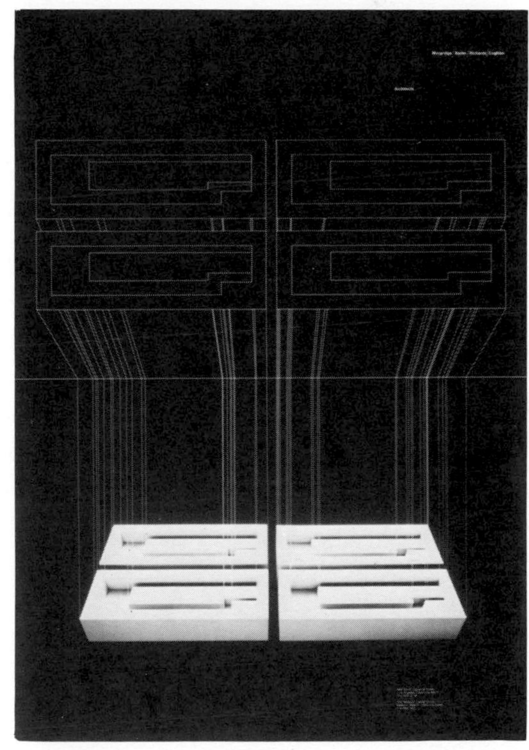

524

522
Art Director Harold J. Shields
Writer John Davis
Director (Creative) Austin P. Kelley
Agency Austin Kelley Advertising, Inc.
Client Big Canoe Corp.

523
Art Director Lee Elliot
Writer Lee Elliot
Designer Ken Carson
Artist Howard Duffy
Agency The Elliot Organization, Inc.
Client Chemical Week

524
Art Director Jann Church Advertis
& Graphic Design, Inc
Designer Jann Church Advertis
& Graphic Design, Inc
Artist Jann Church Advertis
& Graphic Design, Inc
Photographer John Lawder
Agency Jann Church Advertis
& Graphic Design, Inc
Client Morgridge, Bader,
Richards, Coghlan

525

526

525

Art Director Dennis S. Juett
Writers Dennis S. Juett, Barbra Witzer
Designers Dennis S. Juett, Robert Francis
Artists Alan Williams, Michael Sell, Robert Francis, Bill Imhoff
Photographers Tony Sollecito, Rosenberg & Levy, Robert Francis, Dennis S. Juett, Dave Holt, Maria Kwong, Bruce Morr

526

Art Director Jann Church Advertising & Graphic Design, Inc.
Writer Julia Chase
Designer Jann Church Advertising & Graphic Design, Inc.
Photographer John Lawder
Agency Jann Church Advertising & Graphic Design, Inc.
Client George Rice & Sons

527

528

527

Art Director	Walter Lefmann
Writer	Robert DK, Sweeney
Designer	Walter Lefmann
Artist	Walter Lefmann
Photographer	Gene Laurents
Agency	Time
Client	Time Magazine

528

Art Director	Diane M. Cook
Writer	John N. Siddall
Designer	Diane M. Cook
Artist	(Hand Lettering) Reid Icard
Agency	Siddall, Matus & Coughter Inc.
Client	Chesapeake Homes, Inc.

529

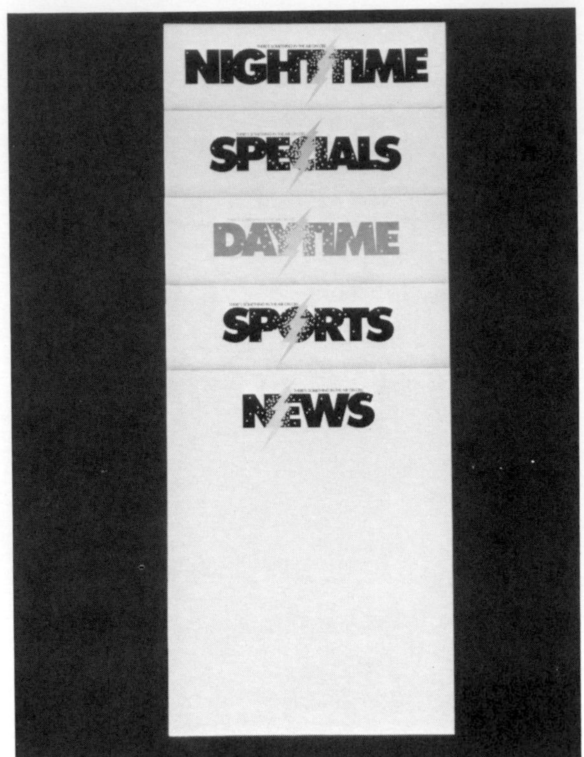

530

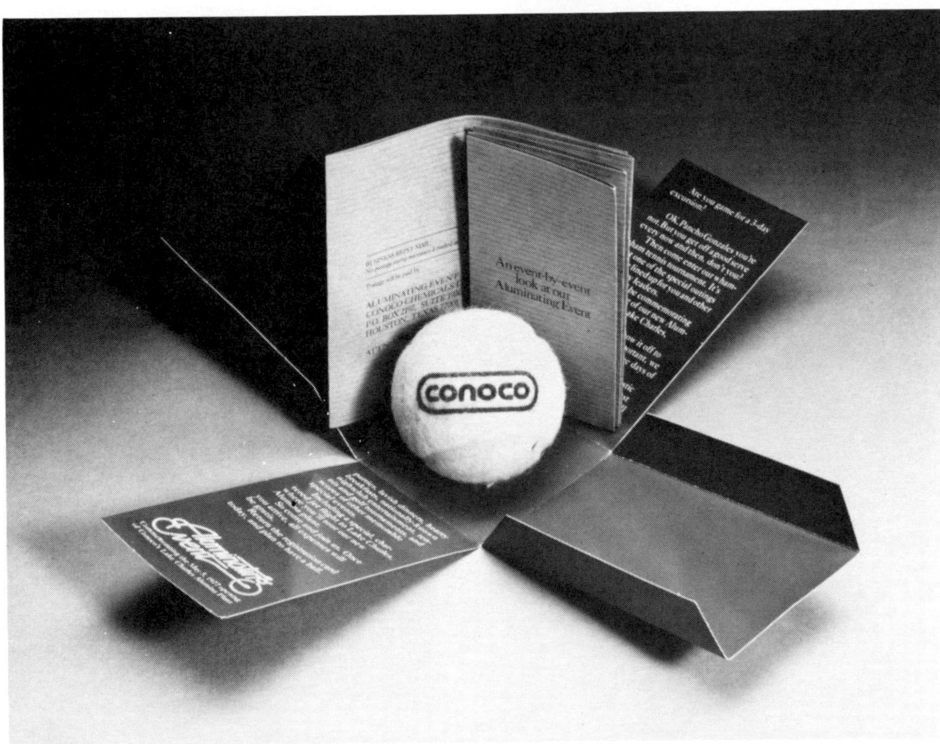

531

529
Art Director Carolyn Zintel
Writer Sandee Cohen
Artist David Wilcox
Agency Hecht, Higgins & Petterson
Client ABC Network Radio

530
Art Director Lou Dorfsman
Designer Tana Klugherz
Artist Tana Klugherz
Agency CBS/Broadcast Group
Client CBS Television Network

531
Art Director Charles Hively
Writer Bob Miller
Designer Charles Hively
Artist Jerry Jeanmard/
Flat Lizard Graphics
Agency Metzdorf Advertising Agency
Client Conoco Chemicals

532 A

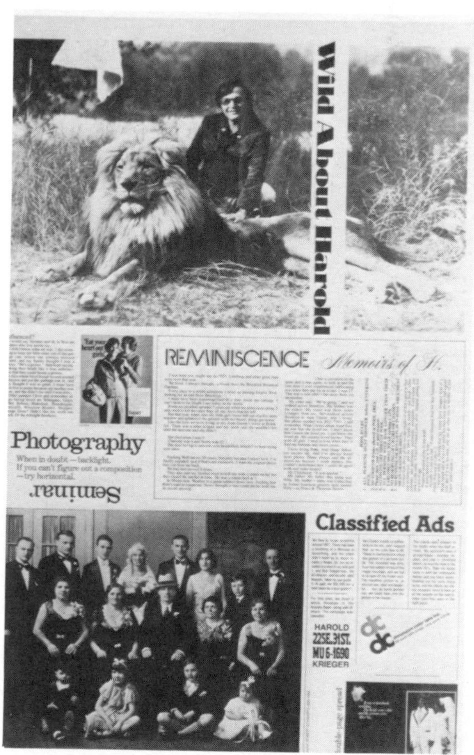

532 B

532A
Art Director Brooke Kenney
Writer Gary LaMaster
Designer Brooke Kenney
Photographer Ken Morrison
Agency Martin Williams Advertising
Client Art Directors/ Copywriters Club of Minnesota

532B
Art Director Eve Butler
Writer Eve Butler
Designer Eve Butler
Photographer Harold Krieger
Agency Advertising of America
Client Harold Krieger Studios

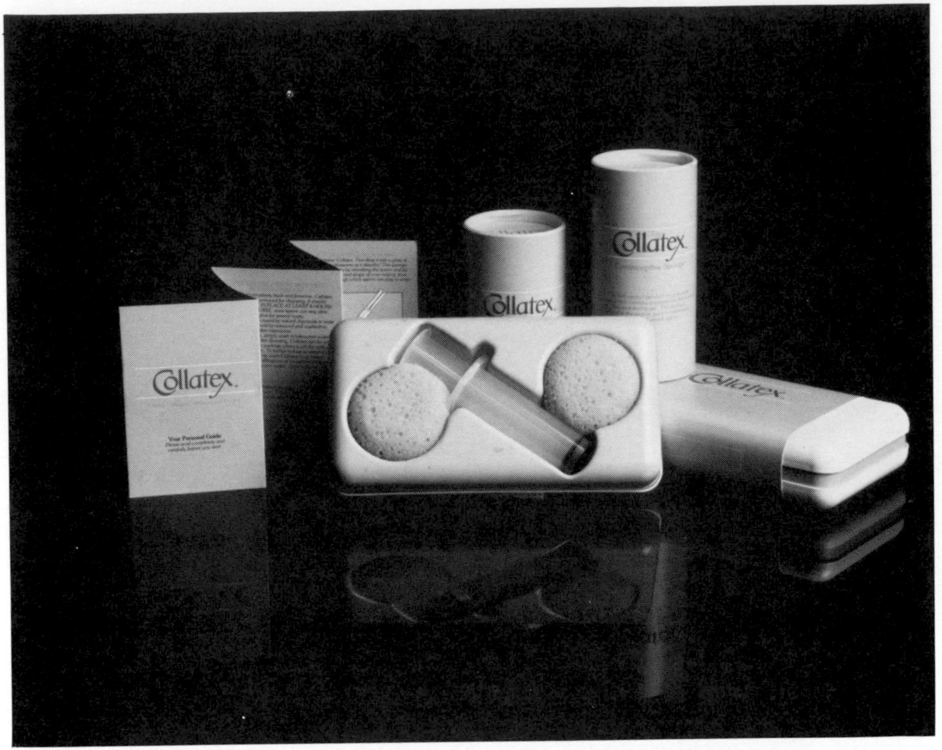

533

534

533

Art Director Jann Church Advertising & Graphic Design, Inc.
Writers Liz Beck
Bruce Vorhauer
Designer Jann Church Advertising & Graphic Design, Inc.
Artist Jann Church Advertising & Graphic Design, Inc.
Agency Jann Church Advertising & Graphic Design, Inc.
Client Vorhauer Laboratories, Inc.

534

Art Director Frank Roth
Designer Becky Venegoni Tower
Artist Linda Solovic
Agency Frank/James Productions
Client Swiss American Import Co.

535

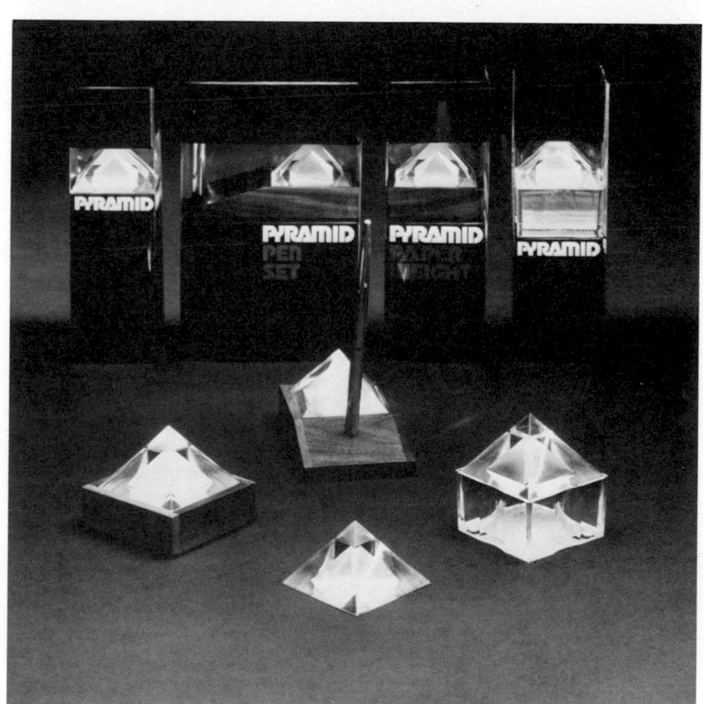

536

535
Art Director Miho
Writer David R. Brown
Designer Miho
Artist Michael Doret
Client Champion Papers

536
Art Director Doug Henry
Writer Steve Hill
Designer Bill Heard
Producer Bob Ubelhor
Production Company Keller-Crescent Co.
Agency Keller-Crescent Co.
Client Ball Giftware

537

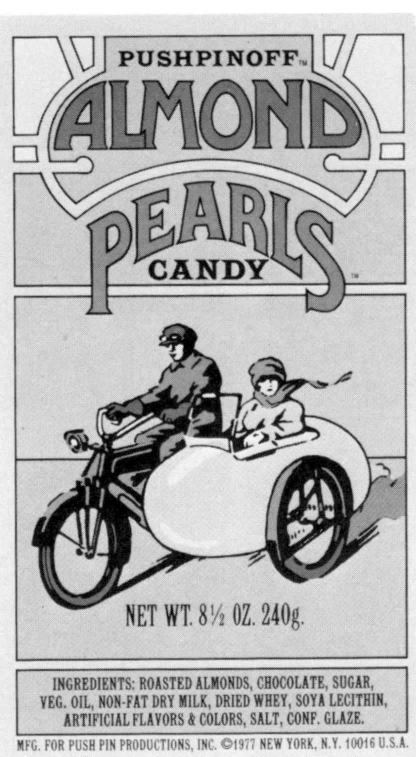

538

537
Designer Seymour Chwast
Artist Seymour Chwast
Agency Push Pin Studios
Client Push Pin Productions

538
Designer Seymour Chwast
Artist Seymour Chwast
Agency Push Pin Studios
Client Push Pin Productions

539

540

541

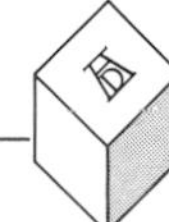

SILVER

SILVER

539
Art Director Michael Peters
Writer Bev Whitehead
Designer Howard Milton
Agency Michael Peters & Partners
Client Winsor & Newton

540
Art Director Michael Peters
Designer Michael Peters
Agency Michael Peters & Partners
Client Winsor & Newton

541
Art Director Michael Peters
Designer Howard Milton
Artists Klaus Schultheis
Angele O'Brien
Bev Whitehead
Photographer Tony Copeland
Agency Michael Peters & Partners
Client Winsor & Newton

542

543

542
Art Director Joseph Schindelman
Writer Ray Myers
Designer Joseph Schindelman
Agency Scali, McCabe, Sloves
Client Buckingham Corporation

543
Art Director Michael Peters
Designer Madeline Bennett
Artist Howard Milton
Agency Michael Peters & Partners
Client Penhaligon's

547

548

547
Art Director Miguel G. Sanchez
Designer Miguel G. Sanchez
Photographer Richard L. Shaefer
Agency Howdy Studio
Client Susan Bennis/Warren Edwards

548
Designer William Mitchell
Artist William Mitchell
Agency Macy's Visual Merchandising Dept,
Client Macy's

549

550

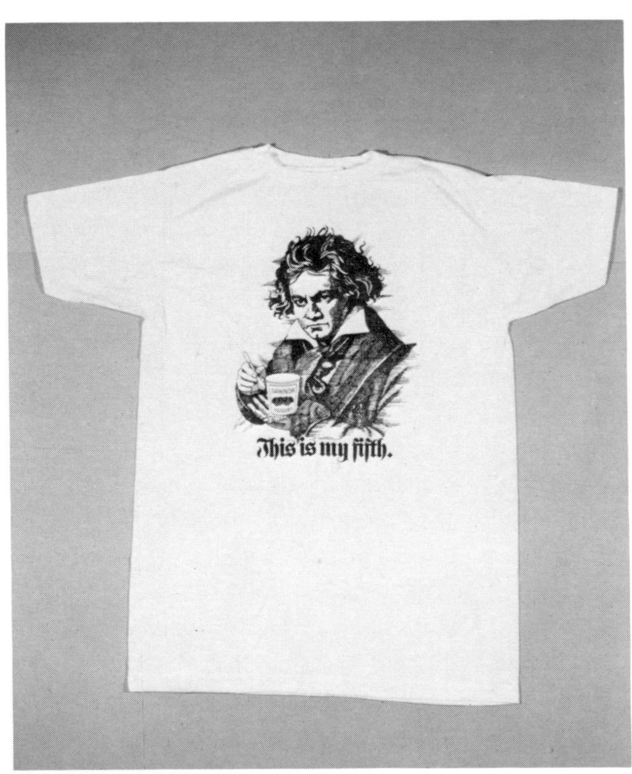

551

549
Designer Seymour Chwast
Artist Seymour Chwast
Agency Push Pin Studios
Client Push Pin Productions

550
Art Director John Lind
Writer Fred Neeper
Designer Bill Sarnoff
Agency CBS/Retail Stores Division
Client CBS/Retail Stores Division

551
Art Director Rob Lopes
Writer Rob Lopes
Agency Marsteller
Client Dannon Yogurt

552

553

554

552
Designer Seymour Chwast
Artist Seymour Chwast
Agency Push Pin Studios
Client Push Pin Productions

553
Art Directors Arthur Eilertson
Larry Long
Designer Larry Long
Photographer Clint Clemens
Agency Gregory Fossella Associates
Client General Electric

554
Art Director Ken Parkhurst
Designer Ken Parkhurst
Artist Jean-Claude Muller
Production Company Advance Paper Box Company
Agency Ken Parkhurst & Associates,
Client Microsonics Corp.

555

556

557

555
Art Director Ed Brodsky
Writers Peggy Haney
Jean Ward
Designer Ed Brodsky
Photographer Four & Five Stock Photos
Production Company Stephen Gould Corporation
Agency Brodsky Graphics Inc.
Client J.C. Penney Company Inc.

556
Art Director Bill Urban
Photographer George Ehrlich
Agency McCann-Erickson
Client Brown-Forman

557
Art Directors Bob Dennard
Mary McDowell Keck
Designer Dan Lynch
Artist Dan Lynch
Photographers Various
Agency The Richards Group, Inc.
Client Dolph Briscoe for
Governor Committee

558

559

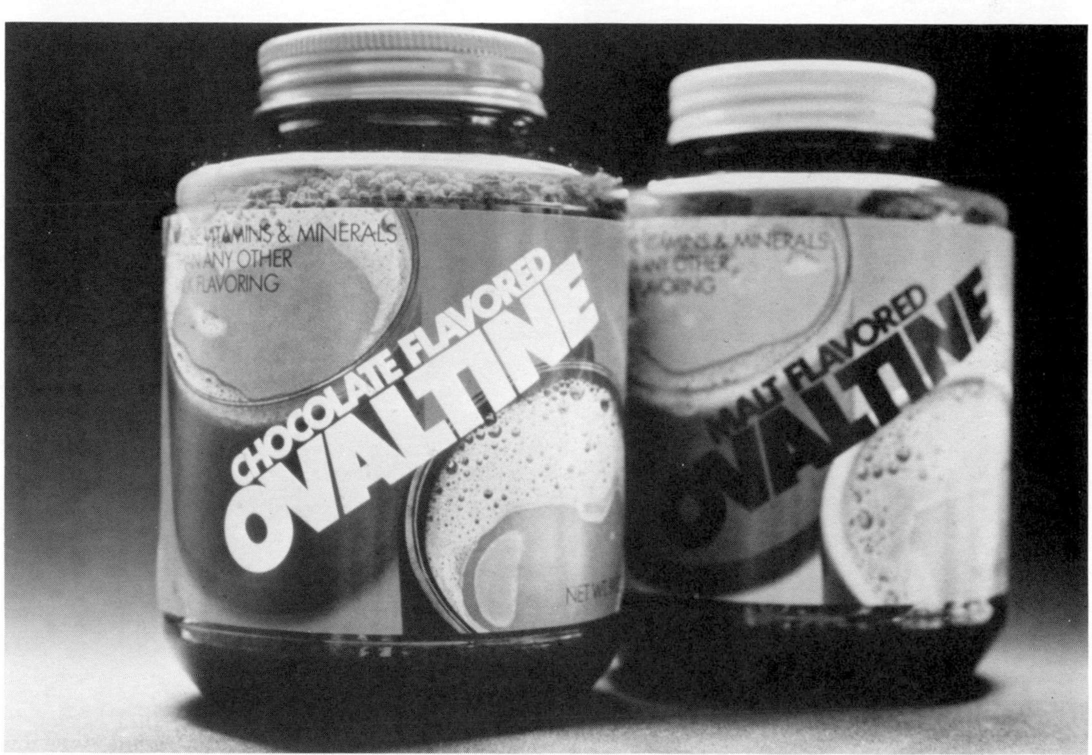

560

558
Art Director Norman Grey
Designer Becky Hollingsworth
Agency Bozell & Jacobs—Atlanta
Client Kosmos International (USA), Inc.

559
Art Director Lyle Metzdorf
Writer Lyle Metzdorf
Designer Lowell Williams
Agency Metzdorf Advertising Agency
Client Continental Oil Company

560
Art Director Stanley Eisenman
Designer Stanley Eisenman
Artist Ken Godat
Photographer George Cochran
Agency Eisenman & Enock, Inc
Client DKG

561

562

561
Art Director John Berg
Photographer Don Hunsetein
Agency CBS Records
Client CBS Records

562
Art Director Ed Lee
Artist Gerard Huerta
Client CBS Records

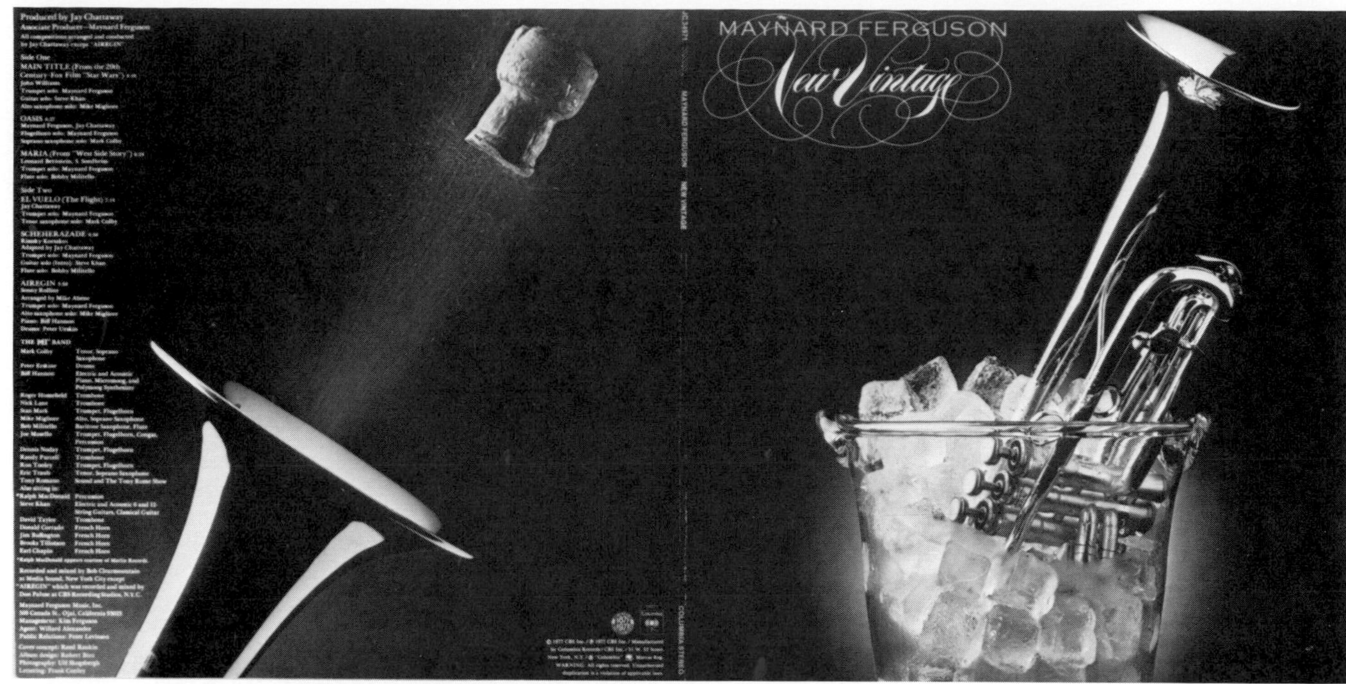

563

564

565

563
Art Director Robert Biro
Designer Robert Biro
Photographer Ulf Skogsbergh
Agency Columbia Records
Client Maynard Ferguson

564
Art Director Paula Scher
Artist David Wilcox
Agency CBS Records
Client CBS Records

565
Art Director Tony Lane
Designer Tony Lane
Artist Bruce Roberts
Photographer Todd Smith
Producer Tom Dowd

566

567

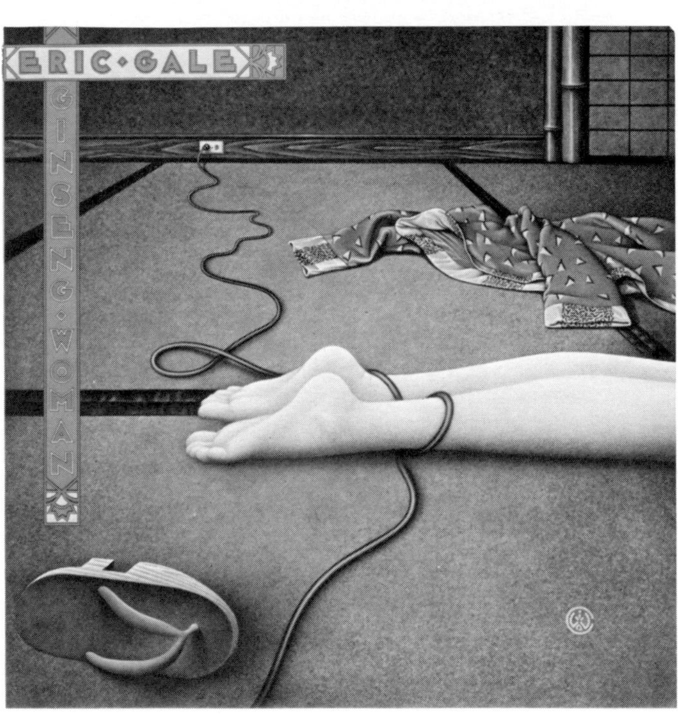

568

566
Art Director Acy R. Lehman
Designer Acy R. Lehman
Artist David Plourde
Agency RCA Records
Client RCA Records

567
Art Director Stephen Ancona
Designer Stephen Ancona
Artist Stephen Ancona
Agency Ancona Design Atelier
Client Dellwood Records

568
Art Directors Andy Engel
Paula Scher
Artist David Wilcox
Agency CBS Records
Client CBS Records

569

570

569
Art Director Michael Sean Walsh
Designer Michael Sean Walsh
Artist Christopher Spollen
Client Pickwick International, Inc.

570
Art Director Henrietta Condak
Artist Ed Sorel
Agency CBS Records
Client CBS Records

571

572

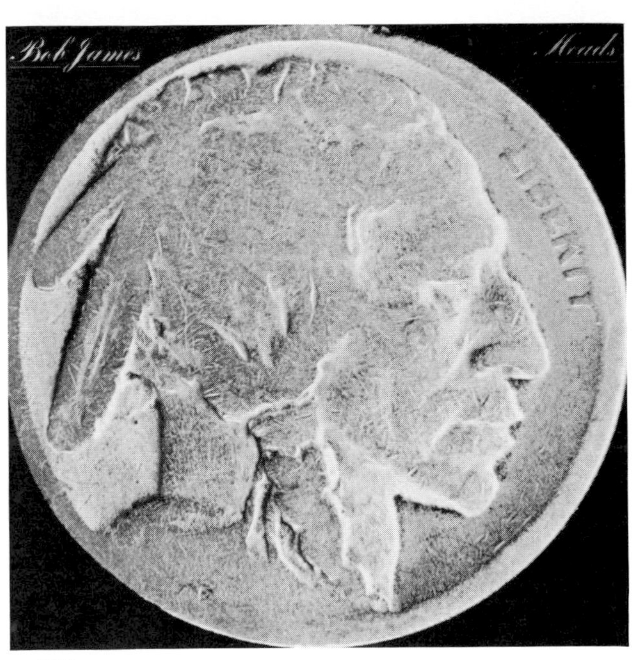

573

571
Art Director Diana Marie Kaylan
Designers Diana Marie Kaylan
Jim Evans
Terry Lamb
Artist Jim Evans
Agency In House
Client Capricorn Records

572
Art Director Bob Defrin
Designer Abie Sussman
Artist Benno Friedman
Photographer Benno Friedman
Agency Atlantic Records
Client Atlantic Records

573
Art Directors John Berg
Paula Scher
Photographer Buddy Endress
Agency CBS Records
Client CBS Records

574

575

576

574
Art Director Paula Scher
Artist Gerard Huerta
Client CBS Records

575
Art Directors John Berg
Paula Scher
Artist Milton Glaser
Agency CBS Records
Client CBS Records

576
Art Director Paula Scher
Artist Stan Mack
Agency CBS Records
Client CBS Records

577

578

577
Art Director Joseph Stelmach
Designer Joseph Stelmach
Artist Joseph Stelmach
Agency RCA Records
Client RCA Records

578
Art Director Joseph Stelmach
Designer Joseph Stelmach
Artist Mike Hodges
Agency RCA Records
Client RCA Records

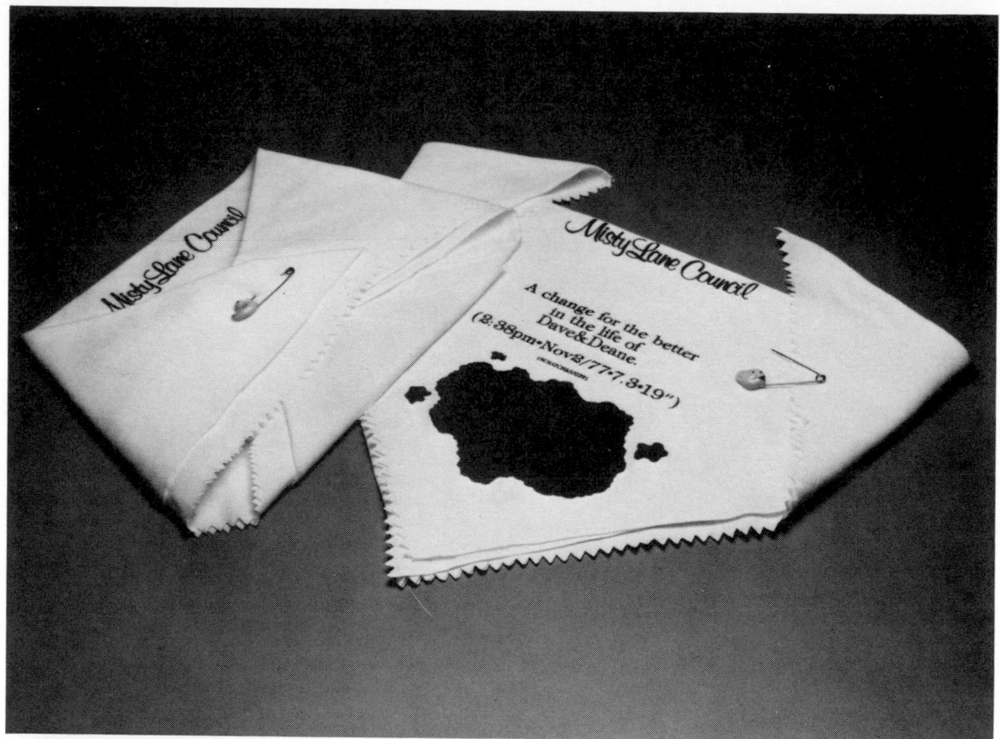

579

580

579
Art Director David Council
Writer Jim Albright
Designer David Council
Agency Albright Council
Client David and Deane Council

580
Art Director Bill Bonnell III
Designers Bill Bonnell III
W. Kaulfuss
Client Container Corporation
of America

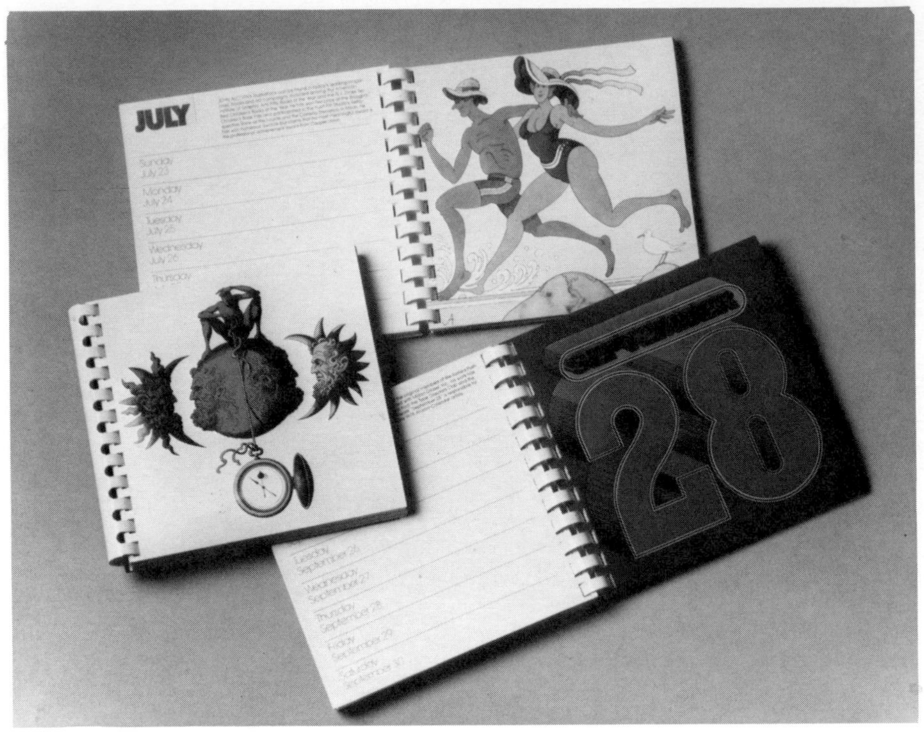

581

582

583

581
Art Directors Marilyn Hoffner
Al Greenberg
Writer Marilyn Hoffner
Designers Marilyn Hoffner
Al Greenberg
Artists Alumni Calendar Artists
Photographers Alumni Calendar Photographers
Client Cooper Union Alumni Association

582
Art Director Jesse Califano
Designers Johannes Regn
Jesse Califano
Artist Johannes Regn
Agency Regn/Califano, Inc.
Client Design Research, Inc.

583
Art Director Roger Huyssen
Designer Gerard Huerta
Client Graphic Desserts

584

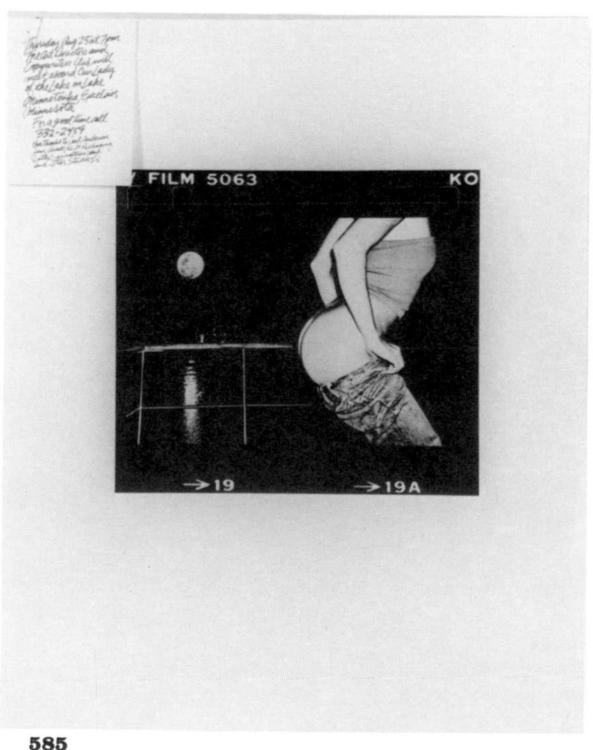

585

586

584
Art Director Tony Rutka
Writer Tony Rutka
Designer Tony Rutka
Agency Diana & Tony Rutka
Client Diana & Tony Rutka

585
Art Director Frank Haggerty
Photographers Jim Arndt
Curt Anderson
Agency Carmichael-Lynch, Inc.
Client Minnesota Art Directors and Copywriters Club

586
Art Director Tom Varisco
Writer Tom Varisco
Designer Tom Varisco
Artist Tom Varisco
Agency Tom Varisco Graphic Designs
Client Greater Typographic Services, Inc.

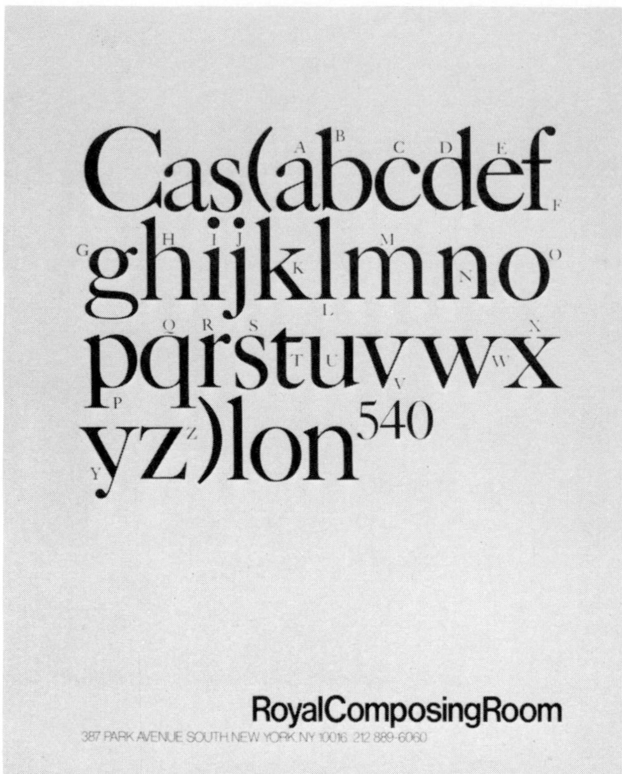

587

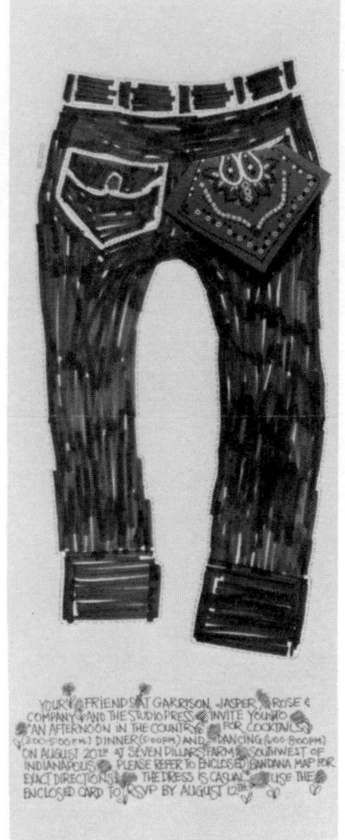

588

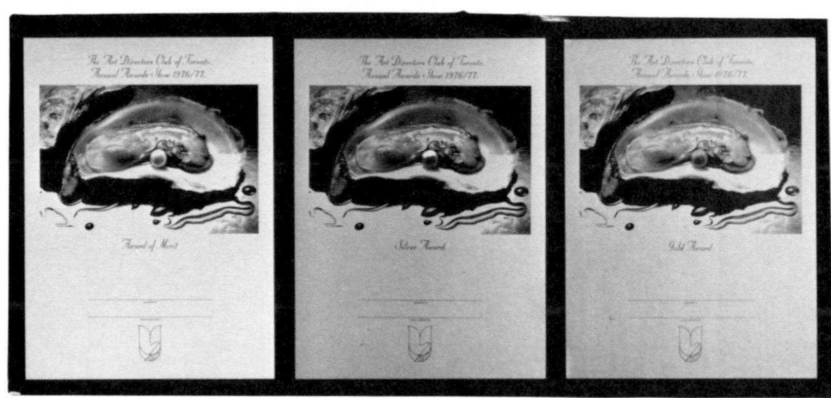

589

587
Art Director Martin Solomon
Designer Martin Solomon
Publisher Royal Composing Room
Client Royal Composing Room

588
Art Director Joseph Smith
Writers Walter Bagot
Doug Lyell
Designer Joseph Smith
Artist Joseph Smith
Agency Garrison, Jasper, Rose & Company
Client Garrison, Jasper, Rose & Co. & The Studio Press

589
Art Director John Cruickshank
Writer Heather Chisvin
Designer John Cruickshank
Artists Ron Hills
Wally Allen
Photographer Villy Svarre
Agency Case Associates Advertising Ltd.
Client Art Directors Club of Toronto

NATIONAL 30¢
ENQUIRER
How to Cope With the Fears of Everyday Life
PAGE 43
LARGEST CIRCULATION OF ANY PAPER IN AMERICA
DALLAS EXCLUSIVE
WOMAN GIVES BIRTH TO BUNDLE OF WOOD
PAGE 2

Find Special Diet Can Protect Smokers' Lungs From Cancer *page 3*

★ ★ ★

Robert Stack's Wife Tells: Why I Believe There's Life After Death *page 14*

★ ★ ★

How to Get Out of Bed on the Right Side and Stay Happy All Day *page 35*

★ ★ ★

The Shocking Truth About Coffee Prices *back page*

★ ★ ★

How to Get Out of a Rut *page 53*

"I WAS BUSHED." That was the initial response of a very tired but happy mother after the big event. When asked by the ENQUIRER if she and her husband were shocked at the new arrival, Shauri responded "You can say that again. Keith and I were expecting a boy." (See Story, Page 2)

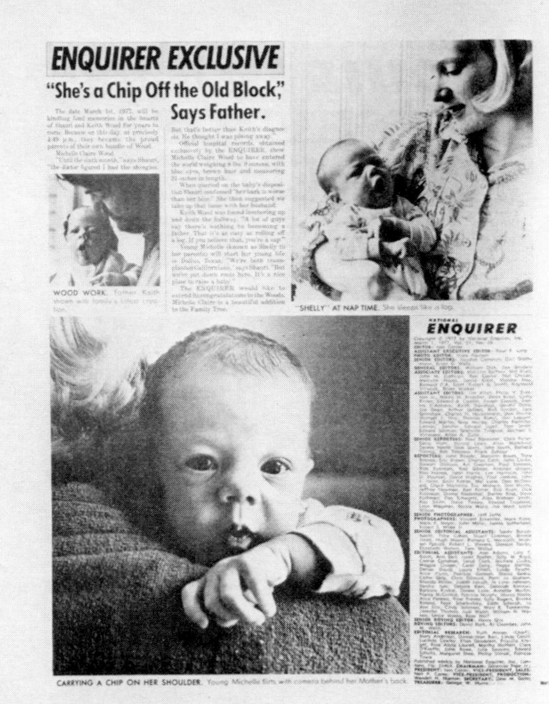

ENQUIRER EXCLUSIVE

"She's a Chip Off the Old Block," Says Father.

WOOD WORK.

"SHELLY" AT NAP TIME.

NATIONAL ENQUIRER

CARRYING A CHIP ON HER SHOULDER. Young Michelle flirts with camera behind her Mother's back.

590

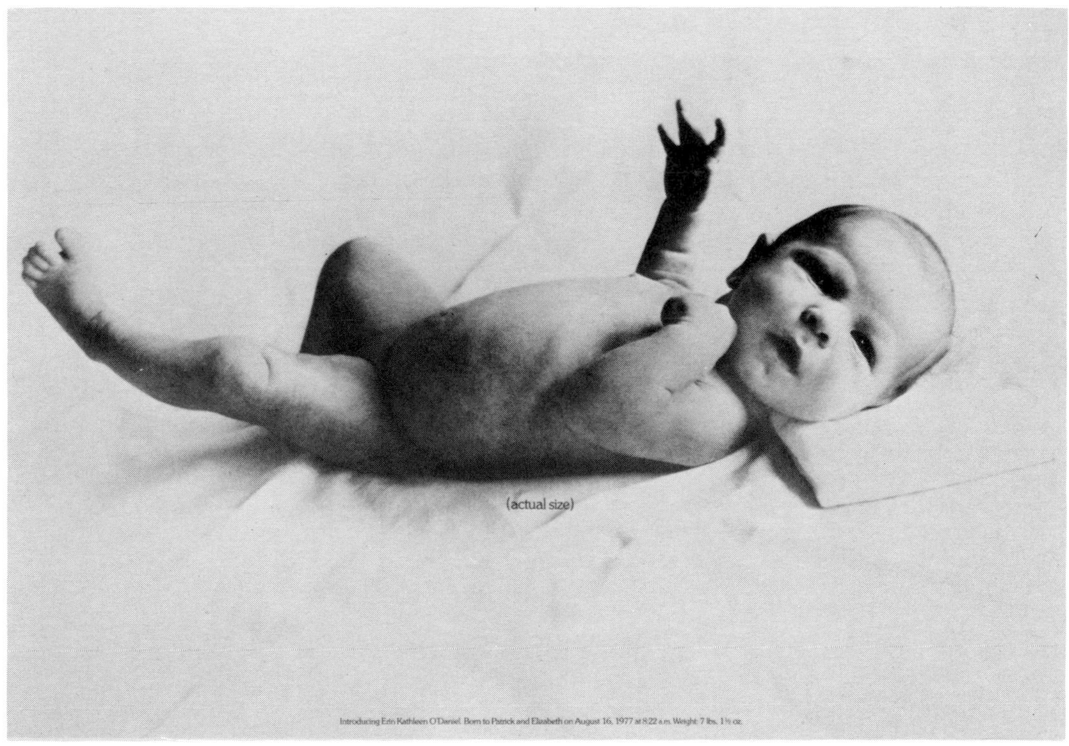

(actual size)
Introducing Erin Kathleen O'Daniel. Born to Patrick and Elizabeth on August 16, 1977 at 8:22 a.m. Weight: 7 lbs. 1½ oz.

591

590
Art Director Mike Washlesky
Writers Mike Washlesky
Jim Hradecky
Designers Mike Washlesky
Don Grimes
Photographers Keith Wood
Shauri Wood
Agency The Richards Group
Client Keith and Shauri Wood

591
Art Director Dick Henderson
Writer James P. Cole
Designer Dick Henderson
Artist Janousek & Kuehl
Agency Cole Henderson Drake, Inc.
Client Mr. and Mrs. Patrick O'Daniel

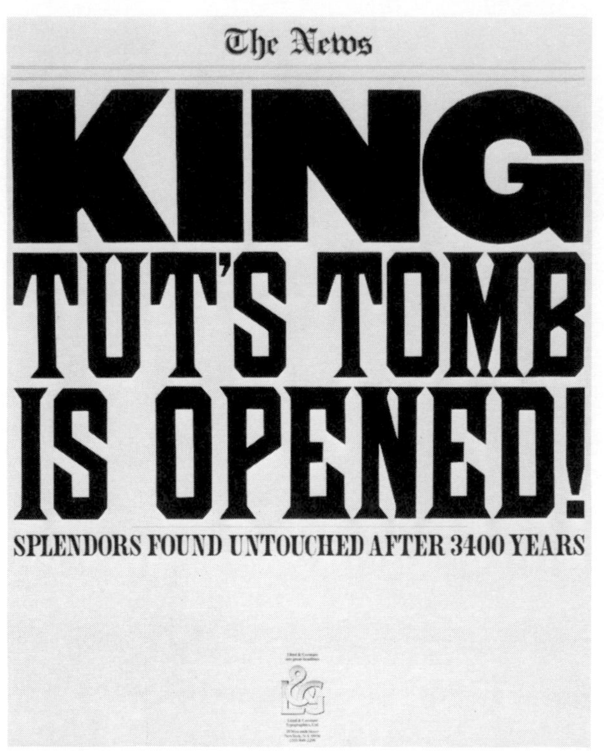

592

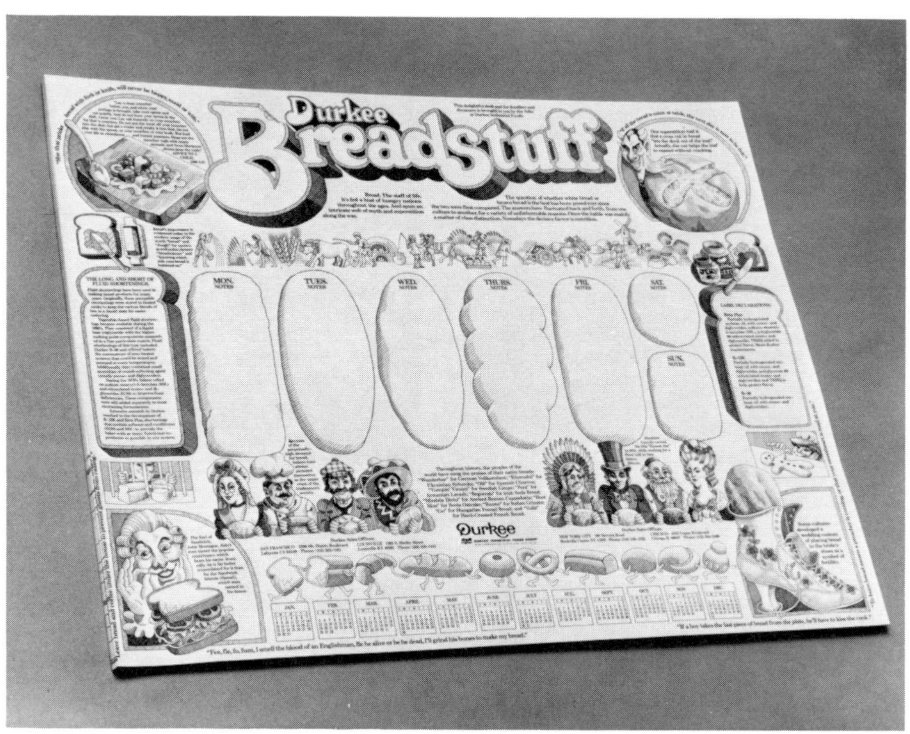

593

592

Art Director	Seymour Chwast
Designer	Richard Mantel
Production Company	Push Pin Studios, Inc.
Client	Lloyd & Germain Typographics, Ltd.

593

Art Director	Bob Rath
Writer	Dennis Okerbloom
Studio	Curilla & Associates
Artist	Dave Fitch
Creative Director	Barry Olson
Agency Production	Lou Vash
Agency	Meldrum and Fewsmith, Inc.
Client	Durkee Industrial Foods Group, SCM Corp.

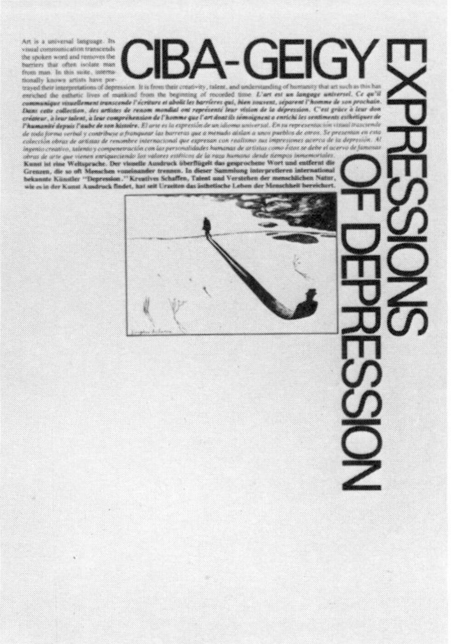

594

595

GOLD

594
Art Director John deCesare
Designer John deCesare
Client Ciba-Geigy Corporation

595
Art Director Gary Schenck
Writer Mary Schenck
Designer Kenneth Plunk
Artist Mary Schenck
Photographer Dan Wadley
Agency Schenck, Plunk & Deason
Client Jaggars, Chiles, Stovall, Inc.

596

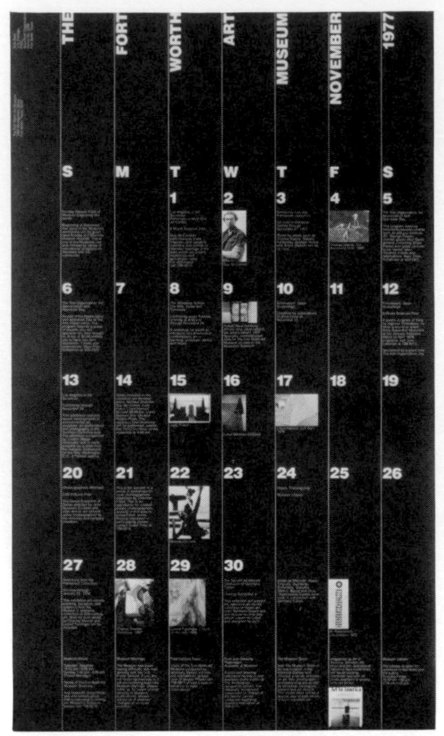

597

IF YOU HAVEN'T GOT ONE YOU CAN'T COME.

And if you have got one, we're gonna hang it on our tree! It's the Second Annual FKB Christmas Tree Ornament Contest and Party. Come join us at 8:00 p.m., December 17th, at 924 Westwood Boulevard, Suite 999. Bring your most creative one (ornament, that is) and help decorate our tree. We'll provide the spirits and goodies. RSVP.

598

596
rt Director Lloyd Crider
Designer Lloyd Crider
Artist Lloyd Crider
Client Anderberg-Lund Printing Co.

597
Art Directors Ivan Chermayeff
Stephan Geissbuhler
Designer Stephan Geissbuhler
Agency Chermayeff & Geismar Associates
Client Fort Worth Art Museum

598
Art Director Michael Kaiser
Writer David Wilkin
Designer Brad Donenfeld
Artist Steve Corey
Agency Finlay, Kaiser & Ballard, Inc.
Client Finlay, Kaiser & Ballard, Inc.

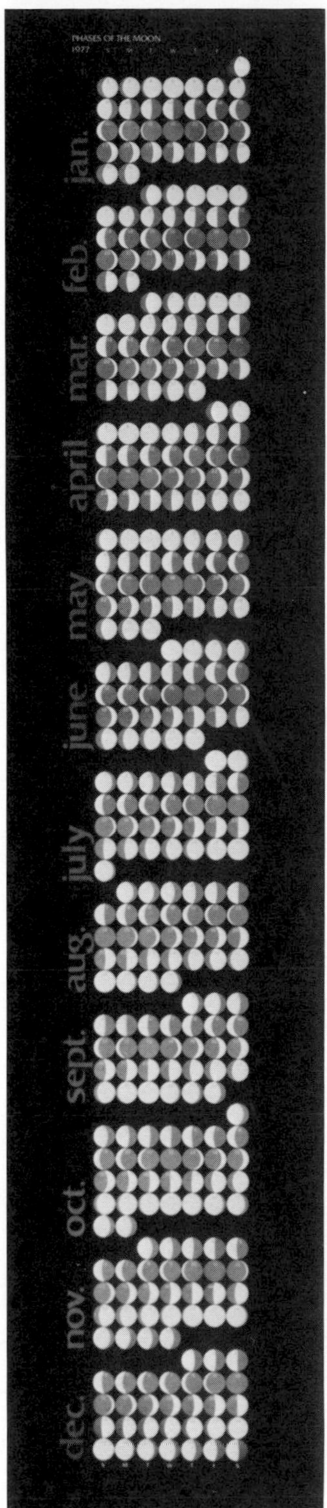

599

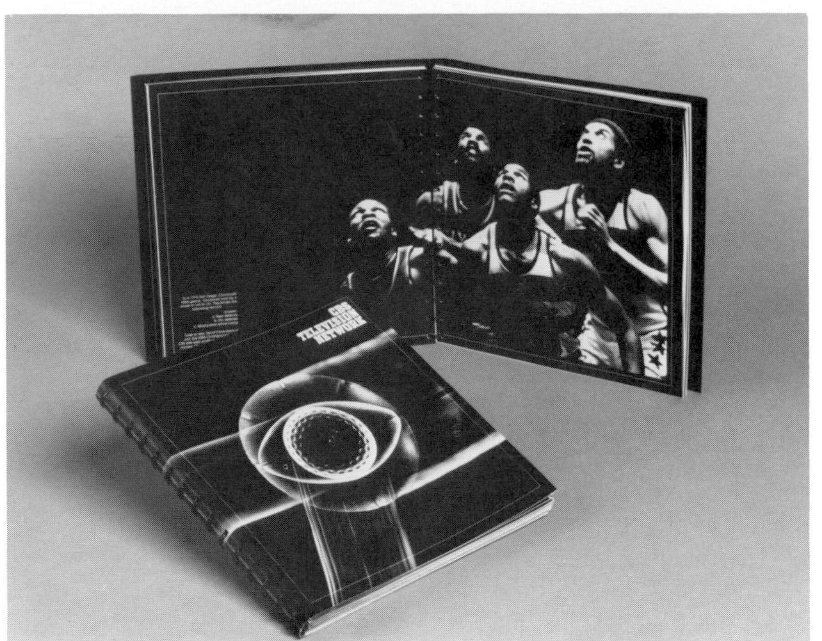

601

602

599

Art Director Carol Vanderhoven Moore
Designer Carol Vanderhoven Moore
Artist Jane Hively Barber
Agency Davis-Delaney-Arrow Inc.
Client Davis-Delaney-Arrow Inc.

601

Art Directors Ed Sobel
David November
Writer Peter Moreau
Designers Ed Sobel
David November
Photographers Jerry Darvin
Pete Mecca
Mel DiGiaccomo
Agency CBS Entertainment Division
Advertising and Promotion
Client CBS Television Network

602

Art Directors Robin Rickabaugh
Heidi Rickabaugh
Les Hopkins
Designer Robin Rickabaugh
Artists Robin Rickabaugh
Terry Daline
Agency Pihas Schmidt Westerdah
Client Tri-Met

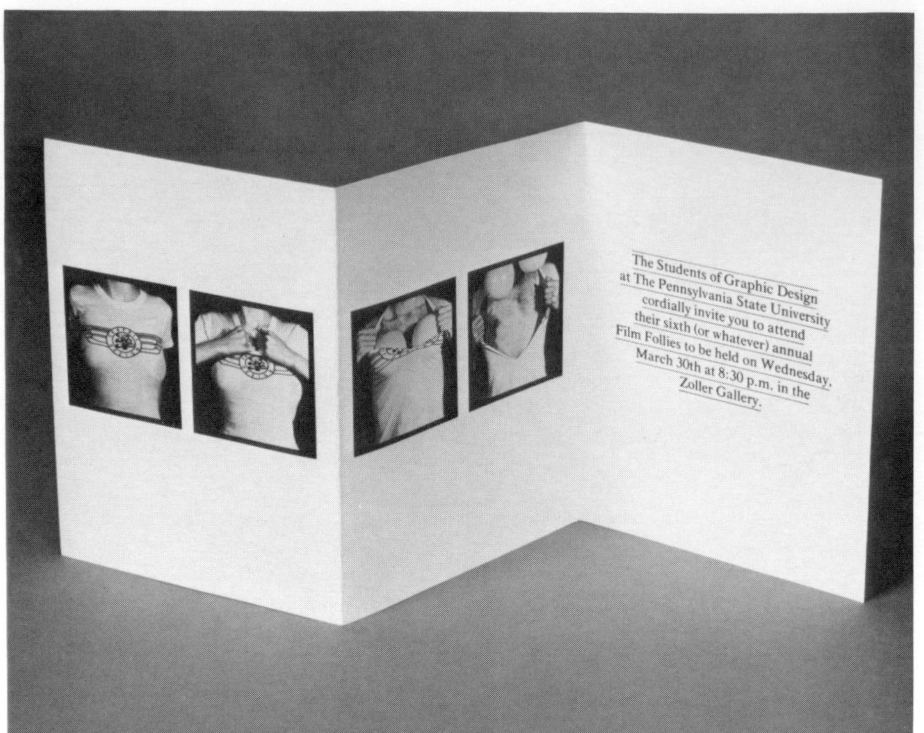

603

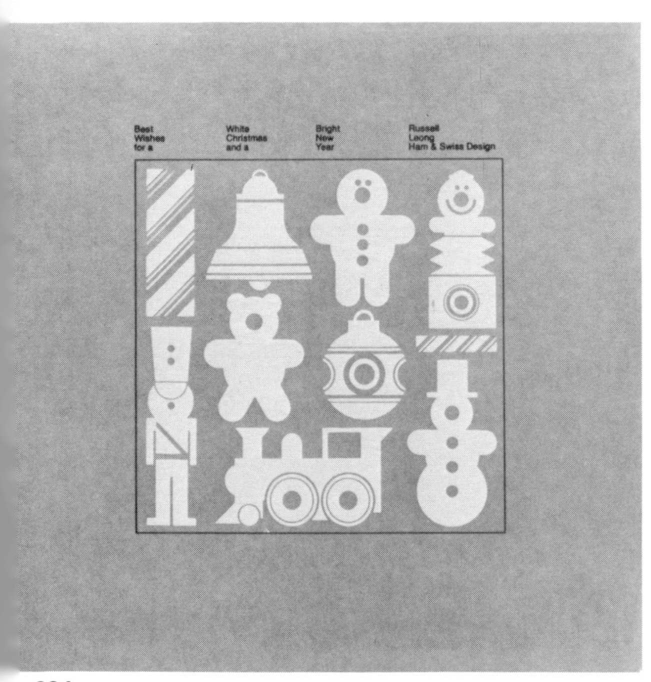

604

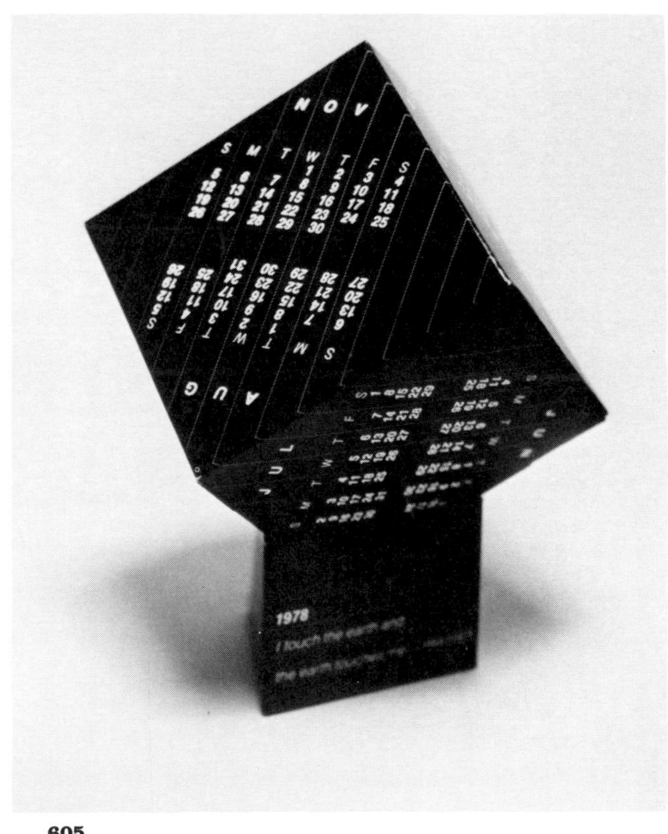

605

603
Art Director Lanny Sommese
Writer Theresa Dawson
Designers Jules Epstein
Steve Zellers
Photographer Bob Borkoski
Agency Lanny Sommese, Free Lance Design
Client Dept. of Graphic Design, Penn State

604
Art Director Russell K. Leong
Writer Russell K. Leong
Designer Russell K. Leong
Artist Russell K. Leong
Agency Ham & Swiss Design
Client Russell K. Leong

605
Art Director Mel Byars
Designer Pierre Asselin
Agency Apple Design, Inc.
Client JC Penney

606

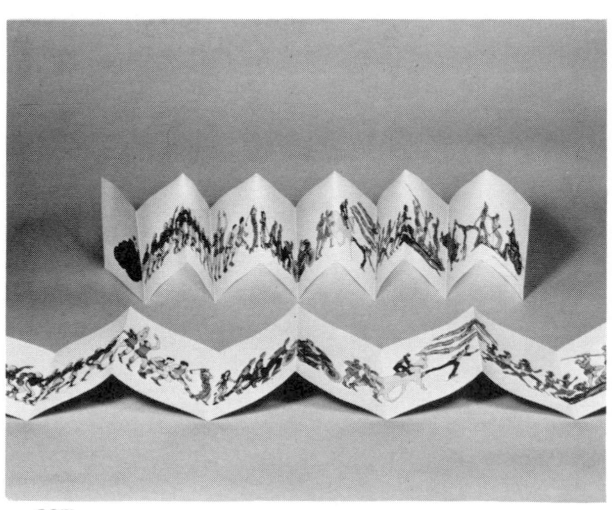

607

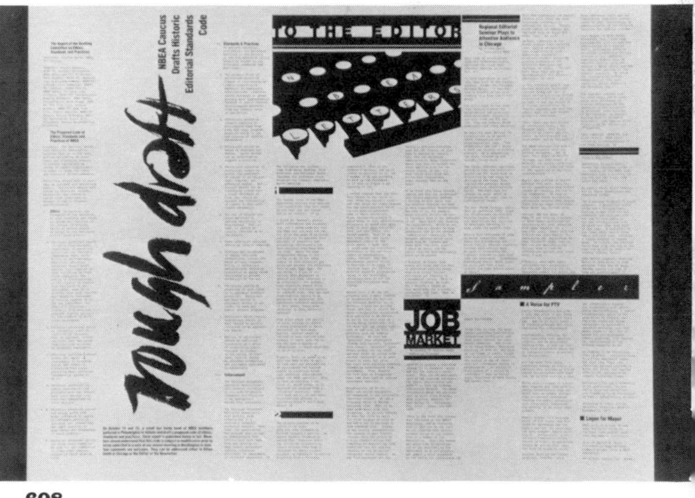
rough draft

NBEA Caucus Drafts Historic Editorial Standards Code

TO THE EDITOR

JOB MARKET

samples

608

606
Art Directors Ivan Chermayeff
Stephan Geissbuhler
Designer Stephan Geissbuhler
Agency Chermayeff & Geismar Associates
Client Fort Worth Art Museum

607
Art Director Chris Lawrence
Designers Chris Lawrence
Tim Lewis
Artist Tim Lewis
Client CBS Sports

608
Art Director Richard Lee Dickinson
Writer Phil Balboni
Designer Richard Lee Dickinson
Artist Richard Lee Dickinson
Agency WCVB-TV Boston
Client National Broadcast Editorial Assoc.

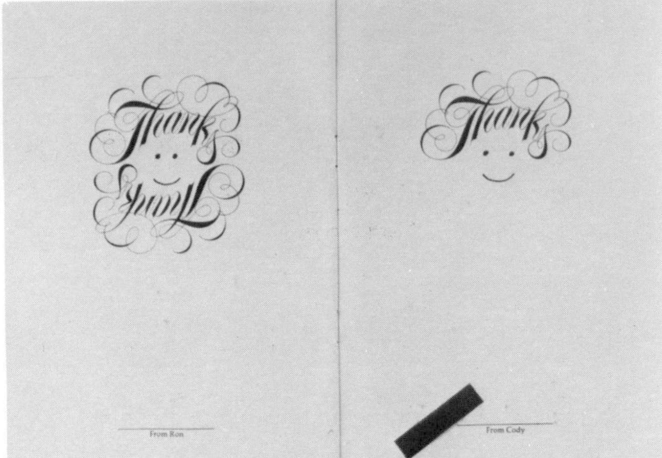

609

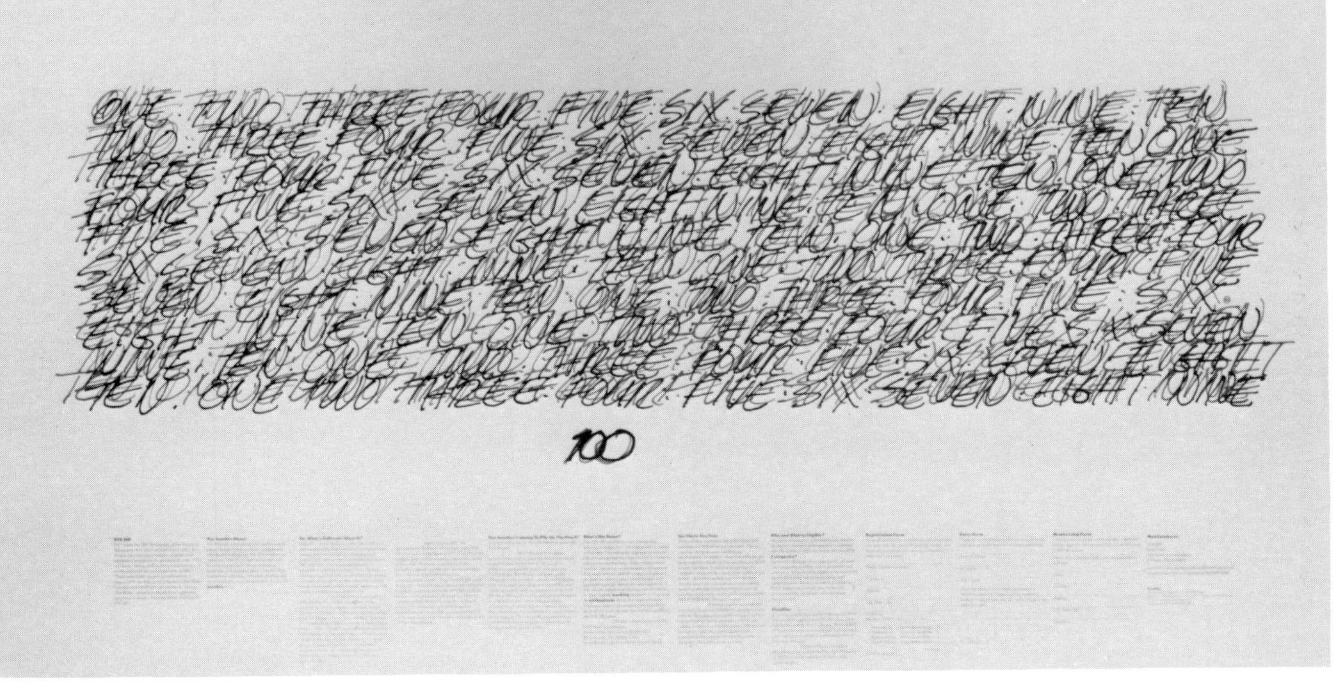

610

609
Art Director Arthur Eisenberg
Writers Arthur Eisenberg
Carol St. George
Designer Ron Hudson
Artist Ron Hudson
Agency Eisenberg & Pannell
Client Eisenberg & Pannell

610
Art Director Joseph M. Essex
Writers Joseph M. Essex
John Bisinger
Designer Joseph M. Essex
Calligrapher Joseph M. Essex
Agency Burson-Marteller/Chicago
Client Society of Typographic Arts

611

612

613

611
Art Directors Chris Hill
Loucks Atelier
Writers Barry Silverman
Chris Hill
Designer Chris Hill
Artist Peggy McDaniel
Agency Goodwin, Dannenbaum, Littman & Wingfield
Client The Michael Family

612
Art Director Gill Fishman
Designers Fredric Golinko
Gill Fishman
Eli Post
Paul Levy
Artists Fredric Golinko
Gill Fishman
Eli Post
Paul Levy
Agency Rainboworld Inc.
Client Rainboworld Inc.

613
Art Director Stuart Leventhal
Designer Stuart Leventhal
Photographer Various
Publisher Merrill Lynch
Client Merrill Lynch

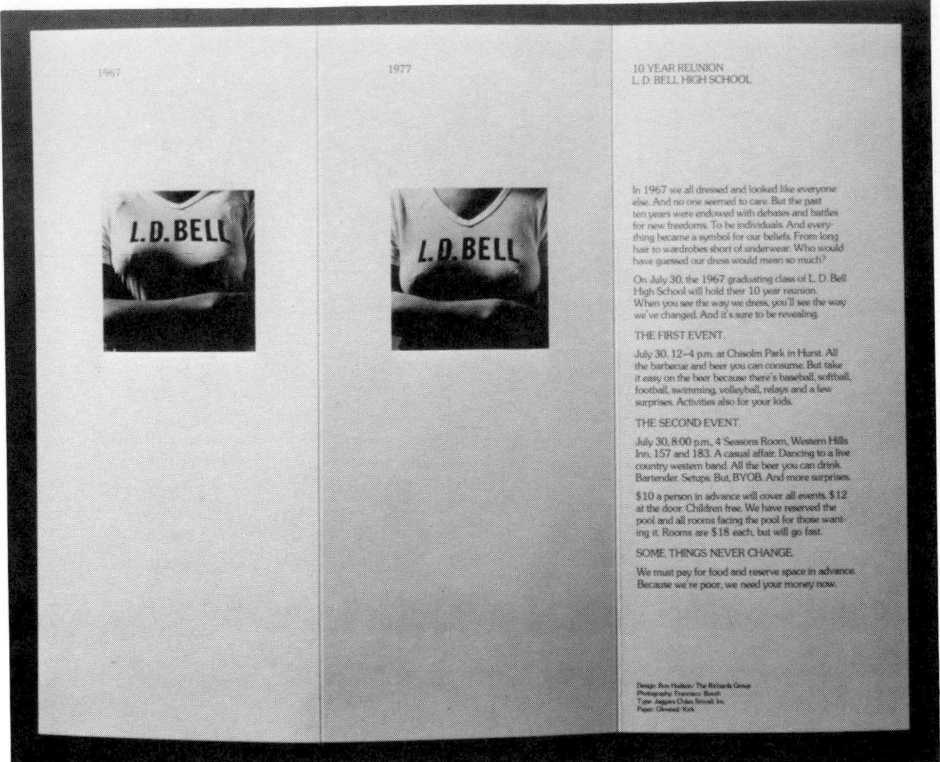

614

615

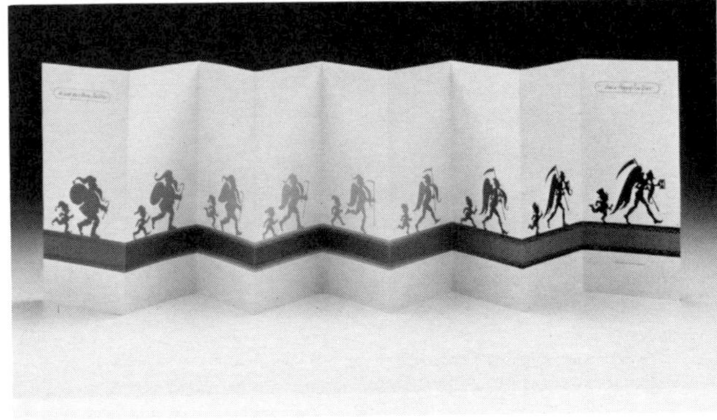

616

614
Art Director Ron Hudson
Writer Ron Hudson
Designer Ron Hudson
Photographer Mike Malloy/Francisco & Booth
Agency The Richards Group
Client L.D. Bell High School, Class of '67

615
Art Director Bruce Davis
Writer Bruce Davis
Designer Bruce Davis
Agency Bruce Henry & Davis Advertising
Client Byrne Smith

616
Art Director Woody Pirtle
Writer Woody Pirtle
Designer Woody Pirtle
Artist Woody Pirtle
Agency The Richards Group, Inc.
Client The Richards Group, Inc.

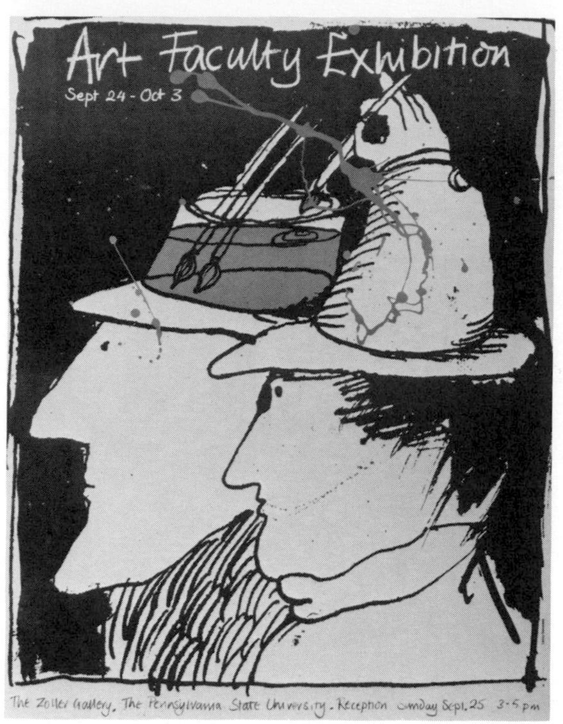

617

618

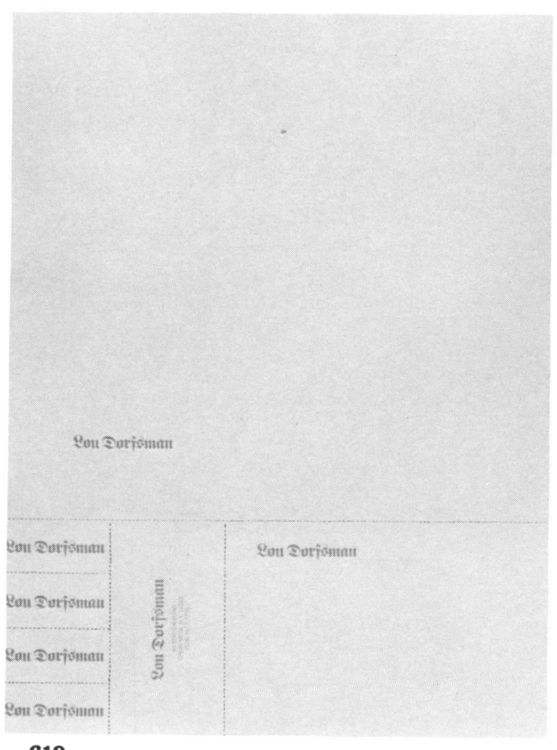

619

617
Art Director Lanny Sommese
Designer Lanny Sommese
Artist Lanny Sommese
Agency Lanny Sommese, Free Lance Design
Client Art Department, Penn State

618
Art Director Henry Wolf
Designer Henry Wolf
Photographer Henry Wolf
Agency LSC&P Design Group
Client Gilbert Paper Company

619
Art Director Lou Dorfsman
Designer Lou Dorfsman
Agency LSC&P Design Group
Client Gilbert Paper Co.

620

621

622

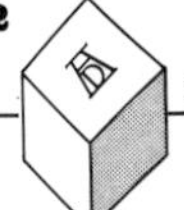

SILVER

620
Art Director Herb Lubalin
Designer Herb Lubalin
Artist Rick Schreiter
Agency Rick Schreiter Design
Client Herb Lubalin

621
Art Director Woody Pirtle
Designer Woody Pirtle
Artist Woody Pirtle
Agency The Richards Group, Inc.
Client Thom Liddell

622
Art Director Robert Burns
Designers Robert Burns
Roger Hathaway
Artist Roger Hathaway
Agency Burns, Cooper, Hynes Limited
Client Alan Littlewood/Architect

623

624

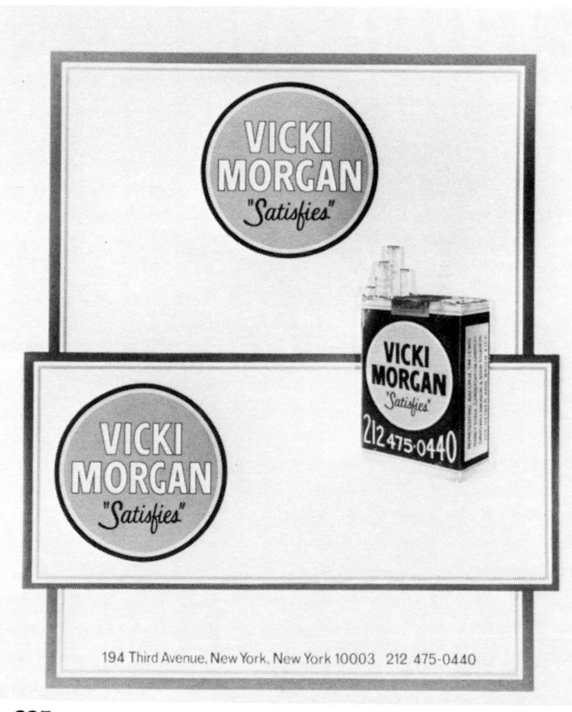

625

623
Art Director Joe Spencer
Designer Joe Spencer
Artist Joe Spencer
Agency Art Throb X
Client Rod Kinder Music Group

624
Art Director Lou Dorfsman
Designer Meg Gates
Artist Meg Gates
Agency CBS/Broadcast Group
Client CBS Television Network

625
Art Director David Willardson
Designers David Willardson
Brian Zick
Artists David Willardson
Brian Zick
Agency Star Studio
Client Vicki Morgan

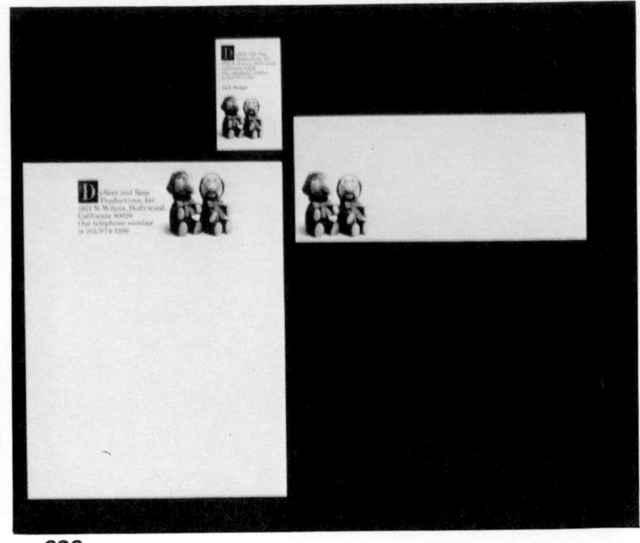

626

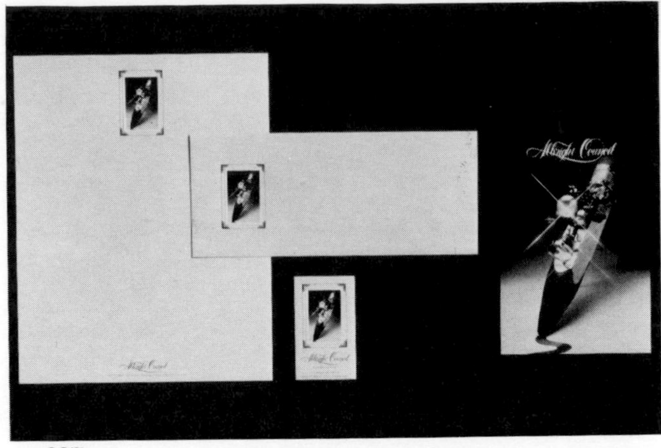

627

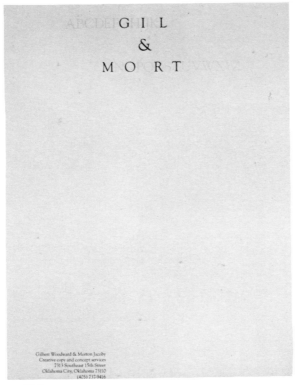

628

626
Art Director Bill Sowder
Designer Bill Sowder
Artist Brent Carpenter
Photographer Dennis Manarchy
Client Desort & Sam Productions

627
Art Director David Council
Designer David Council
Photographer Deryl Duer
Agency Albright Council

628
Art Director Steve Connatser
Designer Steve Connatser
Agency Connatser & Crum
Client Gilbert Woodward & Morton Jacoby

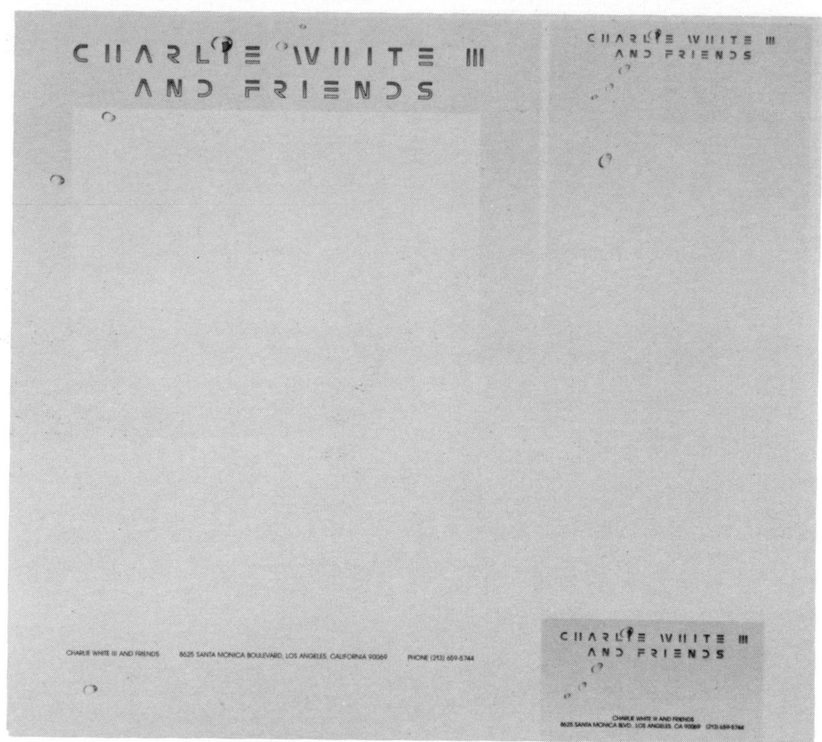

629

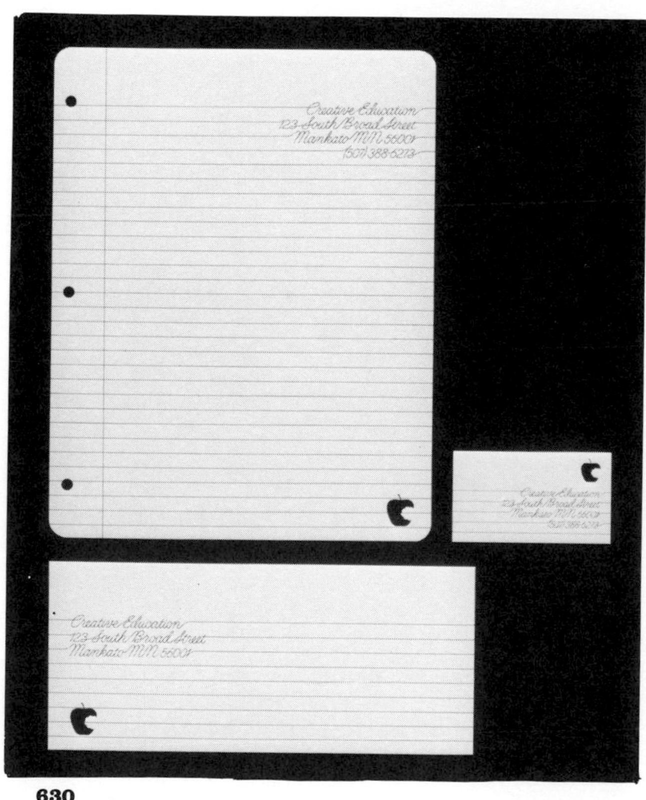

630

631

629
Art Director Charlie White III
Designer Charlie White III
Artist Chuck Schmidt
Agency Charlie White III & Friends
Client Charlie White III & Friends

630
Designer Marty Neumeier
Letterer Jay Flammer
Agency Marty Neumeier Design
Client Creative Education

631
Art Director Lou Dorfsman
Designer Peter Katz
Artist Peter Katz
Agency CBS/Broadcast Group
Client CBS Sports

632

633

634

632
Art Director Steven Sessions
Designer Steven Sessions
Artist Steven Sessions
Producer Steven Sessions
Production Company Beasley Printing Company
Agency Baxter & Korge, Inc.
Client Tom Payne Photography

633
Art Director Frank Schulwolf
Writer Arthur Low
Designer Frank Schulwolf
Photographer Robert Panuska
Agency Frank Schulwolf
Client Arthur Low

634
Art Director John Casado
Designer John Casado
Artists Calvin Hom
Del Rae Hrubes
Agency Casado, Ltd.
Client Casado, Ltd.

635

636

637

635
Art Director Parry Merkley
Designer Adrian Pulfer
Artist Vincent Gonzales
Photographer George M. Brown
Agency Two's Company
Client Pro Musica

636
Art Director Roger Huyssen
Designer Gerard Huerta
Client Graphic Desserts

637
Art Director Lou Dorfsman
Designer Tana Klugherz
Artist Tana Klugherz
Agency CBS/Broadcast Group
Client CBS Radio

638

639

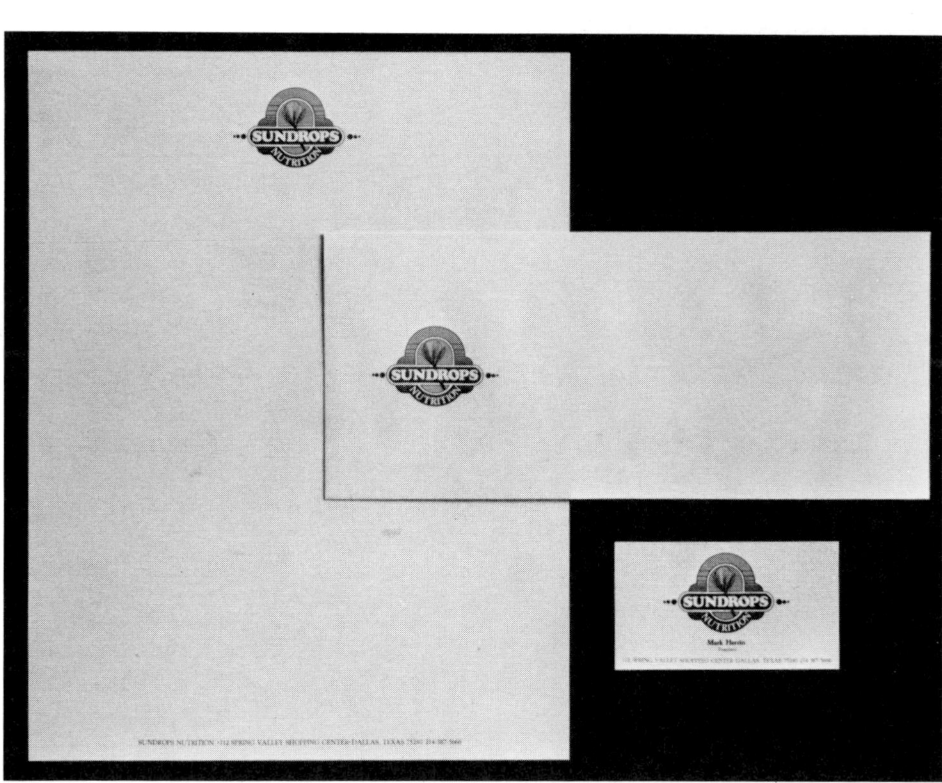

640

638
Art Director Robert Fillie
Designer Robert Fillie
Artist Robert Fillie
Client Jennifer Place

639
Art Director Lou Dorfsman
Designer Tana Klugherz
Artist Tana Klugherz
Agency CBS/Broadcast Group
Client CBS Radio

640
Art Director David Council
Writer Jim Albright
Designer David Council
Agency Albright Council
Client Sundrops Nutrition

641

642

643

641
Art Director Mac Talmadge
Designer Mac Talmadge
Artist Mac Talmadge
Agency Tucker Wayne & Company
Client Doncaster, Inc.

642
Art Director Jann Church Advertising & Graphic Design, Inc.
Designer Jann Church Advertising & Graphic Design, Inc.
Artist Jann Church Advertising & Graphic Design, Inc.
Agency Jann Church Advertising & Graphic Design, Inc.
Client Decima Research

643
Art Director John Casado
Designer John Casado
Artist Calvin Hom
Agency Casado, Ltd.
Client West End Studio

644

645

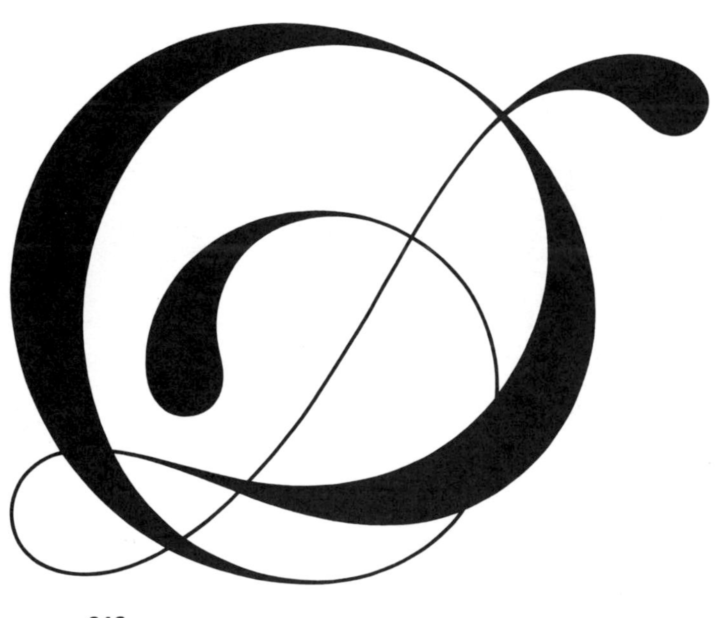

646

644
Art Director Bruce Johnson
Designer Bruce Johnson
Artist Bruce Johnson
Agency The Ink Spot
Client Foremost Lithograph Co.

645
Art Director Michael O. Kelly
Designer Michael O. Kelly
Artist Michael O. Kelly
Agency Murrie White Drummond Lienhart & Assoc.
Client Family Service of South Lake County

646
Art Director Woody Pirtle
Designer Woody Pirtle
Artist Woody Pirtle
Agency The Richards Group, Inc.
Client Dallas Civic Opera

647

648

647
Art Director Don Moravick
Designer Don Moravick
Artist Randy Chaffee
Agency John Scott and others
Client "Maitre D' "

648
Art Director Carolyn Wade Frazier Studio
Designer Marilyn Worseldine
Artists Mary Carol Smith
Carolyn Wade Frazier
Agency Carolyn Wade Frazier Studio
Client Brass Elephant Restaurant

649

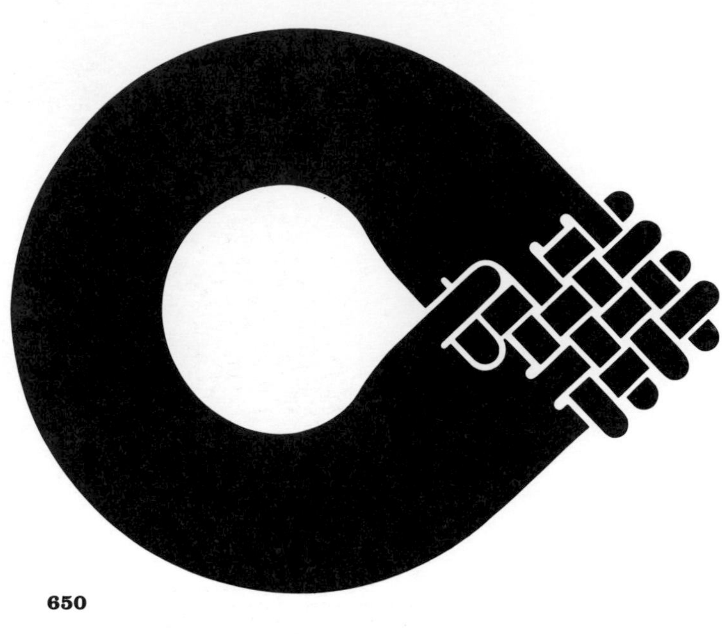

650

651

649
Art Director Peter McGuggart
Designer Peter McGuggart
Agency Compton Adv. Inc.
Client IBM Office Products Division

650
Art Director Don Grimes
Designer Don Grimes
Artist Don Grimes
Agency The Richards Group, Inc.
Client Dallas Handweavers & Spinners Guild Inc.

651
Art Director Cliff Schwandner
Designer Mark Stockstill
Artist Mark Stockstill
Agency Northlich, Stolley, Inc.
Client Delta Queen Steamboat Company

652

653

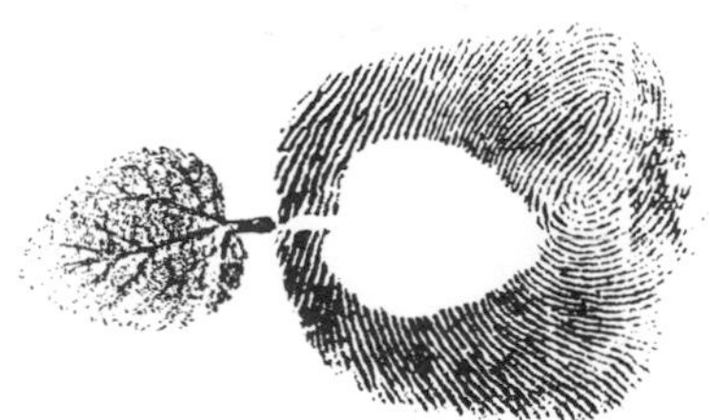

654

652
Art Director George Monagle
Designer Mike Fountain
Artist Mike Cariglio
Agency George Monagle/ Graphic Productions, Ltd.
Client George Monagle/ Graphic Productions, Ltd.

653
Art Director Myron Polenberg
Designer Gerard Huerta
Artist Gerard Huerta
Client Arista Records

654
Art Director Steven Sessions
Designer Steven Sessions
Artist Steven Sessions
Agency Baxter & Korge, Inc.
Client The Green Thumb Plant Store

655

656

AMERICAN
STAGE

657

655
Art Director Janet Rieck
Designer Janet Rieck
Artist Janet Rieck
Client Carl Rieck

656
Art Director Gary Alfredson
Designer Gary Alfredson
Artist Gary Alfredson
Agency Burson-Marsteller/Chicago
Client En Celebracion de Latinos

657
Art Director Herb Lubalin
Designer Herb Lubalin
Agency LSC&P Design Group
Client American Stage Magazine

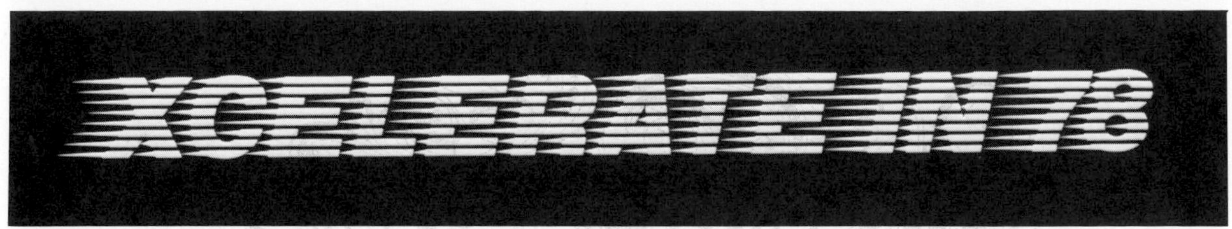

658

659

660

658
Art Director Rick Stubbins
Writer Pat Loporcaro
Designer Rick Stubbins
Artists Dave Kolchuk
Adolph L. Jeff
Agency Xerox Corporation
Client Xerox Corporation

659
Art Director Rick Stubbins
Writer Vincent M. Coughlin
Designer Rick Stubbins
Artist Dave Kolchuk
Agency Xerox Corporation
Client Rochester Downtown Development Corp.

660
Art Director Rose Farber
Designer Rose Farber
Artist Joan Farber
Agency Rose Farber Graphic Design Inc.
Client Harris & Farber Words & Pictures, Inc.

661

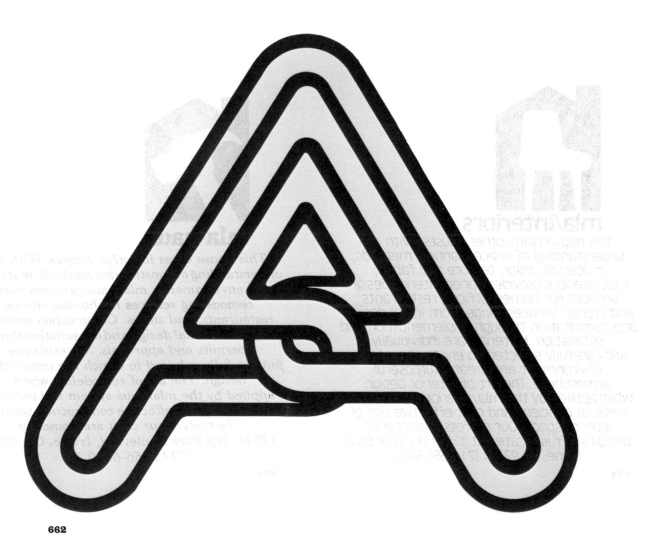

662

661
Art Director Alan Peckolick
Designer Alan Peckolick
Agency LSC&P Design Group
Client Kimberly-Clark Corporation

662
Art Director Joseph M. Essex
Designer Joseph M. Essex
Artists Joseph M. Essex
Peter Crockett
Agency Burson Marsteller
Client Ace Chain Link Fence Inc.

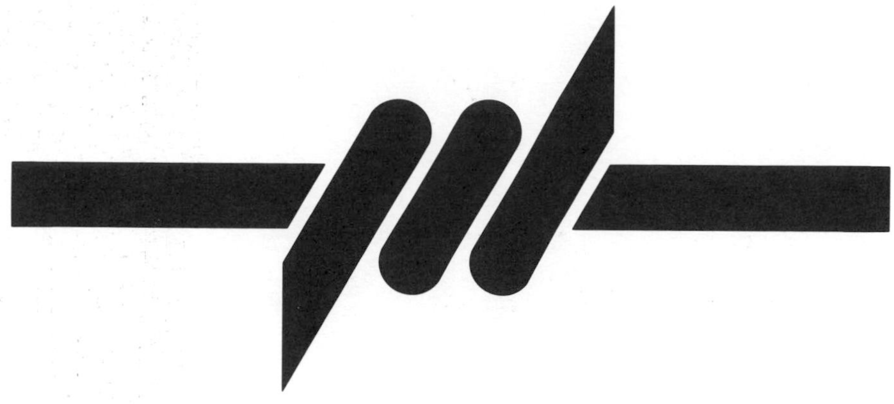

663

mla/interiors

This house plans other houses. With an understanding of space planning methods, materials, color, texture and fabric, mla/interiors provides varied interior design services for homes, offices, restaurants and stores. Services range from initial design and consultation through implementation and installation. Materials are individually and carefully selected to enrich the interior environment and create purposeful atmosphere. The art of interior design when applied by the mla/interiors system will result in efficient and cost-effective use of interior space. Our professional interior design staff is located at 17848 Sky Park Blvd. Irvine, CA 92714 (714) 556-6610.

664

mla·haus

This house cares for other houses. With an understanding of construction methods, materials and environments, mla/haus provides varied remodeling services for homes, offices, restaurants, and stores. Construction services range from initial design and consultation through permits and approvals. Materials are purposefully selected to enrich the intent of the design. The art of remodeling when applied by the mla/haus system will result in efficient and cost-effective construction additions The tools of our craft are housed at 17848 Sky Park Boulevard, Irvine, CA 92714 (714) 556-6610

665

663

Art Director Jann Church Advertising & Graphic Design, Inc.
Designer Jann Church Advertising & Graphic Design, Inc.
Agency Jann Church Advertising & Graphic Design, Inc.
Artist Jann Church Advertising & Graphic Design, Inc.
Client Bixby Ranch Co.

664

Art Director Jann Church Advertising & Graphic Design, Inc.
Writer Jann Church Advertising & Graphic Design, Inc.
Designer Jann Church Advertising & Graphic Design, Inc.
Artist Jann Church Advertising & Graphic Design, Inc.
Agency Jann Church Advertising & Graphic Design, Inc.
Client MLA/Interiors

665

Art Director Jann Church Advertising & Graphic Design, Inc.
Designer Jann Church Advertising & Graphic Design, Inc.
Writer Jann Church Advertising & Graphic Design, Inc.
Artist Jann Church Advertising & Graphic Design, Inc.
Agency Jann Church Advertising & Graphic Design, Inc.
Client MLA/Haus

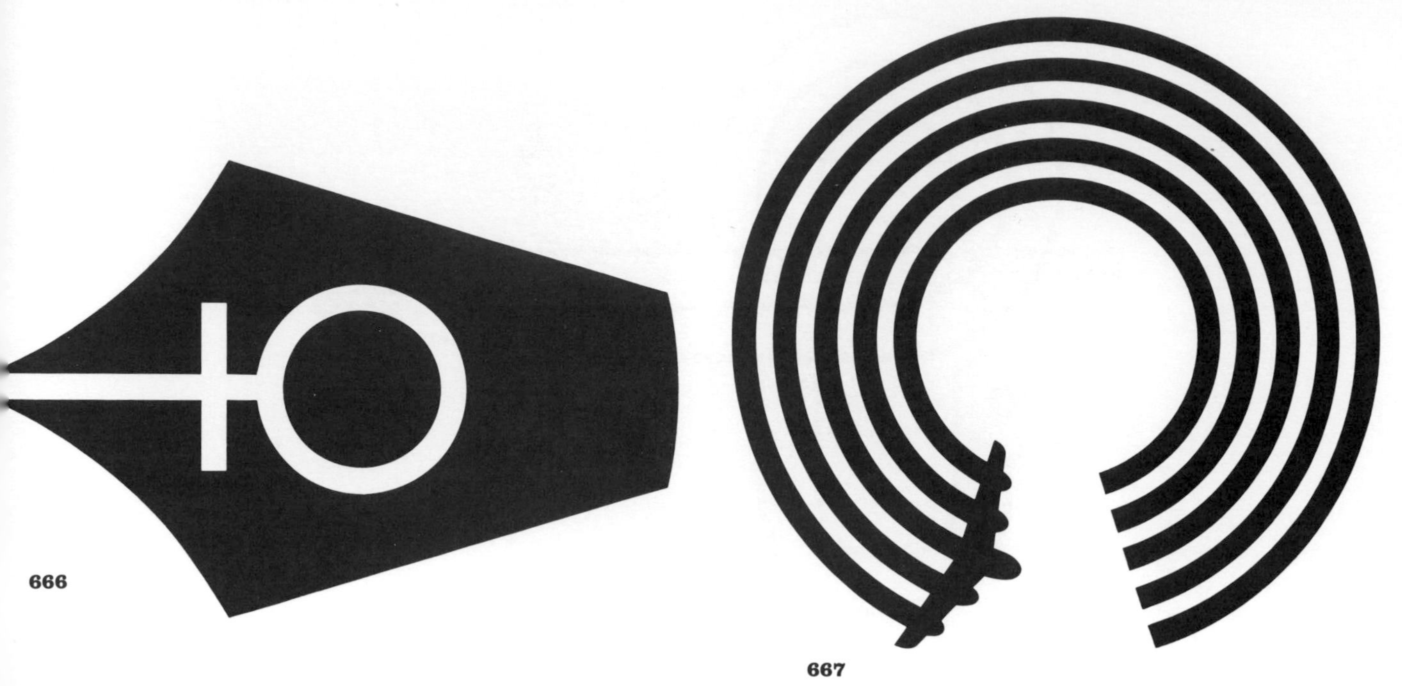

666

667

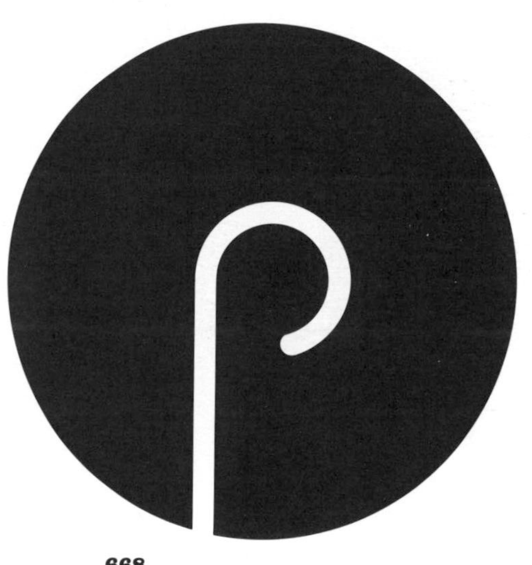

668

666
Art Director D. Bruce Zahor
Designer D. Bruce Zahor
Agency Zahor Design Inc.
Client International Women's Writing Guild

667
Art Director D. Bruce Zahor
Designer D. Bruce Zahor
Agency Zahor Design Inc.
Client Command Travel Inc.

668
Art Director Mel Byars
Designer Mel Byars
Agency Apple Design, Inc.
Client Excelsior Research Inc.

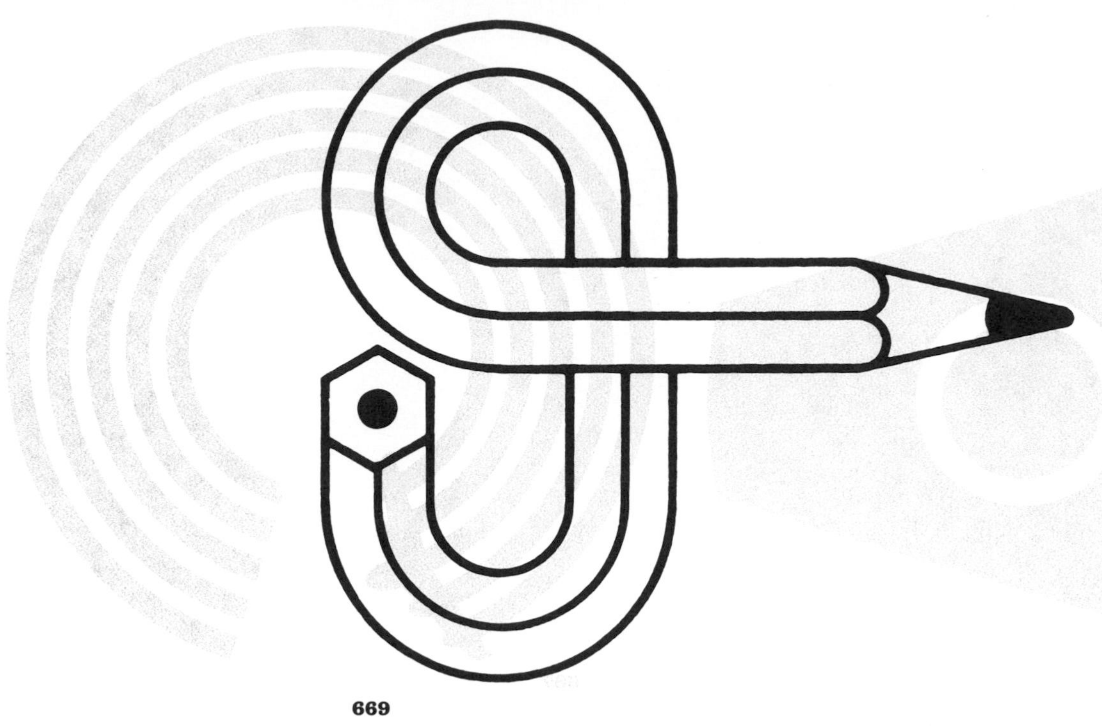

669

670

671

669

Art Director Pat Procaccino
Designer Pat Procaccino
Artist Pat Procaccino
Agency Procaccino's Creative Pencil
Client Procaccino's Creative Pencil

670

Art Director Jann Church Advertising & Graphic Design, Inc.
Designer Jann Church Advertising & Graphic Design, Inc.
Artist Jann Church Advertising & Graphic Design, Inc.
Agency Jann Church Advertising & Graphic Design, Inc.
Client Bayshore/Olmstead Development Corp.

671

Art Director Steven Sessions
Designer Steven Sessions
Artist Steven Sessions
Agency Baxter & Korge, Inc.
Client R & J Ranch

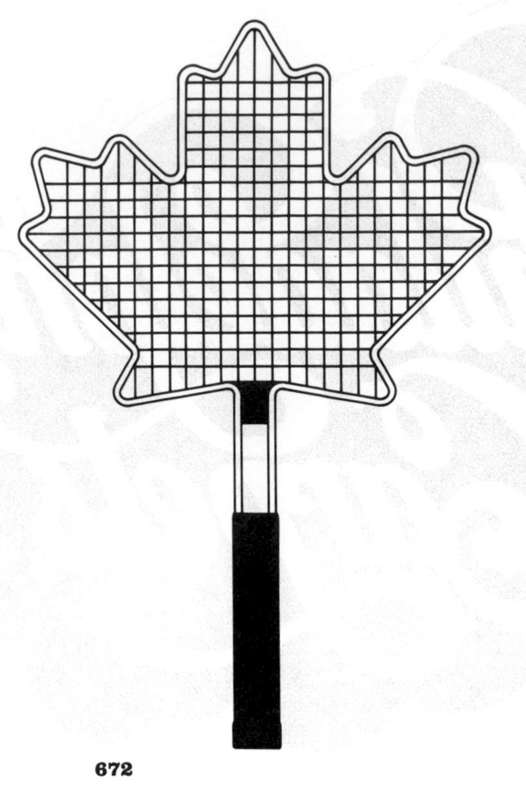

672

672
Art Director Yoshi Sekiguchi
Designer Yoshi Sekiguchi
Artist Yoshi Sekiguchi
Agency Rising Sun Design
Client Maple Bluff Racquet Club

673
Art Director John Casado
Designer John Casado
Artists John Casado
Calvin Hom
Agency Casado, ltd.
Client Holiday Inn

674

675

674
Art Director Mac Talmadge
Designer Mac Talmadge
Artist Mac Talmadge
Agency Tucker Wayne & Company
Client Philadelphia Carpet Company

675
Art Director Lou Dorfsman
Designer Peter Katz
Artist Peter Katz
Agency CBS/Broadcast Group
Client CBS Sports

676

677

678

676
Designer Marty Neumeier
Agency Marty Neumeier Design
Client Western Medical

677
Art Director Frank J. D'Astolfo
Designer Frank J. D'Astolfo
Artists Frank J. D'Astolfo
Richard McGarrity
Client Pittsburgh Psychoanalytic Center, Inc.

678
Art Director Steven Sessions
Designer Steven Sessions
Artist Steven Sessions
Agency Baxter & Korge, Inc.
Client Acme Locksmith

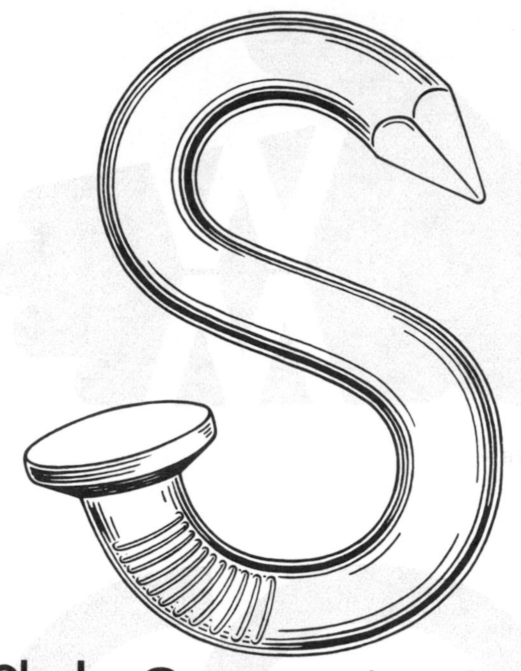

679

680

681

679
Art Director Abraham J. Amuny
Designer Abraham J. Amuny
Artist Larry McIntyre
Agency Art City
Client Shults Const. Co.

680
Art Director James Laird
Designer James Laird
Artist James Laird
Agency James Laird Design
Client Rude Battenfeld

681
Art Director Michael O. Kelly
Designer Michael O. Kelly
Artist Horst Mickler
Agency Murrie White Drummond Lienhart & Assoc.
Client Liedtke Binding & Finishing, Inc.

683

684

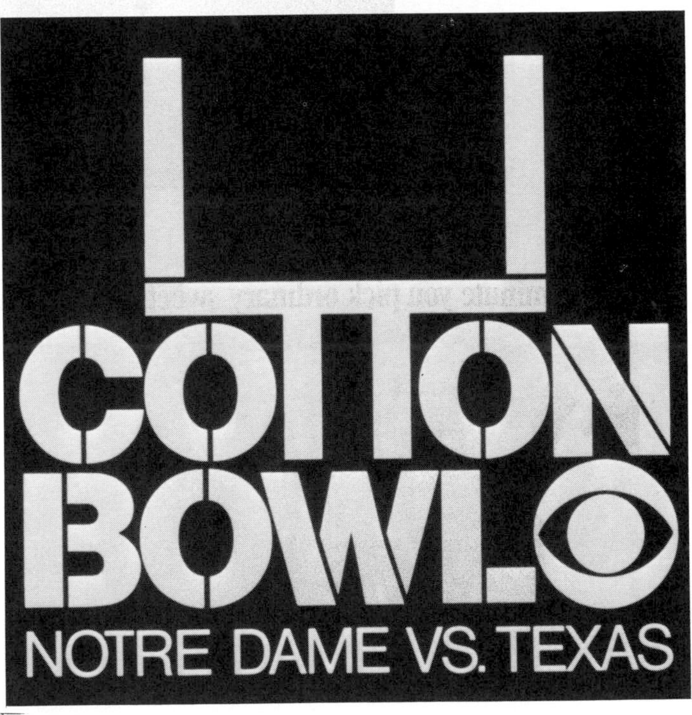

682

682
Art Directors Herman Aronson
Bill Snyder
Designer Alan Brooks
Artist Alan Brooks
Agency CBS Entertainment Advertising and Promotion On-Air Graphics Department
Client CBS Television Network

683
Art Director Robert Delpire
Designer Robert Delpire
Photographer Art Kane
Agency Ideodis
Client Cacharel

684
Art Director Coy Berry
Writers Joe Conwell
Coy Berry
Designer Coy Berry
Photographer Bilecky/McLean, Inc.—John Bilecky
Agency Lawler Ballard Little Advertising
Client Landmark Bank

685

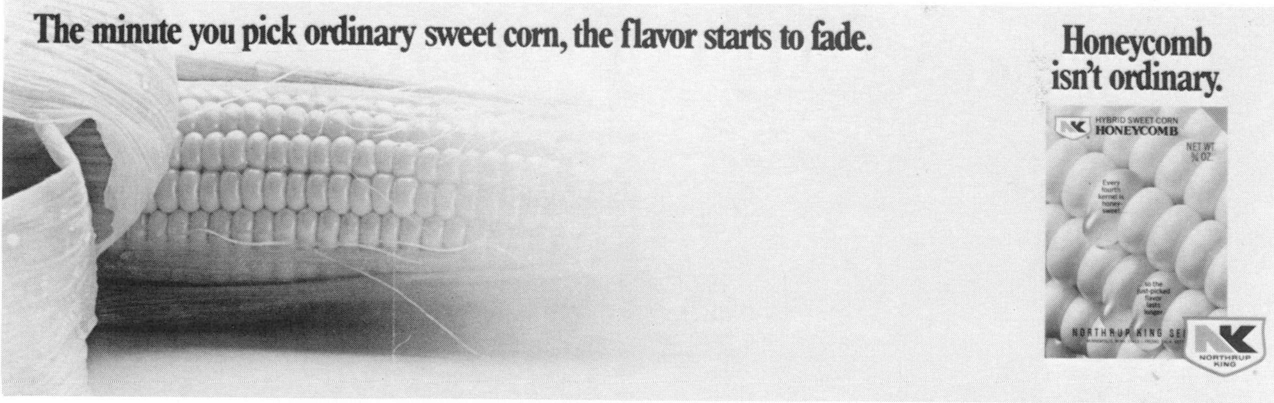

The minute you pick ordinary sweet corn, the flavor starts to fade.
Honeycomb isn't ordinary.
HYBRID SWEET CORN
HONEYCOMB
NORTHRUP KING

686

685
Art Director Jack Looney
Writer Peter Minichiello
Designer Melinda Bush
Artist Melinda Bush
Client Bantam Books

686
Art Director Sue Crolick
Writer Sandra Bucholtz
Designer Sue Crolick
Artist Star Studio
Photographer Bill Gale
Agency Martin Williams Advertising
Client Northrup King Seeds

687

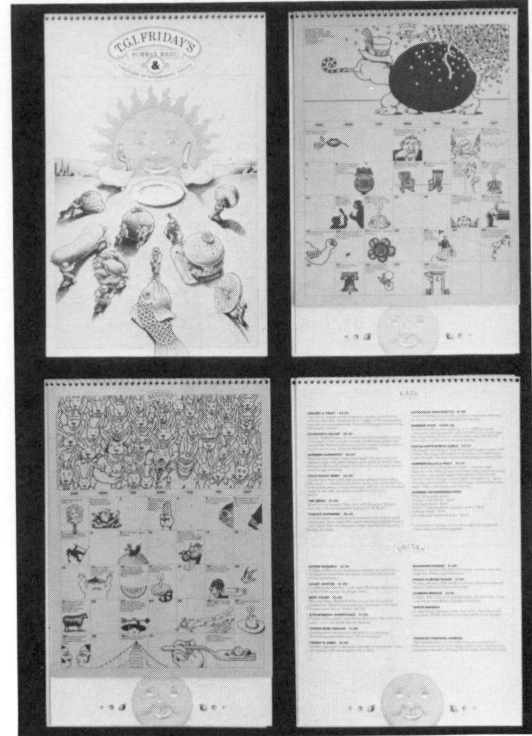

688 A

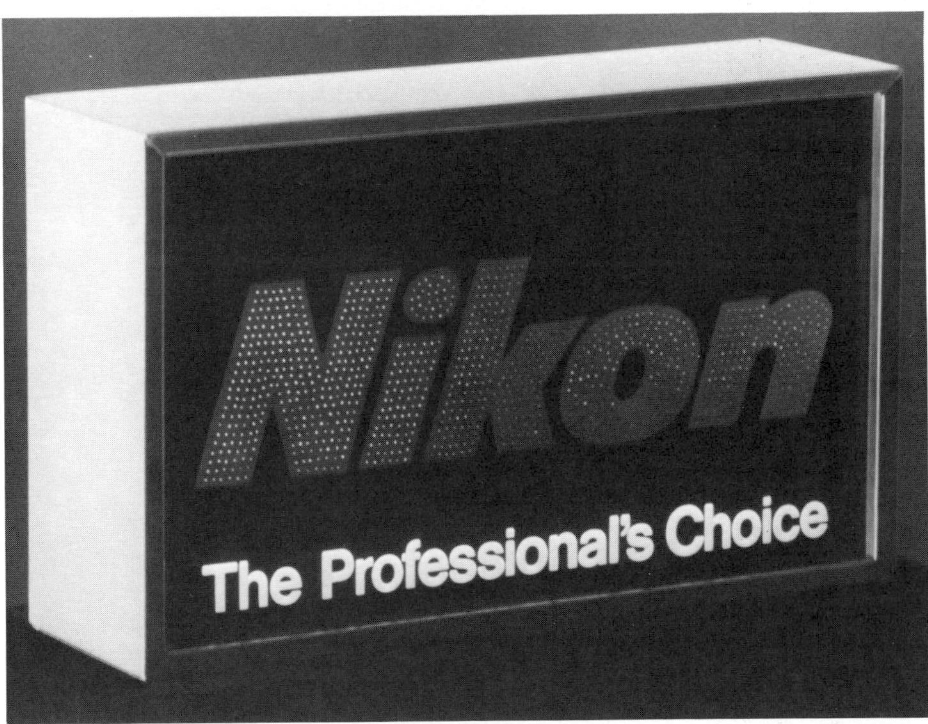

688B

687
Art Director George E. Rumsey
Writer Leonard Burstein
Designers George Rumsey
Roger Lundquist
Artist Roger Lundquist
Agency Rumsey-Lundquist & Associates
Client The Brothers Deli

688A
Art Director Woody Pirtle
Writer Jim Hradecky
Designers Woody Pirtle
Jerry Jeanmard
Artist Jerry Jeanmard
Agency The Richards Group, Inc.
Client T.G.I. Friday's

688B
Designer Louis Abramowitz
Directors Fred Way
Dick Warner
Producer Way Electroptics, Inc.
Client Nikon, Inc.

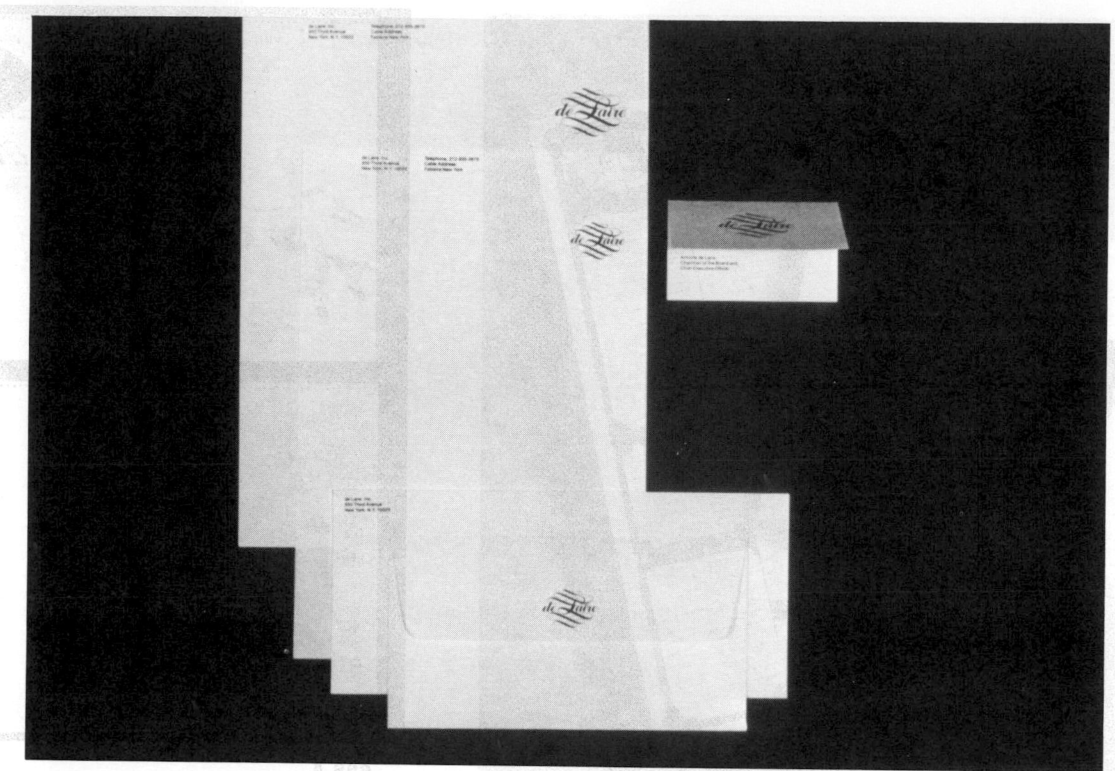

689

690

689

Art Director	**Danne & Blackburn, Inc.**
Designer	**Bruce Blackburn**
Artist	**Tony Stan, Photo-Lettering, Inc.**
Agency	**Danne & Blackburn, Inc.**
Client	**De Laire, Inc.**

690

Art Director	**David Willardson**
Designers	**David Willardson** **Brian Zick**
Artists	**David Willardson** **Brian Zick**
Agency	**Star Studio**
Client	**Vicki Morgan**

Posters

692

691

693

SILVER

691
Artist Doug Johnson
Lettering Gerard Huerta
Client Rosebud Advertising/ Paramount

692
Art Directors Dick Lopez, Ed McCabe
Designers Dick Lopez, Ed McCabe
Agency Scali, McCabe, Sloves
Client Buckingham Corporation

693
Art Director Janet Neff
Writer Tim Sullivan
Designer Janet Neff
Artist Michael Doret
Agency J. Walter Thompson Company
Client Burger King Corporation

Our kind of town.
Aetna Bank
Lincoln, Fullerton and Halsted

694

BERLIN NOW
Art · Music · Literature · Theater · Film · Urbanism
Cultural Aspects of a City
March 12 through April 19 1977
Sponsored by Goethe House New York · For further information call 744 8472

695

696

694
Art Director Bob Sherman
Writer Arnold Paley
Designer Bob Sherman
Photographer Mike Ditlove
Agency Brand Advertising Inc.
Client Aetna Bank

695
Art Director George Tscherny
Writer Staff/Goethe House New York
Designer George Tscherny
Artist George Tscherny
Agency Infoplan International, Inc.
Client Goethe House New York

696
Art Director Murray Klein
Writer Murray Klein
Designer Steve Ohman
Artist Steve Ohman
Agency Smith/Greenland, Inc.
Client Somerset Importers, Ltd.

697

698

699

697
Art Director Stan Jones
Writer Richard Leiter
Designer Stan Jones
Photographer Carl Futura
Agency Doyle Dane Bernbach
Client Southern California Gas Company

698
Art Director Bob Bidner
Writer Ray Baker
Designer Bob Bidner
Artists Bob Bidner, Tony Toscano
Production Company McNaughton Litho.
Agency Ted Bates & Co., Inc.
Client Julius Wile Sons & Co., Inc.

699
Art Director Reinhold Schwenk
Designers Paul Davis, Reinhold Schwenk
Artist Paul Davis
Agency Case & McGrath, I
Client New York Shakesp Festival

700
702

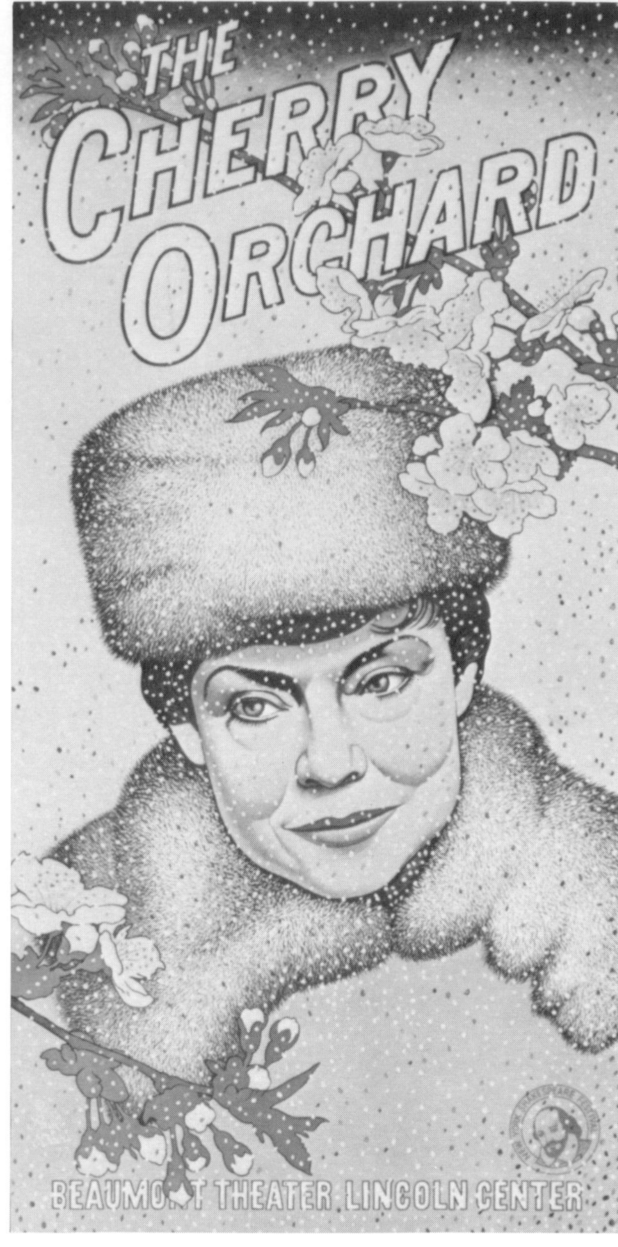

701

700
Art Director Reinhold Schwenk
Designer Reinhold Schwenk
Artist Reinhold Schwenk
Photographer Jean Marie Guyaux
Agency Case & McGrath, Inc.
Client New York Shakespeare Festival

701
Art Director Reinhold Schwenk
Designer Paul Davis
Artist Paul Davis
Agency Case & McGrath, Inc.
Client New York Shakespeare Festival

702
Art Director Reinhold Schwenk
Designers Reinhold Schwenk, Paul Davis
Artist Paul Davis
Photographer Jean Marie Guyaux
Agency Case & McGrath, Inc.
Client New York Shakespeare Festival

703

704

703
Art Director Robert Delpire
Designer Robert Delpire
Photographer Art Kane
Agency Ideodis
Client Cacharel

704
Art Director Tom Cordner
Writer Blake Hunter
Designer Tom Cordner
Artist Tom Cordner
Photographer Peter Sagara
Agency Dailey & Associates
Client So. California Ford Dealers

705

706

705

Art Director	Stan Jones
Writers	Richard Leiter
	Dave Butler
Designer	Stan Jones
Photographer	Carl Futura
Agency	Doyle Dane Bernbach
Client	Southern California Gas Company

706

Art Director	David Bosley
Writers	David Bosley
	Diane Timmerman
Designer	David Bosley
Artist	Lee Bonner
Agency	W. B. Doner & Company
Client	Baltimore Orioles Baseball Club

707

709

708

707
Art Director Steve Lawrence
Designers Steve Lawrence
Christian Piper
Artist Christian Piper
Client Studio 54/Fiorucci

708
Art Director John Johnson
Artist Bruce Wolfe
Agency Paul Pease
Advertising, Inc.
Client Snow Lion

709
Art Director Ken Parkhurst
Designers Ken Parkhurst
Denis Parkhurst
Artist Denis Parkhurst
Production Company Anderson Lithograph Company
Agency Ken Parkhurst & Associates, Inc.
Client Los Angeles County Museum of Art

710

Acapulco
(where else!)

711

In our family business there's three things you don't mind spending your money on. Copper tubing. Fast cars. And a fine pair of warm, dry boots. And that third one is just as important as the first two. When you're crouching down in some gully with your feet in ice-cold ditch water, never moving a muscle for hours, whilst them damn Treasury agents snoop around with their dogs barking and sniffing, well, that's the time you're glad you didn't cut corners on your boots. These boots we bought are fine boots, well made, need no breaking in. But to us, that don't mean so much compared to the way they're waterproof and warm.

Timberland

A whole line of fine leather boots that cost plenty, and should.

712

710
Art Director Charles Rosner
Writer Arthur Einstein, Jr.
Designer Simon Bowden
Photographer Reid Miles
Agency Lord, Geller, Federico, Inc.
Client Steyr Daimler Puch

711
Art Director John Lucci
Writer John Carrigan
Designer John Lucci
Photographer Peter Vaeth
Agency Dancer, Fitzgerald & Sample, Inc.
Client Fonatur

712
Art Director Harry Kerker
Writer Charles Harding
Designer Harry Kerker
Photographer Vince Aiosa
Agency Marvin & Leonard Advertising Co., Inc.
Client Timberland Footwear, Inc.

714

715

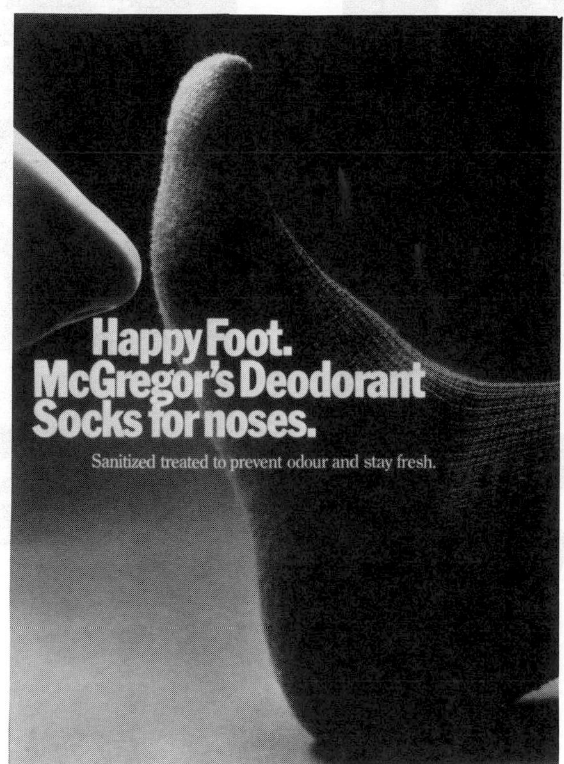

713

713
Art Director Raymond Lee
Writers Raymond Lee
Richard Kurtz
Mark Greenberg
Designer Raymond Lee
Artist Terry O'Connor
Photographer Yosh Inouye
Agency Raymond Lee & Associates Limited
Client McGregor Hosiery Mills

714
Art Director Robert Reitzfeld
Writer David Altschiller
Designer Robert Reitzfeld
Photographer Henry Sandbank
Agency Altschiller, Reitzfeld & Jackson
Client American Beverage Corp.

715
Art Director Robert Reitzfeld
Writer Dick Jackson
Photographer Henry Sandbank
Agency Altschiller, Reitzfeld & Jackson
Client American Beverage Corp.

WRANGLER
WHEN YOU'RE RIDING BY THE SEAT OF YOUR PANTS,
THOSE PANTS BETTER BE WRANGLER.

716

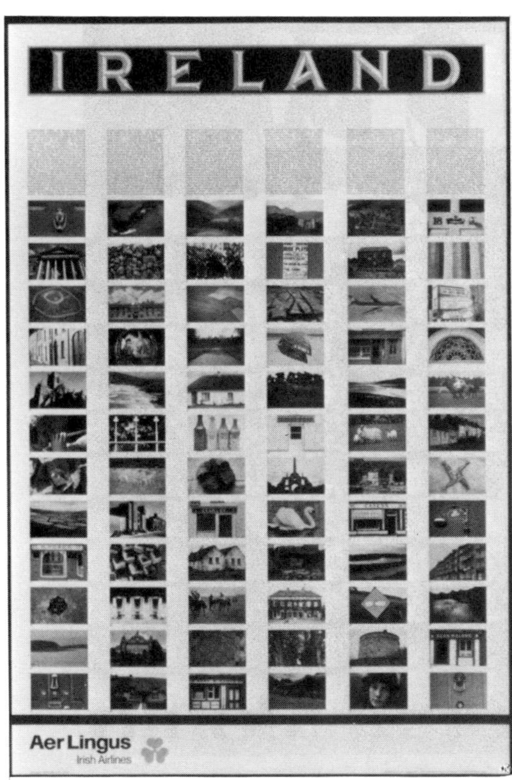

717

718

716
Art Director Merv Shipenberg
Writer Austin Hamel
Designer Merv Shipenberg
Artist Kathy Fineran
Photographer Frank Cowan
Agency Altman, Stoller, Weiss
Client Wrangler

717
Art Director Miho
Writer David R. Brown
Designer Miho
Artist Miho
Photographer Miho
Client Champion Papers

718
Art Directors David Wiseltier
Marv Schneider
Writers Lew Sherwood
Marv Schneider
Designer David Wiseltier
Photographer UPI
Agency KSW&G Advertising
Client New York Daily News

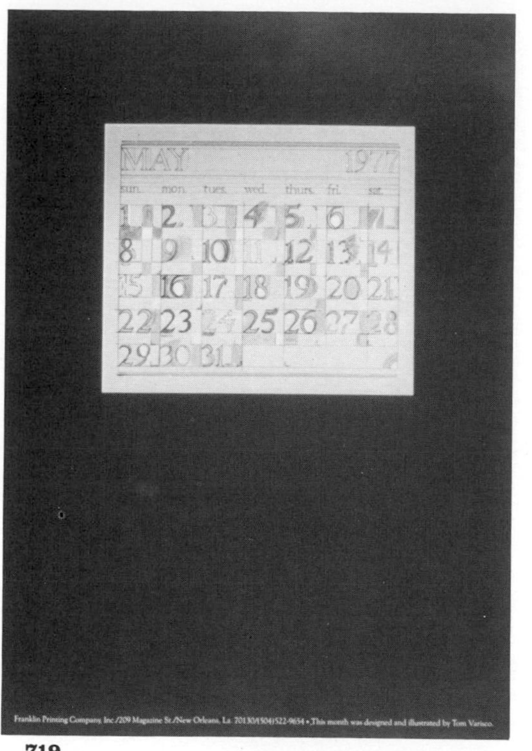

719

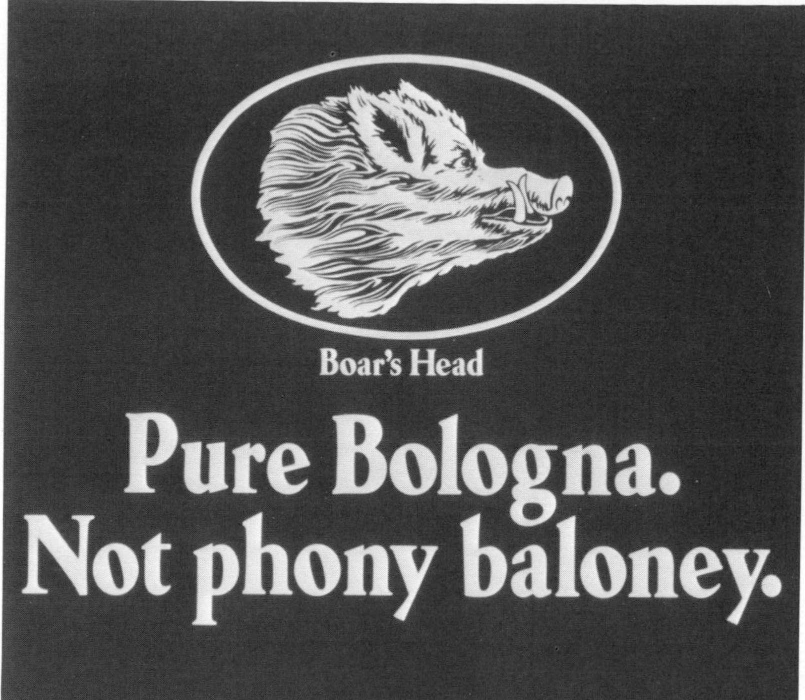

722

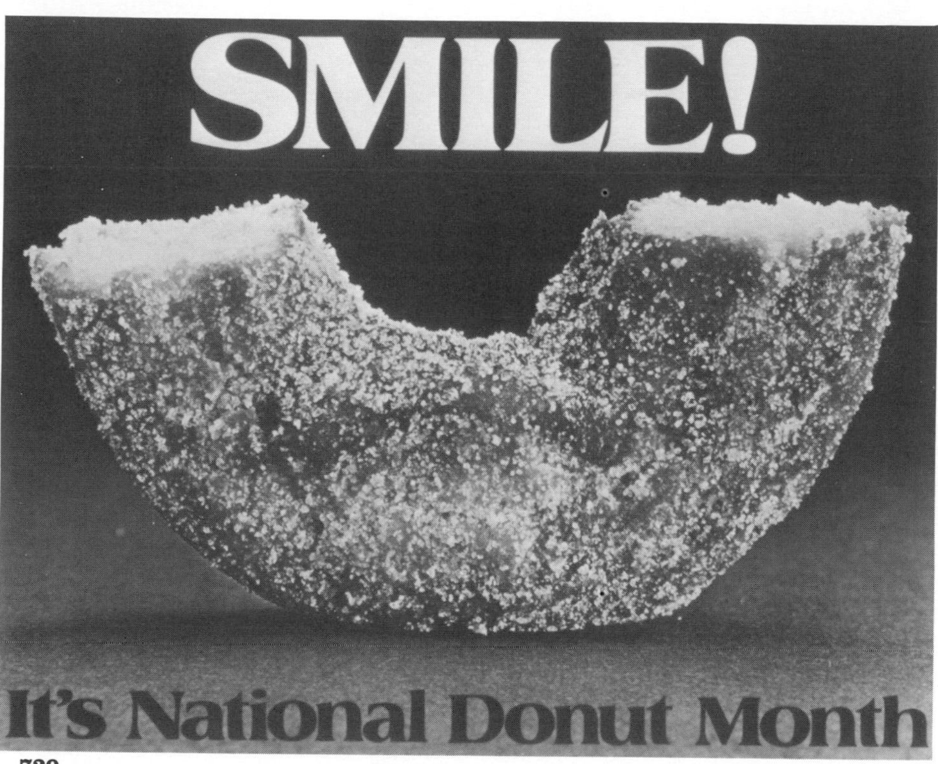

720

719
Art Director Tom Varisco
Writer Tom Varisco
Designer Tom Varisco
Artist Tom Varisco
Agency Tom Varisco Graphic Designs
Client Franklin Printing Co.

720
Art Directors William Pasternak, Jeffrey B. Nucey
Designer Brooks Betts
Photographer Wilson Southam
Agency Inner Thoughts Co., Inc.
Client Victor Friedman (DCA Company)

722
Art Director Robert Reitzfeld
Writer David Altschiller
Designer Robert Reitzfeld
Artist Robert Reitzfeld
Photographer Henry Sandbank
Agency Altschiller, Reitzfeld & Jackson
Client Boar's Head Provisions

723

724

725

723
Art Director Robert Reitzfeld
Writer Dick Jackson
Photographer Henry Sandbank
Agency Altschiller, Reitzfeld & Jackson
Client American Beverage Corp.

724
Art Director Bob Young
Writer John Eickmeyer
Designer Graphicsgroup, Inc./Atlanta
Artist Graphicsgroup, Inc./Atlanta
Agency Tracy-Locke Advertising
Client Haggar Slacks

725
Art Director Victor Della Barba
Writer Sara Bender
Designer Victor Della Barba
Artist Bob Byrd
Agency Lewis & Gilman
Client Bell of Pennsylvania

Call your father.

726

727

728

726
Art Director Victor Della Barba
Writer Sara Bender
Designer Victor Della Barba
Artist Bob Byrd
Agency Lewis & Gilman
Client Bell of Pennsylvania

727
Art Director Jeff Anthony
Writer Mary Jo Leverette
Artist Bill Vuksanovich
Agency N W Ayer/Chicago
Client OAG

728
Art Director Jesse Joseph Zellner
Designers Carol Travis
Jesse Joseph Zellner
Agency Kirkland College
Client Kirkland College

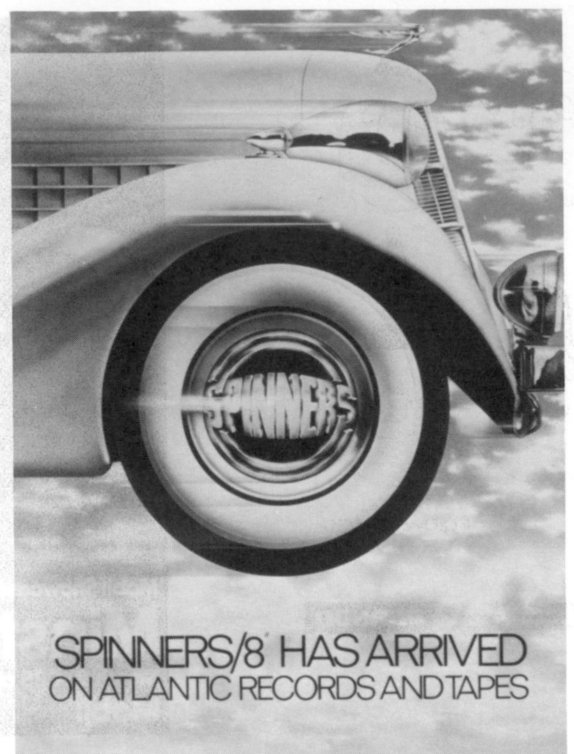

729

Christmas Tree
Films Incorporated · 1144 Wilmette Avenue · Wilmette Illinois 60091 · 312/256-3200

730

731

729
Art Director Bob Defrin
Designer Sandi Young
Artist Brian Zick
Agency Atlantic Records
Client Atlantic Records

730
Art Director Gerry Puglisi
Writer Vivian Bender
Artist David Povelities
Publisher Films Incorporated
Client Films Incorporated

731
Art Director Ron Carmel
Writer Harry London
Designer Ron Carmel
Photographer Allen Polansky
Agency Eisner & Associates, Inc.
Client Shoe Service Institute of America

732

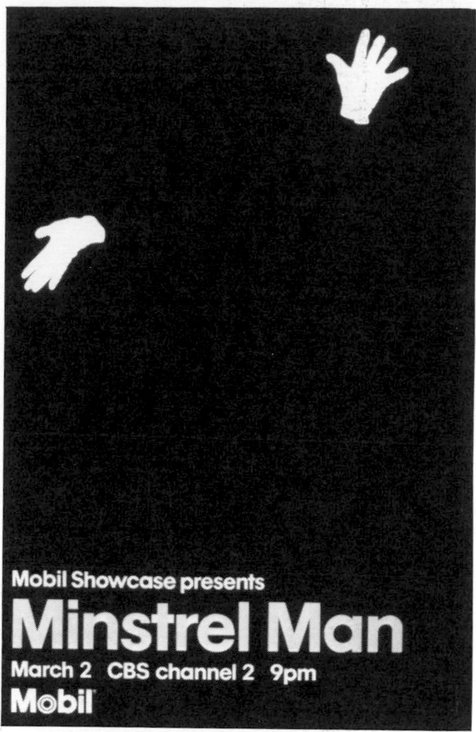

734

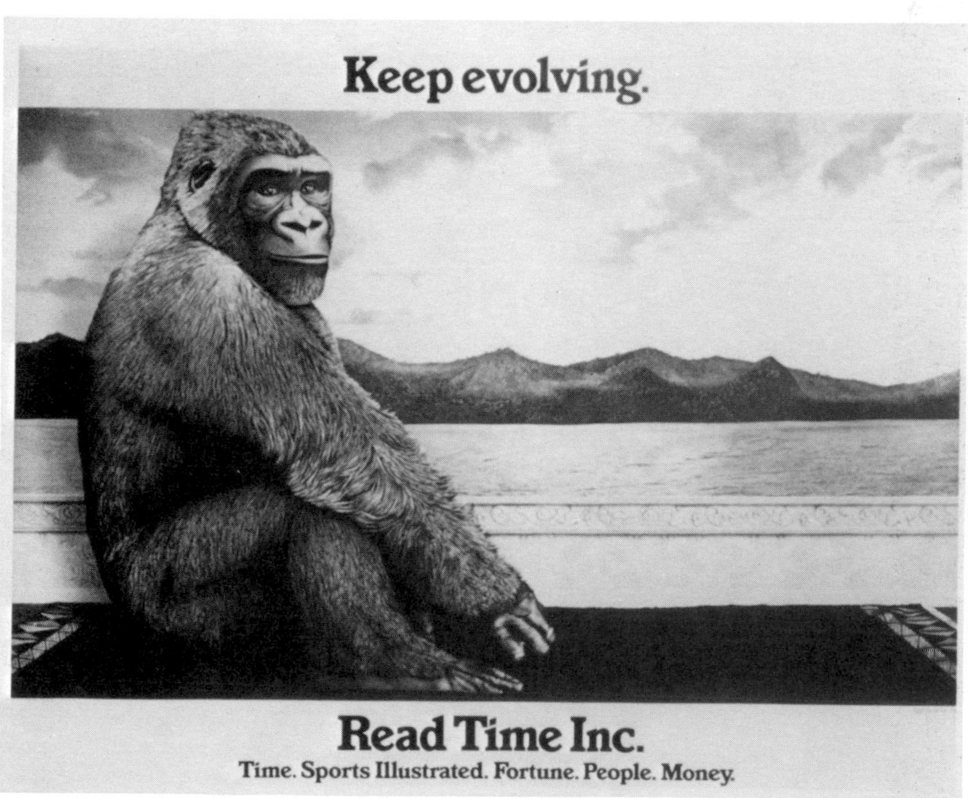

Keep evolving.
Read Time Inc.
Time. Sports Illustrated. Fortune. People. Money.

733

SILVER

732

Art Director	Bob Bidner
Writer	Ray Baker
Designer	Bob Bidner
Artists	Bob Bidner Tony Toscano
Production Company	McNaughton Litho.
Agency	Ted Bates & Co., Inc.
Client	Julius Wile Sons & Co. Inc.

733

Art Director	Bob Czernysz
Writer	Dick Olmsted
Artist	Tom Palmore
Agency	Young & Rubicam
Client	Time Incorporated

734

Art Director	Ivan Chermayeff
Writer	Mobil Oil Corp.
Designer	Ivan Chermayeff
Artist	Ivan Chermayeff
Printer	Crafton Graphics
Agency	Chermayeff & Geismar Associates
Client	Mobil Oil Corporation

735

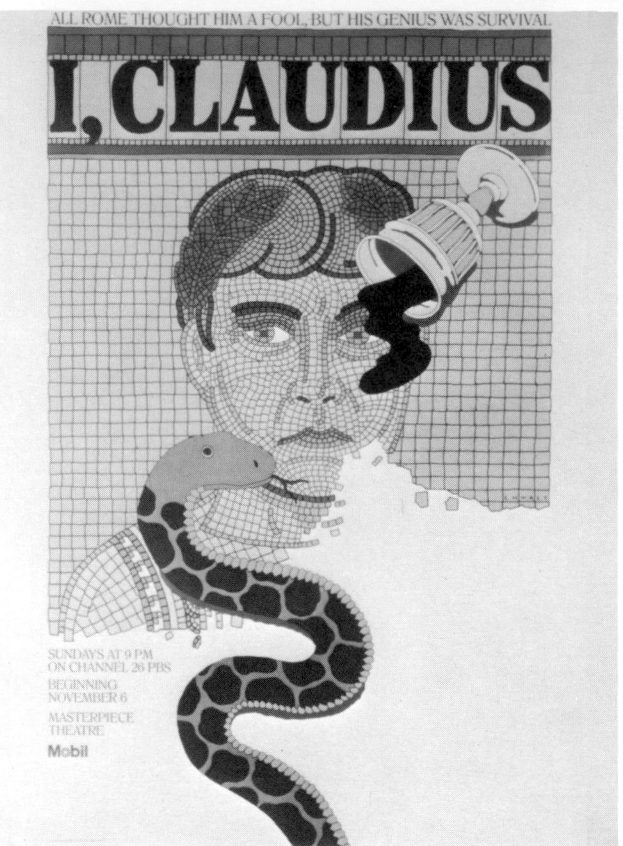

737

735
Art Director Ivan Chermayeff
Writer Mobil Oil Corp.
Designer Ivan Chermayeff
Artist Ivan Chermayeff
Printer Crafton Graphics
Agency Chermayeff & Geismar Assoc.
Client Mobil Oil Corp.

737
Art Director Seymour Chwast
Designer Seymour Chwast
Artist Seymour Chwast
Agency Push Pin Studios
Client Mobil Oil Corp.

738

EDDINGTON
Tosca
THE CLASSIC CHILLER BY PUCCINI ◆ STARRING METROPOLITAN OPERA TENOR MISHA RAITZIN*
OCTOBER 19*, 21*, 22*, 25 ◆◆◆ A BRIGHAM YOUNG UNIVERSITY MUSIC THEATER PRODUCTION
COSPONSORED BY THE BYU MUSIC DEPARTMENT AND ASBYU ◆◆◆ 8:00 PM. IN THE deJONG
CONCERT HALL, HFAC ◆◆ $1.00 FOR BYU STUDENTS, FACULTY, STAFF OR CHILDREN; $3.50 FOR
GENERAL ADMISSION ◆◆◆◆◆ MUSIC TICKET OFFICE, 375-7788 (CAMPUS, EXTENSION 3001)

739

738
Art Director Seymour Chwast
Designer Seymour Chwast
Artist John Collier
Agency Push Pin Studios
Client Mobil Oil Corp.

739
Art Director McRay Magleby
Writer Clayne Robison
Designer Ron Eddington
Artist Ron Eddington
Agency BYU Graphic Communications Dept.
Client Brigham Young University

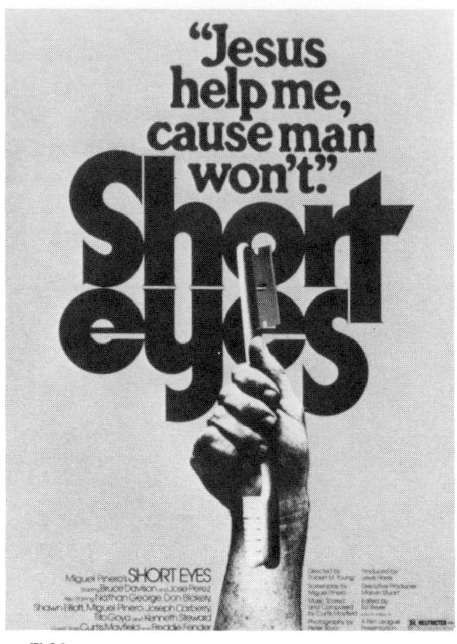

741

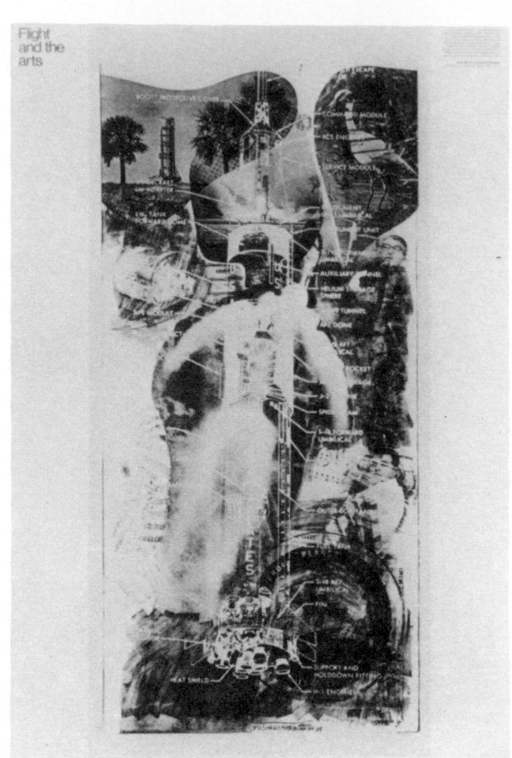

742

740

740
Art Director Neville Smith
Designer Neville Smith
Artist Neville Smith
Producer Viki Ball
Production Company Viki Ball & Associates
Client Folio Graphics

741
Art Director Alan Peckolick
Writer Miguel Pinero
Designer Alan Peckolick
Photographer Carl Fischer
Agency LSC&P Design Group
Client The Film League

742
Art Director James Dean
Writer David Brown
Designers James Miho
Tomoko Miho
Artist Robert Rauschenberg
Photographer Joel Breger
Publisher National Air and Space Museum
Agency Miho Inc.
Client National Air and Space Museum

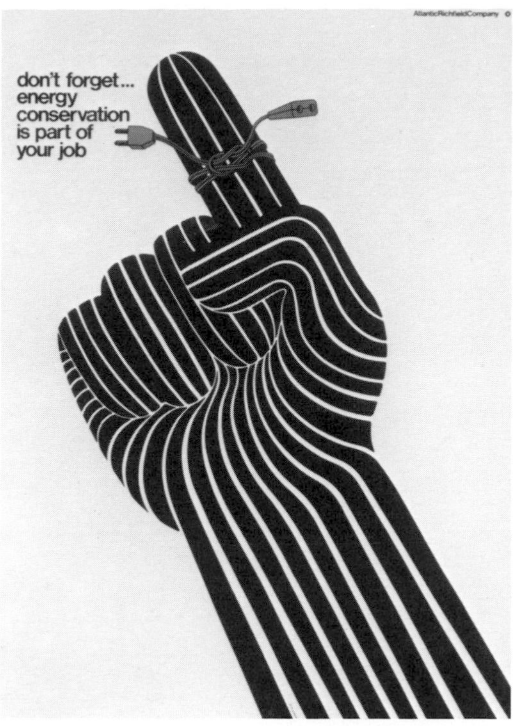

743

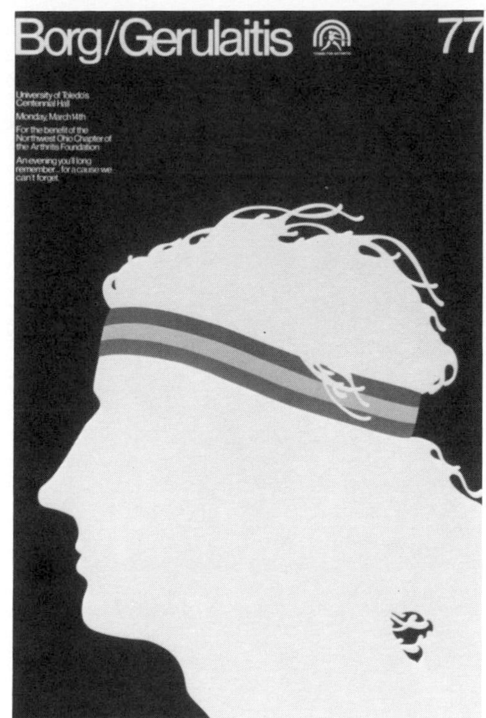

744

THE MARATHON · BODY · MIND · DISEASE PREVENTION

DATE : JULY 23 AT 8AM · PLACE : ORSON SPENCER HALL

745

743
Art Directors Lee Madox
Tom Kamifuji
Writer Mary Asroff
Director Tom Yerxa
Designer Tom Kamifuji
Artist Tom Kamifuji
Agency H. Tom Kamifuji & Associates
Client Atlantic Richfield Co.

744
Art Directors Terry Lesniewicz
Al Navarre
Designers Terry Lesniewicz
Al Navarre
Artists Terry Lesniewicz
Al Navarre
Agency Lesniewicz/Navarre
Client Northwest Ohio Chapter
of the Arthritis Foundation

745
Art Director Adrian Pulfer
Designer Adrian Pulfer
Artist Parry Merkley
Agency Two's Company
Client Governor's Council
on Physical Fitness

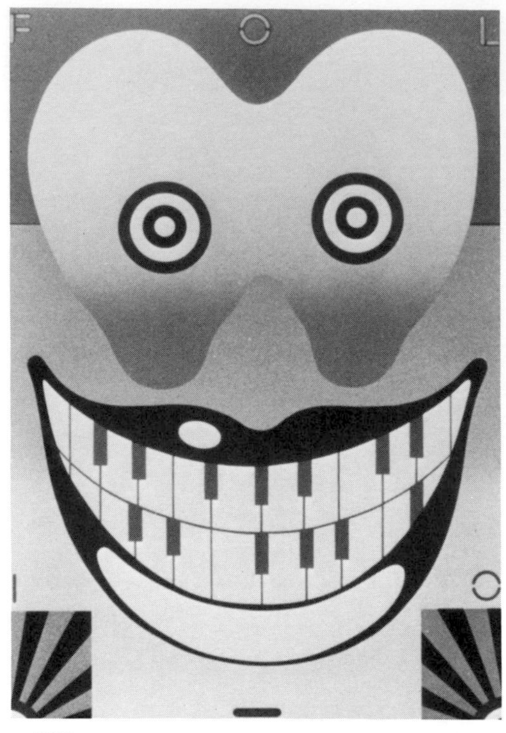

746

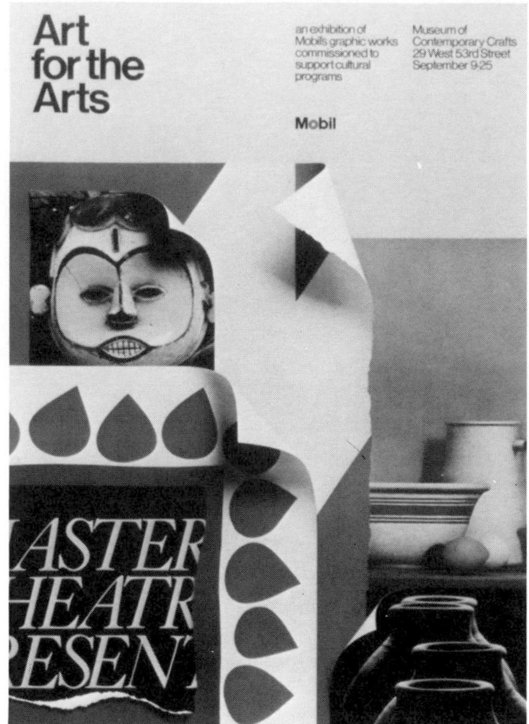

748

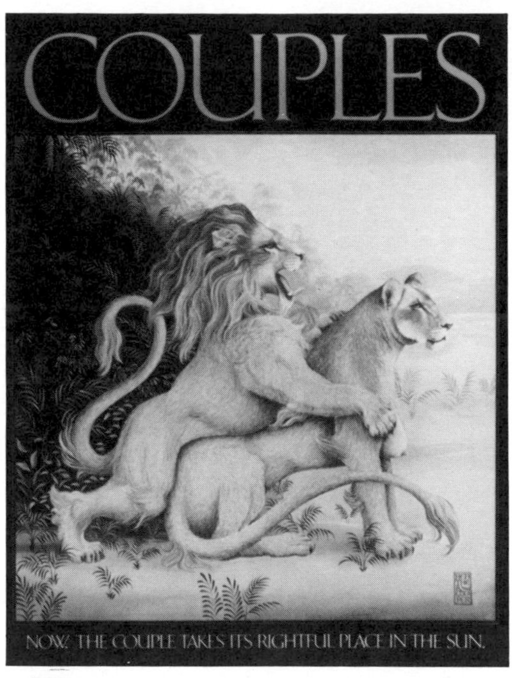

747

746
Director Tom Simons
Writer Jim Pappademas
Agency Hill, Holliday, Connors, Cosmopulos, Inc.
Client Boston Chapter—American Red Cross

747
Art Directors Alan Murphy, Heather Cooper
Designers Heather Cooper, Lawrence Finn
Artist Heather Cooper
Agency Alan Murphy & Associates
Client Couples Hotel—Jamaica

748
Art Director Arnold Saks
Designer Arnold Saks
Photographers Peggy Barnett, Ronald Barnett
Production Company Sanders Printing Corp.
Client Mobil Oil Corp.

749

750

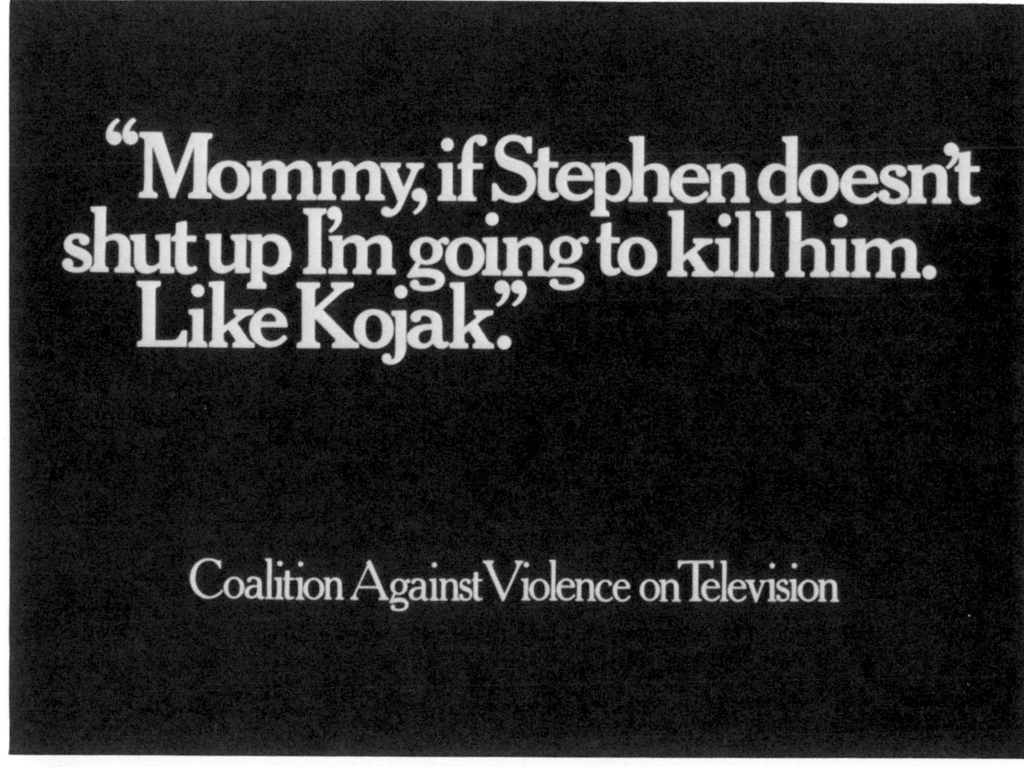

751

749
Art Director Heather Cooper
Designers Heather Cooper
Lawrence Finn
Artist Heather Cooper
Agency Burns, Cooper, Hynes Limited
Client Canadian Opera Company

750
Art Director G. Edward Gibbs
Writer Jim Smith
Designer G. Edward Gibbs
Artist Don Kellermeier
Agency Widerschein/
Strandberg Associates
Client WGTE-TV, Channel 30

751
Art Director Ron Anderson
Writer Tom McElligott
Agency Bozell & Jacobs/Mpls MN
Client Coalition Against TV Violen

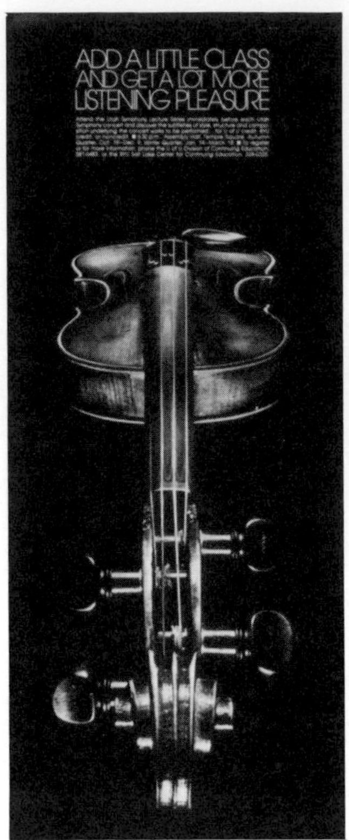

752

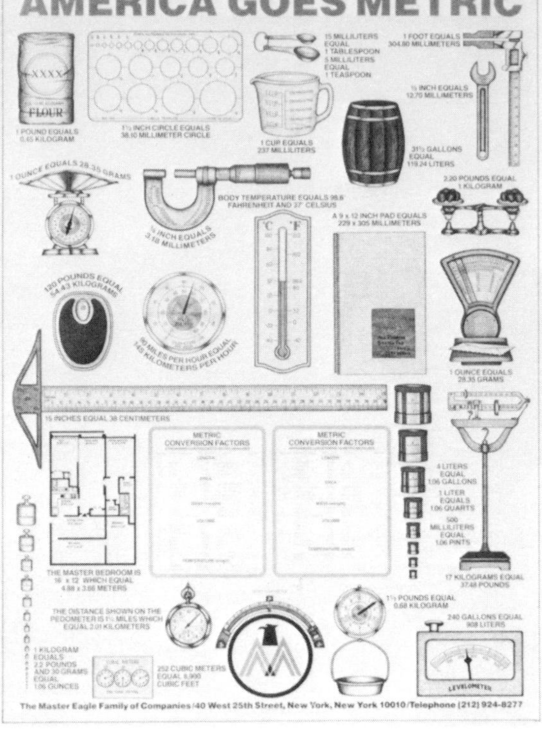

753

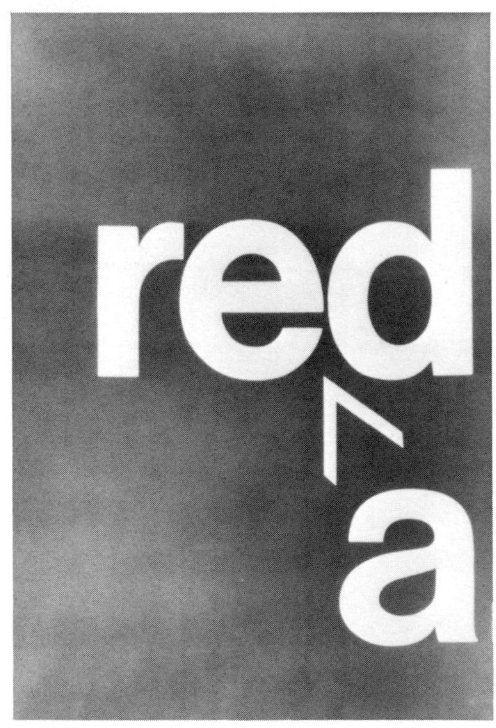

754

752
Art Director Michael B. Richards
Writer Polly Richman
Designer Glade Christensen
Photographer George M. Brown
Agency University of Utah Graphic Design
Client Division of Continuing Education, University of Utah

753
Art Director Penny Coleman
Writers Penny Coleman, Chuck Albano
Designer Penny Coleman
Artist Chuck Albano
Agency School of Visual Arts
Client Master Eagle Family of Companies

754
Art Director John Massey
Designer John Massey
Artist John Massey
Director John Massey
Client American Library Association

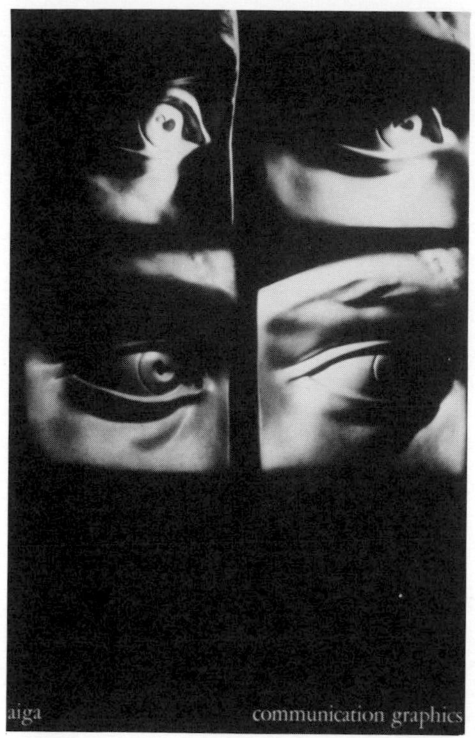

755

756

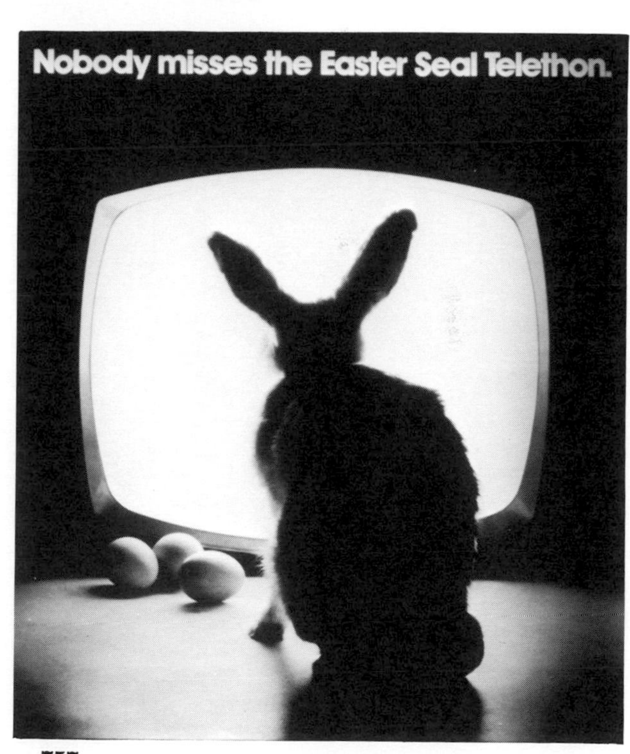

757

755
Art Director James Cross
Designer James Cross
Photographer James Cross
Agency James Cross Design Office, Inc.
Client American Institute of Graphic Arts

756
Designer Victor Di Cristo
Client Tekra Corp.

757
Art Director Gene Mandarino
Photographer Phil Marco
Agency Leo Burnett Company
Client Easter Seals

758

759

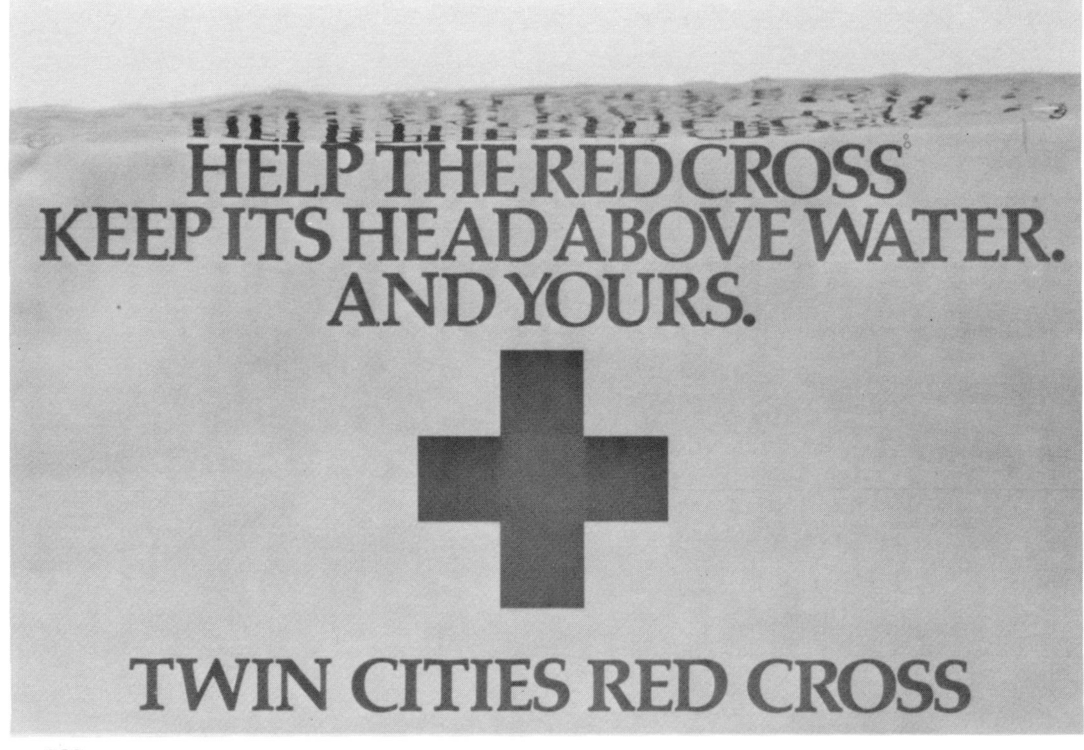

760

758
Art Director Doug Johnson
Writer Doug Johnson
Designer Anne Leigh
Artist James McMullan
Agency Performing Dogs
Client Society of Illustrators

759
Art Director Ron Anderson
Writer Tom McElligott
Agency Bozell & Jacobs
Client Twin Cities Red Cross

760
Art Director Ron Anderson
Writer Tom McElligott
Agency Bozell & Jacobs/Mpls MN
Client Twin Cities Red Cross

YOU DON'T GET THE
NOBEL PEACE PRIZE
FOR SERVING
COFFEE AND DONUTS.

TWIN CITIES RED CROSS

761

YOU CAN'T SQUEEZE BLOOD
FROM A TURNIP.

762

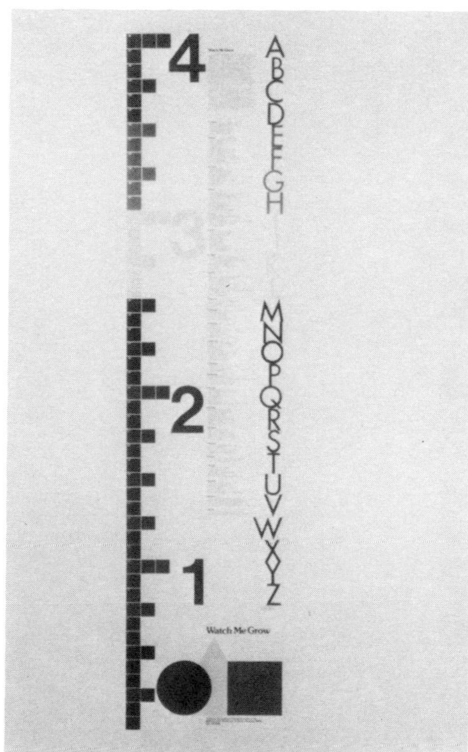
4
ABCDEFGH
3
MNOPQRSTUVWXYZ
2
1
Watch Me Grow

763

761
Art Director Ron Anderson
Writer Tom McElligott
Agency Bozell & Jacobs
Client Twin Cities Red Cross

762
Art Director Ron Anderson
Writer Tom McElligott
Designer Ron Anderson
Photographer Rick Dublin
Agency Bozell & Jacobs
Client Twin Cities Red Cross

763
Art Director Tom Bellucci
Designer Tom Bellucci
Agency The Graphic Attic
Client American Occupational Therapy Foundation

764

765

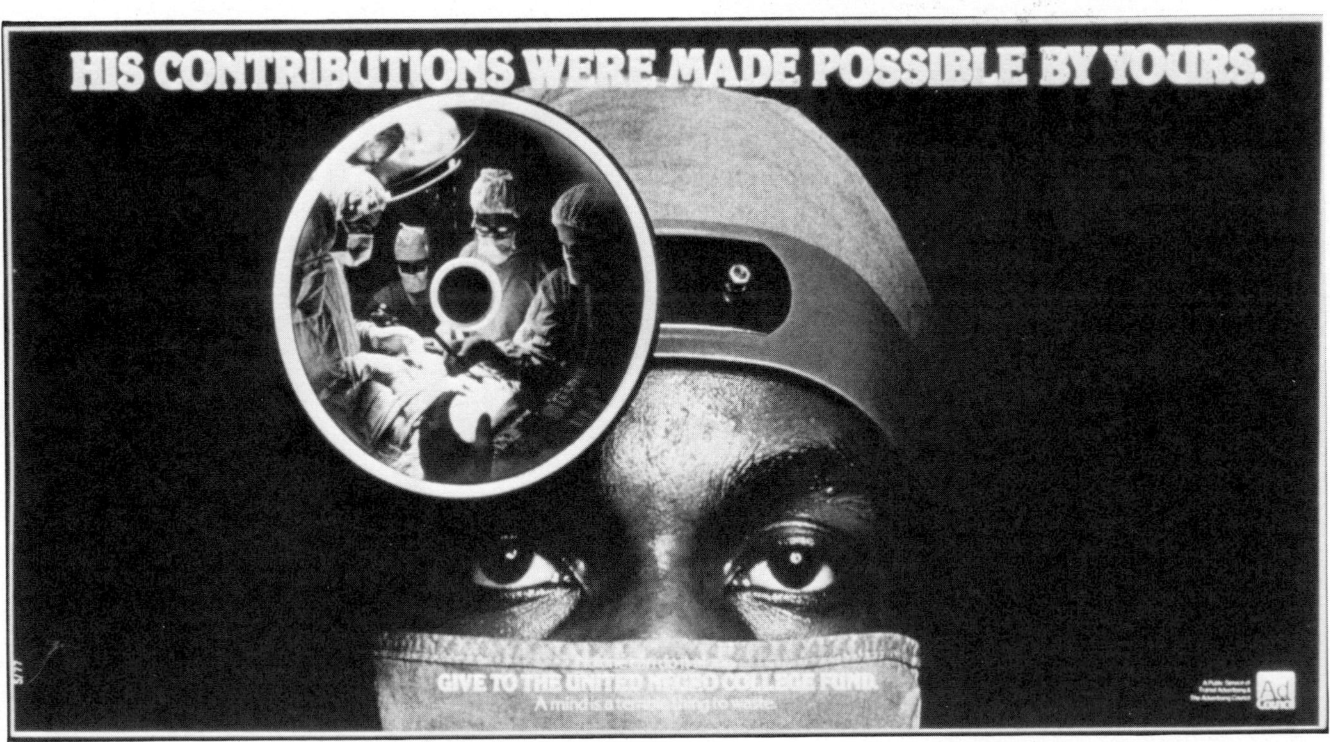

766

764
Art Director Kurt Meinecke
Writer Jane Brewer
Designer Kurt Meinecke
Artist Kurt Meinecke
Agency Stan Gellman Graphic Design, Inc.
Client Washington University

765
Art Director David Hausmann
Writer Tim Radford
Designer David Hausmann
Photographer David Hausmann
Agency National Endowment for the Arts
Client The Conservation Foundation

766
Art Director Edward Rotondi
Writer Dick Olmsted
Photographer Onofrio Paccione
Agency Young & Rubicam
Client United Negro College Fund

Books and Jackets

768

767

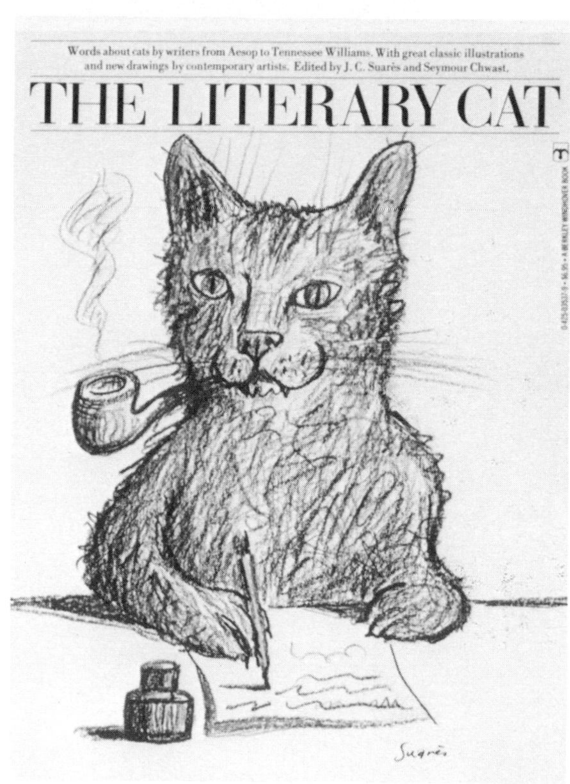

769

767

Art Director Kiyoshi Kanai
Writer Yoshinobu Tokugawa
Designer Kiyoshi Kanai
Artists Kiyoshi Kanai
Peter Siepmann
Photographers Ryoichi Takaku
Masao Tanaka
Publisher Japan Society
Agency Kiyoshi Kanai, Inc.
Client Japan Society

768

Art Directors R. D. Scudellari
Janet Odgis
Writer Mary Gilliatt
Editor Barbra Plumb
Designer Janet Odgis
Photographer (cover) Neal Slavin
(inside) Michael Dunne
Production Connie Mellon
Publisher Pantheon
Client Pantheon Books

769

Designer Seymour Chwast
Editor William E. Maloney
Producer Jean-Claude Suares
Agency Push Pin Studios
Client Push Pin Press

770

771

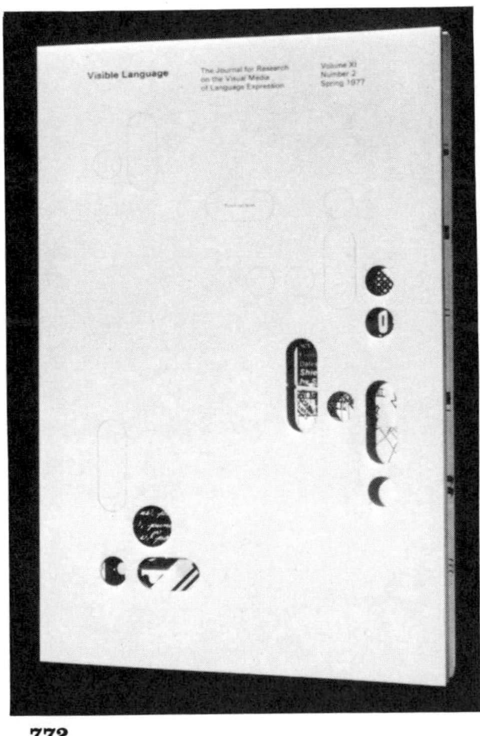

772

SILVER

770
Art Director B. Martin Pedersen
Writer Joseph Gribbins
Designer B. Martin Pedersen
Agency Jonson/Pedersen/Hinrichs
Client Nautical Quarterly Inc.

771
Designer George Delmerico
Writer Roger C. Sharpe
Photographer James Hamilton
Publisher E. P. Dutton

772
Art Director Sharon Poggenpohl
Guest Editor Aaron Marcus
Designers Sharon Poggenpohl
Carter Clock
Diane Hanau-Strain
Nikki Slusser-Krause
Publisher Merald E. Wrolstad
Client Visible Language

774

774
Designer Seymour Chwast
Writer William E. Maloney
Producer Jean-Claude Suares
Publisher Push Pin Press
Agency Push Pin Studios

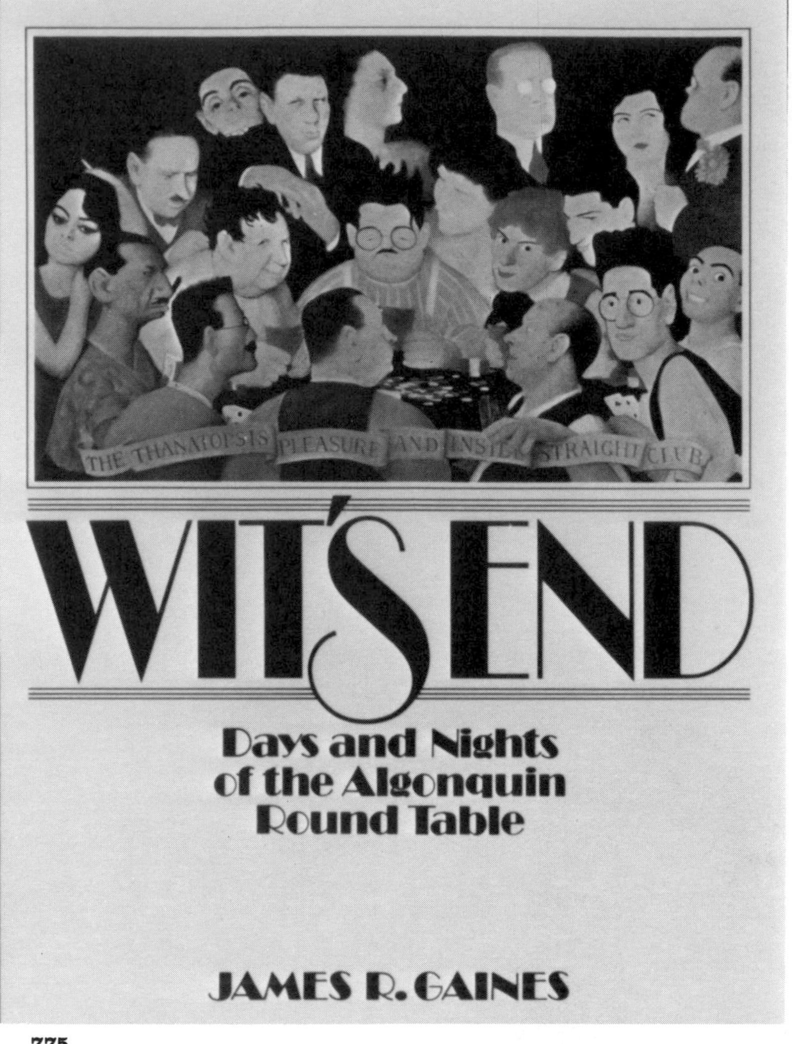

775

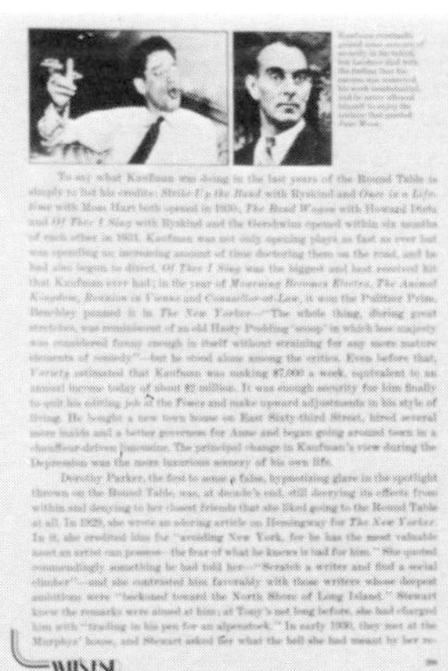

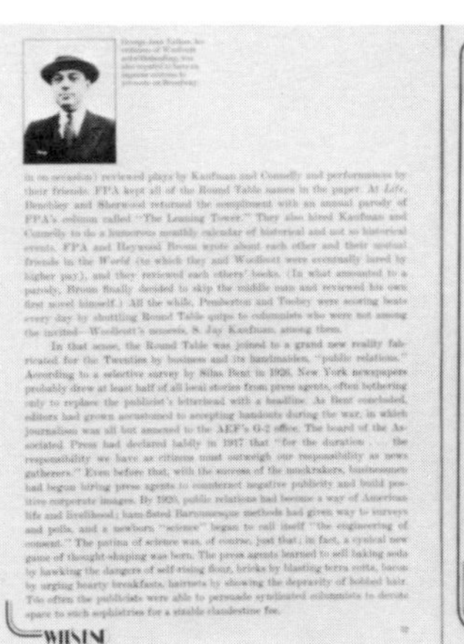

775

Art Director	Harris Lewine
Editor	Dan Okrent
Designers	Book—Stephanie Tevonian
	Jacket—Robert Anthony, Inc.
Publisher	Harcourt Brace Jovanovich, Inc.
Client	Harcourt Brace Jovanovich, Inc.

776

776

Art Director	**Bernie Klein**
Editor	**Toni Morrison**
Designer	**Jim Lambert**
Publisher	**Random House**
Client	**Random House**

777

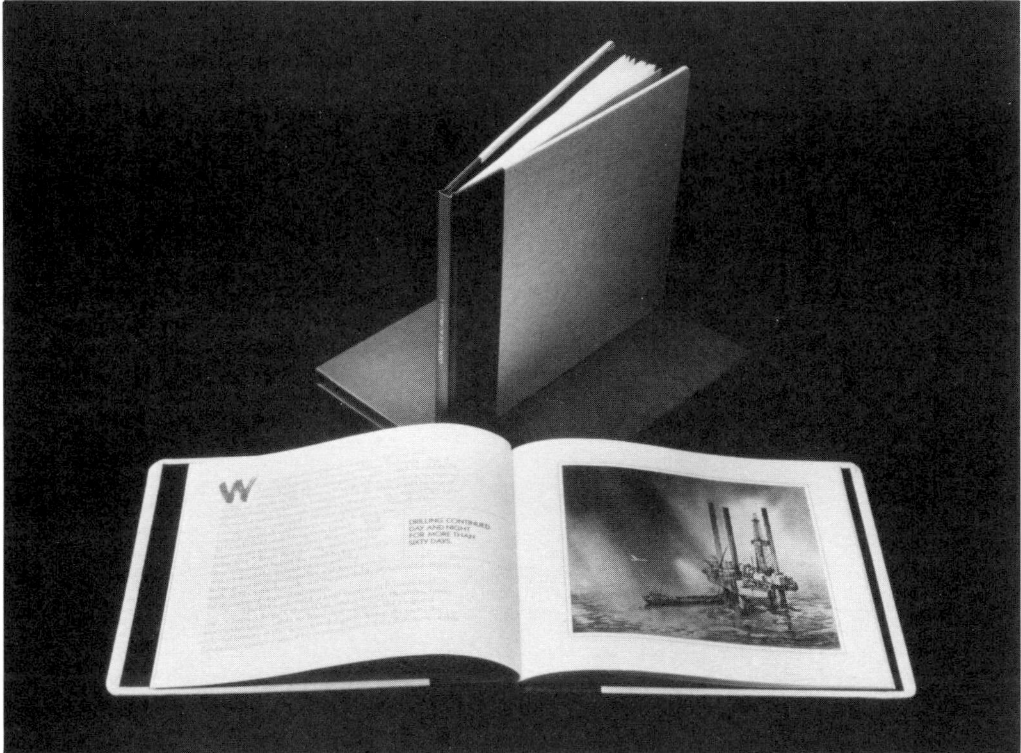

779

777

Art Director	Jaren Dahlstrom
Editor	John Pearson
Designer	Jaren Dahlstrom
Artist	Jaren Dahlstrom
Photographer	John Pearson
Production Company	Universal Printing Co.
Publisher	Addison-Wesley
Agency	Crow-Quill Studios
Client	Addison-Wesley

779

Art Director	Steven Sessions
Writers	Bill Paull Mica McCutcheon
Designer	Steven Sessions
Artist	Norman Baxter
Producer	Steven Sessions
Production Company	Fidelity Printing/Emmott Bookbinding
Publisher	Houston Natural Gas Corporation
Agency	Baxter & Korge, Inc.
Client	Houston Natural Gas Corporation

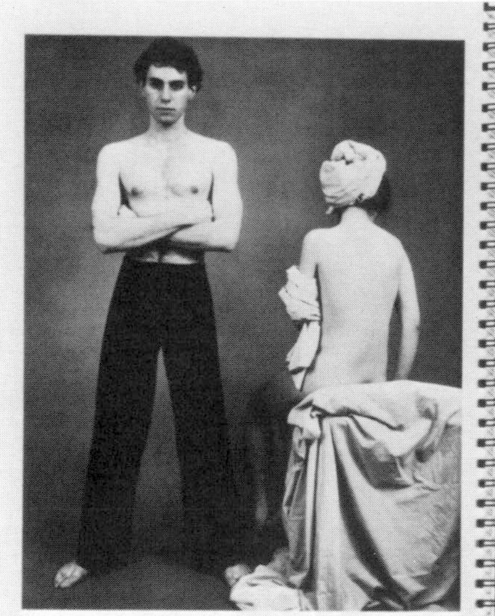

780

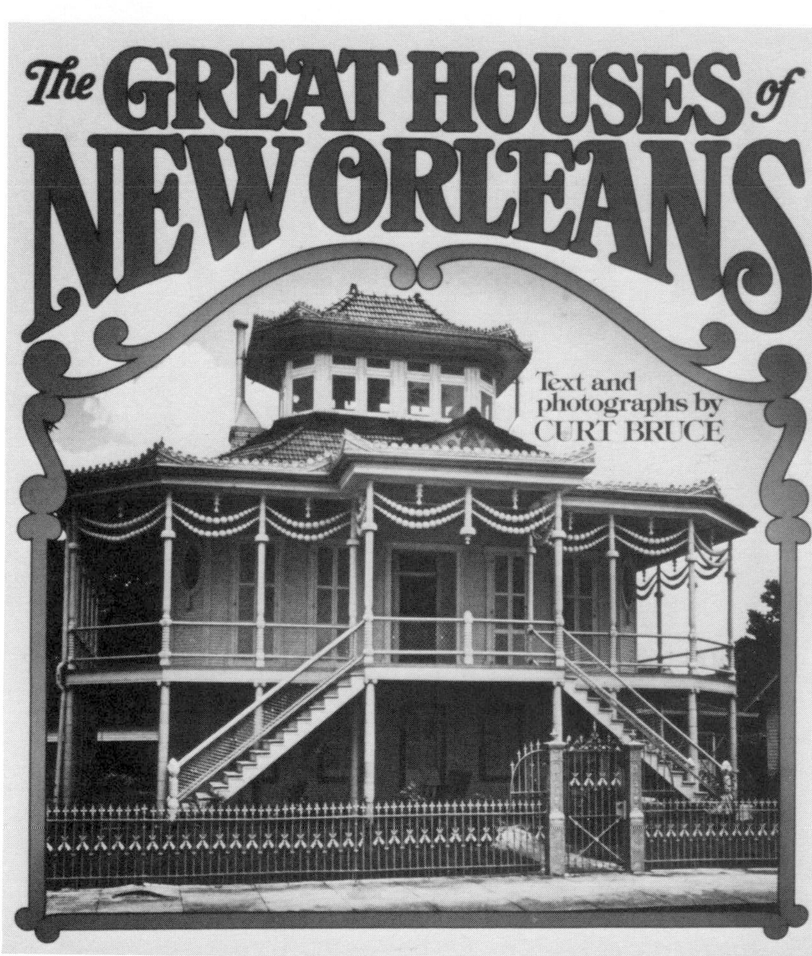

781

780

Art Directors	Lawrence Barth
	Robert Cummings
Designers	Robert Cummings
	Lawrence Barth
Artist	Karen Fredericks/cover
Photographer	Lawrence Barth
Client	The Cooper Union

781

Art Director	Betty Anderson
Writer	Curt Bruce
Editor	Ann Close
Designer	Camilla Filancia
Jacket Design	Ray Cruz
Jacket Art Director	Lidia Ferrara
Photographer	Curt Bruce
Production Manager	Marylea O'Reilly
Publisher	Alfred A. Knopf, Inc.
Client	Alfred A. Knopf, Inc.

782

the piercing, wild cry of the almighty hühn!

Gerhard sprang to his feet, ready to charge in the direction of the fearsome sound, but he couldn't find it. It sounded like there were hühns all around him, and for the first time in his life, Gerard felt real fear. Being regarded as one of the worst hunters in the Südheide Forest, Gerhard now had real doubts about his mission. Maybe all the things the others had said about the hühn were true. Maybe it did have the ability to breath fire. Maybe it was capable of luring hunters deeper and deeper into the wild until they were totally lost. And, oh yes, maybe it could become invisible.

By now Gerhard wasn't just frightened, he was petrified! Finally, human instinct took over, and he turned and ran as hard as he could to his hometown. After he had gone about a mile, he started to slow down, but over his panting breath, he could still hear the hühn. He really wished he had never been so hasty as to try to hunt the hühn alone. The hühn was chasing him, and he couldn't even see it.

As he came within looking distance of Eschede he suddenly felt ashamed. He had planned his hunt with a selfish motive. His main concern should have been for the welfare of his family and friends, not his personal

gain. He was getting just payment for this: he was being driven back to town by the sounds of something he couldn't even see. As he entered the gates of his village he could still hear the dreaded bird. Was this sound going to haunt him for the rest of his life?

783

782	
Art Director	Betty Anderson
Editor	Victoria Wilson
Designer	Virginia Tan
Jacket Art Director/Designer	Lidia Ferrara
Photographer	George Bennett
Production Manager	Marylea O'Reilly
Publisher	Alfred A. Knopf, Inc.
Client	Alfred A. Knopf, Inc.

783	
Art Director	Frank Nichols
Writer	Frank Nichols
Designer	Frank Nichols
Artists	Various
Publisher	ArtHouse Press
Agency	Dodo Graphics
Client	Dodo Graphics

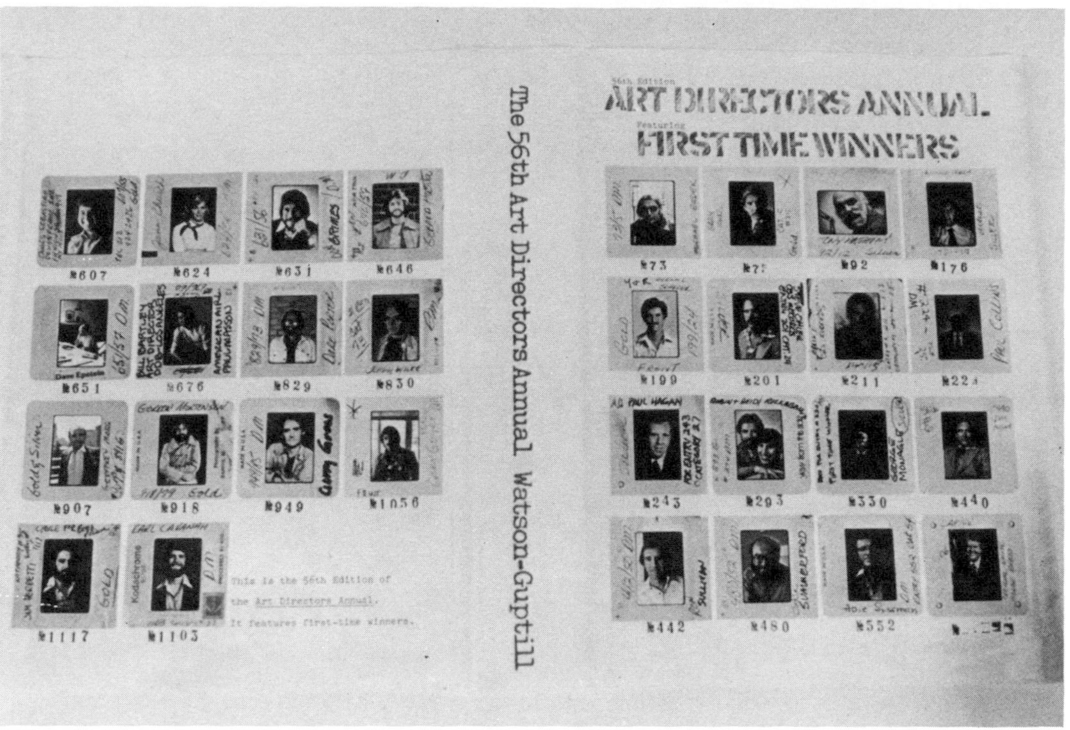

784

785

784

Art Director Lawrence Miller, Design Alliance, Inc.
Writer John McCormick
Editor Jennifer Place
Designer Lawrence Miller
Artists Peter Roth
Ellen Shapiro
Ed Marson
Lou Myers
Phil Marco
Louise Fili
Scott Bivans
Bob Salpeter, Lopez Salpeter
Harvey Bernstein, Design Alliance
Gene Federico, Lord Geller Federico
Don Reilly, Hour Hands, Inc.
Ira Mazer
Herman Estever
Ivan Chermayeff
Photographer Peter Roth
Publisher Watson Guptill Publications
Agency Design Alliance, Inc.

785

Art Director Nai Chang
Writer Michael Crichton
Designer Patrick Cunningham
Publisher Harry N. Abrams, Inc.

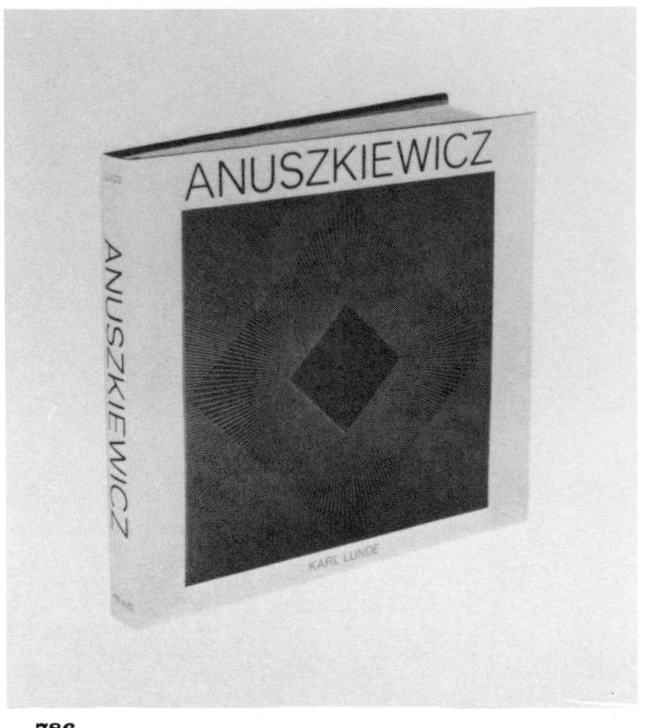

786

787

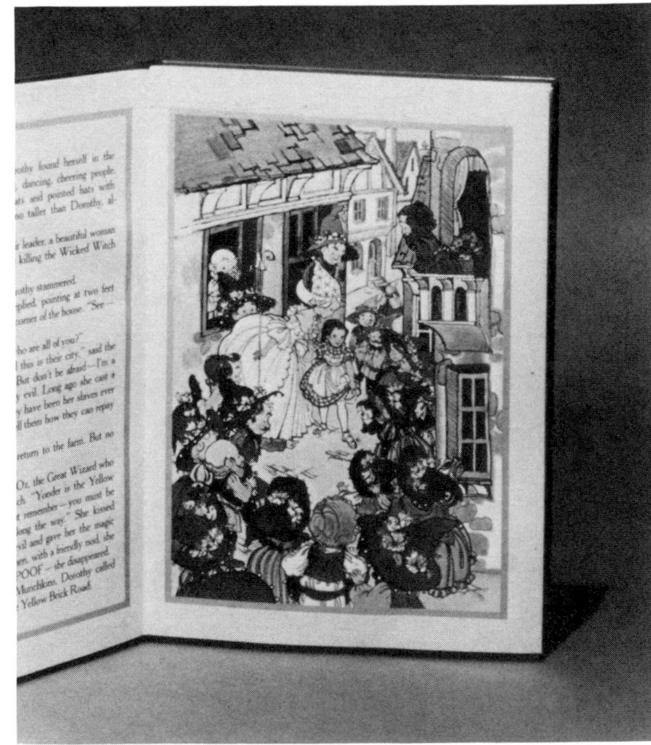

788

786
Art Director Nai Chang
Writer Karl Lunde
Designer Wei Wen Chang
Publisher Harry N. Abrams, Inc.

787
Art Director Nai Chang
Writer David Finn
Designer Ulrich Ruchti
Photographer David Finn
Publisher Harry N. Abrams, Inc.

788
Art Director Bill Hunt
Writer Ed Cunningham
Designer Bruce Baker
Artist Pat Paris
Paper Dimensionals Dick Dudley
Publisher Hallmark Cards
Client Hallmark Cards

789

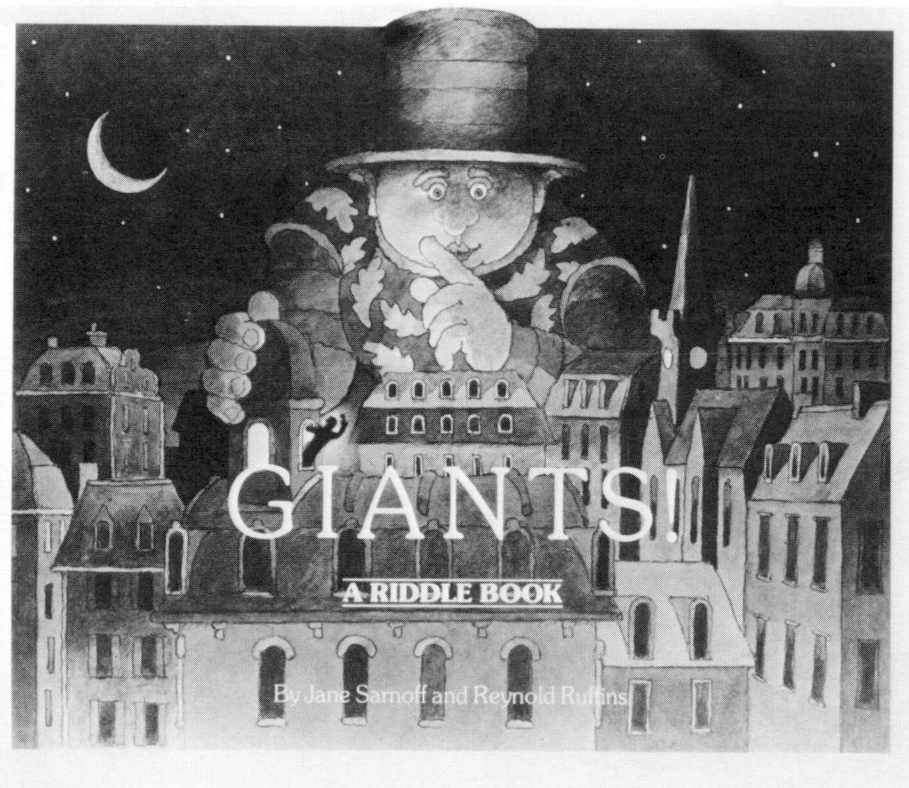

790

789
Art Director May Cutler
Writer John Lim
Designer Rolf Harder
Artist John Lim
Publisher Tundra Books of Montreal

790
Art Director Diana Hrisinko
Writer Jane Sarnoff
Designer Reynold Ruffins
Artist Reynold Ruffins
Publisher Charles Scribner's Sons
Client Charles Scribner's Sons

It's So Nice to Have a Wolf Around the House
Story by Harry Allard
Pictures by James Marshall

791

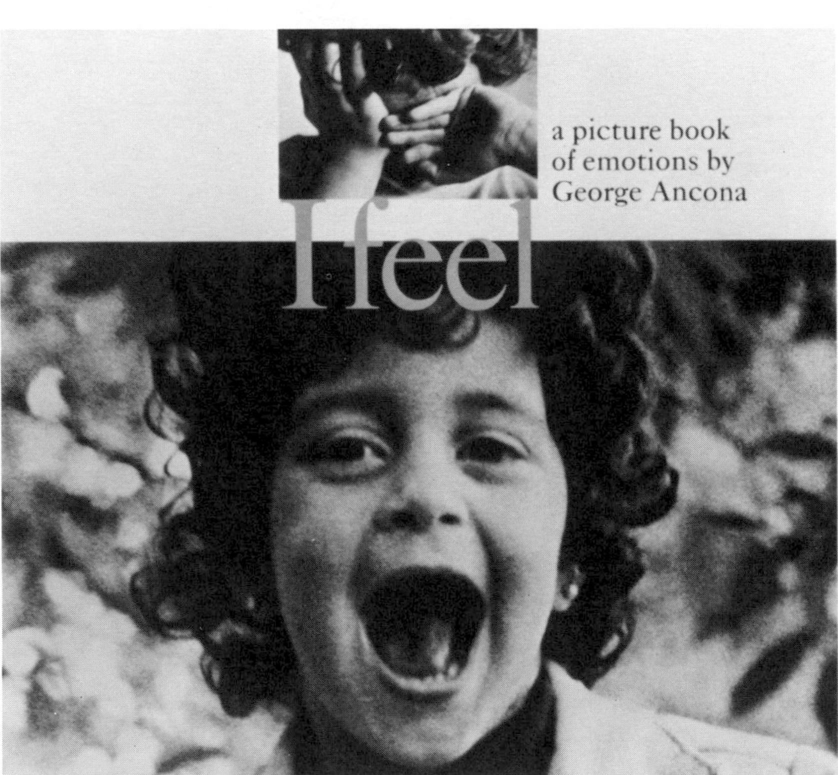

a picture book of emotions by George Ancona
I feel

792

791

Art Director	Diana Klemin
Editor	Joanna Cole
Designers	Joseph Merlo Randall Mize
Artist	James Marshall
Publisher	Doubleday & Company, Inc.
Client	Doubleday & Company, Inc.

792

Art Directors	Riki Levinson George Ancona
Writer	George Ancona
Designer	George Ancona
Photographer	George Ancona
Production Company	George Ancona, Inc.
Publisher	E. P. Dutton

793

794

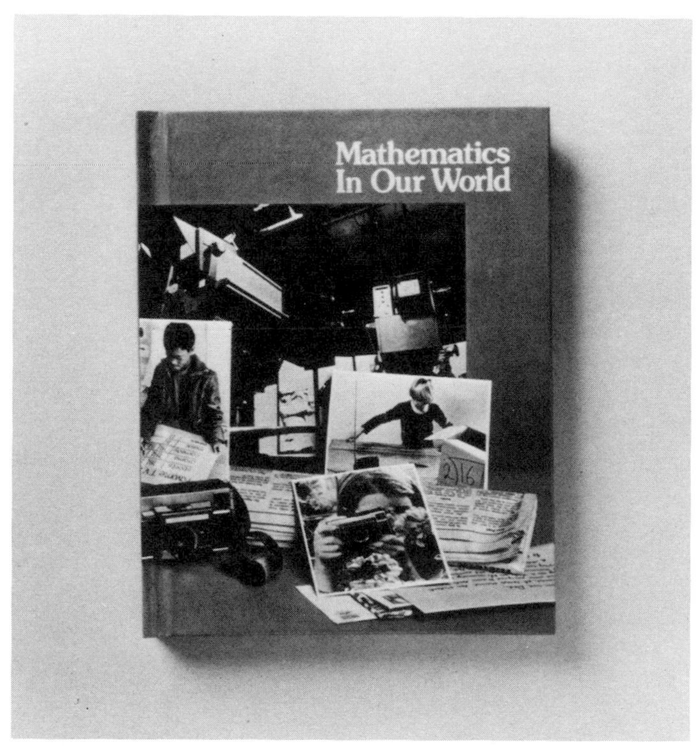

795

793
Art Director Diana Hrisinko
Writer Anne Diven
Designer Diana Hrisinko
Artist Mercer Mayer
Publisher Charles Scribner's Sons
Client Charles Scribner's Sons

794
Art Director Barbara Hennessy
Writer Betsy Maestro
Editor Norma Jean Sawicki
Designers Giulio Maestro
Barbara Hennessy
Artist Giulio Maestro
Publisher Crown Publishers, Inc.
Client Crown Publishers, Inc.

795
Art Director Ann Remen
Writers Robert E. Eicholz
Phares G. O'Daffer
Charles R. Fleenor
Designers Don Fujimoto
Don Taka
Cynthia Bassett
Artists Various
Photographers Various
Publisher Addison-Wesley Publishing Compa
Client Addison-Wesley Publishing Compa

796

797

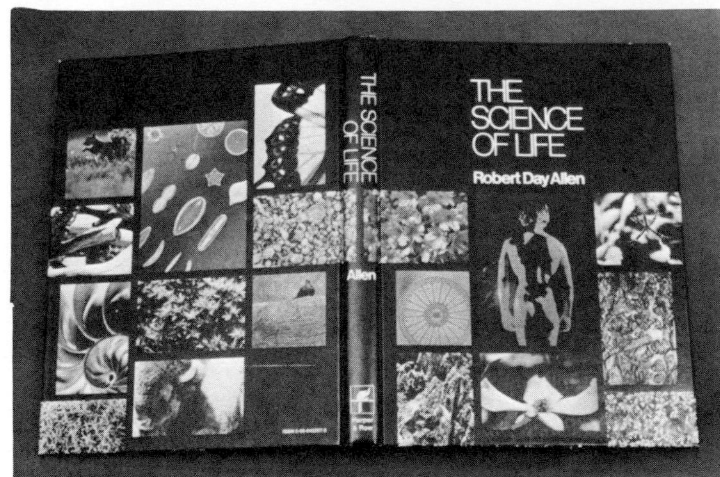

798

796
Art Director Beth Lambert
Writer Del Alberti
Designer Beth Lambert
Artist Beth Lambert
Publisher Expanding Development, Inc.
Agency Cook, Ruef, Spann & Weiser, Inc.
Client Expanding Development, Inc.

797
Art Director Gill Fishman
Writer Michael Markman
Designers Gill Fishman
Fredric Golinko
Publisher American Jewish Historical Society
Agency Gill Fishman Associates
Client American Jewish Historical Society

798
Art Director Howard Leiderman
Designer Emily Harste
Artist J & R Technical Services Inc.
Publisher Harper & Row, Publishers Inc.

799

800

801

799
Art Director Ann Remen
Writer Henry A. Bamman
Designer Design Office/Bruce Kortebein
Artists Nicolas Sidjakov, Wayne Bonnett, Mary Knowles, Kinuko Craft, Pat Maloney, Bob Haydock, Karen Sasaki, Victor Moscoso, Ewald Brewer
Publisher Addison-Wesley Publishing Company
Agency Design Office
Client Addison-Wesley Publishing Company

800
Art Director Harris Lewine
Editor John Ferrone
Designer John Alcorn
Artist John Alcorn
Publisher Harcourt Brace Jovanovich, Inc.
Client Harcourt Brace Jovanovich, Inc.

801
Art Director Dick Athey
Designer Ron Seichrist
Artist Anita Rose
Photographer Ron Seichrist
Agency Webb & Athey, Inc.
Client Kingsmill on the James

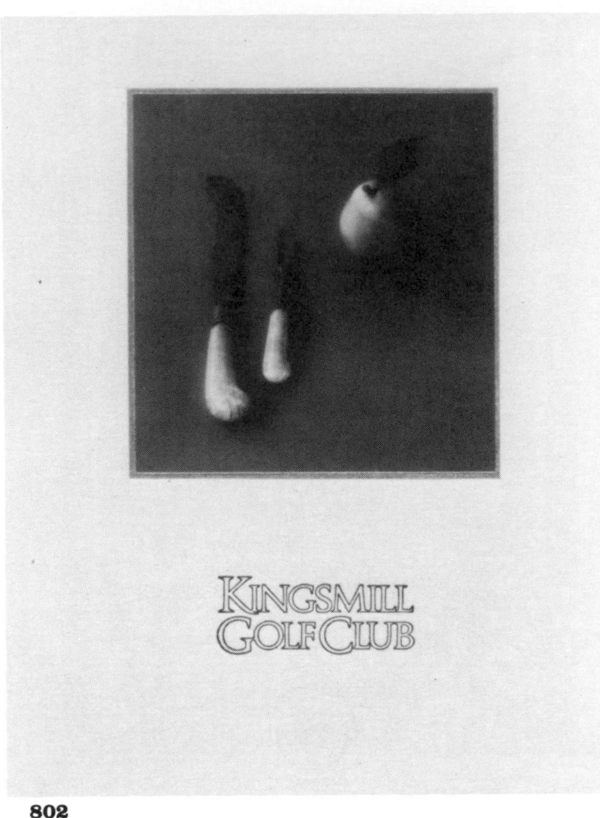
KINGSMILL
GOLF CLUB

802

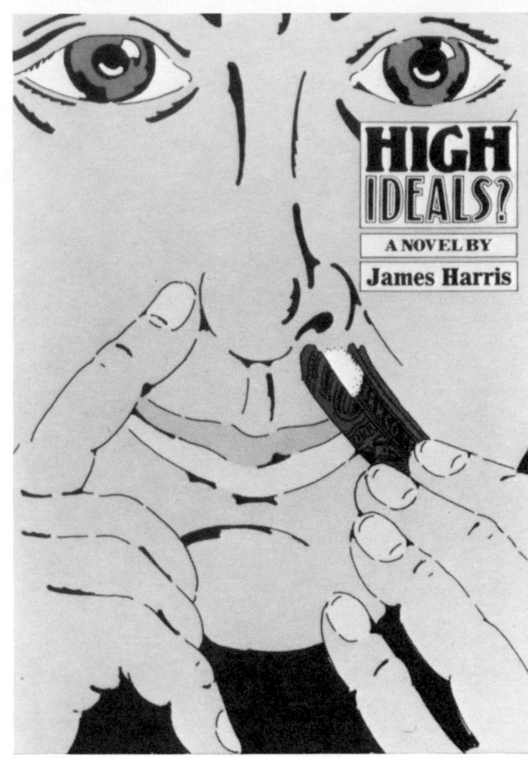
HIGH
IDEALS?
A NOVEL BY
James Harris

803

As though scared off by the Serbian cannon, the fog moved down…and thickened into a great dense skein above the Morava, rolling along the river's meandering course. A mild, bright day rose over the earth, with the sky forming a wide, deep arc above the mountain and the great battle being fought there. An autumn day such as one could not have hoped for…had flown down this morning over Serbia like a wild goose over a newly sown field.

Ivan looked around him, fascinated: the mountains with their snowy white peaks loomed up into the light and blueness, into eternity and peace. The war, the battle, was taking place in the fog, in the foothills, in some pit at the bottom of the earth. The bright light and the intense blue brought tears to his eyes, and he took off his glasses: yes, the war would end in the fog, in the streams. No battle could be fought under this blue sky; one could not kill people in such bright light.
0-15-190448-0

HARCOURT
BRACE
JOVANOVICH

DOBRICA
ĆOSIĆ
A
TIME
OF
DEATH
HBJ

DOBRICA ĆOSIĆ
A TIME OF
DEATH

804

802
Art Director Dick Athey
Designer Ron Seichrist
Artist Anita Rose
Photographer Ron Seichrist
Agency Webb & Athey, Inc.
Client Kingsmill on the James

803
Art Director Harris Lewine
Editor Gayle Benderoff
Designer Seymour Chwast
Artist Seymour Chwast
Publisher Harcourt Brace Jovanovich, Inc.
Client Harcourt Brace Jovanovich, Inc.

804
Art Director Harris Lewine
Editor Drenka Willen
Designer Stan Zagorski
Artist Stan Zagorski
Publisher Harcourt Brace Jovanovich, Inc.
Client Harcourt Brace Jovanovich, Inc.

805

806

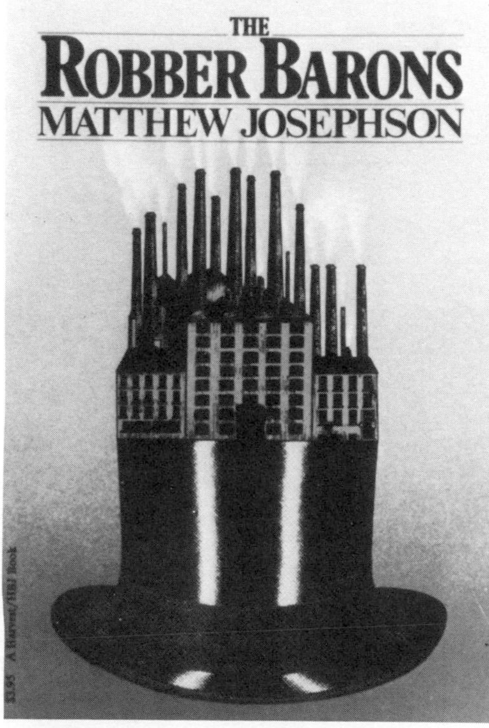

807

805
Art Director Harris Lewine
Editor John Ferrone
Designer Bascove
Artist Bascove
Publisher Harcourt Brace Jovanovich, Inc.
Client Harcourt Brace Jovanovich, Inc.

806
Art Director Harris Lewine
Editor Helen Wolff
Designer Bascove
Artist Bascove
Publisher Harcourt Brace Jovanovich, Inc.
Client Harcourt Brace Jovanovich, Inc.

807
Art Director Harris Lewine
Editor John Ferrone
Designer Richard Mantel
Artist Richard Mantel
Publisher Harcourt Brace Jovanovich, Inc.
Client Harcourt Brace Jovanovich, Inc.

808

809

810

808
Art Director Harris Lewine
Editor Helen Wolff
Designer Bascove
Artist Bascove
Publisher Harcourt Brace Jovanovich, Inc.
Client Harcourt Brace Jovanovich, Inc.

809
Art Director Harris Lewine
Editor John Ferrone
Designer Bascove
Artist Bascove
Publisher Harcourt Brace Jovanovich, Inc.
Client Harcourt Brace Jovanovich, Inc.

810
Art Director Harris Lewine
Editor John Ferrone
Designer Bascove
Artist Bascove
Publisher Harcourt Brace Jovanovich, Inc.
Client Harcourt Brace Jovanovich, Inc.

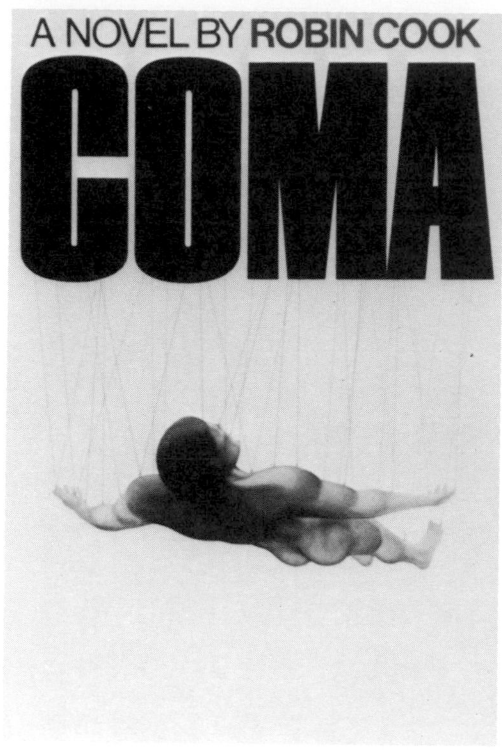

811

812

813

811
Art Director Char Lappan
Artist Paul Bacon
Publisher Little, Brown and Company
Client Little, Brown and Company

812
Art Director Alex Gotfryd
Jacket Typography Abby Goldstein
Artist Ron Becker
Publisher Doubleday & Company, Inc.
Client Doubleday & Company Inc.

813
Art Director Rocco Campanelli
Artist Rocco Campanelli
Agency David Deutsch Associates, Inc.
Client Air Afrique

815

816

815
Art Director Harris Lewine
Editor John Ferrone
Designer Bascove
Artist Bascove
Publisher Harcourt Brace Jovanovich, Inc.
Client Harcourt Brace Jovanovich, Inc.

816
Art Director Harris Lewine
Editor Gene Stone
Designer Harris Lewine
Artist Richard Hess
Publisher Harcourt Brace Jovanovich, Inc.
Client Harcourt Brace Jovanovich, Inc.

817

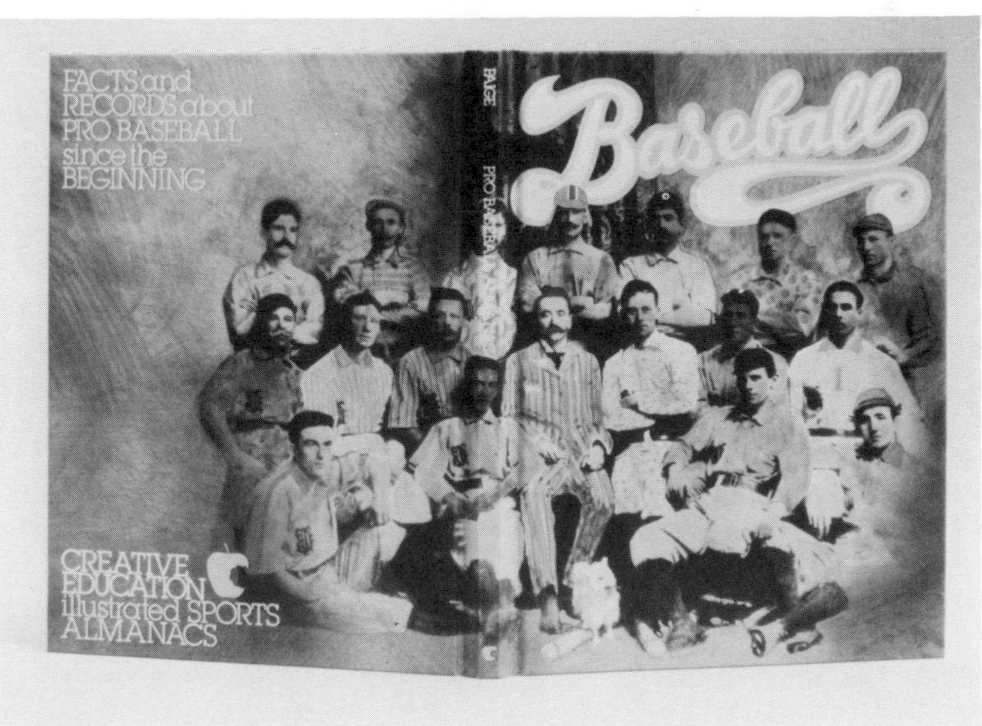

818

817
Art Director R. D. Scudellari
Writer Charles Elliot
Designer R. D. Scudellari
Artist Photo retouching: Joe Ramer
Photographer Felix Nadar
Publisher Alfred A. Knopf
Agency Alfred A. Knopf

818
Art Director Mark Landkamer
Writer Mark Landkamer
Designer Mark Landkamer
Artist John Keely
Publisher Creative Education
Agency Creative Education
Client Creative Education

819

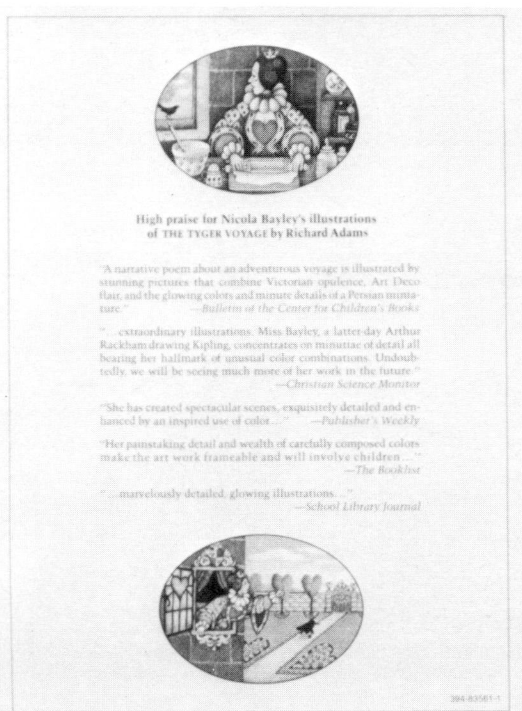

820

819	
Art Director	Marty Neumeier
Writer	Stephen Cosgrove
Designer	Kathleen Trainor
Illustrator	Robin James
Publisher	Creative Education
Agency	Marty Neumeier Design
Client	Creative Education

820	
Art Director	Sallie Baldwin
Editor	Fabio Coen
Designers	Sallie Baldwin
	Spencer Drate
Illustrator	Nicola Bayley
Publisher	Alfred A. Knopf/New York

821

822

823

821
Art Director May Cutler
Writer John Lim
Designer Rolf Harder
Artist John Lim
Publisher Tundra Books of Montreal

822
Art Director Mark Landkamer
Designer Mark Landkamer
Artist Joe Greenwald
Publisher Creative Education
Agency Creative Education
Client Creative Education

823
Art Director Skip Sorvino
Editorial Director Ray Shepard
Designer Christopher Austopchuck
Publisher Scholastic Magazines, Inc.
Agency Scholastic Magazines, Inc.
Client Scholastic Magazines, Inc.

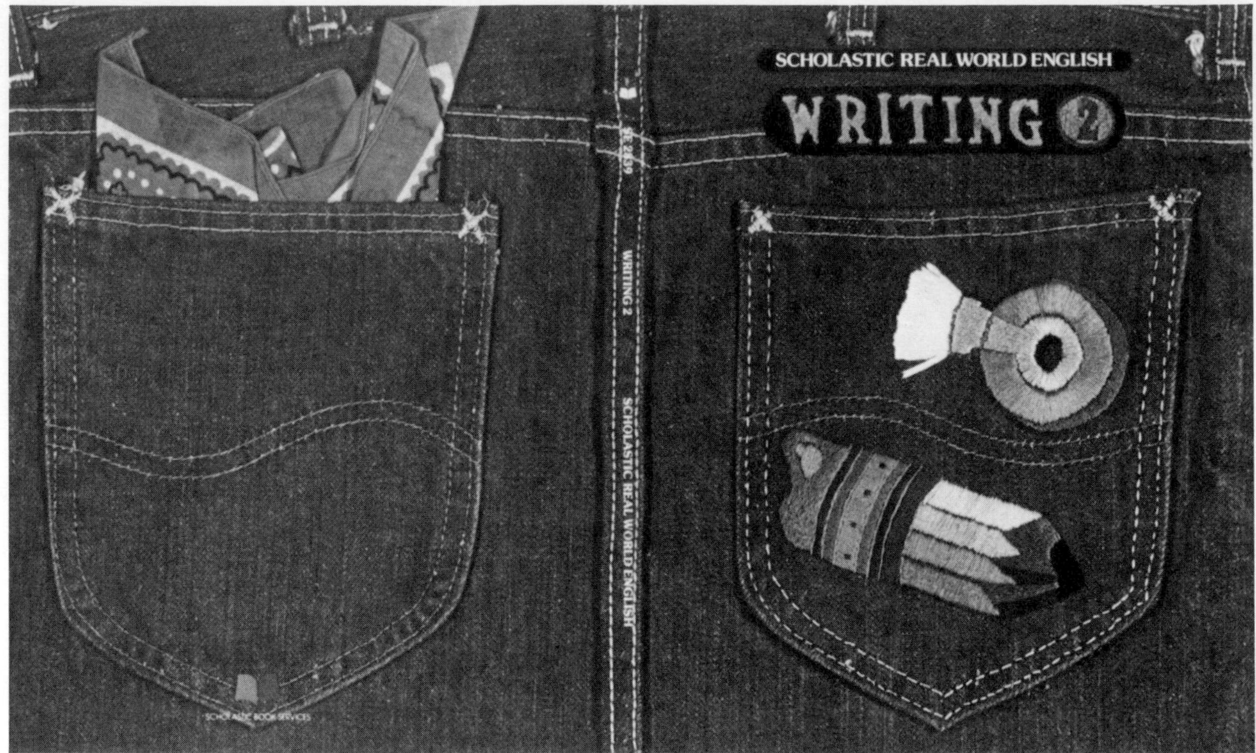

824

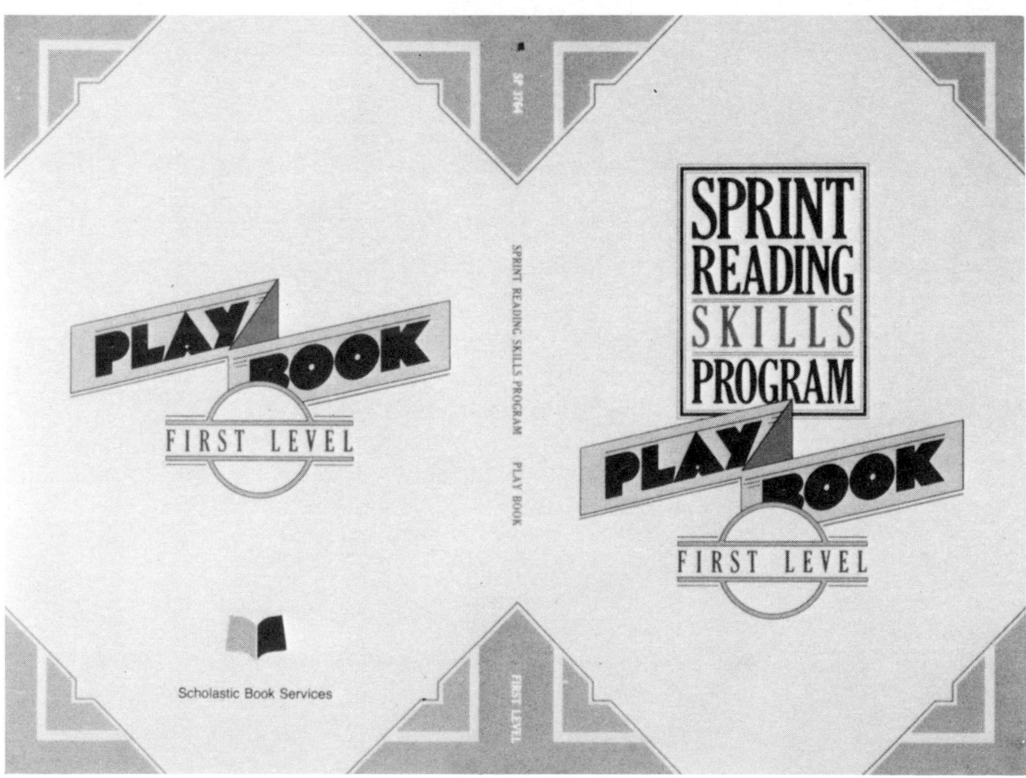

825

824
Art Director Skip Sorvino
Writer Lois A. Markham
Editorial Director Ray Shepard
Designer Skip Sorvino
Artist Richard Lucik
Publisher Scholastic Magazines, Inc.
Agency Scholastic Magazines, Inc.
Client Scholastic Magazines, Inc.

825
Art Director Skip Sorvino
Editorial Director Ray Shepard
Designer Christopher Austopchuck
Publisher Scholastic Magazines, Inc.
Agency Scholastic Magazines, Inc.
Client Scholastic Magazines, Inc.

Art and Illustration

An exquisite setting for a few unique homes. Devil's Elbow.
DEVIL'S ELBOW

826

828

What do you see when you look at $1,100,000,000? You might see enough money to support your family for the next 20,000 years, or enough to support your Uncle Sam for the next 23 hours.

It depends on your perspective.

We see the 5-year, $1.1 billion capital program we announced late in 1973, and we're reminded that, so far at least, we're delivering what we promised, and then some.

We said we'd invest those capital dollars while concurrently reducing our debt-to-equity ratio to 0.6:1, and we have. It's presently 0.5:1.

We said we'd invest 23% in projects that would keep our facilities well maintained, reduce pollution and increase employee safety, and we are.

We said we'd invest 77% in projects that would improve efficiencies and expand capacities, and we are.

We said these latter projects would yield at least 12% after taxes, and we expect they will.

We didn't say we'd simultaneously raise our common stock dividend from 25¢/share/year to $1.10/share/year, but we did.

We didn't say we'd earn an "A" credit rating from both Standard & Poor's and Moody's, but we did.

Today, that $1.1 billion is 62% invested, and the question becomes: what has it bought?

- A 30% increase in pulp and paper capacity.
- An improved product mix; coated paper, for example.
- 500,000 acres of timberland (to add to our already substantial timber base).
- More efficient mills; five new sawmills, for example, to process small diameter logs with little waste.
- Mill energy efficiencies. More waste is now being used to generate power. That's important when you consider that our energy costs have more than doubled in the last three years.
- The capability to further improve our performance. Which is exactly what we intend to do—and that's a promise.

Boise Cascade Corporation

A company worth looking at.

827

826
Art Director Charles Steinbaugh
Designer Charles Steinbaugh
Artist Ed Lindlof
Agency The Drumm Company
Client Diamondhead Corporation

827
Art Director Kirk Hinshaw
Writer David Hill
Designers John Casado
Kirk Hinshaw
Artist Larry Duke
Publisher Oakland National
Agency Dancer, Fitzgerald, Sample, Inc./SF
Client Boise Cascade Corporation

828
Art Director Dolores Gudzin
Designer Dolores Gudzin
Artist Rick McCollum
Agency National Broadcasting Company
Client National Broadcasting Company

Taking money out of mothballs.

One

A customer who manufactured mothballs had a money problem.

From the time he ordered, bought and paid for his raw materials and chemicals in the fall, to the time he could sell, bill and receive revenues in the spring, there was a gap of nearly 180 days.

Not an enviable position to be in.

But one that was a business reality.

First National State bankers, working closely with the mothball maker, recognized the business opportunity that went with the problem.

Helped tailor a package that improved cash flow, offered a line of credit to be tapped *as needed*, and, in close analysis of the business, focused on several ways our customer could make his money go further.

Yes, we're New Jersey's largest commercial banking organization. And yes, we're the leader among New Jersey banks in commercial finance.

But we do a lot more than basic accounts receivables financing.

We start with a Commercial Finance Department staffed with experienced professionals.

Our officers visit your plants. Ask questions to help better understand your business. Involve themselves with how you operate, why you do what you do, and what you hope to accomplish.

In short, when you do business with First National State, you get more than money.

You get an experienced banking team of professionals who know that the best way they can help you meet your objectives is to start looking at a lot more than just your balance sheet.

The programs referred to in this brochure are designed for the corporate borrower with commercial financing needs in excess of $100,000.

829

Losses in Transit

The value of goods and materials has climbed to levels where a company's shipments in transit at any one time can represent a substantial portion of the company's assets. Yet it is estimated that for half of all shipments, companies rely upon the carrier of those goods to bear the risk of loss, theft and damage.

Rail and truck bills of lading—which serve as the contract between the shipper and the carrier—state the carrier's legal liability for loss or damage to goods in their custody. Most of them are for "full value," meaning that the carrier is responsible in the event of loss for the true value of the goods. However, through "released value" bills of lading, carriers can sharply limit their potential liability under certain conditions.

In the case of domestic air carriers for instance, the Civil Aeronautics Board recently ruled that they must raise their minimum liability from 50 cents to $9.07 a pound. Some goods are worth more than $9.07 a pound, of course, and so shippers may then have the option of paying a higher tariff and obtaining full-value coverage.

Many shippers who are paying a tariff that seemingly ensures them of full-value coverage then consider their risk taken care of.

A complete transfer of risk to carriers, however, is simply not possible.

First, the carrier is seldom responsible for "acts of God." It may not be liable, for example, if a tornado, windstorm or flood causes damage to merchandise in its custody. Nor may the carrier be liable for damage caused by riots and strikes.

Second, when damage is not discovered until the package is opened at its destination, recovery from the carrier may be difficult. A carrier with a signed receipt may use it as a defense against con-

Companies that rely on railroads, truckers and airlines to cover any risk to their shipments may find that, in the case of a loss, questions of liability may prevent them from obtaining a full, or even partial, recovery from the carrier.

A brief review by INA of an insurance topic of interest to business executives.

ceded damage claims.

Third, when goods travel by two or more carriers, each may argue that the damage was the fault of the other. In such cases, the shipper must realize that claims can take months to settle.

The effect of payment delays on cash flow is obvious, for the shipment probably will have to be duplicated immediately to satisfy the waiting customer.

Finally, the carrier could suffer financial difficulties that lead to insolvency. Unlikely perhaps, but the bankruptcies of major railroads and trucking lines are indelible reminders that it can happen. In that case, the shipper seeking recovery for damage to goods lines up with the bankrupt company's other creditors.

Limits to carrier responsibility

Options for the shipper

Risk managers, after studying exposures, loss patterns and the costs of transferring risk, may decide that it is preferable for the company to retain

the risk of losses not covered by the carrier. On the other hand, they may decide it is more economical in the long run to turn to an outside insurer, for either full or partial coverage. The shipper can choose between a comprehensive policy that covers all goods in transit or single-trip insurance for high-value shipments.

In either case, the insurer will promptly reimburse the shipper for losses in transit and then seek recoveries due from the carrier. Such recoveries, credited to the company's loss record, help minimize insurance premiums.

For a fuller discussion of transportation insurance, including international shipments, INA has prepared a brochure entitled, "Losses in Transit: Some Professional Considerations." Copies may be requested by writing to INA Corporation, 1600 Arch Street, Philadelphia, Pa. 19101.

The Insurance Company of North America, founded in Independence Hall, Philadelphia, in 1792. Today INA and its affiliated companies operate around the world, with major interests in property and casualty insurance, marine and aviation insurance, life and group insurance, reinsurance and risk management services.

INA insurance products and services are made available through selected independent agents and brokers—professionals with a comprehensive knowledge of insurance needs and solutions.

INA
Insurance Professionals

830

CHARLIE CHRISTIAN
THE MAN WHO ELECTRIFIED JAZZ

THE BLACK PRESENCE IN MUSIC

PEPSI

NUMBER 5 IN A SERIES FROM PEPSI-COLA

831

829
Art Director Jerry Cosgrove
Writer Emile Pragoff III
Designers Jerry Cosgrove
Vicki Navratil
Artist Jerry Cosgrove
Agency Cosgrove Associates Inc.
Client First National State Bank of New Jersey

830
Art Director Richard Kline
Writer Everett Mattlin
Designer Richard Kline
Artist Mel Furukawa
Agency Geer, DuBois Inc.
Client INA (The Insurance Company of North America)

831
Art Director David Krieger
Writer Sam Thorpe
Designers Ted Amber
Mike Psaltis
Ron Canagata
Artist Charles Lilly
Agency Adelante Advertising Inc.
Client Pepsi-Cola Company

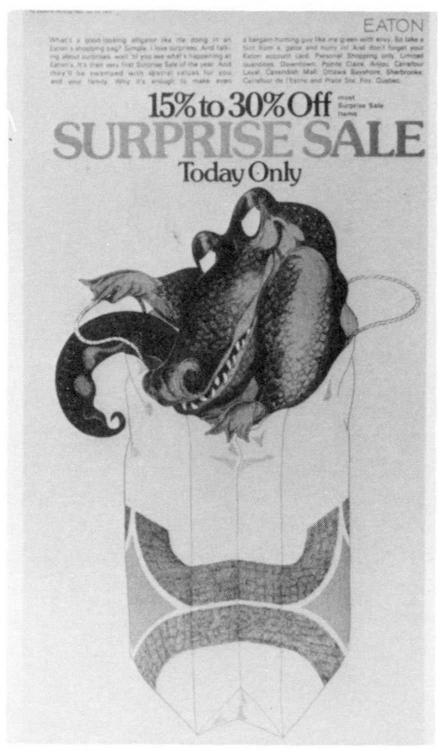

832

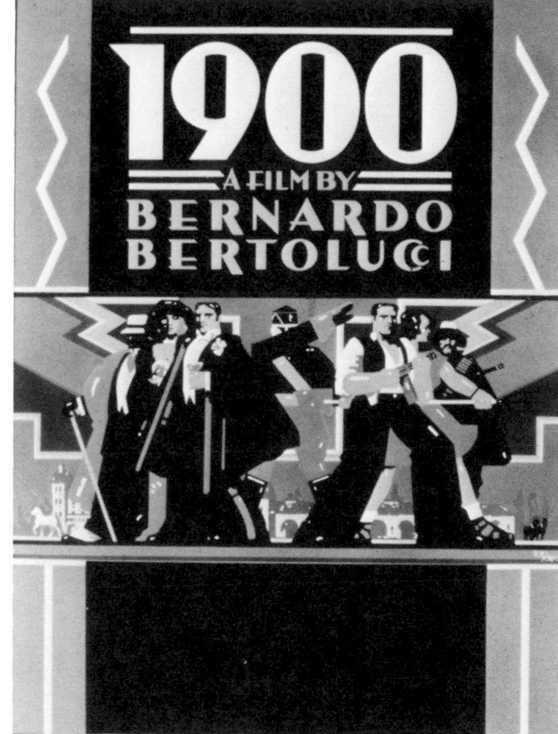

833

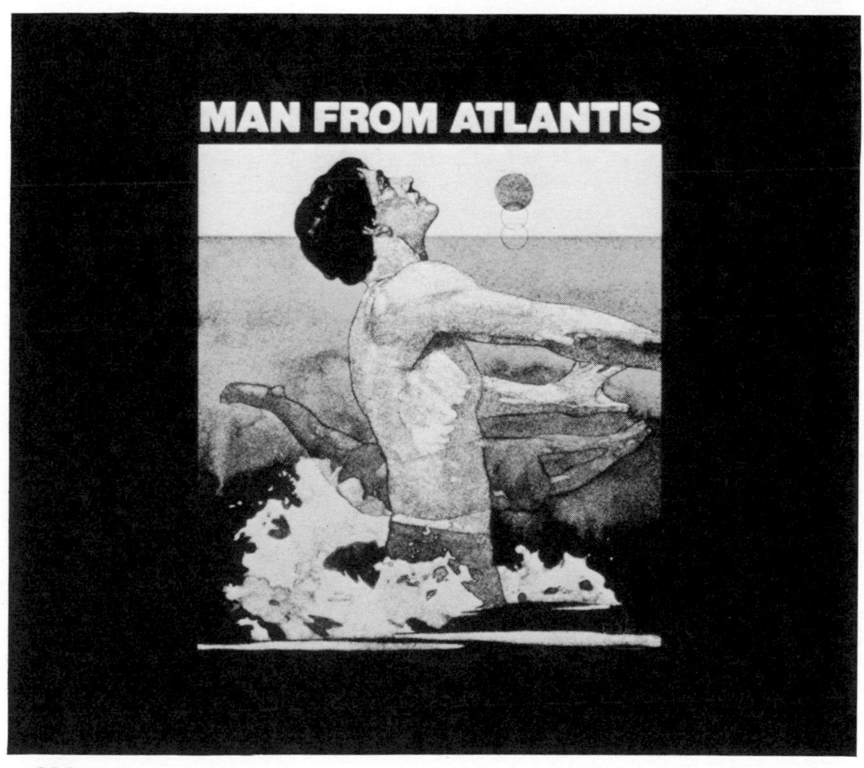

834

832
Art Director Harriet Golfos Santroch
Writer Sandy Gordon
Designer Virginia Poisson
Artist Virginia Poisson
Agency T. Eaton Co. Montreal

833
Art Director Rosebud Advertising
Artist Doug Johnson
Lettering Gerard Huerta
Client Rosebud Advertising/ Paramount

834
Art Director Dolores Gudzin
Designer Dolores Gudzin
Artist Bart Forbes
Agency National Broadcasting Company
Client National Broadcasting Company

Kurt Weill
BARRON STOREY LOOKS GOOD ON MOHAWK

835

PERNOD
"Pernod.
It grows on you."
Enjoy Pernod as a long drink with grapefruit juice, the "Pamplemousse." Also enjoyable with your favorite mixer, or with water and ice in a tall glass. Imported from France. 90 proof.
PERNOD

837

An exhibition of paintings and prints by Robert Bidner, Nov.8 to Dec.3, 1977. Preview Nov. 8, 5:30-8:30 P.M. FAR Gallery, 22 East 80th Street, New York, N.Y.

836

835

t Directors Richard Loomis
Robert Paige
Designer Richard Loomis
Artist Barron Storey
Agency Evans Garber & Paige, Inc.
Client Mohawk Paper Mills, Inc.

836

Art Director Bob Bidner
Writer Bob Bidner
Designer Bob Bidner
Artist Bob Bidner
Production Company Sienna Studio
Agency Bob Bidner
Client Far Gallery

837

Art Director Bob Bidner
Writer Ray Baker
Designer Bob Bidner
Artists Bob Bidner
Tony Toscano
Production Company Quality Engraving
Publishers Time, Inc. and Municipal Publications Inc.
Agency Ted Bates & Co., Inc.
Client Julius Wile Sons & Co., Inc.

838

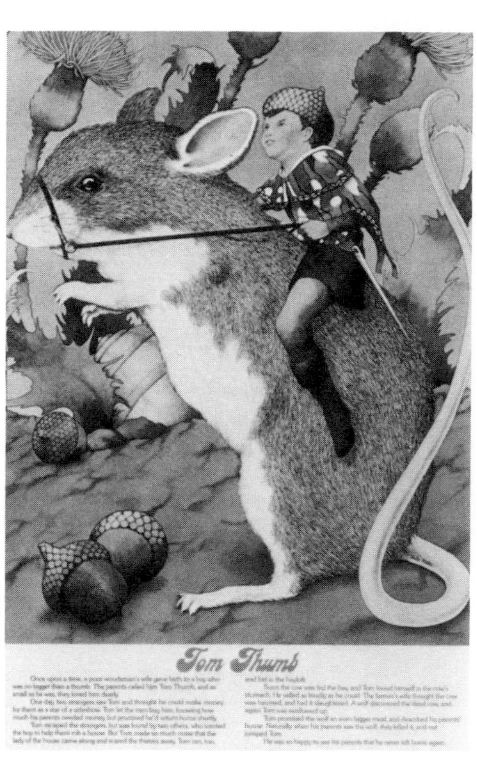

839

840

838
Art Director Jim Clarke
Writer Jim Pappademas
Designer Jim Clarke
Artist Don Ivan Punchatz
Agency Martin Landey, Arlow Adv., Inc.
Client Business-Professional Advertising Assoc.

839
Art Director Anthony V. Leone
Writer Sara E. Bender
Designer Anthony V. Leone
Artist Verlin Miller
Agency Lewis & Gilman
Client Roerig/Pfizer

840
Art Director Anthony V. Leone
Writer Sara E. Bender
Designer Anthony V. Leone
Artist Verlin Miller
Agency Lewis & Gilman
Client Roerig/Pfizer

841

Encore! Bob Peak looks great on
NAVAJO COVER

842

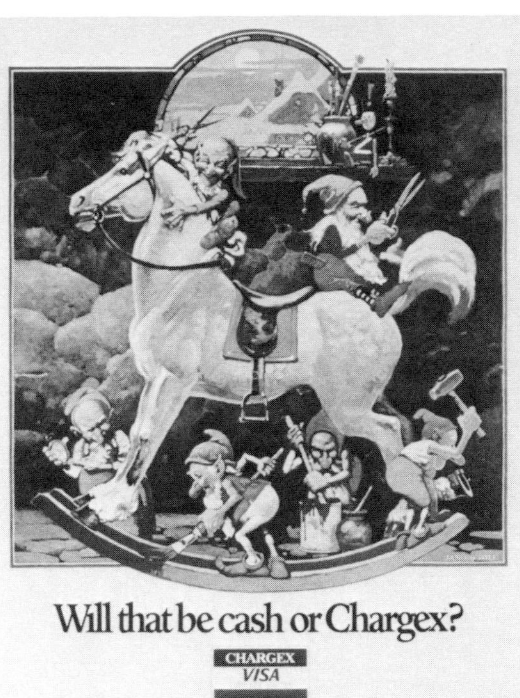

Will that be cash or Chargex?
CHARGEX
VISA
In Canada and around the world.

843

841
Art Director Dolores Gudzin
Designer Dolores Gudzin
Artist Robert Van Nutt
Agency National Broadcasting Company
Client National Broadcasting Company

842
Art Directors Richard Loomis
Robert Paige
Designer Richard Loomis
Artist Bob Peak
Agency Evans Garber & Paige, Inc.
Client Mohawk Paper Mills, Inc.

843
Art Director Terry Iles
Writer Doug Moen
Designer Terry Iles
Artist James Hill
Agency McCann-Erickson
Client The Chargex Plan

844

845

844
Art Director Dick Hane
Writer Ron Newman
Designer Dick Hane
Artist Bob Peak
Agency Stevenson & Associates, Inc.
Client Worthington Compressors, Inc.

845
Art Director Dick Hane
Writer Ron Newman
Designer Dick Hane
Artist Bob Peak
Agency Stevenson & Associates, Inc.
Client Worthington Compressors, Inc.

846

848

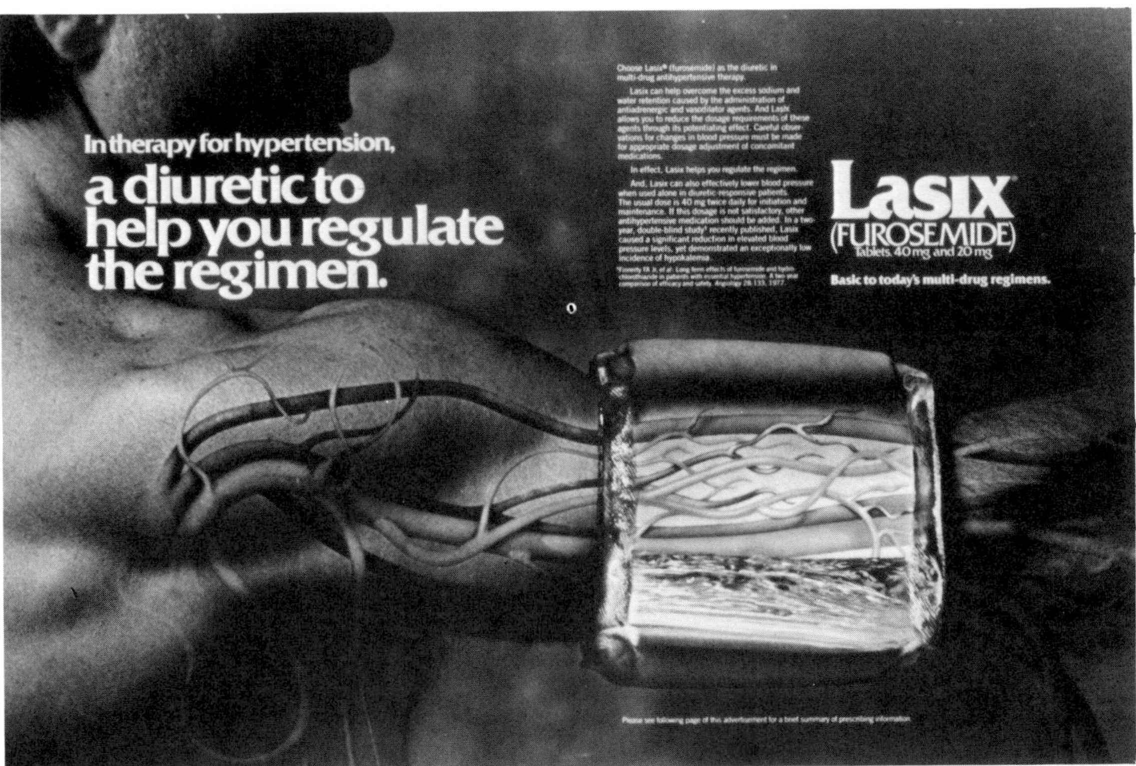

847

846
Art Director Dick Birkey
Designer Don Weller
Artist Don Weller
Agency The Russ Reid Company
Client Myrrh

847
Art Director Walter Scott
Writer Frank Hughes
Designer Charles Schmalz
Artists Lou Bory
Gene Cadore
Photographer Shig Ikeda
Agency William Douglas McAdams
Client Hoechst Roussel

848
Art Director Reinhold Schwenk
Designer Paul Davis
Artist Paul Davis
Agency Case & McGrath, Inc.
Client New York Shakespeare Festival

849

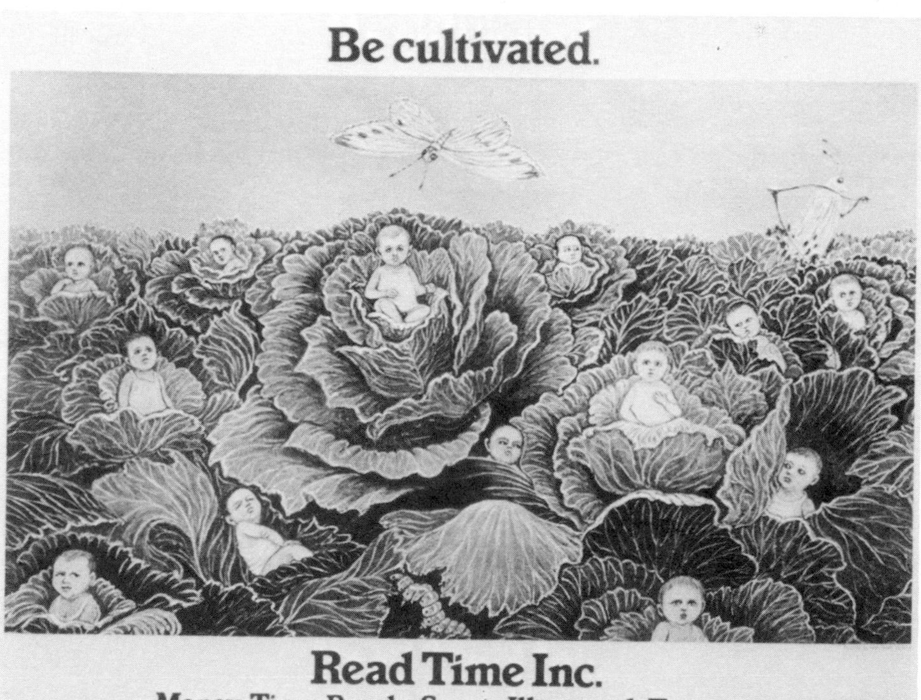

850

849
Art Director Peter Coutroulis
Designer Peter Coutroulis
Artist Wayne McLoughlin
Agency Lerman & Van Leeuwen, Inc.
Client Clinton E. Frank

850
Art Director Bob Czernysz
Writer Dick Olmsted
Artist Jean Jones Jackson
Agency Young & Rubicam
Client Time Inc.

Lisa and Akihiko Seki are delighted to announce the birth
of their first child, a boy, Alexander Tomohiko, on Wednesday,
February 23rd, nineteen hundred and seventy-seven at 5:04 p.m.,
weighing 9 pounds 7½ ounces, 22 inches in height.

851

852

851
Art Director Akihiko Seki
Writer Lisa Seki
Designer Akihiko Seki
Artist Lisa Seki
Client Mr. & Mrs. Akihiko Seki

852
Art Director Rocco Campanelli
Artist Rocco Campanelli
Agency David Deutsch Associates, Inc.
Client Air Afrique

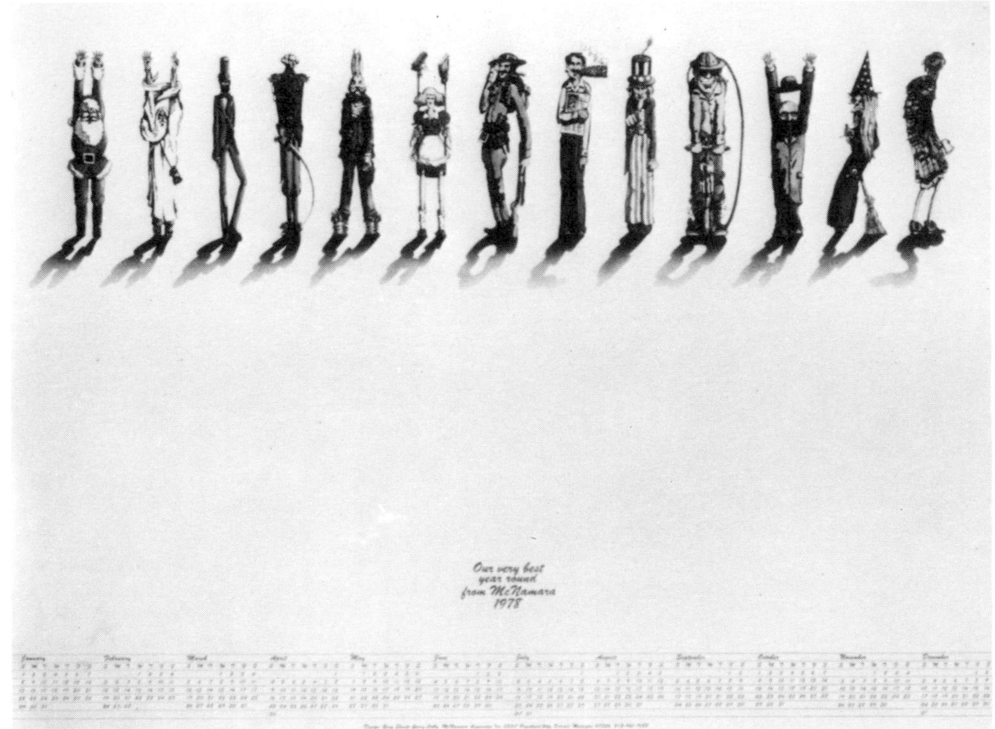
Our very best
year round
from McNamara
1978

853

CHICAGO

854

COUPLES
NOW. THE COUPLE TAKES ITS RIGHTFUL PLACE IN THE SUN.

855

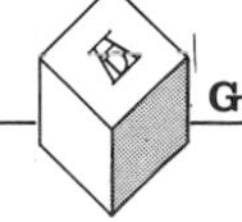

GOLD

853
Art Director Gary Shortt
Designer Gary Shortt
Artist Garry Colby
Agency McNamara Associates, Inc.
Client McNamara Associates, Inc.

854
Art Director Howard Borggren
Designer Bill Choy
Artist Mark McMahon
Agency Handelan Pedersen Inc.
Client Mark McMahon Prints

855
Art Directors Alan Murphy
Heather Cooper
Designers Heather Cooper
Lawrence Finn
Artist Heather Cooper
Agency Alan Murphy & Associates
Client Couples Hotel—Jamaica

856

857

858

856
Art Director Bryan Honkawa
Designer Bryan Honkawa
Artist Bryan Honkawa
Agency The Lilienwall Group/ Honkawa Studio
Client The Queen Mary

857
Art Director Heather Cooper
Designers Heather Cooper, Lawrence Finn
Artist Heather Cooper
Agency Burns, Cooper, Hynes Limited
Client Canadian Opera Company

858
Art Director Tom Kamifuji
Designer Tom Kamifuji
Artist Tom Kamifuji, Karen Okazaki
Agency H. Tom Kamifuji
Client Aizawa Associates

Sleeper of the year!

859

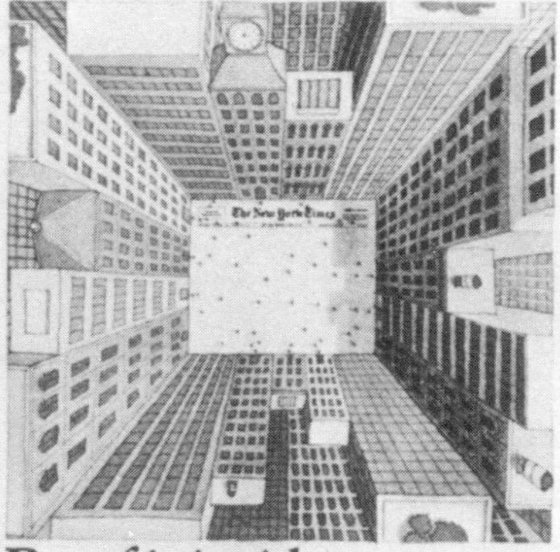

One newspaper at the hub of the world's greatest business and financial community is daily consultant to more of your customers and prospects than any business publication.
Proof is inside.

860

LIFE is one long process of getting tired.
SAMUEL BUTLER

861

859
Art Director Andrew Kner
Writer Jane Klein
Designer Andrew Kner
Artist Dave Epstein
Publisher The New York Times
Client The New York Times

860
Art Director Andrew Kner
Writer Shep Conn
Designer Andrew Kner
Artist Pierre Le-Tan
Publisher The New York Times
Client The New York Times

861
Art Director Walter Lefmann
Writer Velma Francis
Designer Walter Lefmann
Artist Walter Lefmann
Publisher Time Inc.
Agency Time
Client Time Magazine

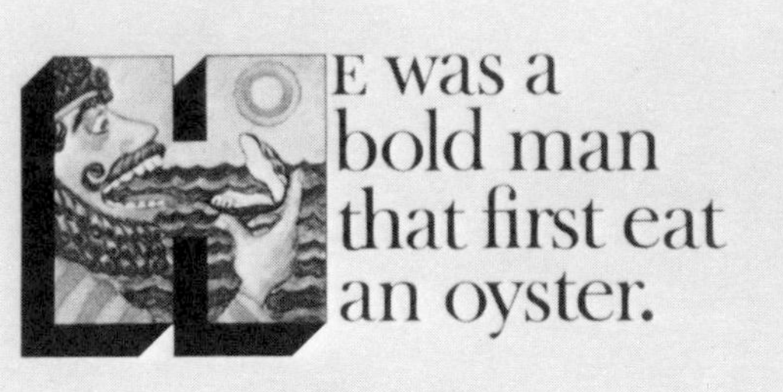

862

863

862

Art Director Walter Lefmann
Writer Velma Francis
Designer Walter Lefmann
Artist Walter Lefmann
Publisher Time Magazine
Agency Time
Client Time Inc.

863

Artist Norm Bendell
Agency Harvey Raymond Inc.
Client Sony Corporation of America

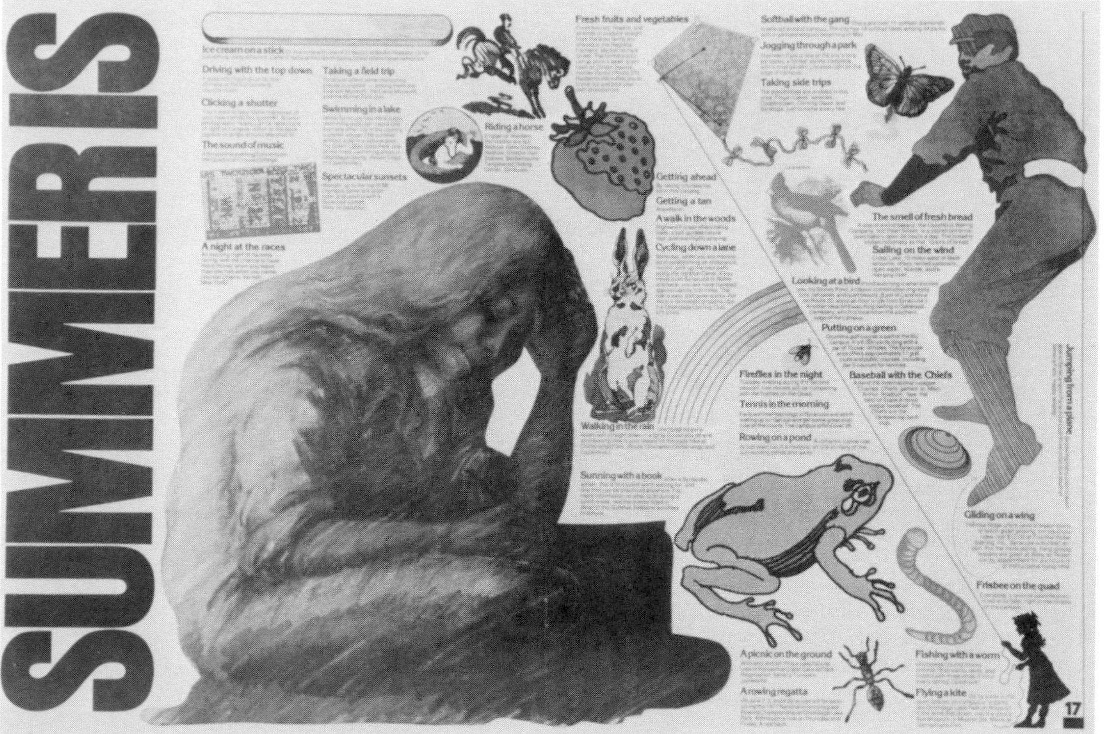

864

865

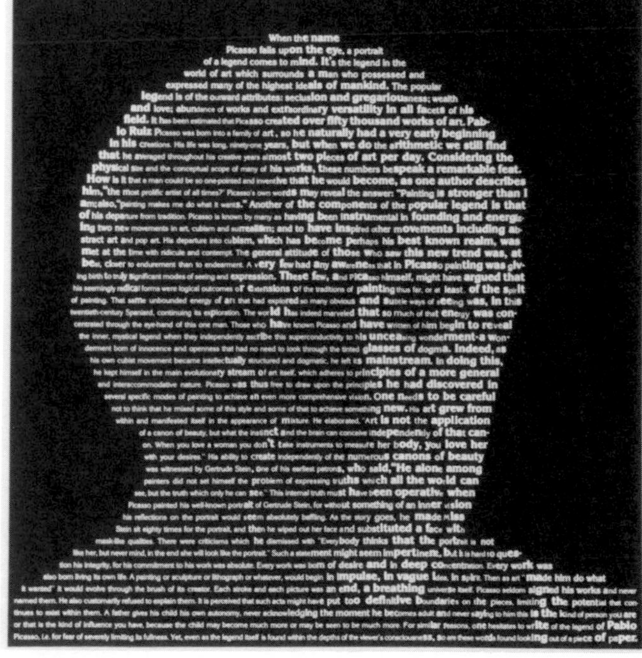

866

SILVER

864
Art Director Don Trousdell
Writer Pat Very & Office of Summer Sessions
Designer Don Trousdell
Artists Don Trousdell, Nancy Stevenson, Paula Havey, Cary Smith, Sandi Glass, Jane Kowalik, Roger Poole, Barbara Sablow
Agency Don Trousdell (Freelancer)
Client Syracuse University, Div. of Summer Sessions

865
Art Director Peter Coutroulis
Writer Albert Lerman
Designer Peter Coutroulis
Artist Roy Carruthers
Agency Lerman & Van Leeuwen
Client House Ad

866
Art Director Paul Siemsen
Writer Paul Siemsen
Designer Paul Siemsen
Artist Paul Siemsen
Client The Graphic Corporatio

867

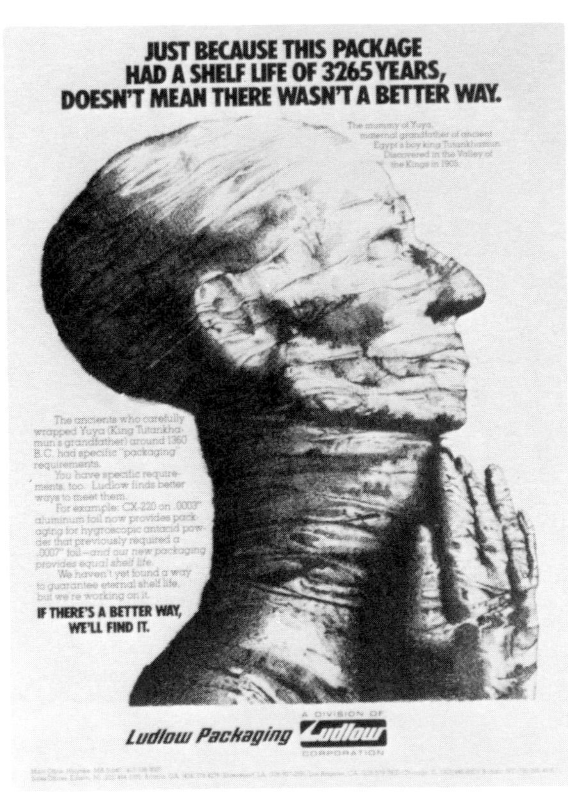

868

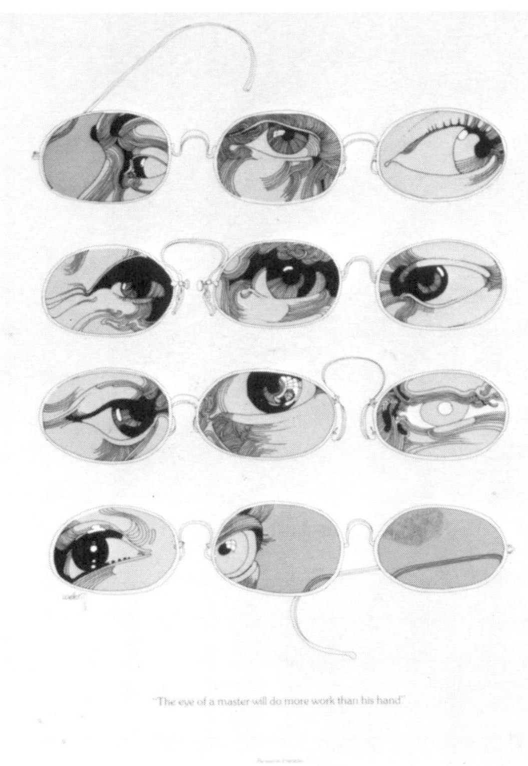

869

867

Art Directors	K. Barnes
	L. Elliot
Writer	L. Elliot
Artist	Victor Valla
Agency	The Elliot Organization, Inc.
Client	Sweet's Division, McGraw-Hill Information Systems

868

Art Director	Russ Veduccio
Writers	Bill Comeau
	Betty Parks
Designer	Russ Veduccio
Artist	John Burgoyne
Agency	Harold Cabot & Co., Inc.
Client	Ludlow Corporation, Packaging Division

869

Art Director	Don Weller
Writer	Benjamin Franklin
Designer	Don Weller
Artist	Don Weller
Publisher	Premier Printing Corp.
Agency	Ron Posthuma
Client	Premier Printing Corp.

870

871

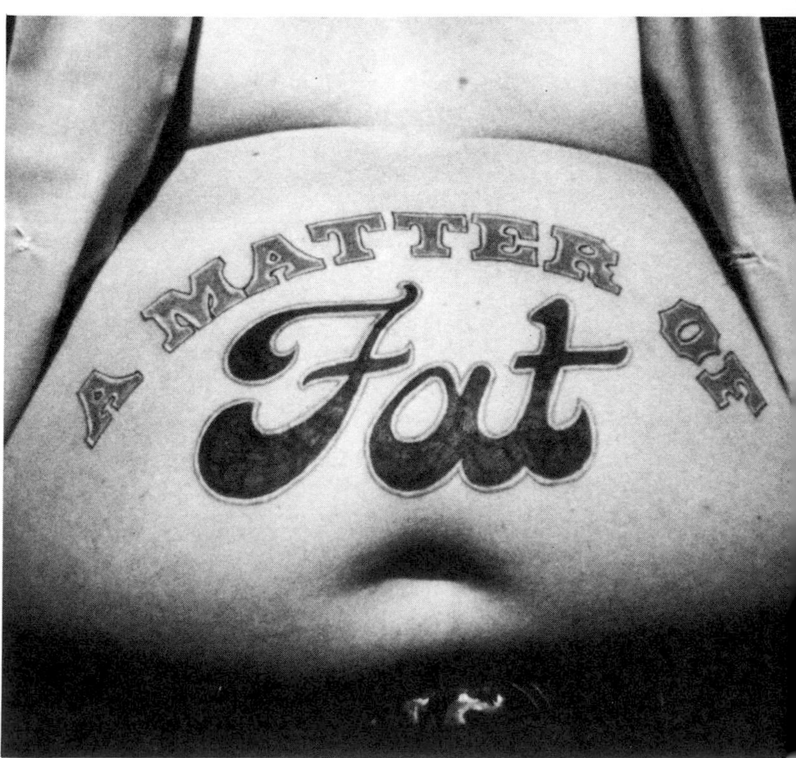

872

870
Art Director William Vollers
Writer Don Brown
Designer Bill Feeney
Artist Jim Spanfeller
Photographer Ty Hyon
Agency Stuart Williams Assoc., Inc.
Client A. H. Robbins

871
Art Director Don Weller
Writer Sheldon Weinstein
Designers Don Weller
Chikako Matsubayashi
Artist Don Weller
Photographer Stan Caplan
Publisher Standard Brands Paint Company
Agency The Weller Institute for the Cure of Design
Client Standard Brands Paint Company

872
Art Director Dennis W. Bender
Designer Dennis W. Bender
Artist Dennis W. Bender
Photographer Dennis W. Bender
Agency WPSX-TV/Wagner Ann
Client WPSX-TV
Programming Dept.

873

875

874

873
Art Director Tom Kamifuji
Designer Tom Kamifuji
Artist Tom Kamifuji
Agency H. Tom Kamifuji
Client Aizawa Associates

874
Art Director Sal Albano
Writer Terry Thomas
Designer Don Kahn/Creative Annex, Inc.
Artist Don Kahn/Creative Annex, Inc.
Photographer Louis Mervar
Agency N. W. Ayer ABH International
Client Department of Defense

875
Art Director Tom Kamifuji
Designer Tom Kamifuji
Artist Tom Kamifuji
Agency H. Tom Kamifuji
Client Aizawa Associates

876

877

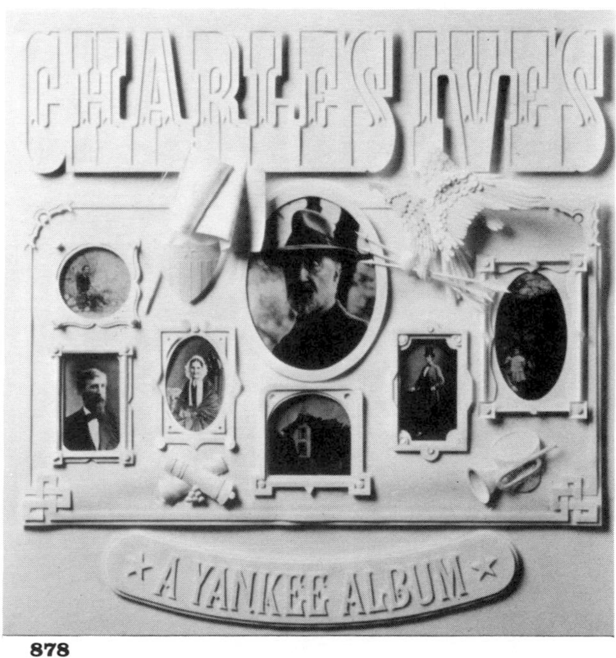

878

876
Art Director Tom Kamifuji
Designer Tom Kamifuji
Artist Tom Kamifuji
Agency H. Tom Kamifuji & Assoc.
Client Tom Kamifuji

877
Art Director Tom Kamifuji
Designer Tom Kamifuji
Artist Tom Kamifuji
Agency H. Tom Kamifuji & Assoc.
Client Tom Kamifuji

878
Art Director Donald Kahn
Designer Donald Kahn
Artist Donald Kahn
Photographer Louis Mervar
Client Walter Horn

879

880

880B

879
Art Director Donald Kahn
Designer Donald Kahn
Artist Donald Kahn
Photographer Louis Mervar
Client Mervar Studio, Inc.

880A
Art Directors David Van Gieson
Nancy MacLean
Writer Conrad Razidlo
Designer David Van Gieson
Photographer Marvy Advertising Photography
Agency Razidlo Advertising
Client Saint Paul Chamber Orchestra

880B
Art Director Frank B. Marshall III
Designer Frank B. Marshall III
Artist Frank B. Marshall III
Agency Frank B. Marshall Graphic Design
Client Frank B. Marshall III

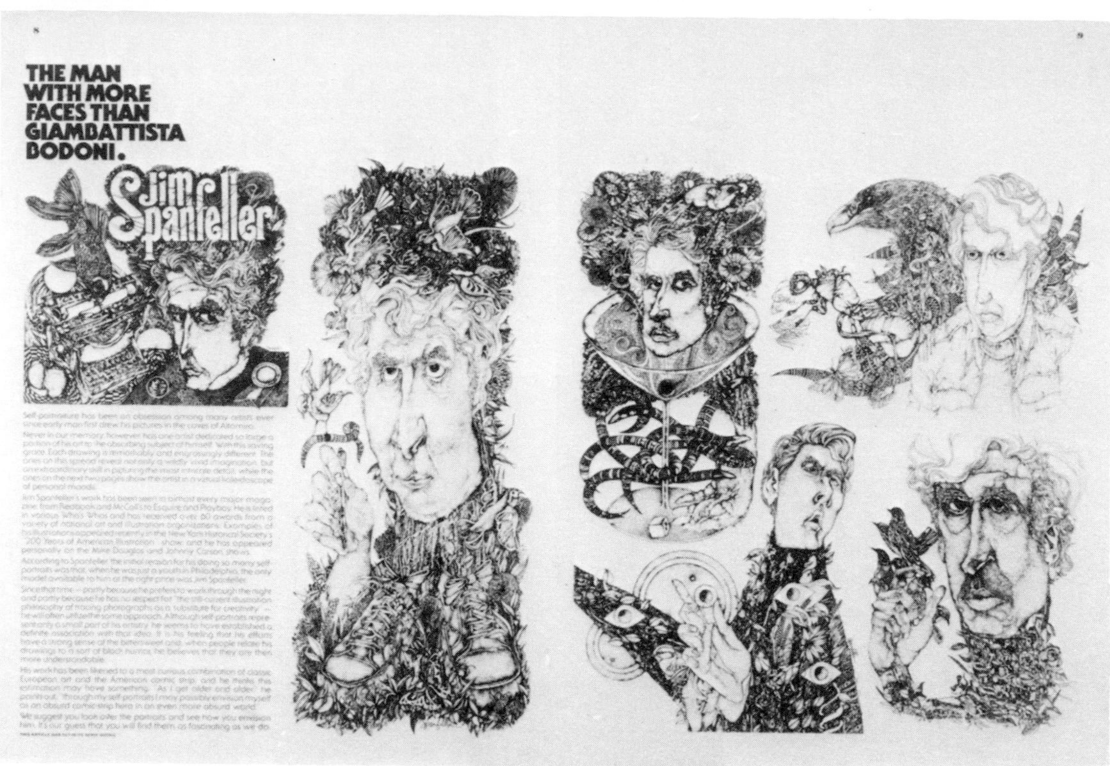
THE MAN
WITH MORE
FACES THAN
GIAMBATTISTA
BODONI.
Jim
Spanfeller

881

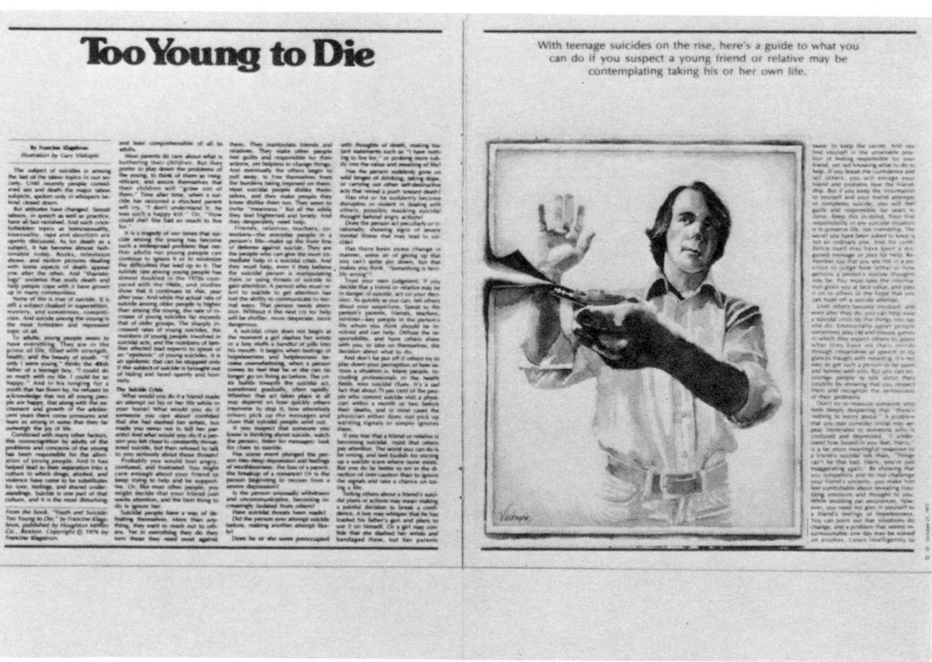

Too Young to Die

With teenage suicides on the rise, here's a guide to what you can do if you suspect a young friend or relative may be contemplating taking his or her own life.

882

881
Art Director Herb Lubalin
Writer Herb Lubalin
Designer Herb Lubalin
Artist Jim Spanfeller
Publisher International Typeface Corp.
Agency LSC&P Design Group
Client International Typeface Corp.

882
Art Director Cliff Gardiner
Writer Stan Green
Artist Gary Viskupic
Agency Newsday Editorial Art Dept.
Client Newsday Inc.

Claimed by Art and Nature

Frederick Law Olmsted
Drawing by Pierre Le Tan

883

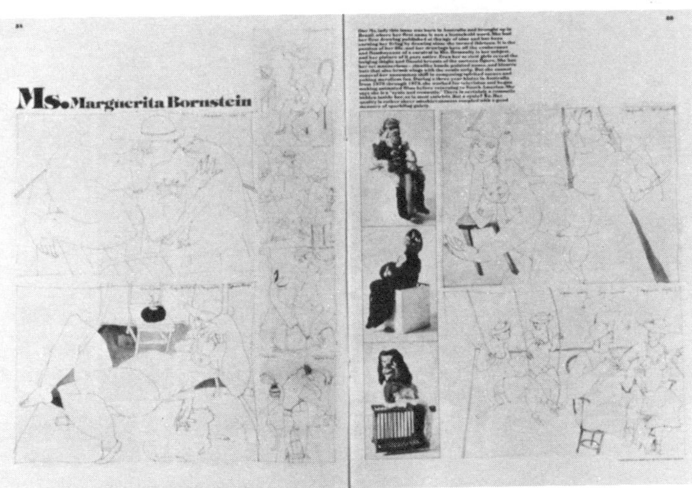

884

885

883
Art Director Steve Heller
Editor Harvey Shapiro
Designer Steve Heller
Artist Pierre Le-Tan
Publisher The New York Times
Agency The New York Times
Client The New York Times

884
Art Director Herb Lubalin
Writer Herb Lubalin
Designer Herb Lubalin
Artist Marguerita Bornstein
Publisher International Typeface Corp.
Agency LSC&P Design Group
Client International Typeface Corp.

885
Art Director Herb Lubalin
Writer Jack Anson Finke
Designer Herb Lubalin
Artist Dian Friedman
Publisher International Typeface Corp.
Agency LSC&P Design Group
Client International Typeface Corp.

886

887

888

886
Art Director Pamela Vassil
Editor David Schneiderman
Designer Pamela Vassil
Artist Brad Holland
Publisher The New York Times
Client The New York Times

887
Art Director Brad Holland
Editor Emily Chewning
Designer Seymour Chwast
Artist Brad Holland
Producer Jean-Claude Suares
Production Company Push Pin Press
Publisher Thomas Y. Crowell Co.

888
Art Director Brad Holland
Editor Emily Chewning
Designer Seymour Chwast
Artist Brad Holland
Producer Jean-Claude Suares
Production Company Push Pin Press
Publisher Thomas Y. Crowell Company

The Curious Double Life of Rosa Multiflora

Is she an innocent garden rose or an ecological villain?
by Robert Schery

889

City Wildlife

From London's foxes to Seattle's blackberries, a surprising variety of wild plants and creatures have adapted to urban life
by Robert Michael Pyle

890

891

889
Art Director Bruce McIntosh
Editor Paul Trachtman
Designer Bruce McIntosh
Artist Bruce McIntosh
Publisher Massachusetts Horticultural Society
Client Horticulture Magazine

890
Art Director Bruce McIntosh
Editor Paul Trachtman
Designer Bruce McIntosh
Artist Bruce McIntosh
Publisher Massachusetts Horticultural Society
Client Horticulture Magazine

891
Art Director Paul Back
Artist Gary Viskupic
Agency Newsday Editorial Art Dept.
Client Newsday Inc.

892

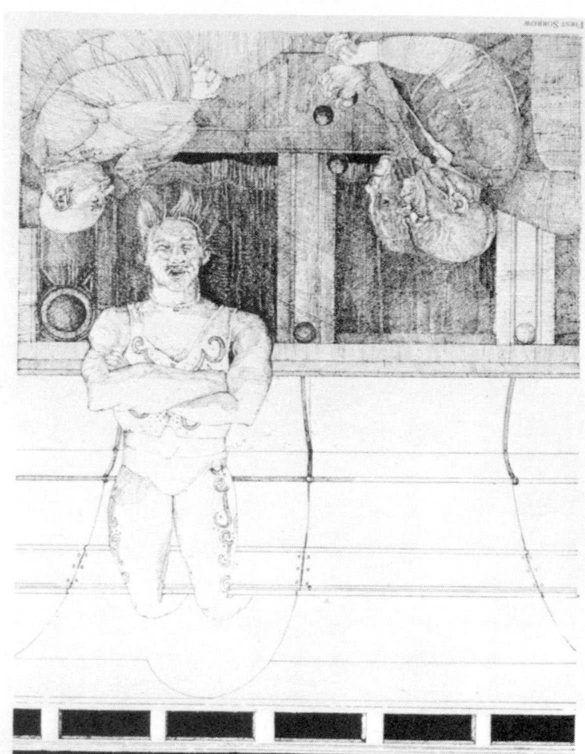

893

894

892
Art Director Noel Werrett
Artist Gary Viskupic
Client Quest/'77 Magazine

893
Art Director Ken Munowitz
Designer Alan E. Cober
Artist Alan E. Cober
Publisher American Heritage Co.
Client Horizon

894
Art Director Pamela Vassil
Editor David Schneiderman
Designer Pamela Vassil
Artist Brad Holland
Publisher The New York Times
Client The New York Times

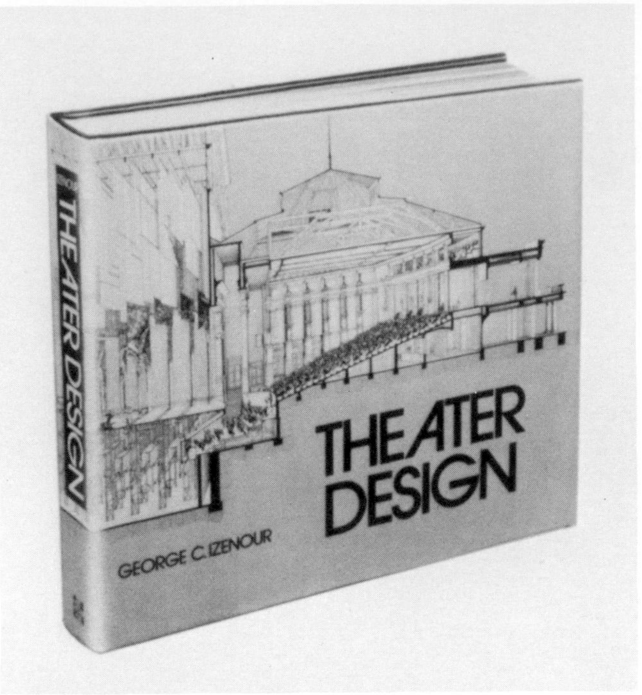

895

896

895

esign Director	Naomi Auerbach
Editors	Jeremy Robinson
	Margaret Lamb
Designer	Naomi Auerbach
Artists	Richard Casler
	W.G. Clark
	William Forrester
	William Hersey
	John Jayner
	David Kiphuth
	Grady Larkin
	Michael Lassell
	Carol Rene Rountree
	Robert Stewart
	Paul Zalon
Production Supervisors	Stephen J. Boldish
	Teresa Leaden
Book Title	Theater Design
Author	George C. Izenour
Publisher	McGraw-Hill Book Company

896

Art Director	Ralph Forbes
Writer	Client
Designer	Ralph Forbes
Artist	Kenneth F. Dewey
Agency	William Douglas McAdams
Client	Hoechst Roussel

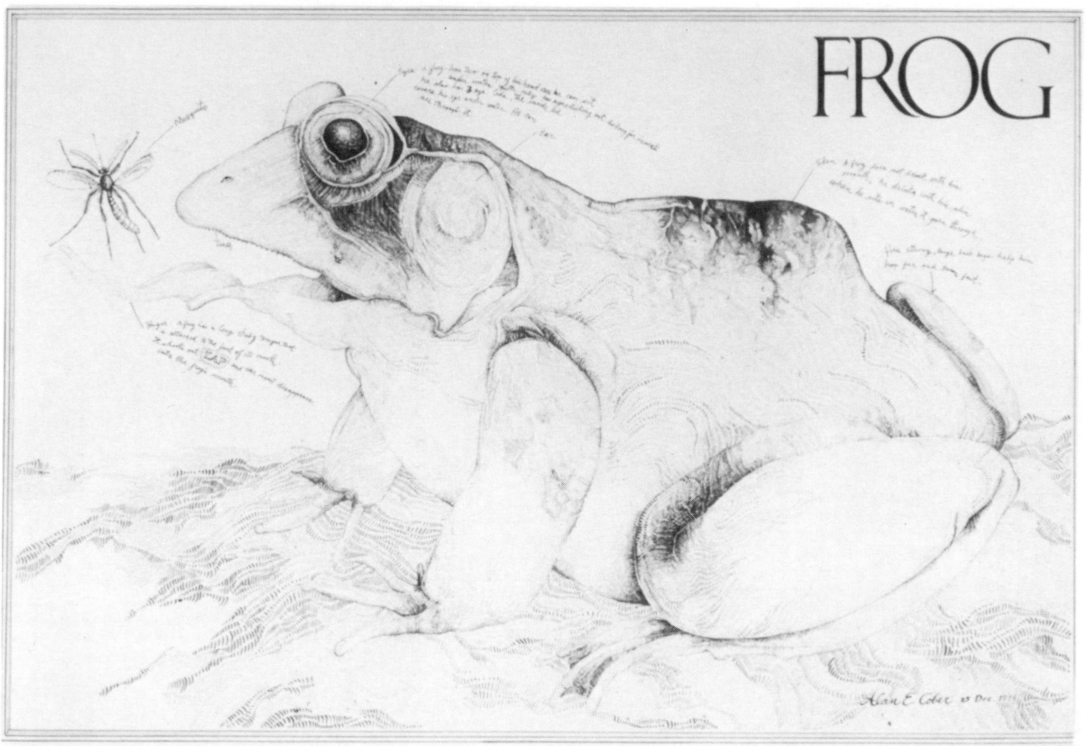

898

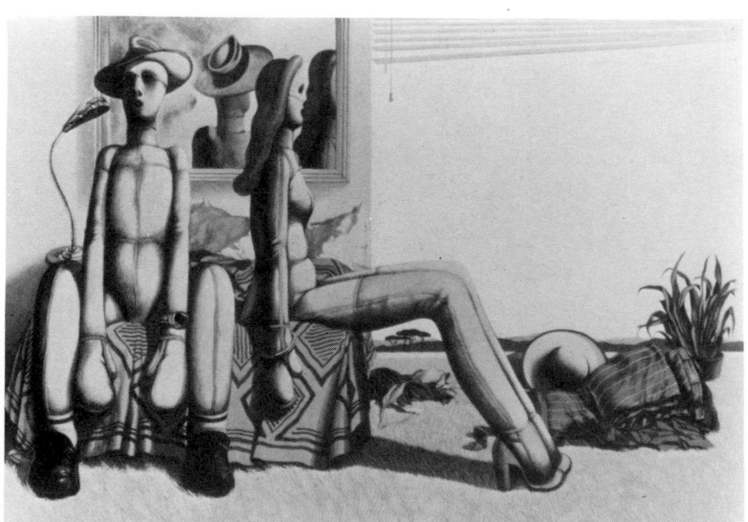

899

897

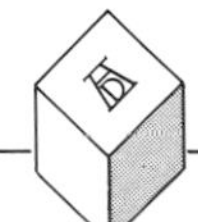

SILVER

897
Art Director Tom Burns
Editor Robert Parker
Designer Tom Burns
Artist Geoffrey Moss
Publisher Touche Ross
Agency Tom Burns Associates
Client Touche Ross

898
Art Directors Carol Carson
Alan E. Cober
Designer Alan E. Cober
Artist Alan E. Cober
Publisher Scholastic Magazines, Inc.
Client Scholastic Magazines, Inc.

899
Art Director Don Menell
Designer George Kenton
Artist Patrick Byrne
Publisher Playboy Enterprises, Inc.

900

901

TO CAP OR NOT TO CAP

THE CASE FOR COSMETIC DENTISTRY

Lauren Hutton's smile has probably done more good for people with crooked teeth than anything else in the world. After all, if a top model can have a gap between her front teeth, why should the rest of us lesser beings worry about any minor imperfections we might have? But a lot of people are bothered, and bothered a lot, by flaws in their teeth—be they major or minor ones. Anything from a slightly discolored front tooth to a severe case of "gapitis" is enough to make them cover their mouths with their hands whenever they talk, smile, or laugh. So, they turn to their dentist, or a specialist he's referred them to, to have cosmetic dentistry done.

But cosmetic dentistry doesn't mean just putting caps on teeth. It also means orthodontia (yes, people in their twenties and thirties *do* get braces put on their teeth); the making and fitting of dentures; the reshaping of a tooth or a segment of the gum; tooth implantation; and, in extreme cases, the repositioning of the teeth and reshaping of the mouth through surgery to correct other medical problems such as headaches, neuralgia, and dizziness, all of which can be caused by a bad bite.

However, most of today's cosmetic dentistry is done for purely cosmetic reasons—people aren't satisfied with their teeth looking the way they do naturally, so they get them capped to make them look more attractive. Caps—or jackets, as dentists call them—can solve the problem of discolored teeth, of teeth that are out of position, of buck teeth,

Photo illustration by Guy Fery; makeup by Pierre Laroche; lips colored with Lumilane Rouge Rouge Lipstick by Orlane

902

900
Art Director Jean-Claude Suares
Writer Emily Chewning
Designer Seymour Chwast
Artist Brad Holland
Producer Jean-Claude Suares
Production Company Push Pin Press
Publisher Berkley Windhover Books

901
Art Director Jean-Claude Suares
Editor Emily Chewning
Designer Seymour Chwast
Artist Brad Holland
Producer Jean-Claude Suares
Production Company Push Pin Press
Publisher Berkley Windhover Books

902
Art Director Rowan Johnson
Designer Claire Victor
Artist Guy Fery
Publisher Bob Guccione
Client Viva International

DOCTOR D'ARQUEANGEL

FICTION BY HARLAN ELLISON

The word *beautiful* simply did not do her justice. She was quantum leaps beyond merely beautiful. Exquisite, perhaps, carried to the nth degree. She sat behind her desk and Romb hoped she wouldn't stand up; he wasn't at all sure he could handle an unobstructed view of her, full-length. She was purely the most breathtaking human being he had ever seen. He thought she would look perfect standing on a pedestal in Thrace somewhere.

"You're staring, Mr. Romb," she said. Gently. With amusement.

He felt his face grow warm. He was in his thirties, very slick, good moves—and he wasn't used to being embarrassed by women. It was usually the other way around. "Oh, excuse me, Doctor; I was thinking about what you said. Then it *is* possible?"

"Oh yes. It's possible. It *can* be done. But it comes at a premium, of course."

"I expected as much," Romb said. He had vague feelings of danger: contracts signed in blood, loss of immortal soul, less nameable tremblings. He wore tinted aviator glasses and his hair had been styled by an Italian. His suit had been purchased in Savile Row. "Just *how* much is the question."

"Ten percent of what you realize."

"I have no idea how much that might be."

"Payment deferred. I can wait. My patients are unfailingly grateful. I've never had to sue for collection."

"Patients? You've used these treatments before."

"Occasionally. When the circumstances have been, er, extraordinary, shall we say. A high degree of confidentiality is, of course, imperative."

He thought about that for a moment. *Imperative* was as inadequate as *beautiful*. He had come to the office of Dr. D'arqueAngel as a final act of desperation. He had heard whispers among a strange group of his acquaintances who were involved with witchcraft . . . a silly bunch of people, really, but on occasion he found them amusing. And they had been talking about her one evening at what they called their "coven," though it was more like a social tea for overage singles than a coven as he had read about such things. The whispers had been incomplete, hardly specific; but if what they said about her was accurate, she might be the answer to his nightmarish dilemma.

Simply stated, it didn't *sound* all that desperate:

Charles Romb wanted to murder his wife.

The actuality of the situation, however, was a quantum leap beyond desperate. Beyond nightmarish. It was, simply stated, a life sentence in a living hell.

"Mr. Romb?"

He realized he had been staring again. These lapses into preoccupation had been coming more and more frequently. He had been staring into the middle distance, thinking about Sandra, thinking how monstrous his even *being here* seemed in retrospect. But he *had* come here, he *was* sitting across the Saarinen desk from her, and he *had* confided his desire . . . to a total stranger.

An exquisite, disturbing stranger he had heard about only in whispers.

"I'm sorry. I still can't believe I'm here saying these things to you. The whole idea is so crazy . . . but I'm so miserable. . . ."

"I understand perfectly, Mr. Romb. You can be completely open with me." She didn't say it, but the unspoken next sentence was, *You can trust me. I'm a doctor.*

"But it works?" He felt like a fool pressing her; she had already said it worked, had said it several times.

"Oh, it works very well indeed. As well as snake venom. Same principle, really." She steepled incredibly slim fingers. He watched her hands in fascination.

"I'm not sure I understand that."

"Consider," Dr. D'arqueAngel said, "if you were to be injected with infinitesimal doses of, say, the venom of the black mamba—*Dendroaspis*

Copyright ©1977 by Harlan Ellison

Only the mistress of eternity could
cure his malady, but the price was higher than he bargained for.

903

904

903	
Art Director	Rowan Johnson
Designers	Bob Guccione
	Claire Victor
	Martha Pearson
Publisher	Bob Guccione
Client	Viva International

904	
Art Director	Joan H. Gramatte
Writer	Raymond Barrio
Artist	Salvador Bru
Publisher	Nuestro Publications
Agency	Bru Associates
Client	Nuestro Publications

"Today, money has replaced sex as the source of our most powerful hang-ups."

HOW MUCH MONEY DO YOU EARN?

by Lynn Sherr

Like most people I know who work for a living, I have always hidden my paycheck stubs. Back in the days when I was a reporter and sat in a big open news room with everyone else and received my weekly pay in a plain brown envelope from the bookkeeper who made the rounds every Friday morning, it was tricky. Somehow I worked out a system whereby I could slit open the flap, peer inside to make sure nothing unusual had been deducted, and slip it into my handbag (zipper compartment) without allowing any alien eyeball to make contact. My desk might accumulate two months' growth of old letters, articles, and out-of-town newspapers, but never among the debris would anyone find a stray paycheck stub. Not mine.

Most of my colleagues operated the same way, because we all succumbed early to one of the most prevalent of American occupational diseases: Don't Let Anyone Know How Much Money You Earn. The reasons for this taboo vary as widely as the incomes themselves. Some people are embarrassed because they think they earn too much; others because they earn too little. Some are avoiding increases in alimony payments; others are trying to ward off the tax collector or less visible burglars. It is a way to protect social status, and to preserve something considerably less tangible.

"It's perfectly natural that you wouldn't want everyone to know how much you make," insists a professional financial consultant who wouldn't tell me how much she earned. "It's like your name. It's a target, something to shoot at. It puts you in a spot. I think of it as a personal question—as personal as, 'Are you sleeping with anyone now?' "

More personal. In an age when sleeping habits are flaunted on the front pages, financial matters are still primly tucked away in the bedroom. According to Dee Dee Ahern, who conducts money management workshops for women across the country and wrote *The Economics of Being a Woman*, "Money has replaced sex as the source of our most powerful hang-ups. Like sex, money means many different things to each of us, and each of its meanings is charged with such awesome emotions as greed, fear, envy, and guilt. We desire money as a means to material comfort, power, freedom, prestige, even love and beauty...But at the same time we desire money, we fear it."

Or, as reporter Nancy Collins put it during a panel on gossip at a journalism convention last fall, "Celebrities will tell you everything and anything about their sex lives, but it's a different story when you ask them how much they make."

The same diffidence seems to be true of less famous workers, like those encountered on the lecture circuit by a psychologist dealing with people's reactions to money. His request that they tell what they earn was constantly greeted with silence, distinct lack of comfort, and then nervous laughter.

When I asked people how much money they earn in the course of preparing this article, I generally encountered a less evasive response. "It's none of your business," they all said. And they all said it with hostility.

There are, of course, individuals whose income becomes known because of a sudden success or a sudden windfall, like a best-selling novel that earns six-figure sums for paperback and movie rights. The figures in one case I know of were $360,000 and $250,000, and even after agents' fees and partnership payoffs, it left a tidy balance for the author. But he told me gently, still pleading for anonymity, "It's embarrassing when your friends read in the paper how much you've made. You walk into a gin mill and get kidded. I'm not a particularly secretive person, but I do like to keep my business personal."

Some working people have no choice in the matter, since their salaries are made public by law, or by policy, or by dogged investigation. Members of trade unions know where their colleagues fit on the wage scale. The

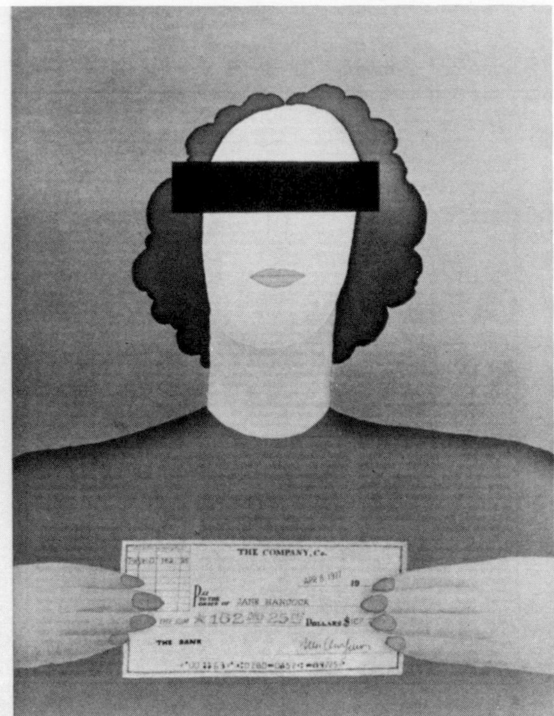

905

THE GREENING OF COWTOWN

by Gary Cartwright

At Fort Worth's Colonial Golf Tournament, all the action is not on the links.

906

905

Art Director	Paul Hardy
Writer	Beatrice Buckler
Designer	Paul Hardy
Artist	Guy Billout
Publisher	Beatrice Buckler

906

Art Directors	Sybil Broyles Jim Darilek
Designers	Sybil Broyles Jim Darilek
Artist	Larry McEntire
Production Company	Texas Monthly
Publisher	Mediatex Communications Corp.
Exhibitor	Texas Monthly

AMERICA HAS BECOME A DOG RUN

SNARL

BY COLMAN McCARTHY

907

909

908

907
Art Director Gordon Mortensen
Editor David Sanford
Designer Gordon Mortensen
Artist Ed Soyka
Publisher James L. Bartlett III
Politics Today
(formerly Skeptic Magazine)
Client Politics Today
(formerly Skeptic Magazine)

908
Art Directors Phyllis Cayton
Robert Ericksen
Writer Robert Rossner
Designers Phyllis Cayton
Robert Ericksen
Beth Whitaker
Artist Alan Henderson
Publisher Progressive Publishing

909
Art Director Don Owens
Editor Don Owens
Designer Alan E. Cober
Artist Alan E. Cober
Publisher Don Owens Publishing Co.
Client Picture Magazine

BY JOHN F. HELLEGERS

THE CONCORDE IS VERY FAST — ALSO LOUD, DANGEROUS AND FINANCIALLY DISASTROUS

BOOM AND BUST

If you're in business to make a profit, the worst thing you can do is lose money. The Ford Motor Company, after a few unhappy seasons with the Edsel, took the car off the market, cut its losses and hoped that people would forget.

In politics, though, the worst thing is to admit an obviously horrendous multibillion-dollar mistake. The admission is too likely to be thrown back in your face at the next election. Far better to brazen it out and hope that any admission can be postponed for your successor. This is why the world is still struggling with the Anglo-French Concorde supersonic transport, or SST, an aircraft into which the British and French governments say they have sunk $3 billion since 1962. (The real sum is probably much larger.) For their money they'll eventually get 16 copies of a plane that's more than twice as loud on takeoff as the loudest subsonic commercial jet (four times louder than a 747). In addition to being a fuel-guzzling financial disaster and a threat to the stratospheric ozone layer, which filters out solar ultraviolet radiation and thus protects us from skin cancer. The Concorde is also a producer of startling sonic booms that have bedeviled residents of southern England and the islands in the English Channel since commercial Concorde service began last year. Luckily, the British and French have agreed not to build any more than 16 Concordes. But no one can figure out how to get rid of them.

That's not for lack of trying; the Concorde is still around despite strenuous behind-the-scenes efforts by its nominal supporters to kill it. As long ago as 1964, the newly elected British government led by

John F. Hellegers is the attorney for the Environmental Defense Fund in Washington, DC.

910

Una Vita Più Nobile

Arctic explorer, dirigible expert, general, teacher— the list is nearly endless. And all these occupations were mastered by one man: Umberto Nobile

By PHILIP NOBILE

911

910
Art Director Gordon Mortensen
Editor David Sanford
Designer Gordon Mortensen
Artist Ed Soyka
Publisher Politics Today (formerly Skeptic Magazine)
Client Politics Today (formerly Skeptic Magazine)

911
Art Director John Ciofalo
Artist George Angelini
Publisher I AM Publishing Corp.
Client I Am Magazine

Why is the Copley Press unique? Name another news organization that had 23 intelligence agents masquerading as "reporters" on its payroll!

THE SPIES WHO CAME IN FROM THE NEWSROOM

BY JOE TRENTO AND DAVE ROMAN

912

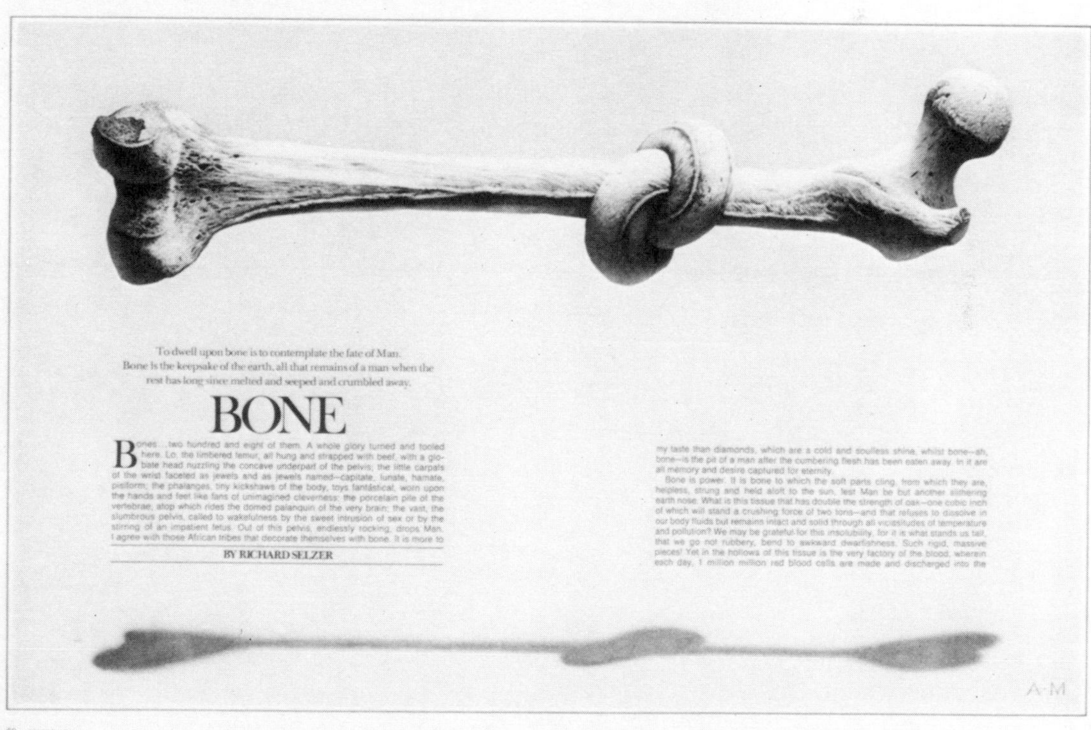

To dwell upon bone is to contemplate the fate of Man. Bone is the keepsake of the earth, all that remains of a man when the rest has long since melted and seeped and crumbled away.

BONE

Bones…two hundred and eight of them. A whole glory turned and tooled here. Lo, the timbered femur, all hung and strapped with beef, with a globate head nuzzling the concave underpart of the pelvis; the little carpals of the wrist faceted as jewels and as jewels named—capitate, lunate, hamate, pisiform; the phalanges, tiny kickshaws of the body, toys fantástical, worn upon the hands and feet like fans of unimagined cleverness; the porcelain pile of the vertebrae, atop which rides the domed palanquin of the very brain; the vast, the slumbrous pelvis, called to wakefulness by the sweet intrusion of sex or by the stirring of an impatient fetus. Out of this pelvis, endlessly rocking, drops Man. I agree with those African tribes that decorate themselves with bone. It is more to my taste than diamonds, which are a cold and soulless shine, whilst bone—ah, bone—is the pit of a man after the cumbering flesh has been eaten away. In it are all memory and desire captured for eternity.

Bone is power. It is bone to which the soft parts cling, from which they are, helpless, strung and held aloft to the sun, lest Man be but another slithering earth nose. What is this tissue that has double the strength of oak—one cubic inch of which will stand a crushing force of two tons—and that refuses to dissolve in our body fluids but remains intact and solid through all vicissitudes of temperature and pollution? We may be grateful for this insolubility, for it is what stands us tall, that we go not rubbery, bend to awkward dwarfishness. Such rigid, massive pieces! Yet in the hollows of this tissue is the very factory of the blood, wherein each day, 1 million million red blood cells are made and discharged into the

BY RICHARD SELZER

913

912
Art Director Joe Brooks
Designer Joe Brooks
Artist Fred Otnes
Client Penthouse International

913
Art Director Joe Brooks
Designers Joe Brooks
Frank De Vino
Bob Luzzi
Artist Alan Magee
Client Penthouse International

914

Former president Nixon, who now spends hours each day in meditation, did not attend. He was busy completing his memoir, which is called God Is My Co-conspirator.

The Feds broke up the Old Gang that perpetrated the most infamous "third rate burglary" in history. But it's hard to keep a bad man down, so here they are, together again at the gala. . . .

WATERGATE REUNION

BY EDWARD SOREL

he closest and most durable relations, we all know, are those hat are forged in the white heat of crisis. People who have been hrough great personal catastrophes—war, natural disasters, estilence, Otto Preminger movies—form a bond of friendship hat is never severed, a feeling of comradeship that never withers espite the passage of many long years.

It should therefore come as no surprise that the doughty band f fellows who were the personification of that national crisis nown as Watergate, who once faced a nation's wrath with little ore than their own consciences and TV Guide, decided to hold a reunion to rekindle their old friendship and nurture their bonds. And it is no surprise that they decided to meet on the fifth anniversary of that fateful night when a persnickety night watchman who worked at the Watergate office building called the police because he'd noticed that, for some remarkable reason, someone kept putting adhesive tape over the door latches.

No one knows whose idea this reunion first was—although any careful judge of character would suspect that it was most probably that old softy John Mitchell, thought by many to be cold and forbidding, known to his colleagues for his warm and tender

915

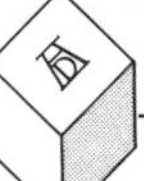 SILVER

914
Art Director Arthur Paul
Writer Asa Baber
Designer Bob Post
Artist Charles Bragg
Publisher Playboy Enterprises, Inc.
Client Playboy Magazine

915
Art Director Joe Brooks
Designers Joe Brooks
Frank De Vino
Artist Ed Sorel
Client Penthouse International

THE MIND OF MARGARET MEAD

How she democratizes greatness

JEAN HOUSTON

It is 5 a.m. In a Manhattan apartment near the American Museum of Natural History, a small, feisty woman of 75 wakes up. She contemplates her dreams and the insights they contained. "Now that's interesting," she muses. "I wonder what that was about?" She observes her mental images—vivid, prolific, teeming from the cornucopia of memory and reflection. She begins to rehearse a critical speech she will soon give on the human uses of science. She remembers an appalling exhibit in Copenhagen: a man tried to create human beings and instead made grotesques. Her body responds to the degradation of treating people as objects—"target populations" . . . "human inventories." She recalls dozens of scientific studies that objectify the human condition. She thinks of her audience and sees them as strangely deficient in music and art, eyes veiled, ears stopped up. A sweep of Beethoven races through her, a sense of standing before the David, *and then looking up at the Sistine ceiling. These images give way to pictures of Early Man, pitiful, helpless, with his arms full of sticks; then to a memory of a New Guinean friend, savage in 1928, intellectual in 1953. Images join images, words appear suited to form, and a complex and potent speech unfolds. The woman decides that it is time to get up and go to work on the typewriter. Her eyes open, and Margaret Mead climbs out of bed.*

This is an essay on human possibilities: that's why it's about Margaret Mead.

For years I have investigated the mystery of why people fail to use their full powers. As director of the Foundation for Mind Research, I have sought clues to this latency in many fields—history, literature, anthropology. Using various techniques, ancient and modern, I have guided hundreds of research subjects on journeys both physical and mental. The evidence clearly suggests that in the human being as he or she presently exists, a great many abilities and ways of functioning have been distorted, inhibited, or altogether blocked. Although the causes and effects vary widely from person to person and from culture to culture, it appears that very few of us have escaped serious crippling. Almost everybody is much less than he or she has the demonstrated capacity to be.

In the course of our research at the Foundation, we have explored ways to unshackle these natural powers in adults and to prevent their initial inhibition in children. Our experiments persuade us that ordinary people, given opportunity and training, can learn to think, feel, and know in new ways, to become more imaginative, and to aspire within realistic limits to a much larger awareness.

Such statements may sound utopian, the fancies of a lobbyist for Atlantis. But nothing is more urgent today than our need to overcome the psychological constraints of tribalism, nationalism, and ecological mayhem. Time is warping, space is shrinking, and we have entered a period of global interdependence in which the human species may not survive if we retain our lethal habits of consumption, aggrandizement, and manipulation. It is time to educate ourselves to the web of kinship and fellow feeling necessary on this endangered planet—to awaken all those dormant potentials that were not necessary to man in his role as conqueror of nature and other people. We are challenged, as never before, to achieve a new humanity and a new way of nurturing the species in harmony with nature and each other.

Which brings us to Margaret Mead.

For some reason that I've mercifully forgotten, I was demonstrating a particularly exotic headstand in an elegant salon in Bath, England.

"Jean!" a voice commanded from the next room. "Stop walking around on your head and tell these people about your experiments with time distortion."

I had only recently met Margaret Mead, and I did as I was told. She took notes, challenging me on fine points and nodding happily as new information was added to her burgeoning storehouse of ideas. The room became crowded and international. A well-known British don drifted over and informed her in unctuous polysyllables that Western civilization was dead.

"Rubbish!"

The don was showered with a barrage of concrete instances in which Western civilization appeared to be in its prime. Suspicion was thrown on the perceptual powers of Oswald Spengler, followed by suggestions for a more syncretic vision that would include a possible flowering of world civilization.

The don backed away, sucking hugely on his unlit pipe.

An old lady appeared, eyes bright and arms filled with flowers. She gave Margaret the flowers and launched into a poignant tale about her youngest son. Margaret listened intently, encouraging her with searching questions. The

JEAN HOUSTON is a psychologist and director of the Foundation for Mind Research in Pomona, New York. She and her husband, Robert E. L. Masters, are coauthors of *Mind Games*.

ILLUSTRATED BY FRED OTNES

916

a dental assistant, and she comes from Cliffside Park, New Jersey . . . I'm . . . I'm going to freeze. Bill . . . **is ri ght!!** *(Applause.)* Um . . . um . . . things that use zippers? **Yes, you got it!!!...Oh my God!** While our lo[vely assis]tant Judy shows us this *dinner for two at the fabulous* six hundred and fifty dollars . . . ? I'm sorry, the ans wer is *Argentina (Oh, fool)* this handsome set of Samsonite luggage and . . . that's right! Higher! Higher! [. . .] recliner that relaxes!) And I have two children, a boy . . . six, and **anything can happen when you're cookin' on a Tappan!** (Mr. Ludden's wardrobe by Botany 500.) Say the magic word and win a hun[. . .]rs **as you sun and fun at the fabulous** Taj Mahal? No, and the box or the curtain . . . um . . . Paul Lynde? *Oh my God!* Ten dollars down and we go to Bennett (ding!) . . . I'm terribly sorry . . . (Products provid[ed in exch]ange for promotional consideration.) **And Eastern...the wings of man.** (And the take-home game.) See you next week!

917

916
Art Director Noel Werrett
Writer Jean Houston
Designers Noel Werrett, Eberhard Luethke
Artist Fred Otnes
Publisher Ambassador Int'l Cultural Foundation

917
Art Director Peter Kleinman
Artist Sue Coe
Publisher National Lampoon, Inc.

CONVERSATION WITH

ROBERT K. BROWN

The King of the Mercenaries talks about his *Soldier of Fortune* magazine, his blood-and-guts encounters with the Viet Cong and Cuban refugees, and why he thinks war is absolute heaven

918

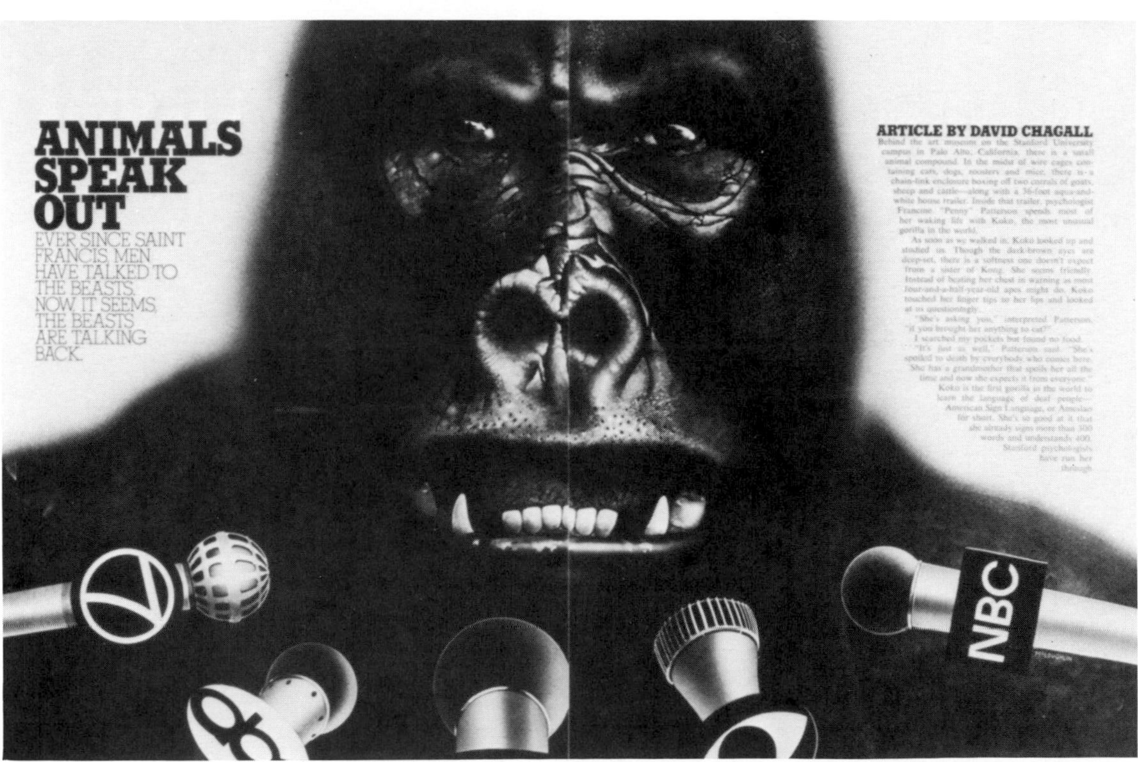

ANIMALS
SPEAK
OUT
EVER SINCE SAINT FRANCIS MEN HAVE TALKED TO THE BEASTS. NOW, IT SEEMS, THE BEASTS ARE TALKING BACK.
ARTICLE BY DAVID CHAGALL
NBC

919

918
Art Directors Michael Brock
George Kenton
Designer Michael Brock
Artist John Collier
Publisher Playboy Enterprises, Inc.
Client Oui Magazine

919
Art Directors Don Menell
Michael Brock
Designer Don Menell
Artist Wayne McLouglin
Publisher Playboy Enterprises, Inc.
Client Oui Magazine

BOOK WORLD

Recordings

The High Price of The Isthmus

Search And Destroy

The Politics Of Cancer

Moving Pictures of the Holocaust

920

BOOK WORLD

Recordings / Gardens

Sacco and Vanzetti: Fifty Years of Doubt

The Flowers Are All Poison

Our Man in Ayer Hitam

Fighting the Apartment Department

921

BOOK WORLD

Recordings

The Way We War

To The Postal Station

Are You Running with Me, Jimmy?

922

920
Art Director K. Francis Tanabe
Editor William McPherson
Designer K. Francis Tanabe
Artist Gary Viskupic
Publisher The Washington Post Book World
Client The Washington Post Book World

921
Art Director K. Francis Tanabe
Editor William McPherson
Designer K. Francis Tanabe
Artist Carlos Llerena-Aguirre
Publisher The Washington Post Book World
Client The Washington Post Book World

922
Art Director K. Francis Tanabe
Editor William McPherson
Designer K. Francis Tanabe
Artist Gary Viskupic
Publisher The Washington Post Book World
Client The Washington Post Book World

Book World

The Alchemical Man

The Woof at the Door

Born Again at the Justice Department

923

924

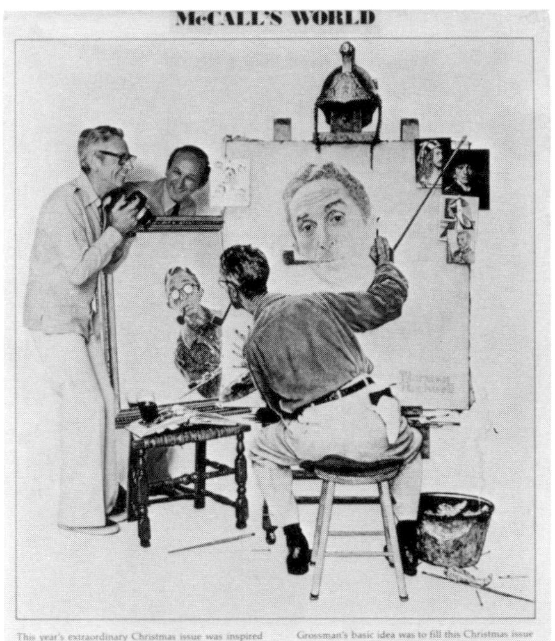

McCALL'S WORLD

This year's extraordinary Christmas issue was inspired by the man whose self-portrait you will recognize above: Norman Rockwell. And superimposed on the painting (in the same humorous spirit as Rockwell, who often painted his own image into his work) are the two men responsible for this tribute to America's most beloved artist: McCall's art director, Alvin Grossman (immediately to the left), who conceived and planned the entire issue, and photographer Otto Storch, at far left, whose

Grossman's basic idea was to fill this Christmas issue with photographs that would duplicate the spirit of Rockwell's paintings—specifically, to create photographic replicas of the nine favorites you will find on the next page. Storch—who once studied with Rockwell at the Art Students' League in New York and later became his friend (in fact, the studio Storch used for many years had once been Rockwell's)—was the ideal choice to attempt the task. Together, the two men visited Rockwell's

925

923
Art Director K. Francis Tanabe
Editor William McPherson
Designer K. Francis Tanabe
Artist Gary Viskupic
Publisher The Washington Post Book World
Client The Washington Post Book World

924
Art Director Carol Carson
Writer Jean Marzolo
Designer Carol Carson
Artist Simms Taback
Publisher Scholastic Magazines, Inc.
Client Scholastic Magazines, Inc.

925
Art Director Alvin Grossman
Designer Alvin Grossman
Photographer Dolores Storch
Publisher The McCall Publishing Company
Client McCall's Magazine

DR. DEMENTO'S HISTORY OF DIRTY DISCS

ARTICLE BY BARRY (DR. DEMENTO) HANSEN

The recent explosion in explicit record lyrics—*vide* Donna Summer's "come tracks," Johnnie Taylor's "move it in, move it out"—is hardly anything new. Neither are the unfettered monologs of such comedians as Richard Pryor and George Carlin. Both "phenomena" actually represent the culmination of 50 years of phonograph erotica, a little-researched aspect of America's audio heritage. It's a fascinating as well as titillating story.

The history of risqué records includes some great names—Redd Foxx, Rusty Warren, Doug Clark and the Hot Nuts, Ruth Wallis—plus a few names one might not expect to show up, such as Ethel Waters and Cliff Edwards, the voice of Walt Disney's Jiminy Cricket. Then there are those wonderful artists whose names I may never know but whose records, with plain white labels, my Uncle Herb kept on the top shelf of his closet.

According to the recording industry, this year is the 100th anniversary of the phonograph recording. The phonograph was a Victorian invention, and for 50 years Victorian standards firmly dictated the lyric content of commercial pop-record releases. Then, in the early Thirties, the Depression almost wiped out the record business. Desperate for a hit, the record companies became

FROM ETHEL WATERS TO RICHARD PRYOR BY WAY OF REDD FOXX

926

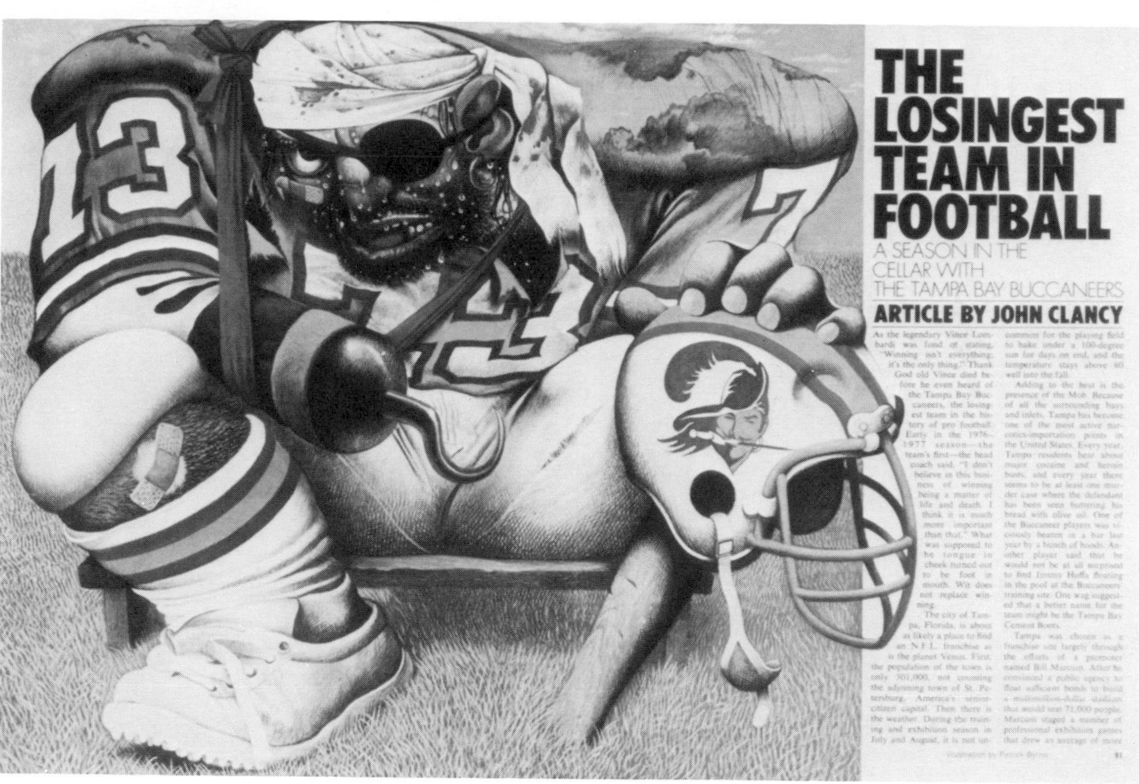

THE LOSINGEST TEAM IN FOOTBALL

A SEASON IN THE CELLAR WITH THE TAMPA BAY BUCCANEERS

ARTICLE BY JOHN CLANCY

As the legendary Vince Lombardi was fond of stating, "Winning isn't everything, it's the only thing." Thank God old Vince died before he even heard of the Tampa Bay Buccaneers, the losingest team in the history of pro football. Early in the 1976–1977 season—the team's first—the head coach said, "I don't believe in this business of winning being a matter of life and death. I think it is much more important than that." What was supposed to be tongue in cheek turned out to be foot in mouth. Wit does not replace winning.

The city of Tampa, Florida, is about as likely a place to find an N.F.L. franchise as is the planet Venus. First, the population of the town is only 301,000, not counting the adjoining town of St. Petersburg, America's senior-citizen capital. Then there is the weather. During the training and exhibition season in July and August, it is not uncommon for the playing field to bake under a 100-degree sun for days on end, and the temperature stays above 80 well into the fall.

Adding to the heat is the presence of the Mob. Because of all the surrounding bays and inlets, Tampa has become one of the most active narcotics-importation points in the United States. Every year, Tampa residents hear about major cocaine and heroin busts, and every year there seems to be at least one murder case where the defendant has been seen buttering his bread with olive oil. One of the Buccaneer players was viciously beaten in a bar last year by a bunch of hoods. Another player said that he would not be at all surprised to find Jimmy Hoffa floating in the pool at the Buccaneers' training site. One wag suggested that a better name for the team might be the Tampa Bay Cement Boots.

Tampa was chosen as a franchise site largely through the efforts of a promoter named Bill Marcum. After he convinced a public agency to float sufficient bonds to build a multimillion-dollar stadium that would seat 71,000 people, Marcum staged a number of professional exhibition games that drew an average of more

Illustration by Patrick Byrne 91

927

926
Art Directors Michael Brock
George Kenton
Designer Jean Pierre Holley
Artist Wilson McLean
Publisher Playboy Enterprises, Inc.
Client Oui Magazine

927
Art Director Michael Brock
Designer George Kenton
Artist Patrick Byrne
Publisher Playboy Enterprises, Inc.
Client Oui Magazine

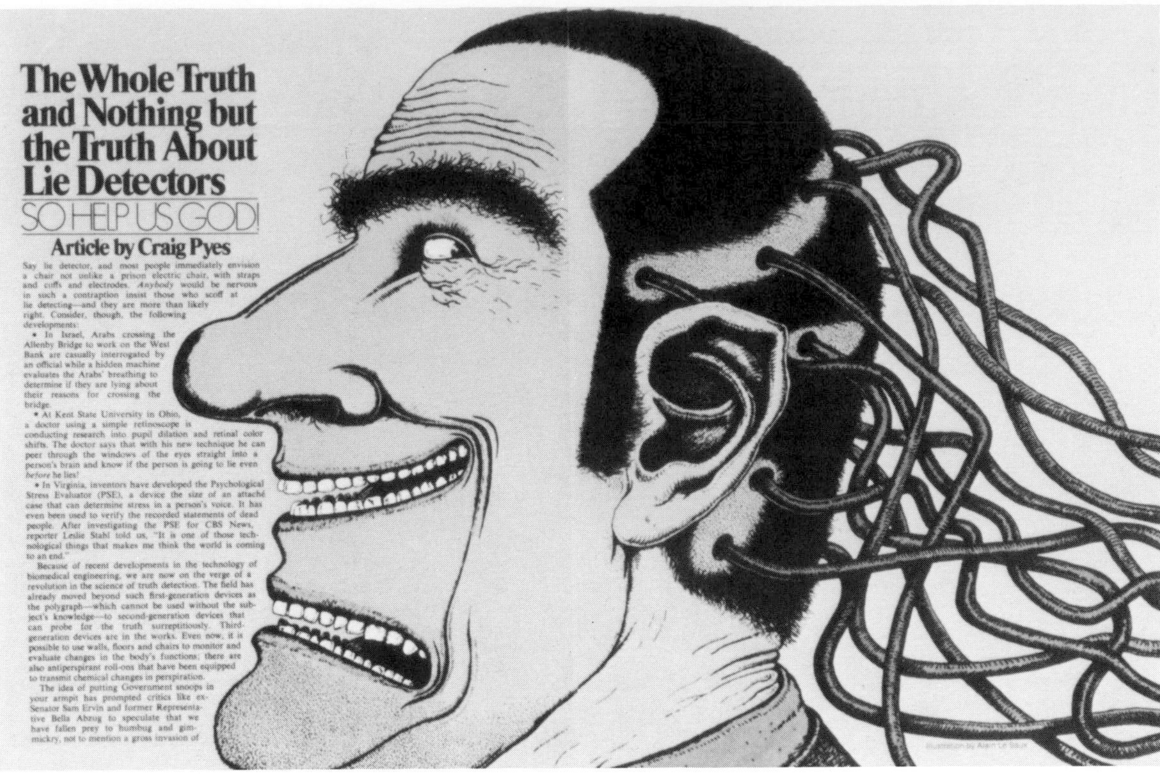

The Whole Truth and Nothing but the Truth About Lie Detectors

SO HELP US GOD!

Article by Craig Pyes

Say lie detector, and most people immediately envision a chair not unlike a prison electric chair, with straps and cuffs and electrodes. *Anybody* would be nervous in such a contraption insist those who scoff at lie detecting—and they are more than likely right. Consider, though, the following developments:

• In Israel, Arabs crossing the Allenby Bridge to work on the West Bank are casually interrogated by an official while a hidden machine evaluates the Arabs' breathing to determine if they are lying about their reasons for crossing the bridge.

• At Kent State University in Ohio, a doctor using a simple retinoscope is conducting research into pupil dilation and retinal color shifts. The doctor says that with his new technique he can peer through the windows of the eyes straight into a person's brain and know if the person is going to lie even *before* he lies!

• In Virginia, inventors have developed the Psychological Stress Evaluator (PSE), a device the size of an attaché case that can determine stress in a person's voice. It has even been used to verify the recorded statements of dead people. After investigating the PSE for CBS News, reporter Leslie Stahl told us, "It is one of those technological things that makes me think the world is coming to an end."

Because of recent developments in the technology of biomedical engineering, we are now on the verge of a revolution in the science of truth detection. The field has already moved beyond such first-generation devices as the polygraph—which cannot be used without the subject's knowledge—to second-generation devices that can probe for the truth surreptitiously. Third-generation devices are in the works. Even now, it is possible to use walls, floors and chairs to monitor and evaluate changes in the body's functions; there are also antiperspirant roll-ons that have been equipped to transmit chemical changes in perspiration.

The idea of putting Government snoops in your armpit has prompted critics like ex-Senator Sam Ervin and former Representative Bella Abzug to speculate that we have fallen prey to humbug and gimmackry, not to mention a gross invasion of

928

MOTHERHOOD
If, When, and How Many?

THE MYTH OF THE ONLY CHILD

by Carol Saline

All the kids in the neighborhood called her "poor Phyllis." Not to her face, of course. Only when she wasn't around. Actually Phyllis was well liked, well groomed, even well off. It was just that she was an only child. Poor Phyllis had no brothers or sisters and we all felt terribly sorry for her. Though we fought like mortal enemies with our siblings, disliked them for grabbing the spotlight, and resented wearing their hand-me-downs, we still pitied poor Phyllis.

Most of our negative attitudes about only children stem from the days when multiples were the norm and an only child signaled to the outside world that something was amiss at home. The couple couldn't produce more than one child, in which case the mother probably felt cheated and deprived. She'd compensate by throwing her life into her one and only, pampering him, doting on his every whim, and eventually smothering him with her excessive caring. Maybe the problem was much deeper. Sexual dysfunction. Gross incompatibility. "Let's have a child to see if we can patch things up." But children are a poor cement and the single product of an unhappy union was truly the pitiable only child. Momma pulled her one way: "Love me. Be my ally." Poppa pulled her in the other direction: "No, love me. Be my ally."

That was the way we were. But we aren't that way any more. Love, marriage, and children in the plural isn't the only road for all couples. Some are saying, "We don't want children," and they aren't automatically labeled as hopelessly selfish or misguided. Others retain the traditional view that having a child is one of the ultimate joys in life, an experience they wouldn't want to miss. So they are deciding in increasing numbers to have only one child and concentrate the thrill of parenting on one tidy package.

They are saying, "We want the pleasures of family life but we don't want to be dominated by kids. We don't want the horrendous expense of several children, the racing around to meet lots of different schedules. We both want careers and we want private time besides to devote to each other and to ourselves." These goals seem quite obtainable by limiting their family to one offspring.

Once we would have shuddered at such self-centered thinking. Now there's evidence it makes a great deal of sense. With one child we are able to come closest to the ideal conditions of what parenting should be. Though each child in a family is unique, the demands of coping with several somehow make us forget that miracle of life. Repetition and its accompanying exhaustion wear down the wonder of it all. But with the only child, there's an exciting newness all the time. Everything is a first. We savor each stage of development, eagerly attend class plays and recitals, zero in on the child's every burgeoning interest. Our attention, divided at best in the harried lives we all lead, is fairly easy to focus on one child. It doesn't have to be doled out in those rarely successful attempts at equal time.

Only children get the best we have to offer materially and emotionally, skimmed off the top perhaps, but never the dregs. There's no one at home with whom the only child has to share toys or a room. Only children rarely wear hand-me-downs, never suffer the discomfort of sporting a boxy coat, long out of style, bought for someone with a much different frame. There are no embarrassing sibling comparisons because there's nobody with whom to compare; they never worry who's the favorite because they haven't any rivals.

No doubt about it. The only child is treated as someone quite special. Whatever he or she does—builds a bridge with an Erector set, makes the finals in the spelling bee—it's considered terrific. Because of the undiluted doses of attention and affection, only children not only feel special, they are pushed to accomplish special things. That's why they are frequently high achievers, well aware they carry the full load of their parents' expectations.

We used to call this kind of kid "spoiled rotten." Our puritan ethic told us it was bad to allow somebody to feel so good about himself. Well, that's changed too. Current psychology recognizes that everybody needs to feel special. Positive strokes and lots of warm fuzzies are the best soil for helping tender egos grow into healthy adults. The only child has a running start in this direction because he or she receives more than the average share of nurturing.

So we can shoot down the myth that only children are somewhat the worse for being spoiled. In the opinion of Philadelphia psychologist Matt Gershenfeld, there's no evidence to support this accusation.

Another myth tattles that only children are dominated by their parents. They are kept under a kind of protective surveillance, their lives orchestrated by baton wielding

929

928
Art Director Michael Brock
Designer Jean Pierre Holley
Artist Alain Le Saux
Publisher Playboy Enterprises, Inc.
Client Oui Magazine

929
Art Director Paul Hardy
Writer Beatrice Buckler
Designer Paul Hardy
Artist Nancy Stahl
Publisher Beatrice Buckler
Client Working Woman Magazine

Swanner's most incredible trip back in time was a visit with the space men to Albert Einstein in his Zurich office.

82 oui

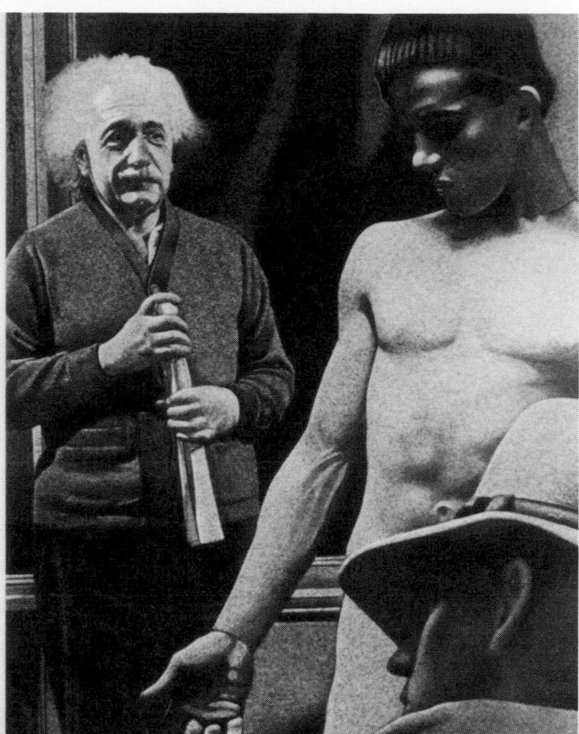

930A

B

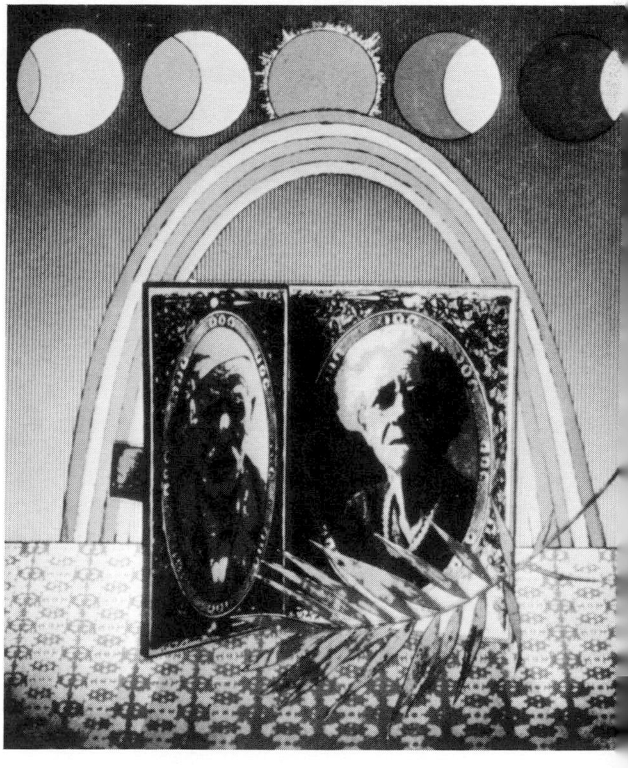

C

930A
Art Directors Michael Brock
George Kenton
Designer Michael Brock
Artist Alex Gnidziejko
Publisher Playboy Enterprises, Inc.
Client Oui Magazine

930B
Art Director Kenneth Dyball
Designer Kenneth Dyball
Artist Kenneth Dyball
Client WCBS-TV News

930C
Art Director Gil Cowley
Designer Gil Cowley
Artist Gil Cowley
Client WCBS-TV/Summer Semester

930 D

930E

930F

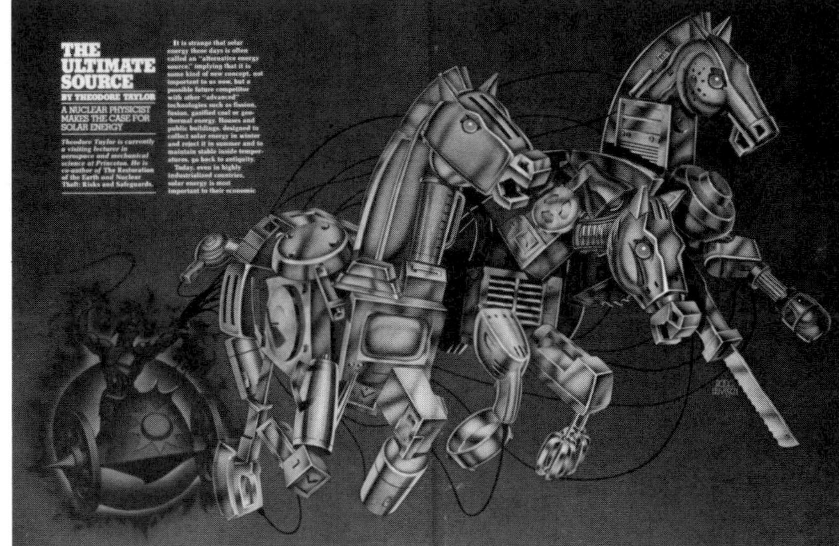

930G

930D
irector Allan H. Drossman
signer Allan H. Drossman
Artist Allan H. Drossman
Client WCBS-TV News

930E
Art Director Kevork Cholakian
Designer Kevork Cholakian
Artist Kevork Cholakian
Client WCBS-TV

930F
Art Director Steve Phillips
Designer Carole Jean Feuerman
Artist Carole Jean Feuerman
Photographer Steve Phillips
Production Company New Times Publishing Co.
Publisher New Times Publishing Co.
Client New Times

930G
Art Director Gordon Mortensen
Editor David Sanford
Designer Gordon Mortensen
Artist Roger Huyssen
Client Politics Today
(formerly Skeptic
Magazine)

931

932

THE ART AND POLITICS OF
GEOFFREY MOSS
With a Foreword by Dan Rather

A Washington Post Book

933

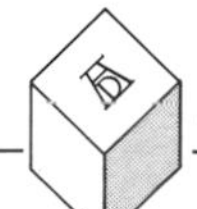
GOLD

931
Art Director Harold Tench
Writer Ron Strauss
Designer Harold Tench
Artist Reid Icard
Photographer Harold Tench
Agency Webb & Athey, Inc.
Client Ithaco, Inc.

932
Designer William Mitchell
Artist William Mitchell
Agency Macy's Visual Merchandising Dept.
Client Macy's

933
Art Director Geoffrey Moss
Editor Sandra Choron
Designer Stanley Drate
Artist Geoffrey Moss
Publisher Hawthorn Books Inc.
Client Hawthorn Books Inc.

934

GOLD

934

Art Directors Marilyn Hoffner
Albert Greenberg
Writer Marilyn Hoffner
Designers Marilyn Hoffner
Albert Greenberg
Artists John Alcorn
Harold Altman
Al Blaustein
Tom Boutis
Gretna Campbell
Edmond Casarella
Remy Charlip
Seymour Chwast
Ray Cruz
Lillian Delevoryas
Lois Dodd
Lou Donato
Audrey Flack
Gerry Gersten
Gregory Gillespie
Milton Glaser
Dimitri Hadzi
Lionel Kalish
Alex Katz
William King
R. B. Kitaj
Lee Krasner
George Leavitt
Herb Lubalin
Richard Lytle
Peppino Mangravite
Kenneth Munowitz
Norman Narotzky
William Negron
Elliot Offner
Clare Romano
Richard Rosenblum
John Ross
Reynold Ruffins
George Segal
Alan, Arthur & Judy Singer
Robert Slutzky
Ed Sorel
Raphael Soyer
Simms Taback
Louis Trakis
Gary Viskupic
Hilde Weingarten
Tom Wesselmann
Christopher Wilmarth
Photographers Carl Fischer
Norman Griner
Art Kane
Jay Maisel
Irving Schild
Neal Slavin
Ben Swedervsky
Publisher The Cooper Union
Alumni Association
Client Cooper Union

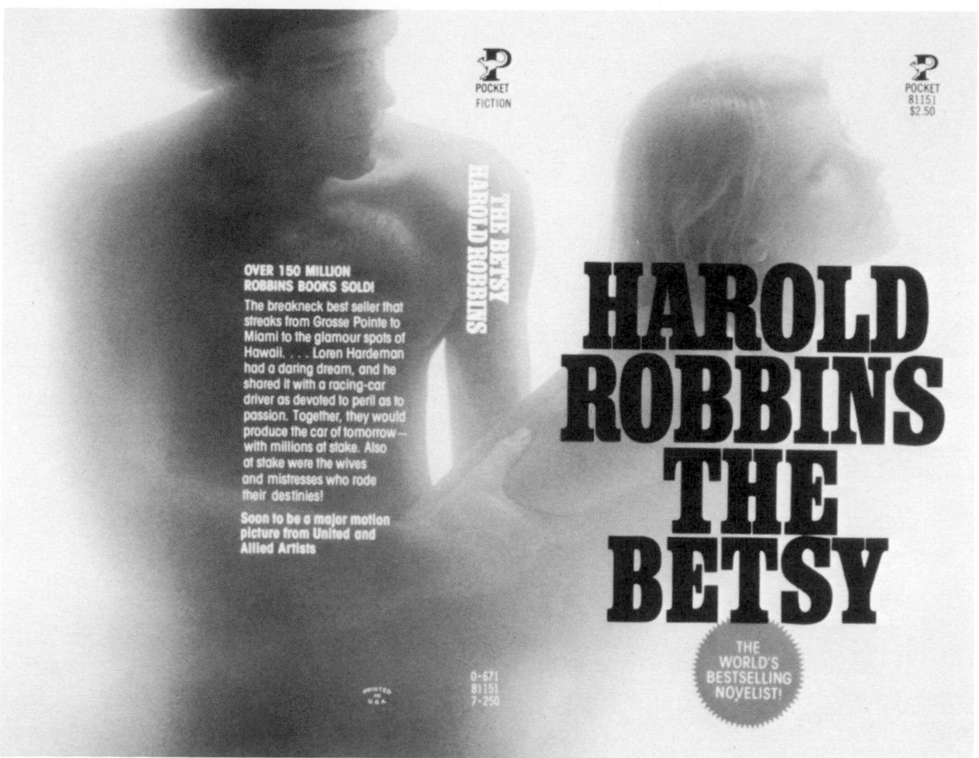

935

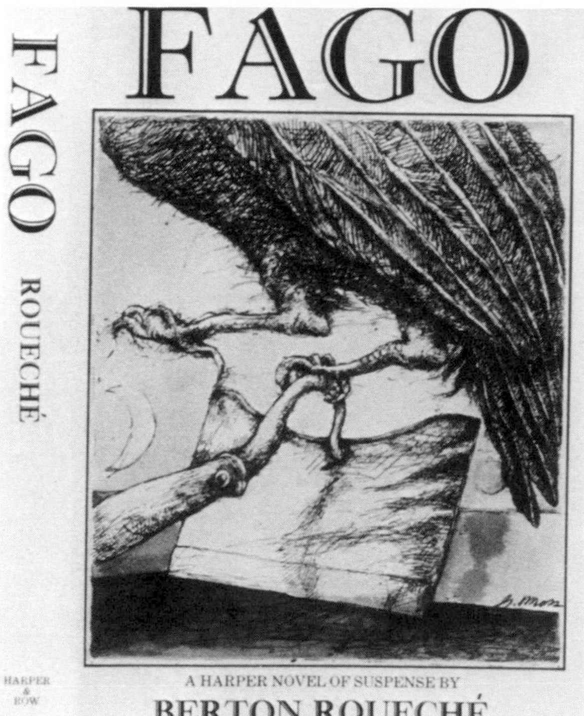

936

Here's Help....for the choking nonsmoker, and the smoker who wants to quit!
Y3680/$1.95/PYRAMID
WE MIND IF YOU SMOKE
Don C. Matchan
BROWN TEETH
BAD BREATH
COUGH! COUGH!

937

935
Art Director Milton Charles
Writer Harold Robbins
Designer Milton Charles
Photographer Mort Engel
Publisher Pocket Books
Client Pocket Books

936
Art Director Geoffrey Moss
Editor Joan Kahn
Designer Geoffrey Moss
Artist Geoffrey Moss
Publisher Harper & Row
Client Harper & Row

937
Art Director Harris Lewine
Editor Barbara Rogasky
Designer Milton Glaser
Artist Milton Glaser
Publisher Jove Books C/O Harcourt Brace Jovanovich, Inc.
Client Jove Books C/O Harcourt Brace Jovanovich, Inc.

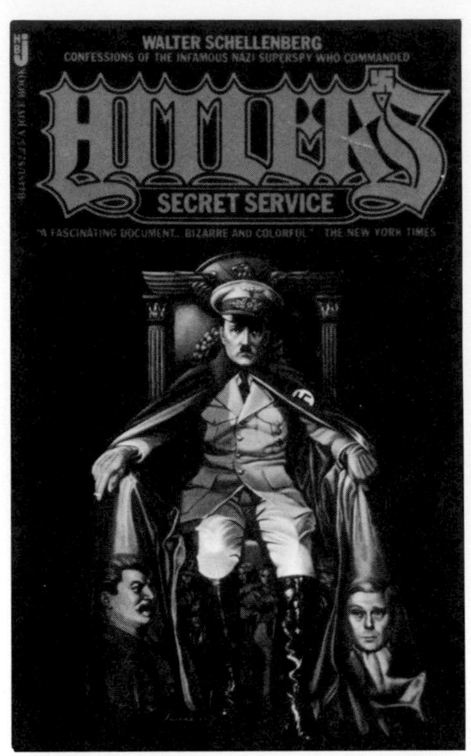

938

940

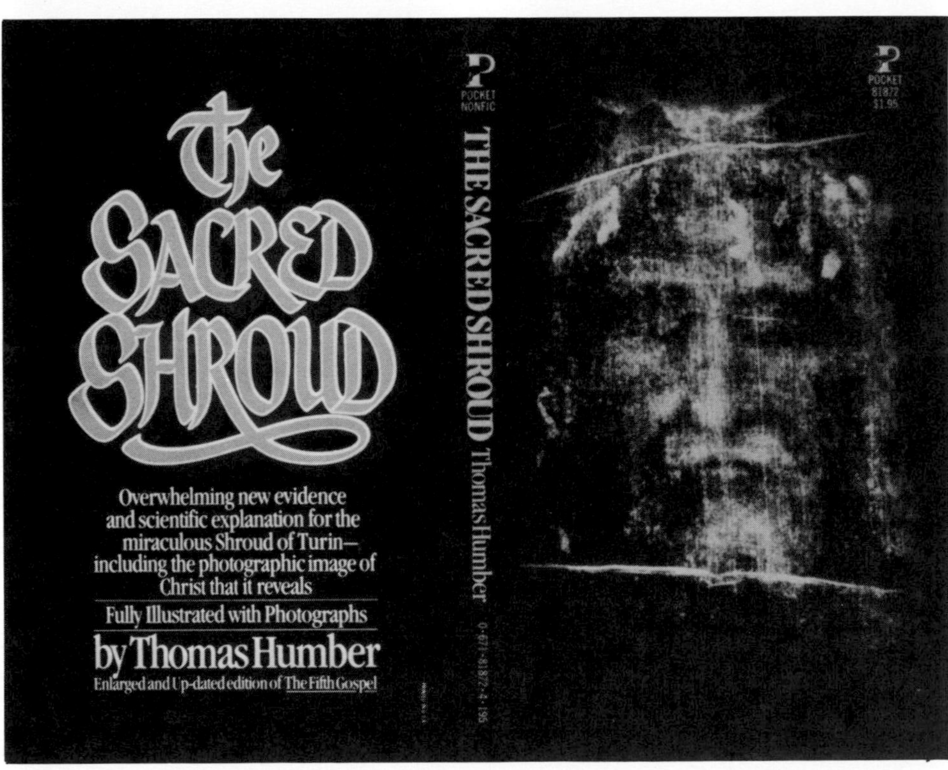

939

938
Art Director Harris Lewine
Editor Barbara Rogasky
Designer Tony Greco
Artist Rowina Morrill
Publisher Jove Books
Client Jove Books

939
Art Director Milton Charles
Writer Thomas Humber
Designer Milton Charles
Letterer Carl Dellacroce
Publisher Pocket Books
Client Pocket Books

940
Art Director Tony Greco
Editor Barbara Rogasky
Designer Tony Greco
Artist Tom Upshur
Publisher Jove Books
Client Jove Books

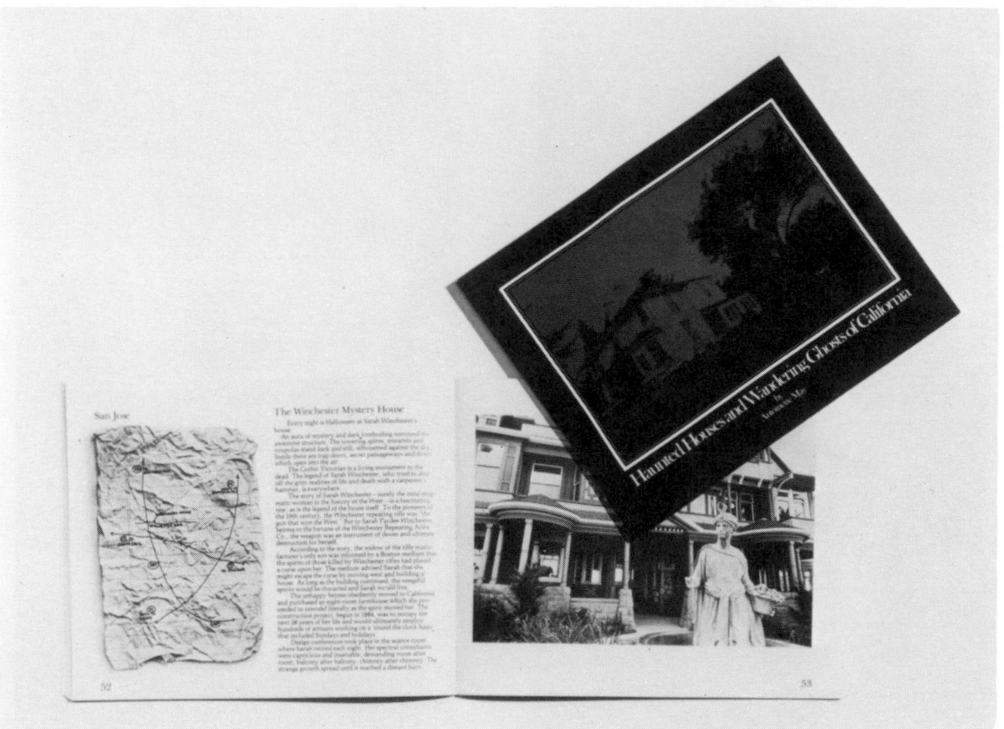

941

941

Art Director	**Carol Fulton**
Writer	**Antoinette May**
Designer	**Carol Fulton**
Artist	**Pat Wilson**
Photographer	**Ron Shuman**
Producer	**Steven Jacobs Design**
Production Company	**Steven Jacobs Design**
Publisher	**Examiner Special Projects**
Agency	**Steven Jacobs Design**
Client	**San Francisco Examiner**

Photography

How the Other Third lives.
parade
It wouldn't be Sunday without a Parade

943

PAN AM
Take an elevator to the airport.
PAN AM

944

All the body money can buy.
parade
It wouldn't be Sunday without a Parade

946

943
Art Director Tony Mandarino
Writer Karl Vollmer
Designer Tony Mandarino
Photographer Tony Mandarino
Agency Frankfurt Communications
Client Parade Magazine

944
Art Director Mark Gershman
Writer Pat Sutula
Photographer Cosimo
Agency Carl Alley
Client Pan Am

946
Art Director Tony Mandarino
Writer Karl Vollmer
Designer Tony Mandarino
Photographer Tony Mandarino
Agency Frankfurt Communications
Client Parade Magazine

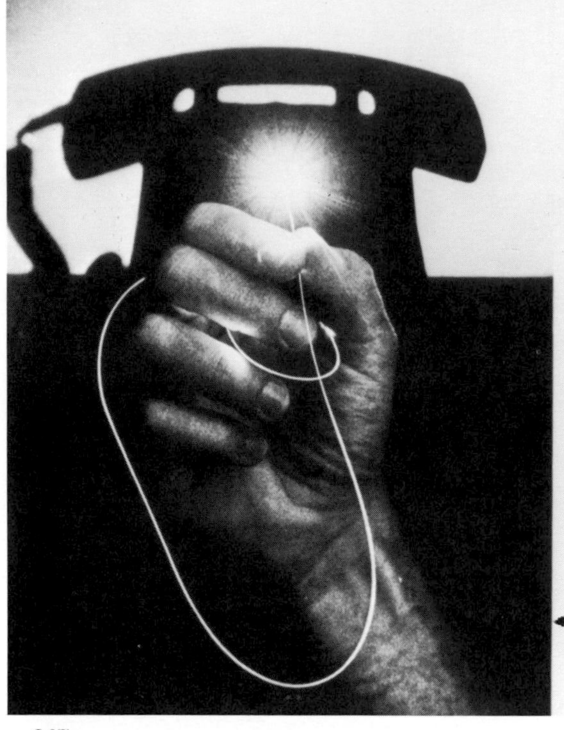

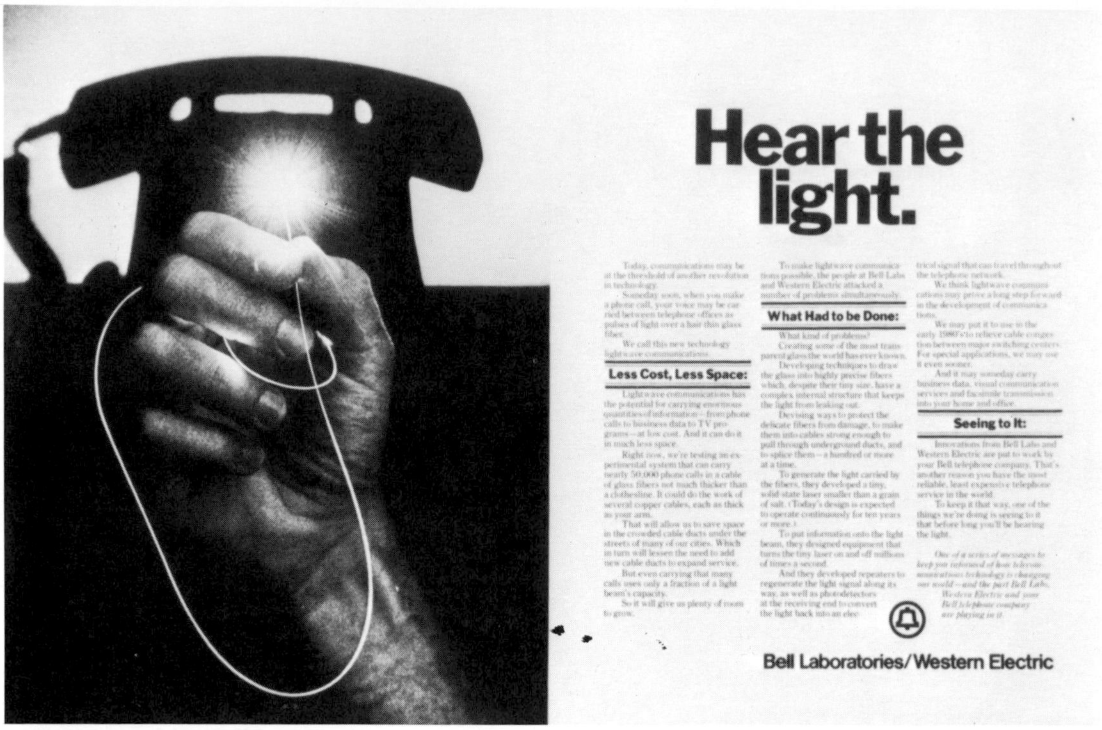

Hear the light.

Today, communications may be at the threshold of another revolution in technology.

Someday soon, when you make a phone call, your voice may be carried between telephone offices as pulses of light over a hair thin glass fiber.

We call this new technology lightwave communications.

Less Cost, Less Space:

Lightwave communications has the potential for carrying enormous quantities of information—from phone calls to business data to TV programs—at low cost. And it can do it in much less space.

Right now, we're testing an experimental system that can carry nearly 50,000 phone calls in a cable of glass fibers not much thicker than a clothesline. It could do the work of several copper cables, each as thick as your arm.

That will allow us to save space in the crowded cable ducts under the streets of many of our cities. Which in turn will lessen the need to add new cable ducts to expand service.

But even carrying that many calls uses only a fraction of a light beam's capacity.

So it will give us plenty of room to grow.

To make lightwave communications possible, the people at Bell Labs and Western Electric attacked a number of problems simultaneously.

What Had to be Done:

What kind of problems?

Creating some of the most transparent glass the world has ever known.

Developing techniques to draw the glass into highly precise fibers which, despite their tiny size, have a complex internal structure that keeps the light from leaking out.

Devising ways to protect the delicate fibers from damage, to make them into cables strong enough to pull through underground ducts, and to splice them—a hundred or more at a time.

To generate the light carried by the fibers, they developed a tiny, solid-state laser smaller than a grain of salt. (Today's design is expected to operate continuously for ten years or more.)

To put information onto the light beam, they designed equipment that turns the tiny laser on and off millions of times a second.

And they developed repeaters to regenerate the light signal along its way, as well as photodetectors at the receiving end to convert the light back into an electrical signal that can travel throughout the telephone network.

We think lightwave communications may prove a long step forward in the development of communications.

We may put it to use in the early 1980's to relieve cable congestion between major switching centers. For special applications, we may use it even sooner.

And it may someday carry business data, visual communication services and facsimile transmission into your home and office.

Seeing to It:

Innovations from Bell Labs and Western Electric are put to work by your Bell telephone company. That's another reason you have the most reliable, least expensive telephone service in the world.

To keep it that way, one of the things we're doing is seeing to it that before long you'll be hearing the light.

One of a series of messages to keep you informed of how telecommunications technology is changing our world—and the part Bell Labs, Western Electric and your Bell telephone company are playing in it.

Bell Laboratories/Western Electric

947

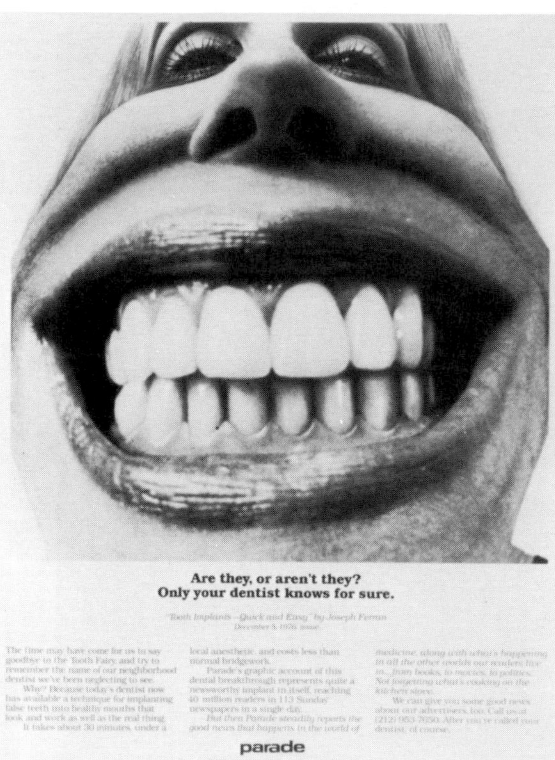

948

949

947
Art Director Joe Frederick
Writer Roger Levinshon
Photographer Carl Fischer
Agency Foote, Cone and Belding Communications, Inc.
Client Western Electric

948
Art Director Tony Mandarino
Writer Karl Vollmer
Designer Tony Mandarino
Photographer Tony Mandarino
Agency Frankfurt Communications
Client Parade Magazine

949
Art Director Robert Reitzfeld
Writer Gerry Scally
Photographer Bob Richardson
Producer Ina Kahn
Agency Trevira® In-House (Hoechst)
Client Kasper

We helped make Joe Torre famous for football.

To our knowledge, he never won one for the Gipper. But, when it's football season in Brooklyn, Joe Torre's the man they call.

Joe owns a sporting goods store in Brooklyn. And he advertises it in the Yellow Pages. Because, while everybody knows Joe Torre the ballplayer, not everybody knows Joe Torre the businessman.

And that's exactly where we help.

When a junior football league went looking for uniforms and equipment, they found Joe in the Yellow Pages. So did a couple of local athletic clubs. Not to mention the sandlotters, schoolyarders, and just plain sports who find Joe in the Yellow Pages every day.

If you figure your business can use that kind of reach, give us a call. We can probably help you too.

We might even help make you famous.

yellow pages

950

You call the shot. We've got the cameras.
Panasonic

951

952

950
Art Director Jorge Perez-Vinalet
Writer John Mezzina
Photographer Carl Fischer
Agency Cunningham and Walsh, Inc.
Client Yellow Pages

951
Art Director Buddy Sykora
Writer Tom Allen
Photographer Dom Quartuccio
Client Panasonic

952
Art Director Jim Begany
Writer Janine Lindloff
Designer Jim Begany
Photographer Frank Maresca
Agency RMI
Client Optyl Corp.

953

Minnesota Symposium on Visual Communication

955

In Saronno, Amaretto is our bambino.

It was in our little town that Amaretto, the drink of love, was born 450 years ago. When a beautiful young woman created an extraordinary liqueur to please the man she loved. To this day, nobody makes love the way we do in Saronno.

Here we still make Amaretto di Saronno as we have for centuries. We allow the flavor to develop until it is soft and full. We take our time—can love be hurried?

The resulting taste is rich and subtle and intriguing. It will not bring a tear to the eye. Such is not love, caro.

Enjoy Amaretto di Saronno as it is, or on the rocks, or with coffee. Try it in any number of exciting mixed drinks. With love, anything goes.

But a word of caution. There is only one Amaretto di Saronno. Remember this. Because if it is not Amaretto di Saronno that you drink, it may not be love after all.

The Bambino.

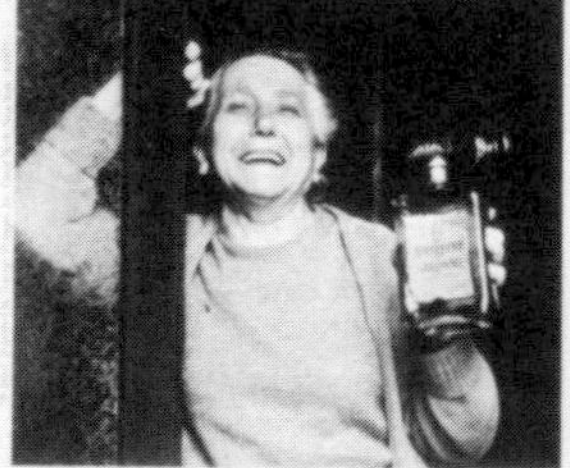

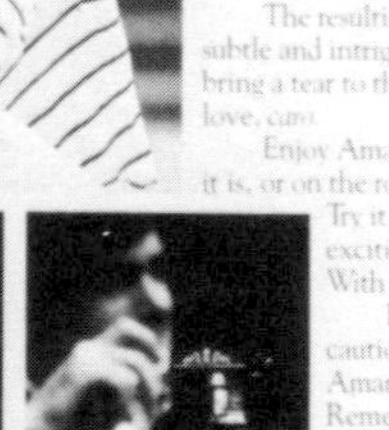

Amaretto di Saronno. Originale.
From the Village of Love.

954

953
Art Director Don Wise
Designer Don Wise
otographer Art Kane
Agency Don Wise & Co
Client Katja designs for Wellman

954
Art Director Tom Heck
Writer Marsha Grace
Designer Tom Heck
Photographers Anthony D. Edgeworth (Still Life by Irene Stern)
Agency Wells, Rich, Greene, Inc.
Client Amaretto Di Saronno

955
Art Director Sue Crolick
Writer Phil Hanft
Designer Sue Crolick
Photographer Kent Severson
Agency Martin Williams Advertising
Client University of Minnesota

956

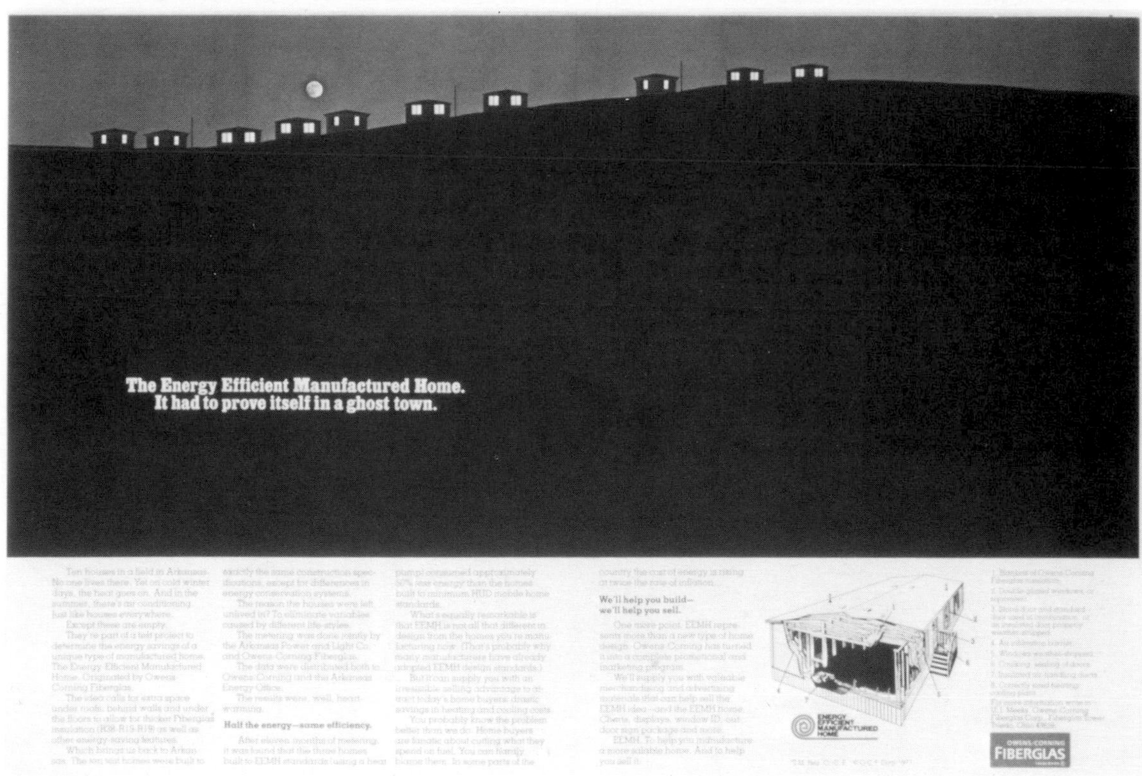

957

956
Art Director Buddy Sykora
Photographer Dom Quartuccio
Client Panasonic

957
Art Director Láurel Emery
Writer David Schneider
Photographer John Olson
Agency Ogilvy & Mather Inc.
Client Owens-Corning

OMNI
Some things in our hotel are more obvious than others.
But our dedication to excellence and elegance is unmistakably expressed in everything we do.
You'll see it in our dramatic architecture, our original art.
In cocktail lounges graced by greenery and great open space. With music everywhere, from quiet contemporary to light piano classics.
And in restaurants committed to the maxim that while a good meal is simply food, a great meal is an inspiration.
Tasteful surroundings and appointments, impeccable service, casual elegance, constant attention to detail.
This is the Omni International Hotel experience.
For reservations, please call 659-0000.
Omni International Hotel, Marietta Street at International Boulevard, Atlanta, Georgia 30303.

958

959

958
Art Director Bill Sweney
Writer Brian McKenna
Designer Bill Sweney
Photographer Jamie Cook
Agency Cole Henderson Drake, Inc.
Client Omni International Hotels, Inc.

959
Art Director Len Fury
Writer Carol Tutundgy
Designer Len Fury
Photographer Phil Marco
Publisher Nabisco
Agency Corporate Annual Reports
Client Nabisco

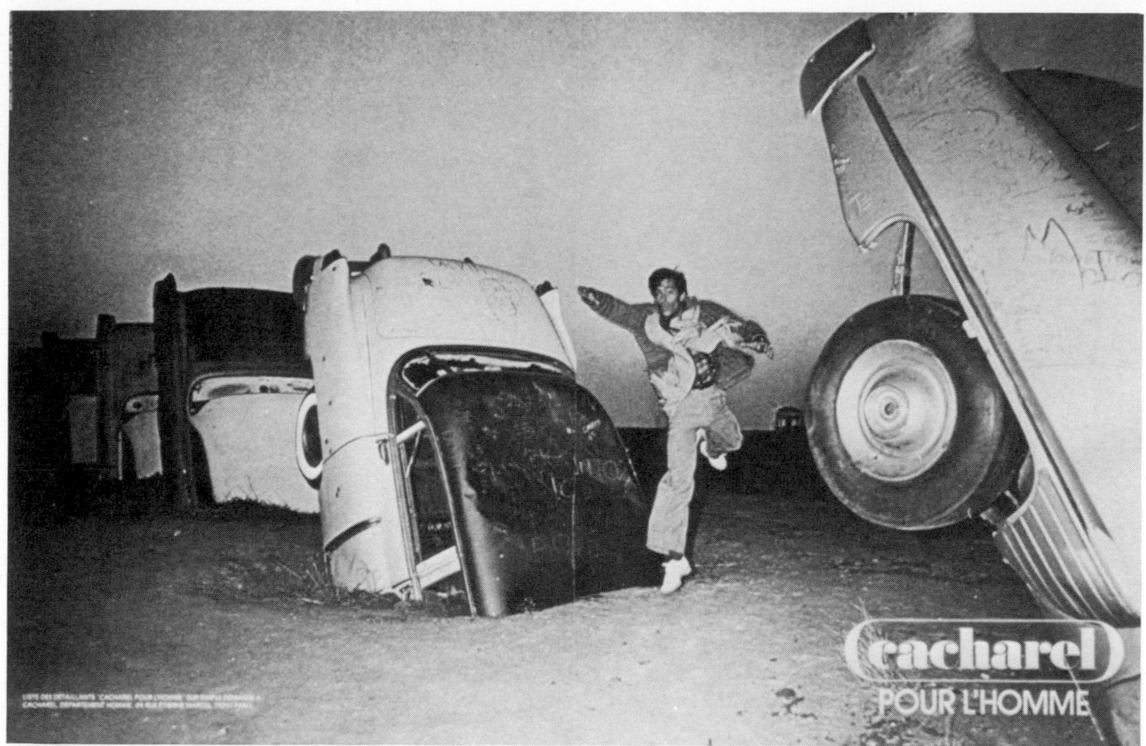

960

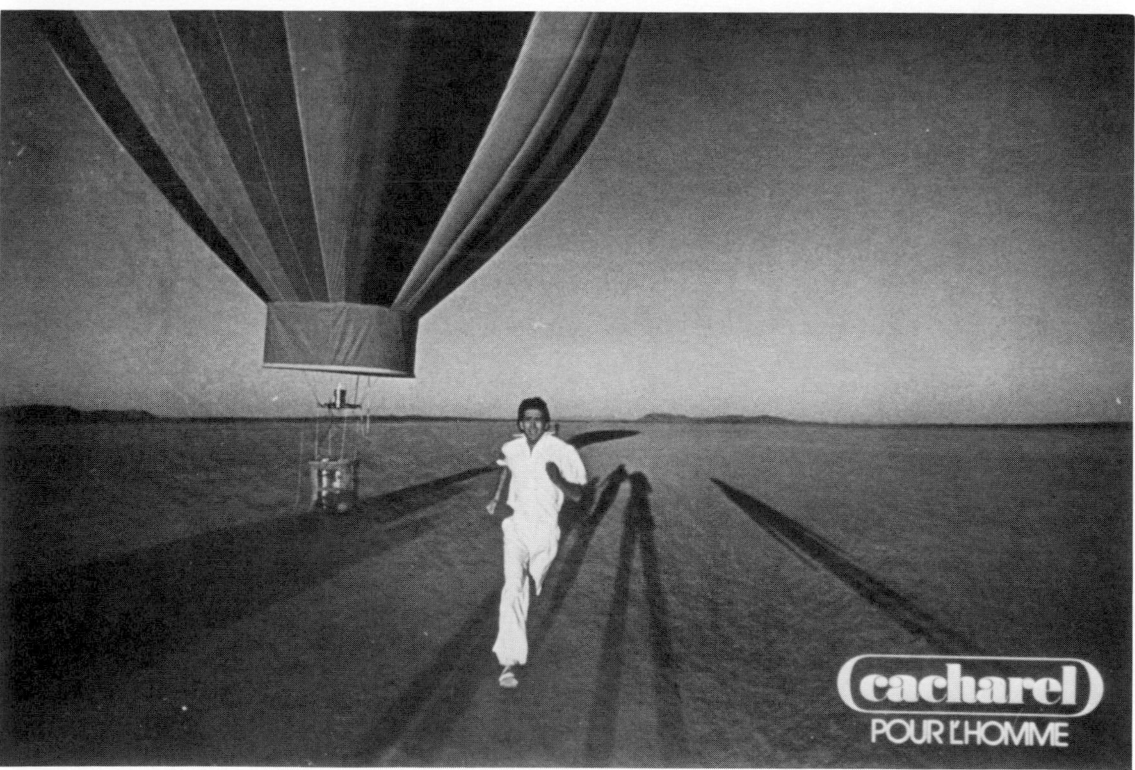

961

960
Art Director Robert Delpire
Designer Robert Delpire
Photographer Art Kane
Agency Ideodis
Client Cacharel

961
Art Director Robert Delpire
Designer Robert Delpire
Photographer Art Kane
Agency Ideodis
Client Cacharel

The Communicators...
...Through our growing network of overseas facilities—branches, representative offices, subsidiaries and correspondents—Manufacturers Hanover offers international customers direct access to virtually any marketplace in the world. Consider the source.
MANUFACTURERS HANOVER
The financial source.Worldwide.

962

The Naturists...
...Pollution control systems provided by our equipment financing/leasing subsidiary, one of the largest in the U.S., gives industry the means to protect the environment for future generations. Consider the source.
MANUFACTURERS HANOVER
The financial source.Worldwide.

963

962
Art Director Mario Giuriceo
Writer Neal McMenamin
Designer Mario Giuriceo
Photographer Marvin Koner
Agency Edwin Bird Wilson, Inc.
Client Manufacturers Hanover Trust Company

963
Art Director Mario Giuriceo
Writer Neal McMenamin
Designer Mario Giuriceo
Photographer Marvin Koner
Agency Edwin Bird Wilson, Inc.
Client Manufacturers Hanover Trust Company

INTRODUCING THE NEW, LARGE
AUDI 5000
AND THE EXTRAORDINARILY GIFTED
ENGINEERS WHO DESIGNED IT.

964

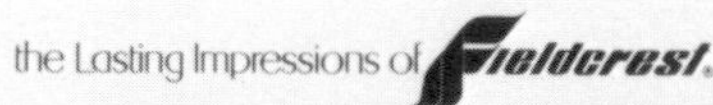

"FESTIVE SPIRIT" BY MISSONI

A new kind of sunshine for the bed and bath.
Milan's leading design team brings a warm and festive feeling
to their newest collection for Fieldcrest.

965

964
Art Director Helmut Krone
Writers Bob Levinson
David Reider
Photographer Carl Fischer
Agency Doyle, Dane, Bernbach, Inc.
Client Audi

965
Art Director Fred Donoher
Photographer Ruszard Horowitz
Agency Fieldcrest
Client Fieldcrest

966

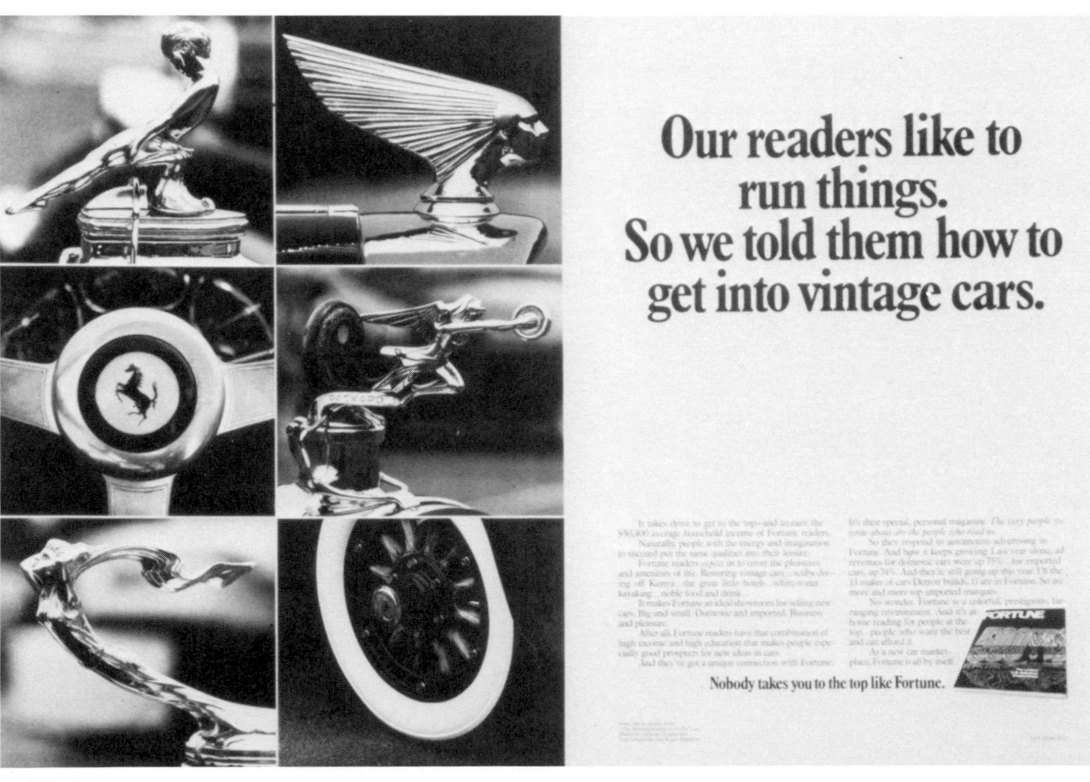

967 A

966
Art Director David Kennedy
Designer David Kennedy
Photographer Art Kane
Agency Benton & Bowles—Chicago
Client Harley Davidson

967A
Art Director Glenn Scheuer
Writer Dick Olmsted
Photographer Editorial Photography
Agency Young & Rubicam
Client Fortune Magazine

B

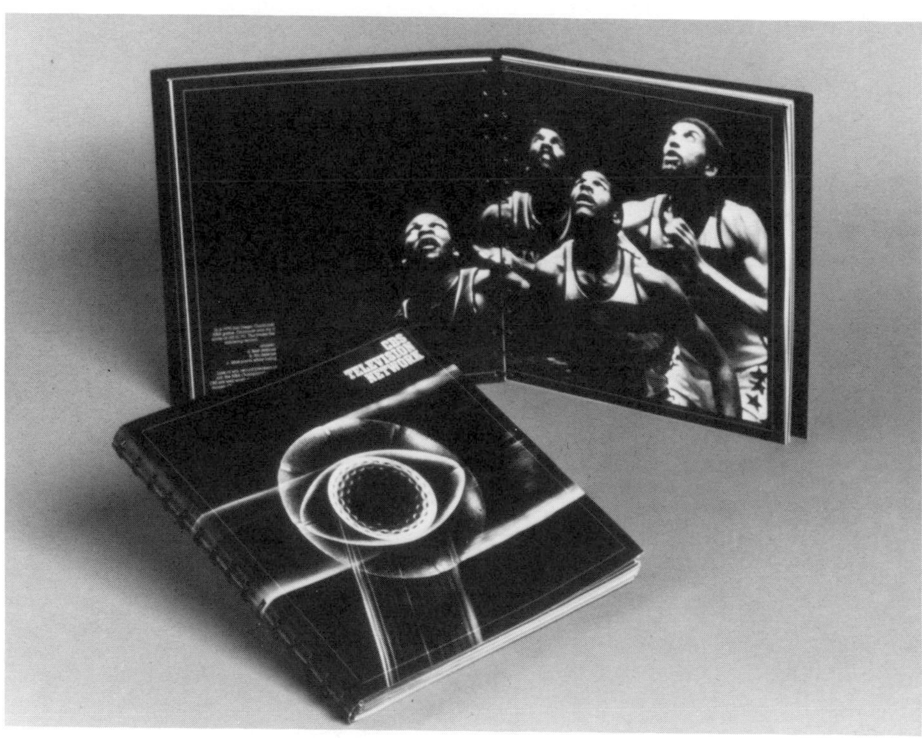

968

967B

Art Director Santo Cambareri
Writers Steve Hunter
Santo Cambareri
Designer Santo Cambareri
Photographer Michael Pruzan
Agency Ketchum, MacLeod and Grove, Inc.
Client Ciba-Geigy Corp.

968

Art Directors Ed Sobel
David November
Writer Peter Moreau
Designers Ed Sobel
David November
Photographers Jerry Darvin
Pete Mecca
Mel DiGiaccomo
Publisher CBS Television Network
Agency CBS Entertainment Division/Advertising and Promotion
Client CBS Television Network

969

970

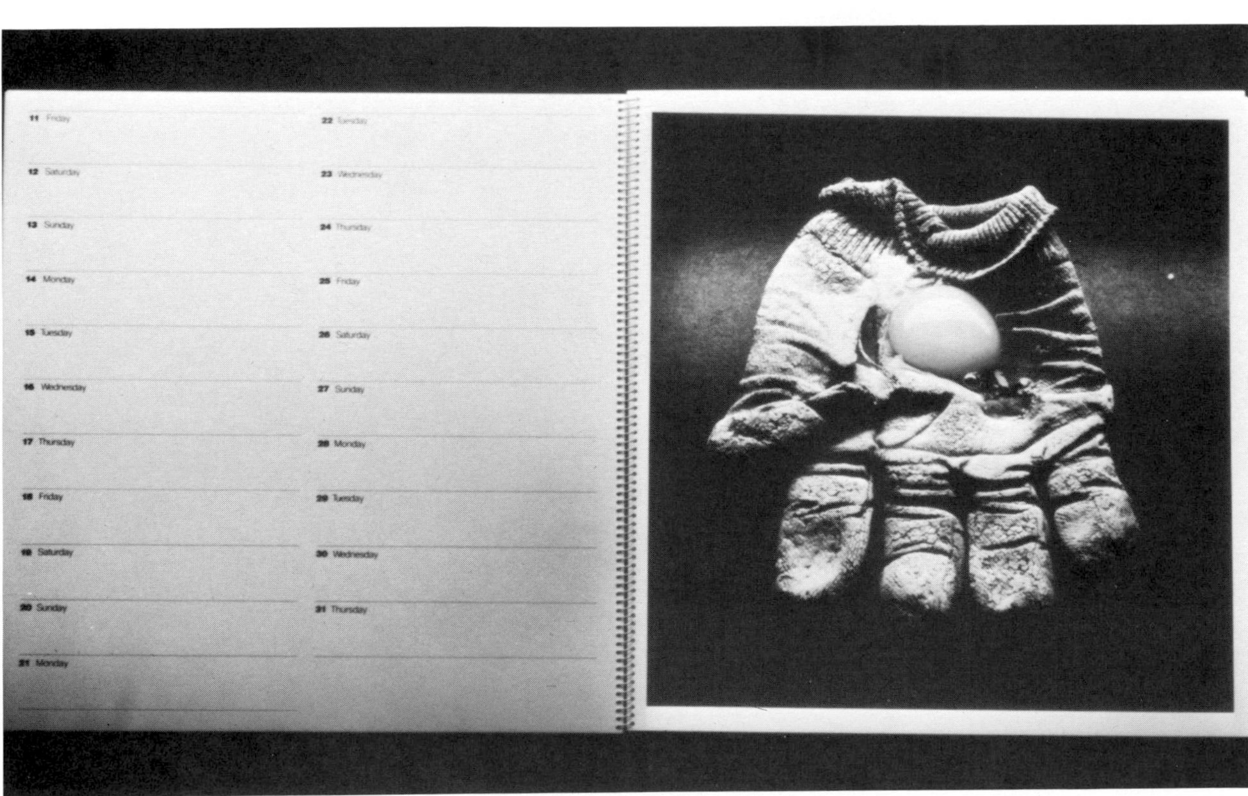

971

969
Art Director Nick Rozsa
Designer John Coy
Photographer Nick Rozsa
Agency John Coy Design
Client Nick Rozsa

970
Art Director André Gillardin
Designer André Gillardin
Photographer André Gillardin
Agency Gillardin Inc.
Client André Gillardin

971
Art Director Phil Marco
Designer Richard Danne
Photographer Phil Marco
Publisher S.D. Scott Printing Company
Client S.D. Scott Printing Company

972

974

973

972
Art Director Len Fury
Writer Carol Tutundgy
Designer Len Fury
Photographer Phil Marco
Agency Corporate Annual Reports Inc.
Client Nabisco, Inc.

973
Designers Alan Mitelman/Design Organization
Photographer John Olson
Client John Olson Productions Inc.

974
Art Director Leslie A. Segal
Writer Rubina Grosso
Designer Leslie A. Segal
Photographer Gary Gladstone
Agency Corporate Annual Reports Inc.
Client Rexham Corporation

975

976

977

975
Art Directors Ike Millman
Daniel S. Lee
Designer Ken Thompson
Photographer Daniel S. Lee
Agency 2010 Advertising, Inc.
Client Revlon, Inc.

976
Art Directors Ike Millman
Daniel S. Lee
Designer Ken Thompson
Photographer Daniel S. Lee
Publisher Art Power
Agency 2010 Advertising, Inc.
Client Revlon, Inc.

977
Art Director John Olson
Writer David Hale
Designers Kit Hinrichs/Jonson
Pedersen Hinric
Photographer John Olson
Client John Olson Productions Inc.

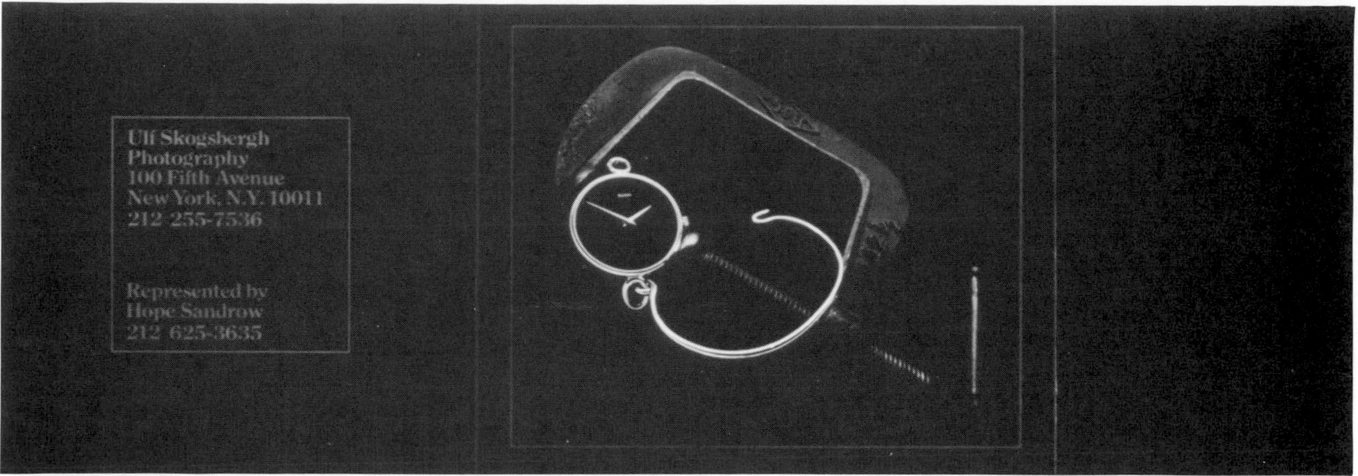

978

979

980

	978		979		980
Designer	Tom Penn	Art Director	Peter Toth	Art Director	Tony Mandarino
Photographer	Ulf Skogsbergh	Writers	Various	Designer	Tony Mandarino
Producer	Tom Penn	Designer	Peter Toth	Photographer	Tony Mandarino
Client	Ulf Skogsbergh	Photographer	Sarah Moon	Agency	Tony Mandarino
		Agency	Deere and Company	Client	Tony Mandarino
		Client	Deere and Company		

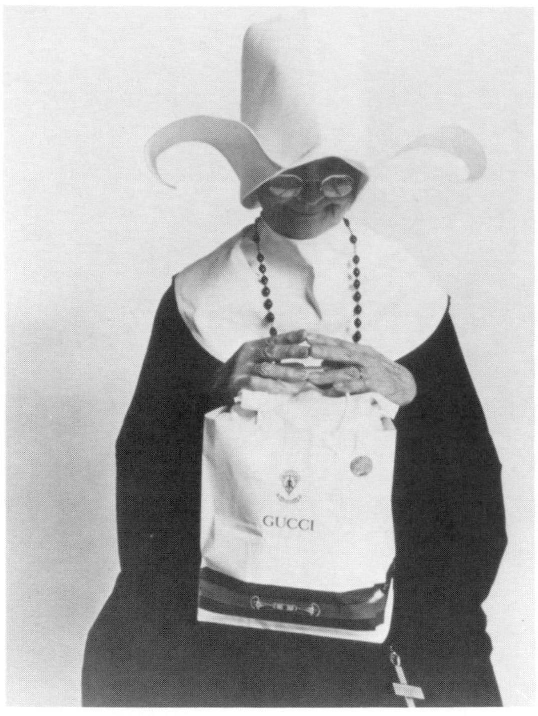

981

982A

982 B

By Geoffrey Stokes

Wagner v. Stein:
Not Just Two Rich Kids

983

981
rt Director Tony Mandarino
Designer Tony Mandarino
tographer Tony Mandarino
Agency Tony Mandarino
Client Tony Mandarino

982A
Art Director Len Fury
Designer Len Fury
Photographer Phil Marco
Agency Corporate Annual Reports, Inc.
Client St. Joe Minerals Corporation

982B
Art Director Clark Maddock
Photographer John Winstanley
Agency D'Arcy-MacManus & Masius, Inc.
Client Dow-Chemical

983
Art Director George Delmerico
Writer Geoffrey Stokes
Designer George Delmerico
Photographer Fred W. McDarrah
Publisher New York Magazine Co.
Client Village Voice

WILL GAY BARS KILL GAY LIB? (P. 21)

the village VOICE

SPECIAL 28-PAGE FASHION INSERT

Rags

THE WEEKLY NEWSPAPER OF NEW YORK · MON. MARCH 14, 1977 · 60¢

WHY WE HATE THE SUBWAYS

BY ALEXANDER COCKBURN & JACK NEWFIELD (P. 11)

Gilda Radner Tells All (P. 51)

DOES IT PAY TO GO BROKE? A GUIDE TO BANKRUPT NEW YORK

BY GEOFFREY STOKES (P. 26)

984

The scene above, conjured up by photographer Jerry Uelsmann, suggests the world of the agoraphobe, who is beset by fears and phantoms and clings to the safety of home. Uelsmann's new work will be exhibited at New York's Witkin Gallery later this month.

985

INTERIORS

"I look at the windows, the source of light. Consciously or unconsciously, people are attracted to clarity, luminescence. Making that experience beautiful is very important."

Joseph D'Urso's work might be likened to an alphabet—a limited number of letters combining to form an infinity of meanings.

INTERIOR DESIGN IN NEW YORK has a long history of decorative excess. What some decorators call "modern" more often than not relies simply on stainless steel and mirrors, avoiding such issues as the nature of apartment spaces and the problems of living in an urban environment. There are few designers, apart from architects, who are searching for a genuine vocabulary of forms appropriate to life in Manhattan. Joseph D'Urso is one of them. Using a surprisingly limited range of materials, he has been responsible for a remarkable series of meticulous and sophisticated residential interiors which reveal the architectural potential of even the most banal set of high rise rooms.

Certain elements are common to all D'Urso projects: high gloss white walls, gray industrial carpets, and industrial fixtures such as door handles, hinges and electrical outlets. But it is in the manipulation of the space as a whole that the variety and richness of his work is revealed. Using and re-using many of the same fixtures and themes, each project becomes in a very real sense a cohesive and completely realized universe. His work might be likened to an alphabet—a limited number of letters combining to form an infinity of meanings. And on the East Side, the D'Urso style is fast becoming the lexicon of Minimalist chic.

As his career has evolved, D'Urso has slowly shaped his own philosophy. He is so intensely involved with his work that he seems at times inseparable from it. And not surprisingly, there are many parallels between his own personality and the spaces he designs. He is a profoundly complex man who expresses himself in a simple, almost spare vocabulary. He has the aristocrat's scorn for excessive comfort and luxury, the bluntness of a man who is absolutely secure in his beliefs, and the sophistication of a pragmatist who is aware of the need for compromise and improvisation. Joseph D'Urso also inspires great loyalty in his clients and his friends—often they become one and the same.

Physically, the bearded, thirty four year-old D'Urso rather resembles the animal from which his name derives, Ursa, the bear. His expression is habitually benign, although wary, and his eyes shine with intelligence. His background is, in fact, a fairly thorough grounding in his profession. He studied for a total of five years at Pratt Institute, four years in interior design and one in architecture. This was followed by a term at The Royal College of Art and a year at Manchester Polytechnic in England. Upon his return to New York in 1967, D'Urso had a one-man show at The Museum of Modern Art and then worked for designer Ward Bennett before setting out on his own in 1968.

"I'll tell you how I deal with a space," he says. "It's really very simple. I concentrate on what exists. The question of apertures is the first priority. I look at the windows, the source of light. Consciously or unconsciously, people are attracted to clarity, luminescence. Making that experience beautiful is very important. Next, I look at the structure of the space. What are its qualities, how are they obscured—and they usually are—and how can they be revealed? There are so many relationships implicit in every space; sometimes only the smallest modifications have to be made—a slit cut into a wall or a column liberated from its context—and everything is transformed. Articulating these relationships is crucial to the way I work."

D'Urso is also excited by the idea of mystery and reticence. "To take one example: most New York apartments are designed so you practically fall into them as soon as you open the front door. I like the device of creating a sort of delay mechanism, an ante room. Sometimes it takes the form of a wall, obscuring the room beyond, so that you have to walk around it to reach it."

Joseph D'Urso's chic interior designs are austere, and yet luminous and luxurious.

34 AVENUE OCTOBER 1977

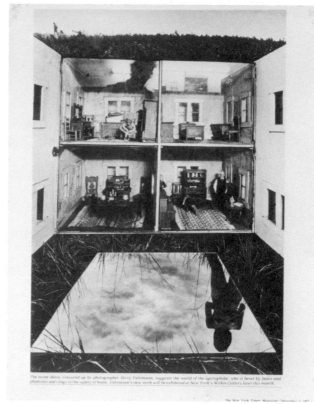

988

984
Art Director George Delmerico
Editor Marianne Partridge
Designer George Delmerico
Photographer Fred W. McDarrah
Publisher New York Magazine Co.
Client Village Voice

985
Art Director Ruth Ansel
Editor Edward Klein
Designer Ruth Ansel
Photographer Jerry Uelsmann
Publisher The New York Times Magazine
Agency The New York Times
Client The New York Times

988
Art Director David Breul
Writer Dick Friedman
Designer Bob Ciano
Photographer Arnold Newman
Publisher Judith Price
Client Avenue Magazine

989

989

Art Director	Ernest Scarfone
Writer	Julia Scully
Photographer	John Benton Harris
Publisher	ABC Leisure Magazines, Inc.
Client	Modern Photography

'I have no regrets'

By Maurice Nadjari

Recently a friend remarked that "all the fight" must be out of me after four grueling years as Special Prosecutor. "Not at all," I replied. "The fight's still there because I still believe in the need for reform." Further, I believe the public maintains a high interest in reform of our institutions, particularly the criminal-justice system, by which I mean the police, the district attorneys and the courts.

There is little public perception, however, of the difficulties involved in investigating and prosecuting official corruption—even among people who might be expected to have some insight. For the most part, crimes of corruption involve "understandings." Seldom are they violent, and a traceable, overt act is as difficult to find as the contrail of a long-vanished jet plane. More often, a wink, a nod or simply the reminder of an obligation may be all that is needed to consummate such a crime, and rarely are there eyewitnesses or victims anxious to testify.

Just such a web of subtlety was apparent to the Knapp Commission, which was appointed in 1970 to investigate corruption in the New York City Police Department. The commission found widespread evidence of organized and systematic corruption at all levels of the department. In addition, it found that narcotics dealers could buy their way out of trouble, criminals could pay for protection, and, worse, that law-enforcement agents subordinated their duties to the pursuit of illegal profit. The unanswered question was how high up did that corruption go.

Acting on the recommendations of the commission, former Gov. Nelson A. Rockefeller in 1972 directed State Attorney General Louis Lefkowitz to appoint a deputy to investigate and prosecute corruption in the criminal-justice system. I was appointed Special Prosecutor, amid much controversy and over the objections of many, including the district attorneys, whose failure to prosecute official corruption had been noted by the Knapp Commission.

This dissension continued until my final removal from office on June 25, 1976. Gov. Hugh Carey had announced he would dismiss me six months earlier, at a time when my office was pursuing its most crucial investigations. Attorney General Lefkowitz, who knew I would not leave voluntarily, gave me six months to complete those cases, but it wasn't enough. When the end of June arrived, the Governor, as I read in The New York Times, offered to allow me to stay on the job—but said he would, at the same time, remove my power to investigate.

I refused the offer, and tried to explain that I had taken the job not to have a job—but to do a job. Since then, the important "political-judicial" cases have been dismissed and the entire establishment is falling over its feet in its urgent desire to please the chief. Small wonder that the office of Special Prosecutor is dying, for what lawyer or prosecutor in his right mind would fail to heed "the Nadjari lesson."

The mechanics of my removal are now relatively unimportant. What is important, in retrospect, is that everybody understands that what really got me was the system. I was unrelenting in pursuit of my legal mandate because in order to be an efficient prosecutor, one has to be unrelenting. The first time a prosecutor backs off an investigation or prosecution because it might be "politically unwise" will not be the last time.

It should also be remembered that our office was not pursuing the classic public enemies, that the crimes under investigation were not murder, robbery and rape. Rather, our mandate was to pursue the corrupt public official, a member of the establishment, and the crime was bribery.

There is no more difficult crime to prosecute than official corruption. Bribes, deals and favors take place behind closed doors and between alert and willing partners. The real victim of official corruption is the public because the very system it has entrusted to others, through the elective or appointive process, is being subverted.

The prosecutor who waits for clearly defined cases to be brought before him will spend long days in mental repose. Prosecutors, as public protectors, cannot choose to be passive about their responsibility. There is too much to be done and, in my case, there was too little time in which to do it.

As the Knapp Commission had shown, the corruption of the police was a cash economy. In our battle against police corruption we were much more successful right from the start. For the crimes were clear-cut. Most often, they involved single bribe transactions, not long-term associations between the "briber" and "bribe taker." The police usually don't have the political friendships with judges that politicians and other judges have.

What is the "system"? It is the political leaders and their minions. They decide who will be the public servants, the judges, the court personnel and the district attorneys. It is also the unethical attorneys who purchase justice and, in turn, are protected from exposure. And it is some honest men and women who want to continue on the bench or at the bar without offending those in power.

We developed our investigations from a number of sources. More often than not, we would begin with an allegation or piece of information from another law-enforcement agency. We regularly received information from the Police Department's Internal Affairs Division and other branches of the Police Department. Quite often, the allegation involved a police officer or other public official of lesser rank. Often it turned out to be unprovable or the original source of the information—such as a confidential informant—was so unreliable that the investigation was dropped after an initial inquiry.

(Continued on Page 67)

Maurice Nadjari, former New York State Special Prosecutor, is now a candidate for District Attorney of Queens County.

990

991

990
Art Director Ruth Ansel
Photographer Neil Selkirk
Publisher The New York Times
Client The New York Times Magazine

991
Art Director Ernest Scarfone
Photographer David Plowden
Publisher ABC Leisure Magazines, Inc.
Client Modern Photography

992

993

992
Art Director Ernest Scarfone
Writer Andy Grundberg
Photographer Paul Caponigro
Publisher ABC Leisure Magazines, Inc.
Client Modern Photography

993
Art Director Ernest Scarfone
Writer Julia Scully
Photographer John Benton Harris
Publisher ABC Leisure Magazines, Inc.
Client Modern Photography

WILL N.Y.'S GREAT SMART HOPE RUN FOR MAYOR?
HENTOFF ON MARIO CUOMO (P. 31)

the village VOICE

THE WEEKLY NEWSPAPER OF NEW YORK 60¢

THE McGARRIGLES:

TWO TOUGH COOKIES WITH SWEET VOICES
BY STOKES & PRINDLE (P. 49)

GAY THEATRE AFTER CAMP
BY ROSS WETZSTEON (P. 87)

Hugh Carey's Welfare Fraud
by Josh Friedman (P. 25)

Cable TV Comes to Queens
by Carol F. Brown (P. 27)

City Hall Debates Sterilization
by Stephanie Harrington and Jane Wholey (P. 20)

Pat Caddell's White House Connection
The Greasy Pole (P. 16)

THE BOYS IN THE BOTTLE
MICHAEL DALY REPORTS FROM THE BOWERY (P. 11)

994

Dog in the Alley, Child in the Sky

A story by John Irving

Father of pretense, orphan of imagination

Janet listened from the kitchen to the story Kemp made up for Pete. Like many of the stories Kemp told Pete and Roger, it began as a story for the children and ended up as a story Kemp seemed to have made up for Kemp.

"There was a dog," Kemp said.

"What kind of dog?" said Pete.

"A big dog," said Kemp.

"What was his name?" Pete asked.

"He didn't have a name," Kemp said. "He lived in a city in Germany, after the war."

"What war?" said Pete.

"World War Two," Kemp said.

"Oh, sure," said Pete, who was five.

"The dog had been in the war," Kemp said. "He had been a guard dog, so he was very fierce and very smart."

"Very mean," said Pete.

"No," Kemp said, "he wasn't mean and he wasn't nice, or sometimes he was both. He was whatever his master trained him to be, because he was trained to do whatever his master told him to do."

"How did he know who his master was?" Pete asked.

"I don't know," Kemp said. "After the war, he got a new master. This master owned a café in the city; you could get coffee and tea and drinks there and read the newspapers. At night the master would leave one little light on, inside the café, so that you could look in the windows and see all the wiped-off tables with the chairs upside down on the tabletops. The floor was swept clean, and the big dog paced back and forth across the floor every night. He was like a lion in his cage at the zoo; he was never still. Sometimes people would see him in there and they'd knock on the window to get his attention; the dog would just stare at them—he wouldn't bark or even growl. He'd just stop pacing and stare, until whoever it was went away. You had the feeling that if you stayed too long, the dog might jump through the window at you. But he never did; he never did anything, in fact, because no one ever broke into that café at night. It was enough just having the dog there."

"The dog looked very mean," said Pete.

"You've got the picture," Kemp said. "Every night was the same for that dog, and every day he was tied up in an alley beside the café. He was tied to a long chain that was tied to the front axle of an old Army truck, which had been backed into the alley and left there—for good. This truck didn't have any wheels. And you know what cinder blocks are," Kemp said. "The truck was set on blocks, so it wouldn't roll on its axles. There was just enough room for the dog to crawl under the truck and lie down out of the rain and the sun. The chain was just long enough so that the dog could walk to the end of the alley and watch the people on the sidewalks and the cars in the street. If you were coming along the sidewalk, you could sometimes see the dog's nose poking out of the alley; that was as far as the chain would reach—no farther. If you tried to pat him, he would duck his head and slink back into the alley. The way he stared at you made you think it would not be a very good idea to follow him into the alley or to try very hard to pat him."

"He would bite you," Pete said.

"Well, you couldn't be sure," Kemp said. "He never bit anyone, actually, or I never heard about it if he did."

"You were there!" Pete said.

"Yes," Kemp said.

"Pete!" Janet called from the kitchen; she always eavesdropped on the stories Kemp told the children. "That is what they mean by 'a dog's life'!"

But Pete said, "Go on with the story. What happened to the dog?"

The responsibilities loomed for Kemp, every time. What is the instinct in people that makes them expect something to happen?

"Go on!" Pete cried impatiently.

Kemp went on. "Well, the dog was either under the truck or at the end of the alley; he never stopped in between. He had his habits (Continued on page 158)

John Irving's short story Almost in Iowa marked his first appearance in Esquire. His novels are Setting Free the Bears, The Water-Method Man and The 158-Pound Marriage. He is this year a Guggenheim fellow.

Photographed by Jeff Perkell

995

994
Art Director George Delmerico
Writer Michael Daly
Designer George Delmerico
Photographer James Hamilton
Publisher New York Magazine Co.
Client Village Voice

995
Art Director Michael Gross
Writer John Irving
Designer Judy Schiern Hecker
Photographer Jeff Perkell
Publisher Esquire Inc.
Client Esquire Magazine

BUSINESS

By birth, temperament, inclination, habit, lifestyle and work pace, Thomas S. Carroll is indeed a true New Yorker, one of a vanishing breed.

He is president and chief executive officer of Lever Brothers Company, the giant manufacturer of soaps, margarine, health and beauty aids that in itself is almost a household word in this country. Since joining the company in 1958, the son of a city cop from Washington Heights, Carroll has helped lead Lever through innovative, aggressive marketing to record sales of over seven-hundred forty-seven-million dollars.

If, back in the fifties, Carroll represented a change in style from his more traditional, Ivy-League corporate counterparts, it may have seemed almost appropriate that the new company headquarters were the controversial but epoch-making Lever House on Park Avenue at 53rd Street, New York's first all-glass "skyscraper," which became the standard architectural style of American Big Business.

Carroll does things his own way. For many years his weekend retreat has been in New Canaan, but after work he goes home to the East Side. When the chief executive officer of a major Manhattan-based company wearies of commuting to his Connecticut or Westchester sanctuary, the result is all too predictable—the company moves, the executive doesn't. Over the past twenty years, according to one recent study, thirty-one chief executives who live in bedroom communities have shifted their companies to their own backyards, spiraling New York taxes and the city's other frustrations. The list of companies that have pulled up stakes sounds like a broker's suggested list of blue chips. In most cases, the chief executive lived eight miles or less from the new company headquarters.

But among the companies that have debated, but voted down, moving to the suburbs is Lever Brothers. Carroll has not only personally resisted the move, but is a prime force in channeling company support, in one way or another, to New York University, Columbia, the New York City Council on Economic Education, the Urban Coalition, and some fifteen other city or volun-

A native New Yorker, Lever Brothers President Thomas Carroll has resisted proposals to move the company out of the city, while pushing for more community involvement.

ARNOLD NEWMAN

996

997

996

Art Director	David Breul
Writer	Peter Carlsen
Designer	Bob Ciano
Photographer	Duane Michals
Publisher	Judith Price
Client	Avenue Magazine

997

Art Director	Ernest Scarfone
Writer	Julia Scully
Photographer	John Benton Harris
Publisher	ABC Leisure Magazines, Inc.
Client	Modern Photography

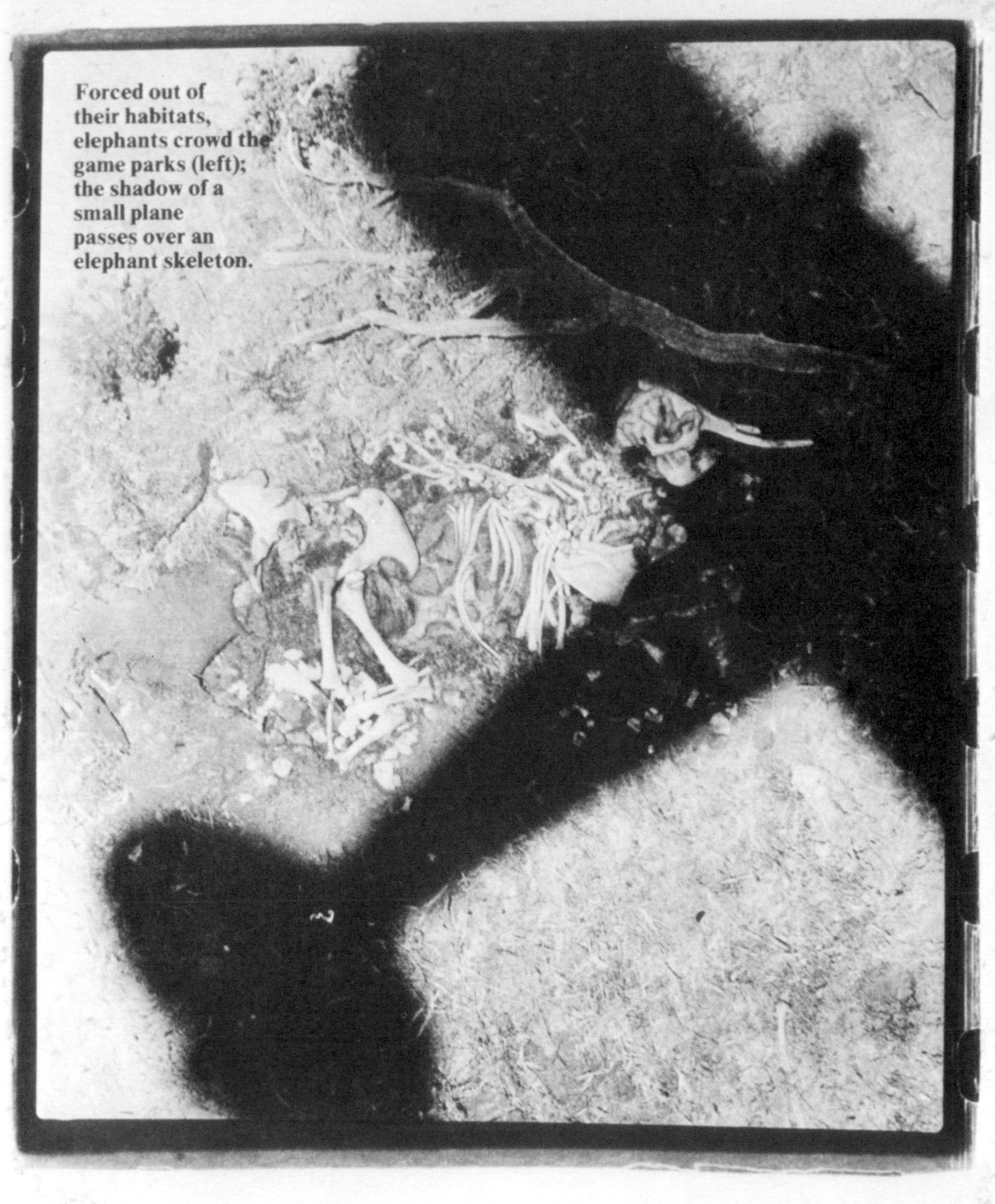

Forced out of their habitats, elephants crowd the game parks (left); the shadow of a small plane passes over an elephant skeleton.

998

998

Art Director Ruth Ansel
Editor Edward Klein
Designer Ruth Ansel
Photographer Peter Beard
Publisher The New York Times
Agency The New York Times
Client The New York Times

1000

999

1001

999
Art Director Ernest Scarfone
Writer Patricia Maye
Photographer John Ortner
Publisher Ehrenreich Photo Optical Ind.
Client Nikon World

1000
Art Director Ernest Scarfone
Writer Pat Maye
Photographer Stephen Castagneto
Publisher Ehrenreich Photo Optical Ind.
Client Nikon World

1001
Art Directors Robin Rickabaugh, Heidi Rickabaugh
Designer Robin Rickabaugh
Photographer Scott Blackman
Publisher Oregon Rainbow Inc.
Client Oregon Rainbow

1002

1003

1002
Art Director Ernest Scarfone
Writer Andy Grundberg
Photographer Charles Knoeckel
Publisher ABC Leisure Magazines, Inc.
Client Modern Photography

1003
Art Director Sunday Hendrickson
Writer Jacqueline McCord
Designer Sunday Hendrickson
Photographer Jean Pagliuso
Publisher George Morrisey
Agency Ziff-Davis Publishing Co.
Client Modern Bride Magazine

1006

DEVIL'S FOOD!

Little black comes back

1005

1004

1004
Art Director Michael Gross
Writer Marilyn Kaytor
Designer Michael Gross
Photographer Salomon-Wahlberg
Publisher Esquire, Inc.
Client Esquire Magazine

1005
Art Director Robert Clive
Writer Beverly Stephen
Designer Tom Ruis
Photographer Tom Arma
Client New York Daily News

1006
Art Director Ernest Scarfone
Writer Andy Grunderg
Photographer John Running
Publisher ABC Leisure Magazines, Inc.
Client Modern Photography

1007

What Famous Designers Have to Say About Faces

By Angela Taylor

1008

1007

Art Director Ernest Scarfone
Writer Julia Scully
Photographer Ken Domon
Publisher ABC Leisure Magazines, Inc.
Client Modern Photography

1008

Art Director Will Hopkins
Writer Angela Taylor
Designer Will Hopkins
Artist Barbara Bordnick
Photographer Barbara Bordnick
Publisher The New York Times
Client The New York Times

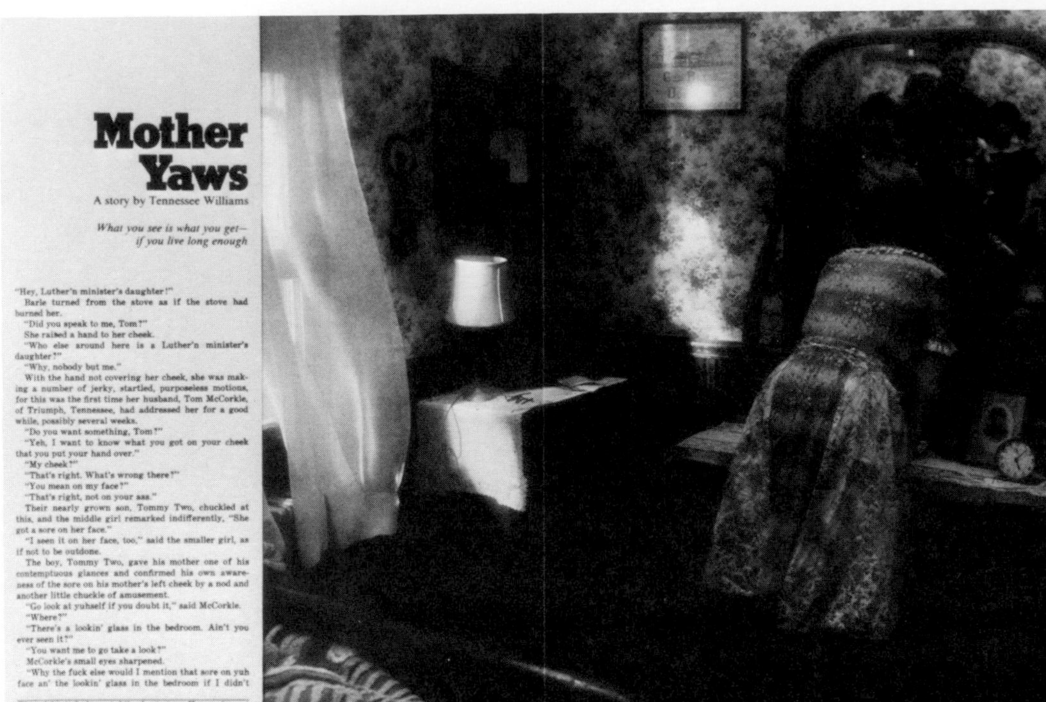

Mother Yaws

A story by Tennessee Williams

*What you see is what you get—
if you live long enough*

"Hey, Luther'n minister's daughter!"

Barle turned from the stove as if the stove had burned her.

"Did you speak to me, Tom?"

She raised a hand to her cheek.

"Who else around here is a Luther'n minister's daughter?"

"Why, nobody but me."

With the hand not covering her cheek, she was making a number of jerky, startled, purposeless motions, for this was the first time her husband, Tom McCorkle, of Triumph, Tennessee, had addressed her for a good while, possibly several weeks.

"Do you want something, Tom?"

"Yeh, I want to know what you got on your cheek that you put your hand over."

"My cheek?"

"That's right. What's wrong there?"

"You mean on my face?"

"That's right, not on your ass."

Their nearly grown son, Tommy Two, chuckled at this, and the middle girl remarked indifferently, "She got a sore on her face."

"I seen it on her face, too," said the smaller girl, as if not to be outdone.

The boy, Tommy Two, gave his mother one of his contemptuous glances and confirmed his own awareness of the sore on his mother's left cheek by a nod and another little chuckle of amusement.

"Go look at yuhself if you doubt it," said McCorkle.

"Where?"

"There's a lookin' glass in the bedroom. Ain't you ever seen it?"

"You want me to go take a look?"

McCorkle's small eyes sharpened.

"Why the fuck else would I mention that sore on yuh face an' the lookin' glass in the bedroom if I didn't

The celebrated playwright's short story Happy August the 10th appeared in these pages a few years ago.

78 ESQUIRE: MAY   Photographed by Larry Robins

1009

Food Taboos

A Consideration in Improved Nutrition

Although great advances have been made in increasing food supplies throughout the world, nutritionists still are faced with the dilemma of starving people who will refuse to eat the nourishing foods—if the foods transgress edicts of their religion, or are taboo.

The reasons cited by historians are diverse. They range from health, to social and economic, to purely ritualistic. Precise origins of food taboos are clouded. The only certainty is that they do exist, are changing only imperceptibly, and are an essential factor in the planning of nutrition programs.

The history of food taboos is the history of man. Where they exist, they are an integral part of a person's psyche; they can dominate him without his ever reasoning why. So overwhelming is this dominance that it has been known to lead to severe depression and ultimately death in those who innocently ate the flesh of a forbidden animal.

To the primitive mind nature was suffused with supernatural spirits which had to be appeased and cajoled continuously. They were feared as much as they were worshipped. Moreover, a "law of similarity" often dictated which animal was to be eaten: most savages believed that they would acquire the qualities of the animals or plants they consumed. Consequently, clumsy, slow, timid animals were unwelcome fare while brave, swift, sagacious animals were relished.

A tribe in Western Africa would not eat the tortoise for fear that its members would run less swiftly. Other tribes avoided the hare because of its timid nature.

8

1010

1009

Art Director	Mike Gross
Writer	Tennessee Williams
Designer	Mike Gross
Photographer	Lawrence Robins
Publisher	Esquire Inc.
Client	Esquire Magazine

1010

Art Director	Brennan/Bouthoorn
Writer	Barney Tolk
Designer	Brennan/Bouthoorn
Photographer	Steve Fukuda
Director	David Ringler
Production Company	Pacific Rotaprint
Publisher	Foremost Foods Company
Agency	Brennan/Bouthoorn
Client	Formost Foods Company

Dental Health: Nutrition's Special Role

Juan M. Navia, Ph.D.
Senior Scientist, IDR
Professor of Dentistry, Biochemistry & Comparative Medicine
Director of Research Training, School of Dentistry
University of Alabama in Birmingham

Nutrition is of special importance to oral tissues.

Researchers now are increasing their recent efforts to define the nutritional needs of developing oral tissues, as well as to understand the oral health implications of a nutritionally inadequate diet.

This emphasis is not only because of the tissue's own specific nutrient requirements, but because the tissues come in contact with foods twice:

- Directly, when foods are masticated in the oral cavity, and
- Systemically, when, after digestion and absorption, nutrients are returned through the circulatory system to nourish and maintain these tissues.

The nutrient composition of foods in the diet therefore can influence teeth at two distinct stages:

- Before eruption, the structure and chemical composition, as well as the eruption time of teeth, may be affected, and
- After the tooth has erupted, nutrients in the diet can enhance the accumulation and metabolic activity of bacterial masses or plaque on the enamel surface. Nutrients may also affect the flow and composition of the saliva which bathes the enamel surface, as well as the bacteria that normally cover the teeth.

The failure of some epidemiological studies to recognize the importance of the different preeruptive and posteruptive effects of dietary nutrients has led to a misunderstanding of the true influence of diet on the etiology and the development of dental caries.

In most oral disease processes, such as caries and periodontal disease, the outcome is usually determined by the interaction of host, microbial, and nutritional factors.

Host factors include, among others, the integrity and perfection of enamel; the morphology of teeth; the size ratio of teeth to mandible; and the chemical and immunological composition of saliva and gingival fluids.

The microbial factor is represented by the bacterial masses in contact with oral tissues. These micro-organisms secrete metabolic products that affect the oral tissues with which they are in close contact.

Under the influence of the nutrient composition of the diet and other undetermined factors, plaque bacteria may develop such a degree of virulence that disease (caries or periodontal disease) can become rampant, if left untreated.

Malnutrition and Caries Susceptibility

Malnutrition at an early age is especially detrimental to developing organs. The teeth, particularly the enamel, begin forming *in utero* and continue to develop during the next 20 years of life. Once formed, enamel cannot be cellularly repaired.

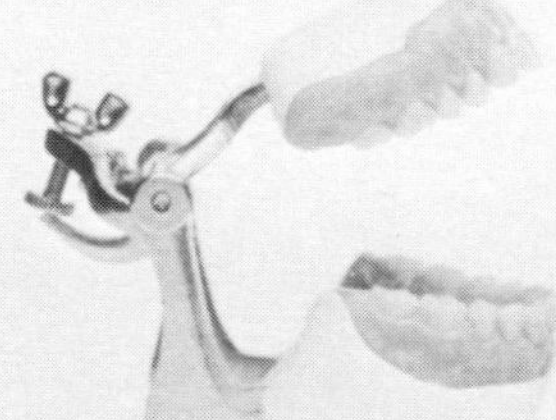

1011

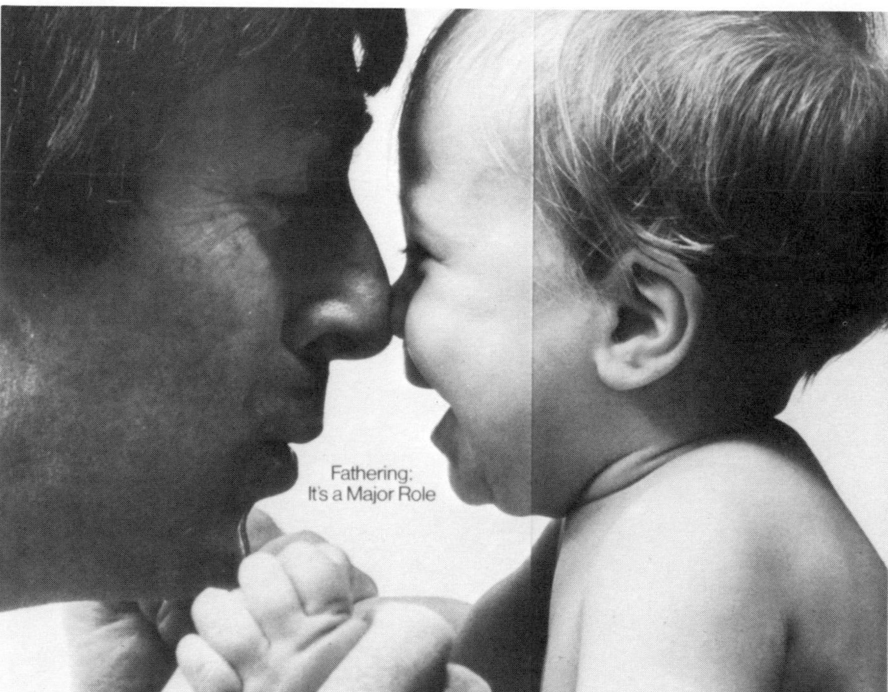

Fathers bring a special dimension to infant care, according to recent studies. In the way they play, and in the way their kids respond.
By Ross D. Parke and Douglas B. Sawin

"FATHERS ARE A BIOLOGICAL NECESSITY but a social accident," Margaret Mead once observed. Contemporary women might take issue with this traditional image of the father as the helpless parent with little talent for or interest in child-rearing. They are likely to argue that the father is just as capable of caring for babies as the mother, and ought to at least share the burdens.

Interestingly, research by developmental psychologists tends to support their view. Our studies of fathers confirm that they are not a social accident at all. They contribute significantly to an infant's social and intellectual growth, although in ways that are different from the mother's. The father is not just a poor substitute for the mother; he makes his own unique contribution to the care and development of infants and young children.

Our observations began seven years ago, in Madison, Wisconsin, with the assistance of Sandra O'Leary, after we convinced reluctant maternity-ward personnel that fathers should be permitted to handle their newborns and not just admire them through a glass window. The fathers were allowed to join mothers and infants in their hospital rooms, where trained observers watched and recorded a wide variety of parenting behaviors in the first two days after delivery. We concluded that the fathers clearly were just as involved with their babies as the mothers—looking and smiling at them, holding and kissing.

There were several questions that remained from this early study. First, since both mother and father were in the room, the high degree of father-infant interaction might have been due to the supporting presence of the mother, who might encourage the father's involvement and provide physical assistance and verbal instructions. Second, most of the fathers had attended Lamaze childbirth classes and had been present during the delivery. They therefore might have been more interested in their parental role and more likely to involve themselves with their infants than other fathers. Third, the men we

109

1012

1011
Art Director Brennan/Bouthoorn
Writer Barney Tolk
Designer Brennan/Bouthoorn
Photographer Robert Arnold
Director David Ringler
Production Company Pacific Rotaprint
Publisher Foremost Foods Company
Agency Brennan/Bouthoorn
Client Foremost Foods Company

1012
Art Director Carveth Kramer
Writer Howard Muson
Photographer Carl Fischer
Publisher Ziff-Davis Publishing Company
Client Psychology Today

1013

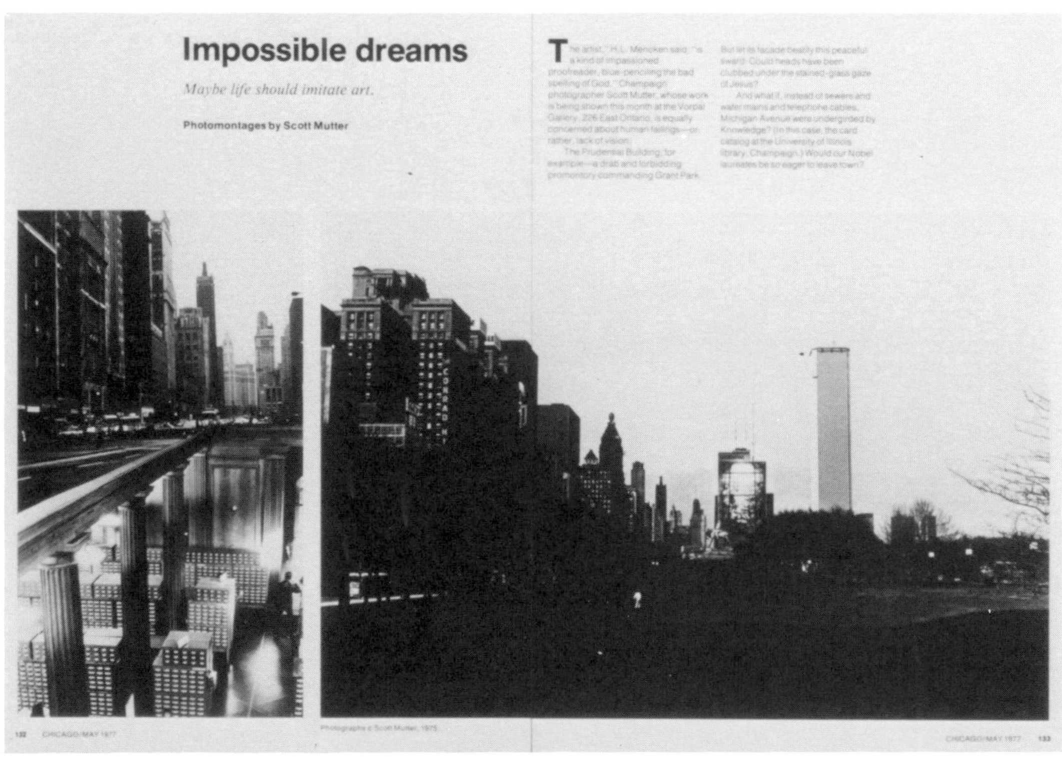

Impossible dreams

Maybe life should imitate art.

Photomontages by Scott Mutter

The artist," H.L. Mencken said, "is a kind of impassioned proofreader, blue-penciling the bad spelling of God." Champaign photographer Scott Mutter, whose work is being shown this month at the Vorpal Gallery, 226 East Ontario, is equally concerned about human failings—or, rather, lack of vision.

The Prudential Building, for example—a drab and forbidding promontory commanding Grant Park. But let its facade beatify this peaceful sward: Could heads have been clubbed under the stained-glass gaze of Jesus?

And what if, instead of sewers and water mains and telephone cables, Michigan Avenue were undergirded by Knowledge? (In this case, the card catalog at the University of Illinois library, Champaign.) Would our Nobel laureates be so eager to leave town?

122 CHICAGO/MAY 1977

Photographs © Scott Mutter, 1975.

CHICAGO/MAY 1977 123

1014

1013
Art Director Emma Landau
Designer Massimo Vignelli
Photographer Terrence Moore
Publisher American Heritage Publishing Co.

1014
Art Director Jack Lund
Writer Mike Greenberg
Designer Jeff Pilarksi
Photographer Scott Mutter
Publisher WFMT Inc.
Client Chicago Magazine

BRAVO BASIL

Discover the aromatic summer herb that adds excitement to everything from tomatoes to pasta. *by Doris Tobias*

Sweet basil is a delight to see and sniff, whether you grow it in your garden or on a sunny windowsill, or buy fragrant, leafy bunches from a produce store. And it's one of the versatile herbs you can use with both hot and cold dishes. Be sure to keep an ample supply of this seasoning for all seasons on hand, not only in summer but the rest of the year too.

Although there are many varieties, the sweet basil, Ocimum basilicum, is the most widely used. The plant has small, bright green leaves and a zesty, mintlike bouquet. Basil and fresh ripe tomatoes are classic lovers, but its flavor also adds romance to sauces, meats, fish, and pasta.

Fresh basil will keep in the refrigerator for several days. Rinse under cold water, shake thoroughly and wrap loosely in paper toweling, then place the basil, toweling and all, in a plastic storage bag and keep in the vegetable crisper. To store longer, ...

1015

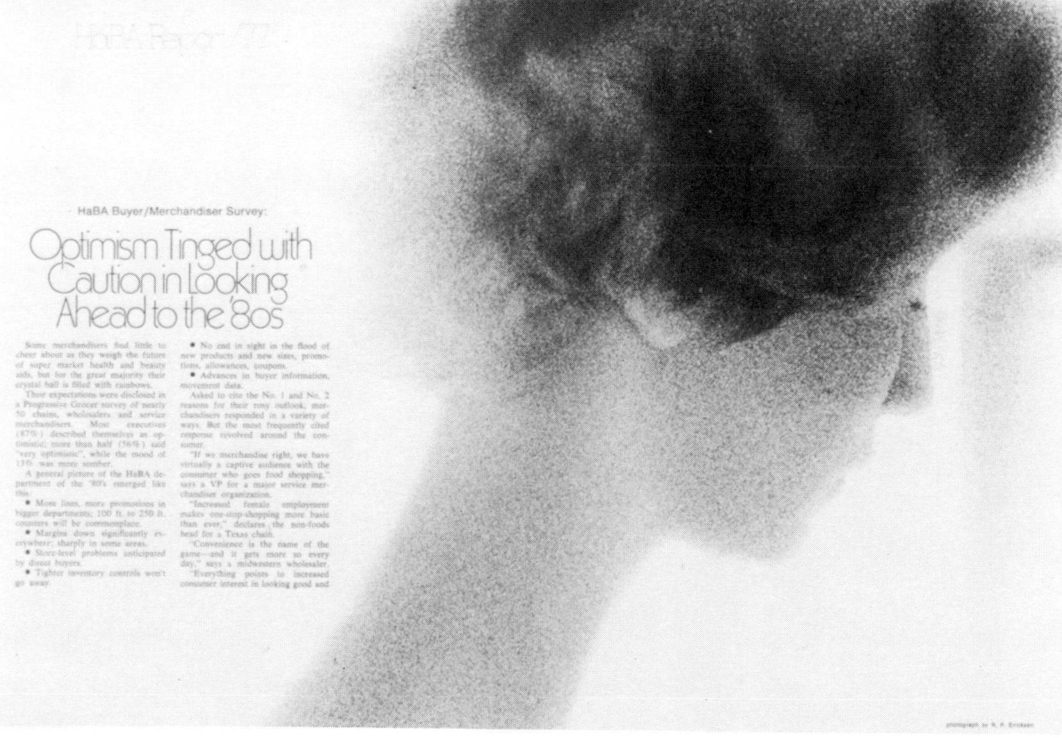

HaBA Report/77

HaBA Buyer/Merchandiser Survey:

Optimism Tinged with Caution in Looking Ahead to the '80s

Some merchandisers find little to cheer about as they weigh the future of super market health and beauty aids, but for the great majority their crystal ball is filled with rainbows.

Their expectations were disclosed in a Progressive Grocer survey of nearly 50 chains, wholesalers and service merchandisers. Most executives (87%) described themselves as optimistic; more than half (56%) said "very optimistic", while the mood of 13% was more somber.

A general picture of the HaBA department of the '80's emerged like this:

- More lines, more promotions in bigger departments; 100 ft. to 250 ft. counters will be commonplace.
- Margins down significantly everywhere; sharply in some areas.
- Store-level problems anticipated by direct buyers.
- Tighter inventory controls won't go away.
- No end in sight in the flood of new products and new sizes, promotions, allowances, coupons.
- Advances in buyer information, movement data.

Asked to cite the No. 1 and No. 2 reasons for their rosy outlook, merchandisers responded in a variety of ways. But the most frequently cited response revolved around the consumer.

"If we merchandise right, we have virtually a captive audience with the consumer who goes food shopping," says a VP for a major service merchandiser organization.

"Increased female employment makes one-stop-shopping more basic than ever," declares the non-foods head for a Texas chain.

"Convenience is the name of the game—and it gets more so every day," says a midwestern wholesaler.

"Everything points to increased consumer interest in looking good and

1016

1015	
Art Director	Richard Ference
Writer	Doris Tobias
Designer	André Gillardin
Photographer	André Gillardin
Client	American Home Magazine

1016	
Art Director	Robert P. Ericksen
Writer	Glenn H. Snyder
Designer	Robert P. Ericksen
Photographer	Robert P. Ericksen
Publisher	Progressive Publishing
Client	Progressive Grocer

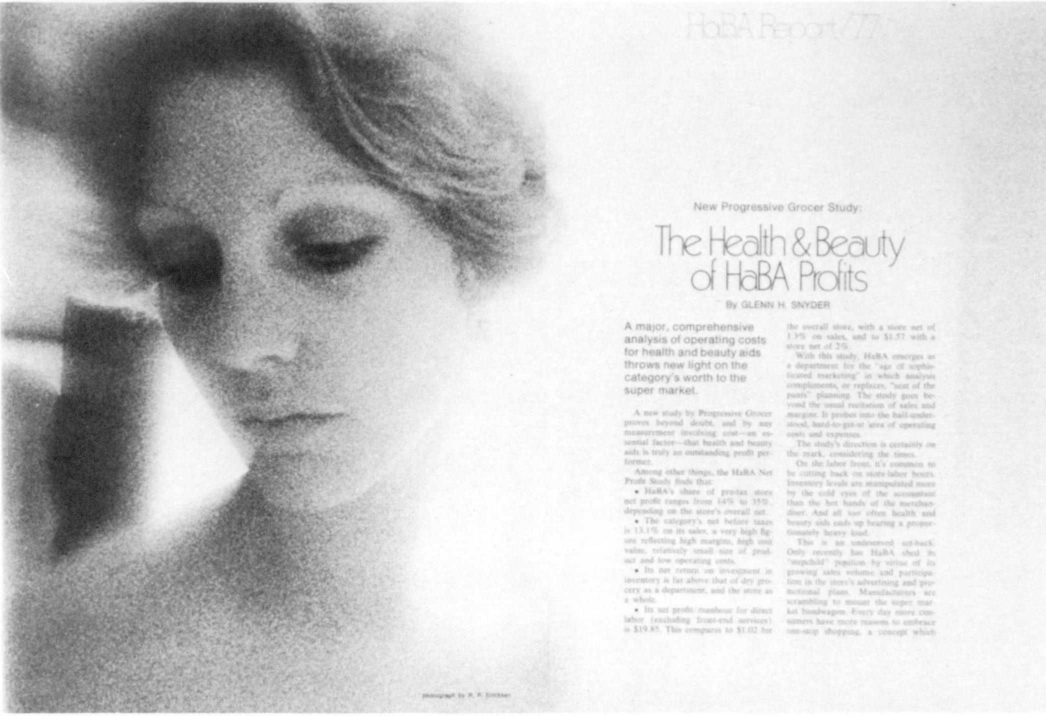

HaBA Report/77

New Progressive Grocer Study:

The Health & Beauty of HaBA Profits

By GLENN H. SNYDER

A major, comprehensive analysis of operating costs for health and beauty aids throws new light on the category's worth to the super market.

A new study by Progressive Grocer proves beyond doubt, and by any measurement involving cost—an essential factor—that health and beauty aids is truly an outstanding profit performer.

Among other things, the HaBA Net Profit Study finds that:

- HaBA's share of pre-tax store net profit ranges from 14% to 35%, depending on the store's overall net.
- The category's net before taxes is 13.1% on its sales, a very high figure reflecting high margins, high unit value, relatively small size of product and low operating costs.
- Its net return on investment in inventory is far above that of dry grocery as a department, and the store as a whole.
- Its net profit/manhour for direct labor (excluding front-end services) is $19.85. This compares to $1.02 for the overall store, with a store net of 1.3% on sales, and to $1.57 with a store net of 2%.

With this study, HaBA emerges as a department for the "age of sophisticated marketing" in which analysis complements, or replaces, "seat of the pants" planning. The study goes beyond the usual recitation of sales and margins. It probes into the half-understood, hard-to-get-at area of operating costs and expenses.

The study's direction is certainly on the mark, considering the times.

On the labor front, it's common to be cutting back on store-labor hours. Inventory levels are manipulated more by the cold eyes of the accountant than the hot hands of the merchandiser. And all too often health and beauty aids ends up bearing a proportionately heavy load.

This is an undeserved set-back. Only recently has HaBA shed its "stepchild" position by virtue of its growing sales volume and participation in the store's advertising and promotional plans. Manufacturers are scrambling to mount the super market bandwagon. Every day more consumers have more reasons to embrace one-stop shopping, a concept which

1017

Border Hoppers

CHECKING THE TRAFFIC IN ILLEGAL ALIENS

BY MELANIE WIRKEN

1018

1017

Art Director	Robert P. Ericksen
Writer	Glenn H. Snyder
Designer	Robert P. Ericksen
Photographer	Robert P. Ericksen
Publisher	Progressive Publishing
Client	Progressive Grocer

1018

Art Director	Gordon Mortensen
Editor	David Sanford
Designer	Gordon Mortensen
Lettering	Gerard Huerta
Photographer	Barrie M. Schwortz
Publisher	Politics Today (formerly Skeptic Magazine)
Client	Politics Today (formerly Skeptic Magazine)

1021

1020

1019

1019
Art Director Gordon Mortensen
Editor David Sanford
Designer Gordon Mortensen
Photographer Barrie M. Schwortz
Publisher Politics Today (formerly Skeptic Magazine)
Client Politics Today (formerly Skeptic Magazine)

1020
Art Director Jack Lund
Writer Allen Kelson
Designer Jack Lund
Photographer Arthur Seigel
Publisher WFMT Inc.
Client Chicago Magazine

1021
Designer Don Johnson
Photographer John Olson
Agency Johnson & Simpson
Client Interpace Corp.

"hondo"–meaning deep

It was dawn and the tide was rising—the critical moment. Maneuvered by eight tugs, the barge *Oceanic 93* swung into the channel of San Francisco Bay. Its strange cargo, looking like an enormous steel box kite and weighing 7,000 tons, was the lower half of an oil production platform destined for the Hondo field in the Santa Barbara Channel.

Cautiously the tugs slide the mammoth structure beneath the Oakland Bay Bridge, clearing it with 28 feet to spare, and headed for the Golden Gate Bridge and their last narrow passage. Ahead lay a 36-hour, 340-mile voyage along the Pacific coast to Santa Barbara, site of one of the most important offshore oil producing areas on the Pacific coast.

In oil industry terminology, the platform section under tow was a part of the "jacket," the underwater steel framework which, when fastened to the sea floor by pilings, supports the production decks safely above water. The lower section

21

1022

Itel Rail implements its business solutions approach through continual expansion of its equipment and service base. Building upon its original point of entry in leasing boxcars to short line railroads, Itel Rail has developed its present ability to supply general purpose boxcars, general service gondolas, and piggyback trailers under per diem leases and all types of rail equipment under full service operating or tax-leveraged leases.

Itel Rail actively broadens its knowledge of the industry through the operation of company-owned short line railroads. The expertise acquired enables Itel Rail to offer services as comprehensive as the building and certificating of short line railroads connecting customers' facilities to a main line, in addition to providing all railcars and handling equipment.

1023

1022

Art Director	John J. Conley
Designer	John J. Conley
Photographer	Charles Moore
Publisher	Exxon Corp.
Client	Exxon Corp.

1023

Art Directors	Lynn Becker
	Steve Burns
Writer	Lynn Becker
Designers	Hildy Burns
	Steve Burns
Photographers	Hildy Burns
	Steve Burns
Embossing Dies	Daniel's Engraving Company
Printer	Anderson Lithograph Co.
Type	Spartan Typography
Agency	Burns Becker Burns, Inc.
Client	Itel Corporation, Rail Division

ANYONE CAN
SHAKE HIS ASS, BUT, PLEASE,
LETS MAKE CIVILITY PREVAIL
Photography by Jean-Paul Goude/Pierre Houles
Here are clothes that will make music with your skin. Mike's white vest and pants ($125) are from Tiger of Sweden, his shirt ($65) is by Stenstrom of Sweden, his tie ($20) is from Cerruti CXIII and his classic white bucks ($40) are from Intercuero/Cole-Haan. Anita, the rumba queen, wears a black Norma Kamali jump suit ($285) and Charles
Jourdan shoes and is bejeweled, as are all the women here, by Patricia Von Musulin. Dominique, showing how she hails taxis, uses her Norma Kamali skirt ($375) as a prop, her red-silk Betsy Gonzalez for S. Onata blouse ($96) for warmth and her Goody Two Shoes silk sandals for stability. Donald's tux ($360), shirt ($43) and tie ($15) are all from Polo by Ralph

1025

1025
Art Director Don Menell
Designer Michael Brock
Photographers Jean-Paul Goude
Pierre Houles
Publisher Playboy Enterprises, Inc.
Client Oui Magazine

1026

1027

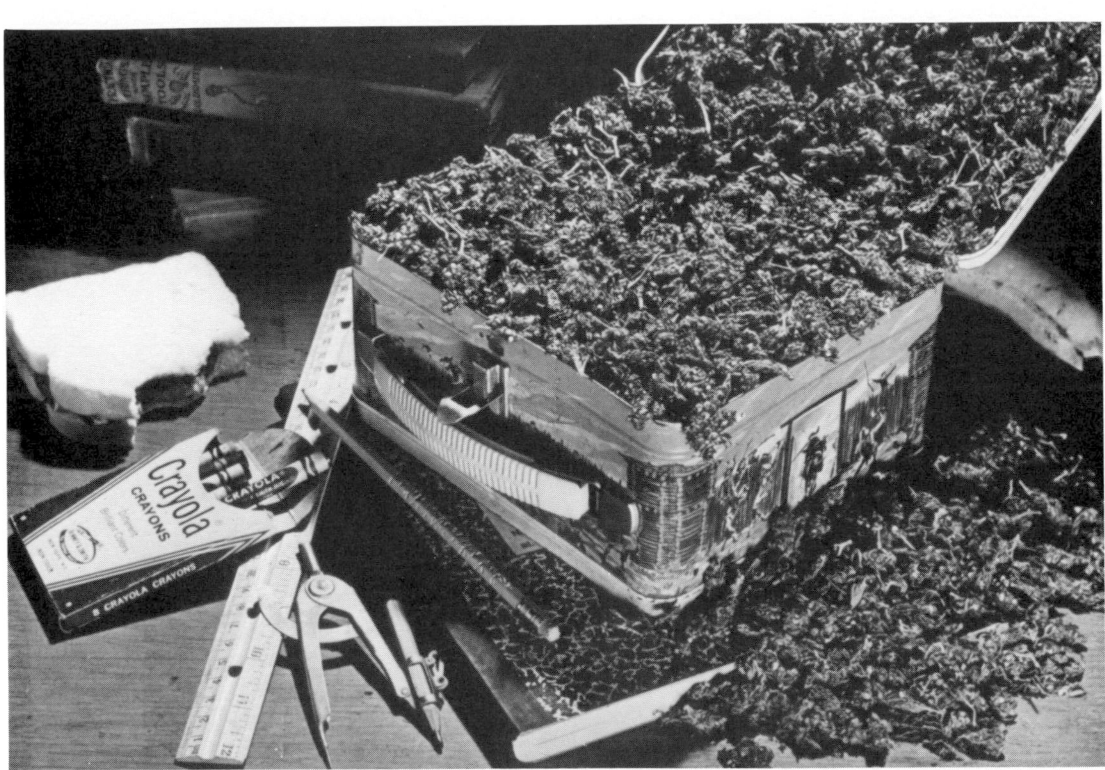

1028

1026
Art Director George W. Coderre
Photographer David Morton
Publisher Reinhold Publishing Company
Client Progressive Architecture Magazine

1027
Art Director Peter Belliveau
Writer Alan Theodore
Designer Neil Ferrara
Photographer Al Frencekevich
Agency William Douglas McAdams
Client Ciba-Geigy Corp.

1028
Art Director T. Courtney Brown
Photographer Steve Cooper
Publisher Trans-High Corp.
Client High Times Magazine

1029

1031

Goat Cheeses, Tame to Tangy

Below, some of the fromages de chèvre available in New York City, starting with the mildest.

1. Capricette: Very mild, creamy, and spreadable. Pure goat.
2. Chevrotin, Chevreton: One-and-a-half-pound cylinder, mild but uninteresting. Pure goat.
3. Banon: See page 45.
4. Montrachet: Ten-ounce log, pleasantly tart and salty, comes either white or coated with ashes (slightly sharper). A creamier version is sold in cups. Pure goat.
5. Lezay logs: Large logs or trapezoidal loaves; may be all white or have an orange or ash coating. They are typically firm, chalky, and pleasantly tangy. Pure goat.
6. Ste. Maure: A small log, six to ten ounces. It is one of the most popular goat cheeses in France. Develops a surface creaminess as it ripens. Pure goat.
7. St. Saviol, Bucheron: Large logs with a light rind, chalky center, creamy edges, and a tangy but rich goat flavor. Pure goat.
8. Capricorne: A wheel with a hole in the middle. It's moderately sharp and salty, but very fresh. Except for surface mellowing, the texture is fairly dry. Pure goat.
9. Géant du Poitou: Medium-sized wheels that ripen and run like Brie. The cheese has a sharp, goaty tang. Pure goat.
10. Pyramide: Pyramid shape, available white or coated with ashes. Very assertive. Pure goat.
11. Crottin de Chavignol: Small, hard, sharp-tasting disks. For the educated palate. Pure goat.

Nos. 12 and 13 are flavored with herbs, pepper, and olives. Dealers thought these appealed to the novice rather than the experienced eater of goat cheese.

12. La Chevrette: Available in six-ounce logs or large logs sold by the pound in plain, herb, pepper, and olive. They are not pure goat, and the texture is smooth but not fluent. The salty olive or the sharp pepper is fairly good, but to me the herb tasted somewhat sour.
13. Royal Provence: Of the two flavored goat cheeses, I prefer this one in the olive or pepper variety. For one thing, it's prettier, the outside of the wheel studded with olives or crushed pepper. The rich, salty olive or the snappy pepper is delicious with cocktails. Not pure goat.

1030

1029
Art Director Tom Bentkowski
Photographer Carl Fischer
Publisher New York Magazine Corp.
Client New York Magazine

1030
Art Director Joan Dworkin
Photographer Niki Ekstrom
Publisher New York Magazine Co.
Client New York Magazine

1031
Art Director Walter Bernard
Photographer Carl Fischer
Publisher New York Magazine Co.

ner (A History of Building Types, Princeton University Press, 1976) the Nervi of the age, projected 1840s forerunners of the long span exhibition hall. The Palais de l'Industrie at the 1855 exhibition spanned 156 ft, breaking the Crystal Palace's record. The Galerie des Machines at the 1878 exhibition spanned 121 ft without tie bars, through the introduction of long-span girders. Dutert and Contamin's 1889 Galerie des Machines for the Paris Exhibition carried technology to its most dramatic with its 364-ft span. By the same token the Eiffel Tower of the same year was to institutionalize the unification of technological advancement and tourism.

Even as a building type the exhibition hall was of particularly French derivation. France had mounted the first national industrial exhibition in 1798, then proceeded to stage nine more from 1801 to 1844.

The pedestrian as protagonist

The exhibition hall, with its sibling building types, the market and the shopping arcade, were made for pedestrians wending their way through a lavish display of commodities. Beginning with the arcades where luxury goods were sold ("art in service of the salesman" as Walter Benjamin later observed), then exhibition halls ("places of pilgrimage to the fetish commodity") Paris became a movable feast through which the flâneur, Baudelaire's browsing aesthetic, sauntered.

Benjamin and Sigfried Giedion have both insightfully observed that the exhibitions, from the time of their inception in 1798, served a psychological and social purpose: the creation of a public festival to mollify the alienated working classes with the glitter of distraction and entertainment. The festival form, Giedion argues, had to

1032

□ It was hot on the way to Las Vegas. In Barstow at ten at night, it was 85 degrees, but with the windows open and the car at eighty, the air was cool on my hands, and the sky was full of stars. Then, for no reason, with the sky still black and starry and the road still straight, it began to get hot. Hotter. 11 P.M. "Baker, California, Gateway to Death Valley." 105 degrees. I was driving with a radical feminist librarian, and we began to wonder why we were going to Vegas at all. Why? When it was obviously going to be hot as hell. Why did I want to go? Well, I was going to talk with single mothers in Las Vegas, to learn what their life was like. They were single mothers, so was I. Maybe the similarities didn't end there.

I never associated Las Vegas with motherhood, I guess. I had some vague image of dayless, nightless casinos and everything a come-on—but motherhood? I thought of Vegas as a kind of low-class place for people with shallow values and beehive hairdos who were *not like me*—a place where poor suckers were conned out of their cash, and entertainers like Frank Sinatra and Elvis Presley sang to people who didn't know we had *ever* gotten into the sixties, much less out of them. Low-life. Quick marriages. Quick divorces. Flashing signs. Sin, in short. *Sin!* All the things that frighten me, that have nothing to do with my life—nothing to do with me.

Or do they? Who are those women there, those single mothers? Are they like me? Now that I have fallen from grace, no longer successful, no longer the assistant dean's wife in the Neutra house with the swimming pool and the guest house and the endless visitors and the Sunday omelet brunches. (But, after all, was it every really like that? The pool didn't work, and it grew green, and mosquitoes laid their eggs on it, and the grass grew between the bricks, and the landlord went mad, and his wife died of cancer, and water leaked into the darkroom, and the Christmas tree caught fire and exploded.)

Still, a fall from grace, from the success of ten years together and my having been a professional and his having a good job and the baby being clever—how am I different from all these women? Are they fallen women, too? Or were they always down there? And what is down?

The road climbed and it got cooler there in the blackness, and then Cassiopeia swung around clockwise on us, from 1 to about 2, and the air started getting hotter again and we started a slow slide down a long hill. Then the ground lights were there, brighter than the starlight, and then the big flashing signs, like directions at Kennedy Airport: TWA—green; American Airlines—a blue; only these said DUNES! and SAHARA! and FLAMINGO! THE CHECKMATES! and JOHNNY CARSON AT THE SANDS!

It seemed like we ought to go through customs, but nobody stopped us and nobody noticed we were there. When we saw the time-heat sign up on the top of the Hilton, it was 11:59 at night and 98 degrees.

Our first stop was the Dunes, but at first we didn't stop. We drove down the Strip and looked at the big signs—the biggest signs in the world. Lake Mead translated into strobes, into Roman palaces, flamingo-pink uterine tracts, constantly sloughing off excess tissues, filling up again, sloughing off. Lake Mead transformed into desert mirages, into a million golden nuggets. Water turned into fire. Night turned into day. Lakes, dams, energy, power, transformers, electricity. The librarian who used to live in a commune with mostly Marxists, tell me that Lake Meade is the only natural resource in practically all of Nevada. If men had not found a way to harness its power to light casinos all night long, there would be no industry here at all. But there is something else here in this desert where even water turns into fire, and my friend feels it, too. Sin. Hell-fire and damnation.

Something almost comforting about this preserved pocket of childhood sin, 1950s sin, where there is still such a thing as heaven and hell, laws and outlaws; where gambling and prostitution are still wicked for sure, and the world hums with the sweet promise of Mary Magdalenes and prodigal sons. Where I live there is only Yang flowing into Yin and back with the speed of a soft-boiled-egg timer. Gamblers and prostitutes and rock-and-roll superstars are big-time stock market businessmen. Everybody swings.

At Circus, Circus, the air conditioner was broken. We came in from the hot night air and it was raining, water streaming down on the front desk, and the girls handing out room keys and wearing newspapers on their heads and frantically phoning some repairman who would not answer. Through the rain, we saw the forest of slot machines and heard the pealing of jackpot bells. We went to our room.

Outside the window was one of the stranger sights I have ever seen. The sky was black. There was a concrete moat, and beyond that a white pebbled rooftop, sloping upward, at about eye level. Two huge light fixtures anchored on the roof sent powerful beams of light up to the sky. Along the moat, absolutely motionless, were hundreds and hundreds of small brown grasshoppers. Higher up, moving slowly, stealthily, squadrons of fat black bee-

(continued on page 237)

No Place to Be a Single Mother

Las Vegas—that glittery Gomorrah of sin, sexism, and high-priced pleasures—doesn't sound like a place for a lone woman with children. So what are so many single mamas doing there?

By Victoria Hodgetts

1033

1032
Art Director George W. Coderre
Photographer Tim Street Porter
Publisher Reinhold Publishing Company
Client Progressive Architecture

1033
Art Director Linda Cox
Writer Helen Gurley Brown
Photographer Carl Fischer
Publisher The Hearst Corp.
Client Cosmopolitan Magazine

1034

1035

1034

Art Director James Eisenman
Writer Sean Callahan
Designer Will Hopkins
Artists Michael O'Neill—Vodka, Rum, Wine
J. Barry O'Rourke
Photographer Michael O'Neill—Vodka, Rum, Wine
Publisher The Hearst Corp.
Client Sports Afield Magazine

1035

Art Director Ernest Scarfone
Writer Patricia Maye
Photographer Richard Steedman
Publisher Ehrenreich Photo Optical
Client Nikon World

1036

1037

1036
Art Director Ernest Scarfone
Writer Patricia Maye
Photographer Lloyd Englert
Publisher Ehrenreich Photo Optical
Client Nikon World

1037
Art Director Ernest Scarfone
Writer Patricia Maye
Photographer Darrell E. Arnold
Publisher Ehrenreich Photo Optical
Client Nikon World

1038

1039

1038
Art Director Ernest Scarfone
Writer Patricia Maye
Photographer Day McCoy
Publisher Ehrenreich Photo Optical
Client Nikon World

1039
Art Director Ernest Scarfone
Writer Patricia Maye
Photographer Co Rentmeester
Publisher Ehrenreich Photo Optical
Client Nikon World

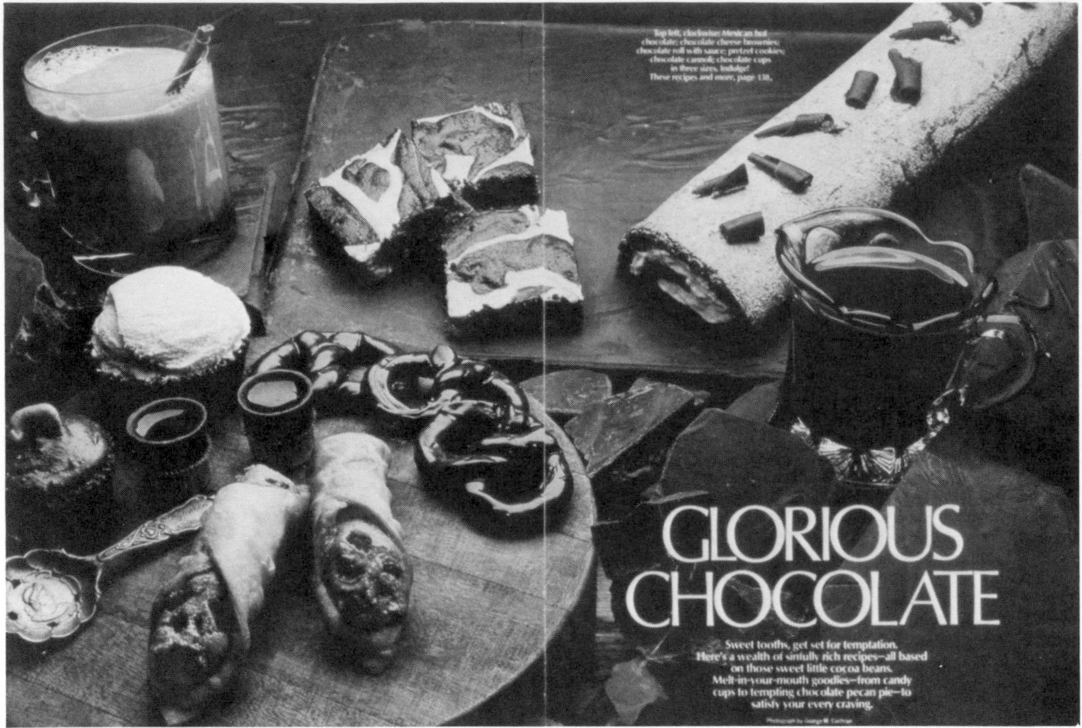

GLORIOUS
CHOCOLATE

Sweet tooths, get set for temptation.
Here's a wealth of sinfully rich recipes—all based
on those sweet little cocoa beans.
Melt-in-your-mouth goodies—from candy
cups to tempting chocolate pecan pie—to
satisfy your every craving.

1040

THE BATTLE OVER CHILDREN'S RIGHTS

By David Ferleger

In most states, parents can commit their kids to mental institutions. Should children have the right to be heard independently? That's the question for the courts.

1041

1040
Art Director Donald A. Adamec
Writer Lys Margold
Designer Donald A. Adamec
Photographer George M. Cochran
Agency Ladies' Home Journal

1041
Art Director Neil Shakery
Photographer Mark Kozlowski
Publisher Ziff-Davis Publishing Company
Client Psychology Today

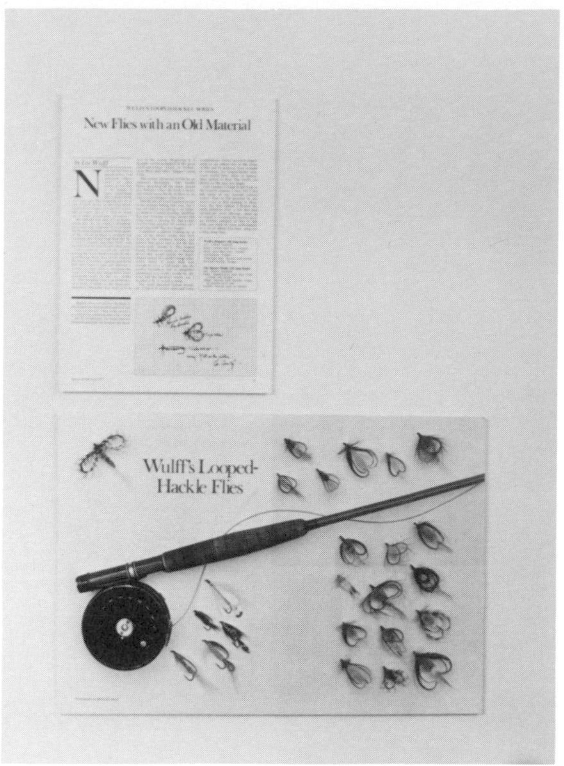

1042

1048

1042
Art Director James Eisenman
Writer Lee Wulff
Designer Bern White
Photographer Wesley Balz
Publisher The Hearst Corp.
Client Sports Afield Magazine

1048
Art Director Don Longabucca
Designer Mike Stromberg
Photographer Cosimo
Publisher MacMillan
Client MacMillan

Television

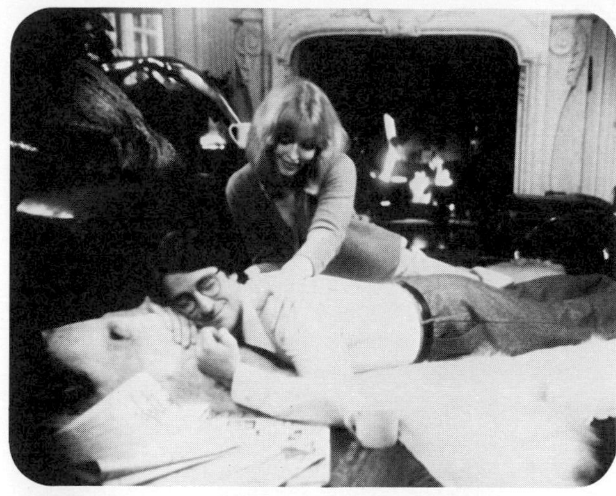

PATTERNS
30-second

ANNCR: Since Van Heusen introduced solid color Qiana shirts, millions of men are saying ...

GUY: Mmm ...

ANNCR: Now we're introducing another feeling in Qiana shirts.

GIRL: Dot-dot-dot.

ANNCR: Patterns.

GUY: Mmm.

ANNCR: Geometrics.

GIRL: Squares never turned me on like this.

GUY: Ahh. . Feast your eyes on these.

ANNCR: Van Heusen's new shirts in patterned Qiana. It's another new feeling in shirts.

GIRL: One ... two ...

GUY: Go back to one ...

GIRL: One ... two ...

1049

Art Director	Ray Alban
Writer	Melissa Huffman
Director	Steve Horn
Producer	Ken Yagoda
Production Company	Steve Horn
Agency	Scali McCabe Sloves
Client	Phillips-Van Heusen

BOX
30-second

ANNCR: Landmark Bank is giving you a present.

MUSIC: All-Day, All-Night Marianne.

(VO): She's Fast

MUSIC: Just the Landmark Bank has Marianne.

(VO): She's easy to use.

MUSIC: Bank by day, bank by night now you can.

(VO): She's always open.

MUSIC: Just the Landmark Bank has sweet Marianne.

(VO): And she's yours.

MUSIC: Just the Landmark Bank has sweet Marianne.

(VO): If you bank at Landmark.

1050
Art Director Clyde Hogg
Writer Tony Burke
Director Joe Sedelmaier
Producer Clyde Hogg
Music Doppler, Atlanta
Production Company Sedelmaier Films
Agency Lawler Ballard Little Advertising
Client Landmark Bank

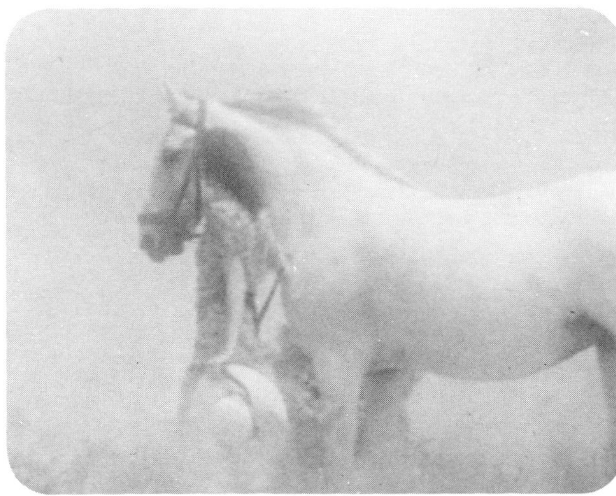

BOAT III

30-second

ANNCR (VO): Come to find the beautiful fragrance of Jontue.

Sensual . . . but not too far from innocence.

Jontue.

The beautiful fragrance . . .

Sensual . . .

but not too far from innocence.

Jontue from Revlon.

Wear it and be wonderful.

1051

Art Director	David Leddick
Writer	David Leddick
Director	Ed Vorkapich
Producer	John Greene
Music	Crescendo Prod. (Michael Cohen, Composer)
Production Company	Lipson Film Associates
Agency	Grey
Client	Revlon, Inc.

EXPLOSION
30-second

ANNCR (VO): A revolutionary camera idea explodes on the scene.

Minolta has taken the best features of 35mm reflex cameras and combined them with the simplicity and light weight of cartridge cameras.

The result, a remarkable camera with built-in zoom and close-up lenses. And through-the-lens viewing. It sets itself automatically. It's the world's only 110 Zoom SLR.

And it's dynamite.

1052

Art Director	Marce Mayhew
Writer	Editing Concepts
Designer	Marce Mayhew
Director	Herbert Loebel
Producer	Marc Mayhew
Music	Dick Lavsky
Production Company	Herbert Loebel
Agency	Bozell & Jacobs, Inc.
Client	Minolta Corporation

SKATEBOARD
30-second

ANNCR (VO): It's got four wheels . . .

ANNCR: and reflexes so quick,

ANNCR: it almost seems alive.

ANNCR: It is perfectly balanced . . .

ANNCR: to perform, and perform and perform.

ANNCR: It is the wide-open sports car, MG Midget.

ANNCR: A moving experience.

ANNCR: The lowest-priced authentic sports car on the market.

ANNCR: MG Midget.

ANNCR: Strong. Honest. Fun. Young.

ANNCR: MG Midget from British Leyland.

1053
Art Director Marce Mayhew
Writer Tom Murphy
Designer Marce Mayhew
Director Cal Bernstein
Producer Marc Mayhew
Music Tom Dawson
Production Company Dove Films
Agency Bozell & Jacobs, Inc.
Client British Leyland Motors Inc.

SUPERMARKET
30-second

WOMAN: The first time I bought these, Frank said . . .

WOMAN: Myra, you know how I feel about those chips in a can . . .

WOMAN: Frank, I said, these new Stackables are from Wise!

WOMAN: So he tries one.
(As Frank) Nice golden color . . . good crunch . . .

WOMAN: Verrrrrry tasty!!

WOMAN: Now, he's disappointed when I don't buy 'em.

ANNCR (VO): Try New Stackables from Wise.

ANNCR (VO): You won't be disappointed.

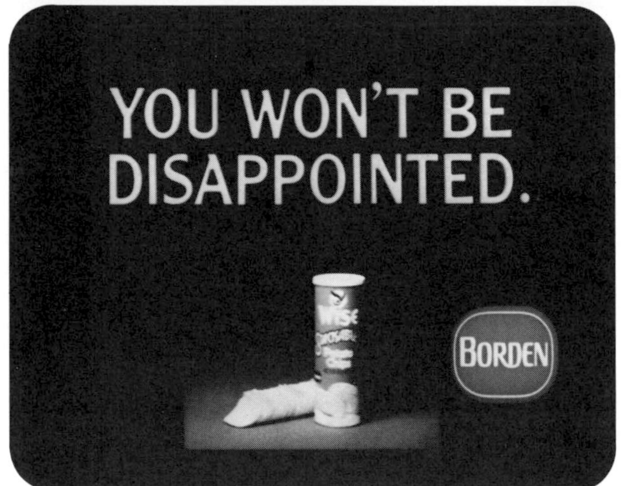

1054
Art Director Ed McCabe
Writer Brian Olesky
Director Steve Horn
Producer Marc Mayhew
Production Company Steve Horn Productions
Agency Bozell & Jacobs, Inc.
Client Wise Foods

SUPER GLUE
30-second

This drop is too little to cover the head of a match.

Yet this is enough adhesive, super-strong, super-fast, to lift 2½ tons. It's Duro Super Glue.

A drop will do, to mend

jewelry,
ceramics,
rubber,
and glass.

In only ten seconds.

It truly is super-strong and super-fast.

Super Glue. A drop will do.

Super Glue.

A product of Loctite technology.

1055
Art Director Bob Kwait
Writer Mike Marino
Director Maggie Condon
Producer Donna Solpa
Production Company N. Lee Lacy (New York)
Agency Wyse Advertising
Client Woodhill/Permatex

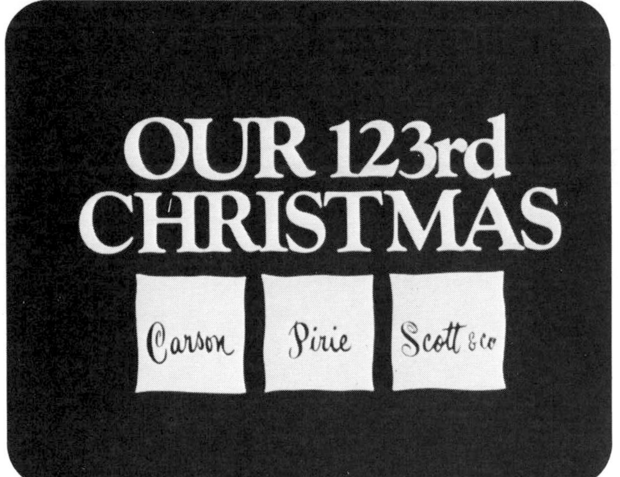

CRITICS CHOICE
30-second

INTERVIEWER: (VERY CONDESCENDING) Tell me, what did you think of Santa at Carsons?

DAMIEN: I found him very believable.

TOMMY: A beautiful human being.

JARA: Didn't promise more than he could deliver.

KIP: I found him totally responsive to my needs.

DANIELLE: Very believable.

RENE: He asked some penetrating questions.

ANNCR (VO): For 124 Christmases, our management, our sales people, even our Santa has been playing to rave reviews.

DANIELLE: He's a man I can trust.

1056
Art Director Barry Vetere
Writer Jan Zechman
Director Tim Newman
Producer Janet Collins
Production Company Jenkins Covington Inc.
Agency Zechman and Associates
Client Carson Pirie Scott & Co.

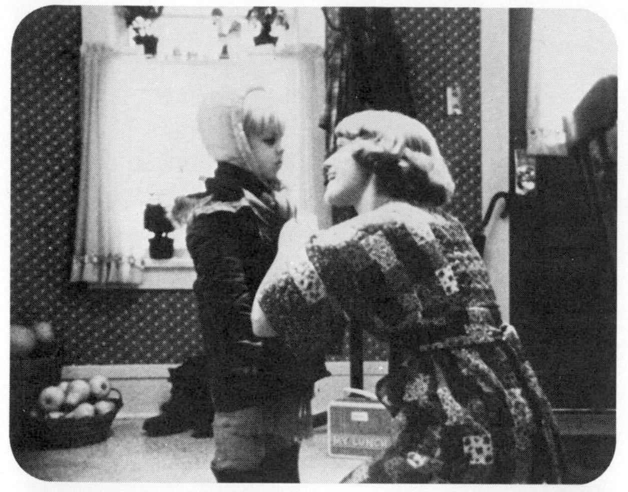

WIN SOME LOSE SOME
30-second

MOTHER (LOVINGLY): Bob Gregory says it's going to be very cold . . .

BOB GREGORY (VO): Hello, I'm Bob Gregory. You know, when I report the weather for Channel 13, I like to give you more than just the raw numbers. I want you to know what to wear, how to dress the kids for school—useful things like that. Giving weather reports that help people have won me a few friends . . . and lost me a few.

ANNCR (VO): Bob Gregory. Weekdays on Newscenter 13. With Paul Udell.

1057
Art Director Barry Vetere
Writer Jan Zechman
Director George Gootsan
Producer Janet Collins
Music Dick Boyell
Production Company Filmfair Inc.
Agency Zechman and Associates
Client WTHR-TV

WELCOME BACK
30-second

MAYOR (OVERLY ELOQUENT): Mr. Hambrick, it is with great joy that we herald your return to Cleveland. And may I say . . .

HAMBRICK: Ah, I'm sorry. That was John Hambrick who worked in Cleveland. I'm his brother, Judd.

MAYOR: Oh. Kill the banners!

ANNCR (VO): Some Clevelanders still confuse our new anchorman, Judd Hambrick, with his brother. But once you've sampled Judd on Newscenter 8, we think you'll agree. Cleveland has never seen an anchorman the likes of Judd Hambrick.

MAYOR: "Sorry".

1058
Art Director John Sapienza
Writer Jan Zechman
Director Richard Chambers
Producer Janet Collins
Production Company Chambers & Associates
Agency Zechman and Associates
Client WJKW-TV

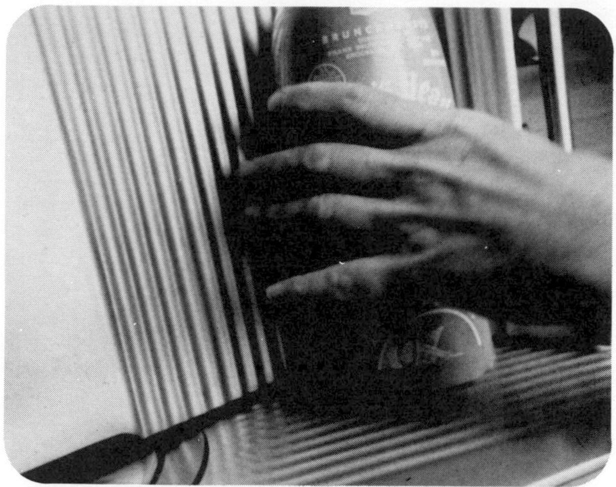

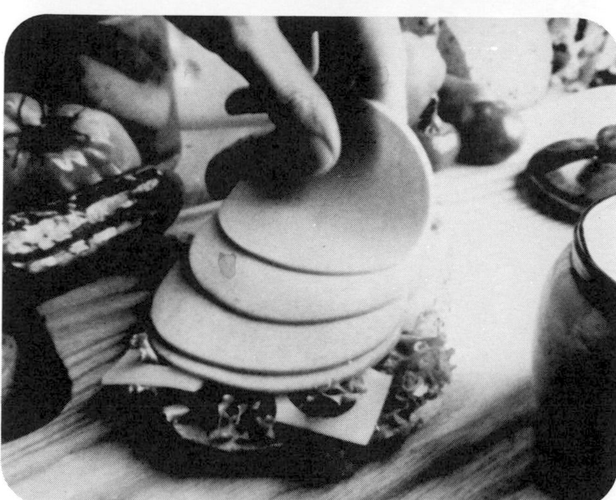

1059
30-second

This commercial is pure baloney.

Boar's Head bologna.

Unlike some bologna, we don't add soy or corn starch.

We don't add cereal.

We don't add extenders.

We don't add artificial color.

Boar's Head bologna is made from pure beef and pork. And not beef and pork by-products, either.

We wouldn't purany meat in our bologna that you wouldn't put on your own table.

Boar's Head.

Pure bologna, Not phony baloney.

1059

Art Director	Robert Reitzfeld
Writers	Dick Jackson
	David Altschiller
Designer	Robert Reitzfeld
Photographer	Henry Sandbank
Director	Henry Sandbank
Producer	Robert Reitzfeld
Music	Worner Levenson
Production Company	Sandbank Films
Agency	Altschiller, Reitzfeld & Jackson
Client	Boars Head Provisions

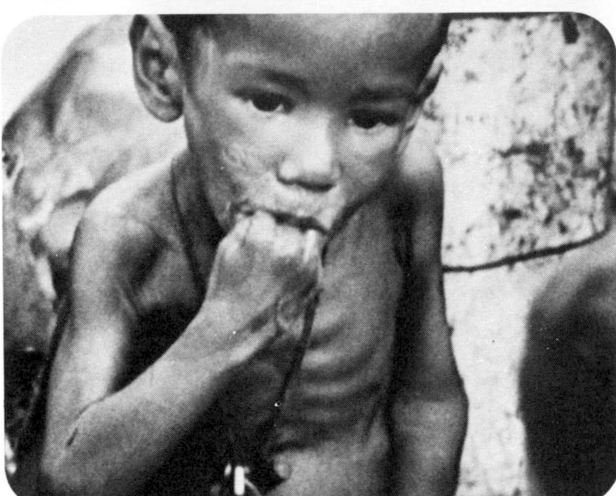

PEOPLE #2
30-second

People. They're curious creatures.

Sometimes fascinating

Powerful

Tragic

Glamorous

Frightening

Funny

People and what makes them tick. They're important to your world.

That's why we care enough to write about them.

All the things you care about, you'll learn more about in The Dallas Morning News.

1060
Art Director Chuck Bua
Designer Chuck Bua
Writer Barbara Harwell
Director Lou Puopolo
Producer Chuck Bua
Music Lucas McFall
Production Company Lou Puopolo
Agency Kerss, Chapman, Bua & Norsworthy, Inc.
Client The Dallas Morning News

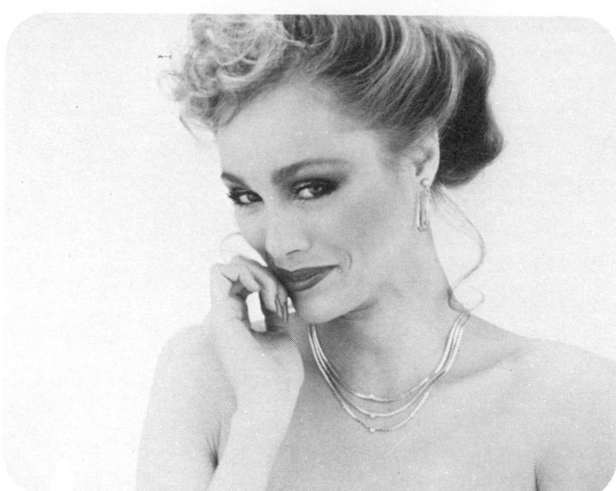

NAPIER
30-second

ANNCR (VO): Napier is sexier . . .

Napier is wittier . . .

Napier is merrier . . .

For giving or getting fabulous jewelry . . .

Napier is timelier.

1061
Art Director Gene Federico
Writers Gene Federico
Olivia Trager
Designer Gene Federico
Director William Helburn
Producer Robert Kronenberg
Music Corelli, Jacobs
Production Company William Helburn Productions
Agency Lord, Geller, Federico, Inc.
Client The Napier Company

BUBBA SMITH
30-second

BUBBA: I had my own way of tackling. I used to grab the whole backfield. Then I threw guys out until I found the one with the ball. When I started drinking beer, I did the same thing and this is the one I'm holding onto. Lite Beer from Miller. It has a third less calories than their regular beer. It's less filling and it tastes terrific, too.

I also love the easy opening can.

VO: Lite Beer from Miller. Everything you always wanted in a beer. And less.

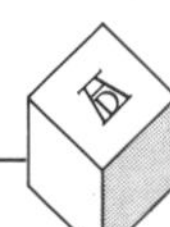

GOLD

1062

Art Director Bob Engel
Writer Charlie Ryant
Director Bob Giraldi
Agency Producer Bob Engel
Production Company Bob Giraldi Productions
Agency McCann-Erickson, Inc.
Client Miller Lite (Miller Brewing Co.)

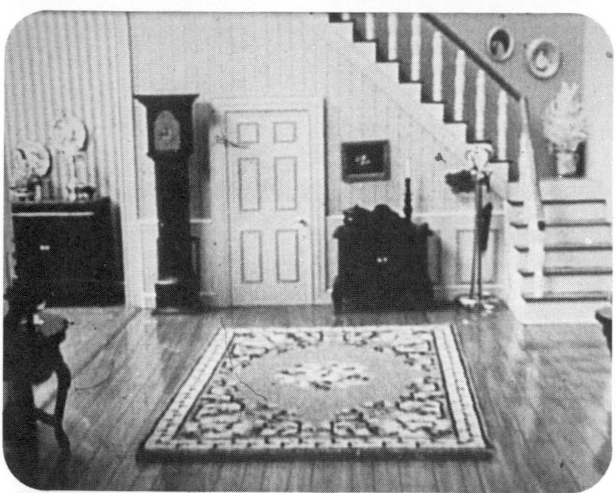

FORGET YOUR MOVE
30-second

NARRATOR: At best, moving is something you'd like to forget.

And you can when you remember to call Bekins.

Bekins got to be a big moving company by doing everything to make little moves, as well as the big ones trouble-free and totally forgettable.

So when it's time for you to move Remember Bekins and you can forget your move.

1063

Art Director	Logan Broussard
Writer	Steve August
Editor	Mike Hardin (MCI)
Director	Jim Beresford
Producer	Dan Wells
Production Company	The Shooting Gallery
Agency	The Bloom Agency
Client	Bekins Van Lines

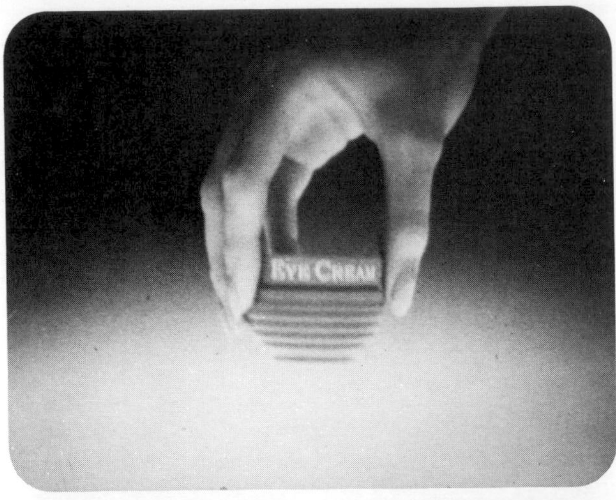

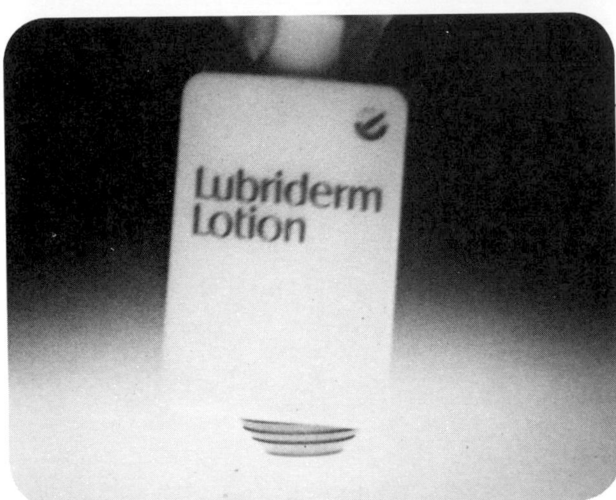

ONE BOTTLE
30-second

VO: I used to use an expensive under-eye cream. Now Lubriderm is all I need.

And I gave up my costly makeup moisturizer. Lubriderm is light enough to absorb beautifully.

And I replaced my high-priced night cream. Lubriderm is rich enough to protect my skin for hours. And my old body lotion?

I found one with almost twice the moisturizers. One bottle of Lubriderm Lotion.

ON CAMERA: It's simply all your skin needs, for all your skin needs.

1064

Art Director	Al Weintraub
Editor	Peter Stasse, Starmark
Director	Henry Sandbank
Producer	Marillyn Leaman
Music	Phil Kelley (score)
Production Company	Sandbank Films
Agency	The Bloom Agency
Client	Texas Pharmacal

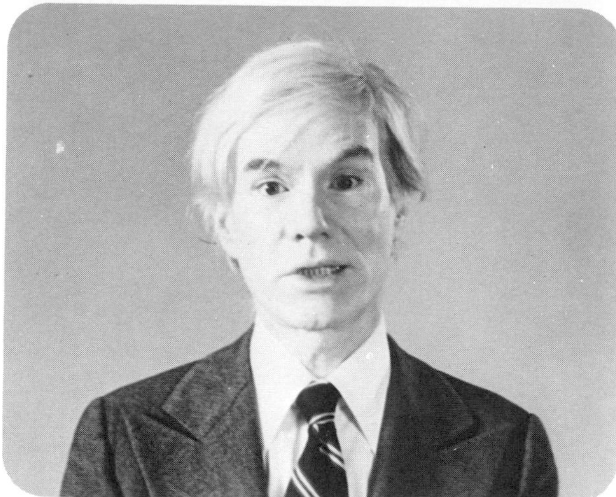

U.S. NEWS & WORLD REPORT
30-second

JOHN SWEET: Have you ever met anybody who actually reads U.S. News & World Report?

JOHN SWEET: "Only 8 million very selective people do. Have you ever wondered why they do?"

CAROL GERTZ: "No fashion."

JOHN NEWCOMBE: "No sports."

JOE ARMSTRONG: "No fun."

ANDY WARHOL: "No gossip."

JIMMY WALKER: "No jokes."

TRUMAN CAPOTE: "Not stylish."

JOHN SWEET: "I'm John Sweet, President and Publisher of U.S. News and World Report. Our philosophy is simple.

"We spare our readers unimportant news. We spare our advertisers unimportant readers."

1065
Art Director J. Ryder
Writer D. Staley
Photographer M. Pateman
Producer J. Goodhue
Production Company The Movie House
Agency Ted Chin & Company, Inc.
Client U.S. News & World Report

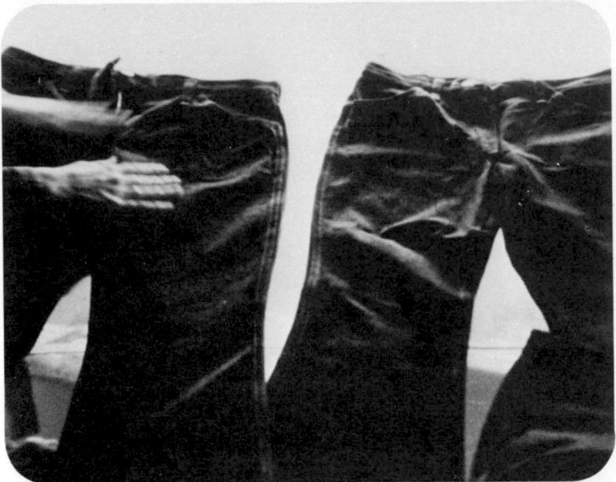

SAME JEANS
30-second

ANNCR (VO): You can buy these denim jeans at fine department stores everywhere. They're not cheap. But they're a good value.

You can buy these jeans at our stores, just as often as we're able to get them. They're top-quality, too. In fact, they're exactly the same jeans.

The difference is that we sell them for a lot less. And we can do it for one simple reason. (SOUND EFFECTS: SOUND OF SCISSORS SNIPPING LABEL.)

At Plain Value Stores, jeans aren't the only thing we sell for less.

1066

Art Director	Norman Grey
Writer	Tom McNeer
Director	Jim Collins
Prod. Co. Producer	Jim Rogers
Agency Producers	Norman Grey Tom McNeer
Production Company	Jayan Films, Atlanta
Agency	Bozell & Jacobs/Atlanta
Client	Plain Value Stores

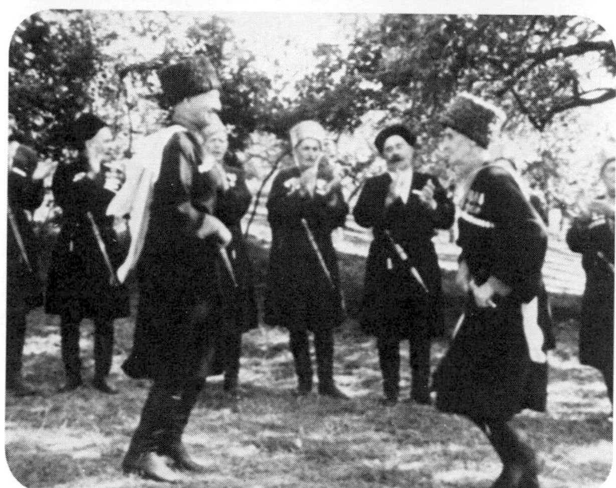

GEORGIAN CHORUS
30-second

VO: In Soviet Georgia, where they eat a lot of yogurt, a lot of people live past 100. Of course, many things affect longevity, and we're not saying Dannon yogurt will help you live longer. But Dannon is a wholesome, natural food that has active cultures. Many other yogurts don't. By the way, Temur Vanasha thought Dannon was really fine yogurt. He ought to know. He's been eating yogurt for 105 years.

1067
Art Director Joe Goldberg
Writer Peter Lubalin
Director Bob Gaffney
Producer Arlene Hoffman
Production Company Bob Gaffney Productions
Agency Marsteller
Client Dannon Yogurt

AIRPLANE
30-second

These new jumbo jets are pretty amazing. When you're sitting here, it's easy to forget how much ingenuity it takes to get 200 tons of airplane off the ground. And how much aluminum. Without aluminum, a plane like this would never leave the runway.

Aluminum has made an entire era of commercial aviation possible. You use it whenever you fly, even when you mail a letter. And there's no substitute.

ANNCR: Aluminum. You need it whether you know it or not.

1068

Art Director Bill Mullen
Writer John Sealander
Director Mike Van Ackeren
Producer Bill Mullen
Production Company Van Ackeren Productions
Agency Kraft Smith Advertising
Client Western Aluminum Producers

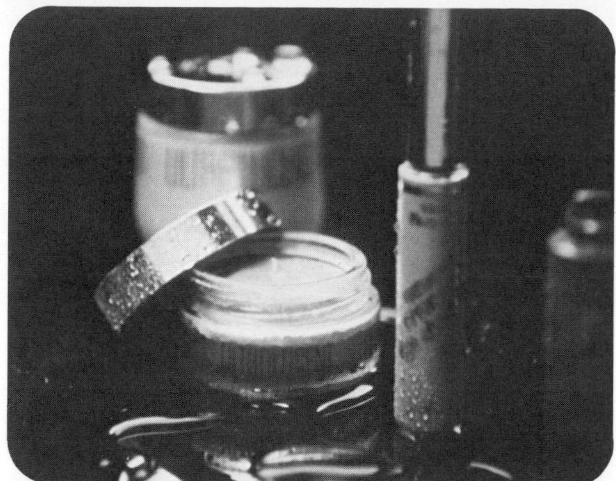

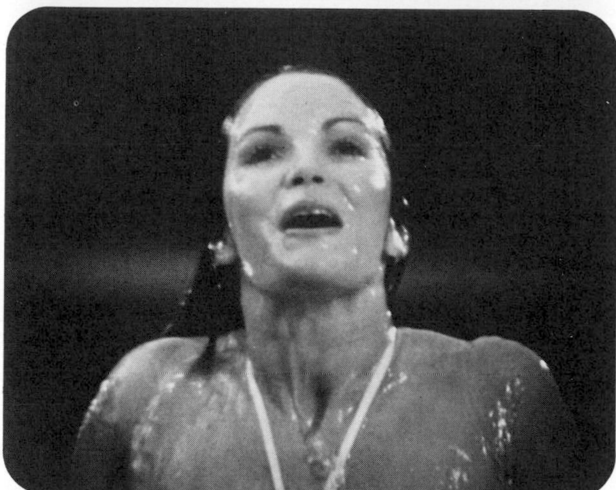

SWIMMING POOL
30-second

VO: It happened on April 15, 1976, before filming, Jackie put on her Max Factor Waterproof Makeup, her Blush, her Creme-on Eyeshadow and her Superlashmaker comb-on Mascara. And went to work.

She came out of the water fifteen times without a touch-up. And take after take, her look stayed soft and natural ... and beautiful.

Our Waterproof Face.
Performance Tested. And only by Max Factor.

1069
Art Director Bob Kuperman
Writer Pacy Markman
Director Jack Cole
Producer Paula Del Nunzio
Music John Tartaglia Productions
Production Company Lee Lacy Productions
Agency Wells, Rich, Greene/West
Client Max Factor

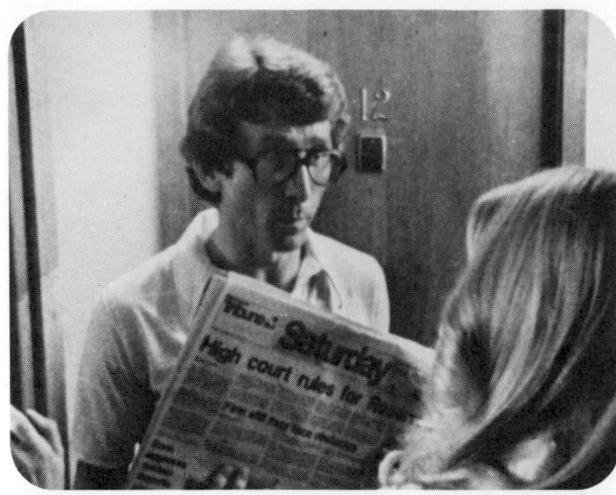

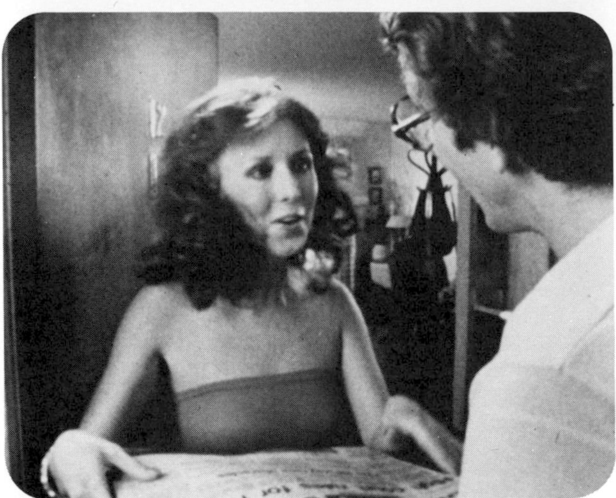

HI, THERE
30-second

MAN: Hi, there. I'm a Star subscriber and I think I got your Saturday Tribune by mistake.

WOMAN: No, no. You see, the morning Tribune and the evening Star have combined into one big edition on Saturday morning.

MAN: Is that a fact?

WOMAN: Ya, see, there's a new Saturday Star magazine and two more new sections.

MAN: Well, you know, why don't we just kinda get together and you can tell me all about it? You know I've always ... (FADE OUT)

MAN: Hi, there. I'm a Star subscriber and I think I got your Saturday Tribune by mistake.

WOMAN: (LAUGHING) No, no. You see the morning Tribune and the evening Star have combined ... (FADE UNDER)

ANNCR (VO): The Minneapolis Star. The Minneapolis Tribune. The newest news in town.

MAN: (TO WOMAN) Is that a fact?

1070
Art Director Pat Burnham
Writer Steve Kahn
Director Fred Tumler
Producer Fred Tumler
Production Company Film Factory
Agency BBDO/Minneapolis
Client The Minneapolis Star/Minneapolis Tribune

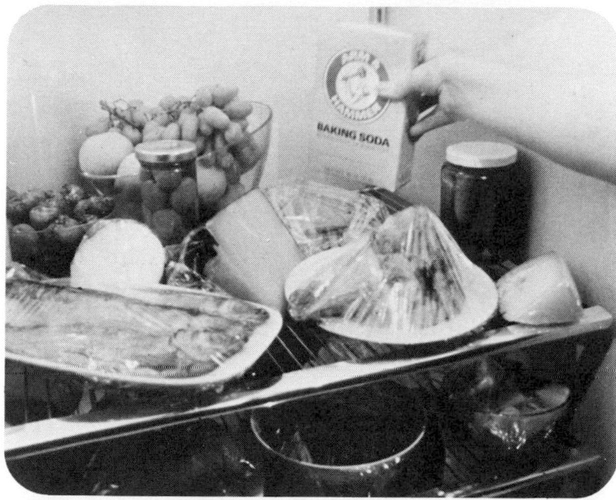

INTERVIEWS
30-second

ANNCR: When was the last time you changed the Arm & Hammer Baking Soda in your refrigerator?

1ST WOMAN: . . . About four months ago.

2ND WOMAN: Last spring.

3RD WOMAN: 197? . . .

ANNCR: Arm & Hammer Baking Soda helps keep your refrigerator sweet-smelling, but it can't last forever. So for best deodarizing results, every two months put in a fresh box and pour the old box down the drain, to keep it sweet-smelling too.

4TH WOMAN: The last time I changed it? Was I supposed to change it?!

1071

Art Director Bruno Brugnatelli
Writer Gerald Weinman
Director Bob Vietro
Producer Irene Taffel
Production Company Bob Vietro & Co.
Agency Kelly Nason, Univas Inc.
Client Church & Dwight

ICE
30-second

VO: They say Sam Breakstone could turn cream sour ... by just looking at it.

SAM: Where's my ice?

VO: Unfortunately, it wasn't that easy.

SAM: We need that ice because when we make sour cream we cool it and heat it and cool it ... until I say it's the best sour cream ... money can buy!

VO: In his day, Sam Breakstone was one of the most demanding men alive. But if Sam weren't so demanding ... his sour cream wouldn't be so good.

1072
Art Director Lars Anderson
Writer Irwin Warren
Designer Lars Anderson
Director Dick Loew
Producer Wayne Lachman
Production Company Gomes-Loew
Agency Richard K. Manoff Inc.
Client Kraft, Inc./Dairy Group

HORSE/BOAT
30-second

ANNCR (VO): Come to find the beautiful fragrance of Jontue.

Sensual . . .

. . . but not too far from innocence.

Jontue.

The beautiful fragrance . . .

Sensual . . .

. . . but not too far

from innocence.
Jontue from Revlon.

Wear it and be wonderful.

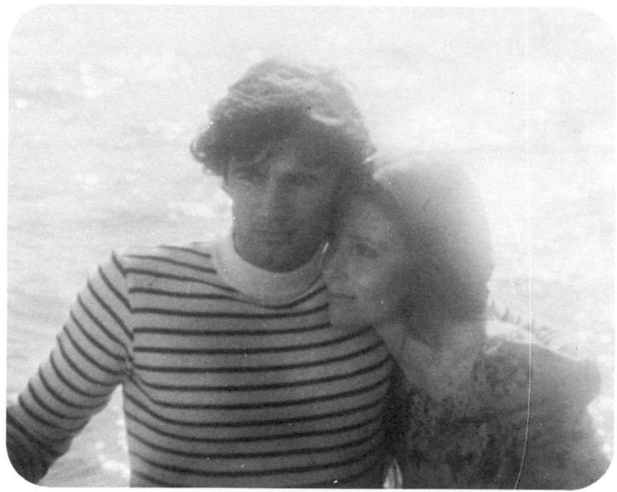

1073

Art Director	David Leddick
Writer	David Leddick
Director	Ed Vorkapich
Producer	John Greene
Music	Crescendo Prod. (Michael Cohen, Composer)
Production Company	Lipson Film Assoc.
Agency	Grey Advertising
Client	Revlon, Inc.

PATENT OFFICE
30-second

ANNCR: The people who work in the Patent Office see a lot of new ideas every day . . .

. . . but very few as appetizing as this one. That's because at Arthur Treacher's, the fish is more than delicious . . .

In fact, it's so special . . . so unique . . .

We've even been awarded a U.S. Government patent for the way we fix it.

Next time you're hungry for something different . . . try the place that's famous for it . . .

Arthur Treacher's, we are something else! And we've even got the patent to prove it.

1074
Art Director Bob Reed
Writer Carl Koehler
Editor Steve Bodner
Director Denny Harris
Executive Producer Vic Lewis
Producer Bill D'Elia
Production Company Denny Harris, Inc.
Agency Sawdon & Bess Advertising
Client Arthur Treacher's Fish & Chips

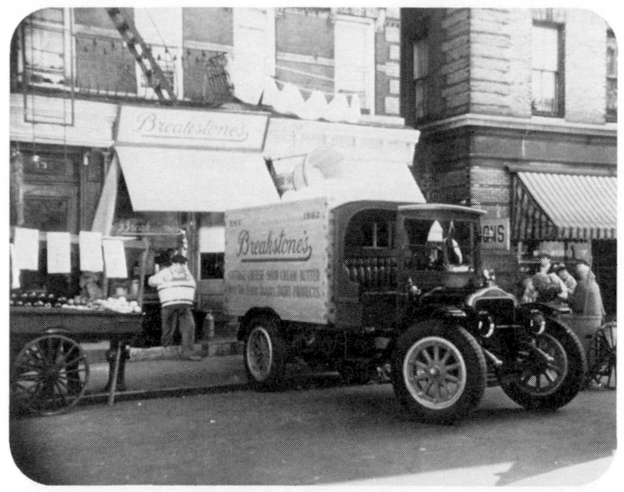

Breakstone's
CALIFORNIA CREAMED STYLE
COTTAGE CHEESE
Since 1882

TRUCK
30-second

VO: When Sam Breakstone delivered his cottage cheese, fast . . . was not fast enough.

WORKER: Who does old man Breakstone think he is?! Hurry . . . hurry . . . hurry . . . my cottage cheese must arrive fresh. You'd think it was gold!

SAM: Cover my cottage cheese you numbskull!

WORKER: Yes, Mr. Breakstone.

SAM: (MIMICKS) Yes, Mr. Breakstone. Out!

VO: In his day, Sam Breakstone was one of the most demanding men alive. But if Sam weren't so demanding . . . his cottage cheese wouldn't be so good.

1075

Art Director Lars Anderson
Writer Irwin Warren
Designer Lars Anderson
Director Dick Loew
Producer Wayne Lachman
Production Company Gomes-Loew
Agency Richard K. Manoff Inc.
Client Kraft, Inc./Dairy Group

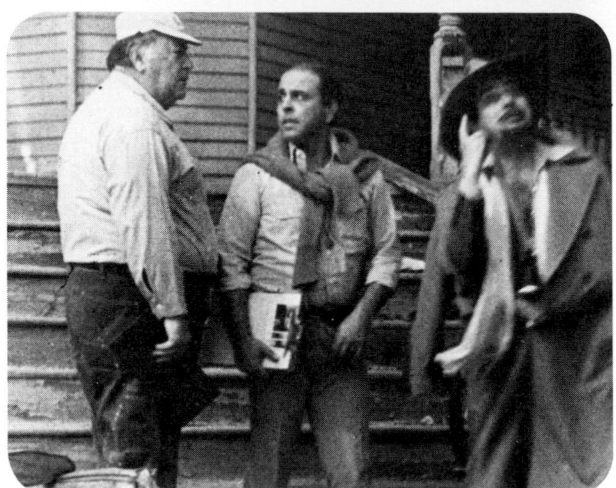

DIRECTOR
30-second

DIRECTOR: Haunted house . . . fantastic. Old paint . . . fantastic. The texture, the patina . . .

ASSISTANT: Ya like this house, chief?

DIRECTOR: Fantastic! We shoot in the morning.

ASSISTANT: Morning!

DIRECTOR: House fantastic, director fantastic . . .

ASSISTANT: Look at that old paint, and nutsy wants it ready by morning.

PAINTER: Better use Olympic Overcoat.

ANNCR (VO): Overcoat's made 'specially to keep old paint under cover for good . . . with a tough acrylic finish that'll last for years. (Next day at dawn painters swarm over house with ladders and paint furiously. Assistant sets up lights and reflectors just as director drives up.)

PAINTER: Hi, Skipper!

DIRECTOR: (LOOKING AT HOUSE) Where's my old paint?

PAINTER: Under cover for good, chief.

DIRECTOR: Fantastic.

ANNCR (VO): Olympic Overcoat helps keep old paint under cover for good!

1076

Art Director	Bill Mullen
Writer	Jim Aaby
Director	N. Lee Lacy Associates
Producer	Bill Mullen
Production Company	N. Lee Lacy Associates
Agency	Kraft Smith Advertising
Client	Olympic Stain

LIGHTFINGER HARRY
30-second

ANNCR (VO): When Lightfinger Harry robs your house, chances are, he'll open the door like this!

ANNCR: Most burglars don't pick locks. They force them open. This is Superguard Lock. The others are ordinary front door locks. And we're going to hit each door with half a ton of force. Watch.

Superguard holds fast! It's the world's strongest door lock. And you can install it yourself with a screwdriver. So if you want to prevent break-ins, start with a lock that won't break. Superguard!

1077

Art Director Ed Mandell
Writer Ed Mandell
Designer Mike Elliot
Director Mike Elliot
Producer Ed Mandell
Production Company E.U.E/Screen Gems
Agency Richard & Edward's Inc.
Client Ideal Security Hardware Corporation

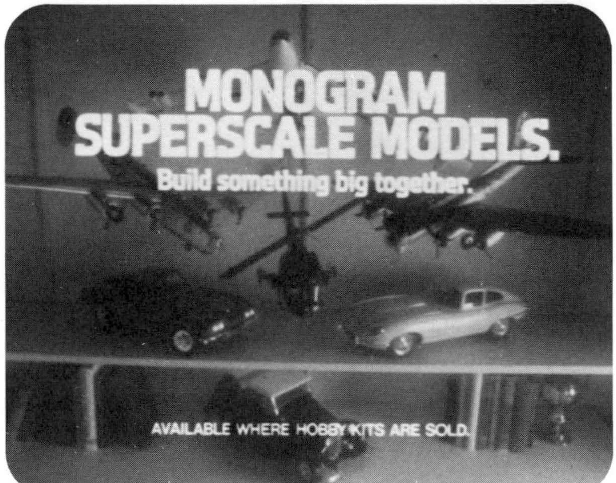

SOMETHING SPECIAL HAPPENS
30-second

DAD: Time to attach the ignition wires, Mitch.

SON: Right, dad. Here . . . I can do it.

DAD: A monogram '32 Ford Street Rod. What a beauty.

Sure was worth the time.

SON: I like the way the steering works, and this windshield is neat.

DAD: Nice job, Mitch . . . and look at the size of this thing.

SON: Let's start the B-29 tomorrow night.

DAD: I hear it's got a 35″ wingspan.

ANNCR: Something special happens when a father and son get together over a Monogram Super Scale Model.

SON: Dad!

ANNCR: Monogram Super Scale Models. Build something big together.

1078

Art Director Arnold Rosenthal
Writers Mark Friedman
Arnold Rosenthal
Director/Cameraman Joe Sedelmaier
Producer Arnold Rosenthal
Production Company Sedelmaier Film Productions, Inc.
Agency Garfield-Linn & Co.
Client Monogram Models, Inc.

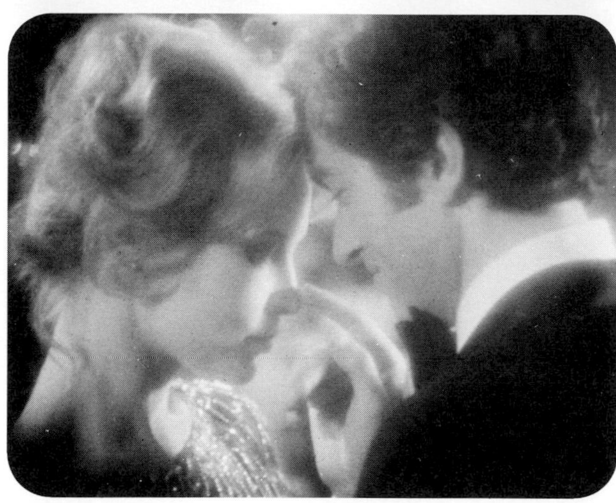

AS TIME GOES BY
30-second

SHE: Ummm, Ciara . . . what does it remind you of?

HE: You smell terrific

ANNCR: Ciara by Charles Revson . . . the thoroughly female fragrance.

ANNCR: What will it remind you of.

ANNCR: Find out.

1079

Art Director	Martin Stevens
Writer	Rita Connor Grisman
Director	Ed Vorkapich
Producers	Martin Stevens
	Carolyn Axelrod
Music	Hupfeld/Warner Bros.
Production Company	Len Lipson Associates
Agency	Revlon, 50th Floor Workshop
Client	Ultima II

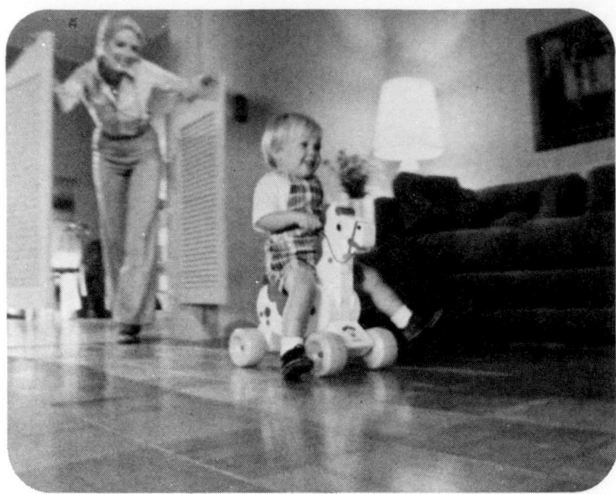

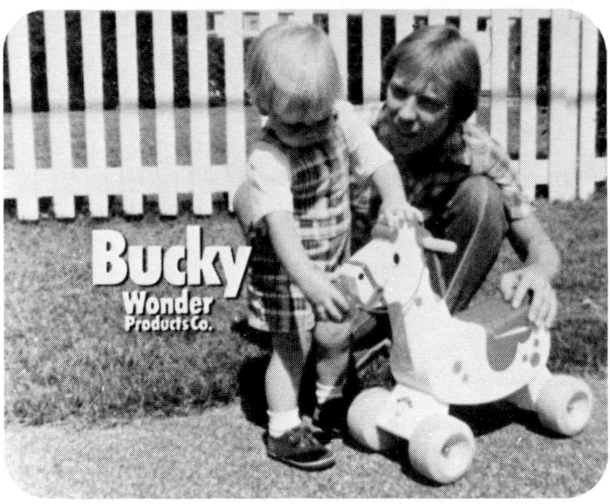

BUCKY
30-second

And they're off!
It's Bucky on the inside . . .
it's Bucky the Wonder Horse on the outside . . .
it's Bucky with the feet that kick forward when you pull his head . . .
it's Bucky that whinnies when you pull his reins . . .
it's Bucky with the big safe wheels!
And in the stretch it's Bucky and daddy . . .
it's daddy and Bucky neck and neck . . .
it's Bucky the Wonder Horse by a nose!
Bucky . . . for kids 18 months to 3 years old.
Bucky from Wonder Products.

1080

Art Director Bill Wurtzel
Writers Ron Wagner
Bill Wurtzel
Director John Sterner
Producer Bill Wurtzel
Production Company Du Rona
Agency Hicks and Greist
Client Creative Playthings

KARATE
30-second

SPOKESMAN: We're at the World Seido Karate Organization to test the strength of Elmer's Glue-All.

We cut a board in half, then glued it together with Elmer's. Because when it comes to wood and most porous materials . . . Elmer's is incredibly strong. Is Elmer's strong enough to stand up to Master T. Nakamura?

Look! The Elmer's bond held. Elmer's was stronger than the wood itself.

MASTER NAKAMURA: Strong glue.

SPOKESMAN: Exactly.

VO: Elmer's Glue-All. Stronger than you'll ever need for most household jobs.

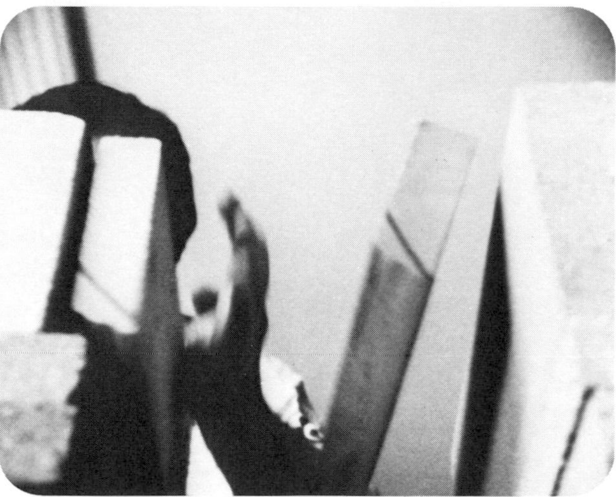

1081

Art Director	Bob Sullivan
Writer	John Hahn
Director	Tibor Hirsch
Producer	Bob Emerson
Production Company	Tibor Hirsch
Agency	Conahay & Lyon, Inc.
Client	Borden Inc.

ARNOLD'S BRICK OVEN WHITE BREAD
30-second

"Whole eggs. Arnold Brick Oven Bread. Open kettle molasses, grade-A-milk, 93 score butter, golden honey. Arnold's Brick Oven Bread. Unbleached flour, the finest ingredients, the finest taste—Arnold's."

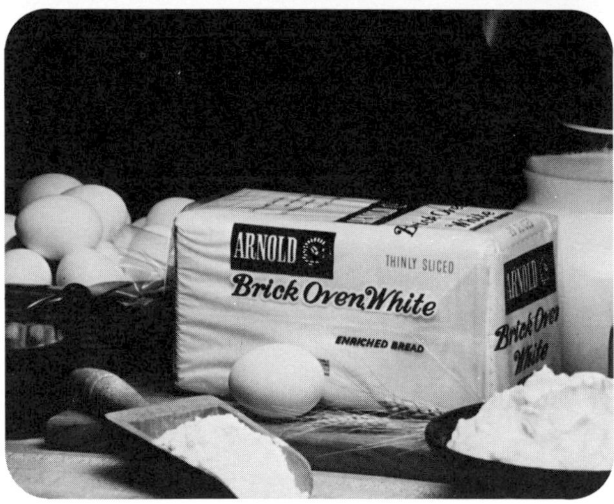

1082

Art Director Larry Hansen, W.E. Long Advertising
Designer Morton Goldsholl
Photographers Nick Kolias
Harry Goldsholl
Director Morton Goldsholl
Producer Bob Rowe, Goldsholl Assoc. Inc.
Music Composer: Michael Thomas (Ideal Concept)
Production Company Goldsholl Associates Inc.
Agency W.E. Long Advertising/Chicago
Client Arnold's Bread & Holsum Bakery, Inc.

ALBERT & ETHEL
30-second

VO: Albert, how about some crunch Caramel Nut Ice Cream?

WIFE: (WARNING) Now Albert!

VO: Or Creamy Strawberry . . . or Vanilla Fudge Twirl!

WIFE: Albert!

VO: But Ethel . . . it's Light n' Lively Ice Milk.

WIFE: (SUSPICIOUS) It sure tastes like ice cream to me.

VO: (WARMLY) It's made with the same good things as ice cream. Except it has less than half the fat.

VO: Light n' Lively. The ice creamy ice milk.

MAN: You got that, Ethel?

WOMAN: (SHEEPISHLY) Yeah.

1083

Art Director Dan Weiss
Writer Joan Eaton
Creative Director Agi Clark
Director Bill Hudson
Producer Maury Penn
Production Company Bill Hudson Films
Agency N W Ayer ABH International
Client Sealtest Foods

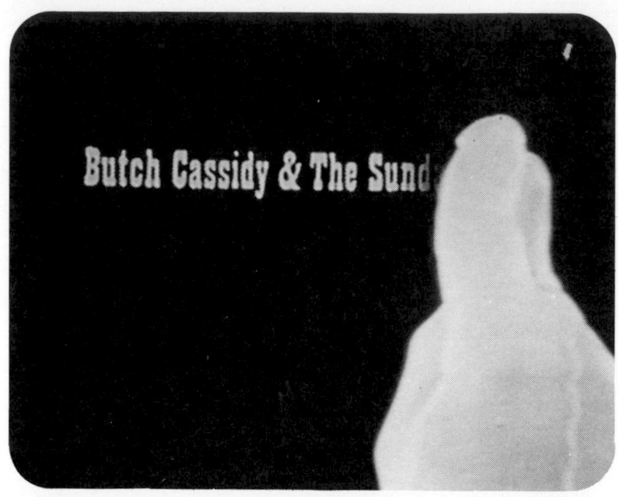

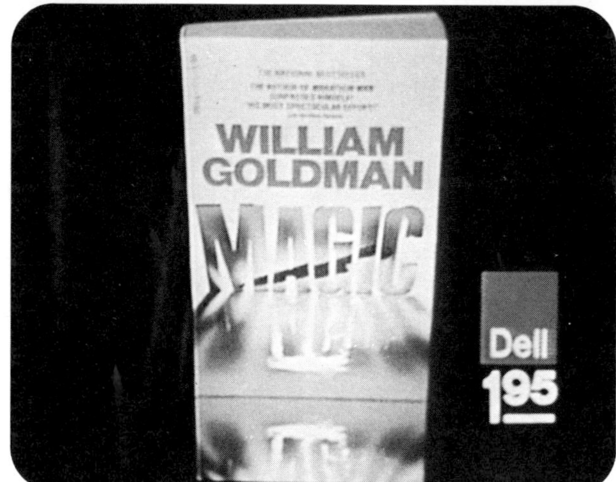

MAGIC
30-second

He wrote Butch Cassidy and the Sundance Kid.

A story touched with magic.

He wrote the screenplay for A Bridge too Far.

Magic.

He wrote Marathon Man.

Magic again.

But nothing William Goldman has ever written compares with the most terrifying novel of psychological suspense you have ever read.

Magic. By William Goldman.

The nerve-shattering bestseller from Dell.

1084
Art Director Philip Cimo
Writer Lou D'Angelo
Production Company Chimera Productions
Agency Franklin Spier Inc.
Client Dell Publishing Co., Inc.

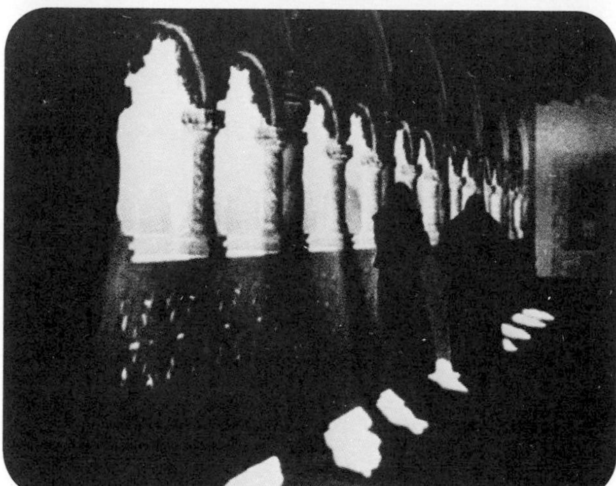

CENTER OF THE WORLD
30-second

VO: In the sixteenth century, Spain was the center of the world.

And it's easy to see why.

These are the things that make Spain, Spain.

And they're just for starters.

1085

Art Director	Haruo Koriyama
Writer	Jon B. Fischer
Cinematography	Tibor Hirsch
Director	Tibor Hirsch
Producer	Esther Iwanaga
Music	Charlie Morrow
Production Company	T.H.T. Productions, Inc.
Agency	Dentsu Corporation of America
Client	Spanish National Tourist Office

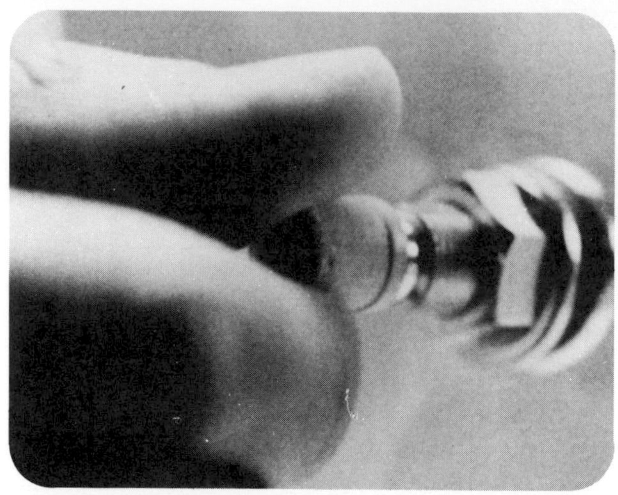

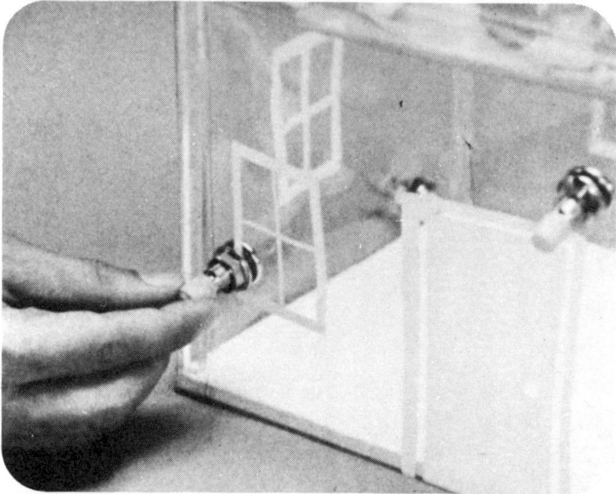

INFLATABLE HOUSE
30-second

ANNCR (VO): Every winter, heated air inside most homes leaks out.

Through tiny spaces that <u>ordinary</u> insulation often misses.

But every home Ryan builds is not only insulated, it's <u>super-sealed</u>.

At every critical point. To save energy and money.

You see, Ryan believes a house shouldn't just keep the outside, out.

It should also keep the inside . . . in.

1086

Art Director Robert F. Guirlinger
Writer Chris Perry
Producer Bob Long
Production Company CPC Associates
Agency Howard Swink Advertising, Inc.
Client Ryan Homes, Inc.

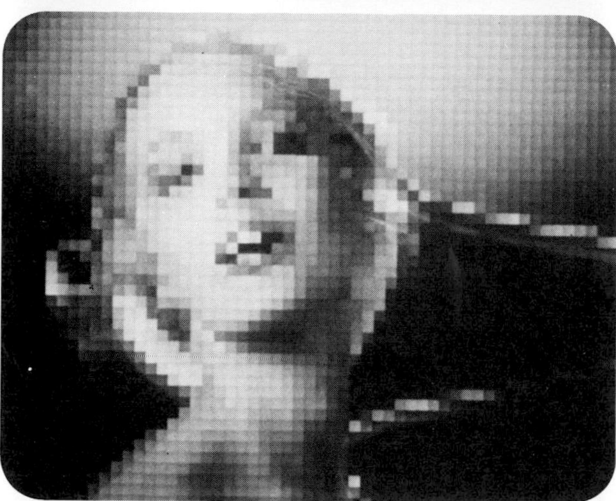

BEAUTIFUL LIFE
30-second

"Introducing the new face hygiene, and a beautiful life for your skin. Revlon Formula II. A non-fragrance cleanser and moisturizer with a gentle, electrical attraction for your skin.

The cleanser attracts dirt and oil so gently, your face actually feels softer. The moisturizer bonds with your skin smoothing on hours of protection.

The new face hygiene—Revlon Formula II. New, from The Revlon Research Group."

1087

Art Directors Olaf Moetus
Hal Martin (Leo Burnett Co.)
Photographers (live action) Fred Levinson & Co.
(special effects) Harry Goldsholl
Director Fred Levinson & Co., Morton Goldsholl
Producers Bob Rowe (Goldsholl)
Jerry Chodera (Leo Burnett)
Music Jerry Swayzee, Swayzee & Friends
Production Company Goldsholl Assoc. Inc./Fred Levinson & Co.
Agency Leo Burnett Co.
Client Revlon

BUDDIES
30-second

BOY: Me and Billy is best friends.

BILLY: Some times we fight a lot

BOY: But mostly we have fun. Today we were fightin'

BILLY: My Mom patched us with Curad

BOY: Billy's Ma says Curad is "ouchless" and helps boo-boos heal fast. See, it sticks to your skin, but don't stick to your sore. That's why Billy's Ma likes Curad, 'cause it helps boo-boos heal fast.

BOTH BOYS: We like Curad 'cause it don't ouch us.

CURITY
curad
"OUCHLESS"
Helps boo-boos
heal fast.

1088
Art Director Celester Santee
Writer Howie Stabin
Director Mike Cuesta
Producer Andy Doyle
Production Companies Myers & Griner/Cuesta, Inc.
Agency Kenyon & Eckhardt Advertising, Inc.
Client Colgate-Palmolive

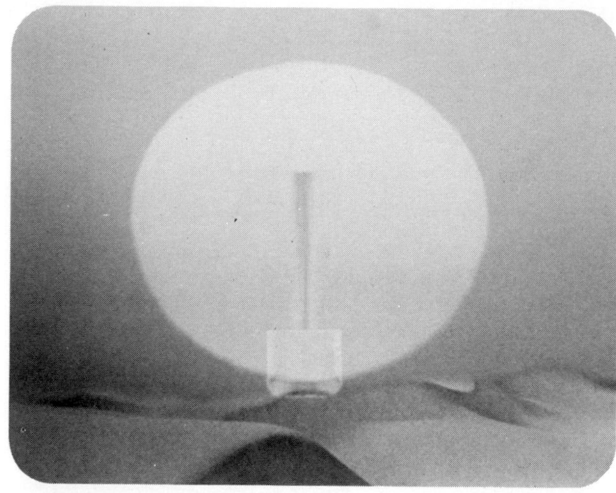

NATURAL CHOICE
30-second

ANNCR (VO): Sand. It's natural. Inexpensive.

And America's got plenty.

That's good. Because only one soft drink container is made from this natural element.

The glass bottle.

Which means soft drinks taste naturally great in glass. Right to the bottom.

And since glass begins with sand, old bottles can be melted down into new bottles.

So for the natural soft drink container, make the only natural choice. Glass.

1089
Art Director Frank Brugos
Writer Andrew Kresch
Director Herb Loebel
Producer Frank Brugos
Music Michael Small
Agency Dancer Fitzgerald Sample
Client Glass Packaging Institute

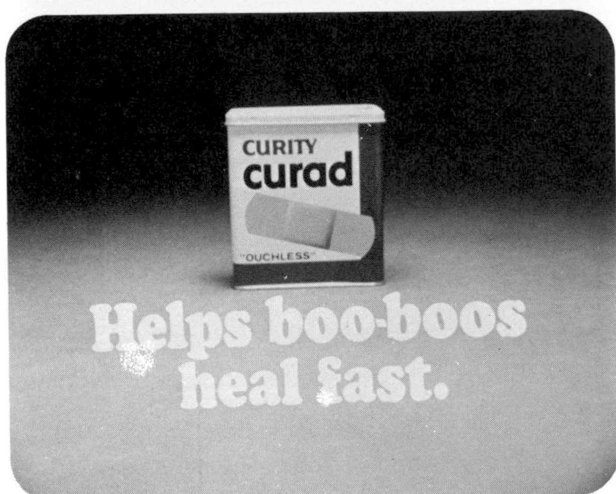

BIKE REV
30-second

BOY: This is my new bike. I got it for my birthday. This is my new hurt, I got with my new bike. My mom put a Curad on it. My Mom says Curad is "ouchless" and helps boo-boos heal fast. See, it sticks to my skin, but it don't stick to my sore. That's why my Mom likes Curad, 'cause it helps boo-boos heal fast, I like Curad 'cause it don't ouch me.

1090

Art Director	Celester Santee
Writer	Howie Stabin
Director	Mike Cuesta
Producer	Andy Doyle
Production Companies	Myers & Griner, Cuesta, Inc.
Agency	Kenyon & Eckhardt
Client	Colgate-Palmolive

STAND-UP
30-second

MAN: Introducing the Panhandler from Proctor-Silex. It cooks hamburgers and hotdogs like these appliances. Crepes and omelettes like these appliances. Fries bacon like a bacon maker. It even pops corn.

So you can buy this multi-purpose appliance for just under $100. Or you can buy ours for about $30 or less.

1091

Art Directors	Lou Carvell
	Ken Amaral
Writer	Jim McKennan
Director	Dick Loew
Producer	Lesleigh Latcham
Production Company	Gomes-Loew
Agency	Richard K. Manoff Inc.
Client	Proctor-Silex

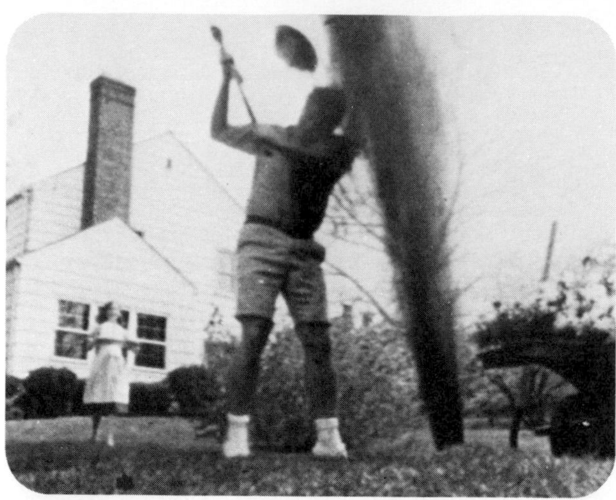

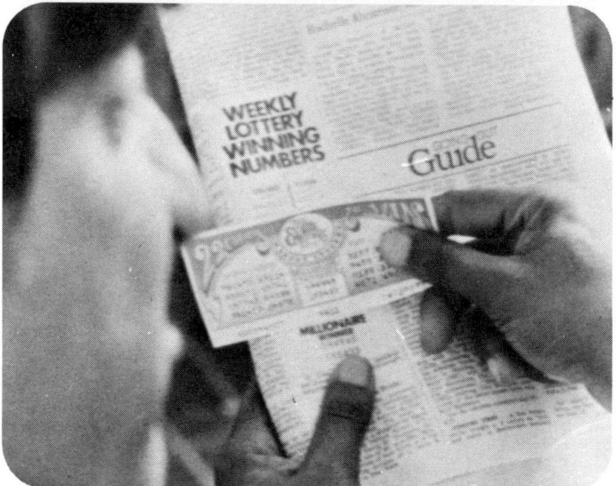

SHORTCUT
28-second

In the game of life, there have always been those who found the shortcut.

That lucky handful who didn't have to wait for their rewards.

But now, anyone can have that same advantage, in The Empire Stakes Weekly Lottery, where a doll r buys you 22 chances to win.

In The Empire Stakes Weekly Lottery, no one has a better chance than you.

1092

Art Director Paul Jervis
Writer Marc Shenfield
Director Neil Tardio
Producer Kyle M. Dennis
Production Company Lovinger, Tardio & Melsky
Agency Smith Greenland, Inc.
Client New York State Lottery

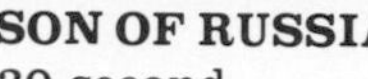

SON OF RUSSIA
30-second

ANNCR (VO): Eat yogurt every day for 90 or 100 years and you really become an expert. That's why we're proud the Soviet Georgians loved Dannon. But then, it's a lot like their yogurt. All natural, not just natural flavor. No preservatives, no starch, no color additives. With plenty of active cultures. Many other American yogurts simply aren't made that way. As for 81 year old Goodge Kvitzinia and his older brother, Upta, they loved Dannon yogurt. Why? They said it's just like Momma's.

1093
Art Director Elliot Matlin
Writer Steve Kasloff
Director Bob Gaffney
Producer Arlene Hoffman
Production Company Bob Gaffney Productions
Agency Marsteller
Client Dannon Yogurt

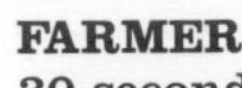

FARMER
30-second

FARMER: I remember Clarence Birdseye from 1936.

When it came to picking corn for his new frozen foods process, he was mighty particular.

VO: So he hands me seeds, he selected it himself.

I planted his seeds, and you know what?

'Cause his seeds were better, my corn was sweeter.

OC: Has been ever since. We still plant for Birdseye.

ANNCR (VO): If you're as fussy as Clarence Birdseye, serve your family the vegetables that bear the name of the father of frozen foods.

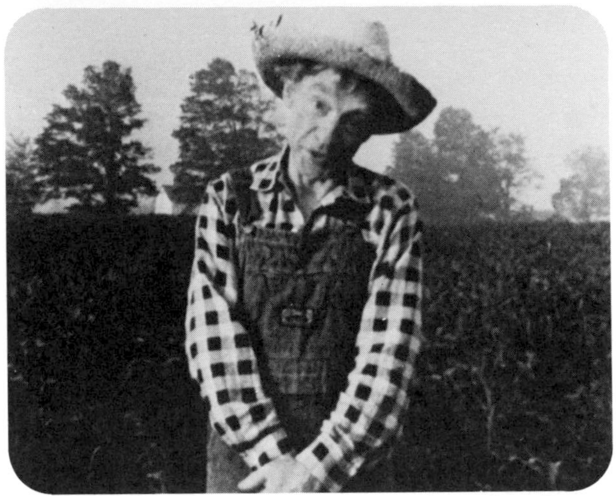

1094

Art Director Stew Birbrower
Writers Stew Birbrower
Mike Becker
Producer Phyllis Landi
Production Company Steve Horn
Agency Young & Rubicam
Client General Foods Birdseye

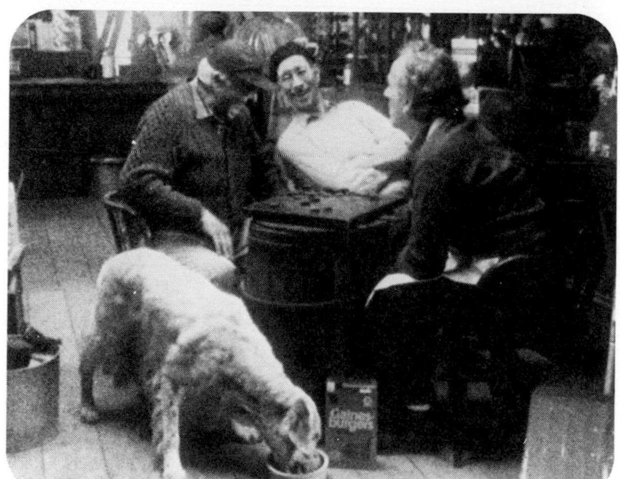

COUNTRY GENERAL STORE
30-second

ANNCR (VO): Pardon me . . . what kind of dog food does your dog eat?

STORE OWNER: Young fellow, there's two things I know; checkers and dogs.

Dogs like canned dog food . . .

'Specially Herman here.

ANNCR (VO): Do you think he'd like Gainesburgers?

KIBITZER: Well, he might . . .

STORE OWNER: Ed, leave this to me. Dogs like food that's moist and meaty.

ANNCR (VO): But Gainesburgers are. Moist and meaty, see . . .

STORE OWNER: Go ahead, but . . .

ANNCR (VO): . . . and they taste terrific.

KIBITZER: And you don't know nothin' about checkers neither.

ANNCR (VO): Gainesburgers dog food . . . the canned dog food without the can.

1095

Art Director	Mike Miller
Writer	Tom Thomas
Producer	Ralph Ward
Production Company	Giraldi
Agency	Young & Rubicam
Client	General Foods/Gainesburger

LIKE FATHER, LIKE DAUGHTER

30-second

ANNCR: This is Secretariat.
And this is his daughter.
From all appearances, it's a case of like father, like daughter.

And some day, at Aqueduct or Belmont Park, perhaps she'll come into her inheritance. To know what that's like, you've got to be there.

1096

Art Director Ira Madris
Writer Rick Johnston
Director Michael Gottlieb
Producer Diane Maze
Production Company Len Lipson Associates
Agency McCann-Erickson, Inc.
Client The New York Racing Association

FRANCINE NEFF
30-second

FRANCINE NEFF: Do you know me? I was Treasurer of the United States, so many people know my name but not me. That's why I carry the American Express Card.

It's welcome all over—and that makes me welcome all over. Sure, it's super to have my signature on 6 billion dollars, but for traveling and entertaining, . . .

it's a lot better to have my name right here.

ANNCR (VO): To apply for an American Express Card Call 800-528-8000.

NEFF: The American Express Card. Don't leave home without it.

1097

Art Directors Mark Ross
Mel Rustom
Writers Bill Taylor
Mark Ross
Director Neil Tardio
Producer Mel Rustom
Production Company Lovinger, Tardio, Melsky
Agency Ogilvy & Mather Inc.
Client American Express Co.

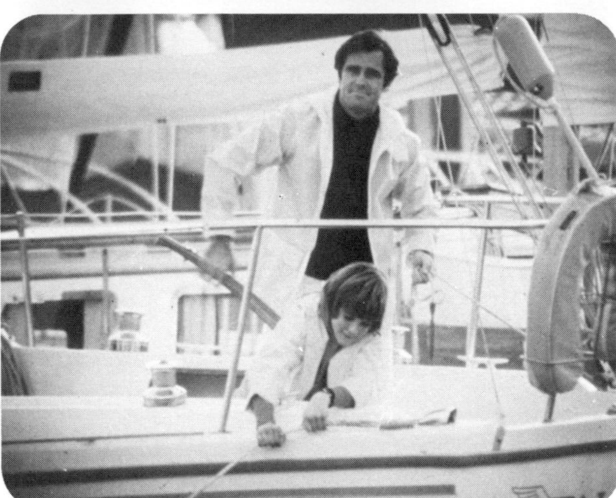

Talk to us now.
You could thank us later.
PaineWebber.

SAILBOAT
30-second

MAN: When you work hard to makemoney, one of the most important things a brokerage house can do is help you keep it.

Thank you, Paine Webber.

WOMAN: Thank you, Paine Webber.

GIRL: Thank you, Daddy!

FATHER: Thank you, Paine Webber.

ANNCR: Paine Webber can't assure you that you'll make money, but call us about our brokerage services and you might say . . .

MAN: Thank you, Paine Webber.

ANNCR: Talk to us now. You could thank us later. Paine Webber.

1098

Art Director Andrew Langer
Writer Marshall W. Karp
Director Steve Horn
Producer Diane Jeremias
Music Warner-Levinson
Production Company Steve Horn, Inc.
Agency The Marschalk Co., Inc.
Client Paine Webber

Read the label,use only as directed

PARTY
30-second

SINGING: That was some party, dancing all night.

End up eating pizza by dawns early light.

I can't help it if I like to live.

But living like that means something's got to give.

I gotta get me Alka-Seltzer. Fast, Fast.

Plop, Plop, Fizz, Fizz. Oh, What A Relief It is. Fast, Fast.

OC: Upset stomach and headache, meet the Plop, Plop, Fizz, Fizz.

SINGERS: Oh, what a relief it is. Fast, Fast, Fast.

1099

Art Director	Bob Wilvers
Writer	Paul Margolies
Photographer	Ed Brown
Director	Michael Ulick
Producer	Sandy Breakstone
Production Company	Rick Levine Productions
Agency	Wells, Rich, Greene
Client	Miles Laboratories

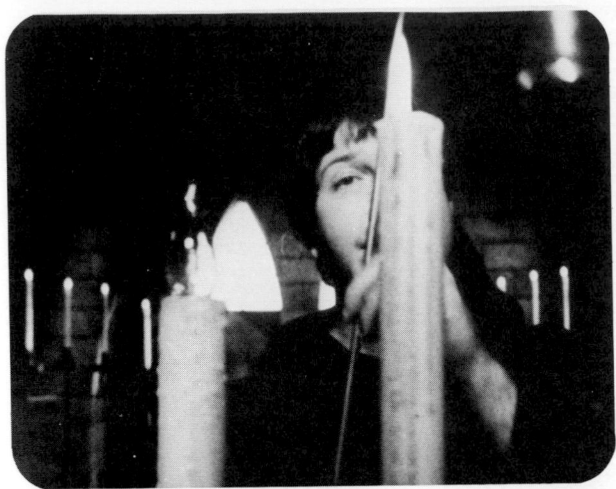

GRO LUX
30-second

ANNCR (VO): The Sylvania Blue Dot Flicker Light.

ANNCR (VO): The Sylvania Blue Dot Mood Light.

ANNCR (VO): You can get Sylvania Blue Dot quality . . .

ANNCR (VO): . . . in everything to flicker lights . . .

ANNCR (VO): . . . to Gro-Lux Lights.

ANNCR (VO): We're a lot more . . .

ANNCR (VO): . . . than something . . .

ANNCR (VO): . . . to read by.

1101
Art Director Ron Arnold
Writer Daryl Warner
Photographer Ed Brown
Director Michael Ulick
Producer Phil Bodwell
Production Company Rick Levine Productions
Agency Doyle Dane Bernbach
Client GTE Sylvania

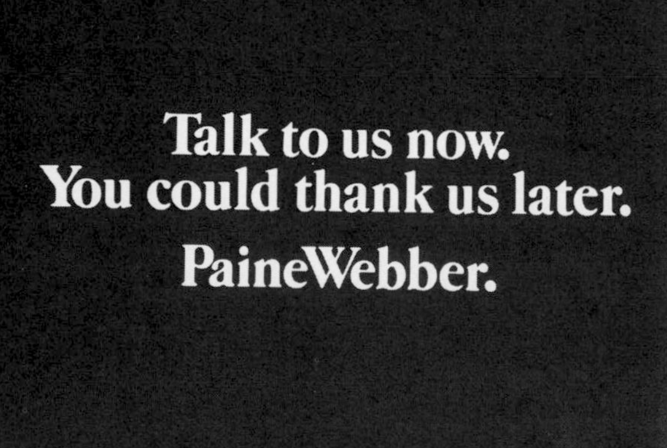

STABLES
30-second

MAN: Sometimes, the most important thing a brokerage house can do, is help you keep the money you already made.

Thank you, Paine Webber.

MS. BACALL: Thank you, Paine Webber.

WOMAN: Thank you, Charles.

MAN: Thank you, Paine Webber.

VO: Paine Webber can't assure you that you'll make money, but call us about our brokerage services, and you might say . . .

WOMAN: Thank you, Paine Webber.

VO: Talk to us now. You could thank us later. Paine Webber.

1102

Art Director	Andrew Langer
Writer	Marshall W. Karp
Director	Steve Horn
Producer	Diane Jeremias
Music	Warner-Levinson
Production Company	Steve Horn, Inc.
Agency	The Marschalk Company, Inc.
Client	Paine Webber

FLYING
30-second

SINGER: Well, I bought a pair

of Levis
and they've really been around

I've taken them camping

and I've laid them on the ground
they've come with me to parties

and they've climbed up a tree

and they've been to school so often

that they're nearly as smart as me.
But after years and years of wearing

my levis in and out

I couldn't help but notice

that the knee wore out.

So I sewed on a patch

and a flower here and there

they looked so good again
I could take them anywhere.

Now I'm using them as cut-offs

and flying in the air.
But I really think it's time

that I got another pair.

You can live in Levis.

1103

Art Director Brian Harrod
Writer Allan Kazmer
Director Lester Bookbinder
Producer Karen Hayes
Music Music Track
Production Company Trudel Productions Ltd.
Agency McCann-Erickson Canada
Client Levi's Canada

KODAK EK6 INSTANT CAMERA

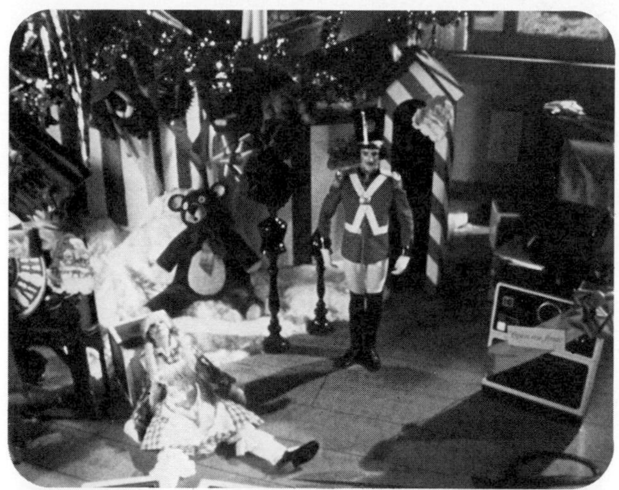

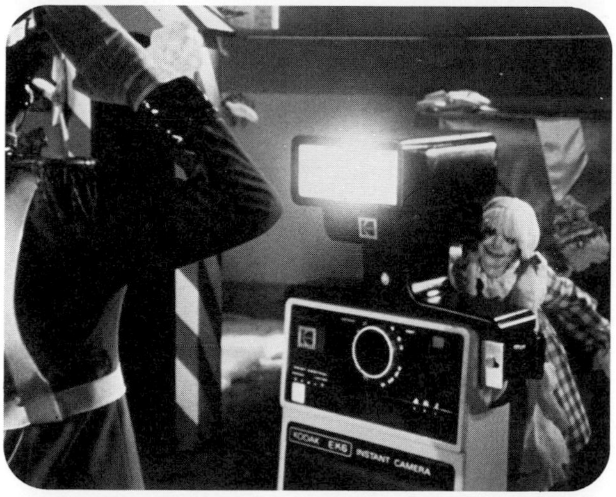

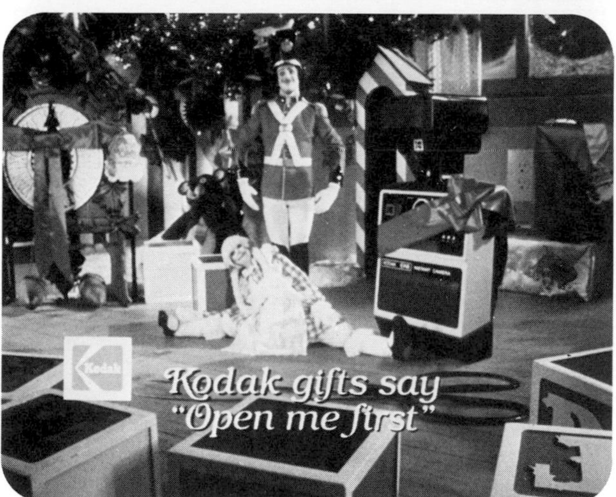

Kodak gifts say
"Open me first"

TOY SOLDIERS REV 2
30-second

MUSIC: In and under.

ANNCR (VO): The magic of Christmas comes to life . . . in instant color by Kodak. The EK6—the only motorized instant camera that gives you this . . .

bright, brilliant color by Kodak. You can capture all the enchantment . . .

and color of Christmas instantly. There's instant color. And there's instant color by Kodak.

CHILD: Look, what Santa Claus brought!

1104

Art Directors	John Kamerer
	Bernard Owett
Writers	Ruth Downing Karp
	Grant Monsarrat
Director	Stu Hagmann
Producers	Tom Hall
	Bernard Owett
Music	Pinder Lane Productions—New York City
Production Company	E.U.E/Screen Gems—Burbank
Agency	J. Walter Thompson Company
Client	Eastman Kodak Company

OUT OF THE MOUTHS OF BABES
30-second

VO: Matchbox announces 10 cars America has been waiting for.

BOY: We're looking for a family car that's sporty enough for me.

GIRL: Yet practical for me.

2ND BOY: I need a car that's built the way I use it: tough.

VO: Like every Matchbox car, each of our 78's has a sticker price of about a buck.

3RD BOY: I want a car that lets me express the real me. No matter who you are, Matchbox has the car that says you.

SILVER

1105

Art Director Bill Kamp
Writer John Russo
Designer Bill Kamp
Director John Sterner
Producer Merle Bloom
Music Michael Small
Production Company Andre Durona
Agency Levine, Huntley, Schmidt, Plapler & Beaver, Inc.
Client Lesney Products Corp.

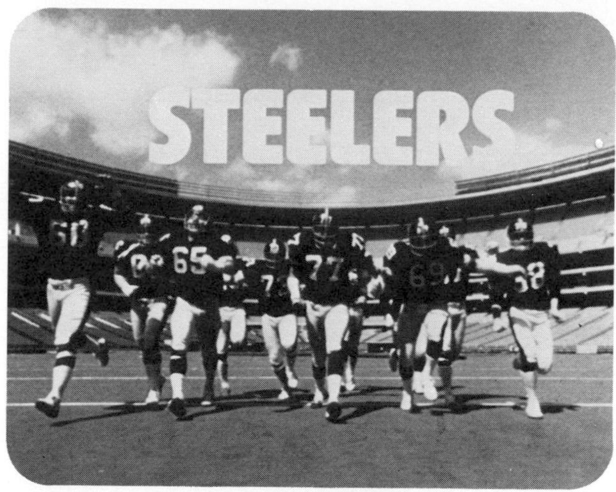

SAMSONITE VS. STEELERS
30-second

ANNCR: Samsonite . . .
versus . . .
The Pittsburgh Steelers.

PLAYER: That's one tough bag.

ANNCR: Samsonite makes over 400 styles of tough bags.
Samsonite's got your bag.

1106

Art Director	John Kamerer
Writers	Len Dia
	Cynthia Milliken
Director	Sid Myers
Producer	Wyn Walshe
Music	Stock ("Blue Danube")
Production Company	Myers & Griner, Cuesta
Agency	J. Walter Thompson Company
Client	Samsonite Corporation

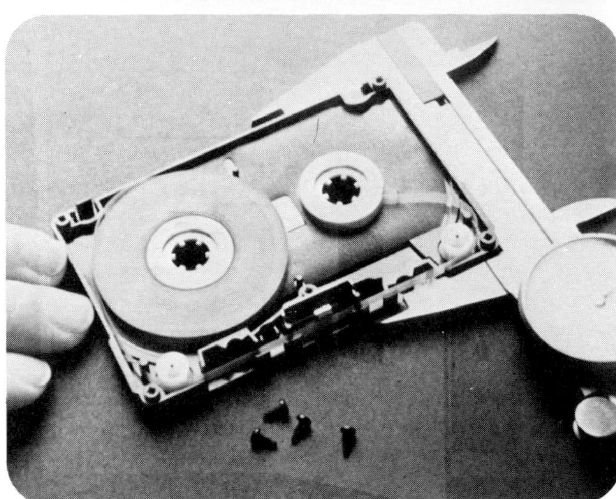

QUALITY
30-second

ANNCR: This is Maxell recording tape. It costs more than most other cassettes because it's made better. Maxell is the only tape that comes with this special non-abrasive head cleaner. Maxell casings are held together by steel screws. And they're finished to tolerances 25% higher than industry standards. So while other manufacturers give you a price that sounds good, Maxell gives you a tape that sounds good.

1107
Art Director Earl Cavanah
Writer Ron Berger
Designer Earl Cavanah
Director Henry Sandbank
Producer Carol Singer
Production Company Henry Sandbank Productions
Agency Scali, McCabe, Sloves
Client Maxell Corporation of America

TROY
30-second

ANNCR (VO): This is an electronic typewriter.

The Xerox 850 Display Typing System.

Push a button, and a full page of text appears on a screen.

You can correct spelling, rearrange paragraphs, even change margins instantly.

Then it automatically types out on paper. Letter perfect.

If your business deals with thousands of words each day, remember this one. Xerox.

1108

Art Directors Allen Kay
Tony Angotti
Writers Allen Kay
Steve Penchina
Director Paul Herriet
Producer Sydelle Rangell
Production Company E.U.E.
Agency Needham, Harper & Steers
Client Xerox Corp.

THE LESSON
30-second

ANNCR: Tonight, Arthur you're going to learn how to drink from a glass. Oh! Arthur. That's OK pal, it's alright. Alright, Arthur—no problem—let's try again. A paper towel so strong and absorbent you can wring it out without wearing it out. In tests it actually stood up to a washing machine. Here's Viva. Here's Bounty. And here's Bolt.

FATHER: You're doing it. Arthur, you're doing it. You're not doing it, Arthur. Bolt, the World's most cloth-like paper towel.

1109

Art Director	John Danza
Writer	Mike Drazen
Director	Neil Tardio
Producer	Tanya English
Production Company	Lovinger, Tardio, Melsky
Agency	Scali, McCabe, Sloves
Client	American Can Company

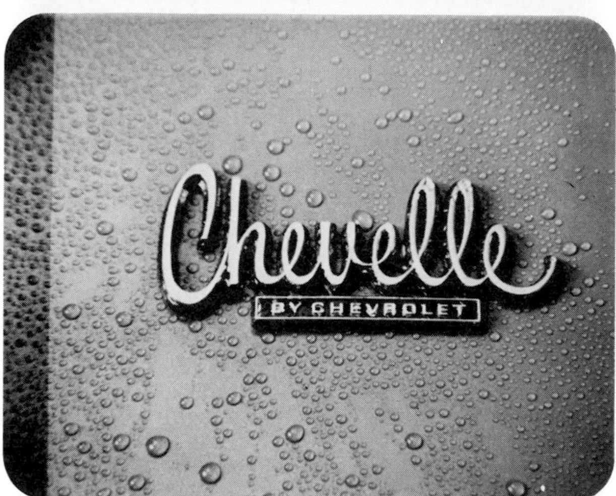

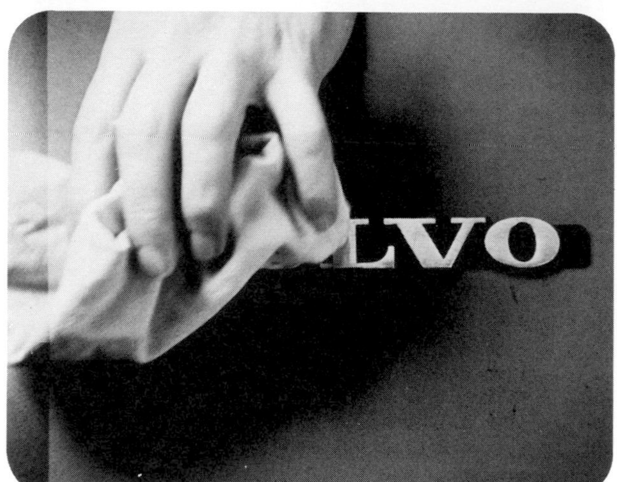

GENERIC-DETROIT II
30-second

Between them, G.M., Ford, Chrysler and American Motors make 56 different cars.

That means they have 56 opportunities to satisfy you.

Yet a recent nationwide survey has shown . . .

. . . that Volvo owners are more satisfied with their cars . . .

. . . than the owners of any G.M., Ford, Chrysler or American Motors car.

We're very proud of that.

SUPER: The car for people who think.

1110

Art Director John Danza
Writer Larry Cadman
Designer John Danza
Director Henry Sandbank
Producer Tanya English
Music HEA
Production Company Henry Sandbank
Agency Scali, McCabe, Sloves
Client Volvo of America Corp.

MORE BREAST MEAT WORKSHOP
30-second

FRANK PERDUE: I froze the breed of chicken most chicken companies sell and one of my Perdue chickens of the same weight to prove a point. Watch, even though they weigh the same my chicken has more meat on its breast than the other one. That's just one more thing that makes my Perdue chickens stand out. They've got the biggest breasts in the business.

1111

Art Director	Sam Scali
Writer	Ed McCabe
Designer	Sam Scali
Director	Franta Herman
Producer	Karen Spector
Production Company	Televideo
Agency	Scali, McCabe, Sloves
Client	Perdue Farms Inc.

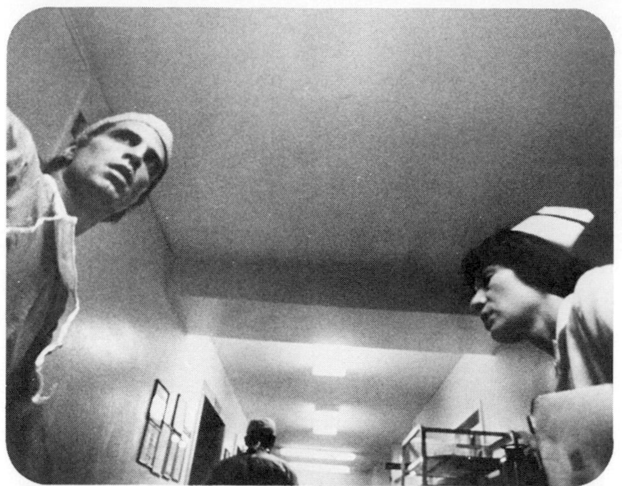

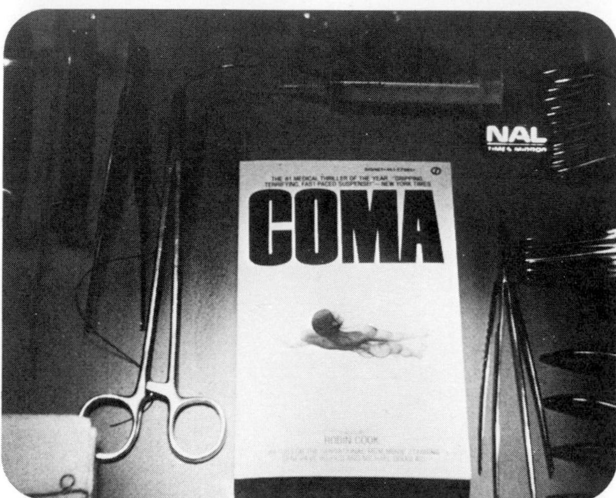

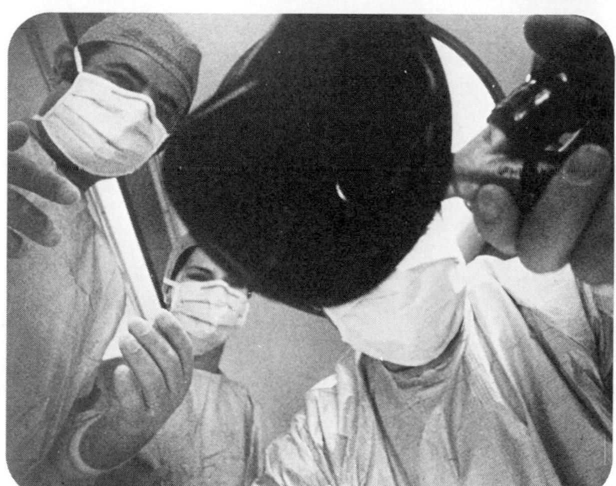

COMA
30-second

VO: Every patient facing surgery suffers from fear.

Because nothing requires more trust than putting your life into the hands of another person.

Even if that person is a doctor.

"Coma," the new Signet paperback, is the story of Susan Wheeler, a young medical student who discovers a group of doctors that have no intention of curing their patients.

1112
Art Director Bob Phillips
Writer Frank Anton
Director Mike Cuesta
Producer Don Trevor
Production Company Myers & Griner, Cuesta
Agency Levine, Huntley, Schmidt, Plapler & Beaver, Inc.
Client Signet Books

PRISON
30-second

BOSS: Did you bring the escape plans, Louie?

LOUIE: Right here, boss.

BOSS: It's too big, Louie. Get out of here!

ANNCR (VO): Naturally, the new Xerox 3107 copier makes regular size copies.

But it also makes large copies of large documents

and small copies of large documents.

BOSS: O.K. boys, Louie came through.

BOSS: One for you, Mugsy. Here's one for you, Fingers.

BOSS: Here's one for you, Warden . . . Warden??!!

1113

Art Director Tony Angotti
Writer Steve Penchina
Director Paul Herriet
Producer Sydelle Rangell
Production Company E.U.E.
Agency Needham, Harper & Steers
Client Xerox Corporation

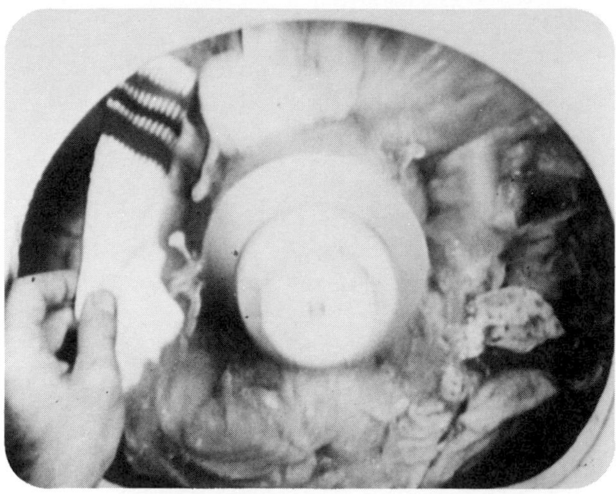

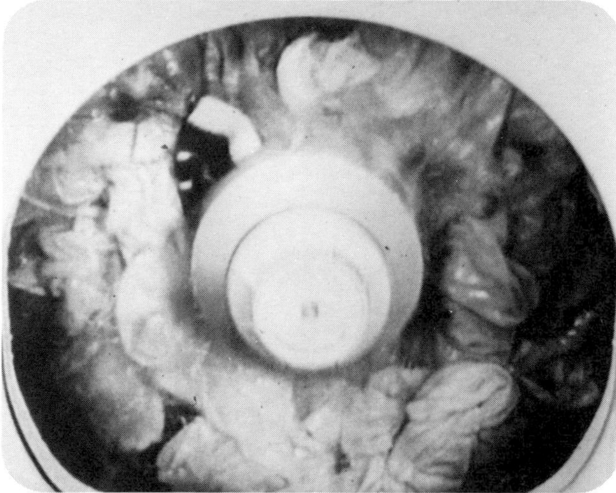

SOCK REV. I
30-second

ANNCR (VO): One key to getting clothes cleaner is getting them to the bottom of the washer as often as possible.

Watch what happens when we put a sock in this Frigidaire washer.

Watch what happens when we put it in the best selling brand's best washer.

It's not surprising that independent laboratory tests proved . . .

All Frigidaire jet cone washers clean better than their best washer.

FRIGIDAIRE.
ENGINEERED BY GENERAL MOTORS.

1114

Art Director	Steve Singer
Writer	Allen Kay
Director	Henry Sandbank
Producer	Sydelle Rangell
Production Company	Sandbank Films, Inc.
Agency	Needham, Harper & Steers
Client	Frigidaire

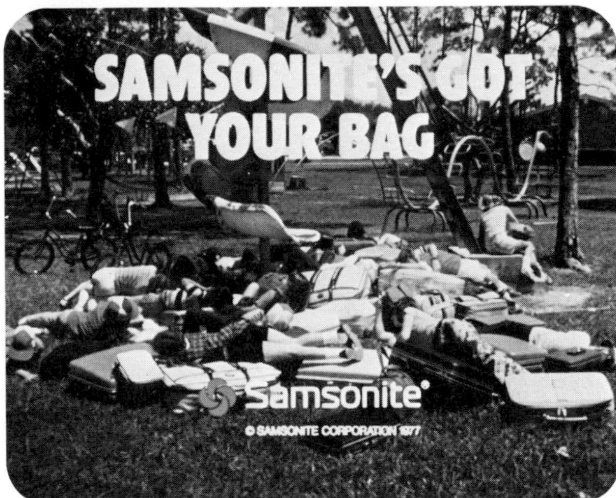

SAMSONITE VS. THE 3RD GRADE
30-second

ANNCR: Samsonite . . .
versus . . .

the Gulliver School
third grade, Florida

CHILD: That's one tough bag!

ANNCR: Samsonite makes over 400 styles of tough bags.

Samsonite's got your bag.

1115

Art Director John Kamerer
Writers Len Dia
Cynthia Milliken
Director Sid Myers
Producer Wyn Walshe
Music Stock ("1812 Overture")
Production Company Myers & Griner, Cuesta
Agency J. Walter Thompson Company
Client Samsonite Corporation

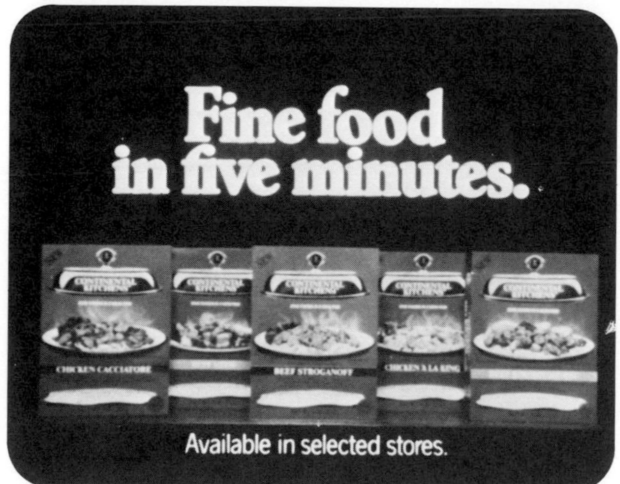

PHONE
30-second

ANNCR: One of these men will be tasting one of Continental Kitchens' new non-frozen entrees.

The other, a leading frozen brand.

Continental Kitchens' entree comes in our revolutionary Flavor Seal pouch.

It isn't frozen or refrigerated. So you just heat for five minutes . . .

and serve.

MAN: It's delicious.

ANNCR: How does the frozen entree taste? We'll know in about twenty minutes, when it's done. Call 800-543-9635 and we'll tell you.

VO: New Continental Kitchens' non-frozen entrees.

Fine food in five minutes.

1116
Art Director Allen Kay
Writers Lois Korey
Alan Fraser
Director Paul Herriet
Producer Sydelle Rangell
Production Company E.U.E.
Agency Needham, Harper & Steers
Client ITT Continental Baking

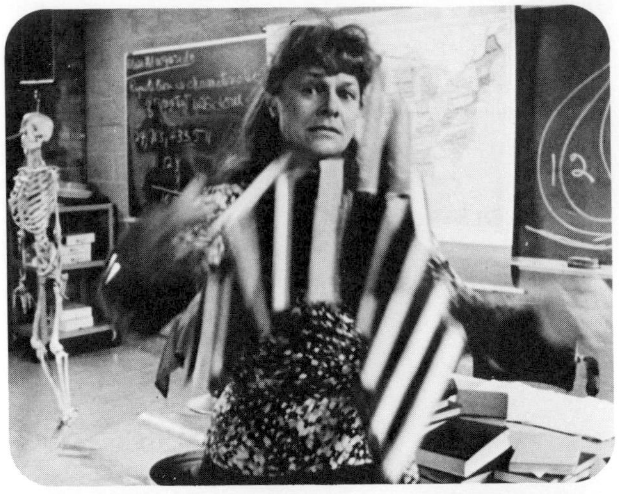

MISS MARGARIDA REVISED
30-second

MISS MARGARIDA (OC): Miss Margarida wants to see all of you in Miss Margarida's class . . .

What you will learn in Miss Margarida's class is not in these!

And don't think you're going to get sex education.
You want Miss Margarida to undress in front of you, don't you?
Fat chance!

But Miss Margarida doesn't want to be hard on you . . .

Miss Margarida wants to show you the way.

ANNCR (VO): Joseph Papp presents Estelle Parsons in Miss Margarida's Way at the Ambassador Theatre. Call 265-1855. Charge it . . .

MISS MARGARIDA: And be on time.

1117

Art Director	Reinhold Schwenk
Writers	Bob Schulman Joel Goodman
Director	Bill Mason
Producers	Marilyn Cook Janet Davidson
Production Company	Mason/Stearns
Agency	Case & McGrath Inc.
Client	New York Shakespeare Festival

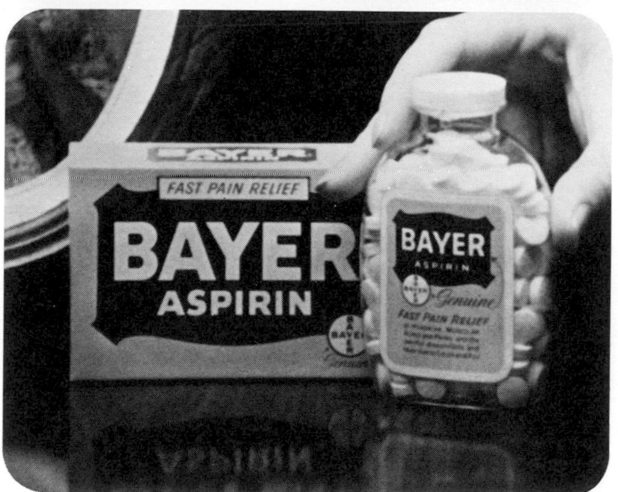

GENERATIONS
30-second

GIRL (OC): In my family, we've known for generations . . . to relieve the aches and fever of colds and flu . . . get rest . . . drink fluids . . . and take Bayer Aspirin.

MAN (OC): . . . Rest . . . fluids . . . Bayer Aspirin . . .

ANNCR (VO): Generations of cold and flu sufferers have known it. Generations of doctors have recommended it. Rest, fluids, aspirin. And the number one aspirin is Bayer.

1118
Art Director Dom Marino
Writer Lore Parker
Designer Dom Marino
Director Steve Horn
Producer Eileen Rodgers
Production Company Steve Horn Productions
Agency Doyle Dane Bernbach
Client Bayer Sterling Drug

MUNICH, GERMANY

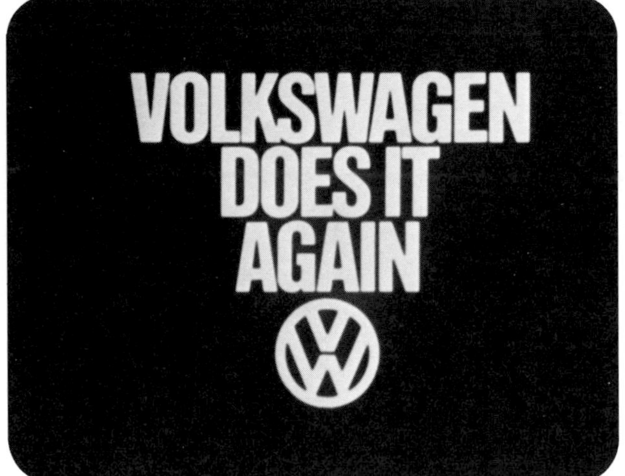
VOLKSWAGEN
DOES IT
AGAIN

MUNICH TRADE-IN
30-second

MAN: I can also afford . . . not to.

SINGERS: Volkswagen (MUSIC) . . . Does it again.

1119

Art Director Bert Steinhauser
Writer Robert Levenson
Designer Bert Steinhauser
Director Rick Levine
Producer Jim deBarros
Music Tom Dawes
Production Company Rick Levine Productions
Agency Doyle Dane Bernbach
Client Volkswagen

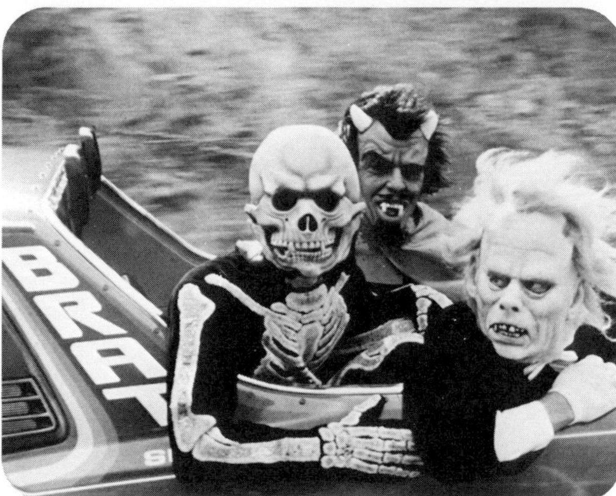

FUN IN THE SUN
30-second

SUPER: Introducing the Subaru Brat. Fun on wheels.

VO: The Subaru Brat is a new kind of car, that shifts from front wheel to four wheel drive at the flick of a lever.

And the Brat's back is wide open. And so is the fun you can have in its 2 outdoor seats.

SUPER: The Subaru Brat. Fun on wheels.

1120

Art Director	Allan Beaver
Writer	Larry Plapler
Designer	Allan Beaver
Producer	Don Trevor
Music	Michael Small
Production Company	Rick Levine Productions

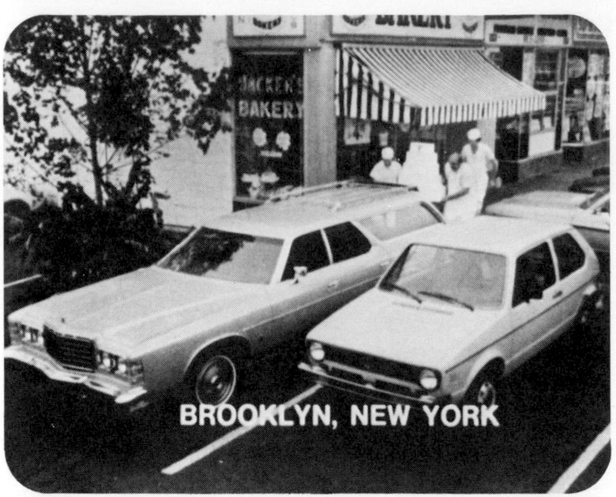
BROOKLYN, NEW YORK

VOLKSWAGEN
DOES IT
AGAIN

BAKER
30-second

MAN: Neither can I.

MAN: I bought the wagon because it was big and the Rabbit because it was small.

MAN: Now the big car is smaller than the Rabbit and the Rabbit is bigger than the big car. Makes me crazy.

VO: What do you say about the Rabbit now?

MAN: Let 'em eat cake.

SINGERS: Volkswagen—(SFX: WEDDING BELLS) Does it again.

1121

Art Director Bert Steinhauser
Writer Robert Levenson
Designer Bert Steinhauser
Director Rick Levine
Producer Jim deBarros
Music Tom Dawes
Production Company Rick Levine Productions
Agency Doyle Dane Bernbach
Client Volkswagen

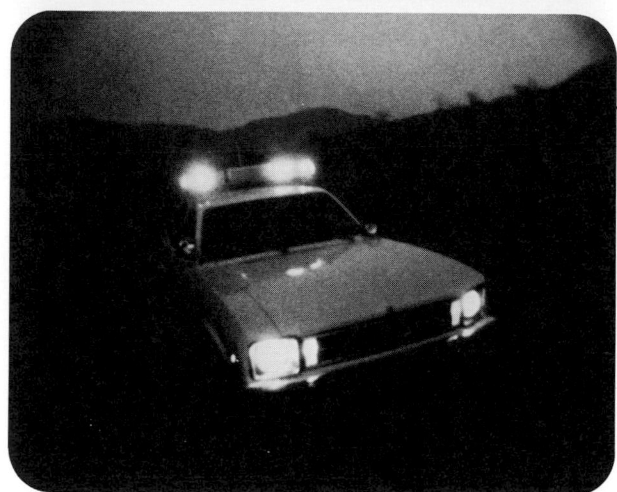

CADILLAC
30-second

ANNCR (VO): We put Mobil 1 into a taxi, drove it 5,000 miles . . . took that used oil, drove it another 5,000 miles in a police car . . . drove it 5,000 more miles in a Cadillac and found that after 15,000 miles without an oil change, Mobil 1 protected the engine as well as new ordinary motor oil.

Mobil 1 . . .

the oil that saves you gas, saves you oil changes.

1122

Art Director	Roy Grace
Writer	John Noble
Designer	Roy Grace
Artist	Roy Grace
Director	Carroll Raver
Producer	Susan Calhoun
Production Company	Carroll Raver Productions
Agency	Doyle Dane Bernbach
Client	Mobil Oil Corporation

GTE
GENERAL TELEPHONE
Call us.

BUILD A ROOM
30-second

ANNCR (VO): GTE decorator phones . . .

You can build a room around them.

1123

Art Director Bob Starr
Writer Eilene Weiss
Designer Bob Starr
Director Paul Harriet
Producer Phil Bodwell
Production Company Independent Artists
Agency Doyle Dane Bernbach
Client General Telephone

MUD PUDDLE
30-second

ANNCR (VO): Some people carry American Tourister's Verylite . . . because it's beautiful.

Some carry the Verylite because it's roomy.

And then . . . there are people who carry the Verylite . . . because it's very light.

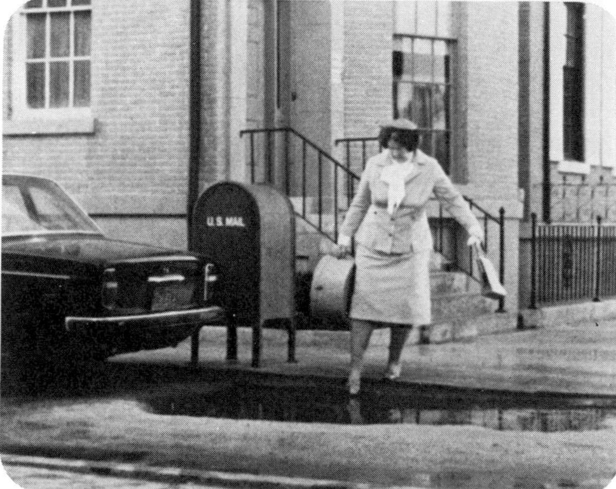

1124

Art Director Roy Grace
Writer Marcia Bell Grace
Designer Roy Grace
Artist Roy Grace
Director Howard Zieff
Producer Susan Calhoun
Music Susan Hamilton
Production Company Independent Artists
Agency Doyle Dane Bernbach
Client American Tourister

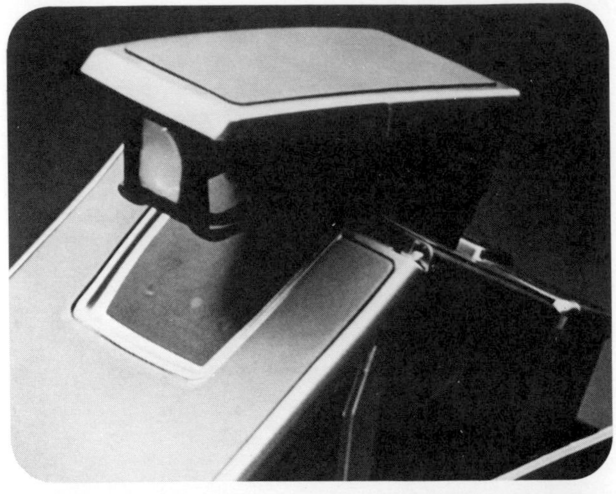

GREAT CAMERA REV.
30-second

ANNCR (VO): How much should you expect from a great camera?

Polaroid's SX-70 lets you shoot

automatically,

very close,

or very far away,

in lots of light,

or hardly any,

shoot every second and a half

and have beautiful pictures in minutes.

No other camera in the world, does it all.

The SX-70 Alpha 1.

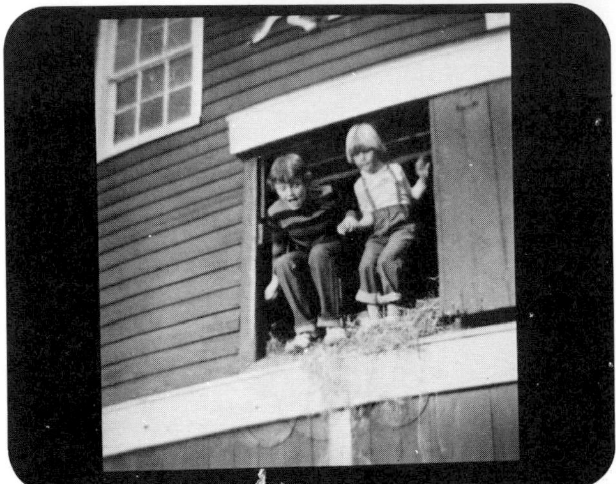

1125

Art Director	Bob Tucker
Writer	Phyllis Robinson
Director	Steve Horn
Producer	Joe Scibetta
Production Company	Steve Horn Productions
Agency	Doyle Dane Bernbach
Client	Polaroid

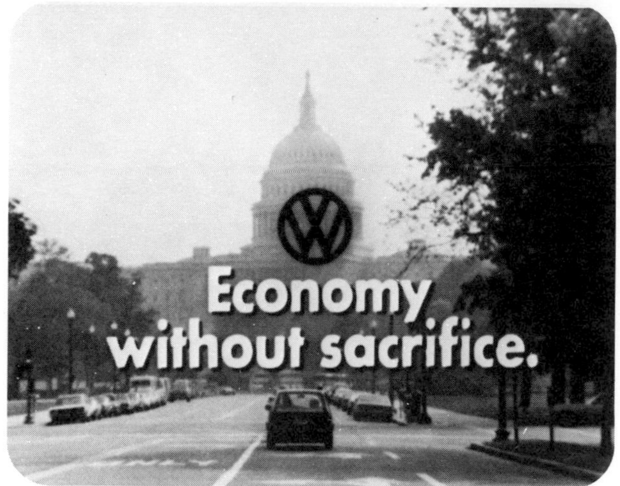

ENERGY PROPOSAL
30-second

VO: Volkswagen presents an energy proposal for government:

For the Secretary of Interior we propose a Dasher Wagon with one of the roomiest interiors in its class.

For the Secretary of State, who's always zipping to airports, our Scirocco sports car which zips from 0 to 50 in 7.5 seconds.

And for our treasurer, who understands big economy, our big economy Rabbit.

Now that's an energy proposal without sacrifice!

1126

Art Director John Eding
Writer Douglas Houston
Director Bob Giraldi Productions
Producer Jim deBarros
Music Lucas McFall
Production Company Bob Giraldi
Agency Doyle Dane Bernbach
Client Volkswagen

GM/RABBIT
30-second

MAN: Now, let's see if I read the ad right. In General Motors five-car showdown, they tested their Buick Opel against the Toyota Corolla . . .

. . . the Subaru DL, the Datsun B-210 . . .

. . . and the Volkswagen Rabbit.

There were four different tests. O.K.

Now. GM did the tests.

But . . . the overall winner was the VW Rabbit.

Oh. O.K., General Motors, you convinced me.

I'll buy the Rabbit.

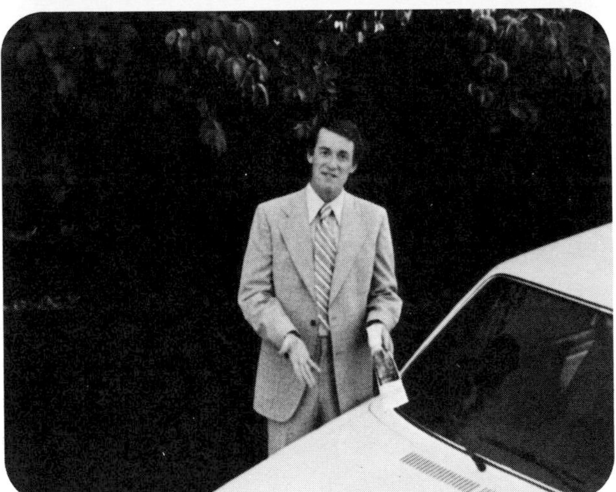

1127
Art Director Gordon James
Writer Diane Till
Director Bob Roughsedge
Producer Nancy Campbell
Production Company Both Coasts Productions
Agency Doyle Dane Bernbach
Client Volkswagen

BANK
Actual closed-circuit picture.

"IT'S A SONY."

PENNSYLVANIA
30-second and 25/30-second

VO: On June 8th, 1973, in Pottstown, Pennsylvania, a TV set was put

in a bank window as a promotion. The set was left running for over two years, twenty-four hours a day. With not so much as an adjustment.

Which translates to over 16 years of daily prime-time viewing. What kind of set was it?

That's right, it's a Sony.

1128
Art Director John Caggiano
Writer Mike Mangano
Designer John Caggiano
Director Rick Levine
Producer Jim deBarros
Agency Doyle Dane Bernbach
Client Sony

TESTIMONIAL II
30-second

ANNCR (VO): This is a testimonial for Tickle . . .

The anti-perspirant with the big wide ball.

It's so effective at helping stop perspiration . . .

. . . so effective at helping stop odor . . .

. . . it's given people a unique way of saying it works for them.

How do we know? If Tickle wasn't working, who'd be laughing?

Staying drier is nicer . . . with a little Tickle.

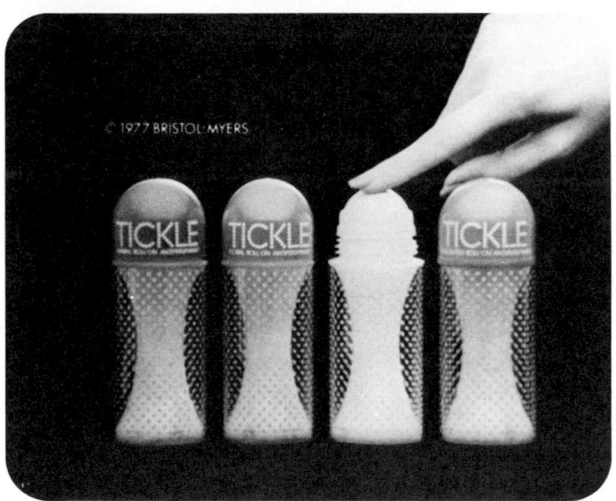

1129

Art Director Roy Grace
Writer Tom Yobbagy
Designer Roy Grace
Photographer Ken Sinclair
Director Bill Helburn
Producer Rosemary Barre
Production Company William Helburn Productions
Agency Doyle Dane Bernbach
Client Bristol-Myers Co.

CASSEROLE
30-second

VO: If there's one thing terrific with macaroni and cheese . . .

VO: Hamburger . . .

Chicken and rice . . . or hamsteak . . .

VO: It's an S.O.S. soap pad. With its special . . .

. . . grease-dissolving soap . . .

VO: S.O.S. cleans even the dirtiest pots and . . . pans in a hurry. Because nothing . . .

. . . gets off . . .
. . . burnt-on . . .
. . . stuck-on . . .
. . . splattered-on . . .
. . . messes faster . . .
. . . or easier . . .

VO: S.O.S. There's nothing better after a meal.

1130

Art Director Roy Grace
Writer Diane Rothschild
Designer Roy Grace
Photographer Mathew Brady
Director Mathew Brady
Producer Eileen Rogers
Music Tom Dawes
Production Company Mathew Brady Productions, Inc.
Agency Doyle Dane Bernbach
Client Miles Laboratories

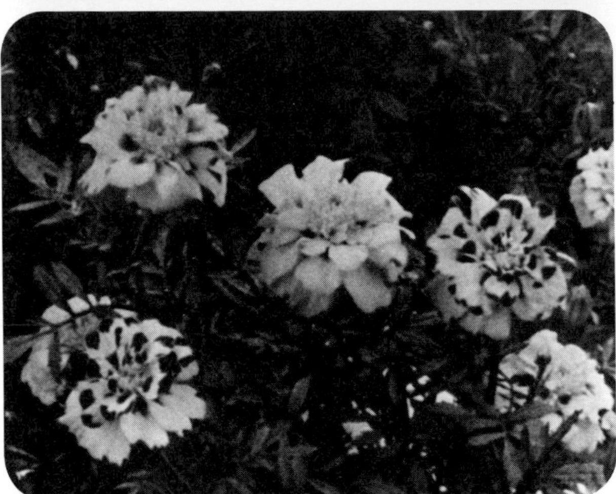

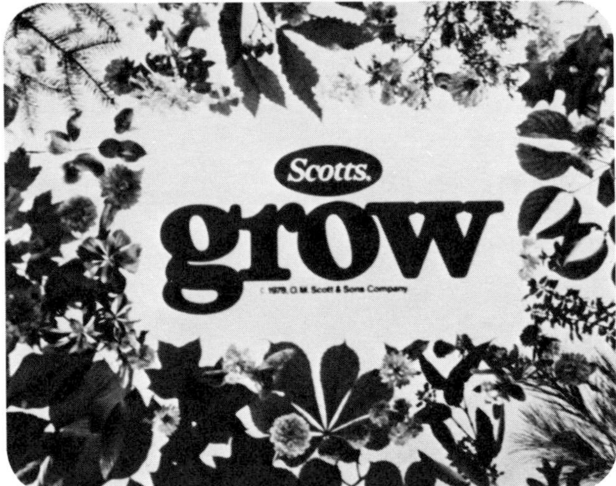

FLOWER FIREWORKS
30-second

ANNCR (VO): This is Scotts Grow Flowers Fertilizer. Sprinkle some around your flowers,

wait a few weeks . . .

And watch the fireworks.

CROWD (VO): Ooooo.

ANNCR: Compared with not fertilizing you'll get more marigolds.

CROWD: Ahhhh.

CROWD: Ohhhh.

ANNCR: Jazzier geraniums.

CROWD: Ahhhh.

ANNCR: Prettier petunias

CROWD: Ooooo. (APPLAUSE)

ANNCR: Scotts Grow Flowers Fertilizer. Put some in your garden . . . and enjoy the show.

CROWD: (WILD APPLAUSE)

ANNCR: Scotts Grow Fertilizers. For flowers, shrubs, and trees.

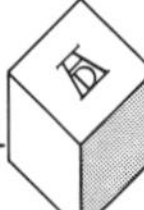

SILVER

1131

Art Directors Bill Arzonetti
Wally Arevalo
Writer Walt Hampton
Director David Quaid
Producer Wally Hill
Production Company Bianchi Films
Agency Doyle Dane Bernbach
Client O.M. Scott

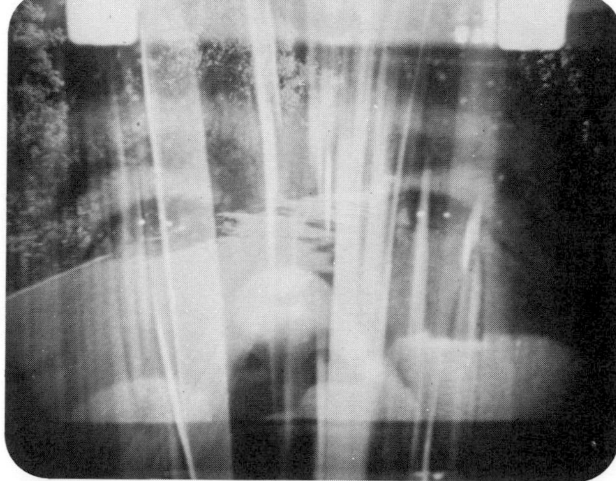

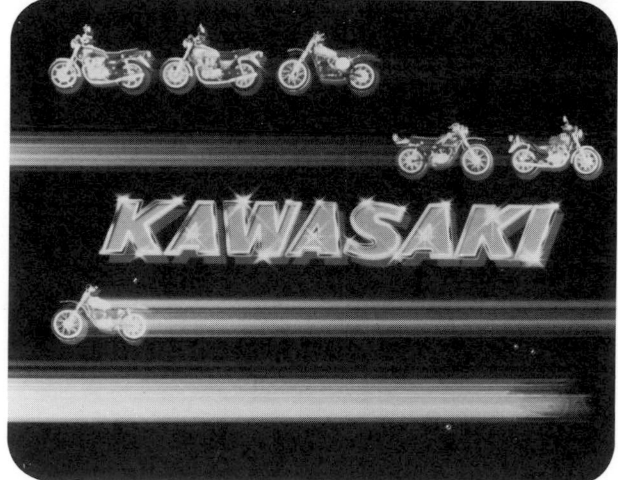

ULTIMATE TRIP
30-second

JINGLE: Kawasaki let's the good time roll.

Kawasaki introduces a full line of fast, dependable four stroke road bikes that'll take you down any road the mind can travel.

TAG: Kawasaki. We know why you ride.

1132

Art Director	Richard Taylor
Editor	Bob Abel
Designers	Richard Taylor Hal Cohen
Photographers	Jim Dickson Don Baker
Directors	Bob Abel Richard Taylor
Producers	Bob Abel Tom Hall
Music	Dan Dalton
Production Company	Robert Abel & Associates
Agency	J. Walter Thompson (LA)
Client	Kawasaki

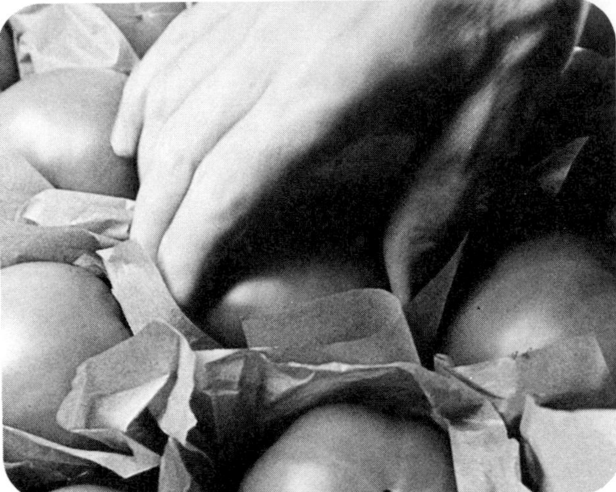

Fresher food delivered at supermarket prices.
THE GROCERY WAGON®

FRESHER FOOD
30-second

ANNCR: There's a new way to shop for food that's better than any supermarket yet it doesn't cost more. It's called the Grocery Wagon. You get meat that isn't dried out because it's cut to your order, fresh fruits and vegetables that haven't been picked at by 50 people before you, breads and rolls that are never stale, they're baked fresh every night. . . . Of course, when you have food delivered by the Grocery Wagon, there is one thing you have to give up . . . your weekly trip to the supermarket.

1133
Art Director Ron Becker
Writer Ron Berger
Director Henry Sandbank
Producer Bertelle Selig
Production Company Sandbank Films
Agency Ally & Gargano
Client Phone & Shop Systems, Inc.

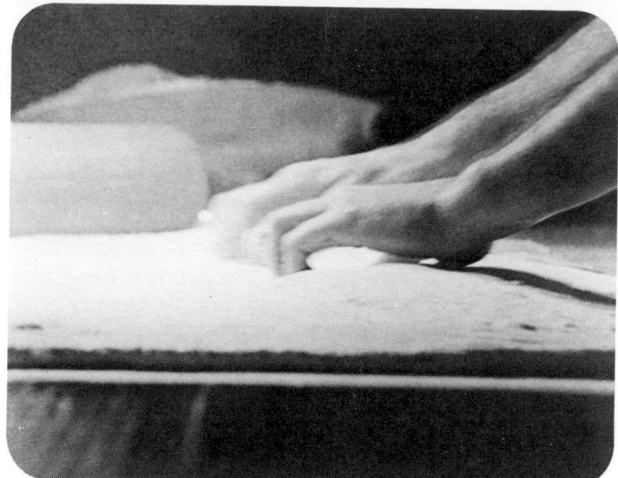

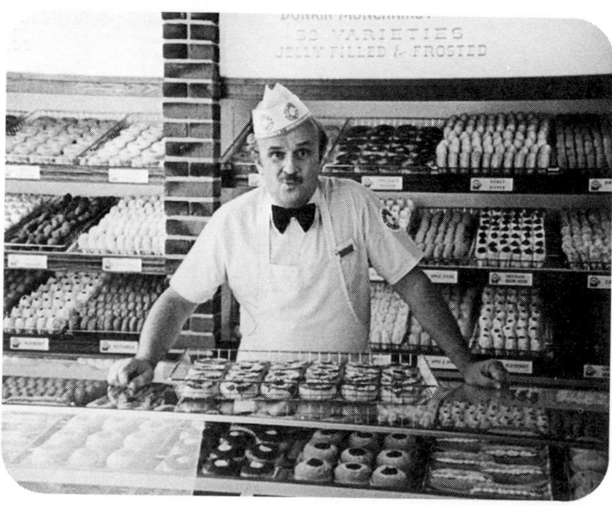

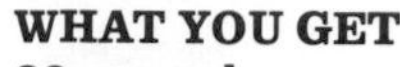

WHAT YOU GET
30-second

SPOKESMAN: The donuts you find in a supermarket are usually made by machine. At Dunkin' Donuts, we make ours by hand. In the store you have 5 or 6 varieties to choose from. We give you 52. In the supermarket, you don't really know how old the donuts are. We make donuts night and day. Why do we do all this? Because it's easier for you to buy donuts in the supermarket than to make a special stop at Dunkin' Donuts. So we make it worth the trip.

1134

Art Director	George Euringer
Writer	Patrick Kelly
Designer	George Euringer
Director	Steve Horn
Producer	Maureen Kearns
Music	Jonico Productions
Production Company	Steve Horn Productions
Agency	Ally & Gargano
Client	Dunkin' Donuts

PASS IT ON
30-second

BOSS: Wimpus, if this package isn't in Peoria by tomorrow morning, it's your job.

WIMPUS: Freeman, if this package isn't in Peoria by tomorrow morning, it's your . . .

FREEMAN: Simpson, if this . . . package isn't in Peoria by tomorrow morning . . .

SIMPSON: Harley, if this package is not in Peoria by tomorrow . . .

HARLEY: Belnap, if this package . . .

ANNCR: If more people knew enough to call Federal Express in a situation like this, it sure would save everybody a whole lot of grief.

CLERK: Call Federal.

ANNCR: Federal Express

ANNCR: When it absolutely, positively has to be there overnight.

1135

Art Director George Euringer
Writer Patrick Kelly
Director Joe Sedelmaier
Producer Maureen Kearns
Production Company Sedelmaier Film Prod./Chicago
Agency Ally & Gargano
Client Federal Express

OUT OF TOWNERS
30-second

ANNCR: A lot of people come a long way to shop at Barneys. So when they get back home from New York they bring back more than memories. A rancher from Nevada brought back seven Lanvin suits. A Turkish pasha brought home two suits by Oxford. A Japanese diplomat carried home some English tweeds by Burberry. And for a basketball player from Bulgaria it was one dozen Yves St. Laurent shirts. When you build the world's finest men's store, the word gets around.

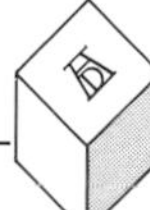

SILVER

1136

Art Director Amil Gargano
Writer David Altschiller
Director Steve Horn
Producer Janine Marjollet
Music Michael Small
Production Company Steve Horn Productions
Agency Ally & Gargano
Client Barney's

P.S.
30-second

ANNCR: Dear Germany, you make the best beer in the world.

Dear France, your champagne is first rate.

Dear England, your tea is the best there is.

And Dear Japan, your color TVs are the standard worldwide.

Signed, Italy.

Ah, P.S., we'll make the sports cars.

1137

Art Director Barry Vetere
Writer Patrick Kelly
Director Tony Petrucelli
Producer Maureen Kearns
Production Company Petrucelli Films
Agency Ally & Gargano
Client Fiat Motors of N. America

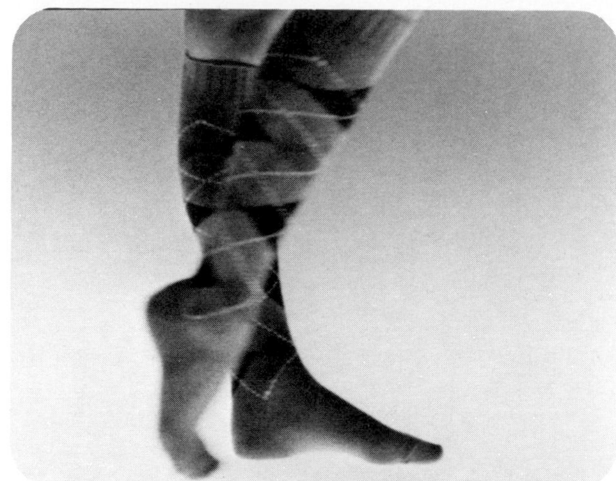

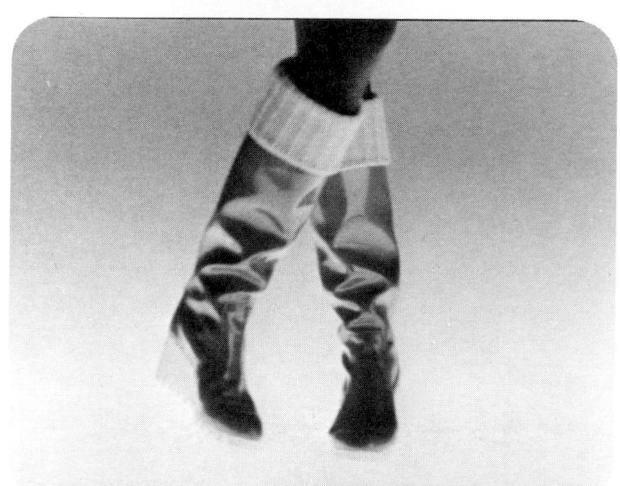

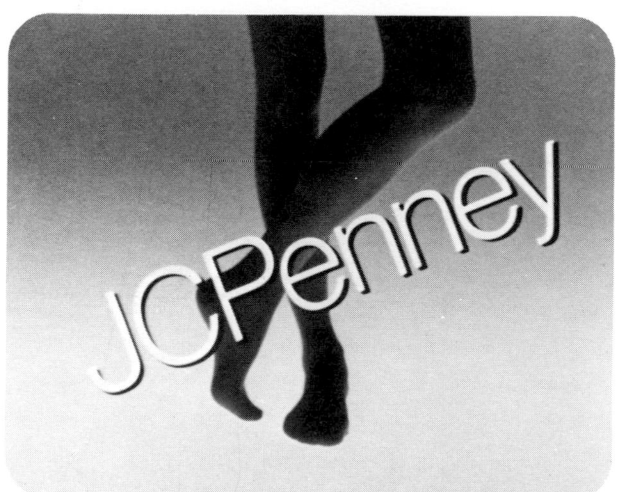

FASHION PROJECT (LEGWORKS)
30-second

ANNCR (VO): Legworks . . . At JC Penney it means the works for your legs. Kicky knee-hi's in a kaleidoscope of colors and a welter of woofs and weaves. The long and the short of it, matching or clashing in a rainbow of shades. Leg warmers all stripey or straight. Wear 'em under. Slip 'em over. And to top it off, boot toppers that do just that. Get the works. The legworks at JC Penney.

1138

Art Director	Tom Conrad
Writer	Joe DellaFemina
Director	David Stickles
Producer	Greg Califano
Music	Corelli Jacobs
Production Company	RGR
Agency	McCaffrey & McCall
Client	JC Penney

WORKING WOMAN
30-second

WOMAN SINGING (VO): I've been good and I've been sweet I've had a long hard day and boy I'm beat . . .

. . . but I'm gonna have an AXVIANNE NIOHT.

ANNCR (VO): Prince Matchabelli brings you Aviance, an exciting perfume that lasts far into the night. And what a way to start it.

WOMAN SINGING (VO): I'm gonna have an Aviance night . . .

MAN SINGING (VO): Oh yeah we're gonna have a Aviance night . . .

MAN-WOMAN SINGING (VO): Oh yeah we're gonna have an Aviance night.

1139

Art Director Jim Handloser
Writer Sharon Hartwick
Photographer Andre Bartkowiak
Director Edward Bianchi
Producers Linda Tesa
Carolyn Hailey
Music HEA—Walter Raim
Production Company Bianchi Films
Agency DellaFemina Travisano
Client Prince Matchabelli

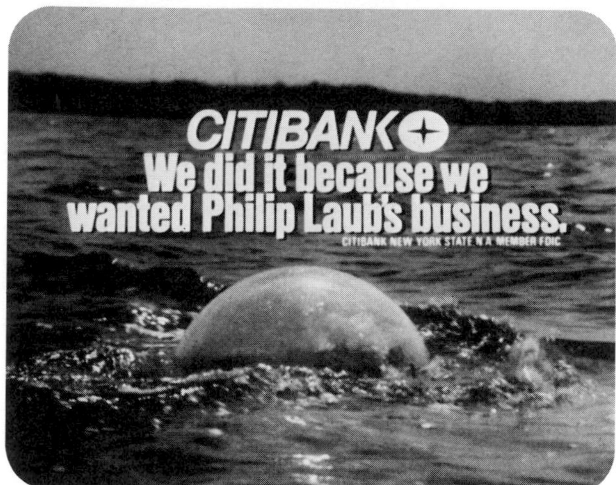

SUBMARINE LOAN
30-second

PHILIP LAUB: I'm kind of a private person.

So when I needed a loan to buy a submarine,

no one appreciated Citibank's private loan lounge more than I did.

LOAN OFFICER: Now what was that loan for?

PHILIP LAUB: I'd like to buy a submarine.

(VO): Yeah! They laughed a little, but Citibank gave me that loan in 24 hours. They explained my credit report to me. And said as long as my credit was good they didn't care if I bought a nuclear submarine.

(CHUCKLES) I wonder what they go for.

1140

Art Director	Rob Lopes
Writer	Joe O'Neill
Photographer	Alan Metzger
Director	Edward Bianchi
Producers	Sandy Breakstone Bob Rabinowitz
Production Company	Bianchi Films
Agency	Wells Rich Greene
Client	Citibank

ELOPEMENT
30-second

MAN (VO): Oh love of my life . . . are you ready?

WOMAN: Tonight? I thought it was next week.

ANNCR (VO): When your hair needs a quick touchup, you need America's favorite curling iron.

Clairol's Crazy Curl.

With Crazy Curl, you get a handful of 10-second steam curls.

And, when the occasion demands it, very fast touchups.

MAN: You're not Lorraine.

WOMAN: You're not Allen.

(PAUSE)

MAN: Hey . . . uh . . . you busy tonight?

ANNCR (VO): Clairol Crazy Curl.

1141

Art Director Bill Foster
Writer Ted Littleford
Designer Bill Foster
Director George Gomes
Producer Ed Murphy
Music Mega Music
Production Company Gomes/Lowe
Agency Foote, Cone & Belding
Client Clairol, Inc.

FOUR OFFICES
30-second

WOMAN: What is it!? Mr. Blake.

ANNCR (VO): Do you need special ringing that tells you who's calling?

MAN: Page twelve Harry . . .

ANNCR (VO): Do you need to make conference calls but can't?

MAN: Are you getting this, Stanley?

ANNCR (VO): Whatever you need in a business phone system, you need Western Electric Business phones from your Bell Telephone Company.

ANNCR (VO): They work for you.

WOMAN: Mr. Martin it's your Computer Dating Service.

ANNCR (VO): Not against you.

ANNCR (VO): Nobody makes telephones like Western Electric.

1142

Art Director	Joe Frederick
Writer	Jim Murphy
Designer	Joe Frederick
Director	George Gomes
Producer	Ed Murphy
Production Company	Gomes/Lowe
Agency	Foote, Cone & Belding
Client	Western Electric

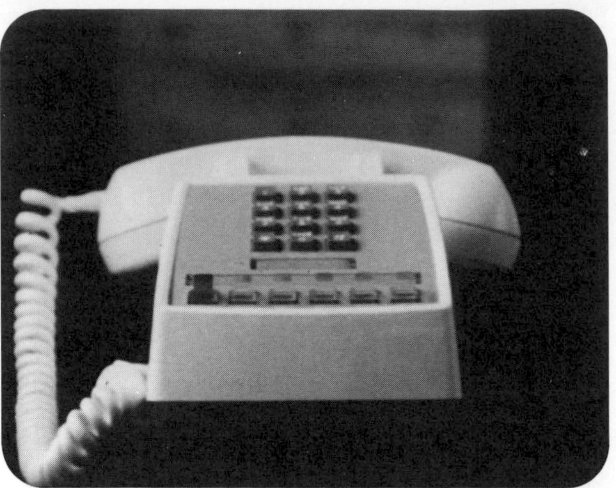

BLUE DANUBE
30-second

ANNCR (VO): At Western Electric before we put any new telephones into production we put them through a few tests.

ANNCR (VO): Nobody makes telephones like Western Electric.

1143

Art Director Bill Foster
Writer Ted Littleford
Designer Bill Foster
Director Henry Sandbank
Producer Ed Murphy
Music Dick Lavsky
Production Company Sandbank
Agency Foote, Cone & Belding
Client Western Electric

EXCERPTS/TONY NOMINEE
30-second

LADY-IN-RED (OC): You have been of no assistance.

I want you to know this was an experiment to see how selfish I could be . . .

if I could really carry on to snare a possible lover . . .

if I was capable of debasin' myself for the love of another . . .

if I could stand not bein' wanted when I wanted to be wanted and I cannot . . .

ANNCR (VO): For Colored Girls . . . Tony Award Nominee Best Play 1977.

Credit card reservations 246-5969.

1144

Art Director Reinhold Schwenk
Writer Bob Schulman
Editor Chris Dixon
Director Tony Lover
Producers Marilyn Cook
Kimberly Hoeck
Production Company Liberty Studios
Agency Case & McGrath Inc.
Client New York Shakespeare Festival

UH-OH! THE BOSS REVISION II
30-second

EUNICE (OC): Uh-oh! The Boss!

BOSS (OC): Why is it everyone looks so busy . . . but nothing ever gets done!?!?!

FRANCES (OC): Sir . . . It's your after shave. It always gets here ten seconds before you do . . .

Can I make a suggestion?

BOSS: Suggest . . .

FRANCES: Mennen Skin Bracer After Shave . . .

It's got a nice clean smell . . . not too perfumey.

It won't arrive before you do.

BOSS: (SLAP! SLAP!) Thanks, this company needed that . . .

BOSS: Aha!!!!

ANNCR (VO): Skin Bracer doesn't get there . . . 'til you do.

1145

Art Director Reinhold Schwenk
Writer Gene Case
Director Adrian Riso
Producer Kimberly Hoeck
Production Company Centrex Productions
Agency Case & McGrath, Inc.
Client The Mennen Company

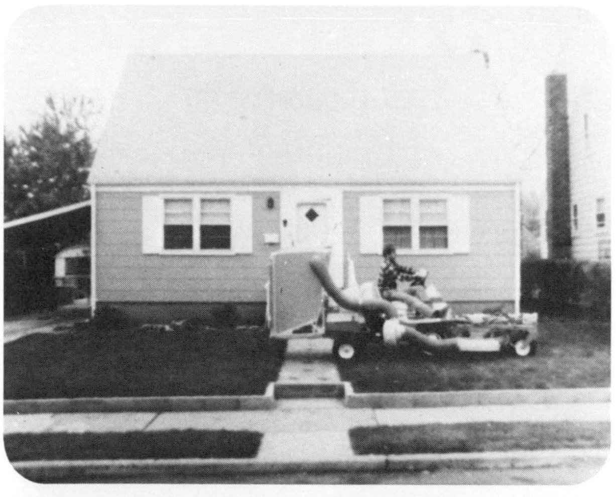

NEEDS
30-second

VO: A lot of companies say they have just what you need . . .

and wind up selling you just what they have.

That's not how it is with Xerox.

We're the only company that has eighteen different copiers and duplicators to choose from.

So with Xerox . . .

you never have to live with more than you want,

you never have to live with more than you want,

or settle for less than you need.

1146

Art Director Allen Kay
Writers Lois Korey
Lester Colodny
Director Sid Myers
Producer Sydelle Rangell
Production Company Myers, Griner, Cuesta, Inc.
Agency Needham, Harper & Steers
Client Xerox Corp.

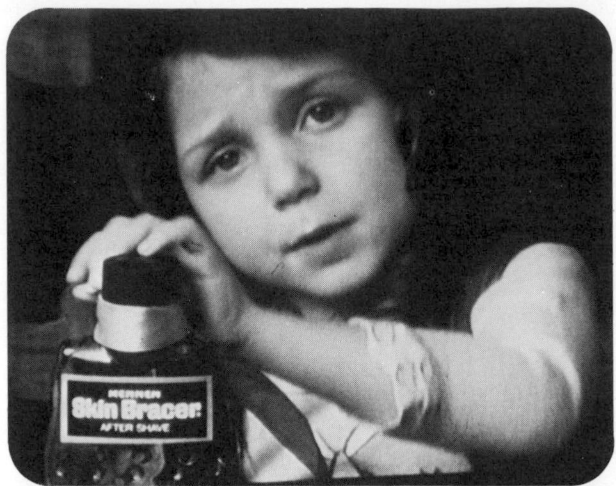

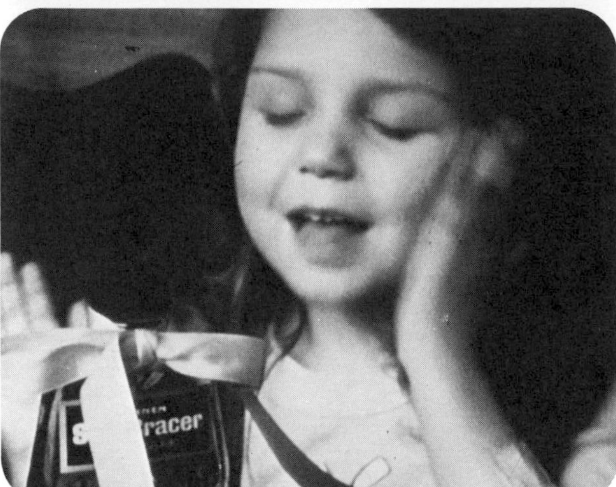

CLOSE CONFESSIONS—FIRST LOVE
30-second

GIRL: I love you, Daddy . . . 'Cause you bought me a bike 'Cause you protect me from cavities An' 'cause you explain instead of hit

and mostly 'cause you're my daddy . . . So I bought you this Skin Bracer for a present, Daddy . . .

'Cause you like to use it in the morning to slap on you . . . slap slap . . . for waking up . . .

and Skin Bracer smells good so when you hug me—it makes it pleasant . . .
Here . . .

1147
Art Director Marvin Fireman
Writer Ilon Specht
Director Adrian Riso
Producer Kimberly Hoeck
Production Company Centrex Productions
Agency Case & McGrath, Inc.
Client The Mennen Company

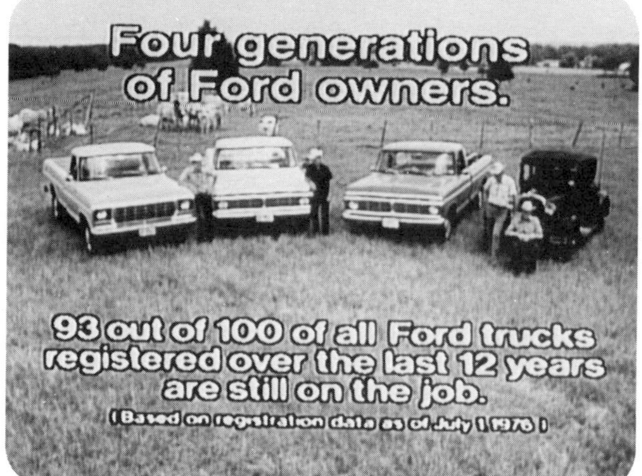

Four generations
of Ford owners.
93 out of 100 of all Ford trucks
registered over the last 12 years
are still on the job.
(Based on registration data as of July 1 1976)

VAN CRAM II
30-second

ANNCR (VO): We'd like to show you how roomy a Ford van is . . .

. . . so we asked 104 students to try to get in. Guess how many made it?

Now, this is Ford's new Free-Wheeling Van with a long wheel base. It comes with options like a custom interior . . .

Super paint job . . . port holes . . .

. . . and trick wheels.

How many got in, Dean?

DEAN (OC): According to my count—all 104. It's the first time they ever got together on anything!

ANNCR (VO): We don't recommend you overload your van like this—but if you're really into vanning . . .

. . . you're into—

ALL KIDS: FORD!

1148

Art Director	John Sands
Writer	Joe Feke
Photographer	R. Brooks
Director	Ray Corwin
Producer	John Sands
Production Company	Ray Corwin Productions
Agency	J. Walter Thompson Company
Client	Ford Motor Company

THE ORGANIZATION
30-second

VO: On February 1, the Organization was formed. The Dedicated Datsun Dealers of Southern California. And they would do anything . . . anything . . . to protect you from slipshod service and flimflammery.

If for any reason a Dealer isn't dedicated, the Organization takes care of him. On Friday Datsun Dealer, Jim Lacey, forgot to rotate Mr. Markman's tires. We didn't like that. Goodbye, Jim.

A Datsun Dealer's dedicated. Or else.

1149

Art Directors	George D'Amto Bob Kuperman
Writers	Herb Greene Pacy Markman
Director	Stan Dragotti
Producer	Bob Kuperman
Music	Stock
Production Company	Petersen Co.
Agency	Wells Rich Greene/West
Client	Southern California Datsun Dealers Assn.

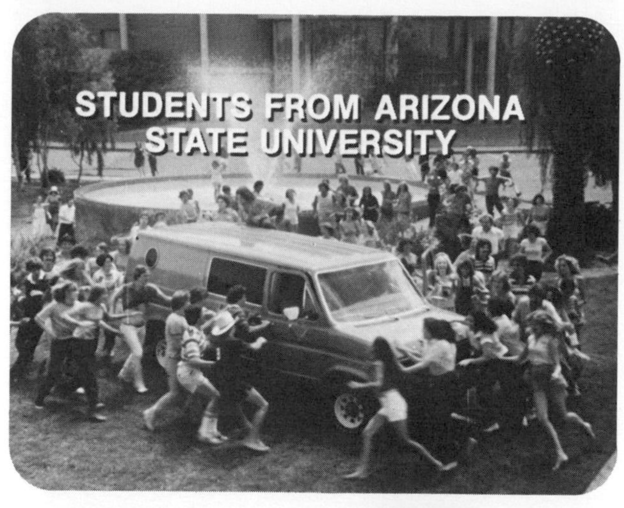

NEW FOUR GENERATIONS
30-second

CLAY: I drive a Ford Pickup 'cause my Daddy told me they were built tough.

Right, Daddy?

HARRELL: Right! And I drive a Ford Pickup 'cause my Daddy told me they were built tough.

Right, Daddy?

CHARLES: Yup! And I drive a Ford Pickup 'cause my Daddy told me they were built tough.

Right, Daddy?

WILL: Yup! My daddy came to Texas in a covered wagon so I had to learn about Fords on my own.

WILL: I'm a smart old bird, ain't I? (heh heh heh)

ANNCR (VO): Of all Ford Trucks registered over the last 12 years 93 out of 100 are still on the job!

1150

Art Director	George Schoenberger
Writer	Ed Hiestand
Photographer	Donald Morgan
Director	M. Cowan
Producer	Don Ayers
Production Company	Johnson and Cowan
Agency	J. Walter Thompson Company
Client	Ford Motor Company

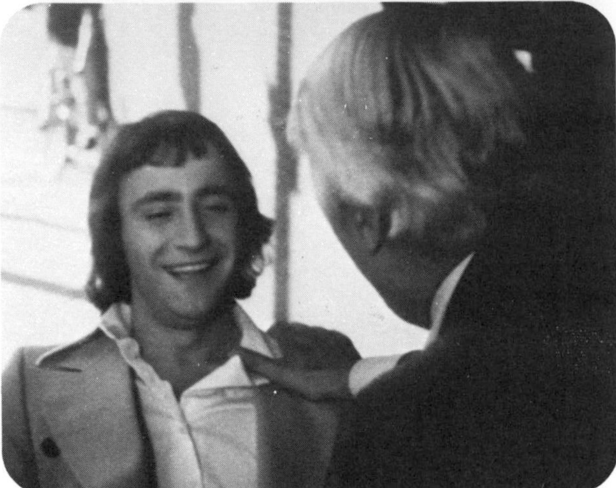

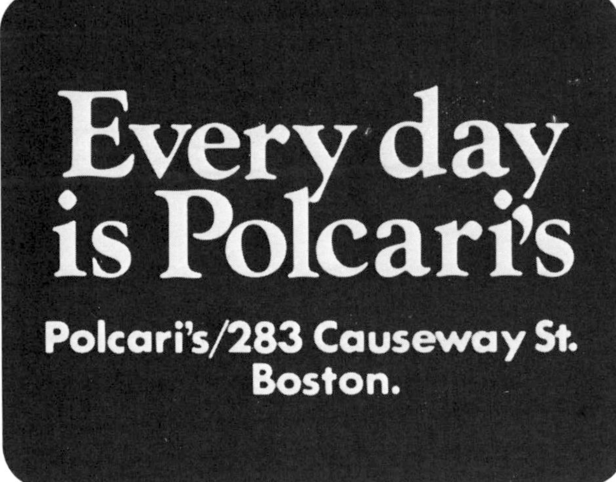

ANTHONY MARTINGETTI
30-second

VO: Now, you may not recognize him. But that's Anthony Martingetti,

the boy who used to run home through the North End of Boston for spaghetti every Wednesday.

Wednesday may still be Spaghetti Day in the North End.

But if you've ever wondered where Anthony ate the rest of the week, the answer is here at Polcari's on Causeway Street.

JOHN POLCARI: Hey Anthony, where were you on Wednesday?

VO: Every day is Polcari's

1151

Art Director	Dick Pantano
Writers	Tony Winch
	S. McGuire
Director	Barry Bransfield
Producer	Dan Driscoll
Production Company	September Productions
Agency	Hill, Holliday, Connors, Cosmopulos, Inc.
Client	Polcari's Restaurant

SPEAK OUT ALIMONY
30-second

ANNCR: Judge rewrites law. Alimony for men. The people speak out!

JONELLA BARNETT: I think it's wonderful. I mean women's lib has done everything else they might as well give them alimony too!

HELENE BAYME: I think it's unfair. You've changed the rules in midstream. Women got married never expecting to have to support their husbands!

BOB GOSSETT: I don't think anyone should get alimony. You should just call it a draw, split up and go your separate ways . . .

ANNCR: Speak out! Help make things happen!

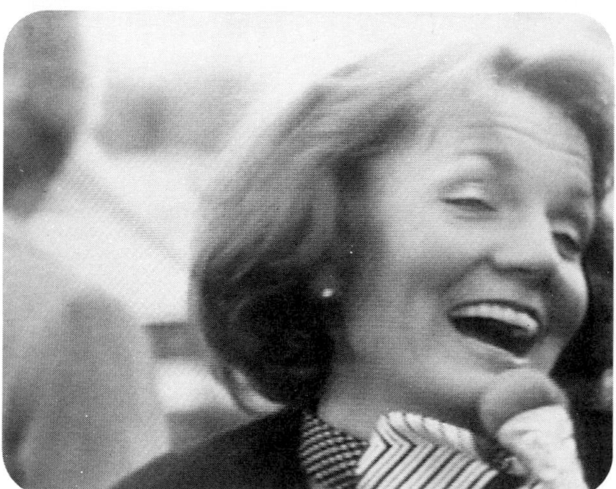

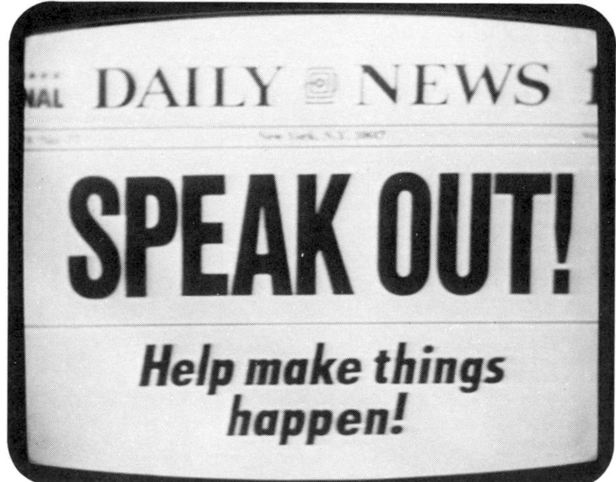

1152

Art Director David Wiseltier
Writers Lew Sherwood
Marvin Schneider
David Wiseltier
Director Lew Sherwood
Producer Chris Vitale
Production Company Avon Productions
Agency KSW&G Inc.
Client The Daily News

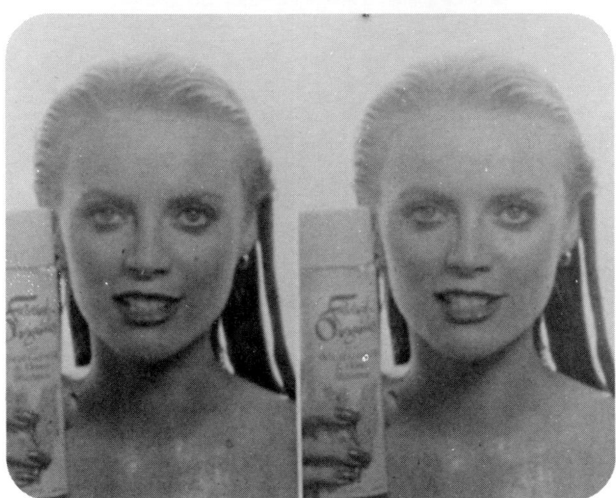

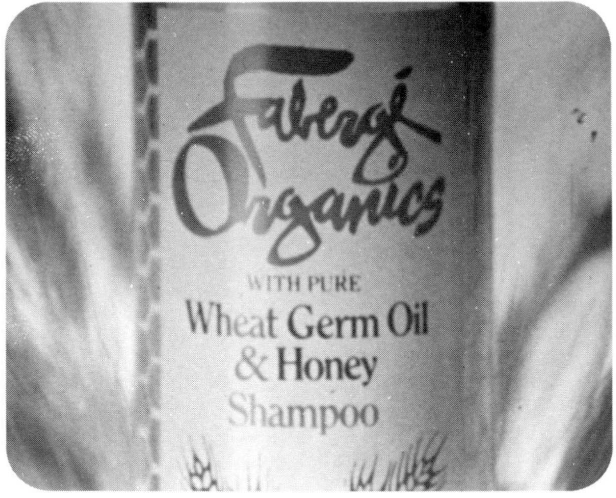

KRISTINA—FRIENDS
30-second

KRISTINA: I told two friends about Faberge Organics Shampoo with pure wheat germ oil and honey. And they told two friends. And so on . . . and so on . . .

ANNCR: That'll be your reaction, too. You'll want to tell your friends about super-rich Faberge Organics Shampoo. For fresh-smelling hair with super shine and super body, give it a try. You'll tell two friends about it. And they'll tell two friends . . . And so on . . . and so on . . . and so on.

ANNCR: Faberge Organics Shampoo with pure wheat germ oil and honey.

1153

Art Director Irwin Goldberg/Creative Director/Exec. Producer
Editor Barry Geier
Director Richard Heimann
Producer Joan Gringer
Production Company RHA, Inc.
Agency Nadler and Larimer, Inc.
Client Fabergé, Inc.

FOUNDING FATHER
30-second

ANNCR: An important announcement for the mothers of America from the father of Mr. Bubble.

MR. B.: I am sitting in perhaps the most significant breakthrough in bubble bath history.

We know you want bubbles—so we've made Mr. Bubble powder bubblier.

We know you want mild—so we've made Mr. Bubble milder—not just a little milder, but milder than Ivory bath soap.

We didn't get to be America's number one kid's bubble bath by just sitting around on our bubbles.

SUPER: Milder than Ivory bath soap.

1154

Art Director Ralph Ammirati
Writer Martin Puris
Designer Ralph Ammirati
Producer Ozzie Spenningsby
Agency Ammirati Puris AvRutick
Client Gold Seal Company

FRENCH
30-second

SINGERS: NoNoNoNo

ANNCR: When you're

SINGERS: (UNDER) NoNoNoNo NoNoNo NoNo

ANNCR: watching your weight, too much of

SINGERS: (UNDER) NoNo YesYesYes NoNo

ANNCR: even a good thing can be a No, No.

SINGERS: (UNDER) YesYes NoNoNoNoNoNoNoNo
YesYesYesYes

ANNCR: That's why there's Diet Rite Cola.

SINGERS: (UNDER) YesYesYesYesYesYesYesYes
NoNoNoNo

YesYesYes

NoNoNoNo YesYesYesYesYesYes

ANNCR: One calorie

SINGERS: (UNDER) Yes Yes Yes

ANNCR: Diet Rite

Cola.

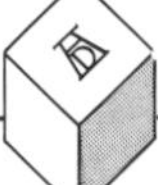

GOLD

1156

Art Director John Plucinski
Writer Mara Blum
Director Bob Giraldi
Agency Producer Angelo Antonucci
Music Lucas-McFaul
Production Company Bob Giraldi Productions
Agency Leo Burnett, Inc.
Client Royal Crown Cola

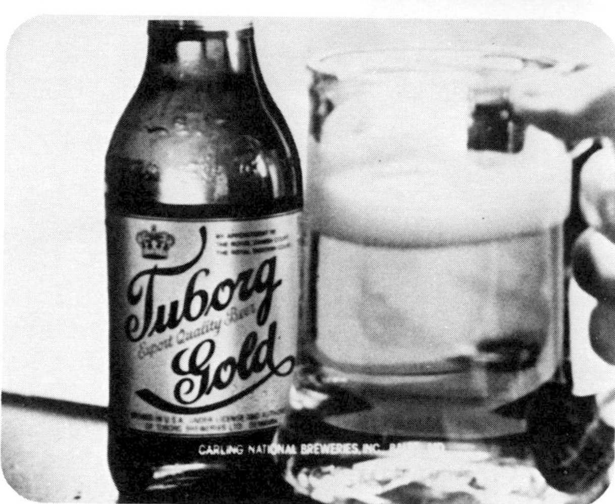

SCROLL
30-second

ANNCR (VO): Tuborg Gold.

By appointment to the Royal Danish Court since the reign of Frederick the Ninth.

Proclaimed, the Golden Beer of Danish Kings!

Today, this light beer of noble heritage is brewed in America.

and Tuborg Gold is affordable to everyone.

In fact, for about what you'd pay for the king of beers, you can now have Tuborg Gold. The Golden Beer of Danish kings.

1157

Art Directors Eugene Azzam
Mario Bognanni
Editor Dennis Hayes
Writers Robert Urquhart
Andy Gillinson
Director Elbert Buhdin
Producer Jeff Kliman
Music Grant/Murtaugh
Production Company Ampersand
Agency W. B. Doner & Company
Client Carling National Breweries

TRUCK
30-second

VO: When Sam Breakstone delivered his cottage cheese, fast . . . was not fast enough.

WORKER: Who does old man Breakstone think he is?! Hurry . . . hurry . . . hurry . . . my cottage cheese must arrive fresh. You'd think it was gold!

SAM: Cover my cottage cheese you numbskull!

WORKER: Yes, Mr. Breakstone.

SAM: (MIMICKS) Yes, Mr. Breakstone. Out!

VO: In his day, Sam Breakstone was one of the most demanding men alive. But if Sam weren't so demanding . . . his cottage cheese wouldn't be so good.

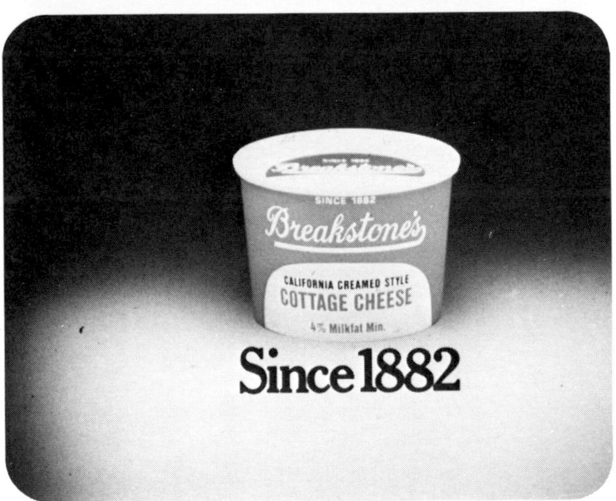

1158

Art Director Lars Anderson
Writer Irwin Warren
Designer Lars Anderson
Director Dick Loew
Producer Wayne Lachman
Production Company Gomes-Loew
Agency Richard K. Manoff Inc.
Client Kraft, Inc./Dairy Group

CYRANO
30-second

ROGER: A most gracious welcome to The Old Country . . . where you will discover culinary delights . . . entertainment of the first rank . . . and a realm of old world adventure.

ROGER: Imagine . . . all this wonderment right under one's nose.

1159

Art Directors	Carl Lampe Marv Gold
Writers	John Stevenson John Nieman
Director	Joe DeVoto
Producer	Vince Coryell
Music	Perry Botkin Jr. Productions
Production Company	Joel Productions
Agency	Gardner Advertising Company
Client	Busch Gardens Division/Anheuser-Busch Inc.

BOXER
30-second

DOC: Only 2 miles to go, Slugger.

SLUGGER: That's easy for you to say, Doc . . . you got The Advantage.

DOC: Uh, I certainly do. The Advantage is a new tire from B.F. Goodrich. It's everything Goodrich has ever learned about making tires. And they made the first American radial.

SLUGGER: Goodrich . . . Hey, remember when I was fightin' the Kid, and looked up in the fifth, and got KO'd? I was lookin' at their blimp! The Goodrich blimp.

DOC: A winner . . . he's not.

ANNCR (VO): B.F. Goodrich. The Other Guys.

1160
Art Director Alan Kupchick
Writer Robbie Goolrick
Director Rick Levine
Producer Vinnie Infantino
Production Company Levine Productions
Agency Grey
Client B.F. Goodrich

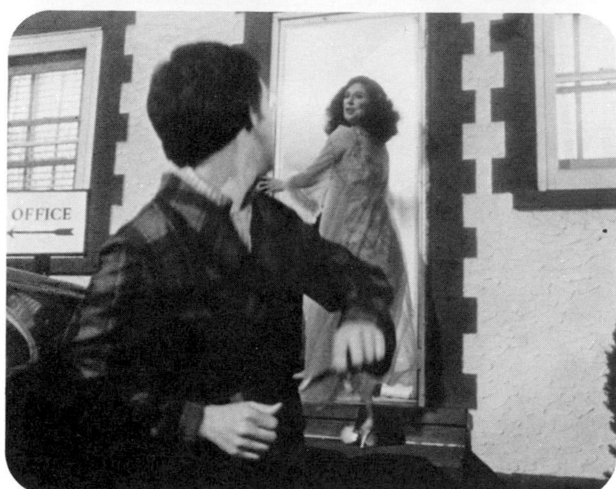

NEWLYWEDS
30-second

WIFE: What're you doing, Cookie Face?

HUSBAND: I'm checking the air pressure in my Goodrich radials, Snugglebunny.

WIFE: At midnight? On your honeymoon?

HUSBAND: We've got a long drive to Niagara Falls tomorrow. If we don't have the right amount of air in our tires, it could be unsafe. And, my Goodrich dealer told me the tires would last longer.

WIFE: Goodrich! You should have married that Goodrich blimp.

ANNCR (VO): Tires you can trust. B.F. Goodrich. The Other Guys.

HUSBAND: But, Honey . . .

WIFE: What?

HUSBAND: Goodrich doesn't have a blimp!

1161

Art Director Alan Kupchick
Writer Robbie Goolrick
Director Jeff Lovinger
Producer Maura Dausey
Production Company Lovinger, Tardio, Melsky
Agency Grey
Client B.F. Goodrich

RONDO/STICK FIGHTING
30-second

ANNCR: These men are working up a Rondo thirst.

When they get done, they're not gonna want a soda they have to sip. They're gonna want a Rondo.

Rondo's lightly carbonated, so you can slam it down fast.

Rondo has a clean citrus taste that's never sticky.

Rondo.

The Thirst Crusher.

1162

Art Director Bob Versandi
Writer Phil Slott
Editor Jerry Bender
Photographer Fred Levinson
Director Fred Levinson
Producers David Frankel
Roy Tonnseno
Music Charlie Callelo
Production Company Fred Levinson & Company
Agency Ted Bates & Company
Client Cadbury Schweppes, U.S.A., Inc.

BURRITO
30-second

CHINESE MAN: Most definitely not an egg roll.

JEWISH MATRON: It's coitainly not a knish.

ITALIAN MAN: And it's not a pizza pie, either. What, what is it?

VO: Jack In The Box Restaurants introduces the Jack Burrito: It's beef, bean, & cheese filling in a golden fried tortilla.

JEWISH MATRON: Now you're cookin' Jack.

SONG: Ji-Ji-Ji-Jack
Ji-Ji-Ji-Jack
Ji-Ji-Ji-Jack
Jack in the Box
We're really cookin' Jack.

1163

Art Directors Bruce Campbell
Stan Dragoti
Bob Kuperman
Writers Chuck Kollewe
Charlie Moss
Pacy Markman
Director Stan Dragoti
Producer Paula Del Nunzio
Music Elsmere Productions (Steve Karmen)
Production Company Peterson Productions
Agency Wells, Rich, Greene/West
Client Foodmaker (Jack in the Box)

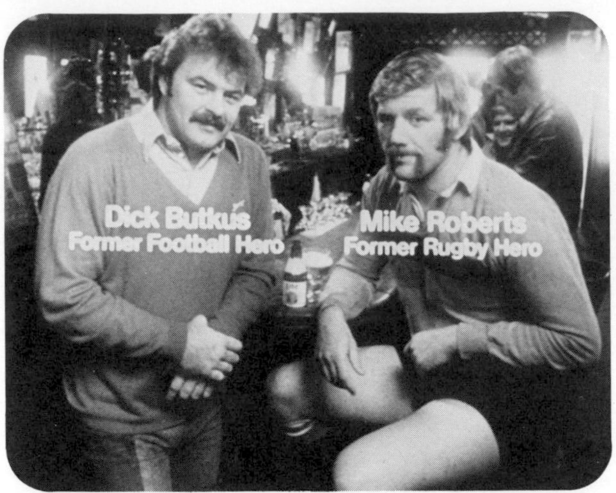

RUGBY PLAYER
30-second

DICK BUTKUS: Mike, I'll never like rugby. But I do love those cute little shorts.

ANNCR (VO): Lite Beer from Miller. Everything you always wanted in a beer. And less.

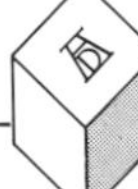

SILVER

1164

Art Directors R. Lenz
R. Engel
Writers C. Ryant
R. Meury
Director Bob Giraldi
Producers R. Johnson
J. Paperno
R. Engel
Production Company Bob Giraldi Productions
Agency McCann-Erickson, Inc.
Client Miller Brewing Company

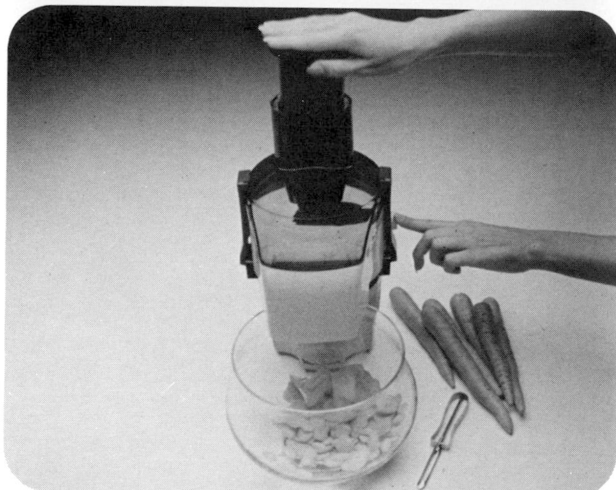

30 SECOND SALAD
30-second

ANNCR (VO): La Machine presents the 30 second salad.

MUSIC

ANNCR (VO): A salad in 30 seconds. Now that's fast food.

La Machine. By Moulinex. The incredible food preparation system from France.

GOLD

1165

Art Director	Joe Sedelmaier
Writer	Jeff B. Gorman
Editors	Peggy De Lay
	Henry Hoda
Director/Cinematographer	Joe Sedelmaier
Production Company	Sedelmaier Film Productions
Agency	Marketing Communications International
Client	Moulinex/La Machine

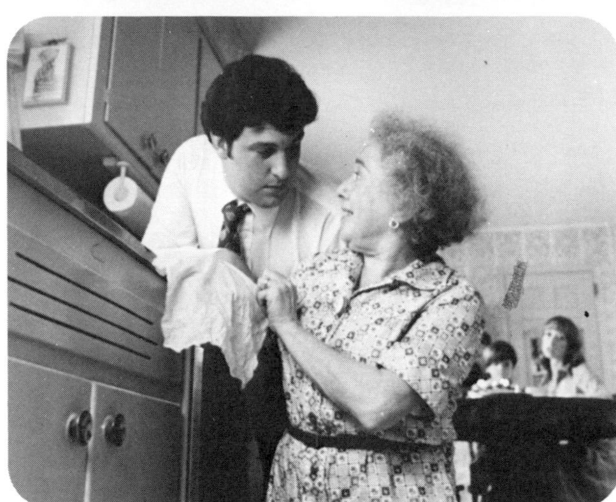

GRANDMA
30-second

SON: Ma, we didn't invite you here to clean the kitchen.

MOTHER: I don't mind.

SON: At least take another paper towel. You've been using that one for a half-hour.

MOTHER: It's perfectly fine.

SON: Ma, it's disposable.

MOTHER: But it's still good.

ANNCR: A disposable paper towel so close to cloth that in tests, it actually stood up to a washing machine. Here's Viva. Here's Bounty. And here's Bolt.

SON: Drop it, Ma.

MOTHER: It's still good

SON: Drop it

MOTHER: It's still good

ANNCR: Bolt. The world's most cloth-like paper towel.

1166

Art Director John Danza
Writer Mike Drazen
Designer John Danza
Directors Neil Tardio
Joe Pytka
Producer Tanya English
Production Companies Lovinger, Tardio, Melsky/STF
Agency Scali, McCabe, Sloves
Client American Can Company

NEAT-O
30-second

BILL COSBY: Whenever something was real good when I was a child

I'd always say Neat-o

And when the good guy would catch the bad guy and put him in jail, I'd say Neat-o.

My mother would make some Jell-o pudding

I would say

CHILD: Neat-o.

ANNCR (VO): Kids love pudding and Jell-o brand is the one kids have loved for 40 years.

COSBY: So what do you think of Jell-o pudding?

CHILDREN: Neat-o.

COSBY: What do you think if a dragon breathed on your toes?

CHILDREN: Neat-o.

COSBY: Really?

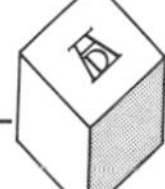

GOLD

1167

Art Directors Bob Ryzner (Elmo & Neato)
Jeff Whitchel (Butter Pecan)
Writers Jean Zerries (Elmo & Neato)
Harold Kaplan (Butter Pecan)
Producers Ted Storb (Elmo & Neato)
Ed Pollack (Butter Pecan)
Production Company Bianchi
Agency Young & Rubicam
Client General Foods/Jell-O Pudding

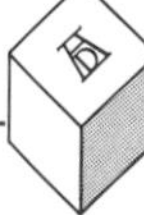
SILVER

1168

Art Directors Bob Ryzner
Charlie Carpenter
Writers Richard DePascal
Jean Zerries
Producers Ed Pollack
Ted Storh
Production Company Bianchi
Agency Young & Rubicam
Client General Foods/Jello Pudding

JOCKEYS
30-second

1ST ANNCR (VO): It's a match race between Rose Furlong with New York Telephone's Touch-Tone Phone,

and long shot Bromberg with a Rotary Phone.

Touch-Tone claims to be faster and more convenient to dial.

And it comes in Rose's favorite color.

And they're off!

And it's Rose Furlong . . . by a length.

2ND ANNCR (VO): To order Touch-Tone service,

call your local telephone business office.

CHORUS (VO): We bring New York people together.

1169

Art Director	Ted Shaine
Writer	Larry Spector
Producer	John Clark
Production Company	Myers & Griner, Cuesta
	The Peterson Company
Agency	Young & Rubicam
Client	New York Telephone

JOCK
30-second

(SINGS): Band Aid brand sticks where it's supposed to but it doesn't stick where it's not supposed to.

(SINGS): Band Aid sticks where it's supposed to, but it doesn't stick where it's not supposed to

VO: The adhesive on a Band Aid brand adhesive bandage from Johnson & Johnson sticks, but, now there's a special non stick cushion pad that doesn't stick

This pad won't pull the scab off like ordinary gauze bandages can

(SINGS): Bandaid sticks were it's supposed to, but it doesn't stick where it's not supposed to.

1170

Writer Mike Becker
Producer Phyllis Landi
Production Company Sunlight
Agency Young & Rubicam
Client Johnson & Johnson

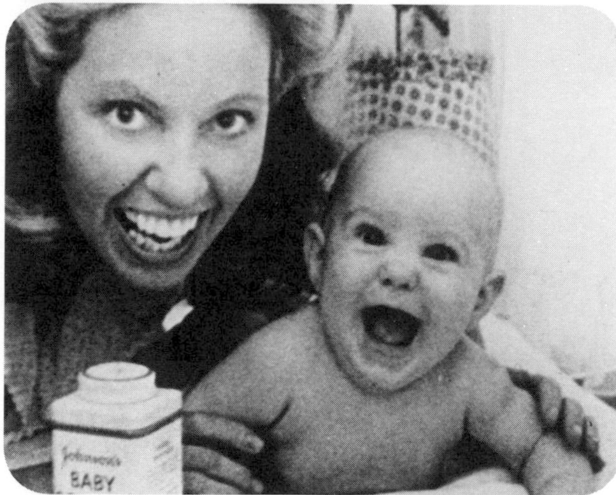

WINTER
30-second

AUDIO: When I was a little girl one of the nicest things I remember was feeling soft and loved with Johnson's Baby Powder.

CHORUS SINGS: From the start of your life it's been a part of your life, a special comfort to you and loving feeling to you. It's a feeling you never outgrow. Johnson's Baby Powder is a feeling you never outgrow.

VO: Pure Johnson's powder from Johnson & Johnson

GIRL: It's a feeling you never outgrow.

1171
Art Director Clark Frankel
Writer Ellen Perless
Producer Mike Schapiro
Production Company Langley/Sann
Agency Young & Rubicam
Client Johnson & Johnson

FLOATING SUITCASE
30-second

ANNCR (VO): American Tourister's Verylite soft luggage is so beautiful, you look good holding on to it.

But . . .

hold on to it because the Verylite isn't just beautiful.

The Verylite is . . . very light.

1172

Art Directors	Roy Grace Jack Mariucci
Writer	Marcia Bell Grace
Designers	Roy Grace Jack Mariucci
Artists	Roy Grace Jack Mariucci
Photographer	Steve Horn
Directors	Steve Horn Howard Zieff
Producer	Susan Calhoun
Music	Susan Hamilton
Production Companies	Steve Horn Inc./Independent Artists
Agency	Doyle Dane Bernbach
Client	American Tourister

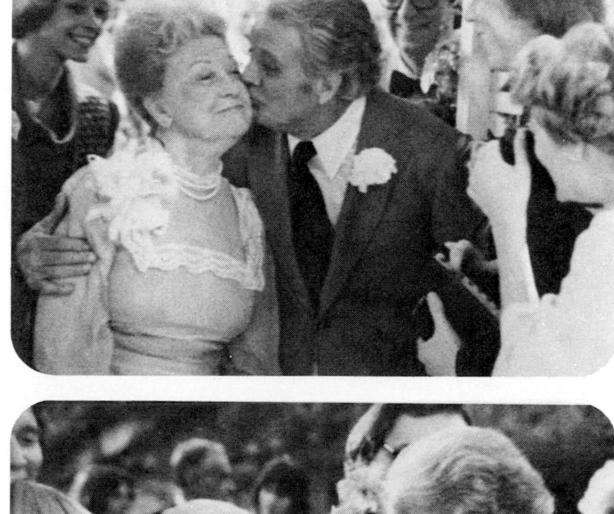

GOLDEN ANNIVERSARY
30-second

GM (VO): This is the first Saturday your father hasn't played golf since 1927.

D (VO): Oh, Mom!

GF (VO): I seem to marry this girl every 50 years.

MINISTER (VO): OK, you may now k—

GM (VO): Kiss the bride.

ANNCR (VO): The minute (MUSIC STOPS A SECOND)

ANNCR (VO): The maker (MUSIC STOPS A SECOND)

ANNCR (VO): Its Polaroid's new Minute maker for beautiful color in just 60 seconds.

1173

Art Director	William Taubin
Writer	Jack Dillon
Designer	William Taubin
Director	Steve Horn
Producer	Mootsie Elliot
Production Company	Steve Horn
Agency	Doyle Dane Bernbach
Client	Polaroid

JAPANESE RABBIT
30-second

VO: Sir, with all those good Japanese cars why did you buy a Volkswagen Rabbit?

MAN: (ANSWERS IN JAPANESE)

VO: But what makes the Rabbit so great?

MAN: (ANSWERS IN JAPANESE)

VO: It is roomy—

VO: But how about the Rabbit's engineering?

MAN: (MAN ANSWERS IN JAPANESE)

VO: Well, how advanced is it?

MAN: (MAN ANSWERS IN JAPANESE)

VO: Ah, space, performance, engineering.

VO: That must be why the Rabbit is the . . .

VO: . . . best selling imported car in Japan.

SINGERS: Volkswagen . . . does it again.

1174

Art Director Bert Steinhauser
Writer Robert Levenson
Designer Bert Steinhauser
Director Rick Levine
Producer Jim deBarros
Music Tom Dawes
Production Company Rick Levine Productions
Agency Doyle Dane Bernbach
Client Volkswagen

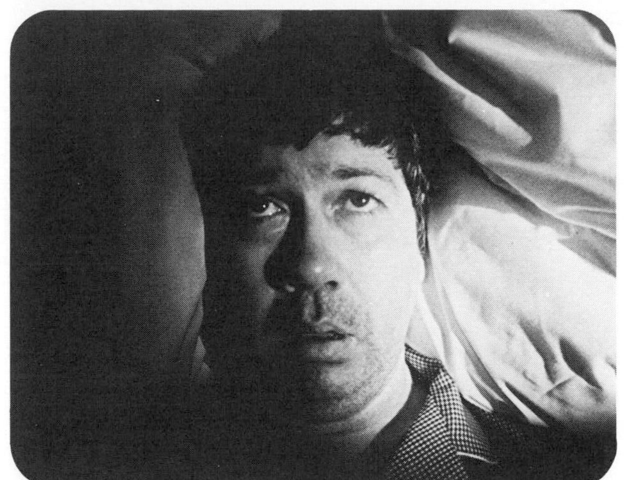

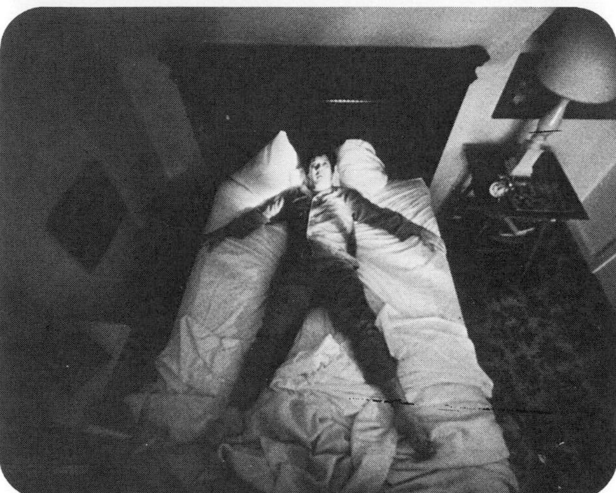

TOSSING & TURNING
30-second

ANNCR: This guy is expecting a package in the morning.
Right now, its 2,000 miles away.
And if it isn't on his desk by noon tomorrow, he's had it.

Too bad he doesn't know that Federal Express will pick up, fly and deliver almost anyplace in the country overnight for a reasonable price. Unfortunately, this guy had never heard of us. Fortunately, the guy on the other end had. Federal Express. When it absolutely, positively has to be there overnight.

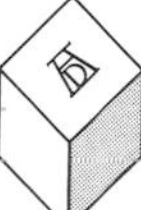

SILVER

1175

Art Director George Euringer
Writer Patrick Kelly
Director Joe Sedelmaier
Producer Maureen Kearns
Production Company Sedelmaier Film Prod./Chicago
Agency Ally & Gargano
Client Federal Express

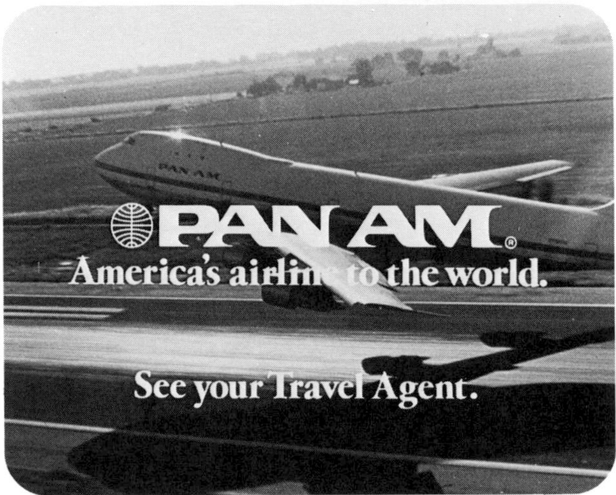

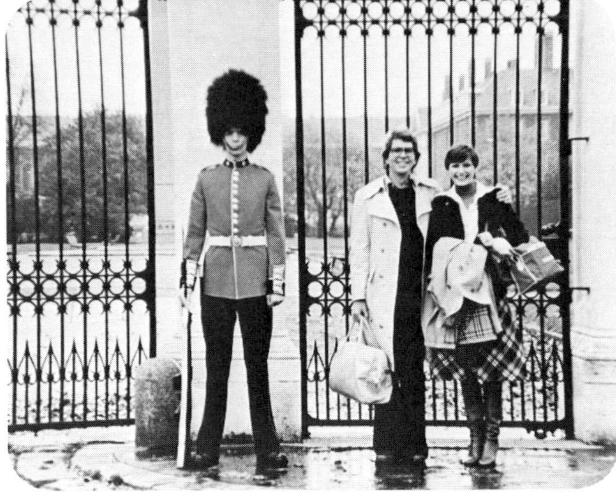

COWBOYS
30-second

ANNCR: Every day, Pan Am brings people like this closer to people like this. And places like this closer to places like this. To bring the rest of the world a little closer to America. Or America a little closer to the rest of the world.

SINGERS: We're America's airline to the world . . . Pan Am.

1176
Art Director Michael Tesch
Writer Tom Messner
Director Tibor Hirsch
Producer Maureen Kearns
Music Joe Brooks
Production Company Tibor Hirsch Productions
Agency Ally & Gargano
Client Pan American World Airways

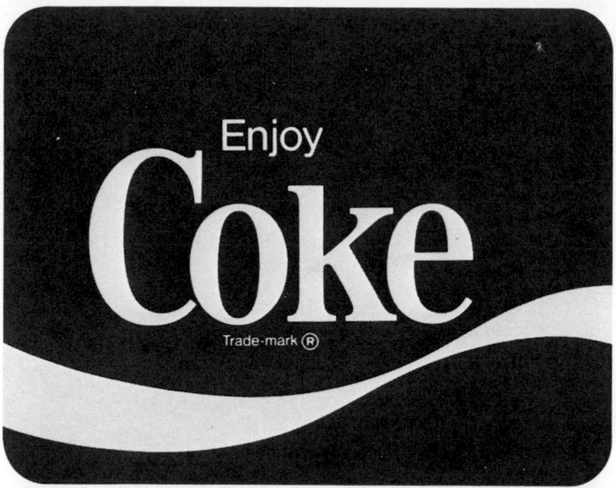

RYAN
30-second

NURSE: This is nonsense.

INT.: I beg your pardon.

NURSE: I am a nurse. In fact I am the top industrial nurse in this state. And this whole test is nonsense.

INT.: We just want you to choose.

NURSE: I don't want to choose either one of them. I'm a Coke drinker. I have been since the war. I served in the Pacific and I was top nurse there too. Them boys was an inspiration to me. And in the heat of the jungle nothing but Coke would do. Say, you ever been in the service?

INT.: Well, I . . .

NURSE: You look like a slacker to me.

ANNCR: There's more to Coke. Coke adds life.

SUPER: Coke adds life.

1177

Writer Rick Johnston
Director Dick Clark
Producer Jill Paperno
Production Company Nice Movies
Agency McCann-Erickson, Inc.
Client Coca-Cola USA

BUTCH
30-second

ANNCR (VO): They still call him Butch.

The first time he faced Catfish Hunter in Yankee Stadium, he hit a homerun to win the game.

The first time against Jim Palmer, another homer.

At 20, Butch Wynegar was the youngest player ever to play in the All-Star game.

Butch says he loves baseball so much, if he had to, he'd play for nothing.

OWNER CAL GRIFFITH: I really like that kid.

VO: It's a whole new ball game at the Met.

1178

Art Director	Tom Weyl
Writer	Phil Hanft
Director	Steve Griak
Producers	Tom Weyl Phil Hanft
Music	Cookhouse
Production Company	Wilson-Griak
Agency	Martin/Williams
Client	Minnesota Twins

Ford

75TH ANNIVERSARY

Ford wants to be your car company.

CAR BODY DESTRUCTION
30-second

BILL COSBY: The Ford Motor Company Car-Body-Destruction-Test.

This Lincoln Continental body was just welded together.

Now . . . would you believe it? These guys are tearin' it apart. It's their job, it really is.

Every week they take Ford, Mercury and Lincoln bodies and they tear them apart to see that the welds hold.

They tear them all apart . . . only way to know how tough they're put together.

It's simple. Ford wants to be your car company.

1179

Art Director	Celester Santee
Writers	Howie Stabin
	Bruce Montgomery
	Frank Mecca
Director	Dave Norman
Producer	Andy Doyle
Production Company	Jefferson Productions
Agency	Kenyon & Eckhardt Advertising, Inc.
Client	Ford Motor Company

SON OF MONK
30-second

BROTHER DOMINIC: I have a confession to make.

Last year, the Abbot asked me to do an impossible job—

copy 500 sets of this manuscript.

I did it—

but I used the Xerox 9200.

Now, he wants it copied on both sides. And he wants it fast. (SHOWS MANUSCRIPT)

This is going to take another miracle!!

WORKMAN: Where do you want it, Brother Dominic?

BROTHER DOMINIC: Right here.

ANNCR: The Xerox 9400 with automatic 2 sided copying.

Will miracles never cease?

1180

Art Directors Tony Angotti
Allen Kay
Writers Steve Penchina
Lois Korey
Lester Colodny
Allen Kay
Directors Bob Bean
Sid Myers
Jeff Lovinger

Producer Sydelle Rangell (for all three)
Production Companies Bean/Kahn
Myers & Griner, Cuesta
Lovinger, Tardio, Melsky
Agency Needham, Harper & Steers
Client Xerox Corp.

1181

AUNT MILLIES "COCKTAIL PARTY"
??-second

I paid $150 for a cocktail party, and all anybody noticed was the mustard.

super...

Kosciusko Mustard

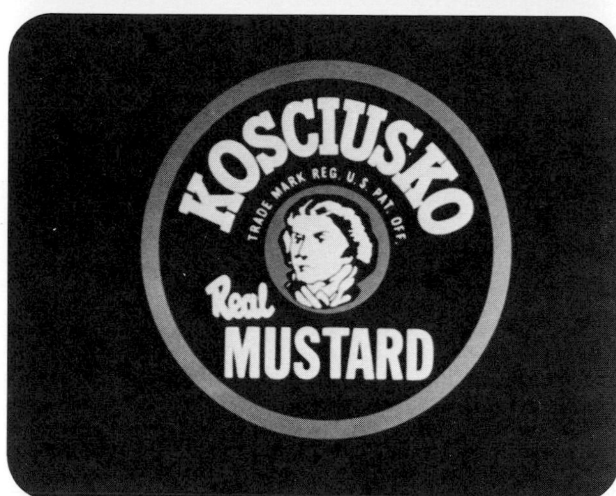

1181

Art Director	Robert Reitzfeld
Writer	Dick Jackson
Designer	Robert Reitzfeld
Photographer	Henry Sandbank
Director	Robert Reitzfeld
Producers	Robert Reitzfeld
	Dick Jackson
Production Company	Flickers, Inc.
Agency	Altschiller, Reitzfeld & Jackson, Inc.
Client	Kosciusko Mustard/Aunt Millies Sauces

LABEL
10-second

ANNCR: We put our favorite tuna recipe on every can we sell.

Bumble Bee. It's so good you can eat it plain.

1182

Art Director Lars Anderson
Writer Irwin Warren
Designer Lars Anderson
Director Elbert Budin
Producer Wayne Lachman
Music Original/Jimmy Curtiss
Production Company Ampersand Productions
Agency Richard K. Manoff Inc.
Client Bumble Bee Seafoods—
(Division of Castle & Cooke, Inc.)

TELEPHONE BOOTH
8-second

Script is an improvisation of screams.

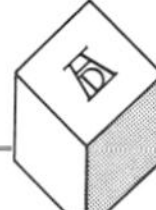

SILVER

1183

Art Director Paul Jervis
Writer Marc Shenfield
Director Elliot Resnick
Producer Kyle M. Dennis
Production Company Cailor/Resnick
Agency Smith/Greenland
Client New York State Lottery

STILL THE ONE
2-minute

A montage of images based on the number 1.

SONG: We've been together since way back when
And this year's going to be a winner again
And we want you to know
After all is said
We're still the one you can turn to for a friend

Still the one
You can turn to for cheer
Still the one
That wants you near
You're still having fun and we're
Still the one.

Animation Art Director	Harry Marks
Editors	Phil Datry
	Richard Audd
Animation Designers	John David Moore
	Harry Marks
Animation Artist	Michael Gibson
Live-Action Photographer	Michael Jones
Director	Roger Flint
Producers	Larry Sullivan
	Harry Marks
Music	John & Johanna Hall
Production Company	Roger Flint Productions
Publisher	Siren Songs Inc.
Agency	Sullivan & Marks Inc.
Client	American Broadcasting Co.

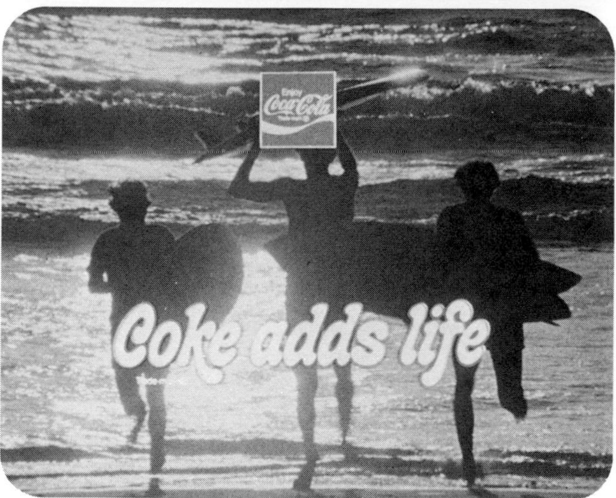

ENDLESS SUMMER
60-second

SFX: Coca-Cola music throughout

SFX: We've made it!

1186
Art Director A. Scully
Producer Paul Frahm
Production Company Steve Horn Productions
Agency McCann-Erickson, Inc.
Client Coca-Cola USA

ALUMNI
60-second

SPILLANE: We have assembled here a most congenial group . . . brought together by their love for a truly great beer. Right group?

GROUP: Right.

SPILLANE: It's Lite Beer from Miller. Right, Group?

GROUP: Right.

SPILLANE: They think the best thing about it is it's less filling. It has a third less calories than their regular beer. Right, Group?

HALF OF THE GROUP: Right.

OTHER HALF OF THE GROUP: Wrong.

HORNUNG: The best thing about it is that it tastes great.

FORD: No Hornung . . . it's less filling.

DAVIDSON: Sez who?

NIETCHKTE: Sez me.

BUONICONTI: Hey, take it from me. It tastes great.

BUTKUS: Who are you?

JONES: You won't think this fight is no joke, when you come to and your nose is broke.

BUTKUS (TO DANGERFIELD): No wonder you don't get no respect.

DANGERFIELD: I tell ya I don't deserve no respect.

HEINSOHN: You still don't know nothing about beer.

RUDOLPH: I thought I threw you out of this bar last year.

MARTIN: I feel very strongly both ways. I never argue.

GIRL: Hi Mickey.

SPILLANE: Hi doll.

GIRL: What's a nice guy like you doing in a fight like this?

SPILLANE: Waiting for you doll.

GROUP: (Mumbles and burbles of a dying argument as they all fall in and follow the girl)

THRONEBERRY (ALONE AT BAR, BEMUSED): I still don't know why they wanted me to do this commercial.

ANNCR: Lite Beer from Miller. Everything you always wanted in a beer. And less.

SILVER

1187

Art Directors Robert Engel
Robert Lenz
Writer Charles Ryant
Director Bob Giraldi
Producer Robert Engel
Music Bob Giraldi Productions
Agency McCann-Erickson, Inc.
Client Miller Brewing Company

PLANT
60-second

ANNCR (VO): The demand for electricity rises about the same time every weekday.

Businesses open and begin using electricity . . .

Factories are going full blast . . .

And people at home are running appliances . . .

The trouble is, everyone wants electricity at the same time: Daytime, Monday through Friday. So, back-up power plants, using more expensive fuels, have to help handle the extra load.

And the daytime demand for electricity is going up, so even more power plants will have to be built. It's all very costly for everyone.

Wisconsin Electric is working hard to hold down these costs. And you can help. If you can wait till the evening or anytime over the weekend to run appliances like your washing machine, dryer, dishwasher . . . you'll help reduce that costly daytime demand.

So, try to turn it on at night or on weekends instead . . . we'll all be better off during the day.

1188

Art Directors	Dennis W. Frankenberry Steve Laughlin
Writers	Dennis W. Frankenberry Steve Laughlin
Designer	Hal Silvermintz
Director	Hal Silvermintz
Producer	Dennis W. Frankenberry
Music	Mac McKinney
Production Company	Perpetual Motion
Agency	Frankenberry, Laughlin, Bernstein & Persa, Inc.
Client	Wisconsin Electric Power Company

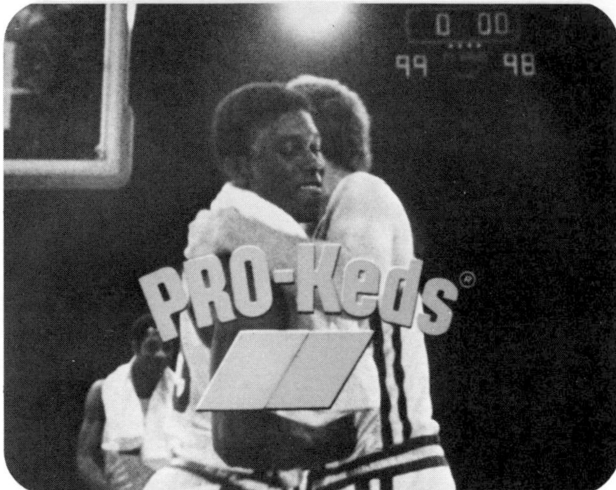

MOMENTS
60-second

ANNCR (VO): We at Pro-Keds ...
... would like you to know ...
... there's a movement ...
... a foot.
SINGERS: It looks so easy on TV ...
... the ball just doesn't seem to bounce your way ...
... Usually you're all thumbs.
... Sometimes that magic comes ...
... Look at you, you've made the perfect play ...
CHORUS: You've put it all together.
... for a moment you're the rookie of the year ...
... That moment is so sweet ...
... with those Pro-Keds on your feet ...
... Pro-Keds for all those moments you feel like a pro.
ANNCR (VO): America is moving to Pro-Keds ...
... because Pro-Keds ...
... are built to leap ...
... jump, run, cut ...
... kick and drive comfortably ...
... possible, and that's what ...
... the Pro-Keds movement is all about.
SINGERS: Pro-Keds for all those moments ...
... you feel like a pro ...
... Pro-Keds for all those moments ...
... you feel like a pro.

1189
Art Director Matt Basile
Writer Doug MacGibbon
Photographer Ed Brown
Director Michael Ulick
Producer Diane Flynn
Production Company Rick Levine Productions
Agency Young & Rubicam
Client Uniroyal/Keds

TAP DANCE
60-second

CHOREOGRAPHER: Okay girls. Let's work on the piano number. We have one hour.

PRODUCER: Oh no, they're not dancing on those pianos. They're $10,000 Baldwins.

GIRLFRIEND: That's $30,000 worth of pianos!

PRODUCER: Forty.

ASSISTANTS: Don't worry, sir. We put a St. Regis masking material on top.

ANNCR (VO): The St. Regis masking material protecting these pianos . . .

. . . is a latex coated plastic film.

One of our many masking materials made . . .

. . . to protect prefinished surfaces during manufacture.

And just one of the surprising products from . . .

St. Regis' highly sophisticated coating technology.

PRODUCER: On with the show!

1190

Art Director Herm Siegel
Writer Stafford Ordahl, Jr.
Designer Robert Ramsay
Director Fred Levinson
Producer John Held
Music Sidray Enterprises Inc.
Production Company Fred Levinson & Co.
Agency Cunningham & Walsh Inc.
Client St. Regis Paper Company

REFRIGERATION
60-second

EDISON: I think I mind the heat more now than I used to. I can remember visiting my grandfather's farm when I was little. We children would play in his icehouse. All cool and dark and smelling of sawdust. He'd fill it with ice in the winter, and hope it would last all summer. If the ice didn't last, his milk would sour and his butter go rancid. And that was a catastrophe. Electricity has changed all that. Right now—1928—electric refrigeration is going into homes all over America. And the company I helped start—General Electric—has had a lot to do with that. Oh, the idea of electric refrigeration has been around quite a while. But developing a machine that was practical for the home—well, that was a different matter. Making the machine quiet and reliable . . . so it would run without fuss for years and years . . . that's what General Electric has done. It didn't come easy. Here . . . let me show you something . . . just take a look at that. (SHOWS OLD GE AD IN NATIONAL GEOGRAPHIC, READS HEADLINE) "Fifteen years of development." Well, these things never come easy. Working on my electric light bulb taught me that. But I suspect that pretty soon you won't find an icebox or an icehouse anywhere in this whole country. And that will be the end of playing in icehouses on hot summer days. But I'm probably a little old for that anyhow.

1191

Art Director Len McCarron
Writer Bill Stone
Set Designer Stephen Hendrickson
Director Norman Griner
Producer Tom Anderson
Production Company Myers & Griner, Cuesta
Agency BBDO
Client General Electric

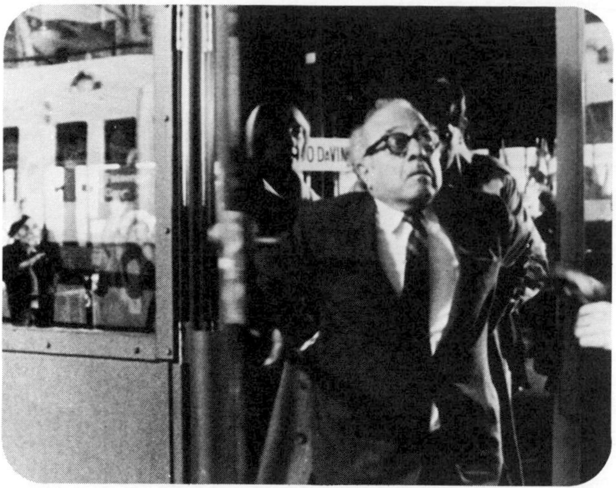

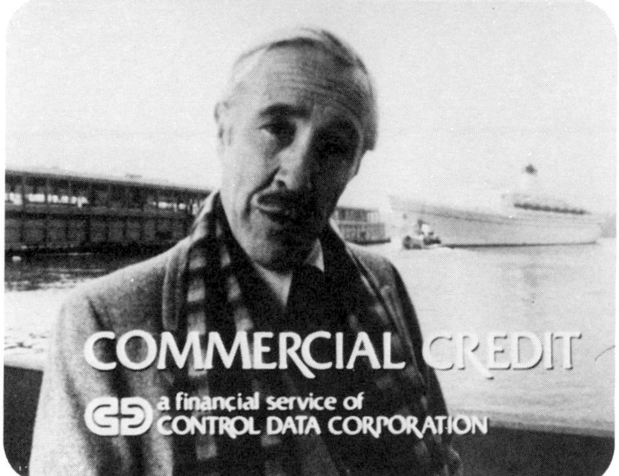

GOODBYE PAPA
30-second

MR. ROBARDS (VO THEN VOC): He came to America with only the clothes on his back.

SON (VOC): Good trip, Papa. Take care.

ROBARDS: Raised a family. Built a new life.

PAPA: Grazie, Dominic.

ROBARDS: His one wish was to see the place of his birth . . . once more.

SON: Papa.

ROBARDS: His son borrowed twenty-three hundred dollars from Commercial Credit to pay for the trip.

Yes, Commercial Credit—the same company that lends millions of dollars to help business—lends even more money to help people.

So when you need a personal loan, Commercial Credit will find ways to help you.

1193

Art Director	Stan Sweeney
Writers	Bob Urquhart
	Al Buono
Editor	Dennis Hayes
Director	Dominick Rossetti
Producer	Arnold Blum
Music	Lucas/McFaul
Production Company	Rossetti Films
Agency	W. B. Doner & Company
Client	Commercial Credit

CHRISTMAS CARD
60-second

ANNCR (VO): Gene Barry. This Christmas card was sent to you by the people at Miller High Life. Merry Christmas.

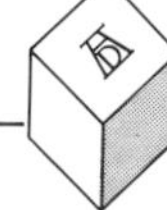

GOLD

1194

Art Director Robert Lenz
Writer Robert Meury
Director Bob Gaffney
Producers Linda Mevorach
Sally Smith
Production Company Bob Gaffney Productions
Agency McCann-Erickson, Inc.
Client Miller Brewing Company

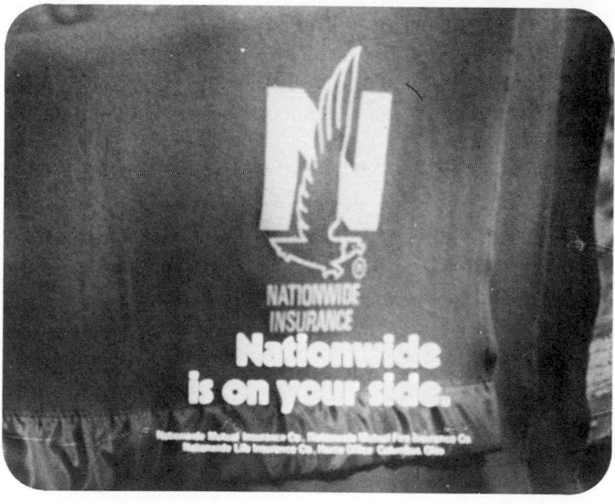

STORY OF LIFE
??-second

Life. It's a story of waiting. Of hoping. Of working. Of planning. Of learning. Of growing. At Nationwide, we want to be part of your story. That's why we offer so many different kinds of life insurance. To help you save for all you've worked for. And planned for. And hoped for. For all your life.

1195
Art Director Ray Fitzgerald
Writer Gary Kott
Director Bob Eggers
Producer Ray Fitzgerald
Music Steve Karmen
Production Company Petersen Co.
Agency Ogilvy & Mather
Client Nationwide Insurance

IMPRESSIONS—I
30-second

BEGIN THEME MUSIC, "TRY TO REMEMBER."

ANNCR (VO): A lot of people left impressions on your life, remember?

CONTINUE MUSIC.

ANNCR (VO): Lots of people left impressions on your life. Don't let them fade away. Show them you still care with Long Distance.

MUSIC UP THEN FADE.

1196

Art Director Jeff Odian
Writer Dick Keith
Director Fred Levinson
Producers Roy Townshend (F.L. & Co.)
Carol Dawn (N W Ayer)
Music Elliot Lawrence
Production Company Fred Levinson & Co.
Agency N W Ayer & Sons, Inc.
Client AT&T Long Lines "Impressions"

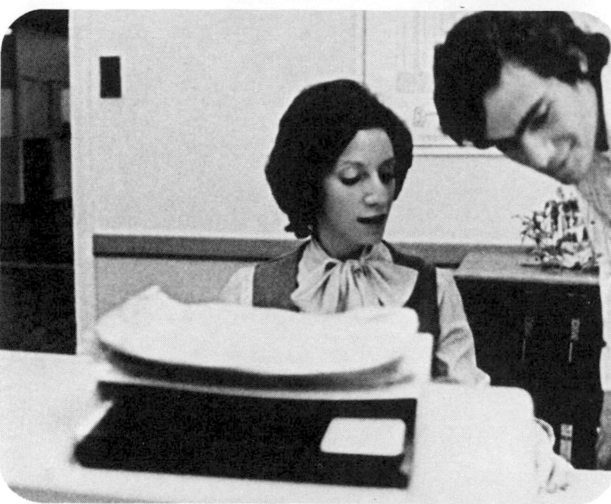

RODRIGUES FAMILY
2-minute

SON (VO): We're a family of seven.

We arrived in this country in the year 1962.

We moved to California.

That's my father, Graciana Rodrigues.

My father, he always wanted to start his own business.

Once he saved a little money he came over to the produce market to buy Spanish foods.

Foods that people that spoke Spanish would buy from him.

He decided to open up a place.

The first day, he took in 65 cents, so my mother was telling him, "I told you it wasn't going to work."

But he was very persistent, he would start at six o'clock in the morning and go to about nine, ten o'clock at night.

The business started growing.

HELPER: Buy five, get one free.

SON (VO): The little stores were constantly asking us to carry a bigger line of products.

There came a point where we couldn't do any more.

Roberto was the first to come up with the idea of getting some kind of machine that would do our inventory.

Through one of the other companies, he heard of IBM System 32.

We were all so excited. The day we got the machine we said that would be the end of our problem finally.

Now, Richard tells Maria to do the statements and she can get statements out in 30 minutes. Maybe 800 customers.

We use the System 32 for almost everything, especially inventory.

Working as a family is a lot of fun right now.

Before we were very scared of expanding because we figured if we couldn't control the way we did our business,

there was no way we could go ahead and open up a new place.

But now my father is having some big ideas again.

FATHER: I say we open in San Francisco. Yea.

SON (VO): My father, he's some man.

ANNCR (VO): IBM. Helping people find the answers.

1197

Art Director	Tony Oliveto
Writer	George Adels
Director	Denny Harris
Producers	George Adels Tony Oliveto
Production Company	Denny Harris Production
Agency	Conahay & Lyon
Client	International Business Machines

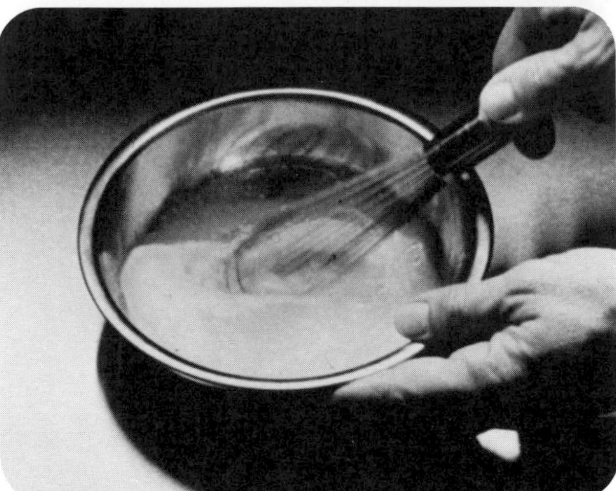

RHAPSODY
60-second

MALE SINGER: You, you're the one

we're cookin' for.
Our best is fresh food

you'll adore.
Our Grade A
eggs cooked

on the spot.

With pure pork sausage sizzling hot.

SINGERS: It's breakfast,
McDonald's breakfast,
made from the very best ingredients.
We do it all for you.

MALE SINGER: We start out with
an English muffin
Then add cheese

and egg

And something really good
Canadian bacon.

Yes, that's how we go 'bout makin'

SINGERS (VO): Breakfast,

McDonald's breakfast.
Made from the very best ingredients

We do it all for you.

MALE SINGER: Now
when you want
a morning treat,

hotcakes and sausage

they taste neat.

Made fresh from batter

they taste better

topped with butter

Yes indeed it's

SINGERS: Breakfast,

McDonald's breakfast,

Made from the very best ingredients

We do it all for you.

At McDonald's, we do it all for you.

We do it all for you.

1198

Art Director Sal D'Onofrio
Writer Mike Cafferata
Production Company N. Lee Lacy
Agency Needham, Harper & Steers
Client McDonald's Corporation

CROSS COUNTRY
60-second

MAN: I drink Dr Pepper and I'm proud.

I used to be alone in a crowd.

But now you look around these days,

There seems to be a Dr Pepper craze. I'm a pepper, he's a pepper, she's a pepper.

ALL SING: We're a pepper. Wouldn't you like to be a pepper, too?

I'm a pepper, he's a pepper, she's a pepper.

If you drink Dr Pepper you're a pepper, too.

MAN: Us Dr Peppers are an interesting breed,

An original taste is what we need.

Ask any pepper and he'll say,

ALL SING: Only Dr Pepper tastes that way.

MAN SINGS: I'm a pepper, he's a pepper, she's a pepper,

ALL SING: We're a pepper. Wouldn't you like to be a pepper too.

I'm a pepper he's a pepper, she's a pepper. We're a pepper.

Wouldn't you like to be a pepper, too?

Be a pepper. Drink Dr Pepper.

MAN: Come on.

ALL SING: Be a pepper.

Drink Dr Pepper.

Be a pepper. Drink Dr Pepper . . .

1200

Art Director Frank DeVito
Writer Jane Warshaw
Producer Phyllis Landi
Production Company Sunlight
Agency Young & Rubicam
Client Dr Pepper

CELEBRITIES
60-second

ZSAZSA GABOR: If you have my right ZIP code then, you've got my number, Darling it is 90024.

ED BYRNES: For the woman who has everything except my correct ZIP code, it is 90213.

HENNY YOUNGMAN: Speaking of correct ZIP codes, take my wife's it's 10019.

CHARLIE CALLAS: I'll only tell my ZIP code to redheads and brunettes.

ELKA SOMMERS: If you tell me your ZIP code I'll tell you mine.

CHARLIE CALLAS: Elkie, Elkie, Elkie huh! In your case I'll make an exception mine is 07024.

ELKA SOMMERS: My correct ZIP is 90024 got it.

CHARLIE CALLAS: Who -ooooo

HENNY YOUNGMAN: How do you remember your own ZIP code, practice, practice.

ED McMAHON: I always use the right ZIP code
I never forget my ZIP,
I forgot my ZIP.

ISSAC HAYES: (SINGS AND PLAYS) It ain't hip to forget your ZIP mine is 38107. If you don't use a ZIP it slows everything down, but the right ZIP's the best way to move the mail around.

LOGL: Zip up your mail with the right ZIP code.

1201

Art Director	Paul Gold
Writer	Roberta Seltzer
Producers	Paul Gold
	Roberta Seltzer
Production Company	Mason/Stearns
Agency	Young & Rubicam
Client	U.S. Postal Service

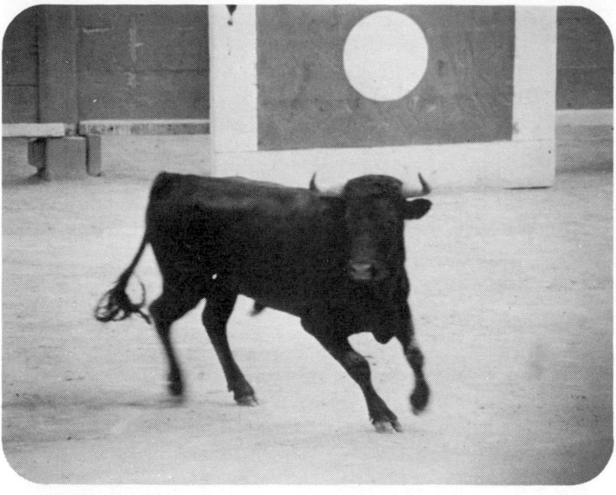

THE BULLFIGHT
60-second

ANNCR (VO): El toro . . .
and the matador.

ANNCR: And between them, two sheets of St. Regis plastic. Altogether only 10/1000's of an inch thick.

Can the bull get through to the bullfighter?

Watch.

ANNCR (VO): How could these two thin sheets of plastic hold back a charging bull? Each sheet is actually made of two different high performance plastics . . . extruded simultaneously.

But this is just one of the surprising plastics St. Regis makes.

As a leading maker of plastic film, we can engineer plastic sheets to do all kinds of unexpected things.

And this is what St. Regis is all about: bringing technology into the marketplace in every product we make.

St. Regis serving Man and Nature to the benefit of both.

1202

Art Director Herm Siegel
Writer Stafford Ordahl, Jr.
Designer Robert Ramsay
Director Fred Levinson
Producer John Held
Music Music House
Production Company Fred Levinson & Co.
Agency Cunningham & Walsh Inc.
Client St. Regis Paper Company

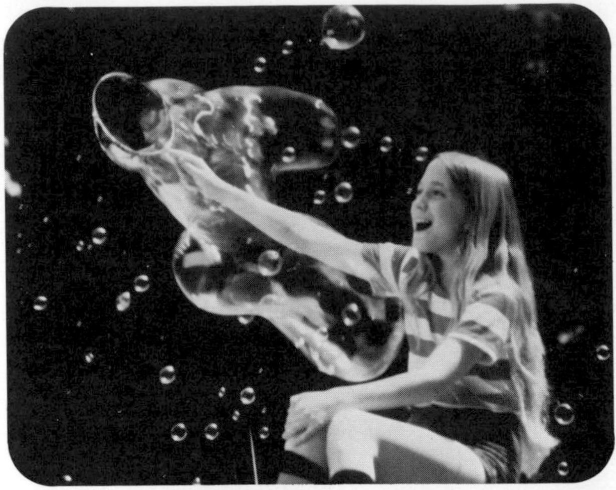

PERFECT TIME
60-second

SINGERS: You,
you're the one
Wakin' up to golden sunshine.
You, you're the one
Fillin' every day with fun times.
You're who we like to please
With good food and a smile.
We can make you feel at ease
When you stay with us a while.
You, you're the one
You're why we're always near
You, you're the one
It's you we like to hear.
You're who we're cookin' for
Each and every day.
You're who we're lookin' for
So come on by our way.
At McDonald's
We do it all for you.

1203
Art Director Dennis Kromm
Writer Nancy Jordan
Production Company DeSort & Sam Productions
Agency Needham, Harper & Steers
Client McDonald's Corporation

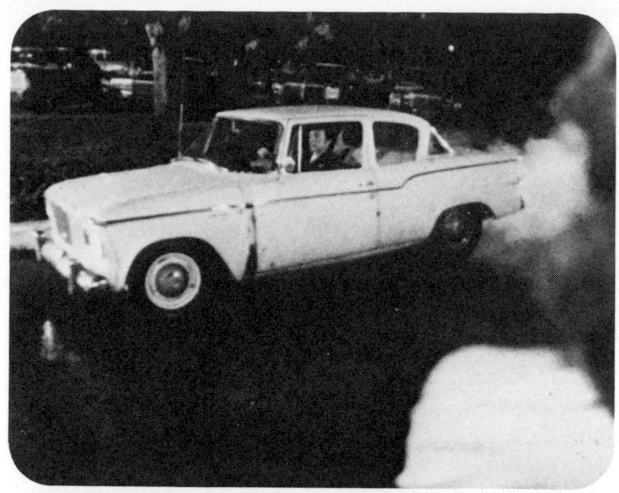

CONWAY/AUTO LOAN
60-second

CONWAY: (TO HEAD VALET) 13

HEAD VALET: Yes sir . . . 13

CARHOP: Yoo yoo!

MISS CONWAY: Hi, how are you? Just fine thank you.

LADY: I wanna see who has the nerve to get into that . . .

CARHOP: Anybody get hurt in that wreck?

HEAD VALET: 13?

CONWAY: No mine's a cocoa convertible . . .

BANK MAN: You know, I could probably get that guy the money for a new car in 24 hours.

CONWAY: Legally?

BANKMAN: Sure, I work for Manufacturers Hanover. We make more auto loans than any bank in New York . . .

CONWAY: Yeah, but you wouldn't get that guy a loan . . . would ya!

BANKMAN: We don't make any money turning people down . . .

CONWAY: Can you give me . . . I mean, ah . . . him a special deal?

BANKMAN: If that guy qualifies for his loan and has a checking and savings account

with Manufacturer's Hanover,

we'll reduce the annual percentage rate on his loan.

CONWAY: You gettin' this?

BANKMAN: Nice talking to you . . . I'll see you . . .

CONWAY: See you tomorrow! At the bank!

HEAD VALET: Cocoa convertible?

CONWAY: Ah, a yellow taxi.

ANNCR (VO): Manufacturers Hanover. It's banking the way you want it to be.

1204

Art Director Ed Rotondi
Writer John LaRock
Producer Steve Labovsky
Production Company Gomes-Loew
Agency Young & Rubicam
Client Manufacturers Hanover Trust

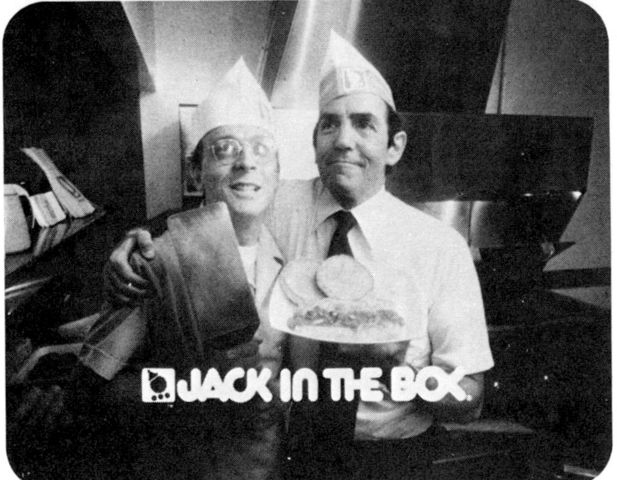

TRAINEE/MUSIC
60-second

VO: At some restaurants, learning to cook hamburgers is the beginning and the end. At Jack in the Box restaurants, it's only the beginning.

TRAINEE: How did I do?

MANAGER: Fine. Now on to the taco.

TRAINEE: On to the taco?

MANAGER: Not quite.

TRAINEE: I did it.

MANAGER: French fries.

MANAGER: Onion rings.

MANAGER: Fine. Steak sandwich.

VO: At Jack in the Box restaurants, our kids have learned to cook more than great hamburgers.

VO: When we tell you we're really cookin', we're really cookin'

MANAGER: I think you're ready.

TRAINEE: A double Jumbo Jack.

SONG: Ji-Ji-Ji-Jack
Ji-Ji-Ji-Jack
Ji-Ji-Ji-Jack
Jack in the Box.

We're really cookin' now.

1205

Art Directors Bob Kuperman
Stan Dragotti
Writer Pacy Markman
Director Stan Dragotti
Producer Paula Del Nunzio
Music Elsmere Music Co./(Steve Karmen)
Production Company Petersen Co.
Agency Wells, Rich, Greene/West
Client Foodmaker

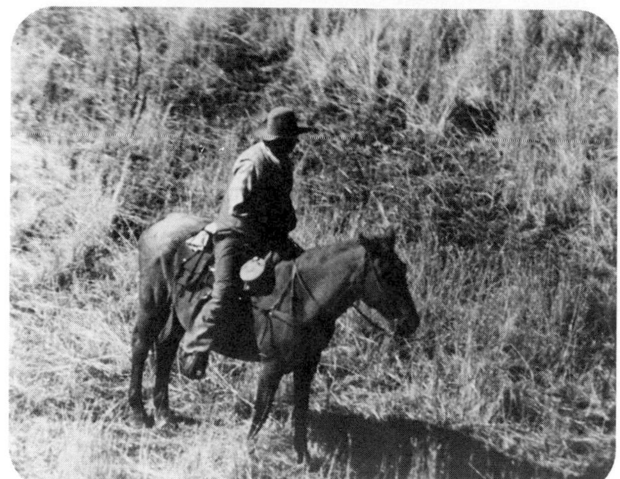

OPERA/WYOMING C-'78 II
1-minute

SFX: (PROMINENT ARIA)

SFX: (ARIA UNDER)

ANNCR (VO): It's Saturday afternoon, all over America.

And millions of people are sitting back and enjoying something that's become a very special part of their lives. Grand opera.

Broadcast live from the Metropolitan Opera HXOUSE IN New York, home of America's only national opera company.

For 38 years, Texaco has been bringing this glorious music performed by the world's great opera stars . . .

to local radio stations from Bath, Maine to Laramie, Wyoming.

COWBOY: (SINGS OVER RADIO VOICE)

ANNCR (VO): Texaco has been proud to broadcast this magnificent music all over America, and bring delight to so many.

Texaco we've been helping the Met make beautiful music for 38 years.

1207

Art Director	Joseph Gregorace
Writer	Peter Nord
Producer	Paul McDonough
Music	Roy Eaton
Production Company	Dick Miller
Agency	Benton & Bowles Inc.
Client	Texaco Inc.

A TIME TO SEW: A TIME TO REAP
60-second

INSTRUMENTAL INTRODUCTION TO "THE TIMES OF YOUR LIFE."

SINGER (VO): Good morning, yesterday
You wake up
and time has slipped away
And suddenly it's hard to find
The memories you left behind
Remember
Do you remember
The laughter and the tears
The shadows of misty yesteryears
You get the yearning now and then
To bring the moments back again
Remember
Will you remember
The times of your life

ANNCR (VO): Kodak film. For the times of your life.

1208

Art Director Warren Aldoretta
Director Fred Levinson
Producers Roy Townshend (F.L. & Co.)
Warren Aldoretta (J.W. Thompson)
Music Roger Nichols
Production Company Fred Levinson & Co.
Agency J. Walter Thompson
Client Kodak "A Time to Sow"

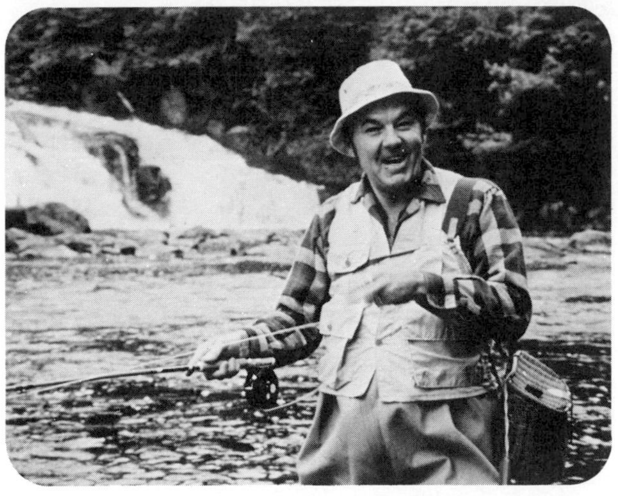

TOURISM/TELEPHONE/60
60-second

FISHERMAN FROM NEW HAMPSHIRE: I live in New Hampshire, but I love New York.

HIKER FROM WEST VIRGINIA: I live in West Virginia, but I love New York.

MAN ON BEACH FROM CAPE COD: I live on Cape Cod, but I love New York.

HORSEBACK RIDER FROM NORTH CAROLINA (VO): I live in North Carolina, but I love New York.

New York's resorts and vacation places are surrounded by some of the most exciting outdoor country in the world.

Over four thousand beautiful lakes and rivers. Forty-two of the highest peaks in the East. One hundred and twenty seven miles of spectacular sand and surf.

That's why outdoor lovers from the Carolinas to Canada love to vacation in New York.

CAMPER FROM BROOKLYN: I live in Brooklyn, but I love New York.

SINGERS: I love New York. (What a great vacation.)

1209

Art Director	Gerry Ranson
Writer	Peter Ognibene
Photographer/Cameraman	Mike Zingale
Director	Mike Zingale
Producer	Don Kohn
Music	"I Love New York" by Steve Karmen
Production Company	Lou Puopolo, Inc.
Agency	Wells, Rich, Greene
Client	New York State Commerce Department

BLOCK PARTY
30-second

ANNCR (VO): In Morgan Park recently, an elderly couple held a party for their friends. Not their old friends, they'd all moved, or passed away. But their new friends, the children who'd moved into the neighborhood.

Unfortunately, they couldn't see how happy the party made the kids, because they're blind. Yet when you think about it, they saw things very clearly.

Now this wasn't the big story of the day. But we felt it was an important one. And that's why it was on Eyewitness News.

1211
Art Director Gary Johns
Writer Mike Faems
Director Bob Giraldi
Producer Enid Katz
Production Company Bob Giraldi Productions
Agency N W Ayer/Chicago
Client WLS-TV, Chicago

THE PROFESSOR
60-second

PROFESSOR: Let us now take a look into the future of train travel.

Lights, please.

I foresee the day . . .

when swift passenger trains powered by efficient turbine engines . . .

will glide smoothly from city to city.

These Turboliners will have climate control systems that regulate air temperature so that passengers . . .

will be cool in the summer and warm in the winter.

And sliding doors between cars will open with the touch of a toe.

AUDIENCE: Poppycock! Balderdash!

PROFESSOR: Seats will recline with the push of a button.

Hot meals will be available cooked in a flash in microwave ovens.

There will be plush service in a Turbo Club.

And I predict that these trains of the future . . .

will provide the fastest, most comfortable means of land travel . . .

in the year 2000.

WOMAN: What an imagination.

MAN: 2000??? Never!!!

ANNCR (VO): The Turboliner won't arrive in 2000.

Because it's here today. Amtrak's new Turboliner now running between New York, Albany and Buffalo.

Take a ride into the future today!

1212

Art Director	Dick Levy
Writers	Allen Kay
	Matthew Forbes
Director	Steve Horn
Producer	Gloria Gengo
Production Company	Steve Horn Productions
Agency	Needham, Harper & Steers Adv. Inc.
Client	National Passenger Railroad

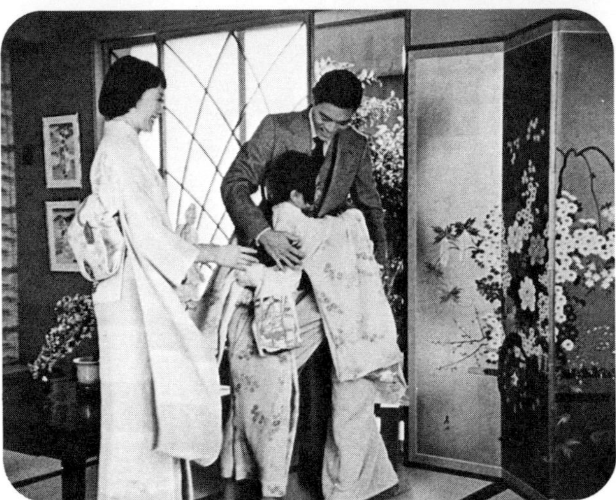

OUT OF TOWNERS
60-second

ANNCR: A lot of people come a long way to shop at Barneys

So when they get back home from New York they bring back more than memories.

A rancher from Nevada brought back seven Lanvin suits. A Turkish pasha brought home two suits by Oxford.

A Japanese diplomat carried home some English tweeds by Burberry. And for a basketball player from Bulgaria it was one dozen Yves St. Laurent shirts.

When you build the world's finest men's store, the word gets around

---

1213

Art Director Amil Gargano
Writer David Altschiller
Director Steve Horn
Producer Janine Marjollet
Music Michael Small
Production Company Steve Horn Productions
Agency Ally & Gargano
Client Barney's

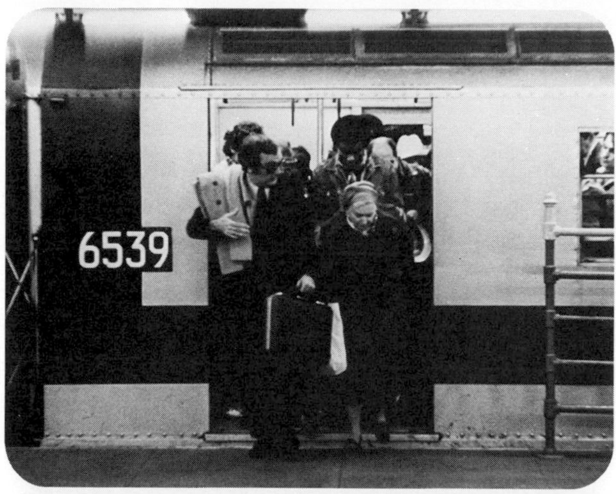

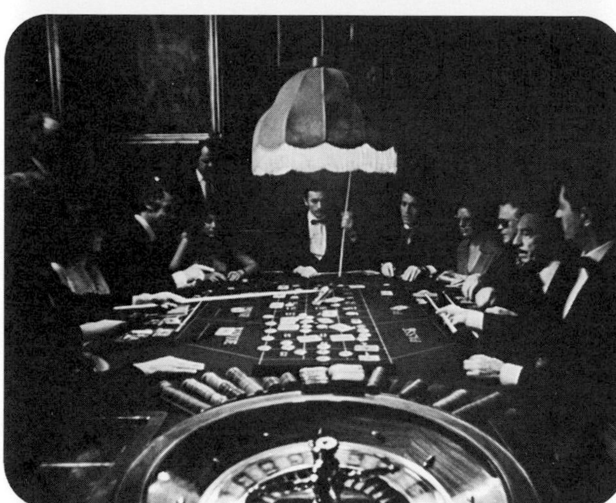

PEOPLE, PLACES
60-second

ANNCR: Every day, Pan Am brings people like this . . . closer to people like this . . . and connects places like this . . . with places like this.

And people like this.

CROUPIER: Siete rojo

ANNCR: . . . with people like this.

We bring the rest of the world a little closer to America and America a little closer to the rest of the world.

CLASS: My country 'tis of thee . . .

GROUP IN PUB: God save the Queen.

CHEERLEADERS: Give me an "O" . . .

CROWD: Ole!

ANNCR: It's what we started out to do with our very first flight.

And it's why today, we can take you direct to more places from the U.S. than anybody else.

SINGERS: We're America's airline to the world . . . Pan Am.

1214
Art Director Michael Tesch
Writer Tom Messner
Director Tibor Hirsch
Producer Maureen Kearns
Music Joe Brooks
Production Company Tibor Hirsch Productions
Agency Ally & Gargano
Client Pan American World Airways

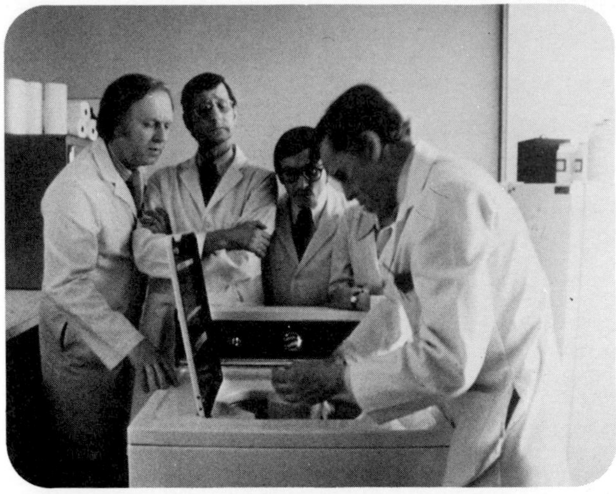

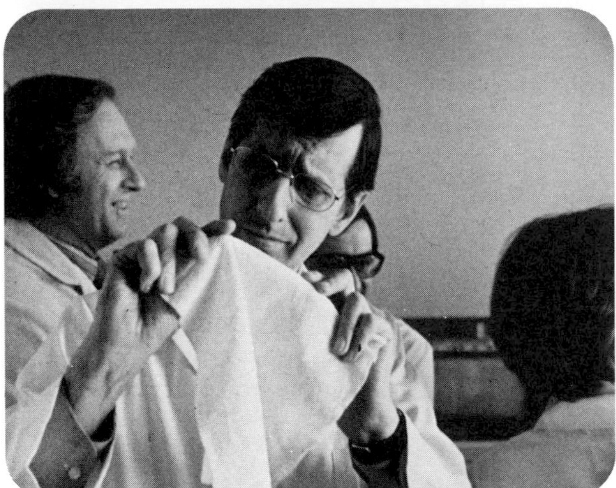

LABORATORY II

60-second

RESEARCH SCIENTIST: My colleagues and I have recently completed work on what has to be the most important advance in paper towels since the paper towel itself.

What we discovered is a whole new way of making paper that produces a paper towel that comes amazingly close to cloth.

A towel far stronger and more absorbent than towels made the conventional way.

The guys in the advertising department are calling it Bolt. Get it . . . like in bolt of cloth.

Of course, along with all great discoveries come a few skeptics, like Fredricks, here.

"If this Bolt is so much like cloth," he said, "why don't we test it in a washing machine?"

Shall we?

Well, here is Viva

Here is Bounty

And here, Fredricks, is amazing . . . new Bolt.

ANNCR: Introducing Bolt. The world's most cloth-like paper towel.

1215

Art Director John Danza
Writer Mike Drazen
Designer John Danza
Director Joe Pytka
Producer Tanya English
Production Company STF (Sandler Tape & Film)
Agency Scali, McCabe, Sloves
Client American Can Company

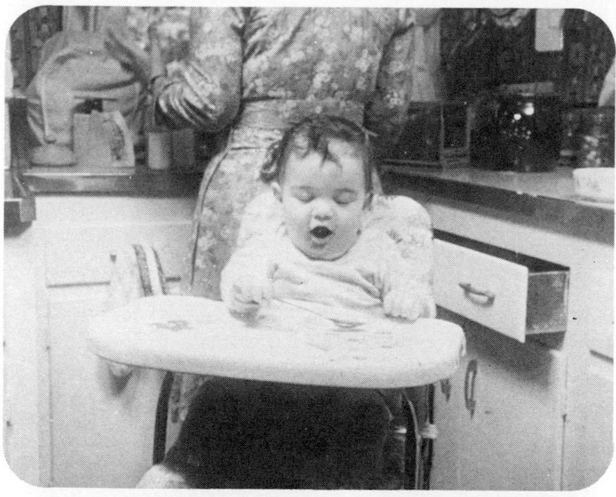

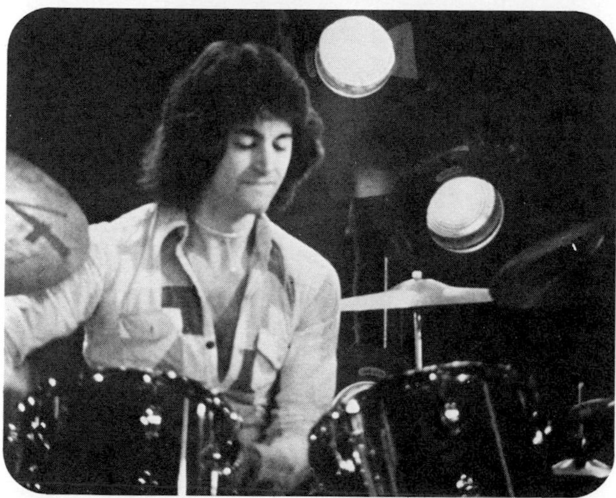

DRUMMER
60-second

ANNCR: Nobody decides to be a drummer.

MOM: Ralph, please.

ANNCR: You just find yourself drumming.

MOM: Ralph, please!

ANNCR: It doesn't make you instantly popular.

GIRL: Ralph, please.

ANNCR: And no one asks you to play their favorite tunes.

DAD: Ralph, please.

ANNCR: But with endless practice . . .

SISTERS: Ralph, please.

ANNCR: And fanatical persistence . . .

MOM AND DAD: Ralph, please.

ANNCR: You get there. Your drumming isn't just noise anymore. And you're not the only one who thinks so.

GIRL: Oh Ralph, please.

ANNCR: When a lifetime of work has gone into playing a piece of music,

Pioneer thinks you should hear all of it. So we designed high fidelity components not to add

anything or take anything away. That's why we've become a #1 today with people who care about music.

Pioneer. We bring it back alive.

1216

Art Director Stan Schofield
Writer Phil Peppis
Designer Stan Schofield
Director Bob Giraldi
Producer Ken Yagoda
Production Company Giraldi Productions
Agency Scali, McCabe, Sloves
Client U.S. Pioneer Electronics

TUTHILL
60-second

ANNCR: He was a man who never danced, never sang, never performed for an audience.

Yet, since 1891, his talent has thrilled millions.

TUTHILL: A little more to the left.

1ST WORKMAN: Right, sir.

ANNCR: His name was William Tuthill. His gift, architecture. And his masterpiece, Carnegie Hall. Perhaps the only music hall in the world,

where every person in the audience can hear every note. No matter how softly it's played.

2ND WORKMAN: Mr. Tuthill. We're about finished sir.

TUTHILL: Mr. O'Reilly,

here you don't have to shout.

ANNCR: The same commitment to perfect sound that went into building Carnegie Hall

goes into every high fidelity component Pioneer makes.

That's what's made Pioneer #1 today

with people who care about music.

Pioneer. We bring it back alive.

1217

Art Director	Stan Schofield
Writer	Bruce Feirstein
Designer	Stan Schofield
Director	Bob Giraldi
Producer	Ken Yagoda
Production Company	Giraldi Productions
Agency	Scali, McCabe, Sloves
Client	U.S. Pioneer Electronics

SONNY ROLLINS
60-second

ANNCR: In nineteen fifty nine, after twelve years of success,

a great jazz saxophonist decided he wasn't good enough,

Sonny Rollins dropped out of the music business.

Night after night he stood alone on the Brooklyn Bridge and practiced.

For months, he blew his music to the stars.

And when he felt the time was right,

Sonny Rollins came back to his public.

Since then his records have earned the highest acclaim.

And today, Sonny Rollins is, at last "good enough."

This uncompromising dedication to music is something Pioneer understands.

So we design our hi-fi components to let you get everything out of music that a musician puts into it.

That's what's made us number one today with people who care about music.

Pioneer. We bring it back alive.

1218

Art Director	Bob Needleman
Writers	Phil Peppis
	Ed McCabe
Designer	Bob Needleman
Director	Steve Horn
Producer	Ken Yagoda
Production Company	Steve Horn Productions
Agency	Scali, McCabe, Sloves
Client	U.S. Pioneer Electronics

SECRET AGENT
60-second

SECRET AGENT: Sir . . .

MAN (OFF/C): It's about time you're here.

MAN (O/C): Another late night, I presume? . . . Well, let's get started . . .

MAN: The first thing we have for your assignment is this microcassette taperecorder . . .

S.A.: Ingenious! Did you design this, sir?

MAN: Well, no . . . Actually, it's a Sony.

MAN: Next is this radio with 32 worldwide bands. Can tune in just about anyplace.

S.A.: Extraordinary! Who gets the credit for this one? . . .

MAN: Ehhh . . . this is a Sony, too.

MAN: . . . You'll also need this ultra compact portable video camera and we're going to mount this 5″ color TV in your car along with this Betamax Deck for playback.

S.A.: Remarkable! . . . Are they . . .

MAN: Yes . . .

. . . They're Sony also.

S.A.: Excuse me, sir, but did you just walk into a store and buy these? . . .

MAN: Well . . . yes! . . .

S.A.: Keep up the good work, sir.

VO: If it's a little extraordinary . . .

VO: . . . chances are . . . it's a Sony.

1219
Art Director John Caggiano
Writer Mike Mangano
Designer John Caggiano
Director Rick Levine
Producer Jim deBarros
Music Lee Schumer
Agency Doyle Dane Bernbach
Client Sony

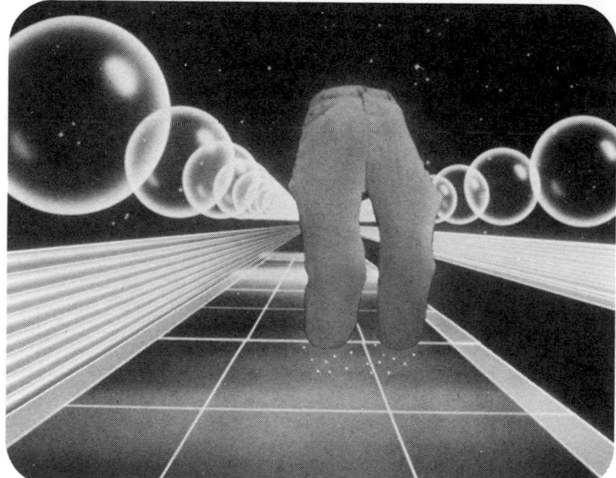

BRAND NAME
60-second

C'mon old Trademark, time for your walk

Where will you take me—sure wish you could talk

I know what you'd tell me, how your family began

With the same Levi's blue jeans worn by this man.

Hey, here comes more Levi's; red, yellow, and blue

Free wheeling kiddos are wearing them too!

And what a surpise—

Look who's been window shopping for clothes

Yeah, a gal in her Levi's instinctively knows of your special appeal.

Enough of this kissing, little registered mark,

Time that we meet some guys by the park

Dressed in your sportswear—your newest addition

Sums it up fellah: Levi's Panatela.

Hey, Trademark, this looks like the place where tomorrows begin

Your family's future—sure looks like it should

That's right, little trademark—

Levi's don't have to be blue—just have to be good!

1220

Art Director Chris Blum
Editors Bob Abel, Hal Cohen
Designer Richard Taylor
Artists Richard Taylor, Con Pederson, Wayne Kimbell
Music Ken Nordine
Photographers Ed Martin, Don Baker, Richard Corbin, Ron Saks
Directors Bob Abel, Richard Taylor
Producers Bob Abel, Ove Tilling, Dick Kerns
Production Companies Robert Abel & Assocs., E.U.E/Screen Gems
Animators Ed Verraux, Sari Gennis, Dan Thompson
Agencies Foote, Cone & Belding/Honig
Client Levi Strauss

TUTHILL
60-second

ANNCR: He was a man who never danced, never sang, never performed for an audience.

Yet, since 1891, his talent has thrilled millions.

TUTHILL: A little more to the left.

1ST WORKMAN: Right, sir.

ANNCR: His name was William Tuthill. His gift, architecture. And his masterpiece, Carnegie Hall. Perhaps the only music hall in the world.

where every person in the audience can hear every note. No matter how softly it's played.

2ND WORKMAN: Mr. Tuthill. We're about finished sir.

TUTHILL: Mr. O'Reilly,

here you don't have to shout.

ANNCR: The same commitment to perfect sound that went into building Carnegie Hall

goes into every high fidelity component Pioneer makes.

That's what's made Pioneer #1 today

with people who care about music.

Pioneer. We bring it back alive.

1221

Art Directors Stan Schofield
Bob Needleman
Writers Phil Peppis
Ed McCabe
Bruce Feirstein
Designers Stan Schofield
Bob Needleman

Directors Bob Giraldi
Steve Horn
Producer Ken Yagoda
Production Companies Giraldi Productions
Steve Horn Productions
Agency Scali, McCabe, Sloves
Client U.S. Pioneer Electronics

REFRIGERATION
2-minute

I think I mind the heat more now than I used to. I can remember visiting my grandfather's farm when I was little. We children would play in his icehouse, all cool and dark and smelling of sawdust. He'd fill it with ice in the winter and hope it would last all summer. If the ice didn't last, his milk would sour, or his butter would go rancid, and that was a catastrophe. Electricity has changed all that. Right now, 1928, electric refrigeration is growing in the homes all over America, and the company I helped start had a lot to do with that. Oh, the idea of electric refrigeration has been around quite a while. But developing a machine that was practical for the home, well that was a different matter. Making the machine quiet and reliable so it would run without fuss for years and years, that's what General Electric has got, and it didn't come easy. Here, let me show you a subject. Just take a look at that. Fifteen years of development. Well, these things never come easy. Working on my electric light bulb taught me that. But I suspect that pretty soon you won't find an icebox or an icehouse anywhere in this whole country, and that will be the end of playing in icehouses on hot summer days. But I'm probably a little old for that anyhow.

1222

Art Director Len McCarran
Writer LeShaw
Photographer Norman Griner
Director Norman Griner
Producer Tom Anderson
Production Company Myers & Griner, Cuesta
Agency BBDO International, Inc.
Client General Electric

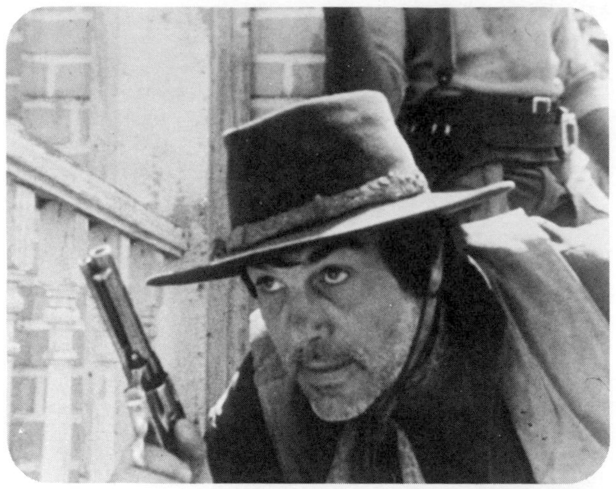

STUNTMAN
60-second

ANNCR: Stuntman.

You get the bruises instead of the glory.

You hit the deck and bite the dust till your bones ache.

Then you pick yourself up and do it again.

OFF CAMERA: (VOICE OF ASSISTANT DIRECTOR) OK Cut! That's a wrap everybody!

SHERIFF: Let's go buddy.

BANDIT: Boy, am I dry.

ANNCR: But now comes Miller Time. Time to wrap it up and reach for

the best tasting beer you can find.

Miller High Life.

America's quality beer since 1855.

SINGER: (LYRIC) If you've got the time, we've got the beer.

Miller tastes too good to hurry through.

When it's time to relax.

We've got the beer.

VOCAL GROUP: (LYRIC) Miller Beer

1223

Art Directors	Henry Holtzman
	Robert Lenz
Writer	Ken Schuman
Directors	Conrad Hall
	Dick Miller
Producers	Sally Smith
	Dick Standridge
Production Companies	Wexler Hall
	Wakeford, Orloff
Agency	McCann-Erickson, Inc.
Client	Miller Brewing Co.

CHURCH
1-minute

SFX: (NATURAL . . . DISTANT BELL . . . MUSIC)

SFX: (UNDER)

ANNCR (VO): In the summer of 1974, just one year before she was going to be married . . .

Osteo-genic Sarcoma, a form of bone cancer, struck 19-year old . . .

Eva Menetti.

SFX: (NATURAL)

Doctors, using research supported by money you gave the American Cancer Society, tried everything possible to save . . .

her life. One year later, on June 28th . . .

on the day she had planned to be married . . . Eva Minetti became . . .

Eva Ball . . .

(WEDDING MUSIC LOUD)

and walked down the aisle right on schedule.

(MUSIC)

ANNCR (VO): Thanks to your help . . .

we can now save almost half the people who get cancer.

Don't quit on us now.
We're almost half-way there!

1224
Art Director Jon Guliner
Writer Chet Lane
Producer Joanne McShane
Production Company Steve Horn
Agency Benton & Bowles Inc.
Client American Cancer Society

I AM AMERICA
30-second

Only part of me is Black.

Part is Red.

Part is Yellow.

And part of me is White.

I am also part Jew.

Part Catholic.

Part Buddhist. I am America.

I am Swedish, (VOICES CONTINUE BUT UNDER ANNOUNCER)

ANNCR: This is

I am Italian.

ANNCR: Your America.

I am Irish.

ANNCR: If you're full of

Mexican

ANNCR: Brotherly love.

. . . if you're full of brotherly hate . . . this is what your America will become,

ALT: This will be your America if you're full of brotherly hate.

ANNCR (VO): Prejudice is something America can live without.

1225

Art Director	Rosenwasser
Writer	Bob Veder
Production Company	Myers & Griner, Cuesta
Agency	Grey
Client	Anti-Defamation League

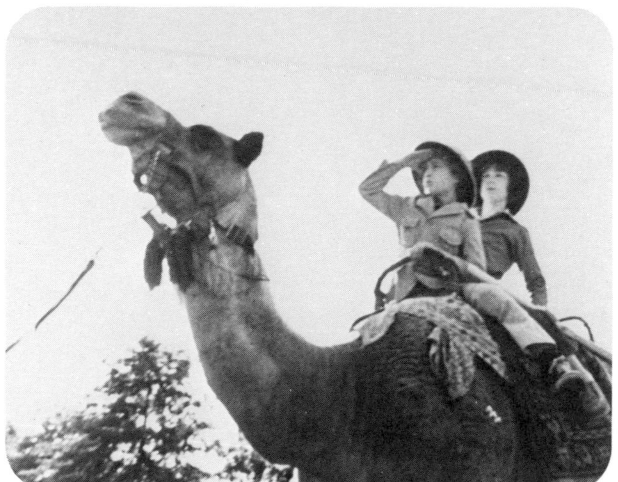

THE GREAT EXPLORER
60-second

LITTLE BOY (VO): Today, I, the great explorer, decided to rescue the lost professor. I grabbed my trusty rifle bearer, and directed my bi-plane deep into the jungle.

OC: I hope our fuel lasts . . .

VO: We first fell upon a sinister world of reptiles.

GIRL OC: He thinks we're lunch.

BOY OC: Courage!

VO: Undaunted, we pressed through a tropical rain forest. Strange birds eyed us suspiciously.

BOY OC: Only 500 more miles.

VO: We plunged into a world of darkness filled with night creatures. Unfortunately, I had to hold my trusty rifle bearer's hand. At last, obtaining a camel, we rode until . . .

OC: I'm here, Professor Schtunkfossel!

PAL OC: It's Norman Crimp, you creep! Got any bubble gum?

VO: As the sun set over the Bronx, I realized, yet another mssion was successfully completed.

1226A

Art Director Richard Brown
Writer Melissa Huffman
Director Andy Jenkins
Production Company Jenkins-Covington
Agency Scali, McCabe & Sloves
Client Bronx Zoo

CLASSROOM
60-second

PROFESSOR: Jensen? (VOICE CALLS OUT "HERE") Lincoln?

LINCOLN: Present, sir.

PROFESSOR: You're new here, aren't you?

LINCOLN: This is my first year in college.

PROFESSOR: But you're listed as a second year government student.

LINCOLN: I'm interested in government administration and I've done a lot of studying . . . sort of on my own.

PROFESSOR: Oh? Then tell us about the Kansas-Nebraska Act of 1854.

LINCOLN: The Kansas-Nebraska Act . . .

ANNCR (VO): If you've been learning on the job, in the military, through independent study, many colleges think you deserve credit for it. Take College Level Examinations and earn college credit.

PROFESSOR: Not bad, Lincoln. Now can anybody tell us something about the battle of Vicksburg?

ANNCR (VO): Get a head start on college. Send a postcard to CLEP, Box 1901, Radio City Station, New York. Get college credit for what you've learned in life.

1226B

Art Directors Brett Shevack
Dennis D'Amico
Writers Laurence Dunst
Dick Tarlow
Director Mike Cuesta
Producer Robin Sherman
Production Company Myers & Griner, Cuesta
Agency Daniel & Charles Associates, Ltd.
Client College Level Examination Board

WHO CARES ABOUT NEW YORK CITY?
20-second

VO: Who cares about New York City?

ROBERT KLEIN: I care. I'm Robert Klein. New York? Well, you can be what you want! You can even, (LOOKING OFF SCREEN) Hey, how are ya? You can even sing on the street! Boo, daa-daa, boo, daa-daa-dee . . .

1227

Art Director	Christine Jurzykowski
Writers	Teletronics International Cinetudes Film Productions, Ltd.
Designer	Neal Marshad
Photographer	Jeff Lion Weinstock (DP)
Director	Neal Marshad
Producer	Christine Jurzykowski
Actor	Robert Klein
Production Company	Cinetudes Film Productions, Ltd.
Agency	Cinetudes Film Productions, Ltd.
Client	Citizens Committee for New York City, Inc.

DIRTY COILS
30-second

SUPER: R-2 D-2, star of "Star Wars." R-2 D-2 says . . . Hello, I am not a native New Yorker,

but I'd like to help you with your energy situation.

Take this refrigerator.

It has condensor coils on the bottom or back.

When they're dirty, your refrigerator uses more power to stay cold. Unplug it for a couple of minutes and vacuum the coils once a month. You'll save energy, and money.

We thank you and the earth thanks you.

SUPER: It doesn't take much energy to save energy.

1228
Art Director Rick Browning
Writer Bonnie Allen
Director Richard Moore
Producers Mel Kane
Richard O'Neill
Production Company STF (Sandler Tape & Film)
Agency Doyle Dane Bernbach
Client New York State Alliance to Save Energy

DIMMIT
30-second

SUPER: R-2 D-2, star of "Star Wars". R-2 D-2 says . . .

Sometimes you earth people use more energy than you need.

Let me shed a little light on the subject . . .

. . . with a solid state dimmer switch.

You can turn it up for reading . . .

. . . down for eating . . .

. . . or way down for whatever.

It makes your energy bills smaller.

Your light bulbs last longer.

And the earth last longer.

So you may never have to worry about this.

SUPER: It doesn't take much energy to save energy.

1229

Art Director Rick Browning
Writer Bonnie Allen
Director Richard Moore
Producers Mel Kane
Richard O'Neill
Production Company STF (Sandler Tape & Film)
Agency Doyle, Dane & Bernbach
Client New York State Alliance to Save Energy

ROOTS
60-second

ANNCR (VO): She grew up in the Bronx, in an orthodox home.

She went to the city schools, the city college. A scholarship sent her to Columbia Law.

She married, worked as a lawyer, had babies,

raised a family, worked—in tenants' rights

cases, labor law, and the early, hopeless

struggles in the kangaroo courts of the South.

She was elected to Congress, shook it to its foundations, and when the dust settled she was one of its leaders.

She made the honor roll of our generation—Nixon's enemies list—and helped launch his impeachment.

Peace, women's rights, human rights—

she was always there, out front, taking the risks.

Loud? Oh Yes! But her loudness helped turn more losing causes into winning causes than a hundred mousier voices. And her greatest cause is New York City. And we need her strength,

her flamboyance,

her fighting spirit

like never before.

Let's make Bella the Mayor.

1230

Art Director	Gene Case
Writer	Gene Case
Editor	Chris Dixon
Director	Arnold Beckerman
Producer	Kimberly Hoeck
Production Company	Beckerman/Mansfield
Agency	Case & McGrath Inc.
Client	Bella Abzug for Mayor Committee

FIGHTER
60-second

ANNCR (VO): A lot of men are running for Mayor. But not one of them is a fighter like . . . Bella.

BELLA: We all want to fight to keep the middle class in the City of New York. And the fundamental of that is to be able to live in housing that we can afford.

It's the tenants who had to conduct their own fights. And that's one of the reasons why I think we need some change in the City of New York! (APPLAUSE)

ANNCR (VO): Now this is a Mayor.
In-exhaust-ible . . .

Ir-resist-able . . .

BELLA: I know when to be soft . . .

(LAUGHTER UNDER)

ANNCR (VO): And nobody pushes her around.

BELLA: . . . and when to be tough! And how to get things done.

ANNCR (VO): And Bella proved it . . . The House of Representatives voted her one of its three most influential members . . .

BELLA (VO): This city needs a leader, somebody who knows how to create a spirit.

. . . And people have to say, 'My God! She's right! I'm going to follow her!' I've had that happen to me before. I think I can do it for the City!

ANNCR (VO): We need a fighter in City Hall like we never needed one before.

Come on . . .

Let's make Bella the Mayor.

1231

Art Director	Gene Case
Writer	Gene Case
Editor	Chris Dixon
Photographer	Arnold Beckerman
Director	Arnold Beckerman
Producer	Kimberly Hoeck
Production Company	Beckerman/Mansfield
Agency	Case & McGrath
Client	Bella Abzug for Mayor

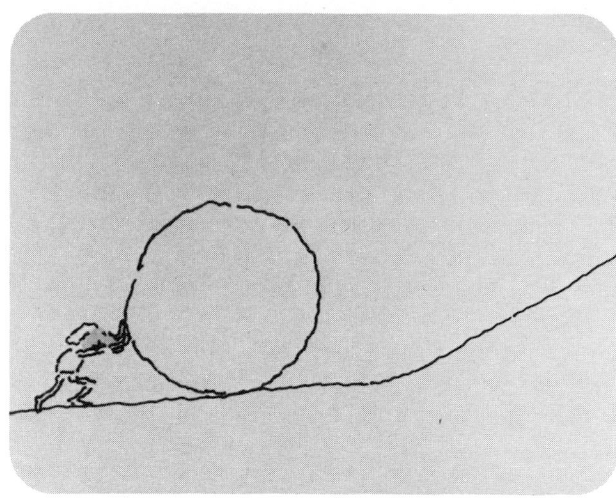

1232
30-second

Gonna Make It Yes I Can
Got Some Friends and Got A Plan
Only Winners Need Apply
We Can Do It
If We Try Work To Winners We
Can Do It If We Try
Gether Ev'ry one
Mov-in Gether Ev'ry one
Movn-Tains can be Done
We're The Moun-tains can be Done
Winners
The Winners
Winners Winners
3

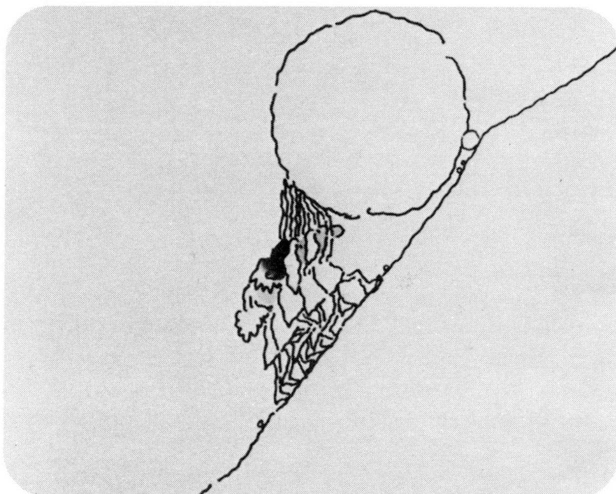

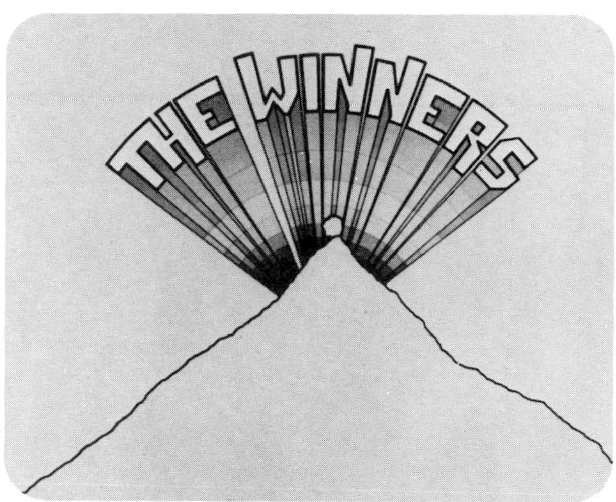

1232

Art Director	Lou Dorfsman
Designers	Lou Dorfsman
	R. O. Blechman
Artist	R. O. Blechman
Director	R. O. Blechman
Producer	R. O. Blechman
Music	Scott-Textor Production
Production Company	R. O. Blechman, Inc.
Agency	CBS/Broadcast Group
Client	CBS Television Network

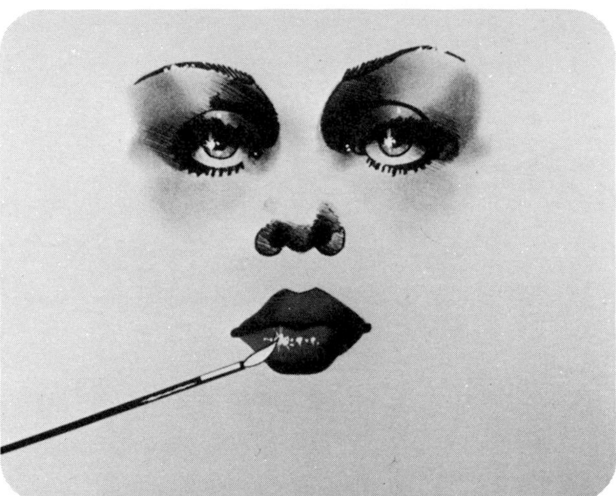

COSMETIC TAG
5-second

COSMETIC TAG: Bring your face to Bloomingdale's. We'll teach it the act of make-up.

FRAGRANCE: Discover the finishing touch to your look. Your scent at Bloomindale's.

1233

Art Director	Bill Casale
Writer	Marty Regen
Designer	Bill Casale
Artist	Michael Vollbrichdt
Director	Buz Potemkin
Producers	Catherine Land Regina Ebel
Music	Dick Lausky Michael Cohen
Production Company	Perpetual Motion Pictures Inc.
Agency	Grey
Client	Bloomingdale's

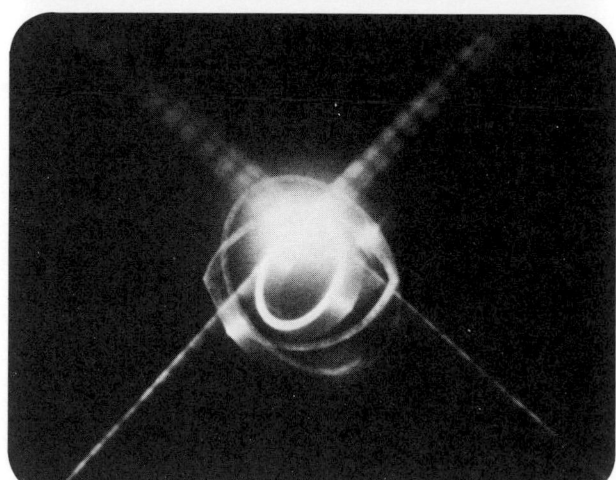

THE CBS 6:30 MOVIE
22-second

FRAMES: #1 Bronze rings slowly spin together toward the camera.

#2 Rings come together to form CBS eye.

#3 Zoom through eye to reveal a field of glints that start to form logo.

#4 Logo revealed.

1234

Art Director	Tom Gericke
Designers	John LePrevost
	Tony Valdez
	Tom Gericke
Photographers	Ray Mercer & Co.
	Hogan & Lee Images
Director	Tom Gericke
Producer	Tom Gericke
Music	Thom Bell
Production Company	KNXT-TV
Agency	KNXT-TV
Client	KNXT-TV

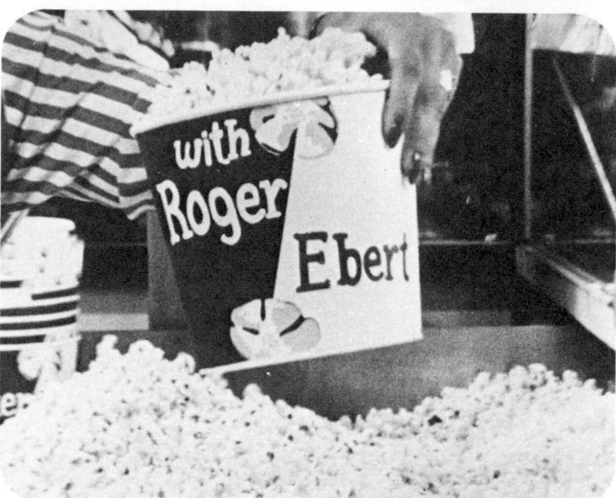

SNEAK PREVIEWS
40-second

Music—theme
Music—theme
Music—theme
Music—theme w/SOF
Music—theme w/SOF
Music—theme w/Sound Effects
Music—theme w/SOF
Music—theme w/SOF
Music—theme
Music—theme w/SOF
Music—theme w/SOF
Music—theme w/Sound Effect
Music—theme w/Sound Effect
Music—theme w/SOF
Music—theme w/SOF
Music—theme w/SOF
Music—theme

1235A
Art Director Patterson Denny
Artist Carolyn Gleeson
Photographer Cal Langenberg
Director Patterson Denny
Producer Thea Flaum
Music "Showing Off"
Agency WTTW-TV Chicago
Client Television program "Sneak Previews"

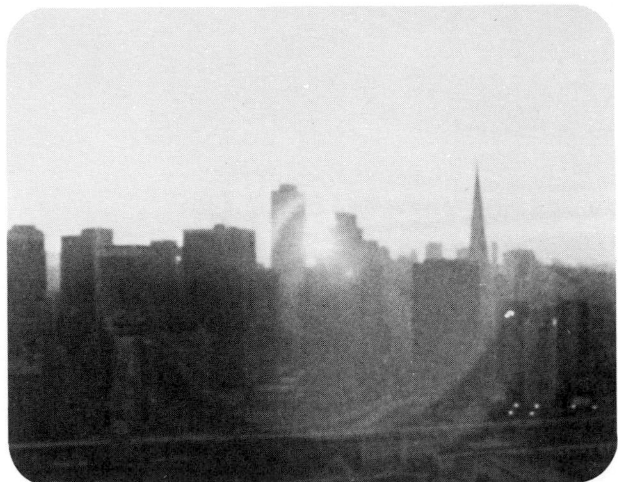

T.V. SIGN ON—SIGN OFF
90-second

MUSIC: Single piano playing "Star Spangled Banner"

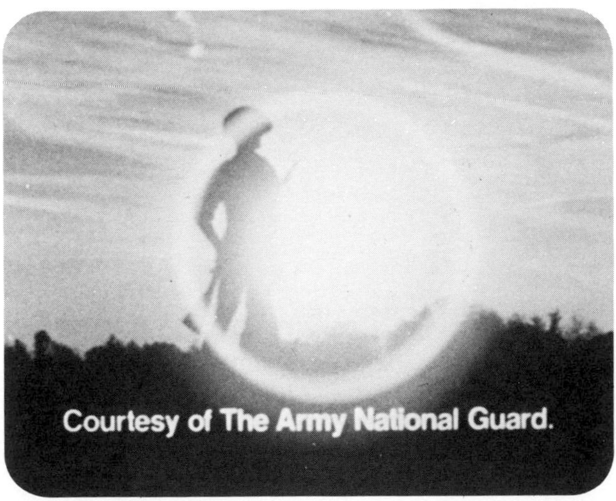
Courtesy of The Army National Guard.

1235B

Art Director Stan Sweeney
Writer Lou Gunshol
Editor Bob Smallheiser/First Edition
Directors Ron Scheffer
Paul Kramer
Producer Ed Pollack
Music Stock
Production Company The Production Company
Agency W. B. Doner & Company
Client The National Guard Bureau

SEASONS
40-second

A) Channel 2 welcomes you to Spring.

B) Channel 2 welcomes you to Summer.

C) Channel 2 welcomes you to Fall.

D) Channel 2 welcomes you to Winter.

1236

Art Director Jerry Greenberg
Writer Jerry Greenberg
Designer Milton Glaser
Artist Milton Glaser
Director Staff
Producer Harold Friedman
Music Vivaldi
Production Company Harold Friedman Consortium
Client WBBM-TV Channel 2 Chicago

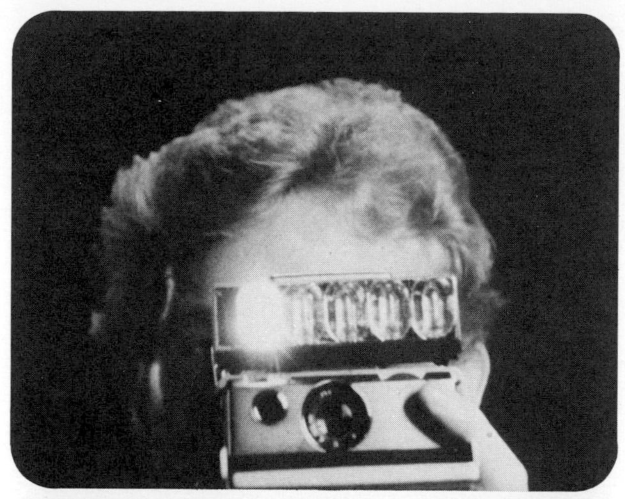

LONDON CONVENTION OPENING
2-minute, 45-second

Opens with man in the distance, walking towards the viewer, slowly getting closer.

He stops, raises a small camera to his face and snaps a series of five flash photos.

He pulls the undeveloped picture from his camera.

A series of 5 undeveloped photos are shown being passed from hand to hand.

The 5th undeveloped photo remains on the screen and it slowly develops into a still shot of the group BOSTON. The still shot changes to a live performance of the same group doing "More Than A Feeling."

Photo dissolves into TEDDY PENDERGRASS doing "I Don't Love You Anymore."

Photo dissolves into TED NUGENT doing "Cat Scratch Fever."

Photo dissolves into HEART doing "Barracuda."

Photo dissolves into KANSAS doing "Carry On Wayward Son."

Photo dissolves into EARTH, WIND, & FIRE doing "Saturday Nite."

Photo dissolves into BOZ SCAGGS doing "Lowdown."

Photo dissolves into AEROSMITH doing "Back In The Saddle."

Photo dissolves into BARBRA STREISAND doing "My Heart Belongs To Me."

Last shot is of photo reading:
AT CBS RECORDS
ARTIST DEVELOPMENT
IS OUR ART
With Streisand music playing under.

1237
Art Director Arnold Levine
Writer Arnold Levine
Designer Arnold Levine
Artist Arnold Levine
Photographer Ted Churchill
Director Arnold Levine
Producer Bonnie Brand
Production Company CBS Records
Publisher CBS Records
Agency CBS Records
Client CBS Records

ADC FILM

Music Under

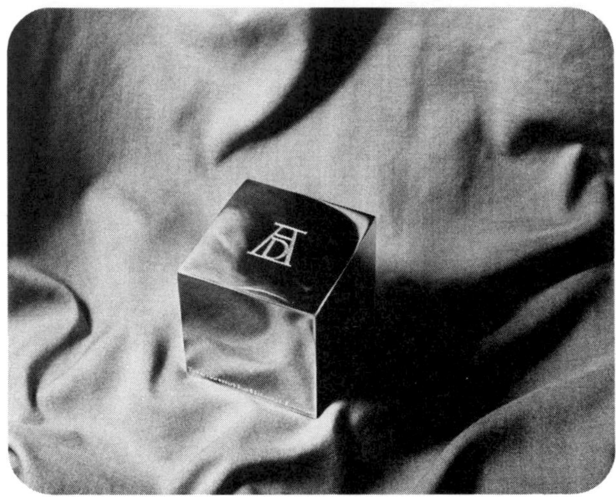

1238

Art Directors	Herb Lubalin Bernie Owett
Designers	Herb Lubalin Bernie Owett
Cameraman	Dick Rauh
Directors	Herb Lubalin Bernie Owett
Production Company	Completion Inc.
Agency	LSC&P Design Group
Client	The Art Directors Club

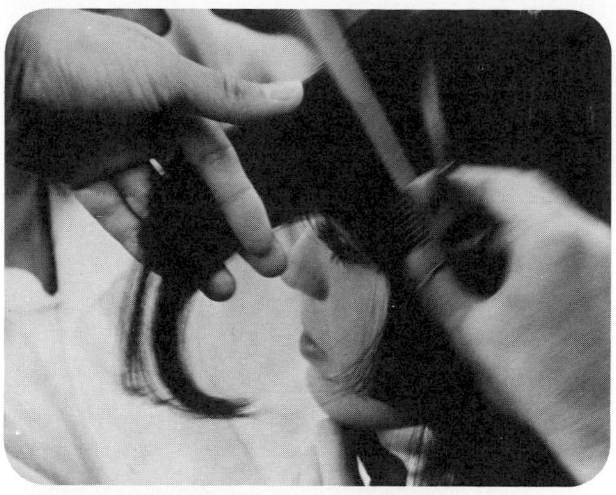

MARIE
60-second

A teenage Marie Osmond is transformed into an elegant young woman.

DONNY OSMOND: Marie
You've done some changing
Marie
Some rearranging
Marie
The transformation's wild!
That child! I've known has grown!!
Your smile
So sweet and sassy
Your style!
A chic and classy new gal!
But still my pal
That's Marie

MARIE: That's me

DONNY: Marie

1239

Art Director Richard Avedon
Editor Richard Audd
Artist Jack Horton
Director Richard Avedon
Producers Larry Sullivan
Harry Marks
Music Irving Berlin
Earl Brown (lyric)
Production Company Richard Avedon Productions
Agency Sullivan & Marks Inc.
Client ABC-TV

ABC COMEDY SPECIAL
10-second

Man is attacked by a duck which comes from his television set. He subdues the duck by throwing a pie at the television.

Music, effects.

1240

Art Director Harry Marks
Writer Leonard Glasser
Designer Leonard Glasser
Artist Leonard Glasser
Director Leonard Glasser
Producer Leonard Glasser
Production Company Sullivan & Marks Inc.
Agency Sullivan & Marks Inc.
Client ABC-TV

Hall of Fame

1972	M. F. Agha
	Lester Beall
	Alexey Brodovitch
	A. M. Cassandre
	René Clarke
	Robert Gage
	William Golden
	Paul Rand
1973	Charles Coiner
	Paul Smith
	Jack Tinker
1974	Will Burtin
	Leo Lionni
1975	Gordon Aymar
	Herbert Bayer
	Heyworth Campbell
	Alexander Liberman
	L. Moholy-Nagy
	Cipe Pineles
1976	E. McKnight Kauffer
	Herbert Matter
1977	Saul Bass
	Herb Lubalin
	Bradbury Thompson
1978	Thomas M. Cleland
	Lou Dorfsman
	Allen Hurlbuert
	George Lois

This year's elections to the Art Directors Club Hall of Fame include three men active in the field and one deceased.

Lou Dorfsman, George Lois and Allen Hurlburt continue at the work which earned them their places in the Hall.

Thomas Maitland Cleland died in 1964. His election signals the beginning of an effort on the part of the Hall of Fame committee to honor the greats of the early years of the profession. The Hall of Fame being a recent institution, the committee feels that a danger exists of underestimating the value of the work done by the pioneers.

So it was decided to set aside one place each year to be awarded to a candidate who has finished his life's work at the time of the election.

The following sixteen pages will be different in format from the rest of this book, because we have asked each new member of the Hall of Fame to design his own four-page spread. How better to show the work which earned them the highest honor their peers can bestow?

The four-page spread on Thomas M. Cleland was designed by Bradbury Thompson, and written by John McCormick, with photography by Sharon Good.

Committee Members:
Herb Lubalin, Chairman
Gennaro Andreozzi
Robert O. Bach
William Brockmeier
William Buckley
Aaron Burns
Cipe Pineles Burtin
David Davidian
David Deutsch
William Duffy
Lee Epstein
Michael Fenga
Carl Fischer
Arthur Hawkins
Walter Kaprielian
Eugene Milbauer
Tony Palladino
Dick Ross
Ernest Scarfone
Eileen Hedy Schultz
Robert S. Smith
Bradbury Thompson

Thomas M. Cleland, self-portrait, 1940

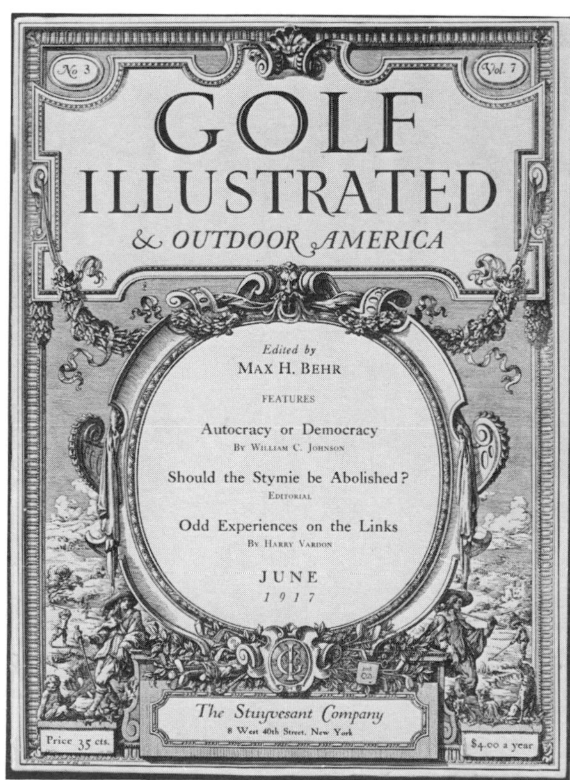

Golf Illustrated magazine, cover, 1917

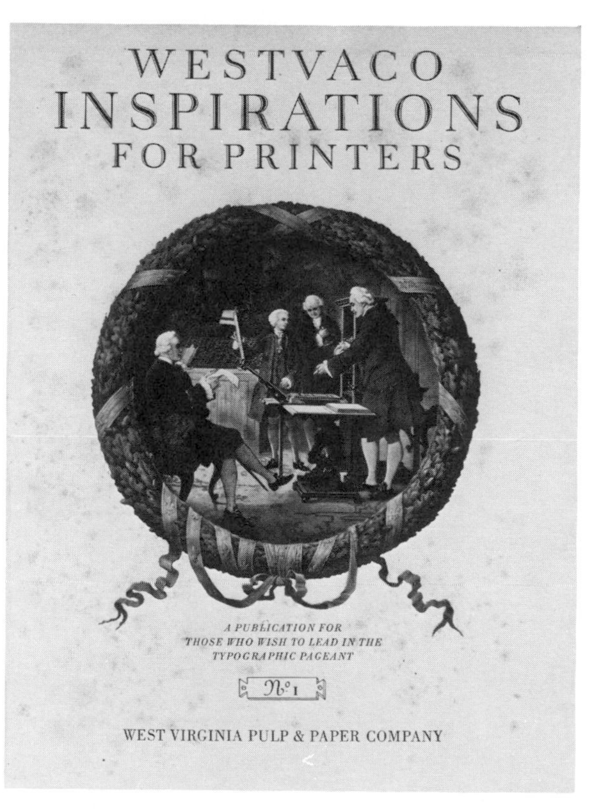

Westvaco Inspirations, No. 1, format and cover, 1925

THOMAS M. CLELAND

Thomas Maitland Cleland was among the first practitioners of the new profession of art directing. A complete art director, he was a well-developed artist, typographer, editor and printer who designed whole pages and whole booklets. His advertisements and marketing booklets for Locomobile and Cadillac automobiles are typical of his elegant and enduring work.

While those less specialized times required great versatility of every art director, Cleland was unusual among them. His personal papers are replete with correspondence and articles which picture him as a painstaking designer, artist and craftsman, whose knowledge of his several disciplines was encyclopedic.

Born in Brooklyn in 1880, Thomas Cleland set his career course at the age of fifteen when he enrolled in a course in applied ornament at The Artist-Artisan Institute of New York. While still a young man, he "... owned and operated three different picayune printing plants, all of them notable as exceptionally unprofitable enterprises ..." However, he credited these experiences with teaching him his expert knowledge of the printing trades.

One of Cleland's talents was type designing. He created Della Robbia, still in common use, in 1903. And the type which you are now reading was closely adapted from the ATF Garamond, which he designed with M.F. Benton in 1917. A superb illustrator as well, Cleland expended extraordinary effort in pursuit of perfection, once spending six years to design and illustrate one book.

In 1907–08, as the art director of McClure's Magazine, Cleland completely redesigned the periodical. Later, he was retained by Fortune Magazine to design the magazine and to act as its art director. The cover of Fortune's first issue, February 1930, is still cited as a masterpiece of classical design. In 1937, Cleland planned a new typographic style for Newsweek and later designed the newspaper PM, probably the first time a complete newspaper was ever truly designed.

Cleland was not easy to work with. His knowledge of the printing and typography trades enabled him to give detailed instruction to printers on how to do their jobs, and his insistence on perfection made meeting deadlines an uncertain task. Publisher George Macy wrote to Cleland in 1942, "The history books will, of course, refer to you as a sensitive and conscientious artist; and those adjectives will look wonderful after you and I have departed this earth. But just think how much simpler your life would be, not only your life in the past, but your life in the future, if you were a trifle less sensitive and a trifle less conscientious."

From the beginning, Cleland's work was recognized for its excellence and precision, and he received many honors both formal and informal. The American Institute of Graphic Arts, The Art Directors Club and the Harvard Business School, among others, recognized his work, and his design of PM earned him the Ayer Award.

And he was a writer of no mean talent. His critical comments about trends which he saw as diminishing his craft were made less biting by his wit and self-deprecating good humor.

Cleland's attitude toward art and technology might make him an expensive anomaly in today's world of business art, but his contributions to the art direction of his time were unsurpassed and will remain as a tribute to a consummate and complete art director.

Fortune magazine, No. 1, format and cover, 1930

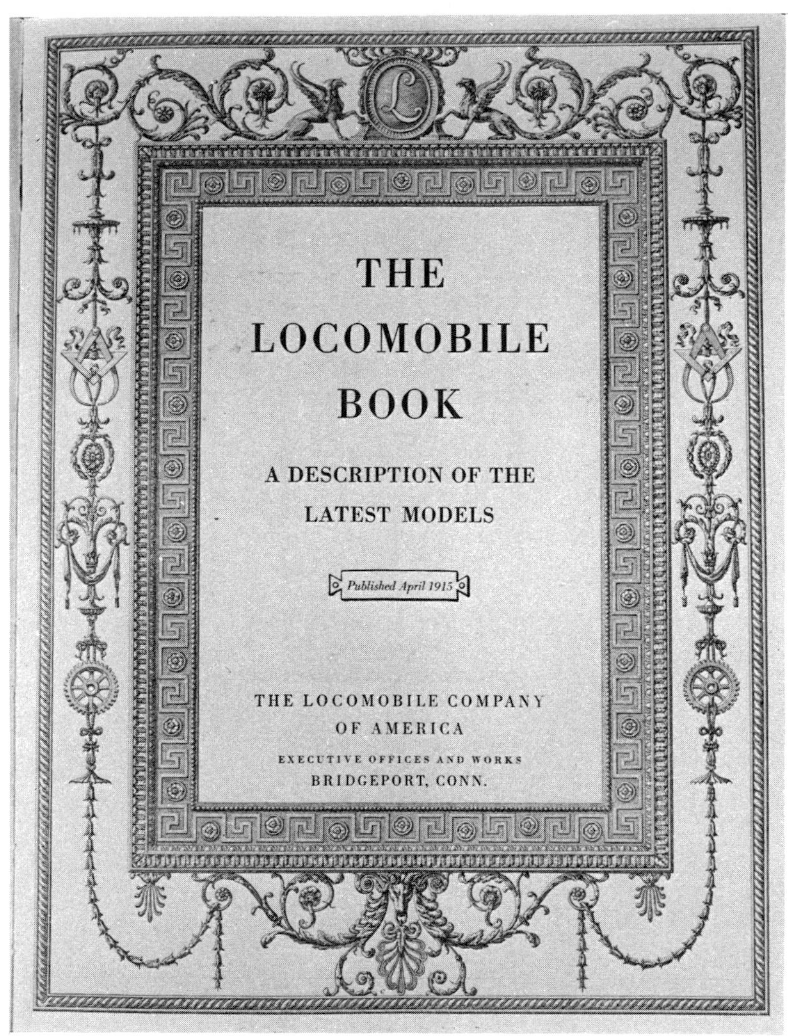

Locomobile booklet, cover, 1915

Locomobile booklet, cover, 1917

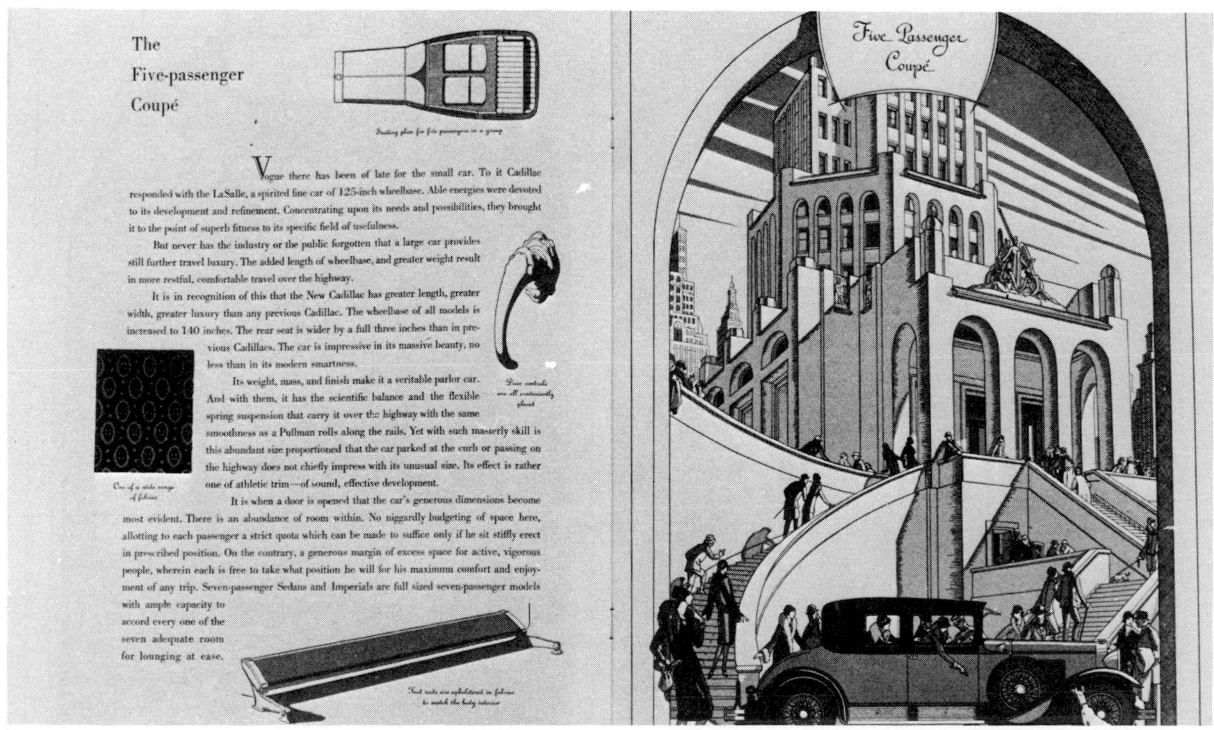

The
Five-passenger
Coupé

Vogue there has been of late for the small car. To it Cadillac responded with the LaSalle, a spirited fine car of 125-inch wheelbase. Able energies were devoted to its development and refinement. Concentrating upon its needs and possibilities, they brought it to the point of superb fitness to its specific field of usefulness.

But never has the industry or the public forgotten that a large car provides still further travel luxury. The added length of wheelbase, and greater weight result in more restful, comfortable travel over the highway.

It is in recognition of this that the New Cadillac has greater length, greater width, greater luxury than any previous Cadillac. The wheelbase of all models is increased to 140 inches. The rear seat is wider by a full three inches than in previous Cadillacs. The car is impressive in its massive beauty, no less than in its modern smartness.

Its weight, mass, and finish make it a veritable parlor car. And with them, it has the scientific balance and the flexible spring suspension that carry it over the highway with the same smoothness as a Pullman rolls along the rails. Yet with such masterly skill is this abundant size proportioned that the car parked at the curb or passing on the highway does not chiefly impress with its unusual size. Its effect is rather one of athletic trim—of sound, effective development.

It is when a door is opened that the car's generous dimensions become most evident. There is an abundance of room within. No niggardly budgeting of space here, allotting to each passenger a strict quota which can be made to suffice only if he sit stiffly erect in prescribed position. On the contrary, a generous margin of excess space for active, vigorous people, wherein each is free to take what position he will for his maximum comfort and enjoyment of any trip. Seven-passenger Sedans and Imperials are full sized seven-passenger models with ample capacity to accord every one of the seven adequate room for lounging at ease.

Cadillac booklet, spread, 1928

Westvaco Inspirations, cover, 1939

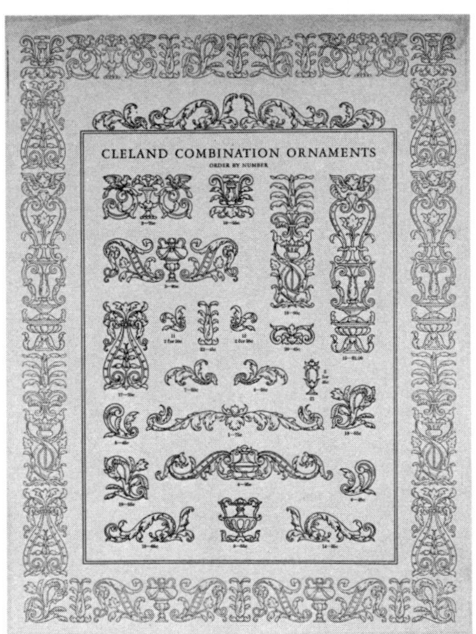

ATF Cleland ornaments, ca. 1923

Trademark designs, ca. 1920

It was in 1944, while Lou Dorfsman was serving with a public relations unit of the U.S. Army in Dallas, Texas, that he discovered CBS—in that year's Art Directors Club Annual, of all places. CBS was well represented by intelligent and provocative work of high graphic standards, evidence of what was even then a long-standing corporate tradition of design excellence and logic.

Lou made up his mind to work there. After all, hadn't he just won the first and second prizes for poster design in a national U.S. Army art contest?

At war's end, Lou applied to CBS and became a staff designer. Lou describes working conditions at CBS as "a designer's hothouse, conducive to personal growth."

And grow he did!

His responsibilities began with radio, grew to embrace TV. His responsibilities have

JEROME
SNYDER
ARTIST
WRITER
CRITIC
GOURMET
NOTARY
PUBLIC

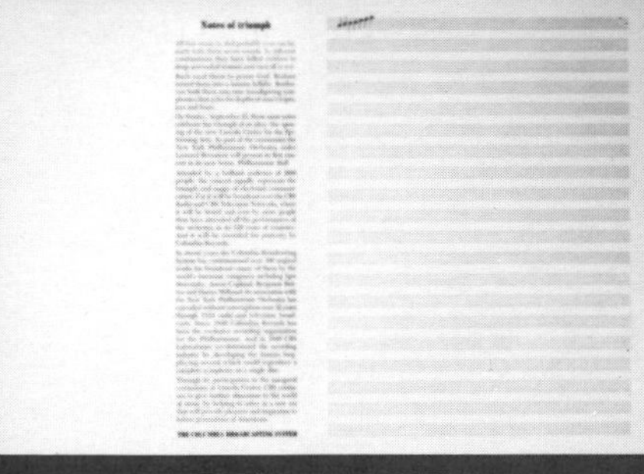

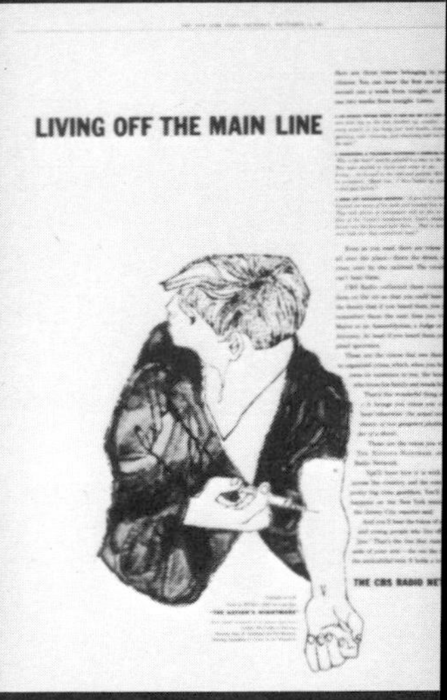

Nixon watches Kosygin.
Kosygin watches Mao.
Mao watches Ho.
Ho watches Ky
(Who watches Thieu).
Nasser watches Dayan.
Dayan watches DeGaulle.
DeGaulle watches Nixon.
Cronkite watches Everybody.

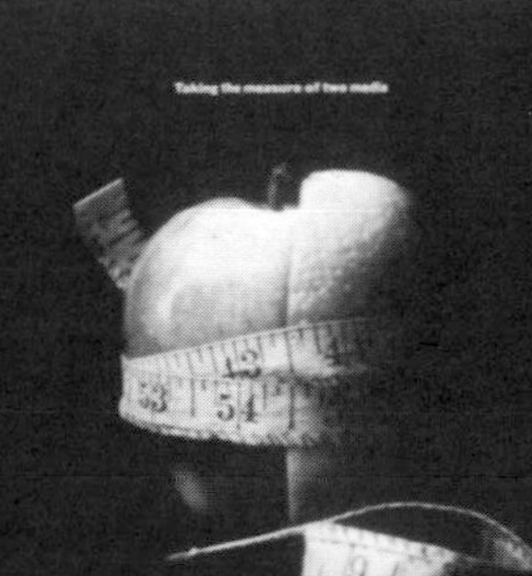

First of a seven-part series

"Black History: Lost, Stolen or Strayed."

OF BLACK AMERICA

10 TONIGHT CBS NEWS 2

You always said you wanted grandchildren.

Change. You can see it coming on The Five CBS Stations

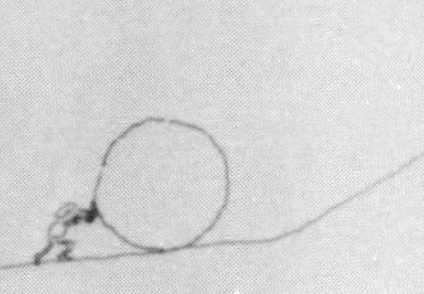

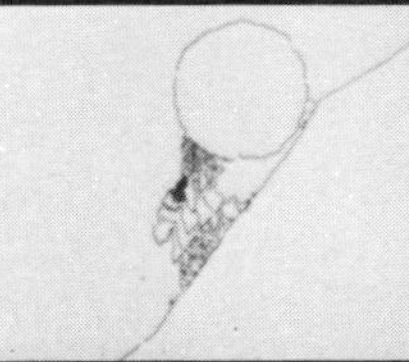

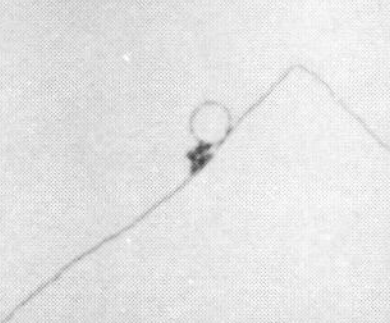

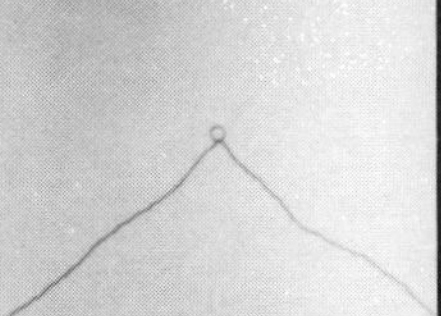

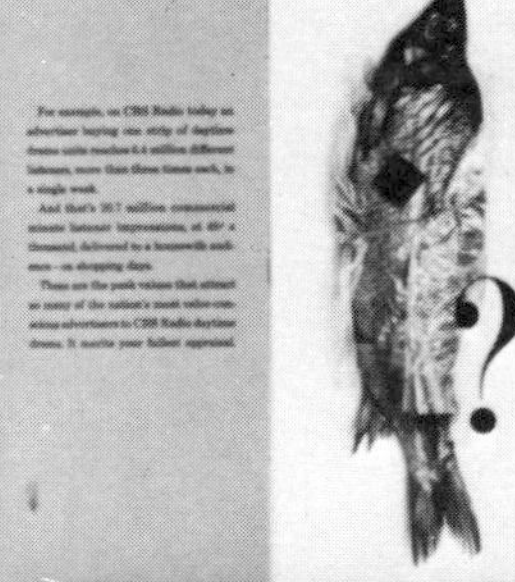

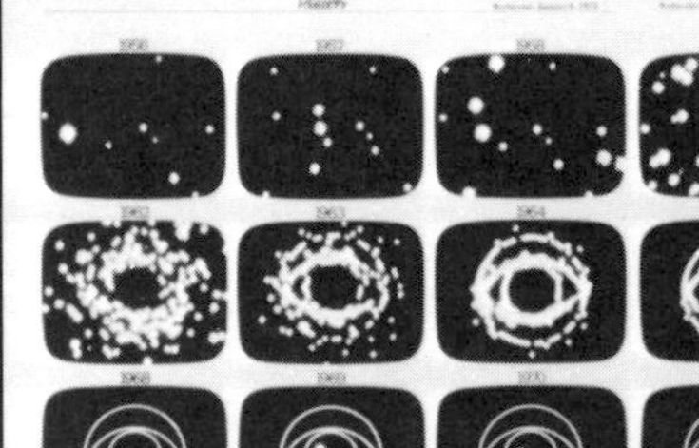

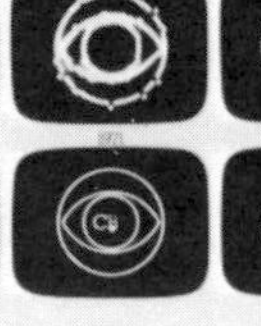

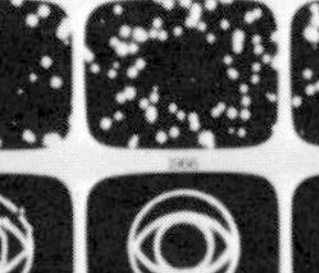

Year after year CBS outshines them all... the number one network for 19 star-studded years in a row.

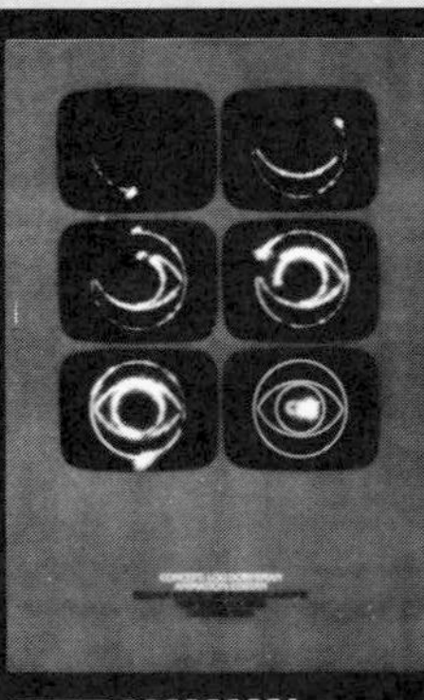

FRANK STANTON
WE CITE YOU, SIR, FOR
HIGHEST ACHIEVEMENT IN THE
PUBLIC INTEREST AND IN THE FORWARD PROGRESS
OF THE BROADCAST MEDIA

A flood of money, from
$100 checks to a nickel
pasted on a board.

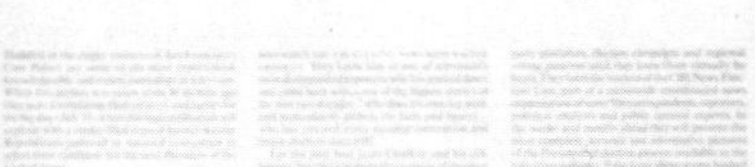

10

11

12

WHITE VS WHITE
WHITE VS BLACK
BLACK VS BLACK
BLACK VS WHITE
WHITE VS YELLOW
YELLOW VS YELLOW
YELLOW VS BROWN
BROWN VS BROWN

WATCH THE
WORLDWATCHERS
CBS NEWS

(We did it!)

The CBS Television Network

expanded over the years and now include all corporate design as well.

A believer in the elegance of simplicity, Lou considers that his concepts and visual expressions of twenty-five years ago to be valid today, except for typographic style.

Hall of Famer Herb Lubalin, Lou's classmate at Cooper Union, tells us that all of his work has been influenced by what Lou has done throughout the years.

Milton Glaser calls Lou "quite simply, the best corporate designer in the world."

Hall of Famer Saul Bass, when he heard he would be asked for a comment, left for Europe for five weeks!

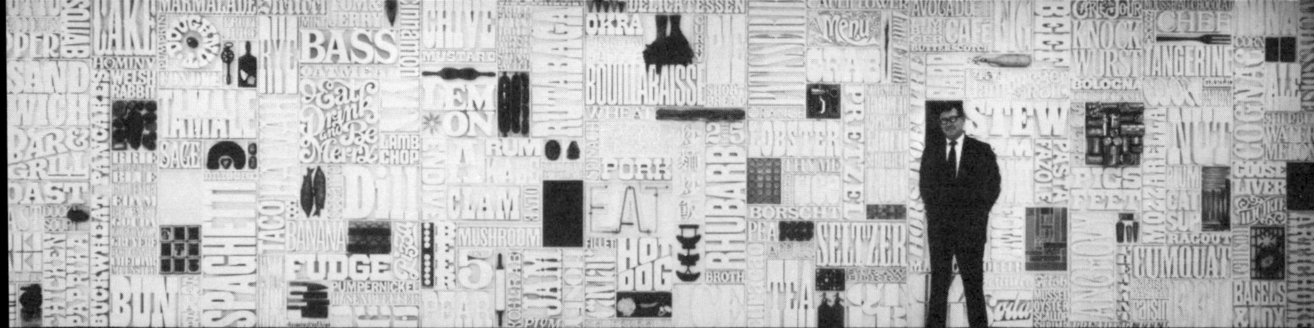

Allen Hurlburt

photo by William Joli

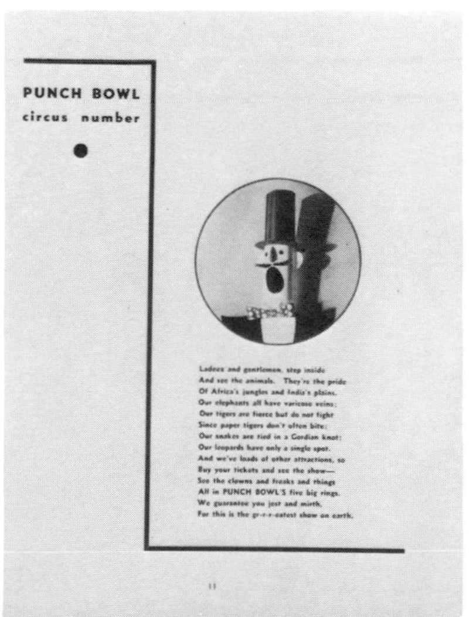

PUNCH BOWL
circus number

Ladies and gentlemen, step inside
And see the animals. They're the pride
Of Africa's jungles and India's plains.
Our elephants all have varicose veins;
Our tigers are fierce but do not fight
Since paper tigers don't often bite;
Our snakes are tied in a Gordian knot;
Our leopards have only a single spot.
And we've loads of other attractions, so
Buy your tickets and see the show—
See the clowns and freaks and things
All in PUNCH BOWL'S five big rings.
We guarantee you jest and mirth,
For this is the gr-r-r-eatest show on earth.

11

1932 early magazine layout

Allen Hurlburt is best known for his magazine design and his creative use of photographic images during the sixties and magazines were his principal design focus almost from the beginning. Born in 1910, by the time he was 21 years old he was both editor and designer of *Punch Bowl* at the University of Pennsylvania. It was only a college magazine, but it was good enough to elicit a note of praise from Dr. Agha, art director of *Vanity Fair,* when Punch Bowl did a parody of that magazine. That same year he had his first encounter with the work of Alexey Brodovitch at an exhibition at the N.W. Ayer gallery, and although he never worked or studied under either of these men, they both came to exert a profound influence on his development as a designer.

His design education was unorthodox, to say the least, consisting of a carefully orchestrated series of elective courses in drawing, architectural rendering, and psychology combined with a Wharton School major in advertising. In 1932 he graduated with a BS degree into a world of breadlines and nearly non-existent job opportunities for graphic designers.

After a few years as a free lance magazine cartoonist his career began in earnest when he became assistant designer with the publisher of eight business magazines including *Advertising & Selling* and the *American Printer.* Within a year he was art director of all eight of them.

Allen Hurlburt's career like many others was interrupted by the war and he served for three years in the infantry receiving a battlefield commission in France. On his return in 1946 he became art director of the National Broadcasting Company and participated in the important formative years of television graphics and promotion. In 1951 he moved to a position of administrative art director under Paul Rand at the Weintraub agency. Although he soon learned that advertising was not his central interest, he would have considered meeting and working with Paul

the Outrageous

"There's only one thing that really means anything to me and that's the Hell's Angels patch I wear. I can get me anything else—a new bike, a new old lady or money—but I can't get me another patch." "We've had a few deaths this year, but otherwise, it's been a good year. By that I mean we haven't had much police harassment." ". . . It's like being brothers. Like, every man in the club's your brother." "Power. That's what it feels like when we ride in. On a three-day weekend, we might have one-fifty, two-hundred bikes out on a run. People all get excited when they see us coming, and—I don't know—it's beautiful." ". . . You know what it is, it's a mind-blower. They come around with movie cameras. It's really beautiful." "If somebody messed up one of our brothers, it would be complete retaliation. An eye for an eye." ". . . My brothers—that's my whole life. My brothers. It's all I've got."

continued

1968 *Look* spread: photo Irving Penn

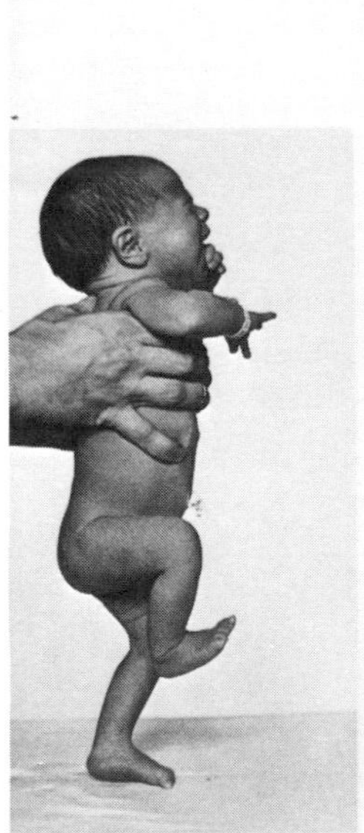

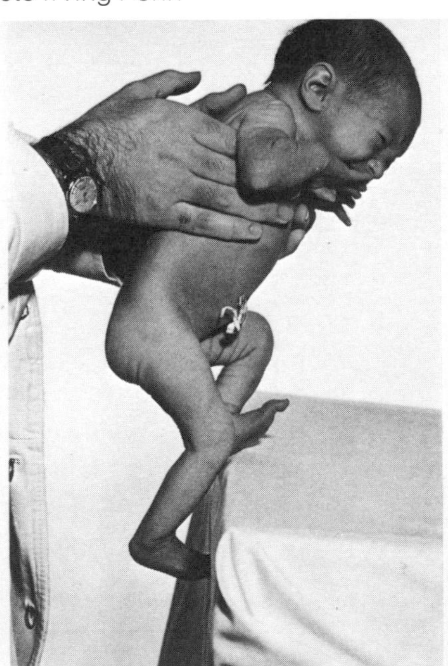

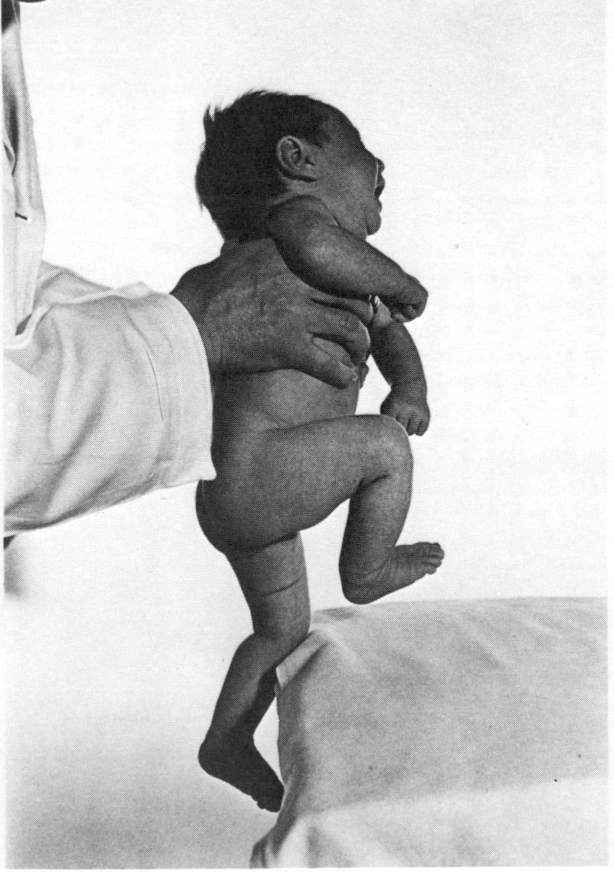

A baby is born knowing how to "walk," but soon "forgets."

Nobody knows why, but newborn babies have a walking reflex. The baby at the left is only two days old, yet when his foot is touched to the table, he lifts it as if he were stepping forward. When the baby's shin is touched to the edge of the table (above), he lifts his leg to overcome the obstacle. At six weeks (right), a baby still does this. By 12 weeks, he should lose these reflexes, if his development is normal. While such neurological tests have value, doctors are cautious in drawing conclusions about young babies: most wait till 16 weeks before making a judgment.

continued

56

1966 *Look* spread: photo Robert Freson

Rand reward enough if he had not met someone even more important there—his wife, Regina.

The high point of his career was the years he spent at *Look* magazine between 1953 and 1971 including fifteen years as its art director. At *Look,* under the leadership of Gardner Cowles and the inspired editorial direction of Dan Mich, Hurlburt's innovative page design and understanding use of photographs and artwork made *Look* one of the most respected magazines in the design world.

Throughout his career Allen Hurlburt received a wide measure of recognition for his work. He was honored with over a dozen Art Directors Club gold medals for his designs at NBC and *Look;* he was awarded the golden T-square as art director of the year by the National Society of Art Directors in 1965 and he received the American Institute of Graphic Arts gold medal in 1973. In commenting about his awards he points out with characteristic directness, "Of course, a lot of it was being in the right place at the right time, but I was also fortunate that so many people—staff, photographers, and artists—often did their best work for me."

It was natural that his own do-it-yourself design education and his continuing curiosity about the design process would lead to his involvement in education. He was program chairman of the International Design Conference at Aspen on "Design Sources and Resources" in 1966. He has served as a trustee, senior lecturer, and curriculum consultant at Parsons School of Design. He has written three books: *Publication Design,* first published in 1971 with a revised edition in 1977; *Layout,* published in 1977 and already in its third printing; and his newest book *The Grid* scheduled for publication in 1978.

Allen Hurlburt is a life member of the Art Directors Club, a fellow of the Royal Society of Arts, and a member of the Alliance Graphique Internationale. Since 1974 he has lived in London with his wife Regina and his daughter Susan, where he continues his teaching, writing and design research.

1947 NBC folder: art Joe Kaufman

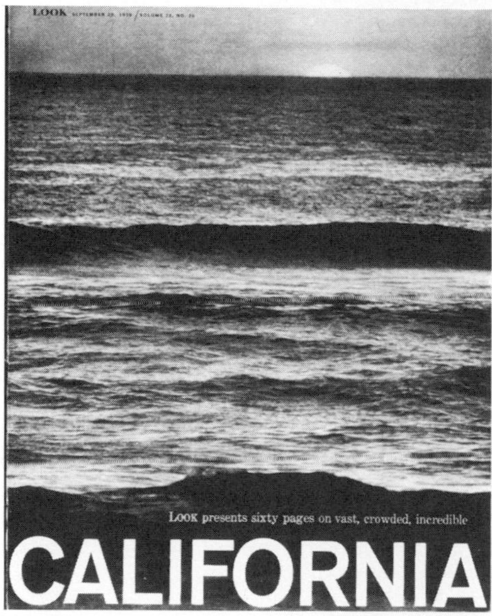

1959 *Look* page: photo Cal Bernstein

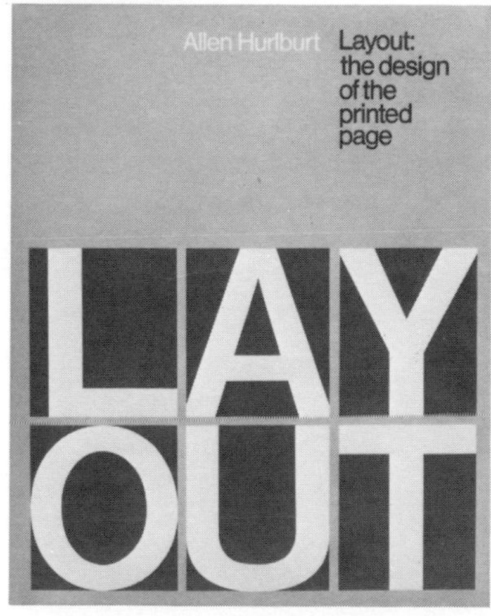

1977 cover for book on design

THE SIXTIES

OUR UNBELIEVABLE DECADE

WHAT OTHER TEN YEARS have been so loaded with tragedy, triumph and change? As America hurtles into the Seventies, the mood is very different from what it was in 1960—complacent. Like most of us, I've been shook up, torn apart and exhilarated during the Sixties. I was shaken by assassination after incredible assassination. I was torn to see generation against generation, man against man, white against black. My ears ached with the echo of protest. Protest. PROTEST! And I was lifted up, out of myself, purged, when the impossible *happened*—three men made it to the moon. (The Mets and the moon the same year!)

We are caught in the riptide of two revolutions that started in the Sixties: the young struggling to overthrow the bureaucracy-bound Establishment and the blacks to possess their long-overdue rights. NOW. There has been a determination to cut through the crap, as the young insist on saying. But it has caused some traditions to be ruthlessly jettisoned. The hippie phenomenon, a protest against the fakery and money-mindedness of middle- and upper-class life, has also been a convenient poncho for the lazy and the nogoodnik to hide under. School protests became so widespread it was obvious some were protesting for the sake of protesting. The revolt against censorship of any kind bared breasts and bottoms of all shapes and sizes, few of them worthy of exposure. It also plopped us into a mud bath of pornography. Some of the costumes worn by the young, including mine, made a stroll in the park a hilarious experience. Ladies' pants-suits, including mine, and male hair became symbols of personal freedom—while in Vietnam the war ground on, in Appalachia a child starved, in Hollywood a girl walked out of a window because she was high on LSD.

The decade had started so bright-hopefully. When John Fitzgerald Kennedy was inaugurated that windy January day in 1961 (with Robert Frost, bareheaded in the cold, reading a poem), he brought class, cool and culture with him to the White House. He started the Peace Corps. Jackie invited Casals to play. The President made a mistake—Cuba—and he promised South Vietnam assistance against Communism. But the young believed.

After less than three years in office, he was shot and killed riding in an open car down a sun-drenched Dallas avenue. Jackie (right, with his brother Robert, Caroline and John) buried him in Arlington as, on TV, the nation watched—and wept. PATRICIA COFFIN

12 LOOK 12-30-69 PRODUCED BY PATRICIA COFFIN AND ALLEN HURLBURT

1969 *Look* spread: photo Marvin Newman

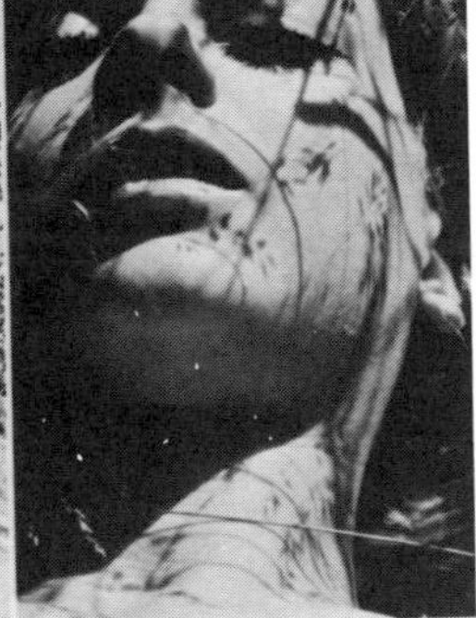

All snowflakes . . . and all women are alike, yet different

Beauty. Snowfall in the forest; the loveliness of women; the exciting forms and colors of modern life. If you delight in the many faces of beauty, then you understand why beauty is "its own excuse for being" in *Look* Magazine and why *Family Circle* Magazine is so deeply involved in the beautiful world of women.

Cowles Communications *EDUCATION THROUGH INFORMATION: A TOTAL APPROACH.*

Cowles (pronounced *Coals*) enriches and extends human experience through *Look*, *Family Circle* and *Venture* Magazines; through television and radio, newspapers, professional and business publications, a growing list of books for in-school and continuing adult education; and through *Xograph* 3-dimensional reproductions.

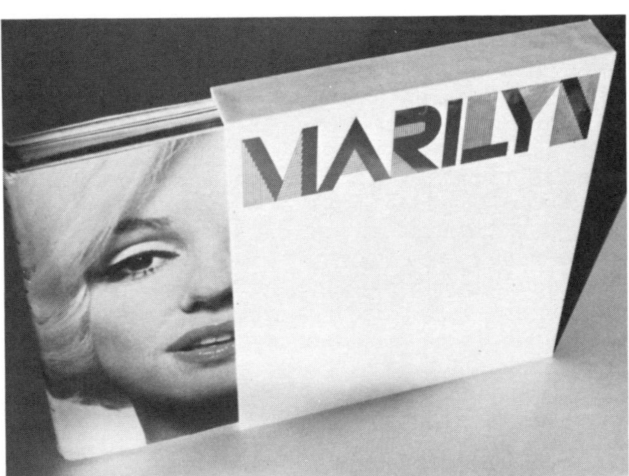

1973 *Marilyn:* cover photo Bert Stern

1971 CCI advertisement:
photos Ernst Haas, Irving Penn

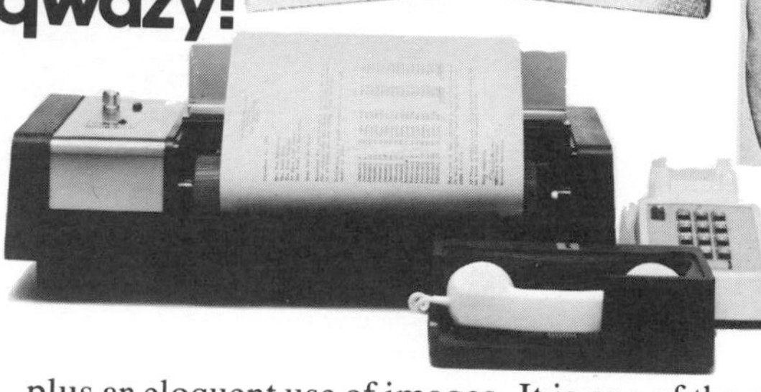

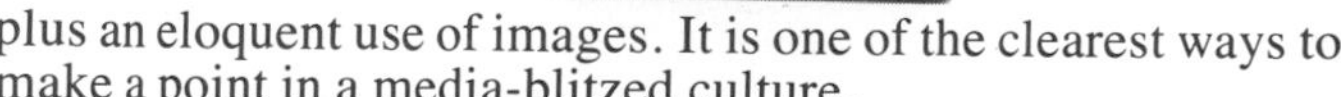

A guide to George Lois

(From the widely praised introduction by Bill Pitts to the widely praised "The Art of Advertising" by George Lois. Pitts and Lois have worked together in three agencies that have borne Lois's name, including the maverick art director's newest agency, Lois Pitts Gershon.)

Everything begins with the word, especially with George Lois, an art director by craft, an advertising man by profession. He has stretched the limits of his craft and challenged the ways of his profession by using pictures as words, words as pictures, and pictures with words as no creative personality before him. He has pushed the role of art director from artisan of design to the shaper of ideas. He is probably America's most resourceful art director and surely its most prolific. If one can agree with Marshall McLuhan that "historians and archaeologists will one day discover that the ads of our time are the richest and most faithful daily reflections any society ever made of its entire range of activities," the work of George Lois says volumes about America of the fifties, sixties and seventies.

His 1963 Esquire cover of Sonny Liston as Santa Claus (note the prehistoric year) has been called "one of the greatest social statements of the plastic arts since Picasso's Guernica."

His 1969 campaign for Braniff gave to the language, for better or worse, "When you got it, flaunt it!"

His passionate, volunteer 1975 battle for Rubin Hurricane Carter made Lois a lightning rod that drew down bolts of criticism from friends and colleagues and clients. Disarming, disturbing work that keeps piercing the curtain of communications overkill.

Is it advertising?

Is it commercial art?

It it commercial?

Is it art?

It is certainly vintage Lois, the pointed message that riddles our defenses and roils the juices, an artful distillation of words plus an eloquent use of images. It is one of the clearest ways to make a point in a media-blitzed culture.

George Lois is the son of an immigrant Greek florist whose name was Haralampos. Vasilike was his mother's name. His two older sisters are Hariclea and Paraskeve. He was born and raised as a true Greek Orthodox youth (including membership in The Sons of Pericles) in the Irish Kingsbridge section of the upper Bronx, between the shadows of the Broadway I.R.T. el and St. John's Catholic Church.

Endowed with a Rabelaisian memory ("Don't bullshit a bullshitter" is one of his maxims), Lois recalls his coming of age among the Irish as a ten-year donnybrook that left half the male Gael population of the north Bronx disfigured with broken noses and, to be sure, with a grudging respect for the Greek outlander. ("I count nine broken noses of my own," he swears.)

He went on to Pratt Institute instead of the family store, but his formal education ended during his second year when one of his professors, Herschel Levit, who was quick to notice that the crooked-nosed street kid was too advanced in his talent for what Pratt could offer, sent him to see Reba Sochis, the owner of a stylish design studio. She examined Lois' portfolio of schoolwork and promptly hired him. Lois thus dropped out of Pratt and went to work for the uncompromising Miss Sochis, where he learned the disciplines of his craft. His career was interrupted by the war in Korea, where he was wounded by shrapnel, preceded by frequent incarcerations in various Army stockades for incorrigible behavior, notably toward authority. Lois (according to Lois) was the ultimate impenitent rebel.

When he returned from Asia he resumed his career and headed resolutely toward the center of commercial action. The florist's kid knew what he wanted: a career as a trailblazing art director. Lois got what he wanted, and has indeed managed to alter the form and substance of his craft and profession.

Amid the cultured and the powerful of corporate America, he has clung doggedly to his Bronx brogue, his schoolyard diction and his largely self-nurtured image as something of a "crazy man," while heading up the fourth successful advertising agency of his career, creating campaigns with an uncommon quotient of audacity for a variety of corporations.

If one were to choose a single word to characterize the Lois

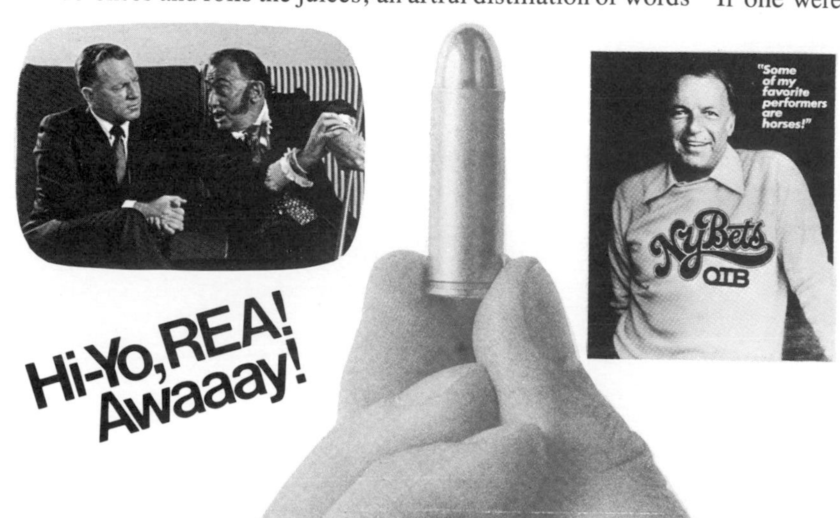

Hi-Yo, REA!
Awaaay!
"Some of my favorite performers are horses!"
NyBets
OTB

Counting today, I have sat in prison 3,135 days for a crime I did not commit.

If I don't get a retrial, I have 189 years to go. 6 months ago the "eye-witnesses," who testified they saw me leaving a bar in which 3 people had been killed, admitted they gave false testimony. Despite this, the judge who sentenced me won't give me a retrial. Why?

RUBIN "HURRICANE" CARTER, NO. 45475
TRENTON STATE PRISON

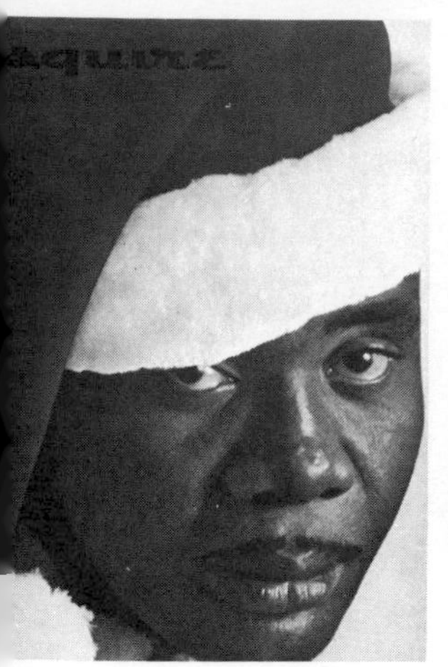

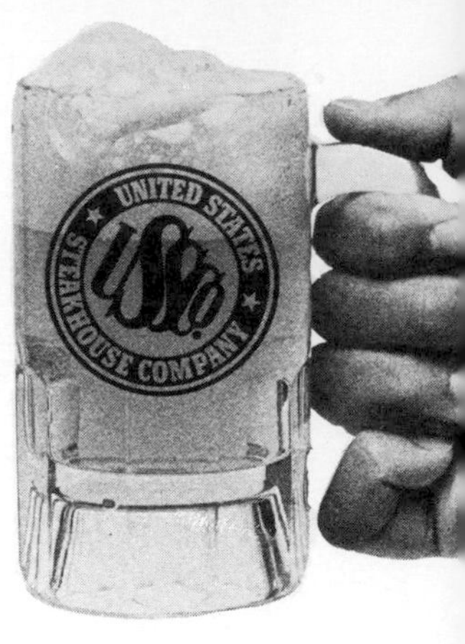

approach it would be *simplify*. In a milieu where fools and frauds *do* run ideas up flagpoles to see if someone salutes, where clients are understandably conservative and admen are predictably cautious, where committees reign and lawyers restrain, the heathen from Kingsbridge has been infusing such alien qualities as clarity, intelligence and taste into American advertising.

While others have succeeded brilliantly in the advertising agency business (Bernbach, Ogilvy, Reeves, Burnett, Wells), the success of Lois has been the achievement of an art director. This seemingly fluke development came about through ego, personal force, demonic drive, indefatigability and an almost savage competitive passion. But beyond these qualities of personality, a fierce talent has governed his career and has inspired a remarkable body of work. The art of Lois, that audacious blending of image and word, that fury to communicate, is a logical happening in the history of advertising art.

Gradually but surely during the post World War II years a counterculture began to find expression on Madison Avenue through a new creative generation, a rebellious coterie of art directors and copywriters who understood that visual and verbal expressiveness were indivisible, who bridled under the old rules that consigned them to secondary roles in the admaking process under the dominion of noncreative technocrats.

A new species of advertising art was becoming discernible. It was strikingly graphic and visually "alive." It was entirely different from what had gone before. A creative upheaval was gathering force. This new expressiveness was structured as a work method in 1948 when William Bernbach founded Doyle Dane Bernbach. In his new agency, an art director and a copywriter worked as a creative pair. The idea of using artist-writer teams as the prime source of advertising was positively revolutionary. From this union the New Advertising was born. Madison Avenue would never be the same.

The creative rock on which Bill Bernbach built his new agency was the art director Bob Gage. Indeed, many of the ad industry's most gifted art directors, such as Helmut Krone and William Taubin, also homed in at DDB, where Bernbach had precipitated what advertising people now generally accept as the Creative Revolution.

This dramatic breakaway was furthered through the 1960s by more than a few artists and writers who started new ad agencies and demonstrated by their success that the art of advertising was substantially more than making layouts or crafting exquisite designs. Power had come to the people who made the ads. It was a yeasty time to be an art director with a rage to communicate, to blaze trails.

In January 1954, Private George H. Lois, U.S. Army, US51161237, newly returned from Korea, threw a punch (according to Lois) at a fat Cracker sergeant in Camp Brunswick, New Jersey. A few days later the Army returned Lois to civilian life with an honorable discharge. (I have seen the document.)

He went to work as an art director for Bill Golden at CBS, a designer's paradise with an atmosphere of the atelier that he left after a few years to make his mark in the roughhouse world of advertising. In 1957 he was hired by Lennen & Newell, a gigantic, conventional ad agency. His career there was brief and explosive. After several months of fruitless hard work, Lois evidently took furious exception to the way his work was being manhandled by the account group on American Airlines. In a by now legendary Madison Avenue episode, he overturned a potentate's desk (there are live witnesses) in a paroxysm of outrage against the Philistines of Lennen & Newell.

By the ripe age of twenty-six, Lois was evolving into a composite persona of Zorba the Greek, Joyce Cary's Gulley Jimson of "The Horse's Mouth" and Elliott Baker's possessed poet Samson Shillitoe of "A Fine Madness."

He went to work for Sudler & Hennessey under the gentle and supremely talented Herb Lubalin, where he settled down, but not for long. For the ambitious Greek, pharmaceutical advertising reached too parochial an audience. Lois wanted action on the consumer front.

After a year he was hired by Bob Gage at Doyle Dane Bernbach. During his one year in Bill Bernbach's creative paradise, he won three gold medals in the annual competition of the New York Art Directors Club for his work on Volkswagen, Chemstrand, and for Goodman's Matzos, a campaign he sold by threatening to jump from a third story window, climaxed by his heraldic cry, "You make the matzoh, I'll make the ads!"

In 1960, at age twenty-eight, he left Bernbach's agency to

WARNING:
IF YOU LIVE WITHIN FIVE MILES OF A HIGHWAY, A RAILROAD, A HARBOR OR A STORAGE TANK...
MOVE!
PENTHOUSE

Dear Dick Tiger:

Here's why I think
I deserve
a crack at your
middleweight crown:
The last time we fought,
I beat you!

Respectfully,
Joey Archer

Dear Dick Tiger:

The Middleweight
Champion should meet
the best middleweight
(not a welterweight).
I'm a middleweight,
and I licked every man
I ever fought, including you.

Respectfully,
Joey Archer

P.S.
(How about a fight, Dick?
I'm going broke
on these ads.)

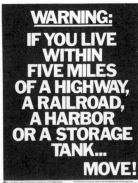

become co-founder of Papert, Koenig, Lois. Although DDB had been on the scene for a dozen years by then, and had become the ad agency for Polaroid, Volkswagen, Chemstrand and other auspicious advertisers, this first creative agency was perceived by the Madison Avenue establishment as a freak, if not *the* freak, in the business. When Lois left DDB to start PKL, he was bucking a stone wall of skepticism. Madison Avenue's conventional wisdom in 1960 allowed for only one "creative" ad agency in America.

Starting from zero, PKL grew to a forty million dollar agency in seven years. Consistent with his unorthodoxy, Lois became the first modern art director to launch a "big business." And in 1962, PKL became the first modern ad agency to go public. (Old established agencies later followed this brash creative shop's excursion into capitalism.) The Lois breakaway demonstrated to creative men and women in the ad world that it was possible to lay one's talents on the line and become a commercial success. Other creative agencies quickly proliferated, following PKL's example, and many flowered.

In 1963, Lois was named Art Director of the Year by the New York Art Directors Club. The previous recipient, his former boss Herb Lubalin, observed at that time, "Nobody has the right to be so young and so successful."

In 1967 the restive Lois left PKL with copywriter Ron Holland and marketing man Jim Callaway to start all over again. PKL had grown too fat and comfortable for his tastes. Something, he felt, probably their having become a public corporation, had altered the soul of his wonderfully successful agency. "I'm thirty-five and too young to die," was his parting shot.

His new ad agency, Lois Holland Callaway, was soon repeating the rapid success of PKL. In 1969 Ad Age named Lois as one of 1968's top ten newsmakers. (He was the only art director among the ten, which included one Robert Haldeman of J. Walter Thompson, who was recognized by Ad Age because he "helped put Nixon in the White House.") In 1971, he was elected president of the New York Art Directors Club. In 1972, Lois completed his tenth year as the art director who created those brash and prophetic covers for Esquire.

In 1977 he stunned Madison Avenue—again. Lois quit LHC to become president of an industrial/corporate agency called Creamer FSR, Inc. During a whirlwind 15 months Lois pushed the agency into prominence by attracting more than $30 million in billings. This once obscure agency changed its name to Creamer Lois and became known as one of the hottest creative shops on the advertising scene. A profound dispute about *style,* however, led to Lois's departure. (Lois, to be sure, was pro-style.) Undaunted, the prolific maverick promptly started a fourth agency to bear his name, Lois Pitts Gershon. Just 60 days after its formation it had grown to $12 million. "I'll keep doing it until I get it right," observed the incorrigible art director, apparently getting it right.

Now at 47, Lois can look back on a body of work that surges forward from the post World War II years of design innocence to somewhere beyond McLuhan's perceptions, when the message, not the medium, is again the message. Lois has evolved an audacious art, a kind of language: that fusion of image and word, that emphasis on idea and concept, that obsession with results, that will to move from ad to action, that respect for any medium if the message has muscle, that determination to make things happen and get things done. If the creative revolution took advertising beyond design, Lois has shoved communication beyond advertising.

He cleaned up the printed advertisement and toughened its message. His very early ads of a generation ago are forthright in meaning, deceptively simple in design, liberated from decorative litter. But even then, they were the stunning inventions of an artist with an irrepressible instinct to *disarm.*

When television became the prime medium, Lois preserved his print style against the cinematography that was carried over from movies. Backgrounds were eliminated. Scenes were shot as clean and clear as Little Orphan Annie cartoons (or a Fang mask). The camera held on faces and silhouettes. "Slightly moving stills" is the phrase he uses to describe his TV commercials.

He has used celebrities a great deal because they bring to mind immediate associations. He has featured enough athletes in his spots to fill a small stadium, because they are embodied myths. Headlines must sound like speech, like the words and cadences people actually use, not like copy. Copy has to read like images, not abstractions.

He sheared away all the trivia, all the trash, and he got down to essentials. But above everything else, from his work for Reba

Sochis to his latest campaign, coming up with the unexpected always mattered most.

This influential adman/art director is the product of many influences. From the purity and mystery of African sculpture, a lifelong Lois love, through the comics, and right up to twentieth century painting and sculpture, the advertising art of Lois draws many of its techniques.

"Parlor primitive" he was dubbed by New York magazine for his remarkable collection that literally dominates his Greenwich Village apartment. Lois lives with his wife Rosemary, his sons Harry and Luke (20 and 16), his cat Zeus, a Greek vase, Cycladic figures, Eskimo masks, Maori sculpture, an Easter Island skeleton figure, a Northwest Coast rattle, Fang heads, bannerstones, Asmat shields, fertility dolls, stone pipes, ivory fetishes, flaring headdresses, cult objects, reliquary heads, ceremonial staffs and assorted primitive statuary, including a four foot Uli (a rarity of Oceanic art from the Pacific island of New Ireland, a wooden male god with pagan Halloween eyes, large breasts and an erect penis, painted and pigmented over generations to a magical luster).

Unexpected, mystical, profoundly simple, geometrically enthralling—these common chords of primitive art that hypnotized Picasso and led to Cubism—these same sources of wonder surround an ad agency art director named George Lois as he watches King Kong on TV in his Manhattan apartment.

Warren Robbins, director of Washington's Museum of African Art, expressed his "extraordinary thanks" to Lois for his "sensitive and knowing organization" of the 243 page Collection book on the 1971 deHavenon exhibition, while Gaston deHavenon described Lois as a person "who knew and loved the collection so well that he was able to work its unique aesthetic transformation."

In 1968 he designed a catalogue and installation at D'Arcy Gallery for rare Karawari sculptures. The catalogue is now a collector's item. His installation set a new standard for sculpture exhibitions.

As a high school student, Lois was mesmerized by the American painter Stuart Davis. Davis dramatically simplified forms and reduced them to a system of flat planes and geometric shapes. Davis was also permanently gripped by the dynamism of New York City. He was a precursor of the modern art director, endowed with peripheral vision that could visually collect subway signs and tabloid headlines and passing trucks and so many of the nuances of daily life. He painted while playing the radio and reading newspapers. Davis was a multi-media personality at the sunrise of that era.

Brancusi the Rumanian peasant mystic was another Lois favorite since his high school years. There is a sturdy coherence to this attraction. Bird in Flight, Sleeping Muse, The Kiss, Prayer, The Seal, The Fish are all the boldest possible simplifications of form, while producing an overwhelming, entirely unexpected emotional response.

And years before Georges de La Tour became suddenly known in 1974 (after one of his handful of paintings, "Magdalen in the Mirror," was bought by the National Gallery of Art for eight million dollars), Lois was urging me to study his work. One day he brought in a French volume of de La Tour's paintings. They were stark scenes without backgrounds, forms of intense simplicity, lights and darks in concentrated juxtaposition. From Uccello to Corbusier, from Della Francesca to Man Ray, from Bellini to Bauhaus, from Oceanic art to Arthur Dove, Lois soaked in the details and saw the essence of their work.

Look at any layout or storyboard by Lois and you'll find a gameboard to his eclectic obsessions. The face of a Lois woman is strikingly similar to Ella Cinders, that oval eyed innocent of the comics. Or are her arcs of hair closer to a BaKota reliquary figure from Gabon? The male figure in his concept layouts is a ringer for Dick Tracy. Or is it the flat-chinned face of a Cycladic idol? His drawings of people, male and female, are two-dimensional renderings of Elie Nadelman's painted cherry wood carvings. Or are they more like the Greek vase paintings of a sixth century B.C. amphora? Invariably, his work reaches out for an unexpected effect, that common denominator of primitive art.

To a much larger extent than meets the eye, the works of George Lois derive from an unconscious connection with primitive myth and art. His unashamedly commercial career has produced a body of work that recaptures and recycles the common experience of video age Americans. This unexpected transformation of cultural matter clarifies our out-of-focus times—in *advertising!* These works of a modern art director may one day be seen as the work of an artist.

Club Activities

David Davidian, President.

When I took office one year ago, I had a pretty clear understanding of what was required to run the Club. After all, I had served on the Board and on various committees for more years than I care to count. As President, I would preside at Board meetings to decide what should be done—I had pretty firm ideas about that, too—and then I would select committee chairmen, tell them and the Club staff what to do, and PRESTO!, it would be done. Little did I know!

I have learned, this first year, that being President of the Art Directors Club is not all beer and skittles.

Somewhere along the way, the Club had become a good-sized business. And nobody noticed. Until our predecessor Board recognized that fact and made the decision to hire professional management with a mandate to develop a professional staff.

So the past year has been devoted primarily to organization—or reorganization, if you prefer. We have examined our programs and identified our needs. We have recruited professional management and trained competent staff. And the staff has assumed the burden of administering committee functions—a formidable task! h have the highest respect for my predecessors who discharged all these responsibilities without the

strong staff support now available. I cannot imagine how they did it!)

Later on, you will read separately about each of the Club's activities, but here I would like just to mention a few of our major accomplishments and even a new direction or two:

The most exciting of these is the new Publishing Division, whose first project is the 57th Annual. Notice the Art Director's Club emblem on the spine of this book. Our new professional staff makes it possible to undertake such projects.

And speaking of staff, we have recognized that the Competition, Exhibition and an expanded Traveling Show are a year-round endeavor and so have engaged a full-time Exhibition Manager.

Our financial picture is healthier than a year ago, a fact attributable solely to the institution of better controls on income and expense. Also on that subject, we have retained a new accounting firm which will prepare monthly financial statements.

Our new staff has even devised ways to expand the menu at the Club—in spite of the indadequate food preparation facilities. Hot buffet every Tuesday, Wednesday and Thursday. Add the Penthouse Pounders every Tuesday and the twenty-odd Wednesday special programs and the Club becomes a great place for lunch.

The Japanese Graphic Idea Exhibition was new this year, and the Visual Communicators Education Fund awarded its first scholarships. A very busy Portfolio Review Program made a further contribution to the Club's educational activity.

Add to this the 88 new members who joined and we see an active and satisfying year—at least for me and the others who participate. And we wonder, those of us who are active, why there are so few of us. We certainly don't need extra work to occupy our time, so there must be other reasons for us to be as involved as we are. And there are, but they are difficult to explain. There is a feeling—of participation, of belonging, of service, of influence, of pride—all of these and more. These satisfactions are here for the taking. The Club is the weaker, and its members the poorer, when they do not participate.

The Art Directors Club, or any association, is only as strong, aggressive and innovative as its members.

So come on up!

Board Of Directors

David Davidian, President
William O. Taubin, First Vice President
Richard Ross, Second Vice President
Robert C. Reed, Secretary
Eugene Milbauer, Treasurer
Meg Crane, Assistant Secretary-Treasurer

Executive Committee

Donald Adamec
Gladys Barton
Lee Epstein
Michael Fenga
Charles Rosner
Jessica Weber

LEFT TO RIGHT: Treasurer Gene Milbauer, Michael Fenga, First Vice President William Taubin, Vice-Treasurer / Secretary Meg Crane, Lee Epstein, President David Davidian, Jessica Weber, Secretary Robert Reed, Gladys Barton and Charles Rosner. Don Adamec and Second Vice President Dick Ross were unable to attend.

Staff

Executive Director:
Diane Herzman
Exhibition Manager:
Martin de Maat
Consultant:
John McCormick
Exhibition Staff:
Sheila Augusta
Daniel Sheehan
Administrative Staff:
Sharon Good
Gloria Mingo
Bea Piskrich
Rose Pesce
James Shewalter

Advisory Board

Every President of the Club, present and past, is a member of the Advisory Board. The collective wisdom of this group, every member of which has been recognized by his peers as a leader, smooths the path of each new administration by providing continuity with the Club's past, immediate and distant. The current Board's personal knowledge of Club activities extends back to the Presidency of Stuart Campbell in 1929.

The Advisory Board traditionally handles the plans for the Annual Awards Presentation and such other items as are referred to them by the Executive Board.

Activists always, these past Presidents do not always wait for a referral from the Executive Board, but often act on their own initiative to communicate the thoughts of their considerable constituency.

Advisory Board

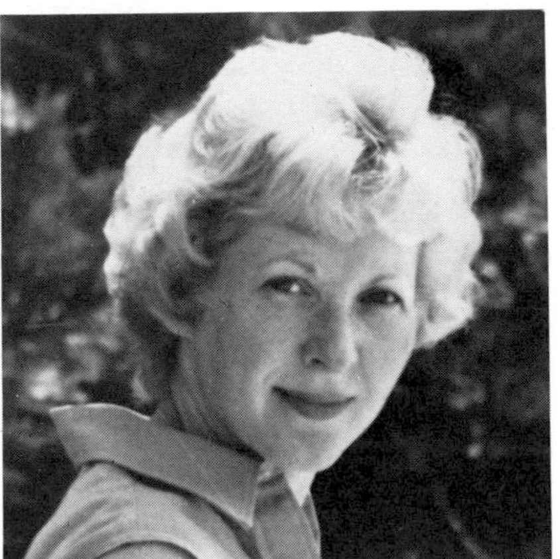

Eileen Hedy Schultz

Eileen Hedy Schultz, Chairwoman
Gordon C. Aymar
Frank Baker
Robert H. Blattner
William P. Brockmeier
William H. Buckley
Stuart Campbell
David Davidian
Lou Dorfsman
Edward B. Graham
Walter Grotz
Arthur Hawkins
John Jamison
George Lois
Herb Lubalin
Garrett P. Orr
John Peter
Lester Rondell
Paul Smith
Robert S. Smith
Loren B. Stone

Membership

Bill Duffy, Chairman of the Membership Committee, presided over deliberations which led to the approval of 88 new members last year.

With a more understandable application designed by Lorraine Allen and two letters of invitation written by Toby Moss, Bill hopes to do as well or better next year.

For readers interested in joining the Club, here are the requirements:

REGULAR MEMBERS—Individuals who are twenty-one years of age, have been Art Directors for at least two years, and live or work within a 75-mile radius of New York City. Initiation fee is $50 and annual dues $150.

NON-RESIDENT MEMBERS—Those regular members who live and work more than 75 miles from New York City. Initiation fee is $25 and annual dues are $75.

ASSOCIATE MEMBERS—Those members who are not primarily Art Directors but who are otherwise connected with the arts, for example, painters, illustrators, photographers, designers and writers. Fees are the same as for Regular Members.

JUNIOR MEMBERS—Those between the ages of 21 and 25 with one year of work in the graphic arts industry who live and work within 75 miles of New York City. No initiation fee; dues are $25.

AFFILIATE MEMBERS—

Corporate—Corporations engaged in the communications or graphic arts industries. Initiation fee is $250; dues are $750.

Institutional—University, college or college level art school with study programs in graphic arts or communications or which operates an art museum.

Professional—Professional association in communications or graphic arts.

For Institutional and Professional members, initiation is $125; dues $500.

William R. Duffy

Committee Members:

William Duffy, Chairman

Lorraine Allen
Edward Barbini
Donald Duffy
Michael Fenga
Blanche Fiorenza
Roy La Grone
Richard MacFarlane
Toby Moss
Allan Philiba
Ray Robertson

Portfolio Review

Chairman Sal Lazzarotti, whose energy in pursuit of art students in need of guidance is frightening, inspired students from far and wide to come and have their work examined.

Schools represented were:

- Cooper Union
- Fashion Institute of Technology
- High School of Art and Design
- New York City Community College
- Parsons School of Design
- Pratt Institute
- Pratt Phoenix School of Design
- School of Visual Arts
- Kean College, Union, New Jersey

Sal Lazzarotti

Committee Members:

Sal Lazzarotti, Chairman

Co-Chairmen:

George Hartman—Magazine and Newspaper Editorial

Jack Tauss—Magazine and Newspaper Advertising

Wendy Morgan—Promotion and Graphic Design

Sam Reed—Television

Participating Art Directors:

Pat Addiss
Robert Anthony
Gladys Barton
Allan Beaver
James Bell
Sy Berkley
Ed Brodsky
Joe Brooks
Bob Bruce
Jim Clarke
Robert Clive
John Conley
Richard Cummings
Ethel Cutler

Kent State University, Ohio
Kutztown State College, Pennsylvania
Moore College of Art, Philadelphia
Rhode Island School of Design, Providence
Trenton State College, New Jersey
University of Massachusetts, Amherst

Sal left nothing to chance. He invited all interested art directors to a luncheon at the Club. There, deliberations centered on the need to communicate to the art schools, in a constructive manner, whatever negative impressions the reviewing art directors received from the students. Future programs will be planned to develop specific impressions of each school's performance and to inform the school of the results, good or bad. The hope is that this kind of feedback will eventually influence the art school curriculum.

Scholarships

On another educational front, the scholarship arm of the Club, the Visual Communicators Education Fund, again received a generous contribution from Mrs. Lila Acheson Wallace, co-founder of Reader's Digest, whose devotion to the arts has assisted so many deserving students and institutions. From this grant, the Fund awarded ten scholarships of $1,000 to students of local art schools. Two hundred portfolios were submitted to the School Art League, whose judges selected sixty finalists. Bill Taubin, President of the Fund, David Davidian, President of the Art Directors Club, and Kurt Haiman, Chairman of the Scholarship Committee, formed a panel to judge the finalists. They awarded the scholarships to:

Alice Cheung—High School of Art and Design
Luciano Genao—William Cullen Bryant High School
Alise Loebelsohn—John Dewey High School
David Pickman—John Dewey High School
Bruce Polin—South Shore High School
Irene Rofheart—John Dewey High School
Percy Scott—City College
Andrea Scrima—New Dorp High School
Loren Sosna—High School of Art and Design
Carmen Zeif—Hillcrest High School

and granted Certificates of Merit to:

David Cohen—Beach Channel High School
Chris Riccardi—Port Richmond High School
Anna Wong—High School of Art and Design

The Fund is off and running; but, by its nature, it is always in need of funds. Please send personal or company contributions—either way, they are tax-deductible—to the Visual Communicators Education Fund at The Art Directors Club, 488 Madison Avenue, New York, New York 10022.

Chel Dong
Bill Duffy
Don Duffy
Zen Eidel
Henry Epstein
Lee Epstein
Atalay Evcimen
Mike Fenga
Blanche Fiorenza
Bill Gold
Eric Gluckman
Kurt Haiman
George Hartman
Bob Kopelman
Howard LaMarca
Steve Laudani
Sal Lazzarotti
Beverly Littlewood
Dave MacInnes
Sam Magdoff
Gene Milbauer
Larry Miller
Wendy Morgan
Geoffrey Moss
Bernard O'Connor
Jack Odette
Theo Pettus
Robert Pliskin
Anny Queyroy
Sam Reed
Ray Robertson
Herb Rosenthal
Eileen Hedy Schultz
Dorris Shaw
Robert S. Smith
Harold Sosnow
Dean Stefanides
Wendy Stehling
Linda Stillman
Jack Tauss
Dick Thomas
Frank Vitale
Theo Welti
Ron Wickham
Bruce Zahor
Milton Zelman
Alan Zweibel

Visual Communicators Education Fund Officers and Committee:

William Taubin

Kurt Haiman

William O. Taubin—President
David Davidian—Vice President
Robert Reed—Secretary
Kurt Haiman—Scholarship Chairman

Judging

57th Chairman Arnie Arlow was assisted by Judging Section Chairmen Harvey Gabor (TV), Herbert M Rosenthal (Promotion & Graphics), David Deutsch (Print Ads) and Meg Crane and Sheldon Cotler (Editorial) in handling the preliminary and final judging. They supervised a panel of sixty judges, who labored at the Club, and at Ogilvy & Mather for TV, for seven nights to select the 1200-plus pieces which were awarded places in the Exhibition and which appear in this volume.

Twenty entries were given Gold Awards, thirty-four received Silver Awards, and Distinctive Merit Certificates were granted to fifty-eight. Winners were announced at the Opening Reception which took place at the Union Carbide Gallery, Park Avenue at 48th Street, on the evening of July 10, first day of the Exhibition, which was shown at the Gallery through July 28.

The tremendous task of receiving and opening the packages, sorting and filing the 9,000 entries, and preparing the necessary records and reports, was performed at the Club by a dozen local art students under the supervision of Exhibition Manager Martin de Maat. Martin and his crew went on to manage the mechanics of the judging process so that Arnie Arlow and his chairmen could concentrate on the entries.

Tony Palladino designed the Exhibition and the poster, a simple black-on-white composition which Tony insisted be placed for the general public in subway stations and public places all over midtown. The Exhibition drew visitors far in excess of any Exhibition in recent memory. Under Tony's guidance, the Club staff mounted the Exhibition for hanging, in space donated as usual by Pioneer-Moss, Inc.

Concurrent with the main show, the staff assembled three additional exhibitions which, with the New York show, will be shown throughout the U.S. and the world.

As usual, IDEA Magazine will sponsor showings of the entire exhibition in Tokyo and other major Japanese cities. President David Davidian will show the TV reel at an advertising communications seminar held in conjunction with the Tokyo exhibition.

And this year will see the first appearances of the Traveling Show in India and the Philippines.

The domestic scene is even busier, with the full mounted New York Exhibition scheduled to be shown at the Federal Building in downtown Manhattan, then by the Art Institutes of Atlanta, Pittsburgh and Denver, and by the Lowe Art Gallery of Syracuse University. Smaller shows will be seen at the Art Institute of Fort Lauderdale, Ryder Gallery in Chicago, in Dallas and Houston, Texas, and Newport Beach, California.

Entries from thirty-eight states, 9,000 of them, attest to the every-growing reputation of the Art Directors Club Annual Competition as a prestigious professional event in the field of communications arts.

Judging

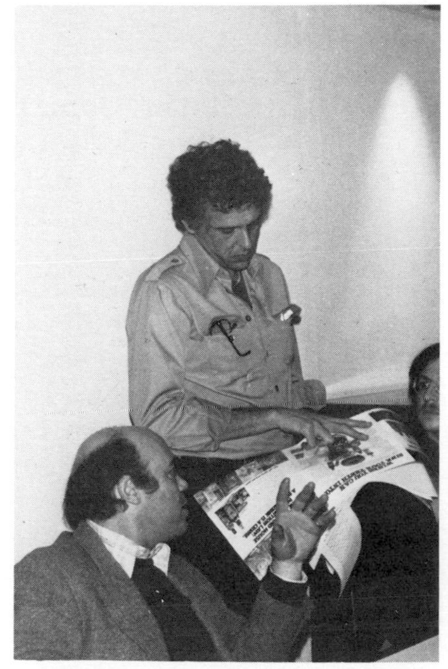

Kurt Haiman and Arnie Arlow

Judging

Ira Sturtevant

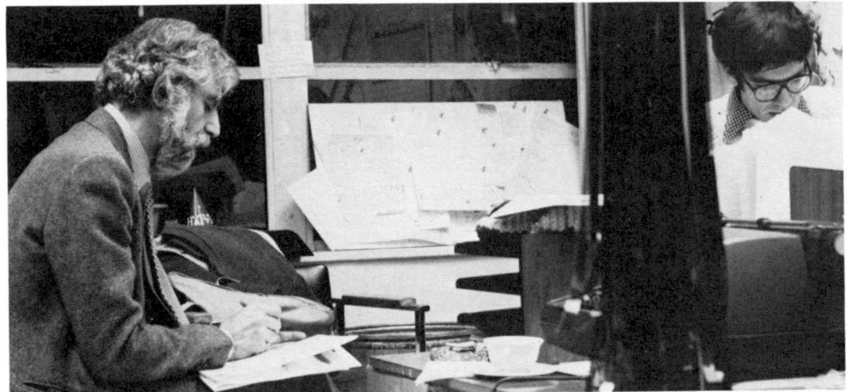

David Davidian and Martin de Mae

Judging

Awards and Exhibition

David Davidian and Geoffrey Moss

ADC Award Cube

Tony Palladino Exhibition Designer

Exhibition

Exhibition

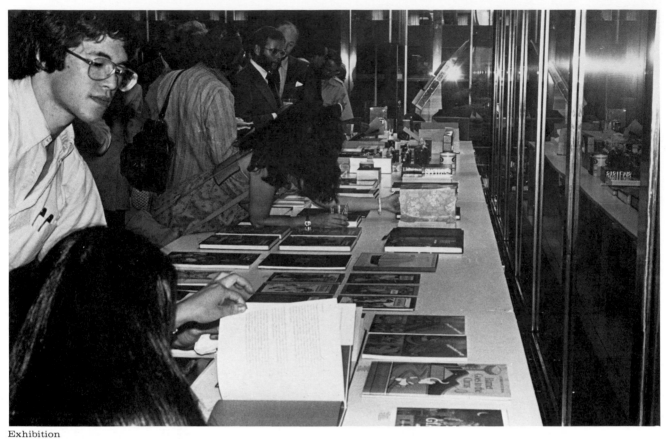

David Davidian and Clem McCarthy

Amie Arlow and Lou Dorfsman
Presenters

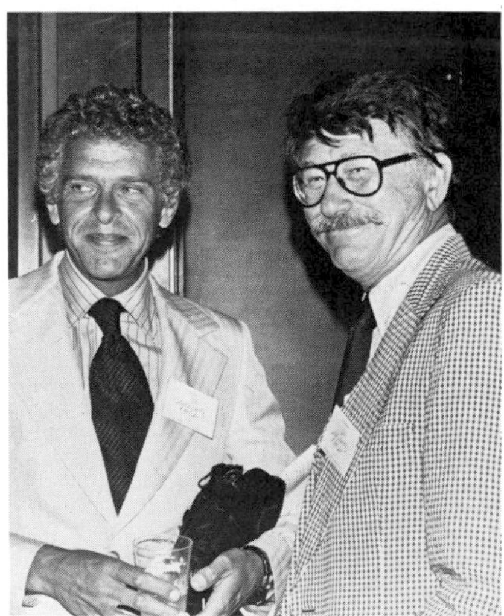

The Club gallery has had an unusually busy season, with exhibitions of: Original illustrations and pen and ink drawings by Bill Charmatz; Illustrations and designs of Jacqui Morgan; Original art for editorial illustrations for Skeptic Magazine, now called Politics Today; Posters, illustrations and prints of Polish artist Jan Sawka; Collages of Jeffrey Schrier; Book jackets, postage stamps and posters by German graphic artist Toni Eichenberg.

Committee Members:
Meg Crane
Alan Peckolick

Above, Bill Charmatz
Upper left, Toni Eichenberg

Above, Jan Sawka
Lower left, Jan Sawka

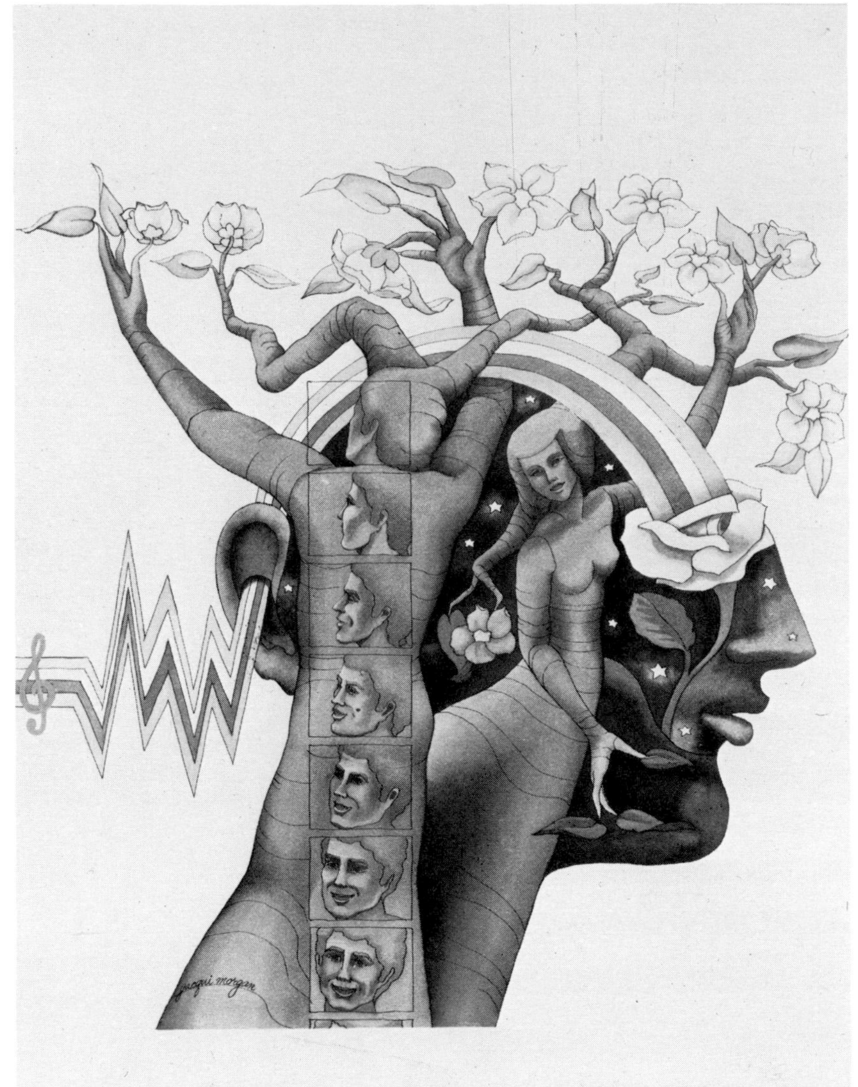

Above, Bill Charmatz

Upper left, Jacqui Morgan

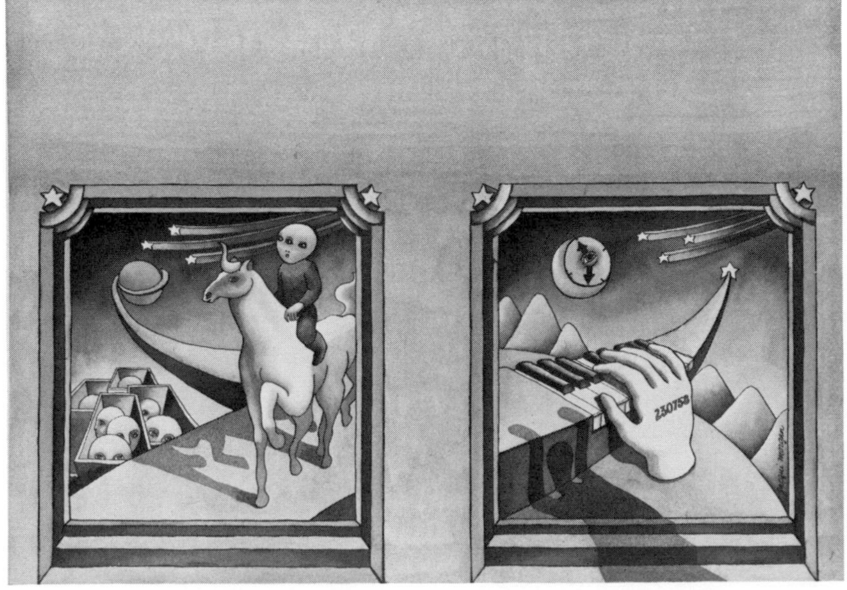

Above, Jeff Schrier

Lower left, Jeff Schrier

For over a year, the Club worked with the Japanese Graphic Idea Exhibition Committee to organize an exhibition of posters, books, packaging and advertising designed by Japan's foremost graphic designers and art directors. This salute to that nation's top photographers and illustrators opened at Nikon House and later appeared at the Master Eagle Gallery and the Nippon Club.

Japanese
Exhibition Poster

Shinichiro Tora
Exhibition Chairman

Art Directors Club member Shinichiro Tora, Exhibition Chairman, was assisted by Gene Milbauer as Exhibition Director, Meg Crane as Exhibition Co-Director and Jitsuo Hoashi, Promotion Art Director.

Shin sees the Exhibition as the first in a series of design-idea exchanges between Japan and the United States, as well as with other countries.

Japanese
Exhibition Poster

Eugene Milbauer
Exhibition Director

Meg Crane
Exhibition Co-Director

Dick Ross, Special Programs Committee Chairman, is also the prime mover behind Jazz Tuesday. As leader, drummer and master of ceremonies, Dick is the most familiar of the loyal troupe of volunteers who pack the house every Tuesday luncheon with their trills, arpeggios and riffs. As if that were not enough to keep him occupied, Dick arranged Wednesday luncheon programs featuring such diverse attractions as helicopter traffic reporter George Mead, Gloria Steinem of Ms. Magazine, Jack Zander's animation techniques and the dog in the Breakstone commercials.

A highlight of the year was the elegant luncheon prepared and served by the Club staff to forty invited guests, to honor Shinzo Takahashi, Chairman of the Board, Hiromo Yoshimura, President, and other executives of Mainichi Broadcasting System of Japan.

The A-Deviates:
Dick Ross, drums
Elliot Abrams, piano
Jim Gribbon, trumpet
Don Phillips, saxophone
Bobby Pratt, trombone & piano
Bob Sparkman, clarinet
Dick Walberger, bass

The A-Deviates

Other programs featured:

Charles McCabe—Manufacturers Hanover, The Superjock Bank
Joel Harnet—Because You Didn't I Did
"Emerald Isle of Guadaloupe"—Travel
Stu Silver—The Met and Me
Howard Lamarka—European Advertising Seminar
Running Fences—By Maysles Films
George Vales—Artist is King
Holiday Magic—Our Christmas Luncheon
George Wolf—Off-Track Betting
Visual Artists & Galleries Association, Inc. (VAGA)—Martin Bressler
Anselmo Spring—Photographer

Dick Ross and Irene Schleider

Robert O. Anderson is honored by The Art Directors Club not for his leadership in industry, which is chronicled in publications with circulation wider and purposes less narrow than ours. It suffices here to say that from a modest beginning he constructed one of the corporate giants of America and manages it with unsurpassed enlightenment.

Our appreciation of Mr. Anderson arises from his manifest understanding of the role of art and artist in corporate management.

His involvement with art in business was stimulated in 1953 when he joined the Aspen Institute for Humanistic Studies, of which he assumed the chairmanship in 1960.

Herbert Bayer, a member of the Art Directors Club Hall of Fame, who has been associated with Robert Anderson as friend and collaborator since the early days at Aspen, tells us that Anderson has placed the artist/designer on a par with his top corporate executives.

Personally a lover of art with instinctively clear artistic judgment, Anderson has a large private collection, as do many wealthy businessmen. But Anderson has used art extensively in his business operations, as early as 1954, when he bought the Wilshire Oil Company in California and had his gas stations designed as part of a corporate graphic style.

When he joined Atlantic, became its chairman and acquired Richfield Oil, he expanded the role of the artist in business. Through design consistency, he created the image of a modern company in all visual manifestations, in its gas stations, its various offices throughout the country and its sponsorship of television programs. The Arco Foundation supports special exhibitions and art schools and, through its Arco Center for Visual Art, provides free gallery space to artists.

For his use of art to increase corporate profits and for his use of corporate profits to support art, The Art Directors Club salutes Robert O. Anderson.

Robert O. Anderson
Chairman,
Atlantic Richfield Company

Index

ADC MEMBERS

Adamec, Donald
Adams, Gaylord
Adams, George
Addiss, Patricia
Adler, Peter
Adorney, Charles
Agha, M. F.
Aldoretta, Warren
Allen, Lorraine
Allner, Walter
Ambrose, Joseph
Ammirati, Carlo
Andreozzi, Gennaro
Andresakes, Ted
Anthony, Al
Anthony, Robert
Arlow, Arnold
Aronson, Herman
Asano, Tadashi
Augenbraun, Seymour
Aymar, Gordon C.

Bach, Robert O.
Baer, Priscilla
Baker, Frank
Barbini, Edward F.
Barron, Don
Bartel, Clyde W.
Barton, Gladys
Basile, Matthew
Beaver, Allan
Bee, Noah
Bell, James Jr.
Belliveau, Peter
Bennett, Edward J.
Benson, Laurence Key
Berg, John
Berkowitz, Seymour
Berliner, Saul
Bernstein, Ted
Berry, Park
Bevil, Serge
Birbrower, Stewart
Blank, Peter
Blattner, Robert
Blend, Robert
Block, David S.
Blod, Francis
Blomquist, Art
Blomquist, Jane M.
Bode, Robert
Bonder, Ronne
Booth, George W.
Boothroyd, John Milne
Bossert, William
Bourges, Jean
Bowman, Harold A.
Bowser, Robert
Boyd, Doug
Braguin, Simeon
Brandt, Joan
Brattinga, Pieter
Brauer, Fred J.
Braverman, Al
Brock, Michael
Brockmeier, William P.
Brodsky, Ed
Brody, Marc
Brody, Ruth
Brooke, John D.
Brooks, Joe
Brophy, Stephen J.
Bruce, Robert
Bruderer, Rolf B.
Brugnatelli, Bruno
Brussel-Smith, Bernard
Brzoza, Walter
Bua, Chuck
Buckley, William H.
Burns, Aaron
Burns, Herman F.
Burton, Cipe P.

Cadge, Bill
Campanelli, Rocco E.
Campbell, Stuart
Cappiello, Tony
Carlu, Jean R.
Carnase, Thomas
Cascio, Salvatore
Cavalieri, Verna
Cerullo, Edward C.
Charles, Irene
Cherry, John V.
Chin, Kay
Christie, Alan
Church, Stanley
Chwast, Paula
Chwast, Seymour
Civale, Frank
Clarke, James V.
Clemente, Thomas F.
Cline, Mahlon
Cline, Mattlyn W.
Clive, Robert
Closi, Victor
Coiner, Charles
Coll, Michael
Collins, Benjamin F.
Conley, John J.
Cooney, Robert A.
Corchia, Al
Corvington, Mark
Costa, Ernest
Cotler, Sheldon
Cowman, Irving
Craddock, Thomas
Craig, James Edward
Crane, Meg
Cranner, Brian A.
Crozier, Robert
Cummings, Richard
Cummins, Jerry
Cupani, Joseph
Cutler, Charles
Cutler, Ethel R.

Dadmun, Royal
Dahlmann, William F.
D'Anna, Russell
Dallenbach, Bilal
Dane, Norman
Da Rold, Thierry
David, Stephanie
Davidian, David
Davis, Herman
Davis, Philip
deCesare, John A.
Defrin, Bob
Del Sorbo, Joseph
Del Vecchio, Pat
Demner & Merlicek
Deppe, Florian R.
Deutsch, David
Devito, Francis J.
Diehl, Carolyn
Diehl, Edward P.
Dignam, John F.
Dixon, Kenwood
Dolobowsky, Robert
Donald, Peter
Dorfsman, Louis
Dorian, Marc
Doyle, Wesley J.
Dubin, Morton
Duffy, Donald H.
Duffy, William R.
Dusek, Rudolph
Duskin, Ken

Eckstein, Bernard
Edelson, Carol Herman
Edgar, Peter
Egensteiner, Don
Eichenberg, Antonie
Eidel, Zeneth
Eisenman, Stanley
Elton, Wallace W.
Emery, Rod A.
Enock, David
Epstein, David
Epstein, Henry
Epstein, Lee
Ermoyan, Suren

Fabiani, Titti
Farber, Robert
Farnum, Michelle
Farrell, Abe
Fass, Harry
Favale, Joseph P.
Federico, Gene
Feitler, Bea
Fenga, Michael
Fernandez, George R.
Finegold, Rupert J.
Finn, William F.
Fiorenza, Blanche
Firpo, Gonzalo
Fischer, Carl
Fitzgerald, John E.
Flock, Donald P.
Foster, Robert
Fraioli, John
Frankel, Ted
Frankfurt, Stephen O.
Franznick, Philip E.
Freedman, Mel
Freyer, Frederic B.
Friedlander, Joel
Friedman, Martin
Frost, Oren S.
Fujii, Satoru
Fujita, Neil
Fury, Leonard W.

Gabor, Harvey
Gage, Leighton David
Gage, Robert
Garber, Charles A., PhD
Garlanda, Gene
Gatti, David
Gauss, Joseph T.
Gavasci, Alberto
Georgi, Carl H.
Gering, Joseph
Germakian, Michael
Giammalvo, Nick
Gibson, Wayne
Gibbs, Edward
Gillis, Richard B.
Ginsburg, Frank C.
Giusti, George
Glaser, Milton
Gluckman, Eric
Goennel, Heidi
Goff, Seymour
Gold, William
Goldberg, Irwin
Goldowsky, Eli
Graham, John
Greenberg, Albert
Greenberg, Nancy
Greenwell, Robert L.
Greller, Fred
Griffin, John
Griner, Norman
Grotz, Walter
Grunfeld, Maurice
Gruppo, Nelson
Guffey, Dionne M.
Guild, Lurelle
Guild, Rollins S.

Hachmann, Hank
Hack, Robert H.
Haiman, Kurt
Halpern, George
Halvorsen, Everett
Hamilton, Edward
Hamway, Ed
Handleman, Michael
Hanson, Thurland
Harris, Ken
Harrod, Brian
Hartelius, Jr., Paul
Hartman, George
Hautau, Janet
Hawkins, Arthur
Hayes, Dorothy E.
Heff, Saul
Heiffel, Eugene
Heller, Shelley L.
Helleu, Jacques

ADC MEMBERS

Hemmick, Bud
Heyman, Wes
Hipwell, Grant
Hirsch, Peter
Hoashi, Jitsuo
Hodes, Ronald
Hoffner, Marilyn
Holeywell, Arnold C.
Holtane, George
Hopkins, Leslie
Hopkins, William
Hovanec, Joe
Howard, Hoyt
Howard, Kenneth M.
Howard, Mark
Hurd, Jud
Hurlburt, Allen
Hyatt, Morton

Iger, Martin
Irwin, William A.
Ishii, Skip

Jaccoma, Edward
Jackson, Robert T.
Jacobs, Harry
Jaggi, Miritz S.
Jagisch, Ronald A.
Jamison, John
Jenks, Neilan F.
Johnson, Rowan G.
Jones, Bob
Joslyn, Roger
Jossel, Leonard
Julia, Christian

Kambourian, Ron
Kanai, Kiyoshi
Kaprielian, Walter
Katsui, Mitsuo
Katzen, Rachel
Kaufmann, M. Richard
Kearns, William J.
Keil, Tom S.
Kent, Nancy
Kenzer, Myron W.
Kittel, Frederick H.
Kleckner, Valerie
Klein, Judith
Klyde, Hilda Stranger
Kner, Andrew
Knoepfler, Henry
Kolomatsky, Eugene
Komai, Ray
Koos, John
Kopelman, Robert F.
Kosarin, Norman
Kovar, Constance
Krauss, Oscar
Kreller, Janet Leigh
Krikorian, George
Kurnit, Shep
Kurz, Anna

LaGrone, Roy E.
Laird, James E.
Lamarca, Howard
Lamarque, Abril
Lambray, Maureen
Larkin, John
Lavey, Kenneth H.
Lazzarotti, Sal
Lee, Daniel
Leeds, Don
Leeds, Martin
Leon, Norberto
Leonard, Jack
Leslie, Robert L.
Leu, Olaf
Levine, Richard L.
Levinson, Julian P.
Levy, David
Leydenfrost, Robert
Leyhausen, Manfred
Liberman, Alexander Conde
Liebert, Victor
Lipuma, Sal
Littlewood, Beverly
Lockwood, Richard
Lois, George
Longo, Vincent
Longyear, William
Lotito, Rocco
Lowry, Alfred
Lubalin, Herb
Lucci, John
Ludekens, Fred
Luden, Richard
Luria, Dick
Lurin, Larry
Lyon, Robert W., Jr.

Macdonald, John
MacFarlane, Richard
MacInnes, David H.
Macri, Frank
Magdoff, Sam
Magnini, Louis
Mahler, Maurice
Mancino, Anthony
Marshall, Al
Marshall, Frank B. III
Martin, Raymond M.
Martinott, Robert T.
Marquez, Andrea
Massey, John
Mathew, Marce
Matsubara, Masaki
Matyas, Theodore
Mazzella, Dennis
McCaffrey, Bill
McCallum, Robert
McCarthy, Clem
McCauley, Rita M.
McCoy, Kevin G.
McGinnis, George
McOstrich, Priscilla
Medina, Fernando
Meeker, Albert
Menell, Don
Merlicek, Franz
Mesnick, Eve
Messina, Joe
Messina, Mario Giulio
Metzdorf, Lyle
Michael, Jan
Milbauer, Eugene
Miller, Gerald
Miller, Lawrence
Milligan, John
Minko, William
Miyauchi, Haruo
Mizerek, Leonard J.
Mohamad, Michael
Mohtares, Alexander
Molomut, Ivan
Morang, Kenneth E.
Morgan, Burton A.
Morgan, Wendy Jo
Moriber, Jeffrey
Morris, Mitzi
Morrison, William R.
Morton, Thomas
Moss, Geoffrey
Moss, Tobias
Moy, George
Mutter, Ralph J.

Nakamura, Makoto
Nappi, Nick
Nassau Community College, The Art Department at
Nichols, Raymond
Nicolo, Frank
Nissen, Joseph
Noda, Ko
November, David
Nussbaum, Edward

Obsatz, Leonard
O'Dell, Robert
Odette, Jack W.
O'Hehir, Joseph
Okladek, John
Olivo, Garry
Orden, A. Robin
Orr, Garrett P.
Ottino, Larry
Owett, Bernard S.

Paccione, Onofrio
Pachman, David
Paladino, Joanne
Palladino, Tony
Pallas, Brad
Pan, Lilly Filipow
Parenio, Ralph
Parker, Paul E., Jr.
Paslavsky, Ivan
Pasternack, Bob
Pearl, Leonard
Peck, Penny
Peckolick, Alan
Pento, Paul
Pereira, Brendan C.
Perel, Jules
Pessalano, John
Peter, John
Peterson, Robert L.
Petrocelli, Robert
Peyton, Philip
Pfeffer, Elmer
Phelps, Stewart J.
Philiba, Allan
Philips, Gerald M.
Pioppo, Ernest
Piotrowsky, Eugene
Place, Jennifer
Platt, Melvin
Pliskin, Robert
Podeszwa, Ray
Pollenberg, Myron
Pompiean, Thomas
Ponzian, Joel
Portuesi, Louis
Post, Anthony J.
Pozsonyi, Anthony
Pride, Benjamin
Prigoff, Mark
Pulise, Santo

Quarrell, Richard
Queyroy, Anny
Quilles, Mario
Quon, Mike

Radtke, Gary
Rafalaf, Jeffrey
Rand, Paul
Read, C. Richard
Reed, Robert C.
Reed, Samuel
Reed, Sheldon
Reeves, Patrick A.
Reinke, Fred
Reinke, Herbert O.
Reisinger, Dan
Renning, David J.
Ribetti, Robert
Ricotta, Edwin C.
Rieger, Howard J.
Ritter, Arthur
Rizzo, Dominic
Robbins, Morris
Robertson, Raymond
Robinson, Clark L.
Rocker, Harry
Rockwell, Harlow
Romano, Andy
Romeo, Anthony
Rondell, Lester
Rosenblum, Morris L.
Rosenfeld, Jerry
Rosenthal, Herbert M.
Rosner, Charlie
Ross, Andrew
Ross, Don
Ross, James Francis
Ross, Richard
Roston, Arnold
Rothenberg, Marjorie Grace
Rothman, Irwin
Rubenfeld, Lester
Rubenstein, Mort

Rubin, Randee
Russell, Henry N.
Russell, Dr. Stella Pandwell
Russo, John
Rustom, Mel
Ruther, Don
Ruzicka, Thomas

Sadiz, Ahmad
St. Louis, Leonard A.
Saks, Robert
Salpeter, Robert
Samerjan, George
Sant'Andrea, Jim
Sargent, John
Sauer, Hans
Scali, Sam
Scarfone, Ernie
Schaible, Timothy
Schenk, Roland
Schiller, Lawrence
Schleider, Irene
Schmidt, Klaus F.
Schneider, William
Schreckinger, Sy
Schreiber, Martin
Schultz, Eileen Hedy
Schuster, Rand
Scocozza, Victor
Scott, Ruth
Segal, Leslie
Seidler, Sheldon
Sellers, John L.
Shakery, Neil
Shaw, Dorris
Shaw, Wesley
Shear, Alexander
Sheldon, William
Shiffman, Orit
Shipenberg, Myron
Shomer, Harvey
Shubeck, Barbara
Siano, Jerry
Siegal, Donald J.
Silverstein, Louis
Simpson, Milt
Sirowitz, Leonard
Skinner, Thomas H.
Skolnik, Jack
Slaughter, O. Paul
Smith, Paul
Smith, Robert S.
Smokler, Jerry
Sobel, Edward
Solomon, Martin
Sosnow, Harold
Sotto, Olga
Spelman, Hoyt
Srebnick, Jean
Stabin, Mel
Stapelfeldt, Karsten
Stauf, Alexander
Stech, David
Stehling, Wendy
Steinbrenner, Karl H.
Stenzel, Al

Stern, Charles
Stern, Charles M.
Sternglass, Lila
Stewart, Daniel E.
Stewart, Richard
Stillman, Linda
Stolz, Steward
Stone, Bernard
Stone, Loren
Storch, Otto
Strosahl, William
Sturtevant, Ira F.
Sussman, Abie
Sweret, Michael
Sykes, Philip
Szczesny, Francis S.

Taibi, Anthony
Takao, Teruaki
Talarczyk, Robert
Tanaka, Soji George
Tanassy, Tricia
Tarallo, Joseph
Tardiff, Melissa K.
Tashian, Melcon
Taylor, Arthur R.
Taubin, Bill
Tauss, Jack George
Tesoro, Ciro
Theon, Petter K.
Thomas, Bradbury
Thomas, Richard
Thorne, Richard Lee
Tillotson, Roy W.
Tinker, John Hepburn
Todd, Robert S.
Todero, John
Toland, Truman
Toledo, Harold
Tolle, Gerald
Tora, Schinichiro
Tortoriello, Don
Toth, Peter
Touart, Ellen
Towles, Edward L.
Trasoff, Victor
Treidler, Adolph

Urbain, John
Urrutia, Frank

Venti, Tony
Vitale, Frank A.
Von Collande, Constance

Wagener, Walter
Wagner, Charles W.
Wahler, Alan
Waivada, Ernest
Wall, Robert C.
Wallace, Joseph O.
Walton, Mark
Wassyng, Sy
Watson, Judith
Watt, James C.
Watts, Ronald E.

Wayne, Joel
Weber, Jessica
Weihs, Kurt
Weinberger, William
Weithas, Art
Weitz, Joseph S.
Wells, Sidney A.
Welti, Theo
Wetzel, Ron
Wheaton, Ned
White, Courtland T.
White, Peter A.
Wickham, Ronald V.
Wilbur, Gordon M.
Wilde, Richard
Wilkison, David E.
Williamson, Jack
Wilvers, Bob
Winkler, Horst
Witalis, Rupert
Wolf, Henry
Wurtzel, William K.

Yamamato, A. Hidehito
Yamamoto, Yoji
Yamashita, Masakazu
Yao, Takeo
Yonkovig, Zen
Yuranyi, Steve

Zahor, Bruce
Zwiebel, Alan

INDEX

Art Directors

Writers

INDEX

Designers

Editors

Directors

INDEX

Producers

INDEX

Music

Production Companies

Artists & Photographers

INDEX

INDEX

INDEX

Agencies

INDEX

Publishers

Alphabetized Clients A-I

INDEX

INDEX

INDEX